Garage Sale & Flea Market

ANNUAL

FIRST EDITION

CASHING IN ON
TODAY'S LUCRATIVE COLLECTIBLES MARKET

NOSTALGIA PUBLISHING C·O·M·P·A·N·Y

The current values in this book should be used only as a guide. They are not intended to set prices, which vary from one section of the country to another. Auction prices as well as dealer prices vary greatly and are affected by condition as well as demand. Nostalgia Publishing Co., Inc. does not assume responsibility for any losses that might be incurred as a result of consulting this guide.

On the cover top to bottom, left to right:

Pin, Hobé tri-colored genuine gemstones, bezel set in filigree gold-tone, 2¾x1½", circa 1948, $175.00-225.00.

Doll, Judy Garland as Dorothy in "The Wizard of Oz," wood composition w/ jointed legs and arms, manufactured by Ideal Toy & Novelty, 18" tall, 1939, $320.00.

Reindeer and Santa, made in West Germany by Steiff, 1950's, 10" reindeer - $75.00-85.00; small reindeer - $50.00-55.00; Santa - $140.00-160.00.

Salad plate, amber, Mayfair pattern, produced by Federal Glass Co., 6¾", $10.00.

Perfume lamps, DeVilbiss, 7" tall - $100.00-200.00; 12" tall - $200.00-250.00.

Cinderella, ceramic with high glaze finish, marked "Goldscheider;" 12" tall, circa 1940s, $150.00-175.00.

Coffeepot, teacup and saucer made by Fiesta. Depending on color, prices range as follows: coffeepot - $75.00-145.00; teacup - $16.00-28.00; saucer - $1.00-7.00.

Tray, Coca-Cola, girl w/menu, 10½x13¼", mid 1950's, $25.00-45.00.

• • • ● • • • ● • • • ● • • ● • • • ● • • • ● • • • ● • • • ● • • • •

Nostalgia Publishing Co. Inc.
P.O. Box 277
La Center, Kentucky 42056

• • • ● • • • ● • • • ● • • • ● • • • ● • • • ● • • • ● • • • •

A Word from the Editor

It has been repeated many times that there are twenty million collectors in the United States today. I would suspect that this figure is vastly understated. Almost everyone has a collecting interest of one sort or another. Anywhere you might go, no matter how small, nearly any town has one grocery store, one filling station, and, yes, one antique shop. Every state in the union has its share of nationally advertised (and very well attended) flea markets; scores of antique malls and co-ops have sprung up all over the country — even along interstates; antique shows both general and specialized are held with mind-boggling frequency; and junk stores are everywhere! There are hundreds, maybe even thousands of collector's clubs with members interested in specific subjects such as dolls, glassware, pottery, guns, knives, quilts, trains, toys, advertising memorabilia, and sports cards. Scores of magazines, tabloids and tradepapers are published that are devoted entirely to antiques and collectibles, and garage sales have become a way of life. For those seriously interested in getting into the fast-growing field of collecting, there are literally hundreds of very good books on every subject imaginable. Make no mistake about it, this industry is big and getting bigger every year. I hope that this book will whet your appetite and stimulate your interest to the point that you will want to become more involved.

Cashing In on Today's Lucrative Collectibles Market

The collectibles market, as any veteran can tell you, has gone through a drastic change in the past decade. If you've found it difficult to relate to 18th or 19th century antiques and if terms like 'trammel' or 'firkin' leave you totally confused, forget it! The things that are moving the fastest today are items that you (or your parents) grew up with — familiar things that you'll remember right away, or at best need only a gentle mental nudging to recall. Remember the cookie jar on grandma's kitchen counter? It's barely noteworthy nowadays to hear that one of the rare ones has sold for $1,000 or more.

Sports card buying and selling is big business. I can remember attending a flea market in Memphis, Tennessee, in the early seventies. A fellow in his twenties came through the front door wheeling an army footlocker on a two-wheeled dolly. I asked him what he had in his trunk. He replied that it was crammed to the top with baseball cards. I asked, 'How much?' 'I'll take a hundred dollars, footlocker and all,' he answered. I offered him fifty, but he kept on rolling. Thirty minutes later he came back by flashing a smile and a hundred dollar bill. I can't even imagine what those cards would be worth today!

Slot cars, Matchbox toys, Tonka toys, and Fisher-Price toys are in great demand; the rhinestone jewelry that glittered at many a senior prom in the fifties carries dazzling price tags today; and even those character glasses you got free from the fast food restaurants a few years ago are valuable. There are salt and pepper shakers from the thirties and forties that originally sold for less than a dollar a pair that today sell for more than a hundred dollars. None of these items are rare or even hard to find. All the information you need to get in on the 'thrill of the hunt,' the 'reward of the find,' the 'buy of the century' you'll find in the following pages. Whether you see yourself simply as a collector or someone wanting to supplement your income in tough economic times, you'll want to read on!

The thousands of current values found in this book will increase your awareness of today's wonderful world of buying, selling, and collecting antiques and collectibles. Use it to educate yourself with regard to both new collectibles and some of the already well-established fields to the point that you'll be the one with the foresight to know what and how to buy at garage sales and flea markets, as well as where and how to turn those 'sleepers' into cold cash if that is your goal. Let me warn you now, though, it's very easy to become a dyed-in-the-wool collector who finds himself unwilling to part with anything! It's often said in jest (but how true it seems to be) that once you've accumulated three — Soakies, cap guns, model kits or whatever — you've become a collector. But as anyone in the business will tell you, even when the general economic growth is down, values of antiques and collectibles often climb at an astonishing rate; so hanging on to things you enjoy for even just a few years will generally be very profitable.

To be able to zero in on today's new collectibles, obviously you have to first take the time to recognize those items you'll be looking for, and this means study. In most of our subject narratives, other books are recommended that will provide you with a more in-depth study into various fields. These books, compiled and written by many of today's experts and leading authorities, will help beginners as well as seasoned collectors and dealers to develop a feel for the market. You'll find your money well spent if you'll begin immediately to build a substantial library on a broad range of subjects.

Be assured that there is much pleasure to be had and money to be made by the informed, well-read and experienced persons dealing in 'today's collectibles' and 'tomorrow's antiques.' No one can remember it all, so at least in the beginning you might want to concentrate your efforts in areas that you find most interesting and that are especially appealing to you. Soon you'll realize that items other than those you've chosen seem vaguely familar as well, and you'll want to do some further research. Armed with your newly acquired knowledge, make a few trips to a good flea market or antique mall. You'll soon discover which collectibles are more prevalent in your area; and before you know it, you'll be able to zip through those garage sales and flea markets, snapping up the bargains ahead of those less informed than yourself.

Where To Find the Bargains

Once you're mentally prepared, you need to plan your rounds. Garage sales are great fun and absolutely wonderful for finding bargains. But knowing what you're looking for is no advantage unless you get there first! Even non-collectors are drawn to much the same merchandise as you will be, and at garage sale prices they're going to snatch it up, enjoy it for awhile, and then probably recycle it in their own garage sale.

Your local paper no doubt will list many of the sales in your area. Local cable channels may also carry garage sale advertising. Most people hold their sales on the weekend, but some may start earlier in the week, so be sure to turn to the classifieds daily. Write them down and try to organize them by areas — northwest, northeast, etc. At first, you'll probably need your city map, but you'll be surprised at how quickly the streets will become familiar to you.

As the cat burglars say, 'case the joint.' Upper middle-class neighborhoods generally have the best sales and the best merchandise. When you've decided where you want to start, go early! If the ad says 8:00, be there at 7:00. This may seem rude and pushy, but if you can bring yourself to do it, it will pay off. And chances are when you get there an hour early, you won't have been their first customer. If they're obviously not ready for business when you get there, just politely inquire if you may look. If you're charming and their nerves aren't completely frayed from trying to get things ready, chances are they won't mind.

Scan the tables before you even move, then head toward the most likely-looking area. Don't be afraid to ask for a better price if you feel it's too high, but most people have already priced garage sale merchandise so that it will sell. ('Permanent' garage sales are another matter; those you'll soon learn to avoid like the plague!) Make a mental note of anything interesting that you didn't buy — for instance, items too pricey that the owner wouldn't come down on so early in the day, or things you couldn't decide on at the time. Then move on to the next sale. After you've finished your initial rounds, you may want to check back. Often by noon, at least by mid-afternoon, veteran garage sale buyers are finished with their rounds and attendance becomes very thin. Owners are usually haunted with visions of having to drag the stuff back in the house or have about decided to give it to Goodwill, so any offer you make at this point may be music to their ears!

I have a friend that makes two trips to every garage sale in the area. One trip very early before the advertised time and the second about closing time at the end of the last day. The early trip is to 'pick the cherries' that might be underpriced, and the late trip is to make an offer for the entire remaining inventory. He owns and operates a barn called 'Sam's Junktique.' Sam does quite well with an annual taxable income well into the six-figure range.

When you shop, learn to check for marks. This is especially true of pottery, silver, costume jewelry, and some glassware. A friend of mine recently sold a $1.50 garage sale bowl for a cool $200.00 within minutes of taking it to a dealer. Most people wouldn't have given the piece a second look, but she was mentally prepared and the heavy green bowl caught her eye. The mark? Teco! McCoy vases are easily found, but because that company used a variety of marks, you may have to study a bit to recognize them all. My find of the summer was an orange vase marked Cowan. My investment? $1.00. My profit? $79.00. You can do it, too.

Tag sales are common in the larger cities. They are normally held in lieu of an auction, when estates are being dispersed, or when families are moving. Sometimes only a few buyers are admitted at one time, and as one leaves another is allowed to take his place. Again, it's the early bird who has the best chance. I know of one fellow that camps out in his van for hours before the sale opens, and he can tell many tales of just how well this strategy works for him. Be prepared to pay higher prices, since it's customary to have tag sale items appraised before values are set. Still, bargains can and do turn up at this type of sale.

Of course, flea markets are a wonderful source for finding under-valued 'goodies,' and they provide a hands-on learning experience for which there is no substitute. You'll learn to look around for the bargains. Normally you'll find a wide range of prices for the same item. This is because flea market dealers are themselves so different. They'll range from very knowledgeable collectors who are 'thining out' and veterans who are 'hip' to the flea market ambiance to the fellow who only sets up on rare occasion and makes no attempt to stay in touch with the market. Some won't keep up with the constant price changes and rather than spring for the price of a new edition will use outdated books to price their merchandise.

But of this there is no doubt, the competition among flea market buyers is stiff, so don't expect to arrive late in the morning and find the bargains still there. Being early is a virtue you'll want to live by. If you have a friend, you can cover the tables in half the time if you'll split up. The very serious pairs can be seen at any large flea market talking via walkie-talkie with each other. But the competition only adds fun to the challenge and a boost to the 'high' you'll get knowing you've found that great buy.

Flea market prices aren't set in stone. Even though many dealers may put 'high book' prices on their merchandise, they realize that at this level of the buying/selling chain, many of their sales will be to other dealers who can't buy at 'retail' and expect to make a profit, or to collectors who may view 'so-so' examples as things they could live without unless found at a bargain. So don't be afraid to ask for a better price. Most will expect it; it's part of the transaction. A courteous attitude and a smile can sometimes save you big bucks.

If there is a consignment auction house in your area, check it out. These are usually operated by local auctioneers, and the sales they hold in-house often involve low-income estates. You won't find something every time, so try to investigate the merchandise ahead of schedule to see if it's going to be worth your time to attend. Competition is probably less at one of these than in any of the other types of sales we've mentioned, and wonderful buys have been made from time to time.

Your very own attic (or your parents' — certainly your grandparents') is a great place to start your search. I've always said 'Thank goodness for yesterday's savers who put things away in closets, boxes, and attics, for without them we wouldn't have a collectibles market.' Check the Yellow Pages in your phone book for 'Resale Shops,' and be sure to visit Goodwill stores when you're traveling. I've been able to buy good records very inexpensively this way, and when we visited the west coast last year I found a wonderful Florence figurine for only $35.00. I have a friend who always checks for the Robert Wood prints she likes, and a young couple I know have been able to accumulate an entire set of the brown Pfaltzgraff dinnerware at very little expense.

Holding Your Own Garage Sale

Are you with me so far? Have I convinced you that there's profit to be made and enjoyment to be had in the collectibles market? If so, you're next concern might be how to get started without straining the family budget. OK, here's my suggestion. Have a garage sale.

Surely you have things that are no longer useful. Offer to clean out Uncle Al's attic or basement while you're at it. Unless you're unbelievably young, you should have items with some collector value yourself — Hot Wheels, Barbie dolls, Kiss posters, Avon bottles...whatever. Advertise your sale, being sure to mention 'antiques' and 'collectibles.' To attract buyers, it's very important to be able to write a good ad.

Unless you come up with tons of merchandise, chances are you'll do just as well with a one-day sale as you would by running it longer. In fact, serious buyers will hit you early, just as I suggested you do, and you'll see a drop off in buyers within a few hours after you open. In addition to ads in your local papers and on your town's cable TV chanel, you can usually put up signs. Check to see if there are ordinances that restrict you in regard to where they may be tacked up. In many places, signs may be posted on telephone poles, but this is not always the case. You may have to drive a stake into the ground to support your sign. In any case, use posterboard or some equally stiff cardboard and be sure to print in letters large enough to be read from passing cars. I'm not personally aware of any states that collect sales tax on garage sales, but you might want to check to make sure.

The majority of sales begin on Friday or Saturday, and usually attract a larger crowd than those starting on Thursday, simply because busy people sometimes don't feel it worthwhile to get out for only a few sales. Then the majority that make it their habit to get out on the weekend avoid them altogether, because by then they're second-day sales.

Sort and price your items. Remember that garage sale buyers expect to find bargains. Take into consideration that by having your own sale your overhead is minimal, you're enjoying the comfort of being at home, and price accordingly. If you're toying with the idea of renting mall space or trying flea market selling and you have a few items you know are very collectible, don't give them away, either. Use masking tape or gummed labels for price tags. Unless you've invited a friend or a neighbor to bring their stuff over, you won't need to remove them as they sell — the profits are all yours. If others are involved, you'll have to keep tabs. Initial your tags and have everyone else do the same. It's good to have someone to help you, but don't let things get out of hand. I once had a sale where eighteen friends brought in a 'few things.' We had a great-looking sale, but no one did well. You can have too much merchandise.

Clothing, with the exception of children's things, won't sell well unless it is cheap. If you have in-style, like-new adult clothing that you can't bring yourself to price so low, you could check around for a resale or consignment shop. These shops normally to set their values at about one-third of the original price. A $150.00 (when new) suit will carry about a $50.00 price tag. You couldn't begin to ask this at a garage sale. One obvious reason is that consignment stores are organized much like department stores. Items are nicely displayed on racks, well cleaned and pressed, the store is well-lit, and there is somewhere for prospective buyers to try clothing on before making a purchase. No $50.00 suit is a bargain if it doesn't fit when you get it home. Their cut will be about 30%, but it will be worth it.

Make sure your items of clothing are clean, mended, and at least relatively unwrinkled. Try to get your better things on hangers. If you're going to have to stack some items on tables, don't expect to get much out of them — most people don't mind going through a few stacks, but if your table is piled high, unless there are some good bargains there, veteran shoppers anxious to get on to the next sale won't spend much of their time pawing through it.

On the day of the sale, put out a large sign in your front yard so you'll be easy to find. Hang some balloons around. You might want to put up another sign saying 'Clothing ½-Price After 12:00.' If your sale is in your garage rather than your yard, put a card table right outside the door so your buyers have space to circulate and can pay you as they leave. Be prepared with plenty of change. If you have joint sale with a neighbor, set up a ledger or tablet with two columns (or one for each seller involved) and write each purchase in the appropriate column. You'll need paper or plastic bags, maybe a few cardboard boxes.

After the sale, pack any good collectibles that didn't sell until you've decided on your next strategy. Sort out the better items of clothing for Goodwill or a similar charity, unless your city has someone who will take your leftovers and sell them on consignment. This is a fairly new concept, but some of the larger cities have such 'bargain centers.'

I never said it was easy, but come on now, it was fun, wasn't it? And now you have a nice little nest egg to finance a bit of prudent garage sale and flea market buying.

Where and How To Sell

Now that you've accumulated a few goodies (if you can bring yourself to part with them), you'll need to decide on the best way to move your merchandise. The first thing you need to determine is approximate value, since this is usually the deciding factor. In addition to this one, there are several other very fine price guides on the market. One of the best on the market is *Schroeder's Antiques Price Guide*, another is *The Flea Market Trader*. Both are published by Collector Books. *The Antique Trader Antiques and Collectibles Price Guide*, *Warman's Antiques and Their Prices*, and *Kovel's Antiques and Collectibles Price List* are others. You may want to invest in a copy of each.

It's very important that you learn to check for condition. Nothing has more bearing on value than condition. I'll go into this in more depth later. Once you have arrived at an estimated value, you'll have to ask yourself, 'Do I want a fast turnover for less money, or am I willing to put in extra time and effort for the maximum return?' My friend with the Teco bowl opted for selling her piece to a dealer for an immediate cash sale. (Remember? She got $200.00 for it.) Retail value for her item was approximately $275.00, leaving her a wonderful profit and the dealer room to make some money as well. Had she had other merchandise, she might have taken it to a flea market, paid the set-up fee, and found a collector willing to pay her price (less bargaining adjustments). She might have placed it in a consignment shop, but the normal consignment fee is 30%. An item that expensive might have been slow to sell, and after the fee was deducted she wouldn't have been any further ahead. Another avenue she might have taken would be to consign it to a special pottery auction where it could possibly have realized an even higher price than the $275.00 she had estimated. The bowl was not particularly spectacular, so she decided not to gamble.

There were two other recourses she might have taken. Could she have made contact with a collector eager to add this piece to his or her collection, she probably would have asked the full retail price and got it. Or she might have run a 'mail bid' in one or several of the many papers available to the antiques and collectibles trade. If you'll turn to the back of this book, you'll see we list several, as well as names and addresses of collectors who are actively trying to add to their collections. Later I'll give you some advice on how and where to place your ad for a mail bid.

There are some wonderful stories that circulate from time to time among collectors and dealers about absolutely spectacular 'finds' — the sooty oil painting purchased at a remote country auction that eventually found its way through a well-known eastern gallery bringing hundreds of thousands of dollars; the rare mechanical bank or tin toy that realized a small fortune at auction . . . you yourself could someday make one of those lucky finds. Once you've become aware of such possibilities, have trained yourself to be observant, and are willing to get out and scour the countryside, it's simply a matter of being at the right place at the right time. The odds are certainly better than your winning the lottery! If after you've done your homework you believe you've found a windfall, you'll want to get an official appraisal. Many of the larger auction galleries have such a service. We list several of these in the back along with the trade papers.

But by and large, the things you're going to find will realistically fall into the $100.00 and under range. This is the type of merchandise that sells best at flea markets or consignment shops, and it will move much faster than high-dollar items, so you can get an early return on your investment. Believe me, it is entirely possible to add substantially to your income by dealing in these less expensive items. As you gain experience in both your buying and selling, you'll see that this can become a reality.

Selling by Mail

Many people have excellent results through sale ads in trade papers or by locating and contacting specialized buyers by mail. There are several ways you can approach this option. You may want to place an ad, listing your merchandise, noting its condition, and giving a specific value. Many trade papers can be picked up free at antique stores or co-ops (another name for an antique mall), or you can usually request a free copy directly from the editors. One of the best is *The Antique Trader Weekly* (P.O. Box 1050, Dubuque, Iowa 52004). It deals with virtually any and all types of antiques and collectibles and has a very large circulation. If you have glassware, china, or pottery from the Depression era, you should have very good results through *The Depression Glass Daze* (Box 57, Otisville, Michigan 48463.)

If you have several items and the cost of listing them all is prohibitive, simply place an ad saying (for instance) 'Several pieces of Royal Copley (toy soldiers, cast iron ware, or whatever) for sale, send SASE (this means stamped, self-addressed envelope) or call for list.' Be sure to give your correct address and/or phone number.

When you're making out your list or talking with a prospective buyer by phone, try to draw a picture with words. Describe any damage in full; it's much better than having a disgruntled customer to deal with later, and you'll be on your way to establishing yourself as a reputable dealer. Sometimes it's wise to send out photographs. Seeing the item exactly as it is will often help the prospective buyer make up his or her mind. Send a SASE along and ask that your photos be returned to you so that you can send them out again, if need be. A less expensive alternative is to have your item photocopied. This works great for many smaller items, not just flat shapes but things with some dimension as well. It's wonderful for hard-to-describe dinnerware patterns or for showing their trademarks.

A third type of ad is called a 'mail bid.' If you've made that 'buy of a lifetime' or an item you've hung onto for a few years has turned out to be a scarce, highly sought collectible, a mail bid is often the best way to get top dollar for your prize. This is how you'll want your ad to read: 'Mail Bid. Popeye cookie jar by American Bisque, slight wear (or 'mint' — briefly indicate condition), closing 6/31/93, right to refuse' (standard self-protection clause meaning you will refuse ridiculously low bids), and give your phone number. Don't commit the sale to any bidder until after the closing date, since some may wait until the last minute to try to place the winning bid.

Be sure to let your buyer know what form of payment you prefer. Some dealers will not ship merchandise until personal checks have cleared. This delay may make the buyer a bit unhappy, so you may want to request a money order or a cashier's check.

Be very careful about how you pack your merchandise for shipment. Breakables need to be well protected. There are several things you can use. Plastic bubble wrap is excellent, or scraps of foam rubber such as carpet padding (check with a carpet-laying service or confiscate some from family and friends who're getting new carpet installed). I've received items wrapped in pieces of egg-crate type mattress pads (watch for these at garage sales). If there is a computer business near you, check their dumpsters for discarded foam wrapping and other protective packaging. It's best not to let newspaper come in direct contact with your merchandise, since the newsprint may stain certain types of items. After you've wrapped them well, you'll need boxes. Find smaller boxes (one or several, whatever best fits your needs) that you can fit into a larger one with several inches of space between them. First pack your well-wrapped items snuggly into the smaller box, using crushed newspaper to keep them from shifting. Place it into the larger box, using more crushed paper underneath and along the sides, so that it will not move during transit. Remember, if it arrives broken, it's still your merchandise, even though you have received payment. You may want to insure the shipment; check with your carrier. Some have automatic insurance up to a specified amount.

After you've mailed it out, it's good to follow it up with a phone call after a few days. Make sure the box arrived in good condition and that your customer is pleased with the merchandise. Most people who sell by mail allow a 10-day return privilege, providing their original price tag is still intact. You can simply initial a gummed label or use one of those pre-printed return address labels that most of us have around the house.

For very large or heavy items such as furniture or slot machines, ask your buyer for his preferred method of shipment. If the distance involved is not too great, he may even want to pick it up himself.

Flea Market Selling

This can either be lots of fun, or it can turn out to be one of the worst experiences of your life. Personally, even though I can remember a late fall event where the temperatures dipped so low that we froze in our coveralls and had to build fires in trash barrels to warm our cold hands, I still enjoy them. But you are at the mercy of the elements, so be sure to listen to weather reports so that you can dress accordingly.

You'll see some inventive shelters you might want to copy. Even a simple patio umbrella will offer respite from the blazing sun or a sudden downpour. I've recently been seeing flea market stands catering just to the needs of the dealer — how's that for being enterprising! Not only do they carry specific items the dealers might want, but they've even had framework and tarpaulins for shelters they'll erect right on the spot!

Be sure to have plastic table covering in case of rain and some large clips to hold it down if there's much wind. The type of clip you'll need depends on how your table is made, so be sure to try them out before you actually have need for them. Otherwise your career as a flea market dealer may be cut short for lack of merchandise!

Price your things, allowing yourself a little bargaining room. Unless you want to collect tax separately on each sale (for this you'd need lots of small change), mentally calculate the amount and add this on as well. Sell the item 'tax included.' Everybody does.

Take snacks, drinks, paper bags, plenty of change, and somebody who can relieve you occasionally. Collectors are some of the nicest people around. I guarantee that you'll enjoy this chance to meet and talk with lots of them, and often you can make valuable contacts that may help you locate items you're especially looking for yourself.

Learning To Judge Condition

Nothing affects value more than condition. Most people, especially inexperienced buyers and sellers, have a tendency to overlook some flaws and to overrate merchandise. Mint condition means that an item is complete and undamaged; in effect, just as it looked the day it was made. Glassware, china, and pottery may often be found in mint condition, though signs of wear will downgrade anything. Unless a toy is still in its original box and has never been played with, you seldom see a mint-condition toy. Paper collectibles are almost never found without deterioration or damage. Most price guides will list values that apply to glass and ceramics that are mint (unless another condition is specifically indicated within some descriptions). Other items are usually evaluated on the assumption that they are in the best as-found condition common to that particular area of collecting. Grade your merchandise as though you were the buyer, not the seller. If, for instance, a vase has a tiny flake off the underside of the foot, it wouldn't be unreasonable to discount it to 'near mint' and reduce the price by 10% to 15%. A bit larger chip on the lip is another matter. Realistically, you wouldn't want to buy it, and unless it's a rare item, neither will anyone else. You might discount this damage by 60% to a 'very good' status. It may sell and it may not. The first rule of buying is 'Don't put your money in damaged goods.'

How To Use This Book

Our format is simple. We've organized our topics alphabetically, following the most simple logic, usually by manufacturer or type of product. Exceptions to this may occur when a subject is better served by having its own narrative. For instance, rather than let 'Barbie' get lost in the 'Dolls' category, she has her own space. And rather than put Jadite glass — which is so much in demand — in the 'Kitchen Glassware' category, we've dealt with it separately. We've used cross-references when this happens, and I think on the whole you'll be able to find things very easily. Only very standard abbreviations have been used, and you'll find our line descriptions are very easy to read and understand.

Many of our narratives contain references to wonderful books that can provide you with more information concerning the subjects you're especially interested in. They're written by many of today's experts and leading authorities and are a must for every seller, buyer, dealer, collector, or any individual who is just trying to develop a feel for the market.

If you'll turn to the back of the book, you'll find names and addresses of individuals who are actively seeking to buy in specific areas; their interests are listed as well. Please remember that you must include an SASE (stamped, self-addressed envelope) when you contact them, if you want a reply. Some may have given their phone numbers, but please don't call them collect. And if you call and get their machine, suggest that they call you back collect.

Auction houses are listed as well. If you have an item you feel might be worth selling on consignment, be sure to contact one of them. Many have appraisal services; some are free while others charge a fee dependant on number of items and time spent. We suggest you first make a telephone inquiry before you send in a formal request.

In Summation

Whether you're wanting to supplement your income on a spare-time basis or actually considering a career move, buying and selling antiques and collectibles is certainly a viable alternative to many other options and certainly worth your consideration. Just this weekend in my area I've managed to pick up four items that book for a total of $470.00 for only $11.75. I found a Roseville 'Autumn' shaving mug (unmarked) for $10.00, a Rosemeade pheasant flower frog for $1.25 (actually that was for two of them, but one was broken), and two Imperial Cape Cod goblets at fifty cents. Last weekend I bought a McCoy 'El Rancho' coffeepot and warmer for $32.50. It books for $100.00 to $150.00. I also bought a TV lamp for $5.00 that I've often seen nearer to $50.00. I saw several other items that money could be made on, but not being a regular flea market dealer myself (I'm one who gets very possessive of things once I bring them home), I chose to let them lay. I don't expect to do that well every time I go out, but there's always a chance that I might, and after desk-sitting for five days a week, I enjoy the outdoors and the opportunity to talk to the dealers. Collecting is a hobby that I would recommend to everyone — it's a great leisure-time interest for a couple or even an entire family to share. Try it! You'll like it! Join with the hundreds of thousands already enjoying the hunt for 'today's collectibles, tomorrow's antiques.'

Abbreviations

MIB - Mint in (original) box
M - Mint Condition
NM - Near Mint Condition
EX - Excellent Condition
VG - Very Good Condition
G - Good condition

A B C Plates

These are earlier than most collectibles we've included, but ABC plates are the type of items that are often passed down, so you may have one that you're curious about. Most were made in the Staffordshire area of England during the 1800s, but some are from this century as well. Among the most valuable are those with sign language and those that are sports related or depict a famous person. There's a series with Franklin's maxims that are especially nice, and normally (unless overriding factors are present) those with colors added over the transfer are more desirable.

Ceramic, 5", 'Now I Have a Cow,' transfer print w/multicolor details, Franklin Maxim, Staffordshire $145.00

Ceramic, 5", 'Shepherd Boy,' scene w/his dog & goat, transfer print..$80.00

Ceramic, 5½", 'Harvest Home,' scene w/hay wagon, transfer print, marked Meakin $85.00

Ceramic, 6", 'Robinson Crusoe,' pink transfer print, marked Brownhills, England $115.00

Ceramic, 6", 'Zebra,' transfer print w/polychrome details, Staffordshire $95.00

Ceramic, 6", kittens jumping rope, sign language embossed along rim, marked Aynsley $200.00

Ceramic, 6", young English newsboy w/newspapers, transfer print w/polychrome details, Meakin....................$125.00

Ceramic, 6½", 'Nations of the World,' transfer print w/polychrome details, marked Brownhill......................$185.00

Ceramic, 6¾", 'Sioux Indian Chief,' brown transfer print, Allerton, England $115.00

Ceramic, 7", 'A Fishing Elephant,' two small girls & elephant w/fishing poles, pink transfer print, marked Allerton..$100.00

Ceramic, 7", boys knock hat off of a napping man, black transfer..$100.00

Ceramic, 7", 'Titmouse,' bird on branch on left side, alphabet on right, transfer print w/polychrome details $90.00

Ceramic, 7", boy riding in cart, red transfer print, Staffordshire..$150.00

Ceramic, 7", riders on bucking horses, blue transfer print, Staffordshire $145.00

Ceramic, 7½", man & boy riding on burro, transfer print, Staffordshire $125.00

Ceramic, 8", 'Rule of Three,' lettered banner above three Black men w/glasses raised, Staffordshire $200.00

Glass, 6", duck & ducklings, glass, attributed to Crystal Glass Company $50.00

Glass, 6", elephant carrying people in howdah, clear.$70.00

Glass, 6", rabbit in foliage in center, clear......................$50.00

Glass, 7", 'Christmas Eve,' Santa Claus stands at chimney, clear...$70.00

Tin, 5", 'Jumbo,' elephant embossed in center, Central Stamping...$50.00

Tin, 8", 'Hey Diddle Diddle,' scene w/cow, cat, & dog from nursery rhyme $85.00

Tin, 8", 'Who Killed Cock Robin?'...............................$95.00

Tin, 8½", 'Peter Rabbit,' animals & ABCs embossed around rim...$70.00

Abingdon Pottery

You may find smaller pieces of Abingdon around, but it's not common to find many larger items. This company operated in Abingdon, Illinois, from 1934 until 1950, making not only nice vases and figural pieces but some kitchen items as well. Their cookie jars are very well done and popular with collectors. They sometimes used floral decals and gold to decorate their wares; a highly decorated item is worth about 25% more than the same shape with no decoration. Some of their glazes also add extra value. If you find a piece in black, bronze, or red, you can add 25% to those as well.

If you talk by phone about Abingdon to a collector, be sure to give him the mold number on the base. To learn more about Abingdon cookie jars, we recommend *The Collector's Encyclopedia of Cookie Jars* by Joyce and Fred Roerig.

Ashtray, turquoise, box form, #488, 1936-38..............**$45.00**
Ashtray, white, elephant form, #509, scarce **$100.00**
Ashtray, 5" dia, black & yellow, leaf shape, #660........**$35.00**
Bookends, pink, modeled as sea gulls, #305 ....**$55.00**
Bookends, 5¾", modeled as colts, #363 ....**$65.00**
Bowl, small, pink, hibiscus, #527, 1941-48.................**$35.00**
Bowl, 16", blue, Tai Leaf, #529 ....**$30.00**
Bowl, 9½", turquoise matt, sunflower, #383, 1936-38..**$80.00**
Bud vase, 5½", light green, Fern Leaf, #427, 1937-38..**$75.00**
Candle holders, double, white, Astor, #451, 1936, pr.....**$44.00**
Candlesticks, white, Classic, #126, pr **$35.00**
Cookie jar, Baby, blue, #561 ....**$300.00**
Cookie jar, Hippo, cream w/hand-painted decoration, #549..**$225.00**
Cookie jar, Hippo, pink, #549...................................**$190.00**
Cookie jar, Hobby Horse, fired-on decoration, #602.**$185.00**

Cookie jar, Humpty Dumpty, fired-on decoration, #663 ....**$185.00**
Cookie jar, Little Old Lady, cream w/hand-painted decoration, #471...**$525.00**
Cookie jar, Little Old Lady, light green, no decoration, #471 ....**$195.00**
Cookie jar, Pineapple, #664.......................................**$60.00**
Cornucopia, blue w/decoration, #569D **$25.00**
Goblet, green, Swedish, #322.....................................**$45.00**
Pitcher, 2-qt, red matt, ice lip, #200...........................**$25.00**
Pitcher, 8", white, Fern Leaf, #430, 1937-38 ....**$135.00**
Planter, 6", molded as a fish, 6" **$37.50**
Teapot tile, turquoise gloss, geisha, #400....................**$80.00**
Vase, copper brown, Chang, #310, 1934-36, rare......**$275.00**
Vase, large, white, Volute, #412, 1937-40...................**$125.00**
Vase, 10", turquoise matt, Delta, #104 ....**$28.00**
Vase, 5½", white, box form, #402, 1937-38 ....**$70.00**
Vase, 6", light blue, Beta, #110 ....**$30.00**
Vase, 6", white, Alpha, #109......................................**$18.00**
Vase, 8", white matt, wheel handle, #466 ....**$25.00**
Vase, 9", white, Athenia Classic, #315, 1934-36 ....**$36.00**
Wall pocket, deep red, double morning-glory, #375...**$55.00**
Wall pocket, white, acanthus, #648, rare.....................**$60.00**

Advertising Collectibles

This field is so vast, we can only attempt to introduce you to it briefly. Watch for condition; it's very important here. A mint condition item may bring twice what the same item in only very good condition will, and often (unless they're rare or especially sought after) things that are damaged are very slow to sell. If you are drawn to tin containers, tobacco-related tins are normally the most desirable, but peanut butter or talcum tins with beautiful ladies and children are very collectible as well.

Items with character logos are always good. There's the Red Goose Shoe's goose, RCA's Nipper, the Campbell Kids, and Buster Brown, just to name a few. You'll find ash trays, dolls, pin-back buttons, and tons of other small items from the past few decades that have a market value of $50.00 or less, and these are the types of things that make up a good percentage of today's sales. Even the collector-type tins made during the past ten years are selling well for flea market dealers who seem to price them in the $3.00 to $25.00 range. They say that especially tins marked 'West Germany' (since that no longer exists) are moving.

There are several books we recommend: *Huxford's Collectible Advertising* by Sharon and Bob Huxford, *The Book of Moxie* by Frank Potter, *American Sporting Advertising, Vol I, Posters and Calendars* by Bob and Beverly Strauss, *Antique Advertising Encyclopedia, Vol 1 and Vol 2* and *Antique Advertising Handbook* both by L-W Promotions, *Advertising Dolls Identification and Value Guide* by Joleen Ashman Robinson and Kay Sellers, *Pepsi-Cola Collectibles* by Bill Vehling and Michael Hunt, and *The Collector's Guide to Key-Wind Coffee Tins* by James H. Stahl.

See also Airline Memorabilia, Automobilia, Avon, Beer Cans, Bubble Bath Containers, Cereal Boxes, Character and Promotional Drinking Glasses, Coca-Cola Collectibles, Cookbooks, Cracker Jack Collectibles, Dairy Bottles, Decanters, Fast Food Toys and Figurines, Gas Globes and Collectibles, Keen Kutter, Labels, Pez Candy Containers, Pin-Back Buttons, Planters Peanuts, Playing Cards, Posters, Soda Bottles, Soda Fountain Collectibles, Typewriter Ribbon Tins, Vending Machines, Watch Fobs.

Banks

Bokar Coffee, tin, EX..**$12.50**
Burgermeister Beer, 3¼", metal can form, bright colors, 1952, unused **$7.50**
Campbell's Tomato Soup, mug, torches each side of logo, 'Joseph Campbell Company' on front...................**$10.00**

Campbell's Tomato Soup, 11", soup can form, plastic, 1980s, M **$10.00**

Del-Monte, clown **$22.00**

Dodge Saves, 3¼", shaped like an oil barrel, tan & red **$24.00**

Electrolux, Pay-N-Save, from 1980 Olympics, MIB **$35.00**

Eveready Batteries, black cat figural, vinyl, 1981, EX ..**$15.00**

Frigidaire, 4x2", refrigerator form, white paint on pot metal, EX **$36.00**

Kentucky Fried Chicken, 13", Colonel Sanders, EX **$15.00**

Metz Beer, barrel shape, embossed ceramic, EX **$25.00**

North American Steak Sauce, 3½x2" dia, tin can form, 1950s, M **$6.00**

Olympia Beer, can shape w/horseshoe, EX **$10.00**

RCA, 4x5", embossed logo on top, red plastic, M **$40.00**

Rival Dog Food, small, tin, VG **$12.00**

Royal Triton Union Oil, 3x2", can form, tin, 1950s, M ...**$8.00**

Southern Comfort, rifleman aiming at bottle of product, mechanical, EX **$65.00**

Calendars

Budweiser, 17", reclining woman w/embossed Art Nouveau border, 1932, EX **$50.00**

De Laval Cream Separators, 22x12", goat pulling child in a carriage, 1928, framed, EX **$175.00**

Dodge & Plymouth, Boy Scouts by Norman Rockwell, C&F Motor Sales, 1954, EX **$25.00**

Dr Pepper, 1949, NM **$55.00**

Hercules Powder, 31x13", WWI Anniversary, soldier & dog, VG **$150.00**

Kik Cola, 33x16", little girl sitting on beach ball w/glass of Kik, 1954, NM **$45.00**

Metropolitan Life Insurance, 6½x6½", 157-year perpetual, 1800-1957, celluloid revolving-wheel type, EX **$20.00**

Nehi, 29x17", portrait of a woman, includes historical events, matted & framed, 1936, EX **$185.00**

Pepsi-Cola, lady in rocker & two men, 1944, EX **$60.00**

Singer Sewing Machines, 26x22", Indian on die-cut animal skin is surrounded by calendar sheets, paper, framed, EX **$80.00**

Squirt, 16x22", tin border, 1948, NM **$28.00**

Swift & Company, 25", farmyard animals & birds, 1902, December pad only, EX $395.00

Texaco Sky Chief, paper litho, 1940, EX **$50.00**

Clocks

Bud Light Beer, 13x13", lighted, 1986, EX **$35.00**

Canada Dry, 16" sq, logo in center, plastic w/metal frame, EX **$40.00**

Friskies, winking dog, light-up, 1950s, M **$175.00**

Lucky Strike Tobacco, 14" dia, Roman numerals, RA Patterson Tobacco Company, EX **$550.00**

Mauser Mill Co, 6x4½", electric, cathedral shape, painted tin, working, EX **$48.00**

Orange Crush, 36x19", regulator, round numbered dial w/reverse-painted glass below advertised products, EX **$200.00**

Pabst Blue Ribbon Beer, 11x12", metal figural, bartender & beer bottle beside round face, electric, EX **$85.00**

Pepsi-Cola, 18" dia, plastic & metal, 1950s **$165.00**

Rival Dog Food, 'Time To Buy Rival Dog Food' in center, red, blue, & black on white, wood frame, EX **$90.00**

Star Brand Shoes, 4", round face on rectangular base, metal frame, 1920s, EX **$45.00**

7-Up, glass front, wood frame, 1950s, NM **$145.00**

Coffee Cans

Arco, 1-lb, key-wind lid, NM **$45.00**

Avon Club, 1-lb, 6x4" dia, couple on horseback & distant clubhouse on paper label, VG **$250.00**

Eagle Brand, 1-lb, 6x4" dia, eagle logo, VG.................**$55.00**
Hills Brothers, 1-lb, red, key-wind lid, 1936, VG.........**$26.00**

Jewel Private Blend, 1-lb, VG...................................$20.00
Maxwell House, 1-lb, key-wind lid, EX.......................$15.00
Oak Hill, 1-lb, coffee cup in large oval, EX.................$40.00
Old Master, 1-lb, 6x4" dia, 'B' on shield trademark, press lid, EX...**$65.00**
Royal Dutch, round, Royal Dutch logo, slip lid, EX....**$40.00**
Sanka, 1-lb, key-wind lid, EX.......................................$20.00
Savoy, 9", coat-of-arms label w/cream background, press lid, EX...**$45.00**

Displays

Adam Hats, 17", Baby Snooks, die-cut cardboard, EX ..**$30.00**
Baby Ruth Candy Bars, holder, 10x5x6", candy bar on front, EX..**$35.00**
Brownie Laundry Wax, 6x10x7", Palmer Cox Brownies on label, cardboard w/slanted glass front, VG...........**$30.00**
Campbell's, 15", girl sitting at desk w/earphones, using tape recorder, cardboard, 1988 ....$10.00
Campbell's, 22", blonde girl w/globe & pointer, cardboard, 1978, M **$10.00**
Clark's Teaberry Gum, glass pedestal dish, EX...........**$55.00**
Dr Scholl's Zino-Pads, 5x13", glass in wood & metal case w/back light, EX...**$70.00**
Gardgum Clorophyl 10¢ Gum, carton of twenty packages, soldier illustration, 1950s, EX **$17.50**
Hinds Cream, 34x59", portico w/ladies & products, cardboard trifold, EX...**$65.00**
Konjola Medicine, 34x47", bottle & cure rate chart, cardboard w/die-cut letters, EX **$150.00**
Michelin, 60", Michelin man holding up steel-belted tire, plastic figural, EX...**$800.00**
Ology Cigars, 25x37", man w/golf club, yellow lettering, die-cut easel-back, EX...**$170.00**
Pepsi-Cola, 15x17", counter-top, lettering on scroll wrapped around Pepsi bottles, die-cut, 1930s, NM...**$240.00**

Pureoxia Ginger Ale, 28x38", elephant riding in a Rolls Royce, die-cut cardboard, rare, EX.....................**$125.00**
Smith Brothers Cough Drops, 34x12", die-cut figures of the Smith Brothers, cardboard, EX..........................**$150.00**
Valley Forge Beer, boxers, plastic die-cut, EX............**$50.00**

Woodland Mills, 14x12x11", pictures man driving shoe car at Shoe Lace Service Station, G................$400.00
Wrigley's Spearmint Gum, 4x6", Wrigley man on lid, 'Perfect Gum, Flavor Lasts,' cardboard, 1930s, NM...........**$50.00**

Dolls

Alka-Seltzer, 'Speedy,' 20", cloth, 1984 Anniversary edition, VG...**$50.00**
Aunt Jemima, 'Uncle Moses,' 12", blue & white striped pants & yellow jacket, cloth, 1950, EX **$16.50**
Babbit's Cleanser, 'Babbit,' 15", composition & cloth, 1916, EX **$250.00**
Bazooka Bubble Gum, 'Bazooka Joe,' stuffed cotton, 1973, EX...**$16.00**
Blue Bonnet Margarine, 'Miss Blue Bonnet,' 10", cloth w/yarn hair, original bag, 1980s, EX.....................**$14.00**
Brach's Candy, 'Bracho Clown,' 17", cloth, VG...........**$10.00**
C&H Sugar, 'Hawaiian Girl,' 16", cloth, 1973, VG.......**$12.50**
Campbell's Soups, cheerleader, 1957, EX....................**$40.00**
Chiquita Bananas, 16", 1974, EX **$20.00**
Close-Up Toothpaste, 'Dumbo the Elephant,' 8", vinyl, 1974, EX...**$25.00**
Del Monte, 'Sweet Pea,' 9", plush, original tag, EX **$15.00**
Franklin Life Insurance Company, 'Ben Franklin,' 13", cloth, in original bag, M..**$20.00**
General Mills, 'Count Chocula,' 1975, EX....................**$20.00**
Good & Plenty, 'Choo-Choo Charlie,' 10", beanbag doll w/vinyl face & hands, EX......................................**$20.00**
Green Giant, 'Jolly Green Giant,' 16", leaf tunic & hat, cloth, 1966, EX...**$12.00**
Hardee's, 'Gilbert Giddy-Up,' 14", cloth, 1971, EX **$12.00**
Kellogg's, Alligator, 10½", stuffed fabric.....................**$45.00**
Kellogg's, 'Linda Lou,' 12", vinyl, 1962, EX **$10.00**

Mohawk Carpets, 'Tommy,' 15", cloth, Chase Bag Company, 1970s, EX...**$15.00**

Nestle, 'Little Hans the Chocolate Maker,' 13", Chase Bag Company, 1970s, VG.......................................**$60.00**

Pizza Hut, 'Pizza Pete,' EX..............................**$35.00**

Popeye Puffed Wheat, 'Popeye,' 15", cloth, 1974-76, EX...**$8.00**

Quaker Oats, 'Puffy,' 16", cloth, 1930s, EX...............**$195.00**

Starkist Tuna, 'Charlie Tuna,' 8", vinyl, EX.................**$18.00**

Match Holders

Billings-Chapin Paints, 5x4", colorful paint can, tin litho, NM...**$275.00**

Congress Beer, 5x5x3", case of Congress Beer w/logo above, tin litho, VG...............................**$185.00**

Dutch Boy Paint, 7x3x1", Dutch boy holding can, embossed die-cut tin, VG...............................**$180.00**

Gale Manufacturing Company, 5x3", colorful factory scene, tin litho, VG...............................**$140.00**

Juicy Fruit, portrait of the founder, 'The Man Juicy Fruit Made Famous,' tin litho, NM.....................**$250.00**

Lax-Ets, 5x3", open tin of Lax-Ets, tin litho, EX...........**$50.00**

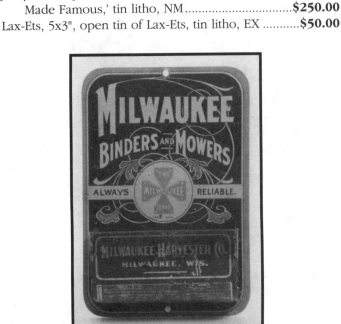

Milwaukee Binders & Mowers, 5x3", tin litho, EX.$100.00

New Process Gas Range, 3x2", silver image on red background, EX..**$125.00**

Smith Wallace Shoe Company, 5x3", blue w/red & black lettering, tin, VG...**$90.00**

Pocket Tins

Bagley's Old Colony Mixture, 5x3", portrait of a woman on both sides, slip lid, EX.......................**$75.00**

Granulated 54 Tobacco, leaf on blue & yellow, M....**$125.00**

Model Tobacco, red & silver, EX...........................**$25.00**

Regal Cube Cut Smoking Tobacco, 4x4", lions, unique rolled cover, rare, VG...............................**$125.00**

Repeater Fine Cut Tobacco, 3x4", man on a horse, rounded corners, EX.......................................**$35.00**

Smith's Dyspepsia Tablets, portrait of the founder & fancy graphics, EX...**$65.00**

Shot Glasses

Callum Shot, Havre, Montana, red-painted letters on frosted glass, 3"...**$4.00**

Carlisle Rye, clear lettering on frosted pennant design, EX...**$15.00**

Empire Rye, 'Empire Rye, Melchers' Best' etched in large letters, rare, M.......................................**$20.00**

Fox Home Liquor Store, black-painted lettering & fox, 3"...**$4.00**

Golden Spring Whiskey, etched lettering w/entwined GB monogram, EX.......................................**$16.50**

Gopher Distributing Co, 'Direct To Consumers At Wholesale, 124 E Third St, St Paul Minn,' etched in large letters, EX...**$15.00**

Hi-way Liquors, Frederick, Maryland, red-painted letters, 2½"...**$4.00**

Kentucky Tavern Straight Whiskey, 'Jas Thompson & Bro, Louisiville Ky' etched in large letters w/fancy scrolls, EX...**$16.00**

Mart Hayes Wines & Liquors, '...101 S Division St, Grand Rapids Mich' etched in sharp letters, M.................**$18.00**

Montreal Malt Rye, product name etched in large letters, bright gold rim, EX.......................................**$20.00**

Old Grand-Dad Whiskey, product name etched in thick letters, cut panels around side of base, EX..............**$20.00**

Roy's Liquor Store, Roy Winjum Prop, Fairbault, Minnesota, 2¼"...**$4.50**

Silver Hill Rye, 'T Hoffer & Co, New Albany Ind' etched in block letters & script, EX.............................**$18.00**

Trost Brothers, 'Good Cheer, Louisville Ky' etched in large letters w/fancy scrollwork, gold rim, M.................**$25.00**

Signs

Arrow Shirts, 29x23", windblown couple in a rowboat, cardboard, framed, EX.......................................**$75.00**

B-1 Soda, 14x14x6", blinking light-up type, Art Deco style, 1950s...**$35.00**

Bartels Beer, 18" dia, blue & white logo, tin, EX.........**$95.00**

Beech-Nut Chewing Tobacco, 15x11", die-cut tin figural package, bright reds & blues, 1910-20, M..........**$115.00**

Borden, 15" dia, Elsie in a daisy, cardboard, EX..........**$45.00**

Budweiser Beer, 26x15", red & gold eagle & hops, tin, 1960s...**$12.00**

Clabber Girl Baking Powder, 12x34", tin, double-sided, 1940s, NM...**$55.00**

Clayton & Russell's Ginger Cordial, 8x15", reverse-painted glass w/gold leaf lettering & filigree border, EX.**$125.00**

Cooper Tires, 14x25" oval, knight's head in armour embossed on metal, 1950s...............................**$35.00**

Crispettes Popcorn, 8x14", girl eating popcorn, cardboard, 1930s, EX...**$20.00**

Dad's Root Beer, Elizabeth Montgomery, cardboard, 1960, M...**$35.00**

Dolly Madison Ice Cream, 37x27", Dolly Madison w/several flavors of ice cream, die-cut cardboard, EX..........**$25.00**

Du Pont, 23x15", men duck hunting from a boat, paper, VG..........**$55.00**

Evinrude, 14x26", moonlit fishing scene, tin, 1930, EX..........**$390.00**

Firestone, 4x16", cream, blue, & orange, tin, EX..........**$65.00**

Ford, 24", 'Property of Ford Motor Company' on back, double-sided porcelain, EX..........**$250.00**

Funk's Hybrid Corn, 10x15", ear of corn (embossed) & large 'G' logo, tin, 1940s, EX..........**$12.00**

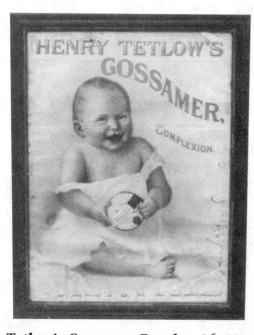

Henry Tetlow's Gossamer Powder, 26x20", paper litho, G..........$250.00

Homelite Chainsaws, 10x28", white embossed letters on red, tin, 1940s, EX..........**$15.00**

Ivory, 28x22", shelves of product & busy clerks, cardboard, VG..........**$100.00**

Johnson Outboard Motors, 27x39", green winged horse on red banner, dealer's name on attachment, tin, 1950, EX..........**$550.00**

Kist Beverages, bottle on right side, 'Get Kist Today' on left, self-framed tin, 1940s, NM..........**$75.00**

Kist 5¢ Root Beer, 14x26", girl in shorts, cardboard w/in tin frame, 1939, EX..........**$60.00**

Knox Gelatine, 21x15", woman w/box of gelatine & display of desserts, cardboard, framed, EX..........**$195.00**

Lone Star Beer, 18x14", red shield on white w/gold, tin over cardboard, 1950s, NM..........**$16.00**

Luden's Cough Drops, 7x8", open box of cough drops, die-cut tin, VG..........**$250.00**

Ma's Root Beer, 12x10", cardboard, 'Drink Old Fashion Ma's Root Beer,' 1940s, EX..........**$6.50**

Mentholatum, 19x15", girl w/injured boy, die-cut tin, EX..........**$185.00**

Milky Way, 33x20", boy astronaut, planets, & glasses of milk, 'Off For The Milky Way,' die-cut cardboard, 1950s, M..........**$90.00**

Moxie, 36" long, 'Drink Moxie' in oval, flanged, 1960s, EX..........**$250.00**

New Home Sewing Machine, 20x24", factory buildings in Orange Mass, paper over cardboard, EX..........**$50.00**

Nichol Kola, 15x15", bottle cap design, tin, EX..........**$60.00**

Pabst Brewing Company, 34x46", colonial man in library w/steins of beer, cardboard, 1936, framed, EX.....**$60.00**

Pears Soap, 10x8", children being bathed, paper, framed, EX..........**$60.00**

Pennzoil, 9x30", red arrow & 'Expert Lubrication' on white background, porcelain, 1930-40, EX..........**$165.00**

Pepsi-Cola, 48x17", bottle of Pepsi & card w/ribbon, 'More Bounce To The Ounce,' tin, 1950s, EX..........**$220.00**

Pepsi-Cola, 6x17", red & blue on white, embossed tin, 1920s, framed, NM..........**$260.00**

Pepsi-Cola, 8x12", Black girl w/bottle, celluloid & tin, oval, 1960s, EX..........**$60.00**

Pepsi-Cola, 14x14", reverse-painted glass with metal frame, 1958-63, NM..........$85.00

Pippins Cigars, 10x20", lettering & apple on blue background, embossed tin, EX..........**$95.00**

Red Man Cigars, 10x6", woman in yellow, paper litho, framed, EX..........**$40.00**

Schlitz Beer, 15x22", glass, brass back-lit frame, EX...**$150.00**

Seagram's, 11", 3-D, plastic, electric, #7 w/crown on top, 'Sure,' EX..........**$8.50**

Sherwin-Williams Paints, 30x20", man at table w/poker chips, logo on table top, paper, framed, EX.......**$260.00**

Standard Beer, 10x26", white lettering on red background, light-up w/hanging chain, EX..........**$70.00**

Standard Feeds, 11x11", tin barn shape, red, yellow & gray paint, 1940s, EX..........**$15.00**

Texaco Motor Oil, 11x21", product name & logo in corners, text on both sides, tin, 1947, NM..........**$80.00**

Union 76 Gasoline, 11½" dia, orange & blue, porcelain, 1950s, M..........**$25.00**

Wonder Bread, 12x20", large loaf of bread, embossed tin, EX..........**$95.00**

7-Up, 13x30", Pop Art w/logo under rainbow, tin, 1974, EX $28.00

7-Up, 5½x12", 'Enjoy a 7-Up Float' & large arrow, cardboard, EX..$2.50

7-Up, 8x12", swimsuit bottle & sepia picnic photo, 1950, EX...$7.50

Thermometers

B-I Soda, 17x5", red w/blue stripes, embossed tin, 1951, EX $22.50

Cobbs Creek Whiskey, 38", 1936, EX $65.00

Columbian Rope Company, 8" dia, litho face w/brass holder, EX..$25.00

Cott Ginger Ale, tin, 1940s, EX.................................$40.00

Dr Pepper, 26", bottle shape, tin, NM $150.00

Goldstein's Sons, 15x4", painted wood w/arched top, metal hanger, Metals Smelters & Refiners, EX................$30.00

Hills Brothers Coffee, man in flowered robe & turban, porcelain, round top, 1930-40, NM.....................$275.00

Mission Orange, 5x17", soda bottle on blue background, 'Real Fruit Juice, Naturally Good,' tin, EX $40.00

Moxie, man pointing, 'Drink Moxie,' tin w/rounded corners, EX $100.00

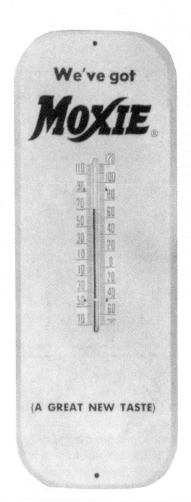

Moxie, painted tin, 1960s **$25.00**

Nesbitt's Orange, bottle cap logo & scholar, 'Don't Say Orange, Say Nesbitt's,' rounded corners, EX.........$40.00

Orange-Crush, 29", bottle figural, tin, EX...................$50.00

Pepsi-Cola, 27x7", bottle cap, 'The Light Refreshment' at bottom, tin, 1950s, EX..$35.00

Prestone Anti-Freeze, 36x9", 'You're Safe...And You Know It' at bottom, porcelain, 4-color, 1940s, NM $90.00

Red Rock Cola, 27x7", painted metal, 1939, EX..........$50.00

Sanilac Cattle Spray, 19x9", cows in pasture, wood, 1930s, EX $400.00

Wolfschmidt Vodka, round w/glass face, 1950, NM....$25.00

Tins

A&P Paprika, 3⅛x1⅝", red w/gold lettering & large logo, EX...$9.50

Ammen's Powder, baby's face on paper label, EX......$10.00

Angelus Marshmallows, 5-lb, cream, gold, green, & red, round, EX $30.00

Bat Chewing Tobacco, 7x7x3", Philly baseball logo on plug, black, red, & yellow, EX.....................................$35.00

Buick Rear Axle Lubricant, 6x4" dia, 'Buick' printed over logo, 1962, VG $35.00

Buster Brown All Spice, round, Buster & Tige on paper label, press lid, EX..$30.00

Chevron Starting Fluid, 5x4" dia, ether mix for race cars, 1954, M $8.00

Crystalized Pineapple, 3x5½x1½", VG **$38.00**

Eagle Brand Dry Cleaner, 5x3", American Shoe Polish Company, EX...$125.00

Elephant Salted Peanuts, 10-lb, 11x8" dia, logo on paper label, press lid, EX..$125.00

Girard Educators Cigars, 6x6" dia, portrait of the founder of Girard College, slip lid, EX.....................................$75.00

Golden Shell Motor Oil, 5-qt, 10x7", 'Golden Shell' on red shell w/orange highlights, 1935-45, EX $65.00

Hippo Cigars, 6x6", 'Get the Habbit,' VG $35.00

Jackie Coogan Peanuts, 7x7" dia, Jackie Coogan riding an elephant, press lid, VG $125.00

Johnsons Baby Powder, 9-oz, VG...............................$12.50

Lakritsia Licorice, children on yellow background, Halva, slip lid, EX..$35.00

Liberty Bell Salted Peanuts, 10x8" dia, Liberty Bell logo, press lid, VG..................................$65.00

Lipton Tea, 7x9", workers picking tea, EX.................$70.00

Little Warrior Band-Aids, 4x3", children in Indian costumes, 1950s, full, M.................................$10.00

Mennens Baby Powder, 4-oz, VG......................$8.00

Miller's Pretzels, little baker on both sides of large pretzel, 'Perfect Health Food,' EX.......................$25.00

Mohican Cream Cheese, 30-lb, Indian logo over cattle scene, press lid & bail, VG..............................$135.00

Nabob Baking Powder, 12-oz, cake & product name, press lid, EX.................................$15.00

National Licorice Lozenges, glass front, lettering & ornate graphics on reverse, hinged lid, EX......................$35.00

Owl Chop Teas, 9x7x5", owl logo, hinged lid, VG.....$90.00

Pansies Salted Peanuts, 10-lb, 11x8", logo on paper label, press lid, EX...........................$125.00

Phillips 66 Outboard Motor Oil, 9x3½" dia, 1940, EX..$22.00

Riley's Bunny-Bons, rabbit scenes on all sides, slip lid, EX............................$135.00

Royal Baking Powder, 12-oz, 1938, EX.................$15.00

Squirrel Peanut Butter, 7x5", logo & ornate graphics, press lid, VG.............................$125.00

Stapels Prepared Wax, 3" dia, pictures a beehive, EX...$8.50

Tortoise Shell Tobacco, rectangular w/rounded corners, embossed turtle & lettering on tortoise shell background, EX.............................$50.00

Venus Pencils, 7x2x1", Venus & pencil, VG.............$12.00

Tip Trays

American Brewing Company, 4" dia, Indian princess seal for Liberty Beer, NM..................................$140.00

Bartholomay's Tam O' Shanter Ale, 4" dia, Scotsman holding a glass of beer, EX..............................$80.00

Best Electric Iron, 4", EX $58.00

Crescent Mapleine, 4½", VG......................$45.00

Dotterweich Brewing Company, 4" dia, glass & bottle, 'Beer, Ales, & Porter' on rim, rare, VG.................$55.00

Dr Pepper, 3", Black child eating watermelon, EX....$275.00

Germania Brewing Company, 4" dia, little girl w/roses in her hair, 'Chammer's High Grade Bottled Beer,' M.................................$225.00

King's Puremalt, 6x4", waitress w/tray & bottle, Panama Pacific International Expo Medal at bottom, oval, 1915, EX.................................$40.00

Merit Separator Company, cream separator & lettering, embossed tin, fluted edges, EX.....................$175.00

Pepsi-Cola, 6x4", decorative border, Charles Shonk litho, 1908, EX $325.00

Pilsener Brewing Co, 4" dia, bottle & glass, 'Cleveland Ohio,' NM.................................$45.00

Popel-Giller Company, 4" dia, girl holding roses & sipping beer, NM.................................$125.00

Rockford Watches, girl sitting in front of a tree, ornate border, die-cut, EX.................................$40.00

Schlitz Beer, 4" dia, logo & lettering, EX.................$55.00

Stegmaier Brewing Company, 4" dia, factory scene, 'Wilkes Barre Pa' on rim, EX.................................$85.00

Trade Cards

A&P, 8x7", Ben Franklin drinking tea, EX.................$25.00

Bay State Fertilizer, potato man facing right, M.............$8.00

Borden's Milk, girl drinking a glass of milk w/pug dog at her feet, NM.................................$8.50

Clark's Spool Cotton, two boys flying a kite, NM.........$4.50

General Electric, blue-tinted irons w/astronomical background, EX $12.00

Home Insurance Company, girl standing by tree, NM..$6.50

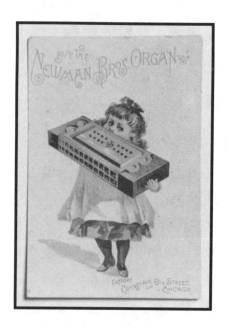

Newman Bros Organs, 4¾x3⅛", little girl w/large harmonica.................................$6.00

Prudential Life Insurance, salesman at door, NM..........$8.00

Quaker Bread, Santa in window & children reading, NM $12.00

Soapine, 5", whale w/sailor, die-cut, NM.....................$7.50

Tulip Soap, two girls playing in the sand, NM..............$5.50

Waring Aluron Irons, hand using product, EX............$18.00

Trays

Bartels Beer, 13" dia, early diamond logo, deep-dish style, VG.................$175.00

Dr Pepper, 10½x13½", EX.................$125.00

Ebling's Beer & Ale, 13" dia, woman holding glass of beer, deep-dish, 1934, VG.................$45.00

Frank's Fruits & Beverages, branch of cherries in center, lettering on rim, EX.................$15.00

Haberle's, 12" dia, eagle logo & list of products, deep-dish, 1950s, NM.................$20.00

Narragansett Ale, 13" dia, 'Narragansett' diagonally in center, decorative rim, EX.................$25.00

Premier Beer, 10x13", still life w/lobster & beer, EX...$40.00

Yellowstone Whiskey, 13x11", bottle & waterfall, VG.$65.00

Miscellaneous

A&W Root Beer, mug, 4", glass, EX.................$4.50

Airway 88, tie tack, metal, 1950s.................$1.50

Alka-Selzer, booklet, 'Know Your Presidents,' undated (1940s), VG.................$3.00

Arm & Hammer, leaflet, 'A Friend In Need,' blue cover, 28 pages, 1933, EX.................$4.50

Arm & Hammer, match safe, gutta percha, EX.................$60.00

Bell Roasted Coffee, pocket mirror, 2" dia, EX.................$20.00

Betty Crocker, insert, 'Collector's Casseroles, Oven Casserole Recipes From Hamburger Helper,' 8 pages, 1970s, EX.................$4.50

Black Cat Polish & Cake Club, bill hook, 2" dia, celluloid & tin, 1940s.................$3.50

Bond Bread, blotter, shows portable TV, 1939, EX.....$12.00

Borden, booklet, 'Bouillon Is Basic,' 32 pages, 1978, EX.................$3.50

Boston Belting Company, paperweight, 3", glass, EX.$10.50

Breyers, ashtray, 90th Anniversary, 1866-1956, EX.....$20.00

Campbell's, spoon, silverplate w/boy or girl figural handle, 1968, pr.................$25.00

Campbell's, thermal mug, boy's face on one side, girl on the other, NM.................$5.00

Campbell's Soup, bowl, 'M'm M'm M'm Good' in red lettering on white, Correlle, 1981 premium.................$8.50

Campbell's Soup, mug, Corning, late 1980s, M in box..$6.00

Campbell's Soup, placemat, girl & boy stirring soup, rectangular.................$6.00

Campbell's Tomato Soup, refrigerator magnet, soup can shape, 1989, M in wrapper.................$3.50

Campbells, booklet, 20-page, 'Light Eating Menu Planner,' 1979, M.................$5.50

Canada Dry, bottle opener, 3¼" long, steel, flat metal cap lifter.................$3.00

Canadian Club, whiskey pitcher, ceramic, EX.................$10.00

Carhartt, window decal, 6x9", red, white, & blue w/heart-shaped background, 'From Mill To Millions,' NM...$7.50

Carson Pirie Scott, shoe horn, NM.................$10.00

Castle Steel Distributors, playing cards, white & orange w/black castle logo, complete.................$7.50

Chesterfield Cigarettes, bridge pad, cameo lady backs, 1950s, NM.................$15.00

Clark's ONT Spool Cotton, thimble, logo over scene of girl hanging clothes on line, gold bands, Franklin USA, EX.................$16.00

Clark's Spool Cotton, cabinet, 8x22x16", oak w/two lettered glass drawer inserts, VG.................$225.00

Clark's Teaberry Gum, ruler, ca 1937, EX.................$4.00

Cliquot Club, bottle opener, 3¼" long, flattened wire type, minor rust.................$5.00

Deca Vitamins, tape measure, blue & white on celluloid, retractable, 1951, VG.................$12.50

Diamond Brand Children's Shoes, whirligig, colorful airplane, cardboard & wood, 1950s, EX.................$15.00

Domino Sugar, box, Domino logo on inside of lid, blue metal, hinged lid & clasp, EX.................$15.00

Dr Pepper, fan, 6-pack, green & red, EX.................$60.00

Du Pont Sporting Powder, envelope, 4x7", colorful bird on a railing, VG.................$40.00

Duncan Yo-Yo, 29¢, on original card, M.................$8.00

Duffy's Pure Malt, mirror, 2", chemist testing product, celluloid, EX.................$15.00

Eagle Lock Company, cabinet, 20x16x12", wood & glass w/three shelves, ca 1920s, EX.................$140.00

ER Heller Milling Co, flour sack, 20x10", rooster pulling child in a wagon, paper, EX.................$20.00

Ethyl Gasoline, pump sign, Anti Knock Compound logo, 1940, VG.................$45.00

Ex-Lax, sample tin, M.................$15.00

Fab, tape measure.................$25.00

Firestone, ashtray, tire shape w/glass insert, EX.........$15.00

Ford, puppet, Ford logo, straw hat, 1975, EX.................$16.00

Ford Motor Co, blotter, 6x3", 'Ford Trucks Last Longer,' color, unused, M.................$5.00

Frisch's Big Boy, ashtray, 3" dia, Frisch's boy holding up a hamburger, glass.................$30.00

Frosty Treat Ice Cream, waxed cup, ½-pt, ice skaters on lid, 1950s, M..**$1.00**

General Electric, ashtray, embossed flourescent bulb w/platinum ends on white ceramic, M **$50.00**

Gerber, spoon, 6", 'Gerber 50 Years of Caring,' stainless steel, EX..**$16.00**

Gold Dust Washing Powder, shipping box, 12x19x14", multiple images of the Gold Dust twins, VG **$110.00**

Goodrich Tires, ashtray, tire shape, EX....................**$13.50**

Harley-Davidson Motorcycles, wine cooler bottle, 8", old motorcycle shown, 1980s **$6.50**

Heinz Pickles, lapel pin, 1" miniature pickle w/pin-back, 1940s **$2.00**

Heinz Tomato Juice, glass tumbler, 5", white fired on clear **$18.00**

Hershey's, chocolate mold, four rows of candy bars, tin, EX **$180.00**

Hires Root Beer, belt buckle, 'Drink Hires Root Beer,' EX.**$5.50**

Hoover Boulder Dam, tape measure, 2" dia, photo litho of dam, celluloid, EX..**$18.00**

Illinois Herb Co, almanac, 1941, EX **$12.50**

Independent Stove Company, paperweight, elephant figural, cast iron w/embossed lettering, EX **$45.00**

Jack Daniels Whiskey, key chain, 3", plastic man figural, 1950..**$2.50**

John Deere, tape measure, celluloid, EX....................**$14.00**

Kikkoman Soy Sauce, fan, bamboo stick, 1940s, EX...**$15.00**

Kool Aid, canteen, plastic, M **$10.00**

Log Cabin Syrup, container, 2x2" dia, plastic wigwam, yellow lettering, 1950s, rare **$6.50**

Lucky Strike, pocket mirror, 2" dia, cowboy standing beside window sign, 1920s, EX..**$25.00**

Marksman Cigars, box, 3x5x1", men shooting guns, cardboard, VG **$25.00**

Milky Way, candy box, 1941..**$15.00**

Minute Maid, monkey mask, w/original envelope **$16.00**

Modox, soda glass, 5x5x3", Indian head, embossed 'Drink Modox,' NM..**$55.00**

Morton Salt, pencil clip, celluloid, EX......................**$7.50**

Morton Salt, pocket mirror, 4" dia, EX......................**$25.00**

Moxie, fan, girl in a bonnet, EX................................**$25.00**

Moxie, mug, 3" dia, girl transfer in center, china, flared foot, EX **$120.00**

Mr Delish, popcorn box, bellhop pictured, 1950s **$1.50**

NuGrape, menu board, 'NuGrape' & bottle above board, rounded corners, EX..**$45.00**

Old Grand-Dad Whiskey, ink blotter, 6x3", whiskey bottles & product name, M..**$12.50**

Orange Crush, paperweight, 3x4", bottle & lettering, 'Orange-Crush, Lemon-Crush, Lime-Crush,' glass, NM **$150.00**

Orange Crush, patch, cloth, M **$6.50**

Pearl Bear, post card, 'What Me Worry?,' color, 1951, unused **$15.00**

Pepsi-Cola, coaster, 4" dia, 'Pour Your Own...The Perfect Mixer,' 1940s, EX..**$6.50**

Pepsi-Cola, lighter, bottle shape, metal, 1950s, EX......**$35.00**

Pepsi-Cola, pencil, mechanical, 1950s, EX..................**$50.00**

Pepsi-Cola, pin, 'Drink Pepsi-Cola, Delicious, Healthful,' marked Pepsi-Cola Co, New York **$13.50**

Pepsi-Cola, push bar, 3x30", bottle cap logos, 'Have A Pepsi' in center, 1950s, EX..**$75.00**

Pet Milk, can opener..**$10.00**

Pillsbury Flour, bin, pictures Dough Boy, 1960s **$10.00**

Post Grape Nut Flakes, flip movie book, 1½x2½", 1949, EX **$15.00**

Q-Tips, playing cards, in original box........................**$15.00**

Rakestraw's Dairy Products, bottle seal opener, 4½", heavy wire **$5.00**

Ralston Purina, ashtray, 6" dia, shaped like a dog's feeding bowl w/logo on white background, ceramic, EX.**$40.00**

Red Goose Shoes, clicker, yellow w/Red Goose logo, 1950s, M **$12.50**

Red Goose Shoes, shoe horn, metal, EX......................**$12.00**

Remington Kleanbore, banner, 50x56", game hunter shooting a lion, 'Come On In & Shoot,' canvas, VG **$75.00**

Reynolds Wrap, pamphlet, 'New Holiday Know How For Use With Reynolds Wrap,' 16-page, Acme Markets, 1967, EX **$7.50**

Robin Hood Flour, statue, 1930s, M **$20.00**

Sambo's Restaurant, coaster, Bicentennial, EX..............**$4.50**

Sambos Restaurant, token, 1½" dia, 'Free Coffee,' multicolor paint on wood **$2.00**

Schlitz Beer, coaster, 3½", lady on globe, metal, 1960s, M **$2.50**

Schmidt's Meats, ashtray, oval, EX................................**$8.00**

Schweppes Ginger Ale, push bar, 3x30", black, gold, & white on green, porcelain, NM **$55.00**

Seagram's, booklet, 'Fun At Cocktail Time,' 1934, EX.**$12.00**

Sears & Roebuck, booklet, 'Century of Progress,' pop-up, 1933, EX **$12.00**

Shell, radio, miniature, gas pump figural **$40.00**

Shredded Whole Wheat, crate, 21x33x17", wood w/cardboard inserts, EX..**$25.00**

Snow White Flour, sack, 8x14", color picture of Snow White, 1940s, NM **$2.50**

Squirt, chalkboard, 28x20", boy & bottle at top, painted tin w/embossed letters, 1959, EX **$25.00**

Squirt, duffle bag, inflatable, M....................................**$15.00**

Starkist Tuna, wristwatch, Charlie Tuna, 1971, M......**$125.00**

Sweet Cuba Chewing Tobacco, store bin, 12x18x14", yellow w/red & black lettering, slant top, VG **$175.00**

Ted's Root Beer, pocket mirror, baseball player & bottle, EX...**$15.00**

Tip Top Bread, fan, 1950, EX **$6.50**

Victory Candies, bucket, 7x7" dia, wood w/Statue of Liberty on paper label, VG **$16.00**

Welch's, decal, 12", grape wreath, EX **$12.00**

Westinghouse, salt & pepper shakers, washer & dryer figurals, pr..**$20.00**

Winchester, potato sack, 36x22", 100-lb, burlap, 3-color overprint of Conestoga wagon w/Winchester rifle, EX **$12.50**

Winchester Arms, envelope, illustrated, NM **$45.00**

Winston Cigarettes, ashtray, embossed tin **$8.50**

Wurlitzer Juke Box, coaster, 4½" dia, Johnny One Note, 1940s, M...**$2.00**

Zoom, paper airplane, Zoom Girl, original package ..$6.00

7-Up, inflatable can, 1970s, EX **$25.00**

Airline Memorabilia

Items from commercial airlines such as dinnerware, flatware, playing cards, and pins and buttons worn by the flight crew represent a relatively new field of collector interest. Anything from before WWII is rare and commands a high price. Advertising material such as signs, models of airplanes from travel agencies, and timetables are included in this area of collecting as well.

Air Atlanta, coffee mug, china, name & logo on side....**$6.50**

Air Rhodesia, route map, 1960s **$5.50**

Continental, Junior Pilot wings, metal, gold w/center decal, 1966 ....**$16.00**

Delta, 'Welcome Aboard' packet, contains information & DC 9-32 emergency card, 1969................................**$5.50**

Delta, coffee mug, china, 'Delta Air Lines' in script ...**$4.00**

Delta, hat badge, gold w/blue & white enamel, ca 1929-53 ....**$100.00**

Eastern, emergency card, plastic, DC-9-31, Mar 1976....**$5.00**

Lufthansa, flight map, Europe to North America, early 1960s **$4.00**

North Central, cocktail list, plastic, March 1972 ....**$5.00**

Pan American, Junior Clipper pilot wings, metal, gold & blue **$6.50**

Pan American, Junior Flyer wings, plastic, gold & blue ..**$5.50**

Pan American, playing cards, white logo on blue background, NM **$7.00**

Piedmont, route map & bar menu, plastic envelope, 1970s...**$4.50**

Presidential, flight attendant wings, gold w/blue enamel **$28.00**

South African Airways, stationery, plastic folder............**$8.00**

Southern, shot glass, 10th Anniversary, gold, 1959 .....**$30.00**

TWA, coach menu, Transcontinental, 1970s **$3.50**

TWA, playing cards, Lockheed 1049G, 1955, complete deck, M $15.00

United, air atlas, DC-8 pictured on cover, September 1964 ....**$5.00**

United, emergency card, plastic, DC-8, August 1973.....**$6.00**

United Airlines, playing cards, 'Fly the Friendly Skies of United' on blue background, NM **$6.00**

Western, Junior Pilot wings, plastic, red & gold, 1950s.**$8.00**

Akro Agate

Everybody remembers the 'Aggie' marbles from their childhood; this is the company that made them. They operated in West Virginia from 1914 until 1951, and in addition to their famous marbles they made children's dishes as well as many types of novelties — flowerpots, powder jars with scotty dogs on top, candlesticks, and ashtrays, for instance

— in many colors and patterns. Though some of their glassware was made in solid colors, their most popular products were made of the same swirled colors as their marbles. Nearly everything they made is marked with their logo: a crow flying through the letter 'A' holding an Aggie in its beak and one in each claw. Some children's dishes may be marked 'JP,' and the novelty items may instead carry one of these trademarks: 'JV Co, Inc,' 'Braun & Corwin,' 'NYC Vogue Merc Co USA,' 'Hamilton Match Co,' and 'Mexicali Pickwick Cosmetic Corp.'

In the children's dinnerware listings below, you'll find values for 'Concentric Ring (Rib).' Concentric Rib is a line that varies only slightly from Concentric Ring, and prices are the same for both.

For further study we recommend *The Collector's Encyclopedia of Akro Agate Glassware* by Gene Florence.

Children's Dishes

Chiquita, creamer, 1½", opaque green $5.00
Chiquita, cup, 1½", transparent cobalt........................$12.00
Chiquita, plate, 3¾", baked-on colors.........................$6.00
Chiquita, saucer, 3⅛", opaque green $2.00
Chiquita, teapot, 2¾", transparent cobalt, w/lid..........$20.00
Chiquita, 16-pc set in original box, opaque green $67.50
Concentric Ring (Rib), cereal, 3⅜", all colors...............$22.50
Concentric Ring (Rib), creamer, 1¼", green or white $7.50
Concentric Ring (Rib), cup, 1¼", lavender $30.00

Concentric Ring (Rib), cup, 1¼", pumpkin............$15.00
Concentric Ring (Rib), plate, 3¼", blue (illustrated) .$6.00
Concentric Ring (Rib), saucer, yellow (illustrated)..$4.50
Concentric Ring (Rib), plate, 3¼", turquoise $6.00
Concentric Ring (Rib), teapot, 2⅞", all colors, w/lid ...$40.00
Concentric Ring (Rib), 21-pc large set in original box, all colors $365.00
Interior Panel, cereal, 3⅜", lemonade & oxblood........$30.00

Interior Panel, cereal, 3⅜", solid colors.....................$22.50
Interior Panel, creamer, 1¼", cobalt or pumpkin.........$25.00
Interior Panel, creamer, 1⅜", lemonade & oxblood $35.00
Interior Panel, cup, 1¼", solid colors..........................$18.00
Interior Panel, plate, 3¼", solid colors.........................$7.50
Interior Panel, plate, 4¼", lemonade & oxblood..........$20.00
Interior Panel, saucer, 3⅛", lemonade & oxblood.......$12.50
Interior Panel, sugar, 1⅜", lemonade & oxblood, w/lid..$55.00
Interior Panel, sugar bowl, 1¼", cobalt or pumpkin, no lid..$25.00
Interior Panel, sugar bowl, 1⅜", cobalt or pumpkin, w/lid..$40.00
Interior Panel, teapot, 2⅝", solid colors, cobalt, or pumpkin, w/lid...$40.00
Interior Panel, 21-pc set, original box, solid colors...$335.00
J Pressman, cereal, 3⅛", baked-on colors......................$8.00
J Pressman, creamer, 1½", transparent blue...............$35.00
J Pressman, plate, 4¼", transparent brown or green ...$12.00
J Pressman, saucer, 3¼", baked-on colors....................$5.00
J Pressman, teapot, 2¾", transparent blue...................$65.00
J Pressman, 16-pc set in original box, transparent brown or green..$300.00
Marbleized (any pattern), cereal bowl, 3⅜", oxblood & white..$27.50
Marbleized (any pattern), creamer, 1¼", blue & white..$35.00
Marbleized (any pattern), cup, 1¼", oxblood & white ..$32.50
Marbleized (any pattern), plate, 3¼", green & white...$12.50
Marbleized (any pattern), saucer, 2⅜", blue & white ..$12.00
Marbleized (any pattern), sugar bowl, 1⅜", green & white or oxblood & white, w/lid...$40.00
Marbleized (any pattern), teapot w/lid, 2⅝", green & white..$45.00
Marbleized (any pattern), 21-pc large set in original box, blue & white $515.00
Miss America, creamer, large, orange & white............$75.00
Miss America, cup, large, decaled..............................$45.00
Miss America, plate, large, white $20.00
Miss America, saucer, large, green.............................$25.00
Miss America, sugar bowl, large, orange & white, w/lid..$110.00
Miss America, teapot, large, decaled, w/lid $135.00
Miss America, 17-pc large set in original box, white.$475.00
Octagonal, cereal bowl, 3⅜", all colors, closed or open handle...$11.00
Octagonal, cereal, 3⅜", lemonade & oxblood $25.00
Octagonal, creamer, 1½", lemonade & oxblood..........$30.00
Octagonal, creamer, 1¼", all colors, open handle.......$17.50
Octagonal, cup, 1½", all colors, open handle $15.00
Octagonal, cup, 1¼", all colors, closed handle...........$25.00
Octagonal, pitcher, 2⅞", all colors, open handle.........$20.00
Octagonal, plate, 3⅜", all colors, closed handle $7.00
Octagonal, plate, 4¼", all colors.....................................$7.00
Octagonal, sugar bowl, 1¼", all colors, no lid, open handles $17.50
Octagonal, sugar bowl, 1½", all colors, open handles .$27.50
Octagonal, sugar bowl, 1½", lemonade & oxblood, no lid..$35.00
Octagonal, teapot, 2⅜", all colors, lid, open handle....$17.50

Octagonal, teapot, 2⅝", lemonade & oxblood, w/lid, closed handle **$67.50**
Octagonal, tumbler, 2", all colors..................................**$12.00**
Octagonal, 21-pc large set in original box, all colors, open handles **$245.00**
Raised Daisy, creamer, 1⅛", opaque solid colors **$80.00**
Raised Daisy, cup, 1⅛", opaque solid colors **$35.00**
Raised Daisy, plate, 3", opaque solid colors **$15.00**
Raised Daisy, saucer, 2½", opaque solid colors...........**$10.00**
Raised Daisy, sugar bowl, 1⅛", opaque solid colors ...**$80.00**
Raised Daisy, tumbler, 2", opaque solid colors............**$25.00**
Raised Daisy, 13-pc set in original box, opaque solid colors **$235.00**
Stacked Disc, creamer, 1¼", pink.................................**$20.00**
Stacked Disc, cup, 1¼", yellow **$45.00**
Stacked Disc, pitcher, 2⅞", solid green or white **$10.00**
Stacked Disc, plate, 3¼", opaque solid colors..............**$5.00**
Stacked Disc, sugar bowl, 1¼", no lid, pink **$20.00**

Stacked Disc, teapot, 3⅜", cobalt w/custard lid $32.50
Stacked Disc, tumbler, 2", solid green or solid white **$4.50**
Stacked Disc, 8-pc set in original box, solid opaque colors **$55.00**

Other Lines of Production

Apothecary jar, black, embossed w/JV Co Inc.............**$50.00**
Ashtray, Goodrich tire **$35.00**
Ashtray, 4", marbleized, embossed 'Akro Agate Ware' **$65.00**
Ashtray, marbleized, leaf shape **$4.50**
Ashtray, marbleized, shell shape...................................**$4.00**
Ashtray, Victory, 8-pointed star shape.......................**$200.00**
Ashtray, 5¼" sq, black **$60.00**
Basket, marbleized, one high arched handle............**$250.00**
Bell, 5¼", pumpkin (color)...**$100.00**
Bowl, small solid colors, embossed ivy.........................**$7.50**
Bowl, 5¼", Stacked Disc, solid colors **$25.00**

Bowl, 6", solid colors, 3-footed...................................**$18.00**
Candlestick, 3¼", marbleized, pr **$150.00**
Cup & saucer, demitasse; blue & white marbleized....**$15.00**
Cup & saucer, demitasse; marbleized.........................**$12.50**
Cup & saucer, demitasse; solid green...........................**$5.00**
Finger bowl, marbleized...**$10.00**
Flowerpot, 2½", Banded Dart, solid colors **$15.00**
Flowerpot, 3", Ribs & Flutes, cobalt or pumpkin, scalloped top...**$7.50**
Flowerpot, 3", Ribs & Flutes, marbleized, smooth top ..**$5.00**
Flowerpot, 4", Stacked Disk, marbleized.......................**$7.50**
Flowerpot, 5½", Ribs & Flutes, solid colors, scalloped top **$15.00**
Lamp, opaque blue, pineapple molded body...........**$100.00**
Planter, 11½x7", solid colors, 8-sided w/even numbers of darts in relief **$100.00**
Planter, 6", solid colors, oval.......................................**$3.50**
Planter, 8" rectangular, factory decorated...................**$35.00**
Planter, 8" rounded rectangle form, pumpkin (color), high scalloped top...**$25.00**
Powder jar, marbleized, apple shape **$275.00**
Powder jar, marbleized, embossed ivy leaves, w/lid...**$50.00**
Powder jar, marbleized, embossed Mexican, Mexicali, w/hat-form lid **$30.00**
Powder jar, marbleized, ribbed, w/lid.......................**$27.50**
Puff box, Colonial Lady, 1939-1942, lime green...........**$225.00**
Puff box, Scotty dog on lid, 1939-1942, transparent colors..**$325.00**
Shaving mug, blue, mortar & pestle shape, embossed w/JV Co Inc **$25.00**
Urn, 3¼", marbleized, square footed **$10.00**
Vase, 3¼", marbleized, cornucopia style **$8.00**
Vase, 3¼", marbleized, hand shape **$15.00**
Vase, 6¼", marbleized, scalloped top..........................**$60.00**
Vase, 6¼", solid colors, smooth top.............................**$65.00**
Vase, 8", Ribs & Flutes, cobalt or pumpkin...............**$125.00**
Vase, 8¾", cobalt or pumpkin, seven embossed darts ..**$60.00**
Vase, 8¾", solid colors, seven embossed darts...........**$30.00**

Aluminum

This is an exciting, relatively new field of collecting, and your yard sale outings will often yield some nice examples at very little expense. You'll find all types of serving pieces and kitchenware, most of which will be embossed with fruit or flowers. Some will have a hand-hammered texture; these pieces are generally thought to be from the fifties, though aluminum ware was popular from the late 1930s on. The best buys are those with a backstamp; a good one to watch for is Wendell August Forge. Russel Wright and Royal Hickman were two highly renowned designers of dinnerware and ceramics that used this medium for some of their work; items signed by either are very collectible.

Ashtray, 6½" dia, six incised flowers, Buenilum **$5.00**

Bowl, 11½x9", chrysanthemums, Continental, w/lid, EX $20.00

Bowl, 7½" dia, pine cone design, shallow w/fluted edges, Wendell August Forge $25.00

Bread tray, 11" oval, bamboo pattern w/bamboo handles, Everlast $20.00

Buffet server, holds 1½-qt baking dish, hammered lid w/floral knob, server has floral handles, Rodney Kent.$28.00

Cake saver, 12", embossed rose & leaf design, World Hand Forged...$7.50

Candlesticks, 7⅝", acanthus leaf base, Continental, pr...$23.50

Celery tray, 18", ruffled rim, twisted handle.................$12.50

Coasters & caddy, coasters have tulip design, caddy handle w/simple floral design, unmarked, set of eight $20.00

Coffee urn, Buenilum, w/stand & warmer...................$58.00

Console set, bowl & pair of short candlesticks; tulip design, Farberware...$15.00

Goblet, water; hammered design, flared top, no mark ..$8.00

Ice bucket, 8", heavily hammered, double walled w/rubber seal, handles & knob on lid, Canterbury Arts $50.00

Pitcher, water size, heavy strap handle, Everlast.........$20.00

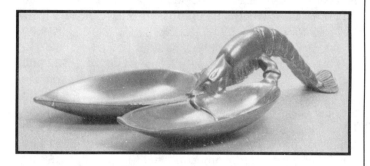

Relish tray, lobster form, signed by Royal Hickman for Bruce Cox..**$40.00**

Silent butler, 6½" dia, hammered w/incised flowers, twisted handle, Buenilum Hand Wrought.........................$20.00

Sugar bowl & creamer, hammered design, sugar bowl w/lid & handles, Everlast $18.00

Tidbit tray, 6" dia, dogwood pattern w/fluted edges & hammered looped handle, Designed Aluminum $8.00

Tray, 14x9", flying geese & cattails, Wendell August Forge $17.50

Tray, 25½x13½", pine cones, Everlast $30.00

Vase, 12", dogwood & butterfly pattern, weighted hammered base w/slightly flared top, Arthur Armour.$90.00

Animal Dishes

Glass dishes with animal and bird figures on the lids are a common sight at flea markets today, but you'll need to study the subject thoroughly to be able to tell the old ones from the new. Many were made in the late 1800s and the early years of this century. Some of the smaller ones were sold to food processors who filled them with products such as mustard or baking powder. Several companies have recently made reproductions. In the 1960s, Kemple made a cat, duck, dove, fox, hen, lamb, lion, rabbit, rooster, and turkey; Westmoreland was making some in the 1980s, and some you'll see were made yesterday! Beware. *Covered Animal Dishes* by Everett Grist will help you in your study.

Bird on round basket, milk glass, Vallerysthal.............$85.00
Boar's head, 9½", milk glass, Atterbury.....................$975.00
Camel, 6¼", resting, blue opaque, Westmoreland.....$155.00
Cat, 5½", milk glass, unmarked McKee $175.00
Cat on lacy base, milk glass, Westmoreland $95.00
Cow, 5½", milk glass, two McKee marks $1,050.00
Deer on fallen tree base, milk glass, Flaccus.............$250.00
Dog, 5½", recumbent, milk glass, marked McKee.....$350.00
Duck, 11", milk glass w/amethyst head, Atterbury....$500.00
Duck on cattail base, 5½", milk glass, unmarked $85.00
Egg on sleigh, 5½", milk glass, Westmoreland $65.00
Elephant, 5½", milk glass, unmarked McKee.........$1,300.00
Entwined fish, 6" dia, milk glass, on lacy base, Atterbury...$165.00
Fish, large, milk glass, Challinor, Taylor, & Company ..$185.00
Fox, 6¼", milk glass, lacy base, Atterbury, dated $150.00
Frog, milk glass, unmarked McKee $550.00
Frog, 5½", milk glass, one McKee mark $650.00
Hand & dove, dated $110.00
Hen, 6", clear, straight head, Indiana Glass $10.00
Hen on basketweave, blue, Westmoreland..................$85.00
Hen on basketweave, 2", Vallerysthal $35.00
Hen on cattails, 5½", milk glass $65.00
Hen on lacy base, milk glass w/amethyst head, Atterbury...$295.00
Hen w/chicks, 5½", milk glass, two McKee marks....$365.00
Horse, 5½", milk glass, two McKee marks $250.00
Irish Setter on square base, green, attributed to Flaccus $195.00
Lamb, 5½", milk glass, two Mckee marks $225.00

Lion, 6", amber, marked 'IG' (Indiana Glass) inside head, patent dated August 6, 1889..................$95.00

Lion on picket base, blue, Westmoreland....................$85.00
Lion on square scroll base, 5½", milk glass.................$65.00
Mother eagle, milk glass, Challinor, Taylor, & Company $295.00
Mother eagle, milk glass, Westmoreland, WG mark....$75.00
Mule-eared rabbit, picket base, blue, Westmoreland ..$85.00
Owl head, 5½", milk glass, marked McKee...............$875.00
Pig, 5½", milk glass, two McKee marks..................$1,200.00
Pintail duck, 5½", milk glass, Westmoreland...............$55.00
Quail on scroll base, milk glass $65.00
Rabbit, milk glass, marked Vallerysthal.....................$135.00
Rabbit, 5½", milk glass, two McKee marks $350.00
Rabbit on egg, small, Vallerysthal............................$225.00
Rat on egg, pink, Vallerysthal $175.00
Rooster on basketweave, 8", milk glass, Challinor, Taylor, & Company $135.00
Snail on strawberry, 5¼", milk glass, Vallerysthal........$85.00
Squirrel, 5½", milk glass, unmarked McKee...............$145.00

Swan, basketweave base, amber $165.00
Swan, 5½", milk glass, head down, marked McKee.....$335.00
Swan, 5½", milk glass, head down, unmarked McKee ..$185.00
Turkey, clear & frosted, Cambridge............................$55.00
Turtle, large, amber $125.00

Art Deco Collectibles

During the period from about 1925 until 1950, popular taste and fashions favored architecture, home furnishings and decorations, jewelry, appliances, and even automobiles with sleek aerodynamic lines, cubist forms, or sweeping curves. Lightning bolts, slender nudes, sleek grayhounds, and geometrics were prefered decorative motifs. Chrome, vinyl, and plastic were high style, though at the other end of the spectrum, lush fabrics and exotic woods were used as well. When Art Deco furnishings began showing up in some of our leading home decorating magazines a few years back, collector demand for authentic pieces started to increase. Many moderately priced items are around today,

but signed pieces often carry high-dollar price tags.

For further study we recommend *The Collector's Guide to Art Deco* by Mary Frank Gaston.

See also Chase.

Ashtray, floor; 24", cast metal, nude standing on ball w/square base, her arms reaching up to support tray, Frankart $700.00
Ashtray, 5" dia, round blue glass tray w/chrome sailboat, FD Company, American $60.00
Belt buckle, enameled crescents in shades of green between bands of gold trim, gold clasp, German...............$20.00
Bookends, 7", metal w/brass finish, Scottie dogs sitting on hind legs on 2-tiered square bases, Frankart, pr.$245.00
Bracelet, enameled black & green elongated diamond shapes connected w/sterling silver, ca 1920s........$85.00
Candle holders, 5½", frosted blue glass, sailboat form, pr $55.00

Centerpiece, 9½", brass, abstract figures in dancing pose support bowl, 1930s, no mark..............$250.00
Cheese dish, 14" dia, chrome, round banded plate w/dome lid & black ribbed knob, Chase $115.00
Cigarette dispenser, 4½", wedge-shaped burled maple wood, top of wedge slides up to display cigarettes $170.00
Cigarette holder, 9", Bakelite.....................................$24.00
Clock, digital; 19" long, bronze, clock case w/rounded corners sits on long flat base, ca mid-1930s, Silvercrest.....$225.00
Clock, mantel or shelf; ebony-trimmed walnut case w/Roman numerals, hinged chrome-trimmed glass front, British $200.00
Clock, mantel or shelf; 11½x10", gold-painted dog resting on top of green ceramic chrome-trimmed base, unmarked $125.00
Clock, mantel; 8¼x14½", mahogany & walnut footed case w/inlaid numbers & black trim, German $450.00

Cocktail, 6½" clear glass bowl & base w/black glass nude figure stem, Cambridge Glass Company, Ohio...**$140.00**

Cocktail shaker, 12", chrome, etched border of stylized grapes & leaves on body, cork-lined spout cover, unmarked **$50.00**

Compact, yellow & black enameled rectangle w/Egyptian design, French..............**$125.00**

Compote, 3x6½" dia, porcelain, orange, black, & white abstract designs on gold lustre background, Noritake..............**$75.00**

Evening bag, deep orange enameled mesh w/black chain strap, ca early 1920s, Whiting & Davis, New York **$85.00**

Figurine, 10", pot metal & ivorene female figure in Spanish attire posed on marble base..............**$225.00**

Figurine, 9½", ceramic, pair of spotted leopards on oval base, early 1920s, Hutschenreuther, German......**$750.00**

Flatware, stainless steel w/red Bakelite handles, 4-pc setting..............**$25.00**

Flower frog, 7", dancing nude, ceramic, German........**$55.00**

Jewel box, Limoges porcelain, elongated octagonal shape w/green & gold abstract floral design, French....**$225.00**

Magazine rack, 15½x11", bronze w/silver finish, nude & greyhound in frolicking pose against circular design **$800.00**

Necklace, black beads set between orange & clear plastic cubes..............**$15.00**

Newspaper holder, 11¼x8½", cut-out copper-finish metal, circle design w/boy hawking paper, 'Paper' lettered below..............**$45.00**

Perfume bottle, black glass w/silver lattice-work band near top, w/stopper, French..............**$100.00**

Pin, five square-cut blue glass stones set in gold-plated metal stylized floral design..............**$40.00**

Pipe stand, bronze, nude posed in diving position on a rectangular base, unmarked..............**$140.00**

Pocket lighter, tortoise shell rectangular shape w/chrome trim, elongated diamond in center, Ronson..........**$75.00**

Salad fork & spoon, chrome w/yellow celluloid handles, Chase, set..............**$45.00**

Swan, chrome, used to hold picks for onions & olives, on pedestal base, S-shaped neck w/red bead for head, unmarked **$25.00**

Table lamp, 11½", light blue-green glass shaped as the planet Saturn tilted on cone-shaped base, 1939 World's Fair..............**$350.00**

Watch pendant, 1¼", green & black enamel pentagon shape w/silver trim, band of stylized flowers on back, Borel..............**$275.00**

Autographs

'Philography' is an extremely popular hobby, one that is very diversified. Autographs of sports figures, movie stars, entertainers, and politicians from our lifetime may bring several hundred dollars, depending on rarity and content, while John Adams' simple signature on a document from 1800, for instance, might bring thousands. A signature on a card or photograph is the least valuable type of autograph; a handwritten letter is the most valuable, since in addition the signature, you get the handwritten message as well. Content is also important. Depending upon what it reveals about the personality involved, it can make a major difference in value.

Many times a polite request accompanied by an SASE to a famous person will result in receipt of a signed photo or a short handwritten note that might in several years be worth a tidy sum!

Obviously as new collectors enter the field, the law of supply and demand will drive the prices for autographs upward, especially when the personality is deceased. There are forgeries around, so before you decide to invest in expensive autographs, get to know your dealers.

Ali, Muhammad; signed black & white photo, action shot, 8x10" **$30.00**

Ally, Kirstie; in-person signed color portrait **$40.00**

Alpert, Herb; signed card **$7.00**

Anderson, Harry; inscribed signed color photo from 'Night Court,' red ink **$8.00**

Arafat, Yassir; signed photo, 1982, 4x7"..............**$150.00**

Armstrong, Neil; signed card, 3x5" **$30.00**

Arnold (Barr), Roseanne; in-person signed color photo of cast, signed only by Roseanne..............**$45.00**

Arthur, Bea; signed photo, bust portrait from 'Maude' TV series $8.00

Averill, Earl; signed index card, 3x5" $8.00

Axton, Hoyt; signed color photo, 'Gremlins' trading card, signed on reverse $6.00

Bailey, Pearl; signed black & white photo, deceased Black singer, 3x5" $12.00

Banks, Ernie; signed commemorative envelope, 50th-Anniversary of All Star Game, 1983 ....$50.00

Barlick, Al; signed United States Post Office post card, w/postmark $10.00

Barton, Clara; signature cut from letter, EX $195.00

Basinger, Kim; in-person signed photo, full-length portrait, wearing a bathing suit $45.00

Bates, Alan; signed photo, original still from 'King of Hearts,' 1967 ....$12.00

Benson, Robby; inscribed signed photo, actor in 'The Chosen,' 5x7" $6.00

Berra, Yogi; signed color photo, 8x10" $20.00

Boyington, Pappy; inscribed signed black & white photo, ca 1945 ....$95.00

Brooks, Garth; in-person signed color photo, half-length portrait, wearing famous cowboy hat $45.00

Brooks, Mel; signed photo, 'Silent Movie' scene $10.00

Burgess, Meredith; signed bust-length photo, actor, 1970s $12.00

Caan, James; signed photo, original still from 'Alien Nation,' 1988 ....$20.00

Cagney, James; signed half-bust portrait photo, M $75.00

Candy, John; signed photo, original still, scene from 'Who's Harry Crumb?,' 1989 ....$12.00

Carey, Mariah; in-person signed photo, contemporary singing star $60.00

Cartwright, Angela; inscribed signed photo of cast of 'Lost in Space' $8.00

Chong, Tommy; signed color photo, original still from 'Still Smokin'' $12.00

Cochran, Mickey; signed United States Post Office post card, w/postmark $200.00

Connery, Sean; signed photo, original still from 'The Next Man,' 1976 ....$35.00

Connors, Chuck; inscribed signed photo of 'The Rifleman' $8.00

Curtis, Jamie Lee; signed bust-length portrait from 'Anything but Love' $8.00

Danson, Ted; in-person signed color 'Cheers' photo, young $30.00

DeMille, Cecil B; signed check, April 26, 1957 ....$165.00

Depp, Johnny; in-person signed color portrait of 'Edward Scissorhands' star $40.00

DiMaggio, Joe; signed color photo $65.00

Domino, Fats; signed color photo, 8x10" $30.00

Douglas, Kirk; inscribed signed photo from 'Cast a Giant Shadow,' 1966 ....$25.00

Dreyfus, Richard; signed photo, close-up 'Goodbye Girl' portrait $15.00

Eastwood, Clint; signed color photo, original still from 'Firefox,' 1982 ....$12.00

Ebsen, Buddy; inscribed signed photo, 'Jed Clampett' $8.00

Estevez, Emilio; inscribed signed photo, original still from 'Young Guns,' 1988 ....$12.00

Fawcett, Farrah; signed photo, nude (though covered) color portrait $17.50

Fisher, Carrie; signed color photo scene from 'Star Wars' shown w/R2D2 ....$15.00

Fisk, Carlton; signed color photo $16.00

Garner, James; signed color portrait as 'Maverick' $12.00

Gleason, Jackie; inscribed signed photo as 'Soldier in the Rain' $65.00

Gobel, George; inscribed signed photo, 8x10" $10.00

Goldberg, Whoopi; signed photo as 'The Color Purple' star $12.00

Goulet, Robert; inscribed signed photo $15.00

Harris, Neil Patrick; in-person signed color photo from TV series 'Doogie Howser, MD' $35.00

Hepburn, Audrey; signed photo, 'My Fair Lady' star ...$35.00

Hines, Gregory; signed photo, original still, 'Eve of Destruction' $10.00

Hoover, Herbert; signed letter, dated September 7, 1939, M $150.00

Horne, Lena; inscribed signed close-up photo, singer ...$6.00

Horsley, Lee; inscribed signed photo, still from 'Paradise,' signed 'Lee' $8.00

Jackson, Bo; signed commemorative envelope, 'Most Valuable Player,' 1989 ....$75.00

Jimmy the Greek, signed photo, 8x10" $20.00

Johnson, Don; in-person signed color photo of 'Miami Vice' star $40.00

Johnson, Lady Bird; signature on White House letterhead, personal 1-page letter, 1964 ....$47.50

Kahn, Madeline; signed photo, original color still from 'City Heat,' 1984 ....$8.00

Keach, Stacy; signed photo, still from 'Fat City,' 7x9" $8.00

Kelley, Deforrest; inscribed signed photo as 'Dr McCoy' of 'Star Trek' $8.00

Kelly, Gene; inscribed signed photo from 'Singing in the Rain,' showing Kelly dancing around lamppost ...$12.00

Kissinger, Henry; signed black & white photo, 8x10".$20.00

Krupa, Gene; inscribed signed photo, 8x10" $25.00

Laurel, Stan; two signed photos, the 1st 5x7", 1930, EX, both for $500.00

27

Lewis, Al; signed photo as 'Granpa Munster' from the 1960s 'The Munsters' TV series.................................$12.00

Lopez, Al; signed United States Post Office post card, w/postmark..$25.00

Lynn, Loretta; inscribed signed color photo.................$8.00

Mancini, Henry; signed photo, seated by piano, 8x10".$30.00

Martin, Steve; signed photo, original still from 'LA Story,' 1991 ....$10.00

Mason, Marsha; signed photo, original lobby card from 'The Goodbye Girl,' 11x14", M $15.00

McDowall, Roddy; inscribed signed photo as 'Book Worm' on 'Batman'..$8.00

McQueen, Butterfly; signed photo of 'Prissy' in 'Gone with the Wind'...$22.50

Merman, Ethel; signed photo, early, 5x7" $45.00

Mize, Johnny; signed index card, 3x5" $5.00

Moore, Clayton; inscribed signed photo of 'Lone Ranger' pictured w/'Tonto' & 'Silver' $12.00

Moore, Roger; in-person signed color half-length photo as 'James Bond,' holding pistol pointing at the camera...$55.00

Moranis, Rick; inscribed signed photo of 'Honey I Shrunk the Kids' star..$8.00

Musial, Stan; signed United States Post Office post card, w/postmark..$35.00

Newman, Paul; signed close-up color portrait............$45.00

Nielsen, Leslie; signed photo, original movie poster, 'Airplane,' 1980, 22x28", VG $20.00

Nimoy, Leonard; inscribed signed color photo as 'Mr Spock' from 'Star Trek' TV series $20.00

Nolte, Nick; inscribed signed photo of a bearded Nolte from 'Prince Of Tides,' 1990s $8.00

Norris, Chuck; signed photo, original still from 'Lone Wolf McQuade'...$8.00

O'Connor, Hugh; inscribed signed promotional photo, star of 'In the Heat of the Night' $8.00

O'Toole, Annette; signed half-length color photo, very sexy..$22.50

Parton, Dolly; signed full-length color portrait, performing..$12.00

Pearl, Minnie; signed Christmas card..........................$15.00

Pesci, Joe; in-person signed color close-up portrait $37.50

Pfeiffer, Michelle; in-person signed bust-length color portrait $50.00

Phillips, Lou Diamond; in-person signed close-up bust portrait..$40.00

Post, Emily; signed card, 5x3".....................................$16.00

Post, Markie; inscribed signed bust-length portrait........$6.00

Price, Vincent; signed color photo as 'Egghead' from 'Batman' series...$12.00

Rashad, Phylicia; inscribed signed bust-length portrait .$6.00

Rather, Dan; inscribed signed color photo, CBS anchorman $6.00

Reagan, Ronald; signed letter in his handwriting, regarding business matter for GE Theatre, 1958.......$500.00

Reese, Pee Wee; signed color photo, 8x10"................$30.00

Reynolds, Debbie; signed photo, original still from 'The Singing Nun' $8.00

Roberts; Robin; signed color photo, 8x10"..................$12.00

Romero, Caesar; signed photo as 'The Joker' $8.00

Russell, Jane; signed bust-length color photo.............$15.00

Ryan, Nolan; signed index card, 3x5"..........................$10.00

Savage, Fred; inscribed signed color photo of 'Wonder Years' TV series star...$15.00

Sheedy, Ally; signed half-length color photo, actress..$10.00

Short, Martin; signed photo, original still from 'Three Amigos,' 1986...$8.00

Skaggs, Ricky; signed color photo, singer...................$12.00

Skerritt, Tom; inscribed signed close-up photo from 'Alien'...$8.00

Stallone, Sylvester; in-person signed action-scene photo from 'Paradise Alley,' signed 'Sly Stallone'...........$55.00

Stewart, James; signed photo, original still from 'Shanendoah,' 1965 ....$15.00

Streisand, Barbra; signed photo, actress/director of 'Prince of Tides'..$40.00

Sutherland, Kiefer; in-person signed color 'Young Guns' portrait, on horseback $40.00

Swayze, Patrick; in-person color bust-length portrait, 'Ghost' & 'Point Break' star.................................$50.00

Takei, George; inscribed signed photo as 'Sulu' from 'Star Trek' TV series..$6.00

Tandy, Jessica; signed color photo of 'Driving Miss Daisy' star...$17.50

Terry, Bill; signed black & white photo $25.00

Tiegs, Cheryl; inscribed signed photo, three-quarter length portrait $8.00

Tiny Tim, signed photo, in singing pose, 8x10" $25.00

Tomlin, Lily; signed bust-length photo..........................$8.00

Torme, Mel; signed half-length photo, in tuxedo $8.00

Travolta, John; signed original movie poster from 'Saturday Night Fever,' 22x28", VG $25.00

Turner, Janine; signed photo of 'Northern Exposure' TV series star...$10.00

Turner, Kathleen; signed photo, bust-length portrait ..$17.50

Urich, Robert; signed photo, 'Spencer For Hire' portrait.$8.00

Vinton, Bobby; signed photo, singer, 5x7"....................$6.00

Wagner, Jack; signed photo, 'Santa Barbara' star..........$6.00

Walston, Ray; signed photo as 'Uncle Martin' from 'My Favorite Martian' TV series $8.00

Weller, Peter; inscribed signed color photo, 'Robo-Cop' star..$8.00

Williams, Robin; signed photo, full-length portrait as 'Mork from Ork'...$20.00

Winger, Debra; in-person signed bust-length color photo, 'An Officer & a Gentleman' & 'Terms of Endearment' star $40.00

Yeager, Chuck; signed photo, 10x8" $30.00

Automobilia

A specialized field that attracts both advertising buyers and vintage car buffs alike, 'automobilia' refers to auto-related items and accessories such as hood ornaments, gear shift and steering wheel knobs, owner's manuals, license plates, brochures, and catalogs. Many figural hood ornaments bring from $75 to $200 — some even higher. Things from the thirties through the fifties are especially popular right now.

Ashtray, Goodrich Silvertown, tire shape w/embossed swirl glass insert, 'The Safest Tire Ever Built' w/Goodrich logo **$30.00**

Ashtray, Pennsylvania Rubber Company, tire shape w/green glass insert **$40.00**

Blotter, Amoco, print of a Rockwell illustration, 1939, EX **$20.00**

Brochure, 10x8", 10-page, shows all of the 1962 Cadillac lines, M **$15.00**

Brochure, 11x8½", 12-page, color illustrations of the 1960 Chevrolet lines **$26.00**

Brochure, 7x10", 4-page, illustrating seven models of the 1961 Chevy II **$8.00**

Catalog, 16-page, showing full line of the 'Patrician Series #400' of the 1955 Packard, original jacket, NM.....**$225.00**

Extinguisher, Texaco, brass, 1930s, EX........................**$50.00**

Flashlight, Shamrock Oil, EX...**$10.00**

Fold-out, Dodge, 'Action Car of America,' 1953....$35.00
Fold-out, 20x14", shows sixteen of the 1953 Chevrolets including details of the new power steering & transmission **$10.00**

Gearshift knob, 2" dia, orange, brown, tan, & white swirls, M **$60.00**

Gearshift knob, 2" dia, oval, orange to off-white, G **$35.00**

Grease tube, Texaco Starfak, metal, 1940s, MIB..........**$20.00**

Key chain flashlight, tan & black, eagle in flight above 'Buick' printed in block letters **$15.00**

Magazine, 'Motor Life,' September, 1917, 112 pages in black & white w/some color, M....................................**$60.00**

Map rack, Sinclair, 1950s, M...**$25.00**

Mask, 'Chevrolet Man,' 11", die-cut paper, November 7 on hat, 1940s, EX...**$35.00**

Matchbox holder, Goodyear & Exide Batteries...........**$50.00**

Medallion, 1¼" dia, 1938 Plymouth, brass, '1928-1938 Climaxing 10 Years of Great Cars'.............................**$30.00**

Oil can, Havoline, 'Advanced Custom Made' in red, white, & blue, VG **$10.00**

Oil can, 1-gal, Veedol-Forzol, 'The Economy Oil Made for Fords' printed in orange on black can w/handle & spout **$70.00**

Oil can, 1-qt, Gulfpride Motor Oil, blue letters on white, red, & blue background **$20.00**

Oil can, 1-qt, Kendall Dual Action Motor Oil, red letters on white background **$38.00**

Oil can, 1-qt, Quaker State Motor Oil, white letters on dark green background **$20.00**

Oil pail, 5-gal, Wolf's Head, 1970s..............................**$10.00**

Owner's manual, 118-page booklet for the 1953 Buick, EX **$40.00**

Owner's manual, 24-page instruction booklet for the 1912 Ford Model-T, NM...**$50.00**

Paperweight, oval, brass, for the 1963 Henry Ford Centennial, Henry w/his first car on one side, script on reverse **$55.00**

Pin-back button, 1¼" dia, gold, green, purple & white celluloid w/the McFarlan Six logo **$45.00**

Pin-back button, 1¼" dia, red & white celluloid, 'I Want a Maxwell' **$50.00**

Post card, photo of 1907 Oldsmobile touring car, EX ...**$8.00**

Price list, 84-page list of Chevrolet parts & prices, 1912, EX **$30.00**

Radiator cap, 4" long, whippet dog figure **$130.00**

Sign, 12x18", Sky Chief Gasoline, red, black, & white letters on red background w/green striped top, 1953, EX **$120.00**

Sign, 14x12", Mobil Premium, white background w/red & blue letters, EX...**$115.00**

Sign, 20x28", Delco Battery, 2-sided, blue & white, pictures battery..**$65.00**

Tar patch kit, Texaco, 1960s, EX...................................**$8.00**

Tire-holding stand, Mobile, EX **$35.00**

Tray, 18x12", stainless steel, 'Ford' & old V-8 logo embossed in corner, from plant cafeteria..............................**$70.00**

Watch fob, Buick, blue & white enamel on brass, 'Buick Valve in Head Motor Cars' **$65.00**

Autumn Leaf Dinnerware

A familiar dinnerware pattern to just about all of us, Autumn Leaf was designed by Hall China for the Jewel Tea Company who offered it to their customers as premiums. In fact, some people refer to the pattern as 'Jewel Tea.' First made in 1933, it continued in production until 1978. Pieces with this date in the backstamp are from the overstock that was in the company's warehouse when production was suspended. There are matching pitchers, tumblers, and stemware all made by the Libbey Glass Company, and a set of enameled cookware that came out in 1979. You'll find blankets, tablecloths, metal canisters, clocks, playing cards, and many other items designed around the Autumn Leaf pattern. All are collectible.

Since 1984, the Hall Company has been making items for the National Autumn Leaf Collectors Club. So far, these pieces have been issued: a teapot (their New York style); a restyled vase; candlesticks; a teapot, sugar bowl and creamer set; a sugar packet holder; a tea-for-two set; a Solo tea set; a donut jug; and a large oval casserole. All are plainly marked and dated.

Limited edition items (by Hall) are being sold by China Specialties, a company in Ohio; but once you become familiar with the old pieces, these are easy to identify, since the molds have been redesigned or were not previously used for Autumn Leaf production. So far, these are the pieces I'm aware of: the Airflow teapot and the Norris refrigerator pitcher (shapes not found among the originals), a square-handled beverage mug, and a restyled Irish mug.

For further study, we recommend *The Collector's Encyclopedia of Hall China* by Margaret and Kenn Whitmyer.

Baker, oval, Fort Pitt	$90.00
Bean pot, 1-handle	$400.00
Bean pot, 2¼-qt, handles	$135.00
Bowl, cereal; 6"	$10.00
Bowl, coupe soup	$12.00
Bowl, cream soup; handles	$18.00
Bowl, fruit; 5½"	$4.00
Bowl, mixing; 6¼", 7½", 9", set of three	$55.00
Bowl, Royal Glas-Bak, set of four	$45.00
Bowl, salad	$14.00
Bowl, stackette, 18-oz, 24-oz, 34-oz, set of three graduated sizes, w/lids	$75.00
Bowl, vegetable; 10", w/lid, oval	$35.00
Bowl, vegetable; 10½", divided	$75.00
Bowl, vegetable; 9" dia	$75.00
Bowl, vegetable; 10", oval, w/lid	$35.00
Bowl cover set, plastic, 8-pc, seven assorted covers in pouch	$50.00
Bread box, metal	$175.00
Butter dish, 1-lb	$275.00
Butter dish, ¼-lb	$150.00
Butter dish, ¼-lb, square top	$400.00
Cake plate, 9½"	$12.00
Cake safe, 4½x 10½", metal, side decorated only	$30.00
Cake safe, 5x10", metal, motif on top & sides	$35.00
Cake stand, metal base, original box	$150.00
Candy dish	$350.00
Canister, metal, w/copper lid, set of four, round	$175.00
Canister, metal, w/ivory plastic lid, round	$10.00
Canister, 7", metal, w/matching lid, round	$25.00
Canister, 8½" & 4½", metal, set of four, square	$135.00
Casserole, Royal Glas-Bake, w/clear glass lid, deep	$25.00
Casserole, Tootsie-handle, w/lid	$22.00
Casserole/souffle, 10-oz	$10.00
Cleanser can, 6", metal, square	$300.00
Clock, original works	$350.00
Coaster, 3⅛", metal	$4.00
Coffee dispenser/canister, 10½x19" dia, metal, wall-hanging type	$150.00
Coffee maker, 5-cup, all china, w/china insert	$250.00
Coffee maker, 8", 9-cup, w/metal dripper	$35.00
Coffee percolator, electric, all china	$225.00
Cookie jar, Tootsie	$165.00
Creamer, New Style	$8.00

Creamer, 4¼", Old Style	$15.00
Cup & saucer	$8.00
Cup & saucer, St Denis	$22.00
Custard cup	$4.00
Flatware, silverplate, ea	$15.00
Flatware, stainless, ea	$10.00
Fruit cake tin, metal	$10.00
Golden Ray base, use w/candy dish or cake plate	$25.00
Gravy boat	$18.00
Hot pad, oval	$12.00
Hurricane lamp, Douglas, w/metal base	$200.00
Kitchen utility chair, metal	$450.00
Mixer cover, Mary Dunbar, plastic	$25.00
Mug, beverage	$45.00
Mug, Irish coffee	$85.00
Mustard jar, 3½"	$55.00
Napkin, ecru muslin	$25.00
Pickle dish or gravy liner, 9", oval	$18.00
Picnic thermos, metal	$250.00
Pie baker, 9½"	$18.00
Pitcher, utility; 6", 2½-pt	$15.00
Placemat, paper, scalloped	$25.00
Plate, 10"	$12.00
Platter, 11½"	$15.00
Platter, 13½"	$18.00
Playing cards, regular or Pinochle	$125.00
Range set, shakers & covered drippings jar	$35.00
Sauce dish, serving; Douglas, Bakelite handle	$125.00
Shakers, Casper (shaped), pr	$18.00

Stack set, three units w/lid	**$60.00**
Sugar bowl, New Style	$12.00
Sugar bowl, 3½", Old Style	$18.00
Tablecloth, plastic	$150.00
Tablecloth, 54x54", cotton sailcloth w/gold stripe	$75.00
Tablecloth, 56x81", ecru muslin	$150.00
Teakettle, metal enamelware	$150.00
Teapot, Aladdin	$38.00

Teapot, Newport...$135.00
Teapot, 7", long spout $45.00
Toaster cover, plastic, fits 2-slice toaster $25.00
Towel, dish; pattern & clock motif $45.00
Towel, tea; 16x33", cotton $35.00
Trash can, metal, red $100.00
Tray, metal, oval $55.00
Tray, tidbit; 2-tier $35.00
Tray, tidbit; 3-tier $55.00
Tray, 19½x11¼", glass w/wood handle $95.00
Tumbler, 10-oz, gold frost etched, flat $30.00
Tumbler, 10-oz, gold frost etched, footed $45.00
Tumbler, 13-oz, Brockway $18.00
Tumbler, 14-oz, 5½", frosted $12.00
Tumbler, 15-oz, gold frost etched, flat $45.00
Tumbler, 16-oz, Brockway $20.00
Tumbler, 6½-oz, gold frost etched, footed $45.00
Tumbler, 9-oz, Brockway $16.00
Tumbler, 9-oz, 3¾", frosted $18.00
Vase, bud; 6" $175.00
Warmer base, oval $150.00
Warmer base, round $110.00
Warmer base, w/candles, round, MIB $125.00

Avon

You'll find Avon bottles everywhere you go! But it's not just the bottles that are collectible — so are jewelry, awards, magazine ads, catalogs, and product samples. Of course the better items are the older ones (they've been called Avon since 1939 — California Perfume Company before that), and if you can find them mint in box (MIB), all the better.

See also Cape Cod.

Ammoniated Toothpaste, white & green tube w/green screw cap, 1949-55, MIB..............................$9.00
Baroque Cream Sachet, 2-oz round white milk glass jar w/gold footed bottom & gold dome top, various fragrances, 1974..$6.00
Bear Cookie Jar, brown ceramic, 1985.............$20.00
Chesapeake Collection Tray, 12" dia green metal tray, 'Mallards in Flight' on back, 1981-82 ....$5.00
Clean as a Whistle Bubble Bath, 8-oz red & white plastic figure w/red whistle cap, 1960-61............................$12.00
Cockatoo Pomander, 8½", blue scented wax, Floral Medley fragrance, 1972-73...............................$8.00
Cologne Cruet, 8-oz clear glass cruet shape w/glass stopper, sits on small plate, various fragrances, 1973-74 ....$14.00
Compact, square, turquoise & gold metal, 1936, MIB.....$25.00
Country Pump, 10-oz clear glass pump w/white plastic top, holds body lotion, 1975.............................$4.00
Decorator Soap Miniatures, 1956-66, M..........$8.00
Deep Woods Cologne, 8" gray Rolls Royce form w/plastic silver grill & top, label on bottom, some paint flecks $20.00
Double Dare Nail Polish, 1-oz glass bottle w/black cap, red paper label w/white lettering, 1946-47.................$12.00

Empress Lipstick, blue, green, & gold diamond design metal case, 1970-71, MIB $5.00
Forever Spring Toilet Water, 2-oz clear glass bottle w/green lettering & yellow tulip cap, 1951-56.....................$16.00
Fragrance Bell, 2-oz hobnail milk glass bell w/gold looped handle, various fragrances, 1973-74.........................$6.00
Gardenia Perfume, ⅜-oz clear glass bottle w/flower-shaped cap, paper or painted label, 1948-52 ....$45.00
Golden Promise Perfume, clear bottle w/gold ball-shaped cap, gold label w/red lettering, 1947....................$55.00
Holly Jolly Day Set, three 2-oz white plastic bottles w/red caps, green & white box, choice of toiletries for men, 1963 ....$18.00
Indian Tepee, 4-oz amber glass decanter in shape of a tepee w/brown plastic cap, Wild Country or Avon Spicy, 1974-75...$4.00
Key Note Perfume, ¼-oz glass key w/gold plastic cap, various fragrances, 1967 MIB $25.00
King Pin, 4-oz white glass bowling pin w/red label, Wild Country or Bravo after shave, 1969-70 ....$6.00
Klean Air, 12-oz blue & white labeled spray can w/white cap, mint scent, 1956-58 ....$5.00
La Belle Telephone, 1-oz, clear glass telephone w/gold cap, various fragrances, 1975-76 ....$8.00
Lilac Soap, box holds three oval-shaped lavender soaps w/embossed floral design & 'Lilac' on each bar, 1968-77 ....$8.00
Lotion Sachet, ½-oz fan-shaped clear glass bottle w/blue cap, Persian Wood & Here's My Heart, 1958..........$5.00
Mallard Duck, 6-oz green glass decanter w/silver head, various after shave fragrances, 1967-68 ....$12.00
Miss Lollypop Ice Cream Puff Talc, 3½-oz yellow ice cream cone-shaped bottom w/pink puff top, 1968-70, MIB $6.00
Nearness Body Powder, round frosted glass bottle w/blue cap & label, 1956-58 ....$12.00
Occur! Perfumed Bath Oil, 6-oz black plastic bottle w/gold ball-shaped cap, gold letters painted on bottle, 1964-65 ....$6.00
Purse Petite Cologne, 1½-oz embossed clear glass w/gold cap & trim, gold chain strap, various fragrances, 1971 ....$6.00
Rapture Perfume, ½-oz glass teardrop-shaped bottle w/metal leaves around base, teardrop-shaped gold metal cap, 1966-69 ....$12.00
Remember When Gas Pump, 4-oz red painted glass w/white & red plastic gas globe cap, Deep Woods or Wild Country, 1976-77 ....$8.00
Santa's Team Set, two 4-oz bottles of after shave & deodorant for men, blue box w/white reindeer, 1964.....$25.00
Snow Flake Cologne Bottle, ⅛-oz embossed glass w/white ball-shape cap, various fragrances, 1957-58.........$12.00
Spinning Top Bubble Bath, 4-oz white & red top w/yellow spinner, 1966-67 ....$8.00
Sweet Honesty Perfume, 3½" gray glass burro, label on bottom, head removes to expose lucite cap.............$50.00
Sweet Honesty Perfume, 5⅛" thermos jug form in red plaid, red plastic cap, M in original red plaid box.........$22.50

Sweet Remembrance, 3¼" round porcelain box w/lid, 'Valentines Day 1982' on bottom, foil-wrapped chocolate inside **$9.00**

Tai Winds Cologne, 7" 1936 MG car, red enamel on glass w/white plastic hood, MIB..........................**$45.00**

To a Wild Rose Bath Oil, 4-oz white glass bottle w/pink ball-shaped cap, paper label, 1956-59.................**$12.00**

Topaz Perfume, ¼-oz glass Deco-style bottle w/glass stopper, gold label w/tulip design, other fragrances, 1934-39..**$95.00**

Unforgettable Perfume, 4¼", clear glass urn w/pedestal foot, intaglio-cut stopper, gold enameling...................**$45.00**

Wild Flowers Fragrance Candle, shaped as a yellow black-eyed Susan w/brown center, 1975-76, MIB.............**$7.00**

Wild Turkey, 6-oz amber glass decanter w/silver & red plastic head, Wild Country or Deep Woods after shave, 1974-76...**$9.00**

Wishful Thoughts, 5½" blue & white porcelain figurine of a girl blowing on a flower, 1982-83.........................**$12.00**

Wishing Cologne Mist, 2½-oz white gold-trimmed plastic bottle w/half-dome cap, gold wishbone on bottle neck, 1963-70...**$4.00**

You're the Berries Candy Jar, 5" clear glass fruit jar w/berry-print cloth lid, for hard candy, 1984 ....**$5.00**

Young Hearts Honey Bun Set, 2½-oz glass toilet water w/pink cap & gold pomade lipstick in blue & pink round box, 1953..**$55.00**

Young Hearts Talc, 1⅔-oz round cardboard shaker canister, 1952-53 ....**$22.00**

Azalea Dinnerware

Although this line of dinnerware was made earlier than most of the collectibles we're dealing with, it was made in huge quantities, and you're likely to find a piece or two now and then. It was manufactured by the Noritake Company from 1916 until about 1935 and was offered through the catalogs of the Larkin Company who gave it away as premiums to club members and home agents.

Collectors use the catalog order numbers Larkin assigned to each piece. There were more than seventy items in the dinnerware line as well as six pieces of matching, hand-painted crystal.

Bowl, oatmeal; 5½", #55...**$28.00**
Bowl, vegetable; 9¼", #172, oval...............................**$58.00**
Bowl, 10", #12..**$42.50**
Butter tub, #54, w/insert..**$48.00**
Candy jar, #313 ....**$695.00**
Casserole, #16, w/lid **$125.00**
Celery/roll tray, 12", #99...**$55.00**
Creamer, 3⅛", & sugar bowl, 3⅝", #7 ....**$45.00**
Creamer, 5¾" & sugar bowl, 6½", #122 ....**$158.00**
Cup & saucer, #2..**$17.50**
Cup & saucer, bouillon; 3½", #124 ....**$24.50**
Egg cup, #120...**$60.00**
Mustard jar, #191...**$60.00**

Pitcher, milk jug; 1-qt, #100 ....**$195.00**
Plate, dinner; 9¾", #13...**$28.00**
Plate, grill; 10¼", #338, 3-compartment.....................**$165.00**
Plate, 7⅝", sq, #315...**$85.00**
Platter, 12", #56...**$58.00**
Relish, #171, 2-part...**$58.00**
Relish, #450, loop handle, 2-part................................**$425.00**
Shakers, 2½", individual size, #126, pr **$27.50**
Shakers, 3½", #11, bell form, pr..................................**$30.00**
Spoon holder, #339, 2-pc **$35.00**
Tea tile, 6", #169..**$48.50**
Teapot, 4½", #400, gold finial **$495.00**
Vase, 5½", #187, footed fan form...............................**$185.00**
Whipped cream set, #3, 3-pc **$38.50**

Banks

There are several types of collectible banks: mechanical — these are the ones with parts that move when the coin is inserted; still; advertising; and registering — those that tabulate the amount of money as you deposit it. This is a very diverse field, with literally thousands of shapes and variations available. If you find yourself drawn toward collecting banks, careful study and observation of the market is a must. Reproductions, though not very good ones, abound at flea markets all over the country. Since many of these banks were produced from the 1870s until about 1940, pass right on by any bank with paint that is too bright. Examine their construction; parts fit together well in the old banks. If the parts fit loosely and the designing is crude, they're new.

Prices for old banks continue to accelerate rapidly. Several of the auction houses we list in the back, especially those that specialize in toys, will often hold large cataloged bank auctions. Condition is of the utmost importance; good paint can mean the difference of hundreds of dollars. And they must be complete and original to bring top price. Repaired banks or those with replaced parts are worth much less.

Although the mechanicals are at the top of the price structure, still banks are widely collected as well. Cast iron examples are preferred, but lead banks are coming on, and tin and pottery banks are attracting more and more collector interest.

There are a number of good books on the market for further study; among them are: *The Dictionary of Still Banks* by Long and Pitman, *The Penny Bank Book* by Moore, *The Still Bank Book* by Norman, *Penny Lane* by Davidson, *The History of Antique Mechanical Toy Banks* by Al Davidson, and *The Collector's Encyclopedia of Toys and Banks* by Don Cranmer. In our listings, 'M' numbers refer to the Moore book, 'L' to the book by Long and Pitman, 'N' to the Norman book, and 'D' to Davidson's.

See also Advertising Collectibles.

Mechanical Banks

Always Did 'Spise a Mule, painted cast iron, Black boy seated on bench staring at mule, elongated base, J&E Stevens, EX...**$1,200.00**

Artillery, 5", D-12, variant of soldier standing next to mortar, round trap, produced from 1900-1932 by J&E Stevens, EX...$2,100.00

Bill E Grin, 4½", D-33, head-&-shoulder form of man grinning, yellow or white in color, no trap, J&E Stevens...$600.00

Bird on the Roof, 6½", D-36, japanned or silver-painted cast iron, stylized bird perched on house roof, J&E Stevens...$2,200.00

Boy Robbing Bird's Nest, 4½", D-51, painted cast iron, boy in tree, ca 1906, J&E Stevens, EX.................$4,500.00

Boy Scout Camp, 9⅞", D-52, painted cast iron, scout in tepee, one w/flag, one at campfire, 1912-17, J&E Stevens, EX...$4,500.00

Boys Stealing Watermelons, 6½", D-53, cast iron, two Black boys & dog in his house on base, attributed to Kyser & Rex...$3,400.00

Bucking Mule, 4½", D-58, cast iron, japanned (figure may be painted), man astride mule on rectangular base, Judd, EX...$1,100.00

Bull Dog Bank, 7", D-64, coin rests on nose of bulldog sitting w/blanket on box, some variations, J&E Stevens, G...$1,320.00

Bull Tosses Boy in Well, D-67, painted or bronzed brass, bull charges boy, EX.........................$880.00

Butting Buffalo, 8", G-36, cast iron, VG.............$2,000.00

Cabin Bank, 3½", D-93, Black man standing at door of cabin w/slanted roof, yellow & green variations, J&E Stevens, EX...$550.00

Chief Big Moon, 10", D-108, cast iron, squaw seated at tepee, color variations, J&E Stevens, EX.........$4,950.00

Chimpanzee Bank, 6", D-110, cast iron, clothed chimp w/book inside domed building, color variations, Kyser & Rex, EX...$5,280.00

Circus Ticket Collector, 5½", D-115, cast iron, ticket taker standing in front of barrel, color variations, Judd, EX...$935.00

Clown & Dog, 7", D-123, red, yellow, & black tin litho, ca 1920s, Germany...$1,870.00

Clown on Globe, 9", D-227, clown astride black globe on yellow or tan base which may be removable or have Stevens trap...$1,980.00

Confectionary Bank, 8½", D-131, cast iron, figure at candy counter on half-circle base, variations, Kyser & Rex, EX...$8,800.00

Creedmoor Bank, 10", D-137, painted cast iron, figure shooting at target posted on tree, variations, J&E Stevens, EX...$2,600.00

Dapper Dan, 10", D-145, tin, wind-up, dancing Black man on rectangular base advertising Dapper Dan show, 1020s, Marx, EX...$660.00

Dinah, 7", D-153, painted cast iron, bust & head form of a Black lady whose mouth receives coins, variations, Harper, VG...$400.00

Eagle & Eaglets, 8", D-165, painted cast iron, mother & her young on oval base, J&E Stevens, EX.............$715.00

Elephant & Three Clowns, 5¾", D-170, cast iron, elephant may be white or gray w/red or blue blanket, J&E Stevens, G...$1,700.00

Elephant Howdah, D-173, bronze painted iron & wood, man pops out of box on elephant's back, variations, Enterprise, EX...$715.00

Frog on Rock, 3¾", D-203, painted cast iron, frog may have rivet in lower jaw, Kilgore...$700.00

Frog on Round Base, 4½", D-204, cast iron, many color variations, J&E Stevens, EX...$750.00

Hall's Excelsior, 5½", D-228, cast iron & wood, figure pops out of top of building to receive coins, J&E Stevens, EX...$495.00

Hindu, 6", D-239, painted cast iron, bust & head of Hindu man whose mouth receives coins, variations, Kyser & Rex...$1,200.00

Hold the Fort (Five Holes), 6½", D-240, cast iron, gray or tan fortress w/cannon & flag on red or black base, EX...$2,860.00

Horse Race, D-247, cast iron & sheet metal, Black man w/flag overseeing horse race on flanged base, J&E Stevens, EX...$4,500.00

Indian Shooting Bear, 10¼", D-257, painted cast iron, kneeling Indian pointing gun at standing bear, Stevens, EX...$2,100.00

Jonah & the Whale, 10½", D-282, cast iron, Jonah in boat facing whale, rectangular base, 1890s, Shepard Hardware, EX...$3,200.00

Lighthouse, 10½", D-298, cast iron, red tower w/black house & rocks on 6-sided base, some variations, EX.$1,300.00

Little Jocko Musical Bank, D-303, white metal monkey figure dancing on sheet metal base, ca 1910-20, Strauss, EX...$3,200.00

Magician Bank, 8", D-315, painted cast iron, magician stands at table on stepped base, J&E Stevens, VG......$6,800.00

Mammy & Child, 9", D-318, mammy in yellow dress feeds baby lying on her lap, paint variations, Kyser & Rex, EX...$8,500.00

Mason Bank, D-321, cast iron, man carrying hod faces brick layer standing behind red brick wall, Shepard, EX...$6,500.00

Memorial Money Bank (Liberty Bell), D-322, eagle, perched on top of Liberty Bell suspended above base, Enterprise, EX...$440.00

Milking Cow, 10", G-168, painted cast iron, seated figure milking cow by fence, footed base, variations, J&E Stevens, VG.....................$3,000.00

Monkey & Coconut, 8½", D-332, painted cast iron, monkey in sitting position holding coconut, J&E Stevens, EX.....................$2,500.00

Monkey Bank, 8", D-334, organ grinder in red & yellow faces monkey who puts coins in organ, green base, Hubley, EX.....................$600.00

Mosque, 9½", D-340, figure standing on top of building, variations, Judd, VG.....................$850.00

Mule Entering Barn, 8½", D-342, painted cast iron, barn may be gray or light green, J&E Stevens, EX...........$1,750.00

Octagonal Fort, 10¾" long, D-363, painted cast iron, cannon facing fort on elongated base, VG.....................$6,050.00

Organ Bank, 3¾", D-363, painted cast iron, monkey in red jacket sits atop footed crank organ, Kyser & Rex, EX.....................$935.00

Organ Bank, 8", D-369, cast iron, monkey positioned between cat & dog on footed crank organ, Kyser & Rex, EX.....................$935.00

Owl Turns Head, 7½", D-375, cast iron, brown owl on brown tree-branch base, color & metal variations, J&E Stevens, EX.....................$715.00

Paddy & the Pig, 8", D-376, cast iron, Paddy sitting in grass w/pig between his legs, J&E Stevens.....................$3,500.00

Panorama Bank, 6½", D-377, building shape, put coin in slot & see picture sequence, color variations, J&E Stevens, EX.....................$5,200.00

Patronize the Blind Man & His dog, 7", cast iron, fine original paint, coin door missing.............$6,000.00

Peg-Leg Begger, 5½", D-380, cast iron, begger seated on square base w/hat, Judd, EX.................$2,500.00

Rabbit in Cabbage, 4", D-408, brown or white cast iron rabbit w/green & brown base, Kilgore, VG paint....$700.00

Rabbit in Cabbage, 4½", D-408, brown or white rabbit, nickel-plated coin trap, brown is earlier version, Kilgore, NM.....................$350.00

Rooster, 6½", D-419, painted cast iron, dark brown rooster w/red head on green base, gold variation, Kyser & Rex, EX.....................$550.00

Snap It, 4", D-445, japanned cast iron, 8-sided building, there are polychromed versions, ca 1885-1890, Judd, VG.....................$495.00

Squirrel & Tree Stump, D-452, squirrel holds acorn that deposits the coin into tree stump, Mechanical Novelty Works, EX.....................$1,760.00

Stump Speaker Bank, 9½", D-453, cast iron, Black man in top hat stands on red box, black or brown face, Shepard, EX.....................$2,100.00

Tabby Bank, 4¾", D-454, cast iron, white cat sits on egg waiting for chick to hatch, round pedestal base, VG.....................$240.00

Tammany Bank, 5½", D-455, cast iron, chubby man sits in red chair, variations, J&E Stevens, EX...............$660.00

Teddy & the Bear, 7", D-459, cast iron, man points gun at bear as he pops out of tree trunk, J&E Stevens, EX.....................$3,000.00

Telephone, 6½", D-462, nickel-plated or bronze cast iron sheet metal depicting early pay phone, J&E Stevens, EX.....................$700.00

Thrifty Tom, 9", D-468, tin, wind-up, 'Thrifty Tom' stands on 'Jigger Bank' base, Ferdinand Strauss Corp, EX..$715.00

Trick Dog, 8½", D-481, cast iron, dog stands ready to jump through hoop held by clown, 6-part base, Shepard, VG.....................$460.00

Trick Dog, 8½", D-482, cast iron, dog stands ready to jump through hoop held by clown, solid base, Hubley, EX.....................$600.00

Trick Pony, 7", G-272, cast iron, circus pony stands before trough on rectangular base, 1880s, J&E Shepard, 1880s, EX.....................$2,800.00

Uncle Sam, 11½", D-493, cast iron, 'Uncle Sam' stands by carpetbag on box w/embossed eagle, Shepard Hardware.....................$2,420.00

Watchdog Safe, 6½", D-560, cast iron, resting dog embossed on front of black floor safe, J&E Stevens, VG.....$715.00

Weeden's Plantation, 5½", D-562, tin, wind-up, two Black figures performing, one standing, one seated playing banjo.....................$2,090.00

William Tell, 10½", D-565, cast iron, William Tell stands ready to shoot apple from boy's head, 1896, J&E Stevens, EX.....................$1,875.00

World's Fair, 8", D-573, gold or polychromed cast iron, Indian offers Columbus peace pipe, J&E Stevens, EX.....................$825.00

Zoo, 4¼", D-576, cast iron, figures appear in windows of red building w/gold roof, attributed to Kyser & Rex, EX.....................$2,650.00

Registering Banks

Bean Pot, 3", M-951, cast iron, 5¢, VG paint.............$270.00

Beehive, 5½", M-681, painted cast iron, 10¢ register, American manufacturer, light wear **$440.00**

Donald Duck, tin, 10¢ register, Disney, 1930s, NM.....**$90.00**

Dopey, one of seven dwarfs, 10¢ register, 1938, Disney, EX..**$60.00**

Honeycomb, C-105, 5¼"..**$100.00**

Junior Cash, 4¼", M-930, nickel-plated cast iron, light rust...**$50.00**

Keep 'Em Rolling, battleship litho, 10¢ register, EX ..**$100.00**

Kettle, 3½", painted nickel-plated cast iron, 5¢ register..**$25.00**

New York World's Fair, M-1566, tin, 1¢ register..........**$55.00**

Pail, 2¾", M-912, cast iron, 1¢ register, worn paint ...**$220.00**

Popeye, 10¢ register, NM **$65.00**

Prudential, 7¼", nickel-plated cast iron, worn label, EX..**$425.00**

Pump & Bucket, 6½", D-401, painted cast iron, 10¢ register, EX **$2,000.00**

Radio, 5" dia, tin litho, English, VG **$25.00**

Spinning Wheel, 4½" sq, tin litho w/two scenes, West Germany **$25.00**

Trunk, 5", M-947, nickel-plated cast iron, Phoenix 10¢ register, worn black paint **$95.00**

TV Bank, 4", tin litho, various denominations, West Germany **$15.00**

Wee Folks Money Box, 5" sq, tin litho, England **$50.00**

Still Banks

$100,000 Money Bag, M-1262, cast iron, NM paint ...**$575.00**

Arabian Safe, 4½", M-882, cast iron w/multicolored wash, Kyser & Rex, EX...**$400.00**

Aunt Jemima, 5¼", M-175, painted white metal, w/basket, EX..**$65.00**

Baseball Player on Base, 5⅞", M-22, lead, EX............**$110.00**

Bear Stealing Honey, 7", M-1308, cast iron, japanning w/gold, EX **$175.00**

Billiken, 4⅛", M-74, cast iron, traces of gold paint....**$320.00**

Billy Bounce, 4¾", M-14, painted cast iron, Wing, EX **$650.00**

Boston Bulldog, 4⅜", M-413, painted cast iron, bulldog is seated, EX paint **$235.00**

Boston State House, 5⅛", M-1210, painted cast iron, EX paint **$4,600.00**

Boy Scout, 5¾", M-47, painted cast iron, w/buckle & scarf, EX **$325.00**

Boy with Empty Pockets, 3⅞", M-274, painted lead, EX paint **$850.00**

Brementown Musicians, 5⅜", M-649, lead, EX **$1,200.00**

Bulldog, 4⅜", M-357, gold-painted cast iron **$65.00**

Bulldog with Collar, 3", M-399, painted lead.............**$275.00**

Bungalow, 3¾", M-999, painted cast iron, EX............**$375.00**

Camel, 4¾", M-768, cast iron, EX................................**$200.00**

Capitolist, 5", M-5, cast iron **$1,500.00**

Cash Register Savings, M-1538, painted cast iron, EX .**$900.00**

Church Towers, 6¾", M-956, cast iron.......................**$625.00**

Circus Elephant, 3⅞", M-462, painted cast iron, EX...**$350.00**

City Bank with Teller, 5¼", M-1009, painted cast iron, EX **$350.00**

Clown with Crooked Hat, 6¾", M-210, painted cast iron, EX **$2,000.00**

Columbia Bank, 8¾x7x7", cast iron, silver finish, Kenton, G $465.00

Crosley Radio, 5⅛", M-819, painted cast iron, Kenton, EX..**$650.00**

Cupola, 4", M-1146, cast iron, red paint w/multicolored trim...**$115.00**

Dog on Drum, 4⅛", M-359, cast iron, paint traces.......**$75.00**

Dolphin, 4½", M-33, cast iron, paint traces, Grey Iron Casting..**$450.00**

Donkey, 3⅞", M-488, painted cast iron, w/blanket, Kenton, EX..**$750.00**

Dutch Boy, 6¾", M-17, painted cast iron, Grey Iron Casting, VC...**$575.00**

Eggman, 4", M-108, painted cast iron, Arcade, EX...**$2,200.00**

Eiffel Tower, 10½", M-1075, painted cast iron, EX **$925.00**

Elephant, 3⅛x4", cast iron, worn finish, G...........$35.00

Elephant, 3⅛", M-487, painted cast iron, w/blanket, Kenton, EX **$650.00**

Elephant, 4¼", M-445, painted cast iron, elephant is seated, EX **$550.00**

Ferdinand the Bull, 5⅛", M-290, painted compositon, Crown, VG..**$50.00**

Ferris Wheel, 4½", M-1606, nickel-plated cast iron ..**$1,025.00**

Fidelity Trust Vault, 6½", M-903, painted cast iron, JB Smith, EX **$1,100.00**

Fido on Pillow, 4", M-443, painted cast iron.............**$300.00**

Flatiron Building, 8¼", M-1159, painted cast iron, Kenton, EX **$1,250.00**

Floral Safe, 4½", M-885, cast iron w/gold wash, Kyser & Rex **$165.00**

Flower Girl, 4¾", M-1650, painted lead, EX.............**$725.00**

Football Player, 5⅞", M-11, painted cast iron, Williams **$400.00**

Four Tower, 5¾", M-1121, cast iron, brown japanning w/gold, EX **$185.00**

Foxy Grandpa, 5½", M-320, painted cast iron, Hubley...**$450.00**

General Butler, 6½", M-54, painted cast iron, EX **$850.00**

Gingerbread House, 3⅞", M-1029, painted cast iron, EX **$800.00**

Give Me a Penny, 5¾", L-733, cast iron, Wing Manufacturing **$175.00**

Globe on Wire Arc, 4⅝", M-785, Arcade, EX.............**$275.00**

Golliwog, 6¼", M-85, cast iron, England, EX **$475.00**

Good Luck Horse Shoe, 4¼", M-508, painted cast iron, EX **$300.00**

Goose, 3¾", M-614, painted cast iron.........................**$180.00**

Gun Boat, 8½", M-1462, cast iron painted blue, white, & brown, EX **$850.00**

Harleysville Bank, 5¼" long, M-1017, painted cast iron ..**$30.00**

Horse, 4", M-508, black & gold-painted cast iron, Arcade...**$110.00**

Horse, 4¾", M-506, cast iron, gold paint, prancing ...**$185.00**

Independence Hall, 10⅛", M-1242, cast iron, EX.......**$565.00**

Kewpie, 5", M-292, painted papier-mache **$35.00**

Keyless Safety Deposit, 5⅞", cast iron, metal finish w/nickel dials...**$50.00**

Labrador, 4⅝", M-412, cast iron, black & gold paint ...**$245.00**

Liberty Bell, 3¾", M-793, steel w/wooden yoke **$15.00**

Lindburgh Bust, 6¼", L-779, aluminum **$50.00**

Lion, 4¾", M-760, silver-painted cast iron, on wheels.**$65.00**

Lion, 5", M-754, black-painted cast iron, VG...............**$65.00**

Lost Dog, 5⅜", M-407, cast iron **$575.00**

Main Street Trolley, 6⅝" long, M-1469, gold-painted cast iron, EX..**$375.00**

Mammy with Hands on Hips, M-176-A, painted cast iron, EX **$95.00**

Mary with Lamb, 4⅜", M-164, painted cast iron.........**$325.00**

Mickey Mouse with Mandolin, 4⅝", M-203, painted white metal **$145.00**

Minute Man Soldier, L-864/M-44, VG **$475.00**

Monkey, 4¼", M-744, painted white metal..................**$75.00**

Mosque, 4¼", M-1177, cast iron, VG...........................**$95.00**

Mourner's Purse, 5", L-1481, lead, 1902.....................**$50.00**

Mutt & Jeff, 5⅛", M-157, gold-painted cast iron.........**$140.00**

New Deal, 4¾", M-148, bronze, Roosevelt bust.........**$225.00**

Organ Grinder, 6½", M-216, cast iron w/steel base...**$150.00**

Owl, 5", M-598, painted cast iron, 'Be Wise, Save Money,' EX **$165.00**

Pagoda, 5", M-1153, cast iron, silver w/gold overpaint.**$265.00**

Pig, 4¼" long, bronze-painted lead, grin on face **$25.00**

Policeman, 5⅝", L-820, painted cast iron, Arcade......**$325.00**

Presto, 4⅛", M-1167, silver-painted cast iron w/gold dome **$65.00**

Professor Pug Frog, 5¼", M-311, cast iron w/metallic green & gold paint **$450.00**

Punch & Judy, 4⅜", M-1299, tin, EX **$70.00**

Quilted Lion, 5", M-758, cast iron w/gold & red paint **$225.00**

Rabbit, 3⅜", M-567, painted cast iron, white w/muticolored details, EX...**$85.00**

Radio, 3¼", M-821, painted cast iron, black w/gold trim, EX..**$100.00**

Santa, 6", L-843, cast iron, standing w/tree, Hubley, EX..**$145.00**

Save & Smile Money Bank, 4⅛", M-24, painted cast iron **$365.00**

Scottie, 2⅞", M-430, black-painted cast iron................**$60.00**

Shell Out, 2½", L-1178, cast iron **$350.00**

Sidewheeler, 7½" long, M-1459, blue- & red-painted cast iron, EX...**$170.00**

Soldier, 6", M-45, gold- & red-painted cast iron **$145.00**

Space Heater with Bird, 6½", M-1087, cast iron w/dark bronze finish **$65.00**

Spitz, 4", M-409, cast iron w/gold paint traces..........**$175.00**

St Bernard, 5⅝", M-429, cast iron w/paint traces, w/pack...**$35.00**

Stag, 9½", M-737, nickel-plated cast iron, EX..............**$65.00**

State Bank, 3⅛", M-1085, cast iron w/metallic japanning & bronze trim **$95.00**

Statue of Liberty, 6", M-1164, gold-painted cast iron.**$115.00**

Sun Bonnet Sue, 7⅜", M-257, painted cast iron, modern **$75.00**

Tank, 4⅜" long, M-1437, gold-painted cast iron, USA.**$115.00**

Three Monkeys, 3¼", M-743, bronze- & gold-painted cast iron, 'See No Evil...,' EX..**$335.00**

Top Hat, 4¼", M-1391, tin, black, 'College' on band, EX..**$200.00**

Turkey, 3½", M-587, black-painted cast iron................**$40.00**

US Mail, 4¾", M-835, silver- & red-painted cast iron, VG **$60.00**

Villa, 5½", M-959, cast iron, dark brown japanning w/gold, 1882 ....**$350.00**

Von Hindenburg, 9¼", M-152, dark brown-painted lead, EX..**$350.00**

Washington Monument, 6⅛", M-1048, gold-painted cast iron..**$125.00**

Wire-haired Terrier, M-422B, painted cast iron, VG **$75.00**

Wireless Bank, 6⅝", N-5980, cast iron **$75.00**

Woolworth Building, 8", M-1041, gold-painted cast iron .**$95.00**

Yellow Cab, 4", L-1570, cast iron, VG **$400.00**

Barbie and Her Friends

If you compare our Barbie doll values to those in many other price guides, you'll notice they are much lower. This is because we have priced them as you'll probably be finding them: not mint in box as most other guides do, but nude and in good condition. A doll that is mint in box may be worth from three to five times our listed values. If you need to price a MIB Barbie (or one of her companions), refer to one of these fine books: *The Wonder of Barbie* and *The World of Barbie Dolls* by Paris and Susan Manos; or *The Collector's Encyclopedia of Barbie Dolls and Collectibles* by Sibyl DeWein and Joan Ashabraner.

Barbie was first introduced in 1959, and soon Mattel found themselves producing not only dolls but tiny garments, fashion accessories, houses, cars, horses, books, and games as well. Today's Barbie collectors want them all. Though the early Barbies are very hard to find, there are many of her successors still around; don't overlook Ken, Skipper, or any of her other friends.

Our values are given just for the doll, but we've included information within parentheses describing originial clothing and accessories that each doll came out with, in case you're lucky enough to find some of those. In the section on accessories, values are for mint condition items; worn examples are generally worth at least 50% less.

Barbie, Ballerina (white tutu & gold crown, posing stand & red bouquet included), swivel-jointed head & arms, 1976 ....$20.00

Barbie, Ballerina on Tour (white tutu & gold crown, plus two additional outfits), swivel-jointed head & arms, 1976 ....$20.00

Barbie, Beautiful Bride, blond hair, twist waist, bendable knees, 1976..$25.00

Barbie, Busy (blue denim top & long patchwork skirt), long blond hair, hands open & close, 1972..................$50.00

Barbie, Color Magic (1-pc diamond pattern swimsuit, hair color-changing solution included), 1966............$250.00

Barbie, Deluxe Quick Curl (free Jergen's beauty kit included), blond hair, twist waist, bendable knees, 1976...$10.00

Barbie, Fashion Queen (1-pc gold & white striped swimsuit, beach bandana, three wigs & stand), 1963 ....$35.00

Barbie, Funtime (1-pc tangerine swimsuit), pink skin, 1975 ....$20.00

Barbie, Genuine, 1961, complete Enchanted Evening #983; 1962 Ken, painted hair, Tuxedo #787, fully dressed pair, M $450.00

Barbie, Gold Medal Skater (US Olympic-styled outfit & gear, also included was a doll-size medal), 1975..........$10.00

Barbie, Hawaiian (floral bikini w/matching skirt & lei, grass skirt, ukulele, & sailboat included), limited edition, 1975 ....$25.00

Barbie, Live Action (motorized stage included), long blond hair, rooted eyelashes, swivel joints, 1971 ....$25.00

Barbie, Living (1-pc gold & silver swimsuit), 1970......$25.00

Barbie, Malibu (1-pc swimsuit), suntanned skin & long blond hair, twist waist, bendable knees, 1971-72.$10.00

Barbie, Malibu Forget-Me-Nots, promotional offer from Kellogg's, 1972..$10.00

Barbie, Quick Curl (long pink & white checked dress), blond hair, twist waist, bendable knees, 1973......$10.00

Barbie, Spanish Talking (2-pc red vinyl swimsuit & net jacket), 1970 ....$25.00

Barbie, Sun Valley (w/ski gear included), 1974..........$10.00

Barbie, Sweet 16 (pink & white party dress, make-up compact & barrettes included), twist waist, bendable knees, 1974 ....$20.00

Barbie, Talking (2-pc swimsuit w/gold midi-coat), new straight-facing eyes, rooted eyelashes, bendable knees, 1971 ....**$25.00**

Barbie, Talking Busy (blue bibbed hot pants w/rose shirt & hat, green belt & boots), short blond hair w/bangs, 1972 ....**$50.00**

Barbie, Twist 'N Turn (salmon vinyl bikini w/white net cover-up), rooted eyelashes, bendable knees, 1967..**$35.00**

Barbie, Walk Lively (red top & pants w/tan suede double belt, red shoes & yellow bag), long blond hair, 1967..**$20.00**

Barbie (red swimsuit), bubble-cut hair, painted lips & nails, 1962 ....**$50.00**

Christie, Twist 'N Turn (1-pc pink & yellow swimsuit), 1970 ....**$35.00**

Francie, Hair Happenin's (blue mini-dress, four blond hair pieces included), bendable knees, 1970..............**$35.00**

Francie, Quick Curl (long yellow dress w/short sleeves), brunette hair, bendable knees, twist waist, 1973 ..**$20.00**

Francie (1-pc patterned swimsuit w/teal background), tan skin, rooted eyelashes, bendable legs, 1966 ....**$35.00**

Julia, Twist 'N Turn (2-pc nurse's uniform), 1969........**$25.00**

Ken, Busy (red tank top & blue jeans), brown molded hair, bendable elbows, 1972..................................**$25.00**

Ken, Funtime (blue swimming trunks), pink skin, dark brown hair, 1976..**$15.00**

Ken, Genuine (red swimming trunks & sandals), short flocked hair, plastic w/movable head, arms, & legs, 1961 ....**$50.00**

Ken, Live Action (motorized stage included), bendable knees, loosely jointed waist, 1971 ....**$20.00**

Ken, Malibu, suntanned skin, yellow painted hair, bendable knees, 1971..**$10.00**

Ken, Sun Valley (dressed for skiing w/ski gear included), 1974 ....**$10.00**

Ken, Talking (red jacket & trunks), brown-painted Edwardian hair style, bendable knees, 1969 ....**$25.00**

Ken, Talking Busy (red pants w/red & blue shirt), brown hair, bendable elbows, 1972 ....**$35.00**

Ken, Walk Lively (blue short-sleeved shirt & plaid pants, walk 'n turn stand included), bendable knees, 1972..**$15.00**

Ken (red swimming trunks & blue jacket), painted crew-cut hair, bendable legs, 1965..............................**$100.00**

Ken (red swimming trunks & red & white striped beach jacket), painted crew-cut hair, 1962......................**$12.00**

Midge (1-pc multicolored striped swimsuit), blond hair, bendable legs, 1965..**$150.00**

Midge (2-pc multicolored swimsuit & high-heeled shoes), freckle faced w/blue eyes, rooted Saran hair, 1963.**$20.00**

PJ, Groovy Talking (floral mini-dress), blond hair, real eyelashes, bendable legs, 1969 ....**$20.00**

PJ, Malibu (1-pc lavender swimsuit, glasses & towel included), suntanned skin, blond hair, 1972.........**$10.00**

PJ, Twist 'N Turn (1-pc pink swimsuit & sunglasses), 1970 ..**$25.00**

Skipper, Funtime (2-pc yellow swimsuit), pink skin, long blond hair, bendable knees & twist waist, 1967 ..**$15.00**

Skipper, Quick Curl (long blue & white checked dress), blond hair & freckles, twist waist, bendable knees, 1973 ....**$10.00**

Skipper, Twist 'N Turn (1-pc swimsuit w/orange, red, & purple checked top & solid orange bottom), 1969 ....**$15.00**

Skipper (1-pc blue swimsuit w/red & white trim), bendable knees, 1965..**$35.00**

Skipper (1-pc red & white swimsuit, brass headband), vinyl plastic w/movable legs, arms, & head, 1964.........**$12.00**

Skooter, Funtime (2-pc blue swimsuit), dark red hair, blue eyes, 1976 ....**$50.00**

Skooter (navy shorts w/red & white polka dot top), suntanned skin, bendable legs, 1966..........................**$20.00**

Stacey, Twist 'N Turn (1-pc red swimsuit w/button trim), rooted eyelashes, molded teeth, bendable knees, 1968 ....**$35.00**

Steffie, Walk Lively (rose, black, & white jumpsuit, walk 'n turn stand included), long brunette hair w/flip ends, 1972 ....**$25.00**

Truly Scrumptious, Talking (old-fashioned pink & rose satin dress w/fancy hat), bendable legs, 1969 ....**$250.00**

Accessories

Autograph book, Barbie, 1962 ....**$20.00**

Barbie Baby-Sits, pink plastic accessories & dress, 1974-76 ....**$15.00**

Bunk Beds, Skipper & Skooter, 1967 ....**$150.00**

Case, Ken & Allan, from France, hard to find......$100.00

Classy Corvette, Barbie, 1976.....................................**$125.00**

Diary, Barbie, 1963 ....**$25.00**

Dream Boat, Barbie, 1975 ....**$50.00**

Dream Room, Skipper, 1965-66 ....**$300.00**

Dress-Up Kit, Barbie, by Colorforms **$10.00**

Fashion Embroidery, Barbie & Ken **$25.00**

Fashion Hangers, Barbie, 1969-74 ....**$10.00**

Fashion Shop, Barbie, 1962-1964..............................**$200.00**

Fashion Stage, Barbie, 1971 ....**$45.00**

Friend Ship, Barbie, 1973 ....**$45.00**

Game, Queen of the Prom, Barbie, 1961-62 ....**$35.00**
Gift set, Barbie, Ken, & Midge on Parade, 1964 ....**$400.00**
Gift set, Midge's Ensemble, 1964 ....**$400.00**
Horse, 'Dancer,' Barbie, 1971-72 ....**$75.00**
Jumbo Trading Cards, Barbie & Ken, 1962 ....**$45.00**
Make-up case, Barbie, 1963 ....**$20.00**
Motor Roller w/Funtime Barbie **$100.00**
Olympic Ski Village, Barbie, 1975.............................**$45.00**
Outfit, Barbie, Bicentennial Dress.............................**$35.00**
Outfit, Barbie Beautiful Bride, 1966..........................**$150.00**
Outfit, Barbie London Tour, 1965..............................**$60.00**
Outfit, Barbie Sweet Dreams, 1961 ....**$25.00**
Outfit, Ken, American Airlines Captain, 1964..............**$50.00**
Outfit, Ken, Dress Suit **$75.00**
Outfit, Ken, Here Comes the Groom, 1965................**$110.00**
Outfit, Midge, Orange Blossom, 1962.........................**$40.00**
Outfit, Skipper, Land & Sea, 1964.............................**$30.00**
Pool Party, Barbie, 1974-92 ....**$25.00**
Record tote, Barbie, 1961 ....**$18.00**
Sun 'N Fun Buggy, Barbie, 1971-72...........................**$100.00**
Suzy Goose Vanity & Bench, Barbie, 1963-65 ....**$20.00**
Suzy Goose Wardrobe, Skipper, 1965 ....**$35.00**
Sweet-16 necklace, Barbie, 1974................................**$10.00**
Swing-A-Rounder Gym, Skipper, 1972 ....**$40.00**
Ten Speeder, Barbie, 1974 ....**$15.00**
Theatre, Barbie & Ken, 1964....................................**$300.00**

Barware

This field covers cocktail shakers, decanters, ice buckets, and the like that were designed to use in mixing and serving drinks. These items are diverse enough that they appeal to a variety of tastes and collecting interests. Some examples are from the Depression era, some carry advertising messages, and others are very Deco or ultramodern, made of chrome, Bakelite, and aluminum.

A recent issue of Harper's Bazaar carried a two-page photo-illustrated article with some wonderful examples of cocktail shakers from the 1920s and '30s. Nationwide exposure of this type has always attracted the interest of collectors; undoubtedly we can expect a flury of activity in this area.

Kitchen Glassware of the Depression Years and *The Collector's Encyclopedia of Depression Glass* both by Gene Florence show several examples of glass decanters.

Cocktail cup, 3½x2¼", #90067, chrome w/blue glass insert, marked Chase..**$15.00**
Cocktail glass, 6½", Cambridge, black glass nude stem w/clear glass bowl & base **$150.00**
Cocktail mixer, white graphics on cobalt, Hazel Atlas, 'Ships' pattern, w/stirrer **$22.50**
Cocktail set, 12", zeppelin shaped w/nested stirrers, shaker & ice bucket, chrome, marked Germany, ca 1920, M **$1,400.00**
Cocktail shaker, cobalt, barbell shape w/chrome lid ..**$95.00**

Cocktail shaker, penguin figural, Art-Deco styling, Napier..**$350.00**
Cocktail shaker, transparent green, etched grape designs around sides **$20.00**
Cocktail shaker, transparent red, barbell shape w/chrome trim & lid **$85.00**

Cocktail shaker, transparent red, lady's high-heeled boot form **$250.00**
Cocktail shaker, 11½", #90034, chrome w/black trim, marked Chase..**$45.00**
Cocktail tray, 15⅞x5⅜", #09013, chrome, marked Chase **$18.00**
Decanter, 10", transparent green Depression glass, 'Cameo' pattern, w/stopper **$120.00**
Hors d'oeuvre server, chrome swan holds picks for olives & onions, unmarked...**$25.00**
Ice bucket, amber, Paden City, 'Party Line' pattern.....**$27.50**
Ice bucket, black amethyst, w/rattan handle & glass lid **$75.00**
Ice bucket, transparent green, Paden City, 'Cupid' pattern **$150.00**
Ice bucket, transparent red, Anchor Hocking, w/clear glass handle...**$35.00**
Ice bucket, transparent red, Cambridge, 'Mt Vernon' pattern, tab handles **$85.00**
Ice bucket, yellow transparent glass, Fenton, w/rattan handle & glass lid **$125.00**
Ice crusher/bucket, 8½", 'Ice-O-Mat,' chrome, marked Bucketeer Rival Mfg Co, egg shaped w/crank handle & hinged lid **$75.00**
Ice tub, transparent green, tab handles....................**$18.00**
Ice tub, 4¾", transparent pink, Paden City, 'Cupid' pattern **$135.00**
Jigger, double; 2½", chrome...................................**$12.50**

Jigger & stirrer combination, 9", has bottle opener in curve at jigger end, silverplate **$15.00**

Liqueur set, 14", bowling ball form w/bowler as finial, marbleized plastic & chrome, dispenser w/six glasses inside **$100.00**

Soda dispenser, 9½", ovoid chrome body on round footed base, simple Art-Deco styling, marked Soda King USA **$35.00**

Stirrer, 11", chrome spoon w/plastic knob on twisted handle...**$15.00**

Tray, 16x11½", cobalt glass in rectangular chrome base, attributed to Norman Bel Geddes.....................**$250.00**

Tumbler, old-fashioned; 3⅜", Hazel Atlas, 'Ships' pattern **$14.00**

Whiskey, 1½-oz, cobalt, Hazel Atlas, 'Moderntone' pattern **$22.00**

Whiskey, 2", 1-oz, transparent green, Jeannette Glass Co, 'Hex Optic' pattern...**$7.00**

Whiskey, 2¼", white graphics on cobalt, Hazel Atlas, 'Ships' pattern **$105.00**

Baseball Cards

Collecting memorabilia from all kinds of sports events has been a popular hobby for years. Baseball has long been known as the 'national pastime' with literally millions of fans who avidly follow the sport at every level from 'sandbox' to the major leagues. Of those fans, if only one in ten became a collector, the number would be staggering.

There's no doubt that among today's collectors baseball card buying and selling represents a huge percentage of the activity in this field. Hundreds have been printed and many are worth less than 20¢, but a good card can often represent a significant investment. It wouldn't be unusual to have to pay as much as $50.00 for an early Topps or Bowman superstar, and a 1952 Topps Mickey Mantel books today at $18,000.00, though this is probably a minimum value. Some of the more valuable cards have been reproduced, so beware. Except for only a few, the entire 1952 Topps set was reissued in the early 1980s, but these are clearly marked. You'll need a good price guide before you start to collect; one of the best is *Gene Florence's Standard Baseball Cards Price Guide*.

If you are totally unfamiliar with cards, you'll need to know how to determine the various manufacturers. 1) Bowman: All are copyrighted Bowman or B.G.H.L.I., except a few from the fifties that are marked '. . . in the series of Baseball Picture Cards.' 2) Donruss: All are marked with the Donruss logo on the front. 3) Fleer: From 1981 to 1984 the Fleer name is on the backs of the cards; after 1985 it was also on the front. 4) Score & Sportflics: Score written on front, Sportflics on back of each year. 5) Topps: 1951 cards are baseball game pieces with red or blue backs (no other identification). After that either Topps or T.G.C. appears somewhere on the card. 6) Upper Deck: Marked front and back with Upper Deck logo and hologram.

Learn to judge the condition of your card, since its con-

dition is a very important factor when it comes to making an accurate evaluation. Superstars' and Hall of Famers' cards are most likely to appreciate, and the colored photo cards from the thirties are good investments as well. Buy modern cards by the set while they're inexpensive; who knows what they may be worth in years to come. Any of today's rookies may be the next Babe Ruth!

Al Benton, 1952, #374, Topps, EX....................**$175.00**
Al Corwin, 1954, #137, Bowman, EX.....................**$12.00**
Al Evans, 1949, #132, Bowman, VG.......................**$3.50**
Al Kaline, 1956, #20, Topps, VG.........................**$22.50**
Albie Pearson, 1961, #288, Topps, M....................**$2.50**
Allie Clark, 1949, #150, Bowman, EX.....................**$18.00**
Allie Gair, 1954, #179, Topps, M.........................**$15.00**
Alvin Davis, 1984, #30, Fleer, M...........................**$8.00**
Augie Galan, 1949, #230, Bowman, M **$75.00**

Barney, McCosky, 1952, #300, Topps, VG **$13.75**
Barry Larkin, 1986, #34, Sportflics, M **$2.00**
Bert Blyleven, 1971, #26, Topps, M.......................**$40.00**
Bill Bruton, 1960, #37, Topps, M **$3.50**
Bill Fischer, 1961, #553, Topps, VG.......................**$7.00**
Bill Kunkel, 1962, #147, Topps, M.........................**$3.00**
Bill Melton, 1972, #90, Topps, M **$2.00**
Bill Miller, 1952, #403, Topps, M **$175.00**
Bill Rigney, 1960, #225, Topps, M.........................**$3.00**
Bill White, 1963, #290, Topps, M.........................**$5.00**
Billy Cox, 1952, #232, Topps, VG **$7.00**
Billy Cox, 1953, #26, Bowman, M.........................**$30.00**
Billy Gardner, 1955, #249, Bowman, M..................**$25.00**
Billy Martin, 1960, #173, Topps, M **$10.00**
Bo Jackson, 1988, #260, Fleer, M **$2.50**
Bo Jackson, 1990, #697, Score, EX........................**$3.00**
Bo Jackson, 1991, #19, Donruss Leaf prototype, M.....**$15.00**
Bob Aspromonte, 1960, #547, Topps, EX....................**$7.50**
Bob Bonner, 1982, #21, Topps, VG........................**$18.00**
Bob Boone, 1973, #613, Topps, M **$40.00**
Bob Bowman, 1957, #332, Topps, M.......................**$18.00**
Bob Del Greco, 1953, #48, Topps, EX....................**$10.00**

Bob Dillinger, 1951, #63, Bowman, EX......................**$20.00**
Bob Floyd, 1969, 3597, Topps, EX.............................**$85.00**
Bob Friend, 1966, #519, Topps, M.............................**$8.00**
Bob Lemon, 1951, #53, Bowman, VG **$12.50**
Bobby Brown, 1952, #105, Bowman, EX **$25.00**
Bobby Shantz, 1952, #219, Topps, VG **$9.00**
Bobby Young, 1954, #149, Bowman, M......................**$12.00**

Boog Powell, 1965, #3, Topps, EX......................$14.00
Boog Powell, 1967, #243, Topps, M **$4.00**
Bret Saberhagen, 1984, #103, Fleer, M **$40.00**
Brett Butler, 1992, #18, Donruss, M **$2.00**
Bruce Edwards, 1951, #116, Bowman, EX **$14.00**
Bryan Harvey, 1987, #87, Score, M **$1.50**
Bubba Morton, 1962, #554, Topps, VG **$5.00**
Cal Ripken, 1990, #197, Donruss, M **$5.00**
Cal Ripken Jr, 1982, #176, Fleer, M **$50.00**
Carl Yastrzemski, 1961, #287, Topps, VG.................**$37.50**
Carl Yastrzemski, 1981, #294, Donruss, M..................**$1.50**
Carlton Fisk, 1981, #224, Fleer, EX **$1.75**
Cecil Fielder, 1986, #386, Topps, NM **$7.50**
Cecil Fielder, 1986, #512, Donruss, EX......................**$15.00**
Cecil Fielder, 1987, #31, Fleer, EX **$3.00**
Chico Cardenas, 1968, #23, Topps, M **$1.20**
Chico Carrasquel, 1952, #251, Topps, M **$45.00**
Chico Fernandez, 1955, #270, Bowman, VG.................**$4.50**
Chuck Estrada, 1962, #560, Topps, EX......................**$20.00**
Chuck Harmon, 1957, #299, Topps, NM **$15.00**
Chuck Knoblauch, 1991, #37, Fleer Ultimate Update, M..**$1.50**
Chuck Knoblauch, 1991, #396, Donruss Leaf, M **$3.00**
Chuck Schilling, 1962, #345, Topps, M........................**$2.00**
Cleon Jones, 1967, #165, Topps, M.............................**$1.60**
Cliff Chambers, 1954, #126, Bowman, EX **$8.00**
Cliff Fannin, 1951, #36, Topps, M **$25.00**
Cory Snyder, 1986, #653, Fleer, EX...........................**$20.00**
Curt Barclay, 1958, #21, Topps, VG **$1.75**
Curt Simmons, 1954, #79, Bowman, EX **$8.00**
Dale Murphy, 1977, #476, Topps, VG **$11.50**
Danny O'Connell, 1960, #192, Topps, M......................**$3.00**
Danny Tartabull, 1986, #178, Sportflics, VG.................**$2.25**
Darryl Strawberry, 1984, #599, Fleer, M **$42.00**

Darryl Strawberry, 1987, #118, Donruss, M **$1.00**
Dave Magadan, 1987, #648, Fleer, M **$1.00**
Dave Parker, 1991, #3, Donruss, M.............................**$3.00**
Dave Philley, 1952, #226, Topps, VG **$7.00**
Dave Righetti, 1986, #141, Sportflics, M.......................**$1.00**
Denny McLain, 1970, #400, Topps, M.........................**$2.00**
Derrell Griffith, 1966, #573, Topps, M.......................**$12.50**
Dick Ellsworth, 1964, #1, Topps, M............................**$20.00**
Dick Gernert, 1962, #536, Topps, EX **$8.00**
Dixie Walker, 1953, #190, Topps, M..........................**$16.00**
Don Drysdale, 1962, #398, Topps, M **$12.00**
Don Kessinger, 1967, #419, Topps, M **$2.00**
Don Kline, 1965, #56, Topps, M **$1.20**
Don Landrum, 1965, #596, Topps, VG **$2.50**
Don Lee, 1964, #493, Topps, M **$3.00**
Don Leppert, 1963, #243, Topps, M............................**$3.00**
Don Mattingly, 1986, #2, Sportflics, M.........................**$1.25**
Don Mattingly, 1991, #22, Donruss, M........................**$12.00**
Doug Rader, 1967, #412, Topps, M............................**$3.00**
Duke Snider, 1950, #77, Bowman, M.......................**$260.00**
Dusty Rhodes, 1955, #1, Topps, VG **$10.00**
Dwight Evans, 1974, #351, Topps, EX........................**$16.00**
Dwight Gooden, 1985, #190, Donruss, M **$14.00**
Dwight Gooden, 1987, #159, Sportflics, M **$1.25**
Ed Mathews, 1962, #30, Topps, VG **$4.00**
Eddie Bressoud, 1966, #516, Topps, M **$5.00**
Eddie Yost, 1953, #116, Bowman, EX **$45.00**
Ellis Burks, 1987, #5, Sportflics Rookie, M **$1.00**
Elston Howard, 1963, #60, Topps, M...........................**$6.00**
Enos Slaughter, 1951, #58, Bowman, VG **$14.00**
Eric Davis, 1984, #533, Fleer, M................................**$16.00**
Eric Davis, 1985, #325, Donruss, M **$15.00**
Eric Davis, 1985, #533, Fleer, EX **$16.00**
Eric Lindros, 1990, #100, Score, M **$7.00**
Ernie Banks, 1958, #310, Topps, M...........................**$80.00**
Ernie Oravetz, 1957, #179, Topps, VG.........................**$2.00**
Felix Millan, 1967, #89, Topps, M...............................**$1.60**
Fernando Valenzuela, 1981, #140, Fleer, M..................**$2.00**
Ferris Fain, 1950, #13, Bowman, VG..........................**$12.50**
Floyd Baker, 1949, #119, Bowman, EX **$14.00**
Frank Thomas, 1956, #153, Topps, M.........................**$12.00**
Frank Thomas, 1990, #320, Bowman, M **$3.00**
Frank Thomas, 1990, #663, Score, EX..........................**$6.00**
Fred Gladding, 1965, #27, Topps, M............................**$1.20**
Fred Hutchison, 1953, #219, Topps, M.........................**$3.00**
Fred McGriff, 1987, #621, Donruss, EX........................**$3.50**
Gary Scott, 1991, #4, Donruss Leaf bonus card, M **$4.00**
George Bell, 1984, #148, Fleer, M...............................**$1.50**
George Bell, 1984, #73, Donruss, EX...........................**$3.00**
George Brett, 1975, #228, Topps, VG **$50.00**
George Brett, 1977, #580, Topps, M...........................**$25.00**
Georges Maranda, 1960, #479, Topps, M.....................**$4.00**
Gerry Arrigo, 1967, #488, Topps, M............................**$5.00**
Gino Cimoli, 1965, #569, Topps, M............................**$10.00**
Greg Luzinski, 1971, #439, Topps, M...........................**$3.00**
Hank Aaron, 1955, #179, Bowman, EX **$225.00**
Hank Aaron, 1958, ##0, Topps, VG............................**$52.50**
Hank Aaron, 1970, #500, Topps, M............................**$50.00**

Hank Aguirre, 1970, #699, Topps, M $3.00

Hank Allen, 1967, #569, Topps, VG $125.00

Hank Borowy, 1950, #177, Bowman, EX $18.00

Harold Baines, 1981, #346, Fleer, EX.........................$2.50

Harold Baines, 1981, #347, Topps, M $3.50

Harry Byrd, 1958, #154, Topps, VG $1.00

Harvey Haddix, 1959, #184, Topps, M $4.00

Henry Rodriguez, 1991, #8, Donruss Leaf bonus card, M ..$2.00

Howie Koplitz, 1964, #372, Topps, M $3.00

Howie Pollet, 1951, #7, Topps, M...............................$6.00

Irv Noren, 1953, #45, Bowman, EX $20.00

Jack Aker, 1971, #593, Topps, M.................................$1.50

Jack Daniels, 1953, #83, Bowman, EX........................$20.00

Jack Harshman, 1955, #104, Topps, VG $2.25

Jackie Robinson, 1950, #22, Bowman, VG.................$165.00

Jeff Bagwell, 1991, #14, Donruss, M.........................$15.00

Jeff Bagwell, 1991, #30, Donruss Rookie, M $3.00

Jeff Bagwell, 1991, #79, Fleer Ultimate Update, M.........$5.00

Jeff Pendleton, 1985, #534, Donruss, EX $3.00

Jeff Reardon, 1984, #279, Donruss, M.........................$1.00

Jessie Barfield, 1982, #203, Topps, M $2.00

Jim Bouton, 1962, #592, Topps, EX...........................$50.00

Jim Bunning, 1971, #574, Topps, EX...........................$5.00

Jim Davis, 1956, #102, Topps, VG $2.00

Jim Dyck, 1953, #177, Topps, M $16.00

Jim Gentile, 1963, #260, Topps, NM $2.50

Jim Hickman, 1970, #612, Topps, M $1.40

Jim Maloney, 1964, #3, Topps, M................................$8.00

Jim Palmer, 1967, #475, Topps, VG $110.00

Jim Palmer, 1983, #77, Donruss, M $1.00

Jim Palmer, 1984, #576, Donruss, M $3.50

Jim Pendleton, 1962, #432, Topps, EX..........................$4.00

Jim Robertson, 1955, #177, Topps, M $18.00

Jimmie Hall, 1964, #73, Topps, M................................$1.75

Jocko Thompson, 1949, #161, Bowman, M.................$75.00

Joe Adcock, 1963, #170, Topps, EX.............................$24.00

Joe Black, 1955, #156, Topps, M.................................$30.00

Joe Carter, 1984, #41, Donruss, M...............................$35.00

Joe Carter, 1985, #443, Fleer, EX.................................$6.00

Joe Collins, 1952, #202, Topps, VG $8.75

Joe DeMaestri, 1954, #147, Bowman, EX $12.00

Joe Garagiola, 1952, #27, Bowman, M $70.00

Joe Hoener, 1973, #653, Topps, M...............................$2.00

Joe Jay, 1962, #58, Topps, M.......................................$2.00

Joe L Morgan, 1974, #85, Topps, M $5.00

Joe Morgan, 1984, #80, Fleer Update, M $6.00

Joe Pactwa, 1976, #589, Topps, M...............................$2.00

Joe Tipton, 1952, #134, Topps, VG...............................$7.00

Johnny Bench, 1984, #0, Donruss, M $10.00

Johnny Callison, 1962, #17, Topps, M $2.00

Johnny Groth, 1950, #243, Bowman, EX........................$12.50

Johnny Logan, 1954, #80, Bowman, M $10.00

Johnny Pesky, 1952, #15, Topps, M..............................$65.00

Johnny Riddle, 1955, #98, Topps, M.............................$9.50

Johnny Wyrostek, 1955, #237, Bowman, EX $12.50

Jose Canseco, 1986, #39, Donruss, M $80.00

Jose Canseco, 1990, #108, Donruss, EX $3.50

Jose Canseco, 1991, #441, Score Dream Team, M $2.00

Jose Rijo, 1984, #100, Topps, M $5.00

Jose Rijo, 1984, #99, Fleer Update, M $16.00

Juan Marichal, 1970, #67, Topps, EX $4.00

Julio Franco, 1983, #525, Donruss, EX $10.00

Julio Gotay, 1968, #41, Topps, M.................................$1.20

Kal Daniels, 1986, #27, Donruss Rated Rookie, M........$3.00

Karl Drews, 1952, #352, Topps, VG..............................$45.00

Karl Spooner, 1956, #83, Topps, VG.............................$2.00

Keith Hernandez, 1976, #542, Topps, M $5.00

Kelly Gruber, 1986, #16, Donruss, EX $2.00

Ken Griffey Jr, 1991, #3, Score bonus card, M $4.00

Kevin McReynolds, 1984, #34, Donruss Rated Rookie, M .$7.00

Kirby Puckett, 1985, #438, Donruss, VG.......................$8.00

Kirby Puckett, 1991, #21, Donruss, VG $2.50

Kirk Gibson, 1981, #481, Fleer, M...............................$3.00

Larry Anderson, 1978, #703, Topps, EX $12.50

Larry Jackson, 1956, #119, Topps, M $12.00

Larry Yellen, 1964, #226, Topps, M $1.80

Lew Burdette, 1956, #219, Topps, M $18.00

Lloyd Merriman, 1952, #78, Bowman, M $15.00

Lou Brock, 1968, #520, Topps, EX...............................$24.00

Louis Aloma, 1954, #57, Topps, VG.............................$7.50

Mark Grace, 1988, #641, Fleer, EX...............................$4.00

Marquis Grissom, 1990, #107, Donruss Leaf, M $2.50

Matt Batts, 1953, #22, Bowman, EX.............................$30.00

Matt Williams, 1988, #101, Fleer, M $4.00

Matt Williams, 1988, #118, Score, M $1.50

Maurice McDermott, 1952, #119, Topps, VG...............$7.00

Maury Wills, 1972, #437, Topps, M..............................$2.00

Max Avis, 1963, #228, Topps, M $45.00

Mel Parnell, 1953, #19, Topps, M.................................$18.00

Mel Stottlemyre, 1971, #615, Topps, M.........................$3.00

Mickey Mantle, 1955, #202, Bowman, VG $115.00

Mickey Mantle, 1961, #406, Topps, M $40.00

Mickey Mantle, 1963, #173, Topps, M $60.00

Mickey Mantle, 1975, #200, Topps, M $5.00

Mike Brumley, 1964, #167, Topps, VG.........................$6.25

Mike Greenwell, 1986, #178, Sportflics, M $9.50

Mike Greenwell, 1987, #585, Donruss, M....................$4.50

Mike Hegan, 1967, #553, Topps, M $30.00
Mike Schmidt, 1974, #283, Topps, VG.........................$25.00
Mo Vaugn, 1991, #7, Donruss Leaf bonus card, M $8.00
Nellie Fox, 1964, #81, Topps, M $7.00
Nolan Ryan, 1982, #90, Topps, M $8.00
Nolan Ryan, 1986, #258, Donruss, M............................$4.00
Ollie Brown, 1966, #524, Topps, M $28.00
Pat Dobson, 1967, #526, Topps, M $5.00
Pete Rose, 1968, #230, Topps, EX................................$30.00

Pete Rose, 1983, #100, Topps, EX $2.00
Pete Rose, 1984, #102, Fleer, EX..................................$20.00
Phil Niekro, 1969, #355, Topps, M................................$7.00
Phil Plantier, 1991, #348, Score, M...............................$1.50
Ralph Branca, 1951, #20, Topps, EX...........................$45.00
Ralph Houk, 1950, #465, Topps, VG $3.00
Ralph Kiner, 1950, #33, Bowman, M $120.00
Ray Barker, 1967, #583, Topps, VG $4.50
Ray Katt, 1960, #468, Topps, M $4.00
Rich Beck, 1955, #234, Topps, M $5.00
Richie Ashburn, 1952, #53, Bowman, EX.....................$50.00
Richie Ashburn, 1955, #130, Bowman, M $24.00
Rick Reichardt, 1970, #720, Topps, EX $6.00
Rickey Henderson, 1982, #113, Donruss, M..................$5.00
Rickey Henderson, 1990, #160, Donruss Leaf, M...........$3.00
Rickey Henderson, 1991, #4, Score, M $2.00
Rip Repulski, 1954, #115, Topps, VG $4.00
Rob Clemente, 1967, #242, Topps, M $8.00
Rob Deer, 1985, #648, Fleer, M $1.50
Roberto Alomar, 1988, #122, Fleer Update, M $4.00
Roberto Kelly, 1988, #212, Fleer, M..............................$1.50
Rod Carew, 1983, #90, Donruss, M................................$1.00
Roger Clemens, 1985, #273, Donruss, EX....................$10.00
Roger Clemens, 1987, #159, Sportflics, M......................$1.25
Roger Craig, 1965, #411, Topps, EX..............................$4.00
Roy McMillan, 1952, #238, Bowman, EX.....................$32.00
Roy McMillan, 1973, #257, Topps, M............................$2.00
Roy Smalley, 1957, #397, Topps, M $6.00
Ryne Sandberg, 1983, #507, Fleer, M...........................$35.00
Sam Jeffroe, 1952, #27, Topps, NM..............................$48.00

Sam Mele, 1965, #506, Topps, M $4.00
Sammy Ellis, 1965, #507, Topps, EX.............................$2.50
Sandy Alomar, 1991, #17, Donruss Leaf prototype, M...$5.00
Sandy Amoros, 1955, #75, Topps, M.............................$16.00
Scott Erickson, 1991, #36, Fleer Ultimate Update, M $2.00
Sheldon Jones, 1950, #83, Bowman, VG $4.50
Sherm Lollar, 1955, #201, Topps, EX...........................$12.50
Sid Gordon, 1954, #11, Bowman, M..............................$8.00
Stan Bahnsen, 1967, #93, Topps, M...............................$3.00
Stan Lopata, 1950, #206, Bowman, M...........................$18.00
Steve Avery, 1990, #109, Score, EX...............................$3.50
Steve Avery, 1990, #481, Donruss, EX..........................$20.00
Steve Barber, 1964, #450, Topps, M...............................$3.00
Steve Bilko, 1952, #287, Topps, VG $14.00
Steve Carlton, 1983, #155, Fleer, M................................$1.00
Steve Decker, 1991, #16, Donruss, M $4.00
Steve Sax, 1982, #21, Fleer, M..$4.00
Terry Pendleton, 1985, #236, Fleer, M............................$4.00
Tex Clevenger, 1963, #457, Topps, EX...........................$7.50
Tim Laudner, 1982, #766, Topps, M $3.50
Tino Martinez, 1991, #24, Donruss, EX..........................$6.00
Toby Atwell, 1952, #356, Topps, M...........................$175.00
Toby Atwell, 1954, #123, Bowman, M $8.00
Tom Glavine, 1988, #638, Score, M.................................$1.50
Tom Seaver, 1984, #106, Fleer, M.................................$25.00
Tom Upton, 1952, #71, Topps, VG...............................$14.00
Tommie Agee, 1969, #364, Topps, M $1.00
Tommy Davis, 1960, #509, Topps, VG $5.00
Tony Gwynn, 1983, #360, Fleer, VG...............................$4.50
Tony LaRussa, 1968, #571, Topps, NM...........................$3.50
Tony Phillips, 1992, #25, Donruss, M $2.00
Travis Fryman, 1991, #54, Donruss Leaf stadium card, black
   & white, M..$2.00
Vern Bickford, 1950, #47, Bowman, M.........................$50.00
Vern Bickford, 1950, #57, M...$50.00
Vince Coleman, 1985, #29, Fleer Update, EX.................$7.50
Wade Boggs, 1984, #151, Donruss, EX.........................$15.00
Wade Boggs, 1984, #392, Fleer, EX..............................$10.00
Wade Boggs, 1984, #392, Fleer, VG...............................$2.50
Wade Boggs, 1986, #3, Sportflics, M $2.50
Wally Moon, 1958, #201, Topps, M $4.00
Walt Bond, 1960, #552, Topps, EX $8.00
Will Clark, 1987, #95, Sportflics, M................................$2.00
Willie Jones, 1954, #143, Bowman, M $12.00
Willie Mays, 1959, #317, Topps, EX.............................$15.00
Willy McCovey, 1968, #5, Topps, M $4.00
Woody Fryman, 1966, #498, Topps, M..........................$5.00
Woody Held, 1967, #251, Topps, M $1.50
Yogi Berra, 1960, #480, Topps, M.................................$80.00
Zeke Bella, 1959, #254, Topps, EX $2.50
Zollo Versailles, 1964, #15, Topps, M............................$2.00

Baskets

   Old baskets were made not only of splint, but willow, vines, grasses, leaves, and roots of small trees were used also. They were sometimes designed for special chores.

Egg gathering, cotton harvesting, sewing, and market baskets are only a few of the types you may find. It's very hard to tell the origin of a basket, since weaving techniques were much the same from all parts of the country. The style of their construction and the material from which they were made are the most reliable indicators. Age is difficult to determine, since any basket that has been exposed to the elements very quickly takes on the patina of an antique one. Because old baskets have become very scarce and as a result expensive, contemporary basketweavers have stepped in to satisfy demand. It's often nearly impossible to tell the difference, so unless you're sure, buy only baskets that you'll personally enjoy and assess them on their esthetics and workmanship. We've listed just a few here to give you a basic idea of their values.

For more information we recommend *The Collector's Guide to Country Baskets* by Don and Carol Raycraft.

Ash splint, 15" dia, cat's ear points on rounded-out square bottom **$95.00**

Buttocks, 12", oak splint, well made **$160.00**
Buttocks, 5", 1-egg size, reed & cane, contemporary, signed & dated **$60.00**
Buttocks, 6x8x10", half-round..................................**$180.00**
Cheese, 22", round rim w/hexagonal base & straight sides, 1825 ....**$265.00**
Clam-gathering, 16x14", wire base w/splint top, 1850s.**$345.00**
Egg, 10x10x14", oak splint, 1890s, VG **$65.00**
Egg, 8x9x9", oval w/checkered pattern, NM...............**$75.00**
Gathering, 13", oak, walnut-dyed bands, handles **$85.00**
Laundry, 21" dia, wide splint, rim handles...................**$65.00**
Laundry, 28", bentwood rim handles, wood runner foot, EX..**$110.00**
Lunch basket, 15" long, green & white woven splint, swing handles **$200.00**
Market, 11x12x18", painted green, ca 1910, EX..........**$50.00**

Melon rib, 7x13" dia, decorative design at handle **$100.00**
Nantucket, 10" dia, ca 1900..**$600.00**
Nantucket, 5x8x10", oval turned base, swing handles, EX...**$1,100.00**
Nantucket, 8x12", turned base, swing handle, signed William Appleton...**$1,700.00**
Picnic, 15x20x15", willow w/ash handles & lid, brass hinges...**$75.00**
Potato field, heavy wire, bail handle..........................**$20.00**
Rye straw, 12½", w/lid..**$55.00**
Rye straw, 2¾x12¾", bowl form **$45.00**
Swing handle, 9x15", varnished, marked WJ Rich.....**$375.00**

Bauer Pottery

Undoubtedly the most easily recognized product of the Bauer Pottery Company who operated from 1909 until 1962 in Los Angeles, California, was their colorful 'Ring' dinnerware (made from 1932 until sometime in the early sixties). You'll recognize it by its bright solid colors: Jade Green, Chinese Yellow, Royal Blue, Light Blue, Orange-Red, Black and White; and by its pattern of closely aligned ribs. They made other lines of dinnerware as well; they're collectible, too, although by no means as easily found.

They also made a line of Gardenware vases and flowerpots for the florist trade. To give you an idea of their values, a 12" vase from this line would bring about $75.00.

To further your understanding of Bauer, we recommend *The Collector's Encyclopedia of California Pottery* by Jack Chipman.

California Art, ewer, 10", light blue **$50.00**
California Art, hippo figurine, 3¼x4½", pastel matt glaze **$150.00**
Gloss Pastel Kitchenware, teapot, 8-cup, yellow, in-mold mark...**$60.00**
Hi-Fire, flower bowl, 5", orange-red............................**$25.00**
Ring, baking dish, black, w/lid **$55.00**
Ring, bowl, mixing; #24, yellow **$25.00**
Ring, casserole, individual; 4", orange-red...................**$75.00**
Ring, jug, light blue, ball form **$80.00**
Ring, mug, yellow..**$65.00**
Ring, plate, bread & butter; 6", dark blue **$12.00**
Ring, plate, salad; 7½", black **$45.00**
Ring, salt & pepper shakers, orange-red, pair.............**$15.00**
Ring, teapot, 6-cup, yellow, w/lid **$60.00**
Ring, tumbler, 6-oz, yellow **$15.00**
Ring, vase, 8", dark blue...**$40.00**
Ring, water jug, green, w/lid **$200.00**
Tracy Irwin, vase, 13", pastel colors, #678 ....**$40.00**
Tracy Irwin, vase, 8", pastel colors, #502 ....**$30.00**

Beatles Collectibles

Possibly triggered by John Lennon's death in 1980, Beatles' fans, recognizing that their dreams of the band ever reuniting were gone along with him, began to collect memorabilia of all types. Recently some of the original Beatles material has sold at auction with high-dollar results. Handwritten song lyrics, Lennon's autographed high school textbook, and even the legal agreement that was drafted at the time the group disbanded are among the one-of-a-kind multi-thousand dollar sales recorded.

Unless you plan on attending sales of this caliber, you'll be more apt to find the commercially produced memorabilia that literally flooded the market during the sixties when the Fab Four from Liverpool made their unprecedented impact on the entertainment world. A word about their records: they sold in such mass quantities that unless the record is a 'promotional,' made to send to radio stations or for jukebox distribution, they have very little value. Once a record has been played very often and has lost much of its originial gloss, becomes scratched, or has writing on the label, its value is minimal. Even in near-mint condition, $4.00 to $6.00 is plenty to pay for a 45 (much less if its worn) unless the original picture sleeve is present. The exception to this is the white-labeled Swan recording of 'She Loves You/I'll Get You,' which in great condition may go as high as $50.00. The picture sleeves are usually valued at $30.00 to $40.00, except for the rare 'Can't Buy Me Love,' which is worth ten times that amount. Beware of reproductions!

We recommend *The Beatles, A Reference and Value Guide* by Michael Stern, Barbara Crawford, and Hollis Lamon.

Album, foldout w/many pictures, on chain..........$60.00
Band-Aid Dispenser, dated 1966..................................$12.50
Bank, drum shape w/photos, marked NEMS, 1964, M..**$7.50**
Bubble bath container, Paul, Colgate, EX.................$130.00
Bubble gum cards, 1960s, 175-pc set, M......................$55.00
Calendar, 16x10", McCartney Back in the USSR, 1990, EX $50.00
Charm, Paul, plastic record (illustrated)...............$15.00
Coloring book, 'The Beatles,' Saalfield, 1966, NM.......$55.00
Disk-Go record case, EX..$65.00
Game, 'Flip Your Wig,' Milton Bradley, 1964, NM........$80.00
Hairbrush, in original package.....................................$25.00
Halloween costume, John, 1960s, in original box.....$125.00
Lobby card, 41x27", 'Candy,' w/Ringo, EX...................$25.00
Lunch box, w/thermos, NM..$275.00

Magazine, 'Life,' Paul & Linda on cover, April 4, 1971, EX...**$10.00**
Magazine, 'People,' Paul on cover, June 7, 1976, EX..**$12.00**
Magazine, 'Post,' John on cover, December 1964, EX.**$12.50**
Model, Ringo, Revell, built..**$58.00**
Nodder, 1960s, set of 4, original package, M, rare....**$600.00**
Notebook binder..**$80.00**
Paperback, 'Help!,' 1965, EX..**$12.50**
Pennant, 30", red, white & blue wool, 1964, EX.........**$15.00**
Pin-back button, 2½", 'I Needed Help! So I Got My Beatles Movie Tickets!'...**$14.00**
Poster, London Palladium Royal Command Performance, 1964, marked NEMS...................................**$20.00**
Poster, 21x32½", black-light psychedelic portraits w/Maharishi Mahesh Yogi, ca 1965, G.................................**$70.00**
Poster, 25x12", color head portraits, cardboard, 1964, unframed, G...**$40.00**
Poster, 27x41", Liztomania, Ringo Starr, 1975.............**$12.00**
Puzzle, 'Beatles Yellow Submarine,' Jaymar, 1968, 650-pc, in original box..**$65.00**
Puzzle, 'Yellow Submarine,' 100-pc, in orginal box, EX..**$80.00**
Record, 45rpm, 'And I Love Her/If I Feel,' Capitol, #5235, EX, w/picture sleeve..............................**$50.00**
Record, 45rpm, 'I Want To Hold Your Hand/I Saw Her Standing There,' Capitol, swirl label, w/picture sleeve, EX..**$38.00**
Scrapbook, 10x12", color photo cover, softcover, NEMS, 1964, G...**$30.00**
Skateboard, 19x6", Surf Skater Co, photo decals & logo name on wood, 1965, in original box.................**$125.00**
Song sheet, 'Yes It Is'...**$30.00**
Souvenir booklet, 12x12", Raydell Publishing, 1966, USA Ltd Tour, 1966, 32 pages, M...........................**$47.50**
Souvenir booklet, 8½x11¾", 'Hard Day's Night,' Whitman, 1964, 32-pg, VG..**$25.00**
Switchplate cover, 'Yellow Submarine,' EX.................**$27.50**
Ticket stub, Shea Stadium, August 23, 1966.................**$25.00**
Tie tack, head portrait, 1964, on original full-color display card, set of 4, M...**$75.00**
Tour book, Ringo Starr All-Starr Band, 'US Tour,' 1989, EX..**$12.00**
Tour book, US, original 1964 issue, 24-page..............**$18.00**
Toy, 'Yellow Submarine,' Corgi, VG............................**$95.00**
Wallet, portraits & names on opposing sides, red & white, M..**$100.00**
Wallet, 4½x3¾", tan, complete w/file, mirror, comb, NM..**$125.00**
8-Track tape, Beatles 1967-1970, Apple, set of 2, EX..**$32.00**

Bedroom and Bathroom Glassware

This type of glassware was produced in large quantities during the Depression era by many glasshouses who were simply trying to stay in business. They made puff jars, trays, lamps, and vanity sets for the bedroom; towel bars, soap dishes, and bottles of all types for the bath. These items came in much the same color assortment as the Depression glass dinnerware that has been so popular with collectors for more than twenty years. For the most part, it's not terribly expensive, though prices for items that can be traced to some of the more prestigious companies such as Heisey, Cambridge, Fostoria, or Akro Agate are already climbing.

For more information we recommend *Bedroom and Bathroom Glassware of the Depression Years* by Margaret and Kenn Whitmyer.

Atomizer, 4", ivory, 8-panel w/black panel outline, Cambridge...**$50.00**

Atomizer, 6½", ebony w/gold encrusted decor, Cambridge...**$100.00**

Barber bottle, cranberry, Vertical Stripe, Fenton.......**$100.00**

Bath bottle, 2½" sq, crystal w/red dot decor, red glass stopper...**$10.00**

Bathroom set, four crystal bottles w/embossed labels, plastic tops, wooden tray..**$75.00**

Clock, crystal w/pressed glass body, round................**$35.00**

Clock, 6½", pink, embossed leaf design.....................**$100.00**

Cold cream jar, marbleized orange, black glass or celluloid lid, Akro Agate...**$100.00**

Cold cream jar, 4½", pink, metal lid, 4-footed, 'Dubarry-Richard Hudnut' on label...**$25.00**

Cologne, 6", milk glass, Paneled Grape pattern w/gold decor, Westmoreland...**$50.00**

Doorknob, crystal w/cut design, oval.......................**$55.00**

Dresser set, cobalt, flower embossed in bottom of tray **$125.00**

Guest set, pitcher & six tumblers, pitcher: 7"; tumblers: 3½", crystal, enameled basket & gold decor.............**$150.00**

Jewel box, 6", milk glass w/Jenny Lind figure in beaded oval, oval, Fostoria #833.................................**$50.00**

Lamp, 'Prima Donna,' fired-on blue, glass shade.........**$45.00**

Lamp, 'Victorian Lady,' frosted green w/metal base & shade...**$125.00**

Lamp, fired-on blue, sailboat shape...........................**$35.00**

Lamp, transparent green, embossed flowers, ball shape...**$25.00**

Lamp, 6¼", milk glass, English Hobnail, Westmoreland #555/1...**$45.00**

Lamp base, Waffle, transparent pink....................**$60.00**

Lotion bottle, 4¾", 'Ardena Velva' from Elizabeth Arden, black w/gold label, glass stopper.........................**$45.00**

Manicure set, 6" long, green, acid-etched design on cover, frosted base, heart shape, marked EW Inc, Chicago Ill...**$70.00**

Night light, frosted crystal, covered wagon shape.....**$130.00**

Night light, opaque beige, football shape....................**$90.00**

Perfume, amber w/metal collar & stopper, Cambridge #575...**$40.00**

Perfume, 5", mulberry, beehive stopper, Cambridge #585...**$40.00**

Perfume, 5", peachblow w/wheel-cut decor, 8-sided scalloped stopper, Cambridge #198...........................**$55.00**

Perfume, 6", blue w/gold leaf & white enamel hand-painted decor, Fostoria #2322....................................**$85.00**

Perfume lamp, 5", crystal w/prisms, Irice paper label, Czechoslovakia...**$85.00**

Perfume lamp, 8½" square multicolored glass insert w/nudes in silhouette, container below, cover for perfume, DeVilbiss...**$190.00**

Pin box, 5", milk glass, plain, oval, Fostoria #829.......**$35.00**

Pin tray, emerald, Winged Scroll pattern w/gold decor, Heisey...**$90.00**

Powder jar, 'Court Jester,' black w/jester head finial, round base w/twelve square tab-like feet........................**$80.00**

Powder jar, 'Lovers,' frosted pink, couple embracing as lid finial, 5" oval base w/variegated vertical ridges ..**$90.00**

Powder jar, marbleized orange w/embossed ivy, dome lid, Akro Agate...**$50.00**

Powder jar, opaque yellow, vertically ribbed, 3-footed, Akro Agate...**$35.00**

Powder jar, 4½" dia, 'Babs I,' frosted green, lady's head & shoulders as lid finial, 3-footed.............................**$55.00**

Powder jar, 4½" dia, 'Crinoline Girl,' frosted pink, lady holding bouquet & hat as lid finial, embossed bows on base **$90.00**

Puff box, pressed glass w/embossed silverplated top, Heisey...**$75.00**

Puff box, 3½" dia, opaque blue, colonial lady bust as finial on dome lid, base completes skirt, Akro Agate **$65.00**

Puff box, 4", cranberry opalescent, Coin Dot w/crystal lid, Fenton #1485..**$80.00**

Puff box, 4" dia, topaz w/hand-painted decor, dome lid, Cambridge #582 ....**$30.00**

Puff box, 6½x3½"dia, opaque pink, embossed Scotties around base, seated Scotty finial on dome lid, Akro Agate **$55.00**

Soap holder, 4x6", frosted pink, seated nude figural ..**$40.00**

Towel bar, pink, metal clips...................................**$30.00**

Trinket box, black w/hand-painted flowers on lid, Westmoreland **$20.00**

Trinket box, emerald, Winged Scroll pattern w/gold decor, Heisey..**$70.00**

Trinket box, 3x3½x4", marbleized green, treasure chest shape w/dome lid, Akro Agate **$75.00**

Vanity box, cranberry, enameled flowers, hinged, Wave Crest...**$130.00**

Beer Cans

In the mid-1930s, beer came in flat-top cans that often carried instructions on how to use the triangular punch-type opener. The 'cone-top' can was patented about 1935, and in the 1960s both types were replaced by the aluminum beer can with the pull-tab opener. There are hundreds of brands and variations available to the collector today. Most are worth very little, but we've tried to list a few of the better ones to help you get a feel for the market.

Condition is very, very important! Collectors grade them as follows: 1) rust-free, in 'new' condition; 2) still no rust, but a few scratches or tiny dents are acceptable; 3) a little faded, minor scratching, maybe a little rusting; 4) all of the above only more pronounced. Our prices are for cans in Grade 1 condition. Billy Beer? Unopened it's worth only about $1.00 a can.

ABC, 12-oz, pull top, red & white **$4.50**
American Dry, 12-oz, flat top.......................................**$60.00**
Aspen Gold, 10-oz, pull top, blue label w/gold band...**$2.00**
Ballantine, 12-oz, pull top, gold & white **$4.00**
Berghoff 1887, 16-oz, pull top, red & gold on white ..**$18.00**
Blatz, 16-oz, pull top, light brown, dark brown label ...**$4.00**
Blatz Bock, 12-oz, pull top, red & gold......................**$12.00**
Budweiser, 12-oz, flat top, red & white........................**$7.50**
Busch Lager, 12-oz, flat top..**$65.00**
Butte Lager, 12-oz, flat top, red, white, & gold...........**$25.00**
Cascade, 12-oz, pull top, blue & white **$2.50**
Colt Beer, 12-oz, pull top, white & blue **$12.50**

Coors, 12-oz, flat top, gold & black............................**$65.00**
Dodger, 12-oz, flat top, white & red...........................**$50.00**
DuBois, 12-oz, pull top, gold & white...........................**$6.50**
Duquesne Pilsener, 12-oz, cone top............................**$42.50**
Edelweiss, 12-oz, pull top **$3.00**
Falstaff, 12-oz, flat top, white & gold...........................**$5.00**
Falstaff Draft, 12-oz, pull top **$22.50**
Genesee, 12-oz, flat top, red & white..........................**$10.50**
Goebel Luxury, 12-oz, flat top, red, black, & gold **$10.00**
Golden Crown, 11-oz, flat top, gold label w/red & white lettering...**$8.00**
Grain Belt, 12-oz, flat top, brown & gold on white.......**$5.50**
Hauenstein, 12-oz, cone top, red w/white label.........**$24.00**
Hop'n Gator, 12-oz, pull top, white.............................**$2.00**
Land of Lakes, 12-oz, flat top, blue & white **$20.00**
Michelob, 11-oz, pull top, gold w/embossed lettering..**$2.00**
Miller Malt Liquor, 15-oz, pull top, red w/white lettering..**$5.00**
Oertel's 92, 12-oz, cone top, silver w/silver 92 on black **$20.00**
Pabst, 7-oz, pull top, red, white, & blue on silver........**$1.50**
Pioneer, 12-oz, flat top, brown on white **$25.00**
Schlitz, 16-oz, flat top, silver & white w/blue bull........**$8.00**
South Pacific, 12-oz, pull top, exotic bird **$15.00**
Stag Premium Dry, 12-oz, cone top............................**$22.50**
Storz, 12-oz, flat top, red & gold on white.................**$12.50**
Wooden Shoe, 12-oz, cone top, EX..........................**$100.00**

Belleek

This is a very complex field, but since it is still being made and you just might find a single example or two occasionally, you need to be at least aware of what Belleek is and its range of values. Belleek has been produced in Ireland since the middle of the 19th century. Tablewares, vases, figurines, and decorative pieces have been made in a variety of patterns and finishes. It is a very thin, translucent porcelain, and it is marked. These marks have changed over the years, so it's easy for a knowledgeable person to arrive at a reasonably accurate date of production. Dating is very important, since an early piece will often bring triple the value of the same piece in current production. Though marks varied, all contain a wolfhound, a round tower, a harp, and a shamrock. The first three marks were black; they were in use from 1863 until 1947; green marks have been in use since then, and in 1980 a gold mark was added.

American companies made belleek as well, though it is very scarce and was discontinued in 1930. If you'd like to study it, we recommend *American Belleek* by Mary Frank Gaston. Irish Belleek is thoroughly covered in the book *Belleek, The Complete Collector's Guide and Illustrated Reference* by Richard Degenhardt.

Bearded Mask, creamer, small, 1863-1890, pearl/plain.**$175.00**
Bird's Nest, basket, 3¾", 4-strand, pearl/plain **$380.00**
Bird's Nest, tree stump vase, 1965-1980, handpainted...**$1,500.00**

Calawite, candle extinguisher & stand, 3½", 1863-1890, pearl/plain..**$750.00**

Celtic Tea Ware, plate, 6½", 1926-1946, hand-painted & gilted...**$60.00**

Celtic Tea Ware, teacup & saucer, 1926-1946, hand-painted & gilted...**$125.00**

Chinese Tea Ware, sugar bowl, 3", 1863-1890........**$225.00**

Diamond, flowerpot, 3½", 1965-1980, pearl/plain.......**$40.00**

Dolphin, chamberstick, 1980-current, hand-tinted & gilted...**$300.00**

Echinus, bowl, 8½", 1965-1980, footed, pearl/plain..**$450.00**

Echinus Tea Ware, creamer, 3", 1863-1890, hand-painted...**$350.00**

Echinus Tea Ware, mustache cup, 2½", 1863-1890, hand-gilted..**$325.00**

Feather, vase, small, 1955-1965, cob lustre.................**$35.00**

Fern & Flower, wall bracket, 11", 1863-1890, pearl/plain...**$1,000.00**

Figurine, leprechaun, 5½", 1926-1946, pearl/plain....**$250.00**

Figurine, pig, large, 1891-1926, cob lustre..............**$200.00**

Figurine, spaniel on cushion, 3", 1965-1980, pearl/plain..**$75.00**

Figurines, boy & girl basket bearers, 1965-1980, pearl/plain, pr...**$750.00**

Five O'Clock Tea Ware, teapot, 4½", 1891-1926, hand-tinted...**$500.00**

Florence, jug, small, 1980-current, hand-tinted & gilted.**$75.00**

Grass, mug, 2½", 1955-1965, cob lustre......................**$75.00**

Grass Tea Ware, honey pot & stand, 6½", 1863-1890, hand-painted & gilted..**$700.00**

Heart, basket, 6½", No 3, 4-strand, hand-painted......**$455.00**

Heart, plate, 6¼", No 3, 1955-1965, cob lustre............**$35.00**

Hexagon, 10", cake plate, 4-strand, pearl/plain.........**$450.00**

Hexagon Tea Ware, luncheon tray, 1891-1926, hand-tinted...**$1,000.00**

Indian Corn, spill vase, 6¼", 1863-1890, pearl/plain.**$250.00**

Institute Tea Ware, platter, 10½" dia, 1863-1890, pearl/plain...**$375.00**

Ivy Trunk, stump spill, 5", 1863-1890, hand-painted.**$250.00**

Limpet Tea Ware, dinner plate, 10½", 1965-1980, cob lustre...**$70.00**

Limpet Tea Ware, plate, 8", 1926-1946, pearl/plain.....**$65.00**

New Shell Tea Ware, biscuit jar, 7", 1965-1980, cob lustre...**$90.00**

Octagon, flowerpot, 4½", 1965-1980, cob lustre..........**$48.00**

Primrose, 4¾", butter plate, 1926-1946,......................**$75.00**

Rathmore, vase, 7½", 1965-1980, cob lustre................**$70.00**

Ribbon, vase, 8", 1926-1946, flowered, pearl/plain...**$250.00**

Scroll Tea Ware, teacup & saucer, 1891-1926, hand-tinted & gilted...**$200.00**

Shamrock Ware, biscuit jar, 6½", 1965-1980, hand-painted shamrocks..**$130.00**

Shamrock Ware, box, 3¾", 1891-1926, hand-painted shamrocks, oval...**$175.00**

Shamrock Ware, kettle, large, 1891-1926, hand-painted shamrocks...**$475.00**

Shamrock Ware, milk jug, small, 1926-1946, hand-painted shamrocks, round...................................**$120.00**

Shamrock Ware, teapot, 6¾", 1926-46, hand-painted shamrocks...**$300.00**

Shell Tea Ware, teacup & saucer, 1891-1926, pearl/plain...**$150.00**

Sycamore, plate, 4½", 1955-1965, cob lustre..............**$21.00**

Toy Shell, creamer & sugar bowl, 1955-1965, cob lustre...**$60.00**

Wall plaque, 8x9", 'Praise Ye the Lord,' 1863-1890, hand-painted...**$600.00**

Betty Boop Collectibles

Personality-related collectibles belong to one of the largest and fastest growing areas of interest today, and Betty Boop certainly has her share of devotees. She was created in the early 1930s by the Fleischer Studios and during the decade appeared in almost one hundred black and white cartoons. Her dog was Bimbo, and her clown friend was KoKo. Most of the early cels (an original drawing required to produce an animated movie) are gone, but those from the color remakes of the sixties are still available and range in value from $125.00 to about $400.00. Many Betty Boop items were produced in the thirties; in fact, they have been made sporatically ever since. In the eighties, Vandor came out with a line of ceramics, but these were marked with the Vandor designation.

Ashtray, lustre-glazed ceramic, 1930s, EX.................**$120.00**

Autograph, Max Fleischer..**$200.00**

Bridge card set, pictures Betty & Bimbo, EX...............**$35.00**

Buckle, celluloid, 1930s...**$45.00**

Calendar, 1987, 16-month, M...**$15.00**

Candy bar box, 8x11½", marked Fleischer Studios, 1920s...**$125.00**

Candy dish, 3¾", Betty in red dress on heart form, marked Vandor, 1983, M...**$25.00**

Decal, for shirt, 1950s..**$12.00**

Doll, Betty, composition head, wood jointed body, marked 'Fleischer Studios,' 12", M $650.00
Doll blanket, marked Max Fleischer Studios...............$80.00
Figurine, jointed wood w/original black dress, marked Kallus, EX...$850.00
Figurine, 3", Betty, bisque, Japan, 1930s, VG............$125.00
Figurine, 3", Bimbo playing the violin, bisque, 1930s, NM $35.00
Figurine, 4", Betty playing the French horn, bisque, 1930s $50.00
Figurine, 4", Koko the Clown, bisque, ca 1930, NM....$60.00
Handkerchief, 9", 1930s...$35.00
Movie reel, 'Spanish Town,' Duracolor, 1930s............$48.00
Pin, Betty w/chained dog, silverplated, ca 1930s, G .$100.00
Pocket watch, Ingraham, die-embossed back, 1934, in original box, M $500.00
Record, 'Betty Boop Scandals of 1974,' 33⅓ rpm, Mark 56 Records, #658, NM $40.00
Score pad, 4", pictures Betty & Bimbo, 1930s, M $45.00
Sheet music, 'Poor Cinderella,' dated 1934, EX............$65.00
Socks, original label, 1930s, pr....................................$95.00
String holder, 10" across, string comes out of mouth, chalkware...$135.00
Tea set, 11-pc, service for four, lustreware, in original box $375.00
Toy, 7", celluloid, wind-up, marked Japan $600.00
Wall pocket, figure of Betty, Fleischer Studios $125.00
Wall pocket, 6", glazed ceramic w/photo on front, EX $120.00

Big Little Books

The Whitman Publishing Company started it all in 1933 when they published a book whose format was entirely different than any other's. It was very small, easily held in a child's hand, but over an inch in thickness. There was a car-

toon-like drawing on the right hand page, and the text was printed on the left. The idea was so well accepted that very soon other publishers — Saalfield, Van Wiseman, Lynn, World Syndicate, and Goldsmith — cashed in on the idea as well. The first Big Little Book hero was Dick Tracy, but soon every radio cowboy, cartoon character, lawman, and space explorer was immortalized in his own adventure series.

When it became apparent that the pre-teen of the fifties prefered the comic book format, Big Little Books were finally phased out; but many were saved in boxes and stored in attics, so there's still a wonderful supply of them around. You need to watch condition carefully when you're buying or selling.

Adventures of Huckleberry Finn, 1948, VG $24.00
Adventures of Tom Sawyer, 1934, EX $48.00
Air Fighters of America, 1941, NM.............................$30.00
Alley Oop & Dinny, 1935, EX....................................$45.00
Andy Panda & Pirate Ghosts, 1949, VG......................$15.00
Bambi's Children, 1943, M..$55.00
Big Chief Wahoo, Whitman, 1938 (illustrated).....$25.00
Blondie, Baby Dumpling & All, 1941, VG...................$25.00
Blondie, Cookie & Daisy's Pups, 1943, VG.................$22.50
Blondie & Bouncing Baby Dumpling, 1940, VG $17.50
Brer Rabbit, Song of the South, 1945-47, EX...............$50.00
Buck Jones & the Two-Gun Kid, 1937, VG.................$20.00
Buffalo Bill & Pony Express, 1934, VG.......................$25.00
Captain Easy, Soldier of Fortune, 1934, VG $37.50
Chester Gump at Silver Creek Ranch, 1933, EX...........$40.00
Chester Gump in City of Gold, 1935, G $12.00
Chitty Chitty Bang Bang, 1968, movie edition, VG........$7.50
Dan Dunn, Underworld Gorillas, 1941, G...................$15.00
Dick Tracy & Boris Arson Gang, 1935, M $55.00
Dick Tracy & the Phantom Ship, 1940, VG.................$40.00
Dick Tracy Returns, 1939, VG...................................$25.00
Donald Duck, Ghost Morgan's Treasure, 1946, EX $70.00
Donald Duck, Off the Beam, 1943, EX........................$50.00
Donald Duck Gets Fed Up, 1938, G...........................$15.00
Flash Gordon, Fiery Desert Mongo, 1948, EX.............$45.00
Flash Gordon in Jungles of Mongo, 1938, EX.............$65.00
Foreign Spies, Doctor Doom & the Ghost Submarine, 1939, NM $60.00
G-Men on the Job, 1935, VG.....................................$20.00
Gene Autry, The Hawk of the Hills, 1942, VG............$30.00
Gene Autry in Land Grab Mystery, 1948, EX $30.00
Green Hornet Strikes!, 1940, NM $55.00
Inspector Charlie Chan of the Honolulu Police, 1939, VG..$50.00
Invisible Scarlet O'Neil Versus the King of Slums, 1946, G $12.00
Jackie Cooper in Gangster's Row, 1938, EX................$37.50
Junior Nebb Joins the Circus, 1939, VG $15.00
Junior Nebb on the Diamond Bar Ranch, 1938, G $12.50
Just Kids, 1937, G...$35.00
Kazan, King of the Pack, 1940, VG............................$35.00
Kit Carson & Mystery Riders, 1935, VG $27.50
Last Days of Pompeii, 1935, VG.................................$37.50

Li'l Abner Among the Millionaires, 1939, EX...............$50.00
Little Orphan Annie & the Haunted Mansion, 1941, VG.$40.00
Lone Ranger & His Horse Silver, 1935, NM...................$55.00
Lone Ranger & the Silver Bullets, 1946, NM $45.00
Lone Ranger on the Barbary Coast, 1944, NM............$60.00
Mandrake the Magician, 1935, EX...............................$50.00
Mandrake the Magician, Flame Pearls, 1946, EX $50.00
Maximo, The Amazing Superman & the Super-Machine,
    1941, EX...$45.00
Mickey Mouse, Lazy Day Mystery, 1947, EX...............$45.00
Mickey Mouse & Pluto the Racer, 1936, VG $60.00
Nancy & Sluggo, 1946, NM $60.00
New Adventures of Tarzan, 1935, VG $27.50
Phantom, Desert Justice, 1941, EX.............................$50.00
Pilot Pete, Dive Bomber, 1941, VG.............................$25.00
Plainsman, 1936, VG..$37.50
Pluto the Pup, 1938, NM $50.00
Popeye & Castor Oyl the Detective, 1941, VG............$55.00
Radio Patrol, 1935, EX...$35.00
Red Barry Ace Detective, Hero of the Hour, 1935, VG ..$30.00
Red Ryder & the Secret Canyon, 1948, NM.................$30.00
Riders of Lone Trail, 1937, EX.....................................$30.00
Roy Rogers, King of the Cowboys, 1943, EX $30.00
Roy Rogers at Crossed Feather Ranch, 1945, EX $35.00
Secret Agent X-9 & the Mad Assassin, 1938, VG..........$37.50
Shadow & the Living Death, 1940, VG $65.00
Snow White & the Seven Dwarfs, 1938, NM $75.00
Speed Douglas & the Mole Gang, 1941, NM...............$30.00
Tailspin Tommy & the Lost Transport, 1939, NM $55.00
Tailspin Tommy in the Great Air Mystery, 1936, VG...$22.50
Tarzan & Journey of Terror, 1950, EX $30.00
Terry & the Pirates, War in the Jungle, 1946, NM.......$40.00
Tim McCoy on the Tomahawk Trail, 1937, VG $30.00

**Tom Mix & His Circus on the Barbary Coast, Whitman,
    1940, VG $20.00**
Tom Mix & the Hoard of Montezuma, 1937, NM $45.00
Tom Mix & Tony Jr in Terror Trail, 1935, VG.............$27.50
Tom Mix in the Range War, 1937, NM $30.00
Uncle Ray's Story of the United States, 1934, G..........$15.00
Walt Disney's Dumbo of the Circus, 1941, NM...........$60.00

Wash Tubbs & Captain Easy Hunting for Whales, 1938,
    G $15.00
Wash Tubbs in Pandemonia, 1934, G $15.00
West Point of the Air, 1935, VG..................................$22.50
Will Rogers, 1935, VG...$32.00
Windy Wayne & His Flying Wing, 1942, VG $22.50
Zane Grey's King of Royal Mounted, 1936, VG..........$45.00
Zip Saunders, King of the Speedway, 1939, NM.........$50.00

Black Americana

If you see a crowd around a flea market table, it's a
good bet they've found a Black Americana dealer. It's a field
that encompasses a vast array of items — sheet music, salt
and pepper shakers, cookie jars, and advertising items, to
name only a few. Many of the cookie jars have become so
valuable that they're being reproduced; so are salt and pepper shakers, so beware.

For further study, we recommend *Black Collectibles Sold
in America* by P.J. Gibbs.

See also Sheet Music, Post Cards.

Ashtray, ceramic, pup watches boy in blue shorts shoot
    craps, 'Come Seven' on base, 1940s, M $50.00
Ashtray, chalkware, boy eating watermelon, EX $65.00
Ashtray, square, glass, 'Coon Chicken Inn' $40.00
Bank, ceramic, mammy shape w/cream-colored dress & yel-
    low turban, Japan, EX..$35.00
Bank, pot metal, mammy w/laundry basket, EX.......$110.00
Banner, 12" long, 'Aunt Jemima Pancake Jamboree,'
    M $250.00
Beer mug, ceramic, Muscle Moe, EX...........................$65.00
Book, 'Who's Who in Colored America, NY,' 1930-32,
    EX $75.00
Book, 8½x11", cardboard cover, 'Deluxe Edition 1946' of
    'Little Black Sambo,' 16 pages illustrated w/color plates,
    EX $70.00
Box, colorful red & yellow design w/lady in center & 'Big
    Bertha Hair Dressing' printed below $15.00
Candy jar, amber glass head shape w/hand-painted blue
    hat & features, metal screw-on cap at base of neck,
    1920s, NM $200.00
Cigar box, 2¼x15½x6¾", 'Cochran's Sampler' box features
    black bellboys offering cigars, 1930s-40s, EX $130.00
Clock, metal body, Li'l Hannibal graphics on face, West-
    clox..$400.00
Coffee bag, 'Old Plantation Coffee,' Black man moving cof-
    fee sack w/steamship beyond.................................$8.00
Compact, 3x5", enameled metal, lid has cream background
    w/musicans playing various instruments, G..........$30.00
Cookbook, 'Aunt Caroline's Dixieland Recipes,' 1922,
    EX $22.00
Cookie jar, plastic, Aunt Jemima, EX+........................$290.00
Cookie jar, 10½", ceramic, mammy in blue head scarf,
    white-dotted red dress, 1980s, M......................$130.00
Cookie jar, 14", ceramic, little girl named 'Spice,' white dress
    w/pink hair bow, 1980s, JC Penney $75.00

Cookie jar, 9", pottery, mammy holding a basket of flowers, Abingdon...**$675.00**

Cookie jar, 9", pottery, mammy style w/white head scarf & dress, brown face, hands, & shoes, 1940s, National Silver Co **$280.00**

Crate label, 4x13", 'Small Black Zinfandel,' depicts nude boy, 1930s, EX...**$15.00**

Decanter, 7½", pottery, butler in black jacket & white pants raising wine bottle to pour, removable head, 1930s **$430.00**

Dish towel, cotton, mammy washing clothes in the outdoors in red, light blue, & yellow on white background, 1940-50s...**$35.00**

Doll, 14", stocking body w/embroidered features, button eyes, 1930s, EX..**$30.00**

Dolls, 18" & 19", cloth w/stitched features and yarn hair, no mark, 1940s, EX, pr.....................$75.00

Door knocker, natural wood w/red knob, Cotton Club souvenir, EX..**$22.00**

Drinking glasses, 12-oz, whimsical dice players, 1950s, set of six...**$75.00**

Egg cup, 3¼", plastic, 'Robertson Golden Shred Golliwog' **$75.00**

Figure, 48", painted wood, jockey, 1950s, EX............**$145.00**

Figurine, ceramic, mammy w/basket, marked Royal Crown, Germany **$75.00**

Figurine, 2½", ceramic, chubby boy w/tummy ache, Japan **$30.00**

Figurine, 3¼", bisque, w/monkey behind tree, Germany...**$145.00**

Figurine, 5", ceramic, native scratching head.............**$25.00**

Figurine, 6", ceramic, native w/grass skirt & drum, 1950s **$25.00**

Figurine, 6x8", couple in canoe w/few clothes on, gold trim, 1940s **$60.00**

Fishing plug, naughty Sambo, 1950, MIB...................**$25.00**

Flour bag, 50-lb, boy sitting on logo eating cake, 'Mammy's Pride,' 'Larabee Flour Mills Co,' 1940s.....................**$95.00**

Game, 12" figure of Black man w/open mouth, ring toss, ca 1900, EX **$200.00**

Hotpad holder, painted wood, young girl, EX............**$18.00**

Humidor, ceramic, mammy's head shape, M.........**$275.00**

Incense burner, 6¼", pot metal, boy on pot w/wide mouth, MN **$65.00**

Lamp, 7", pottery, lady's head w/elaborate hair & brown skin **$95.00**

Lawn ornament, 20-lb, cast iron, boy w/watermelon, 1955, fine repaint **$135.00**

Magazine, 'Negro South,' 1946, EX **$6.00**

Measuring spoon holder, chalkware, mammy figural, old **$45.00**

Mechanical pencil, Bakelite, Blackamoor figural, EX..**$75.00**

Memo pad holder, 9", chalkware, wall mount, mammy in yellow & green w/hand on side of face, broom in crook of arm, 1940s **$45.00**

Menu, 'Coon Chicken Inn' **$150.00**

Noisemaker, tin w/wooden handle, spinning top has yellow background w/clown playing harmonica.............**$30.00**

Pail, lithographed tin in red & yellow featuring a mammy advertising 'Luters Pure Lard' **$40.00**

Pamphlet, WWI government issue of 'Negro & Flag,' EX **$18.50**

Pancake batter shaker, yellow plastic, Aunt Jemima ...**$65.00**

Paper towel holder, wooden, mammy at side.............**$115.00**

Paperweight, mammy in snow scene............................**$75.00**

Pegboard, 9x5¾", painted die-cut wood, mammy shape, EX **$90.00**

Pencil sharpener, 1" dia, metal, man figural w/blade in mouth **$200.00**

Pincushion, 4½", litho on wood, mammy figural, skirt cushion **$35.00**

Pitcher, 5½", white ceramic, square shape w/rounded corners, Black lady posing w/bottle of Canadian Club, 1960s **$65.00**

Planter, 5", girl by stump w/watermelon, Interco........**$45.00**

Plaque, 4x4", chalkware, boy & girl eat watermelon **$45.00**

Plaque, chalkware, Sambo **$25.00**

Post card, embossed full-color humorous illustration of a Black woman standing by seated 'Poor Old Joe,' EX **$25.00**

Pot holder, 5", cotton, embroidered angel, 1950s **$21.00**

Pot holder caddy, chalkware, boy & girl under umbrellas, pr..**$60.00**

Roly Poly, 7", papier-mache, marked Germany, M........**$250.00**

Salt & pepper shakers, ceramic, mammy's head in white scarf, butler's head w/gray hair, white collar & red tie **$70.00**

Salt & pepper shakers, 2½", ceramic, man's head w/slanted orange hat & red lips, separate watermelon slice, 1935-40s **$50.00**

Salt & pepper shakers, 2½", ceramic, seated girl & boy in red & yellow, she holds flowers, he holds a basket, 1980s **$28.00**

Salt & pepper shakers, 2½", topless natives w/baskets on their heads, in blue or red skirts, EX **$36.00**

Salt & pepper shakers, 2½", wood, mammy & farmer, he in yellow overalls & red shirt, she in orange dress, EX **$40.00**

Salt & pepper shakers, 3", ceramic, natives in yellow grass skirts kissing, girl has bow in her hair, Japan **$40.00**

Salt & pepper shakers, 3", mammy w/pink lips & white head scarf, chef w/pink lips & white hat, 1945-50s **$50.00**

Salt & pepper shakers, 4½", plaster, colorful calypso players in yellow hats w/red bands...................................**$45.00**

Salt & pepper shakers, 5½", native girl & boy w/cone-shaped bodies & flat circular heads, looped ear-rings **$45.00**

Salt & pepper shakers, 5½", native lady made of black wire holding wooden drums **$55.00**

Sheet music, 3 pages, 'Swingin' on the Swanee Shore,' 1936, M..**$10.00**

Shoe horn, man's head at tip of long handle...............**$30.00**

Shot glass, shows figures under palms, 'Here's Looking at You'...**$6.00**

Smoking stand, 34x7½x7½", painted cast iron, butler figural, VG...**$475.00**

Soap dish, painted cast iron, mammy w/basket on head, EX...**$165.00**

Soda bottle, 14", clear glass w/embossed mammy, 1910-20, Mammy Beverage Co..**$400.00**

Spice set, each shaker 4", painted hard plastic, marked F&F Mold & Die Works, Dayton, Ohio, 1930s..$140.00

Spoon rest, 6x6½", whimsical native face in brown, yellow, & dark pink glaze **$70.00**

Syrup, 5", Aunt Jemima premium, F&F, EX..................**$40.00**

Syrup bottle, unopened, from Cotton Club, 1940s **$45.00**

Tablecloth, 48x48", figures eating watermelon, EX **$95.00**

Teapot, ceramic, clown's head, Japan........................**$45.00**

Toaster cover, 18", mammy doll w/cotton-stuffed body, 1940s, EX **$25.00**

Toby pitcher, 3½", girl figural in white w/orange & yellow...**$40.00**

Token, brass, slave auctioneer, dated 1846, EX..........**$55.00**

Toothpick holder, 'Coon Chicken Inn'.......................**$195.00**

Trade card, features dancing Black boy w/cotton balls advertising 'Jas S Kirk & Co Soap Makers,' EX......**$15.00**

Trade card, titled 'Domestic Amenities' w/Uncle Rastus & Aunt Dinah conversing, 'Ariosa Coffee Plant' on reverse, EX...**$25.00**

Wall pocket, 5¾", ceramic, boy w/big red smiling lips in blue hat w/white dots, 1940-50s..........................**$140.00**

Wall pocket planter, 5", ceramic, mammy in white dress & red head scarf sitting on green stove, 1940-50s **$55.00**

Black Cats

Kitchenware, bookends, vases, and many other items designed as black cats were made in Japan during the 1950s and exported to the United States where they were sold by various distributors who often specified certain characteristics they wanted in their own line of cats. Common to all these lines were the red clay used in their production and the medium used in their decoration — their features were applied over the glaze with 'cold (unfired) paint.' The most collectible is a line marked (or labeled) Shafford. Shafford cats are plump and pleasant looking. They have green eyes with black pupils; white eyeliner, eyelashes, and whiskers; and red bow ties. The same design with yellow eyes was marketed by Royal, and another fairly easy-to-find 'breed' is a line by Wales with yellow eyes and gold whiskers. You'll find various other labels as well. Some collectors buy only Shafford, while others like them all.

When you evauate your black cats, be critical of their paint. Even though no chips or cracks are present, if half of the paint is missing, you have a half-price item. Remember this when using the following values which are given for cats with near-mint to mint paint.

For further study we recommend *Collectible Cats, An Identification & Value Guide* by Marbena Jean Fyke.

Ashtray, 3x4", full body, green eyes & gold trim, flat....**$7.50**

Ashtray, 3-D head, open mouth w/cigarette rest, Shafford **$18.00**

Bookends, 7", kitten w/paw against book, pr **$10.00**

Cookie jar, large face w/green eyes, red bow tie, Shafford **$85.00**

Creamer, 5½", yellow eyes, gold whiskers & eyebrows, red bow tie, lifted paw is the spout, Wales **$22.00**

Cruet, 7", slim w/wide red polka dot bow tie, tail handle **$12.00**

Cruets, 8", one has O eyes for oil, other has V eyes for vinegar & red hairbow, sitting upright, Shafford, pr....**$50.00**

Decanter, 8", sitting upright w/right paw lifted & holding bottle which is the spout, w/label, Shafford **$50.00**

Decanter, 9", upright w/lift-off head, green eyes, red bow tie & allover red polka dots, plus six shot glasses, set..**$25.00**

Marmalade & jelly, two heads w/loop handle in center, w/label, Shafford..**$50.00**

Napkin ring, 2⅜", ring forms body **$6.00**

Planter, upright, full figure, no handle, rare, Shafford.**$35.00**

Salt & pepper shakers, 3¾", salt is upright, pepper has tilted head, Shafford, pr **$25.00**

Salt & pepper shakers, 5½", upright, wide gold bow tie w/red polka dots on side of neck, tail handle, pr ..**$8.00**

Spice set, 6-pc, cat's face on 3" square jar, wooden rack, Shafford **$125.00**

Sugar bowl, full-figure crouched cat, w/label, no lid, Shafford **$20.00**

Teapot, cat head w/two spouts & chambers, green eyes, red bow tie, rattan-wrapped handle, Shafford............**$65.00**

Teapot, 5", panther-like sleek face w/gold slanty eyes, paws form spout, upright body $20.00
Teapot, 5¾", fat body, Shafford $40.00
Teapot, 6½", fat body, w/label, Shafford.................$45.00
Toothpick holder, small cat on book by vase, marked Occupied Japan $12.00
Wall pocket, 5½", green eyes, red bow tie, pocket at back $65.00

Black Glass

Although black glass was made as early as the 1600s, the glass you'll find today is almost certain to be of this century, possibly from the Depression era, when it was made by many companies. It was sometimes molded in relief, etched, or enameled.

To learn more about this subject, we recommend *The Collector's Guide to Black Glass* by Marlena Toohey.

Ashtray, 5½", Deco chrome skater on top....................$75.00
Ashtray, 6", elephant, 1920s-30s, Greenburg................$25.00
Bottle, 3½x5¼", shoe form, screw cap, ca 1880-1910..$50.00
Bowl, 9¼", cupped, footed, shallow, ca 1921.............$27.50
Cake plate, 9½", Do-Si-Do, handled, LE Smith $25.00
Candelabrum, 6x7", 3-light, 1930s, US Glass..............$95.00
Comport, 8½", Chatham openwork rim, US Glass....$82.50
Creamer & sugar bowl, 1925-30, #5029, pr $38.50
Kitchen shakers, 4¾", ca 1932, #533, Lancaster Glass, pr $24.00
Relish, ornate metal frame, 3-part, ca 1925-35 ....$33.00
Salad plate, 1932, #1517, Morgantown $8.00
Tray, 10", 3-footed, #1871/7, Lancaster Glass..............$25.00
Tumbler, 12-oz, clear bowl w/black domed foot, ca 1925-35 ....$13.50
Vase, 3", white enamel dot decor, ca 1925-35.............$18.00

Window box, 3x8", embossed classical figures $50.00

Blair Dinnerware

Interest in collecting American dinnerware is strong right now, has been for quite sometime, and shows no indi-cation of slacking off. Blair is a company only recently dis-covered by collectors, so prices are still often low. They operated in Ozark, Missouri, only briefly, opening in 1946 and closing sometime during the fifties. Blair himself was a modernistic painter-turned-potter, and his dinnerware designs reflect his approach to art. He favored square shapes over round, straight-sided hollowware pieces, and simple color combinations and patterns. His work was sold through some of the country's leading department stores, Neiman-Marcus and Marshall Field among them.

His most popular pattern and the one most easily found today was Gay Plaid. The concept was very simple: inter-secting vertical and horizontal brush strokes in brown, dark green, and chartreuse on white. He used twisted rope-like handles and applied leaves as knobs on lids. Yellow Plaid was simlilar; the same colors were used with yellow added. Rick-Rack featured hand-painted zigzags and diagonals. Bamboo was a bit more artistic with a stalk of bamboo and a few large leaves, and Autumn featured leaves as well. A departure from his earlier lines and the hardest to find today, Bird (except for still using the colors he obviously prefered — browns, white, and green) is different in that he used red clay for the body of the ware and the primitive bird designs were carved in the clay (a process called sgraf-fito) rather than hand painted.

You'll have no problem identifying this dinnerware, since it is clearly marked 'Blair, Decorated by Hand.'

For further study, we recommend *The Collector's Ency-clopedia of American Dinnerware* by Jo Cunningham.

Autumn, bowl, small......................................$10.00
Autumn, cup...$10.00
Bamboo, coffee server, w/lid...........................$35.00
Bamboo, creamer..$15.00
Bamboo, plate, dinner; square.........................$12.00

Bamboo, plate, rectangular $12.00
Bamboo, plate, 8", square $8.00
Bird, bowl, vegetable; divided $30.00
Bird, plate, dinner.......................................$15.00
Bird, plate, 6" $15.00
Gay Plaid, casserole, w/lid.............................$30.00

Gay Plaid, cup & saucer..............................$12.00
Gay Plaid, pitcher, water; twisted handle, w/ice lip....$40.00
Gay Plaid, salt & pepper shakers................$12.00
Gay Plaid, tumbler.....................................$12.00
Rick-Rack, bowl, cereal..............................$12.00
Rick-Rack, cup & saucer.............................$20.00
Rick-Rack, sugar bowl, w/lid.......................$15.00
Yellow Plaid, plate, serving; divided............$25.00

Blenko Glass

This type of handmade glassware has been made for over seventy years in Milton, West Virginia. It often has a bubbly appearance, or it may look crackled. Vibrant colors and unusual shapes are characteristic of Blenko Glass. One of the most common items around is the 12" long fish; it has an open mouth and a split tail. These are usually valued at about $20.00 or so.

Beaker, 9½", ruby, flared form w/irregular rim...........$18.00
Bowl, 14" dia, green optic, ribbed w/wide flared rim..$35.00
Cruet, 9", chartreuse, tall pointed stopper, #919C $25.00
Decanter, 1½-qt, crystal w/ringed neck, cut stopper.....$25.00
Goblet, 10-oz, amethyst, double knop stem.............$22.00
Mug, 5½", clear w/applied colored rings & handle ..$15.00
Pitcher, 7½", ruby, optic ribbed, w/ice guard spout, ruby reeded handle $20.00
Plate, 8", ruby, rolled rim $12.00
Rosette vase, 11", emerald green, molded circles at base $60.00
Sherbet, 5", ruby w/crystal air-twist stem, ruby foot ...$25.00
Tumbler, 10-oz, emerald green, applied rosettes on slim lower half $18.00
Vase, 12", light blue w/seed bubbles, gourd shape w/flared rim...$40.00
Vase, 7", dark amethyst w/applied spiral decoration $50.00
Vase, 7½", dark amethyst, ball shape w/flared rim $50.00

Blue and White Stoneware

Though it hasn't been made since the 1930s, blue and white stoneware is a popular collectible today and carries price tags hefty enough that reproductions are everywhere, so we wanted to forewarn you. Beware of too bright colors, sloppy workmanship, and anything that looks unused. This was strictly utilitarian pottery, and it would be a rare piece indeed that showed no signs of wear. It was made as early as the turn of the century by many of the well-known potters of the era, among them Roseville, Brush McCoy, and Uhl.

For further study, we recommend *Blue and White Stoneware* by Kathryn McNerney.

Bean pot, Boston Baked Beans, Flemish, w/lid........$290.00
Bowl, mixing; 10½", Feathers.....................$125.00

Bowl, 10", Wedding Ring...........................$125.00
Bowl, 9½", Apricot...................................$85.00
Bowl, 9½", Daisy on Waffle $90.00
Butter crock, Apple Blossom, original lid & bail......$225.00
Butter crock, Eagle, original lid & bail..............$450.00
Butter crock, 10" dia, Vintage, Robinson Clay Products, EX $105.00
Butter crock, 5", Daisy & Trellis, original lid & bail ..$175.00
Butter crock, 6½", Butterfly, original lid & bail.........$175.00
Canister, Basketweave, Coffee, original lid..............$195.00
Canister, Diffused Blue, Tea, original lid $125.00
Coffeepot, 9½", devil on body, embossed 'Blanke's Coffeepot' on lid.....................................$350.00
Cookie jar, Brickers, original lid $245.00
Cookie jar, Flying Birds, original lid.............$350.00
Humidor, stippled w/bird dog on side, flower finial, w/lid..$150.00
Mug, Basketweave $95.00
Mug, Cattails $125.00
Mug, Flying Bird $175.00
Mug, plain $65.00
Pickle crock, Blue Bands, advertising, bail handle, 5-gal $150.00
Pie plate, Star Mfg...................................$145.00
Pitcher, Acorns..$115.00
Pitcher, Barrel, & six mugs.......................$395.00
Pitcher, Basketweave & Flowers................$175.00
Pitcher, Blue Band, plain...........................$80.00
Pitcher, Blue Band Scroll...........................$160.00
Pitcher, Eagle $450.00
Pitcher, Flowers, stenciled.........................$100.00
Pitcher, Grapes on Waffle.........................$165.00
Pitcher, small, Fishscale & Wild Rose.........$95.00
Pitcher, Swirl...$155.00
Pitcher, Wild Rose...................................$275.00
Pitcher, 10", American Beauty Rose...........$175.00
Pitcher, 11", two old men, dog's-head spout, ...$200.00
Pitcher, 6", Rose & Fishscale $165.00

Pitcher, 7", Dutch Boy & Girl $165.00
Pitcher, 7½", Cattails $175.00
Pitcher, 7½", Cherry Cluster $225.00

Pitcher, 8½", Grape Cluster on Trellis $165.00
Pitcher, 8½", Leaping Deer...$225.00
Pitcher, 8½", Lovebirds, pale color $275.00
Pitcher, 8¾", Diffused Blue, M $100.00
Pitcher, 9", Stag & Pine Trees.......................................$295.00
Pitcher, 9x7", Butterfly..$250.00
Salt crock, Apricot, original lid....................................$135.00
Salt crock, Butterfly, original lid $185.00
Salt crock, Eagle w/Arrow, original lid......................$325.00
Salt crock, Grape on Basketweave, original lid.........$150.00
Salt crock, Peacock, original lid...................................$350.00
Salt crock, Wildflower, original lid $175.00
Slop jar, Bow Tie $125.00
Slop jar, Fishscale & Wild Rose....................................$150.00
Soap dish, Beaded Rose $120.00
Soap dish, Fishscale & Wild Rose $95.00
Soap dish, Indian in War Bonnet.................................$195.00
Spittoon, Peacock & Fountain......................................$275.00
Toothbrush holder, Fishscale & Wild Rose $70.00
Umbrella stand, 21", oak leaves & animals, NM $350.00
Vase, Swirl, cone shape..$300.00
Wash set, Fishscale & Wild Rose, 5-pc........................$600.00
Wash set, Rose on Trellis, 2-pc.....................................$300.00
Water cooler, Blue Band, original lid...........................$175.00
Water cooler, Rachel at the Well, original lid $500.00

Blue Ridge Dinnerware

Blue Ridge has long been popular with collectors, and prices are already well established; but that's not to say there aren't a few good buys left around. It was made by a company called Southern Potteries, who operated in Erwin, Tennessee, from sometime in the latter thirties until the mid-fifties. They made literally hundreds of patterns, all hand decorated. Some collectors prefer to match up patterns, while some like to mix them together for a more eclectic table setting.

One of the patterns most popular with collectors (and the most costly) is called French Peasant. It's very much like Quimper with simple depictions of the little peasant fellow with his staff. They made many lovely floral patterns, and it's around these where most of the buying and selling activity is centered. You'll also find roosters, plaids, and simple textured designs, and in addition to the dinnerware, some vases and novelty items as well.

Nearly every piece is marked 'Blue Ridge,' though occasionally you'll find one that isn't. Watch for a similar type of ware often confused with Blue Ridge that is sometimes (though not always) marked Italy.

The values suggested below are for the better patterns. To evaluate the French Peasant line, double these figures; for the simple plaids and textures, deduct 25% to 50%, depending on their appeal.

If you'd like to learn more, we recommend *Southern Potteries, Inc., Blue Ridge Dinnerware,* by Betty and Bill Newbound.

Ashtray, individual $13.00
Bonbon, china, divided, center handle $85.00
Bowl, cereal or soup; 6" $9.00
Bowl, fruit; 5" $4.00
Bowl, mixing; 8½" $28.00
Bowl, soup; 8", flat $10.00
Bowl, vegetable; 9", divided, oval $22.50
Bowl, 8", round...$13.00
Box, Sherman Lily...$550.00
Butter dish, w/lid, ¼-lb..$40.00
Cake lifter $22.50
Candy box, w/lid, round...$95.00
Casserole, w/lid...$40.00
Celery, china, leaf shape...$30.00
Child's cereal bowl...$28.00
Child's mug $20.00
Child's plate $28.00
Chocolate pot, china, pedestal.....................................$150.00
Cigarette box, w/four trays $110.00
Coffeepot...$100.00
Creamer, china $45.00
Creamer, regular...$8.00
Cup & saucer, demitasse; china $30.00
Cup & saucer, regular..$13.00
Dish, baking; 13x8"..$27.50
Egg cup, double..$32.50
Egg dish, deviled..$32.50
Gravy boat...$17.00
Gravy tray..$17.00
Jug, batter; w/lid..$65.00
Jug, syrup; w/lid...$80.00
Lamp, china..$500.00
Lazy susan...$500.00
Pie baker $25.00
Pitcher, china, fancy $95.00
Plate, cake; 10½"..$28.00
Plate, china, artist signed..$500.00
Plate, Christmas or Turkey $60.00
Plate, dinner; 10" $17.00
Plate, party; w/cup well & cup $22.50
Plate, salad; 8½" $7.00
Plate, salad; 8½", bird decor...$50.00
Plate, 12", aluminum edge...$19.00
Plate, 7½", square...$9.00
Platter, Thanksgiving Turkey $195.00
Platter, 11" $11.00
Platter, 13" $17.00
Platter, 15" $22.00
Platter, 17½", artist signed $770.00
Ramekin, 5", w/lid $20.00
Relish, china, deep shell..$50.00
Relish, china, loop handle...$65.00
Relish, china, maple leaf shape......................................$45.00
Salad fork $28.00
Salad spoon...$28.00

Salt & pepper shakers, apple shape, pr........................$11.00

Salt & pepper shakers, Blossom Top, pr...............$32.50
Salt & pepper shakers, range, pr $32.50
Server, center handle..$28.00

Snack tray, 11½", Martha, w/French pheasant.....$85.00
Sugar bowl, demitasse..$28.00
Sugar bowl, regular, w/lid..$13.00
Tea tile, round or square...$32.50
Teapot, demitasse $80.00
Teapot, earthenware..$70.00
Tidbit, 2-tier..$30.00
Toast, covered..$90.00
Tray, china, flat shell $55.00
Tray for chocolate pot, china..$385.00
Tray, Mod Leaf (illustrated w/salt & pepper shakers)..$65.00
Vase, bud...$85.00
Vase, tapered..$85.00

Vase, 5½", china, round...$60.00
Vase, 7¼", china, handles..$65.00
Vase, 8", boot...$70.00
Vase, 9¼", ruffled top $80.00

Blue Willow Dinnerware

Blue Willow dinnerware has been made since the 1700s, first by English potters, then Japanese, and finally American companies as well. Tinware, glassware, even paper 'go-withs' have been produced over the years — some fairly recently, due to ever-popular demand. It was originally copied from the early blue and white wares made in Nanking and Canton in China. Once in awhile you'll see some pieces in black, pink, red, or even multicolor.

For further study, we recommend *Blue Willow Identification and Value Guide* by Mary Frank Gaston.

Ashtray, Royal $12.00
Ashtray, 4" dia, English, unmarked, advertisement for 'Schweppes Table Waters' $30.00
Ashtray, 5" long, Japan, fish figural $27.00
Baking dish, 2½x5" dia, Japan, Oven Proof...............$30.00
Bank, 7" high, Japan, modeled as three stacked pigs .$45.00
Bank, 9¼" long, kitten figural $250.00
Batter jug, 9", Hazel Atlas, frosted glass, plastic lid...$140.00
Biscuit jar, Made in Japan, Moriyama, cane handle...$125.00
Biscuit jar, 4½", Adderley, Two Temples II pattern, cane handle...$145.00
Biscuit jar, 6", Japan, unmarked, metal handle..........$140.00
Bone dish, 6¼", English, Bourne & Leigh, cresent shape...$45.00
Bone dish, 7½x4½", Wood & Sons, crescent shape $37.00
Bowl, berry; Royal $3.00
Bowl, cereal; Royal $7.00
Bowl, salad; 4x9", English, square $80.00
Bowl, serving; large or small, Royal, each $15.00
Bowl, soup; Royal...$8.00
Bowl, vegetable; Royal, oval..$18.00
Bowl, vegetable; 6x12", Allerton; covered, scalloped edge, interior & exterior pattern $225.00
Bowl, vegetable; 8" dia, Allerton, scalloped edge $60.00
Bowl, vegetable; 8¾x7", English, unmarked, rectangular w/tab handles...$55.00
Bowl, 10", English, unmarked, reticulated sides, for chestnuts $580.00
Bowl, 15" dia, Japan, unmarked, large size for making bread dough, reversed Traditional center pattern.........$160.00
Bowl, 3½x9", English, illegible mark, w/lid (this type of bowl is called a 'Muffin' dish)..............................$140.00
Bowl, 3x11", Cambridge Glass Company, console type, glass, Traditional pattern in green enamel.........$180.00
Bowl, 5x9¼", John Tams Ltd, pedestal base $135.00
Bowl, 8½", English, Josiah Wedgwood, pierced for draining berries or cucumbers, w/underplate, octagonal .$650.00
Butter dish, Japan, w/cover, holds ¼-quarter lb $55.00
Butter dish, ¼-lb, Royal $20.00

Butter dish, 3½x8", Josiah Wedgwood, w/lid $160.00
Butter dish, 3x8", English, unmarked, w/lid $90.00
Butter warmer, Japan, unmarked....................$40.00
Cake plate, 9", unmarked, handles, butterfly border.....$90.00
Cake plate; 9½", Shore & Coggins, Mandarin center pattern w/dagger border $55.00
Cake stand, 4", unmarked, Traditional pattern $240.00
Candelabra, 11", American, Shenango China, brass & ceramic w/matching side dishes.........................$190.00
Candle holder, unmarked, Ship's Light.......................$75.00
Candle holder, 5" dia, Gibson & Sons, chamberstick type w/scalloped edge & gold trim $160.00
Candle holders, 5½", unmarked, Two Temples II Simplified pattern, multicolored Willow, pr $215.00
Canister set, Japan, Flour, Sugar, Coffee, & Tea $250.00
Carafe & warmer, 10", Japan......................$185.00
Casserole, Royal, w/lid $40.00
Cheese & cracker dish, 10" dia, Cambridge Glass Company, unmarked, enameled pattern w/gold trim $160.00
Cheese dish, Wiltshaw & Robinson, Carlton Ware $165.00
Child's tea set, plastic w/original box, Ideal Toys $70.00
Child's toy tea set, 15-pc, American, plastic, Traditional center pattern w/butterfly border $45.00
Cigar lighter, B & Co, London, metal stand & fittings, two cylindrical ceramic containers...........................$400.00
Clock, 8-day, Traditional pattern, German works......$115.00
Coaster, 4" dia, English, advertisement for 'Tennent's Pilsener Beer' $25.00
Coaster/tip tray, 4" dia, ad for 'Yorkshire Relish'.........$25.00
Coffee jar, 6", Japan, for instant coffee, collar.............$45.00
Coffee jar, 6", Japan, for instant coffee, plastic measuring spoon & holder on side of jar $30.00
Coffeepot, 6½", unmarked, graniteware, straight sides ..$75.00
Coffeepot, 7", Japan.......................$70.00
Comb holder, 4½x6½", English, red Willow $115.00
Compote, 3½x9" dia, Doulton, flow blue Willow......$250.00
Compote, 3x6" dia, Shenango China $45.00

Condiment cruet set, 7½" overall, Japan.............$225.00

Condiment shaker, 2", Taylor, Tunnicliffe & Company, pierced silver lid....................$43.00
Cookie jar, 9", American, McCoy, made in form of a pitcher $40.00
Creamer, 2", England, scalloped edge $33.00
Creamer, 4x6", unmarked, Two Temples II pattern, footed, butterfly border $70.00
Creamer, 5x7", English, unmarked, fitted w/stopper, cow figural....................$900.00
Creamer & sugar bowl, Royal, w/lid $12.00
Creamer & sugar bowl, 5", Ashworth, Canton pattern, squared forms....................$70.00
Cup, punch; 3", English, unmarked, Two Temples II pattern, pedestal foot, butterfly border $50.00
Cup, tea; 3", Made in Occupied Japan, polychrome variant pattern....................$30.00
Cup, tea; 4¾", John Meir & Son $27.00
Cup, 3", Homer Laughlin, unmarked, short pedestal base, used for serving custard $15.00
Cup, 4x4½" dia, Japan, unmarked, oversize, for chili..$35.00
Cup & saucer, Royal $5.00
Cuspidor, 7½", Doulton, large rounded body............$220.00
Drainer, meat; 16", English, unmarked, Mandarin pattern w/dagger border, rectangular shape $300.00
Ginger jar, 5", Arthur Wood, England............$30.00
Gravy boat, 7", Wood & Sons $55.00
Gravy boat, 8", Ridgways $65.00
Gravy boat & undertray, Royal $15.00
Hot pot, 6", Japan, electric $45.00
Jardiniere, 4½x8", Tams Ware, 10-sided rim $200.00
Knife rest, 4", unmarked, Traditional border pattern.$125.00
Ladle, 8", unmarked, Traditional center pattern $115.00
Lamp base, 10", Wedgwood & Company, mounted on brass band....................$160.00
Match safe, 2", Shenango China Company....................$70.00
Mug, Royal $12.50
Mustard pot, 2½", unmarked, barrel shape $65.00
Napkin ring, 1½", unmarked....................$70.00
Oil & vinegar set, 6", Japan, pr $55.00
Pepper pot, 3¾", unmarked, rounded body & top, short pedestal foot....................$190.00
Pie plate, Royal $10.00
Pie plate, 10", Made in Japan $55.00
Pie server, 10", Made in Japan $30.00
Pitcher, 5", Edge, Malkin, & Co, Mandarin pattern w/dagger border $90.00
Pitcher, 6", Allerton, scalloped border......................$115.00
Pitcher, 7", Doulton $165.00
Planter, 9¼" long, Lipper & Mann Inc, Japan, kitten figural....................$250.00
Plate, grill; Made in Japan, Moriyama...........................$25.00
Plate, grill; 10½" dia, Made in Japan, Traditional center & border patterns....................$20.00
Plate, grill; 10¾" dia, Booths $25.00
Plate, hot water; 9½x8¼", Booths $225.00
Plate, soup; 9" dia, Shenango China...........................$25.00
Plate, 10" dia, Burgess & Leigh, scroll & flower border .$20.00
Plate, 10½", Royal....................$4.00

Plate, 13" dia, Buffalo China, Traditional pattern.........$80.00
Plate, 6", Royal $5.00
Plate, 6½", HM Williamson & Sons, square shape.......$15.00
Plate, 7½", Royal..$6.00
Plate, 7¼" dia, unmarked, reticulated edge...............$160.00
Plate, 8¾" dia, Booths, octagonal shape.....................$45.00
Plate, 9", Ashworth, Canton pattern............................$30.00
Plate, 9½" dia, Buffalo Pottery, scalloped edge $40.00
Platter, fish, 20½x11½", Minton, gold trim, elongated
    hexagon shape...$550.00
Platter, Royal, oval $18.00

Platter, 10", Japan $30.00
Platter, 12¾x9½", Made in Occupied Japan $40.00
Platter, 14x11¼", William & Samuel Edge $215.00
Platter, 7x10", Greenwood China, 8-sided...................$55.00
Pudding mold, 4½", England, incised mark $55.00
Salad fork & spoon, 11¼", ceramic & silverplate.....$160.00
Salt & pepper shakers, Royal, pr $14.00
Sugar shaker, 5", Made in Japan $70.00
Teapot, Royal $65.00
Tumbler, juice; 3½", Japan, ceramic, pr......................$20.00
Tureen, 6x10", Japan, unmarked, scalloped footed
    base $140.00
Tureen, 6x9", English, unmarked, w/ladle................$350.00

Bookends

You'll find bookends in various types of materials and designs. The more inventive their modeling, the higher the price. Also consider the material. Normally bronze and brass examples are higher than cast iron, though elements of design may override the quality of material. If they are signed by the designer or marked by the manufacturer, you can about triple the price. Those with a decidedly Art Deco appearance are often good sellers, so are cast iron figurals in good paint.

Amish couple, 4½", cast iron, pr.................................$35.00
Cottage, 4", Ancestral Home of George Washington, brass,
    pr...$35.00

Dancer, 7½", bronze, Deco style, heavy, pr..............$150.00
Drunkard, bronzed metal, pr $17.50
Dutch boy & girl, 5", brass, Frankart, pr $125.00
End of Trail, bronzed metal, dated 1930, pr..............$42.50
Flowers, chalkware, pr...$15.00
Gazelle, 8", bronze, leaping form on marble base, M
    Osmond, pr...$285.00
Goldfish, 5¾", fantasy form, cast brass, pr $85.00
Hartford Fire Insurance Company, bronze, dated 1935,
    pr $100.00
Horse head figural, stylized, Frankart, pr..................$120.00
Lady at birdbath, 5¼", cast iron, pr............................$32.00
Lady's head, bronze finish, Frankart, pr....................$155.00
Liberty bell, gold-painted aluminum, pr.....................$15.00
Lincoln delivering Gettysburg Address, bronzed metal,
    pr $45.00
Nude holds drapery overhead, 8", bronze on marble base, H
    Molins, pr $350.00
Nude man wrestling lion, 6", bronzed iron, Deco style,
    pr $40.00
Old Ironsides, 5", copper-plated cast iron, heavy, pr..$60.00
Peacock, bronze, pr...$40.00
Roman soldier w/horse, cast iron, Deco style, pr........$30.00

Sailboats, 7", marked Bronze Art, pr $125.00
Setter dog lying by gate, metal, pr.............................$25.00
Spanish galleon in full sail, 4½", EX multicolor paint on cast
    iron, pr..$40.00

Books

Books have always occupied the mind's imagination. Before television lured us out of the library into the TV room, everyone enjoyed reading the latest novels. Western, horror, and science fiction themes are still popular to this day — especially those by such authors as Louis L'Amour, Steven King, and Ray Bradbury, to name but a few. Edgar Rice Burrough's Tarzan series and Frank L. Baum's Wizard of Oz books are regarded as classics among today's collectors. A first edition of a popular author's first book (especially if it's signed) is especially sought after, so is a book that 'ties in' with a movie or television program.

On the whole, ex-library copies and book club issues (unless they are limited editions) have very low resale values.

For further information we recommend *Huxford's Old Book Value Guide* by Sharon and Bob Huxford. This book is designed to help the owners of old books evaluate their holdings, and it also lists the names of prospective buyers.

See also Children's Books, Paperback Books, Cookbooks.

Abbey, Edward; Cactus Country, NY, Time-Life, 1973, 1st edition, NM...**$40.00**

Adoff, Arnold; All the Colors of the Race, NY, Lothrop Lee, 1982, 1st edition, w/dust jacket, NM **$25.00**

Allen, Gracie; How To Become President, NY, Duell Sloan & Pearce, 1940, 1st edition, w/VG dust jacket, NM **$65.00**

Allen, Woody; Side Effects, NY, Random House, 1980, 1st edition, w/dust jacket, M......................**$40.00**

Asimov, Isaac; Foundation & Empire; NY, Gnome Press, 1952, 1st edition, w/VG dust jacket, M...............**$165.00**

Asimov, Isaac; The End of Eternity, Garden City, Doubleday, 1955, 1st edition, w/dust jacket, NM **$200.00**

Auel, Jean; The Clan of the Cave Bear, NY, Crown, 1980, 1st edition, w/dust jacket, NM **$60.00**

Auster, Paul; Moon Palace, NY, Viking Press, 1989, 1st edition, w/dust jacket, M **$30.00**

Baldwin, James; No Name in the Street, NY, 1972, 1st edition, w/dust jacket, M **$25.00**

Barthelme, Donald; Snow White, NY, Atheneum, 1967, 1st edition, w/dust jacket, NM **$75.00**

Barthelme, Frederick; Two Against One, NY, Weidenfeld & Nicholson, 1988, 1st edition, w/dust jacket, M **$25.00**

Bayler & Carnes; Last Man Off Wake Island, Indianapolis, 1943, 1st edition, VG **$25.00**

Beattie, Ann; Spectacles, NY, Workman Press, 1985, 1st edition, w/dust jacket, M **$35.00**

Betts, Doris; The Scarlet Thread, NY, Harper, 1964, 1st edition, author's 3rd book, w/NM dust jacket, M **$75.00**

Black, Adams & Charles; The Royal Air Force in Action, London, Black & Black, 1941, 101 photos, VG.....**$20.00**

Blake, Christopher; The Fair Ladies of Chartres St, New Orleans, Beale Press, 1965, 1st edition, NM **$30.00**

Block, Lawrence; The Burglar Who Painted Like Mondrian, NY, Arbor House, 1983, 1st edition, w/dust jacket, M...**$25.00**

Boucher, Anthony; The Case of the Baker Street Irregulars, NY, 1940, 1st edition, w/NM dust jacket, M........**$175.00**

Bowen, Elizabeth; To the North, NY, Knopf, 1933, w/dust jacket, NM **$150.00**

Bradbury, Ray; Something Wicked This Way Comes, London, Rupert Hart Davis, 1st UK edition, w/dust jacket, M **$85.00**

Bradbury, Ray; Stories of Ray Bradbury, NY, Knopf, 1980, 1st edition, w/price-clipped dust jacket, M...........**$45.00**

Bradley, Marion Zimmer; The Mists of Avalon, NY, Knopf, 1982, 1st edition, w/dust jacket, NM.....................**$50.00**

Brautigan, Richard; Revenge of the Lawn, NY, Simon & Schuster, 1971, w/dust jacket, NM **$60.00**

Brautigan, Richard; The Tokyo-Montana Express, London, Jonathan Cape, 1981, 1st UK edition, w/dust jacket, M...**$30.00**

Buck, Pearl S; Stories for Little Children, NY, John Day, 1940, 1st edition, Weda Yap illustrated, w/EX dust jacket, NM...**$150.00**

Buechner, Frederick; The Return of Ansel Gibbs, NY, Knopf, 1958, 1st edition, author's 3rd book, w/dust jacket, NM...**$50.00**

Burgess, Anthony; Nothing Like the Sun, NY, Norton, 1964, 1st US edition, w/price-clipped dust jacket, NM.**$50.00**

Burke, Martyn; Laughing War (Vietnam novel), Garden City, Doubleday, 1980, w/dust jacket, NM.....................**$50.00**

Burnett, WR; Mi Amigo: A Novel of the Southwest, NY, 1959, 1st edition, w/dust jacket, M **$50.00**

Burnett, WR; The Goodhues of Sinking Creek, NY, 1934, 1st edition, JJ Lankes illustrated, w/dust jacket, NM...**$55.00**

Burroughs, Edgar Rice; Tarzan & the Foreign Legion, Edgar Rice Burroughs Publishing, 1947, w/dust jacket, NM...**$75.00**

Burroughs, William Jr; Kentucky Ham, NY, Dutton, 1973, 1st edition, w/dust jacket, M.............................**$50.00**

Burroughs, William S; Junkie, New English Library, Olympia Press, 1st edition, signed, w/wrappers, VG **$150.00**

Burroughs, William S; Naked Lunch, NY, Grove Press, 1959, 1st edition, w/dust jacket, G **$75.00**

Burroughs, William S; Naked Lunch, NY, Grove Press, 1959, 1st edition, signed, w/dust jacket, VG.................**$200.00**

Cabell, James Branch; Between Dawn & Sunrise, NY, McBride, 1930, 1st ed, w/G dust jacket, EX........**$50.00**

Cain, James M; Sinful Woman, Cleveland, World, 1948, 1st edition, w/NM dust jacket, M **$75.00**

Caldwell, Taylor; Melissa, NY, Scribners, 1948, 1st edition, inscribed & signed, w/VG dust jacket, M.............**$45.00**

Calloway, Cab; Of Minnie the Moocher & Me, NY, Crowell, 1976, 1st ed, w/worn dust jacket, NM **$25.00**

Campbell, Ruth; Small Fry & Winged Horse, Volland, 1927, Tenggren illustrated, EX **$35.00**

Carr, JD; In Spite of Thunder, NY, 1960, 1st edition, w/NM dust jacket, M...**$30.00**

Carr, John Dickson; The Devil in Velvet, NY, Harper, 1951, 1st edition, w/dust jacket, M **$40.00**

Carver, Raymond; Cathedral, NY, Knopf, 1983, 1st edition, w/dust jacket, M...**$50.00**

Carver, Raymond; What We Talk About When We Talk About Love, 1981, 1st ed, w/dust jacket, M ...**$75.00**

Cass, EC; The Book of Fencing, Lothrop, 1930, 1st edition, VG...**$40.00**

Catlin, George; O-Kee-Pa: A Religious Ceremony & Other Customs of the Mandans, New Haven, 1967, Centennial Edition, NM $30.00

Chandler, Raymond; The Little Sister, Houghton Mifflin, 1949, w/G dust jacket, VG $150.00

Christie, Agatha; They Came to Baghdad, London, Crime Club, 1951, 1st UK edition, w/dust jacket, VG......$60.00

Christie, Agatha; Towards Zero, London, Crime Club, 1944, 1st edition, w/VG dust jacket, NM $65.00

Christopher, John; The Little People, NY, Simon & Schuster, 1966, 1st edition, w/dust jacket, NM.....................$25.00

Clark, Walter Van Tilburg; The Ox-Box Incident, NY, 1940, 1st edition, w/VG dust jacket, NM......................$100.00

Coblentz, Stanton A; The Sunken World, Los Angeles, Fantasy Publishing, 1948, 1st edition, w/dust jacket, NM $35.00

Cohen, Octavius Roy; The Townsend Murder Mystery, NY, 1933, 1st edition, w/dust jacket, VG $32.50

Corman, Avery; Kramer Versus Kramer, NY, Random House, 1977, 1st edition, w/dust jacket, NM....................$30.00

Cornwell, Patricia D; Body of Evidence, NY, Scribners, 1991, advance reading copy, M $45.00

Cowper, Richard; The Twilight of Briareus, NY, John Day, 1974, 1st US edition, w/dust jacket, M $30.00

Crawford, Max; Waltz Across Texas, NY, 1975, 1st edition, author's 1st novel, w/NM dust jacket, M $30.00

Crichton, Michael; The Andromeda Strain, NY, Knopf, 1969, 1st edition, w/VG dust jacket, NM.....................$50.00

Crichton, Michael; Travels, Franklin Library, 1988, 1st edition, signed, full leather binding, M.....................$65.00

Crispin, Edmund; Sudden Vengeance, NY, Dodd Mead, 1950, 1st US edition, w/worn dust jacket, EX.......$25.00

Crumley, James; The Last Good Kiss, NY, Random House, 1978, 1st edition, w/NM dust jacket, M $35.00

Culver & Grant, The Book of Old Ships, Garden City, Doubleday, 1935, 1st edition, illustrated, w/NM dust jacket, M $30.00

Darrah, William C; The World of Stereographs, Gettysburg, 1977, 1st edition, signed, 300 illustrations, w/dust jacket, M $45.00

Davies, Robertson; Fifth Business, NY, Viking, 1970, 1st edition, w/dust jacket, NM $45.00

Deighton, Len; Funeral in Berlin, NY, Putnam, 1964, 1st edition, w/dust jacket, VG.............................$75.00

Derleth, August; The House on the Mound, NY, Duell Sloan & Pearce, 1958, 1st edition, signed, M.................$60.00

Dinesen, Isak; Out of Africa, NY, Random House, 1938, 1st edition, w/dust jacket, VG.............................$85.00

Dinesen, Isak; Winter's Tales, NY, Random House, 1949, 1st edition, w/dust jacket, VG............................$50.00

Disney, Doris Miles; Fire at Will, Garden City, Doubleday, 1950, 1st edition, w/dust jacket, VG.....................$25.00

Dobie, J Fank; The Mustangs, Boston, 1952, 1st edition, w/VG price-clipped dust jacket, M........................$40.00

Dobie, J Frank; Guide to Life & Literature of the Southwest, Austin, 1943, 1st edition, w/wrappers, NM........$125.00

Dos Passos, John; The Big Money, NY, Harcourt Brace, 1936, 1st edition, w/dust jacket, VG....................$85.00

Duncan, David Douglas; The Silent Studio, NY, WW Norton, 1976, 1st US edition, w/dust jacket, NM..............$55.00

Eastman, Max; Kinds of Love, NY, Scribners, 1931, 1st edition, w/NM dust jacket, M $65.00

Eberhart, Mignon G; Hasty Wedding, NY, Doubleday Doran, 1st edition, w/dust jacket, VG $45.00

Eddy, Mary Baker; Science & Health, no place, 1934, leather binding, EX..$20.00

Ellington, Duke; Music Is My Mistress, Garden City, Doubleday, 1973, 1st edition, w/dust jacket, NM $75.00

Ellory, James; The Black Dahlia, NY, Mysterious Press, 1987, 1st edition, w/NM dust jacket, M $35.00

Ellroy, James; Clandestine, London, 1984, 1st edition, inscribed, w/dust jacket, M $60.00

Farrar, EF; Old Virginia Houses Along the James, NY, 1957, 1st edition, folio, NM $27.50

Faulkner, William; A Fable, NY, Random House, 1954, 1st edition, w/dust jacket, VG....................................$60.00

Faulkner, William; The Collected Stories of William Faulkner, NY, Random House, 1950, 1st edition, w/dust jacket, VG..$125.00

Faulkner, William; The Reivers, NY, Random House, 1962, 1st edition, w/dust jacket, NM $30.00

Faulkner, William; The Town, NY, Random House, 1957, 1st edition, w/dust jacket, NM..............................$100.00

Fisher, Vardis; Tale of Valor, NY 1958, 1st edition, w/dust jacket, VG $22.50

Fleming, Ian; From Russia with Love, London, Jonathan Cape, 1957, 1st edition, w/dust jacket, VG $100.00

Fleming, Ian; Goldfinger, NY, Macmillan, 1959, 1st edition, w/dust jacket, VG $50.00

Fleming, Ian; Octopussy & the Living Daylights, London, Jonathan Cape, 1966, 1st UK edition, w/dust jacket, NM..$40.00

Fleming, Ian; Spy Who Loved Me, London, Jonathan Cape, 1962, 1st edition, w/dust jacket, VG $45.00

Fleming, Ian; The Golden Gun, London, Jonathan Cape, 1st UK edition, w/dust jacket, NM..............................$45.00

Flynn, Errol; My Wicked, Wicked Ways; NY, Putnam, 1959, 1st edition, 438 pages, w/dust jacket, NM.............$85.00

Fowle, Art E; Flat Glass, Libbey Owens, 1924, 1st edition, illustrated, 71 pages, EX $20.00

Francis, Dick; Across the Board, NY, Harper, 1975, 1st edition, w/dust jacket, NM $65.00

Fuller, R Buckminster; Nine Chains to the Moon, Philadelphia, 1938, 406 pages, gilt cloth binding, EX........$50.00

Gardner, Erle Stanley; Case of the Careless Cupid, NY, Doubleday, 1968, Book Club edition, w/dust jacket, VG $7.50

Gardner, Erle Stanley; Human Zero, NY, William Morrow, 1981, 1st edition, w/dust jacket, EX.....................$30.00

Gardner, Erle Stanley; Perry Mason Omnibus, no place, no date, Book Club edition, w/dust jacket, EX...........$7.50

Gardner, Erle Stanley; The Case of the Amorous Aunt, NY, William Morrow, 1963, 1st edition, w/dust jacket, NM..$50.00

Gardner, Erle Stanley; The Case of the Grinning Gorilla, NY, William Morrow, 1st edition, w/dust jacket, VG...$45.00

Gardner, Erle Stanley; The Case of the Lonely Heiress, NY, William Morrow, 1948, w/dust jacket, VG **$25.00**

Gingerich, M; The Mennonites in Iowa, Iowa City, 1939, 1st edition, 419 pages, VG **$65.00**

Goldsmith, Oliver; The Vicar of Wakefield, David McKay, 1929, Arthur Rackham illustrated, w/dust jacket, VG **$75.00**

Goldwater, Barry; Arizona Portraits, no place, 1946, 1st edition, NM **$75.00**

Gordon, Caroline; The Malefactors, NY, Harcourt, 1956, 1st edition, w/dust jacket, NM **$65.00**

Gores, Joe; Hammett, NY, Putnam, 1975, 1st edition, w/dust jacket, M **$45.00**

Grau, Shirley Ann; The House on Coliseum Street, NY, Knopf, 1961, 1st edition, w/dust jacket, NM **$45.00**

Greene, Graham; Dr Fischer of Geneva, NY, Simon & Schuster, 1980, 1st edition, w/dust jacket, EX **$15.00**

Greene, Graham; In Search of a Character, NY, Viking, 1961, 1st US edition, w/VG dust jacket, M **$45.00**

Greene, Graham; The End of the Affair, London, Heinemann, 1951, 1st edition, w/dust jacket, G **$50.00**

Greene, Graham; The Orient Express, Garden City, Doubleday, 1933, 1st edition, w/dust jacket, VG **$175.00**

Gresham, William Lindsay; Nightmare Alley, NY, Rinehart, 1946, 1st edition, author's 1st book, w/dust jacket, NM **$45.00**

Grey, Zane; Forlorn River, NY, Harper, 1927, 1st edition, VG **$20.00**

Grey, Zane; Horse Heaven Hill, NY, Harper, 1959, 1st edition, w/dust jacket, VG **$60.00**

Grey, Zane; The Maverick Queen, NY, Harper, 1950, 1st edition, w/dust jacket, G **$60.00**

Grey, Zane; The Ranger, NY, Harper, 1960, 1st edition, w/dust jacket, VG **$55.00**

Grey, Zane; Thunder Mountain, NY, Harper, 1935, 1st edition, w/dust jacket, VG **$30.00**

Grey Owl; Tales of an Empty Cabin, NY, Dodd Mead, 1936, 1st edition, w/dust jacket, EX **$95.00**

Gruelle, Johnny; Raggedy Ann & Andy & the Camel with the Wrinkled Knees, Indianapolis, Bobbs Merrill, 95 pages, VG **$16.00**

Gurganus, Allan; The Oldest Living Confederate Widow Tells All, NY, Knopf, 1989, 1st edition, w/dust jacket, NM **$45.00**

Hammett, Dashiell; Adventures of Sam Spade, no place, Tower Publishing, 2nd edition, w/dust jacket, VG **$7.50**

Hammett, Dashiell; Big Knockover, NY, Random House, no date, 2nd edition, w/dust jacket, VG **$15.00**

Hammett, Dashiell; Dain Curse, NY, Knopf, 1929, 1st edition, w/dust jacket, NM **$150.00**

Haney, L; Naked at the Feast, NY, 1981, 1st edition, illustrated, 338 pages, w/dust jacket, VG **$37.50**

Hare, Cyril; Best Detective Stories of Cyril Hare, London, Faber, 1959, 1st edition, w/dust jacket, NM **$35.00**

Harris, Thomas; Black Sunday, NY, Putnam, 1975, 1st edition, author's 1st book, w/dust jacket, M **$100.00**

Hashimoto, M; Sunk (Japanese submarines in WWII), NY, 1954, 1st edition, w/dust jacket, M **$35.00**

Hassler, WW; Commander of the Army of the Potomac, 1962, Baton Rouge, 1st edition, w/dust jacket, M.**$40.00**

Heinl, RD; Soldiers of the Sea, Annapolis, 1962, 1st edition, w/NM dust jacket, M **$100.00**

Heinlein, Robert A; The Green Hills of Earth, 1951, Chicago, Shasta, 1st edition, w/dust jacket, NM **$150.00**

Hemingway, Ernest; Across the River & into the Trees, NY, Scribnesr, 1950, 1st edition, w/dust jacket, VG **$65.00**

Hemingway, Ernest; Green Hills of Africa, NY, Scribners, 1935, 1st edition, w/dust jacket, EX **$450.00**

Hemingway, Ernest; Nick Adams Stories, NY, Scribners, 1972, 1st edition, w/dust jacket, EX **$50.00**

Hemingway, Ernest; The Old Man & the Sea, NY, Scribners, 1952, 1st edition, w/dust jacket, EX **$150.00**

Hemingway, Ernest; Winner Take Nothing, NY, Scribners 1933, 1st edition, w/dust jacket, EX **$400.00**

Hianes, William Wister; The Winter War, Boston, Little Brown, 1961, 1st edition, w/NM dust jacket, M **$35.00**

Hiassen, Carl; Double Whammy, NY, Putnam, 1987, 1st edition, w/dust jacket, M **$30.00**

Hilton, James; So Well Remembered, Boston, Atlantic-Little Brown, 1945, 1st edition, w/dust jacket, NM **$30.00**

Hoban, Russell; Turtle Diary, NY, Random House, 1975, 1st edition, w/dust jacket, NM **$45.00**

Holme, CG; Decorative Art, London & NY, The Studio, 1936, folio, 140 pages, VG **$20.00**

Howard, Maureen; Not a Word About Nightingales, NY, Atheneum, 1962, 1st edition, author's 1st book, w/dust jacket, NM **$50.00**

Hurley, Jack F; Portrait of a Decade...Documentary Photography in the Thirties, Baton Rouge, 1972, w/dust jacket, NM **$50.00**

Huxley, Aldous; Music at Night; London, Chatto & Windus, 1931, 1st edition, w/dust jacket, VG **$50.00**

Huxley, Elspeth; The Walled City, Philadelphia, 1949, 1st edition, w/dust jacket, VG **$17.50**

Irving, John; The Cider House Rules, Franklin Library, 1985, 1st edition, signed tipped-in leaf, gilt-stamped leather, M **$75.00**

Jackson, Jon A; The Blind Pig, NY, Random House, 1978, 1st edition, author's 2nd book, w/dust jacket, M..**$45.00**

Jacobi, Carl; Revelations in Black, Arkham House, 1947, 1st edition, author's 1st book, w/dust jacket, M **$45.00**

Jerome, VJ; The Paper Bridge, NY, Citadel, 1966, 1st edition, w/dust jacket, M **$35.00**

Johnson, Dorothy M; All the Buffalo Returning, NY, 1979, 1st edition, w/dust jacket, M **$30.00**

Johnson, Harold; Who's Who in Major League Baseball, Buxton, 1933, 1st edition, scarce, VG **$300.00**

Kaminsky, Stuart; Murder on the Yellow Brick Road, NY, St Martins, 1977, 1st edition, w/NM dust jacket, M...**$45.00**

Kaufman, Bel; Up the Down Staircase, Englewood Cliffs, Prentice-Hall, 1964, advance reading copy, orange wrappers, M **$85.00**

Kent, Rockwell; Goethe's Faust, New Directions, 1941, 1st edition, w/dust jacket, M **$50.00**

Kerouac, Jack; Visions of Gerard, Farrar Straus, 1st edition, w/dust jacket, G **$100.00**

King, Martin Luther Jr; Where Do We Go from Here?; NY, 1967, 1st edition, w/dust jacket, VG **$35.00**

King, Stephen; Danse Macabre, Everest House, 1981, 1st edition, w/dust jacket, VG..................**$40.00**

King, Stephen; Misery, NY, Viking, 1987, 2nd edition, w/dust jacket, EX **$15.00**

King, Stephen; Pet Sematary, NY, Doubleday, 1983, 1st edition, w/dust jacket, EX **$35.00**

King, Stephen; Skeleton Crew, no place, Scream Press, 1985, 1st edition (1/1000), signed, w/box, NM............**$300.00**

King, Stephen; The Shining, NY, Doubleday, 1977, 1st edition, w/dust jacket, EX **$225.00**

King, Stephen; Thinner, no place, no date, Book Club edition, w/dust jacket, VG **$5.00**

Kosinski, Jerzy; Steps, NY, Random House, 1968, 1st edition, w/dust jacket, NM..................................**$65.00**

Kotzwinkle, William; ET: The Extra-Terrestrial; NY, Putnams, 1982, 1st edition, w/dust jacket, NM....................**$85.00**

L'Amour, Louis; Fair Blows the Wind, NY, Dutton, 1978, 1st edition, w/dust jacket, M..........................**$125.00**

L'Amour, Louis; Haunted Mesa, no place, Bantam, 1987, no edition given, w/dust jacket, VG **$20.00**

L'Amour, Louis; How the West Was Won, NY, Random House, 1962, Photoplay & 1st edition, EX **$12.50**

Lagerkvist, Par; The Sibyl, NY, Random House, 1958, 1st edition, w/dust jacket, NM **$45.00**

Lampell, Millard; The Long Way Home, NY, Messner, 1946, 1st edition, w/dust jacket, M **$45.00**

Lawrence, Hilda; Blood upon the Snow, NY, Doubleday, 1944, Book Club edition, VG **$10.00**

Lawrence, TE; Seven Pillars of Wisdom, NY, Doubleday, 1935, 1st edition, w/dust jacket, VG **$125.00**

Lawrence, TE; The Letters of TE Lawrence, Doubleday, 1939, 1st edition, edited by David Garnett............**$50.00**

Le Carre, John; Honorable Schoolboy, NY, Knopf, 1977, 1st US Trade edition, w/dust jacket, EX..................**$35.00**

Le Carre, John; Little Drummer Girl, London, Hodder Stoughton, 1983, 1st UK Trade edition, w/dust jacket, EX..**$40.00**

Le Carre, John; Smiley's People, NY, Knopf, 1980, 1st US Trade edition, w/dust jacket, EX **$30.00**

Le Carre, John; Spy Who Came in from the Cold, NY, Coward McCann, no date, 3rd edition, w/dust jacket, ex-library, EX..**$10.00**

Lessing, Doris; In Pursuit of the English, NY, Simon Schuster, 1961, 1st edition, w/dust jacket, VG **$60.00**

Lewis, Sinclair; The God-Seeker, NY, Random House, 1949, 1st edition, w/VG dust jacket, NM..................**$45.00**

Lewis, Sinclair; Works of Art, NY, Doubleday Doran, 1934, 1st edition, w/dust jacket, M **$50.00**

Lindbergh, Charles; Of Flight & Life, NY, 1948, 1st edition, w/dust jacket, VG **$37.50**

Long, Huey; My First Days in the White House, Harrisburg, 1st edition, w/dust jacket, VG **$65.00**

Lopez, Barry; Arctic Dreams, NY, Scribners, 1986, 1st edition, w/dust jacket, EX **$45.00**

Lopez, Barry; River Notes, no place, Sheed Andrews & McMeel, 1979, 1st edition, w/dust jacket, EX........**$65.00**

Lovecraft, HP; Marginalia, Arkham House, 1944, 1st edition, w/dust jacket, VG **$150.00**

Ludlum, Robert; The Scarlatti Inheritance, NY, World, 1971, correct 1st issue, author's 1st book, w/dust jacket, NM..**$150.00**

MacDonald, John D; The Deep Blue Good-Bye, Philadelphia, 1975, 1st edition, w/NM dust jacket, M......**$100.00**

MacDonald, Ross; Black Money; NY, Knopf, 1966, 1st edition, w/dust jacket, NM **$250.00**

MacDonald, Ross; The Far Side of the Dollar, NY, 1965, 1st edition, w/dust jacket, M..........................**$125.00**

Maltz, Albert; The Cross & the Arrow, Boston, Little Brown, 1944, 1st edition, w/dust jacket, NM...................**$50.00**

Mapplethorpe, Robert; Lady Lisa Lyons, NY, Viking, 1983, 1st hardcover edition, w/dust jacket, EX............**$350.00**

Marquis, Don; Archy's Life of Mehitabel, Garden City, Doubleday, 1933, 1st edition, w/dust jacket, NM......**$100.00**

Matthews, Jack; The Charisma Campaigns, NY, Harcourt Brace Javonovich, 1972, 1st edition, inscribed, w/dust jacket, EX..**$50.00**

Matthiessen, Peter; In the Spirit of Crazy Horse, NY, Viking, 1983, 1st edition, w/NM dust jacket, M **$100.00**

Matthiessen, Peter; Indian Country, NY, Viking, 1984, 1st edition, w/dust jacket, EX **$45.00**

Maugham, WS; Of Human Bonadage, New Haven, 1939, Ltd Edition Club, John Sloan illustrated & signed, 2 volumes w/slipcase..**$400.00**

Maxwell, William; The Chateau, NY, Knopf, 1961, 1st edition, w/dust jacket, NM **$40.00**

McElroy, Joseph; Ancient History: A Paraphrase; NY, Knopf, 1971, 1st edition, w/M dust jacket, M...................**$65.00**

McMurtry, Larry; Moving On, NY, Simon & Schuster, 1970, 1st edition, w/dust jacket, G **$40.00**

McMurtry, Larry; Some Can Whistle, NY, Simon & Schuster, 1979, 1st edition, signed, w/dust jacket, NM........**$45.00**

McMurtry, Larry; The Last Picture Show, NY, Dial Press, 1966, 1st edition, w/dust jacket, NM **$300.00**

Michaels, Barbara; Sons of the Wolf, NY, 1967, 1st edition, w/dust jacket, M..**$75.00**

Michener, James A; Centennial, NY, Random House, 1974, 1st edition, w/NM dust jacket, NM **$40.00**

Michener, James A; The Source, NY, Random House, 1965, 1st edition, w/NM dust jacket, M **$50.00**

Millay, Edna St Vincent; Conversation at Midnight, NY, 1937, 1st edition, w/dust jacket, VG..................**$27.50**

Milne, AA; Pooh Party Book, NY, Dutton, 1971, 1st edition, Shepard illustrated, 146 pages, w/dust jacket, VG ..**$15.00**

Milne, AA; Winnie the Pooh, NY, 1st US edition, VG .**$75.00**

Montross, Lynn; The United States Marines: A Pictorial History; 1st edition, w/dust jacket, M **$30.00**

Moorcock, Michael; End of All Songs, NY, Harper, 1st edition, 1976, w/dust jacket, EX..................**$15.00**

Moore, Brian; Fergus, NY, Holt, 1970, 1st US edition, w/NM dust jacket, M **$30.00**

Moore, CL; Judgement Night; Gnome Press, 1952, 1st edition, w/dust jacket, VG..................**$85.00**

Morrison, Jim; The Lords & the New Creatures, NY, Simon & Schuster, 1970, 1st edition, w/dust jacket, NM ...**$100.00**

Murphy, Audie; To Hell & Back, NY, 1st edition, signed, w/dust jacket, EX $70.00

Nash, Ogden; Primrose Path, NY, Simon & Schuster, 1935, 1st edition, w/dust jacket, EX $175.00

Nin, Anais; Novel of the Future, NY, Macmillan, 1968, 1st edition, 214 pages, w/dust jacket, EX...................$50.00

Nutting, Wallace; Connecticut Beautiful; Garden City, Doubleday, signed, w/G dust jacket, VG $42.50

O'Brien, Tim; The Nuclear Age, NY, Knopf, 1985, 1st edition, signed, w/dust jacket, EX $50.00

O'Neill, Eugene; Moon for the Misbegotten, NY, Random House, 1952, 1st edition, w/dust jacket, EX..........$75.00

O'Neill, Eugene; Mourning Becomes Electra, NY, 1931, 1st edition, w/price-clipped dust jacket, M..............$125.00

O'Neill, Eugene; The Iceman Cometh, NY, Random House, 1946, 1st edition, w/dust jacket, G $40.00

Olson, Charles; Human Universe & Other Essays, NY, Grove, 1967, w/NM dust jacket, M $40.00

Parry, Albert; Tatoo: Secrets of a Strange Art Practiced Among Natives of the US, NY, 1933, 1st edition, 174 pages, VG $85.00

Percy, Walker; Love in the Ruins, NY, Farrar, 1971, 1st edition, w/M dust jacket, M..$45.00

Peters, Elizabeth; Street of the Five Moons, NY, 1978, 1st edition, w/dust jacket, M..$50.00

Plante, David; The Ghost of Henry James, Boston, Gambit, 1970, 1st US edition, author's 1st book, w/dust jacket, M $85.00

Plath, Sylvia; Winter Trees, NY, Harper, 1972, 1st US edition, w/VG dust jacket, NM $45.00

Pohl, Frederick; The Seventh Galaxy Reader, NY, Doubleday, 1964, 2nd edition, w/dust jacket, VG $15.00

Porter, Katherine Anne; Ship of Fools, Boston, Little Brown, 1962, 1st edition, w/dust jacket, NM....................$30.00

Porter, Katherine Anne; The Leaning Tower & Other Stories, NY, Harcourt Brace, 1944, 1st edition, w/dust jacket, VG $75.00

Price, Vincent; I Like What I Know: Visual Autobiography; NY, 1959, 1st edition, w/dust jacket, VG..............$20.00

Queen, Ellery; A Multitude of Sins, NY, Dial Press, 1978, 1st edition, w/dust jacket, VG.....................................$15.00

Queen, Ellery; Double, Double; Boston, Little Brown, 1950, 1st edition, w/dust jacket, M $60.00

Queen, Ellery; The Brown Fox Mystery, Boston, Little Brown, 1955, 4th edition, w/dust jacket, VG $15.00

Queen, Ellery; The Red Chipmunk Mystery, Philadelphia, Lippincott, 1946, 1st edition, w/dust jacket, EX....$45.00

Queneau, Raymond; The Blue Flowers, NY, Atheneum, 1967, 1st edition, w/dust jacket, M $25.00

Rand, Ayn; Atlas Shrugged, NY, Random House, 1957, 1st edition, G...$65.00

Rand, Ayn; Atlas Shrugged, NY, Random House, 1957, 1st edition, w/dust jacket, VG...................................$200.00

Rechy, John; City of Night, NY, Grove Press, 1963, 1st edition, author's 1st book, w/NM price-clipped dust jacket, M $45.00

Rice, Anne; Queen of the Damned, NY, 1988, 1st edition, w/dust jacket, EX...$75.00

Roberts, Kenneth; Trending into Maine, Boston, 1938, 1st edition, Andrew Wyeth illustrated, w/dust jacket, EX $65.00

Rockwood, Roy; Bomba at Moving Mountain, Grosset Dunlap, no date given, reprint edition, w/dust jacket, VG $7.50

Rockwood, Roy; Lost on the Moon, no place given, Whitman Publishing, reprint edition, w/dust jacket, VG $20.00

Rohmer, Sax; Brood of the Witch Queen, NY, Doubleday Page, 1924, 1st edition, VG $45.00

Rohmer, Sax; Daughter of Fu Manchu, NY, Doubleday Doran, 1931, 1st edition, G $15.00

Saarinen, Eliel; The City: Its Growth, Decay, & Future; NY, 1943, 1st edition, inscribed, 340 pages, M.............$45.00

Salten, Felix; Bambi's Children, Indianapolis, Bobbs Merrill, 1939, 1st edition, w/G dust jacket, NM $40.00

Sandburg, Carl; Remembrance Rock, NY, Harcourt Brace, 1948, 1st edition, w/dust jacket, VG $40.00

Santee, Ross; Lost Pony Tracks, NY, 1953, 1st edition, w/dust jacket, VG $25.00

Scherf, Margaret; Don't Wake Me Up While I'm Driving, Garden City, Doubleday, 1977, 1st edition, w/dust jacket, NM...$35.00

Schwartz, Delmore; The World Is a Wedding, New Directions, 1st edition, w/dust jacket, VG....................$50.00

Scott, Sir Walter; Ivanhoe, Limited Edition Club, 1951, Edward A Wilson illustrated & signed, 2 volumes w/slipcase, EX...$60.00

Seale, Bobby; Seize the Time, NY, Random House, 1970, 1st edition, w/dust jacket, NM $35.00

Sell & Weybright; Buffalo Bill & the Wild West, NY, 1955, 1st edition, illustrated, w/VG dust jacket, NM......$35.00

Seuss, Dr; Five Hundred Hats of Bartholomew Cubbins, NY, Vanguard, 1938, 1st edition, w/dust jacket, VG....$40.00

Shambaugh, B; Amana That Was & Is, Iowa City, 1932, 1st edition, 502 pages, VG $45.00

Silverberg, Robert; Lost Cities & Vanished Civilizations, Chilton, 1962, 1st edition, w/dust jacket, VG........$28.00

Simak, CD; Time Is the Simplest Thing, no place given, Doubleday, 1961, 1st edition, w/dust jacket, EX ..$60.00

Simak, CD; Visitors, no place given, Del Rey, 1st edition, w/dust jacket, EX...$20.00

Sinclair, Upton; Co-Op: A Novel of Living Together; NY, Farrar, 1936, 1st edition, w/dust jacket, NM..........$65.00

Sinclair, Upton; The Gnomobile, NY, Farrar, 1936, 1st edition, w/dust jacket, NM $75.00

Smith, George O; Path of Unreason, Gnome Press, 1st edition, w/dust jacket, VG...$30.00

Sontag, Susan; Under the Sign of Saturn, NY, Farrar Straus, 1980, 1st edition, w/dust jacket, M $45.00

Stegner, Wallace; Remembering Laughter, Boston, Little Brown, 1937, 1st edition, author's 1st book, w/dust jacket, NM...$50.00

Steinbeck, John; Grapes of Wrath, NY, Viking, 1939, 1st edition, original binding, w/dust jacket, EX.........$1,200.00

Steinbeck, John; Grapes of Wrath, NY, Viking, 1939, 1st edition, w/dust jacket, VG......................................$500.00

Steinbeck, John; The Wayward Bus, NY, Viking Press, 1947, 1st edition, w/dust jacket, VG..............$60.00

Stewart, GR; The Opening of the California Trail, Berkeley, 1953, w/dust jacket, NM....................$45.00

Stimson, Mary; Marijuana Mystery, Philadelphia, Dorrance, 1st edition, w/dust jacket, VG.............$100.00

Stone, Robert; A Flag for Sunrise, NY, Knopf, 1981, 1st edition, w/dust jacket, M......................$40.00

Stone, Robert; Children of Light, NY, Knopf, 1986, 1st edition, inscribed & signed, w/dust jacket, M............$25.00

Stout, Rex; Death of a Doxy, NY, Viking, 1966, 1st edition, w/dust jacket, VG........................$15.00

Stout, Rex; The Doorbell Rang, NY, 1965, 1st edition, w/dust jacket, VG...........................$27.50

Stuart, Jesse; The Thread That Runs So True, NY, 1949, no edition given, signed, 293 pages, w/dust jacket, VG..............$32.50

Taber, Gladys; Stillmeadow Cookbook, Philadelphia, 1965, 1st edition, w/dust jacket, VG.............$35.00

Taine, John; Seeds of Life, Reading, Fantasy Press, 1951, 1st edition, w/dust jacket, NM..............$35.00

Tarkington, Booth; Growth, Garden City, Doubleday, 1927, 1st edition, w/VG dust jacket, NM...............$45.00

Tarkington, Booth; Seventeen, no place given, Grosset Dunlap, reprint edition, VG.....................$5.00

Tarry & Alland; My Dog Rinty, NY, Viking Press, 1946, 1st edition, photographs, lacks dust jacket, ...$50.00

Taylor, Elizabeth; At Mrs Lippincote's, NY, Knopf, 1945, 1st US edition, author's 1st book, w/dust jacket, NM.$30.00

Taylor, John; Pondoro, NY, 1955, 1st edition, w/dust jacket, VG.............................$42.50

Theroux, Paul; Jungle Lovers, Boston, Houghton Mifflin, 1971, 1st edition, w/dust jacket, NM.............$75.00

Theroux, Paul; Old Patagonian Express, no place given, Houghton Mifflin, Book Club edition, 404 pages, EX.........................$10.00

Theroux, Paul; The Kingdom by the Sea, Boston, Houghton Mifflin, 1983, 1st edition, signed, w/dust jacket, NM.........................$65.00

Thomas, Dylan; A Child's Christmas in Wales, New Directions, 1954, 1st edition, w/dust jacket, VG...........$40.00

Thomas, Dylan; Adventures in the Skin Trade, New Directions, 1953, 1st edition, w/dust jacket, VG...........$55.00

Thomas, Dylan; Under Milk Wood, New Directions, 1954, 1st edition, w/dust jacket, VG................$50.00

Thompson, Kay; Eloise, NY, 1955, 1st edition, w/worn dust jacket, VG.............................$100.00

Thoreau, HD; Walden, Heritage Club, 1939, Thomas Nason illustrated, cloth binding, EX...................$25.00

Tolstoy, LN; Anna Karenina, Limited Edition Club, 1933, Nikolas Piskariov illustrated & signed, 2 volumes w/slipcase, EX.........................$75.00

Tomlinson, HM; Gallion's Reach, London, Heinemann, 1927, 1st UK edition, w/dust jacket, G...............$40.00

Tomlinson, HM; Gifts of Fortune, NY, Harpers, 1926, 1st edition, w/dust jacket, G....................$35.00

Turner, G; Victory Rode the Rails, Indianapolis, 1953, 1st edition, w/dust jacket, VG..................$47.50

Twain, Mark; Adventures of Huckleberry Finn, Limited Edition Club, 1942, TH Benton illustrated & signed, w/slipcase, VG.........................$200.00

Tyler, Anne; Breathing Lessons, NY, Knopf, 1988, 1st edition, w/dust jacket, EX.....................$35.00

Tyler, Anne; The Accidental Tourist, NY, Knopf, 1985, 1st edition, signed on tipped-in page, w/dust jacket, M.........................$150.00

Updike, John; Bottom's Dream, NY, Knopf, 1969, 1st edition, w/dust jacket, NM....................$100.00

Updike, John; Marry Me, Franklin Library, 1976, 1st edition, leather binding, EX.....................$65.00

Updike, John; Rabbit Run; Franklin Library, 1977, limited edition, signed, full leather binding, NM.............$85.00

Updike, John; Rabbit Is Rich, NY, Knopf, 1981, 1st edition, signed, w/dust jacket, EX...................$100.00

Updike, John; Tossing & Turning, NY, Knopf, 1977, 1st edition, signed, w/dust jacket, M...............$75.00

Vargas Llosa, Mario; Time of the Hero, NY, Grove Press, 1966, 1st edition, w/dust jacket, EX.............$45.00

Verne, Jules; Clipper of the Clouds, Association of Booksellers, 1962, w/dust jacket, EX................$12.50

Verne, Jules; Secret of the Island, no place given, Bernard Hanison, 1st edition, w/dust jacket, VG..............$25.00

Verne, Jules; 20,000 Leagues Under the Sea; no place given, Grosset Dunlap, reprint edition, VG...............$7.50

Vidal, Gore; Kalki, NY, Random House, 1978, 1st edition, w/dust jacket, VG..........................$20.00

Vonnegut, Kurt; Happy Birthday Wanda June, NY, Delacorte, 1971, 1st edition, w/dust jacket, EX...........$50.00

Wagoner, David; Staying Alive, Bloomington, Indiana University Press, 1966, 1st edition, w/dust jacket, M..$35.00

Walker, Alice; The Color Purple, no place given, Harcourt Brace, 1982, inscribed, w/dust jacket, .$100.00

Walker, Alice; The Temple of My Familiar, NY, 1989, 1st edition, signed, w/dust jacket, M...............$40.00

Ward, Lynd; Frankenstein, NY, 1934, 1st edition, illustrated, w/dust jacket, VG.....................$145.00

Ware, Caroline F; Greenwich Village 1920-30, Boston, 1935, 1st edition, 496 pages, VG................$40.00

Warren, RP; World Enough & Time, NY, Random House, 1950, 1st edition, signed, w/dust jacket, EX........$125.00

Waugh, Evelyn; Helena, London, Chapman Hall, 1st UK edition, w/dust jacket, EX.....................$125.00

Waugh, Evelyn; Love Among the Ruins, London, Chapman & Hall, 1953, 1st edition, w/dust jacket, NM........$65.00

Waugh, Evelyn; Loved Ones, Boston, Little Brown, 1948, 2nd edition, 164 pages, EX...................$25.00

Waugh, Evelyn; Men at Arms, Boston, Little Brown, 1952, 1st US edition, w/price-clipped dust jacket, NM...$75.00

Waugh, Evelyn; The End of the Battle, Boston, Little Brown, 1961, 1st US edition, w/VG dust jacket, NM........$45.00

Way, Isabel Stewart; Seed of the Land (Midwest farm novel), NY, Appleton, 1935, 1st edition, w/dust jacket, NM.........................$45.00

Wells, Helen; Cherry Ames Army Nurse, no place given, Grosset & Dunlap, reprint edition, w/dust jacket, VG.........................$7.50

Wells, HG; Early Writings in Science & Science Fiction; University of California, 1975, 1st edition, ...$25.00

Wells, HG; War of the Worlds, no place given, Whitman, 1954, reprint edition, VG $7.50

Welty, Eudora; Selected Stories of Eudora Welty, NY, Modern Library, 1954, 1st edition, w/dust jacket, NM .$75.00

Welty, Eudora; The Golden Apples, NY, Harcourt Brace, 1949, 1st edition, w/dust jacket, VG...................$100.00

Weston, CW & Edward; California & the West, NY, 1940, 1st edition, VG $50.00

Wharton, Edith; Twilight Sleep, NY, Appleton, 1927, 1st edition, VG $45.00

White, TH; Breach of Faith: Fall of Richard Nixon; NY, no publisher given, 1975, 1st edition, VG..................$10.00

White, TH; The Godstone & the Blackmor, NY, Putnam, 1959, 1st US edition, w/dust jacket, NM................$45.00

Wiggin, Kate Douglas; Rebecca of Sunnybrook Farm, no place given, Grosset & Dunlap, no date given, Photoplay edition, VG...................$15.00

Williams, Tennessee; Cat on a Hot Tin Roof, New Directions, no date given (1955), 1st edition, signed, w/dust jacket, EX...........................$200.00

Williams, William Carlos; The Build-Up, NY, Random House, 1952, 1st edition, w/dust jacket, VG.........$35.00

Wister, Owen; The Virginian, no place given, Grosset & Dunlap, no date given (1930), reprint edition, 506 pages, VG $8.50

Wodehouse, PG; Crime Wave at Blandings, NY, Sun Dial, 1937, no edition given, VG $30.00

Wodehouse, PG; Full Moon, NY, Doubleday, 1947, 1st edition, VG $40.00

Wodehouse, PG; Laughing Gas, Toronto, McClelland Stewart, 1936, 1st Canadian edition, VG $50.00

Wodehouse, PG; Most of PG Wodehouse, NY, Simon & Schuster, 1960, 1st edition, w/dust jacket, VG......$30.00

Wodehouse, PG; Wodehouse on Crime, Ellery Queen Mystery Club, 1981, 1st edition, w/dust jacket, EX $20.00

Wolfe, Gene; Citadel of the Autarch, NY, Timescape, 1983, 1st edition, w/dust jacket, M $45.00

Wolfe, Thomas; Bonfire of the Vanities, NY, Farrar Straus, 1987, 1st edition, w/dust jacket, EX.......................$50.00

Wolfe, Thomas; From Death to Morning, NY, Scribner, 1935, 1st edition, 1st issue, w/dust jacket, EX $300.00

Wolfe, Thomas; Look Homeward, Angel: A Play; NY, Scribner, 1958, 1st edition, w/dust jacket, EX $60.00

Wollheim, DA; Mike Mars at Cape Canaveral, Doubleday, 1961, 1st edition, signed, w/dust jacket, VG.........$25.00

Woolf, Virginia; Granite & Rainbow, London, no publisher given, 1958, 1st edition, w/dust jacket, VG...........$70.00

Woolrich, Cornell; Rendezvous in Black, NY, 1948, 1st edition, w/NM dust jacket, M $75.00

Wouk, Herman; The Caine Mutiny, NY, Doubleday, 1952, 1st edition, signed, w/dust jacket, EX $100.00

Writers Program of America, New Hampshire: A Guide to the Granite State; Boston, 1938, w/pocket map, VG...........................$27.50

Writers Program of America, New York City Guide, 1939, 708 pages, w/pocket map, NM $35.00

Wyeth, Betsy; The Wyeths, NY, no publisher given, 1971, 1st edition, w/dust jacket, EX................................$50.00

Zappa, Frank; The Real Frank Zappa Book, NY, Poseidon Press, 1989, 1st edition, signed, illustrated, w/dust jacket, M $100.00

Zelazny, Roger; Courts of Chaos, NY, Doubleday, 1978, 1st edition, w/dust jacket, EX $35.00

Zelazny, Roger; Damnation Alley, NY, Putnam, 1969, 1st edition, w/dust jacket, EX $50.00

Bottle Openers

A figural bottle opener is one where the cap lifter is an actual feature of the model being portrayed — for instance, the bill of a pelican or the mouth of a 4-eyed man. Most are made of painted cast iron or aluminum, though some were chrome or brass plated. Some of the major bottle opener producers were Wilton, John Wright, L&L, and Gadzik. They have been reproduced, so beware of any examples with 'new' paint. Condition of the paint is an important consideration when it comes to evaluating an opener. There are some rare ones — faces of a winking boy, a skull, an Amish man, a coyote, and an eagle (these are wall mounts); 3-dimensional stand-up figures of college students and cheerleaders, a girl in a bathing suit, a dodo bird, and a beer drinker with an apron string opener. These are worth from $100.00 to $400.00 or so (if the paint is good) to the right collector.

Alligator, 6", cast iron w/worn multicolor paint, open mouth, long..$50.00

Black face, 4½x4", chrome $90.00
Bull's head, 5", cast iron, curved tail handle...............$30.00
Cowboy at signpost, cast iron...................................$120.00
Donkey, 3¼", cast iron w/multicolor paint, seated w/head upright $35.00
Elephant, 5", cast iron w/worn multicolor paint, seated upright $25.00
Flamingo, cast iron, EX paint, Wilton....................$95.00

Four-Eyed man, cast iron, G paint, Wilton...................**$50.00**
Goat, 4½", cast iron, EX paint, horns are opener **$55.00**
Lobster, 3½", cast iron w/worn red paint.....................**$25.00**
Monkey, cast iron w/black paint **$235.00**
Parrot, 5", chrome w/corkscrew **$65.00**
Parrot on tall perch, 5", cast iron w/worn paint **$40.00**
Pelican, 3½", cast iron, EX paint **$50.00**

Ram, 4", sitting upright, cast iron w/worn paint .$35.00
Rooster, 3", cast iron w/multicolor paint.....................**$85.00**
Sea gull on stump, brass..**$38.00**
Sea horse, brass...**$25.00**
Squirrel on log, 2", cast iron, EX paint **$75.00**
Truck shape, Grimm Bros Auto Glass **$20.00**

Bottles

You could spend thousands of dollars and come home with very few bottles to show for your money. As you can see in our listings, certain types of old bottles (many bitters, historical flasks, and the better antique figurals, for instance) are very expensive, and unless you're attending one of the big bottle auctions in the East, you're not too likely to see these around. But flea markets are full of bottles, and it's very difficult to know how to start buying.

Mold seams are a good indicator of age. Bottles from ca 1800 normally will have seams that stop at the shoulder. From about 1875 until approximately 1890 the seam ended between the shoulder and the top of the neck. The line crept gradually on up until about 1910, when it finally reached the top of the neck. Bottles have been reproduced, but 'dug' bottles with these characteristics are most certainly collectible.

Color is an important consideration when collecting old bottles. Aqua, amethyst, yellow, and pink tints are desirable, and deep tones are better yet. When old clear glass is exposed to the sun, it will often turn amethyst (because of its manganese content), so this can also be an indicator of age as well.

Unlike many antiques and collectibles, bottles with imperfections are appreciated for flaws such as crooked necks, bubbles in the glass, or whittle marks (caused from blowing glass into molds that were too cold for the molten glass to properly expand). But glass that is stained, cloudy, or sick (having signs of deterioration) is another matter entirely.

Check for mold marks. Three-mold bottles were made in one piece below the shoulder, while the top was made in two. This type of bottle is very old (from the first half of the 19th century) and expensive. Colored examples command premium prices!

There are several types of old bottles — some will have an applied lip (a laid-on-ring), while others are simply 'sheared' (snapped off the blow pipe, reheated, and hand tooled). Pushed-up bottoms (called 'kick-ups' by collectors) were made that way so that they could be easier packed in layers. The necks of the bottom layer of bottles would easily fit into the pushed-up bottoms of the layer on top. A 'blob seal' is a blob of applied glass that has a die-stamped product or company name.

If you find yourself interested in collecting bottles, you'll need to study. Go to bottle shows, talk to dealers, and read all you can. There are several books available on this subject: *Collecting Barber Bottles* by Richard Holiner, *The Standard Old Bottle Price Guide* by Carlo and Dorothy Sellari, and *Bottle Pricing Guide* by Hugh Cleveland.

See also Coca-Cola, Dairy Bottles, Decanters, Perfume Bottles, and Soda Bottles.

Apothecary, Ammonium Chloride Parke Davis & Co (worn paper label), 8", dark amber, original wooden lid.........**$6.50**
Apothecary/utility, 11", blown, medium green, smooth mouth, open pontil, stain **$250.00**
Barber, 10", Bay Rum label under glass, milk glass **$275.00**
Barber, 6¾", thumbprint, turquoise, rolled mouth, pontil scar..**$50.00**
Barber, 7", emerald green w/multicolor florals on ribbed body, smooth mouth, pontil scar, 7" **$250.00**
Barber, 7½", hobnail, cranberry opalescent **$70.00**
Barber, 7⅜", amethyst w/Mary Gregory-type girl, rolled mouth, pontil scar...**$250.00**
Barber, 8½", Coin Spot, teal blue.............................**$120.00**
Barber, 8⅛", clear w/white opalescent swirled ribs, Bay Rum hand painted in red..**$110.00**
Barber, 8⅛", milk glass w/yellow overlay, raised enameling, sheared mouth, smooth base **$350.00**
Beer, Ballantine's Beer, 12", 1-qt, dark amber, original paper labels, ca 1947, EX..**$5.00**
Beer, Birkhoffer Brewing Co Minneapolis Minn (B in triangular shape), blob top, EX **$3.50**
Beer, Briscombe's, 8½", brown & tan pottery, inside threads **$8.00**

Beer, Gentleman Brewing Co Milwaukee, man drinking (embossed), amber **$12.50**

Beer, Grand Prize Beer, Gulf Brewing Co..., 9", paper label on clear, crown top.....................................**$6.00**

Beer, Kessler Malt Extract, 8½", amber, applied top, squat style...**$8.00**

Beer, National Brewing Co Chicago This Bottle Property of...Registered Not To Be Sold, 9", aqua, blob top.**$10.00**

Beer, Rose Neck Brewing Co Richmond VA, 9¾", aqua, embossed star, crown top **$4.00**

Beer, Schwarzenbach Brewing (embossed), 12½-fluid oz, light amber, ca 1905-20.....................................**$5.00**

Bitter's, O'Leary's 20th Century, 8⅝", medium amber, tooled mouth, smooth base **$75.00**

Bitters, Allen's Congress, 10", dark emerald green, rectangular **$85.00**

Bitters, Angostura Bitters (on shoulders), 8½", amber, cylindrical shape **$40.00**

Bitters, Atwood's Jaundice, 6⅛", aqua, 12-sided, applied mouth, pontil scar **$65.00**

Bitters, Boerhave's Holland, 8", bluish-aqua, rectangular...**$50.00**

Bitters, Bourbon Whiskey, 9⅜", deep reddish-puce, applied mouth, smooth base **$210.00**

Bitters, Brazilian Aromatic Stomach, 11", amber, cylindrical shape **$40.00**

Bitters, Brown's Iron Bitters, honey amber, some stain ..**$15.00**

Bitters, Chartreuse Damiana NY, 9⅜", yellow-amber, applied mouth, smooth base, stained **$90.00**

Bitters, Columbo Peptic, 9½", amber...........................**$25.00**

Bitters, Dr Bell's Blood Purifying, 9½", amber, rectangular...**$50.00**

Bitters, Dr FFW Hogguers Detroit MI, 9¼", amber, applied mouth, smooth base **$325.00**

Bitters, Dr Landley's Root & Herb Boston, 8¼", medium amber, applied mouth, smooth base.................**$100.00**

Bitters, Dr Soule's Hop Bitterine 1872, 9½", yellow w/embossed florals, applied mouth, smooth base.....................**$140.00**

Bitters, Dr Van Hopfs Curacoa Bitters Des Moins Iowa, amber, NM...**$35.00**

Bitters, Fratelli Baranch Milano, 13½", light green, cylindrical shape **$15.00**

Bitters, Great English Remedy Dr Bell's Blood Purifying, 9⅝", amber **$65.00**

Bitters, Hart's Virginia Aromatic, 7⅝", clear, rectangular..**$65.00**

Bitters, Hartwig Kantorowicz Berlin, 9", amber, applied mouth, smooth base **$125.00**

Bitters, Marshall's Best Laxative & Blood Purifier, 8⅝", amber **$65.00**

Bitters, Mishler's Herb, 9", amber, ruled marker, 'Table Spoon Graduation, Dr SB Hartman & Co,' faint haze & wear **$40.00**

Bitters, Oregon Grape Root, 10", clear, cylindrical shape **$45.00**

Bitters, Oswego 25 Cents, 7", medium amber, tooled mouth, smooth base **$75.00**

Bitters, Peruvian Bitters (monogram), amber...............**$65.00**

Bitters, Purdy's Cottage, 9", amber, rectangular...........**$95.00**

Bitters, Star Kidney & Liver, 8⅞", amber, tooled mouth, smooth base **$75.00**

Bitters, Wood's Tonic Wine Cincinnati OH, 9½", aqua, applied mouth, smooth base, crude...................**$150.00**

Bitters, 12", amber, original label on lady's leg form...**$50.00**

Bitters, 9¾", Electric Brand, amber, sq **$15.00**

Blob seal, Burger Spital Wurzburg, 7½", amber, applied ringed lip, European $90.00

Calabash, Jenny Lind, aqua, embossed lady, Glassworks, Glasshouse, S Huffsey, applied mouth, open pontil $55.00

Chestnut flask, 4½", blown, yellowish-amber, rolled mouth, pontil scar..**$250.00**

Chestnut flask, 6⅛", blown, olive-yellow, rolled mouth, pontil scar **$110.00**

Cosmetic, Carpenter Morton Co Colorite, 4", amethyst .**$2.00**

Cosmetic, Colgate & Co Perfumers, 3¾", amethyst........**$5.00**

Cosmetic, Creme Simon, 2¼", milk glass.......................**$3.50**

Cosmetic, Fitch, EW Ideal Dandruff Cure, 6½", sun-turned amethyst **$12.50**

Cosmetic, Haber's Magic Hair Coloring, 6", cobalt **$8.00**

Cosmetic, Imperial Hair Regenerator, 4½", aqua, shield w/crown in center..**$5.00**

Cosmetic, Krank's Cold Cream, 2¾", milk glass.............**$5.50**

Cosmetic, Meade & Baker Carbolic Mouth Wash Antiseptic Gargle, 5", amethyst **$3.50**

Cosmetic, New Bros Herpicide for the Scalp, 7", clear..**$3.50**

Cosmetic, Purola Complexion Beautifier, 5¼", cobalt ...**$6.50**

Cosmetic, Sozodont for Teeth & Breath, 2¼", clear.......**$2.00**

Cosmetic, Watkin's Garda Cream (on cap) **$4.00**

Druggist, AG Noid Dispensing Druggists Canton SD, eagle (embossed), clear...**$5.50**

Druggist, EC Bent, Dell Rapids SD (in script), NM **$5.00**

Druggist, LE Highly Hot Springs SD, NM **$5.00**

Druggist, Rhodes & Troxell Prescription Druggists, Cheyenne Wyo (large monogram), tall **$15.00**

Figural, Black waiter, 15", black glass head w/painted features, frosted body..**$445.00**

Figural, monkey, 4½", milk glass, Trade Mark embossed, tooled mouth, smooth base, EX.........................**$130.00**

Figural, pig, 7", Rosebaum Bros Old Kentucky Whiskies, unglazed pottery...**$275.00**

Figural, pineapple, 9", medium amber, applied mouth, smooth base..$140.00

Food, Burnett's Standard Flavoring Extracts, 5", aqua ...**$3.00**

Food, catsup, Cayuga County...NY, 10", aqua w/yellow-green swirls, applied mouth, smooth base...........**$55.00**

Food, catsup, HJ Heinz, 9¼", amethyst **$4.00**

Food, chile powder, Gebhardt Eagle, 5½", amethyst.....**$3.50**

Food, clam bouillon, Scott & Gilbert Co, 4", amethyst ..**$4.00**

Food, Croft's Milk Cocoa, Croft & Allen, Philadelphia, 6¼", clear, screw top w/original tin lid..................**$4.00**

Food, Spark's Horseradish, 7", aqua **$3.00**

Food, jelly, 6", deep purple..**$8.00**

Food, Minute Maid Orange Juice, 7¼", clear, maid embossed on two sides, screw-on lid **$3.00**

Food, mustard, Clock, 4½", clear, figural clock **$10.00**

Food, mustard, deep purple, barrel shape.....................**$6.00**

Food, mustard, NW Opermann Factory, 4¾", aqua, rolled mouth, pontil scar.....................................**$190.00**

Food, olive oil, San Juan, 6½", wax sealer **$7.00**

Food, olive oil, Sylmar Brand, 3¼", clear **$2.00**

Food, peppersauce, Evangeline, 5¼", amethyst............**$4.00**

Food, peppersauce, Hirsch's Pepper Sauce, 7¼", pink .**$2.00**

Food, peppersauce, 8½", amethyst, twenty-six rings.....**$6.50**

Food, salad dressing, Durkee ER & Co, 8", clear...........**$1.50**

Food, Tropicana Grapefruit Juice, 8¼", red lettering on clear, screw-on lid...**$4.50**

Household, Bragg's Arctic Liniment, aqua, pontiled, some stain...**$5.00**

Household, Champlin's Liquid Pearl, milk glass, M.....**$10.00**

Household, hydrogen peroxide, Gold Medal Quality, 8", amber...**$5.00**

Household, liniment, Centaur Liniment, 5", aqua **$3.00**

Household, oil, Lubricant Rust Preventive, 5", aqua......**$5.00**

Household, sewing machine oil, Pure Sperm Sewing Machine Oil, 5¼", amethyst....................................**$1.50**

Household, shoe polish, Benton Holladay & Co, 4⅞", aqua...**$4.50**

Household, shoe polish, Gilt Edge Shoe Polish, 4", green **$10.00**

Ink, Carter's, 9¾", cobalt, cathedral shape, original spout & labels...**$95.00**

Ink, Carter's No 8 (on base), 3-oz, 2¾", sun-colored amethyst **$4.00**

Ink, Doulton Lambeth, 4½", brown pottery, w/pouring spout on lip...**$15.00**

Ink, Harrison's Columbian, 1⅝", aqua, 8-sided, rolled mouth, pontil scar...**$70.00**

Ink, Higgins Drawing Ink (embossed on bottom), 3", clear, paper label, rubber stopper, round..................**$1.00**

Ink, Kirkland's Writing Fluid, 2¼", aqua......................**$5.00**

Ink, Laughlin's & Bushfield Wheeling VA, 2⅞", aqua, 8-sided **$95.00**

Ink, Sanford's Fountain Pen Ink, 2" sq base, 1½" chimney, clear w/thick base, machine made **$7.50**

Ink, 2½", sun-colored amethyst, plain type...................**$5.00**

Ink, 2¾", light blue, cone shape **$7.50**

Medicine, Abernathy's Ginger Brandy, 10½", amber, cylindrical shape **$5.00**

Medicine, Anderson's Dermador, 4¼", aqua, applied mouth, pontil scar...**$45.00**

Medicine, Angier's Petroleum Emulsion, 7", aqua, oval ..**$2.50**

Medicine, Barker Moore & Mein Medicine Co, 6", aqua, rectangular...**$5.00**

Medicine, Bauer's Instant Cough Cure, 7", aqua, rectangular **$12.50**

Medicine, Birney's Catarral Powder, 2½", clear, cylindrical shape **$2.50**

Medicine, Blood & Liver Syrup, 10", aqua **$2.50**

Medicine, Brigg's Pills Never Fail To Cure, 2½", aqua, stained **$7.50**

Medicine, Bromo-Nervine, 4¾", cobalt, oval **$4.50**

Medicine, Brown's Essence of Jamaica Ginger, 5¾", aqua, oval **$6.50**

Medicine, Chamberlain's Summer Fever Cure **$12.00**

Medicine, Charles H Fletcher Castoria, 5¾", aqua, rectangular, cork top **$2.00**

Medicine, Citrate Magnesia, 8½", clear, flat collar, porcelain stopper **$18.00**

Medicine, Citrate of Magnesia, Chas T George, Harrisburg PA, 7¼", clear, double ring collar **$22.50**

Medicine, Cuticura Treatment for Affections of the Skin, 6½-oz, light aqua, square **$5.00**

Medicine, Dr Agnew's Cure for the Heart, clear, 7½"..**$12.00**

Medicine, Dr Alexander's Lung Healer, 6½", aqua, rectangular, cork top, some cloudiness **$7.50**

Medicine, Dr Cole's Catarrh Cure, 2⅞", aqua, NM **$6.00**

Medicine, Dr Greene's Nervura, aqua, w/NM label **$15.00**

Medicine, Dr Kilmer's Swamproot Kidney Cure, 4¼" **$4.50**

Medicine, Dr Miles Medical Co, 8¼", aqua, rectangular, cork top **$4.00**

Medicine, Dr Miles New Heart Cure, 8", aqua **$8.00**

Medicine, Dr S Pitcher's Castoria, 5⅞", aqua, rectangular, cork top, some cloudiness **$4.50**

Medicine, Dr Shoop's Family Medicine, Racine Wis, aqua, M **$7.00**

Medicine, Dr Vanderpool's Headache & Liver Cure, 7¾", aqua **$15.00**

Medicine, Fletcher's Castoria Laxative, 7", clear **$1.50**

Medicine, Foley's Kidney & Bladder Cure, 7¼", amber.**$7.50**

Medicine, Glover's Imperial Mange Cure, amber **$6.50**

Medicine, Great South American Nervine Tonic & Stomach & Liver Cure (monogram), inside stain **$37.50**

Medicine, Haywood's Bitterless Chill Tonic, label **$6.00**

Medicine, Healy & Bigelow Indian Sagwa, Indian w/full headdress (embossed), aqua, stained **$10.00**

Medicine, Howard's Vegetable Cancer & Canker Syrup, 8½", amber, rectangular **$12.00**

Medicine, Joseph's Spirit of Camphor, applied mouth, label, M **$3.00**

Medicine, Kendall's Spavin Cure, 5", amber, 12-sided...**$9.00**

Medicine, Listerine, Lambert Parmacal Company, 5½", clear, cylindrical shape, applied mouth, cork top **$5.00**

Medicine, Melvin & Badger Apothecaries, 6¾", cobalt, 6-sided **$10.00**

Medicine, Mrs E Kidder's Dysentery Cordial Boston, 6½", aqua, applied mouth, pontil scar **$60.00**

Medicine, Otto's Cure for Throat & Lungs, 6", clear **$7.50**

Medicine, Paine's Celery Compound, 9½", dark amber ..**$12.50**

Medicine, Pinex, 6", aqua, rectangular, applied mouth, cork top **$2.50**

Medicine, Red Star Cough Cure, 5¾", aqua, hazy **$3.50**

Medicine, Rosewood Dandruff Cure, 6½", hazy **$6.50**

Medicine, Russian Rheumatic Cure, Rochester NY, 6¾", clear **$35.00**

Medicine, Samitol for the Teeth, milk glass **$10.00**

Medicine, Sharp & Dohme Baltimore, 2½", dark amber, 6-sided, cork top **$5.00**

Medicine, Sloan's Liniment Kills Pain, clear, applied mouth, M **$2.00**

Medicine, Sloan's Sure Colic Cure, 4¾", clear **$7.00**

Medicine, Snow & Mason Croup & Cough Syrup, 5½", aqua, cylindrical shape **$2.50**

Medicine, US Veterans Bureau, 6⅝", clear w/paper label, oval, cork top, crude **$5.00**

Medicine, Veronica Medical Water, amber, light stain...**$6.00**

Medicine, Warner's Safe Cure (embossed at neck), 9½", amber, applied mouth, smooth base **$110.00**

Medicine, Warner's Safe Kidney & Liver Cure, aqua, oval **$6.50**

Medicine, Warner's Safe Rheumatic Cure, 9½", amber, applied mouth, smooth base, light stain $75.00

Medicine, Wistar's Balsam of Wild Cherry, 5", blue.......**$7.50**

Medicine, 6½", blown, olive-amber, rectangular w/beveled corners **$100.00**

Mineral water, Abilena Natural Cathartic Water, 10", amber, M **$5.00**

Mineral water, Allen Springs, 11½", aqua, applied top..**$6.00**

Mineral water, AP New Almaden Vichy Water California, olive-amber, applied mouth, M **$14.00**

Mineral water, B&C San Francisco, cobalt, applied mouth, cylindrical shape **$35.00**

Mineral water, John Ryan Excelsior, 'Union Glassworks Phil' on back, 7½", cobalt blue, blob top, iron pontil...**$80.00**

Mineral water, Kissinger Mineral Wasser, 12", light green, slender form **$4.00**

Mineral water, Perrier, 8½", clear, bowling-pin form.......**$4.00**

Mineral water, Poland Water, 9½", medium green, cylindrical w/crown cap **$4.00**

Mineral water, Richardson's, 12", amber, cylindrical **$8.00**

Mineral water, Witter Springs, 10", clear, cylindrical **$4.00**

Nurser, Acme Graduated, 1¼" dia, circle on top **$45.00**

Poison, Carbolic Acid, Use w/Caution, 5", cobalt, 6-sided **$12.50**

Poison, Dick's Ant Destroyer, 6", clear **$20.00**

Poison, Lattice & Diamond pattern, 7½", cobalt, tooled mouth, smooth base, original label **$85.00**

Poison, owl on mortar & pestle, 9⅜", cobalt, 3-sided ...**$525.00**

Poison, skull & crossbones, 3¼", cobalt **$60.00**

Poison, Sulpholine, cobalt, rectangular, ribbed, 4¼" ...**$20.00**

Poison, Triloids, cobalt, triangular w/ribs **$12.50**

Poison, 2½", amber, square w/raised ridges **$3.50**

Ross's Royal Belfast Ginger Ale Ireland, 10", round w/diamond-shaped label & applied top, medium green glass **$4.00**

Scent, 6", cobalt, 12-sided, flared mouth, smooth base ..**$65.00**

Scent, 9⅛", milk glass, square w/roped corners & stars, tooled mouth, smooth base....................................**$75.00**

Snuff, 4⅛", green...**$22.00**

Snuff, 4¾", olive-amber **$27.50**

Spirits, Ameliorated Schiedam Holland Gin, 9", amber ..**$22.00**

Spirits, Bellows & Co New York & Chicago, 11", clear, cylindrical w/blob seal **$15.00**

Spirits, Bininger's Old Dominion Wheat Tonic, 10", olive-green...**$80.00**

Spirits, Bonny Bros Louisville Ky, aqua, wheat (embossed) **$5.00**

Spirits, Chapin & Gore, amber, barrel shape **$37.50**

Spirits, Chianti Wine, 36" (approximately), emerald green, wicker holder **$15.00**

Spirits, Dallemand & Co Creme Rye, 2¾", sample size, amber **$8.00**

Spirits, Duffy Malt Whiskey (monogram), amber...........**$5.00**

Spirits, Gaelic Old Smuggler Scotch Whiskey (label), 8¾", aqua, cork top **$7.50**

Spirits, Gordon's Dry Gin London England (embossed vertically), 9", aqua, boar's head on bottom, cork top...**$9.00**

Spirits, Harmony Medium Sherry, 16", amber, guitar figural...**$12.00**

Spirits, HB Kirk & Co, 11¼", dark amber, three Indian heads (embossed) on shoulder....................................**$25.00**

Spirits, Sunny Brook the Pure Food Whiskey, 11½", clear, cork top **$12.50**

Spirits, Warranted Flask, 7¾", clear, coffin shape, applied neck, double collar, strapped sides **$6.00**

Whiskey, UDL Old Rye, 11", amber w/paper label........**$16.00**

Boy Scout Collectibles

The Boy Scouts of America was organized in 1910. It was originated in England by General Baden-Powell and was inspired by his observations during the Boer War. He believed boys wanted and needed to learn about outdoor-related activities. The first Boy Scout Jamboree was held in Washington DC in 1937. Today people who are or have been active in Scouting are interested in all types of items that relate to its history; for example: patches, uniforms, pins, medals, books and magazines, Jamboree items, Explorer items, pictures, and paper items.

Badge, Eagle, type one, Boy Scout Association on square tan khaki cloth, 1920 ....**$50.00**

Badge, First Class, scout on square tan cloth, 1920.....**$10.00**

Badge, Scoutmaster, tan square cloth w/green emblem, 1920 ....**$40.00**

Book, Cave, 'Official Boy Scout Hike Book,' 1st edition, 1913 ....**$15.00**

Bracelet, charm; sterling, Cub Scout, w/rank charms..**$15.00**

Buckle, 'Be Prepared,' two side loops, 1911...............**$35.00**

Calendar, small, Rockwell cover, 1930-40 ....**$12.50**

Card, membership; 3-fold, in slipcase, 1920-30 ....**$3.00**

Coin, brass, Boy Scout Association, scout w/staff, 1915..**$10.00**

Diary, red linen cover, Boy Scout Association, 1st edition, 1913 ....**$50.00**

Game, action; Ten Pins, 1920.....................................**$20.00**

Game, board; 'The Scout Trail,' 1916, Milton Bradley.**$22.00**

Knife, hunting; Remington, RS34, 1930 ....**$60.00**

Knife, utility; Official Remington, RS-3333, 4-blade.....**$50.00**

Medal, sterling w/enamel tips, Sea Scout Quartermaster, 1950 ....**$25.00**

Membership card, plastic, 4-page type, dated 1915.....**$10.00**

Neckerchief, red or blue, full square, 1937 Jamboree .**$40.00**

Pamphlet, small, 'Lone Scout Handbook,' 1918...........**$15.00**

Patch, Eagle, type one, on tan square, 1920 ....**$35.00**

Patch, 3", George Washington on twill, 1950 Jamboree..**$25.00**

Patch, 3", white felt, 1937 National Jamboree..............**$50.00**

Pennant, large, 1937 National Jamboree **$30.00**

Pin, green enamel, Scoutmaster, round, 1940.............**$20.00**

Pin, 1½", brass or silver, First Class, 1940...................**$10.00**

Poster, 24x40", Rockwell illustration w/logo, 1937 National Jamboree **$75.00**

Statue, pot metal, Scout Presentation, scout w/hat, 1930..**$25.00**

Watch, 1st issue, Boy Scout Association logo, band, 1950, in working order **$15.00**

Brass

Because it has become so costly to produce things from brass (due to the inflated price of copper, one of its components), manufacturers have largely turned to plastics and other less-expensive materials. As a result, nearly anything made of brass is becoming collectible.

If you'd like a source for further study, we recommend *Antique Brass and Copper Identification and Value Guide* by Mary Frank Gaston.

Andirons, 19x8¼", baluster type on cabriole base, screw-on steeple finial, pr **$150.00**

Candelabrum, 12", 5-light, Art Nouveau style w/swirling arms, embossed fleur-de-lis at base, pr.............**$250.00**

Candelabrum, 20x16", 3-light, English origin, mid-1800s, EX...$350.00

Candlestick, 7¼", octagonal base w/notched corners, Queen Anne period, 1720s, pr.........................$350.00

Candlestick, 7x2½", English, octagonal base, mid-1800s, pr..$250.00

Coal tongs, 10½" long, simple scissors style $45.00

Fire dog, 8", spherical base w/embossed flower & leaf designs, European, mid-1800s, pr.................$350.00

Fireplace fender, 24" long, double row of reticulation as decoration, English, EX $150.00

Kettle, 11", for making jam, American Brass Kettle Company...$80.00

Kettle, 7x13", iron bail, American, mid to late 1800s, EX $225.00

Ladle, 13½", w/iron handle, marked FBS Canton OH..$75.00

Lamp, 17½", desk type w/black metal shade on cast brass body, American, 1920s, EX $250.00

Match box, 3½", high hinged lid................................$28.00

Steam pressure gauge, 6" dia, Ashton Boston.............$20.00

Teapot, footed English style, amber glass handle, mid-1800s, few dings, EX.....................................$300.00

Teaspoon, American, simple style, worn, 1800s..........$12.50

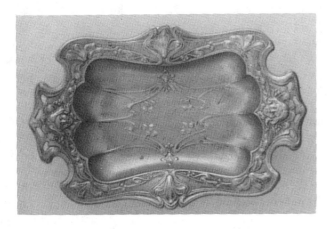

Tray, 9x14", embossed Art Nouveau designs $75.00

Trivet, 7½x24", folding type, for fireplace, EX...........$550.00

Wall sconce, 19x15", embossed bird & scenic decoration, English $325.00

Sascha Brastoff

California has always been a big producer of dinnerware and decorative pottery items, and those from the thirties, forties, and fifties are attracting lots of collector interest right now. Designer wares such as those by Sascha Brastoff, Marc Belaire, and their contemporaries are especially in demand. Brastoff's career was diversified, to say the least. Although he is best-known in our circles for his high-style ceramic, enamelware, and resin pieces which even then (1940s-50s) were expensive, he was also a dancer, costume designer, sculptor, painter, and jeweler.

Brastoff's wares are signed in two ways. If the item was signed with his full signature, it was personally crafted by Brastoff himself. These are much more valuable than items simply stamped 'Sasha B,' a mark used on production pieces that were made by his staff under his supervision. Unless our listings contain the phrase 'full signature,' values that follow are for pieces with the 'Sasha B' stamp.

Jack Chipman has written a book on California potteries in which he devotes a chapter to Brastoff. It is entitled *The Collector's Encyclopedia of California Pottery*; we highly recommend it for further study.

Ashtray, 3¼x5½", domed shape, signed Sascha B............$25.00

Ashtray, 5½", artichoke form, enamelware, signed Sascha B..$25.00

Ashtray, 6¼", leaf form, enamelware, signed Sascha B..$25.00

Bowl, cereal; 6", Night Song, stamped mark...............$20.00

Bowl, 2¼x10", abstract ballerina, 3-footed, signed Sascha B..$60.00

Cigarette holder, satin-matt gold glaze, Sascha B...........$30.00

Cigarette lighter, green pepper (vegetable) form, satin-matt gold glaze, signed Sascha B $35.00

Compote, 10", gold & multicolored stripes on white $40.00

Dish, 3½" sq, Alaska, polar bear, signed Sascha B.......$20.00

Figurine, 10½", horse, platinum on matt pink, ca 1957, signed Sascha B $150.00

Figurine, 7x9", poodle, satin-matt crackle glaze, signed Sascha B $125.00

Pipe, 5½x5¾", head of a lady & gold swirls on white, signed Sascha B $30.00

Plate, dinner; 11", Winrock, stamped mark..................$25.00

Plate, 10½", Star Steed, ca 1959, signed Sascha Brastoff...$200.00

Vase, 12", abstract design, signed Sascha B $80.00

Vase, 13", Alaska, Eskimo dressed in parka, signed Sascha B $100.00

Wall mask, 9½", native portrait, one of a series, signed Sascha B $125.00

Brayton Laguna

Brayton was the potter, Laguna Beach, California, his residence. Durlin Brayton began making dinnerware in the 1920s and is credited for being the one to introduce the concept of the mixed, solid-color dinnerware lines made later by Bauer and Homer Laughlin (the manufacturer of Fiesta). His pieces were rather crudely designed, and it is said that he simply erected stands and sold the ware in his front yard or carried it in the trunk of his car to wherever people were apt to congregate.

When he married in 1936, his wife helped him develop his business into a larger, more lucrative enterprise. They started producing quality figurines, some of them licensed by Walt Disney Studios. They also made vases, cookie jars, various household items, and larger figurines that they refered to as sculptures. Some of their decorating was done by hand, some by the airbrush-painting method. Finishes varied and included a white crackle as well as a woodtone (stained) bisque among their more standard glazes.

All of their marks include either the word 'Brayton,' 'Laguna,' or both, except for the stamp used on their Pinocchio series. These pieces were marked 'Geppetto Pottery' in an oval. Not everything they made was marked, though, simply because very often there wasn't enough room. But there will be an incised or painted decorator's initial to clue you, and as you see and handle more of the ware, you'll be able to recognize Brayton's unique style.

The company did quite well until after WWII, when vast amounts of Japanese imports spelled doom for many small American potteries. They closed in 1968.

For further study, read *The Collector's Encyclopedia of California Pottery* by Jack Chipman.

Figurine, abstract man w/cat, 21", satin-matt black, ca 1957, in-mold mark **$150.00**

Figurine, calf, 6" long, purple **$25.00**
Figurine, Chinese boy & girl, childhood series, set of two **$80.00**

Figurine, crane, 10", brown stain w/white crackle glaze accents **$38.00**
Figurine, donkey, 7¼x10" **$50.00**
Figurine, fox, from English Hunter with Fox & Hounds set, late 1930s **$35.00**
Figurine, Hillbilly Shotgun Wedding, 9" tallest, stamped marks, 6-pc set **$300.00**
Figurine, Mexican man, 9" **$80.00**
Figurine, Mexican peasant couple, 12½", textured bisque & high-gloss glaze, in-mold mark **$80.00**
Figurine, Pluto, howling, 6", Walt Disney **$150.00**
Figurine, Rosita, 5½", childhood series by Frances Robinson, stamped mark **$40.00**
Figurine, Toucan, 9", polychromed high-gloss glaze, 1950s-60, in-mold mark **$80.00**
Figurine, 9", Fighting Pirates, colored & crackle glazes, ca 1956, set of two **$275.00**
Mug, handle, solid color, plain, early, incised mark **$25.00**
Pitcher, 7¼", solid color, plain, loop handle, incised mark **$80.00**
Teapot, 5½", solid color, plain, w/lid **$100.00**
Tile, 4½" sq, incised cats on roof, primary colors in black border **$55.00**
Tile, 8x8", abstract tree, flowers & mushroom in solid border, multicolored, incised mark **$80.00**
Vase, bud; 8", realistic snake entwined about light blue body, incised mark **$80.00**

Breweriana

'Breweriana' is simply a term used by collectors to refer to items (usually freebies) distributed by breweries to advertise their products. Some people prefer pre-prohibition era bottles, pocket mirrors, foam scrapers, etched and enameled glasses, mugs, steins, playing cards, post cards, pin-back buttons, and the like; but many collectors like the more available items from the past few decades as well. Some specialize either in breweries from a particular state, specific items such as foam scrapers (used to clean the foam off the top of glasses or pitchers of beer), or they might limit their buying to just one brewery.

The book we recommend for this area of collecting is *Back Bar Breweriana* by George J. Baley.

Ashtray, Coors, ceramic, EX **$6.00**
Blotter, Schlitz, pictures woman holding glass of beer, EX...**$6.50**
Bottle opener, Miller, 1955, EX..............................**$35.00**
Calendar, 17", Budweiser, paper, reclining woman w/embossed Art Nouveau border, 1932, EX.........**$50.00**
Charger, 16" dia, tin, pictures couple w/man adding beer to fondue pot, EX...**$150.00**
Charger, 18" dia, Bartel's Brewing Company, tin, pictures bouquet of flowers on a ledge, logo on reverse, EX...**$20.00**
Coaster, Lowenbrau, 1964 World's Fair, EX **$4.50**
Display, Pabst Brewing Company, metal, waiter's arm holding a Pabst Blue Ribbon sign, EX **$95.00**
Display, 16", Blatz, metal figural, man w/barrel body holding mug of beer, EX..**$85.00**
Drinking glass, FW Cook Brewing Company, etched factory scene, NM...**$55.00**
Drinking glass, 6", Miller, 'Miller High Life' on paper label, EX..**$20.00**
Foam scraper, Meister Brau, celluloid, EX **$18.00**
Foam scraper, Rubsams & Horman Brewing Company, EX **$16.00**
Mug, 5", Budweiser, ceramic, embossed wagon & Clydesdales, M **$175.00**
Puzzle, 6" sq, 9-pc, Pabst Brewing Company, cardboard, colonial man in library drinking steins of beer, double-sided, EX...**$35.00**
Salt & pepper shakers, Budweiser, plastic, can form, pr..**$5.00**

Sign, Jetter Brewing Co, 32" long, tin litho, blemishes & rust spotting..**$175.00**

Sign, 11" dia, Hampden Brewing Company, tin, unattractive man w/tray, 'Who Wants the Handsome Waitor,' 1934, EX **$100.00**
Sign, 11x14", Bartel's Brewing Company, paper, factory scene, EX **$85.00**
Sign, 12x14", Michelob, light-up, NM **$25.00**
Sign, 15x20", Greenway's Brewery, cardboard, girl in profile, EX **$325.00**
Sign, 16x20", Hoster Brewing Company, tin, drunken monk leaning on beer barrels, oval, EX..........................**$90.00**
Sign, 9x17", Anheuser-Busch, paper, 1 of 5 frontier images by August A Busch, titled 'Attack on an Immigrant Train,' EX...**$100.00**
Stein, 7", Budweiser, embossed wagon & Clydsdales in birch trees, beaded rope top & bottom, M **$150.00**
Stein, 9", Stroh's, logo w/Alps scene in relief, EX..........**$7.50**
Stencil, 11x17", Stag Brewing Company, brass, block letters, barrel form, EX...**$25.00**
Tip tray, 4" dia, New Lebanon Brewing Company, tin, colorful logo in center, Lebanon PA, NM **$85.00**
Tip tray, 4" dia, Seitz Brewing Company, tin, brown & gold w/eagle logo on wide center band, EX...............**$185.00**
Tip tray, 4" dia, tin, Narragansett Brewing Company, 'Narragansett' diagonally w/logo below, EX...................**$55.00**
Tray, 11x13", Breidt City Brewery, American Maid taking bottles from cooler, EX.....................................**$95.00**
Tray, 12" dia, American Brewing Company, tin, Indian princess seal, Liberty Beer, Rochester NY, NM.....**$135.00**
Tray, 12" dia, National Brewing Company, tin, star logo on gold background, EX..**$55.00**
Tray, 12" dia, Oneida Brewing Company, porcelain, pictures Shenandoah, chief of the Oneidas, EX...............**$100.00**
Tray, 12" dia, Rising Sun Brewing Company, tin, deep-dish, girl on crescent moon w/a Seeber Special beer, EX **$225.00**
Tray, 12" dia, Stegmaier Brewing Company, tin, factory view & trains, 'Drink Stegmaier's Gold Medal Beer,' EX......**$50.00**
Tray, Thos Ryan's Consumers Brewing Co, 12", tin litho, wear **$100.00**
Tumbler, 3⅛", Coors, 'Coors Banquet' in orange, M **$8.00**

Breyer Horses

Breyer horses have been popular children's playthings since they were introduced in 1952, and you'll see several at any large flea market. The earlier horses had a glossy finish, but after 1968 a matt finish came into use. You'll find domestic animals as well. They are evaluated by condition, rarity, and desirability; some of the better examples may be worth a minimum of $150.00.

Bronco, #190, bucking, 1966-74...................................**$50.00**
Buffalo, #76 ....**$17.50**
Donkey, #81, brown, 1958-76......................................**$20.00**
Five-gaiter, #52, 1963-86...**$30.00**
Foal, #130, alabaster, running, 1963-74 ....**$30.00**
Foal, #165, black Appaloosa, recumbent, 1969-84.......**$15.00**
Foal, #166, buckskin, recumbent **$28.00**

Foal, #168, black Appaloosa, scratching, 1970-77........**$15.00**
Foal, #81, Clydesdale..**$12.00**
Indian pony, #175, brown, 1970-77.....................................**$75.00**
Indian pony, #176, buckskin w/war paint, 1970-73 ..**$150.00**

Moose, circa 1985...**$25.00**
Mustang, #86, gray Appaloosa, 1963-67 ....**$150.00**
Old-timer gray mare, #205, w/harness & blinders.......**$35.00**
Saddle-bred weanling, special run................................**$70.00**
Shetland pony, #23, bay...**$12.50**
St Bernard, #328, 1972-81...**$35.00**
Stallion, #210, dark red roan, running..........................**$75.00**
Stallion, #211, white Arabian..**$25.00**
Stallion, #87, buckskin mustang w/black mane, tail & hooves, pink nose...**$45.00**
Stock horse mare, black paint, special run **$35.00**
Western horse, #110, gray w/chain reins & slip-on saddle, prancing...**$35.00**
Western horse, #115, leopard Appaloosa w/slip-on saddle, prancing...**$50.00**
Yellow mount, #51, 1970-82...**$20.00**

British Royalty Commemoratives

While seasoned collectors may prefer the older pieces using circa 1840 (Queen Victoria's reign) as their starting point, even present-day souvenirs make a good inexpensive beginning collection. Ceramic items, glassware, metalware, and paper goods have been issued on the occasion of weddings, royal tours, birthdays, christenings, and many other celebrations. Food tins are fairly easy to find, and range in price from about $30.00 to around $75.00 for those made since the 1950s.

For more information, we recommend *British Royal Commemoratives* by Audrey Zeder.

Advertising card, Victoria & relatives...........................**$35.00**
Baby plate, 1x7½" dia, George V, 1935 Jubilee, Shelley ..**$175.00**
Bank, Charles & Diana's wedding **$30.00**

Bank, Elizabeth, red mailbox shape, tin......................**$20.00**
Bank, George VI coronation, red mailbox shape, tin..**$25.00**
Beaker, Elizabeth's 1959 Canada visit, blue decoration on glass **$25.00**
Bell, Charles & Diana, 5", pink dress & red jacket......**$25.00**
Bell, Charles & Diana's wedding, multicolor portrait, wooden handle **$40.00**
Bowl, 9½", glass, Elizabeth's coronation, pressed or cut..**$35.00**
Bust, Victoria, 5½", amber celluloid on black base ...**$195.00**
Calendar, 8½x4¾", Princess Elizabeth, 1949 ....**$40.00**
Covered dish, Elizabeth's coronation, cobalt, embossed portrait, Wedgwood...**$75.00**
Cup & saucer, Elizabeth's coronation, black & white portrait of Charles & Anne **$150.00**
Cup & saucer, Queen Mother's 90th birthday, multicolored portrait **$40.00**
Dish, 4x6x2", glass, Victoria 1887, pressed or cut **$125.00**
Dolls, 11", Charles & Diana in wedding clothes, Goldberger, pr...**$75.00**
Label, Victoria's portrait, 'Sunkist Orange'..................**$15.00**
Loving cup, Charles & Diana's wedding, limited edition, Royal Doulton...**$100.00**
Magazine, Charles & Diana's wedding, 'Country Life'.**$25.00**
Magazine, Elizabeth's 60th birthday, 'Radio Times' **$20.00**
Medal, Charles & Diana's wedding, Elizabeth on back..**$10.00**
Medal, Elizabeth II Jubilee, 1½", Queen on horse.........**$10.00**
Medal, Victoria 1900, portrait, 1½", w/Boer War generals...**$90.00**
Miniature, Charles & Diana, plastic figures, 4½"...........**$25.00**
Miniature, Elizabeth's album w/pictures, 1½x1" **$20.00**
Mug, Elizabeth's coronation, sepia portrait, multicolored flags..**$35.00**
Mug, George V, relief portrait, hammered pewter.........**$65.00**
Mug, Queen Mother's 90th birthday, multicolored, gold rim...**$30.00**
Mug, Victoria's 1897 Jubilee, blue portrait or design, JC & N...**$175.00**
Newspaper, Victoria's 1901 death, w/pictures & narrative..**$45.00**
Novelty, Charles & Diana's wedding, 12", plastic ruler .**$5.00**
Novelty, Elizabeth, 'Splitting Image' key chain **$5.00**
Novelty, Elizabeth's coronation, hand mirror, color portrait..**$25.00**
Novelty, Victoria, brewery bottle, 12", relief portrait.**$100.00**
Novelty, Victoria, velvet frame, four generation portraits..**$250.00**
Paper dolls, Diana, Golden, 1985 ....**$10.00**
Plate, Diana, 10½", three portrait versions, LE Royal Doulton..**$175.00**
Plate, Edward VII memorial, 4", multicolored portrait, black wreath...**$75.00**
Plate, Elizabeth's 60th birthday, 4¼", multicolored portrait, Coalport...**$20.00**
Plate, George VI's coronation, blue relief portraits, Wedgwood, pr...**$300.00**
Plate, Queen Mother's 90th birthday, 8", multicolored portrait..**$30.00**

Plate, three royal ladies' August birthdays, 8", blue rim ..**$30.00**
Post card, Diana at Nottingham in 1985 ....**$2.50**
Post card, Diana paper doll **$3.00**
Post card, Princess Bea's christening, black & white **$2.50**
Post card, Princess Diana's 30th birthday, limited edition of five hundred **$10.00**
Post cards, Charles & Diana's wedding, set of twelve .**$30.00**
Print, Victoria on throne wearing black, 12x17", 19th century **$25.00**
Spoon, Diana in black dress, silverplated **$10.00**
Teapot, Queen Mother's 90th birthday, 2-cup, multicolored portrait **$50.00**
Textile, Edward VII, 6x5", woven silk in oval frame .**$150.00**
Textile, Elizabeth's 1977 Jubilee, linen towel **$20.00**
Thimble, Queen Mother's 90th birthday, enameled peepshow **$30.00**

Tin, Charles & Diana, 5½", St Paul's Cathedral Commemorative $22.00

Tin, 7", Elizabeth's Coronation, Honer Toffee $35.00

Tin, Princess Elizabeth, Trooping Colours, Huntley & Palmer **$75.00**
Tin, Victoria w/young & old portrait & three generations, hinged **$195.00**
Toby mug, George V & Queen Mary, pr **$495.00**
Tray, Charles & Diana wedding, 6x7", multicolored engagement portrait **$25.00**
Tray, Elizabeth's coronation, 13" dia, multicolored royal couple, faux wood **$45.00**

Bubble Bath Containers

If you haven't already seen these for sale in flea markets or co-ops, no doubt you were a bit incredulous when you read the title for this section. Yes, these figural plastic bottles are among today's hottest just-for-fun collectibles. They were popular in the 1960s, made in the likenesses of a vast range of cartoon characters. The Colgate-Palmolive Company produced the majority of them — they're the ones marked 'Soaky' — and these seem to be the most collectible. Each character's name is right on the bottle. Other companies followed suit; Purex also made a line, so did Avon.

The prices below are for bottles in excellent to near-mint condition. Be sure to check for paint loss, and look carefully for cracks in the brittle plastic heads of the Soakies.

Alvin, 11", Colgate-Palmolive, Soaky, 1963, NM **$25.00**
Atom Ant, 9½", Purex, EX paint **$45.00**
Augie Doggie, 10", Purex, ca 1965, VG **$38.00**
Baba Louie, Purex, M w/card **$35.00**
Barney Rubble, Purex, MIB **$35.00**
Batman, Soaky, NM **$75.00**
Bozo the Clown, 10", 1960s, vinyl w/hard plastic removable head, EX paint **$25.00**
Bugs Bunny, 1960s, M **$25.00**
Casper, 10", vinyl w/hard plastic removable head, blue facial details, 1960s **$20.00**
Creature, 10", Universal Pictures copyright, metallic green w/tan stomach & orange fish, 1960s, EX **$90.00**
Deputy Dawg, 10", 1966, yellow & brown w/white muzzle, EX **$20.00**
Dino (of the Flintstones), Purex, MIB **$45.00**
Dopey, Colgate-Palmolive, Soaky, ca 1960s **$10.00**
Frankenstein, 10", Colgate-Palmolive, Soaky, 1960s, NM **$95.00**
Fred Flintstone, Purex, MIB **$35.00**
Jiminy Cricket, Purex, full, w/base **$35.00**
Lippy the Lion, Purex **$30.00**
Mickey Mouse, Colgate-Palmolive, Soaky **$12.00**
Mighty Mouse, 1965, NM **$25.00**
Mr Jinks w/Pixie & Dixie (at either side), 10", Purex, ca 1962, EX **$17.50**
Mummy, 10", Colgate-Palmolive, Soaky, 1963 ....**$75.00**
Mush Mouse, 7", Purex, tan vinyl w/purple accents, EX **$45.00**

Popeye, Colgate-Palmolive, Soaky..............................$35.00
Porky the Pig, EX...$18.00
Punkin' Puss, 11½", Purex, M in box........................$45.00
Ricochet Rabbit, 10½", Purex, has movable arm, ca 1965, NM...$65.00
Rocky the Squirrel, Colgate-Palmolive, Soaky..............$30.00
Santa Claus, Purex, full, w/base.............................$24.00
Secret Squirrel, 10", Purex, light wear, EX.................$48.00
Smokey the Bear, NM..$15.00
Snagglepuss, 8", Purex, 1960s, paint wear, EX.............$22.50
Spouty Whale, 10" long, Purex, blue w/black & white eyes & yellow details, 1965, NM...................................$60.00
Superman, Avon, 1978, NM...................................$15.00
Superman, Colgate-Palmolive, Soaky $65.00
Sylvester the Cat, NM..$15.00
Tennessee Tuxedo, NM..$20.00
Theodore (Chipmunk), 11", Colgate-Palmolive, 1963 .$20.00
Thumper (rabbit from Bambi), NM..........................$18.00
Top Cat, 10", Colgate-Palmolive, Soaky, ca 1960s $22.00
Wally Gator, Purex, M w/card $40.00
Winsome Witch, 10½", Purex, ca 1968 ....$32.00
Wolfman, 10", Colgate-Palmolive, Soaky, 1963, M $75.00
Woody Woodpecker, Colgate-Palmolive, Soaky..........$15.00
Yakky Doodle, 6", Purex, some scuffing, EX..............$40.00

Butter Pats

Tiny plates made to hold individual pats of butter were popular in Victorian times; as late as the 1970s, some were still being used by hotels, railroads, and steamship lines. They're becoming a popular item of collector interest because they are so diversified (you'll find them in china, silverplate, pewter, and glass), their small size makes them easy to display, and right now, at least, their prices are relatively low.

The new collector might choose to concentrate on pats made of a particular material or those from only one manufacturer or country. Don't confuse them with children's toy dishes, coasters, or small plates intended for other uses; and don't buy them if they're at all damaged.

Blue Willow, 3", Made in Japan mark $10.00
Ceramic, daffodil decal on yellow, square shape, American $4.50
Commercial type, Union Pacific Railroad, Harriman Blue, vitrified china $24.00
Commercial type, 3½", Astor Hotel, vitrified china, top-marked logo $7.50
Commercial type, 3¼", Grindley, Hotel Ware, green & orange bands...$3.00
Commercial type, 3¼", San Diego Hotel, vitrified china, top marked logo $7.50
Copeland Spode, 3", Old Salem, blue & white...........$12.00
Cut glass, Cypress $32.50
Cut glass, signed Hawkes....................................$27.50
Early American pattern glass, Daisy & Button, crystal, square shape..$7.50

Early American pattern glass, Tree of Life, blue $27.50
Flow Blue, Scinde, Alcock...................................$25.00
Haviland, 2⅝", wild flowers, scalloped rim..............$12.00
Haviland Limoges, shadow leaves & pink roses..........$9.50
Heisey glass, Ipswich, Sahara, square shape $19.00
Ironstone, Tea Leaf pattern, Meakin........................$12.50
Ironstone, 2½" square, brown scenic transfer, unmarked $10.00
Ironstone, 3", Anglais, brown transfer of Holyrood Palace $12.00
Majolica, 2 overlapping leaves.............................$50.00
Majolica, 3", Pansy, Etruscan...............................$37.50
Nippon, 3¾", hand-painted pine cones, M-in-wreath mark...$8.50
Pewter, 3", plain, beaded edge $6.00
Rosenthal, 3⅝", Carmen, hand-painted forget-me-nots .$7.50
Shelley, Bridal Rose, 6 flutes...............................$22.50
Silverplate, acanthus leaf border............................$12.50
Silverplate, Webster, embossed floral & shell border, woman & churn in center...$12.50
Spode, Fleur-de-Lis, brown & white $6.50
Sterling, plain w/rolled edge.................................$14.50
Sterling, 3¼", Gorham, embossed rose border, monogram center, square $22.50
Vernon Kilns, Gingham $5.00

Camark Pottery

You may occasionally find a piece of pottery marked 'Camark,' though it's fairly scarce. This was an Arkansas company based in the city of Camden, from whence came its name — 'Cam' from the city, 'ark' from the state. They operated from the mid-twenties until they closed in the early 1960s, mainly producing commercial wares such as figurines, vases, and novelty items, though artware was attempted for the first few years they were in existence. This early artware, marked 'Lessell' (for John Lessell, the decorator) or 'Le-Camark' is very similar to lines by Weller and Owens, and when a piece comes up for sale, it is usually tagged at somewhere between $300.00 to $500.00, depending on its size and decoration.

Basket, 4½x5", flared form w/handles, green $10.00
Basket, 5x3", embossed florals on cream...................$12.00
Candle holder, triple; leaf form, white $12.00
Centerpiece bowl, w/flower frog modeled as a bird.......$25.00
Ewer, 16", multicolored hand-painted irises................$35.00
Figurine, 8", cat beside fishbowl, white gloss glaze $20.00
Planter, 8", double-swan figural, black glaze.............$15.00
Shakers, blue w/S & P letters, pr $10.00
Teapot, 8", swirled mold, w/warmer..........................$18.50
Vase, 12", gold lustre palm trees on bronze, ...$450.00
Vase, 5", yellow leaf form, flared split top, footed, #827...$7.50
Vase, 7", geometric design at flared top & base, matt green glaze, #406...$12.00
Vase, 8½", Old English, plum & cream scenic design, signed Le-Camark, early $300.00

Cambridge Glassware

If you're looking for a 'safe' place to put your investment dollars, Cambridge glass is one of your better options. But as with any commodity, in order to make a good investment, knowledge of the product and its market is required. There are two books we would recommend for your study, *Colors in Cambridge Glass,* by the National Cambridge Collectors Club, and *The Collector's Encyclopedia of Elegant Glass* by Gene Florence.

The Cambridge Glass Company (located in Cambridge, Ohio) made fine quality glassware from just after the turn of the century until 1958. They made thousands of different items in hundreds of various patterns and colors. Values hinge on rarity of shape and color. Of the various marks they used, the 'C in triangle' is the most common. In addition to their tableware, they also produced flower frogs representing ladies and children and models of animals and birds that are very valuable today. To learn more about them, you'll want to read *Glass Animals and Figural Flower Frogs from the Depression Era* by Lee Garmon and Dick Spencer. (See also Glass Animals.)

Apple Blossom, amber, ash tray, 6", heavy..............**$150.00**
Apple Blossom, amber, pitcher, 50-oz, footed, flattened sides..**$175.00**
Apple Blossom, amber, stem, parfait; #1006..............**$95.00**
Apple Blossom, amber, tray, sandwich; 11", center handle **$37.50**
Apple Blossom, blue, comport, 7"..........................**$80.00**
Apple Blossom, blue, plate, sandwich; 12½", 2-handled..**$55.00**
Apple Blossom, crystal, bowl, baker; 10"................**$25.00**
Apple Blossom, crystal, bowl, console; 12½"............**$30.00**
Apple Blossom, crystal, creamer, ftd **$12.50**
Apple Blossom, crystal, plate, bread & butter; 6" **$5.00**
Apple Blossom, crystal, platter, 11½" **$35.00**
Apple Blossom, crystal, stem, sherbet; 6-oz, #3400, footed **$9.00**
Apple Blossom, crystal, tumbler, 12-oz, footed **$17.50**
Apple Blossom, pink, bowl, fruit; 11", tab handled.....**$75.00**
Apple Blossom, pink, tumbler, 12-oz, #3025 ....**$37.50**
Apple Blossom, yellow, candlestick, 1-light, keyhole .**$25.00**
Apple Blossom, yellow, plate, dinner; 9½" **$65.00**
Apple Blossom, yellow, stem, water; 8-oz, #3130 ....**$30.00**
Apple Blossom, yellow, tumbler, 12-oz, #3135, footed.**$32.50**
Candlelight, crystal, bowl, 12", 4-footed, flared **$62.50**
Candlelight, crystal, bowl, 7", #3900/130, 2-handled...**$30.00**
Candlelight, crystal, cake plate, 13½", #3900/35, 2-handled **$55.00**
Candlelight, crystal, candy dish, w/lid, #3900/165, round.**$95.00**
Candlelight, crystal, comport, 5⅜", #3121, blown........**$57.50**
Candlelight, crystal, creamer, #3900/41 ....**$20.00**
Candlelight, crystal, cruet, w/stopper, 6-oz, #3900/100.**$95.00**
Candlelight, crystal, cup, #3900/100 ....**$95.00**
Candlelight, crystal, hurricane lamp, #1617 ....**$120.00**
Candlelight, crystal, ice bucket, #3900/671 ....**$100.00**
Candlelight, crystal, mayonnaise, 3-pc, #3900/129 ......**$57.50**
Candlelight, crystal, plate, dinner; 10½", #3900/24......**$65.00**

Candlelight, crystal, plate, salad; 8", #3900/22.............**$15.00**
Candlelight, crystal, relish, #3900/120, 5-part..............**$57.50**
Candlelight, crystal, relish, 7", #3900/124, divided, 2-handled..**$35.00**
Candlelight, crystal, stem, cocktail; 30-oz, #3111........**$27.50**
Candlelight, crystal, stem, cordial; 1-oz, #3776 ....**$65.00**
Candlelight, crystal, stem, oyster cocktail; 4½-oz, #3111 ...**$27.50**
Candlelight, crystal, stem, tall sherbet; 7-oz, #3111 .....**$22.50**
Candlelight, crystal, stem, water; 10-oz, #3111 ....**$30.00**
Candlelight, crystal, sugar bowl, #3900/41 ....**$17.50**
Candlelight, crystal, tumbler, iced tea; 12-oz, footed, #3111 ....**$25.00**
Candlelight, crystal, tumbler, juice; 5-oz, #3776...........**$18.00**
Candlelight, crystal, vase, #1309, globe......................**$52.50**
Candlelight, crystal, vase, 12", #1238, footed, keyhole..**$87.50**
Caprice, blue, ash tray, 2¾", #213, 3-footed, shell.......**$10.00**
Caprice, blue, bowl, almond; 2", #95, 4-footed **$40.00**
Caprice, blue, bowl, relish; 12", #126, 4-part, oval....**$135.00**
Caprice, blue, candy dish, w/lid, 6", #168, divided...**$110.00**
Caprice, blue, creamer, medium, #38.........................**$15.00**
Caprice, blue, ice bucket, #201...............................**$150.00**
Caprice, blue, pitcher, 32-oz, #179, ball shape..........**$300.00**
Caprice, blue, salt & pepper shakers, #91, ball, pr...**$100.00**
Caprice, blue, sugar bowl, large, #41 ....**$15.00**
Caprice, blue, tumbler, whiskey; 2½-oz, #300 ....**$25.00**
Caprice, blue, vase, 6½", #338, crimped....................**$175.00**
Caprice, crystal, bonbon, 6" sq, #133, footed............**$14.00**
Caprice, crystal, bowl, salad; 10", #57, 4-footed **$32.50**
Caprice, crystal, candlestick, #74, 3-light.................**$30.00**
Caprice, crystal, cigarette box, w/lid, 4½x3½", #208 ...**$22.00**
Caprice, crystal, comport, 6", #130 ....**$22.00**
Caprice, crystal, decanter, w/stopper, 35-oz, #187....**$125.00**
Caprice, crystal, marmalade, w/lid, 6-oz, #89 ....**$45.00**
Caprice, crystal, oil, w/stopper, 3-oz, #101 ....**$22.00**
Caprice, crystal, plate, lemon; 6½", #152, handled **$11.00**
Caprice, crystal, stem, wine; 2½-oz, #301, blown........**$27.50**
Caprice, crystal, tray, 9-oz, #42, oval **$18.00**
Caprice, crystal, tumbler, juice; 5-oz, #301, blown **$13.00**
Caprice, crystal, vase, 9½", #340, crimped **$150.00**
Caprice, pink, ash tray, 5", #216 ....**$25.00**
Caprice, pink, bowl, 9½", #52, 4-footed, crimped **$67.50**
Caprice, pink, cake plate, 13", #36, footed **$300.00**
Caprice, pink, cigarette holder, 3x3", #204, triangular.**$40.00**
Caprice, pink, mustard, w/lid, 2-oz, #87 ....**$135.00**
Caprice, pink, plate, dinner; 9½", #24 ....**$125.00**
Caprice, pink, stem, cordial; 1-oz, #300, blown **$125.00**
Caprice, pink, stem, fruit cocktail; 4½-oz, #7 ....**$75.00**
Caprice, pink, stem, low oyster cocktail; 4½-oz, #300, blown **$50.00**
Caprice, pink, tumbler, old-fashioned; 7-oz, #310, flat..**$100.00**
Caprice, pink, tumbler, 2-oz, #188, flat **$50.00**
Chantilly, crystal, bowl, celery or relish; 9", 3-part......**$25.00**
Chantilly, crystal, bowl, 11½", tab handled, footed **$32.50**
Chantilly, crystal, butter dish, w/lid, round................**$125.00**
Chantilly, crystal, cake plate, 13½", tab handled.........**$32.50**
Chantilly, crystal, candlestick, 6", 3-light **$37.50**
Chantilly, crystal, candy box, w/lid, footed **$125.00**
Chantilly, crystal, candy box, w/lid, round................**$55.00**

Chantilly, crystal, cocktail icer, 2-pc $55.00
Chantilly, crystal, comport, 5⅜", blown.................$37.50
Chantilly, crystal, creamer $14.50
Chantilly, crystal, decanter, footed $150.00
Chantilly, crystal, hurricane lamp, candlestick base ..$110.00
Chantilly, crystal, ice bucket, w/chrome handle.........$65.00
Chantilly, crystal, mayonnaise, w/liner, two ladles, divided $40.00
Chantilly, crystal, oil, w/stopper, 6-oz, handled $55.00
Chantilly, crystal, plate, bread & butter; 6½" $6.50
Chantilly, crystal, salt & pepper shakers, flat, pr $27.50
Chantilly, crystal, stem, claret; 4½-oz............................$40.00
Chantilly, crystal, stem, cordial; 1-oz, #3600 ....$45.00
Chantilly, crystal, stem, low sherbet; 7-oz, #3625 ....$16.00
Chantilly, crystal, stem, tall sherbet; 6-oz, #3775 ....$17.50
Chantilly, crystal, stem, water; 10-oz, #3600 ....$20.00
Chantilly, crystal, stem, wine; 2½-oz, #3775................$30.00
Chantilly, crystal, tumbler, juice; 5-oz, #3779, footed..$15.00
Chantilly, crystal, vase, 12", keyhole base...................$50.00
Crown Tuscan, candlestick, 4", dolphin & shell, w/foot, pr $100.00
Crown Tuscan, candy dish, 3-compartment, w/lid......$65.00
Crown Tuscan, dish, 11", shell form, 3-footed............$75.00

Crown Tuscan, swan, 9" long.............................$165.00
Crown Tuscan, vase, cornucopia; 10".........................$55.00
Decagon, cobalt blue, bowl, vegetable; 11", round.....$30.00
Decagon, cobalt blue, bowl, almond; 6", footed $35.00
Decagon, cobalt blue, plate, salad; 8½" $10.00
Decagon, cobalt blue, tumbler, 8-oz, footed................$22.00
Decagon, cobalt blue, comport, 7" $30.00
Decagon, green, bowl, cranberry; 3¾", flat rim..........$12.00
Decagon, green, cup...$6.00
Decagon, green, mayonnaise, w/liner & ladle.............$18.00
Decagon, green, sugar bowl, scalloped edge $9.00
Decagon, Moonlight Blue, bowl, fruit; 5¾", flat rim......$6.00
Decagon, pink, bowl, bouillon w/liner $7.50
Decagon, pink, bowl, vegetable; 10½", oval...............$16.00
Decagon, pink, ice bucket $35.00
Decagon, pink, stem, cordial; 1-oz $40.00
Decagon, pink, tray, service; 13", 2-handled...............$20.00
Decagon, red, basket, 7", 2-handled, upturned sides ..$20.00
Decagon, red, bowl, vegetable; 9½", oval...................$27.50

Decagon, red, creamer, footed $20.00
Decagon, red, plate, grill; 10"...................................$14.00
Decagon, red, stem, water; 9-oz................................$30.00
Diane, crystal, basket, 6", footed, 2-handled...............$16.00
Diane, crystal, bitters bottle.....................................$125.00
Diane, crystal, bowl, baker; 10" $40.00
Diane, crystal, bowl, celery or relish; 12", 3-part........$32.50
Diane, crystal, bowl, celery or relish; 9", 3-part..........$30.00
Diane, crystal, bowl, cereal; 6"..................................$25.00
Diane, crystal, bowl, cream soup, w/liner, #3400........$27.50
Diane, crystal, candlestick, 1-light, keyhole..............$17.50
Diane, crystal, candy box, w/lid, round.....................$75.00
Diane, crystal, cocktail shaker, metal top...................$90.00
Diane, crystal, comport, 5⅜", blown.........................$35.00
Diane, crystal, creamer, #3400, scroll handle.............$15.00
Diane, crystal, decanter, cordial; short foot $175.00
Diane, crystal, hurricane lamp, w/prisms, keyhole base...$175.00
Diane, crystal, ice bucket, chrome handle $65.00
Diane, crystal, plate, bread & butter; 6½"....................$5.00
Diane, crystal, plate, torte; 13", 4-footed $35.00
Diane, crystal, salt & pepper shakers, glass tops, footed, pr...$32.00
Diane, crystal, stem, cocktail; 3-oz, #1066..................$16.00
Diane, crystal, stem, cordial; 1-oz, #3122...................$55.00
Diane, crystal, stem, tall sherbet; 7-oz.......................$15.00
Diane, crystal, tumbler, iced tea; 12-oz, footed $25.00
Diane, crystal, tumbler, juice; 5-oz, #1066..................$12.50
Diane, crystal, tumbler, juice; 5-oz, footed.................$27.00
Diane, crystal, tumbler, water; 9-oz, #3106, footed $11.00
Diane, crystal, tumbler, 12-oz, sham bottom $32.00
Diane, crystal, vase, bud; 10".....................................$35.00
Diane, crystal, vase, 12", keyhole base........................$65.00
Diane, crystal, stem, claret; 4½-oz, #1006...................$25.00
Elaine, crystal, basket, 6", 2-handled, upturned handles.$15.00
Elaine, crystal, bowl, bonbon; 5¼", 2-handled.............$13.00
Elaine, crystal, bowl, pickle or relish; 7", 2-part $16.00
Elaine, crystal, bowl, 12", 4-footed, flared..................$35.00
Elaine, crystal, candlestick, 6", 3-light........................$35.00
Elaine, crystal, comport, 5⅜", #3500 stem $39.00
Elaine, crystal, hurricane lamp, candlestick base........$110.00
Elaine, crystal, ice bucket, chrome handle $60.00
Elaine, crystal, mayonnaise, w/liner & ladle $30.00
Elaine, crystal, pitcher, upright $175.00
Elaine, crystal, plate, bread & butter; 6½" $7.00
Elaine, crystal, plate, salad; 8"..................................$15.00
Elaine, crystal, plate, torte; 13", 4-footed....................$30.00
Elaine, crystal, salt & pepper shakers, flat, pr.............$27.50
Elaine, crystal, stem, claret; 4½-oz, #3121 ....$30.00
Elaine, crystal, stem, cocktail; 3½-oz, #3104 ....$50.00
Elaine, crystal, stem, cordial; 1-oz, #3104..................$120.00
Elaine, crystal, stem, low parfait; 5-oz, #3121 ....$25.00
Elaine, crystal, stem, low sherbet; #1402.....................$14.00
Elaine, crystal, stem, tall sherbet; 7-oz, #3500.............$15.00
Elaine, crystal, stem, wine; 2½-oz, #3500 ....$27.50
Elaine, crystal, tumbler, iced tea; 12-oz, #1402, tall foot..$27.50
Elaine, crystal, tumbler, juice; 5-oz, #3121, footed $19.00

Elaine, crystal, tumbler, juice; 5-oz, #3500, footed **$17.00**
Elaine, crystal, tumbler, water; 10-oz, #3500, footed...**$18.00**
Elaine, crystal, vase, 9", footed, keyhole **$45.00**
Gloria, crystal, basket, 6", 2-handled, sides up **$16.00**
Gloria, crystal, bowl, cereal; 6", square **$12.00**
Gloria, crystal, bowl, vegetable; 9½", 2-handled..........**$55.00**
Gloria, crystal, candlestick, 6", pr **$35.00**
Gloria, crystal, plate, bread & butter; 6" **$6.00**
Gloria, crystal, sugar shaker, w/glass top...................**$125.00**
Gloria, crystal, tumbler, water; 10-oz, #3135.............**$12.00**
Gloria, crystal, vase, 11", neck indent.......................**$50.00**
Gloria, green, bowl, console; 12", 4-footed.................**$50.00**
Gloria, green, bowl, cranberry; 3½", 4-footed.............**$40.00**
Gloria, green, comport, 6", 4-footed...........................**$35.00**
Gloria, green, plate, dinner, square **$70.00**
Gloria, green, stem, tall sherbet; 6-oz, #3135.............**$16.00**
Gloria, green, tray, relish; 2-part, center handle **$35.00**
Gloria, green, tumbler, 12-oz, footed, #3120 ....**$30.00**
Gloria, green, vase, 10", keyhole base **$95.00**
Gloria, pink, bowl, bonbon; 5½", 2-handled **$21.00**
Gloria, pink, bowl, cream soup; w/round liner...........**$35.00**
Gloria, pink, ice pail, metal handle w/tongs................**$75.00**
Gloria, pink, stem, cocktail; 3½-oz, #3035 ....**$27.00**
Gloria, pink, tray, pickle; 9", tab handled **$25.00**
Gloria, pink, vase, 14", keyhole base, flared rim.......**$135.00**
Gloria, yellow, bowl, cereal; 6", round.......................**$25.00**
Gloria, yellow, cake plate, 11", footed, square **$110.00**
Gloria, yellow, salt & pepper shakers, w/glass tops, tall, pr...**$70.00**
Gloria, yellow, stem, water; 9-oz, #3120 ....**$25.00**
Gloria, yellow, tumbler, juice; 5-oz, footed, #3115......**$20.00**
Gloria, yellow, vase, 11"...**$95.00**
Imperial Hunt Scene, amber, bowl, cereal; 6" **$25.00**
Imperial Hunt Scene, amber, decanter......................**$225.00**
Imperial Hunt Scene, amber, stem, cordial; 1-oz, #1402.**$55.00**
Imperial Hunt Scene, amber, tumbler, 2½-oz, #3085, footed..**$30.00**
Imperial Hunt Scene, black, bowl, 8"........................**$60.00**
Imperial Hunt Scene, black, finger bowl, w/plate **$35.00**
Imperial Hunt Scene, black, stem, cordial; 1-oz...........**$150.00**
Imperial Hunt Scene, black, tumbler, 5-oz, #3085, footed..**$25.00**
Imperial Hunt Scene, crystal, bowl, cereal; 6" **$15.00**
Imperial Hunt Scene, crystal, creamer, footed **$15.00**
Imperial Hunt Scene, crystal, plate, 8"......................**$12.00**
Imperial Hunt Scene, crystal, stem, sherbet; 6½-oz, #1402 ....**$35.00**
Imperial Hunt Scene, crystal, tumbler, 7-oz, #1402, flat .**$20.00**
Imperial Hunt Scene, emerald green, bowl, 8½", 3-part ..**$45.00**
Imperial Hunt Scene, emerald green, ice bucket.........**$75.00**
Imperial Hunt Scene, emerald green, wine; 2½-oz......**$55.00**
Imperial Hunt Scene, green, candlestick, 2-light, keyhole **$35.00**
Imperial Hunt Scene, green, mayonnaise, w/liner **$50.00**
Imperial Hunt Scene, green, stem, low sherbet; 6-oz, #3085 ....**$22.50**
Imperial Hunt Scene, green, tumbler, 8-oz, #3085, footed..**$25.00**

Imperial Hunt Scene, pink, candlestick, 3-light, keyhole .**$55.00**
Imperial Hunt Scene, pink, pitcher, w/lid, 63-oz, #3085..**$250.00**
Imperial Hunt Scene, pink, stem, water; 9-oz, #3085 ..**$45.00**
Imperial Hunt Scene, Willow Blue, comport, #3085 ...**$30.00**
Imperial Hunt Scene, Willow Blue, pitcher, w/lid, 76-oz, #711 ....**$225.00**
Imperial Hunt Scene, Willow Blue, tumbler, 2½-oz, #1402, flat **$25.00**
Mt Vernon, amber, ash tray, 3½", #63.......................**$8.00**
Mt Vernon, amber, bottle, toilet; 7-oz, #18, square **$65.00**
Mt Vernon, amber, bowl, fruit; 5¼", #6 ....**$10.00**
Mt Vernon, amber, bowl, sweetmeat; 8½", #105, 4-part, 2-handled..**$30.00**
Mt Vernon, amber, bowl, 12", #117, crimped, rolled edge **$32.50**
Mt Vernon, amber, bowl, 12", #129, rolled edge, flanged.**$32.50**
Mt Vernon, amber, box, w/lid, 4½", #15, footed, round ..**$35.00**
Mt Vernon, amber, cake stand, 10½", #150, footed.....**$35.00**
Mt Vernon, amber, candlestick, 8", #35 ....**$25.00**
Mt Vernon, amber, celery, 11", #98 ....**$17.50**
Mt Vernon, amber, comport, 4½", #33........................**$12.00**
Mt Vernon, amber, creamer, #8, footed.....................**$10.00**
Mt Vernon, amber, decanter, w/stopper, 40-oz, #52 ...**$70.00**
Mt Vernon, amber, hurricane lamp, 9", #1607 ....**$70.00**
Mt Vernon, amber, pitcher, ball; 80-oz, #95...............**$90.00**
Mt Vernon, amber, plate, bread & butter; 6⅜", #19.......**$4.00**
Mt Vernon, amber, relish, 12", #104, 5-part................**$30.00**
Mt Vernon, amber, relish, 12", #80, 2-part.................**$30.00**
Mt Vernon, amber, salt & pepper shakers, #28, pr......**$22.50**
Mt Vernon, amber, sauce boat & ladle, #30-445, tab handled...**$55.00**
Mt Vernon, amber, stem, low sherbet, 4½", #42 ....**$7.50**
Mt Vernon, amber, stem, oyster cocktail; 4-oz, #41.......**$9.00**
Mt Vernon, amber, sugar bowl, #8, footed **$10.00**
Mt Vernon, amber, tray for individual sugar & creamer, #4 ....**$10.00**
Mt Vernon, amber, tumbler, 14-oz, #14, barrel shape.**$20.00**
Mt Vernon, amber, tumbler, 5-oz, #56.......................**$12.00**
Mt Vernon, amber, vase, 7", #54, footed **$35.00**
Mt Vernon, crystal, ash tray, 4", #68 ....**$12.00**
Mt Vernon, crystal, bowl, ivy ball or rose; 4½", #12, footed **$27.50**
Mt Vernon, crystal, bowl, pickle; 8", #65...................**$17.50**
Mt Vernon, crystal, bowl, salad; 10½", #120.............**$25.00**
Mt Vernon, crystal, box, w/lid, 4", #17, square...........**$30.00**
Mt Vernon, crystal, candlestick, 4", #130 ....**$10.00**
Mt Vernon, crystal, celery, 10½", #79.......................**$15.00**
Mt Vernon, crystal, coaster, 3", #60, plain **$5.00**
Mt Vernon, crystal, comport, 6", #34.........................**$15.00**
Mt Vernon, crystal, decanter, 11-oz, #47 ....**$50.00**
Mt Vernon, crystal, mustard, w/lid, 2½-oz, #28 ....**$22.00**
Mt Vernon, crystal, pitcher, 86-oz, #91.....................**$110.00**
Mt Vernon, crystal, plate, salad; 8½", #5.....................**$7.00**
Mt Vernon, crystal, salt & pepper shakers, short, #88, pr **$20.00**
Mt Vernon, crystal, stem, water; 10-oz, #1 ....**$15.00**
Mt Vernon, crystal, stem, wine; 3-oz, #27 ....**$13.50**

Mt Vernon, crystal, sugar bowl, #86 ....$10.00

Mt Vernon, crystal, tumbler, water; 10-oz, #3, footed .$15.00

Mt Vernon, crystal, tumbler, whiskey; 2-oz, #55..........$10.00

Mt Vernon, crystal, tumbler, 12-oz, #13, barrel shape.$15.00

Mt Vernon, crystal, vase, 6", #119, crimped $20.00

Nude stem, ash tray, carmen......................................$225.00

Nude stem, brandy, amber..$100.00

Nude stem, brandy, cobalt $115.00

Nude stem, brandy, crystal...$115.00

Nude stem, candlesticks, amber, pr............................$550.00

Nude stem, claret, royal blue $125.00

Nude stem, cocktail, amethyst $90.00

Nude stem, cocktail, dark green $90.00

Nude stem, comport, 8", amethyst bowl............$125.00

Nude stem, goblet, water; crystal $115.00

Nude stem, ivy ball, dark green..................................$200.00

Nude stem, sauterne, topaz...$500.00

Portia, crystal, basket, 2-handled, upturned sides $16.00

Portia, crystal, bowl, cranberry; 3½" square................$20.00

Portia, crystal, bowl, grapefruit or oyster; 6"..............$17.00

Portia, crystal, candlestick, 6", 'fleur-de-lis,' 2-light......$35.00

Portia, crystal, cocktail shaker, w/stopper...................$90.00

Portia, crystal, hurricane lamp, w/prisms...........$125.00

Portia, crystal, mayonnaise, w/liner & two ladles, divided $40.00

Portia, crystal, plate, dinner; 10½" $60.00

Portia, crystal, saucer, square or round $3.00

Portia, crystal, stem, claret; 4½-oz, #3124.................$27.50

Portia, crystal, stem, wine; 2½-oz, #3121.....................$27.50

Portia, crystal, stem, wine; 2½-oz, #3130.....................$25.00

Portia, crystal, tumbler, bar; 2½-oz, #3121 ....$30.00

Portia, crystal, tumbler, iced tea; 12-oz, #3124............$22.00

Portia, crystal, vase, flower; 13" $85.00

Portia, crystal, vase, bud; 10" $35.00

Portia, crystal, vase, 9", keyhole foot..........................$60.00

Rose Point, crystal, ash tray, stack set on metal pole, #1715 ....$195.00

Rose Point, crystal, basket, 6" sq, #3500/55, footed, 2-handled..$37.50

Rose Point, crystal, bowl, cream soup; w/liner............$135.00

Rose Point, crystal, bowl, fruit; 5¼", #3400/56............$42.50

Rose Point, crystal, bowl, nut; 3", #3400/71, 4-footed.$76.50

Rose Point, crystal, bowl, 12", #3500/118, footed, oblong...$145.00

Rose Point, crystal, candelabrum, #1338 ....$55.00

Rose Point, crystal, candlestick, 5", #3400/646, 1-light, keyhole...$30.00

Rose Point, crystal, candy box, w/lid, 8", 3-part, #3500/57 ....$72.50

Rose Point, crystal, cheese dish, w/lid, 5", #980........$400.00

Rose Point, crystal, cocktail shaker, w/metal top, 46-oz, #98 ....$135.00

Rose Point, crystal, comport, 5½", #3900/136, scalloped edge $52.50

Rose Point, crystal, cup, after dinner; #3400/69........$225.00

Rose Point, crystal, hurricane lamp, #1617, candlestick base..$175.00

Rose Point, crystal, marmalade, w/lid, 7-oz, #157, footed..$165.00

Rose Point, crystal, mustard, 4½-oz, #1329, footed ...$295.00

Rose Point, crystal, oil, w/stopper, 6-oz, #3900/100, loop handled...$110.00

Rose Point, crystal, plate, dinner; 10½", #3400/64.....$125.00

Rose Point, crystal, relish, w/lid, 14", #3500/142, 4-part, 2-handled...$400.00

Rose Point, crystal, pitcher, 9"............................$250.00

Rose Point, crystal, stem, cocktail; 3-oz, #3500............$35.00

Rose Point, crystal, stem, low sherbet; 7-oz, #3106.....$25.00

Rose Point, crystal, tray, sandwich; 11", #3400/10, center handle...$135.00

Rose Point, crystal, tumbler, 12-oz, straight sided $50.00

Rose Point, crystal, tumbler, 13-oz, #3900/115 ....$40.00

Rose Point, crystal, urn, w/lid, 10", #3500/41 ....$450.00

Rose Point, crystal, vase, 10", #400, ball bottom........$150.00

Rose Point, crystal, vase, 8", #797, flat, flared............**$120.00**
Valencia, crystal, ash tray, 3¼", #3500/124, round.......**$10.00**
Valencia, crystal, bowl, cereal; 6", #3500/37 ....**$20.00**
Valencia, crystal, candy dish, w/lid, #3500/103 ....**$85.00**
Valencia, crystal, relish, 6½", #3500/69, 3-part............**$20.00**
Valencia, crystal, stem, tall sherbet; #1402 ....**$15.00**
Valencia, crystal, stem, wine, #1402 ....**$30.00**
Valencia, crystal, tumbler, 13-oz, #3400/100 ....**$20.00**
Valencia, crystal, tumbler, 5-oz, #3500, footed **$12.50**
Wildflower, crystal, basket, 6", #3400/1182, 2-handled ..**$25.00**
Wildflower, crystal, bowl, celery or relish; 9", #3900/125, 3-part...**$25.00**
Wildflower, crystal, butter dish, ¼-lb, #3900/52 ....**$165.00**
Wildflower, crystal, cake plate, 13½", #3900/35, 2-handled **$32.50**
Wildflower, crystal, candlestick, 5", #3400/646............**$25.00**
Wildflower, crystal, cocktail icer, #968, 2-pc.............**$65.00**
Wildflower, crystal, creamer, #3900/41 ....**$12.50**
Wildflower, crystal, ice bucket, #3900/671, w/chrome handle **$65.00**
Wildflower, crystal, mayonnaise, #3900/129, w/liner & ladle **$30.00**
Wildflower, crystal, salt & pepper shakers, #3900/1177, pr...**$32.50**
Wildflower, crystal, stem, claret; 4½-oz, #3121 ....**$38.00**
Wildflower, crystal, stem, tall sherbet; 6-oz, #3121......**$17.50**
Wildflower, crystal, tumbler, juice; 5-oz, #3121 ....**$15.00**
Wildflower, crystal, vase, flower; 11", #278, footed.....**$42.00**

Cameras

To make good investments when buying cameras, several criteria are involved. Those that hold their values best and have a better resale potential are usually the more unusual, more obscure models in fine condition. Most camera buffs build their collections around either a particular type of camera (those with the same sort of shutter, for instance), or they might limit their buying to cameras made by only one company. But even if you can afford to buy only inexpensive, mass-produced cameras, you'll find it to be a very interesting hobby. You can (many do) add viewers, photography supplies and advertising, projectors, and accessories of all types to round out your collection.

Argus C20, same basic body style as A4 in brown plastic, includes rangefinder, NM **$18.00**
Argus C44, 35mm wide angle lens, ca 1951, EX..........**$40.00**
Balda Jubilette, made for 30th anniversary of Balda-Werk, folding 35mm w/Compur shutter, ca 1938, EX.....**$35.00**
Balda Juwella II, folding type, Pronto shutter, ca 1938, EX **$37.50**
Bell & Howell Electric Eye 127, metal box style w/automatic diaphragm, black leatherette w/silver enamel, late 1950s **$22.50**
Bentzin Plan Primar, folding type, 1920s, 6x9cm, NM .**$60.00**
Blair Tourist Hawkeye Special, red bellows, sliding front, ca 1897, EX **$200.00**

Boston Hawk-Eye Detective, brass knob works bellows, EX..**$185.00**
Butcher Carbine, folding model w/removable panel in back, common shutter & lens, NM **$35.00**
Canon Canonflex, removable finder, base-plate trigger wind, ca 1959-60, EX....................................**$120.00**
Canon L-1, chrome, cloth shutter curtains, no self timer, EX..**$165.00**
Coronet Ambassador, metal & Bakelite, box style w/fixed-focus lens, ca 1955, NM....................................**$17.50**
Eastman Kodak Autosnap, gray plastic, eye-level type w/automatic exposure, uses 127 film, 1960s, NM.**$10.00**
Eastman Kodak Bantam Special, black-lacquered metal case, Teague design, 1936, NM...............**$185.00**
Eastman Kodak Beau Brownie #2A, rose, NM in leather carrying case **$100.00**
Eastman Kodak Brownie Starflash, black case, 1950s, M.**$7.50**
Eastman Kodak Winner, red plastic pocket 110 type w/emblem: Kodak Official Sponsor of the 1988 Olympic Games, M..**$12.00**
Graflex Super Speed Graphic, 101mm lens, Kodak Flash Supermatic shutter, 1947-1970, 4x5", M.............**$120.00**

Kodak Rangefinder '35' $35.00
Minolta, Arcadia, folding hand type w/metal body, complex leaf shutter, ca 1931, EX.................**$265.00**
Minolta Uniomat, 35mm rangefinder, automatically controlled shutter speeds, 1960, M **$60.00**
Minox B, built-in meter, black body, manufactured from 1958 to ca 1971, NM **$165.00**
Nikon S2, 24x36mm format, rangefinder, rapid wind lever, crank rewind, chrome w/black dials, M.............**$325.00**
Olympus Pen FT, 38mm lens, semi-silvered mirror, self timer, EX..**$175.00**
Petie, vanity case/camera, Kunick/Frankfurt, 1958, EX..**$565.00**
Rochester Standard View, rear focus, mahogany w/brass fittings, reversible back, 8x10", 1890s, EX.............**$195.00**
Sears Tower Automatic 127, flash & meter built in white plastic body, horizontal style, ca 1960s, M...........**$15.00**

Spartus Press Flash, box type w/built-in flash reflector, Bakelite body, takes roll film, ca 1946, EX...........**$17.50**

United Features Snoopy-Matic, dog on house figural, 126 roll film, 1966, MIB..........**$110.00**

Universal Buccaneer, 35mm w/chronomatic shutter 10-300, flash sync, built-in extinction meter, Bakelite body, ca 1945, M..........**$27.50**

Yashika 44LM, built-in light meter, knob advance, gray body, ca 1962, NM..........**$88.00**

Zeiss Continette, 45mm Lucinar lens, self timer, rigid mount, ca 1960, EX..........**$40.00**

Zeiss Icon Contessa, folding type, 35mm, 1950s, NM..**$215.00**

Zeiss Ikonta A, Novar 80mm front-cell focus lens, Compur shutter, ca 1933-1940, NM..........**$68.00**

Candlewick Glassware

This is a beautifully simple, very diverse line of glassware made by the Imperial Glass Company (a division of Lenox Inc., Bellaire, Ohio) from 1936 until the company closed in 1982. It was named for the tufted needlework done by the Colonial ladies in early America. Rows of small crystal balls surround rims of bowls and plates, foot rings of tumblers, and decorate the handles of pitchers. Some pieces have stems of stacked balls. Though most was made in crystal, a few pieces were made in color as well, while others had a gold wash. Imperial made two etched lines, Floral and Valley Lily, that utilized the Candlewick shapes; both are very scarce.

Among the hardest-to-find items are the desk calendar (made as gifts for company employees and customers), the chip and dip set, and the dresser set containing a cologne bottle, powder jar, clock, and mirror.

There were more than 740 items in all, and collectors often use the company's mold numbers to help identify all those variations and sizes. Gene Florence's *Collector's Encyclopedia of Elegant Glassware* has a chapter that gives this line of glassware very good coverage.

From the 1940s through the sixties, Hazel Atlas produced sherbets, cocktail glasses, wines, and water goblets that are being mistaken for Candlewick, so beware. You'll find these in malls and antique shops, priced and labeled as Candlewick. They were made with a crystal, green, amber, or ruby top on a crystal foot ringed with small glass balls. But the flared part of the foot is ribbed, unlike any Candlewick foot, so you can tell the difference. These are becoming very collectible in their own right, but they're certainly not worth Candlewick prices, and you won't want them in your collection. Gene Florence calls them 'Boopie' and indicates values in the $3.00 to $7.00 range for crystal and in the $7.00 to $17.00 range for colors.

Ashtray, 3¼", #400/172, heart shape..........**$9.00**
Ashtray, 3¼", #400/651, square..........**$30.00**
Basket, 5", $400/273, 5", beaded handle..........**$185.00**
Bowl, baked apple; 6", #400/53X, rolled edge..........**$27.50**
Bowl, boullion; #400/126, 2-handled..........**$40.00**

Bowl, butter & jam; 10½", #400/262, 3-part..........**$70.00**
Bowl, cream soup; 5", #400/50..........**$40.00**
Bowl, fruit; 5", #400/1F..........**$12.00**
Bowl, mint; 6", #400/51F, w/handle..........**$18.00**
Bowl, pickle or celery; 7½", #400/57..........**$25.00**
Bowl, pickle or celery; 8½", $400/58..........**$20.00**
Bowl, relish; 13½", #400/209, 5-part..........**$75.00**
Bowl, relish; 7", #400/234, divided, square..........**$100.00**
Bowl, vegetable; 8", #400/65/1, w/lid..........**$250.00**
Bowl, 9", #400/73H, w/handle, heart shape..........**$110.00**
Cake stand, 10", #400/67D, low foot..........**$50.00**
Candle holder, 3½", #300/79R, rolled edge..........**$10.50**
Candle holder, 5", #400/40HC, heart shape..........**$40.00**
Candy box, #400/140, w/lid, beaded, footed..........**$200.00**
Candy box, 7", #400/259, w/lid..........**$125.00**

Cigarette urn, four ashtrays, & tray, flying ducks etching, set..........**$265.00**
Clock, 4", round..........**$250.00**
Coaster, #300/226, w/spoon rest..........**$13.00**
Cocktail, seafood; #400/190, w/beaded foot..........**$50.00**
Compote, 5½", #400/45, 4-bead stem..........**$22.00**
Creamer, 6-oz, #400/30, beaded handle..........**$7.50**
Cup, coffee; #400/37..........**$7.50**
Decanter, 18-oz, #400/18, w/stopper..........**$350.00**
Fork & spoon set, #400/75..........**$35.00**
Hurricane lamp, #400/152, flared & crimped edge, 3-pc..........**$140.00**
Icer, seafood or fruit cocktail; #400/53/3, 2-pc..........**$95.00**
Marmalade set, #400/1989, w/lid & spoon, beaded foot, 3-pc..........**$40.00**
Mustard jar, #400/156, w/spoon..........**$30.00**
Oil, 4-oz, #400/278, handled, bulbous bottom..........**$65.00**
Pitcher, juice or cocktail; 40-oz, #400/19..........**$165.00**
Plate, bread & butter; 6", #400/1D..........**$8.00**
Plate, dinner; 10", #400/10D..........**$35.00**
Plate, luncheon; 9", #400/7D..........**$12.50**
Plate, salad; 7", #400/3D..........**$8.00**
Plate, salad; 8", #400/5D..........**$9.00**
Plate, service; 12", #400/13D..........**$27.50**
Plate, 10", #400/72E, 2-handled, upturned sides..........**$22.50**

Platter, 13", #400/124D $90.00
Rose bowl, 7", #400/142K $110.00
Salad set, plate (round), bowl (flared), fork, & spoon;
    #400/75B...$85.00
Salt & pepper shakers, #400/247, chrome tops, beaded foot,
    straight sides...$16.00

Salt & pepper shakers, 5", bulbous w/beaded pedestal
    foot, pr...$45.00
Salt dip, 2¼", #400/19 ....$9.00
Sauce boat, #400/169...$95.00
Snack jar, #400/139/1, w/lid, beaded foot $400.00
Stem, claret; #3800 ....$30.00
Stem, cordial; 1-oz, #3800 ....$40.00
Stem, parfait; 6-oz, #3400 ....$45.00
Stem, tall sherbet; 5-oz, #400/190 ....$15.00
Stem, water; 10-oz, #400/190 ....$18.00
Stem, wine; 5-oz, #4000...$25.00
Sugar, #400/18, domed foot..$110.00
Tray, condiment; 5¼ x9¼", #400/148.........................$40.00
Tray, fruit; 10½", #400/68F, center handle $50.00
Tumbler, cocktail; 3½-oz, #400/18..............................$38.00
Tumbler, cocktail; 3-oz, #400/19, footed....................$15.00
Tumbler, iced tea; 14-oz, #400/19 ....$20.00
Tumbler, juice; 5-oz, #3400, footed $15.00
Tumbler, old fashioned; 7-oz, #400/18........................$30.00
Vase, bud; 5¾", #400/107, beaded foot......................$45.00
Vase, 10", #400/22, beaded foot, straight sides..........$140.00
Vase, 8", #400/87F, beaded handle, fan form $35.00

Candy Containers

Most of us can recall buying these glass toys as a child, since they were made well into the 1960s. We were fascinated by the variety of their shapes then, just as collectors are today. Looking back, it couldn't have been we were buying them for the candy, though perhaps as a child those tiny sugary balls flavored more with the coloring agent than anything else were enough to satisfy our 'sweet tooth.'

Glass candy containers have been around since our country's centennial celebration in 1876 when the first two, the Liberty Bell and the Independence Hall, were introduced. Since then they have been made in hundreds of styles, and some of them have become very expensive. The leading manufacturers were in the East — Westmoreland, Victory Glass, J.H. Millstein, Crosetti, L.E. Smith, Jack Stough, T.H. Stough, and West Bros. made perhaps 90% of them — and collectors report finding many of them in the Pennsylvania area. Most of them are clear, but you'll find them in various other colors as well.

If you're going to deal in candy containers, you need a book that will show you all the variations available. The books called *An Album of Glass Candy Containers* (there are two volumes) by Jennie Long, are excellent references. They use a numbering system that has become universal among collectors. Numbers in our listings refer to Jennie's books.

Because of their popularity and considerable worth, many of the original containers have been reproduced. Beware of any questionable glassware that is slick or oily to the touch. Among those that have been reproduced are: Amber Pistol (#144), Auto (#355 and #377), Carpet Sweeper (#242 and #243), Chicken on Nest (#12), Display Case (#246), Dog (#24), Drum Mug (#255), Fire Engine (#386), Happifats on Drum (#89), Independence Hall (#76), Jackie Coogan (#90), Kewpie (#91), Mail Box (#254), Mantel Clock (#114), Mule and Waterwagon (#38), Peter Rabbit (#55), Piano (#289), Rabbit Pushing Wheelbarrow (#47), Rocking Horse (#58), Safe (#268), Santa (#103), Santa's Boot (#233), Station Wagon (#378), and Uncle Sam's Hat (#168). Others are possible.

Papier-mache and composition candy containers were made primarily in Germany, often for a particular holiday. They can be very detailed, and some of the larger ones are very expensive.

Our values are given for glass candy containers that are undamaged, in good original paint, and complete (with all original parts and closure). Repaired or repainted containers are worth much less. Papier-mache and composition are seldom found in mint condition, and we have tried to give a condition code or description in each listing.

See also Christmas, Easter, Halloween.

Acorn, #221 ....$600.00
Amos & Andy, G paint, #77 ....$450.00
Barney Google on Pedestal, #78................................$220.00
Basket, flower design, #224 ....$35.00
Battleship, #337..$25.00
Bear Sitting, #454 ....$175.00
Bottle, Baby Dear, #64...$10.00
Bus, Rapid Transit; G paint, #345 ....$550.00
Candlestick, #201 ....$300.00
Candy Cane, Mercury Glass; #613 ....$80.00
Car, Coupe, Long Hood #1, #357 ....$150.00
Car, Limousine, 4-door, G paint, #348.......................$600.00

Charlie Chaplin, Smith, G paint, #348 ....$450.00
Chicken in Sagging Basket, #8...................................$65.00
Clock, Mantel; closure, paper face, NM paint, #116......$140.00
Coal Car on Tender, original wheels, #396................$300.00
Defense Field Gun, original gun, #142....................$300.00
Dirigible, Los Angeles; #322.................................$175.00
Dog, Mutt, #20..$50.00
Dog w/Top Hat, #480...$25.00
Don't Park Here, #314...$185.00
Fairy Pups, #23..$60.00
Fire Engine, Little Boiler, #383.............................$75.00
Flatiron, closure, original paint, #249 ....$400.00
Gas Pump, #316..$225.00
Horn, 3-valve, w/mouthpiece, #281............................$175.00
Hot Doggie, clear, w/paint, #14..............................$450.00
House, closure, original paint, #75..........................$150.00
Jackie Coogan, G paint, #90..................................$115.00
Kiddies' Band, complete, #277................................$200.00
Lamp, Hobnail; w/shade, #209.................................$250.00
Lamp, Valentine; all original, #556 ....$450.00
Lantern, Barn Type #1, #177..................................$95.00
Lantern, crossette-ribbed base, #198.........................$15.00
Lantern, glass reflector, #185...............................$18.00
Lantern, oval panels, #570...................................$30.00
Little Express, #405...$625.00
Locomotive, double square windows, original closure, #414..$125.00
Locomotive, Little Gem, #587.................................$625.00
Lucky Lindy Candy Air Mail, #666.............................$250.00
Lynn Doll Nurser, #72..$28.00
Maud Muller Milk Carrier, #69 ....$175.00
Mounted Policeman, closure, original paint, #551 .$1,800.00
Mug, Child's Tumbler, closure, #256 ....$200.00
Naked Child, Victory Glass, #94..............................$65.00
Opera Glass, brass frame, #260 ....$125.00
Piano, w/paint, #289...$225.00
Play Nursing Set, complete, #259 ....$130.00
Pocket Watch, 'Jeannette' on paper face, #457.........$450.00
Rabbit Family, original paint, #43...........................$750.00
Rabbit in Egg Shell, gold paint, #48.........................$75.00
Rabbit Running on Log, gold paint, #42.......................$200.00
Refrigerator, Victory Glass Co, #266.......................$1,800.00
Rocking Horse #1, #58 ....$350.00
Rooster Crowing, original paint, #56.........................$225.00

Taxi, 12-Vent, #366..$95.00

Telephone, large glass receiver, blue glass, #580........$85.00
Telephone, Victory Glass #1, #298 ....$200.00
Valise, #220...$450.00
Wagon or Stagecoach, #441....................................$125.00
Watch, complete w/fob, #122..................................$375.00
Watch, no fob, #122..$200.00
Wheelbarrow, closure, #273...................................$85.00
Windmill, shaker top, original blades, #445..............$250.00

Papier-mache

Chef on egg, 5", painted composition, Germany, EX..$250.00
Fish, 7½", painted papier-mache, glass eyes, Germany, VG...$235.00
George Washington on stump, 4½", metal axe, EX...$285.00
Irish girl, 4", flesh face, green hat, scarf & shoes.......$110.00
Pug dog, standing, 3½", standing, painted composition, glass eyes, long, VG.......................................$260.00
Rabbit, 12", fur covering, in twig cart w/nests of carrots, Germany...$1,800.00
Rabbit, 16", glass eyes, minor repaint, Germany, 1900 .$250.00
Rabbit, 5", seated, w/glasses, painted composition, repaint, Germany..$395.00
Turkey, 6½", composition, hair wattle, head lifts off, Germany..$175.00

Canes

If you want to collect canes, your collection could certainly be diversified. There are canes that are simple and primitive, while others have hidden compartments that house a collapsible umbrella, a portable bar, or even a weapon. Some had complicated patented mechanisms of one sort or another.

Materials used in cane-making are just as varied. Glassblowers made canes that were carried in parades and proudly displayed as evidence of their artistic abilities. Natural formations of tree branches and roots, precious metals, and man-made compositions were also used.

Ash wood, 35", man's head carved on walnut handle, black paint, 1900...$250.00
Birch, 35½" w/intarsia floral inlay handle $60.00
Celluloid heads of three bears entwined on handle, rosewood shaft..$200.00
Cholla cactus, 36", overall natural piercing, root-end handle..$45.00
Ebony shaft, horn tip, 8", horn handle, 36½"............$200.00
Glass, 32", cranberry cased w/clear, swirled interior ribbing..$150.00
Glass, 33", honey amber spirals, rope swirls at base.$145.00
Glass, 36", blue & brownish-amber central core, twisted, EX..$200.00
Glass, 42", blue & black spiral twist, mushroom knob, baton style...$400.00
Glass, 44", blue & brown swirls...............................$80.00
Glass, 44", red, white & blue spiral threading $115.00

Glass, 52", aquamarine w/gold mica, baton tip.........**$195.00**

Hickory, 36", w/silver boar's head handle final, horn tip **$125.00**

Horn w/amber inserts, 36", steel core **$100.00**

Ivory dog's head handle, glass eyes, sterling mask, bamboo shaft **$850.00**

Japanese bamboo, painted fans, stained root end w/band motif..**$60.00**

Leather disks on steel rod, 35", steel tip, horn handle ..**$90.00**

Picnic type, 34", four parts for utensils & flask, metal tip **$250.00**

Pussy willow, 37½", 1½" sterling-capped handle........**$65.00**

Rhinocerous hide, 35", shaped & varnished, solid w/bent handle...**$125.00**

Rosewood, 36", w/gold-filled bands, horn tip & handle **$300.00**

Rosewood w/cat's eye handle, sterling ferrule w/crown bezel **$275.00**

Tortoise Veneer, 33", braided silver knob.................**$250.00**

Whalebone, 34", turned whale ivory knob, EX **$225.00**

Whalebone, 36", ebony separator, turned ivory knob handle, EX **$300.00**

Wood, 32", long ivory handle w/ebony & ivory separators..**$100.00**

Wood, 36", rope-carved shaft, turk's head knot handle, EX **$165.00**

Cape Cod

You can't walk through any flea market or mall now without seeing tables of this ruby red glassware. It has been issued by Avon since the seventies, the small cruet and tall candlesticks, for instance, filled originally with one or the other of their fragrances, the wine and water goblets filled with scented candlewax, and the dessert bowl with guest soap. Many 'campaigns' since then have featured accessory tableware items such as plates, cake stands, and a water pitcher, and obviously it has been a very good seller for them, judging from the sheer volume of it around and the fact that they still feature some pieces in their catalogs.

I've found some nice pieces at garage sales, so I've bought it with an eye to the future, since it was so cheap. The dealers I've talked with about it tell me that it moves sporadically. I expect it to come into its own. The glassware is of good quality, there's a nice assortment of items in the line, and it's readily available. Even at mall prices, it's not expensive. That's about all it takes to make a collectible.

Bell, 6½", marked 'Christmas 1979' on bottom **$18.00**

Bowl, dessert...**$7.50**

Bowl, serving; 8¾" dia..**$14.00**

Bowl, soup; 1½ x7½" dia...**$12.50**

Butter dish, 7" long, holds ¼-lb stick, w/lid.................**$17.50**

Cake plate, 3½ x10¾" dia **$30.00**

Candle holder, hurricane type w/clear straight-sided chimney **$20.00**

Candle holder, 3¾" dia, squat form, each **$6.00**

Creamer, 4", footed **$7.50**

Cruet, 5-oz...**$10.00**

Cup, 3¼" **$7.00**

Decanter, 10½-oz, w/stopper **$15.00**

Dessert server, 8", wedge-shaped stainless steel w/red plastic handle..**$12.00**

Goblet, champagne; 5¼" **$12.50**

Goblet, water...**$10.00**

Goblet, wine (illustrated) **$6.00**

Mug, 5", w/pedestal foot **$10.00**

Napkin rings, set of 4 ....**$20.00**

Pitcher, water; 8¼", w/foot..**$30.00**

Plate, dessert...**$5.00**

Plate, dinner; 11" **$15.00**

Platter, 10¾x13½"...**$20.00**

Saucer, 3¼" **$3.00**

Shaker, may or may not be dated 'May 1978' on bottom, each...**$6.00**

Sugar bowl, 3½", footed **$7.50**

Tumbler, 3¾", footed **$7.00**

Tumbler, 5½", straight sided...**$8.50**

Vase, 8", footed..**$15.00**

Cardinal China Company

This was the name of a distributing company who had their merchandise made to order and sold it through a chain of showrooms and outlet stores in several states from the late 1940s through the 1950s. (Although they made some of their own pottery very early on, we have yet to find out just what they themselves produced.) They used their company name to mark cookie jars (some were made by the American Bisque Company), novelty wares, and kitchen items, many of which you'll see as you make your flea market rounds. Their primary colors were yellow and green, and their spoon holders came complete with colorful plastic measuring spoons.

The Collector's Encyclopedia of Cookie Jars by Joyce and Fred Roerig shows a page of their jars.

Cookie jar, Castle, #307 ....$75.00
Cookie jar, French Chef, #305...................................$95.00
Cookie jar, Little Girl, #301 ....$85.00
Cookie jar, Safe $65.00

Measuring boy, holds plastic cup & measuring spoons $18.50
Salt & pepper shakers, Chinese couple figurals, pr.....$18.00
Salt & pepper shakers, Chinese couple, pr (illustrated) $22.00
Scissors holder, nest w/chicken figural $25.00
Spoon holder, flowerpot form w/basketweave base...$12.00
Spoon rest, 4-petaled flower form $4.00
Spoon rest, sunflower form (illustrated) $10.00
Sprinkler bottle, Chinaman figural...............................$22.50
String holder, chicken figural $25.00

Carnival Chalkware

From about 1910 until the fifties, winners of carnival games everywhere in the United States were awarded chalkware figures of Kewpie dolls, the Lone Ranger, or any one of a vast assortment of animals and birds. The earliest were made of plaster with a pink cast. They ranged in size from about 5" up to 16".

They were easily chipped, so when it came time for the carnival to pick up and move on, they had to be carefully wrapped and packed away, a time consuming, tedious chore. When stuffed animals became available, concessionists found that they could simply throw them into a box without fear of damage, and so ended an era.

Today, the most valuable of these statues are those modeled after Disney characters, movie stars, and comic book heroes.

Chalkware figures are featured in the book *The Carnival Chalk Prize* written by Thomas G. Morris, who has also included a fascinating history of carnival life in America.

Bell Hop, 13", figure w/hand to pill-box cap, curly hair, C June Yates Jenkins Nov 21, 1946, M.....................$25.00
Captain Marvel, 14½", man in cape, no mark, ca 1940-1950, M...$45.00
Christ on the Cross, 13", two praying angel figures at foot of cross, unmarked, 1940s, M....................................$25.00

Hula Girl, 12½", topless girl w/removable grass skirt, hands to hair, no mark, 1940-50, M................................$30.00
I Love Me Girl, 11¼", hand painted, pink chalk w/mohair wig, ca 1915-1930, M...$75.00
Indian Boy, 8½", boy in full headdress w/arms folded, unmarked, 1935-45, M...$15.00
Lone Ranger, 14½", bow-legged figure in cowboy hat, ca 1938-50, M..$40.00
Mae West, 13", curvy lady in strapless gown, copyrighted JY Jenkins on November 22, 1934, M........................$65.00
Maggie, 9½", lady w/arms folded, tight bun hairdo, King Features Syndicate, ca 1920-35, M........................$75.00
Majorette, 12", girl w/short ruffled skirt & marching boots, marked El Segundo Novelty Co, 1949, M.............$25.00
Mexican Girl, 14½", girl in Mexican-style clothes & sombrero, hand painted, copyrighted JY Jenkins, July 27, 1925, M $85.00
Mickey Mouse, 8½", early-style face, hands in back, unmarked, ca 1930-35, M.......................................$75.00
Pekingese Dog, 7¼x10½", tail over back, no marks, 1935-45, M $20.00
Pinocchio, 13½", large bow tie, no copyright mark, ca 1940s, M..$35.00
Popeye, 13½", one arm across chest, wooden pipe, King Features Syndicate, original artist: EC Segal, 1929-50, M $65.00
Reclining Nude, 5½", marked Rosemead Statuary Co, 1955, M $20.00
Ruth, 15", lady w/scarf around hair, wearing bloomers, copyrighted by Jenkins, May 26, 1924, M..........$120.00
Sitting Kewpie, 6", hand painted, pink chalk, w/or w/out mohair wig, ca 1915-1930, M $45.00

Superman, 16", glitter trim, no marks $125.00

Carnival Glass

From 1905 until late in the twenties, many companies (Northwood, Fenton, Imperial, Millersburg, Dugan, and others) produced huge quantities of this type of press-molded iridescent glassware. Because it was so inexpensive, lots of it was given away at carnivals, and that's where it got its name. Even today you're apt to find a piece stuck away in Grandma's cabinet or at a tag sale, so we want you to be at least a little familiar with it. It's been widely reproduced over the past twenty-five years, and even the new glass is collectible. A few of the companies that have reproduced it are Indiana Glass, Westmoreland, and Imperial. Just be sure you know what you're buying. It's one thing to buy 'new' glass if you like it, but if you have your heart set on the genuine article, you certainly don't want to make mistakes.

To educate yourself so that this doesn't happen, attend antique shows, go to the better shops in your area, and get to know reputable dealers. Read and study *The Standard Encyclopedia of Carnival Glass* by Bill Edwards. You'll soon find yourself confident and able to recognize both old carnival glass as well as the newer reproductions.

See also Indiana Carnival, Westmoreland, Imperial.

African Shield (English), toothpick holder, marigold ..**$45.00**
Apple & Pear Intaglio (Northwood), bowl, marigold, 10"..**$75.00**
Apple Panels (English), creamer, green **$36.00**
Arcs (Imperial), bowl, green, 8½" **$45.00**
Art Deco (English), bowl, marigold, 4" **$32.00**
Astral, lamp shade, marigold..**$45.00**
Austrian Swan (Crystal), bowl, amethyst, 9" **$100.00**
Banded Panels (Crystal), sugar bowl, amethyst..........**$45.00**
Banded Portland (US Glass), puff jar, marigold...........**$60.00**
Banded Rib, tumbler, marigold....................................**$20.00**
Beaded, hatpin, amethyst..**$24.00**
Beaded Panels (Imperial), bowl, marigold, 8" **$40.00**
Beaded Swirl (English), compote, marigold.................**$45.00**
Bells & Beads (Dugan), bowl, blue, 7½"......................**$55.00**
Big Basketweave (Dugan), basket, amethyst, small **$40.00**
Bird w/Grapes, (Cockatoo), wall vase, marigold.........**$64.00**
Blackberry (Northwood), bowl, marigold, footed, 9"..**$47.00**
Blackberry Bramble (Fenton), compote, amethyst **$60.00**
Blossoms & Band (Imperial), bowl, amethyst, 10" **$42.00**
Bow & English Hob (English), nut bowl, blue **$55.00**
Broken Arches (Imperial), punch cup, marigold.........**$25.00**
Bubbles, hatpin, amethyst..**$36.00**
Bumblebees, hatpin, amethyst.....................................**$26.00**
Butterfly, pin tray, marigold **$35.00**
Butterfly & Berry (Fenton), bowl, amethyst, footed, 5"...**$40.00**
Butterfly & Tulip, bowl, marigold, footed, 10½"........**$475.00**
Cane (Imperial), pickle dish, marigold.......................**$25.00**
Captive Rose (Fenton), bowl, marigold, 10" **$37.00**
Carnival Honeycomb (Imperial), bowl, marigold, handled, 6"..**$30.00**
Cattails, hatpin, amethyst..**$26.00**
Checkers, bowl, marigold, 9" **$32.00**
Cherry & Cable Intaglio (Northwood), bowl, marigold, 10" **$36.00**

Cherry Blossoms, tumbler, blue...................................**$28.00**
Chippendale Souvenir, sugar bowl, amethyst............**$80.00**
Circle Scroll (Dugan), bowl, marigold, 5"...................**$40.00**
Cobblestones (Dugan), bowl, marigold, 5" **$38.00**
Columbia (Imperial), vase, green.................................**$45.00**
Corinth (Westmoreland), bowl, teal **$60.00**
Crackle (Imperial), punch cup, green **$16.00**
Crackle (Imperial), spittoon, marigold, large **$38.00**
Cut Arcs (Fenton), vase whimsey, white **$70.00**
Dahlia (Dugan), bowl, marigold, footed, 5"................**$40.00**
Daist & Plume (Northwood), candy dish, amethyst **$55.00**
Daisy in Oval Panels (US Glass), sugar bowl, marigold.**$50.00**
Diamond & Daisy Cut (US Glass), compote, amethyst .**$60.00**
Diamond & File, bowl, marigold, 7".............................**$35.00**
Diamond & Rib (Fenton), vase, blue, 12" **$32.00**
Diamond & Sunburst (Imperial), bowl, amber, 8".......**$55.00**
Diamond Checkerboard, bowl, marigold, 9"................**$35.00**
Diamond Checkerboard, cracker jar, marigold............**$75.00**
Diamond Flutes (US Glass), creamer, marigold...........**$35.00**
Diamond Lace (Imperial), bowl, amethyst, 10"...........**$65.00**
Diamond Ovals (English), compote, marigold.............**$35.00**
Diamond Point Columns (Imperial), bowl, marigold, 4½"..**$20.00**
Diamond Prisms (English), compote, marigold **$45.00**
Diamond Star, vase, marigold, 8"..................................**$60.00**
Diamond Top (English), creamer, marigold.................**$32.00**
Dogwood Sprays (Dugan), bowl, amethyst, 9"............**$50.00**
Dots & Curves, hatpin, amethyst **$42.00**
Dotted Daisies, plate, marigold, 8" **$65.00**
Double Dolphins (Fenton), bowl, pastel, flat, 10" **$60.00**
Drape & Tassel, lamp shade, white...............................**$40.00**
Dutch Mill, plate, marigold, 8" **$35.00**
Dutch Twins, ash tray, marigold...................................**$45.00**
English Hob & Button (English), bowl, green, 10" **$90.00**
Engraved Grapes (Fenton), pitcher, marigold, tall.......**$85.00**
Estate (Westmoreland), mug, marigold, rare................**$85.00**
Fanciful (Dugan), bowl, pastel, 8½" **$60.00**
Fashion (Imperial), fruit bowl, green, w/base **$85.00**
Fashion (Imperial), punch cup, amethyst....................**$35.00**
Feather Stitch (Fenton), bowl, blue, 8½" **$60.00**
Feathered Arrow (English), bowl, marigold, 8½".........**$40.00**
Feathers (Northwood), vase, marigold, 12"..................**$28.00**
Fentonia, bowl, green, footed, 5" **$42.00**
Fern (Northwood), bowl, marigold, 6½".......................**$46.00**
Field Thistle (US Glass), bowl, marigold, 6" **$45.00**
File (Imperial & English), bowl, marigold, 5" **$30.00**
Fine Cut & Roses (Northwood), candy dish, amethyst, footed..**$60.00**
Fine Cut Rings (English), bowl, marigold, oval **$40.00**
Fishscale & Beads (Dugan), plate, marigold, 7"..........**$40.00**
Flared Wide Panel, atomizer, marigold, 3½"...............**$90.00**
Flora (English), float bowl, blue **$75.00**
Floral, hatpin, amber **$50.00**
Floral & Grape (Dugan), hat, marigold **$35.00**
Floral & Wheat (US Glass), bonbon, amethyst, stem...**$45.00**
Flower & Beads, plate, amethyst, 6-sided, 7½".........**$110.00**
Flower & Frames (Dugan), bowl, pastel, 8" **$95.00**
Flute (Northwood), bowl, amethyst, 5" **$26.00**

Footed Drape (Westmoreland), vase, marigold $40.00
Four Flowers, bowl, blue, 6¼" $65.00
French Knots (Fenton), hat, peach opalescent $42.00
Frosted Ribbon, pitcher, marigold $80.00
Fruit Lustre, tumbler, marigold.................................$38.00
Gambier (Crystal), mug, marigold $45.00
Garden Path (Dugan), bowl, fruit; amethyst, 10".........$95.00
Garland (Fenton), rose bowl, marigold, footed $45.00
Golden Flowers, vase, marigold, 7½" $48.00
Golden Oxen, mug, marigold $48.00
Grape (Imperial), wine, green $35.00
Grape & Gothic Arches (Northwood), creamer, blue..$80.00
Grape Leaves (Northwood), bowl, marigold, 8¾" $60.00
Greek Key (Northwood), bowl, amethyst, 8½"...........$90.00
Hawaiian Lei (Higbee), sugar bowl, marigold $65.00
Headdress, compote, blue.......................................$46.00
Heavy Diamond (Imperial), bowl, marigold, 10"........$32.00
Heisey Flute, punch cup, marigold...........................$28.00
Hexagon & Cane (Imperial), sugar bowl, marigold,
     w/lid $65.00
Hobstar (Imperial), berry bowl, marigold, 10"............$35.00
Hobstar & Arches (Imperial), bowl, smoke, 9" $52.00
Holly (Fenton), hat, green.......................................$38.00
Horseshoe, shot glass, marigold $42.00
Intaglio Daisy (English), bowl, marigold, 4½".............$26.00
Intaglio Feathers, cup, marigold $25.00
Interior Rays, sherbet, marigold...............................$35.00
Interior Swirl, spittoon, peach opalescent...................$95.00
Inverted Strawberry, bowl, amethyst, 5"....................$50.00
Jacobean Ranger (Czech & English), wine, marigold ..$28.00
Knotted Beads (Fenton), vase, green, 4"....................$40.00
Lattice & Points, vase, amethyst...............................$42.00
Leaf Rays (Dugan), nappy, marigold.........................$28.00

Melon Rib (Imperial), tumbler, marigold....................$24.00
Nuggate, pitcher, blue, 6"..$90.00
Optic Flute (Imperial), bowl, smoke, 5"......................$28.00
Optic Tree (Fenton), cup, marigold............................$28.00
Peach (Northwood), bowl, white, 5"..........................$60.00
Peach Blossom, bowl, amethyst, 7½".........................$70.00
Peacock & Urn (Fenton), goblet, marigold, rare.........$60.00
Peacock at the Fountain (Northwood), cup, blue $40.00
Peacock Tail (Fenton), bonbon, green.....................$40.00
Persian Medallion (Fenton), compote, amethyst.........$57.00
Pineapple (English), compote, blue $52.00
Question Marks (Dugan), bonbon, ice green $75.00
Rambler Rose (Dugan), tumbler, marigold.................$30.00
Rib & Panel (Fenton), vase, marigold........................$45.00
Rose Bouquet, creamer, marigold.............................$54.00
Rosetime, vase, marigold...$85.00
Rosettes (Northwood), bowl, marigold, dome base, 9".$58.00
S-Band (Australian), compote, amethyst $65.00
S-Repeat (Dugan), creamer, amethyst, small............$60.00
Salamanders, hatpin, amethyst................................$45.00
Scale Band (Fenton), tumbler, blue...........................$35.00
Scales (Westmoreland), bonbon, teal $60.00
Scroll Embossed Variant (English), ash tray, amethyst, han-
     dled, 5" $60.00
Seco Lily, vase, marigold, bulbous............................$85.00
Serrated Ribs, salt & pepper shakers, marigold, pr ...$100.00
Signet, (English), sugar bowl, marigold, w/lid, 6½" $70.00
Singing Birds (Northwood), creamer, marigold..........$80.00
Single Flower (Dugan), bowl, blue, 8" $70.00
Small Rib (Dugan), compote, green $40.00
Smooth Panels (Imperial), bowl, pastel marigold, 6" ..$35.00
Smooth Rays (Imperial), bonbon, marigold...............$26.00
Soda Gold Spears (Dugan), bowl, clear, 8½".............$40.00
Spiderweb (Northwood), candy dish, smoke, w/lid....$35.00
Spiral (Imperial), candlestick, green $75.00
Star & File (Imperial), decanter, marigold, w/stopper.$110.00
Star Medallion (Imperial), butter dish, marigold........$100.00
Star Spray (Imperial), bowl, pastel, 7" $30.00
Stars & Bars, wine, marigold....................................$40.00
Stippled Rambler Rose (Dugan), nut bowl, blue,
     footed..$75.00
Strutting Peacock (Westmoreland), creamer, green,
     w/lid $60.00
Three-In-One (Imperial), plate, smoke, 6½" $80.00
Tree of Life (Imperial), plate, marigold, 7½"...............$37.00
US Diamond Block (US Glass), compote, peach opalescent,
     rare...$75.00
War Dance (English), compote, marigold, 5"..............$75.00
Water Lily & Cattails (Fenton), tumbler, marigold.......$95.00
Wild Strawberry (Dugan), bowl, marigold..................$85.00
Wreath of Roses (Fenton), bonbon, marigold.............$36.00
Zip Zip (English), flower frog, marigold $54.00

Lion (Fenton), bowl, marigold, 7" $85.00
Lotus & Grape (Fenton), bowl, green, flat, 7".............$50.00
Luster, tumbler, marigold $40.00
Maple Leaf (Dugan), sugar bowl, green.....................$70.00
Mayflower, compote, pastel $60.00

Cat Collectibles

I have no doubt that every cat-lover in America is in some small way a 'cat' collector. More than any other species, cats have enjoyed tremendous popularity over the years. They were revered in Ancient Egypt and the Orient, and from Biblical times up to the present day they have been modeled in marble, bronze, pottery, and porcelain. They have been immortalized in paintings and prints and used extensively in advertising.

There are several 'cat' books available on today's market, if you want to see great photos of some of the various aspects of 'cat' collecting, you'll enjoy reading *Collectible Cats, An Identification & Value Guide,* by Marbena Fyke.

Advertising card, Mason & Hamlin Organ Co, girl, cat, dog, & doll at piano **$9.00**
Animal dish, cat on lacy base, milk glass, marked Westmoreland **$95.00**
Animal dish, 5", cat on hamper, white agate, marked Greentown..**$400.00**
Ash receiver, upright figure of a cat, howling, pink glaze, unmarked Red Wing...**$60.00**
Bank, 5", seated cat w/bow, pot metal **$50.00**
Book, 'Big Book of Cats,' Grosset & Dunlap Publishing, 1954, VG **$12.00**
Candy container, 3", pressed paper figure of a cat, 1930s, EX **$115.00**
Carnival chalkware, 12", tall slim stylized figure of a cat, unmarked **$15.00**
Cologne bottle, seated cat, milk glass w/blue flower & ribbon bow, marked Avon.......................................**$10.00**
Cookie jar, cat wearing overalls, marked Enesco, M...**$36.00**
Cookie jar, cat wearing hat, marked Taiwan **$35.00**
Creamer, 5", seated cat, marked Royal Bayreuth.......**$150.00**
Doorstop, seated cat, old black & white repainted cast iron, 9½" **$85.00**
Doorstop, 7½x8", sleeping cat, worn painted cast iron, marked Hubley **$250.00**
Earrings, figure of a cat, Catalin, pr **$30.00**
Figurine, Figaro, marked Brayton Laguna.................**$175.00**
Figurine, 2½", kitten, marked K-12 & Royal Doulton....**$95.00**
Figurine, 4½", seated w/slanted aqua jeweled eyes, marked 'C' in circle, USA...**$4.00**
Figurine, 5¼", standing w/slanted aqua jeweled eyes & pink collar, marked #107...**$6.00**
Figurine, 7x16" long, recumbent panther-like body, shiny green glaze, marked Gonder **$200.00**
Figurine, 8¾", seated, white w/bow & pink rose, marked Cordey..**$200.00**
Handkerchief, 14x14", Chessie shown in center & all corners **$35.00**
Lamp, TV; 11½", seated twin Siamese, marked Lane & Co on bulb recess **$45.00**
Mug, 2¾", cats at play, multicolored transfer on porcelain, unmarked, ca 1890s..................................**$60.00**
Nutcracker, 4½", nickel-plated brass figure of a cat **$45.00**
Pin, figure of a cat, w/danglers, 1-color Catalin **$95.00**
Pin, small figure of a cat, Catalin, resin wash w/glass eye **$60.00**
Planter, 8", black cat w/pink bow tie, marked Royal Copley **$28.00**

Post card, 'A Merry Halloween,' girl w/black cat on black, by Clapsaddle, VG **$28.00**
Post card, 'No Ma'am We Ain't Seen Your Birdie,' three seated kittens w/upturned eyes, by Grace Wiederseim **$15.00**
Shakers, Siamese cats wearing bows, bisque, marked Napco, pr..**$10.00**
String holder, ceramic cat face....................................**$18.00**

Tea set, Siamese mother as upright pot, kittens as covered sugar bowl and creamer, red bow ties, marked Japan..$65.00
Toy, 4", standing Tabby, stuffed mohair w/button marked Steiff..**$60.00**
Whimsey, Cat 'n the Fiddle, Red Rose Tea, Wade, 1971-79 ....**$15.00**

Cat-Tail Dinnerware

Cat-Tail was a dinnerware pattern popular during the late twenties until sometime in the forties. So popular, in fact, that ovenware, glassware, tinware, even a breakfast table set was made to coordinate with it. The dinnerware was made primarily by Universal Potteries of Cambridge, Ohio, though even a catalog from Hall China circa 1927 shows a 3-piece coffee service, and there may have been others. It was sold for years by Sears Roebuck and Company, and some items bear a mark with their name.

The pattern is unmistakable: a cluster of red cattails (usually six, sometimes one or two) with black stems on creamy white. Shapes certainly vary; Universal used a minimum of three of their standard mold designs, possibly more. If you're trying to decorate a forties vintage kitchen, no other design could afford you more to work with. To see many of the pieces that are available and to learn more about the line, read *The Collector's Encyclopedia of American Dinnerware* by Jo Cunningham.

Bowl, 5¼" **$2.75**
Bowl, 6", on Old Holland shape **$6.00**
Bowl, 8½" **$8.00**
Butter dish, 1-lb, w/lid...**$40.00**
Cake server...**$25.00**
Casserole, 8¼", w/lid **$22.00**

Cup & saucer...$12.00
Custard, individual $5.50
Jug, refrigerator; w/angular handle & stopper............$25.00
Pitcher, milk $20.00
Pitcher, red & black on clear glass, w/ice lip $95.00
Plate, dinner; on Laurella shape, marked Universal Potteries..$10.00
Plate, serving; on Laurella shape, marked Universal Potteries..$30.00
Plate, 6"..$2.50
Plate, 9"..$5.00
Platter, 11½" $12.00
Saucer, on Old Holland shape, marked Wheelock........$4.00
Scales, kitchen; decal on white-painted metal, small ..$35.00
Sugar bowl, handled..$6.00
Tablecloth, NM..$75.00
Teapot, on Laurella shape, w/lid $27.00
Tray, utility; 11½" $15.00
Tumbler, iced tea; red & black graphics on clear glass $30.00
Tumbler, marked Universal, scarce $37.00

Catalin Napkin Rings

Plastic (Catalin) napkin rings topped with heads of cartoon characters, animals, and birds are very collectible, especially examples in red and orange; blue is also good, and other colors can be found as well.

Angelfish...$25.00
Band, 2", plain, amber, red, or green, each $5.00
Camel, w/inlaid eye..$66.00
Chicken or bird $15.00
Cottontail rabbit $20.00
Donald Duck, w/decal $58.00
Elephant, w/ball on head $30.00
Elephant #1 ....$23.00
Mickey Mouse $55.00
Penguin...$40.00

Popeye $85.00
Rocking horse $40.00
Schnauzer dog...$20.00

Scotty dog...$18.00

Catalina Island

Located on the island of the same name some twenty-five miles off the Los Angeles coastline, this pottery operated for only ten years after it was founded in 1927. The island was owned by William Wrigley, Jr. (the chewing gum tycoon) who with his partner David Renton established the pottery with the purpose in mind of providing year-round employment for residents while at the same time manufacturing brick and tile to use in the island's development. Using the native red clay, they went on to produce garden ware, vases, decorative accessories, and eventually dinnerware. They made a line of hand-painted plates featuring island motifs such as birds, flying fish, and Spanish galleons that are today highly collectible. They developed some remarkable glazes using only oxides available on the island. Even though the red clay proved to be brittle and easily chipped, at Mr. Wriggley's insistence, they continued to use it until after he died in 1932. To make a better product, they began importing a tougher white-burning clay from the mainland; ironically the added expense was a major contributing factor to their downfall. In 1937 the company was sold to Gladding McBean.

Various types of marks were used over the years, but without enough consistency to indicate a production date. Marks are 'Catalina' or 'Catalina Island.' Paper labels were also used. Pieces marked 'Catalina Pottery' were produced by Gladding McBean.

If you'd like to learn more about this pottery, refer to *The Collector's Encyclopedia of California Pottery* by Jack Chipman.

Ashtray, 3¼x5½", standing polar bear, Monterey brown glaze $275.00
Ashtray, 4", goat figural $200.00
Bookend, 5x4", kneeling monk figural, Descanso green glaze, ca 1932..$300.00
Candleabra, 5x10½", modeled as two seals $300.00
Catalina Island, cup & saucer.......................................$45.00
Catalina Island, pitcher, Toyon red, cylindrical body, ice lip...$150.00
Catalina Island, plate, dinner; 10", solid color, plain w/wide flat rim $35.00
Catalina Island, plate, salad; 7½"................................$25.00
Catalina Island, plate, 11¼", coupe shape...................$35.00
Catalina Island, punch cup...$20.00
Plate, decorative; 10½", underwater scene................$300.00
Plate, decorative; 11", geometric abstract Moorish design, blue, white, rust & black colors, ca 1932...........$300.00
Plate, decorative; 11½", Old Mexico, hand-painted wagon against sunset landscape, impressed mark, ca 1932..$500.00
Plate, decorative; 14", Submarine Garden, as underwater porthole scenic view, impressed mark...............$600.00
Rope Edge, saucer $10.00

Rope Edge, sugar bowl, w/lid......................................**$35.00**
Tea tile, 6x6", solid medium blue, incised Mayan or Inca-type design, early 1930s...........................**$175.00**
Tray, 11¼" dia, turquoise, rolled edge......................**$100.00**
Vase, 8½", solid blue, plain artware style, stepped side handles, early 1930s..................................**$300.00**
Wall pocket, seashell form, turquoise, incised mark...**$150.00**

Catalogs

Catalogs from before 1950 are collectible in their own right, but from a standpoint of the information they contain, collectors from many fields find them a wonderful source for research. Several factors contribute to the value of old catalogs: age, condition, extent of the illustrations they contain (and the amount of color used), the commodity they deal with (and how collectible it is today), and how large it is. Manufacturer's catalogs are more valuable than those put out by a jobber.

Badges, loose cover, 1925, 44 pages, VG...................**$50.00**
Arthur Honen, dolls & toys, 1950, 172 pages, EX........**$35.00**
Bass Still Camera, 1939, 72 pages, EX **$6.00**
Corn King Manure Spreader, 1905, 24 pages, G..........**$15.00**
Crown Overalls, 1927, 32 pages, 4x9" **$20.00**
Disston Saws, Tools, Files, 1924, 48 pages..................**$13.00**
Elliot Co, surveying & drafting materials, 1948, 393 pages, VG...**$25.00**
Frederick Herrschner Lingerie, 1920, 24 pages, VG **$12.00**
Gimson & Coltman Hosiery Machinery, 1880, 16 pages, VG...**$19.00**
Glass & Mirrors by National Glass Association, 1942, 32 pages...**$17.50**
Gummey, McFarland Tinners' Supplies, 1913, 156 pages, VG...**$19.00**
Hallicrafters Radios, 1944-45, 31 pages, EX..................**$8.00**
Heaney Magical Goods, 1924, 96 pages, G...................**$20.00**
Hub Cycles, 1919, 68 pages **$55.00**
Jenkins Band Instruments, 1912, 196 pages, EX..........**$90.00**
Kodak Cameras, 1911, 64 pages, 5½x8", EX................**$40.00**
Krauss Cultivators, 1911, 63 pages, EX........................**$28.00**
Lionel Trains, 1947, 32 pages, EX................................**$35.00**
Lyons Ejector Cigarette Cases, 1930, 3 pages **$8.00**
Mickey Mouse Merchandise, 1939, 98 pages, VG......**$185.00**
Milton Bradley Games & Toys, 1950, 52 pages, VG **$8.00**
Montgomery Ward, 1914, 648 pages, EX.......................**$25.00**
Montgomery Ward, Plumbing, 1920s, 11x8½" **$38.00**
Myers Pump & Water Systems, 1932, EX......................**$12.00**
Oklahoma City Hardware, 1938, 810 pages, EX **$60.00**
Olson Rugs, 1931, 51 pages, VG..................................**$11.00**
Ranger Bicycles, 1918, 64 pages, EX **$70.00**
Ringen Stoves, steel & iron ranges, 1905, 56 pages, EX..**$25.00**
Sears Roebuck Sporting Goods, 1908, EX....................**$50.00**
Snap-On Tools, 1934, EX..**$40.00**
Sunray Gas Stoves, 1915, 48 pages, 7x10", EX............**$25.00**
Terrestrial Telescopes & Accessories, 1892, 25 pages .**$50.00**

Thompson Boats, 1937, 32 pages, EX **$45.00**
Trolley Car Air Brakes, 1903, 56 pages, EX.................**$40.00**
Universal Stoves & Ranges, 1927, 86 pages, EX..........**$45.00**
Wards Airline Radios, 1940, 22 pages...........................**$11.00**
Williams Hardware, 1940, 532 pages, EX.....................**$30.00**

Ceramic Arts Studios

American-made figurines are very popular now, and these are certainly among the best. They have a distinctive look you'll soon learn to identify with confidence, even if you happen to pick up an unmarked piece. They were first designed in the forties and sold well until the company closed in 1955. (After that, the new owner took the molds to Japan, where he made them for only a short time.) The company's principal designer was Betty Harrington, who modeled the figures and knicknacks that so many have grown to love. In addition to the company's mark, 'Ceramic Arts Studios, Madison Wisconsin,' many of the character pieces she designed also carry their assigned names on the bottom.

The company also produced a line of metal items to accessorize the figurines; these were designed by Liberace's mother, Zona.

Though prices continue to climb, once in awhile there's an unmarked bargain to be found, but first you must familiarize yourself with your subject! BA Wellman has compiled *The Ceramic Arts Studio Price Guide* as well as an accompanying video tape that we're sure you'll enjoy if you'd like to learn more.

Ashtray, hippo, 3½" **$36.00**
Bank, Skunky, 4"..**$68.00**
Bank, Tony, razor disposal, 4¾" **$38.00**
Bell, Lillibelle, 6½" **$60.00**
Bell, Winter Belle, 5¼"..**$52.00**
Bowl, Bonita, 3¾" **$30.00**
Bowl, shallow, rectangular or scalloped, 2¼" **$18.00**
Caddy, mountain goat, 5¼"...**$85.00**
Candle holder, angel, Hear No Evil, 5"........................**$32.00**
Figurine, Alice & white rabbit, 4½", 6", pr..................**$95.00**
Figurine, angel, stanging w/star, 5½"...........................**$26.00**
Figurine, angel w/candle, 5"..**$30.00**
Figurine, Aphrodite & Adonis, 7¾", 9", pr.................**$295.00**
Figurine, Archibald the dragon, 8"..............................**$125.00**
Figurine, Bashful, 4¾"..**$30.00**
Figurine, bunny, 1¾" **$24.00**
Figurine, child w/towel, 5"..**$55.00**
Figurine, Colonial man & lady, 6¾", 6½", pr...............**$65.00**
Figurine, Comedy & Tragedy, 10", pr.........................**$140.00**
Figurine, Cupid, 5"...**$55.00**
Figurine, dachshund, standing & laying, 3½", 2½", pr.**$42.00**
Figurine, Daisy, standing, 5¼".....................................**$45.00**
Figurine, Egyptian man & woman, 9½", pr.................**$185.00**
Figurine, Fire man & woman, 11¼", pr **$165.00**
Figurine, Flute lady, standing, 8½"...............................**$75.00**
Figurine, Frisky lamb w/garland, 2¾".........................**$12.00**

Figurine, fruit bearer, 7", & child, pr **$45.00**
Figurine, Guitar man, sitting, 6½" **$75.00**
Figurine, harem girl on stomach, 6" long **$28.00**
Figurine, Harry & Lillibeth, 6½", pr **$50.00**
Figurine, horse mother & spring colt, 4¼", 3½", pr **$65.00**
Figurine, Indian boy & girl, 3", 3¼", pr **$40.00**
Figurine, kitten w/bow, washing, white, 2" **$16.00**
Figurine, kitten washing paw, white, 2" **$16.00**
Figurine, leopards, fighting, 3½", 6¼", pr **$55.00**
Figurine, Little Jack Horner, 4½" **$25.00**
Figurine, Madonna w/Bible, 9½" **$55.00**
Figurine, Madonna w/Child, 1-pc, 6½" **$65.00**
Figurine, mermaid mother on rock, 4" **$42.00**
Figurine, Mr & Mrs Monk, 4", 3½", pr **$56.00**
Figurine, Muff & Puff, 3", pr **$42.00**
Figurine, Peter Pan & Wendy, 5¼", pr **$95.00**
Figurine, pixie girl, kneeling, 2½" **$25.00**
Figurine, Poncho & Pepita, 4½", pr **$48.00**
Figurine, Promenade man & woman, 7¾", pr **$95.00**
Figurine, red devil imp, sitting **$62.00**
Figurine, shepherd & shepherdess, 8½", 8", pr **$110.00**
Figurine, St Francis of Assisi, 7" **$42.00**
Figurine, toadstool, 3" **$16.00**
Figurine, Violin lady, standing, 8½" **$75.00**
Figurine, Winter Willy, 4" **$32.00**
Figurine, zebra, 5" **$40.00**
Figurine, Zulu man & woman #1, 5¼", 7", pr **$175.00**
Jug, Aladdin, 2" **$32.00**
Jug, Buddha, ewer form, 3½" **$28.00**
Jug, George Washington, 2¾" **$28.00**
Jug, rose motif, 2¾" **$26.00**
Lamp, Aphrodite & Adonis, rotating disk, pr **$385.00**
Lamp, Flutist on base **$165.00**
Lamp, Zorina on base **$95.00**
Planter, Lorelei on seashell, 6" **$68.00**
Planter, square flowerpot shape, 1" **$18.00**
Planter head, Barbie, 7" **$55.00**

Planter head, Svea & Sven, 6", 6½", pr **$85.00**
Plaque, Attitude & Arabesque, 9½", pr **$68.00**
Plaque, Chinese lantern man & woman, 8", pr **$75.00**
Plaque, Comedy & Tragedy masks, 5¼", pr **$60.00**
Plaque, Goosie Gander & Mary Contrary, 4½", 5", pr .**$85.00**
Plaque, Grace & Greg, 9½", 9", pr **$80.00**
Plaque, Harlequine & Columbine, 8", pr **$140.00**
Plaque, mermaid, 6" **$55.00**
Salt & pepper shakers, Black Sambo & tiger, 3½", 5" long,
   pr **$165.00**
Salt & pepper shakers, boy in chair, 2¼", pr **$42.00**
Salt & pepper shakers, Chirp & Twirp, 4", pr **$45.00**
Salt & pepper shakers, Dutch boy & girl, 4", pr **$26.00**
Salt & pepper shakers, fish, up on tails, 4", pr **$25.00**
Salt & pepper shakers, fishing boy & farm girl, 4¾", pr.**$48.00**
Salt & pepper shakers, Nip & Tuck, 4¼", 4", pr **$38.00**
Salt & pepper shakers, ox & covered wagon, 3" long,
   pr **$45.00**
Salt & pepper shakers, Paul Bunyan & evergreen tree, 4½",
   2½", pr **$48.00**
Salt & pepper shakers, Santa & tree, 2¼", 2½", pr **$38.00**
Salt & pepper shakers, snuggle bear mother & baby, brown,
   4¼", pr **$38.00**
Salt & pepper shakers, snuggle kangaroo mother & child,
   4¾", pr **$42.00**
Salt & pepper shakers, spaniel dogs (mother & puppy), 2¼",
   1¾", pr **$32.00**
Salt & pepper shakers, sultan & harem girl, 4¾", 4½",
   pr **$75.00**
Salt & pepper shakers, Suzette on pillow, 3", pr **$40.00**
Salt & pepper shakers, Willing & Lover Boy, 4¾", pr .. **$65.00**
Shelf sitter, Bali boy & girl, 5½", pr **$75.00**
Shelf sitter, Banjo girl, 4" **$38.00**
Shelf sitter, canary, left & right, 5", pr **$38.00**
Shelf sitter, Chinese boy & girl, 4", pr **$35.00**
Shelf sitter, Collie mother, 5" **$25.00**
Shelf sitter, Dutch boy & girl, 4½", pr **$35.00**
Shelf sitter, Pete & Polly, birds, 7½", pr **$62.00**
Shelf sitter, Tuffy, white cat, 5¼" **$35.00**
Vase, bud; Bamboo, no figure, 6" **$20.00**
Vase, bud; Ting-a-Ling on bamboo, 6" **$28.00**
Vase, rose motif, round, 2¼" **$20.00**

Cereal Boxes

   Yes, cereal boxes — your eyes aren't deceiving you. But think about it. Cereal boxes from even the sixties have to be extremely scarce. The ones that are bringing the big bucks today are those with a well-known character emblazoned across the front. Am I starting to make more sense to you? Good. Now, say the experts, is the time to look ahead into the future of your cereal box collection. They recommend going to your neighborhood supermarket to inspect the shelves in the cereal aisle today! Choose the ones with Batman, Quisp, Ninja Turtles, or some other nineties phenomenon. Take them home and (unless you have mice) display them unopened, or empty them out and fold them up along the seam lines. If you want only the old boxes, you'll probably have to find an old long-abandoned grocery store, or pay prices somewhere around those in our listings when one comes up for sale.

Store displays and advertising posters, in-box prizes or 'send-a-ways,' coupons with pictures of boxes, and shelf signs and cards are also part of this field of interest.

The prices given below are for mint condition boxes, either still full or folded flat.

If you want to learn more about this field of collecting, we recommend *Toys of the Sixties* by Bill Bruegman.

1935, Post Toasties, Mickey Mouse on front, Walt Disney cutouts on back $500.00
1953, General Mills Sugar Smiles $95.00
1953, Ralston Wheat Chex, Space Patrol's Captain Strong on front $400.00
1957, scale model police car prize from Post Grape Nuts Flakes...$150.00
1960, Kellogg's Corn Flakes, 1-year birthday Yogi Bear, limited edition, w/Yogi birthday comic book inside, M $500.00
1960, Kellogg's Oks, Yogi Bear on front....................$300.00
1960, Kellogg's Ok's, Yogi Bear w/'Best in Oats' slogan on front, EX $200.00

1960, Kellogg's Rice Krinkles, shows So-Hi (Oriental mascot) w/bowl of cereal & baseball trading card offer on front..$150.00
1960, Post Sugar Crisp, running Sugar Crisp Bear holds over-flowing cereal bowl, w/baseball trading cards offer on front..$60.00
1961, General Mills Frosty-O's, reclining Frosty-O's Bear balancing bowl on boot on front, EX.........................$50.00
1961, General Mills Twinkles, Elephant storybook ...$300.00
1963, Kellogg's Fruit Loops, Toucan Sam w/'OOT-fray OOPS-lay' slogan on front, EX.............................$55.00
1963, Kellogg's Sugar Smacks, Quick Draw McGraw w/game offer on front, NM.................................$200.00
1963, Quaker Cap'n Crunch, pirate ring premium advertised, NM $95.00
1964, Kellogg's Cocoa Krispies, Snagglepuss on front, cut-out classic antique car trading cards on back, NM $250.00
1964, Post Crispy Critters, shows animal-shaped cereal pieces jumping through hoop held by Linus the Lion-hearted, M $75.00

1965, Kellogg's Apple Jacks, w/black & white comic page of Apple Jacks kid fighting bullies, NM $65.00
1965, Quaker Quake, Quake (earth-digging miner mascot) on front, cereal discontinued in 1975, NM.........$300.00
1977, Cheerios, Star Wars offer $50.00
1980, General Mills Cheerios, Lone Ranger deputy kit offer on back w/'Legend of Lone Ranger' movie promotion, NM $30.00
1986, Ghostbusters, w/hologram $5.00
1987-88, Wheaties, Lakers team $28.00
1990, Corn Chex, w/Snoopy bank...................................$5.00
1990, Fruity Pebbles, w/Fred Flintstone toy..................$5.00
1991, Ralston Addams Family, figural flashlight shrink-wrapped on front...$12.00

Character and Promotional Drinking Glasses

In any household, especially those with children, I would venture to say, you should find a few of these glasses. Put out by fast-food restaurant chains or by a company promoting a product, they have for years been commonplace. But now, instead of glass, the giveaways are nearly always plastic. If a glass is offered at all, you usually pay 99¢ for it.

You can find these for small change at garage sales, and at those prices, pick up any that are still bright and unfaded. They will move well on your flea market table. Some are worth more than others. Among the common ones are Camp Snoopy, B.C. Ice Age, Garfield, McDonald's, Smurfs, and Coca-Cola. The better glasses are those with super-heroes, characters from Star Trek and thirties movies such as 'Wizard of Oz,' sports personalities, and cartoon characters by Walter Lantz and Walt Disney. Some of these carry a copyright date, and that's all it is. It's not the date of manufacture.

Many collectors are having a good time looking for these glasses; if you want to learn more about them, we recommend *The Collector's Guide to Cartoon and Promotional Drinking Glasses* by John Hervey.

Applause, California Raisins, tumbler, 5⁵/₁₆", shows wraparound scene of dancing & singing raisins, straight sided, 1989..$5.00
Arby's, BC Ice Age, tumbler, 5¼", shows Fat Broad (woman w/snake coiled on club), marked Field Enterprises 1981...$10.00
Arby's, Christmas (Holly & Berries), tumbler, 5", leaves & berries above red stripe at base, gold trim at top, 1983 ....$5.00
Arby's, Monopoly, tumbler, 4¾", shows square marked 'Go To Jail,' 1985...$20.00
Arby's, Movie Stars, tumbler, 5⅝", shows Mae West bust portrait & '4 of 6,' straight sided w/indented base, 1979 ....$10.00
Arby's, Norman Rockwell Summer Scenes, tumbler, 6¼", 'Gramps at the Plate,' straight sided, 1987..............$5.00

Arby's, Norman Rockwell Winter Scenes, tumbler, 4", 'A Boy Meets His Dog' w/Pepsi logo, heavy bottom, 1979 ....$10.00

Burger Chef, Men of Mount Rushmore, 5¼", shows bust portrait of Abraham Lincoln, dated 1975, indented base $10.00

Burger King, Denver Broncos, tumbler, 5⅝", shows portrait of Lyle Alzado, straight sided w/indented base, dated 1977 ....$10.00

Burger King, Empire Strikes Back, tumbler, 5⅞", shows Darth Vader, heavy rounded base, one of set of four, 1980...$5.00

Burger King, Star Wars, tumbler, 5⅝", shows characters in soft pastels on thin glass, marked w/Coca-Cola logo, 1977..$5.00

Capitol Records Inc, Bozo the Clown & His Buddies, tumbler, 5¼", shows Bozo head portrait w/Belinda, 1965 ....$10.00

Coca Cola, Magnificent Ladies, tumbler, 5½", logo w/calendar girl's portrait, flared top, one of series of six..$10.00

Coca-Cola, Bicentennial Heritage, tumbler, 6⅛", shows George Washington & 'Times That Try Men's Souls,' 1976...$5.00

Coca-Cola, Historic Missions, tumbler, 5½", shows San Antonio De Valero, straight sided w/indented base..$10.00

Coca-Cola, Holly Hobbie Happy Talk, tumbler, 5⅞", shows couple & 'Happiness Is Meant To Be Shared,' indented base $5.00

Coca-Cola, King Kong, tumbler, 5⅝", shows Kong battling serpent, straight sided w/indented base, 1976........$2.00

Coca-Cola, Norman Rockwell Saturday Evening Post, tumbler, 'After the Prom (5-25-57),' w/logo, pedestal base $5.00

Coca-Cola, Olympics, Sam the Eagle, tumbler, 6¾", shows Sam kayak racing, straight sided, one of set of twelve, 1980...$5.00

Coca-Cola, Popeye's Kollect-A-Set, tumbler, 5⅞", shows full-length Olive Oyl w/logo, ¾" indented base, 1975..$5.00

Coca-Cola, Santa, tumbler, 6", shows Santa w/finger to mouth & small dog, marked '1 of 3' w/logo, round bottom $2.00

Country Time Lemonade, Saturday Evening Post (Rockwell), tumbler, 5⅞", 'Grandpa's Girl (1923),' sloped indented base $5.00

Dr Pepper, Happy Days, tumbler, 6⅛", shows name above character & '1977 Paramount Pictures,' blank back, Libbey Glass $5.00

Dr Pepper, Star Trek, tumbler, 6⅛", shows any one of four characters & '1976 Paramount Pictures' w/Dr Pepper logo $30.00

Dr Pepper, Star Trek, tumbler, 6⅛", shows Captain Kirk firing phaser gun, indented base, dated 1978 ....$30.00

Godfather's Pizza, The Goonies, tumbler, 5⅝", shows Data on waterslide, marked 'Warner Bros,' 1988 ....$5.00

Hardee's, The Chipmunks, tumbler, 5⅞", shows Chipettes in oval on front, marked 'Bagdasarian Productions,' 1985...$5.00

Hardee's, Ziggy, tumbler, 5⅞", shows Ziggy w/umbrella & 'Be Nice to Little Things,' indented base, 1979 ....$5.00

Kraft's Jelly, Peanuts, tumbler, 6", shows Charlie Brown flying kite & 'copyright United Features Syndicate 1950,' 1988..$5.00

Little Ceasar's, Detroit Tigers, tumbler, 6", shows Lopez, Gibson & Morris, flared top w/indented base, dated 1984 ....$20.00

LK's (motel & restaurant chain), Pierre the Bear, tumbler, 5", shows pastel-color seasonal scene w/verse, 1979 ..$10.00

McDonald's, Camp Snoopy, tumbler, 6", shows Snoopy & 'Civilization Is Overrated!' in landscape, round bottom, 1983..$5.00

McDonald's, Great Muppet Caper, tumbler, 5⅝", shows Happiness Hotel & bus, straight sided w/indented base, 1981..$5.00

McDonald's, McDonaldland Action, tumbler, 5⅝", shows Big Mac on roller skates, indented base, Libbey Glass Co, 1977 ....$10.00

Pepsi, DC Comics Super Heros, tumbler, 6⁵⁄₁₆", shows Aquaman in action pose, thick bottom, Brockway Glass Co, 1978 ....$10.00

Pepsi, Hanna Barbera, tumbler, 6¼", Josie & the Pussycats band w/Pepsi logo, thick, Brockway Glass Co, 1977 ....$20.00

Pepsi, Moon Behind Super Heros, tumbler, 6¼", shows Flash, thick base, Brockway Glass Co, 1976.........$20.00

Pepsi, PAT Ward Productions, tumbler, 6¼", shows Boris Badenov w/logos, thick base, Brockway Glass Co $20.00

Pepsi, Popeye's Famous Fried Chicken, tumbler, 6", shows portrait & 'Brutus Thru the Years' w/Pepsi logo, indented base $20.00

Pepsi, Ringling Bros, tumbler, 6¼", shows elephant's head & 'World's Biggest Menagerie,' marked Federal Glass, 1975 ....$30.00

Pepsi Super Series (moon set), tumbler, Supergirl .$15.00
Pepsi Super Series (moon set), tumbler, Wonder Woman (illustrated) $20.00

Pepsi, Superman the Movie, tumbler, 5⅝", 'From Kal-El the Child to Man of Steel,' indented base, 1979..........**$10.00**

Pepsi, Warner Bros, tumbler, 6¼", shows single character w/name in white letters on front, Brockway Glass Co, 1973 ....**$10.00**

Pepsi, Warner Bros Action, tumbler, 5⅞", shows Buggs Bunny being shot at by Daffy Duck, round bottom, 1979.................**$5.00**

Pizza Hut, ET, tumbler, 6", shows ET in closet w/stuffed animals, marked 'Be Good' & 'Universal Studios,' 1982 ....**$2.00**

Pizza Hut, The Flintstone Kids, tumbler, 6", shows Barney's portrait, marked 'Hanna-Barbera,' rounded bottom, 1986.................**$2.00**

RC Cola, Portland Players Oregon NBA, tumbler, 6¼", shows Bill Walton portrait, straight sided, 1979 ....**$20.00**

Schwartz Peanut Butter, World Wrestling Federation, tumbler, 4½", shows Jake the Snake, Canadian.............**$5.00**

Sneaky Pete in Alabama, Al Capp, tumbler, 6¼", shows full-figure Daisy May, Brockway Glass Co, 1975.........**$50.00**

Taco Bell, Star Trek II Search for Spock, tumbler, 5⅝", shows 'Enterprise Destroyed,' double creased bottom, 1984.................**$5.00**

United Oil, Baseball Past Greats, tumbler, 5", shows full-figure Babe Ruth & 1936, round bottom, 1988 ....**$20.00**

Universal City Studios, Battlestar Galactic, shows Apollo w/trademark of Universal Studios, dated 1979...........**$5.00**

Walt Disney, All Star Parade, tumbler, 4¼", action graphics & 'Three Little Pigs,' medium weight, tapered, 1939..**$50.00**

Walt Disney, Cinderella, tumbler, 4⅝", shows Cinderella w/coach & horses, w/Libbey Glass Co logo **$20.00**

Walt Disney, Disneyland Series, tumbler, 5⅛", shows Mickey Mouse, Coca-Cola & Federal Glass Co logos **$30.00**

Walt Disney, Donald Duck, tumbler, 4¾", shows Donald cooking & nephews on back w/banner at top, 1930s **$90.00**

Walt Disney, Jungle Book, tumbler, 6¼", shows Bagheera (blue leopard), thick, Brockway Glass Co, 1977...**$50.00**

Walt Disney, Mickey Mouse Club Film Strip, tumbler, 5", shows Mickey on skates, straight sided w/indented base **$10.00**

Walt Disney, Mickey Through the Years, mug, shows Mickey in Fantasia (1940) on milk glass w/blue Pepsi logo................**$10.00**

Walt Disney, Mickey's Christmas Carol, tumbler, 6⅛", shows Scrooge Mc Duck w/Coca-Cola logo, flared, ...**$10.00**

Walt Disney, Single Character, mug, shows Minnie w/name & Pepsi logo in black on milk glass **$10.00**

Walt Disney, Single Character, mug, shows Pluto w/name on clear glass, heavy pedestal base **$10.00**

Walt Disney, Single Character, tumbler, 6", shows full-figure Donald Duck, rounded bottom, 1979...................**$10.00**

Walt Disney, Sleeping Beauty, tumbler, 5", shows Prince Phillip to the rescue, slighly curved heavy base, 1958 ....**$20.00**

Walt Disney, Snow White & Seven Dwarfs Music, tumbler, 4¾", shows Happy w/cymbal, Libbey Glass Co mark, ca 1930s **$70.00**

Walt Disney, The Rescuers, tumbler, 6¼", shows Bernard holding lantern, w/Pepsi logo, thick, Brockway Glass Co, 1977................**$30.00**

Walt Disney, Wonderful World, tumbler, 6", shows Alice in Wonderland & White Rabbit w/Pepsi logo, rounded bottom **$10.00**

Welch's Jelly, Howdy Doody, tumbler, 4¼", shows 'Doodyville Elephant Squirts Clarabell,' marked Kagran, early 1950s **$20.00**

Welch's Jelly Co, Archies, tumbler, 4¼", 'Archie Takes the Gang for a Ride,' embossed face in bottom, 1971................**$5.00**

Welch's Jelly Co, Howdy Doody, tumbler, 4⅛", shows banner 'Ding Dong Dell Ring for Welch's...' at top, 1953 ....**$10.00**

Wendy's, Cleveland Browns, tumbler, 6¼", shows head portrait of Brian Sipe in star, dated 1981 ....**$10.00**

Wendy's, New York Times, tumbler, 4⅛", shows headline 'Columbia Returns,' straight sided w/heavy base, 1981................**$5.00**

7-Up, Indiana Jones, tumbler, 5¾", shows him w/sword, straight sided w/creased bottom, dated 1984........**$10.00**

7-11, Marvel Comics, tumbler, 5⅝", shows Captain America & Falcon, straight sided w/indented base, 1977...**$10.00**

9 Lives, Morris the Cat, tumbler, 5", shows Morris & 'Morris On Glass Is Like Sterling on Silver,' indented base **$10.00**

Character Collectibles

Any popular personality, whether factual or fictional, has been promoted through the retail market to some degree. Depending upon the extent of their popularity, we may be deluged with this merchandise for weeks, months, even years. It's no wonder, then, that the secondary market abounds with these items or that there is such wide-spread collector demand for them today. There are rarities in any field, but for the beginning collector, many nice items are readily available at prices most can afford. Western heroes, TV and movie personalities, superheroes, comic book characters, and sports greats are the most sought after.

For more information, we recommend *Character Toys and Collectibles* by David Longest and *Toys of the Sixties* by Bill Bruegman.

See also Beatles Collectibles, Betty Boop Collectibles, Bubble Bath Containers, Character and Promotional Drinking Glasses, Character Watches, Dionne Quintuplets, Disney Collectibles, Elvis Presley Memorabilia, Gone with the Wind, Movie Stars, Paper Dolls, Peanuts Collectibles, Pez Candy Containers, Popeye Collectibles, Puzzles, Radio Personalities, Rock 'n Roll Memorabilia, Shirley Temple, Star Trek Memorabilia, Star Wars Trilogy Collectibles, Three Stooges Memorabilia, TV and Movie Characters, Western Heroes, Wizard of Oz Collectibles.

Amos & Andy, table clock, 1935...............................**$245.00**
Andy Gump, face mask, Listerine premium, 1930s **$35.00**

Barney Google, salt & pepper shakers, 3", 1940s, pr ..**$60.00**

Batman, fork & spoon set, Imperial Knife, 1966, on original card **$40.00**

Blondie, paint book, Whitman, #605, NM..................**$25.00**

Buck Rogers, badge, Chief Explorer, M **$200.00**

Buck Rogers, catalog, '25th Century Equipment Merchandise,' Daisy, 1930s, NM....................................**$65.00**

Buck Rogers, game, 16x16", 'Buck Rogers & His Cosmic Rocket Wars,' 1934, NM......................................**$125.00**

Buck Rogers, map, 18x25", 'Buck Rogers' Map of the Solar System,' rare, EX **$400.00**

Buck Rogers, paint book, 11x14", Whitman, 1935, unused, NM **$70.00**

Buck Rogers, patch, Solar Scout, rare, minimum value...**$1,200.00**

Buck Rogers, pencil box, red & blue, 1935, EX...........**$60.00**

Buck Rogers, ring, initial letter..............................**$380.00**

Bugs Bunny, alarm clock, talking, 1974, in original box **$35.00**

Bugs Bunny, toothbrush holder, figural, copyrighted by Warner Bros **$40.00**

Captain America, badge, Sentinels of Liberty, NM **$330.00**

Captain America, coloring book, 1966, M....................**$15.00**

Captain Marvel, key chain, 1944, NM..........................**$60.00**

Captain Marvel, tie clip, Fawcett Publications, 1946, .**$25.00**

Captain Midnight, badge, Flight Commander, rare ..**$1,500.00**

Captain Midnight, radio premium, Code-O-Graph, 1947...**$45.00**

Captain Video, rocket launcher set, 8x10", NM **$85.00**

Charlie McCarthy, egg cup, lustreware, 1930s...........**$185.00**

Charlie the Tuna, pencil sharpener, in original box....**$25.00**

Chester Gump, book, 'Finds Hidden Treasure,' Whitman, 1934, EX..**$40.00**

Cinnamon Bear, badge, silver star, EX **$80.00**

Colonel Sanders, figurine, 6½", composition, 1954 .....**$65.00**

Dr Seuss, doll, Horton Hatches Egg **$37.50**

Dr Seuss, music box, 5" sq, lithographed Cat-in-the-Hat scenes, Mattel, 1970, EX....................................**$90.00**

Dr Seuss Cat in the Hat, alarm clock, NM.................**$165.00**

Elsie the Cow, creamer, 6x6", pottery........................**$45.00**

Elsie the Cow, ice cream dish, footed, w/logo **$30.00**

Felix the Cat, bead game under glass, 3" **$32.00**

Felix the Cat, game, 9x17", Milton Bradley, 1960, NM .**$38.00**

Felix the Cat, pencil box, 1939, NM **$70.00**

Felix the Cat, pencil case, w/rulers, 1934, NM............**$95.00**

Felix the Cat, yarn holder..**$30.00**

Flash Gordon, space compass, in original package.....**$75.00**

Frankenstein, costume, Ben Cooper, 1-pc suit w/plastic mask, 1963, in original box.................................**$40.00**

Frankenstein, mask, full head size, rubber, EX...........**$35.00**

G-Man, ring, Radio Club..**$20.00**

Goldilocks, poster, 18x29", Vaudeville act, 1920s........**$22.50**

Green Hornet, ring, secret compartment, premium **$750.00**

Green Lantern, costume, Ben Cooper, 1-pc w/plastic mask, 1967, in original 8x12" box, M **$60.00**

Green Sprout, alarm clock, talking, NM **$50.00**

Gumps, ginger ale bottle, 7", bottled by Bon-Ton Beverages **$75.00**

Happy Hooligan, book, 'Story of Happy Hooligan,' McLoughlin Brothers, 1932, EX............................**$50.00**

Happy Hooligan, target set, Milton Bradley, 1925, NM..**$275.00**

Henry, wind-up, celluloid figurine on trapeze, distributed by Borgfeldt, NM...**$500.00**

Huckleberry Hound, pin-back button, 3" dia, 'Huckleberry Hound for President,' 1960....................................**$15.00**

Humphrey, doll, 'The Happy Blacksmith, Joe Palooka's Pal' on his apron, plastic face, cloth body, M............**$115.00**

Humpty Dumpty, game, Lowell Games, original box....**$15.00**

Joe Palooka, bank/candy container, Little Max, 1950s, in original box **$25.00**

Denny Dimwit, nodder doll, 11", composition, copyright 1948, M **$70.00**

Dick Tracy, sparkle paint set, Kenner, 1962, in original box, M **$85.00**

Joe Palooka, toy, Humphrey Mobile, Wyandotte Toy Co, lithographed metal, EX..**$225.00**

Katzenjammer Kids, coloring book, 1930s, M..............**$55.00**

Katzenjammer Kids, game, 7x10", 'Katzenjammer Kids Hockey Game,' 1950...**$45.00**

Kayo, figurine, 1¼", hand-painted lead, 1930s, M.......**$35.00**

King Kong, game, 10x20", Ideal, trap him atop Empire State Building, 1963, M..**$100.00**

Li'l Abner, figurine, 3", lead, 1940s.............................**$22.00**

Little Lulu, rag doll, 15", by Marge, c 1944, EX............**$120.00**

Little Lulu, valentine, 1950s, EX..................................**$22.50**

Little Orphan Annie, decoder, 1940............................**$24.00**

Little Orphan Annie, puzzle, 1930s, in original box....**$30.00**

Little Orphan Annie, wall pocket, lustreware, EX.....**$175.00**

Maggie & Jiggs, salt & pepper shakers, ceramic, pr....**$45.00**

Marky Maypo, bank, 9x6", figural, colored vinyl, Standard Milling Co, 1960s, EX.....................................**$47.50**

Melvin Purvis, manual, Post Toasties premium, EX.....**$38.00**

Mickey McGuire, salt & pepper shakers, Toonerville, ceramic, Japan, pr...**$40.00**

Moon Mullins, coloring book, McLoughlin Brothers, 1930s, EX..**$48.00**

Moon Mullins, figure, 2", hand-painted lead, 1930s, M..**$35.00**

Mr Magoo, doll, 11", advertising General Electric.......**$18.00**

Mutt & Jeff, cigar box, lithographed paper on wood, 1920s...**$80.00**

Oswald the Rabbit, plate, 7", glazed ceramic, 1930s-40s..**$40.00**

Pal the Dog (Skeezix character), doll, 7", oilcloth, EX..**$65.00**

Pappy Yokum, doll, Barry Toys, vinyl, EX..................**$80.00**

Prince Valiant, pin-back button....................................**$25.00**

Prince Valiant, playset, castle & fort, Marx, 1950s, in original box, EX..**$150.00**

Schmoo, pin-back button, Sealtest premium, NM........**$15.00**

Schmoo, planter, 1948..**$30.00**

Schmoo, tumbler, by Al Capp, orange graphics on clear glass, 1949, M...**$20.00**

Scrappy, tumbler, 5", 1935...**$25.00**

Smokey the Bear, doll, 16", inflatable vinyl, in original package...**$28.00**

Smokey the Bear, poster, 13x18", Think, 1974, M.......**$15.00**

Spuds Mackensie, key chain, 1¼x2", plastic, 1985, promotion item for Anheuser Busch...............................**$4.00**

Tarzan, coloring book, 1952, M....................................**$35.00**

Three Little Pigs, toothbrush holder, porcelain, NM....**$70.00**

Twiggy, tote bag, 11x14", Mattel, photo on yellow vinyl, 1967, M...**$50.00**

Uncle Walt, bookmark, 3", 1940s..................................**$15.00**

Uncle Wiggily, mug, Ovaltine premium, 1934, EX.......**$55.00**

Yellow Kid, cigar box, EX...**$400.00**

Yellow Kid, ice cream mold...**$125.00**

Character Watches

There is a growing interest in comic character watches and clocks produced from about 1930 into the fifties and beyond. They're in rather short supply simply because they were made for children to wear (and play with). They were cheaply made with pin-lever movements, not worth an expensive repair job, so many were simply thrown away. The original packaging that today may be worth more than the watch itself was usually ripped apart by an excited child and promptly relegated to the wastebasket.

Condition is very important in assessing value. Unless a watch is in like-new condition, it is not mint. Rust, fading, scratching, or wear of any kind will sharply lessen its value, and the same is true of the box itself. Beware of dealers who substitute a generic watch box for the original. Remember that these too were designed to appeal to children, and (99% of the time) were printed with colorful graphics.

Some of these watches have been reproduced, so beware. For further study, we recommend *Comic Character Clocks and Watches* by Howard S. Brenner.

Pocket Watches

Buck Rogers, Ingraham, in colorful box w/insert ..**$1,000.00**

Dan Dar, Ingersoll, double animation, 1953, EX.......**$165.00**

Dizzy Dean, New Haven, 1935, EX.............................**$90.00**

Donald Duck, Ingersoll, 1939, in original box...........**$550.00**

Jeff Arnold, Ingersoll, animated (right hand moves pistol), 1953, M..**$275.00**

Lone Ranger, New Haven, 1939, in original box w/fob..**$350.00**

Mickey Mouse, Ingersoll, die-debossed back, 1933, in original box w/enameled fob, M..................................**$400.00**

Mickey Mouse, Ingersoll, die-debossed back (beware of repoductions), 1933, EX.......................................**$165.00**

Mickey Mouse, Timex, electric, 1968, in original box, M..**$175.00**

Popeye, New Haven, 1935, EX..................................**$180.00**

Roy Rogers, Bradley, 1959, embossed portrait fob, M....**$150.00**

Three Little Pigs, Ingersoll, die-debossed back, 1934, in original box w/enameled fob...................................**$700.00**

Three Little Pigs, Ingersoll, die-debossed back, 1934, M..**$450.00**

Wristwatches

Babe Ruth, Exact Time...**$275.00**

Bambi, Ingersoll, one of ten in birthday series, MIB...**$250.00**

Bugs Bunny, sold exclusively by Rexall Drugs, Warner Bros, 1951, M...**$125.00**

Charlie the Tuna, 1977, in original box, M..................**$45.00**

Cinderella, Timex, 1958, $7.95 original price, in original box w/small Cinderella figurine watch holder, M......**$125.00**

Cinderella, 1955, in original box, M...........................**$100.00**

Donald Duck, US Time, gold-tone case, $8.95 original price, in original box, M...**$175.00**

Gene Autry, Wilane, 1948, in original box, M...........**$250.00**

Gene Autry, Wilane, 1948, M......................................**$125.00**

Hopalong Cassidy, US Time, 1950, in original box w/small model of a saddle, M...**$135.00**

Howdy Doody, Patent Watch Co, moving eyes, EX....**$60.00**

Li'l Abner, New Haven, animated (waving flag moves back & forth), 1947, in original box, M.......................**$175.00**

Mickey Mouse, Bradley, 1978-79, M..........................**$100.00**
Mickey Mouse, Ingersoll, gold-plated case, 1947......**$200.00**

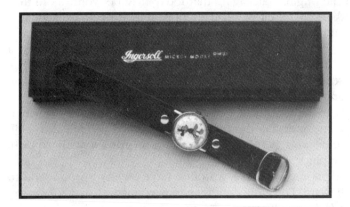

Mickey Mouse, Ingersoll/Timex, 1968-71, in original box, EX..**$125.00**

Porky Pig, Ingraham, 1949, original inner display card & box, M..**$200.00**
Porky Pig, Sheraton, 1972, in original package.........**$200.00**
Puss 'N Boots, Nuhope, 1949, in original box, M......**$100.00**
Robin, Timex, 1978, in original box............................**$50.00**
Robin Hood, Viking, 1938, in original box, M...........**$150.00**
Roy Rogers, original band, 1951, NM.......................**$110.00**
Snoopy, playing tennis, NM..**$35.00**
Snow White, 1957, NM..**$60.00**
Space Ranger, Ingraham, in original box, M.............**$250.00**
Tom Corbett, Ingraham, 1951, in original package...**$150.00**
Wile E Coyote, Sheraton, 1972, in original package..**$250.00**
Zorro, cellophane on hat, 1957, in original box........**$185.00**

Chase Brass and Copper Company

In the thirties, this company began to produce quality products styled in the new 'modernist' style that had become so dominant in the European market. They turned to some of the country's leading designers, Russel Wright and Rockwell Kent among them, and developed a wonderful assortment of serving pieces, smoking accessories, and various other items for the home which they marketed at prices the public could afford. They favored chromium over more expensive materials such as silver, copper, brass, and nickel plate (though these continued to be used in limited amounts). Handles were made of Bakelite or some other type of plastic, and many pieces had glass inserts.

Many newlyweds received Chase products as wedding gifts, and now sadly they've reached the time in their lives where they're beginning to unload some of the nice things they've held onto for years. So it's not uncommon to find some very good examples on the market today. Many show little or no sign of use. Most are marked; if you don't find it right away, look on the screws and rivets. Sets may contain only one marked piece. Unmarked items should be carefully evaluated to see if they meet the high Chase standards of quality. It's best to compare them with pictures of verified pieces or similar items that are marked to be sure.

Automatic lighter & tray, 4" lighter sits in middle of 6½" tray, chromium w/red or black, #846...........**$85.00**
Bacchus pitcher, 10¼x8¾", 3-pt, polished copper or chromium, thumbprint design by Gerth & Gerth, #90036..**$175.00**
Bookends, 7⅜x4", brass or satin nickel on black nickel base, modernistic cat form, Von Nessen design, #17042, pr.....................................**$515.00**
Breakfast set, 4¼" sugar bowl, 3⅛" creamer on 11⅜x5" tray, polished chromium, Gerth & Gerth, #26003.......**$175.00**
Candy jar, 1¾x4", polished or satin copper or polished chromium, Von Nessen design, #NS-316...........**$120.00**
Cheese server, 14" dia tray w/smaller lid that covers center, polished chromium, Gerth & Gerth design, #09009...**$150.00**
Compote, 3⅛x6½", satin copper, octagonal shape, footed, #15002...**$80.00**
Cordova flowerpot, 3¾x4½", brass or copper, will conceal clay pot, #04013B.................................**$32.00**

Creamer & sugar bowl, w/11½" tray, polished chromium, #26008..**$125.00**
Cube cigarette holder, 3¾x2¼x2¼", red w/white interior & polished chromium disk, Von Nessen design, #17070...**$160.00**
Curl candlestick, 9" high w/3¼" base, satin brass or satin copper, Riemann design, #21007, rare............**$1,500.00**
Delphic serving spoon & fork, 13⅛", polished chromium & white plastic, #9088 & #90089.............................**$150.00**
Dinner gong, 8¼x6¼", chromium or polished copper & bronze, Gerth & Gerth design, #11251................**$155.00**
Fiesta flower bowl, 6x8" (on 4" wooden base), polished chromium w/black base, #29002......................**$265.00**

French watering can, 8¼x23" (from handle to tip of spout), polished copper & brass, Gerth & Gerth design, #05001....................**$175.00**

Fruit basket, 4¾x12½", intertwined wire in copper & white, ball feet, Lurelle Guild design, #27028................**$125.00**

Fruit bowl, 3x9½", polished chromium or copper, beaded rim, Von Nessen design, #17007....................**$120.00**

Ice bowl & tongs, 7" dia, chromium or polished brass & copper combination, designed by Russel Wright, #28002 ....**$250.00**

Jam set, 5¼x6⅜", polished chromium lid & tray w/glass hobnail jar, glass spoon, #90018 ....**$250.00**

Lighthouse lamp, 6⅛", satin brass or satin nickel, electric candle in lighthouse form, #16002....................**$90.00**

Liqueur set, six 2⅜" cups on 6" dia tray, polished chromium w/blue glass bottom on tray, #90046 ....**$450.00**

Magazine rack, 14x11⅛x8⅛", English bronze or copper & white, Lurelle Guild design, #27026 ....**$125.00**

Nut bowl, 10" dia, polished chromium & walnut, center screw-type nutcracker, holds four picks, #90084..**$65.00**

Pretzel bowl, 2⅝x7", polished copper or chromium, #15004....................**$75.00**

Salem water pitcher, 9¾x7⅜", polished copper w/white tinned lining, Gerth & Gerth, #90004 ....**$175.00**

Salver, 20" dia, satin copper, three evenly placed steps to center, #90010 ....**$65.00**

Snuffer ash tray, 2¼x6½" dia, polished chromium w/black fish center, #845 ....**$75.00**

Sunday Supper candle holders, 1¾x3⅜" dia, black nickel, polished copper, or satin nickel, set of four, #24002 ....**$55.00**

Tavern pitcher, 10¼x8¾", polished copper w/white tinned lining & brass handle, #17026 ....**$950.00**

Tiffin tray, 18x12", polished chromium, satin copper or polished copper, black handles, Von Nessen design, #17027 ....**$190.00**

Triple flower stand, 14½x16", copper & brass, holds three 5¾" pots (included), #11228....................**$175.00**

Tripod ash tray, satin copper & brass or English bronze & copper, 3-legged, three cigarette rests, #301....**$130.00**

Trojan plate, 12" dia, chromium or satin copper, grooved edges, flat handles, #09004 ....**$125.00**

Trowel, 10" long, polished brass w/black handle, Von Nessen design, #90015 ....**$250.00**

Tulip candlestick, 4½", satin brass & copper combination or polished copper, Von Nessen design, #NS-639 ..**$235.00**

Vanity mirror, 2⅜" dia, buffed & plated metal w/multicolor enameling on back w/etched design, #90043 ....**$95.00**

Weathervane, 12x12", brass, arrow pivots on solid brass point, non-rusting, #90030 ....**$325.00**

Children's Books

There's lots of interest in children's books. Some collectors limit themselves to specific authors or subject matter while others prefer to concentrate on the illustrators. As with any book, first editions are the most valuble, and condition is extrememly important.

Note: In our listings, some of the dates are in parenthesis. This means that this date, though accurate, is not printed in the book.

A Frog He Would A-Wooing Go, Chamberlain Press, 1981, limited edition (1/125), unpaginated, issued without dust jacket **$85.00**

A Is for Anna Belle, Walck Inc, 1954, illustrated by Tasha Tudor, w/dust jacket, VG....................**$15.00**

ABC, Atheneum, 1975, 1st edition, illustrated by Elizabeth Cleaver, 55 pages, issued without dust jacket, NM **$17.50**

African Adventure, Golden Press, 1965, Kathy Martin #13, pictorial binding, last title in series, VG................**$8.00**

Alphabatics, Bradbury Press, 1986, 1st edition, author illustrated by Suse MacDonald, 55 pages, w/dust jacket, NM....................**$25.00**

Alphabears, An ABC Book; Holt Rinehart & Winston, 1984, 1st edition, illustrated by Hague, 32 pages, w/dust jacket, NM....................**$25.00**

Alphabestiary, Lippincott, (1966), 1st edition, illustrated by Milton Hebald, 56 pages, w/slipcase, NM............**$45.00**

Alphabet Dreams, Prentice Hall, 1976, 1st edition, illustrated by Judith Brown, 48 pages, w/dust jacket, NM **$15.00**

Alphabet of Garden Flowers, London, Pelham Books, 1987, illustrated by Marie Angel, 65 pages, w/dust jacket, NM....................**$25.00**

An American ABC, Macmillan, 1941, 1st edition, author illustrated by Maud & Miska Petersham, 53 pages, VG....................**$55.00**

Aviation Book, McLoughlin Bros, 1927, #2556, photo illustrated, unpaginated, 6x12", EX....................**$12.00**

Beasts from a Brush, Pantheon, (1955), limited 1st edition, author illustrated by Kepes, 32 pages, w/dust jacket, NM....................**$55.00**

Betty Gordon on No-Trail Island, Cupples & Leon, 1931, #14, w/dust jacket, last title listed, VG **$12.50**

Birds' Christmas Carol, Wiggin, Houghton Mifflin, 1912, illustrated by Katherine Wireman, 90 pages, G.....**$18.00**

Brian Wildsmith's ABC, Watts, 1963, 1st American edition, Kate Greenaway Medal Winner, signed, w/dust jacket, NM **$65.00**

Bunny Hopwell's First Spring, Wonder Books, 1954, #614, 1st edition, NM **$7.50**

Cats' XYZ, Dutton, 1961, 1st American edition, illustrated by Derrick Sayer, 128 pages, w/dust jacket, NM........**$25.00**

Celestino Piatti's Animal ABC, Atheneum, 1966, 1st American edition, author illustrated, 26 pages, w/dust jacket, NM **$75.00**

Cherry Ames: Cruise Nurse; Grosset Dunlap, #9, rust tweed binding, w/dust jacket, lists to Island, VG..............**$6.00**

Cherry Ames: Island Nurse; Grosset Dunlap, 1960, pictorial binding w/green spine, lists to Staff Nurse, VG....**$10.00**

Child's Garden of Verses, Stevenson, Saalfield, 1924, VG....................**$12.00**

Counting Book, Wonder Books, 1957, #692, NM........**$10.00**

Dorothy & the Wizard of Oz, L Frank Baum, EX ..$200.00

Down-Adown-Derry, A Book of Fairy Poems; Holt, (1922), illustrated by Dorothy Lathrop, 195 pages, gilt cloth binding, VG.....................................$65.00

Ed Emberley's ABC, Little Brown, 1978, 1st edition, 58 pages, w/dust jacket, NM $25.00

Edward Lear's ABC, Salem House, (1986), 1st edition, illustrated by Carol Pike, 32 pages, w/dust jacket, NM.....................................$17.50

Egyptian Cat Mystery, Grosset & Dunlap, 1961, Rick Brant #16, w/dust jacket, last title on all lists, VG $30.00

Elf, Chester the Little Pig, Rand McNally, 1951, #452, 1st edition, VG $3.00

Elf, Cowboy Eddie, Rand McNally, 1950, #437, NM $4.50

Elf, Five Little Bears, Rand McNally, 1955, #496, 1st edition, VG $7.50

Elf, Pillowtime Tales, Rand McNally, 1956, #552, 1st edition, 25¢ original price, VG.....................................$6.00

Elf, Teddy Bear of Bumpkin Hollow, Rand McNally, 1948, #561, 1956 edition, 25¢ original price, VG $8.00

Elf, Teddy the Terrier, Rand McNally, 1956, #558, 1st edition, 25¢ original price, VG $6.50

Frog Went A-Courtin', Harcourt Brace, (1955), 1st edition, Caldecott Medal Winner, illustrated by Rojankovsky, 32 pages.....................................$50.00

Gandy Goose, Wonder Books, 1957, #695, illustrated by CBS Television, VG.....................................$4.50

Gems from Mother Goose, McLoughlin Bros, 1911, illustrated by Noble Ives, unpaginated, 10x12", VG $27.50

Girl Scouts at Penguin Pass, Cupples & Leon, 1953, #1, w/dust jacket, lists to #3, VG $12.00

Guinea Pig ABC, Dutton, 1983, 1st edition, author illustrated by Kate Duke (1st book), 32 pages, ...$25.00

Hardy Boys' Detective Handbook, Grosset & Dunlap, 1959, w/dust jacket, lists to Desert Giant, VG.................$18.50

Helen Oxenbury's ABC of Things, Watts, 1972, 1st American edition, 56 pages, w/dust jacket, NM $35.00

Hilltop Boys on Lost Island, World, 1931, 177 pages, silver letters on red cloth, w/dust jacket, VG....................$7.00

History of the Alphabet, Royal Typewriter Co, (1930), 1st edition, author illustrated by Michael Lipman, 41 pages, VG.....................................$40.00

Hoofbeats on the Turnpike, Cupples & Leon, 1944, Penny Parker #11, w/dust jacket, lists to #15, VG............$15.00

Horse for Johnny, Bookman, Wonder Books, 1952, #754, 39¢ original price, unpaginated, VG $3.50

Hunting for Hidden Gold, Grosset & Dunlap, 1928, Hardy Boys #5, w/dust jacket, lists to Broken Blade, VG ..$12.50

Hunting of the Snark, Watts, (1970), 1st American edition, Kate Greenaway Medal Winner, 48 pages, w/dust jacket, M $45.00

I Am Cherry Alive, The Little Girl Sang; Harper Row, (1979), 1st edition, illustrated by Cooney, 32 pages, w/dust jacket.....................................$30.00

I Saw a Ship A-Sailing, Macmillan, 1972, 1st edition, author illustrated by Janina Domanska, 35 pages, w/dust jacket, NM.....................................$45.00

Jabberwocky, Warne, (1977), 1st American edition, illustrated signed by Jane Zalben, 32 pages, NM $45.00

Jambo Means Hello, A Swahili Alphabet Book; Dial, 1974, 1st edition, Caldecott Honor Book, w/dust jacket, NM $45.00

Jenny Dean: The Secret of the Invisible City; Grosset & Dunlap, Science Fiction Mysteries #4, VG $4.50

Johnny Crow's Garden, Frederick Warne, (1903), 1967 reprint, 64 pages, w/dust jacket, M....................$35.00

Kate Greenaway's Mother Goose, Huntington Library, 1974 facsimile edition, introduction by James Thorpe, 31 pages, NM $15.00

Kellogg's Story Books of Games, Kellogg Co, 1931, #4, 8x10", G $20.00

Land of Oz, L Frank Baum, A Sequel, EX (illustrated) $200.00

Little Black Sambo, Whitman, 1950, 32 pages, 5½ x6", VG $15.00

Little Chameleon, World, (1966), 1st edition, illustrated by Rainey Bennett, 39 pages, w/dust jacket, EX........$20.00

Little Hill, Harcourt Brace, (1949), 1st edition, author illustrated by Harry Behn, 58 pages, w/dust jacket, NM..........$35.00

Little Red Riding Hood, Whitman, 1937, #917, 9x13", VG.$8.00

Maida's Little Houseboat, Grosset & Dunlap, 1943, w/dust jacket, NM.....................................$10.00

Marcel Marceau Alphabet Book, Doubleday, 1970, 1st edition, photographs by Milton Greene, 62 pages, w/dust jacket, NM.....................................$25.00

Mike Mars at Cape Canaveral, Doubleday, 1961, #3, w/dust jacket, VG $6.00

Morning Is a Little Child, Harcourt Brace & World, (1969), 1st edition, illustrated by Anglund, 32 pages, w/dust jacket.....................................$35.00

Mother Goose, Saalfield, (1938), illustrated by Fred Lohman, 8 full-page color plates, w/dust jacket, G $85.00

Mother Goose, The Baby's Bouquet; Warne, ca 1900, illustrated by Walter Crane, 56 pages, VG $95.00

Mother Goose, Whitman, 1934, #989, illustrated by Ruth E Newton, unpaginated, 9½x13", VG......................$9.00

Mother Goose Riddle Rhymes, Harcourt Brace, (1953), 1st edition, illustrated by Low & Low, 48 pages, w/dust jacket, VG $45.00

Mother Goose Treasury, Coward McCann, (1966), 1st American edition, Kate Greenaway Medal Winner, 220 pages, VG.....................................$75.00

My Poetry Book, Wonder Books, 1954, #621, NM **$5.00**

Mystery of the Muffled Man, Little Brown, 1962, Secret Circle Mystery #5, w/dust jacket, VG............................**$7.00**

Nicola Bayley's Book of Nursery Rhymes, Knopf, (1975), 1st edition, author illustrated by Nicola Bayley, w/dust jacket...**$35.00**

Night & the Cat, Macmillan, 1950, 1st edition, illustrated by Tsuguharu Foujita, 55 pages, w/dust jacket, VG ..**$65.00**

Nonesense & Wonder, Poems & Cartoons of Edward Lear; Brandywine Press/Dutton, 1977, 1st edition, 244 pages, w/dust jacket, NM...**$35.00**

Nursery Rhymes, Chartwell, 1978, 1st edition, illustrated by Frances Livens, 61 pages, w/dust jacket, NM........**$12.50**

Old Ballad of the Babes in the Wood, Walck, (1972), 1st edition, illustrated by Ardizzone, 31 pages, w/dust jacket, NM...**$35.00**

Once Upon a Rhyme, Faber & Faber, (1982), 1st edition, illustrated by Jill Bennett, 157 pages, NM **$20.00**

Peacock Pie, Knopf, (1961), 1st edition, illustrated by Barbara Cooney, 117 pages, w/dust jacket, VG **$45.00**

Peek-a-Boo!, Viking, (1981), 1st American edition, illustrated by Janet Ahlberg, 32 pages, NM............................**$20.00**

Pied Piper of Hamelin, Rand McNally, (1910), 1927 reprint, illustrated by Hope Dunlap, 56 pages, NM **$45.00**

Puss in Boots, McLoughlin Bros, 1897, Cinderella Series, illustrated by R Andre, unpaginated, 8x11", VG ...**$35.00**

Robin Hood & His Merry Men, McLoughlin Bros, 1932, #177, illustrated by GA Davis, 48 pages, 7x9½", VG **$7.50**

Robinson Crusoe, McLoughlin Bros, 1897, Kriss Kringle Series, illustrated, unpaginated, 7x9", VG.............**$30.00**

Scout Patrol Boys & the Hunting Lodge Mystery, World, 1933, 118 pages, silver letters on red cloth, w/dust jacket, VG **$7.50**

Secret of Wildcat Swamp, Grosset & Dunlap, 1952, Hardy Boys #31, w/dust jacket, last title listed, VG **$25.00**

Sesame Street ABC Book of Words, Random House, (1988), 1st edition, illustrated by Harry McNaught, 40 pages, NM **$12.50**

Steve Canyon: Operation Snowflower; Grosset & Dunlap, 1959, #2, w/dust jacket, VG **$20.00**

Stormy, Whitman, 1954, Cozy Corner Book, illustrated by Disney Productions, VG..**$7.50**

Story of Appleby Capple, Harper, (1950), 1st edition, author illustrated by Anne Parrish, 184 pages, w/dust jacket, NM **$65.00**

Strange Monsters of the Sea, McGraw Hill, 1979, 1st edition, illustrated by Paul Galdone, 42 pages, w/dust jacket, NM **$15.00**

Summer's Coming In, Holt Rinehart & Winston, 1970, 1st edition, illustrated by Adrienne Adams, 48 pages, w/dust jacket...**$30.00**

Tell-a-Tale, Donald Duck Full Speed Ahead, Whitman, 1953, illustrated by Disney Studios, unpaginated, 6x6½", NM...**$6.50**

Tell-a-Tale, Little Beaver, Whitman, 1954, unpaginated, 6x6½", VG..**$4.00**

Tell-a-Tale, Runaway Pancake, Whitman, 1956, illustrated by Ben Williams, unpaginated, 6x6½", EX..................**$4.00**

Tell-a-Tale, Surprise for Howdy Doody, Whitman, 1951, Kagran Corp, unpaginated, 6x6½", G **$6.00**

Tell-a-Tale, Tweety, Whitman, 1953, illustrated by Warner Bros Cartoons Inc, unpaginated, 6x6½", EX............**$6.00**

Ten Rabbits, Potter, Wonder Books, 1957, #648, 25¢ original price, NM **$4.50**

The Boy Scout Explorers at Headless Hollow, Cupples & Leon, 1957, w/dust jacket, VG **$10.00**

The Clue in the Jewel Box, Grosset & Dunlap, 1943, Nancy Drew #20, B printing, w/dust jacket, VG **$40.00**

The Curlytops & Their Pets, Cupples & Leon, 1921, #6, w/dust jacket, lists to #14, VG..................................**$6.50**

The G-Men Trap the Spy Ring, Grosset & Dunlap, 1939, illustrated by Paul Laune, w/dust jacket, NM........**$10.00**

The Lone Ranger in Wild Horse Canyon, Grosset & Dunlap, 1950, #12, w/dust jacket, lists to #13, VG.............**$20.00**

The Motor Boys on Thunder Mountain, Cupples & Leon, 1924, #22, w/dust jacket, VG **$15.00**

The Outdoor Chums in the Big Woods, Grosset & Dunlap, 1911, w/dust jacket, VG...**$6.50**

The Outdoor Girls at Spring Hill Farm, Grosset & Dunlap, 1927, w/dust jacket, last title listed, VG................**$20.00**

The Owl & the Pussy Cat, Macmillan, (1983), 1st edition, illustrated by Hilary Knight, 32 pages, w/dust jacket, NM **$20.00**

The Secret Tunnel Treasure, Little Brown, 1962, Secret Circle Mystery #4, w/dust jacket, VG **$7.00**

The Sign of the Twisted Candles, Grosset & Dunlap, 1933, Nancy Drew #8, 3rd printing, VG **$20.00**

There Was a Wise Crow, Follett, (1969), 1st edition, illustrated by Joseph Low, 32 pages, w/dust jacket, VG..**$25.00**

Through the Air to Alaska, Grosset & Dunlap, 1930, Ted Scott #12, w/dust jacket, last title listed, VG **$22.50**

Tom Swift & His Giant Robot, Grosset & Dunlap, 1954, #4, pictorial binding, G...**$6.00**

Tom Swift & His Sky Racer, Grosset & Dunlap, w/color dust jacket, lists to Great Oil Gusher, VG.....................**$50.00**

Tom Swift in the City of Gold, Grosset & Dunlap, 1912, w/dust jacket, lists to House on Wheels, VG........**$45.00**

Trixie Belden & the Gatehouse Mystery, Whitman, 1951, w/dust jacket, VG..**$8.00**

Tucky the Hunter, Crown, 1978, 1st edition, calligraphic illustrations by Marie Angel, 44 pages, w/dust jacket, NM **$35.00**

Tuggy the Tugboat, Wonder Books, 1958, #696, NM....**$7.00**

Twelve Days of Christmas, Wonder Books, 1956, #651, illustrated by WT Mars, NM...**$6.00**

Uncle Tom's Cabin, Donohue, ca 1900, #182, Young Folks Edition, illustrated, 64 pages, 7½x10", NM...........**$45.00**

Useful & Instructive Poetry, Macmillan, 1954, 1st edition, introduction by Derek Hudson, w/dust jacket, NM **$75.00**

Utter Zoo Alphabet, Meredith Press, (1967), 1st edition, author illustrated by Edward Gory, w/dust jacket, VG...**$45.00**

West of Boston, Viking, 1956, 1st edition, author illustrated by James Daugherty, 95 pages, cloth, VG............**$20.00**

Whispering Box Mystery, Grosset & Dunlap, 1948, Rick Brant #5, w/dust jacket, lists to Scarlet Lake, VG....**$8.00**

Z Was Zapped, Houghton Mifflin, 1987, 1st edition, author illustrated, signed by Chris Van Allsburg, w/dust jacket, NM **$45.00**

Children's Dinnerware

Little girls have always enjoyed playing house, and glassware and chinaware manufacturers alike have seen to it that they're not lacking in the dinnerware department. Glassware 'just like Mother's' was pressed from late in the 19th century until well into the 20th, and much of it has somehow managed to survive to the present. China was made in England, Japan, and the United States in patterns that ranged from nursery-rhyme themes to traditional designs such as Blue Willow and Tea Leaf. Both types are very collectible today.

For further study, we recommend *Children's Glass Dishes, China, and Furniture, Vols 1 and 2,* by Doris Anderson Lechler and *Collector's Encyclopedia of Children's Dishes* by Margaret & Kenn Whitmyer.

China

A Mother's Affection, mug, 2⅝", girl on swing, blue on white **$95.00**

Blind Man's Bluff, mug, 2½", multicolor transfer, Staffordshire **$80.00**

Blue Willow, tea set, serves four **$65.00**

Bower, tea set, black & white, 16-pc, Edge Malkin...**$475.00**

Children Fishing, mug, bird whistle handle, Germany, 1900 ....**$45.00**

Circus Tricks, tea set, luster on porcelain, serves four, Germany **$150.00**

Clown w/Duck & Dog on Ball, tray, 4¼", Japan **$5.00**

Cornwallis Resigning His Sword, mug, 2", pink lustre rim **$450.00**

Donald Duck, tea set, orange rims, 10-pc, Made in Japan, 1940 ....**$165.00**

Elephant Lustre, teapot, 3¼" **$17.00**

Fishers, dinner set, brown & white, 19-pc, Malkin, England, EX...**$365.00**

Gaudy Ironstone, teapot, 4½", England......................**$70.00**

Goddess of War, mug, 2½", purple transfer, Staffordshire..**$95.00**

Humphrey's Clock, tea set, blue, 12-pc, England......**$250.00**

Kite Flyer, dinner set, 16-pc, ca 1860 ....**$600.00**

Kittens, tea set, 19-pc, Bavaria **$300.00**

Merry Christmas, creamer, 2⅞", green lustre, Germany, 1902...**$23.00**

Mickey, Donald, & Elmer, tea set, teapot 5", no mark, made in Japan **$110.00**

Nursery Scenes, teapot, 4½", Germany......................**$35.00**

Old Curiosity Shop, platter, 5", Ridgway, England **$25.00**

Pagoadas, plate, 3⅞", England **$10.00**

Peg in the Ring, mug, 2¾", girls play game, multicolor transfer...**$75.00**

Plate, 5", pink & blue floral rim on white, Nippon........**$5.00**

Shave for a Penny, mug, 2¼", black transfer & pink lustre trim **$180.00**

Stick Spatter, plate, 5⅜", Staffordshire, England..........**$12.00**

Tom Tom the Piper's Son, bowl, cereal **$30.00**

Glassware

Acorn, butter dish, 4"...**$185.00**

Amazon, sugar bowl, w/lid...**$60.00**

Arches, mug, 3x2¾" **$45.00**

Baby Flute, bowl, berry; small **$7.00**

Beautiful Lady, cake stand **$32.00**

Birds & Flowers, lemonade set, 3-pc, England..........**$200.00**

Braided Belt, sugar bowl, floral on milk glass...........**$185.00**

Button Arches, butter dish, 2⅛" **$150.00**

Button Panel, butter dish, gold flashing.....................**$110.00**

Button Panel, sugar bowl, 4⅝", w/lid..........................**$85.00**

Chimo, sugar bowl, w/lid..**$75.00**

Clear & Diamond Panels, creamer, 2¾", blue.............**$40.00**

Clear & Diamond Panels, creamer, 2¾", green...........**$45.00**

Colonial, punch bowl, 3¼"..**$45.00**

Dewdrop, creamer, 2¾", clear......................................**$60.00**

Dewdrop, spooner, 2¾", blue..**$75.00**

Diamond Band, mug, 2¼x1¼" **$45.00**

Diamond Ridge, butter dish **$175.00**

Drum, sugar bowl, 3½", w/lid......................................**$115.00**

Dutch Kinder, candlestick, 3", blue opaque **$135.00**

Fancy Cut, butter dish, teal **$195.00**

Fancy Cut, spooner, 2¼"...**$28.00**

Fancy Cut, table set **$150.00**

Fish, platter, 5¼x4½", oval, Federal Glass.................**$300.00**

Floral Twigs, mug, 3¾x3", amber **$55.00**

Frances Ware, pitcher, 4¾", amber or blue stain.......**$115.00**

Galloway, pitcher, 3⅞", gold trim **$32.00**

Grape Vine w/Ovals, spooner, 1⅞".................................**$45.00**

Hawaiian Lei, creamer...**$25.00**

Hobnail w/Thumbprint, tray, 7⅜"..................................**$55.00**

Horizontal Threads, butter dish, 1⅞", red flashed **$100.00**

Inverted Strawberry, punch bowl, 3¾" **$60.00**

Lamb, butter dish, 3⅛", milk glass.............................**$185.00**

Lamb, sugar bowl, 4⅛", milk glass, lamb finial..........**$155.00**

Large Block, creamer, 3", blue opaque **$45.00**

Leaf & Grape, decanter set, etched, 5-pc **$225.00**

Lion, butter dish, 4¼", frosted.....................................**$165.00**

Little Bo Peep, plate..**$35.00**

Little Ladders, banana stand...**$45.00**

Menagerie, creamer, 3¾", amber **$145.00**

Menagerie, spooner, 2⅝", blue....................................**$135.00**

Michigan, spooner, 3", clear w/flashing.......................**$70.00**

Mirror & Fan, decanter, gold flashed............................**$60.00**

Nursery Rhyme, mug, 3½", Humpty Dumpty, amber..**$35.00**

Nursery Rhyme, punch bowl, 3¼", cobalt..................**$425.00**

Oval Star, tray, 7¼" **$85.00**

Pattee Cross, punch cup, 1¼".......................................**$25.00**

Pennsylvania, creamer, 2½", green **$75.00**

Pennsylvania, sugar bowl, 4", green w/gold, w/lid...**$190.00**

Pert, butter dish, 2¾" **$125.00**

Petite Hobnail, pitcher, color $235.00
Rooster, sugar bowl, clear or milk glass w/lid..........$165.00
Rose in Snow, mug, 3½x3" $45.00
Sawtooth, sugar bowl, w/lid $45.00
Standing Lamb, sugar bowl, 5⅛", frosted, w/lid $450.00
Stippled Diamond, sugar bowl, color, w/lid..............$145.00
Stippled Raindrop & Dewdrop, sugar bowl, 3", w/lid ..$75.00

**Stork, mug, forest green, peafowl embossed on back,
Degenhart 'D in heart' mark $20.00**
Sultan, butter dish, 3¾", chocolate $600.00
Sunbeam, butter dish...$145.00
Tulip & Honeycomb, creamer.................................$20.00
Two Band, sugar bowl, w/lid $55.00
Wee Branches, butter dish.....................................$135.00
Wild Rose, creamer, 1¾", milk glass........................$55.00
Wild Rose, punch bowl..$100.00

Chocolate Molds

Molds used to shape chocolate are usually tin, though copper and occasionally even pewter molds were made as well. They are quite often very detailed (on the inside, of course), and variations are endless. Some are as simple as an Easter egg, others as complex as a rabbit hunter equipped with his gun and pouch or a completely decorated Christmas tree.

These seem to be regional; if you live in the East, you're bound to see them.

Bear, walking, lg..$235.00
Bell, lg..$55.00
Blacksmith's tongs, 5", 2-part, no mark, ca 1910 ....$27.50
Bugs Bunny, 2x5¼"...$55.00
Bugs Bunny, 9½", Warner Bros, ca 1950s $100.00
Bulldog, 3x3"...$50.00
Candy bars, makes 14, cast metal, Wilbur Candy Co ..$20.00
Champagne bottle, #84, 2-part, 5½x3"........................$25.00

Chicken, 4", #2031, dolphin stamp $32.50
Chimney sweep on roof w/ladder, 4½ x2¾", metal, no
    mark $100.00
Christmas tree, half-mold.......................................$65.00
Clovers, two rows on 10x4" tray...............................$52.50
Dog, begging, sm...$55.00
Donkey, 4½x5"..$50.00
Dutch shoe, fancy, sm $80.00
Easter basket, lg $75.00
Elephant, 2x4½"...$45.00
Father Christmas, sm..$98.00
Father Christmas on donkey, sm $115.00
Fish, 7x14"..$75.00
Girl w/finger in mouth, Reiche & Co, 5".....................$60.00
Hen, nesting, lg...$65.00
Jester, 2-part, 11x5"...$75.00
Lamb, aluminum, 7x6"...$12.50
Penguin, sm...$45.00
Pig, smiling, 2½x3½"..$50.00
Pig, 2½x4½"...$58.00
Rabbit, sitting w/basket, 15", alloy, #4032, Laurosch, 1930s-
    40s $60.00
Rabbit pulling chick in egg, 2½x5" $40.00
Rabbit sitting, hinged & clamped, 5" $40.00
Rabbit standing w/basket on back, 16x5½" hinged
    frame $110.00
Rabbit w/basket on back, 9x4", tinned metal, Eppelsheimer
    Co, 1935...$55.00

Rabbit w/basket on his back, 9½", double....................$150.00
Rabbit w/cart, 9", cast aluminum, single hinge, flat bot-
    tom...$32.50
Rabbit w/egg on back, four in frame $150.00
Rooster, 10", steel & copper alloy, #62, Weygandt, ca
    1950s..$130.00
Rooster pulling chick in egg $78.00
Santa Claus, sm $70.00
Santa Claus, 6½", nickel-plated metal, #15554, Holland
    Handcrafts, 1983...$40.00
Santa Claus, 7¼", nickel-plated metal, B-M #44, ca
    1920s $110.00
Santa's boot, 2-part, 4½x3¾" $48.00
Soccer player, 2-part, 7¾x5" $68.00

St Nicholas w/staff in bishop's robes, 2-part, 4x2¼"....**$70.00**

Swan, 3¼x3½", tinned metal, #1756, Paris **$80.00**

Swiss man, 2-part, 4x2¼"...**$38.00**

Telephone receiver **$50.00**

Turkey, half-mold **$45.00**

Turkey, 4½", tinned nickel silver, #8635, Germany, ca late 1940s-early 1950s **$38.00**

Turkey, 4x4½", metal, #15292, Holland......................**$60.00**

Violin, 10½x3¾", metal, #40034, Anton Reiche.........**$130.00**

Weightlifter, sm...**$90.00**

Wolf, 2-part, 5x4" **$45.00**

Yule log **$60.00**

Christmas Collectibles

Christmas is nearly everybody's favorite holiday, and it's a season when we all seem to want to get back to time-honored traditions. The stuffing and fruit cakes are made like Grandma always made them, we go caroling and sing the old songs that were written two hundred years ago, and the same Santa that brought gifts to the children in a time long forgotten still comes to our house and yours every Christmas Eve.

So for reasons of nostalgia, there are thousands of collectors interested in Christmas memorabilia. Some early Santa figures are rare and may be very expensive, especially when dressed in a color other than red. Blown glass ornaments and Christmas tree bulbs were made in shapes of fruits and vegetables, houses, Disney characters, animals, and birds. There are Dresden ornaments and candy containers from Germany, some of which were made prior to the 1870s, that have been lovingly preserved and handed down to our generation. They were made of cardboard that sparkled with gold and silver trim.

Artificial trees made of feathers were produced as early as 1850 and as late as 1950. Some were white, others blue, though most were green, and some had red berries or clips to hold candles. There were little bottle brush trees, trees with cellophane needles, and trees from the sixties of aluminum.

Collectible Christmas items are not necessarily old, expensive, or hard to find. Things produced in your lifetime have value as well. To learn more about this field, we recommend *Christmas Collectibles* by Margaret and Kenn Whitmyer, and *Christmas Ornaments, Lights, and Decorations* by George Johnson.

Advertising trade card, Christmas scene, John F Patton Company, early 1900s, EX, scarce **$22.50**

Advertising trade card, Christmas scene, Woolson Spice Company, early 1900s, EX............................**$12.50**

Bank, 6", Santa, painted cast iron, American, early 1900s **$185.00**

Bank, 8½", Santa troll, plastic w/cotton beard & flannel suit, Sweden, 1960s, M **$65.00**

Bank, 9", Santa, brown-glazed pottery, embossed Merry Christmas **$140.00**

Book, Santa Claus & the Lost Kitten, Whitman, 1952, EX **$5.00**

Bookmark, Noel & elves, woven silk, NM................**$45.00**

Bubble light, variety of sizes, colors & styles, 1940s to 1950s, minumum value of each being $2.00 & ranging up to **$10.00**

Bulb, baby in basket, tan w/striped blanket...............**$95.00**

Bulb, Humpty Dumpty on wall, multicolor paint on milk glass, EX **$68.00**

Bulb, 2", Matchless Star, glass (plastic up to 50% less), 1930s **$15.00**

Bulb, 2", Santa, 2-faced, red & black paint on milk glass **$30.00**

Bulb, 2½", clown's head, double-faced, multicolor paint on clear glass, EX.......................................**$40.00**

Bulb, 3", bell w/three Santa faces, multicolor paint on milk glass, VG...**$22.00**

Bulb, 3", clown on ball, yellow ruffle, red suit, EX.....**$65.00**

Bulb, 3", Dick Tracy, EX multicolor paint on milk glass **$140.00**

Bulb, 3", pig, multicolor paint on milk glass.............**$110.00**

Bulb, 3", Santa, red & green w/pink bag **$25.00**

Bulb, 3", three men in a tub, bright multicolor paint ..**$60.00**

Bulb, 3½", woman w/cross, multicolor paint on milk glass, EX...**$42.50**

Bulb, 3⅛", Orphan Annie, EX multicolor paint on milk glass, marked c 1935....................................**$55.00**

Bulb, 4", cat, bright multicolor paint on milk glass.....**$37.50**

Bulb, 4", cross w/star, yellow & pink paint, EX..........**$35.00**

Bulb, 4", dog, brown & red paint on milk glass..........**$45.00**

Bulb, 4", girl w/red rose, green blouse, EX **$70.00**

Bulb, 5½", Santa, bright multicolor paint....................**$75.00**

Bulb, 7", star, Noma, EX in original box **$50.00**

Bulb, 9", Father Christmas, Japan, MIB **$100.00**

Bulb, 9", Santa, bright colors on milk glass **$115.00**

Cake pan, 10x11", Christmas tree shape, tin, rolled rim, EX **$30.00**

Candle clip, 1½", angel enameled on tin, double sided, early 1900s, EX **$35.00**

Candle clip, 2¼", Father Christmas enameled on tin, double sided, early 1900s, EX.............................**$95.00**

Candle clip, 3", spring style w/flower bud glass shade, unsilvered, early 1900s **$32.00**

Candle clip, 3½", spring style, glass shade top serves as candle holder, clips to tree, early 1900s....................**$60.00**

Candy container, 2", snowball, celluloid, EX **$25.00**

Candy container, 2", top hat, Dresden, red silk w/silver rosettes, EX...**$250.00**

Candy container, 2½x3", drum, Dresden, vertical gold stripes, silver star..**$95.00**

Candy container, 2x3", opera glasses, Dresden **$185.00**

Candy container, 3", ball, papier-mache, bright multicolored paint..**$42.50**

Candy container, 3", house, red & green painted glass..**$75.00**

Candy container, 3", Santa on sled, composition, Germany, EX **$165.00**

Candy container, 3", star medallion, Dresden, cardboard & glitter..**$110.00**

Candy container, 5", donkey, composition, gray paint, EX details, head lifts off, Germany $135.00

Candy container, 6", cornucopia, foil w/celluloid Santa head on front..$22.00

Candy container, 6", elf, spun glass, w/Dresden horn, on composition snowball, Germany $65.00

Candy container, 6", snowman, mica covered, Germany, EX $35.00

Candy container, 7", Santa, clay face, mesh candy bag, red flannel suit, Japan, 1930s...$30.00

Candy container, 7", snowman, composition, EX........$50.00

Candy container, 9", snowman, mica-covered cardboard w/wool carrot nose, Germany $50.00

Chocolate mold, 9", Santa w/basket, tin, hinged............$90.00

Costume, Santa suit, red cotton, cowl hood, mask face, ca 1900, EX $350.00

Decoration, 26x18", Santa's head, plaster of Paris, EX paint $165.00

Feather tree, 26", red composition berries on limb tips, round wooden base, Germany, 1920s-30s, EX ...$155.00

Feather tree, 72", red composition berries, decorated white square base, 1930s, EX...$500.00

Fence, 2¼x27" square, wood, original green paint, gate at front, EX in original box....................................$95.00

Fence, 24" square, wood, wicker uprights, EX original paint..$150.00

Fence, 56" long, wood, brown & green paint, 4-section, Germany, EX $65.00

Figure, 10", Santa, papier-mache face & boots, Japan, EX $95.00

Figure, 17", Santa, plastic, hole in back for bulb to be inserted, 1960s, NM..$30.00

Figure, 21", Santa, pressed cardboard, velvet-covered suit, Whitman, EX $22.50

Figure, 3", Santa in sleigh w/reindeer, bisque, Germany, EX...$115.00

Figure, 3½x4", Santa, celluloid, on metal tricycle, NM .$55.00

Figure, 4", Santa on skis, celluloid, 1930s, EX.............$80.00

Figure, 5", Santa, celluloid, red & white, 1920s-40s.....$30.00

Figure, 6", Santa, plaster face, pressed cotton body, Japan $35.00

Figure, 9", Santa, felt w/rubber face, jointed, EX........$30.00

Garland, 110", round glass beads, 1950s, EX $20.00

Garland, 112", green & gold glass beads, EX..............$25.00

Garland, 120", paper bells, Father Christmas lithograph, Germany, 1920s..$48.00

Garland, 18", slim multicolor glass beads separated by round gold-colored beads, early type, EX............$25.00

Kugel, 2" to 5", round glass ball, late 1800s, each.......$35.00

Kugel, 2¾", glass grape cluster, any color, early 1900s, each..$100.00

Kugel, 4½", textured glass ball, any color, late 1800s, each..$135.00

Kugel, 6", glass oval, any color, late 1800s, each $55.00

Kugel, 6" to 9", glass ball shape, any color, late 1800s, each..$80.00

Kugel, 7½", glass grape cluster, any color, early 1900s, each..$115.00

Lamb, 5½", composition w/wooden legs, woolly covering, EX..$78.00

Lamp, 8", Santa figural, plastic, holding bubble light in hand, 1950s, EX......................................$25.00

Lamp, 8½", plastic & tin, 1950s, Glo-Light Corporation of Chicago...$15.00

Lamp, 8½", Santa figural, plastic & tan, Glo-Light Corporation, 1950s, NM $12.00

Lights, Noma, Mazda, string of fifteen, EX..................$35.00

Nativity scene, 20x15x14", fold-out cardboard lithograph, Germany, 1900s, EX...$75.00

Ornament, chromo figure on a wire-wrapped ball, 1900s $60.00

Ornament, 1½", bell, pressed cotton, M........................$6.00

Ornament, 1½", house, cardboard, bright paint & mica, Czechoslovakia...$15.00

Ornament, 1½", pear, pressed cotton, NM $7.50

Ornament, 1¼" doll face, mold-blown glass, hand-painted face & eyes on pearly white, 1930s-40s, EX........$100.00

Ornament, 12", candy cane, red & white chenille w/green chenille bow $7.50

Ornament, 2", apple w/face, mold-blown, EX multicolor paint, 1910s **$95.00**

Ornament, 2", basket, Dresden, tan...........................**$110.00**

Ornament, 2", drum, coated cardboard, bright colors.**$12.00**

Ornament, 2½", baby w/pacifier, mold-blown glass, NM multicolor paint, 1900s **$95.00**

Ornament, 2½", bear, mold-blown glass, gold w/black details **$110.00**

Ornament, 2½", fox, Dresden, brown & tan, NM **$315.00**

Ornament, 2½", orange, pressed cotton, M..................**$15.00**

Ornament, 2½", star shape, soft tin & lead w/faceted glass beads...**$20.00**

Ornament, 2¾", elf's head, mold-blown glass, red & black details on pearly white, 1920s, EX.........................**$75.00**

Ornament, 3", bear w/extended legs, mold-blown glass, early 1900s, EX original.......................................**$165.00**

Ornament, 3", bird w/cherries in mouth, mold-blown glass, silvered...$45.00

Ornament, 3", birdcage, metal 'wire' type w/small metal bird inside, EX..**$25.00**

Ornament, 3", boy, mold-blown, pink details on pearly white, EX **$50.00**

Ornament, 3", elk, Dresden, tan & brown, EX **$200.00**

Ornament, 3", girl in bag, mold-blown glass, yellow hair, pink bag **$75.00**

Ornament, 3", girl w/golden hair, mold-blown glass, green bow, yellow hair, painted features on pearly white, 1920s **$75.00**

Ornament, 3", Indian's head, mold-blown glass, matt face, black hair, feathers **$185.00**

Ornament, 3" long, fish, mold-blown glass, silvered (illustrated) $30.00

Ornament, 3", pine cone, mold-blown glass, green paint.**$35.00**

Ornament, 3", spaniel, mold-blown glass, silver w/green ears & legs, red bow..**$55.00**

Ornament, 3", Uncle Sam, mold-blown glass, blue coat & hat, red striped pants..**$235.00**

Ornament, 3½", clown on the moon, mold-blown glass, pearly white, early 1900s.....................................**$65.00**

Ornament, 3½", clown's head, mold-blown glass, multicolor paint on pearly white, NM **$60.00**

Ornament, 3½", Goldilocks, mold-blown glass, red, green & yellow on pearly white, 1930s, NM **$75.00**

Ornament, 3½", old man in pine cone, mold-blown glass, gold w/pink & red details, 1930s, EX...................**$60.00**

Ornament, 3½", scottie w/bow, mold-blown glass, red & green w/black details, 1910s...............................**$75.00**

Ornament, 3½", snowman, mold-blown glass, frosted body, painted features & broom, 1950s **$18.00**

Ornament, 4", bell, chenille w/celluloid Santa face on side, EX...**$40.00**

Ornament, 4", bell, wire-wrapped glass w/Dresden paper leaf, 1900s...**$50.00**

Ornament, 4", bell w/crown top, mold-blown glass, silvered, mid-1930s, EX..**$60.00**

Ornament, 4", Dresden, black & white horse **$300.00**

Ornament, 4", flower girl, mold-blown glass, flesh face, gold hair, multicolor flowers, EX..............................**$145.00**

Ornament, 4", mandolin, wire-wrapped glass.............**$50.00**

Ornament, 4", turnip, pressed cotton, M....................**$12.00**

Ornament, 4½", angel, scrap face & wings w/circular spun glass halo & robe **$20.00**

Ornament, 4½", devil, mold-blown glass, yellow eyes, red mouth, black features, NM **$365.00**

Ornament, 4½", Mary Pickford w/extended legs, mold-blown glass, white w/gold, EX............................**$265.00**

Ornament, 4½", wreath, Dresden, gold w/red, Santa lithograph, 1900s **$75.00**

Ornament, 4x6¼", coach, Dresden, silver paper, EX.**$220.00**

Ornament, 5", chandelier, wire-wrapped glass, 1900..**$100.00**

Ornament, 5", chromolithograph angel riding blue glass wire-wrapped boat...**$50.00**

Ornament, 5", flowerpot, wire-wrapped glass **$30.00**

Ornament, 5", strawberry, mold-blown glass, yellow & pink on white frost, EX **$70.00**

Ornament, 5½", Santa, mold-blown glass, flesh face, gold tree, chenille legs, EX...**$265.00**

Ornament, 6", angel, scrap face & wings w/crepe paper skirt **$15.00**

Ornament, 6", children as central figures in scrap reserve within tinsel frame, 1900s....................................**$15.00**

Ornament, 6", icicle, pressed cotton.............................**$15.00**

Ornament, 6", owl, Dresden, gold & brown, EX..**$135.00**

Ornament, 6½", Lady Liberty, mold-blown glass, applied real hair, painted details, 1920s, EX.........................**$115.00**

Ornament, 7", angel, wax figure w/brown hair, spun glass wings, original horn...**$160.00**

Ornament, 7", Santa on swan, scrap figure on blown bird, NM...**$100.00**

Ornament, 9", Father Christmas, scrap character w/surrounding tinsel, early 1900s **$90.00**

Ornament, 9", Father Christmas, scrap face, cotton robe, tinsel hanger...**$120.00**

Ornament, 9½", Father Christmas, scrap upper body & feet with spun glass skirt **$70.00**

Post card, 'Best Christmas Wishes,' Winsch, 1913, EX..**$10.00**

Post card, 'Oh Look Who's Here,' Santa & child at door, Raphael Tuck & Sons..**$7.50**

Post card, Santa in long green robe, ca 1910 ....**$6.50**

Print, 8x10", baby on chair beside tree, signed Maud Humphrey, 1898..**$65.00**

Ram, 3½", wooden w/metal horns, Germany, EX **$75.00**

Rattle, 4½", Santa figural, celluloid, multicolor, Occupied Japan, NM **$115.00**

Stove pipe cover, 7", Father Christmas holding small girl & doll lithograph, NM **$65.00**

Toy, 5½", Santa, tin lithographed wind-up type, Chein, 1930s, EX **$90.00**

Tree, 2" to 5", bottle-brush type, 'snow' covered bristles, red base, M **$3.50**

Tree, 8½", bottle-brush type, 'snow' covered, original pressed cotton ornaments, NM **$30.00**

Tree stand, 15x18x18", cast iron, inverted cone on tripod foot, 1920s, EX **$70.00**

Tree stand, 18½x6", turned wood, tripod legs, old green paint, EX..**$78.00**

Tree top light, star form w/five original multicolor bulbs, Noma, late 1930s, EX..**$20.00**

Tree-top star, 8½", tin, gold & red paint, patented 1926 . **$55.00**

Cleminsons Pottery

One of the several small potteries that operated in California during the middle of the century, Cleminsons was a family-operated enterprise that made kitchenware, decorative items, and novelties that are beginning to attract a considerable amount of interest. At the height of their productivity, they employed 150 workers, so as you make your 'rounds,' you'll be very likely to see a piece or two offered for sale just about anywhere you go. Prices are not high; this may be a 'sleeper.'

They marked their ware fairly consistently with a circular ink stamp that contains the name 'Cleminsons.' But even if you find an unmarked piece, with just a little experience you'll be able to easily recognize their very distinctive glaze colors. They're all strong, yet grayed-down, dusty tones. They made a line of bird-shaped tableware items that they marketed as 'Distlefink,' and several plaques and wall pockets that are decorated with mottos and Pennsylvania Dutch-type hearts and flowers.

In Jack Chipman's *The Collector's Encyclopedia of California Pottery*, you'll find a chapter devoted to Cleminsons Pottery; and Roerig's *The Collector's Encyclopedia of Cookie Jars* has some more information.

Butter dish, lady figural **$35.00**

Cookie jar, 'The Way to a Man's Heart,' lovebird finial on lid, marked California Cleminsons Copyright........**$70.00**

Cup & saucer, oversize, lady sitting in rocker reads paper, stamp mark...**$20.00**

Egg cup, double; hand-painted cook in apron w/long spoon..**$20.00**

Gravy boat, Distlefink, bird figural, w/ladle.................**$22.00**

Pie bird, 4½", crowing rooster figural, in-mold mark .. **$15.00**

Pitcher, Distlefink, 9½" **$25.00**

Pitcher, Gala Gray, 7", red figures on gray ground **$22.50**

Plaque, 'Let's Pay Off the Mortgage' painted on square form...**$12.00**

Plate, 9½", crowing rooster in center...........................**$10.00**

Spoon rest, 8½", painted floral design on gray, spoon form **$20.00**

Wall pocket, coffeepot shape......................................**$15.00**

Wall pocket, 7¼", chef's head shape, stamped mark ..**$30.00**

Clothes Sprinkler Bottles

In the days before perma-press, the process of getting wrinkles out of laundered clothing involved first sprinkling each piece with water, rolling it tightly to distribute the moisture, and packing it all down in a laundry basket until ironing day. Thank goodness those days are over!

To sprinkle the water, you could simply dip your fingers in a basin and 'fling' the water around, or you could take a plain old bottle with a screw-on cap, pierce the cap a few times and be in business. Maybe these figural bottles were made to add a little cheer to this dreary job. Anyway, since no one does all this any more, they represent a little bit of history, and collectors now take an interest in them. Prices are already fairly high, but there still may be a bargain or two out there!

Cat w/jewel eyes, 9", taupe w/brown airbrushed spots, seated upright with front legs between back feet, ceramic **$45.00**

Cat w/marble eyes, 8", looking left, ceramic, no mark . **$75.00**

Chinaman, Cardinal China w/label **$22.50**

Chinaman, 8", 'Sparkle Plenty,' ceramic **$32.00**

Clothespin, 8", ceramic **$35.00**

Dutch Boy, 8", hands in pockets, ceramic **$45.00**

Dutch Girl, 8", in hat & apron, arms folded at waist, ceramic **$45.00**

Elephant, red plastic, M..**$25.00**

Elephant, 7½", 'Sprinkles,' trunk up, ceramic $65.00

Merry Maid, 7½", girl w/hands on hips, plastic, Made in USA **$25.00**

Rooster, 10", multicolored & airbrushed, very long neck, ceramic (illustrated)........................$40.00
Siamese cat, Cardinal China $75.00

Clothing and Accessories

Vintage clothing shops are everywhere, have you noticed? And what's especially exciting are the forties, fifties, and sixties items that look so familiar. Hawaiian shirts have been hot for some time, and when padded shoulders became fashionable for women, thirties and forties clothing became very 'trendy.'

While some collectors buy with the intent of preserving their clothing and simply enjoy having and looking at it, many buy it to wear. If you do wear it, be very careful how you clean it, they're not made of polyester!

Apron, printed cotton, fitted bodice with shoulder straps, heart-shaped pockets w/ruffled trim, 1940s, EX ...$15.00
Apron, red polka dots, long farm style, 1950s, EX $15.00
Bathing suit, jersey print, tank-style top with full skirt to mid thigh, 1940s, EX $20.00
Bathing suit, wool, 1-pc, skirted tank-top style, ca 1924, EX $55.00
Blouse, handkerchief linen w/lace inserts, ¾-length lace sleeves, tight wrists, ca 1900, EX $400.00
Bonnet, leghorn w/braided trim, 1830s, EX................$85.00
Bustle, 2-tiered, wire mesh frame, adjustable, EX $115.00
Coat, red cashmere w/silver fox collar, full length, 1940s, EX..$60.00
Dress, black crepe, V neck, ¾-length sleeves, shoulder pads, rhinestones, 1940s, EX $38.00
Dress, cotton, scoop neck, short sleeves, flared mini-length skirt, 1960s, M $40.00
Dress, diagonal front closing, wide shawl collar, drop waist, 1910s, child's size, EX.............................$140.00
Dress, evening; organza w/rhinestones, long skirt, 1940s $50.00
Dress, printed percale, square neck, half sleeves, shoulder pads, flared skirt, button-down-front style, 1940s, EX $35.00
Dress, printed silk, button trim at lowered waist, long sleeves, ca mid-1920s, EX...............................$135.00
Dress, rayon floral, sweetheart neckline, short sleeves, 1940s, EX $35.00
Dress, red calico, Cluny lace insert, tucked hem, child's size...$25.00
Dress, red silk, black trim, drop waist, 1920s, EX........$70.00
Dress, silk, slip-on style w/adjustable collar, long sleeves, sash ties in back, 1920s, EX $175.00
Dress, taffeta, strapless w/large bow accent at shoulder, fully lined long skirt w/attached slip, 1950s, EX.$100.00
Dress, white organdy w/red polka dots, 3-tier skirt, short sleeves, red cloth belt, 1940s, EX.......................$65.00
Dress, wool, stand-up collar, ¾-length sleeves, accordion-pleated skirt, buttons to waist, 1949, EX............$175.00
Dress, wool w/lace at neck & cuffs, boned waist, tasseled flounce, long sleeves, 1880s, EX.......................$650.00

Fur coat, Persian lamb, fur collar, full length, EX......$150.00
Fur coat, raccoon, shawl collar, long sleeves, full length, EX $950.00
Fur muff, natural lamb's wool, EX.............................$25.00
Gown, wedding; ivory satin w/lace, long sleeves, full skirt, 1950s, EX $65.00
Hat, felt w/velvet trim & butterfly-style bow, late 1940s, EX $15.00
Hat, garden; blue organdy with 4" wide brim, 1930s, EX $27.50
Long johns, off-wht cotton, drop seat, 1930s, M..........$15.00
Nickers, wool, buckled at side of band below knee, man's golfing style, 1930s, EX.................................$40.00
Nightgown, peach silk w/much lace, long, NM..........$28.00
Nightgown, white batiste, Empire style w/inset yoke w/floral embroidery, full length, 1920s, EX $175.00
Robe, brown & beige striped taffeta, boned bodice, bell sleeves, ca 1860, EX..$625.00
Shawl, intricate black lace, 1920s, 66x12", EX $65.00
Shoes, high-heeled platform style, late 1940s, EX $32.50

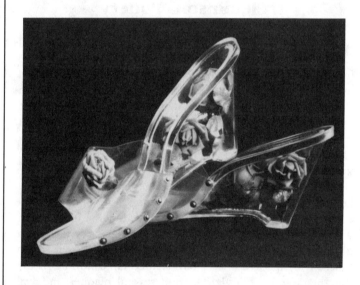

Shoes, lucite w/roses contained in heels & applied to vamp, 1950s $125.00
Shoes, wedgies, open heel & toe, 1949, pr, EX..........$32.00
Suit, gray & white pinstripe wool, wide lapel, double-breasted style, cuffed trousers, 1940s, EX $150.00
Suit, gray wool, fitted jacket, shoulder pads, slim skirt, 1940s, VG $65.00
Suit, navy & white tweed, shawl collar, ¾-length sleeves, flared skirt, 1940s, EX......................................$125.00
Suit, wool, boy's long-sleeve jacket w/knickers, 1930s, EX $65.00
Teddy, silk crepe, lace trim, 1920s, NM $20.00

Coca-Cola Collectibles

Coca-Cola was introduced to the public in 1886. Immediately an advertising campaign began that over the years and to the present day has literally saturated our lives with a never-ending variety of items. Some of the earlier calendars and trays have been known to bring prices well into the four figures. Because of these prices and the extremely wide-spread collector demand for good Coke items, reproductions are everywhere, so beware! Some of the items that have been reproduced are pocket mirrors (from 1905, 1906, 1908-11, 1916, and 1920), trays (from 1899, 1910, 1913-14, 1917, 1920, 1923, 1926, 1934, and 1937), tip trays (from 1907, 1909, 1910, 1913-14, 1917, and 1920), knives, cartons, bottles, clocks, and trade cards. Currently being produced and marketed are an 18" brass 'button,' a 24" brass bottle-shaped thermometer, cast iron toys and bottle-shaped door pulls, Yes Girl posters, a 12" 'button' sign (with one round hole), a rectangular paperweight, a 1949-style cooler radio, and there are others.

In addition to reproductions, 'fantasy' items have also been made, the difference being that a 'fantasy' never existed as an original. Don't be deceived. Belt buckles are 'fantasies.' So are glass doorknobs with an etched trademark, bottle-shaped knives, pocket knives (supposedly from the 1933 World's Fair), a metal letter opener stamped 'Coca-Cola 5¢,' a cardboard sign with the 1911 lady with fur (9x11"), and celluloid vanity pieces (a mirror, brush, etc).

When the company celebrated its 100th anniversary in 1986, many 'centennial' items were issued; they all carry the '100th Anniversary' logo. Many of them are collectible in their own right, and some are already high-priced.

If you'd really like to study this subject, we recommend these books: _Goldstein's Coca-Cola Collectibles_ by Sheldon Goldstein, _Huxford's Collectible Advertising_ by Sharon and Bob Huxford, and _Collector's Guide to Coca-Cola Items, Vols I and II,_ by Al Wilson.

Ashtray, 1936, brass, commemorates Coca-Cola's 50th Anniversary..**$50.00**

Ashtrays, 1950s, ruby glass, set of four shaped as a diamond, heart, club, & spade..................................**$600.00**

Bank, metal, shaped as red & white Coke can............**$10.00**

Bank, plastic, pink w/red fishtail logo on sides...........**$10.00**

Bank, 1950s, dispenser form, battery operated, EX...**$500.00**

Bank, 1950s, shaped as white bottle cap w/'Drink Coca-Cola' encircled in red..**$25.00**

Banner, 1950s, shows Santa with a dog, 'When Friends Drop In, Stock Up For the Holidays,' 20x11", EX.**$20.00**

Blotter, 1938, cardboard, pictures a policeman drinking a Coke, 4x8", NM...**$20.00**

Blotter, 1942, shows a girl on her stomach with her hand under her chin, 'I Think It's Swell,' rectangular, NM...**$8.00**

Blotter, 1953, Sprite boy in the snow with bottles of Coke on the left, 'Good!' lettered on the left, NM............**$4.00**

Blotter, 1960, pictures bottle of Coke on a chart, 'Over 60 Million a Day,' 'Refreshing New Feeling,' NM.........**$6.00**

Book cover, shows a Coke bottle w/button logo plus three scenes on front, back has safety 'ABCs,' EX.........**$12.00**

Bookmark, 1904, paper, Lillian Nordica standing in front of dressing screen, 'Drink Coca-Cola 5¢,' 6¼x2".....**$375.00**

Bookmark, 1906, paper, die-cut owl perched on a branch, 1x3½"...**$750.00**

Bottle, 1960s, clear, 'No Refill,' 10-oz, M.....................**$12.00**

Bottle carrier, 1939, cardboard, depicts the red & white Coca-Cola logo, 7", EX+...**$40.00**

Bottle carrier, 1940s, wood, natural & red, 'Drink Coca-Cola in Bottles,' NM..**$65.00**

Bottle opener, 1930s, chrome corkscrew, 5", NM........**$50.00**

Bottle opener, 1950s, bottle shape, EX+......................**$10.00**

Bottle opener/ice pick, metal w/circular handle, pick end has hook opener, VG+..**$60.00**

Calendar, 1937, paper, colorful image of boy & his dog going fishing, full pad, matted & framed, EX....**$500.00**

Calendar, 1948, metal, red button atop a vertical rectangle w/rounded corners, 'Have a Coke,' 19x8", NM..**$195.00**

Calendar, 1962, die-cut metal, red & green on white w/fishtail logo atop, May pad, 13x10", NM....................**$175.00**

Calendar top, 1918, paper, two ladies on a beach holding a bottle & glass of Coke, pad missing, 28x13".......**$400.00**

Can, 1980s, aluminum, red & white, '4-oz Free,' Max Headroom on back, 16-oz, NM..................................**$3.00**

Chalkboard, 1950s, tin w/rounded corners, lettered oval insert atop, 'Have a Coke' at bottom, 26x18", G...**$50.00**

Channel card, 1953, cardboard, pictures steak dinner & glass of Coke, 'Steak Plate,' 7x24", NM.........................**$30.00**

Channel card, 1960s, cardboard, pictures mountains & a glass of Coke, 'Ham & Cheese & Coke,' 7x24", NM........**$30.00**

Checkers, 1940s, Dragon, Coca-Cola logo on each checker, complete..**$55.00**

Cigarette box, 1936, frosted glass, commemorates Coca-Cola's 50th anniversary...**$475.00**

Cigarette lighter, 1950s, bottle shape, 2"....................**$20.00**

Clock, 1910, wood, boudoir, 'Drink Bottled Coca-Cola,' rare, 3" dia...**$800.00**

Clock, 1939, wood & glass, numbered 1-12 on white background w/red center, 'Drink Coca-Cola in Bottles,' 16x16", NM..**$450.00**

Clock, 1950s, metal & glass counter-top style, red, green, & white w/gold bottle, 15" dia, NM..........................**$425.00**

Clock, 1980 Sessions, wood w/glass face, white, red, & light oak stain, limited edition, 25x17", NM.................**$450.00**

Coaster, 1930, cardboard, red, yellow, & white, depicts a silhouette of a girl, 'Drink Coca-Cola Ice Cold, M.**$5.00**

Coaster, 1950s, green & white, 'Please Put Empties in the Rack,' EX...**$3.00**

Convention cowboy hat, 1937, red band w/date, logo & other lettering...**$200.00**

Cooler, metal w/embossed side panels & tall legs on wheels, shows Coke bottles & logos on the sides, 32x22x17", MN..**$1,250.00**

Cooler, 1940s, 72", MN..**$1,200.00**

Coupons, 1950s, cardboard, shows a 6-pack, 'Save This Valuable Coupon,' 3x4", NM..**$5.00**

Cribbage board, 1940s, wood, beige & red, complete w/box & instructions, 3x10", NM...**$60.00**

Display, 1950s, die-cut cardboard, easel-back, shows children at refrigerator, 'For Santa,' 9x14".................**$135.00**

Display, 1971, die-cut cardboard, shows Santa in front of the Christmas tree holding a Coke & sack, 26x17", NM...**$18.00**

Display dispenser, 1940s, 3-piece rubber w/Coke glass inserted in the bottom, EX $495.00

Display rack, folding wire which holds 6-packs of Coke, logoed top has rounded corners, 47", EX $70.00

Display stand, steel w/round sign atop, 'Take Home a Carton,' '25¢,' 56x16" dia, G.................................$100.00

Doll, Santa, 1950s, M.....................................$150.00

Driver's cap pin, 1950s, metal, 'Drink Coca-Cola'......$175.00

Dry Server, 1929, w/two bottles, 'The Pause that Refreshes,' 3x6", EX $3.00

Fan, 1956, cardboard on wooden stick, shows hand holding bottle, logo on back, 12x8", NM $28.00

Glass, 1923-27, modified flare-shape, etched logo with syrup line, 4", M $35.00

Gum box, wood, faded image of 'Coca-Cola Gum' printed in a key shape on side of box, 6x13x6", G.........$275.00

Hairbrush, 1930s, celluloid, depicts Coca-Cola logo ...$35.00

Ice tongs, 1930s, metal w/yellow wood handle and red lettering..$200.00

Label, paper, for straight 6½-oz Coke bottle.................$75.00

Lamp shade, 1918, leaded glass w/fringed brass, 'Property of the Coco-Cola Company...,' 16" dia, EX $4,500.00

Magazine advertisement, June 1910, both covers of 'The Housewife' magazine showing two women & dog at soda fountain, G $170.00

Magazine advertisement, 1906, pictures a girl in buggy, EX.$23.00

Matchbook, 1930s, 'Refresh Yourself, A Pure Drink of Natural Flavors' $15.00

Menu, 1903, depicts lady in white dress seated holding a glass of coke, 'Soda Menu' on reverse, 6x4" $800.00

Menu board, Coke bottle & 'Drink Coca-Cola' lettered at top of menu, 'Delicious,' 'Refreshing,' 'Good with Food,' EX..$240.00

Message pad cube, 1983, formed as a case of Coca-Cola, 4x6" $5.00

Miniature carton, 1970s, w/six black bottles, 'It's the Real Thing'...$3.00

Miniature case, 1960s, yellow w/twenty-four gold glass bottles, NM..$15.00

Mobile, 1950s, double-sided w/red dangling disk, 'Extra Refreshment,' 19" dia $22.00

Money clip, 1949, brass w/red plastic logo.................$22.00

Napkin, 1911, rice paper, red, white, & blue period logo w/lady in elegant dress, matted, 16x16", MN......$125.00

Needle case, 1924, cardboard, shows a lady w/her hand on her hip enjoying a Coke, 3x2", NM....................$60.00

NFL charm bracelet, 1960s, chain w/four charms......$100.00

Notebook, shows the '1987 Coca-Cola Advertising Schedule,' spiral-bound $8.00

Pedal car, 1940-50, metal w/rubber wheels, red w/white lettering, has been restored, 19x36" $1,200.00

Pencil, mechanical; 1940s, has bottle-shaped metal clip, in original box..$20.00

Pencil, mechanical; 1950s, goldtone, top has floating bottle $18.00

Pencil holder, 1960s, red on white ceramic, urn shape, 8x4", EX+ $190.00

Perfume bottle case, 1920s, sterling silver.................$250.00

Picnic cooler, 1940s, cardboard, red & beige, 'Drink Coca-Cola,' 10x10", EX......................................$65.00

Playing cards, WWII era, cards show three airplanes in silhouette, box shows nurse w/Coke, NM.............$110.00

Playing cards, 1963, white & red, cards show a bottle of Coke, 'Things Go Better With Coke,' 3x2", NM $35.00

Playing cards, 1974, 'Drink Coca-Cola' on stained-glass graphics, in original box, VG $5.00

Pocket mirror, 1908, shows Victorian woman drinking from glass w/soda fountain in background, rare, oval, 3x2", EX $700.00

Pocket mirror, 1920, celluloid, depicts the 'Golden Girl,' has creases in the celluloid, oval, 3x2", EX...............$550.00

Popcorn holder, 1950s, cardboard, red cone shape w/Coca-Cola lettered up the sides.....................................$50.00

Post card, 1930s, depicts the Weldmech Coca-Cola truck $5.00

Post card, 1973, shows the Bobby Allison Coca-Cola race car $4.00

Poster, 1936 reproduction, cardboard, shows a dog entertaining boy, clown, & girl, logo in upper right, 18x27", NM $26.00

Poster, 1936 reproduction, cardboard, shows a sunbather being handed a Coke, round logo on right, 11x27", NM $28.00

Poster, 1960s, shows a boy & girl sitting facing each other, 'The Pause That Refreshes,' 36x20".....................$35.00

Push bar, 1930s, red & white porcelain, 'Drink Coca-Cola,' 16x4"...$200.00

Push bar, 1940s, red, yellow, white porcelain w/black ends, 'Coca-Cola Iced Here,' Canadian, 3x30" $110.00

Push plate, 1938-40, red, yellow, & white porcelain, 'Thanks Call Again for a Coca-Cola,' Canadian, 12x4" $190.00

Puzzle, metal, two interlocking pieces $25.00

Radio, crystal; 1950s, red, has earphone & alligator clip, very rare, 3x2x2", EX **$575.00**

Radio, plastic bottle form $25.00

Radio, 1950s, vending machine, red & white w/'Coca-Cola' across top panel.................................**$225.00**

Radio, 1970s, can style, 'Enjoy Coca-Cola' $30.00

Radio, 1980s, vending machine, red w/'Coke' printed vertically in white on front **$45.00**

Sales training kit, 1955, case w/records & film strips, 19" long, VG **$50.00**

School-teaching kit, 1970s, 'Man & His Environment'.$20.00

Score pad, 1940s, 'American Woman's Volunteer Service'...**$10.00**

Seltzer bottle, blue, w/spigot, EX **$350.00**

Sign, drink rack; red, yellow, & white w/arrow pointing down, 'Take Home a Carton 25¢,' 18" dia, G **$46.00**

Sign, drink rack; 1940s, metal, white, yellow, & red, 'Take Home a Carton,' 12" dia, EX+ **$95.00**

Sign, 1920s, die-cut cardboard, shows a woman w/glass of Coke, 15x10", VG+..................................**$30.00**

Sign, 1930s, embossed metal, Dasco 5-color, 'Drink Coca-Cola,' 6x18" **$225.00**

Sign, 1936, tin, red, white, & green, 'Drink Coca-Cola,' bottle of Coke at left, 12x36", EX+ **$375.00**

Sign, 1939, cardboard, bathing beauty seated on diving board w/a Coke, 50x30", G..................**$125.00**

Sign, 1940, electric, metal w/glass front, 'Serve Yourself' in green on white above 'Drink Coca-Cola,' 10x16", EX **$550.00**

Sign, 1946, metal, bottle w/16" metal disk on top, 40x16" **$400.00**

Sign, 1950s, cardboard, shows hamburgers, hot dogs, & Cokes, 'Family Favorites,' 18x24" **$30.00**

Sign, 1950s, lighted counter, 'Pause, Please Pay When Served' **$650.00**

Sign, 1950s, metal, 'Fountain Service,' 'Drink Coca-Cola,' 12x30", VG **$150.00**

Sign, 1950s, metal, double-sided, depicts early soda fountain dispenser, round corners, 24x24", VG.................**$175.00**

Sign, 1960s, die-cut cardboard, bottle cap form, white on red, 'Drink Coca-Cola,' 13", NM **$65.00**

Sign, 1960s, metal, red fishtail logo w/'Ice Cold' above & bottle of Coke at right on white background, 20x28", NM **$150.00**

Sign, 1960s, tin, paper Coca-Cola cup w/logo, 'Ice Cold,' 'Prepared by the Bottlers of Coca-Cola,' 28", VG..**$75.00**

Sign, 1970s, metal, 'Enjoy Coke,' 'Have a Coke & a Smile,' 17x35" **$30.00**

Sign, 1985, red, white, & black, 'Drink Coca-Cola in Bottles,' 4x17", M..................................**$14.00**

Sign 1920s, cardboard, shows bathing beauty in a robe holding glass of Coke, 32x22", G- **$300.00**

Siren whistle, 1930s, tall thimble shape.....................**$50.00**

Snack bowl, 1930s, light green w/Coca-Cola logo embossed on sides **$500.00**

Straws, 1930s, in red cardboard box w/logo & Coke bottle, EX...**$80.00**

Straws, 1940s, in white, green, & blue box, cut-out heart showing straws w/'Sweetheart Straws' lettered above, VG...**$60.00**

Syrup bottle, applied label w/red lettering on white background, 12", G..................................**$45.00**

Syrup can, white background w/red logoed disk **$125.00**

Tally card, 1940s, tray of Cokes & red disk on tally side, birds pictured on back............................**$35.00**

Thermometer, 1930s, die-cut tin bottle w/white lettering 17", EX...**$100.00**

Thermometer, 1936, tin, red w/gold Christmas bottle, 16x7"...**$175.00**

Thermometer, 1944, masonite, green, yellow, red, & brown, shows a bottle of Coke, 'Thirst Knows No Season,' 17x7", NM **$275.00**

Thermometer, 1956, in the form of a gold bottle, in original box, 9x2", M...**$45.00**

Thermometer, 1960s, plastic, red & white w/red sides, 'Coca-Cola,' 17x6"..................................**$50.00**

Tip tray, 1905, shows a lady holding a glass, 'Delicious, Refreshing,' 4" dia, VG..................................**$200.00**

Tip tray, 1914, pictures 'Betty,' oval, 6x4" G.............**$175.00**

Toy dispenser, 'Item No 16,' 'Toy Coke Dispenser & Four Miniature Glasses' printed on side of original box, EX **$35.00**

Toy grocery cart, 1950s, metal w/heavy cardboard basket depicting grocery items, red wheels...................**$250.00**

Toy top, 1970s, plastic, 'Coke Adds Life...' **$3.00**

Toy, truck, Big Wheels, 1970s, M $100.00

Toy truck, 1940s, Japan, friction-type, tin w/decals, scarce, 4", VG **$90.00**

Toy truck, 1960, Matchbox, yellow, EX.....................**$37.00**

Tray, 1903, pictures Hilda Clark holding a fan & glass, 10" dia, G...**$300.00**

Tray, 1909, shows girl holding glass w/festive scene in background, oval, 13x11", VG+ **$800.00**

Tray, 1916, shows Elaine seated on a box holding a glass of Coke, 19x9", EX **$230.00**

Tray, 1922, pictures Summer girl holding a glass of Coke, 13x11", NM...**$500.00**

Tray, 1925, shows a girl in a fox stole & hat in profile holding a glass of Coke, 13x11", VG.....................**$175.00**

Tray, 1930, pictures the telephone girl, 'Meet Me at the Soda Fountain,' 13x11" **$200.00**

Tray, 1933, pictures Francis Dee in a bathing suit sitting on a ledge holding a Coke, 13x11", G.....................**$150.00**

Tray, 1940, shows a lady enjoying a Coke while fishing, 11x13", EX **$85.00**

Tray, 1948, pictures a smiling blond lifting a bottle of Coke to her mouth, 13x11", NM.........................**$100.00**

Tray, 1950s, shows a girl in hat resting her chin on her left hand & holding a bottle of Coke in right, 13x11" M **$70.00**

Tray, 1957, pictures girl w/umbrella, Canadian, 10½x13¼", EX...$90.00

Tray, 1958, pictures bottle of Coke & birdhouse on a stone ledge, Canadian, 11x13", NM **$75.00**

Tray, 1958, shows a picnic basket on wheels w/bottles of Coke, brown basket-weave border, 14x19", NM ..**$20.00**

Tray, 1961, shows Coke being poured into glass surrounded by pansies, fishtail logo, 'Be Really Refreshed!,' 11x13", NM **$20.00**

Tray, 1973, depicts Santa reading note at fireplace being held down by bottle of Coke (one of many variations), NM **$10.00**

Umbrella, 1930s, cloth on metal pole, shows Coke bottle w/'Ice Cold In Bottles' & 'The Pause That Refreshes,' 72"..**$750.00**

Wallet, 1920s, brown leather, inside says 'Drink Coca-Cola,' 'Delicious & Refreshing,' 9x4", NM **$50.00**

Wallet, 1960s, light tan pigskin w/gold embossed image of Coke bottle & logo, NM...............................**$18.00**

Whistle, 1950s, plastic, 'Merry Christmas,' 'Coca-Cola Bottling, Memphis, Tenn' **$13.00**

Yo-Yo, 1960, red & white plastic, bottle cap form **$10.00**

Comic Books

Though just about everyone can remember having stacks and stacks of comic books as a child, few of us ever saved them for more than a few months. At 10¢ a copy, new ones quickly replaced the old, well-read stacks. We'd trade them to our friends, but very soon, out they went. If we didn't throw them away, Mother did. So even though they were printed in huge amounts, few survive. Today, they're a very desirable collectible. First editions have been known to bring more than $500.00; in fact, Marvel Comics #1 from October, 1939, has a recorded sale of more than $35,000.00.

Factors that make a comic book valuable are condition (as with all paper collectibles, extremely important), rarity, and the quality of its artwork. We've listed some of the more collectible (and expensive) comics, but many are worth very little. You'll really need to check your bookstore for a good reference and value guide before you actively get involved in the comic book market.

Ace Comics, #1, G **$180.00**
Ace Comics, #73, EX..**$55.00**
Action Comics, #112, G **$30.00**
Action Comics, #239, DC Comics, VG **$32.50**
Action Comics, #267, DC Comics, G.........................**$40.00**
Action Comics, #28, VG..**$135.00**
Adventure Comics, #246, G....................................**$12.50**
Adventure Comics, #286, DC Comics, EX **$14.00**
Adventures of Bob Hope, #66, DC Comics, VG **$3.00**
All American Men of War, #13, DC Comics, VG.........**$15.00**
All Star Comics, #13, DC Comics, EX **$525.00**

Amazing Spiderman, #1, G- $200.00
Amazing Spiderman, #18, EX (illustrated)............$25.00
Amazing Spiderman, #1, Marvel, VG........................**$925.00**
Amazing Spiderman, #149, NM................................**$10.00**
Amazing Spiderman, #16, EX..................................**$48.00**
Amazing Spiderman, #38, VG **$18.00**
Aquaman, #32, DC Comics, EX................................**$8.00**
Archie's Madhouse, #1, VG **$24.00**
Archie's Pal, Jughead, #32, VG................................**$4.00**
Astonishing, #16, VG **$12.50**
Atom, The; #9, EX..**$40.00**
Avengers, #9, Marvel, EX.......................................**$50.00**
Baby Huey & Papa, #2, Harvey, 1962, M...................**$55.00**
Batman, #122, VG...**$18.50**
Battlefront, #44, Atlas, VG **$2.25**
Ben Hur, #1052, Dell, 1979, EX **$10.00**

Beware the Creeper, #1, DC Comics, EX $18.00
Beware the Creeper, #2, M..................................$20.00
Black Hood Comics, #19, VG................................$22.00
Brave & Bold, #53, EX......................................$9.00
Brave & Bold, #85, DC Comics, VG..........................$5.00
Buccaneers, #19, Quality, VG $36.00
Bulletman, #5, G..$42.00
Buzzy, #54, VG...$2.00
Calling All Boys, #2, EX..................................$12.00
Captain America Comics, #35, Timely, EX $360.00
Captain America Comics, #55, NM $320.00
Captain Marvel Adventures, #31, VG........................$24.00
Captain Marvel Adventures, #54, Fawcett, VG...........$50.00
Challengers of the Unknown, #38, EX........................$6.00
Crown Comics, #1, VG $30.00
Dale Evans Comics, #16, VG................................$14.00
Daredevil, #37, VG...$4.50
Detective Comics, #103, DC Comics, G......................$22.00
Eighty-Page Giant, #15, DC Comics, VG......................$7.00
Fantastic Four, #10, Marvel, EX..........................$140.00
Fantastic Four, #71, NM...................................$14.00
Felix the Cat, #2, Dell, EX $27.50
Flash, The; #139, VG.......................................$9.00
Four Color, 2nd series, #1077, VG.........................$16.00
Four Color, 2nd series, #1237, EX.........................$57.50
Four Color, 2nd series, #692, Dell, EX.....................$4.00
Frankenstein, #1, VG......................................$48.00
Frankie Comics, #14, VG....................................$5.00
Frontline Combat, #1, VG..................................$60.00
Frontline Combat, #2, G $23.00
Frontline Combat, #5, EX..................................$35.00
Ghost Rider, #3, Marvel, NM $5.00
Harvey Hits, #10, Little Lotta, Harvey, EX $15.00
House of Mystery, #143, VG $12.50
House of Mystery, #154, EX.................................$6.50
House of Secrets, #37, DC Comics, G........................$1.50
House of Secrets, #44, VG..................................$3.50
I Spy, #3, EX...$17.50
Iron Man, #15, Marvel, EX.................................$16.00
It Really Happened, #1, Kit Carson, 1944, EX.............$20.00
Journey Into Mystery, #111, EX............................$10.00
Journey Into Mystery, #117, Marvel, EX $20.00
Journey Into Mystery, #84, M $20.00
Jughead's Fantasy, #3, G...................................$6.50
Jumbo Comics, #77, Fiction House, VG $20.00
Jungle Jim, #12, VG..$3.50
Justice League of America, #10, DC Comics, VG.........$32.50
Justice League of America, #36, EX........................$4.25
Justice League of America, #5, G $20.00
Kerry Drake Detective Cases, #24, VG.......................$6.00
Key Ring Comics, #1, EX...................................$10.00
Kid Komics, #1, VG $180.00
King Comics, #140, EX $20.00
Konga, #14, NM $27.00
Krazy Komics, #1, EX......................................$62.50
Leading Comics, #7, VG $42.00
Little Lulu, #188, NM......................................$9.00
Little Lulu, Four Color, #146, Dell, VG $50.00

Little Lulu & Tubby Annual, #1, VG $42.50
Lone Ranger, #84, Dell, VG................................$6.50
Long Bow, #8, Fiction House, EX $10.00
Looney Tunes & Merrie Melodies, #90, Dell, VG..........$4.00
Mad, #19, EC Comics, EX...................................$45.00
Marvel Mystery, #68, VG...................................$82.50
Marvel Mystery, #73, Timely, EX..........................$275.00
Marvel Tales, 2nd series, #2, EX..........................$29.00
Maverick, #14, EX...$11.00
Menace, #1, EX..$70.00
Mickey Mouse, Four Color, #157, Dell, VG..............$25.00
Mickey Mouse, Four Color, #248, VG........................$22.50
Mickey Mouse, Four Color, #296, VG........................$12.50
Mighty Mouse Comics, 2nd series, #39, G....................$7.00
My Greatest Adventure, #50, VG.............................$3.00
Mystery in Space, #38, Dell, VG...........................$24.50
National Comics, #48, VG..................................$17.00
New Gods, #2, EX...$4.00
Parole Breakers, #1, VG $33.00
Pep Comics, #1, VG $345.00
Phantom Lady, 1st series, #21, VG $115.00
Planet Comics, #12, VG $250.00
Planet Comics, #52, VG $60.00
Popular Comics, #82, EX...................................$45.00
Rangers Comics, #5, Fiction House, VG $40.00
Richie Rich, #1, Marvel, VG...............................$135.00
Ringo Kid Western, #21, VG................................$4.00
Silver Surfer, #5, EX.....................................$12.00
Space Busters, #1, EX $85.00
Space Detective, #1, VG $130.00
Sparky Watts, #1, G.......................................$13.00
Spellbound, #12, VG.......................................$9.00
Strange Tales, #160, Marvel, EX...........................$14.00
Strange Tales Annual, #1, G...............................$27.00
Superboy, #62, G...$5.00
Superboy, #79, DC Comics, G................................$7.50
Superman, #138, DC Comics, EX.............................$29.00
Superman, #238, NM...$6.50
Superman's Girlfriend Lois Lane, #4, DC Comics, EX..$60.00
Suspense Comics, DC Comics, #8, VG $110.00
Tales of Suspense, #49, G..................................$7.00
Tales of Suspense, #69, Marvel, VG........................$4.25
Tales of Unexpected, #1, DC Comics, VG....................$66.00
Tales To Astonish, #57, G..................................$6.00
Tarzan, #71, VG..$4.50
Teen Titans, #26, VG $2.50
Thunder Agents, #7, EX....................................$5.75
Two-Fisted Tales, #28, EC Comics, EX......................$62.00
Uncle Scrooge, #45, Dell, VG...............................$6.00
Unknown Worlds, #29, VG $1.50
USA Comics, #1, VG $585.00
Walt Disney Comics & Stories, #164, Dell, VG $5.00
War Against Crime, #11, EC Comics, VG $100.00
Whiz Comics, #81, Fawcett, EX.............................$19.00
Wings Comics, #46, VG.....................................$18.00
Wings Comics, #62, VG.....................................$16.00
World's Finest Comics, #100, DC Comics, G...............$16.50
World's Finest Comics, #36, G $35.00

X-Men, #159, NM $4.50
X-Men, #26, VG $7.50
Young Allies, #19, VG $62.00
Young Allies, #5, VG $87.00
Young Allies, #8, Timely, VG $80.00
Young Eagle, #2, G $3.50

Compacts

Very new to the collectibles scene, compacts are already making an impact. When 'liberated' women entered the workforce after WWI, cosmetics, previously frowned upon, became more acceptable, and as a result the market was engulfed with compacts of all types and designs. Some went so far as to incorporate timepieces, cigarette compartments, coin holders, and money clips. All types of materials were used, mother-of-pearl, petit point, cloisonne, celluloid, and leather among them. There were figural compacts, those with wonderful Art Deco designs, souvenir compacts, and compacts with advertising messages.

For further study, we recommend *Ladies' Compacts of the 19th and 20th Centuries* by Roselyn Gerson.

Ansico, mother-of-pearl w/rhinestones, square, minimum value $80.00
BB Co, floral cloisonne lid, sterling chain, 1920s, minimum value $250.00
Bracelet, rhinestones & jewels, marked K&K, hinged, minimum value $250.00
Elgin, gold-painted metal, Deco style, fitted w/lipstick case...$125.00
Elgin American, green enameled w/gold-tone designs in relief, minimum value...$65.00
Evans, trunk form lid, gold-tone, ca 1940s, w/watch, minimum value $125.00
France, navy plastic w/Deco-style hand-painted silver bar & wavy lines..$95.00
France, porcelain, hand-painted butterflies on dark green ground, 9¼"...$75.00
France, silver w/overall black enameling, gold medallion, Deco style...$145.00
French, Egyptian figures on yellow w/black trim, Deco style $80.00

French tapestry, roses on black, feather puff inside .$28.00

JV Pilcher, geometric decoration, Art Deco style, 3½", minimum value...$25.00
Mondaine, book form, tooled leather, w/compartments, minimum value $50.00
Petit point carryall, ca 1940s-1950s, w/compartments, minimum value $150.00
Plastic, gold-tone, birds enclosed in dome, minimum value $100.00
R&G Co, floral cloisonne, sterling closure w/chain, minimum value $450.00
Van Cleef & Arpels, paisley decoration on gold-tone, minimum value $85.00
Whiting & Davis, Delysia, colorful mesh, ca 1920s, minimum value $450.00
Yardley, gold-tone & enamel, swivel mirror, ca 1930s, minimum value $40.00

Consolidated Glass

The Consolidated Lamp and Glass Company operated in Coraopolis, Pennsylvania, from 1894 until 1964. At first much of what they made was oil lamps and shades, although they also made Cosmos, a limited line of milk glass tableware decorated with pastel flowers.

By the mid-twenties they were making glassware with 'sculptured' designs, very similar to a line made by a nearby competitor, the Phoenix Glass Company located in Monaca, Pennsylvania. Unless you're a student of these two types of glassware, it's very difficult to distinguish one from the other. The best clue (which is not foolproof) is the fact that most of the time Consolidated applied color to the relief (raised) design and left the background plain, while the reverse was true of Phoenix.

One of their lines was called Ruba Rombic. It has a very distinctive 'cubist' appearance; shapes are free-form with jutting dimensional planes. It was made in strong colors to compliment its Deco forms, and collectors value anything from this line very highly.

Bowl, 12", Catalonian, emerald green (lily bowl)........$40.00
Bowl, 15", Fish, green wash w/frosted design...........$365.00
Lamp, Bittersweet, reverse ruby-stained highlights on crystal...$150.00
Lamp, Dogwood, 3-color, on satin milk glass......$120.00
Plate, 12", Bird of Paradise, green wash.......................$72.00
Plate, 14", Five Fruits, purple wash $150.00
Plate, 15", Ruba Rombic, jungle green $300.00
Plate, 8", Dancing Nymph, frosted................................$70.00
Powder jar, 5", Hummingbird, purple wash.................$70.00
Sundae, Five Fruits, yellow wash................................$25.00
Tumbler, 10-oz, Ruba Rombic, smokey topaz $95.00
Vase, 10", Bird of Paradise, pink wash on fan form..$170.00
Vase, 10", Line 700, gold highlights on custard.........$400.00
Vase, 12", Chrysanthemum, red...............................$285.00
Vase, 7", Florentine, green $185.00
Vase, 7", Katydid, gold iridescent leaves & insects, bulbous...$85.00

Vase, 9½", Ruba Rombic, jungle green........................$265.00

Cookbooks

If you've ever read a 19th-century cookbook, no doubt you've been amused by the quaint way the measurements were given. Butter the size of an egg, a handfull of flour, a pinch of this or that — sounds like a much more time-efficient method, doesn't it? They'd sometimes give household tips or some folk remedies, and it's these antiquated methods and ideas that endear those old cookbooks to collectors, although examples from this circa are not easily found.

Those from the early 20th century are scarce, too, but even those that were printed thirty and forty years ago are also well worth collecting. Food and appliance companies often published their own, and these appeal to advertising buffs and cookbook collectors alike. Some were die-cut to represent the product, perhaps a pickle or a slice of bread. The leaflets we list below were nearly all advertising giveaways and premiums. Condition is important in any area of paper collectibles, so judge yours accordingly.

For further study, we recommend *A Guide to Collecting Cookbooks* by Colonel Bob Allen, and *Price Guide to Cookbooks and Recipe Leaflets* by Linda Dickinson.

American Cookery, James Beard, 1972, hardcover, 877 pages..$30.00
Better Homes & Gardens Cookbook, 1968, hardcover, 160 pages..$10.00
Betty Crocker, Cake & Frosting, 1955, hardcover, 144 pages..$3.00
Campbell Soup, Easy Ways to Delicious Meals, 1967, 203 pages..$6.00
Carnation Cookbook, 1943, 92 pages.........................$3.00
Cheap & Nutritious Cookbook, Gray Panthers, San Francisco, 1987, 130 pages $3.50

Chez Maxim's, 1962 ....$25.00

Chinese Cooking Secrets, Chen, ca 1960, hardcover, 177 pages..$6.50
Clementine Paddleford's Cook Young Cookbook, 1966, 124 pages..$6.00
Come into the Kitchen Cookbook, Price & Price, 1969, 1st edition, 212 pages...............................$25.00
Cookbook for Two, Ida Allen, 1957, 320 pages............$5.00
Creative Cooking Made Easy, Golden Fluffo, 1956, 108 pages..$3.00
Doctor's Quick Inches-Off Diet, Stillman, 1969, 311 pages..$5.00
Duncan Hines Food Odyssey, 1955, hardcover, 266 pages...$12.00
Edwardian Glamour Cooking Without Tears, Hugh, 1960, hardcover, 61 pages...............................$7.00
Encyclopedia of Cookery, Wise, 1948, hardcover, 1,269 pages...$22.00
Fannie Farmer's Boston Cooking School, 1942, hardcover, 830 pages..................................$14.00
Fireside Cookbook, James Beard, 1949, 5th printing, 322 pages...$25.00
First Ladies Cookbook, 1969 ....$10.00
First Ladies Cookbook: Favorite Recipes of All the Presidents, Smithsonian Institute, 1969, hardcover, 228 pages...$10.00
Fondue Cookbook, Callahan, 1968, 104 pages............$4.00
Four Seasons Cookbook, Adams, 1971, hardcover, 319 pages...$12.00
Glorious Eating for Weight Watchers, Wesson, 1961, paperback, 95 pages...............................$4.50
Graham Kerr Cookbook, 1966, hardcover.....................$6.00
Graymoor's Treasury of Meatless Recipes, Smaridge, 1965, 72 pages..................................$3.50
Heloise's Kitchen Hints, 1963, 3rd printing, hardcover, 186 pages..$5.00
How America Eats, Paddleford, 1960 ....$27.50
Kerr Home Canning, Kerr, 1943, 56 pages...................$15.00
Little House Cookbook, Walker, 1979, hardcover, 240 pages..$7.00
LL Bean Game & Fish Cookbook, Cameron, 1983, hardcover, 475 pages...............................$12.00
Marijuana Food: Marijuana Extract Cooking; Drake, 1987, paperback, 160 pages...............................$4.00
Mastering the Art of French Cooking, Julia Childs, 1970, hardcover, 556 pages...............................$15.00
McCall's Cookbook, Random House, 1963, hardcover, 785 pages..$8.00
Mystery Chef's Own Cookbook, Green, 1943, 365 pages..$8.50
Nancy Drew Cookbook, Keene, 1973, 159 pages.........$4.50
Pillsbury Bake-Off, 1955, 6th edition, paperback.......$10.00
Pyrex Prize Recipes, Corning Glass, 1953, 128 pages ..$3.50
Quaker Woman's Cookbook, Lea, 1982, hardcover, 310 pages..$8.00
Savory Suppers, Fashionable Feasts; Williams, 1985, hardcover, 335 pages...............................$12.00
Seasonal Gifts from the Kitchen, Crumpacker, 1983, 1st edition $6.50

The I Hate To Cook Book - More Than 180 Quick & Easy Recipes, Peg Bracken, 1960, 1st edition, hardcover, 176 pages **$10.00**

Time-Life Picture Cookbook, 1958, hardcover, 291 pages...**$20.00**

Traditional Chinese Northern & Western Cuisine, Chen, 1976, signed, 140 pages **$28.00**

Victory Garden Bookbook, Morash, 1982, paperback, 371 pages **$18.00**

White House Chef Cookbook, Verdon, 1967, 1st edition, hardcover, 288 pages...**$10.00**

Yankee Magazine's Favorite New England Recipes, Stamm, 1972, 303 pages **$10.50**

Zane Grey Cookbook, 1976....................................**$20.00**

Zen Cookery, 1966, paperback, 79 pages **$3.50**

Recipe Leaflets

Celebrity Recipes, Helen Dunn, 1961 ....**$3.00**

Coconut Dishes that Everybody Loves, Baker's, 1931, 39 pages **$3.00**

Cook's Tour with Minute Tapioca, 1931, 46 pages........**$2.50**

Cookery Notebook, Mechanics' Institute.....................**$5.00**

Cooking the Cape Cod Way, Heritage Shop, ca 1940, 16 pages **$5.00**

Cox's Delicious Recipes, Cox Gelatin, 1933, 30 pages ..**$2.25**

Fleischmann's Recipes, 1924, 48 pages........................**$2.50**

French Dressings for Your Favorite Salads, Kraft, 1957, 22 pages **$2.00**

Good Things To Eat, Cow Baking Soda, 1936, 32 pages **$3.00**

It's All in Knowing How, Arm & Hammer, 1935, 37 pages **$2.00**

Jell-O, 1932..**$5.00**

Jell-O: What Mrs Dewey Did with the New Jell-O; 1933, 23 pages..**$10.00**

Keep on the Sunny Side of Life, Kellogg's, 1933, 32 pages **$5.00**

Kraft Cookery: Salads, Desserts, Main Dishes, Sandwiches; ca 1960s, Kraft, 12 pages **$3.00**

Making Pickles & Relishes at Home, 1978, 32 pages.....**$1.00**

New Calumet Baking Book, Parker, 1931, 31 pages **$3.00**

Sealtest Food Advisor, New York World's Fair, 1939, 15 pages **$4.50**

Victory Cookbook, Lysol, ca 1936................................**$3.00**

Visions of Sugarplums, Sunsweet, 1959........................**$2.00**

Cookie Cutters and Molds

Although the early tin cookie cutters from the 1700s are nearly all in museums by now, collectors still occasionally find a nice examples of the thinner tin cutters of the late 1800s. What you're more apt to find today, of course, are the plastic and aluminum cookie cutters, many of which we've listed below. Though certainly not in the same class as the handmade tin ones, they are becoming collectible. As cookie bakers become an extinct species (how many do

you know?), cookie cutters will become obsolete. Molds, instead of cutting the cookie out, impressed a design into the dough. To learn more about both (and many other old kitchenware gadgets as well), we recommend *300 Years of Kitchen Collectibles* by Linda Campbell Franklin and *Kitchen Antiques, 1790 to 1940,* by Kathryn McNerney.

Cookie Cutters

Automobile, 4", tin, flat back w/strap handle, ca late 1930s..**$27.50**

Bootjack, 3¼", tin, flat back, American, ca 1910.........**$40.00**

Cat, 4", tin, no handle, marked Davis Baking Powder, ca 1910-20s...**$20.00**

Christmas tree, 4½", light blue plastic, interior detail, Stanley Home Products, 1950s-60s.................................**$2.50**

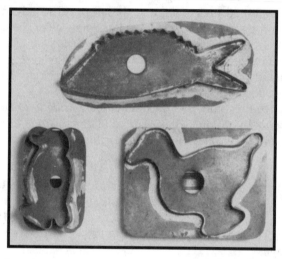

Duck, 3x4", tin, flat back w/strap handle **$27.50**

Cube, 3½x3½", yellow plastic, six simple forms, marked EKCO, 1980 ....**$6.50**

Diamond, 2", stamped aluminum, crimped edges, riveted handle, Mirro, ca late 1920s...................................**$4.00**

Father Christmas w/toy bag, 9½x5", tin, flat back, marked Germany, ca 1900s......................................**$145.00**

Fish, 2¾x5½", tin, flat back w/strap handle (illustrated)...**$37.50**

Gingerbread boy, 5¾", stamped aluminum, shallow details, slits in back form strap handle, 1940s.....................**$5.00**

Gingerbread boy, 5⅞", copper-anodized aluminum, 1960s-70s, on original card **$4.00**

Gingerbread boy, 6x3¾", stamped aluminum, no detail, Mirro, ca 1930..**$6.00**

Heart, 3½", homemade from Maxwell House coffee can, no back or handle, ca 1940s.....................................**$8.50**

Maid Marian, tin, Robin Hood Flour giveaway...........**$12.50**

Mickey Mouse, 4", stamped aluminum, Disney..........**$35.00**

Penguin, 2¾x1¾", tin w/flat back & strap handle (illustrated) **$20.00**

Rabbit, red plastic, no mark, 1970s-80s **$2.00**

Rabbit, 3½", tin, backless, strap handle, ca 1930 ....**$17.50**

Rabbit, 4", tin, no handle, marked Davis Baking Powder, dated 1926...**$20.00**

Rabbit, 6", tin, flat back, ca 1930s.................................**$30.00**

Rolling, card suits, 6⅛", crimped & riveted tin w/green wood handle, 1932 patent.......................**$17.50**

Rolling, six designs, plated cast steel, Germany, ca 1950s...**$15.00**

Rolling, 7¾", heavy cast metal w/wood handle, no marks, ca 1960s-80s...**$8.50**

Santa Claus, 5", light blue plastic, interior details, Stanley Home Products, 1950s-60s...................**$3.00**

Scottie dog, aluminum w/green wood knob handle, ca 1930s-40s..**$8.00**

Twin boy & girl, Avon, in original box.....................**$15.00**

Cookie Molds

Butterfly, 5½", cast iron, flat, oval, Albany, NY, early 19th century...**$160.00**

Pan, 18-cup, tulip or scalloped rounds, cast aluminum, Winton Enterprises, 1980s.............................**$6.00**

Springerle, ceramic, thirty-five designs, German reproduction, ca 1950s..**$32.50**

Springerle board, machine-carved maple, four designs, ca 1910-20s..**$40.00**

Springerle rolling pin, carved wood, sixteen designs, yellow wood handles, ca 1930s...................**$30.00**

Cookie Jars

This is an area where we've seen nearly unprecedented growth in both interest and pricing. Rare cookie jars sell for literally thousands of dollars. Even a common jar from a good manufacturer will fall into the $40.00 to $100.00 price range. At the top of the list are the Black-theme jars, then come the cartoon characters such as Popeye, Howdy Doody, or the Flintstones. Any kind of a figural jar from an American pottery is extremely collectible right now. Who knows when it will level off. Right now we see no signs of this happening.

There were several large producers of jars in this country. One of the largest and best known was McCoy (those jars are listed in our McCoy category). American Bisque was another; they produced jars from 1930 until 1970. Many of their jars have no marks at all; those that do are simply marked 'USA,' sometimes with a mold number. But their air-brushed colors are easy to spot, and collectors look for the molded-in wedge-shaped pads on their bases — these say 'American Bisque' to cookie jar buffs about as clearly as if they were marked.

The Brush Pottery (Ohio, 1946-71) made cookie jars that were decorated with the airbrush in many of the same colors used by American Bisque. These jars in particular took a big jump in prices last year. Their 'Hillbilly Frog' is a fantastic jar, but very rare; it books for a minimum of $1,000.00.

There are lots of wonderful jars by many different companies. Joyce and Fred Roerig's book *The Collector's Encyclopedia of Cookie Jars* covers them all beautifully.

See also Abingdon, McCoy, Shawnee, Red Wing.

Aunt Jemima, marked F&F Mold & Die Works Dayton Ohio, red dress & white apron, M.................**$325.00**

Avon Bear, unmarked, made by California Originals for Avon in 1979, promotional gift.............**$50.00**

Baby Bluebird on Pine Cone, marked Made in USA, 'Metlox Manufacturing Co' paper label, all brown, M........**$75.00**

Baby Elephant, unmarked American Bisque, M........**$110.00**

Balloon Lady, unmarked, lady holding multicolor balloons, rose-colored skirt, M..............................**$125.00**

Bear on Beehive, unmarked, bear finial on yellow hive form w/'Cookies' in brown, M...........................**$22.00**

Betty Boop, marked copyright 1985 King Features Syndicate Inc, fruit on hat, flowers on flared skirt, M.........**$390.00**

Big Bird, marked copyright Muppets Inc, Newcor USA, sitting in nest marked 'Cookies,' M.................**$45.00**

Blackboard Hobo, marked USA, American Bisque, 'Mustn't Forget' & blackboard on front of figure, M........**$190.00**

Casper, marked Harvey Publications Inc USA, M, minimum value...**$500.00**

Cheerleaders, marked Corner Cookie Jar 802 USA, American Bisque, M...**$175.00**

Christmas Tree, unmarked California Originals, golden star finial, M..**$135.00**

Churn, marked Lane USA, brown wood-grained paint, M...**$22.00**

Cinderella, marked JC Napco 1957 K2292, black, yellow, green & white skirt, M.......................**$225.00**

Cinderella Pumpkin, marked W 32 Brush USA, mice finial, 1967, M...**$150.00**

Clover Rabbit, unmarked NS Gustin, green rabbit w/clover at nose, head down, M.........................**$45.00**

Clown, marked Made in Poppytrail Calif, yellow suit w/green buttons, shoes & hat, M.................**$85.00**

Clown, marked W 22 Brush USA, blue pants & bow, M...**$225.00**

Clown on Elephant, marked 896, California Originals, brown elephant w/pink ears, clown finial, M...........**$30.00**

Clown w/Raised Arms, marked USA, American Bisque, M..**$60.00**

Coach, marked Twin Winton San Juan Capistrano Calif USA, yellow & white flower wheels on brown pumpkin-shaped coach, M...**$80.00**

Coffeepot, marked Treasure Craft copyright Made in USA in lid & base, brown w/'Cookies' on gold reserve, M...**$22.00**

Coffeepot, marked USA, American Bisque, M............**$25.00**

Combination Snowman, marked Riddell copyright, teapot on top, cookie jar is base, M.........................**$100.00**

Cookie Canister, marked Marcrest Oven Proof USA, dark brown, M..**$22.00**

Cookie Crock, marked Hull Oven Proof USA.............**$22.00**

Cookie House, marked W 31 Brush USA, green roof, 1962, M..**$60.00**

Cookie Truck, marked USA, American Bisque, M.......**$45.00**

Cookstove Mammy, marked Wihoa's Original Cookie Classic by Rick Wisecarver..., 1988, discontinued, M......**$185.00**

Corn, marked Terrace Ceramics USA 4299, ear of corn figural, yellow w/green shucks, M $55.00

Cow in Overalls, marked USA APCO, red & black details on ivory, M...$22.00

Cow Jumping Over the Moon, marked 806 USA, American Bisque, minimum value, M $250.00

Cow on Moon, marked J 2 USA, Doranne of California, yellow w/black details, late 1950s, M.......................$150.00

Cow w/Can of Milk, marked CJ 107, Doranne of California, white w/red & white neckerchief, pink ears, 1984, M..$60.00

Cow w/Cat Finial, marked W 10 Brush USA, brown with green bell, early 1950s, M $100.00

Cow w/Milk Carton, unmarked, comic figure, black & white w/red kerchief & red milk carton, M....................$35.00

Cylinder w/Bluebirds, unmarked American Bisque, M..$25.00

Cylinder w/Daisies, marked USA, American Bisque, M.$25.00

Daisy, marked Hull 48, yellow daisies on ivory on cylindrical shape, brown ring on lid w/yellow finial........$22.00

Davy Crockett, marked USA, American Bisque, name across chest, M $275.00

Davy Crockett, Regal, M..$450.00

Derby Dan, marked Derby Dan Muggsie The Pfaltzgraff Pottery Co...Designed by Jessop, head figural, hat forms lid, M...$125.00

Dino, marked Metlox Calif USA copyright '87 by Vincent, blue, M $105.00

Dino, marked USA, Hanna-Barbera Productions copyright stamped on base, M $1,100.00

Dino the Dinosaur, American Bisque, M $1,100.00

Dobbin, marked Twin Winton Made in Calif USA 1962, brown w/yellow mane & tail, sitting, straw hat, M...........$50.00

Dog, marked USA, American Bisque, dog lid finial on quilted square jar, M...$50.00

Donald Duck, marked copyright Walt Disney USA, blue hat, red bow tie, yellow beak, feet & hands, M........$375.00

Donald Duck & Pumpkin, marked Walt Disney Productions 805, made by California Originals, blue sailor suit, M $250.00

Donkey & Cart, marked W/33 Brush USA, 1965, M..$275.00

Drum, marked Made in Poppytrail Calif, Metlox, brown w/embossed figures around sides, bisque, M.......$35.00

Duck, marked Hull 966 USA, worn paint at beak & feet $32.00

Dutch Boy, marked USA APCO, red, yellow & black details on ivory, M $32.00

Dutch Girl, marked RRP CO Roseville Ohio, Robinson-Ransbottom, white w/yellow & blue details, M.........$110.00

Eeyore, marked 901 copyright Walt Disney Productions, made by California Originals, smiling face, M...$275.00

Elephant, marked W 8 USA, brush, wearing baby hat, gray w/blue bow, early 1950s, M.............................$450.00

Elephant w/Ball Cap, marked USA, American Bisque, M $80.00

Elsie, unmarked Pottery Guild, Elsie emerging from barrel, M $250.00

Entenmann's Chef, marked B&D copyright, cold-painted red scarf, M $65.00

Ernie, marked copyright Muppets Inc, distributed by Newcor USA, knees drawn up to chest, striped shirt, M $45.00

Ernie, marked copyright Muppets Inc 973, waist-up figure in striped shirt, M $60.00

Ernie (Keebler elf), F&F Mold & Die Works $95.00

Famous Amos, Treasure Craft, Made in USA, M $50.00

Ferdinand, unmarked California Originals, red w/black & white details, M...$80.00

Fishing Hippo, marked Japan, hippo w/fish, brown pants, green hat, M $28.00

Flirty Cat, marked Terrace Ceramics USA 4253, white figure w/light blue eyes, M $50.00

Flower Jar, marked USA, American Bisque, flower reserve on side, flower finial, M.................................$32.00

Franciscan nun, unmarked Hondo Ceramics, made for Marcia of California, brown & white, M....................$150.00

Frango Mint Truck, Made in Italy Expressly for Marshall Field & Company, NM..$65.00

French Poodle, marked USA, American Bisque, M $85.00

Frog w/Bow Tie, marked 2645 USA, California Originals, green with yellow bow tie, M...............................$45.00

Frosty the Snowman, marked RRP Co Roseville O USA, Robinson-Ransbottom, black hat, blue diamond-shaped buttons, M $475.00

Fruit Basket, marked USA 3720, Morton Pottery Co, multi-colored fruit forms lid, green basket body, M.......$30.00

Gingerbread Boy, marked Hull, Crooksville, Ohio, USA, Ovenproof, brown, blue or tan, each....................$50.00

Gingham Dog, unmarked Brayton Laguna, red, white & blue, M $150.00

Gold Medal Cookies, painted tin, M............................$30.00

Goofy's Cookie Co, marked copyright Walt Disney Productions 862 USA, Goofy beside barrel-form jar, M.$400.00

Goose, unmarked Treasure Craft, white w/red bow & holly sprig at neck, yellow beak & feet, M....................$40.00

Goose Woman, marked Brayton Laguna Pottery, lady holds goose, M, minimum value....................................**$300.00**

Grandma, marked California USA, NS Gustin, lady w/rolling pin, cat at feet, M.................................**$95.00**

Grandma, unmarked American Bisque, gold trim, M .**$150.00**

Granny, unmarked Japan, 'If All Else Fails Ask Grandma' on red cap that forms lid, M.................................**$18.00**

Green Pepper, marked CJ 30 USA, Doranne of California, realistic pepper form, 1984, M...............................**$28.00**

Happy Bull, marked Twin Winton copyright Calif USA, brown w/pink flowers around neck, M.............**$25.00**

Heart, mk California Cleminsons copyright, lovebirds finial, yellow heart form w/ruffled base, M.....................**$70.00**

Hen on basket, unmarked Brush, red comb & yellow beak on white, 1969, M...**$100.00**

Hen w/Basket of Eggs, marked CJ 103, Doranne of California, white chicken w/red waddle & comb, blue & white scarf, M...**$45.00**

Hobby Horse, marked 602, paper label: Pigeon Vitrified China Co Barnhart MO USA, made from Abingdon mold, M...**$125.00**

Holstein Cow, marked copyright Otigari, black & white, M...**$65.00**

Hopalong Cassidy, unmarked, Hoppy & horse in reserve on side of barrel form, M, minimum value..............**$400.00**

House, marked Treasure Craft copyright Made in USA, yellow 2-story house w/brown roof, chimney finial, M...**$35.00**

Humpty Dumpty w/Peaked Hat, marked W 29 Brush USA, dark blue details on white, 1962, M...................**$175.00**

Jocko the Monkey, marked RRP Co Roseville O USA, Robinson-Ransbottom, yellow cap forms lid, M...........**$250.00**

Keebler Tree House, unmarked, M.............................**$85.00**

Ketchup Bottle, marked CJ 68 USA, Doranne of California, red bottle w/white cap, 1984, M........................**$38.00**

Kitten & Beehive, marked USA (1958), American Bisque, M...**$35.00**

Kittens & Yarn, marked USA, American Bisque, M..........**$45.00**

Lady Dragon, unmarked, upright figure w/yellow & white apron, M...**$25.00**

Little Audrey, marked USA, American Bisque, M, minimum value..**$2,000.00**

Little Boy Blue, marked K 25 USA, Brush, gold trim, small size, M, minimum value **$650.00**

Little Girl, marked Cardinal USA 301, head form w/freckles, hat forms lid, M...**$85.00**

Little Hen, yellow w/multicolor wing feathers & pink bonnet, M...**$45.00**

Little King, marked DeForest of Calif Copyright 1957, 'Cookie King' on bib, small crown on head, M ..**$150.00**

Little Red Riding Hood, marked Made in Poppytrail Calif, Metlox, yellow hair & basket, M........................**$850.00**

Love Me Dog, marked Maurice of Calif USA, brown dog w/pink tag that says 'Love Me,' M........................**$32.00**

Lunch Box, unmarked Doranne of California, dark blue & light blue, box handle on lid, M **$35.00**

Luzianne Mammy, marked USA, cold paint (underglaze paint is current reproduction), light wear, NM ...**$800.00**

Magic Bunny, marked USA, American Bisque, brown bunny lid on hat form jar, 1959, M.................................**$50.00**

Mammy, marked Made in Taiwan, ceramic F&F reproduction, M...**$35.00**

Mammy, marked Made in Tawian, red dress & white apron, M...**$30.00**

Mammy, marked Weller, holds watermelon, M, minimum value..**$2,500.00**

Mammy, National Silver **$225.00**

Mary Poppins, marked copyright MCMLXIV Walt Disney Productions, penguins dance at hem of skirt, M, minimum value **$375.00**

Mickey Mouse Car, marked copyright Walt Disney Productions...Sears Roebuck & Co 1978 Japan, Mickey in yellow car, M...**$300.00**

Milk Can, mk KJ 10, can figural w/'Cookies & Milk Are Yummy' on side, brown w/red, white & green flowers, M...**$18.00**

Monk, marked Treasure Craft copyright Made in USA, holds scroll saying 'Thou Shalt Not Steal (Cookies),' brown robe, M...**$35.00**

Monk w/Key, unmarked, white w/brown details, M ..**$65.00**

Mosaic Tile Mammy, unmarked, brown & white, relatively common, M...**$550.00**

Mother Goose, marked CJ 16 USA, Doranne of California, green w/black details, late 1960s, M **$125.00**

Mouse, marked 2630 USA, California Originals, comic character in green jacket w/yellow bow tie, M...........**$35.00**

Mrs & Mrs Pig Turnabout, unmarked APCO, hands in pockets **$110.00**

Mrs Claus, marked copyright FF Japan, red dress, holly on apron, M...**$105.00**

Mrs Rabbit, marked USA, American Bisque, green dress, 1959, M...**$130.00**

Musical Santa, unmarked, head form, plays Jingle Bells, M...**$85.00**

Neal the Frog, unmarked California Originals (Sears sold under name of Freddie Frog), green, M...............$35.00

Oriental Lady w/Baskets, unmarked, red jacket, yellow skirt & baskets, yoke across shoulders, M..................$375.00

Oscar the Grouch, unmarked Demand Marketing, green monster in trash can, M..$45.00

Pancake Mammy, marked copyright 1987 CG Carol Gifford, M...$130.00

Panda Bear, marked W21 Brush USA..................$200.00

Panda, marked W 21 Brush USA, blue & yellow on white, 1959, M, minimum value....................................$300.00

Panda Bear, unmarked, Metlox, sitting figure, black & white, M...$75.00

Pearl China Chef, marked Pearl China Co Hand Decorated 22kt gold 639, 'Cookie' on chest, M...................$575.00

Pedestal Jar, marked USA, American Bisque, M..........$18.00

Peek-a-Boo, marked Peek-a-Boo copyright Van Telligen, figure in polka dot pajamas, hands to face, M........$875.00

Penguin, marked Japan, black & white w/yellow bill & feet, red cane & bow tie, M...$28.00

Pig Dancer, unmarked American Bisque, red & black details on white, M...$75.00

Pink Lady, marked w/blue crest stamp on base, M.....$60.00

Pinocchio, marked Walt Disney copyright Productions Cuernavaca Mexico, yellow hat, blue bow tie, M, minimum value...$350.00

Pinocchio w/Fish Bowl, marked copyright Walt Disney Productions 867 USA, holding fish bowl w/jumping fish finial, M..$350.00

Polka Dot Kitty, marked Pat Design ABCO 131 USA, multicolor dots on white cat w/red bow, M..................$50.00

Poodle, marked Sierra Vista Ceramics Pasadena...1956, upright dog, gray & white w/pink bow, black painted features, M...$125.00

Porkey Pig, marked c 1975 Warner Bros Inc Duncan, red & white cap w/black brim, red jacket, sits in green chair, M...$95.00

Professor Owl, marked Japan, flower-shaped eyes, graduation cap on head, 'Cookies' across front, brown, pink & blue, M...$22.00

Pumpkin, marked Holiday Designs, orange w/green stem finial, M...$32.00

Puppy, marked USA (1958), American Bisque, M.......$45.00

Rabbit in Hat, marked DeForest of Calif copyright USA, brown w/pink, white & blue details, M...............$32.00

Raccoon, marked Twin Winton copyright Calif USA, brown w/black mask & rings on tail, M..........................$60.00

Raggedy Andy, marked copyright Maddux, 2108, sitting on drum, red, white & blue paint, M..........................$85.00

Raggedy Ann, marked W 16 USA, Brush, multicolor patches on white dress, 1956, M.....................................$450.00

Ranger Bear, marked Twin Winton...California USA, red collar & cuffs, blue tie w/red dots, black hat forms lid, M...$90.00

Red Riding Hood, unmarked, red cloak & dress, white apron, hands together, basket at elbow, M...........$70.00

Rocking Horse, marked Treasure Craft copyright Made in USA, brown w/yellow flower finial on saddle, M.$40.00

Rooster, marked Gilner G 22, black & white w/red waddle & comb, yellow beak & feet, M.......................$50.00

Rooster, marked Twin Winton...copyright California USA, crowing stance, multicolored tail feathers, , M.....$90.00

Rooster, unmarked American Bisque, yellow w/heavy gold trim, M...$135.00

Sailor Elephant, marked USA, American Bisque, pink ears, blue suit, blue & yellow hat, M............................$70.00

Sailor Mouse, marked with a C through a W, Cumberland Ware, comic character in white hat, M..................$45.00

Santa Head, marked Mallory copyright Inc, smiling face, draped red hat, M...$50.00

Santa in Easy Chair, unmarked, Santa in red suit reads note & sits in green chair, M...$70.00

Schoolhouse, marked USA, American Bisque, bell in lid, M...$40.00

Seal on Igloo, marked USA, American Bisque, M.....$175.00

Sheriff Bear, marked Twin Winton...California USA, blue suit & hat, small club in hand, red star, M..................$90.00

Sitting Bear, marked Maurice of Calif USA, brown w/pink & blue details, M...$30.00

Smiling Pear, marked 6 C 30, Japan, comic figural, eyes painted to look to side, M...$18.00

Snoopy, marked Holiday Designs, not copyrighted, white w/black ears, nose & eye details, M......................$55.00

Space Ship, marked USA, American Bisque, M.........$145.00

Spool of Thread, marked USA, American Bisque, thimble finial, M...$100.00

Sprout, Copyright 1988, Pillsbury Company, Made in Taiwan, M...$45.00

Squirrel on Log, marked USA, Brush, 1965, M...........$80.00

Squirrel w/Top Hat, marked W 15 USA, Brush, early 1950s, M...$200.00

Stove, unmarked, potbellied type, white w/brown feet, pipe, & details, M...$18.00

Strawberry Shortcake, marked MCML XXXIII American Greetings Corp Cleveland OH, sitting w/puppy in lap, M...$125.00

Squirrel on Pine Cone, marked Made in USA, Metlox, gray squirrel finial on brown jar, M..............................$55.00

Superman, marked copyright DC Comics Inc 1978 Calif Original USA 846, red, white & blue, M.............**$250.00**

Teddy Bear, marked Treasure Craft copyright USA, yellow brim on cap, blue bow, brown pads on feet, M...**$40.00**

Telephone, marked Cardinal USA 311, wall type, black & white w/pink finial, M.............................**$60.00**

Tenderheart Bear, marked Tenderheart Bear...American Greetings Corp...4414 Made in Korea 53044, 1984, yellow cap, M..**$65.00**

Tom & Jerry, marked copyright Metro Goldwin Mayer Film Co 1981...Made in Japan, Jerry in window, Tom on roof of house, M **$175.00**

Train, marked Sierra Vista California, smiling face w/blue eyes, brown cab, M.................................**$70.00**

Turkey, unmarked Morton Pottery, realistic style, brown w/red head & waddle, chick finial, M..................**$60.00**

Two-Story House, unmarked, snow-covered house, two stacking sections, snowy roof forms lid, M..........**$55.00**

Umbrella Kids, marked USA 739, American Bisque, M..**$195.00**

Van, marked 843 USA, California Originals, red w/black & white details, M..**$90.00**

Watermelon Mammy, marked copyright 1986 CG Carol Gifford, M...**$130.00**

White Rabbit, paper label: California Originals, white figure w/pink ears & blue at collar, cuffs & hat, M.........**$60.00**

Wilma on Telephone, marked USA, American Bisque, 'Flintstones' is written on chair arm, M **$1,000.00**

Windmill, marked FAPCo, Fredericksburg Art Pottery Co, blue details on white, M...............................**$25.00**

Wonder Woman, marked USA 847 copyright DC Comics Inc 1978, lassoed bank robber, M...........................**$350.00**

1957 Chevrolet, marked Made in Portugal, blue & white w/black tires & details, M..................................**$150.00**

Coors Rosebud Dinnerware

Golden, Colorado, was the site for both the Coors Brewing Company and the Coors Porcelain Company, each founded by the same man, Adolph Coors. The pottery's beginning was in 1910, and in the early years they manufactured various ceramic products such as industrial supplies, dinnerware, vases, and figurines, but their most famous line and the one we want to tell you about was 'Rosebud.'

The Rosebud 'Cook 'n Serve' line was introduced in 1934. It's very easy to spot; after you've once seen a piece, you'll be able to recognize it instantly. It was made in solid colors — rose, blue, green, yellow, ivory, and orange. The 'rose bud' and leaves are embossed and hand-painted in contrasting colors. There are nearly fifty different pieces to collect, and prices are still fairly reasonable.

Advertising sign......................................**$45.00**
Apple baker, 4¾" dia **$20.00**
Bowl, small, tab handles **$10.00**
Bowl, soup; 1-handle................................**$18.00**
Cake knife, 10".......................................**$22.50**

Casserole, 2-pt, straight sides **$20.00**
Cup **$12.50**
Custard cup **$10.00**
Plate, dinner **$15.00**
Plate, 7¼"..**$7.50**
Platter, oval...**$25.00**
Salt & pepper shakers, 2½", pr......................**$24.00**
Saucer **$4.00**
Teapot, 2-cup **$45.00**
Tumbler, footed **$27.50**

Utility jar, w/lid......................................$30.00
Vase, 5½", yellow, impressed design...........**$30.00**

Cordey

Cordey figures were primarily molded; then decorators painted and 'dressed' them, added gold scrollwork and applied flowers, and created characters with 'old-world' charm, busts of lovely young girls, and animals and birds in natural settings. They were made of a type of composition porcelain that their creator, Boleslaw Cybis, called 'Papka.' Lace was often dipped into liquid slip and applied to pantaloons, hats, the bodices of ladies' gowns, etc.

The company was founded in 1942 in Trenton, New Jersey, and operated until sometime in the mid-fifties. Most of the ware is marked and numbered. It was sold through gift shops both here in the United States and abroad.

Ashtray, 5½", Versailles Group, #6035.............**$18.00**
Ballerina, 10¾", dancing position, lace trim, #4101...**$220.00**
Bird, 8½", perched on stump, #2037 ....**$115.00**
Box, 7½" dia, 3 large roses & ruffled lace applied to lid, #6041...**$65.00**
Bust, 6", girl w/hat, #5009 ....**$65.00**
Bust, 7½", lady w/ribbons & roses in hair.........**$75.00**
Bust, 8", Napoleon, #5038 ....**$45.00**
Clock, mantel; 9½", Rococo, Lanshire Electric, #914 .**$250.00**

Clock frame, 11", cherubs, Rococo, #912 ....$225.00
Girl, 10", Yorkshire girl, grapes in folds of dress, standing, #5047 ....$150.00
Lady, 10½", hair in ringlets, lace kerchief, #5082 ....$135.00
Lady, 11", Chinese Mandarin, standing, lace & gilt, #5071 ....$165.00
Lady, 11¼", blue eyes, upswept hair, #5089A $160.00
Lamp, 11½", lady with upswept gray hair, lace, bustle, #5084 ....$140.00
Lamp, 15", Madame DuBarry bust, much lace $250.00
Lamp, 16½", Grape Harvester, #304 ....$150.00
Man, 10½", much lace, standing on scrolled base, #5042 ....$110.00
Man & lady, 11", man w/violin, seated lady, #4129A, pr $300.00
Pheasant, 17", bright colors, very early, #343, rare $260.00
Tray, 13", leaf form $65.00
Vase, 8", Orientals in relief, applied flowers, #7094 ..$160.00
Wall mask, 10", lady's face, #902 ....$200.00

Cottage Ware

Made by several companies, cottage ware is a line of ceramic table and kitchen accessories, each piece styled as a cozy cottage with a thatched roof. At least three English potteries made the ware, and you'll find pieces marked 'Japan' as well as 'Occupied Japan.' From Japan you'll also find pieces styled as windmills and water wheels, though the quality is inferior. The better pieces are marked 'Price Brothers' and 'Occupied Japan.' They're compatible in coloring as well as in styling, and values run about the same. Items marked simply 'Japan' are worth slightly less.

Biscuit jar, 6½x5¼", Maruhon Ware, Occupied Japan ..$75.00
Butter dish, Occupied Japan $55.00
Butter pat, rectangular, Occupied Japan $17.50
Chocolate pot, English $135.00
Cookie jar, 7", Japan $45.00
Cookie jar, 8x6¼", Maruhon Ware $85.00
Creamer, 2⅝", windmill, Occupied Japan $15.00
Creamer & sugar bowl, w/lid, on rectangular tray, Occupied Japan $50.00

Creamer & sugar bowl, 2½", 4½", English $45.00

Cup & saucer, English $40.00
Dish w/lid, small, Occupied Japan $35.00
Egg cup, 1¾" $10.00
Grease jar, Occupied Japan $25.00
Pitcher, water; English $150.00
Sugar bowl, w/lid, 3⅞", windmill, Occupied Japan $25.00
Teapot, 4⅞", windmill, Occupied Japan $45.00
Teapot, 6½", English or Occupied Japan $55.00
Teapot, 6½", Japan $40.00
Tumbler, 3½", set of six, Japan $60.00

Cracker Jack Collectibles

Cracker Jack has been around for over one hundred years. For ninety of those years, there's been a prize inside each box. If you could see the toys from over the years, you'd see the decades of the 20th century unfold. Tanks in wartime, sports cards and whistles in peacetime, and space toys in the sixties. In addition to the prizes, collectors also look for dealer incentives, point of sale items, boxes, cartons, and advertising.

'Cracker Jack' in the following descriptions indicates that the item actually carries the Cracker Jack mark.

Ad, comic book, Cracker Jack $9.00
Ad, Saturday Evening Post, 11x14", 1919, multicolored, Cracker Jack $18.00
Box, ca 1920, red scroll border, Cracker Jack $85.00
Canister, 1-lb, tin, Cracker Jack Coconut Corn Crisp ...$55.00
Canister, 10-oz, tin, Cracker Jack Coconut Corn Crisp ..$65.00
Canister, 10-oz, tin, Cracker Jack Corn Crisp $75.00
Dealer incentive, cart w/two movable wheels, wood dowel tongue, Cracker Jack $33.00
Dealer incentive, corkscrew & opener, 3", metal plated, Cracker Jack & Angelus $65.00
Dealer incentive, Halloween mask, 10", paper, Cracker Jack, NM $24.00
Dealer incentive, magic puzzle, 1934, metal, Cracker Jack, in envelope $14.00
Dealer incentive, palm puzzle, 1½", 1910-14, mirror back, marked Germany RWB, Cracker Jack $110.00
Dealer incentive, post card, 1907, pictures a bear, Cracker Jack $22.00
Dealer incentive, tablet, 8x10", 1929, Cracker Jack ...$195.00
Medal, 1939, salesman award, brass, rare $165.00
Premium, baseball bat, full size, wood, Hillerich & Bradsby, Cracker Jack $125.00
Premium, harmonica, 5⅛", full scale, early, embossed Cracker Jack, rare $650.00
Premium, mirror, oval, Angelus (redhead or blonde) on box, NM $90.00
Premium, recipe book, 1930s, Angelus $22.00
Premium, wings, 3", 1930s, air corps type w/stud back, silver or black, Cracker Jack $75.00
Prize, 'Caution' sign, 1954-60, plastic, yellow $3.00
Prize, assorted animals, 1947, plastic, standup on base, Nosco or Cracker Jack $1.50

Prize, badge, 1¼", pin-back, celluloid, pretty lady w/Cracker Jack label **$98.00**

Prize, badge, 1¼", 1931, cast metal, silver 6-pointed star, marked Cracker Jack Police **$35.00**

Prize, badge, 2⅜", early, tin w/embossed Cracker Jack officer **$110.00**

Prize, bank, 2", early, 3-D book form in red, green, or black, Cracker Jack **$95.00**

Prize, baseball score counter, 3⅜" long, paper, Cracker Jack, NM **$95.00**

Prize, book, 'Bess & Bill on Cracker Jack Hill,' miniature, 1937, paper, series of 12, each............................**$85.00**

Prize, book, 'Birds We Know,' miniature, 1928, paper, Cracker Jack **$65.00**

Prize, book, 'Twigg & Sprigg,' miniature, 1930, paper, Cracker Jack **$85.00**

Prize, boy & dog, die-cut tin w/bend-over tab at top, Cracker Jack **$110.00**

Prize, brooch, early, tin, various designs on cards, Cracker Jack, each **$100.00**

Prize, cash register, 1⅞", early, tin litho, 'More You Eat,' Cracker Jack **$400.00**

Prize, clicker, 1949, 'Noisy Cracker Jack Snapper,' aluminum, pear shape **$32.00**

Prize, comic character, 1936-46, tin, oval standup, Cracker Jack **$85.00**

Prize, decal, 1947-49, paper, nursery rhyme figure, Cracker Jack **$31.00**

Prize, disk, 1½" dia, 1954, plastic w/embossed comic character, series of 12, each............................**$12.00**

Prize, dog, 1954, 3-D, plastic w/hollow base, Cracker Jack, NM...**$4.50**

Prize, fob, 1½", 1954, plastic alphabet letter w/loop on top, 1 of 26..**$2.25**

Prize, fortune wheel, 1¾", 1939-41, 2-pc tin litho, Cracker Jack..$43.00

Prize, fortune wheel, 1¾", paper litho, Cracker Jack...**$68.00**

Prize, game, Midget Auto Race, 3⅜", 1949, paper, Cracker Jack **$25.00**

Prize, hat, Indian headdress, paper, Cracker Jack, ...**$110.00**

Prize, helicopter, 2⅝", 1937, tin w/wood stick, yellow propellor, unmarked...**$18.00**

Prize, horse & wagon, 2⅛", die-cut tin litho, Cracker Jack & Angelus..**$65.00**

Prize, magic game book, 1946, paper w/erasable slate, series of 13, each **$27.00**

Prize, Model T Ford, License: NY 1915 #999, 2", tin, black & white, Cracker Jack, rare **$410.00**

Prize, pocket watch, 1½", 1931, tin, 'Cracker Jack' as numerals, silver or gold...**$58.00**

Prize, rocking horse w/boy, 1½", early, 3-D cast metal, inked..**$22.00**

Prize, sled, 2" long, 1931, tin plated, Cracker Jack **$49.00**

Prize, small box w/electric alarm clock lithograph, 1⅛", tin, unmarked **$75.00**

Prize, small box w/electric stove litho, 1⅛", tin **$90.00**

Prize, soldier, die-cut tin standup, officer, private, etc, unmarked **$17.00**

Prize, spinner, from 1948, plastic, ten designs in various colors..**$1.50**

Prize, top, golf game, 1933, paper w/wood stick center, Cracker Jack **$47.00**

Prize, train, 1941, tin w/lithograph coach, red............**$22.00**

Prize, tray, 2¼x1¾", embossed tin lithograph w/early package **$95.00**

Prize, wheelbarrow, 2½" long, 1931, tin plated, Cracker Jack, NM **$50.00**

Prize, whistle, Razz Zooka, 1949, paper w/C Carey Cloud design, Cracker Jack **$32.00**

Prize, whistle, 1⅜", 1950-53, plastic tube w/animals on top, Cracker Jack..**$8.50**

Sign, large, pictures Santa & prizes, multicolored cardboard, Angelus..**$95.00**

Sign, large, pictures Santa & prizes, multicolored cardboard, Cracker Jack **$165.00**

Sign, 17x22", early, girl w/box of Cracker Jack, 5-color cardboard **$185.00**

Store display, popcorn box, 1923, Cracker Jack..........**$65.00**

Crooksville China

American dinnerware is becoming a very popular field of collectibles, and because many of the more well-established lines such as Fiesta, LuRay, and those designed by Russell Wright have become so expensive, people are now looking for less costly patterns. If you've been at all aware of the market over the past twenty years or so, you know the same thing occurred in the Depression glass field. Lines that we were completely disinterested in during the late sixties have come into their own today.

Crooksville china comes from a small town in Ohio by the same name. They made many lines of dinnerware and kitchen items, much of which carried their trademark, until they closed late in the fifties. One of their more extensive lines is called 'Silhouette,' made in the mid-thirties. It is very similar to a line by Hall China, but you can easily tell the difference. Crooksville's decal is centered by the silhouette of a begging dog. Another nice line is 'House,' so named because of the English cottage featured in the petit point style decal. There are many different floral lines, and don't be surprised if you find the same decal on more than one of their standard shapes.

If you'd like to learn more about the various dinnerware companies we've included in this book, we recommend you read *The Collector's Encyclopedia of American Dinnerware* by Jo Cunningham.

Avenue, sugar bowl, coupe shape, early 1950s, w/lid ..**$8.00**

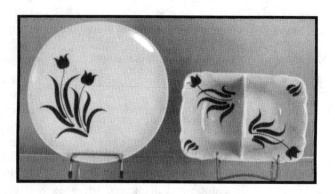

Black Tulip, charger...**$35.00**
Black Tulip, divided bowl (illustrated).................**$35.00**
Blossoms, plate, 6¾", on Fruits form **$5.00**
Blue Blossoms, bean pot, w/lid.................................**$45.00**
Calico Flowers, sugar bowl, on Dartmouth shape.......**$10.00**
Country Home, creamer **$12.50**
Country Home, sugar bowl, w/lid..............................**$15.00**
Flower Fair, plate, dinner; 9".......................................**$8.00**
Hunting, mug, dog decal in oval, barrel form **$15.00**
Hunting, plate, 12", four hunting scene decals, on Iva-Lure shape **$18.00**
Ivy Vine, plate, dinner; 10¼", on coupe shape **$5.00**
Jessie, plate, 6" **$2.00**
Meadow Flowers, plate, dinner; 10¼", coupe shape **$5.00**
Petit Point House, plate, 7¼", on Fruits shape **$8.00**
Petit Point House, plate, 9¾", on Fruits shape.............**$12.00**
Pheasant, plate, 9¾", on La Grande shape...................**$10.00**
Pink Border, plate, dinner; 9"......................................**$8.00**
Posies, cup & saucer, on La Grande shape **$8.00**
Rose Garden, plate, 6" **$2.00**
Rose Garland, gravy boat, w/underliner **$12.00**
Scotch Plaid, plate, dinner; 10¼", on coupe shape........**$6.00**
Silhouette, plate, 8"..**$10.00**
Silhouette, platter, 11½", oval...................................**$17.50**
Silhouette, tumbler, 8-oz **$15.00**
Southern Bell, plate, dinner; 10", on Iva Lure shape **$8.00**
Southern Bell, plate, 6¾", on coupe shape **$4.00**
Spray, plate, dinner; 10¾"...**$8.00**
Spring Blossom, bowl, serving; oval...........................**$15.00**
Spring Blossom, bowl, vegetable...............................**$17.50**
Spring Blossom, creamer..**$12.50**
Spring Blossom, cup & saucer **$12.00**
Spring Blossom, gravy boat.......................................**$17.50**
Spring Blossom, plate, dinner....................................**$12.00**
Spring Blossom, platter, oval **$20.00**

Spring Blossom, sugar bowl, w/lid.............................**$12.50**
Trellis, cup & saucer...**$15.00**
Trellis, pitcher, batter; 8", w/lid **$50.00**
Trellis, plate, 8"..**$8.00**
Trotter, cup & saucer..**$8.00**

Crown Dinnerware

This rather obscure manufacturer of kitchen and dinnerware operated in Evansville, Indiana, from sometime very early in the century until about 1950. Their backstamp varied over the years; sometimes it included the name of the company as well as their location. Often it contained the outline of a crown.

Autumn Leaf, jug, small, w/lid....................................**$65.00**
Bouquet, pie baker, 10", florals off to side of center, fine scalloped rim..**$20.00**
Carriage, bowl, vegetable; carriage & village scene in center, square form w/fine vertically ribbed sides...........**$15.00**
Croyden, gravy boat, floral decal on white...................**$7.50**
Croyden, saucer **$2.50**
Poppy, plate, 9", decal in center of square form, garland border **$5.00**
Windmill, pie baker, 10"..**$20.00**
Windmill, salt & pepper shakers, Oven Ware, pr........**$17.50**

Currier and Ives by Royal

This dinnerware has for the past two or three years been the focus of a great amount of collector interest. It was made by the Royal China company of Sebring, Ohio, and was given away as premiums for shopping at A&P stores. It is decorated with blue and white renditions of early American scenes by Currier and Ives, and so fits not only into the 'country' look now so popular in home decorating but its color schemes as well. Besides the dinnerware, Fire-King baking pans and accessories, glass tumblers, and vinyl placemats were also offered by A&P. Most pieces are relatively easy to find, but the casserole and the teapot are considered 'prizes' by collectors.

Ashtray...**$12.00**
Bowl, cereal; 6⅜", scarce..**$10.00**
Bowl, soup; 8½", flat...**$8.00**
Bowl, vegetable; oval **$18.00**
Bowl, 10"..**$16.00**
Bowl, 6⅜", lug soup..**$15.00**
Bowl, 9"..**$14.00**
Butter dish, ¼-lb...**$20.00**
Casserole, w/lid..**$50.00**
Chop plate, 12"...**$15.00**
Cup & saucer..**$4.00**
Gravy boat, w/ladle & liner..**$20.00**
Mug...**$12.50**
Pie plate, 10" **$12.00**

Plate, 10½"..**$7.50**
Plate, 12"...**$15.00**
Plate, 6"..**$3.00**
Plate, 7⅜"...**$6.00**
Plate, 9"...**$6.50**
Platter, 13"..**$18.00**
Salt & pepper shakers, pr............................**$12.00**
Sugar bowl, w/lid...**$8.00**
Teapot..**$60.00**
Tumbler, juice **$10.00**
Tumbler, old fashioned; 3¼".......................**$10.00**
Tumbler, 4¾", 9-oz.......................................**$8.00**
Tumbler, 5½", 13-oz....................................**$10.00**

Czechoslovakian Glass and Ceramics

Established as a country in 1918, Czechoslovakia is rich in the natural resources needed for production of glassware as well as pottery. Over the years it has produced vast amounts of both. Anywhere you go, from flea markets to fine antique shops, you'll find several examples of their lovely pressed and cut glass scent bottles, Deco vases, lamps, kitchenware, tableware and figurines.

More than thirty-five marks have been recorded; some are ink stamped, some etched, and some molded in. Paper labels have also been used. *Czechoslovakian Glass and Collectibles* by Diane and Dale Barta and *Made in Czechoslovakia* by Ruth Forsythe are two books we highly recommend for further study.

Ceramics

Basket, 3¼", multicolor flowers on dark gray w/black handle & trim **$20.00**
Basket, 4", floral stencil on cream, embossed woven-look decoration at rim & base **$30.00**
Bowl vase, 4½", multicolor mottle w/black design at base & flared rim, black teardrops along body **$80.00**
Coffee mug, 4½", bright multicolor Deco-style flowers on yellow background, black rim & angle handle.....**$45.00**
Creamer, 3", orange & white petal-molded body, green scalloped rim, green vine handle................................**$35.00**
Creamer, 4½", parrot figural, orange beak & back, multicolored wings, black accents **$40.00**
Figurine, 5¼", white goose w/shiny glaze, gold trim & accents **$40.00**
Flowerpot, 4⅝", allover multicolored flowers on white, gold rim, simple cylinder form, marked Erphila Pottery..**$40.00**
Pitcher, 10½", turquoise mottling w/reddish & cream mottling in alternating bands, flared top, ornate handle...**$165.00**
Pitcher, 5¾", bird figural, black & red details on cream body, marked Erphila Art Pottery **$85.00**
Pitcher, 6½", multicolor embossed fruit on maroon ground, angle handle..**$70.00**

Pitcher, 7¾", orange top w/black trim, church scene on body, green base, ornate handle **$50.00**
Planter, 3¼", tan & yellow bird on Deco-style bowl of tan lustreware **$35.00**
Planter, 4", beige w/allover reddish lines, black design at rim & center, ear-shape handles **$55.00**
Plate, 7", majolica, dark green & brownish-yellow leaves form body..**$40.00**
Teapot, 4", white pearl lustreware w/black handle & finial, black accent on spout.............................**$40.00**
Toothpick holder, 3½", white elephant figural, brown eyes, green howdah w/tassels on back **$40.00**
Vase, large rose on brown-to-cream shaded ground, ruffled top, simple handles.............................**$55.00**
Vase, 10¼", beige, black & orange mottling on lustre, black design at base & center, ornate cut-out handles...**$95.00**
Vase, 7¼", yellow shaded to green pearlescent ground w/orange, red & green abstracts, classic form......**$40.00**

Vase, 8", stylized flame motif, Ditmar Urbach Pottery **$250.00**

Glass

Basket, 6½", red, cased, applied black rim & handle..**$75.00**
Berry set, orange, blue & white mottled, cased, applied cobalt handles, 5-pc set....................................**$300.00**
Bowl, red, blue & white mottled, cased, 6-sided bowl on stemmed foot **$85.00**
Bowl, 4", yellow, red & green mottled, cased, small flared foot..**$55.00**
Bowl, 5", black, red cased, flared rim..........................**$75.00**
Candlestick, 3", black, orange cased, wide flared top & foot, pr **$140.00**
Candlestick, 8½", varicolored shades of green, slim form w/wide round foot.......................................**$75.00**
Candlestick, 8¼", black, cased, applied red ring **$70.00**

Candy dish, 7", red, cased, black medallion designs on sides, black knob finial..$85.00

Candy dish, 8", multicolor mottled, cased, applied black 4-footed pedestal base...$120.00

Perfume, approximate size: 6", cut crystal (three styles shown), any $70.00

Perfume, 3", black opaque base w/jeweled decoration & canted corners, black stopper...........................$75.00

Perfume, 4", green crystal pillow form w/intersecting lines, matching pyramidal stopper, marked....................$60.00

Perfume, 4⅛", clear highly cut fan shape, intaglio cut stopper w/lovebirds on branch w/hearts, marked....$145.00

Perfume, 5", clear w/geometric cuttings, black faceted crystal stopper w/dauber, marked $135.00

Perfume, 5¾", blue crystal w/clear 18th-century dancers intaglio on clear stopper w/long dauber, marked.$100.00

Perfume, 5¾", clear highly cut base w/four feet, tall stopper, hole cut in center, w/dauber, marked...................$80.00

Perfume, 5¾", cut amber base, amber intaglio-cut drop stopper..$125.00

Perfume, 6¼", clear cut baluster form urn, tiara-like stopper w/intaglio roses, w/dauber, no mark..................$230.00

Perfume, 6¾", cut base, amethyst drop stopper w/intaglio-cut design...$170.00

Perfume, 7", pink crystal square form, clear stopper w/lady in ball gown intaglio, marked..............................$185.00

Perfume, 7", pink cut crystal, squat hexagon-shaped base w/pink figural bird stopper, w/dauber, marked.$230.00

Perfume, 8½", blue shouldered form, clear geometrically cut stopper w/openwork, w/dauber, marked...........$250.00

Pitcher, blue & red mottled, cased, ruffled rim, applied cobalt handle..$100.00

Pitcher, 10⅛", red, cased, applied black handle, flared cylinder w/collar-type rim...$150.00

Vase, bud; 10", yellow-orange, cased, silver floral decor at rim & bulbous base..$60.00

Vase, bud; 11", green cylinder w/applied 'thorns,' flared cobalt base $145.00

Vase, bud; 8", orange, cased, enamel florals & scrolls, flared foot...$60.00

Vase, jack-in-the pulpit; 13½", yellow, cased, black applied at rim $110.00

Vase, 10", crystal w/alternating frosted panels, scalloped top, flared cylinder form $225.00

Vase, 11¼", orange & yellow mottled w/brown swirls at base, cased, slim form w/slightly flared rim..........$90.00

Vase, 11¾", variegated autumn colors, cased, four clear feet on slim form...$75.00

Vase, 12½", white satin, gold medallions & bands, trumpet neck on shouldered slim form, wide flared base .$150.00

Vase, 4½", varigated colors, cased, gourd form...........$60.00

Vase, 4½", white w/green aventurine design, cased, bulbous w/flared rim & foot...$65.00

Vase, 4½", yellow-orange, cased, brown overlay at base, bulbous shape w/flared rim $50.00

Vase, 4¼", yellow & white mottled, cased, w/metal flower arranger $65.00

Vase, 4¾", tomato red, cased, silver lady on body, silver trim on rim & foot $45.00

Vase, 5", red, cased, black base, applied black trim on flared rim..$70.00

Vase, 6", green w/abstract brown design, cased, ball form, small flared neck...$110.00

Vase, 6½", light green ringed neck w/ruffled rim, mottled overlay base $40.00

Vase, 7", frosted horses embossed on ball form..........$75.00

Vase, 7", maroon, cased, applied amber handles, waisted form $85.00

Vase, 7", red, cased, applied black rim, wide flared rim, pedestal foot...$70.00

Vase, 7½", varicolored red, white & blue, cased, slim form w/gently flared base $65.00

Vase, 7½", variegated colors, cased, applied black 3-footed pedestal base...$80.00

Vase, 7¼", black, cased, enameled bird on silver branch, silver decoration at rim, classic form.....................$140.00

Vase, 7⅞", pale blue, cased, ruffled rim, applied crystal handles...$90.00

Vase, 8", orange, cased, flared cylinder w/applied black serpentine decoration..$85.00

Vase, 8", orange mottled, cased, waisted gourd form w/small foot $70.00

Vase, 8½", crystal w/variegated blue scalloped design, ball form w/small flared rim................................$165.00

Vase, 8½", light blue, cased, applied black trim on ruffled rim, slim flared cylinder form...........................$75.00

Vase, 8½", orange mottled, cased, cobalt handles.......$80.00

Vase, 8¾", orange, cased, ruffled top, silver flower decoration on body, silver trim on rim & foot.............$115.00

Vase, 8⅜", multicolored, cased, applied blue handles below bowl form w/flared rim...$95.00

Vase, 8⅜", yellow & brown variegated design, cased, applied black base w/three buttressed feet $95.00

Dairy Bottles

Between the turn of the century and the 1950s, milk was bought and sold in glass bottles. Until the twenties, the name and location of the dairy was embossed in the glass.

After that it became commonplace to pyro-glaze (paint and fire) the lettering onto the surface. Farmers sometimes added a cow or some other graphic that represented the product or related to the name of the dairy.

Because so many of these glass bottles were destroyed when paper and plastic cartons became popular, they've become a scarce commodity, and today's collectors have begun to take notice of them. It's fun to see just how many you can find from your home state — or try getting one from every state in the union!

For further information, we recommend *Udderly Delightful* by John Tutton.

Adderholdt Brothers Creamery, Gainsville GA, 1-qt, cylindrical, Uncle Sam w/glass, red painted label.............**$67.50**

Barlow Dairy, Sugar Grove PA, 1-qt, square, cow's head on front, painted label....................................**$5.00**

Big Rapids Dairy, Big Rapids MI, 1-qt, square, WWII fighter plane on front, brown painted label.....................**$17.50**

Borden's, ½-gal, cylindrical, 3-armed cactus in square, ochre painted label...**$17.50**

Borden's Elsie, 1-qt, square, Elsie's head on front & back, red painted label **$9.00**

Brookdale Dairy, Seymour CT, 1-qt, cylindrical, farm to home delivery scene, orange painted label **$16.00**

Brookville Dairy Products, Brookville PA, 1-qt, cylindrical, cream top, 'It Whips' on both sides, orange painted label **$27.50**

Burroughs Brothers Walnut Grove Farm, Knightsen CA, 1-qt, cylindrical, cream top, red painted label.............**$20.00**

Clewell's Berwick Creamery, 1-qt, cylindrical, 'God Bless America...' & Statue of Liberty on back, orange painted label **$52.50**

Clover Farm Dairy Co, Memphis TN, 1-qt, cylindrical, red & green painted label, embossed on base **$20.00**

Clover Farms, Norwalk CT, 1-qt, green pyro **$18.00**

Cloverleaf Blue Ribbon Farms, Stockton CA, 1-qt, ribbed cream top, orange painted label **$20.00**

Dairy Dale, Penn Reed Milk Co, Meyersdale PA, 1-qt, cylindrical logo on front, blue painted label.................**$20.00**

Dublin Co-Op Dairies, 1-pt, cylindrical, squat form, 'You Owe It to Your Country...' on back, red painted label...**$30.00**

Dyke's Dairy, Warren PA, 1-qt, cylindrical, 'For Victory Balance Your Meals...' & Uncle Sam's bust, red painted label...**$60.00**

Frederick's Farm Dairy, Conyngham PA, 1-qt, cylindrical, brown painted label...**$17.50**

Gandy's Fine Dairy Products, 1-gal, red pyro, metal handle, 10¾"..**$8.00**

Gillette & Sons Dairy, 1-pt, cylindrical, 'America First Last Always' w/flying eagle, orange painted label **$32.50**

Harlow's Jerseydale Farm, Amherst MA, 1-qt, cylindrical, red painted label...**$15.00**

Harm's Dairy, Savannah GA, 1-pt, cylindrical, tall, boy & girl in scene, green painted label **$15.00**

Highland Dairy Farm, Madera PA, 1-qt, cylindrical, cows & barn, red painted label **$25.00**

Hillcrest Dairy, Cadiz OH, Steubenville OH, 1-qt, red pyro **$12.00**

Hood, 1-gal, square, cow's head on all sides, 'No Deposit' on opposing shoulders, green painted label.........**$22.50**

Hood Dairy Experts, ½-pt, cylindrical, diamond-ribbed neck, embossed...**$12.50**

Janeczek's Wayside Farm, 1-qt, cylindrical, mother & baby on front, orange & green painted label.................**$10.00**

Liberty Milk Co, Buffalo NY, ½-pt, cylindrical, Statue of Liberty on back, embossed..**$10.00**

Lotta Rock Farm, Littleton NH, ½-pt, cylindrical, embossed..**$12.50**

Mason's Dairy, Wadhams NY, 1-pt, wide mouth, red & blue painted label...**$10.00**

ML Fenton, Titusville PA, 1-qt, orange & green pyro ..**$25.00**

Morning Star Dairy, Chattanooga TN, 1-qt, cylindrical, tall, logo in center, embossed **$12.50**

Morningside Farm, ½-gal, cylindrical, cow in sunrise landscape, orange painted label **$12.50**

Nickles Dairy, Lowell MA, 1-qt, square, cow's head, .**$27.50**

Oakhurst Dairy Co, Bathe ME, 1-qt, cylindrical, policeman helps girl across street, orange painted label........**$12.50**

Oatman's Good Homogenized Milk, ½-gal, logo on each shoulder & 'The Brightest Star in the Milky Way' on front, amber..**$8.50**

Party Tonight?, 1-qt, green pyro, cream top.........$15.00

People's Milk Co, 1-qt, cylindrical, tall, logo at center, embossed...**$75.00**

Quinnequack Farm, 1-qt, cylindrical, orange painted label **$17.50**

Reynold's Dairy, 1-qt, square, cow standing, black painted label **$7.50**

Sanitary's Pasteurized Milk & Real Ice Cream, 1-qt, cylindrical, red painted label on front, blue painted label on back **$5.00**

Store bottle, 1-qt, red pyro, (illustrated) **$20.00**

Sundale Dairy, 1-qt, cylindrical, 'Electropoured' on back, green painted label **$12.50**

Sunset Farm Dairy, Woodstock VT, 1-qt, square, orange painted label **$7.50**

Sunshine Dairies, Utica NY, ½-pt, cream top, 'Buy War Bonds' on back, orange painted label **$32.50**

Wanut Crest Farm, Westbook ME, 1-qt, cylindrical, 'Guernsey Milk' in diamond on front, maroon painted label **$15.00**

Wauregan Dairy, 1-pt, cream top, children w/rhyme, black & red painted label **$36.00**

Wells & Lassiter, Jackson TN, 1-qt, cylindrical, 'Keep Physically Fit & Mentally Alert' on back, green painted label **$40.00**

White Springs Farm Dairy, Geneva NY, 1-qt, cylindrical, 'For Security Buy War Bonds' on back, orange painted label **$80.00**

De Vilbiss

The lovely perfume bottles, lamps, and vanity accessories you'll find marked De Vilbiss were not actually made by that company (De Vilbiss made only the metal mounts), but rather by a variety of glasshouses. They were sold by De Vilbiss both here and abroad. You'll find several variations of the company marks as well as some paper labels.

Values hinge on two factors: the type of glass that was used and the design. The most valuable are those made in Aurene glass by Steuben. (Aurene is primarily found in gold or blue and is characterized by its strong iridescence.) Perfumes with figural stems or those with an Art Deco influence are usually near the top of the price scale. Gold-colored glass with a crackled appearance was often used, and the smaller, less-strikingly designed examples made of this type of glass are more common.

A good source for further study is *Bedroom and Bathroom Glassware of the Depression Years* by Margaret and Kenn Whitmyer.

Atomizer, black enameled Art Deco design on pink opaque, mesh cord & bulb **$185.00**

Atomizer, green Hobnail, by Fenton **$42.00**

Atomizer, yellow & black enameled stripes on clear .. **$40.00**

Atomizer, 2¼", clear, brass top w/coral button, in original case marked De Vilbiss **$42.00**

Atomizer, 4", amethyst w/pebbled texture, replaced bulb, w/label **$95.00**

Atomizer, 4¾", gold crackle, beaded flower on top, signed **$65.00**

Atomizer, 6", allover green enameling, original cord & bulb **$70.00**

Atomizer, 6", orange-stained w/footed crystal base **$75.00**

Atomizer, 6¼", allover lavender enameling, original cord & netted bulb **$70.00**

Atomizer, 6¼", ebony, long cord & tasseled bulb **$90.00**

Atomizer, 7", crystal w/gold draped-lady stem **$245.00**

Atomizer, 7", pink, gold caryatid stem, original bulb ... **$275.00**

Atomizer, 7¾", allover green enameling w/much gold, original cord & bulb **$120.00**

Atomizer, 8", clear & white cased baluster form w/enameled flowers & gold, NM **$150.00**

Atomizer, 8", orange w/green iridescent lily pads & vines, no bulb **$175.00**

Atomizer, opaline, jeweled top removes to spray, paper label **$125.00**

Lamp, perfume; 12", black nude silhouette enameled on orange glass insert **$285.00**

Lamp, perfume; 7", black nude silhouette enameled on orange glass insert **$235.00**

Lamp, perfume; 8½", black exotic bird enameled on square glass insert **$135.00**

Perfume bottle, iridescent, black enameled top, stemmed foot, signed **$80.00**

Perfume bottle, small, smoke gray, hand blown **$285.00**

Perfume bottle, 6½", clear w/cut drapery design, slim form w/metal stopper & long glass dauber, signed **$175.00**

Perfume bottle, 7", black & gold abstract enameling, metal stopper w/long glass dauber, signed **$250.00**

Pin tray, black matt w/gold trim **$30.00**

Pin tray, 3¼x5⅝", orange enamel w/black & gold decoration **$25.00**

Vanity set, light blue & crystal frost, 4-pc, rare...........**$70.00**

Decanters

The first company to make figural ceramic decanters was the James Beam Distilling Company, who now own their own china factory here in the United States. They first issued their bottles in the mid-fifties, and over the course of the next twenty-five years, more than twenty other companies followed their example. Among the more prominent of these were Brooks, Hoffman, Lionstone, McCormick, Old Commonwealth, Ski Country, and Wild Turkey. In 1975, Beam introduced the 'Wheel Series,' cars, trains, and fire engines with wheels that actually revolved. The popularity of this series resulted in a heightened interest in decanter collecting.

There are various sizes, the smallest (called miniatures) hold two ounces, and there are some that hold a gallon! A full decanter is worth no more than an empty one, and the absence of the tax stamp will not lower its value either. Just be sure that all the labels are intact and that there are no cracks or chips. You might want to empty your decanters as a safety precaution (many collectors do) rather than risk the possibility of the inner glaze breaking down and allowing the contents to wick into the porous ceramic body.

All of the decanters we've listed are fifths unless we've specified 'miniature' within the description.

Aesthetic Specialties, Cadillac, 1903 model, 1979.......**$38.00**
Aesthetic Specialties Inc, Bing Crosby, 1982...............**$28.00**
Aesthetic Specialties Inc, Model-T Telephone Truck, 1980 ....**$65.00**
Aesthetic Specialties Inc, Stanley Steamer, 1909 model, 1979, black **$42.50**
Beam, Animal Series, Appaloosa, 1974 ....**$13.00**
Beam, Animal Series, Bulldog, 1979...........................**$22.50**
Beam, Animal Series, Setter, 1958...............................**$50.00**
Beam, Centennial Series, Alaska Purchase, 1966 ....**$7.50**
Beam, Executive Series, Blue Cherub, 1960...............**$115.00**
Beam, Executive Series, Majestic, 1966.......................**$32.00**
Beam, Executive Series, Royal Gold Diamond, 1964...**$40.00**
Beam, Fox Series, Rennie the Runner, 1974 ....**$12.50**
Beam, Opera Series, Carmen, 1978 ....**$245.00**
Beam, Organization Series, Ducks Unlimited #2, 1975 ..**$50.00**
Beam, Organization Series, Ducks Unlimited #8, Woody & His Brood, 1982 ....**$37.50**
Beam, Organization Series, Kentucky Colonel, 1970...**$12.00**
Beam, Organization Series, Telephone #3, cradle, 1979 ....**$18.00**
Beam, Organization Series, Blue Goose........................**$5.00**
Beam, Political Series, Donkey, Clown, 1968.................**$7.50**
Beam, Political Series, Donkey & Elephant, Campaigners, 1960, pr..**$30.00**
Beam, Political Series, Elephant, San Diego, 1972.......**$16.00**
Beam, Regal China Series, Texas Hemisfair, 1968 ....**$12.50**
Beam, Sports Series, Bing Crosby National Pro-Am, 1970 ....**$7.00**

Beam, Sports Series, Bob Hope Desert Classic, 14th, 1973 ....**$12.50**
Beam, Sports Series, Hawaiian Open, Pineapple, #7, 1972 ....**$8.50**

Beam, States Series, Arizona....................................$7.00
Beam, States Series, Idaho, 1963.................................**$50.00**
Beam, States Series, Maine, 1970 ....**$55.00**
Beam, States Series, South Carolina, 1970 ....**$5.00**
Beam, Trophy Series, Cardinal, 1968, male.................**$42.50**
Beam, Trophy Series, Coho Salmon, 1976 ....**$15.00**
Beam, Trophy Series, Crappie, 1979............................**$15.00**
Beam, Trophy Series, Pheasant, 1960..........................**$20.00**
Beam, Wheel Series, Chevy Corvette, 1963, red..........**$40.00**
Beam, Wheel Series, Duesenberg, 1934, light or dark blue **$125.00**
Beam, Wheel Series, Fire Chief's Car, 1928...............**$110.00**
Beam, Wheel Series, Ford Paddy Wagon, 1984..........**$55.00**
Beam, Wheel Series, Jewel Tea Wagon........................**$80.00**
Beam, Wheel Series, Passenger Car, 1981....................**$50.00**
Beam, Wheel Series, Stutz Bearcat, 1977, yellow **$38.00**
Beam, Wheel Series, Volkswagen, 1973, blue **$37.50**
Brooks, Animal Series, Bengal Tiger, 1979..................**$32.00**
Brooks, Animal Series, Bucking Bronco, 1974............**$12.50**
Brooks, Animal Series, Elk, 1972 ....**$25.00**
Brooks, Animal Series, Hereford, 1972.........................**$9.00**
Brooks, Animal Series, Razorback Hog, 1970 ....**$15.00**
Brooks, Animal Series, White Tail Deer, 1974 ....**$17.50**
Brooks, Automotive & Transportation Series, Corvette, 1957 Model, 1977...**$115.00**
Brooks, Automotive & Transportation Series, Duesenberg, 1979 ....**$26.50**
Brooks, Automotive & Transportation Series, Lincoln Continental, 1941 model, 1979.....................................**$20.00**
Brooks, Clown Series, Smiley, #1, 1979......................**$30.00**
Brooks, Clown Series, Tramp, 1980.............................**$15.00**
Brooks, Institutional Series, American Legion, 1972....**$15.00**
Brooks, Institutional Series, AMVET Polish Legion, 1908 ..**$8.00**

Brooks, Institutional Series, FOE Eagle, 1979 ....**$20.00**

Brooks, Institutional Series, Kachina #2, Hummingbird, 1973...**$70.00**

Brooks, Institutional Series, Shrine, Clown, 1978 ....**$15.00**

Brooks, Institutional Series, Shrine, Sphinx.................**$10.00**

Brooks, People Series, Gold Prospector, 1970 ....**$5.00**

Brooks, People Series, Sea Captain, 1971.....................**$7.50**

Brooks, Sports Series, Bareknuckle Fighter, 1971.........**$7.50**

Brooks, Ezra, tractor..**$15.00**

Hoffman, Aesop's Fables Series, Androcles & the Lion, 1978...**$25.00**

Hoffman, Car Series, Racecar, Donahue Sunoco #66..**$110.00**

Hoffman, Car Series, Racecar, Rutherford #3, 1974 .....**$75.00**

Hoffman, Cheerleader Series, Dallas Cheerleaders, 1979 ..**$20.00**

Hoffman, College Football Series, Kansas State Wildcats, 1981 ....**$25.00**

Hoffman, Decoy Series, Canada Goose, 1977..............**$17.50**

Hoffman, Helmet Series, Kentucky Wildcats, 1981......**$25.00**

Hoffman, Mr Lucky Series, Mr Baker, 1978..................**$32.50**

Hoffman, Mr Lucky Series, Mr Blacksmith, 1976 ....**$42.00**

Hoffman, Mr Lucky Series, Mr Dancer, 1974, miniature.**$15.00**

Hoffman, Mr Lucky Series, Mr Electrician, 1978 ....**$32.00**

Hoffman, Mr Lucky Series, Mr School Teacher, 1976..**$30.00**

Hoffman, Mr Plumber, 1978...**$30.00**

Hoffman, No Hunting Series, Bears & Cubs **$40.00**

Hoffman, No Hunting Series, Eagle & Fox..................**$50.00**

Hoffman, No Hunting Series, Falcon & Rabbit, 1978 ..**$45.00**

Hoffman, Rodeo Series, Calf Roping, 1978 ....**$32.00**

Hoffman, Rodeo Series, Saddle Bronc Riding, 1978....**$32.00**

Hoffman, Wildlife Series, Bobcat & Pheasant **$28.00**

Lionstone, Bicentennial Series, Betsy Ross..................**$25.00**

Lionstone, Bicentennial Series, George Washington, 1975 ....**$24.00**

Lionstone, Bird Series, Eastern Bluebird, 1972.............**$17.50**

Lionstone, Birds & Waterflowl, Wood Duck, 1981 ......**$55.00**

Lionstone, Birds & Waterfowl, Canvasback Duck, 1981 ..**$40.00**

Lionstone, Birds & Waterfowl, Snow Goose, 1981 ......**$65.00**

Lionstone, Clown Series, Lampy #6, 1979, miniature ..**$17.50**

Lionstone, Clown Series, Monkey Business #1, 1978 ..**$34.00**

Lionstone, Dog Series, Alaskan Malamute, 1977, miniature..**$15.00**

Lionstone, Dog Series, British Pointer, 1975, miniature.**$12.50**

Lionstone, Dog Series, 1977, miniature **$14.00**

Lionstone, European Worker, Cobbler, 1974 ....**$35.00**

Lionstone, European Worker, Watchmaker, 1974........**$30.00**

Lionstone, Fireman, #1, yellow hat, 1972....................**$117.50**

Lionstone, Fireman, #5, 60th Anniversary Emblem, 1979 ....**$27.50**

Lionstone, Oriental Worker, Egg Merchant, 1974 ....**$35.00**

Lionstone, Oriental Worker, Timekeeper, 1974 ....**$35.00**

Lionstone, Western Figures Series, Cowboy, 1969.......**$12.50**

Lionstone, Western Figures Series, Dancehall Girl, 1973.**$55.00**

McCormick, Bicentennial Series, Abe Lincoln, 1976....**$30.00**

McCormick, Bicentennial Series, Benjamin Franklin, 1976, miniature...**$14.50**

McCormick, Elvis Series, #1, Designer, Gold Encore, 1984 ....**$175.00**

McCormick, Elvis Series, #2, 1979..............................**$165.00**

McCormick, Elvis Series, #3, 1980..............................**$30.00**

McCormick, Elvis Series, Aloha, 1981.........................**$125.00**

McCormick, Elvis Series, Gold, 1979 ....**$185.00**

McCormick, Sports Series, Kansas City Chiefs, 1969....**$42.50**

McCormick, Sports Series, Nebraska Football Player, 1972 ....**$38.00**

McCormick, Sports Series, Wisconsin Badgers, 1974...**$15.00**

McCormick, Train Series, Jupiter Engine & Tender, 1969 ....**$28.00**

McCormick, Train Series, Mail Car, 1969.....................**$42.50**

Old Commonwealth, Coal Miner, #3, w/lump of coal ..**$50.00**

Old Commonwealth, Coal Miner #4, Lunchtime, miniature **$22.50**

Old Commonwealth, Coal Miner #5, Coal Shooter......**$40.00**

Old Commonwealth, Coal Miner #5, Coal Shooter, miniature **$22.00**

Old Commonwealth, Irish, Coins of Ireland **$28.00**

Old Commonwealth, Irish, Dogs of Ireland, 1980.......**$20.00**

Old Commonwealth, Irish, Idyll, 1981.........................**$20.00**

Old Commonwealth, Irish, Leprechaun #3, Lucky, 1983...**$30.00**

Old Commonwealth, Wildfowler #1, Hunter, 1978 .....**$42.50**

Old Commonwealth, Yankee Doodle, 1982 ....**$28.00**

Ski Country, Animal Series, Badger, 1981, miniature ..**$17.50**

Ski Country, Animal Series, Burro, Colorado School of Mines, 1973..**$55.00**

Ski Country, Animal Series, Fox Family, 1979..............**$57.50**

Ski Country, Animal Series, Fox on a Log, 1974..........**$80.00**

Ski Country, Animal Series, Skunk Family, 1978, miniature **$18.00**

Ski Country, Bird Series, Baltimore Oriole, 1977 ....**$60.00**

Ski Country, Bird Series, Blue Jay, 1978, miniature **$50.00**

Ski Country, Bird Series, Condor, 1973 ....**$40.00**

Ski Country, Bird Series, Fighting Pheasants, 1977, miniature **$27.50**

Ski Country, Circus Series, Clown Bust, 1974, miniature **$15.00**

Ski Country, Circus Series, Lion, 1976, miniature **$15.00**

Ski Country, Circus Series, Tom Thumb, 1974.............**$22.50**

Ski Country, Indian Series, Ceremonial Antelope Dancer, 1982 ....**$55.00**

Ski Country, Indian Series, Ceremonial Falcon Dancer, 1983...**$75.00**

Ski Country, Indian Series, Cigar Store, 1974..............**$24.00**
Ski Country, Rodeo Series, Barrel Racer, 1979...........**$50.00**
Ski Country, Rodeo Series, Bull Rider, 1980.................**$50.00**
Ski Country, Rodeo Series, Bull Rider, 1980, miniature..**$20.00**
Ski Country, Rodeo Series, Wyoming Bronco, 1979, miniature...**$22.50**
Wild Turkey, Series #3, #7, Turkey & Fox, 1985.........**$70.00**
Wild Turkey, Series 1, #1, male, 1971 ....**$300.00**
Wild Turkey, Series 1, #3, On the Wing, 1982, miniature..**$13.00**
Wild Turkey, Series 1, #6, Striding, 1976.....................**$22.50**
Wild Turkey, Series 1, #8, Strutting, 1983, miniature...**$20.00**
Wild Turkey, Series 3, #10, Turkey & Coyote, 1986....**$88.00**
Wild Turkey, Series 3, #2, Turkey & Bobcat, 1983....**$110.00**
Wild Turkey, Series 3, #4, Turkey & Eagle, 1984, miniature **$37.50**

Wild Turkey, Turkey Lore Series, #1, 1979 ....$42.50
Wild Turkey, Turkey Lore Series, #2, 1980 ....**$42.50**
Wild Turkey, Turkey Lore Series, #4, 1982 ....**$42.50**

Decoys

If you haven't been following the decoy market, you will be amazed to learn that it isn't at all uncommon for an especially fine specimen to bring 5-digit prices at some of the auction houses in the East that specialize in their sale. Many decoys are carved and signed by artists whose talents have become well recognized, just as is true with an artist who works in any other medium. Naturally, many of the more expensive examples are from the first half of the century, though the skill of the carver contributes more to a decoy's value than mere age.

Many decoys were factory made, and even some of these mass-produced birds are very collectible, especially those by Mason, whose rarer species have been known to sell for several thousand dollars on occasion.

Whether you're dealing in artist or factory decoys, condition is all-important. Cracks (especially neck cracks), chips, or shot scars all detract from value. It's very desirable that a decoy retain its original paint. One that has been repainted or whose paint is badly worn must be sharply devaluated.

It only takes one lucky find to bring in a windfall. If Dad or Grandpa were hunters, it could be well worth your time to check out their old discarded decoys. If you'd like to learn more about this fascinating field, we recommend _The Collector's Guide to Decoys, Books I & II,_ by Bob and Sharon Huxford and _Decoys_ by Kangas.

Allen, Charles; bufflehead drake, hollow, mellow patina, artist brand, M condition, 1930s...........................**$450.00**
Anger, Ken; mallard hen, hollow w/incised wings, original paint w/minor wear, EX condition, 1948.........**$1,200.00**
Bliss, Roswell; surf scoter, artist stamp, M condition, 1955..**$300.00**
Brett, Gordon; bluebill hen, EX original scratch paint, artist signed, G condition, 1955 ....**$100.00**
Carney, Armand; bluewinged teal drake, hollow w/relief wing carving, EX condition, 1969 ....**$75.00**
Conklin, Hurley; merganser drake, VG original paint, M condition, 1960...**$400.00**
Corbin, Reed; bufflehead drake, hollow, EX feather paint, signed by artist, M condition, 1969.....................**$750.00**
Cranmer, Bill; shoveler drake, hollow, NM original paint, signed by artist, EX condition, rare, 1953............**$400.00**
Disbrow, Charles; black duck, hollow, original paint w/average wear, 1935...**$500.00**
Down East Decoy Company, black duck, swimming, factory stamp, age line on underside, lightly shot, otherwise M condition **$200.00**
Duplessis, Sylvester; bluewinged teal hen, raised carved wings, original paint w/average wear, gouge in side, 1940s..**$110.00**
Evans Duck Decoy Company, bluebill drake, Mammoth Grade, hollow, original paint, light wear, factory stamp, lightly shot...**$275.00**
Evans Duck Decoy Company, canvasback pr, original paint w/average wear, factory stamp, thin age lines in bodies **$475.00**
Evans Duck Decoy Company, pintail drake, hollow, worn original paint, branded RJL, factory stamp, repairs to head...**$450.00**
Ganung, Lonnie; black duck, turned head, raised primaries, original paint w/minor wear, minor seam separation, 1930s...**$475.00**
Gelston, Thomas; yellowlegs, running, cedar with relief carved wings, old in-use repaint, hit by shot, tiny tail chip..**$500.00**
Gibbs, Harold; black duck, signed by artist, M condition, miniature, 1968...**$200.00**
Gibson, Paul; canvasback drake, original paint w/minor wear, signed by artist, several age lines, 1952 ....**$125.00**

Hayman, Joe; Canada goose, canvas-over-wire, old working repaint w/moderate wear, G condition, 1930s ...**$230.00**

Hays Decoy Factory, black duck, original paint w/moderate wear, hairline crack in underside **$195.00**

Hays Decoy Factory, goldeneye hen, G original paint w/average wear, filler flaking at neck, otherwise EX condition **$200.00**

Hays Decoy Factory, mallard hen, strong original paint w/minor wear, missing one eye, age line on underside **$250.00**

Herein, William; canvasback hen, original paint w/very minor wear, small old repaired neck crack, EX condition $700.00

Herters Inc, bluebill pr, balsa bodies, has a flaw in wood on back, otherwise EX & original condition..............**$90.00**

Herters Inc, crow, balsa body, old repaint w/average wear..**$75.00**

Herters Inc, goldeneye pr, balsa bodies, original paint w/average wear, early, no structural flaws **$165.00**

Jacobsgard, Clarence; mallard hen, NM original paint, signed by artist, EX condition, 1935 ....**$350.00**

Jester, Doug; wood duck drake, standing, signed by artist, EX condition, miniature, 1940..............................**$425.00**

LaFrance, Mitchell; mallard hen, relief wing carving, original paint w/minor wear, several dents & age lines, rare, 1935 ....**$700.00**

Mason Factory, American merganser pr, original paint w/crazing, drake has dry rot at tip of tail............**$900.00**

Mason Factory, black duck, Challenge Grade, original paint w/minor wear, small tail chip, age lines **$350.00**

Mason Factory, black duck, Premier Grade, original paint w/light wear, tail chips w/old touchups, lightly shot **$600.00**

Mason Factory, black duck, Standard Grade, tack eyes, original paint w/average wear, roughness at bill, age lines **$225.00**

Mason Factory, bluewinged teal drake, Standard Grade, tack eyes, original paint w/average wear, early **$375.00**

Mason Factory, brant, Challenge Grade, original paint w/light wear, hairlines in back, early **$1,000.00**

Mason Factory, canvasback drake, Premier Grade, original paint w/average wear, repaint on head, moderately shot **$200.00**

Mason Factory, coot, Challenge Grade, original paint w/average wear, original Challenge stamp, repair to bill...**$1,100.00**

Mason Factory, goldeneye drake, Challenge Grade, original paint w/minor wear, age split in underside.....**$1,500.00**

Mason Factory, greenwinged teal drake, Standard Grade, tack eyes, some original paint, partial overpaint, repairs..**$300.00**

Mason Factory, mallard hen, Premier Grade, original paint w/minor wear, professionally repaired tail chip.**$750.00**

Mason Factory, mallard pr, Standard Grade, glass eyes, original paint w/light wear, professional restoration...**$600.00**

Mason Factory, redhead hen, Premier Grade, snaky head, original paint w/some wear, bill & neck restoration, reglued chip **$475.00**

Mason Factory, willet, tack eyes, old overpaint worn to strong original w/minor wear, rare.....................**$800.00**

McNair, Mark; curlew, feeding, split tail carving, signed by artist, 1979 ....**$650.00**

Mitchell, Madison; black duck, original paint w/average wear, several nail holes in body, 1950s...............**$450.00**

Nichols, Davey; wood duck drake, raised wings, EX original paint, age line in neck, tail chips, 1940s **$1,750.00**

Pierce, Jim; goldeneye drake, preening, artist brand, NM condition, 1970s **$95.00**

Pratt Mfg Company, bluebill drake, old in-use repaint, hairline crack in breast..**$70.00**

Pratt Mfg Company, coot, original paint w/severe flaking at head & breast, no major structural flaws...............**$55.00**

Pratt Mfg Company, mallard pr, hollow, original paint w/minor wear, restored neck crack, oversize.....**$240.00**

Rupple, Walter; tule goose, slightly turned head, hollow w/raised wing tips, signed by artist, EX condition, 1968 ....**$1,100.00**

Schmidt, Ben; bluebill drake, original paint w/average wear, small holes in back, oversized, 1952 ....**$375.00**

Stevens Company, canvasback drake, old in-use repaint w/original on head & back, ca 1880, chips & dry rot on bottom **$750.00**

Stevens Company, redhead drake, repaint, minor age lines **$225.00**

Struebing, Walter; goldeneye drake, old repaint w/traces of original, age line along side, 1930s.....................**$110.00**

Updike, John; black duck, hollow, G original flock paint w/average wear, EX condition, 1930s **$200.00**

Ward, David; curlew, sickle bill, fluted tail, raised wings, M condition, 1980s...**$450.00**

Ward Brothers, black duck, slightly turned head, G original paint, some neck filler missing, 1936 ....**$1,700.00**

Ward Brothers, scaup drake, EX original paint w/some black over paint on head & breast, 1948 ....**$850.00**

Wheeler, Charles; surf scoter, hollow, leather thong & ring, M condition, rare, 1947 ....**$4,500.00**

Wilbur, Charles; mallard hen, hollow, artist brand, M condition, 1950s **$70.00**

Wildfowler Decoy Company, black duck, hollow pine body, worn original paint, Old Saybrook brand, age split in neck **$65.00**

Wildfowler Decoy Company, brant, fine original paint w/minor chipping, Old Saybrook brand............**$475.00**

Wildfowler Decoy Company, Canada goose, sleeping, EX original paint, factory brand, signed C Birdsall/1965, EX condition **$275.00**

Wildfowler Decoy Company, widgeon pr, hollow, inlet bottom board, strong original paint, ca 1939, Old Saybrook brand **$500.00**

Dedham Dinnerware

The Dedham Pottery was located in the city by that name in Massachusetts and from the turn of the century until 1943 produced more than a dozen patterns of blue and white crackle dinnerware in a style that was quite distinctive. All were hand painted by artists who used an ancient decorating method in which the cobalt designs they applied became part of the overall glaze. Some of the most common patterns are Rabbit and Azalea. In addition to their standard lines, special-order designs were made as well; these are very exciting to collectors and highly valued. Pieces decorated with an elephant or Scottie dogs, for instance, may well command prices of several thousand dollars.

Dedham dinnerware is scarce in the country as a whole, but if you live in the East or plan on making a buying trip to the area (it's a wonderful place to 'antique'), you just may be lucky enough to find a piece now and then. And, as you can see from our listings, at these prices, you need to be made aware of it.

Ash tray, 4", Elephant, stamped **$350.00**
Bowl, 1½x7", Rabbit, stamped registered, 5-sided.....**$650.00**
Bowl, 2x4¼", Rabbit, stamped **$200.00**
Bowl, 2x5¼", Polar Bear, stamped **$800.00**
Bowl, 3¼x8", Rabbit, stamped registered..................**$425.00**
Bowl, 4x9", Grape, stamped **$500.00**
Candlestick, 1½x3½", Rabbit, stamped registered, pr..**$575.00**
Creamer, 2¼", Horse Chestnut, stamped....................**$375.00**
Cup & saucer, demitasse; Rabbit, stamped registered..**$275.00**
Cup & saucer, 2½", Rabbit, stamped **$375.00**
Cup & saucer, 3", Rabbit, stamped **$300.00**
Egg cup, single; 1½", Rabbit, unmarked....................**$275.00**
Knife rest, 2½", Rabbit, faint stamp, figural..............**$700.00**
Mug, 4¼", Rabbit, impressed/stamped, NM **$425.00**
Pitcher, 4½", Rabbit, stamped **$650.00**
Plate, 10", Grape, impressed/stamped........................**$275.00**
Plate, 10", Grape, signed Davenport **$350.00**
Plate, 10", Turkey, stamped......................................**$225.00**
Plate, 6", Clover, impressed/stamped **$500.00**
Plate, 6", Magnolia, impressed/stamped, signed Maude Davenport..**$255.00**
Plate, 6", Snow Tree, impressed/stamped, signed Maude Davenport **$225.00**
Plate, 6", Swan, stamped **$400.00**
Plate, 7½", Horse Chestnut, impressed/stamped registered **$285.00**
Plate, 8", Crab, stamped registered, dated 1931........**$650.00**

Plate, 8½", Duck, impressed/stamped.......................**$350.00**
Plate, 8½", Pond Lily, stamped, O Rebus in border...**$275.00**
Plate, 8½", Rabbit, impressed/stamped, O Rebus in border..**$375.00**
Plate, 9¾", Iris, impressed/stamped, signed Maude Davenport, NM **$250.00**

Plate, 8½", Azalea..**$250.00**
Stein, 5", Rabbit, EX..**$225.00**
Sugar bowl, 2½x4", Rabbit, stamped registered........**$300.00**
Tea tile, 4⅝", Rabbit, stamped, dated 1931 ....**$300.00**
Tray, pin; 4", Rabbit, stamped, bunny medallion in center **$275.00**
Tray, 13½" dia, Rabbit, stamped, NM **$900.00**

Degenhart Glass

John and Elizabeth Degenhart owned and operated the Crystal Art Glass Factory in Cambridge, Ohio. From 1947 until John died in 1964 they produced some fine glassware; John himself was well known for his superior paperweights. But the glassware that collectors love today was made after '64, when Elizabeth restructured the company, creating many lovely molds and scores of colors. She hired Zack Boyd, who had previously worked for Cambridge Glass, and between the two of them, they developed almost 150 unique and original color formulas.

Complying with provisions she had made before her death, close personal friends at Island Mould and Machine Company in Wheeling, West Virginia, took Elizabeth's molds and removed the familiar 'D in heart' trademark from them. She had requested that ten of her molds be donated to the Degenhart Museum, where they remain today. Zack Boyd eventually bought the Degenhart factory and acquired the remaining molds. He has added his own logo to them and is continuing to press glass very similar to Mrs. Degenhart's.

Basket Toothpick, Cobalt **$20.00**
Bicentennial Bell, Amethyst **$11.00**
Bicentennial Bell, Crystal...**$6.00**
Bicentennial Bell, Ebony **$5.00**

Bicentennial Bell, Elizabeth's Lime Ice......................$15.00
Bicentennial Bell, Opal...$12.00
Bicentennial Bell, Vaseline...$10.00
Bird Salt & Pepper, Opalescent $35.00

Bird Salt, Forest Green.................................$15.00
Child's Mug, Apple Green...$22.00
Coaster, Amber...$7.00
Colonial Drape & Heart Toothpick, Sapphire.............$15.00
Daisy & Button Salt, Cobalt......................................$15.00
Daisy & Button Toothpick, Cobalt Carnival................$40.00
Daisy & Button Toothpick, Crown Tuscan $25.00
Daisy & Button Toothpick, Light Amberina................$18.00
Forget-Me-Not Toothpick, Bluebell $15.00
Forget-Me-Not Toothpick, Canary $18.00
Forget-Me-Not Toothpick, Caramel $30.00
Forget-Me-Not Toothpick, Lavender Blue...................$25.00
Forget-Me-Not Toothpick, Peach Opaque $18.00
Forget-Me-Not Toothpick, Toffee $25.00
Gypsy Pot Toothpick, Canary $12.00
Gypsy Pot Toothpick, Cobalt, hand stamped $25.00
Gypsy Pot Toothpick, Tomato...................................$35.00

Gypsy Pot Toothpick, Vaseline $18.00
Hands, Crown Tuscan $18.00
Hands, Persimmon...$10.00
Hat, Vaseline, unsigned...$20.00
Heart Box, Brown $22.00
Heart Box, Elizabeth Blue $40.00
Heart Box, Light Chocolate Creme $35.00
Heart Box, Milk Blue $24.00
Heart Toothpick, Caramel $35.00

Heart Toothpick, Ruby $35.00
Heart Toothpick, Seafoam Green $25.00
Hearth Toothpick, Sapphire.......................................$15.00
Hen Covered Dish, Brown Sparrow Slag, 3"...............$40.00
Hen Covered Dish, Caramel Custard, 3".....................$45.00
Hobo Shoe, Blue & White Slag..................................$22.00
Hobo Shoe, Milk Blue, unsigned $20.00
Owl, Amberina..$50.00
Owl, Blue-Green Marble $72.50
Owl, Dark Crown Tuscan...$40.00
Owl, Dark Frosted Jade $50.00
Owl, Fog Opaque $60.00
Owl, Lemon Chiffon $35.00
Owl, Pearl Gray $30.00
Owl, Pink Lady $34.00
Owl, Tangerine, scarce..$125.00
Pooch, Blue Jay Slag...$28.00
Pooch, Buttercup Slag $40.00
Pooch, Caramel Slag $26.00
Pooch, Charcoal $20.00
Pooch, Crystal $12.50
Pooch, Daffodil $18.00
Pooch, Dark Amethyst..$15.00
Pooch, Dark Ivory Slag, scarce $45.00
Pooch, Fawn $22.50
Pooch, Green Caramel Slag..$40.00
Pooch, Green Opalescent..$20.00
Pooch, Gun Metal $22.00
Pooch, Henry Blue...$15.00
Pooch, Ivory Slag $25.00
Pooch, Milk Blue..$18.00
Pooch, Periwinkle $15.00
Pooch, Red $25.00
Priscilla, Blue & White...$100.00
Priscilla, Crystal $50.00
Priscilla, Green Lavender Slag....................................$78.50
Priscilla, Heatherbloom $100.00
Priscilla, Jade Green..$110.00
Priscilla, Orchid...$85.00
Priscilla, Smoky Blue $80.00

Skate Shoe, Sapphire	$30.00
Star & Dewdrop Salt, Opalescent	$18.00
Texas Boot, Amethyst	$18.00
Texas Boot, Baby Green	$20.00
Texas Boot, Peach Blo	$15.00
Tomahawk, Amber	$18.00
Tomahawk, Carnival Blue	$42.50
Tomahawk, Emerald Green	$23.00
Turkey Covered Dish, Amberina	$55.00
Turkey Covered Dish, Gray Slag	$80.00
Wildflower Candy Dish, Crown Tuscan, unmarked	$35.00
Wildflower Candy Dish, Twilight Blue	$38.00

Depression Glass

Since the early sixties, this has been a very active area of collecting. Interest is still very strong, and although values have long been established, except for some of the rarer items, Depression Glass is still relatively inexpensive. Some of the patterns and colors that were entirely avoided by the early wave of collectors are now becoming popular, and it's very easy to reassemble a nice table setting of one of these lines today.

Most of this glass was made during the Depression years. It was inexpensive, mass-produced, and was available in a wide assortment of colors. The same type of glassware was still being made to some extent during the fifties and sixties, and today the term 'Depression Glass' has been extended to include the later patterns as well.

Some things have been reproduced, and the slight variation in patterns and colors can be very difficult to detect. For instance, the Sharon butter dish has been reissued in original colors of pink and green (as well as others that were not original); and several pieces of Cherry Blossom, Madrid, Avocado, Mayfair, and Miss America have also been reproduced. Some pieces you'll see in 'antique' malls and flea markets today have been recently made in dark uncharacteristic 'carnival' colors, which of course are easy to spot.

For further study, Gene Florence has written several informative books on the subject, and we recommend them all: *The Pocket Guide to Depression Glass, The Collector's Encyclopedia of Depression Glass,* and *Very Rare Glassware of the Depression Years.*

Adam, delphite, candlesticks, 4", pr	$200.00
Adam, green, ash tray	$20.00
Adam, green, butter dish, w/lid	$275.00
Adam, green, relish dish, 8", divided	$20.00
Adam, pink, cake plate, 10", footed	$23.00
Adam, pink, pitcher, 32-oz, round base	$45.00
Adam, pink, saucer, 6"	$5.00
Adam, pink, tumbler, iced tea; 5½"	$50.00
Adam, pink, vase, 7½"	$225.00
Adam, pink or green, bowl, cereal; 5¾"	$35.00
Adam, yellow, cup	$85.00
Adam, yellow, plate, salad; 7¾" sq	$85.00
American Pioneer, amber, pitcher, 7", w/lid	$300.00

American Pioneer, amber, plate, 8"	$22.50
American Pioneer, crystal or pink, bowl, 5", handled	$13.50
American Pioneer, crystal or pink, candlesticks, 6½", pr	$57.50
American Pioneer, crystal or pink, coaster, 3½"	$22.50
American Pioneer, crystal or pink, goblet, wine; 4"	$32.50
American Pioneer, crystal or pink, mayonnaise, 4¼"	$52.50
American Pioneer, crystal or pink, sugar bowl, 3½"	$17.50
American Pioneer, green, bowl, console; 10¾"	$55.00
American Pioneer, green, candy jar, 1½-lb, w/lid	$105.00
American Pioneer, green, creamer, 3½"	$20.00
American Pioneer, green, ice bucket, 6"	$50.00
American Pioneer, green, sherbet, 3½"	$17.00
American Pioneer, green, tumbler, juice; 5-oz	$30.00
American Pioneer, green, vase, 9"	$185.00
American Sweetheart, blue, saucer	$22.50
American Sweetheart, blue, tidbit, 8" & 12" tiers	$225.00
American Sweetheart, cremax, bowl, cereal; 6"	$10.00
American Sweetheart, monax, bowl, cream soup	$95.00
American Sweetheart, monax, creamer, footed	$8.50
American Sweetheart, monax, plate, luncheon; 9"	$9.00
American Sweetheart, monax, platter, 13", oval	$55.00
American Sweetheart, monax, salt & pepper shakers, footed, pr	$275.00
American Sweetheart, monax, sugar bowl, open, footed	$7.00
American Sweetheart, pink, bowl, berry; 3¾", flat	$30.00
American Sweetheart, pink, bowl, vegetable; 11", oval	$50.00
American Sweetheart, pink, pitcher, 8"	$425.00

American Sweetheart, pink, plate, dinner; 9¾"	**$30.00**
American Sweetheart, pink, sherbet, 3¾", footed	$15.00
American Sweetheart, pink, tumbler, 4¼"	$60.00
American Sweetheart, pink or monax, tidbit, 8" & 12" tiers	$50.00
American Sweetheart, red, plate, bread & butter; 6"	$40.00
American Sweetheart, red, sugar bowl, open, footed	$75.00
American Sweetheart, smoke & other trims, bowl, berry; 9"	$95.00

American Sweetheart, smoke & other trims, plate, dinner; 9¾" **$60.00**
Anniversary, crystal, butter dish, w/lid **$22.50**
Anniversary, crystal, cake plate, w/metal cover **$14.00**
Anniversary, crystal, relish dish, 8" **$4.50**
Anniversary, iridescent, bowl, berry; 4⅞" **$4.00**
Anniversary, iridescent, cup **$3.75**

Anniversary, iridescent, plate, dinner; 9½" $5.75
Anniversary, iridescent, sugar bowl **$4.00**
Anniversary, pink, bowl, fruit; 9" **$20.00**
Anniversary, pink, cake plate, 12½" **$12.50**
Anniversary, pink, plate, dinner; 9" **$8.00**
Aunt Polly, blue, bowl, 5½", handled **$18.00**
Aunt Polly, blue, butter dish, w/lid **$175.00**
Aunt Polly, blue, creamer **$40.00**
Aunt Polly, blue, pitcher, 8" **$150.00**
Aunt Polly, blue, salt & pepper shakers, pr **$195.00**
Aunt Polly, blue, tumbler, 3⅝" **$22.50**
Aunt Polly, green or iridescent, bowl, berry; 4¾" **$7.00**
Aunt Polly, green or iridescent, bowl, 8⅜", oval **$35.00**
Aunt Polly, green or iridescent, candy dish, w/lid, 2-handled **$57.50**
Aunt Polly, green or iridescent, sugar bowl **$20.00**
Aunt Polly, green or iridescent, vase, 6½", footed **$25.00**
Aurora, cobalt or pink, plate, 6½" **$10.00**
Aurora, crystal, bowl, cereal; 5⅜" **$5.00**
Aurora, green, cup **$7.50**
Aurora, green, saucer **$2.50**
Avocado, green, bowl, relish; 6", footed **$23.00**
Avocado, green, creamer, footed **$30.00**
Avocado, green, plate, luncheon; 8¼" **$17.00**
Avocado, green, tumbler **$195.00**
Avocado, pink, bowl, salad; 7½" **$30.00**
Avocado, pink, bowl, 5¼", 2-handled **$23.00**
Avocado, pink, cake plate, 10¼", 2-handled **$30.00**
Avocado, pink, pitcher, 64-oz **$625.00**

Beaded Block, crystal, pink, green, or amber, sugar bowl **$14.00**
Beaded Block, ice blue, bowl, 5½" sq **$9.50**
Beaded Block, iridescent, vase, bouquet; 6" **$20.00**
Beaded Block, milk white, bowl, 7½", fluted edges **$22.00**
Beaded Block, milk white, pitcher, 5¼", 1-pt jug **$160.00**
Beaded Block, opalescent, bowl, celery; 8¼" **$17.50**
Beaded Block, red, bowl, lily; 4½" **$100.00**
Beaded Block, red, stemmed jelly, 4¼" **$17.00**
Beaded Block, vaseline, bowl, pickle; 6½", handles ...**$17.50**
Block Optic, amber, candlesticks, 1¾", pr **$100.00**

Block Optic, blue, butter dish, 3x5", w/lid $375.00
Block Optic, green, bowl, cereal; 5¼" **$10.00**
Block Optic, green, sandwich server, center handle ...**$47.50**
Block Optic, green, tumbler, 3¼", footed **$20.00**
Block Optic, green, vase, 5¾", blown **$250.00**
Block Optic, green or yellow, plate, luncheon; 8" **$5.00**
Block Optic, pink, bowl, berry; 8½" **$20.00**
Block Optic, pink, plate, dinner; 9" **$25.00**
Block Optic, pink, saucer, 6⅛", w/cup ring **$7.00**
Block Optic, pink, tumbler, 2⅝" **$20.00**
Block Optic, yellow, candy jar, 2¼", w/lid **$50.00**
Block Optic, yellow, cup, four styles, each **$7.50**
Block Optic, yellow, goblet, 7¼", thin **$30.00**
Bowknot, green, bowl, berry; 4½" **$12.00**
Bowknot, green, cup **$6.00**
Bowknot, green, plate, salad; 7" **$9.00**
Bowknot, green, tumbler, 5", footed **$15.00**
Bubble, blue, bowl, berry; 4" **$12.00**
Bubble, blue, sugar bowl **$15.00**
Bubble, crystal, bowl, berry; 4" **$2.50**
Bubble, crystal, plate, dinner; 9⅜" **$4.00**
Bubble, crystal, tumbler, old fashioned; 3¼" **$6.00**
Bubble, green, bowl, cereal; 5¼" **$9.50**
Bubble, green, plate, dinner; 9⅜" **$12.50**
Bubble, green, stem, juice; 5½-oz **$10.00**
Bubble, green or red, saucer **$3.00**
Bubble, pink, cup **$75.00**
Bubble, pink, saucer **$25.00**
Bubble, red, bowl, berry; 8⅜" **$15.00**
Bubble, red, cup **$6.00**
Bubble, red, tumbler, iced tea; 4½" **$10.00**
Cameo, crystal w/platinum rim, bowl, sauce; 4¼" **$5.00**

Cameo, crystal w/platinum rim, cocktail shaker, w/metal lid **$450.00**
Cameo, crystal w/platinum rim, relish, 7½", footed, 3-part **$125.00**
Cameo, green, bowl, cereal; 5½" **$26.00**
Cameo, green, cake plate, 10", 3-footed.................**$17.50**
Cameo, green, cookie jar, w/lid..............................**$42.50**
Cameo, green, sherbet, 3⅛", blown.........................**$13.00**
Cameo, green, vase, 5¾" **$145.00**
Cameo, pink, bowl, berry; 8¼" **$125.00**
Cameo, pink, comport, mayonnaise; 5" wide............**$175.00**
Cameo, yellow, bowl, vegetable; 10", oval **$35.00**
Cameo, yellow, candy jar, 4", w/lid..........................**$65.00**
Cameo, yellow, pitcher, syrup or milk; 5¾"..............**$455.00**
Cameo, yellow, tumbler, 5", flat.............................**$40.00**
Cherry Blossom, delphite, bowl, berry; 8½" **$35.00**
Cherry Blossom, delphite, cup................................**$14.00**
Cherry Blossom, delphite, sugar bowl......................**$16.00**
Cherry Blossom, delphite, tray, sandwich; 10½".........**$16.00**
Cherry Blossom, green, bowl, vegetable; 9", oval **$28.00**
Cherry Blossom, green, creamer..............................**$16.00**

Cherry Blossom, green, pitcher, 7¾", w/foot $65.00
Cherry Blossom, green, salt & pepper shakers, scalloped bottom, pr **$900.00**
Cherry Blossom, green, tumbler, 4¼", patterned at top, flat **$19.00**
Cherry Blossom, pink, bowl, cereal; 5¾" **$25.00**
Cherry Blossom, pink, cake plate, 10¼", 3-footed.......**$24.00**
Cherry Blossom, pink, platter, 11", oval....................**$30.00**
Cherry Blossom, pink, tumbler, 4½", round foot, allover pattern..**$25.00**
Cherryberry, comport, pink or green, 5¾" **$20.00**
Cherryberry, crystal or iridescent, bowl, berry; 4" **$6.00**
Cherryberry, crystal or iridescent, butter dish, w/lid.**$140.00**
Cherryberry, crystal or iridescent, creamer, 4⅝", large ..**$14.00**
Cherryberry, crystal or iridescent, pitcher, 7¾".........**$150.00**
Cherryberry, pink or green, bowl, deep salad; 6½".....**$17.50**

Cherryberry, pink or green, olive dish, 5", handled **$13.00**
Cherryberry, pink or green, plate, salad; 7½" **$12.00**
Chinex Classic, brownstone or plain ivory, bowl, cereal; 5¾"...**$4.50**
Chinex Classic, brownstone, butter dish......................**$50.00**
Chinex Classic, brownstone or plain ivory, plate, dinner; 9¾"...**$4.00**
Chinex Classic, castle decal, bowl, vegetable; 9".........**$30.00**
Chinex Classic, castle decal, sherbet, low footed **$20.00**
Chinex Classic, decaled decoration, bowl, vegetable; 7"..**$18.00**
Chinex Classic, decaled decoration, creamer................**$9.00**
Chinex Classic, decaled decoration, saucer..................**$4.00**
Christmas Candy, crystal, creamer **$8.00**
Christmas Candy, crystal, mayonnaise, w/ladle **$17.50**
Christmas Candy, crystal, sugar bowl **$8.00**
Christmas Candy, teal, bowl, soup; 7⅜".....................**$25.00**
Christmas Candy, teal, plate, dinner; 9⅝"...................**$25.00**
Christmas Candy, teal, sugar bowl.............................**$17.50**
Circle, green or pink, bowl, 4½" **$8.00**
Circle, green or pink, bowl, 8" **$15.00**
Circle, green or pink, goblet, water; 8-oz...................**$9.00**
Circle, green or pink, plate, luncheon; 8¼"................**$4.00**
Circle, green or pink, saucer, w/cup ring..................**$1.50**
Circle, green or pink, sherbet, 3⅛" **$5.00**
Circle, green or pink, tumbler, iced tea; 5" **$16.00**
Circle, green or pink, tumbler, juice; 3½"..................**$8.00**
Circle, pink or green, pitcher, 80-oz.........................**$30.00**
Cloverleaf, black, ash tray, match holder center, 4" **$65.00**
Cloverleaf, black, salt & pepper shakers, pr **$75.00**
Cloverleaf, green, bowl, cereal; 5"............................**$22.00**
Cloverleaf, green, plate, sherbet; 6" **$4.00**
Cloverleaf, green, tumbler, 3¾", flat, flared.................**$35.00**
Cloverleaf, pink, bowl, dessert; 4" **$10.00**
Cloverleaf, pink, cup..**$6.00**
Cloverleaf, pink, sherbet, 3⅝", footed **$5.00**
Cloverleaf, yellow, bowl, cereal; 5" **$27.50**
Cloverleaf, yellow, candy dish, w/lid **$95.00**
Cloverleaf, yellow, tumbler, 5¾", footed.....................**$27.50**
Colonial, crystal, bowl, cream soup; 4½" **$55.00**
Colonial, crystal, goblet, cordial; 3¾" **$17.00**
Colonial, crystal, platter, 12", oval **$14.00**
Colonial, green, bowl, cereal; 5½"............................**$75.00**
Colonial, green, cheese dish....................................**$150.00**
Colonial, green, goblet, claret; 5¼"...........................**$23.00**
Colonial, green, plate, dinner; 10" **$52.00**
Colonial, green, sherbet..**$14.00**
Colonial, pink, butter dish, w/lid.............................**$575.00**
Colonial, pink, mug, 4½"..**$450.00**
Colonial, pink, plate, luncheon; 8½"...........................**$8.00**
Colonial, royal ruby, tumbler, water, 4" **$95.00**
Colonial, royal ruby, tumbler, 5¼".............................**$150.00**
Colonial, white, sugar bowl..**$5.00**
Colonial Block, pink or green, bowl, 4".........................**$6.00**
Colonial Block, pink or green, butter dish...................**$40.00**
Colonial Block, pink or green, candy jar, w/lid..........**$32.50**
Colonial Block, pink or green, powder jar, w/lid........**$15.00**
Colonial Block, white, creamer...................................**$6.00**
Colonial Fluted, green, bowl, berry; 4"........................**$4.50**

Colonial Fluted, green, bowl, large berry; 7½" **$14.00**
Colonial Fluted, green, plate, sherbet; 6" **$2.00**
Colonial Fluted, green, sugar bowl..............................**$4.00**
Coronation, green, bowl, 8"......................................**$100.00**
Coronation, pink, pitcher, 7¾"................................**$200.00**
Coronation, pink, tumbler, 5", footed.........................**$18.00**
Coronation, royal ruby, bowl, nappy; 6½" **$10.00**
Coronation, royal ruby, plate, luncheon; 8½" **$7.00**
Cremax, decaled decoration, creamer **$7.00**
Cremax, decaled decoration, plate, dinner; 9¾" **$8.50**
Cremax, decaled decoration, sugar bowl, open.............**$7.00**
Cremax, ivory, bowl, cereal; 5¾" **$3.00**
Cremax, ivory, plate, bread & butter; 6¼" **$1.50**
Cremax, ivory, saucer **$1.50**
Cube, amber or white, creamer, 2⅝" **$3.00**
Cube, amber or white, sugar bowl, 2⅜" **$2.00**
Cube, green, bowl, dessert; 4½"..................................**$6.00**
Cube, green, pitcher, 8¾"..**$200.00**
Cube, green, tumbler, 4" **$55.00**
Cube, pink, bowl, salad; 6½" **$8.00**
Cube, pink, candy jar, 6½", w/lid **$25.00**
Cube, pink, plate, luncheon; 8" **$4.50**
Cube, pink or green, butter dish, w/lid.......................**$55.00**
Cube, ultramarine, bowl, 4½", deep **$20.00**
Daisy, crystal, bowl, berry; 4½".................................**$4.00**
Daisy, crystal, bowl, vegetable; 10", oval **$9.00**
Daisy, crystal, plate, dinner; 9⅜".................................**$5.00**
Daisy, crystal or green, tumbler, 12-oz, footed............**$18.50**
Daisy, green, bowl, cream soup; 4½" **$5.00**
Daisy, green, cup **$3.50**
Daisy, green, plate, cake or sandwich; 11½"................**$7.00**
Daisy, red or amber, bowl, cereal; 6" **$25.00**
Daisy, red or amber, plate, salad; 7⅜"..........................**$6.50**
Daisy, red or amber, sugar bowl, footed......................**$8.50**
Diamond Quilted, blue, bowl, cream soup; 4¾"............**$16.00**
Diamond Quilted, blue or black, candlesticks, pr.......**$45.00**
Diamond Quilted, blue or black, ice bucket.................**$80.00**
Diamond Quilted, blue or black, plate, luncheon; 8"..**$11.00**
Diamond Quilted, blue or black, sugar bowl **$14.00**
Diamond Quilted, blue or black, vase, fan shape, dolphin
    handles **$65.00**
Diamond Quilted, pink or green, bowl, console; rolled
    edge, 10½"...**$18.00**
Diamond Quilted, pink, compote, 11½", w/lid..............**$62.50**
Diamond Quilted, pink or green, goblet, cordial; 1-oz .**$9.00**
Diamond Quilted, pink or green, pitcher, 64-oz **$42.50**
Diamond Quilted, pink or green, sandwich server, center
    handle...**$20.00**
Diamond Quilted, pink, tumbler, 9-oz, footed.............**$11.00**
Diana, amber, bowl, console/fruit; 11"........................**$12.00**
Diana, amber, platter, 12", oval..................................**$12.00**
Diana, amber, tumbler, 4⅛" **$23.00**
Diana, crystal, ash tray, 3½" **$2.00**
Diana, crystal, creamer, oval **$3.00**
Diana, crystal, salt & pepper shakers, pr....................**$22.50**
Diana, pink, bowl, salad; 9"......................................**$18.00**
Diana, pink, plate, bread & butter; 6"..........................**$1.50**
Diana, pink, sugar bowl, open, oval **$10.00**

Dogwood, green, creamer, 2½", thin, flat **$40.00**
Dogwood, green, sherbet, low, footed.........................**$85.00**
Dogwood, green, tumbler, 5"......................................**$90.00**
Dogwood, monax or cremax, bowl, berry; 8½" **$35.00**
Dogwood, monax or cremax, cup, thin or thick **$35.00**
Dogwood, monax or cremax, plate, salver; 12"..........**$15.00**
Dogwood, pink, cake plate, 13", solid foot.................**$75.00**
Dogwood, pink, plate, bread or butter; 6" **$6.00**
Dogwood, pink or green, bowl, cereal; 5½".............**$20.00**
Dogwood, yellow, plate, luncheon; 8".......................**$50.00**
Doric, delphite, bowl, berry; 4½"...............................**$35.00**

Doric, delphite, pitcher, 6", flat **$950.00**
Doric, green, bowl, cream soup; 5".........................**$225.00**
Doric, green, salt & pepper shakers, pr **$30.00**
Doric, pink, bowl, vegetable; 9", oval **$20.00**
Doric, pink, plate, sherbet; 6" **$3.00**
Doric, pink, tumbler, 4½"...**$40.00**
Doric, pink or green, cake plate, 10", 3-footed...........**$20.00**
Doric & Pansy, crystal, cup **$8.00**

Doric & Pansy, crystal, plate, dinner; 9" **$6.00**
Doric & Pansy, pink or crystal, bowl, berry; 8" **$18.00**
Doric & Pansy, pink or crystal, sugar bowl, open.......**$60.00**

Doric & Pansy, ultramarine, bowl, berry; 4½".............$12.00
Doric & Pansy, ultramarine, butter dish, w/lid.........$450.00
Doric & Pansy, ultramarine, plate, salad; 7"...............$30.00
Doric & Pansy, ultramarine, salt & pepper shakers, pr..$350.00
English Hobnail, amber, pink, or green, candy dish, w/lid, 3-footed $70.00
English Hobnail, amber, pink, or green, marmalade, w/lid...$35.00
English Hobnail, amber, pink, or green, salt & pepper shakers, round or square bases, pr $77.50
English Hobnail, amber, pink, or green, tumbler, iced tea; 4" $16.00
English Hobnail, cobalt, bowl, 8", footed, 2-handled..$95.00
English Hobnail, cobalt, cigarette box.........................$30.00
English Hobnail, cobalt, plate, 8", round or square.....$16.00
English Hobnail, cobalt, wine; 2-oz.............................$44.00
English Hobnail, pink, ash tray, several shapes, each.$20.00
Floragold, iridescent, bowl, fruit; 5½".........................$8.00
Floragold, iridescent, bowl, 4½" sq.............................$5.00
Floragold, iridescent, butter dish, ¼-lb......................$22.50
Floragold, iridescent, creamer.....................................$8.50
Floragold, iridescent, cup & saucer $15.00
Floragold, iridescent, pitcher, 64-oz $32.50
Floragold, iridescent, sugar bowl, w/lid.....................$15.00
Floragold, iridescent, tray, 13½"................................$17.50
Floragold, iridescent, tumbler, 11-oz, footed $17.50
Floral, cremax, bowl, salad; 7½"...............................$125.00
Floral, delphite, bowl, berry; 4" $30.00
Floral, delphite, plate, dinner; 8" $120.00
Floral, green, butter dish, w/lid $80.00
Floral, green, tumbler, juice; 4", 5-oz, footed.............$18.00
Floral, jadite, refrigerator dish, 5" sq.........................$18.00
Floral, pink, candlesticks, 4", pr.................................$65.00
Floral, pink, tray, 6" sq, closed handles.....................$12.00
Floral, pink, tumbler, water; 4¾", footed....................$15.00
Floral & Diamond Band, green, bowl, berry; 4½" $7.50
Floral & Diamond Band, green, compote, 5½"...........$14.00

Floral & Diamond Band, green, plate, luncheon; 8"..$25.00
Floral & Diamond Band, green, sherbet........................$7.00

Floral & Diamond Band, green, tumbler, water; 4" $22.00
Floral & Diamond Band, pink, butter dish, w/lid.....$120.00
Floral & Diamond Band, pink, creamer, 4¾"..............$15.00
Floral & Diamond Band, pink, pitcher, 8"...................$85.00
Floral & Diamond Band, pink, sugar bowl, 5¼".........$12.00
Florentine No 1, ash tray, pink, 5½"...........................$25.00
Florentine No 1, blue, bowl, cream soup; 5" $50.00
Florentine No 1, blue, cup $70.00
Florentine No 1, blue, saucer.....................................$15.00
Florentine No 1, crystal, green, or pink, cup $8.00
Florentine No 1, crystal, green, or pink, sugar bowl, ruffled...$30.00
Florentine No 1, crystal or green, creamer..................$8.50
Florentine No 1, crystal or green, salt & pepper shakers, footed, pr...$35.00
Florentine No 1, pink, candy dish, w/lid $110.00
Florentine No 1, pink, plate, dinner; 10".....................$20.00
Florentine No 1, yellow, salt & pepper shakers, pr.....$50.00
Florentine No 1, yellow or green, butter dish, w/lid.$150.00
Florentine No 1, yellow or pink, bowl, vegetable; 9½", w/lid, oval $55.00
Florentine No 1, yellow or pink, pitcher, 6½", footed..$42.50
Florentine No 1, yellow or pink, plate, grill; 10" $12.00
Florentine No 1, yellow or pink, tumbler, water; 4¾", footed..$18.00
Florentine No 2, blue, comport, 3½", ruffled $50.00
Florentine No 2, crystal, green, or pink, plate, salad; 8½"..$7.00
Florentine No 2, crystal, green, or pink, platter, 11".........$13.00
Florentine No 2, crystal, green, or yellow, pitcher, 7½", cone-footed $28.00
Florentine No 2, crystal or green, bowl, berry; 4½".....$10.00
Florentine No 2, crystal or green, bowl, cereal; 6" $25.00
Florentine No 2, crystal or green, candlesticks, 2¾", pr .$40.00
Florentine No 2, crystal or green, tumbler, water; 4" ..$11.00
Florentine No 2, pink, bowl, cream soup; 4¾" $12.00
Florentine No 2, pink, plate, dinner; 10"....................$13.00
Florentine No 2, pink, tumbler, 4", footed $14.00
Flower Garden w/Butterflies, amber or crystal, candlesticks, 4", pr...$40.00
Flower Garden w/Butterflies, amber or crystal, comport, 4¾x10¼" $45.00
Flower Garden w/Butterflies, amber or crystal, sandwich server, center handle $45.00
Flower Garden w/Butterflies, amber or crystal, tumbler, 7½" $125.00
Flower Garden w/Butterflies, black, bonbon, 6⅝" dia, w/lid...$250.00
Flower Garden w/Butterflies, black, candlesticks, 8", pr $225.00
Flower Garden w/Butterflies, black, cigarette box, 4⅜" long, w/lid...$150.00
Flower Garden w/Butterflies, black, plate, 10", indented $100.00
Flower Garden w/Butterflies, black, vase, 10", 2-handled $225.00
Flower Garden w/Butterflies, blue or canary yellow, comport, 2⅞" $25.00

Flower Garden w/Butterflies, blue or canary yellow, mayonnaise w/plate & spoon, 4¾ x 6¼" (7" plate),footed.**$110.00**

Flower Garden w/Butterflies, blue or canary yellow, tray, 11¾x7¾" **$77.50**

Flower Garden w/Butterflies, pink, green, or blue-green, creamer **$65.00**

Flower Garden w/Butterflies, pink, green, or blue-green, plate, 10" **$40.00**

Flower Garden w/Butterflies, pink, green, or blue-green, saucer...**$25.00**

Flower Garden w/Butterflies, pink, green, or blue-green, vase, 10½" **$125.00**

Flower Garden w/Butterflies, pink or green, candy dish, 6", flat, w/lid **$25.00**

Forest Green, ash tray..**$3.50**

Forest Green, bowl, 7⅜"...**$12.50**

Forest Green, plate, 10" **$25.00**

Forest Green, sugar bowl, flat **$6.00**

Forest Green, tumbler, 10-oz...**$6.50**

Forest Green, vase, 9"..**$6.00**

Fortune, pink or crystal, bowl, berry; 4".......................**$3.50**

Fortune, pink or crystal, bowl, 5¼".................................**$5.00**

Fortune, pink or crystal, cup **$3.50**

Fortune, pink or crystal, plate, luncheon; 8"..................**$8.00**

Fortune, pink or crystal, tumbler, juice; 3½" **$6.00**

Fruits, green, bowl, berry; 5"...**$20.00**

Fruits, green, pitcher, 7", flat bottom **$65.00**

Fruits, green, tumbler, 5" **$95.00**

Fruits, green or pink, plate, luncheon; 8".......................**$5.00**

Fruits, pink, bowl, berry; 8" **$35.00**

Fruits, pink, tumbler, juice; 3½" **$12.00**

Georgian, green, bowl, cereal; 5¾" **$20.00**

Georgian, green, bowl, vegetable; 9", oval **$55.00**

Georgian, green, creamer, 4", footed............................**$13.00**

Georgian, green, cup...**$8.00**

Georgian, green, plate, dinner; 9¼"..............................**$22.50**

Georgian, green, saucer..**$4.00**

Georgian, green, sugar bowl, 4", footed........................**$9.50**

Georgian, green, tumbler, 5¼", flat..............................**$95.00**

Harp, crystal, ash tray/coaster **$4.50**

Harp, crystal, cake stand, 9"...**$20.00**

Harp, crystal, cup...**$12.50**

Harp, crystal, vase, 6" **$17.50**

Heritage, blue or green, bowl, berry; 5".......................**$45.00**

Heritage, crystal, creamer, footed **$20.00**

Heritage, crystal, plate, dinner; 9¼"............................**$10.00**

Heritage, crystal, sugar bowl, open, footed **$15.00**

Hex Optic, creamer..**$5.00**

Hex Optic, pink or green, bowl, berry; 7½"...................**$6.50**

Hex Optic, pink or green, plate, luncheon; 8".............**$5.00**

Hex Optic, pink or green, refrigerator dish, 4x4" **$9.00**

Hex Optic, pink or green, salt & pepper shakers, pr..**$25.00**

Hex Optic, pink or green, tumbler, 7", footed......**$10.00**

Hex Optic, pitcher, 9", footed **$35.00**

Hobnail, crystal, bowl, cereal; 5½"................................**$3.50**

Hobnail, crystal, goblet, iced tea; 13-oz **$7.00**

Hobnail, crystal, tumbler, cordial; 5-oz, footed.............**$5.00**

Hobnail, pink, cup...**$4.00**

Hobnail, pink, plate, luncheon; 8½".............................**$3.00**

Holiday, crystal, pitcher, milk; 4¾"..............................**$15.00**

Holiday, crystal, tumbler, 4½", footed **$7.50**

Holiday, iridescent, tumbler, 4", footed.......................**$10.00**

Holiday, pink, bowl, berry; 5⅛".....................................**$10.00**

Holiday, pink, bowl, vegetable; 9½", oval **$15.00**

Holiday, pink, butter dish, w/lid...................................**$35.00**

Holiday, pink, cake plate, 10½", 3-footed **$80.00**

Holiday, pink, plate, dinner; 9"......................................**$14.00**

Holiday, pink, sugar bowl **$8.00**

Homespun, pink or crystal, bowl, 4½", closed handles ..**$9.50**

Homespun, pink or crystal, butter dish, w/lid.............**$55.00**

Homespun, pink or crystal, plate, dinner; 9¼" **$14.00**

Homespun, pink or crystal, sugar bowl, footed............**$8.00**

Homespun, pink or crystal, tumbler, iced tea; 5¼" **$25.00**

Indiana Custard, ivory, bowl, berry; 5½" **$7.50**

Indiana Custard, ivory, butter dish, w/lid....................**$60.00**

Indiana Custard, ivory, cup **$35.00**

Indiana Custard, ivory, plate, dinner; 9¾" $20.00

Indiana Custard, ivory, sherbet $82.50

Iris, crystal, bowl, berry; 4½", beaded edge $35.00

Iris, crystal, candy jar, w/lid $95.00

Iris, crystal, plate, sandwich; 11¾" $20.00

Iris, iridescent, bowl, soup; 7½" $50.00

Iris, iridescent, goblet, 5¾" $110.00

Iris, iridescent, tumbler, 6", footed $14.00

Iris, pink or green, creamer, footed $75.00

Iris, pink or green, sugar $75.00

Iris, pink or green, vase, 9" $95.00

Jubilee, pink, bowl, 8", 3-footed $225.00

Jubilee, pink, cheese & cracker set $225.00

Jubilee, pink, plate, luncheon; 8¾" $25.00

Jubilee, pink, sugar $30.00

Jubilee, yellow, bowl, fruit; 11½", flat $150.00

Jubilee, yellow, plate, sandwich; 13½" $45.00

Lace Edge, pink, bowl, cereal or cream soup; 6⅜" $15.00

Lake Como, blue scene on white, sugar bowl $25.00

Laurel, blue, bowl, cereal; 6" $18.00

Laurel, blue, plate, dinner; 9⅛" $18.00

Laurel, blue, sugar bowl, tall $25.00

Laurel, green, plate, salad; 7½" $9.00

Laurel, green, salt & pepper shakers, pr $55.00

Laurel, green or ivory, bowl, berry; 5" $6.00

Laurel, ivory, bowl, vegetable; 9¾" $16.00

Laurel, ivory, plate, grill; 9⅛" $11.00

Laurel, ivory, sherbet $11.00

Lorain, crystal or green, bowl, vegetable; 9¾", oval....$35.00

Lorain, crystal or green, cup..$9.00

Lorain, crystal or green, plate, dinner; 10¼" $32.00

Lorain, crystal or green, sugar bowl, footed $13.00

Lorain, yellow, bowl, cereal; 6"..................................$50.00

Lorain, yellow, creamer & sugar bowl..................$40.00

Lorain, yellow, plate, luncheon; 8⅜" $24.00

Lorain, yellow, relish, 8", 4-part $30.00

Lorain, yellow, tumbler, 4¾", footed $25.00

Madrid, amber, ash tray, 6" sq $185.00

Madrid, amber, cake plate, 11¼" $14.00

Madrid, amber, hot dish coaster $35.00

Madrid, blue, bowl, soup; 7" $28.00

Madrid, blue, jam dish, 7" $30.00

Madrid, blue, sherbet...$12.00

Madrid, green, bowl, vegetable; 10", oval...................$15.00

Madrid, green, salt & pepper shakers, 3½", pr............$77.50

Madrid, pink, bowl, sauce; 5" $6.00

Madrid, pink, tumbler, 4¼" $13.00

Manhattan, crystal, ash tray, 4" $10.00

Manhattan, crystal, bowl, salad; 9"............................$17.00

Manhattan, crystal, relish tray, 14", 4-part $16.00

Manhattan, crystal, salt & pepper shakers, 2", pr........$25.00

Manhattan, green or iridized, 10-oz, footed................$10.00

Manhattan, pink, bowl, berry; 5⅜", handled $15.00

Manhattan, pink, comport, 5¾" $25.00

Manhattan, pink, plate, dinner; 10¼".......................$100.00

Mayfair (Federal), amber, bowl, sauce; 5" $7.50

Mayfair (Federal), amber, cup......................................$7.50

Mayfair (Federal), amber or green, plate, dinner; 9½" ..$12.00

Mayfair (Federal), amber or green, saucer $3.00

Mayfair (Federal), crystal, bowl, cream soup; 5"..........$10.00

Mayfair (Federal), crystal, plate, salad; 6¾"..................$4.00

Mayfair (Federal), green, bowl, vegetable; 10", oval ...$25.00

Mayfair (Federal), green, tumbler, 4½" $25.00

Mayfair (Open Rose), blue, bowl, cereal; 5½" $40.00

Lace Edge, pink, comport, 7" $20.00

Lace Edge, pink, cup $20.00

Lace Edge, pink, plate, dinner; 10½" $22.50

Lace Edge, pink, sugar bowl $19.00

Lace Edge, pink, tumbler, 5", footed $60.00

Laced Edge, blue or green w/opalescent edge, bowl, fruit;
4½" $25.00

Laced Edge, blue or green w/opalescent edge, bowl, veg-
etable; 9"...$95.00

Laced Edge, blue or green w/opalescent edge, mayonnaise,
3-pc..$115.00

Laced Edge, blue or green w/opalescent edge, plate, dinner;
10"...$65.00

Laced Edge, blue or green w/opalescent edge, sugar
bowl $35.00

Laced Edge, blue or green w/opalescent edge, tumbler, 9-
oz $50.00

Lake Como, blue scene on white, bowl, cereal; 6" $18.00

Lake Como, blue scene on white, cup, regular $25.00

Lake Como, blue scene on white, plate, dinner; 9¼"..$25.00

Lake Como, blue scene on white, salt & pepper shakers,
pr..$35.00

Mayfair (Open Rose), blue, candy dish, w/lid..........**$250.00**
Mayfair (Open Rose), blue, goblet, water; 7¼", thin.**$135.00**
Mayfair (Open Rose), blue, plate, luncheon; 8½"........**$40.00**
Mayfair (Open Rose), blue, relish, 8⅜"................**$55.00**
Mayfair (Open Rose), blue, tumbler, juice; 3½"..........**$95.00**
Mayfair (Open Rose), green, bowl, vegetable; 7"......**$110.00**

Mayfair (Open Rose), green, bowl, 9" x 3½", 3-leg console $3,750.00

Mayfair (Open Rose), green, celery dish, 10" **$95.00**
Mayfair (Open Rose), green, plate, dinner; 9½" **$65.00**
Mayfair (Open Rose), green, sherbet, 4¾", footed **$140.00**
Mayfair (Open Rose), green, tumbler, water; 4¾" **$165.00**
Mayfair (Open Rose), green or yellow, pitcher, 6"....**$475.00**
Mayfair (Open Rose), green or yellow, platter, 12", open handles **$125.00**
Mayfair (Open Rose), pink, bowl, cream soup; 5" **$38.00**
Mayfair (Open Rose), pink, cake plate, 10", footed **$24.00**
Mayfair (Open Rose), pink, cake plate, 12", handled..**$32.00**
Mayfair (Open Rose), pink, cup **$16.00**
Mayfair (Open Rose), pink, plate, luncheon; 8½" **$20.00**

Mayfair (Open Rose), pink, salt shaker, footed .$2,500.00

Mayfair (Open Rose), pink, sugar bowl, footed **$22.00**
Mayfair (Open Rose), yellow, cookie jar, w/lid.........**$775.00**
Mayfair (Open Rose), yellow, salt & pepper shakers, flat, pr..**$750.00**
Mayfair (Open Rose), yellow, tumbler, 5¼", footed..**$170.00**
Miss America, blue, plate, sherbet, 5¾"...................**$35.00**
Miss America, crystal, bowl, 8", curved inward at top.**$35.00**
Miss America, crystal, cake plate, 12", footed **$22.50**
Miss America, crystal, platter, 12¼", oval **$13.00**
Miss America, crystal, tumbler, juice; 4" **$15.00**
Miss America, green, cup **$10.00**
Miss America, green, salt & pepper shakers, pr **$285.00**
Miss America, pink, butter dish, w/lid **$500.00**
Miss America, pink, celery dish, 10½", oblong **$25.00**
Miss America, pink, pitcher, no ice lip, 8" **$100.00**
Miss America, pink, plate, dinner; 10¼" **$20.00**
Miss America, pink, tumbler, iced tea; 5¾" **$65.00**
Miss America, red, bowl, 11", shallow....................**$650.00**
Miss America, red, goblet, wine; 3¾" **$195.00**
Moderntone, amethyst, bowl, cream soup; 4¾"..........**$16.00**
Moderntone, amethyst, plate, salad; 6¾" **$8.00**
Moderntone, amethyst, platter, 12", oval....................**$35.00**
Moderntone, amethyst, sugar bowl................................**$8.00**
Moderntone, amethyst, tumbler, 12-oz.........................**$75.00**
Moderntone, cobalt, ashtray, 7¾", w/match holder in center **$115.00**
Moderntone, cobalt, butter dish, w/metal lid.............**$95.00**
Moderntone, cobalt, plate, dinner; 8⅞" **$15.00**
Moderntone, cobalt, salt & pepper shakers, pr...........**$40.00**
Moderntone, cobalt, tumbler, 9-oz **$30.00**
Moondrops, amber, bowl, pickle; 7½" **$12.00**
Moondrops, amber, decanter, 11¼"..............................**$50.00**
Moondrops, cobalt or red, ashtray..............................**$30.00**
Moondrops, cobalt or red, bowl, vegetable; 9¾", oval..**$30.00**
Moondrops, cobalt or red, butter dish, w/lid............**$450.00**
Moondrops, cobalt or red, candlesticks, 8½", w/metal stem, pr..**$37.50**
Moondrops, cobalt or red, creamer, 3¾"....................**$15.00**
Moondrops, cobalt or red, gravy boat.......................**$115.00**
Moondrops, cobalt or red, plate, 5⅞" **$9.00**
Moondrops, cobalt or red, sherbet, 4½" **$25.00**
Moondrops, cobalt or red, tumbler, juice; 3", footed ..**$15.00**
Moondrops, crystal, smoke, or black, tumbler, 5⅛" **$13.00**
Moonstone, opalescent hobnail, bowl, dessert; 5½", crimped **$8.00**
Moonstone, opalescent hobnail, bowl, relish; 7¾", divided **$9.50**
Moonstone, opalescent hobnail, cigarette jar, w/lid....**$20.00**
Moonstone, opalescent hobnail, goblet, 10-oz **$17.50**
Moonstone, opalescent hobnail, plate, sandwich; 10".**$20.00**
Moonstone, opalescent hobnail, vase, bud; 5½".........**$12.00**
Moroccan Amethyst, ashtray, 3¼" dia **$5.00**
Moroccan Amethyst, bowl, 6" **$10.00**
Moroccan Amethyst, candy dish, w/lid, short or tall...**$27.50**
Moroccan Amethyst, goblet, water; 5½" **$10.00**
Moroccan Amethyst, goblet, wine, 4" **$9.00**
Moroccan Amethyst, plate, dinner; 9¾" **$7.50**
Moroccan Amethyst, tumbler, juice; 2½" **$7.50**

Moroccan Amethyst, tumbler, water; 4⅝" **$11.00**
Mt Pleasant, black amethyst or cobalt, bonbon, 7".....**$22.00**
Mt Pleasant, black amethyst or cobalt, cake plate, 10½",
footed **$35.00**

Mt Pleasant, black amethyst or cobalt, creamer...$17.00
Mt Pleasant, black amethyst or cobalt, leaf, 11¼".......**$25.00**
Mt Pleasant, black amethyst or cobalt, plate, grill; 9"..**$10.00**
Mt Pleasant, black amethyst or cobalt, sandwich server, cen-
ter handle **$35.00**
**Mt Pleasant, pink, green, black amethyst, or cobalt,
sugar bowl (illustrated)....................................$17.00**
Mt Pleasant, pink or green, bowl, fruit; 4" sq, footed .**$12.00**
Mt Pleasant, pink or green, bowl, 8" sq, 2-handled **$17.50**
Mt Pleasant, pink or green, candlesticks, double, pr...**$25.00**
Mt Pleasant, pink or green, cup **$8.50**
Mt Pleasant, pink or green, mayonnaise, 5½", 3-footed ..**$15.00**
Mt Pleasant, pink or green, plate, 12", 2-handled........**$18.00**
Mt Pleasant, pink or green, sherbet **$9.00**
New Century, green, crystal, pink, cobalt, or amethyst, tum-
bler, 5¼" **$22.00**
New Century, green or crystal, ash tray/coaster, 5⅜"..**$27.50**
New Century, green or crystal, bowl, cream soup; 5"...**$15.00**
New Century, green or crystal, casserole, 9", w/lid.....**$50.00**
New Century, green or crystal, plate, breakfast; 7⅛".....**$7.00**
New Century, green or crystal, plate, dinner; 10"........**$14.00**
New Century, green or crystal, whiskey, 2½" **$13.00**
New Century, pink, cobalt, or amethyst, cup **$18.00**
New Century, pink, cobalt, or amethyst, pitcher,
7¾" **$30.00**
New Century, pink, cobalt, or amethyst, saucer...........**$6.00**
New Century, pink, cobalt, or amethyst, tumbler, 4" ..**$12.00**
Newport, amethyst, bowl, cream soup; 4¾" **$14.00**
Newport, amethyst, plate, luncheon; 8⅞" **$10.00**
Newport, amethyst, platter, 11¾", oval........................**$28.00**
Newport, amethyst, tumbler, 4½" **$28.00**
Newport, cobalt, bowl, berry; 4¾"................................**$13.00**
Newport, cobalt, cup **$9.00**
Newport, cobalt, plate, sandwich; 11½" **$30.00**
Newport, cobalt, salt & pepper shakers, pr **$42.50**
Newport, cobalt, sugar bowl...**$13.00**
Newport, cobalt or amethyst, saucer **$4.00**
No 610 Pryamid, green, tumbler, 11-oz, footed..........**$50.00**
No 610 Pryamid, yellow, bowl, master berry; 8½" **$50.00**
No 610 Pyramid, crystal, bowl, berry; 4¾" **$10.00**
No 610 Pyramid, crystal, tumbler, 8-oz, footed...........**$32.00**

No 610 Pyramid, pink, creamer & sugar bowl......$45.00
No 610 Pyramid, pink, pitcher....................................**$210.00**
No 610 Pyramid, pink or green, creamer.....................**$22.00**
No 610 Pyramid, yellow, sugar bowl............................**$30.00**
No 612 Horseshoe, green, bowl, berry; 4½" **$19.00**
No 612 Horseshoe, green, butter dish, w/lid............**$600.00**
No 612 Horseshoe, green, pitcher, 8½".....................**$220.00**
No 612 Horseshoe, green, plate, grill; 10⅜".............**$52.50**
No 612 Horseshoe, green, plate, luncheon; 9⅜".........**$11.00**
No 612 Horseshoe, green, saucer **$4.00**
No 612 Horseshoe, green, tumbler, 9-oz, footed........**$18.00**
No 612 Horseshoe, green or yellow, bowl, cereal; 6½" .**$19.00**
No 612 Horseshoe, yellow, bowl, vegetable; 8½" **$25.00**
No 612 Horseshoe, yellow, creamer, footed..............**$14.00**
No 612 Horseshoe, yellow, plate, salad; 8⅜" **$9.00**

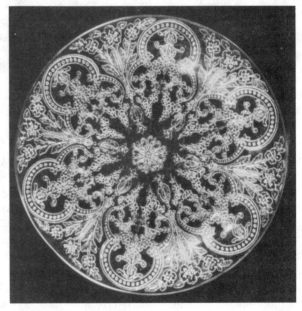

No 612 Horseshoe, yellow, plate, sandwich; 11½" ..$15.00
No 612 Horseshoe, yellow, sugar bowl.......................**$13.00**
No 612 Horseshoe, yellow, tumbler, 12-oz...............**$125.00**
No 616 Vernon, crystal, plate, luncheon; 8"..................**$5.00**
No 616 Vernon, crystal, sugar bowl, footed................**$10.00**
No 616 Vernon, green, creamer, footed **$22.00**
No 616 Vernon, green, plate, sandwich; 11½" **$24.00**
No 616 Vernon, tumbler, 5", footed............................**$30.00**
No 616 Vernon, yellow, cup **$14.00**
No 618 Pineapple & Floral, amber, cup **$8.00**
No 618 Pineapple & Floral, amber or fired-on red, plate,
dinner; 9⅜" **$13.00**

No 618 Pineapple & Floral, crystal, amber, or fired-on red, sherbet, footed **$17.50**

No 618 Pineapple & Floral, crystal, bowl, berry; 4¾"..**$22.00**

No 618 Pineapple & Floral, crystal, bowl, vegetable; 10", oval **$22.00**

No 618 Pineapple & Floral, crystal, creamer, diamond shape **$7.00**

No 618 Pineapple & Floral, crystal, plate, salad; 8⅜" **$7.00**

No 618 Pineapple & Floral, crystal, plate, sandwich; 11½" **$14.00**

No 618 Pineapple & Floral, crystal, platter, relish; 11½", divided..**$18.00**

No 618 Pineapple & Floral, crystal, vase, cone shape.**$35.00**

No 618 Pineapple & Floral, fired-on red, ash tray, 4½".**$18.00**

Normandie, amber, bowl, berry; 5" **$5.00**

Normandie, amber, plate, luncheon; 9¼"......................**$7.00**

Normandie, amber, platter, 11¾" **$15.00**

Normandie, amber, tumbler, juice; 4"..........................**$18.00**

Normandie, amber or iridescent, bowl, vegetable; 10", oval **$14.00**

Normandie, iridescent, cup **$5.50**

Normandie, iridescent, plate, dinner; 11"....................**$14.00**

Normandie, iridescent, sugar bowl **$5.50**

Normandie, pink, bowl, cereal; 6½" **$17.00**

Normandie, pink, pitcher, 8".....................................**$110.00**

Normandie, pink, plate, dinner; 11" **$90.00**

Normandie, pink, salt & pepper shakers, pr...............**$65.00**

Normandie, pink, tumbler, iced tea; 5" **$65.00**

Old Cafe, crystal or pink, bowl, berry; 3¾"..................**$2.50**

Old Cafe, crystal or pink, candy dish, 8", low **$8.00**

Old Cafe, crystal or pink, olive dish, 6", oblong...........**$4.50**

Old Cafe, crystal or pink, pitcher, 80-oz **$80.00**

Old Cafe, crystal or pink, plate, dinner; 10".................**$25.00**

Old Cafe, red, bowl, cereal; 5½"..................................**$9.00**

Old Cafe, red, cup..**$7.00**

Old Cafe, red, sherbet, low footed **$9.00**

Old Cafe, red, tumbler, water; 4"...............................**$15.00**

Old English, pink, green, amber, vase, 12", footed **$50.00**

Old English, pink, green, or amber, bowl, 4", flat.......**$15.00**

Old English, pink, green, or amber, candlesticks, 4", pr..**$27.50**

Old English, pink, green, or amber, creamer...............**$16.00**

Old English, pink, green, or amber, fruit stand, 11", footed **$37.50**

Old English, pink, green, or amber, pitcher, w/lid ...**$110.00**

Old English, pink, green, or amber, sandwich server, center handle...**$47.50**

Old English, pink, green, or amber, tumbler, 5½", footed **$30.00**

Ovide, black, candy dish, w/lid.................................**$40.00**

Ovide, black or green, salt & pepper shakers, pr........**$25.00**

Ovide, green, creamer **$3.00**

Ovide, green, plate, luncheon; 8" **$2.00**

Ovide, white w/decoration, bowl, berry; 4¾"...............**$6.00**

Ovide, white w/decoration, bowl, berry; 8"................**$20.00**

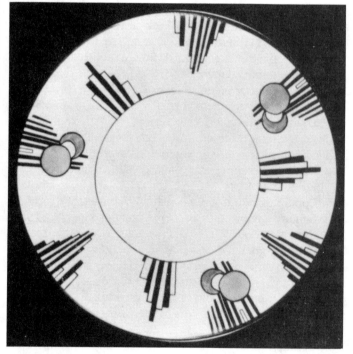

Ovide, white w/decoration, plate, dinner; 9" $18.00

Ovide, white w/decoration, tumbler **$16.00**

Oyster & Pearl, crystal or pink, bowl, fruit; 10½", deep.**$20.00**

Oyster & Pearl, crystal or pink, bowl, 5¼", heart shape, single handle **$6.50**

Oyster & Pearl, red, bowl, 5½", single handle **$11.00**

Oyster & Pearl, red, plate, sandwich; 13½".................**$35.00**

Oyster & Pearl, white w/fired-on green or pink, bowl, fruit; 10½", deep..**$12.00**

Oyster & Pearl, white w/fired-on green or pink, heart shape, single handle **$7.50**

Parrot, amber, bowl, berry; 8".....................................**$70.00**

Parrot, amber, plate, dinner; 9" **$30.00**

Parrot, amber, sugar bowl..**$30.00**

Parrot, amber, tumbler, 4¼" $95.00

Parrot, blue, sherbet, footed cone $100.00
Parrot, green, bowl, berry; 5" $18.00
Parrot, green, butter dish, w/lid................................$275.00
Parrot, green, plate, salad; 7½" $28.00
Parrot, green, platter, 11¼", oblong............................$40.00
Parrot, green or amber, cup $30.00
Patrician, amber, crystal, or pink, jam dish $25.00
Patrician, amber or crystal, bowl, cream soup; 4¾" $14.00
Patrician, amber or crystal, butter dish, w/lid.............$80.00
Patrician, amber or crystal, creamer, footed..................$8.50
Patrician, amber or crystal, plate, salad; 7½"...............$13.00
Patrician, amber or crystal, salt & pepper shakers, pr.$50.00
Patrician, green, bowl, vegetable; 10", oval $30.00
Patrician, green, cookie jar, w/lid................................$400.00
Patrician, green, pitcher, 8", molded handle..............$100.00
Patrician, green, plate, dinner; 10½".............................$30.00
Patrician, green, tumbler, 5½" $38.00
Patrician, pink, bowl, cereal; 6" $20.00
Patrician, pink, plate, luncheon; 9" $8.00
Patrician, pink, sugar bowl..$8.00
Patrick, pink, bowl, fruit; 9", handled..........................$65.00
Patrick, pink, cheese & cracker set................................$85.00
Patrick, pink, mayonnaise, 3-pc...................................$125.00
Patrick, pink, sugar bowl..$35.00
Patrick, yellow, candlesticks, pr.....................................$75.00
Patrick, yellow, goblet, cocktail; 4"..............................$45.00
Patrick, yellow, plate, luncheon; 8" $25.00
Patrick, yellow, tray, 11", center handle $50.00
Petalware, cobalt, sherbet, 4½", low footed.................$30.00
Petalware, cobalt, sugar bowl, footed $30.00
Petalware, crystal, bowl, cream soup; 4½" $4.00
Petalware, floral w/red trim, creamer, footed $25.00
Petalware, floral w/red trim, plate, dinner; 9"............$22.50
Petalware, monax, bowl, berry; 9".................................$15.00
Petalware, monax, plate, salad; 8" $3.00
Petalware, monax, sherbet, 4", low footed....................$6.50

Petalware, pink, bowl, cereal; 5¾".................................$8.00
Petalware, pink, plate, salver; 12"..................................$8.00
Primo, yellow or green, bowl, 4½" $8.50
Primo, yellow or green, cake plate, 10", 3-footed $18.00
Primo, yellow or green, creamer....................................$9.00
Primo, yellow or green, plate, dinner; 10" $14.00
Primo, yellow or green, sherbet....................................$8.50
Primo, yellow or green, tumbler, 5¾"...........................$15.00
Princess, green, ash tray, 4½"..$65.00
Princess, green, butter dish, w/lid $85.00
Princess, green, cookie jar, w/lid..................................$50.00
Princess, green, plate, grill; 9".....................................$11.00
Princess, green, sugar bowl..$9.00
Princess, pink, bowl, cereal; 5" $20.00
Princess, pink, cake stand, 10"......................................$25.00
Princess, pink, pitcher, 7⅜", footed...........................$450.00
Princess, pink, platter, 12", closed handles $20.00
Princess, pink, tumbler, iced tea; 5¼" $20.00
Princess, yellow or apricot, bowl, vegetable; 10" $50.00
Princess, yellow or apricot, coaster $80.00

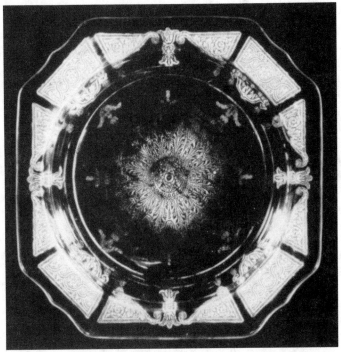

Princess, yellow or apricot, plate, dinner; 9½".....$14.00
Princess, yellow or apricot, salt & pepper shakers, 4½",
  pr $55.00
Princess, yellow or apricot, tumbler, 5¼", footed........$18.00
Queen Mary, crystal, bowl, berry; 5" $3.00
Queen Mary, crystal, butter dish or preserve, w/lid....$20.00
Queen Mary, crystal, comport, 5¾".................................$6.00
Queen Mary, crystal, plate, salad; 8¾"............................$5.00
Queen Mary, crystal, plate, serving tray; 14"...............$10.00
Queen Mary, crystal, salt & pepper shakers, pr...........$17.50
Queen Mary, pink, bowl, cereal; 6" $20.00
Queen Mary, pink, butter dish or preserve, w/lid.......$95.00
Queen Mary, pink, creamer, footed...............................$17.50
Queen Mary, pink, plate, dinner; 9¾"...........................$35.00
Queen Mary, pink, sugar bowl, footed $17.50

Queen Mary, pink, tumbler, 5", footed.....................$35.00
Queen Mary, red, ash tray, 3½" dia $5.00
Queen Mary, red, candlesticks, 4½", double branch, pr...$30.00
Radiance, amber, bowl, relish; 8", 3-part...............$17.50
Radiance, amber, candlesticks, 8", pr $35.00
Radiance, amber, cup, punch.......................................$6.00
Radiance, emerald green, punch bowl liner, 14"...........$30.00
Radiance, ice blue or red, bowl, nut; 2-handled.........$14.00
Radiance, ice blue or red, comport, 6".....................$27.50
Radiance, ice blue or red, condiment set w/tray, 4-pc.$250.00
Radiance, ice blue or red, punch bowl $150.00
Radiance, ice blue or red, sugar bowl.......................$19.00
Raindrops, green, bowl, fruit; 4½" $4.50
Raindrops, green, cup...$5.00
Raindrops, green, plate, luncheon; 8".........................$5.00
Raindrops, green, sugar bowl $6.00
Raindrops, green, tumbler, 5".......................................$8.50
Ribbon, black, bowl, berry; 8" $27.50
Ribbon, black, plate, luncheon; 8" $12.00
Ribbon, black, salt & pepper shakers, pr $37.50
Ribbon, green, bowl, berry; 4" $9.00
Ribbon, green, cup...$4.00
Ribbon, green, sugar bowl, footed $10.00
Ring, blue, plate, luncheon; 8"...................................$27.50
Ring, crystal, bowl, berry; 5" $3.00
Ring, crystal, decanter, w/stopper $20.00
Ring, crystal, sandwich server, center handle $15.00
Ring, crystal, vase, 8"...$15.00
Ring, decorated, butter tub or ice tub $27.50
Ring, decorated, sugar bowl, footed $5.00
Ring, green, salt & pepper shakers, 3", pr................$55.00
Ring, green, tumbler, juice; 3½", footed $7.00
Ring, pink, pitcher, 8½"..$27.50
Ring, red, cup...$17.50
Rock Crystal, cobalt, candelabra, 2-light, pr.............$185.00
Rock Crystal, crystal, bonbon, 7½" scalloped edge $17.50
Rock Crystal, crystal, butter dish, w/lid....................$300.00
Rock Crystal, crystal, creamer, scalloped edge, flat.....$32.50

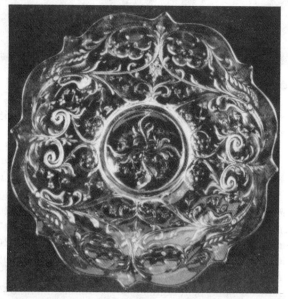

Rock Crystal, crystal, plate, 9", scalloped edge.....$15.00

Rock Crystal, crystal, salt & pepper shakers, pr..........$67.50
Rock Crystal, crystal, tumbler, old fashioned; 5-oz......$15.00
Rock Crystal, red, bowl, 5", scalloped edge.................$37.50
Rock Crystal, red, candlesticks, 5½", pr....................$125.00
Rock Crystal, red, plate, dinner; 10½", scalloped edge ..$150.00
Rock Crystal, red, sugar bowl, 10-oz, open $35.00
Rose Cameo, green, bowl, cereal; 5" $10.00
Rose Cameo, green, plate, salad; 7".............................$9.00
Rose Cameo, green, tumbler, 5".................................$15.00
Rosemary, amber, bowl, berry; 5"................................$5.00
Rosemary, amber, cup $5.00
Rosemary, amber, saucer...$3.00
Rosemary, green, bowl, cereal; 6"..............................$28.00
Rosemary, green, plate, dinner $12.00
Rosemary, green, sugar bowl, footed.........................$11.00
Rosemary, pink, bowl, vegetable; 10", oval $25.00
Rosemary, pink, platter, 12", oval $25.00
Rosemary, pink, tumbler, 4¼".....................................$40.00
Roulette, crystal, pitcher, 8"......................................$22.50
Roulette, crystal, tumbler, old fashioned; 3¼".............$22.50
Roulette, green, bowl, fruit; 9" $12.50
Roulette, green, plate, sandwich; 12" $12.00
Roulette, green, tumbler, iced tea; 5⅛".......................$25.00
Round Robin, green, bowl, berry; 4" $4.50
Round Robin, green, plate, luncheon; 8" $3.00
Round Robin, iridescent, creamer, footed $6.00
Round Robin, iridescent, sherbet.................................$5.00
Roxana, white, bowl, 2⅜x4½".....................................$12.00
Roxana, yellow, bowl, cereal; 6"................................$12.00
Roxana, yellow, plate, 5½"..$7.00
Roxana, yellow, tumbler, 4¼".....................................$14.00
Royal Lace, blue, bowl, vegetable; 11", oval...............$50.00
Royal Lace, blue, butter dish, w/lid..........................$525.00
Royal Lace, blue, cookie jar, w/lid $295.00
Royal Lace, blue, plate, luncheon; 8½".......................$35.00
Royal Lace, blue, sugar bowl, open............................$25.00
Royal Lace, blue, tumbler, 4⅞"...................................$95.00
Royal Lace, crystal, bowl, cream soup; 4¾" $9.50
Royal Lace, crystal, butter dish, w/lid........................$60.00
Royal Lace, crystal, cup $6.00
Royal Lace, crystal, plate, dinner; 9⅞".......................$11.00
Royal Lace, crystal, tumbler, 4⅞" $18.00
Royal Lace, green, bowl, berry; 10" $25.00
Royal Lace, green, cookie jar, w/lid $65.00
Royal Lace, green, pitcher, 48-oz................................$85.00
Royal Lace, green, salt & pepper shakers, pr............$110.00
Royal Lace, green, tumbler, 4⅞" $38.00
Royal Lace, pink, bowl, berry; 5"................................$22.00
Royal Lace, pink, candlesticks, rolled edge, pr...........$45.00
Royal Lace, pink, platter, 13", oval $28.00
Royal Ruby, bonbon, 6½"..$8.00
Royal Ruby, bowl, cereal; 5½" $12.00
Royal Ruby, candle holders, 4½", pr...........................$30.00
Royal Ruby, creamer, footed $8.50
Royal Ruby, crystal w/ruby top, cigarette box/card holder,
   6⅛x4"...$50.00
Royal Ruby, goblet, ball stem..$9.00
Royal Ruby, plate, luncheon; 8½" $7.00

Royal Ruby, sherbet, low footed.................................**$9.00**
Royal Ruby, tray, 6x4½"...**$10.00**
Royal Ruby, tumbler, water; 9-oz..............................**$6.00**
Sandwich (Hocking), crystal, cup, custard, crimped..**$3.50**
Sandwich (Hocking), crystal, plate, dinner; 9"..........**$15.00**
Sandwich (Hocking), gold, bowl, cereal; 6½".............**$12.00**
Sandwich (Hocking), gold, cup, tea or coffee.............**$3.50**
Sandwich (Hocking), green, pitcher, ½-gal, ice lip..**$275.00**
Sandwich (Hocking), green, sugar bowl, w/lid...........**$22.00**
Sandwich (Hocking), ivory, cup, punch......................**$2.00**
Sandwich (Hocking), ivory, punch bowl, 9¾".............**$15.00**
Sandwich (Hocking), ivory, punch bowl stand...........**$12.50**
Sandwich (Hocking), pink, bowl, 8", scalloped..........**$15.00**
Sandwich (Hocking), pink, cookie jar, w/lid...............**$20.00**
Sandwich (Hocking), red, bowl, 6½", scalloped..........**$25.00**
Sandwich (Hocking), red, bowl, 8", scalloped.............**$35.00**
Sandwich (Indiana), amber or crystal, basket, 10".....**$30.00**
Sandwich (Indiana), amber or crystal, decanter, w/stopper...**$20.00**
Sandwich (Indiana), green, bowl, console; 11½"........**$45.00**
Sandwich (Indiana), green, wine, 3".........................**$22.50**

Sandwich (Indiana), pink, plate, dinner; 10½"....$12.00
Sandwich (Indiana), red, creamer..............................**$40.00**
Sandwich (Indiana), red, pitcher, 68-oz....................**$125.00**
Sandwich (Indiana), red, sugar bowl, large................**$40.00**
Sandwich (Indiana), teal blue, bowl, 6", hexagonal....**$12.50**
Sandwich (Indiana), teal blue, plate, sherbet; 6".......**$6.00**
Sandwich (Indiana), teal blue, saucer........................**$4.50**
Sharon, amber, bowl, berry; 5"..................................**$7.50**
Sharon, amber, candy jar, w/lid.................................**$40.00**
Sharon, amber, jam dish, 7½".....................................**$30.00**
Sharon, amber, salt & pepper shakers, pr..................**$37.50**
Sharon, amber, tumbler, 5¼", thin.............................**$45.00**
Sharon, amber, tumbler, 6½", footed.........................**$95.00**
Sharon, amber or pink, butter dish, w/lid..................**$45.00**

Sharon, green, bowl, vegetable; 9½", oval.................**$22.00**
Sharon, green, butter dish, w/lid...............................**$75.00**
Sharon, green, cake plate, 11½", footed.....................**$50.00**
Sharon, green, candy jar, w/lid.................................**$150.00**
Sharon, green, salt & pepper shakers, pr...................**$60.00**
Sharon, green, tumbler, 4⅛", thick............................**$55.00**
Sharon, pink, bowl, cream soup; 5"...........................**$35.00**
Sharon, pink, jam dish, 7½".....................................**$150.00**

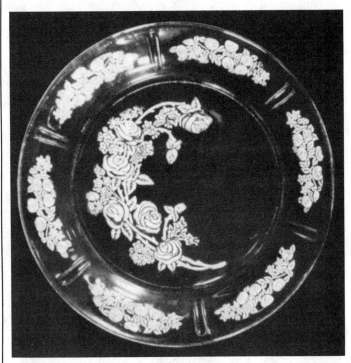

Sharon, pink, plate, dinner; 9½"..........................$16.00
Sharon, pink, sugar bowl...**$12.00**
Sharon, pink or green, plate, salad; 7½"....................**$20.00**
Ships, cobalt w/white decoration, cocktail mixer, w/stirrer...**$22.50**
Ships, cobalt w/white decoration, pitcher, 86-oz, w/lip.**$40.00**
Ships, cobalt w/white decoration, plate, bread & butter; 5⅞"...**$17.50**
Ships, cobalt w/white decoration, plate, dinner; 9".....**$25.00**
Ships, cobalt w/white decoration, tumbler, juice; 3¾"..**$9.50**
Ships, cobalt w/white decoration, tumbler, water; 4⅝".**$9.50**
Sierra, green, bowl, cereal; 5½".................................**$11.00**
Sierra, green, butter dish, w/lid................................**$60.00**
Sierra, green, pitcher, 6½"...**$95.00**
Sierra, green, tumbler, 4½", footed............................**$65.00**
Sierra, pink, bowl, vegetable; 9¼", oval....................**$35.00**
Sierra, pink, cup...**$9.50**
Sierra, pink, plate, dinner; 9"...................................**$14.00**
Sierra, pink, sugar bowl...**$15.00**
Sierra, pink, tumbler, 4½", footed............................**$37.50**
Sierra, pink or green, salt & pepper shakers, pr.........**$35.00**
Spiral, green, bowl, berry; 4¾"..................................**$4.50**
Spiral, green, creamer, flat or footed.........................**$7.00**
Spiral, green, pitcher, 7⅝"...**$27.50**
Spiral, green, plate, luncheon; 8"..............................**$3.00**
Spiral, green, salt & pepper shakers, pr.....................**$27.50**
Spiral, green, sugar bowl, flat or footed.....................**$7.00**

Spiral, green, tumbler, water; 5".................................$7.00
Spiral, green, tumbler, 5⅞", footed $10.00
Starlight, crystal or white, bowl, cereal; 5½", closed han-
dles..$6.00
Starlight, crystal or white, bowl, salad; 11½"..............$16.00
Starlight, crystal or white, creamer, oval......................$4.50
Starlight, crystal or white, plate, dinner; 9" $6.00
Starlight, crystal or white, plate, luncheon; 8½"..........$3.00
Starlight, crystal or white, salt & pepper shakers, pr..$20.00
Starlight, crystal or white, sugar bowl, oval $4.00
Starlight, pink, bowl, cereal; 5½", closed handles $8.00
Starlight, pink, bowl, 8½", closed handles $13.00
Starlight, pink, plate, sandwich; 13" $13.00
Strawberry, crystal, bowl, salad; 6½", deep $13.00
Strawberry, crystalor iridescent , comport, 5¾" $12.00
Strawberry, crystal or iridescent, creamer, small..........$10.00
Strawberry, crystal or iridescent, creamer, 4⅝", large..$30.00
Strawberry, crystal or iridescent, pitcher, 7¾"...........$150.00
Strawberry, crystal or iridescent, sugar bowl, large.....$20.00
Strawberry, pink or green, butter dish, w/lid $140.00
Strawberry, pink or green, creamer, 4⅝"....................$30.00
Strawberry, pink or green, olive dish, 5", handled......$12.00
Strawberry, pink or green, plate, salad; 7½" $12.00
Strawberry, pink or green, tumbler, 3⅝" $25.00
Sunflower, delphite, creamer.......................................$75.00
Sunflower, green, ash tray, 5", center design..............$11.00

Sunflower, green, plate, dinner; 9" $14.00
Sunflower, green, trivet, 7", 3-footed, turned-up edge.$285.00
Sunflower, pink, creamer $14.00
Sunflower, pink, sugar bowl $14.00
Sunflower, pink, tumbler, 4¾", footed.........................$22.00
Sunflower, pink or green, cake plate, 10", 3-footed....$12.00
Swirl, delphite, bowl, cereal; 5¼" $11.00
Swirl, delphite, candle holders, single branch, pr $100.00
Swirl, delphite, platter, 12", oval.................................$30.00

Swirl, delphite, tray, 10½", 2-handled.........................$22.50
Swirl, pink, bowl, console; 10½", footed.....................$17.50
Swirl, pink, candy dish, w/lid $85.00
Swirl, pink, plate, dinner; 9¼"....................................$12.00
Swirl, pink, sherbet, low footed $9.00
Swirl, ultramarine, bowl, salad; 9", rimmed $24.00
Swirl, ultramarine, creamer, footed.............................$12.50

Swirl, ultramarine, pitcher, 48-oz, footed........$1,500.00
Swirl, ultramarine, plate, sandwich; 12½"...................$22.00
Swirl, ultramarine, salt & pepper shakers, pr.............$37.50
Swirl, ultramarine, tumbler, 9-oz, footed....................$30.00
Tea Room, amber, creamer, 4½", footed.....................$60.00
Tea Room, amber, pitcher, 64-oz $400.00
Tea Room, amber, tumbler, 5¼", footed $75.00
Tea Room, crystal, pitcher, 64-oz $275.00
Tea Room, green, bowl, vegetable; 9½", oval..............$60.00
Tea Room, green, finger bowl $45.00
Tea Room, green, marmalade, notched lid.................$177.50
Tea Room, green, plate, luncheon; 8¼" $30.00
Tea Room, green, salt & pepper shakers, pr...............$50.00
Tea Room, green, vase, 9½", ruffled edge...................$90.00
Tea Room, pink, bowl, banana split; 7½", flat base $72.00
Tea Room, pink, creamer, 4½", footed........................$14.00
Tea Room, pink, goblet, 9-oz......................................$57.50
Tea Room, pink, pitcher, 64-oz $120.00
Tea Room, pink, relish, divided...................................$16.00
Tea Room, pink, sugar bowl, 3", flat, w/lid...............$125.00
Tea Room, pink or green, creamer, 3¼" $22.50
Tea Room, pink or green, tumbler, 6-oz, footed........$30.00
Thistle, green, bowl, fruit; 10½"...............................$160.00
Thistle, green, plate, grill; 10¼".................................$18.00
Thistle, pink, bowl, cereal; 5½"...................................$18.00
Thistle, pink, bowl, fruit; 10¼"..................................$250.00
Thistle, pink, cake plate, 13", heavy..........................$100.00
Thistle, pink or green, saucer.......................................$8.50

Thumbprint, green, bowl, cereal; 5" **$4.50**
Thumbprint, green, creamer, footed...........................**$11.50**

Thumbprint, green, cup **$3.00**
Thumbprint, green, plate, dinner; 9¼"...........................**$6.00**
Thumbprint, green, salt & pepper shakers, pr............**$22.50**
Thumbprint, green, sugar bowl, footed **$11.50**
Thumbprint, green, tumbler, 5".....................................**$5.00**
Twisted Optic, blue or yellow, bowl, salad; 7" **$8.00**
Twisted Optic, blue or yellow, cup **$7.00**
Twisted Optic, blue or yellow, plate, salad; 7" **$5.00**
Twisted Optic, blue or yellow, sugar bowl.................**$12.00**
Twisted Optic, pink, green, or amber, bowl, cream soup;
    4¾" **$10.00**
Twisted Optic, pink, green, or amber, candy jar, w/lid ..**$25.00**
Twisted Optic, pink, green, or amber, pitcher, 64-oz .**$27.50**
Twisted Optic, pink, green, or amber, sandwich server, 2-
    handled, flat **$10.00**
Twisted Optic, pink, green, or amber, tumbler, 4½" **$5.00**
Twisted Optic, pink, green, or yellow, cup **$3.50**
Twisted Optic, pink, green, or yellow, plate, luncheon;
    10"..**$8.50**
US Swirl, green, bowl, berry; 4⅜" **$5.00**
US Swirl, green, butter dish, w/lid..............................**$62.50**
US Swirl, green, tumbler, 3⅝" **$8.00**
US Swirl, pink, bowl, berry; 7⅞"..................................**$15.00**
US Swirl, pink, candy dish, w/lid, 2-handled..............**$27.50**
US Swirl, pink, tumbler, 4¾"..**$14.00**
US Swirl, pink or green, pitcher, 8" **$40.00**
US Swirl, pink or green, salt & pepper shakers, pr.....**$40.00**
US Swirl, pink or green, sugar bowl, w/lid.................**$27.50**
Victory, blue or black, bowl, vegetable; 9", oval.........**$70.00**
Victory, blue or black, creamer...................................**$40.00**
Victory, blue or black, plate, bread & butter; 6"..........**$12.00**
Victory, blue or black, plate, dinner; 9" **$32.00**
Victory, blue or black, sherbet, footed.......................**$22.00**
Victory, green, pink, or amber, bowl, cereal; 6½" **$9.50**
Victory, green, pink, or amber, bowl, vegetable; oval **$27.50**
Victory, green, pink, or amber, cheese & cracker set, 12"
    indented plate w/compote **$37.50**
Victory, green, pink, or amber, creamer **$12.00**

Victory, green, pink, or amber, plate, dinner; 9" **$17.50**
Victory, green, pink, or amber, sugar bowl **$12.00**
Vitrock, white, bowl, cream soup; 5½" **$14.00**
Vitrock, white, creamer, oval **$4.00**
Vitrock, white, plate, dinner; 10" **$6.00**
Vitrock, white, saucer **$1.50**
Waterford, creamer, oval **$4.00**
Waterford, crystal, ash tray, 4" **$6.50**
Waterford, crystal, butter dish, w/lid.........................**$23.00**
Waterford, crystal, pitcher, 80-oz, w/ice lip...............**$28.00**
Waterford, crystal, relish, 13¾", 5-part.......................**$15.00**
Waterford, crystal, tumbler, 4⅞", footed....................**$10.00**
Waterford, pink, bowl, cereal; 5½" **$22.00**
Waterford, pink, butter dish, w/lid...........................**$195.00**
Waterford, pink, pitcher, 80-oz, w/ice lip.................**$130.00**
Waterford, pink, sugar bowl **$8.50**
Windsor, blue, creamer **$55.00**
Windsor, blue, plate, dinner; 9"...................................**$55.00**
Windsor, crystal, bowl, cream soup; 5" **$5.00**
Windsor, crystal, candlesticks, 3", pr.........................**$16.00**
Windsor, crystal, creamer **$4.00**
Windsor, crystal, platter, 11½", oval.............................**$5.00**
Windsor, crystal, tumbler, 7¼", footed **$12.00**
Windsor, green, bowl, cream soup; 5" **$22.00**
Windsor, green, creamer **$10.00**
Windsor, green, pitcher, 6¾".......................................**$45.00**
Windsor, green, platter, 11½", oval.............................**$17.00**
Windsor, green, sugar bowl **$25.00**
Windsor, green, tumbler, 4" **$25.00**
Windsor, pink, bowl, vegetable; 9½", oval..................**$18.00**
Windsor, pink, candlesticks, 3", pr **$75.00**
Windsor, pink, pitcher, 4¼".......................................**$100.00**
Windsor, pink, pitcher, 6¾"...**$25.00**
Windsor, pink, plate, dinner; 9"..................................**$12.00**
Windsor, pink, salt & pepper shakers, pr **$32.50**
Windsor, pink, tray, 4" sq..**$32.00**
Windsor, red, pitcher, 6¾" **$400.00**
Windsor, red, tumbler, 4" **$50.00**

Dionne Quintuplets

These famous babies were born on May 28, 1934, in Ontario, Canada, and immediately became the center of worldwide focus. They were the first quintuplets ever delivered who survived longer than a few days. In order to protect them from being exploited as infants, they became wards of King George V. A private nursery was built nearby, equipped with glassed-in viewing areas which were visited by thousands of people every week.

Their parents were very poor people who took advantage of their fame to better themselves financially, allowing the children to endorse a variety of products. By the time they were ten years old, the children returned to live with their parents in a mansion built with money they had earned.

Though many companies made similar dolls, Madame Alexander was the only company ever authorized to market

Dionne Quintuplet dolls. They made more than thirty sets of 'Quints,' from babies up through the toddler stage. Scores of books, toys, and souvenirs of all types were issued over the years, and today all are very collectible.

Of the five, only Yvonne, Cecile, and Annette are alive today. Emily died in 1954 and Marie in 1970.

Book, 'Soon We'll Be Three Years Old,' Whitman Publishing Co, 1936, NM **$25.00**
Bowl, silverplate, EX...**$50.00**
Calendar, 11x9", color drawing, advertising for funeral establishment, 1940, NM.......................................**$20.00**
Doll, 14", Dr Defoe, Madame Alexander, composition, 1937 ....**$1,000.00**
Doll, 17", baby, Madame Alexander, composition w/cloth body...**$500.00**
Doll, 20", toddler, Madame Alexander, composition.**$600.00**
Fan, hand-held cardboard type, North Haledon Bus Lines, 1935, VG **$27.50**
Fan, hand-held type, 'School Days,' EX **$18.00**
Fan, 8x8¾", die-cut cardboard, hand-held type, color portraits w/ad, 1936, M **$22.50**
Hair ribbon, 1936, on original card, M **$75.00**
Photograph album, 'The Complete Story of Their First Two Years,' Dell Publishing Co, 1936, NM, (illustrated) **$35.00**
Post card, Quints w/stuffed toys, dated 1937, EX........**$12.50**
Sheet music, 9x12", 'Quintuplets' Lullaby,' Leo Feist Inc, color photo cover, 1935, EX..................................**$30.00**
Spoon, silverplate, figural handle **$12.50**

Disney

The largest and most popular area in character collectibles is without doubt Disneyana. There are clubs, newsletters, and special shows that are centered around this hobby. Every aspect of the retail market has been thoroughly saturated with Disney-related merchandise over the years, and today collectors are able to find many good examples at garage sales and flea markets.

Disney memorabilia from the late twenties until about 1940 was marked either 'Walt E. Disney' or 'Walt Disney Enterprizes.' After that time, the name was changed to 'Walt Disney Productions.' Some of the earlier items have become very expensive, though many are still within the reach of the average collector.

During the thirties, Mickey Mouse, Donald Duck, Snow White and the Seven Dwarfs, and the Three Little Pigs (along with all their friends and cohorts) dominated the Disney scene. The last of the thirties' characters was Pinocchio, and some 'purists' prefer to stop their collections with him.

The forties and fifties brought many new characters with them — Alice in Wonderland, Bambi, Dumbo, Lady and the Tramp, and Peter Pan were some of the major personalities featured in Disney's films of this era.

Even today, thanks to the re-releases of many of the old movies and the popularity of Disney's vacation 'kingdoms,' toy stores and department stores alike are full of quality items with the potential of soon becoming collectibles.

If you'd like to learn more about this fascinating field, we recommend *The Collector's Encyclopedia of Disneyana* by Michael Stern and David Longest and *Character Toys and Collectibles* and *Toys, Antique and Collectible*, both by David Longest.

Alice in Wonderland, school bag...................................**$60.00**
Babes in Toyland, Big Golden Book, Golden Press, 1961, NM...**$7.00**
Babes in Toyland, Toy Soldier twistable figure, 8", Marx, 1961, EX...**$20.00**
Bambi, ash tray, figural on oval base, Goebel w/stylized bee mark, M **$275.00**
Bambi, cereal bowl, made by Evan K Shaw, 1946 ......**$40.00**
Bambi, Disneykin, Marx Co, in original box, M **$15.00**
Bambi, poster, 27x41", 1975, re-release, marked Walt Disney Productions 1942, EX..**$15.00**
Black Cauldron's King Eidellig, stuffed doll, Tomy, 1985, NM in box **$20.00**
Captain Hook, doll, 12", Sears, 1988, M in box **$30.00**
Clarabelle Cow, pop-up book, Whitman, 1930s, EX ...**$25.00**

Disney book, 8x10", 'Victory March,' Random House Books, 1942, mechanical, EX..........................**$50.00**

Disneyland, souvenir guide, 8½x11½", 1957...........**$25.00**

Donald Duck, ball, Sun Rubber, ca 1940s..................**$38.00**

Donald Duck, bank, painted plastic w/slot in hat, Play Pal Plastics, 1979, M...**$20.00**

Donald Duck, book, 'The Life of Donald Duck,' 1930s, EX..**$75.00**

Donald Duck, bread wrapper, bright colors, 1950s.....**$25.00**

Donald Duck, bubble pipe, painted plastic, Morris Plastic Corp, on original card, M..**$45.00**

Donald Duck, car, hard rubber figure driving hard plastic car, Kohner Co, 1973, M...**$10.00**

Donald Duck, carpet sweeper, painted wood & wire w/original bristles, Ohio Art Co, Walt Disney Enterprises, EX...**$110.00**

Donald Duck, Christmas card, mechanical type, Whitman, 1930s, 5¢ original price w/envelope, G.................**$25.00**

Donald Duck, figurine, 4" long, recumbent, glazed ceramic, Evan K Shaw, EX...**$135.00**

Donald Duck, figurine, 4½", painted bisque, w/violin, EX..**$225.00**

Donald Duck, hairbrush, Hughes Co, marked WD Ent, EX..**$85.00**

Donald Duck, hand puppet, Gund, 1960s, EX...........**$17.00**

Donald Duck, paint box, Transogram & Walt Disney Enterprises, 1938..**$30.00**

Donald Duck, pencil sharpener, celluloid w/metal sharpener inside, EX...**$275.00**

Donald Duck, sand pail, lithographed tin, Ohio Art Co, copyright 1938 WD Enterprises, NM.....................**$90.00**

Donald Duck, Superflex figure, 2½", Lakeside, 1971, M on worn card..**$18.00**

Donald Duck, toothbrush holder, long-billed, two Donald figures joined at shoulders, bisque, Japan, Walt E Disney, NM...**$325.00**

Donald Duck, toothbrush holder, painted bisque w/opening between Donald's hat & right hand, EX.............**$275.00**

Donald Duck, Tricky Trapeze, 2½" figure, Gabriel, 1977, EX..**$5.00**

Donald Duck, umbrella, figural handle w/plaid shade, Louis Weiss Co, EX..**$175.00**

Donald Duck, valentine card, dated 1939, M.............**$25.00**

Donald Duck, wind-up, plastic figure in sombrero w/maracas, 1950s, NM...**$80.00**

Dopey, doll, 9", composition w/velvet clothes, Knickerbocker Toy Co, w/original tag, NM.....................**$225.00**

Dopey, figurine, 6", American Pottery, high-gloss glaze, 1940s, M..**$175.00**

Dopey, hand puppet, composition head w/cloth cap & body, Crown Toys, marked Dopey Walt Disney Ent, NM...**$60.00**

Dopey, hand puppet, 1970s, EX.................................**$10.00**

Dopey, lamp base, figural plaster (modeware), LaMode Studios of New York, marked c 1938 WDE, EX......**$140.00**

Dopey & Happy, bookends, glazed ceramic, S Maw & Sons of England, marked Genuine Walt Disney Copyright Foreign, pr, M...**$220.00**

Dumbo, figurine, 6", American Pottery Co, 1940s, w/original label **$85.00**

Fantasia, miniature plate, pewter, 1980s, M in box **$20.00**

Fantasia, theater program, 10x12½", 1940, 32-page, NM.**$47.50**

Ferdinand the Bull, pencil sharpener, Bakelite w/decal, 1938 ....**$40.00**

Gepetto, paper mask, Gillette premium, 1939, NM **$25.00**

Goofy, snack tray, w/scene of Goofy playing golf, 1950s, M **$25.00**

Jiminy Cricket, figurine, 4", wood composition, Multi Products of Chicago, 1940s.......................................**$75.00**

Jungle Book, Bully PVC figure, 1984, set of 5 in box .**$35.00**

Jungle Book, poster, 1-sheet, 1967, EX **$15.00**

Lady & the Tramp, tape dispenser, heavy metal, 1950s, NM **$32.00**

Little Mermaid, Ariel doll, Applause, 1991, M in shipping box...**$17.00**

Little Mermaid, Ariel doll, Tyco, 1990, M in box..........**$35.00**

Little Mermaid, Ariel PVC figure, Applause, 1991, M.....**$2.75**

Ludwig Von Drake, doll, talking, 1960s, M in original box...**$85.00**

Ludwig Von Drake, doll, 10", missing glasses, EX.......**$35.00**

Ludwig Von Drake, game, 'Tiddley Winks,' Whitman & Walt Disney Enterprises, 1960s.....................................**$20.00**

Mary Poppins, spoon, child's, silverplated, dated 1964..**$15.00**

Merlin, hand puppet, hard plastic head w/cloth body, Gund Manufacturing Co, marked WDP on back of neck, NM...**$15.00**

Mickey & Minnie Mouse, block, wooden, 1⅜x1⅜", 1930s, G **$7.50**

Mickey & Minnie Mouse, serving tray, colorful party lithograph on tin, Ohio Art, 1930s, NM.......................**$75.00**

Mickey & Pluto, ashtray, 3", Mickey w/guitar on lustreware..**$95.00**

Mickey Mouse, airplane, solid rubber, Sun Rubber Co, EX..**$85.00**

Mickey Mouse, alarm clock, reproduction of Bayard 1930s edition, made by Bayard in France, 1970s, M.....**$175.00**

Mickey Mouse, ashtray, seated lustreware figural w/drum on triangular base, Made in Japan, EX.....................**$225.00**

Mickey Mouse, baby rattle, 9", celluloid shows Mickey in relief on rattle w/ring handle, Amloid Co, NM ...**$250.00**

Mickey Mouse, bagatelle, 24", painted wood, Marks Brothers Co, complete w/marbles, EX **$550.00**

Mickey Mouse, bank, leatherette book form, 1930s **$70.00**

Mickey Mouse, bank, painted metal cylinder w/side slot, marked Happynak Series Made in Great Britain, NM..**$150.00**

Mickey Mouse, book, 'Mickey Mouse in Blaggard Castle,' Little Big Book, Whitman, ca 1930s, EX **$60.00**

Mickey Mouse, book, 'The Pop-Up Mickey Mouse,' Blue Ribbon Books Inc, 1933, 3 pop-up scenes, NM..**$175.00**

Mickey Mouse, bottle warmer, Hankscraft Co, in original box, EX...**$15.00**

Mickey Mouse, brush set, painted enamel on wood, Hughes Brush Co, in original box, EX.............................**$175.00**

Mickey Mouse, card game, 'Old Maid,' marked WD, in original box, EX..**$75.00**

Mickey Mouse, cartoon, 'Air Mail,' Movie-Jector reel film, 1930s **$45.00**

Mickey Mouse, charm bracelet, linked die-cut enameled figures, Cohn & Rosenberger Inc, EX $125.00

Mickey Mouse, Christmas light set, eight plastic bells, electric, Noma Light Co, in original box, EX $225.00

Mickey Mouse, clarinet, tin w/Mickey Mouse decal, 1930s $150.00

Mickey Mouse, clicker, lithographed tin, Walt Disney, EX $55.00

Mickey Mouse, compact, enameled tin w/mirror & powder compartment, Cohn & Rosenberger Co, in original box, NM $425.00

Mickey Mouse, doll, stuffed cloth dressed as cowboy, Knickerbocker, 1935, M..............................$500.00

Mickey Mouse, doll, 21", cloth w/composition shoes, Knickerbocker, w/original tag, NM $3,000.00

Mickey Mouse, doll, 5", cloth w/rat-like features, marked Made in England by Dean's Rag Book Co, G $500.00

Mickey Mouse, doll, 6", solid black rubber w/painted features & movable head, Seiberling Latex Products, EX $200.00

Mickey Mouse, dollhouse, 10x14" long, painted fiberboard, OB Andrews Co of Chattanooga, EX...................$165.00

Mickey Mouse, dominoes, solid black, Halsam Co, in original box, EX..$10.00

Mickey Mouse, drum, 8", Ohio Art & Walt Disney Enterprises, 1930s...$200.00

Mickey Mouse, figurine, playing saxophone, bisque, Walt Disney Enterprises, 1940s............................$75.00

Mickey Mouse, figurine, 3", hands on hips, bisque, 1930s $65.00

Mickey Mouse, fishing kit, Hamilton Metal Products, ca 1930s..$85.00

Mickey Mouse, flip movie, 'Mickey Takes Minnie for a Ride,' promotional item from Dodge Car Co, EX............$60.00

Mickey Mouse, game, 'Pin the Tail on Mickey Party Game,' Marks Brothers Co of Boston, in original box, EX.$110.00

Mickey Mouse, hairbrush, EX.......................................$50.00

Mickey Mouse, hairbrush & comb set, Henry Hughes Co, 1930s, in original box, M..................................$150.00

Mickey Mouse, hankerchief, printed cloth, Hermann Handkerchief Co, in original box, NM $200.00

Mickey Mouse, iron-on transfers, McCall's Pattern Co, 1934 ....$85.00

Mickey Mouse, jam jar bank, embossed characters on square glass bottle w/painted tin lid, Glaser Crandall Co, Chicago, G...$75.00

Mickey Mouse, kaleidoscope, colorful graphics on cardboard & metal tube, 1950s, NM $45.00

Mickey Mouse, milk bottle, black graphics on clear glass, 1930s..$65.00

Mickey Mouse, Movie Jector, metal, Movie Jector Co, w/'Winning the Derby' film, original box, EX $650.00

Mickey Mouse, mug, embossed painted porcelain, 'Mickey Mouse Time,' 1950s $35.00

Mickey Mouse, music box, figural plays Mickey Mouse Club theme song, Schmid Co, #203, M $225.00

Mickey Mouse, napkin ring, embossed silver $75.00

Mickey Mouse, necktie, Nuemann Co, 1930s..............$40.00

Mickey Mouse, night light, painted pressed wood w/lithographed tin base & light, Micro-Lite Co, dated 1935, EX $450.00

Mickey Mouse, party horn, cardboard megaphone w/wooden tip, Marks Brothers, EX $100.00

Mickey Mouse, pencil box, cardboard, Dixon USA Company, marked Disney Enterprises, NM $125.00

Mickey Mouse, pencil holder, composition figural w/handhold & well in foot, Dixon Co, EX $425.00

Mickey Mouse, pencil sharpener, 2½", celluloid w/sharpener inside body, NM..$375.00

Mickey Mouse, penny book, 'Uphill Fight,' 1934, EX..$17.50

Mickey Mouse, pin-back button, 'Mickey Mouse Club Copyright 1928-30' & Mickey on lithographed tin, EX..$55.00

Mickey Mouse, planter, Leeds China, 1947 ....$125.00

Mickey Mouse, playing cards, Western P&L Co, 1932, in original box, EX $95.00

Mickey Mouse, pocketknife, Imperial Knife Co, 1930s ..$40.00

Mickey Mouse, pop-up book, 'Silly Symphonies,' 1930s, rare $275.00

Mickey Mouse, porringer, silverplate w/die-cut tab handle, International Silver, 1930s, in original box, M $450.00

Mickey Mouse, potty, child's size, porcelain-clad metal w/Mickey playing piano, Richard Krueger Co, German, EX $450.00

Mickey Mouse, print shop kit, Fulton Specialty Co, complete w/stamp pictures, letters & pad, in original box, NM $100.00

Mickey Mouse, purse, child's size, King Innovations, 1930s $45.00

Mickey Mouse, purse, child's size, mesh w/enameled Mickey pin on front, metal frame & handle, Cohn & Rosenberger, NM $250.00

Mickey Mouse, radio, white Bakelite, Emerson, 1930..$1,200.00

Mickey Mouse, sand pail, 3", Mickey on island, Ohio Art Enterprises, 1930s $125.00

Mickey Mouse, sand sifter, lithographed tin w/arc handle, Ohio Art Co, EX $250.00

Mickey Mouse, scissors, Mickey on handle, 1930s $95.00

Mickey Mouse, sheet music, 'The Wedding Party,' 1930s, EX $50.00

Mickey Mouse, sled, wood, Flexible Flyer, ca 1930s, EX $300.00

Mickey Mouse, snow shovel, lithographed tin, Ohio Art Co, marked copyright Walt Disney, EX.....................$200.00

Mickey Mouse, sparkler, black & white lithograph on tin, lever action, 1932, rare $200.00

Mickey Mouse, spoon, baby size, silverplate, William Rogers & Son, figural handle, M............................$30.00

Mickey Mouse, spoon, child's, silverplated, William Rogers Manufacturing Company $60.00

Mickey Mouse, Superflex figure, 2½", Lakeside Toys, 1971, M on EX card $18.00

Mickey Mouse, switchplate, 5", plastic, 1950s, in original package $22.00

Mickey Mouse, tablet, 1930s, EX.................................$40.00

Mickey Mouse, tool chest, Hamilton Metal Products, 1935 ....$75.00

Mickey Mouse, toothbrush, 1930s, on original card ..**$100.00**

Mickey Mouse, toothbrush holder, hand-painted bisque, bulbous head, Japan, marked 'Mickey Mouse' across stomach, NM **$450.00**

Mickey Mouse, top, lithographed tin, spinning type w/wood knob, Fritz Bueschel Co, EX **$375.00**

Mickey Mouse, Transfer-O-S (used to decorate Easter eggs), Paas Dye Co, Walt Disney Enterprises, M in box .**$50.00**

Mickey Mouse, valentine, 'What's Better than a Kiss?,' Hall Brothers, 1935, EX **$30.00**

Mickey Mouse, wall pocket, lustreware, signed Disney, Japan........................**$235.00**

Mickey Mouse, wall watch, 38", plastic, Elgin Watch Co, ca 1970s-80s, EX **$20.00**

Mickey Mouse, washing machine, lithographed tin w/crank handle, Ohio Art Co, EX........................**$700.00**

Mickey Mouse, watch fob, figure in relief on metal shield w/chain, English, EX **$165.00**

Mickey Mouse, water ball, bathtub float toy, Jolly Blinker Co, in original box, M........................**$25.00**

Mickey Mouse, watering can, 6", Mickey in garden, Ohio Art Co, c Walt Disney, NM $85.00

Mickey Mouse, weather house, painted plastic, Weatherman Co, EX........................**$55.00**

Mickey Mouse, wind-up car, lithograph on tin, Marx, 1950s........................**$110.00**

Mickey Mouse & Pluto, place mat, vinyl, EX **$4.00**

Minne Mouse, valentine, mechanical, hula dancer, Walt Disney Enterprises, 1930s **$35.00**

Minnie Mouse, ash tray, painted ceramic figural w/mandolin, Japan, Walt Disney Enterprises, EX **$250.00**

Minnie Mouse, cup, International Silver, 1930s, EX **$70.00**

Minnie Mouse, cup, 2", china, Patriot China, 1930s.....**$40.00**

Minnie Mouse, egg cup, 3", ceramic, unmarked.........**$95.00**

Minnie Mouse, figurine, 5½", hand-painted bisque, Japan, EX **$475.00**

Minnie Mouse, greeting card, 'Merry Christmas,' Hall Brothers, 1935, EX........................**$38.00**

Minnie Mouse, mug, 4", china, Patriot China Co, EX ..**$60.00**

Minnie Mouse, pincushion, bisque figure pushing wheelbarrow, NM........................**$750.00**

Minnie Mouse, puppet, Gund, 1960s, in original box.**$35.00**

Minnie Mouse, tumbler, 4¾", black graphics on clear glass, Walt Disney **$25.00**

Minnie Mouse, wind-up, washing machine, Precision Specialties, 1950s, in original box **$75.00**

Mowgli, salt shaker, 5", Enesco, ceramic, standing before stump, EX **$23.00**

Peter Pan, doll, Sears, 1988, M in box........................**$20.00**

Peter Pan, marionette, ca 1950s, in original box **$140.00**

Peter Pan, punch-out book, 1950s, NM........................**$55.00**

Pinocchio, alarm clock, Baynard, animated Jiminy Cricket dances above Pinocchio's head, 1964, M.............**$75.00**

Pinocchio, bank, figure riding turtle, composition, Crown Toy, 1939........................**$200.00**

Pinocchio, bread wrapper, 1940s, complete **$40.00**

Pinocchio, paint book, Whitman, 1939, EX................**$45.00**

Pinocchio, puppet, composition head w/cloth body, Crown Toy, 1939........................**$45.00**

Pinocchio, school tablet, Pinocchio & Gepetto cover, 1940, M **$35.00**

Pinocchio, wind-up, 10½", painted composition, George Borgfeldt, EX........................**$425.00**

Pluto, acrobat toy, metal & celluloid, LineMar, 1950s, M........................**$250.00**

Pluto, bank, glazed ceramic, Leeds China Co, M.........**$25.00**

Pluto, figurine, hand-painted chalk, Japan, copyright Walt Disney, M **$25.00**

Pluto, mug, coffee size, 'Pluto the Pup' & picture on front, Patriot China Co, M........................**$95.00**

Pluto, scissors, painted plastic, marked Walt Disney's Cartoon Scissors on original package, M **$15.00**

Pluto, valentine, mechanical, Walt Disney Enterprises, 1930s **$30.00**

Pluto, 4½x6" long, friction toy, plastic, marked WDP, manufactured by Marx, NM $40.00

Red Riding Hood, game, 'Walt Disney's Own Game,' 1930s, complete, EX in original box **$60.00**

Robin Hood, rub-on transfers, Letraset, 1970s, EX **$5.00**
Roger Rabbit, ashtray, Amblin, 1987, M **$20.00**
Roger Rabbit, Baby Herman flexi figure, Lin, 1988, M on card **$30.00**
Roger Rabbit, Bennie the Cab, animate figure, Lin, 1988, M on display card.....................................**$40.00**
Roger Rabbit, Blo-Up Buddy, 36", Lin, 1988, M in package **$15.00**
Roger Rabbit, Golden Book, Golden, 1988, M..............**$6.00**
Roger Rabbit, Jessica flexi figure, Lin, 1988, M on card...**$30.00**
Roger Rabbit, key chain, Amercep, 1987, M on card **$5.00**
Roger Rabbit, party pack for four, Unique, 1987, M in package **$5.00**
Roger Rabbit, PVC figure, Applause, 1987, M...............**$3.00**
Roger Rabbit, Skateboard Bunny, Japan, 1988, M in EX box...**$35.00**
Roger Rabbit, suction-cup doll, 10", 1987, M **$15.00**
Roger Rabbit, umbrella, Amblin, England, 1987, M.....**$48.00**
Roger Rabbit, Whacky Heads, Applause, 1987, M in bag .**$5.00**
Seven Dwarfs, drinking glass, small, shows Bashful in 1-color graphics on clear, Walt Disney, EX..............**$30.00**
Seven Dwarfs, 5½" figure, painted solid hard rubber, Seiberling Latex Co, NM, each **$45.00**
Sleeping Beauty, game, Parker Brothers, 1958, complete in original box, VG...**$25.00**
Sleeping Beauty, paper dolls, Whitman, 1959, EX.......**$35.00**
Snow White, figurine, painted ceramic (used for watch stand), 1960s **$40.00**
Snow White, flour sack, 1950s, common **$8.00**
Snow White, ironing board, 21x27", metal, Wolverine ...**$45.00**
Snow White, paper mask, Gillette premium, dated 1938, EX...**$25.00**
Snow White, sand pail, 5", shows Snow White & dwarfs, Ohio Art, 1938.....................................**$125.00**
Snow White, telephone, NN Hill Brass, 1930s, NM.....**$170.00**
Snow White, toothbrush holder, 5", china, 1938.......**$150.00**
Snow White, toy sink, Wolverine, 1960s.....................**$20.00**
Snow White & the Seven Dwarfs, cake decorations, 1960s, complete set, M..**$15.00**

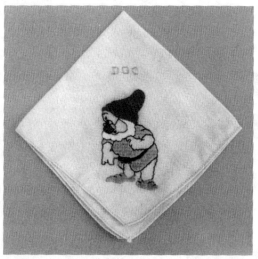

Snow White & the Seven Dwarfs, handkerchief, shows Doc embroidered on linen, ca 1938, M...........$25.00

Snow White & the Seven Dwarfs, sheet music, 'Heigh Ho,' marked Disney, 1938, M.......................................**$25.00**

Snow White & the Seven Dwarfs, valentine, shows dwarfs at door, mechanical, EX......................$25.00
Three Little Pigs, bank, metal book form, 'We Save Our Coins So Who's Afraid...,' Zell Products, marked WE Disney, M **$100.00**
Three Little Pigs, flashlight, Electric Mfg, 1936, EX.........**$75.00**
Three Little Pigs, plate, Patriot China, 1930s, NM........**$38.00**

Three Little Pigs, sand pail, lithographed tin, ca 1930s, M $45.00
Three Little Pigs, toothbrush holder, pigs at piano, bisque figural, copyright Walt Disney, EX......................**$170.00**
Uncle Remus, record set, 78rpm, Capitol, 1947, set of 3 in original sleeve, NM **$27.50**

Uncle Scrooge, bank, Scrooge reclining in bed, ceramic figural, 1961..**$20.00**

Wendy, doll, 11", Sears, 1988, M in box.......................**$20.00**

Wicked Queen (from Snow White), marionette, Alexander Doll Co, 1930s, NM...**$200.00**

Zorro, Halloween costume, Walt Disney, in original box, EX...**$28.00**

Zorro, hankerchief, M...**$20.00**

Zorro, pencil holder & sharpener, 6", ceramic, 1950s.**$65.00**

Zorro, whip set, M Shimmel Sons, 1950s, whip & mask on original card **$70.00**

101 Dalmations, figure, 7½", vinyl, blue eyes, open mouth, blue collar, 1963, M **$32.00**

Dollhouse Furniture

Some of the mass-produced dollhouse furniture you're apt to see on the market today was made by Renwal and Acme during the forties and Ideal in the 1960s. All three of these companies used hard plastic for their furniture lines and imprinted most pieces with their names. Strombecker furniture was made of wood, and although it was not marked, it has a certain recognizable style to it. Remember that if you're lucky enough to find it complete in the original box, you'll want to preserve the carton as well.

Bath scales, ivory, Renwal..**$7.00**

Bed, twin; brown w/molded spread, Renwal **$6.00**

Bed, twin; dark wood, Strombecker, EX.....................**$18.00**

Bedroom set, wooden, Donna Lee, M in box.............**$16.50**

Candelabrum, metal & glass, EX.................................**$25.00**

Chair, dining; Strombecker, set of 4, EX **$40.00**

Chair, parlor; upholstered, Biedermeier.....................**$185.00**

Chair, wing; red w/brown legs, Little Hostess, EX **$12.50**

Chifferobe, Mattel...**$5.00**

Clock, grandfather; w/door, Little Hostess..................**$10.00**

Corner cupboard, dark wood, Tynietoy, EX...............**$80.00**

Dining room set, marked Strombecker Playthings walnut, 7-pc $50.00

End table, cast iron, Arcade, ca 1925...........................**$88.00**

Fireplace, lithograph on tin w/'marble' top, VG.........**$32.00**

Grand piano, cast iron, Arcade, 1920s, VG **$60.00**

Ironing board, pink, Renwal **$7.50**

Lamp, floor; w/cream shade, Strombecker...................**$7.50**

Mirrored dresser, brown, Renwal, w/bench & lamp..$20.00

Parlor set, bentwood, settee, rocker & armchair, EX.**$225.00**

Play pen, pink, Renwal..**$6.00**

Rocker, brown, tall back, Little Hostess, EX................**$12.50**

Sink, bathroom, pink w/blue faucets, Renwal **$7.50**

Sofa, cream & gold, Petite Princess, EX.......................**$25.00**

Sofa, red, Strombecker, EX...**$10.00**

Stove, Little Willie, cast iron, EX **$75.00**

Table, dining; Petite Princess, EX in original box.......**$32.00**

Table, kitchen; green, Strombecker, EX **$10.00**

Table, library; Tootsietoy, 1925, EX............................**$15.00**

Tea cart, brown, Tootsietoy **$20.00**

Telephone, Fantasy; Petite Princess, NM in box.........**$12.00**

Tub, pink & blue, Renwal **$6.00**

Wash stand, painted tin, VG **$32.00**

Dolls

Doll collecting is one of the most popular hobbies in the United States. Since many of the antique dolls are so expensive, even modern dolls have come into their own and can be had at prices within the range of most budgets. Today's thrift shop owners know the extent of 'doll mania' though, so you'll seldom find a bargain there. But if you're willing to spend the time, garage sales can be a good source for your doll buying. Granted most will be in a 'well loved' condition, but as long as they're priced right, many can be redressed, rewigged, and cleaned up. Swap meets and flea markets may sometimes yield a good example or two, depending upon whether the dealer is a professional or someone just trying to peddle his 'junk.'

Modern dolls, those made from 1935 to the present, are made of rubber, composition, magic skin, synthetic rubber, and many types of plastic. Most of these materials do not stand up well to age, so be objective when you buy, especially if you're buying with an eye to the future. Doll repair is an art best left to professionals. But if yours is only dirty, you can probably do it yourself. If you need to clean a composition doll, do it very carefully. Use only baby oil and follow up with a soft dry cloth to remove any residue. Most types of wigs can be shampooed with wig shampoo and lukewarm water. Be careful not to matt the hair as you shampoo, and follow up with hair conditioner or fabric softener. Comb gently and set while wet, using small soft rubber or metal curlers. Never use a curling iron or heated rollers.

In our listings, unless a condition is noted in the descriptions, values are for dolls in excellent condition except for the Cabbage Patch dolls. Those are priced mint in box. (Even if a Cabbage Patch is in super condition but is without its original box, its value would be only about 25% of what we've listed here.)

For further study, we recommend these books, all by Patricia Smith: *Patricia Smith's Doll Values, Antique to Modern; Modern Collector's Dolls* (five in the series), *Vogue Ginny Dolls, Through the Years with Ginny;* and *Madame Alexander Collector's Dolls.* Patikii Gibbs has written the book *Horsman Dolls, 1950 - 1970,* and Estelle Patino is the author of *American Rag Dolls, Straight from the Heart;* both contain a wealth of information on those particular subjects.

See also Liddle Kiddles, Barbie and Friends, Male Action Figures, Squeeze Toys, and Shirley Temple.

Alexander, Alexanderkins Alice in Wonderland, straight leg walker, all original, 1955, minimum value...........**$600.00**

Alexander, Alexanderkins Ballerina, 8", #620-1965, sequined bodice, pink tutu, all original...............................**$300.00**

Alexander, Alexanderkins Little Godey, #491, all original (gown, felt jacket & hat), 1955, up to.................**$1,500.00**

Alexander, Alexanderkins Wendy, straight leg non-walker, all original (body suit, jumper & bonnet), 1954, minimum value **$300.00**

Alexander, Bonnie, 19", vinyl w/rooted blond hair, blue sleep eyes, stuffed vinyl body, all original, 1954............**$175.00**

Alexander, Cissette Bridesmaid, 10", #960-1957, original pink dress & hat, earrings, NM, minimum value.........**$500.00**

Alexander, Genius Baby, 19", vinyl head w/rooted blond hair, flirty sleep eyes, open mouth nurser, all original, 1960 ....**$165.00**

Alexander, India, 7½", hard plastic w/black wig, sleep eyes, jointed knees, all original, 1966 ....**$145.00**

Alexander, Janie Ballerina, 12", #1124-1965, pink sequined bodice w/rhinestones on skirt, all original..........**$400.00**

Alexander, Maggie Mixup, 16½", #1811-1960, all original..**$400.00**

Alexander, Margaret O'Brien, 18", composition, all original, 1946, NM **$750.00**

Alexander, Margaret O'Brien, 21", composition, original blue dress, replaced shoes & socks, 1946-1947...........**$900.00**

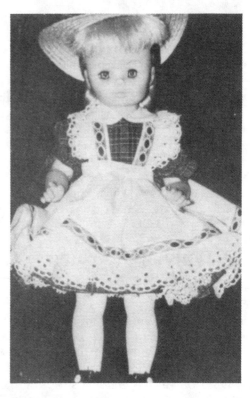

Alexander, McGuffey Ana, 14", #1450-1968, plastic & vinyl, all original **$250.00**

Alexander, Melissa, 16", vinyl head w/rooted hair on plastic body, brown sleep eyes, painted teeth, all original, 1962...**$385.00**

Alexander, Peter Pan, 14", hard plastic, w/saran wig, Maggie face, all original, 1953...............................**$650.00**

Alexander, Polly Pigtails, 14", original plaid dress, straw bonnet **$500.00**

Alexander, Princess, 24", composition, open mouth w/four teeth, original taffeta dress & hat........................**$750.00**

Alexander, Princess Ann, 8", hard plastic w/glued-on wig, blue sleep eyes, jointed knees, all original, 1957........**$1,200.00**

Alexander, Sonja Henie, 21", all composition, all original w/skate button..**$700.00**

Alexander, Southern Belle, 8", hard plastic, jointed knee walker, all original, 1956................................**$1,300.00**

Alexander, Sweet Tears, 13", vinyl w/black rooted hair, sleep eyes, open mouth nurser, all original, 1965.........**$125.00**

American Character, Barbara Sue, 16", vinyl w/1-pc body & legs, disk-jointed arms, all original, 1955, minimum value **$95.00**

American Character, Chuckles, 24", cloth body with vinyl head and limbs, rooted hair, blue sleep eyes, open/closed mouth with two upper teeth, redressed **$85.00**

American Character, Dandy, 12", all composition w/molded curly hair, redressed, 1942....................................**$25.00**

American Character, Hedda Get Betta, 21", 3-sided vinyl head in hard plastic bonnet, vinyl body, all original, 1961 ....**$100.00**

American Character, newborn infant, 18", Bye-Lo type, composition head & hands, cloth body & limbs, molded hair..**$200.00**

American Character, Pretty Penny, 19", hard plastic w/vinyl head, sleep eyes, posable arms, original clothes, 1966...**$60.00**

American Character, Sunny Boy, 21", cloth body, early vinyl head arms & legs, open/closed mouth, all original, 1951...**$100.00**

American Character, Sweet Sue, 31", vinyl head w/rooted hair, plastic body, organdy dress, 1957, M, minimum value **$400.00**

American Character, Sweet Sue Godey Lady, 17", hard plastic, curled/braided wig, walker, all original **$325.00**

American Character, Sweet Susanne, 17", hard plastic, replaced human hair wig, original clothes, 1956.**$350.00**

American Character, Tiny Betsy McCall, 8", hard plastic, jointed knees, rooted hair, all original, minimum value...**$145.00**

American Character, Tiny Tears, plastic & vinyl, rooted hair in skull cap, sleep eyes, molded toes, redressed......**$165.00**

Applause, Raggedy Ann, 12", cloth, all original, 1981.**$25.00**

Arranbee, Angeline, 18", hard plastic w/glued-on mohair wig, sleep eyes, walker body, head turns, all original, 1952 ....**$30.00**

Arranbee, Bride, 14", hard plastic, blue sleep eyes, all original, 1953-54, minimum value **$185.00**

Arranbee, Dream Baby, 21", composition head & limbs w/cloth body, molded painted blond hair, blue tin sleep eyes, open mouth w/two upper teeth, all original, ca 1936 ....$235.00

Arranbee, Francine, 17", hard plastic, glued-on mohair wig, sleep eyes, 2nd & 3rd fingers together, all original, 1955...**$400.00**

Arranbee, Nancy, 17", composition, sleep eyes, glued-on wig, open mouth, original organdy dress, 1937, minimum value **$285.00**

Arranbee, Nancy Lee, 14", composition, sleep eyes, human hair wig, all original, 1939, minimum value........**$225.00**

Arranbee, Nanette, 14", hard plastic, sleep eyes, original 2-pc gray suit, replaced shoes & socks, 1953.........**$250.00**

Arranbee, Nanette, 17", hard plastic, glued-on mohair wig, sleep eyes, all original, 1955, minimum value **$350.00**

Arranbee, Rosie, 19", cloth w/composition swivel head on shoulder plate, composition limbs, sleep eyes, molded hair...**$100.00**

Arranbee, Scarlet, 15", composition w/green sleep eyes, closed mouth, all original, 1940, up to.................**$250.00**

Arranbee, Sweet Angel, 12", vinyl w/blond rooted hair, blue sleep eyes, replaced clothes, 1957.........................**$35.00**

Arranbee, Sweetie Lue, 12", composition, jointed shoulders, hips & neck, eyes painted to side, molded hair, all original **$75.00**

Baby Berry, Mammy Yokum, 21", stuffed vinyl head & gauntlet hands, yarn wig, cloth body & limbs, felt clothes, 1952 ....**$225.00**

Cabbage Patch, baldie w/eye colors other than blue, 1985, M in box, minimum value...................................**$150.00**

Cabbage Patch, Black baldie, 1983, M in box, from $100.00 up to **$125.00**

Cabbage Patch, Black baldie w/freckles, 1983, M in box **$500.00**

Cabbage Patch, Black boy w/shaggy hair & freckles, 1983, M in box...**$600.00**

Cabbage Patch, Black girl w/freckles, 1983, M in box, up to **$800.00**

Cabbage Patch, Black girl w/2 ponytails, 1983, M in box, from $75.00 up to **$100.00**

Cabbage Patch, Black w/pacifier, 1984, M in box, from $175.00 up to **$225.00**

Cabbage Patch, Black w/shag hairdo, 1983, M in box, from $125.00 up to **$150.00**

Cabbage Patch, boy w/freckles & auburn loop hairdo or brunette shag hair, 1983, M in box, each, from $200.00 up to **$300.00**

Cabbage Patch, boy w/freckles & tan shag hair, 1983, M in box...**$150.00**

Cabbage Patch, boy w/red shaggy hairdo, any face mold, 1983, M in box, from $250.00 up to **$600.00**

Cabbage Patch, boy w/red shaggy hairdo & pacifier, 1983, M in box, from $40.00 up to **$500.00**

Cabbage Patch, girl w/brunette ponytail, single tooth, 1985, M in box, from $150.00 up to **$200.00**

Cabbage Patch, girl w/freckles, single auburn ponytail or red braids, 1983, each, from $175.00 up to.........**$300.00**

Cabbage Patch, girl w/freckles & brunette braids or brunette poodle hairdo, 1983, each, M in box **$150.00**

Cabbage Patch, girl w/freckles & gold hair, 1985, M in box..**$75.00**

Cabbage Patch, girl w/single auburn ponytail & pacifier, 1983, M in box **$150.00**

Cabbage Patch, girl w/tan poodle hair & pacifier, 1983, M in box...**$125.00**

Cabbage Patch, gray-eyed girl, 1983, very few made, M in box, from $150.00 up to.......................................**$275.00**

Cabbage Patch, gray-eyed girl, 1985, M in box, from $50.00 up to...**$75.00**

Cabbage patch, no dimples, 1983, M in box, from $50.00 up to...**$75.00**

Cabbage Patch, popcorn hairdo, 1985, M in box, from $100.00 up to..**$125.00**

Cabbage Patch, two dimples & pacifier, 1983, M in box, from $50.00 up to..**$75.00**

Cameo, Baby Mine, 19", all vinyl w/pin-jointed body, sleep eyes, molded tongue & hair, ca 1962 ..$175.00

Cameo, Kewpie, 3½", vinyl w/painted features, marked Kewpie Rose O'Neill Cameo, 1971 ....**$12.00**

Cameo, Miss Peep, 19", pin-jointed shoulders & hips, molded hair, inset brown eyes, earlier version, all original **$95.00**

Cameo, Plum, 18", vinyl w/rooted hair, sleep eyes, dimples, hinged jointed body, all original............................**$90.00**

Cameo, Ragsy Kewpie, 10", vinyl, blue body & bonnet, painted features & hair, nude, 1964.....................**$60.00**

Cameo, Scootles, 19", vinyl, molded hair, closed mouth, all orig w/O'Neill tag, 1964......................................**$300.00**

Chase, baby, 16", stitched fingers, molded hair (brush painted), painted features, redressed, 1940s-1950s................**$225.00**

Deluxe, Candy Fashion, 20", marked A1 HH K92 on head, vinyl w/jointed elbows & knees, human hair, all original, 1957..**$85.00**

Deluxe Reading, Penny Brite, 8", vinyl w/blond rooted hair, painted eyes & dimples, four teeth, all original, 1963...**$12.00**

Deluxe Topper, Baby Bunny, 20", plastic & vinyl, rooted hair, stationary eyes, waves arms & legs, all original, 1969...**$35.00**

Deluxe Topper, Baby Peek & Play, 18", plastic & vinyl, battery operated, all original **$35.00**

Deluxe Topper, Party Time, plastic & vinyl, open mouth nurser, battery-operated to blow noisemaker, all original, 1967...**$35.00**

Deluxe Topper, Tickles, 20", plastic & vinyl, rooted blond hair, sleep eyes, battery operated, original, 1963 ....**$35.00**

Eegee, Bobby, 13", vinyl, deeply molded hair, stationary blue eyes, dimples, original sunsuit, 1955.............**$45.00**

Eegee, Connie, 26", stuffed vinyl w/wire inside legs, rooted hair, sleep eyes, original Mollye Goldman clothes, 1956 ....**$45.00**

Eegee, Honey Lamb, 9½", brown rooted hair, brown painted eyes, plastic & vinyl, 1978-79............$15.00

Eegee, Lil Susan, 16", vinyl & plastic, rooted blond hair, open mouth nurser, all original, 1960 ....**$10.00**

Eegee, Little Debutant, 20", vinyl, rooted hair, sleep eyes, jointed shoulders & hips, original dress, 1957, M.**$60.00**

Eegee, Miss Charming, 19", compositon, glued-on blond wig, sleep eyes, six teeth, 1936, minimum value **$350.00**

Eegee, Musical Baby, 17", plastic & vinyl on cloth body, rooted hair, key-wind music box inside, 1967......**$20.00**

Eegee, Posi-Playmate, 18", vinyl glove hands & head, rooted white hair, foam body, all original, 1969...............**$20.00**

Eegee, Softina Toddles, 17", vinyl w/brown rooted hair, sleep eyes, jointed at neck only, all original.........**$20.00**

Eegee, Susan, 17", vinyl & plastic, rooted blond hair, blue sleep eyes, all original, 1967 ....**$25.00**

Effanbee, Alyssia, 19½", hard plastic walker w/vinyl head, ponytail, separate fingers, all original, 1958..........**$250.00**

Effanbee, Baby Bright Eyes, 19", composition head & limbs on cloth body, molded & painted hair, redressed, 1946...**$285.00**

Effanbee, Baby Wonder, 13", composition w/red molded hair, painted eyes, Patsy body, redressed, 1927 . **$185.00**

Effanbee, Candy Kid, 13", jointed composition, blue sleep eyes, molded hair, all original w/replaced shoes, 1946......................................$250.00

Effanbee, Candy Walker, 24", hard plastic, vinyl head turns, rooted hair, strung arms, 1956, minimum value .. **$185.00**

Effanbee, Gumdrop, 16", plastic & vinyl, rooted blond hair, blue sleep eyes, all original, 1962...........................**$35.00**

Effanbee, Honey Girl, 13½", hard plastic, glued-on wig, sleep eyes, closed mouth, all original, 1949-1955.........**$250.00**

Effanbee, Katie, 8½", vinyl w/molded & painted brown hair, sleep eyes, straight legs, all original, 1957 ....**$65.00**

Effanbee, New Dy Dee Baby, 17", vinyl, rooted blond hair, sleep eyes, open mouth nurser, redressed, 1967..**$28.00**

Effanbee, Patricia, 14", composition, brown human hair wig, all original, 1932..**$300.00**

Effanbee, Patsy Ann, 15", vinyl w/rooted hair, sleep eyes, freckles, all original in sailor dress, 1959 ....**$150.00**

Effanbee, Pum'kin, 10½", all vinyl, freckles, 1966 on.. **$35.00**

Effanbee, Pumpkin Bicentennial Doll, 11", all vinyl w/freckles, original red, white & blue clothes, 1976.........**$90.00**

Effanbee, Sugar Plum Fairy, 11", plastic & vinyl w/dark hair, sleep eyes, all original, w/tag, 1976......................**$65.00**

Effanbee, Suzette, 12", composition, 1939 ....**$200.00**

Effanbee, Sweetie Pie (or Mickey or Baby Bright Eyes), 16", composition, wig, open hands, redressed **$200.00**

Effanbee, Today's Girl, 18", composition head & limbs w/pink cloth body, black yarn hair, original clothes, 1943 ....**$250.00**

Effanbee, WC Fields, 22", composition & cloth, all original, 1938 ....**$695.00**

Fortune Toys, Pam, 7½", hard plastic, walker, molded-on T-strap shoes, redressed, minimum value.................**$50.00**

Half doll, Germany, 12", arms & hands completely away, minimum value **$900.00**

Half doll, Germany, 3", arms & hands attached, common type, minimum value..**$30.00**

Half doll, Germany, 3", arms & hands completely away, minimum value **$125.00**

Half doll, Germany, 3", arms extended, hands attached, minimum value...**$65.00**

Half doll, Germany, 5", arms & hands attached, common type, minimum value..**$40.00**

Half Doll, Germany, 5", arms & hands completely away, minimum value **$250.00**

Half doll, Germany, 5", arms extended, hands attached, minimum value...**$75.00**

Half doll, Germany, 8", arms & hands attached, common type, minimum value..**$55.00**

Half doll, Germany, 8", arms & hands completely away, minimum value **$425.00**

Half doll, Germany, 8", arms extended, hands attached, minimum value...**$95.00**

Half doll, Goebel, 4½", flowers in her hair $250.00

Half doll, Japan mark, 3", minimum value..................**$20.00**

Half doll, Japan mark, 5", minimum value..................**$30.00**

Half doll, Japan mark, 8", minimum value..................**$50.00**

Hasbro, Charlie's Angels Kelly, 8½", 'Spelling-Goldberg...Made in Hong Kong' on back, all original, 1977 ....**$25.00**

Hasbro, Doll House Mother, 7", plastic w/glued-on mohair wig over molded hair, painted-on shoes, all original, 1957 ....**$30.00**

Hasbro, Flying Nun, 5", vinyl w/rooted hair & painted features, all original, 1967 ....**$45.00**

Hasbro, Little Miss No Name, 15", plastic & vinyl, rooted hair, large brown eyes, tear on cheek, all original, 1965 ....**$85.00**

Hasbro, Sweet Cookie, 18", vinyl w/rooted hair, all original, 1972 ....$35.00

Hasbro, 4", Mamas & Papas, vinyl w/rooted hair, all original, 1967, each..$40.00

Hasbro, 9", Black World of Love figure, vinyl w/rooted hair, all original, 1971..$15.00

Horsman, Angelove, 12", plastic & vinyl, made for Hallmark, all original, 1974....................................$40.00

Horseman, Answer Doll, 10", solid vinyl body, rooted hair, head nods..$20.00

Horsman, Baby First Tooth, 16", vinyl & cloth, cry mouth w/one tooth, tears on cheek, all original $50.00

Horsman, Beany, 10", bean bag-type cloth body, vinyl head & hands, rooted hair, painted eyes, 1975..............$15.00

Horsman, Betty Jane, 19", plastic & vinyl, all original.$50.00

Horsman, Betty Joe, 16", plastic & vinyl, all original, 1962 ....$30.00

Horsman, Bootsie, 12", plastic & vinyl, rooted black hair, brown sleep eyes, all original, 1969 ....$10.00

Horsman, Bright Star, 15", hard plastic, all original, 1952..$275.00

Horsman, Brother, 13", vinyl, all original, 13"..............$45.00

Horsman, Buttercup, 14", plastic & vinyl, rooted brown hair, open mouth nurser, original dress, 1963..............$15.00

Horsman, Campbell Kid, 13", composition, 'Dolly Dingle' style face, all original, 1930s-40s........................$400.00

Horsman, Celeste Bride, 13", plastic w/vinyl arms & head, 2nd & 3rd fingers molded together, 1977..........$25.00

Horsman, Cinderella, 11½", plastic & vinyl, eyes painted to side, all original, 1965......................................$45.00

Horsman, Cindy, 15", hard plastic, marked '170' on body, all original, 1950s, minimum value..........................$125.00

Horsman, crawling baby, 14", vinyl, all original, 1967 ..$40.00

Horsman, Ella Cinders, 14", composition & cloth, all original..$375.00

Horsman, Floppy, 18", vinyl w/foam body & legs, all original, 1965 ....$35.00

Horsman, Jackie Coogan, 14", composition & cloth, painted eyes, all original, 1921..................................$500.00

Horsman, Jojo, 12", composition, redressed, 1937, EX..$90.00

Horsman, Kindergarten Kathy, 15", plastic & vinyl, rooted blond hair, sleep eyes, original dress, replaced shoes, 1961 ....$15.00

Horsman, Linda, 36", plastic & vinyl w/long rooted hair, sleep eyes, all original, 1959..............................$100.00

Horsman, Mary Poppins, 12", all original, 1964..........$45.00

Horsman, Mommy's Darling, 18", vinyl w/stuffed cloth body, rooted blond hair, sleep eyes, cryer, ...$30.00

Horsman, Patty Duke, 12", posable arms, all original, 1965 ....$45.00

Horsman, Peggy Pen Pal, 18", #27, has extra joints at waist & elbows, all original, w/writing desk, 1970........$40.00

Horsman, Peterkin Indian, 12", composition head & limbs w/cloth body, all original....................................$225.00

Horsman, Pretty Betty, 16", vinyl, rooted brown hair, sleep eyes, open mouth nurser, redressed, 1954..........$20.00

Horsman, Pudgie, 12½", vinyl, large painted eyes, all original, 1974 ....$40.00

Horsman, Pudgie Baby, 12", plastic & vinyl, redressed, 1978..$15.00

Horsman, Rosebud, 14", composition & cloth, marked w/name, dimples & smile, sleep eyes, wig, all original, 1928 ....$250.00

Horsman, Ruthie, 15½", early stuffed vinyl, molded hair, disk-jointed arms, original clothes, 1953 ....$35.00

Horsman, Ruthie, 20", plastic & vinyl, all original, ca 1960..$38.00

Horsman, Teensie Tot, 11", plastic w/vinyl head & arms, black sleep eyes, all original, 1973 ....$15.00

Horsman, Tuffie, 16", all vinyl, upper lip molded over lower, all original..$85.00

Ideal, Andy Gibb, 7", vinyl, painted eyes, open mouth w/painted teeth, all original, 1978-1980 ....$25.00

Ideal, April Showers, 14", battery operated, head turns, hands make splashing motion, all original, 1968..$30.00

Ideal, Baby Baby, 7", vinyl 1-pc body & limbs, inset blue eyes, dry nurser mouth, original panties, blanket, & bottle $9.00

Ideal, Baby Crissy, 24", pull string to make hair grow, all original, 1973-75..$85.00

Ideal, Bam-Bam, 12", plastic & vinyl, 1963 ....$20.00

Ideal, Betsy Wetsy, 1959, vinyl head w/molded hair, hard plastic torso, separate fingers, redressed..............$50.00

Ideal, Betty Big Girl, 30", plastic w/vinyl arms & head, walker, battery-operated talker in back, all original, 1969 ....$200.00

Ideal, Betty Jane, 14", composition, sleep eyes, open mouth, redressed, 1930s-44..$90.00

Ideal, Bonnie Braids, 13", hard plastic w/vinyl head, all original, 1951 ....$60.00

Ideal, Bride, 15", composition, sleep eyes, blond wig, all original..$175.00

Ideal, child, 14", composition, diamond mark & number, girl w/sleep eyes, open mouth, all original..............$175.00

Ideal, Crissy, 17½", auburn hair, brown sleep eyes, lace dress, 1968-69, all original..................................$145.00

Ideal, Deanna Durbin, 21", black mohair wig, brown sleep eyes, all original, 1939-41, minimum value........$585.00

Ideal, Deluxe Kissy, 22", all original, ca 1962, M.........$85.00

Ideal, Diana Ross, 18", plastic & vinyl, all original $165.00

Ideal, Fanny Brice, 12½", flexible wire in composition hands, head & feet, as Baby Snooks, 1939, minimum value $285.00

Ideal, Flossie Flirt, 22", composition & cloth, flirty eyes, all original..$300.00

Ideal, Giggles Toddler, 18", plastic & vinyl, push arms out & she giggles & tilts head, all original, 1967.............$80.00

Ideal, Goody Two Shoes, 27", talking walker, redressed $70.00

Ideal, Honey Baby, 20", composition head & limbs on cloth body, painted hair, sleep eyes, open mouth w/teeth, redressed $100.00

Ideal, Honey Moon, 15", cloth & vinyl, 1965, NM...........$65.00

Ideal, Honeysuckle, 20", vinyl head w/rooted hair, 1-pc stuffed vinyl body & limbs, blue sleep eyes, all original, 1955 ....$75.00

Ideal, James Arness, 1976, M in box............................$65.00

Ideal, Jiminy Cricket, 9", composition & wood, all original, 1939-40, M..$300.00

Ideal, Joe Stivic, 15", vinyl 1-pc body & limbs, painted eyes, anatomically correct, all original.....................$50.00

Ideal, Judy Garland, 14", composition, all original, 1939 ....$1,000.00

Ideal, Judy Garland, 18", wood composition w/jointed limbs, original clothes, NM.................................$400.00

Ideal, Kissing Thumbelina, 10½", all original, 1962.....$20.00

Ideal, Lindy, 7½", hard plastic, 1-pc body & head, gray sleep eyes, molded lashes, original dress, 1956.............$15.00

Ideal, Mary Hartline, 16", hard plastic, hipped walker, all original, minimum value $350.00

Ideal, Miss Curity, 14", hard plastic, redressed, 1952.....$100.00

Ideal, Miss Revlon, 17", vinyl, rooted brown hair, sleep eyes, jointed waist, all original, 1956 ....$165.00

Ideal, Miss Revlon, 18", blond, original clothes & jewelry, early, NM $165.00

Ideal, Mortimer Snerd, 12", composition & wire, all original, 1939 ....$300.00

Ideal, Pebbles, 8", plastic & vinyl, all original, 1963....$18.00

Ideal, Penny Playpal, 32", plastic & vinyl, rooted red hair, blue sleep eyes, posable head, 1959, NM...........$185.00

Ideal, Pepper, 9", plastic & vinyl, rooted blond hair, painted eyes, closed mouth, all original, 1963 ....$30.00

Ideal, Pinocchio, 11", composition & wood, all original, 1938-41 ....$300.00

Ideal, Sara Ann, 14", hard plastic, saran wig, all original, 1952 on, minimum value..................................$245.00

Ideal, Snoozie, 13", composition & cloth, molded hair, sleep eyes, open yawning mouth, redressed, 1933........$50.00

Ideal, Suzy Playpal, 24", vinyl head & limbs on plastic body, rooted hair, open mouth, original clothes..........$165.00

Ideal, Tabitha, 15", cloth & vinyl, eyes painted to side, all original, 1966...$65.00

Ideal, Tammy, 12", plastic & vinyl, painted features, rooted hair, all original, 1962 ....$50.00

Ideal, Tammy's Mom, 12", plastic & vinyl, eyes to side, all original, 1963...$55.00

Ideal, Thrift Kit Doll, 12", hard plastic w/side-glancing sleep eyes, molded hair, sold to put together & dress $15.00

Ideal, Tiffany Taylor, 18", top of head swivels to change hair color, all original, 1973...$80.00

Ideal, Tiny Kissy, 12", all vinyl, press stomach for puckered mouth, all original, 1962.......................................$45.00

Ideal, Toni, 14", hard plastic w/red nylon wig, sleep eyes, closed mouth, all original w/tag, 1949, minimum value $250.00

Ideal, Tony, 15", strawberry blond, redressed, NM ...$225.00

Ideal, Tony, 21", hard plastic walker w/glued-on nylon wig, all original, 1950-53 ....$350.00

Ideal, Tribly, 20", cloth & vinyl, 3-faced baby, 1951 ..$65.00

Ideal, Upsy Dazy, 15", foam body, stands on head, all original, 1972 ....$20.00

Ideal, Velvet, 16", plastic & vinyl, rooted blond hair w/grow feature, sleep eyes, all original, 1969.................$60.00

Ideal, Velvet Beauty Braider, 15½", lavender floral dress, braiding device for hair, M.................................$75.00

Imperial Crown, Baby Linda, plastic head w/rubber body, red caracul wig, original romper, 1950.................$65.00

Japan, Crawler, 13", plastic & metal body w/vinyl head, battery operated, all original, 1967 ....**$15.00**

Japan, Mary Mary, 7", all vinyl w/rooted black hair, closed mouth, all original, 1968.............................**$3.00**

Jolly Toys, Cutie, 14", vinyl w/rooted hair in ponytails, sleep eyes, open hands, stubby legs, all original, 1965 .**$20.00**

Jolly Toys, Jimmy, vinyl head w/rooted hair, foam body & limbs, vinyl gauntlet hands, 1967, NM...................**$20.00**

Jolly Toys, Linda, plastic & vinyl, rooted black hair, brown sleep eyes, baby legs, all original, 1969 ....**$25.00**

Jolly Toys, Nikki, 13", plastic & vinyl, rooted blond hair, sleep eyes, all original, 1964 ....**$8.00**

Jolly Toys, Playpen Doll, 14", plastic & vinyl, rooted hair, sleep eyes, open mouth nurser, original sleeper, 1967 ....**$5.00**

Kay Sam, Patty Girl, 13", vinyl, molded bun hairdo, panties, socks & shoes, redressed, 1955....................**$6.00**

Kaybee, Love-lee, 16", plastic w/vinyl head & limbs, painted black eyes, original bunny suit, 1966 ....**$12.00**

Kenner, Big Foot, 13", rigid vinyl, all original..............**$20.00**

Kenner, Black Baby Bundles, 16", all original **$28.00**

Kenner, Black Dana, 12½", all original, 1978...............**$40.00**

Kenner, Blythe, 11½", pull string to change color of eyes, all original, 1972..**$45.00**

Kenner, Blythe, 11½", pull string to change color of eyes, redressed, 1972 ....**$20.00**

Kenner, Crumpet, 18", plastic & vinyl, redressed, 1970..**$15.00**

Kenner, Darcy Cover Girl, 12½", posable vinyl, painted features, original Garden Party dress, 1978................**$40.00**

Kenner, International Velvet (Tatum O'Neill), 11½", all original, 1976 ....**$20.00**

Kenner, Sleep Over Dolly, 17", plastic & vinyl, all original gown & cap, w/3¾" Skye doll, 1976....................**$45.00**

Kenner, Strawberry Shortcake, 4¼" to 5", sleep eyes, all original, 1980s **$35.00**

Kenner, Strawberry Shortcake character, 9", all original, 1980s..**$12.00**

Kenner, Stretch Armstrong, 13", extremely stretchable vinyl, molded hair, jointed at neck only.........................**$12.00**

Kenner, Sweet Cookie, 18", all original, 1972..............**$35.00**

Kewpie, Baby, 15", 1-pc stuffed body & limbs, all original, M...**$165.00**

Kewpie, Ragsy, 8", vinyl (1-pc) w/molded-on clothes, heart on chest, 1964 ....**$60.00**

Kewpie, Thinker, 4", vinyl (1-pc), sitting down, 1971.**$15.00**

Kewpie, Ward's Anniversary, 8", 1972, M....................**$80.00**

Kewpie, 9", vinyl, jointed at shoulder, M **$55.00**

Kinckerbocker, Raggedy Ann or Andy, 16", red yarn hair, painted features, tag sewn in seam, all original....**$60.00**

Knickerbocker, Annie, 16", all cloth, curled yarn hair, removable dress w/plush dog in pocket, M.......**$25.00**

Knickerbocker, Annie, 6", vinyl head w/rooted hair & painted features, plastic body, all original, 1982, M in box..**$15.00**

Knickerbocker, Beloved Belindy, cloth, all original, 1954 ....**$300.00**

Knickerbocker, Bozo the Clown, 17", vinyl & cloth, all original **$50.00**

Knickerbocker, Bride & Groom, 6", hard plastic, fully jointed, rattle inside, all original, M in box **$15.00**

Knickerbocker, Carrie, 10½", freckles & painted brown eyes, original 'Holly Hobby' style clothes, all original, 1974 ....**$15.00**

Knickerbocker, child, 15", composition, right arm bent at elbow, all original, 1938 on, minimum value **$225.00**

Knickerbocker, Kewpie, 6", red plush w/vinyl face mask, 1960s, M...**$60.00**

Knickerbocker, Kuddles, 15", all cloth w/yellow yarn hair, original clothes, 1965, M..**$10.00**

Knickerbocker, Little House on the Prairie character, 12", all original, 1978, each..**$20.00**

Knickerbocker, Pinocchio, 13", plush & cloth, all original, M, minimum value **$145.00**

Knickerbocker, Raggedy Ann or Andy, 12", red yarn hair, painted features, tag sewn in seam, all original, 1960s **$165.00**

Knickerbocker, Sooper Snooper, 1959, NM **$60.00**

Knickerbocker, Soupy Sales, 13", vinyl & cloth, non-removable clothes, 1966 ....**$165.00**

Knickerbocker, 11", Missy, all vinyl w/painted eyes, all original, 1975 ....**$8.00**

Knickerbocker, 2-headed doll, 12", one face crying/one face smiling, 1960s...**$20.00**

Knickerbocker, 7", Sunbonnet Doll Mandy, all original w/name on skirt, 1975...**$10.00**

Lenci, Amanda, 20", molded felt face w/hand-painted features, all original, 1982 ....**$500.00**

Lenci, Cristina, 27", molded felt face w/hand-painted features, all original, 1981 ....**$700.00**

Lenci, Laviana, 20", molded felt face w/hand-painted features, all original, 1980 ....**$500.00**

Lenci, Susanna, 20", molded felt face w/hand-painted features, all original, 1978 ....**$500.00**

Marx, Miss Toddler, all plastic, molded hair, paper eyes, battery-operated walker, rollers on bottom of feet, 1965, NM **$40.00**

Marx, Ready Gang Sundown Kid, 1970s, M in box.....**$40.00**

Marx, Twinkie, 5", vinyl w/painted features, shoes & socks, soft plastic clothes, wigs & accessories, complete..**$15.00**

Mattel, Baby First Step, 18", plastic w/vinyl head, rooted hair, sleep eyes, molded-on shoes, battery operated, 1964 ....**$30.00**

Mattel, Baby Go Bye Bye, 12", all original, 1968.........**$20.00**

Mattel, Baby Pattaburp, 13", vinyl w/cloth body, burping mechanism in back, all original, 1963 ....**$30.00**

Mattel, Baby Say 'n See, 17", all original, 1965 ....**$35.00**

Mattel, Baby Teenie Talk, 17", all original, 1965..........**$40.00**

Mattel, Baby Tenderlove, 15", 1-pc dublon foam, rooted white hair, painted eyes, open mouth nurser, all original..**$12.00**

Mattel, Baby Walk 'n See, 18", all original **$35.00**

Mattel, Black Christie, 11½", 1968, minimum value.....**$95.00**

Mattel, Black Dancerina, 24", plastic & vinyl, painted eyes, knop on top of head, all original, 1968.................**$65.00**

Mattel, Bucky Love Notes, 12", press body parts for tunes, all original, 1974...**$28.00**

Mattel, Casper the Ghost, 16", hard plastic head w/stuffed body, pull-string talker, 1964 ....**$30.00**

Mattel, Charlie's Angels character, 11½", marked 1966, all original, 1978...**$15.00**

Mattel, Charmin' Chatty, 25", pull-string talker w/records, all original (Cinderella), 1961, M.............................**$125.00**

Mattel, Chatty Cathy, 10", dark hair, brown eyes, all original, 1962 on...**$95.00**

Mattel, Cheerleader, 13", all original, 1965..................**$20.00**

Mattel, Cheryl Ladd, 12", 1978, M in box **$20.00**

Mattel, Chester O'Chimp, 15", vinyl head & ears, stuffed plush w/wired fingers, eyes twirl, 1964, M **$30.00**

Mattel, Dancerina, 24", all original, 1968.....................**$50.00**

Mattel, Debbie Boone, 11½", all original, 1978............**$25.00**

Mattel, Dr Doolittle, 22½", cloth & vinyl, talker, all original, 1967 ....**$60.00**

Mattel, Dr Doolittle, 6", vinyl, all original, 1967..........**$25.00**

Mattel, Gentle Ben, 18", plush, pull-string talker, plastic eyes, felt tongue, 1967, M.......................................**$35.00**

Mattel, Gorgeous Creature, Mae West-style body w/animal head, all original, 1979 ....**$25.00**

Mattel, Herman Munster, 16", all original....................**$45.00**

Mattel, How the West Was Won Indian, 10", all original, 1971 ....**$30.00**

Mattel, Jimmy Osmond, 10", redressed, 1979..............**$10.00**

Mattel, Kitty O'Neill, 12", vinyl w/painted eyes & teeth, Barbie body w/bendable knees, all original, 1966.....**$30.00**

Mattel, Lone Wolf, 9½", vinyl head w/rooted hair, painted eyes, plastic body, mechanism in back, 1971, M..**$25.00**

Mattel, Mrs Beasley, 16", vinyl & cloth, pull-string talker, all original...**$60.00**

Mattel, Platter Pal, 15", printed cloth, pull-string talker, 1969, M **$15.00**

Mattel, Rockflowers, 6½", all original, 1970.................**$30.00**

Mattel, Scarlet Gem Rose, 4", rooted hair, painted blue eyes, all original, 1976..**$30.00**

Mattel, Scooby Doo, 21", all original, 1964 ....**$85.00**

Mattel, Singing Chatty, 17", pull-string talker, all original, 1964 ....**$45.00**

Mattel, Slugger, 5½", vinyl head w/rooted red hair, painted green eyes, all original, 1975....................................**$10.00**

Mattel, Storybook Kiddles Rapunzel & the Prince, 2", w/storybook & jewelry, 1966, M in heart box................**$45.00**

Mattel, Sweet 16, 11½", vinyl head & rigid plastic, painted brown eyes, all original, 1975, minimum value **$85.00**

Mattel, Truly Scrumptious, 11½", all original, minimum value **$250.00**

Mattel, Wayne Gretzky, M in box **$65.00**

Mattel, Welcome Back Kotter character, 9", all original, 1973 ....**$15.00**

Mego, Camelot character, 8", any one of five in series, all original, 1974...**$20.00**

Mego, Daisy Duke, 8", 1981, M on card.......................**$20.00**

Mego, Diana Ross, 12½", all original, minimum value ..**$45.00**

Mego, Dorothy (Wizard of Oz), all original, 1974 ....**$25.00**

Mego, Falcon, 8", jointed action figure, all original.......**$12.00**

Mego, Farrah Fawcett-Majors, 12½", vinyl head w/green decal eyes, bending knees, all original, 1975.......**$20.00**

Mego, Gorn, 8", Star Trek alien action figure, 1974.....**$15.00**

Mego, Haddie Mod, 11½", all original, 1971 ....**$15.00**

Mego, Incredible Hulk, 12½", 1978, M in box **$80.00**

Mego, Iron Man, 8", fully jointed, original removable clothes **$10.00**

Mego, John Boy Walton, 8", 1974, M in package **$40.00**

Mego, Kiss, vinyl & plastic, rooted hair, jointed waist, bendable knees, all original, 1976................................**$75.00**

Mego, Lainie, 19", jointed waist, battery operated, all original, 1973 ....**$50.00**

Mego, Mary Ellen Walton, Lorimar Productions, all original, 1974 ....**$15.00**

Mego, Dorothy & Toto, 1974, M in box **$40.00**

Mego, Muhammad Ali the Champ, 9½", 1976, M in package **$110.00**

Mego, Ponch (of CHIPS), 8", 1980, M on card............**$20.00**

Mego, Robin Hood, 1974, M in box **$175.00**

Mego, Robin Hood character, 8", any one of four in series, all original, 1971..**$45.00**

Mego, Shirley, 11½", vinyl head w/rooted hair, plastic body, jointed waist, all original, 1977 ....**$25.00**

Mego, Sonny Bono, 12", 1970s, M in Sears box..........**$45.00**

Mego, Wonder Woman (Lynda Carter), 12½", all original, 1975 ....**$20.00**

Mollye, baby, 15", vinyl, redressed, EX.......................**$12.00**

Mollye, baby, 8½", vinyl, all original **$15.00**

Mollye, Baby Joan, 24", cloth w/pressed, hand-painted face mask, all original...**$150.00**

Mollye, child, 15", cloth, all original...........................**$145.00**

Mollye, child, 15", composition, redressed, EX...........**$45.00**

Mollye, child, 16", vinyl, redressed **$25.00**

Mollye, child, 8", vinyl, redressed **$10.00**

Mollye, Cynthia, 15", vinyl head w/rooted hair, 1-pc stuffed body & limbs, original dress, minimum value **$100.00**

Mollye, Dilly, 24", all cloth w/hand-painted face, all original, tag on foot, 1934..**$90.00**

Mollye, Ginger Rogers, 15", composition w/sleep eyes, human hair wig, original taffeta gown & underskirt, minimum value **$350.00**

Mollye, Jeanette McDonald, 27", composition, redressed...**$250.00**

Mollye, Kate Greenaway, 13", stuffed cloth w/hand-painted face, yarn hair, original black silk dress & accessories...**$150.00**

Mollye, of Little Women, 9", vinyl, all original $40.00

Mollye, Mamie Eisenhower, 20", hard plastic w/vinyl head, glued-on wig, all original, minimum value $400.00

Mollye, Princess Margaret Rose, 19", hard plastic w/vinyl head, gold tiara, all original, minimum value $350.00

Mollye, Raggedy Ann or Andy, 15", red yarn hair, printed features, multicolored socks, all original, minimum value $700.00

Mollye, Sherry Ann, 24", composition, all original, tag on wrist, 1944-45 ....$400.00

Mollye, Swedish Girl, 9", all vinyl w/sleep eyes & rooted hair, all original, minimum value $35.00

Mollye, Terrykins, 19", vinyl head w/painted eyes, latex body & limbs, original terry cloth outfit, minimum value $80.00

Mollye, young lady, 16", cloth, all original $185.00

Mollyee, baby, 14", hard plastic, redressed $65.00

Nancy Ann, Margie Ann, 5", bisque, Storybook Doll USA, all original in school dress, minimum value $150.00

Nancy Ann, Muffie, 8", hard plastic, marked Storybook Doll USA Trademark Reg, redressed $85.00

Nancy Ann, 3½" to 4½", bisque, bent-leg baby, marked Storybook Doll USA, all original, minimum value ...$125.00

Nancy Ann, 5", bisque, marked Storybook Doll USA, all original, minimum value $65.00

Nancy Ann, 5", bisque, swivel neck, marked Storybook Doll USA, all original, minimum value $75.00

Nancy Ann, 5", plastic, marked Storybook Doll USA Trademark Reg, all original, minimum value $45.00

Remco, Baby Crawl-A-Long, 20", plastic & vinyl, all original, 1967 ....$20.00

Remco, Baby Laugh a Lot, 16", plastic & vinyl, all original, 1970 ....$20.00

Remco, Baby Stroll-A-Long, 15", plastic & vinyl, rooted hair, sleep eyes, molded shoes, battery operated, 1966 .....$20.00

Remco, Jeannie (I Dream of Jeannie), 6", plastic & vinyl, all original $20.00

Remco, Jumpsy, 14", plastic & vinyl, rooted blond hair, painted blue eyes, battery operated, holds jump rope, 1970 ....$20.00

Remco, Lyndon B Johnson, 1960s, M in box $85.00

Remco, Mimi, 19", plastic & vinyl, battery-operated singer, all original, 1972-73 ....$40.00

Remco, Snugglebun, 16", plastic & vinyl, rooted blond hair, sleep eyes, all original, 1965 ....$15.00

Remco, Tumbling Tomboy, 16", plastic & vinyl, all original, 1969 ....$20.00

Remco, 5½", Heidi, plastic & vinyl, all original $9.00

Royal, Debbie, 15", vinyl w/jointed elbows, strung limbs, dimples, sleep eyes, all original, 1961 ....$60.00

Royal, Joy Bride, 12", vinyl, all original, 1965 ....$45.00

Sun Rubber, Bannister Baby, 17", Lastic-Plastic vinyl w/molded hair, sleep eyes, open mouth nurser, redressed $65.00

Sun Rubber, Betty Bows, rubber w/vinyl head, molded hair & hole for ribbon, sleep eyes, crossed legs, 1953 ......$20.00

Sun Rubber, Gerber Baby, 11", rubber w/molded hair, inset stationary eyes, open mouth nurser, all original, 1956 ....$50.00

Sun Rubber, So Wee, 10", vinyl w/molded hair, stationary eyes, 1-pc body, redressed, 1957 ....$12.00

Terri Lee, Baby Linda, 10", vinyl, painted eyes, all original $185.00

Terri Lee, Terri Lee, 15½", Lastic-Plastic vinyl, molded hair under wig, all original $195.00

Terri Lee, Terri Lee, 18", hard plastic, glued-on white hair, painted features, all original, 1950 ....$185.00

Terri Lee, Walking Tiny Jerry Lee, 10", hard plastic, glued-on caracul wig, sleep eyes, all original, 1950 ....$195.00

Uneeda, Baby Dana, 20", plastic w/vinyl head, dry nurser mouth, all original, 1975 ....$20.00

Uneeda, Baby Trix, 16", vinyl, all original, 1964 ....$20.00

Uneeda, Blabby, 18", vinyl, rooted hair, sleep eyes, press tummy & mouth moves, sucks thumb, cryer, all original, 1962 ....$30.00

Uneeda, Dollikins, 19", vinyl head w/rooted hair, hard plastic body, sleep eyes, pierced ears, all original, 1957 ....$40.00

Uneeda, Freckles, 32", vinyl head w/rooted hair, flirty eyes, plastic body & legs, all original, 1960 ....$65.00

Uneeda, Jennifer, 18", vinyl head w/rooted hair, painted eyes, plastic body & legs, all original, 1971 ....$20.00

Uneeda, Magic Meg, 16", vinyl, 'grow hair,' all original, 1971 ....$20.00

Uneeda, Purty, 15", vinyl, press stomach to make eyes squint, all original, 1961 ....$30.00

Uneeda, Serenade, 21", vinyl, battery-operated talker, all original, 1962 ....$50.00

Uneeda, Suzette, 10", vinyl, painted & molded lashes, all original, M in box $40.00

Uneeda, Sweetum, 22", vinyl head w/rooted hair, 1-pc unjointed latex body, blue sleep eyes, redressed, 1953 ....$8.00

Uneeda, Wiggles, 19", vinyl head w/rooted hair, oilcloth outer body covering w/vinyl limbs, redressed......$45.00

Uneeda, Yummy, 12", vinyl w/rooted hair, sleep eyes, open mouth, press tummy & mouth moves, all original, 1961 ....$15.00

Valentine, Rosebud, 16", plastic w/vinyl head & arms, sleep eyes, all original, 1964 ....$15.00

Vogue, Baby Burps, 14", vinyl, fully jointed, rooted hair, painted eyes, open mouth nurser, all original, 1975 ....$25.00

Vogue, Baby Wide Eyes, 16", vinyl, large brown sleep eyes, all original, 1976 ....$45.00

Vogue, Brickette, 18", rooted hair, sleep eyes, all original, 1979-80 re-issue................$85.00

Vogue, Ginny, 7½", hard plastic, painted blue eyes, original tennis clothes, tag on dress $350.00

Vogue, Ginny, 8", hard plastic, bend-knee walker, redressed................$185.00

Vogue, Ginny, 8", hard plastic w/molded hair, all original (as Red Riding Hood)................$350.00

Vogue, Ginny, 8", original riding habit (all felt), black boots................$300.00

Vogue, Ginny Baby, 7", hard plastic w/glued-on lambs wool wig, sleep eyes, baby legs, all original, minimum value................$550.00

Vogue, Ginny Ballerina, 8", pink satin ribbons, all original **$300.00**

Vogue, Ginny Clown, 8", hard plastic, walker, all original, minimum value **$300.00**

Vogue, Ginny Ice Skater, 8", hard plastic, brown sleep eyes, all original, w/skates **$300.00**

Vogue, Ginny Scotch Highlander, 8", vinyl w/sleep eyes, rooted hair, all original **$50.00**

Vogue, Jan, 10", vinyl head w/rooted hair, sleep eyes, plastic body, high-heel feet, all original, 1957 tag **$75.00**

Vogue, Jeff, 10", vinyl head w/molded & painted brown hair, sleep eyes, plastic body, original suit, 1957..**$50.00**

Vogue, Jill, 10", in original pink skating outfit, 1958 ...**$75.00**

Vogue, Littlest Angel, 11", vinyl w/rooted hair, sleep eyes, toddler legs w/dimpled knees, all original, 1964..**$15.00**

Vogue, Precious Baby, 12", vinyl, rooted hair, sleep eyes, all original, 1975...**$45.00**

Vogue, Toodles, 7½", composition w/painted eyes, all original (China from International group), minimum value **$285.00**

Vogue, Toodles Sailor Boy, 8", composition w/painted eyes, all original, minimum value **$285.00**

Vogue, Welcome Home Baby, vinyl head & limbs on cloth body, painted hair & eyes, closed mouth, redressed...**$125.00**

Vogue, 14", composition, sleep eyes, mohair wig, all original Victorian clothes **$345.00**

Doorstops

There are three important factors to consider when buying doorstops — rarity, desirability, and condition. Desirability is often a more important issue than rarity, especially if the doorstop is well designed and detailed. Subject matter often overlaps into other areas and can appeal to collectors of Black Americana and advertising, for instance, tending to drive prices upward. Most doorstops are made of painted cast iron, and value is directly related to the condition of the paint. If there is little paint left or if the figure has been repainted or is rusty, unless the price has been significantly reduced, pass it by.

Be aware that Hubley, one of the largest doorstop manufacuers, sold many of their molds to the John Wright Company who makes them today. Watch for seams that do not fit properly, grainy texture, and too-bright paint.

For further information, we recommend *Doorstops, Identification and Values,* by Jeanne Bertoia.

Ann Hathaway's Cottage, 6⅜x8⅜", EX paint, Hubley..**$225.00**

Art Deco Mexican Guitar Player, 11¾", worn multicolored paint..**$145.00**

Boston Bulldog, 13", G paint, glass eyes, wedge back, Greenblatt..**$200.00**

Cat, 7", old gold paint, seated, Gary Iron Works, 1925 ..**$65.00**

Cat silhouette, 9½", black paint, paw & tail up **$235.00**

Child in Sailor Suit, 8¾", traces of old multicolored paint, VG..**$285.00**

Cocker Spaniel, 9x7", wedge back, faces front, Metalcrafters, EX **$110.00**

Cottage, 5¾x7½", NM paint, Hubley..........................**$175.00**

Dog by Fence, 6⅝x8⅝", Albany Foundry, VG **$150.00**

Egyptian Camel, 4½", old multicolored paint, recumbent, G **$75.00**

Fireside Cat, 6x10", Hubley, EX............................$165.00

Frog, 3½x6¾", yellow & green paint, full-figured, VG ..**$85.00**

Geese, 8", worn multicolored paint, group of three, Hubley...**$210.00**

Horseshoe, 5x4", wedge back, VG **$115.00**

Lady in Bonnet w/Purse, 10½" $185.00

Lobster, 12½x6½", green & black paint, EX..............**$475.00**

Maiden, 8⅞x3¾", EX paint, light green dress............**$375.00**

Mutt & His Bone, 8¼x5½", green paint.....................**$145.00**

Owl, 5¾", EX paint, side view **$75.00**

Parrot on Perch, 6½", old multicolored paint..............**$40.00**

Penguin, 11", full figure, worn black & white paint, light rust...**$215.00**

Pointer, 15", black & white paint, left leg raised **$85.00**

Rabbit with Top Hat, 9⅞x4¾", EX paint, Albany Foundry..**$450.00**

Rooster, 12", painted $400.00
Saddled Horse on Base, 10½x7⅝", EX paint.............$125.00
Spotted Dog, 7¾x7¾", VG paint, Taylor Cook, 1930, rare $575.00
Steeplechase, 7¼x7½", woman on white horse, EX $375.00
Twin Kittens, 7½", old multicolored paint, G..............$75.00
Two Men in Livery, 9", worn original paint, Fish Mfg Co $625.00
Wolfhound, 15", repaint, no base $85.00

Dryden Pottery

This pottery operated in Ellsworth, Kansas, from 1946 until 1956, when it was relocated to Hot Springs, Arkansas, primarily to benefit from the tourist trade. Their early ware can easily be distinguished from the Arkansas-made pottery, due to the dark clay they used before the move. Most of the pieces found today are small, novelty items, though in the forties the company made dinnerware similar to Fiesta as well as larger hand-thrown collector pieces.

Creamer, #12, miniature, dark green $12.00
Figurine, elephant, 4" long, marked Souvenir..............$20.00
Jug, 3¼", marked KU, maroon $20.00

Mug, face in relief on side $15.00

Pitcher, 6½", #94, brown w/bird handle, w/label........$27.50
Salt & pepper shakers, #73, maroon, Wichita, Kansas..$16.00
Spittoon vase, large, brown & blue, signed ARS, gold sticker $48.00
Vase, #104, black $14.00
Vase, 4", #17, maroon, square.....................................$15.00
Vase, 5", blue, boot form..$15.00
Vase, 5", green & tan, leaf form...................................$18.00
Vase, 5", marked Mankato Kans, maroon, boot form..$13.00
Vase, 7", #75, navy...$13.00

Vase, 9", w/standing deer, 9"...................................$24.00

Duncan & Miller Glassware

Although the roots of the company can be traced back to as early as 1865 when George Duncan went into business in Pittsburgh, Pennsylvania, the majority of the glassware that collectors are interested in was produced during the twentieth century. The firm became known as Duncan & Miller in 1900. They were bought out by the United States Glass Company, who continued to produce many of the same designs through a separate operation which they called the Duncan & Miller Division.

In addition to crystal, they made some of their wares in a wide assortment of colors including ruby, milk glass, some opalescent glass, and a black opaque glass they called Ebony. Some of their pieces were decorated by cutting or etching. They also made a line of animals and bird figures; for information on these, see Glass Animals.

Astaire, goblet, champagne; colors $18.00
Canterbury, cigarette box, crystal, w/silver lid............$40.00
Canterbury, goblet, water; chartreuse..........................$14.00
Canterbury, plate, 12", crystal $35.00
Canterbury, plate, 8", amber $14.00
Canterbury, sherbet, light blue.....................................$7.00
Canterbury, stem, cocktail; 3½", amber, footed $10.00
Canterbury, stem, wine; light blue................................$12.00
Canterbury, sugar bowl, crystal, 9-oz $10.00
Caribbean, bowl, vegetable; 9¼", crystal, handled......$50.00

Caribbean, bowl, 8½", crystal.................................**$22.50**
Caribbean, candy dish, 4x7", crystal, w/lid.................**$35.00**
Caribbean, cocktail shaker, 9", blue, amber, or red ..**$150.00**
Caribbean, pitcher, syrup; 4¼", blue, amber, or red .**$110.00**

Caribbean, pitcher, water; crystal **$350.00**
Caribbean, plate, salad; 7½", crystal **$8.00**
Caribbean, relish, 6" dia, crystal, 2-part........................**$10.00**
Caribbean, relish, 9½", blue, amber. or red, oblong....**$52.50**
Caribbean, stem, sherbet; 4¼", blue, amber, or red **$15.00**
Caribbean, tray, 12¾" dia, crystal.................................**$17.50**
Caribbean, vase, 10", footed, blue, amber, or red **$110.00**
Caribbean, vase, 7½", crystal, ruffled...........................**$25.00**
Fine Rib, pitcher, large, colors **$85.00**
Fine Rib, tumbler, iced tea; colors **$18.00**
Fine Rib, tumbler, juice; colors **$14.00**
First Love, bowl, 12", crystal, flared...............................**$75.00**
First Love, bowl, 13", crystal, scalloped.........................**$75.00**
First Love, compote, crystal..**$30.00**
First Love, goblet, water; tall, crystal **$35.00**
First Love, plate, sandwich; 12", crystal........................**$65.00**
First Love, relish, terrace; 9", crystal, 4-part, handled..**$60.00**
First Love, stem, cocktail; crystal...................................**$30.00**
First Love, sugar bowl, crystal, handled **$20.00**
First Love, vase, cornucopia; crystal **$70.00**
Hobnail, candlestick, crystal...**$12.00**
Hobnail, candy dish, pink or blue...............................**$125.00**
Hobnail, candy dish, 9½", blue opalescent **$65.00**
Hobnail, compote, crystal..**$24.00**
Hobnail, mug, 3¾", crystal w/cobalt handle **$15.00**
Hobnail, top hat, 4", crystal..**$30.00**
Hobnail, tumbler, iced tea; pink or blue, flat...............**$30.00**
Language of Flowers, bowl, 11½", crystal **$35.00**
Language of Flowers, candlesticks, 3", crystal, pr........**$35.00**
Mardi Gras, cake plate, 10", crystal, footed.................**$75.00**
Mardi Gras, creamer, crystal, individual **$25.00**
Mardi Gras, cup, punch; crystal **$8.00**
Murano, bowl, 10x7", milk glass...................................**$17.00**

Murano, bowl, 11½", pink opalescent, crimped **$85.00**
Pall Mall, swan, 7", chartreuse **$57.00**
Sandwich, ash tray, 2⅔", crystal, square.......................**$8.00**
Sandwich, bottle, oil; 5¾", crystal **$50.00**
Sandwich, bowl, fruit; 11½", crystal, footed, crimped .**$50.00**
Sandwich, bowl, salted almond; 2½", crystal **$12.00**
Sandwich, butter dish, ¼-lb, crystal, w/lid..................**$40.00**
Sandwich, candlestick, 5", crystal, 2-light....................**$25.00**

Sandwich, cheese set, 13"platter w/3" compote ...$45.00
Sandwich, cigarette holder, 3", crystal, footed **$27.50**
Sandwich, plate, hostess; 16", crystal............................**$90.00**
Sandwich, relish, 10", crystal, 4-part, handled **$35.00**
Sandwich, stem, oyster cocktail; 2¾", crystal, footed ..**$15.00**
Sandwich, tumbler, iced tea; 5¼", crystal, footed **$17.50**
Sandwich, vase, epergne; 7½", crystal, threaded base...**$165.00**
Sanibel, nappy, fruit; 6½", colors **$20.00**
Sanibel, relish, 12", colors, 3-part, oval **$40.00**
Sanibel, relish, 8¾", blue opalescent, 2-part.................**$35.00**
Ships, plate, 8", amber..**$16.00**
Ships, plate, 8", green...**$18.00**
Spiral Flutes, bottle, oil; 6-oz, colors, w/stopper **$135.00**
Spiral Flutes, bowl, cereal; 6½", colors, small flange...**$25.00**
Spiral Flutes, bowl, cream soup; 4¾", colors, footed...**$15.00**
Spiral Flutes, bowl, nappy; 6", colors, w/lid **$60.00**
Spiral Flutes, cup, seafood sauce; 2½", colors **$22.00**
Spiral Flutes, cup & saucer, colors...............................**$15.00**
Spiral Flutes, pitcher, ½-gal, colors............................**$125.00**
Spiral Flutes, sweetmeat, 7½", colors, w/lid................**$85.00**
Spiral Flutes, tumbler, soda; 4¾", colors.....................**$27.50**
Sylvan, plate, 7¼", crystal **$7.50**
Sylvan, swan, 12½", blue opalescent **$195.00**
Tear Drop, ash tray, 5", crystal..**$8.00**
Tear Drop, bottle, oil; 3-oz, crystal **$20.00**
Tear Drop, bowl, fruit; 7", crystal....................................**$7.00**
Tear Drop, bowl, salad; 9", crystal................................**$25.00**
Tear Drop, bowl, 12", crystal, 4-handled, square **$42.50**
Tear Drop, candy dish, 7½", crystal, heart shape **$22.00**
Tear Drop, celery, 11", crystal, 2-part, handled **$18.00**

Tear Drop, cheese & cracker set, crystal, 2-pc.............$42.50
Tear Drop, compote, 4¾", crystal, footed $12.00
Tear Drop, creamer, 6-oz, crystal................................$6.00

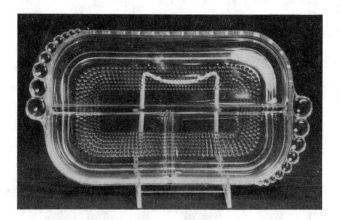

Tear Drop, divided relish tray, 6x12", crystal $25.00
Tear Drop, marmalade, 4", crystal $35.00
Tear Drop, pitcher, milk; 5", crystal.............................$50.00
Tear Drop, pitcher, water; crystal w/silver decor........$125.00
Tear Drop, plate, canape; 6", crystal $10.00
Tear Drop, plate, dinner; 10½", crystal........................$27.50
Tear Drop, plate, torte; 16", crystal, rolled edge..........$37.50
Terrace, ash tray, small, colors, square $28.00
Terrace, plate, dinner; colors, square $65.00
Touraine, goblet, water; crystal..................................$8.00
Willow, sherbet or champagne, 4¾", crystal..............$14.00

Easter Collectibles

The egg (a symbol of new life) and the bunny rabbit have long been part of Easter festivities; and since early in the twentieth century, Easter has been a full-blown commercial event. Post cards, candy containers, toys, and decorations have been made in infinite varieties. In the early 1900s, many holiday items were made of papier-mache and composition and imported to this country from Germany. Rabbits were made of mohair, felt, and velveteen, often filled with straw, cotton, and cellulose.

For more information, we recommend *A Guide to Easter Collectibles* by Juanita Burnett.

Bank, figural vinyl rabbit, marked Huron Products Co, 1960s...$25.00
Candy box, 8½x6x1", colorful scene of rabbit chasing chick on cardboard, 1930s, EX, without contents...........$30.00
Candy container, clear glass rabbit head w/paper features & top hat, Flavour Candy Co, 1950s.....................$25.00
Candy container, 10", papier-mache, rabbit w/glass eyes, EX multicolored paint..$175.00
Candy container, 12", flocked rabbit w/paint palette, German, 1950s $125.00
Candy container, 3" egg, Victorian girls lithograped on tin...$42.50
Candy container, 5", papier-mache, bunny in firetruck, NM $65.00

Candy container, 9", standing papier-mache rabbit w/basket on back, 1940s $55.00
Card, 'Sincere Easter Greetings,' rabbit painting eggs w/chicks looking on, in floral frame w/butterfly, 1930s...$20.00
Coloring book, 'Uncle Wiggily Starts Off, Read the Stories, Color the Pictures,' 1940s $15.00
Cookie cutter set, 'Aunt Chick's Happy Days,' 1950s, in original box..$15.00
Diecut, 6x9¾", chicks w/goblet & violets....................$17.50
Diecut, 7½x7", four chicks in basket, apple blossoms .$14.00
Egg, large, papier-mache, Victorian ladies in park, artist signed, EX...$78.00
Egg, 8½", papier-mache...$40.00
Egg coloring kit, Paas, complete w/dippers, magic crayon & transfers, 1960s, M...$10.00

Musical Easter basket, 2½x4x5¼", cardboard w/plastic handle, Mattel, ca 1955, basket only (filled with ducks & chicks of the period) $20.00
Plate, milk glass, Easter Greetings, chickens & egg in basket...$40.00
Puzzle, 'Bonnie & Bunnie,' Perfect Picture Puzzle, 1940s ..$15.00
Puzzle, 4½", 3-pc painted wood rabbit, marked Made in England, 1940s $10.00
Rabbit, 'Plush Pals,' My Toy Co, plush w/rubber head, w/original tag...$35.00
Rabbit, figural pillow, made from printed fabric panel kit, dressed in print shirt, overalls & cap, 1970s..........$15.00
Rabbit, plush w/felt features & cotton string whiskers, Common Wealth Toy Co, 1950-60................................$25.00
Rabbit, short-haired plush w/straw stuffing, wearing felt tuxedo outfit & bow tie, 1930s..........................$150.00
Rabbit, stuffed plush, musical wind-up, American, 1950s..$50.00
Rabbit, velveteen w/satin-lined ears & neck ruff, wearing felt jacket, embroidered nose & mouth, button eyes, 1930s..$150.00

Rabbit, 15¼", hand-crafted wood w/movable limbs, 1970-80 ....**$25.00**
Rabbit, 5", celluloid, w/basket, EX.............................**$35.00**
Rabbit, 5", painted papier-mache, 1940s **$12.00**
Rabbit, 7", 'Ballerina,' Annalee, 1980s, all original.....**$175.00**

Egg Cups

Egg cups were at one time a standard piece in many lines of dinnerware, but most of them you'll see today are the novelty type that were produced in Japan, Germany, or Czechoslovakia. They take up very little room, so they appeal to apartment dwellers or those of us who simply have no room left for bigger things! They're very inexpensive, and many darling examples can be bought for under $10.00.

Obviously the single-size cup was just right to hold a soft-boiled egg. But if you preferred two for breakfast, you needed a double. You could either have them boiled or poached, and it wasn't considered at all rude to dip your toast points into the soft yolks.

Chinaware, bucket w/hand-painted florals, Portugal **$6.00**
Chinaware, chick beside eggshell, Japan **$4.00**
Chinaware, duck w/spread wings in relief on side, painted details, Occupied Japan...**$15.00**
Chinaware, embossed bluebird on pedestal base, one in series, Goebel, 1988..**$6.00**
Chinaware, hen w/cup in back, painted details & gilt trim on white, marked Occupied Japan......................**$15.00**
Chinaware, Mason's Vista, double **$10.00**
Chinaware, peasant girl, marked Quimper **$25.00**
Chinaware, Rose, Pansy, Forget-Me-Not, small pedestal base, Shelley...**$35.00**
Glass, double, amber, Paden City...............................**$10.00**
Glass, double, clear top w/black foot, no mark **$12.50**
Glass, transparent yellow, Hazel Atlas.........................**$5.00**

Milk glass, 3½", chick form, red painted accents .$20.00

Treen (woodenware), early..**$25.00**

Egg Timers

During the 1930s and '40s, figural egg timers were imported from Japan and Germany, some of which were marked with the country of origin. Later some were marked 'Occupied Japan.' They were made in the likenesses of clowns, Black children, chefs, and birds and animals of many types. They were functional, though; each held or contained in some way a sand-tube timer designed to help you produce the perfect '3-minute egg.'

The sand tubes were made of fragile glass and are often missing. In our listings, values are given for complete timers with tubes intact. Deduct 50% for missing tubes.

Bellboy, 3", kneeling & holding timer in outstretched hand, painted red, marked Germany **$25.00**
Black boy, 3½", plastic head fills w/sand to form timer on ceramic body..**$50.00**
Chef, 4½x4½", painted die-cut wood w/side-glance googly eyes, timer in base, EX **$90.00**
Chef & lady, 3¾", double, marked w/Goebel crown mark, 1935-49 ....**$55.00**
Dog, 3½", sitting on haunches w/timer in left paw, painted red, marked Germany..**$25.00**
Dutch girl, 3½", kneeling w/timer in outstretched hand, marked Germany **$25.00**
Friar Tuck, 3½", double, marked Goebel, ca 1963-69 .**$45.00**
Friar Tuck, 3½", single, marked Goebel, dated 1959...**$45.00**
Mammy, 3", colorful painted porcelain w/tray of fruit, marked Germany **$90.00**
Mammy, 3⅞", painted porcelain in chef hat, marked Germany, ca 1930s, NM..**$125.00**
Mammy, 4", timer in right arm, Occupied Japan.............**$45.00**
Mammy, 7x6", painted wood diecut, extended arm w/pot holder hook..**$110.00**
Parlor maid, 3", talking on telephone w/timer at side, marked Japan **$12.00**
Swami, 3", wearing orange jacket & holding fruit w/thin tube, marked Japan..**$15.00**
Two chicks, 3¾", painted yellow w/red beaks, marked w/1972-79 Goebel mark..**$45.00**

Elvis Presley Memorabilia

Since he burst upon the fifties scene wailing 'Heartbreak Hotel,' Elvis has been the undisputed 'King of Rock 'n Roll.' The fans that stood outside his dressing room for hours on end, screamed themselves hoarse as he sang, or simply danced till they dropped to his music are grown-up collectors today. Many of their children remember his comeback performances, and I'd venture to say that even their grandchildren know Elvis on a first-name basis.

There has never been a promotion to equal the manufacture and sale of Elvis merchandise. By the latter part of

1956, there were already hundreds of items that appeared in every department store, drugstore, specialty shop, and music store in the country. There were bubble gum cards, pin-back buttons, handkerchiefs, dolls, guitars, billfolds, photograph albums, and many others. You could even buy sideburns from a coin-operated machine. Look for the mark 'Elvis Presley Enterprises (along with a 1956 or 1957 copright date); you'll know you've found a goldmine.

Due to the very nature of his career, paper items are usually a large part of any 'Elvis' collection. He appeared on the cover of countless magazines. These along with ticket stubs, movie posters, lobby cards, and photographs of all types are sought after today, especially those from before the mid-sixties.

Though you sometime see Elvis 45s with $10.00 to $15.00 price tags, unless the record is in very good to excellent condition this is just not realistic. In fact, the picture sleeve itself (if it's in good condition) will be worth more than the record. The exceptions are, of course, the early Sun label records that collectors often pay $400.00 to $500.00 for, some of the colored vinyls, promotional records, and EPs and LPs with covers and jackets in excellent condition.

Anklets, nylon stretch type, Chester H Roth Co, two pair in unopened package **$125.00**
Bracelet, dog-tag style, 1960s, NM...............................**$20.00**

Calendar, 1963, color bonus included w/Girl's, Girl's, Girls, album $50.00
Calendar, 1986, M **$8.00**
Calendar, 8½x11", 1980, thirteen color photos, EX........**$6.00**
Concert pin, 3", 'Sincerely Elvis'..................................**$10.00**
Game, 'King of Rock'..**$35.00**
Guitar, 'Love Me Tender,' 4-string, Elvis Presley Enterprises, Emenee, complete in original carrying case **$600.00**

Handkerchief, song hit in each corner, Elvis Presley Enterprises, 1956..$125.00
Hat, black & white gabardine w/drawings & song titles in six colors, w/original tag, 1956, M......................**$100.00**
Key chain, dog-tag style w/stamped portrait & signature **$15.00**
Lobby card, 11x14", 'Girl Happy,' 1965, EX **$30.00**
Lobby card, 11x14", 'King Creole,' 1958......................**$35.00**
Lobby card, 11x14", 'Speedway'....................................**$15.00**
Lobby card, 14x11", 'Love Me Tender,' 1956, EX........**$35.00**
Magazine, 'Elvis Presley Speaks!,' Rave Publishing Corp, 1956, EX...**$40.00**
Magazine, 'Look,' August 7, 1956..................................**$35.00**

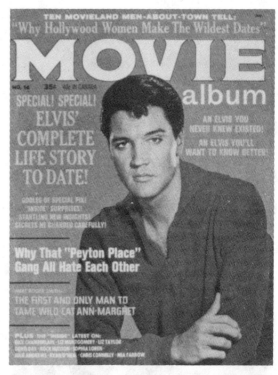

Magazine, 'Movie Album #16,' 1965, contained the article 'Elvis' (complete life story to date), EX.....$25.00
Magazine, 'Photoplay,' July 1957 ....**$35.00**

Magazine, 'Teenage Rock & Roll Review,' Elvis cover, October 1956, NM..**$40.00**

Magazine, 'TV & Movie Screen,' February 1960...........**$15.00**

Menu, 11x14", Elvis cover, menu printed on back, Las Vegas Hilton, 1975, M..**$15.00**

Necklace, dog-tag style, marked Elvis Presley Enterprises, ca late 1950s...**$35.00**

Paper dolls, Elvis & Priscilla, 1st edition, uncut.........**$125.00**

Pennant, 'I Love Elvis,' felt, early..................................**$45.00**

Perfume, Teddy Bear, copyright 1957, Elvis Presley Enterprises, M, sealed..**$125.00**

Photo, 11¾x11¾", color portrait in Arab clothes, from 'Harum Scarum' album (included w/album for limited time)...**$25.00**

Photo, 5x7", black & white w/signature.....................**$300.00**

Pin-back button, 3", 'Best Wishes, Elvis,' color on celluloid, 1956 Elvis Presley Ent, Kim Cioffi, Philadelphia ...**$55.00**

Post card, 3½x5½", Christmas 1967, Elvis portrait in light suit **$20.00**

Press book, 'Roustabout,' 1964, EX..............................**$40.00**

Press book, 12x17", 'Double Trouble,' MGM, 1967, 12 pages, w/11x17" preview flyer, M **$25.00**

Print, 20x16", from painting by June Kelly, color, 1960s ..**$35.00**

Record sleeve, 'Jailhouse Rock'.....................................**$50.00**

Scarf, 28x28", Elvis Summer Festival, portrait in each corner, M **$120.00**

Sheet music, 'Good Luck Charm'...................................**$20.00**

Tape measure, heart shape, promotional item for 1977 Portland Maine concert, EX..**$7.50**

Tour photo album, 8½x11", black & white photos on 16 pages, 1972..**$20.00**

Wallet, vinyl, Elvis Presley Enterprises, All Rights Reserved, 1956 ....**$150.00**

Yearbook, 'The Hound Dog News,' 1956, EX.............**$25.00**

Erphila

Items marked Erphila were imported from various manufacturers by the Philadelphia marketing company, Ebeling and Ruess. They sold porcelain and ceramic items such as art pottery, figurines, kitchenwares, and novelties to which they added their own marks and paper labels.

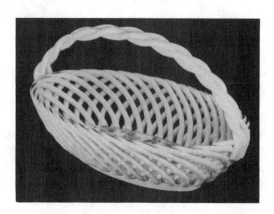

Basket, 2x8½", openweave w/flowers in bottom .$75.00

Basket, 3¾", brown, blue, & green, porcelain, deer handle, Made in Germany **$22.50**

Biscuit jar, yellow, red berries w/leaves on lid...........**$48.00**

Bottle, white porcelain, bulbous, w/gold stopper, Made in Germany **$28.50**

Candlestick, child on base, Made in Germany............**$32.00**

Candlestick, 5¾", red & blue flowers on white, handle, Made in Germany **$22.00**

Creamer, 4", green, white, & black, cat handle, Made in Germany **$45.00**

Creamer, 4½", standing cow, multicolor spots............**$38.00**

Creamer, 5½", black & tan, horse & wagon, w/lid.........**$85.00**

Dish, tartan plaid (2-color), divided, w/handle **$45.00**

Figurine, cat, 10½" long, white w/gold ball, Made in Germany **$120.00**

Figurine, fox, 8½" long, brown, crouching, Made in Germany **$95.00**

Figurine, German shepherd, 6", tan & brown, Made in Germany **$42.00**

Figurine, lion, 3" long, tan, Made in Germany............**$10.00**

Figurine, parrots (pr), 6½", on tree stump, blue & green, Made in Germany **$52.00**

Figurine, pirate, 4", parrot on shoulder, Made in Germany **$15.00**

Figurine, rooster, 11¾", white, silver label **$40.00**

Figurine, spaniel, 6", brown & white, sitting, Made in Germany **$45.00**

Jelly dish, multicolor fruit, w/lid & short spoon, Made in Germany **$25.00**

Mug, 4¼", red, Toby type...**$35.00**

Pitcher, 5½", orange & green flowers **$22.00**

Pitcher, 5½", orange flowers on green, w/lid & underplate..**$35.00**

Planter, 3x5¼", Oriental scene, Italy...........................**$25.00**

Planter, 5", gold & brown, campfire silhouette...........**$50.00**

Plate, 9", Black Forest, grapes on majolica, Made in Germany **$160.00**

Salt & pepper shakers, Dutch man & woman, pr........**$18.00**

Salt & pepper shakers, 5", black dots on white, pr **$30.00**

Sprinkling can, 5½", porcelain, orange poppies on white **$45.00**

Toothpick holder, 3½", black & white dog by tub......**$17.00**

Vase, 10", orange, bulbous, Czech Art Pottery............**$55.00**

Vase, 5⅜", multicolored flowers.................................**$35.00**

Farberware

Louis and Harry Farber established Farber Brothers in 1915 in New York City. They specialized in metalcrafting and in the early days produced hollowware in a variety of finishes. Some were nickle or silverplated, while others were made of solid brass. Fruit bowls, smoking articles, and accessory items of all types were popular.

When chromium plating was developed in the late twenties, the company began to use the new material to a very large extent. They patented a special type of snap-on fastener that allowed metal holders to be used with glass and china inserts. The inserts could be replaced with ease in case of accidental breakage. Their innovations met with immediate approval, and their line of products sold well for years through leading department and gift shops all across the country. But fashion is fickle. By the fifties, the market for chromium-plated ware had fallen off dramatically, and the public once again showed a preference for silverplating. The glass industry had suffered as well during this time, and few companies remained to supply them with their inserts. By 1965, the Farber Brothers' company had closed.

Nearly every piece was marked, but even the few that weren't should be easy to identify, once you become familiar with their patterns. Most of the glassware inserts were made by the Cambridge company, though several other glass companies were involved on a much smaller scale.

When you buy, check for signs of deterioration to the clip-on as well as to the surface. Replating, though it can be done, is often very expensive. If you need to clean a piece, take note of the finish and use an appropriate cleaning product.

Bonbon, 2¼x5½" dia, chrome holder, amethyst glass insert, Cambridge $20.00
Butter dish, 2¼x5½", chrome holder w/etched tulips in each corner, amber glass insert, Cambridge $12.50
Cake basket, 6½x12" dia, chrome frame w/handle, Princess Feather pattern, Westmoreland $20.00
Candlesticks, 6⅝", 4" dia at base, chrome holder w/embossed tulips on base, royal blue glass insert, Cambridge, pr $35.00
Candy dish, 3½x5½" dia, chrome holder, umbrella design on lid, amber glass insert, Cambridge........................$24.00

Centerpiece, compote on tray w/attached candle holders **$125.00**
Compote, 5½x5½" dia, clip-on brass holder, amethyst glass insert, Cambridge..$30.00
Compote, 5¼x5" dia, chrome base & stem, crystal bowl, Caribbean pattern, Duncan & Miller.....................$20.00
Compote, 5¾x5½" dia, screw-on chrome base, ruby flashed glass insert w/crystal stem, Duncan & Miller $16.00

Compote, 7½x5½" dia, chrome holder w/open stem, amethyst glass insert, Cambridge..........................$24.50
Compote, 7x4" dia, chrome holder, frosted glass insert, Lotus pattern, Westmoreland................................$15.00
Cordial, 2⅞", 1-oz, chrome holder, royal blue glass insert, Cambridge $10.00
Cordial, 4", 1-oz, chrome holder, royal blue glass insert, Cambridge $8.50
Cordial, 4¼", 1-oz, brass holder, amethyst flared glass insert, Cambridge $12.50
Decanter, 11¼", 24-oz, chrome holder, faceted stopper, forest green glass insert, Cambridge..........................$28.00
Decanter, 8", 12-oz, chrome holder, amber glass insert, Cambridge $25.00
Pickle dish, 4½x5½", chrome holder, amber glass insert, Cambridge $14.50
Pitcher, 7½", 76-oz, chrome holder, amber glass insert, Cambridge..$45.00
Relish dish, 12½" dia, chrome tray w/clear glass insert, five compartments, Indiana Glass $18.50
Salt & pepper shakers, 3½", chrome holder & tray, royal blue glass insert, Cambridge $25.00
Sherbert, 3¾", 6-oz, chrome holder, amber glass insert, Cambridge, set of six...$14.50
Tumbler, 5", 12-oz, chrome holder, royal blue flared glass insert, Cambridge...$10.50
Wine glass, 4⅛", 4½-oz, footed chrome holder, forest green glass insert, Cambridge................................$10.50

Fast Food Toys and Figurines

Since the late 1970s, fast food chains have been catering to their very young customers through their kiddie meals. The toys tucked in each box or bag have made a much longer lasting impression on the kids than any meal could. Today it's not just kids but adults (sometimes entire families) who're clammoring for them. They're after not only the kiddie meal toys but also boxes, promotional signs used by the restaurant, the promotional items themselves (such as Christmas ornaments you can buy for 99¢, a collector plate, a glass tumbler, or a stuffed animal), or the 'under 3' (safe for children under 3) toys their toddler customers are given on request.

There have been three kinds of promotions: 1) national — every restaurant in the country offering the same item, 2) regional, and 3) test market. While, for instance, a test market box might be worth $20.00, a regional box might be $10.00, and a national, $1.00. Supply dictates price.

To be most valuable, a toy must be in the original package, just as it was issued by the restaurant. Beware of dealers trying to 'repackage' toys in plain plastic bags. Most original bags were printed or contained an insert card. Vacuform containers were quickly discarded, dictating a premium price of $10.00 minimum. Toys without the original packaging are worth only about half or less than those mint in package.

Toys representing popular Disney characters draw

cross-collectors, so do Star Trek, My Little Pony, and Barbie toys. It's not always the early items that are the most collectible, because some of them may have been issued in such vast amounts that there is an oversupply of them today. At the same time, a toy only a year or so old that might have been quickly withdrawn due to a problem with its design will already be one the collector will pay a good price to get.

This is an area that can afford you lots of fun at very low prices, and what else can you collect that you get a free burger with? If you'd like to learn more about fast food collectibles, we recommend *The Illustrated Collector's Guide to McDonald's® Happy Meal® Boxes, Premiums, and Promotions©* by Joyce and Terry Losonsky.

McDonald's Corporation

Bib, Ronald w/bear in highchair, 1986 ....**$1.00**
Boat, rubber-band propelled, 1981 ....**$10.00**
Book, 'Little Golden Poky Little Puppy,' 1982 ....**$5.00**
Bracelet, Star Trek, blue, 1979 ....**$15.00**
Calendar, 'Secret Solver,' 1979 ....**$10.00**
Car, Team McDonald Fry Guy Happy Car, turquoise, 1984 ....**$1.50**
Changeables, Big Mac Sandwich to robot, blue & yellow, 1987 ....**$2.50**
Changeables, Chicken McNuggets to robot, 1987 ....**$2.50**
Comb, Grimace, red, 1980 ....**$1.00**
Cookie cutter, Grimace, red, 1980 ....**$1.00**

Doll, Baby Fozzie Bear, stuffed plush w/green scarf, 1988 ....**$4.00**
Doll, Baby Kermit, red hat & plaid vest, 1988 (illustrated) **$4.00**
Doll, Early Bird, stuffed cloth w/goggles, marked Dakin, 1984 ....**$20.00**
Doll, 21", Ronald w/whistle, vinyl w/cloth body, 1978 ..**$15.00**
Doll, 5", Hamburglar, marked Remco, 1976 ....**$17.50**
Eraser, Hamburglar, black & white, 1984 ....**$2.00**
Game, 'Fishin' Fun w/Captain Crook,' has hook w/eight fish, 1979 ....**$3.00**

Game, Milton Bradley, 1975, complete, in original box, M **$30.00**
Happy Meal box, Olympic Sports I series, 'Boats Afloat,' 1984 ....**$3.00**
Happy Meal box, Olympic Sports II series, 'Hilarious Hurdles,' 1988 ....**$2.00**
Happy Meal box, Sailors series, 'Fishy Crossword,' 1987 ..**$2.00**
Happy Meal box, Star Trek Meal series, Klingons, 1979 .**$17.50**
Pin-back button, 1½", Mac Tonight at keyboard, 1988 ..**$1.50**
Pin-back button, 3½", 'Make It America's Choice...Large Fries,' red, white & blue on tin, 1980s **$2.00**

Other Fast Food Chains

Arby's, box, Kenya w/Babar, giraffe & ostrich, EX **$2.50**
Arby's, car, Babar's World Tour, Zephir in blue & white car, M **$3.50**
Arby's, car, Looney Tunes, Slush Musher (Tasmanian Devil), EX **$2.00**
Arby's, figurine, Looney Tunes, Bugs Bunny as Santa Claus, in original package, M **$4.50**
Arby's, figurine, Looney Tunes, Roadrunner, EX **$2.50**
Arby's, finger puppet, Babar's World Tour, Babar **$3.00**
Arby's, finger puppet, Babar's World Tour, Queen Celeste, pink **$3.00**
Burger King, ball, 1½", Alvin the Chipmunk, rubber, in original package, M **$5.50**
Burger King, book, Golden Jr Classic series, 'My Little Book of Trains,' EX **$2.50**
Burger King, box, Matchbox fire station, ca 1989, NM ..**$2.50**
Burger King, car, Archie series, Veronica in purple car, EX **$3.00**
Burger King, car, Matchbox, Corvette, yellow, in original package, M **$6.00**
Burger King, doll, 13", Marvelous Magical Burger King, NM **$10.00**
Burger King, figurine, Action series, Kid Vid, in original package, M **$4.50**
Burger King, figurine, Beauty & the Beast, Chip the teacup, gray plastic, in original package, M **$8.00**
Burger King, figurine, Belle from Beauty & the Beast, yellow plastic, in original package, M **$7.50**
Burger King, figurine, Bone Age, Fangra, dark brown plastic dinosaur, EX **$3.00**
Burger King, figurine, Capitol Critters series, Max in Jefferson Memorial, in original package, M **$4.50**
Burger King, figurine, Freaky Fella series, plastic w/roll of Life Savers candy, in original package, M **$4.50**
Burger King, figurine, Teenage Mutant Ninja Turtle series, Leonardo, EX **$3.50**
Burger King, figurine, The Simpsons series, Homer w/skunk, in original package, M **$5.00**
Burger King, puppet, Many Faces of Alf series, Cooking w/Alf, NM **$6.00**
Burger King, stickers, Alvin the Chipmunk Adventure, M ..**$2.50**
Burger King, stuffed plush doll, Rodney Reindeer, M ...**$5.00**
Burger King, trick or treat bag, McGruff Crimefighter, 1991, in original package, M **$3.00**

Denny's, car, Dino Racer series, Bamm-Bamm, green, EX....................$3.00

Denny's, cards, Jetson's Space series, Astronomers, in original package, M...................$4.00

Denny's, stuffed plush doll, 4", Flintstones, Betty & Barney Rubble, together in original package, M...................$6.00

Domino's, figurine, Noid series, He Man, in original package, M...................$6.00

Domino's, figurine, Noid series, Hunchback, EX..........$4.50

Frisch's Big Boy, game, 'Bunny Ring Toss,' in original package, M...................$5.00

Hardee's, book, Little Golden Book series, 'Little Red Caboose,' NM...................$5.00

Hardee's, book, Little Golden Book series, 'The Three Bears,' EX...................$2.50

Hardee's, book w/record, Gremlin Adventures series, 'The Gift of the Mogwai,' EX...................$4.00

Hardee's, car, Fender Bender 500 Racers series, Yogi & Boo-Boo in picnic-basket racer, EX...................$3.50

Hardee's, car, Thunder Racers series, Mellow Yellow #51, black & green, M...................$5.00

Hardee's, figurine, Beach Bunnies series, male bunny on skateboard, EX...................$2.50

Hardee's, figurine, Raisin Men series, complete set of 4, EX...................$20.00

Hardee's, figurine, Surfin' Surfs series, Papa on red surf board, EX...................$3.50

Hardee's, stuffed cloth toy, Pound Puppies series, tan w/black ears, EX...................$2.50

Hardee's, stuffed plush doll, Shirt Tales series, Digger, EX...................$3.50

Kentucky Fried Chicken, record, 33rpm, 'Christmas Eve w/Colonel Sanders,' RCA, 1967, in color jacket, EX...................$22.50

Long John Silver's, box, Treasure Chest, ca 1990.........$1.50

Long John Silver's, car, fish form, yellow plastic, M......$2.50

Long John Silver's, kaleidoscope, Sea Watchers series, orange, miniature, EX...................$5.00

Pizza Hut, puppet, Land Before Time series, Ducky, green & yellow rubber, EX...................$5.00

Shoney's, stuffed plush doll, Shoney Bear, EX.............$3.50

Taco Bell, figurine, Hugga Bunch series, Fluffer, stuffed plush, EX...................$3.50

Wendy's, book, World Wild Life series, 'All About Tigers,' EX...................$2.50

Wendy's, box, Yogi Bear & Friends, NM...................$2.50

Wendy's, car, Fast Food Races series, Hamburger, EX..$3.00

Wendy's, figurine, All Dogs Go to Heaven series, Itchy w/green vest & hat, NM...................$3.00

Wendy's, figurine, Meet the Jetsons, Judy on yellow base w/wheels, in original package, M...................$5.50

Wendy's, figurine, 3", California Raisins series, Raisin w/microphone, plastic, EX...................$5.00

Wendy's, finger puppet, Fingles series, green mold w/blue playdough, in original package, M...................$4.50

Wendy's, stuffed plush doll, 7", Furkins series, Farrell wearing plaid shirt & jeans, stuffed plush, M...................$6.00

Wendy's, stuffed plush Koala bear, World Wild Life series, M...................$5.00

Hardee's, stuffed toy, Pound Puppies, MIB............$6.50

Hardee's, toy, 6", Raisin Men series, lady w/yellow shoes, plush, EX...................$3.00

Kentucky Fried Chicken, bank, 9½", figural Colonel Sanders, painted plastic, ca 1968, NM...................$37.50

Fenton Glass

Located in Williamstown, West Virgina, the Fenton company is still producing glassware just as they have since the early part of the century. Nearly all fine department stores and gift shops carry a broad line of their beautiful products, many of which rival examples of finest antique glassware. The fact that even their new glassware has collectible value attests to its fine quality.

Over the years they have made many lovely colors in scores of lines, several of which are very extensive. Paper labels were used exclusively until 1970; since then some pieces have been made with a stamped-in logo.

Numbers in the descriptions correspond with catalog numbers used by the company. Collectors use them as a means of identifying subtle variations, such as a goblet with a particular style of stem. If you'd like to learn more about the subject, we recommend *Fenton Glass, The Second Twenty-Five Years*, by William Heacock.

Aqua Crest, basket, #1923, 10" **$70.00**
Aqua Crest, tidbit tray, 3-tier **$65.00**
Aqua Crest, vase, 4", tulip form **$30.00**
Beaded Melon, bottle, scent; #711, 4½", lime overlay.**$60.00**
Beaded Melon, rose bowl, 3½", blue overlay **$20.00**
Beaded Melon/Peach Crest, basket, 7" **$80.00**
Big Cookies, basket, #1681, jade green.....................**$110.00**
Black Rose, vase, #5155, 10½", hand form...............**$195.00**
Blue Overlay, basket, #1924, 5" dia **$48.00**
Burmese, vase, 11", tulip form **$75.00**
Chinese Yellow, bowl, #1663, 13", oval **$110.00**
Coin Dot, atomizer, French opalescent **$34.00**
Coin Dot, bowl, #203, 6", honeysuckle opalescent **$45.00**
Coin Dot, cruet, #208, 7", French opalescent.............**$75.00**
Coin Dot, tumbler, #1447, 12-oz, cranberry opalescent .**$25.00**
Coin Dot, vase, 7", cranberry opalescent, tricorner **$60.00**
Daisy & Button, cigarette holder, #1900, blue opalescent..**$38.00**
Daisy & Button, console set, #1904, milk glass, 3-pc ..**$40.00**
Dancing Ladies, vase, #901, ruby, scalloped rim.......**$295.00**
Dancing Ladies, vase, #901, 8½", Mongolian Green..**$185.00**
Diamond Lace, epergne, 11", French opalescent.......**$145.00**
Diamond Lace, jug, #192, 6", ruby overlay **$45.00**
Diamond Optic, vase, #1502, 8½", ruby, fan form.......**$38.00**
Dolphin, bowl, #1608, jade green, oval, footed...........**$95.00**
Dolphin, bowl, 6", jade green, handles.......................**$22.00**
Dolphin, compote, 7½", orchid, footed.......................**$55.00**
Dot Optic, plate, 8", blue opalescent **$145.00**
Ebony, bowl, #607, 8", cupped....................................**$60.00**
Emerald Crest, bowl, heart shape **$40.00**
Emerald Crest, flowerpot, #401, 4½", attached saucer.**$45.00**
Flame, candlesticks, #449, 8¾", hexagonal, pr..........**$145.00**
Georgian, claret, #1611, 4½-oz, ruby.........................**$18.00**
Georgian, cup, #1611, 3¼" dia, ruby..........................**$18.00**
Georgian, tumbler, #1611, Moonstone........................**$18.00**
Gold Crest, vase, #1924, 4", double crimped..............**$40.00**
Grape & Cable, bowl, #935, ruby, non-iridescent.......**$48.00**
Hanging Hearts, vase, 14", blue...................................**$150.00**
Hobnail, ash tray, 5½", French opalescent, fan form...**$37.50**
Hobnail, basket, #3837, 7", cranberry opalescent.......**$65.00**
Hobnail, basket, 10", cranberry opalescent...............**$145.00**
Hobnail, basket, 4½", blue opalescent **$45.00**
Hobnail, bone dish, topaz opalescent, crescent form .**$35.00**
Hobnail, bottle, cologne; 4", cranberry opalescent......**$50.00**

Hobnail, bowl, fruit; 12", milk glass, oval **$20.00**

Hobnail, bowl vase, 5x5½", cranberry opalescent ..**$58.00**
Hobnail, candlesticks, 6", blue opalescent, cornucopia form, pr...**$90.00**
Hobnail, candy dish, French opalescent, footed..........**$45.00**
Hobnail, creamer & sugar bowl, small, blue opalescent ..**$45.00**
Hobnail, cruet, 6", cranberry opalescent **$68.00**
Hobnail, goblet, water; blue opalescent.......................**$32.00**
Hobnail, marmalade set, French opalescent, 4-pc.....**$110.00**
Hobnail, pitcher, water; milk glass, crimped **$40.00**
Hobnail, salt & pepper shakers, French opalescent, flat, pr...**$35.00**
Hobnail, salt & pepper shakers, French opalescent, footed, pr...**$70.00**
Hobnail, tumbler, 15-oz, 5", green opalescent.............**$25.00**
Hobnail, vase, #389, 4½", blue opalescent..................**$32.00**
Hobnail, vase, 15", blue opalescent, footed, irregular free-form top...**$75.00**
Hobnail, vase, 5", cranberry opalescent, cupped **$60.00**
Hobnail, vase, 5", topaz opalescent.............................**$40.00**
Hobnail, vase, 6", French opalescent, conical.............**$14.00**
Ivory Crest, candlesticks, #1522, cornucopia form, pr.**$50.00**
Jade Green, bowl, 17", oval, handles **$95.00**
Jade Green, macaroon jar, #1681...............................**$110.00**
Lincoln Inn, cup & saucer, cobalt................................**$25.00**
Lincoln Inn, sherbet, 4¾", cobalt **$25.00**
Lincoln Inn, tumbler, 5¼", ruby, footed **$28.00**
Mandarin Red, ginger jar, #893, gold dragon, ebony lid & foot **$265.00**
Melon Rib, vase, 8½", rose overlay..............................**$20.00**
Melon Rib/Silver Crest, bottle, scent; 7", w/stopper **$32.00**
Ming Green, pitcher, #1653, 10"..................................**$90.00**
Mongolian Green, vase, #847, 5" dia...........................**$70.00**
Peach Crest, basket, #192, 10", milk glass handle **$160.00**
Peach Crest, bowl, #203, 7½" sq.................................**$38.00**
Peach Crest, jug, #192, handle **$55.00**
Peach Crest, vase, 8½", double crimped.....................**$40.00**
Periwinkle Blue, vase, #847, 6½", crimped **$62.50**
Plymouth, goblet, wine; red..**$20.00**

Plymouth, highball, #1620, 8-oz, amber **$18.00**
Polka Dot, salt & pepper shakers, 3", cranberry opalescent, pr...**$65.00**
Rib Optic, creamer & sugar bowl, #1604, green opalescent...**$85.00**
Rose Crest, jug, handle...**$45.00**
Rose Overlay, basket, #1924, 5".................................**$60.00**
Royal Blue, candle holder, #848, 4" dia.....................**$15.00**
Ruby Overlay, bottle, scent; #192A............................**$40.00**
San Toy, bowl, #349, 8½", etched decoration............**$40.00**
Sheffield, bowl, #1800, 12", French opalescent, crimped **$38.00**
Sheffield, tumbler, #1800, 4¼", ruby.........................**$20.00**
Silver Crest, basket, 7½" **$36.00**
Silver Crest, cake salver, 13"......................................**$35.00**
Silver Crest, fruit stand, 11", tall **$20.00**
Silver Crest, plate, 6"..**$10.00**
Silver Crest, tumbler, 6", footed **$25.00**
Silvertone, pitcher, iced tea; #1352, crystal **$70.00**
Silvertone, pitcher, iced tea; #1352, etched...............**$68.00**
Spiral, vase, #3160, 6½", cranberry opalescent **$50.00**
Swan, bonbon, #5, green or pink, each **$20.00**
Swirled Feather, fairy lamp, #2090, cranberry opalescent **$180.00**
Vasa Murrhina, pitcher, small, Autumn Orange..........**$66.00**
Vasa Murrhina, vase, #6457, 7", Rose Mist, fan form...**$60.00**
Vasa Murrhina, vase, #6459, 14", Blue Mist................**$95.00**
Water Lily & Cattail, bowl, purple opalescent, 9" **$68.00**

Wild Rose, vase, 7½", vertically ribbed, white cased, ruffled top, ca 1961-62 ....$50.00
Wistaria, candlesticks, 8", purple iridescent, pr.........**$110.00**
Wistaria, vase, #349, 8", white satin, fan form **$38.00**

Fiesta

You still can find Fiesta, but it's hard to get a bargain. Since it was discontinued in 1973, it has literally exploded onto the collectibles scene; and even at today's prices, new collectors continue to join the ranks of the veterans.

Fiesta is a line of solid-color dinnerware made by the Homer Laughlin China Company of Newell, West Virginia. It was introduced in 1936 and was immediately accepted by the American public. The line was varied; there were more than fifty items offered, and the color assortment included red (orange-red), cobalt, light green, and yellow. Within a short time, ivory and turquoise were added. (Of these 'original' colors, red and cobalt are higher.)

As tastes changed during the production years, old colors were retired and new ones added. The colors collectors refer to as 'fifties' colors are dark green, rose, chartreuse, and gray and today these are very desirable. Medium green was introduced in 1959 at a time when some of the old standard shapes were being discontinued. Today, medium green pieces are the most expensive. Most pieces are marked. Plates were ink stamped, and molded pieces usually had an indented mark.

In 1986, Homer Laughlin reintroduced Fiesta, but in colors different than the old line: white, black, cobalt, rose (bright pink), and apricot. Many of the pieces had been restyled, and the only problem collectors have had with the new colors is with the cobalt. But if you'll compare it with the old, you'll see that it is darker. Turquoise, periwinkle blue, yellow, and seamist green have since been added, and though the turquoise is close, it is a little greener than the original.

New items that have not been restyled are being made from the original molds. This means that you may find pieces with the old mark in the new colors. When an item has been restyled, new molds had to be created, and these will have the new mark. So will any piece marked with the ink stamp. The new mark is a script 'FIESTA' (all letters upper case), while the old is 'Fiesta.' Compare a few, the difference is obvious. Just don't be fooled into thinking you've found a rare cobalt juice pitcher or individual sugar and creamer set, they just weren't made in the old line.

For further information, we recommend *The Collector's Encyclopedia of Fiesta* by Sharon and Bob Huxford.

Ashtray, '50s colors **$52.00**
Ashtray, original colors...**$32.00**
Ashtray, red or cobalt...**$40.00**
Bowl, covered onion soup; cobalt & ivory...............**$275.00**
Bowl, covered onion soup; red **$300.00**
Bowl, covered onion soup; turquoise....................**$1,200.00**
Bowl, covered onion soup; yellow or light green.....**$225.00**
Bowl, cream soup; '50s colors **$40.00**
Bowl, cream soup; medium green, minimum value..**$1,200.00**
Bowl, cream soup; original colors **$25.00**
Bowl, cream soup; red or cobalt.................................**$35.00**
Bowl, dessert; 6", '50s colors......................................**$35.00**
Bowl, dessert; 6", medium green................................**$190.00**
Bowl, dessert; 6", original colors **$25.00**
Bowl, dessert; 6", red or cobalt..................................**$32.00**
Bowl, footed salad; original colors...........................**$160.00**
Bowl, footed salad; red or cobalt **$190.00**

Bowl, fruit; 11¾", original colors	$105.00
Bowl, fruit; 11¾", red or cobalt	$140.00
Bowl, fruit; 4¾", '50s colors	$22.00
Bowl, fruit; 4¾", medium green	$180.00
Bowl, fruit; 4¾", original colors	$18.00
Bowl, fruit; 4¾", red or cobalt	$22.00
Bowl, fruit; 5½", '50s colors	$26.00
Bowl, fruit; 5½", medium green	$50.00
Bowl, fruit; 5½", original colors	$18.00
Bowl, fruit; 5½", red or cobalt	$22.00
Bowl, individual salad; 7½", medium green	$62.00
Bowl, individual salad; 7½", red, turquoise & yellow	$50.00
Bowl, nappy; 8½", '50s colors	$36.00
Bowl, nappy; 8½", medium green	$60.00
Bowl, nappy; 8½", original colors	$25.00
Bowl, nappy; 8½", red or cobalt	$35.00
Bowl, nappy; 9½", original colors	$30.00
Bowl, nappy; 9½", red or cobalt	$40.00
Bowl, Tom & Jerry; ivory w/gold letters	$120.00
Candle holder, bulb; original colors, pr	$52.00
Candle holder, bulb; red or cobalt, pr	$65.00
Candle holder, tripod; original colors, pr	$200.00
Candle holder, tripod; red, cobalt, or ivory, pr	$245.00
Carafe, original colors	$115.00
Carafe, red or cobalt	$135.00
Casserole, '50s colors	$165.00
Casserole, French; standard colors other than yellow	$300.00
Casserole, French; yellow	$160.00
Casserole, medium green	$240.00
Casserole, original colors	$75.00
Casserole, red or cobalt	$115.00
Coffeepot, '50s colors	$150.00
Coffeepot, demitasse; original colors	$135.00

Coffeepot, demitasse; red, cobalt, or ivory	**$165.00**
Coffeepot, original colors	$95.00
Coffeepot, red or cobalt	$120.00
Compote, sweets; original colors	$34.00

Compote, sweets; red or cobalt	$42.00
Compote, 12", original colors	$75.00
Compote, 12", red or cobalt	$95.00
Creamer, '50s colors	$20.00
Creamer, individual; red	$105.00
Creamer, individual; turquoise	$165.00
Creamer, individual; yellow	$42.00
Creamer, medium green	$35.00
Creamer, original colors	$14.00
Creamer, original colors, stick handled	$22.00
Creamer, red or cobalt	$16.00
Creamer, red or cobalt, stick handled	$25.00
Cup, demitasse; '50s colors	$150.00
Cup, demitasse; original colors	$35.00
Cup, demitasse; red or cobalt	$40.00
Egg cup, '50s colors	$85.00
Egg cup, original colors (except ivory)	$32.00
Egg cup, red, cobalt, or ivory	$40.00
Lid, for mixing bowl #1-#3, any color	$275.00
Lid, for mixing bowl #4, any color	$300.00
Marmalade, original colors	$100.00
Marmalade, red or cobalt	$135.00
Mixing bowl, #1, original colors (except ivory)	$55.00
Mixing bowl, #1, red, cobalt, or ivory	$78.00
Mixing bowl, #2, original colors	$40.00
Mixing bowl, #2, red or cobalt	$52.00
Mixing bowl, #3, original colors	$45.00
Mixing bowl, #3, red or cobalt	$55.00
Mixing bowl, #4, original colors	$50.00
Mixing bowl, #4, red or cobalt	$58.00
Mixing bowl, #5, original colors	$58.00
Mixing bowl, #5, red or cobalt	$62.00
Mixing bowl, #6, original colors (except ivory)	$75.00
Mixing bowl, #6, red, cobalt, or ivory	$82.00
Mixing bowl, #7, original colors (except ivory)	$128.00
Mixing bowl, #7, red, cobalt, or ivory	$145.00
Mug, Tom & Jerry; ivory w/gold letters	$45.00
Mug, Tom & Jerry; original colors	$36.00
Mug, Tom & Jerry; '50s colors	$60.00
Mug, Tom & Jerry; red or cobalt	$52.00
Mustard, original colors	$95.00
Mustard, red or cobalt	$130.00
Pitcher, disk juice; gray	$750.00
Pitcher, disk juice; red	$165.00
Pitcher, disk juice; yellow	$30.00
Pitcher, disk water; '50s colors	$150.00
Pitcher, disk water; medium green	$365.00
Pitcher, disk water; original colors	$60.00
Pitcher, disk water; red or cobalt	$85.00
Pitcher, ice; original colors	$60.00
Pitcher, ice; red or cobalt	$75.00
Pitcher, jug, 2-pt; '50s colors	$70.00
Pitcher, jug, 2-pt, original colors (except ivory)	$38.00
Pitcher, jug, 2-pt, red, cobalt, or ivory	$48.00
Plate, cake; light green or yellow	$300.00
Plate, cake; red or cobalt	$365.00
Plate, calendar; 10", 1954 or 1955	$30.00
Plate, calendar; 9", 1955	$35.00

Plate, chop; 13", '50s colors.................................$40.00
Plate, chop; 13", medium green........................$65.00
Plate, chop; 13", original colors.......................$22.00
Plate, chop; 13", red or cobalt.........................$25.00
Plate, chop; 15", '50s colors.............................$45.00
Plate, chop; 15", original colors.......................$25.00
Plate, chop; 15", red or cobalt.........................$32.00
Plate, compartment; 10½", '50s colors.............$30.00
Plate, compartment; 10½", original colors........$20.00
Plate, compartment; 10½", red or cobalt...........$24.00
Plate, compartment; 12", original colors...........$30.00
Plate, compartment; 12", red or cobalt..............$28.00
Plate, deep; '50s colors...................................$35.00
Plate, deep; medium green...............................$58.00
Plate, deep; original colors..............................$24.00
Plate, deep; red or cobalt................................$34.00
Plate, 10", '50s colors.....................................$34.00
Plate, 10", medium green.................................$55.00
Plate, 10", original colors................................$22.00
Plate, 10", red or cobalt..................................$28.00
Plate, 6", '50s colors..$6.00
Plate, 6", medium green...................................$10.00
Plate, 6", original colors...................................$3.50
Plate, 6", red or cobalt......................................$5.00
Plate, 7", '50s colors..$9.50
Plate, 7", medium green...................................$15.00
Plate, 7", original colors....................................$6.00
Plate, 7", red or cobalt......................................$8.00
Plate, 9", '50s colors.......................................$15.00
Plate, 9", medium green...................................$30.00
Plate, 9", original colors....................................$7.50
Plate, 9", red or cobalt.....................................$14.00
Platter, '50s colors..$32.00
Platter, medium green......................................$60.00
Platter, original colors......................................$20.00
Platter, red or cobalt..$28.00
Salt & pepper shakers, '50s colors, pr..............$28.00
Salt & pepper shakers, medium green, pr..........$48.00
Salt & pepper shakers, original colors, pr..........$15.00
Salt & pepper shakers, red or cobalt, pr............$20.00
Sauce boat, '50s colors....................................$40.00
Sauce boat, medium green...............................$60.00
Sauce boat, original colors...............................$28.00
Sauce boat, red or cobalt.................................$38.00
Saucer, '50s colors...$4.50
Saucer, demitasse; '50s colors.........................$34.00
Saucer, demitasse; original colors....................$10.00
Saucer, demitasse; red or cobalt......................$12.00
Saucer, medium green.......................................$7.50
Saucer, original colors.......................................$2.50
Saucer, red or cobalt...$3.50
Sugar bowl, individual; turquoise....................$160.00
Sugar bowl, individual; yellow..........................$65.00
Sugar bowl, w/lid, 3¼x3½", '50s colors............$36.00
Sugar bowl, w/lid, 3¼x3½", medium green.........$55.00
Sugar bowl, w/lid, 3¼x3½", original colors........$22.00
Sugar bowl, w/lid, 3¼x3½", red or cobalt...........$30.00
Syrup, original colors.....................................$165.00

Syrup, red or cobalt.......................................$190.00
Teacup, '50s colors...$28.00
Teacup, medium green.....................................$32.00
Teacup, original colors.....................................$20.00
Teacup, red or cobalt.......................................$25.00
Teapot, large, original colors............................$80.00
Teapot, large, red or cobalt..............................$95.00
Teapot, medium, medium green.......................$260.00
Teapot, medium, original colors........................$70.00
Teapot, medium, red or cobalt..........................$92.00
Teapot; medium, '50s colors...........................$155.00
Tray, figure-8; cobalt.......................................$45.00
Tray, figure-8; turquoise.................................$135.00
Tray, figure-8; yellow.....................................$150.00
Tray, relish; mixed colors, no red....................$130.00
Tray, utility; original colors..............................$22.00
Tray, utility; red or cobalt................................$28.00
Tumbler, juice; Harlequin yellow, dark green, or chartreuse,
    each..$160.00
Tumbler, juice; original colors..........................$20.00
Tumbler, juice; red or cobalt............................$28.00
Tumbler, juice; rose...$30.00
Tumbler, water; original colors.........................$36.00
Tumbler, water; red or cobalt...........................$40.00

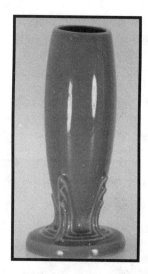

Vase, bud; original colors.................................$38.00
Vase, bud; red or cobalt...................................$50.00
Vase, 10", original colors...............................$350.00
Vase, 10", red or cobalt..................................$425.00
Vase, 12", original colors...............................$425.00
Vase, 12", red or cobalt..................................$535.00
Vase, 8", original colors.................................$265.00
Vase, 8", red or cobalt....................................$350.00

Kitchen Kraft

Bowl, mixing; 10", light green or yellow.............$60.00
Bowl, mixing; 10", red or cobalt........................$70.00
Bowl, mixing; 6", light green or yellow...............$32.00
Bowl, mixing; 6", red or cobalt..........................$38.00
Bowl, mixing; 8", light green or yellow...............$50.00

Bowl, mixing; 8", red or cobalt.....................**$60.00**
Cake plate, light green or yellow.................**$35.00**
Cake plate, red or cobalt.............................**$40.00**
Cake server, light green or yellow..............**$55.00**
Cake server, red or cobalt...........................**$65.00**
Casserole, individual; light green or yellow.............**$90.00**
Casserole, individual; red or cobalt............**$100.00**
Casserole, 7½", light green or yellow.........**$65.00**
Casserole, 7½", red or cobalt......................**$70.00**
Casserole, 8½", light green or yellow.........**$70.00**
Casserole, 8½", red or cobalt......................**$75.00**
Covered jar, large, light green or yellow.................**$160.00**
Covered jar, large, red or cobalt.................**$180.00**
Covered jar, medium, light green or yellow.............**$150.00**
Covered jar, medium, red or cobalt............**$165.00**
Covered jar, small, light green or yellow.................**$145.00**
Covered jar, small, red or cobalt.................**$160.00**

Covered jug, light green or yellow **$140.00**
Covered jug, red or cobalt **$160.00**
Fork, light green or yellow.............................**$45.00**
Fork, red or cobalt.......................................**$50.00**
Metal frame for platter.................................**$20.00**
Pie plate, 10", light green or yellow **$35.00**
Pie plate, 10", red or cobalt.........................**$40.00**
Pie plate, 9", light green or yellow **$30.00**
Pie plate, 9", red or cobalt...........................**$35.00**
Salt & pepper shakers, light green or yellow, pr.........**$60.00**
Salt & pepper shakers, red or cobalt, pr **$70.00**
Spoon, light green or yellow........................**$48.00**
Spoon, red or cobalt....................................**$52.00**
Stacking refrigerator lid, light green or yellow **$40.00**
Stacking refrigerator lid, red or cobalt........**$45.00**
Stacking refrigerator unit, light green or yellow **$25.00**
Stacking refrigerator unit, red or cobalt......**$30.00**

Kay Finch

Wonderful ceramic figurines signed by artist-decorator Kay Finch are among the many that were produced in California during the middle of the century. She modeled her line of animals with much expression and favored soft color combinations. Some of her models were quite large; they range in sizes from 12" down to a tiny 2". She made several animal 'family groups' and, though limited, some human subjects as well.

She used a variety of marks and labels, and though most pieces are marked, some of the smaller animals are not; but you should be able to recognize her work with ease, once you've seen a few marked pieces.

For more information, we recommend *The Collector's Encyclopedia of California Pottery* by Jack Chipman.

Ashtray, incised dog's head, one of a series, plain solid color, flat, stamped mark.......................**$25.00**
Ashtray, 5x7", Song of the Sea **$15.00**
Bank, 10", pig figural w/floral decoration...................**$75.00**
Bank, 5½", English cottage form, dated 1944 ....**$100.00**
Cookie jar, 11¾", Cookie Puss (cat).........................**$175.00**
Figurine, camel, 5" **$85.00**
Figurine, Chanticleer, 10¾", in-mold mark.................**$150.00**
Figurine, Cottontail, 2½", ca 1946 ....**$40.00**

Figurine, dog, 12½", ambrosia glaze **$150.00**
Figurine, elephant, 5"...................................**$45.00**
Figurine, rooster, 8¼".................................**$65.00**
Figurine, Yorky pup, 6¾" **$80.00**
Flower bowl, 2x12¾", modeled as large fish on shell, incised mark.......................................**$25.00**
Salt & pepper shakers, 6", Puss figurals (matches cookie jar), pr.......................................**$45.00**
Vase, 4¼", Santa Claus figural, stamped mark **$45.00**
Vase, 9", solid colored, tapered cylindrical body, 3-footed, incised mark.......................................**$45.00**

Fire-King Dinnerware

This is a new area of collecting interest that you can

enjoy without having to mortgage the home place. In fact, you'll be able to pick it up for a song, if you keep you're eyes peeled at garage sales and swap meets.

Fire King was a tradename of the Anchor Hocking Glass Company, located in Lancaster, Ohio. As its name indicates, this type of glassware is strong enough to stand up to high oven temperatures without breakage. From the early forties until the mid-seventies, they produced kitchenware, dinnerware, and restaurant ware in a variety of colors. (We'll deal with two of the most popular of these colors, peach lustre and jadite, later on in the book.) Blues are always popular with collectors, and Anchor Hocking made two, turquoise blue and azurite (light sky blue). They also made pink, forest green, ruby, gold-trimmed lines, and some with fired-on colors. During the late sixties they made Soreno in avocado green to tie in with home decorating trends.

Bubble (made from the thirties through the sixties) was produced in just about every color Anchor Hocking made. You may also hear this pattern refered to as Provincial or Bullseye.

Alice was an early forties line; it was made in jadite and a white that was sometimes trimmed with blue or red. Cups and saucers were given away in boxes of Mother's Oats, but plates had to be purchased (so they're scarce today).

In the early fifties, they produced a 'laurel leaf' design in peach and 'Laurel Gray' lustres (the gray is scarce), followed later in the decade and into the sixties with several lines made of white glass and decorated with decals — Honeysuckle, Fleurette, Primrose, and Game Bird to name only a few. The same white glass was used for lots of kitchen items such as bowl sets, range shakers, grease jars, etc. decorated in bold designs and colors. (See Kitchen Glassware and Reamers.)

So pick a pattern and get going. These are the antiques of the future! If you'd like to study more about Anchor Hocking's dinnerware, we recommend *Collectible Glassware of the 40s, 50s, and 60s* by Gene Florence.

Alice, cup, embossed florals on white w/blue rim, early 1940s **$7.50**

Alice, plate, 9½", embossed florals on white w/blue rim, early 1940s **$15.00**

Alice, saucer, embossed florals on white w/blue trim, early 1940s **$2.50**

Anchorwhite, bowl, dessert; 4⅞", swirled design, ca 1955-early 1960s **$2.25**

Anchorwhite, plate, dinner; 9⅛", swirled design, ca 1955-early 1960s **$2.75**

Anchorwhite, sugar bowl, swirled design, open handles w/foot, ca 1955-early 60s....................................**$2.50**

Azurite Swirl, bowl, soup; 7⅝", 1956-early 1960s **$4.50**

Blue Mosaic, bowl, dessert; 4⅝", circular mosaic tile design on white, 1967..**$3.50**

Blue Mosaic, bowl, vegetable; 8¼", circular mosaic tile design on white, 1967..**$10.00**

Blue Mosaic, cup, 7½-oz, straight blue sides w/curved handle on white indented base, 1967..........................**$3.50**

Blue Mosaic, plate, dinner; 10", circular mosaic tile design on white, 1967..**$3.00**

Blue Mosaic, plate, salad; 7⅜", circular mosaic design on white, 1967 ....**$3.00**

Blue Mosaic, platter, 9x12", circular mosaic tile pattern on white, 1967 ....**$12.50**

Charm, bowl, salad; 7⅜", Azurite (light blue), square form, Fire-King, 1950-54 ....**$12.50**

Charm, cup, Azurite (light blue), square, Fire-King, 1950-54 ....**$6.50**

Charm, plate, luncheon; 8⅜" square, Azurite (light blue), Fire-King, 1950-54 ....**$7.50**

Charm, saucer, 5⅜" square, Azurite (light blue), Fire-King, 1950-54 ....**$1.50**

Fleurette, bowl, dessert; 4⅝", floral decal on white, 1958-60 ....**$1.50**

Fleurette, bowl, vegetable; 8¼" dia, floral decal on white, 1958-60 ....**$5.00**

Fleurette, plate, salad; 7⅜", floral decal on white, 1958-60 ....**$2.00**

Fleurette, sugar bowl, floral decal on white, 1958-60....**$2.50**

Game Bird, ashtray, 5¼", bird decal on white **$5.00**

Game Bird, bowl, soup; 5", bird decal on white, 1959-62 ....**$5.50**

Game Bird, creamer, bird decal on white, 1959-62 ....**$6.00**

Game Bird, plate, dinner; 9⅛", bird decal on white, 1959-62 ....**$5.00**

Game Bird, tumbler, iced tea; 11-oz, bird decal on white, 1959-62 ....**$6.00**

Golden Anniversary, bowl, vegetable; 8¼" dia, 22k gold trim on swirled sides, 1955-ca 1963................................**$4.75**

Golden Anniversary, plate, serving; 11", 22k gold trim on swirl rim, 1955-ca 1963..**$3.25**

Golden Anniversary, platter, 9x12", 22k gold trim on swirled rim, oval, 1955-ca 1963......................................**$6.00**

Golden Shell, bowl, cereal; 6⅜", scalloped 22k gold trim on white shell design, 1963-late 1970s..........................**$2.00**

Golden Shell, cup, 8-oz, scalloped 22k gold trim at rim, 1963-late 1970s **$3.00**

Golden Shell, plate, dinner; 10", scalloped 22k gold trim on white, 1963-late 1970s..................................**$3.00**

Golden Shell, platter, 9½x13", scalloped 22k gold trim on white, oval, 1963-late 1970s................................**$7.50**

Gray Laurel, bowl, dessert; 4⅞", embossed leaf band around rim, 1952-63 ....**$3.00**

Gray Laurel, creamer, embossed leaf band around sides w/foot, 1952-63 ....**$3.00**

Gray Laurel, plate, dinner; 9⅛", embossed leaf band design about rim, 1952-63 ....**$5.00**

Honeysuckle, platter, 9x12", decal on white, 1958-60...**$8.00**

Honeysuckle, tumbler, iced tea; 12-oz, decal on clear glass, 1958-60..**$5.00**

Honeysuckle, tumbler, juice; 5-oz, decal on clear glass, 1958-60..**$3.00**

Ivory White, platter, 12x9", swirled design, early 1950s-ca 1955 ....**$5.50**

Ivory White, sugar bowl, swirled design, flat base, tab handles, early 1950s-ca 1955 ....**$3.00**

Mugs, 3½", Jadite, Game Bird, & blue **$10.00**
Philbe, bowl, cereal; 5½", crystal **$17.50**
Philbe, bowl, salad; 7¼", pink........................**$45.00**
Philbe, bowl, vegetable; 10", blue, oval **$95.00**
Philbe, cup, crystal...**$35.00**
Philbe, cup, pink or green **$80.00**
Philbe, pitcher, juice; 6", pink or green..............**$600.00**
Philbe, pitcher, 8½", crystal **$350.00**
Philbe, plate, luncheon; 8", pink or green **$25.00**
Philbe, platter, 12", pink or green, w/closed handles .**$60.00**
Philbe, sugar bowl, 3¼", crystal **$35.00**
Philbe, tumbler, iced tea; 6½", blue, footed **$45.00**
Philbe, tumbler, juice; 3½", crystal, footed............**$30.00**
Philbe, tumbler, 5¼", pink or green, footed............**$65.00**
Pie plate, 1½x9" dia, ivory, 1942-50s **$6.50**
Pink Swirl, bowl, vegetable; 7¼", swirled lustre design, 1956-early 1960s **$7.50**
Pink Swirl, plate, dinner; 9⅛", swirled lustre design, 1956-early 1960s **$6.00**
Pink Swirl, platter, 9x12", swirled lustre design, 1956-early 1960s **$12.50**
Primrose, bowl, dessert; 4⅝", floral decal on white, 1960-62 ....**$1.75**
Primrose, bowl, vegetable; 8¼", floral decal on white, 1960-62 ....**$5.50**
Primrose, plate, dinner; 9⅛" dia, floral decal on white, 1960-62 ....**$3.50**
Primrose, platter, 9x12", floral decal on white, 1960-62 ..**$8.00**
Primrose, tumbler, water; 9-oz, floral decal on clear glass, 1960-62................................**$4.00**
Sunrise, plate, dinner; 9⅛", red trim on pink lustre, 1956-early 1960s **$6.00**
Sunrise, platter, 9x12", red trim on pink lustre oval w/swirl design rim, 1956-ca early 1960s **$12.50**
Turquoise Blue, bowl, berry; 4½", 1957-58 .....**$5.00**
Turquoise Blue, bowl, cereal; 5", 1957-58 ....**$8.00**
Turquoise Blue, bowl, vegetable; 8", 1957-58............**$12.50**
Turquoise Blue, cup, 1957-58 ....**$4.00**
Turquoise Blue, divided relish, 7½x11", gold trim ..**$12.00**
Turquoise Blue, egg plate, 9¾", w/gold trim at rim, 1957-58 ....**$12.50**
Turquoise Blue, plate, 9", 1957-58 ....**$6.50**
Turquoise Blue, relish, 11⅛", 3-compartment w/beaded gold trim edge, 1957-58 ....**$10.00**
Turquoise Blue, sugar bowl, 1957-58 ....**$5.00**
Wheat, bowl, vegetable; 8¼", wheat spray on white, 1962-late 1960s................................**$5.50**
Wheat, cup, 8-oz, wheat spray on white, 1962-late 1960s **$3.00**

Wheat, plate, dinner; 10", wheat spray off-center on white, 1962-late 1960s **$3.00**
Wheat, platter, 9x12", wheat spray on white, 1962-late 1960s................................**$8.00**
Wheat, soup; 6⅝", wheat spray in center on white, 1960s-late 1960s **$3.50**
Wheat, sugar bowl, wheat spray on white, handles & lid, 1962-late 1960s **$4.50**

Fire-King Ovenware

Anchor Hocking made ovenware in many the same colors and designs as their dinnerware. Their most extensive line (and one that is very popular today) was made in Sapphire Blue, clear glass with a blue tint, in a pattern called Philbe. Most pieces are still very reasonable, but some are already worth in excess of $50.00, so now is the time to start your collection. Gene Florence's book, *Collectible Glassware of the 40s, 50s, and 60s,* is a good source for more information.

Ivory, baker, individual; 6-oz, round, 1942-50s.............**$2.00**
Ivory, cake pan, 10½x10½", plain, 1942-50s **$10.00**
Ivory, cake pan, 9" dia, plain, 1942-50s.......................**$12.50**
Ivory, casserole, 2-qt, plain, w/lid, 1942-50s...............**$13.00**
Ivory, custard cup, 5-oz, plain, 1942-50s.....................**$2.50**
Ivory, loaf pan, 9⅛", rectangular, tab handles, deep, 1942-50s (also sold as baking pan w/glass lid)..............**$10.00**
Primrose, baking dish, 5x9", floral decal on white, rectangular, w/clear glass lid, 1960-62 ....**$10.00**
Primrose, cake pan, 8", floral decal on white, square, 1960-62 ....**$7.50**
Primrose, casserole, ½-qt, floral decal on white, oval, w/clear glass lid, 1960-62 ....**$12.00**
Sapphire Blue, baker, 2-qt, round, 1942-50s...............**$12.50**
Sapphire Blue, bowl, utility; 6⅞" dia, 1-qt, 1942-50s ...**$10.00**
Sapphire Blue, casserole, 1½-qt, w/knob-handled cover, 1942-50s **$12.50**

Sapphire Blue, casserole, 1-pt, knob-handled cover, 1942-50s **$11.00**
Sapphire Blue, casserole, 2-qt, w/knob-handled cover, 1942-50s (illustrated) **$18.00**
Sapphire Blue, measure, dry; 8-oz, no spout, 1942-50s, rare **$150.00**
Sapphire Blue, measure, liquid; 8-oz, w/spout, 1942-50s **$16.00**
Sapphire Blue, mug, 7-oz, 1942-50s **$21.50**
Sapphire Blue, roaster, 10⅜" long, cover same as bottom (illustrated)................................**$60.00**

Wheat, baking pan, 2x12½x8", wheat sprays on two sides, white, 1962-late 1960s..$10.00

Wheat, baking pan, 5x9", wheat sprays on two sides, white w/clear glass lid, 1962-late 1960s........................$10.00

Wheat, cake pan, 8" dia, wheat spray on white, 1962-late 1960s $7.50

Wheat, casserole, 1½-qt, wheat sprays on white, oval, w/au gratin lid, 1962-late 1960s......................................$12.00

Fishing Lures

This is a hobby that has really caught on over the past five years. There is a national collectors club, newsletters, and several informative books for the serious buyer of old fishing lures.

There have been literally thousands of lures made since the turn of the century. Some have bordered on the ridiculous, and some have turned out to be just as good as the manufacturers claimed. Other than buying outright from a dealer, try some of the older stores in your area — you just might turn up a good old lure. Go through any old tackle boxes that might be around; and when the water level is low, check out the river banks.

If you have to limit your collection, you might want to concentrate strictly on wooden lures, or you might decide to try to locate one of every lure made by a particular company. Whatever you decide, try to get examples with good original paint and hardware.

For further information, we recommend *Old Fishing Lures and Tackle* by Carl F. Luckey.

Al Foss Oriental Wiggler, plastic, glass eyes $12.00

Alcoe Magic Minnow #401, wood, painted eyes, flexible dorsal, ventral, & tail fins..$6.00

Clark's 2600 Series Goofy Gus, metal, pearl w/red eyes, hourglass-shaped body, nose- & tail-mounted propeller spinners $15.00

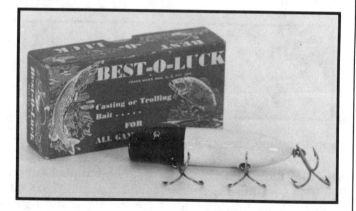

Best-o-Luck, three treble hooks, red & white, in original box $15.00

Creek Chub Champ Spoon, metal, painted eyes.........$20.00

Creek Chub Deluxe Wag Tail, glass eyes, reversible metal lip blade & two belly-mounted double hooks, metal tail fin...$20.00

Creek Chub Jigger, glass eyes, water sonic plug, belly-mounted treble hook & trailing treble hook........$20.00

Creek Chub Plunking Dinger, glass eyes, scale finish w/broom-like hair tail, two treble hooks $15.00

Creek Chub Plunking Diver, wood, glass eyes........$20.00

Creek Chub Weed Bug, glass eyes, frog color, weedless floater w/two single-point trailing hooks.............$30.00

Creek Chub Wiggler, metal, glass eyes, jointed plug w/fluted nickel tail, two belly-mounted treble hooks $8.50

Decker's Plug Bait, wood, no eyes, aluminum propeller blades, three treble hooks....................................$25.00

Decker's Underwater Bait, wood, no eyes, metal propeller spinners, three treble hooks.................................$95.00

Dickens Weedless Wonder, wood, no eyes, screw-eye hook hanger, red feathered tail hook............................$12.50

Dunk's Double Header, flat head w/rotatable metal plate for top or underwater fishing.................................$15.00

Eger's #100 Series Weedless Dillinger, wood, white w/red stripes, single black spinner mounted on wire leader..$4.00

Eger's #300 Series Master Dillinger, wood, white w/red stripes, three treble hooks, nose- & tail-mounted spinners $4.50

Eger's Bull Nose Frog, wood, bulbous nose covered w/real frogskin, three treble hooks $10.50

Fenner's Weedless Automatic Bait, Pyralin, painted eyes, two single hooks...$8.50

Heddon-Stanley Weedless Pork-Rind, Bakelite, glass eyes, wire weed guard & surface attachment.................$20.00

Heddon's #20 Series Dowagiac Minnow, wood, nose-mounted propeller spinner, three treble hooks....$25.00

Heddon's #90 Series Bubble Bug, wood, yellow w/black markings, red painted mouth, yellow feathers......$35.00

Heddon's Crazy Crawler, wood, painted eyes.............$15.00

Heddon's Luny Frog, plastic, painted eyes, frog color..$45.00

Heddon's Moonlight Radiant, wood, glass eyes, bulbous head, four treble hooks....................................$150.00

Heddon's Series #1300 Black Sucker Minnow, glass eyes, rainbow finish, three treble hooks.......................$95.00

Heddon's Series #220 Weedless Widow, wood, bead eyes, bull frog color, detachable double hook on belly..$12.50

Paw Paw Watta Frog, wood, tack eyes $25.00

Paw Paw Weedless Wow, frog finish, rubber legs, fixed double hook...$8.50

Paw Paw Wilson Wobbler, no eyes, rainbow finish, three treble hooks..$5.50

Pepper's Underwater Minnow, wood, yellow glass eyes, reverse gill stripes, three treble hooks...................$65.00

Pflueger's Breakless Devon, metal w/1-blade spinner ..$12.50

Pflueger's Metalized Minnow, three treble hooks, fore & aft propellers...$25.00

Pflueger's TNT, metal, deep-diving metal lip, three treble hooks $20.00

Shakespeare's Bass-Kazoo, metal, no eyes, sloped head, three treble hooks $10.00

Shakespeare's Kazoo, wood, glass eyes, screw-eye hook fastener, three treble hooks $15.00

Shakespeare's Pikie Kazoo, metal w/bendable lip, three treble hooks..**$5.50**
South Bend Min Oreno, wood, tack eyes **$20.00**

South Bend, Surf-O-Reno, yellow..........................$27.50

Florence Ceramics

During the forties, Florence Ward began modeling tiny ceramic children as a hobby at her home in Pasadena, California. She was so happy with the results that she expanded, hired decorators, and moved into a larger building where for two decades she produced the lovely line of figurines, wall plaques, busts, etc. that have become so popular today. The 'Florence Collection' featured authentically detailed models of such couples as Louis XV and Madame Pompadour, Queen Elizabeth and King Arthur, Pinkie and Blue Boy, and Rhett and Scarlett. Nearly all of the Florence figures have names which are written on their bases.

Many figures are decorated with 22k gold and lace. Real lace was cut to fit, dipped in a liquid material called slip, and fired. During the firing it burned away, leaving only hardened ceramic lace trim. The amount of lacework that was used is one of the factors that needs to be considered when evaluating a 'Florence.' Size is another. Though most of the figures you'll find today are singles, a few were made as groups, and once in awhile you'll find a lady seated on a divan. The more complex, the more expensive.

If you'd like to learn more about the subject, we recommend *The Collector's Encyclopedia of California Pottery* by Jack Chipman.

Ballerina, 7", 22k lace-trimmed tutu, stamped mark .**$150.00**
Betty, 4½", reclining mermaid (goes w/bowl)..........**$175.00**
Bowl, 3¼x15¾", seashell form, realistic colors **$45.00**
Brooch, lady's bust **$45.00**
Cynthia, 9¼", blue coat over white dress, 22k gold trim on hat, lace & fur, in-mold mark...............................**$175.00**
Dealer sign, 6¼x5", lady holds large card 'Florence Pasadena Calif,' 22k gold trim, stamped mark....**$300.00**
Flower holder, 7", girl holding skirt, wearing wide-brim hat..**$25.00**
Flower holder, 8¼", girl w/parasol, blue & pink flowers on white dress..**$35.00**

Frame, 4½x6½", applied florals, pink & cream w/gold trim **$45.00**
Girl w/brown hair stands before book planter...........**$35.00**
Kay, 6", 22k gold florals on white gown, overcoat & muff, stamped mark..**$80.00**

Lillian, 7¾", gold trim $100.00
Marie Antoinette, 10", ruffled bodice & tiered skirt, roses w/lace on dress, 22k gold trim, stamped mark ..**$275.00**
Melanie, 7½"...**$65.00**
Priscilla, 7¾", pilgrim lady holds book, light 22k gold trim, stamped mark **$200.00**

Scarlett, 9", lady w/flowers on hat, w/ purse $100.00
Shirley, 8", holds hand-applied compact, rose & fur trim w/22k gold, stamped mark **$150.00**
Victoria, 7x8¼", seated on divan (attached), ribbon, roses & lace trim w/22k gold, in-mold mark...................**$275.00**
Wall pocket, 7", Violet (lady figural), 22k gold trim, stamp mark...**$100.00**

Fostoria

This was one of the major glassware producers of the twentieth century. They were located first in Fostoria, Ohio, but by the 1890s had moved to Moundsville, West Virginia. By the late thirties, they were recognized as the largest producers of handmade glassware in the world. Their glassware is plentiful today and, considering its quality, not terribly expensive.

Though the company went out of business in the mid-eighties, the Lancaster Colony Company continues to use some of the old molds — herein is the problem. The ever-popular American and Coin Glass patterns are currently in production, and even experts have trouble distinguishing the old from the new. Before you invest in either line, talk to dealers. Ask them to show you some of their old pieces. Most will be happy to help out a novice collector. Read *Elegant Glassware of the Depression Era* by Gene Florence. If there is a Fostoria outlet within driving distance, it will be worth your time just to see what is being offered there.

You'll be seeing lots of inferior 'American' at flea markets and (sadly) antique malls. It's often priced as though it were American, but in fact it is not. It's been produced since the 1950s by Indiana Glass who calls it 'Whitehall.' Watch for pitchers with only two mold lines, they're everywhere. (Fostoria's had three.) Remember that Fostoria was handmade, so their pieces were fire polished. This means that if the piece you're examining has sharp, noticeable mold lines, be leery. There are other differences to watch for as well. Fostoria's footed pieces were designed with a 'toe,' while Whitehall feet have a squared peg-like appearance. The rays are sharper and narrower on the genuine Fostoria pieces, and the glass itself has more sparkle and life. And if it weren't complicated enough, the Home Interior Company has recently offered 'American'-like vases, covered bowls, and a footed candy dish that were produced in a foreign country, but at least they've marked theirs. Coin Glass was originally produced in crystal, red, blue, emerald green, olive green, and amber. It's being reproduced today in crystal, green, blue, and red. The green and blue are 'off' enough to be pretty obvious, but the red is close. Beware. Here are some (probably not all) of the items currently in production: bowl, 8" diameter; bowl, 9" oval; candlesticks, 4½"; candy jar w/lid, 6¼"; creamer and sugar bowl; footed comport; wedding bowl, 8¼". Know your dealer!

Numbers included in our descriptions were company-assigned stock numbers that collectors use as a means to distinguish variations in stems and shapes.

American, basket, 7x9", crystal, w/reed handle **$80.00**
American, bottle, cologne; 5¾", crystal, w/stopper **$70.00**
American, bowl, banana split; 3½x9", crystal............**$225.00**
American, bowl, cream soup; 5", crystal, 2-handled ...**$45.00**
American, bowl, fruit; 3x12" dia, crystal, rolled edge.....**$42.50**
American, bowl, preserve; 5½", crystal, w/lid, 2-handled **$80.00**
American, bowl, punch; 14", 2-gal, crystal, high footed base..**$225.00**

American, bowl, relish or celery; 11", crystal, 3-part ...**$30.00**
American, bowl, vegetable; 10", crystal, 2-part, oval...**$25.00**
American, butter dish, ¼-lb, crystal, w/lid **$17.50**
American, cake plate, 10", crystal, 2-handled **$18.00**
American, candlestick, 3", crystal, footed...................**$15.00**
American, candy box, crystal, w/lid, 3-part, triangular..**$65.00**
American, cigarette box, 4¾", crystal, w/lid................**$36.50**
American, comport, jelly; 6¾", crystal, w/lid...............**$30.00**
American, cookie jar, 8⅞", w/lid...............................**$300.00**
American, creamer, 9½-oz, crystal **$11.00**
American, cup, punch; crystal, flared rim **$11.00**
American, decanter, 9¼", 24-oz, crystal, w/stopper.....**$90.00**
American, goblet, claret; 4⅞", 7-oz, #2056 ....**$37.50**
American, goblet, oyster cocktail; 3½", 4-oz, #5056, crystal, w/plain bowl..**$10.00**
American, goblet, sherbet; 3½", 5-oz, #2056½, low.....**$10.00**
American, goblet, sherbet; 4⅜", 4½-oz, #2056, crystal, flared **$9.00**
American, hat, crystal, western style **$175.00**
American, hurricane lamp, 12", crystal, complete **$150.00**
American, ice bucket, crystal, w/tongs.........................**$60.00**
American, jam pot, crystal, w/lid **$50.00**
American, marmalade, crystal, w/lid & chrome spoon .**$35.00**
American, mustard, crystal, w/lid **$27.50**
American, oil, 7-oz, crystal **$32.50**
American, pitcher, 5⅜", 1-pt, crystal, flat....................**$27.50**
American, plate, bread & butter; 6", crystal.................**$12.00**
American, plate, dinner; 9½", crystal **$20.00**
American, plate, torte; 14", crystal **$17.50**
American, sugar bowl; crystal, w/lid **$10.00**
American, tray, appetizer; 10½", crystal, w/six inserts..**$235.00**
American, tray, relish; 6½x9", crystal, 4-part **$40.00**
American, tumbler, juice; 4¾", 5-oz, crystal, #2056 .....**$10.00**
American, vase, bud; 8½", crystal, flared.....................**$20.00**
American, vase, 6½", crystal, flared rim.......................**$15.00**

American, water pitcher, 7" **$55.00**

Baroque, ashtray, crystal..**$7.50**

Baroque, bowl, cream soup; blue..............................**$65.00**

Baroque, bowl, relish; 10", blue, 3-part....................**$30.00**

Baroque, bowl, 12" yellow, flared..............................**$32.50**

Baroque, cake plate, 10", crystal................................**$20.00**

Baroque, candelabrum, 8¼", crystal, 2-light, sixteen lustres..**$85.00**

Baroque, candlestick, 4½", blue, 2-light....................**$55.00**

Baroque, candy dish, yellow, 3-part, w/lid................**$65.00**

Baroque, comport, 4¾", crystal..................................**$15.00**

Baroque, creamer, 3¾", blue, footed..........................**$14.00**

Baroque, cup, yellow..**$20.00**

Baroque, mayonnaise, 5½", crystal, w/liner..............**$15.00**

Baroque, pitcher, 7", blue, w/ice lip........................**$625.00**

Baroque, plate, 7½", yellow..**$10.00**

Baroque, platter, 12", blue, oval................................**$60.00**

Baroque, salt & pepper shakers, yellow, pr..............**$100.00**

Baroque, sherbet, 3¾", 5-oz, yellow..........................**$17.50**

Baroque, sugar bowl, 3½", crystal, footed..................**$6.00**

Baroque, tray, 11", blue, oval......................................**$47.50**

Baroque, tumbler, juice; 3¾", 5-oz, blue....................**$37.50**

Baroque, tumbler, water; 5½", 9-oz, crystal, footed.....**$12.00**

Baroque, vase, 6½", blue..**$125.00**

Century, ash tray, 2¾", crystal......................................**$9.00**

Century, basket, 10¼x6½", crystal, wicker handle.......**$65.00**

Century, bowl, cereal; 6", crystal................................**$22.00**

Century, bowl, salad; 8½", crystal..............................**$22.50**

Century, butter dish, ¼-lb, crystal, w/lid....................**$30.00**

Century, candy dish, 7", crystal, w/lid........................**$32.50**

Century, comport, cheese; 2¾", crystal......................**$17.50**

Century, mustard, crystal, w/spoon & lid....................**$27.50**

Century, pitcher, 7⅛", 48-oz, crystal..........................**$95.00**

Century, plate, dinner; 10½", crystal..........................**$27.50**

Century, plate, luncheon; 8½", crystal........................**$12.50**

Century, salt & pepper shakers, 3⅛", crystal, pr........**$17.50**

Century, stem, cocktail; 4⅛", 3½-oz, crystal..............**$18.00**

Century, sugar bowl, 4", crystal, footed......................**$8.00**

Century, tray, muffin; 9½", crystal, handled..............**$25.00**

Century, tumbler, juice; 4¾", 5-oz, crystal, footed......**$20.00**

Century, vase, bud; 6", crystal....................................**$17.50**

Chintz, bowl, vegetable; 9½", #2496, crystal..............**$65.00**

Chintz, candlestick, 3½", #2496, crystal, double..........**$27.50**

Chintz, candy dish, #2496, crystal, w/lid, 3-part.......**$100.00**

Chintz, celery, 11", #2496, crystal..............................**$32.50**

Chintz, comport, cheese; 3¼", #2496, crystal............**$22.50**

Chintz, cup, #2496, crystal, footed............................**$20.00**

Chintz, dinner bell, crystal..**$100.00**

Chintz, finger bowl, 4½", #869, crystal......................**$40.00**

Chintz, ice bucket, #2496, crystal............................**$125.00**

Chintz, plate, cracker; 11", #2496, crystal..................**$37.50**

Chintz, plate, dinner; 9½", #2496, crystal..................**$45.00**

Chintz, plate, luncheon; 8½", #2496, crystal..............**$20.00**

Chintz, platter, 12", #2496, crystal..............................**$85.00**

Chintz, sauce boat, #2496, crystal, oval......................**$67.50**

Chintz, stem, cordial; 3⅞", 1-oz, #6026, crystal..........**$45.00**

Chintz, stem, sherbet; 4⅜", 6-oz, #6026, crystal, low...**$20.00**

Chintz, sugar bowl, 3½", #2496, crystal, footed..........**$15.00**

Chintz, tray, 11", #2375, crystal, center handle..........**$37.50**

Chintz, tumbler, juice; 5-oz, #6026, crystal, footed......**$25.00**

Chintz, vase, 7½", #4143, crystal, footed..................**$125.00**

Coin Glass, ashtray, green, oblong..............................**$25.00**

Coin Glass, ashtray, 10", blue......................................**$50.00**

Coin Glass, ashtray, 7½" dia, amber............................**$35.00**

Coin Glass, bowl, 8" dia, crystal or olive green (being reproduced in crystal)..**$75.00**

Coin Glass, bowl, 8½", blue, footed, w/lid................**$195.00**

Coin Glass, bowl, 8½", red, footed..............................**$70.00**

Coin Glass, bowl, 9", amber or olive green, oval........**$45.00**

Coin Glass, candle holders, 4½", amber, pr................**$45.00**

Coin Glass, candle holders, 8", red, pr......................**$100.00**

Coin Glass, candy dish, 7", blue, w/lid (being reproduced)..**$50.00**

Coin Glass, candy dish, 7", green, w/lid......................**$75.00**

Coin Glass, candy jar, red....................................$65.00

Coin Glass, cigarette urn, 3⅜", amber, footed............**$25.00**

Coin Glass, cigarette urn, 3⅜", green, footed..............**$35.00**

Coin Glass, cigarette urn, 3⅜", ruby, footed..............**$40.00**

Coin Glass, creamer, blue (being reproduced)............**$22.50**

Coin Glass, creamer, green..**$32.50**

Coin Glass, cruet, 7-oz, amber, w/stopper..................**$70.00**

Coin Glass, cruet, 7-oz, green, w/stopper..................**$150.00**

Coin Glass, cruet, 7-oz, olive green, w/stopper..........**$80.00**

Coin Glass, cup, punch; crystal..................................**$30.00**

Coin Glass, decanter, 10½", amber............................**$120.00**

Coin Glass, decanter, 10½", blue, w/stopper............**$160.00**

Coin Glass, lamp, oil; 16⅝", blue, patio style............**$250.00**

Coin Glass, lamp, oil; 9¾", amber, courting style w/handle..**$100.00**

Coin Glass, lamp, oil; 9¾", blue, courting style w/handle..**$150.00**

Coin glass, nappy, 4½", crystal....................................**$18.00**

Coin Glass, nappy, 5⅜", amber....................................**$25.00**

Coin Glass, pitcher, 32-oz, blue................................**$100.00**

Coin Glass, pitcher, 32-oz, green..............................**$125.00**

Coin Glass, plate, 8", red..**$40.00**

Coin Glass, punch bowl, 1½-gal, crystal....................**$150.00**

Coin Glass, punch bowl base, crystal.........................$150.00
Coin Glass, salt & pepper shakers, 3¼", amber, pr $35.00
Coin Glass, salt & pepper shakers, 3¼", green, pr $90.00
Coin Glass, salt & pepper shakers, 3¼", red, pr $50.00
Coin Glass, sugar bowl, amber, w/lid $35.00
Coin Glass, sugar bowl, blue, w/lid $45.00
Coin Glass, sugar bowl, green, w/lid $60.00
Coin Glass, tumbler, iced tea; 14-oz, crystal $30.00
Coin Glass, tumbler, water; 9-oz, crystal...................$27.50
Coin Glass, vase, bud; 8", blue $50.00
Coin Glass, vase, bud; 8", red $50.00
Coin Glass, vase, 10", crystal, footed $45.00
Colony, ashtray, 3", crystal, round $7.00
Colony, bowl, almond; 2¾", crystal, footed $15.00
Colony, bowl, salad; 7¾", crystal $22.50
Colony, bowl, 10½", crystal, high foot.....................$85.00
Colony, cake plate, 10", crystal, handled $22.00
Colony, candlestick, 7½", crystal, w/eight prisms........$55.00

Colony, candlestick, 9", clear, pr.........................$50.00
Colony, candy dish, ½-lb, crystal, w/lid, footed $60.00
Colony, cheese & cracker, crystal..............................$50.00
Colony, creamer, 3¾", crystal....................................$6.00
Colony, cup, 6-oz, crystal, footed $7.50
Colony, ice bucket, crystal, plain edge.....................$95.00
Colony, mayonnaise, crystal, 3-pc $35.00
Colony, pitcher, milk; 16-oz, crystal $65.00
Colony, plate, bread & butter; 6", crystal.....................$4.00
Colony, platter, 12", crystal.....................................$45.00
Colony, sugar bowl, 3½", crystal.................................$5.00
Colony, tumbler, water; 3⅞", 9-oz, crystal...................$14.00
Colony, vase, bud; 6", crystal, flared $14.00
Colony, wine, 4¼", 3¼-oz, crystal.............................$22.00
Fairfax, baker, 9", amber, oval $15.00
Fairfax, bottle, salad dressing; green $70.00
Fairfax, bowl, centerpiece; 13", amber, oval...............$20.00
Fairfax, bowl, cereal; 6", blue $20.00
Fairfax, bowl, fruit; 5", rose $12.00
Fairfax, bowl, soup; 7", orchid..................................$25.00

Fairfax, butter dish, topaz, w/lid................................$90.00
Fairfax, candlestick, 3", rose....................................$12.50
Fairfax, comport, 7", blue $25.00
Fairfax, cordial, 4", ¾-oz, rose..................................$60.00
Fairfax, cup, after dinner; orchid $22.00
Fairfax, ice bucket, amber.......................................$30.00
Fairfax, oil, green, footed $90.00
Fairfax, pitcher, #5000, topaz.................................$130.00
Fairfax, plate, bread & butter; 6", rose..........................$3.00
Fairfax, plate, chop; 13", amber...............................$14.00
Fairfax, plate, grill; 10¼", orchid $12.00
Fairfax, plate, luncheon; 9½", blue...........................$15.00
Fairfax, platter, 12", green, oval $20.00
Fairfax, relish, 8½", topaz, 3-part...............................$8.00
Fairfax, sherbet, 6", 6-oz, orchid..............................$20.00
Fairfax, sugar bowl, amber, flat $10.00
Fairfax, tray, 11", green, center handle.......................$15.00
Fairfax, tumbler, 6", 12-oz, topaz, footed $18.00
Fairfax, vase, 8", amber $35.00
Fairfax, wine, 5½", 3-oz, blue...................................$30.00
Hermitage, bowl, cereal; 6", #2449½", azure or wisteria ..$14.00
Hermitage, bowl, grapefruit; #2449, amber, green, or topaz,
  w/crystal liner...$35.00
Hermitage, creamer, #2449..$4.00
Hermitage, finger bowl, 4½", #2449½, amber, green, or
  topaz $6.00
Hermitage, mustard, #2449, amber, green, or topaz....$27.50
Hermitage, plate, crescent salad; 7⅜", #2449, azure or wisteria
  ....$25.00
Hermitage, plate, sandwich; 12", #2449, amber, green, or
  topaz $12.50
Hermitage, relish, pickle; 8", #2449, crystal...................$8.00
Hermitage, sherbet, 3¼", 5½-oz, #2449, amber, green, or
  topaz, high foot...$11.00
Hermitage, tumbler, 2½", 2-oz, #2449, crystal...............$5.00
Hermitage, vase, 6", crystal, footed...........................$20.00
June, ashtray, crystal...$23.00
June, bowl, baker; 9", pink or blue, oval......................$85.00
June, bowl, centerpiece; 11", yellow $40.00
June, bowl, cereal; 6", pink or blue $35.00
June, bowl, mint; 5", crystal $11.00
June, candlestick, 2", crystal....................................$10.00
June, candy dish, ½-lb, yellow, w/lid.........................$155.00
June, creamer, pink or blue, footed $25.00
June, finger bowl, yellow, w/liner..............................$25.00
June, goblet, water; 8¼", 10-oz, yellow.......................$35.00
June, ice bucket, crystal...$47.50
June, mayonnaise, pink or blue, w/liner.......................$60.00
June, pitcher, yellow..$300.00
June, plate, bread & butter; 6", pink or blue.................$12.00
June, plate, dinner; 10¼", yellow $55.00
June, sauce boat, pink or blue..................................$275.00
June, tray, 11", crystal, center handle $20.00
June, tumbler, 4½", 5-oz, pink or blue, footed $35.00
June, vase, 8", yellow...$145.00
Kashmir, bowl, baker; 9", blue..................................$45.00
Kashmir, bowl, cream soup; yellow or green.............$22.00
Kashmir, cup, after dinner; yellow or green $35.00

Kashmir, plate, dinner; 10", blue **$50.00**

Kashmir, plate, salad; 7", yellow or green, round **$6.00**

Kashmir, sauce boat, yellow or green, w/liner **$75.00**

Kashmir, stem, water; 9-oz, yellow or green **$20.00**

Kashmir, stem, wine; 2½-oz, blue **$40.00**

Kashmir, vase, 8", blue **$100.00**

Navarre, bowl, 12", #2496, crystal, flared **$60.00**

Navarre, celery, 9", #2440, crystal **$27.50**

Navarre, cordial, 3⅞", 1-oz, #6106 .... **$45.00**

Navarre, creamer, 4¼", #2440, crystal, footed **$20.00**

Navarre, crystal, dinner bell **$30.00**

Navarre, plate, bread & butter; 6", #2440, crystal **$10.00**

Navarre, plate, dinner; 9½", #2440, crystal **$39.50**

Navarre, salt & pepper shakers, 3½", #2375, crystal, footed, pr **$95.00**

Navarre, tumbler, juice; 4⅝", 5-oz, #6106, crystal **$22.50**

Navarre, tumbler, water; 7⅝", 10-oz, #6106, crystal, footed **$30.00**

Navarre, vase, 10", #2470, crystal, footed **$135.00**

Romance, bowl, baked apple; 6", #2364, crystal **$15.00**

Romance, bowl, fruit; 13", #2364, crystal **$50.00**

Romance, candy dish, crystal, w/lid, blown, round **$67.50**

Romance, pitcher, 8⅞", 53-oz, #6011, footed **$225.00**

Romance, plate, sandwich; 11", #2364, crystal **$35.00**

Romance, relish, celery; 11", #2364, crystal **$27.50**

Romance, stem, cocktail; 4⅞", 3½-oz, #6017, crystal ... **$21.50**

Romance, tray, 11¼", #2364, crystal, center handle **$32.50**

Romance, tumbler, 6", 12-oz, #6017, crystal, footed **$25.00**

Romance, vase, 7½", #4143, crystal, footed **$57.50**

Royal, ashtray, 3½", #2350, amber or green **$22.50**

Royal, bowl, cream soup; #2350, blue or black **$30.00**

Royal, bowl, salad; 10", #2350, amber or green **$35.00**

Royal, butter dish, #2350, w/lid **$225.00**

Royal, plate, dinner; 10½", #2350 .... **$27.50**

Royal, sauce boat, amber or green, w/liner **$125.00**

Royal, stem, sherbet; 6-oz, #869, blue or black, low ... **$25.00**

Royal, sugar bowl, #2315, amber, footed, flat **$17.00**

Royal, tumbler, 12-oz, #859, blue or black, flat **$30.00**

Royal, vase, #2324, amber or green, footed urn form . **$75.00**

Seville, bowl, baker; 9", #2350, green **$30.00**

Seville, bowl, cream soup; #2350½, green, footed **$17.00**

Seville, bowl, fruit; 5½", #2350, amber **$10.00**

Seville, candy jar, ½-lb, #2250, amber, w/lid, footed .. **$85.00**

Seville, cocktail, #870, amber **$15.00**

Seville, egg cup, #2350, amber **$30.00**

Seville, ice bucket, #2378, green **$52.00**

Seville, plate, chop; 13¾", #2350, amber **$30.00**

Seville, tray, 11", #2287, green, center handle **$30.00**

Seville, tumbler, 12-oz, #5084, amber, footed **$18.00**

Seville, wine, #870, amber **$22.50**

Trojan, ashtray, large, #2350, pink **$50.00**

Trojan, bowl, cream soup; #2375, yellow **$22.00**

Trojan, candlestick, 3", #2375, pink, flared **$20.00**

Trojan, candy dish, ½-lb, #2394, pink, w/lid **$175.00**

Trojan, cup, after dinner; #2375, yellow **$35.00**

Trojan, goblet, cordial; 4", ¾-oz, #5099, yellow **$70.00**

Trojan, ice bucket, #2375, pink **$75.00**

Trojan, mayonnaise, #2375, yellow, w/liner **$50.00**

Trojan, pitcher, #5000, pink **$375.00**

Trojan, plate, bread & butter; 6", #2375, yellow **$5.00**

Trojan, plate, dinner; 10¼", #2375, pink **$65.00**

Trojan, sauce boat, #2375, yellow **$95.00**

Trojan, sugar pail, #2378, pink **$145.00**

Trojan, tray, 11", #2375, yellow, center handle **$32.50**

Trojan, tumbler, 6", 12-oz, #5099, pink, footed **$32.50**

Trojan, vase, 9", #2369, yellow **$195.00**

Versailles, ashtray, #2350, pink or green **$24.00**

Versailles, bowl, baker; yellow, 10", #2375, yellow **$40.00**

Versailles, candlestick, 2", #2394, pink or green **$20.00**

Versailles, celery, 11½", #2375, blue **$45.00**

Versailles, creamer, #2375½, yellow, footed **$15.00**

Versailles, finger bowl, #869/2283, blue, w/6" liner **$45.00**

Versailles, goblet, cocktail; 5¼", 3-oz, #5098 or #5099, pink or green **$25.00**

Versailles, oil, #2375, blue **$495.00**

Versailles, plate, canape, 6", #2375, yellow **$30.00**

Versailles, sauce boat, #2375, pink or green **$65.00**

Versailles, sugar pail, #2378, blue **$195.00**

Versailles, tumbler, 4½", 5-oz, #5098 or #5099, blue ... **$27.50**

Versailles, vase, 8½", #2385, pink or green, footed, fan form **$110.00**

Vesper, bowl, bouillon; #2350, green, footed **$12.00**

Vesper, bowl, cereal; 6½", #2350, amber, square or round **$20.00**

Vesper, candlestick, 4", #2394, blue **$30.00**

Vesper, creamer, #2350½, green, footed **$14.00**

Vesper, cup, #2350½, amber, footed **$15.00**

Vesper, pitcher, #2350, blue, footed **$475.00**

Vesper, plate, dinner; 9½", #2350, green **$15.00**

Vesper, platter, 12", #2350, amber **$50.00**

Vesper, sherbet, #5093, blue, tall **$25.00**

Royal, candy dish, medium blue, 3-section, w/lid.......$65.00

Royal, candy dish, ½-lb, amber, w/lid, footed **$145.00**

Royal, comport, jelly; 6", #1861½, blue or black **$50.00**

Royal, creamer, #2350½, amber or green, footed **$13.00**

Royal, egg cup, #2350, blue or black **$50.00**

Vesper, sugar bowl, #2315, green, footed...................**$18.00**
Vesper, tumbler, 5-oz., #5100, amber, footed..............**$18.00**
Vesper, vase, 8", #2292, blue **$110.00**

Fountain Pens

Fountain pens have been made commercially since the 1880s. Today's collector usually prefer those from before 1950, but some of the later ones are collectible as well. Pens by major manufacturers are most desirable, especially Conklin, Mont Blanc, Parker, Sheaffer, Swan, Wahl-Eversharp, and Waterman. Extra large and extra fancy pens, such as those with silver or gold overlay, filigree, or mother-of-pearl, are at the top of most collectors' lists and can easily run into several hundreds of dollars, some even thousands. Unless the pen is especially nice and the price is right, avoid buying examples with cracks, missing parts, or other damage.

For more information, we recomend *The 1992 Official P.F.C. Pen Guide* by Cliff and Judy Lawrence.

Chilton, green jade marbleized, gold-filled trim, touchdown filler, 1929, G...**$180.00**
Conklin, black, gold-filled trim, initialed, lever filler, 1934, EX **$100.00**
Conklin, Endura, gold marbleized, gold-filled trim, lever filler, 1930, EX..**$99.00**
Conklin, Endura, gold marbleized, gold-filled trim, lever filler, 1930, EX..**$100.00**
Conklin, No 30P, black chased hard rubber, gold-filled trim, crescent filler, 1920, NM.......................**$170.00**
Eversharp, Skyline presentation, blue, gold-filled metal cap, lady's, 1945, M..**$90.00**
Gold Bond, Stonite, green marbleized, gold-filled trim, 1929, EX...**$90.00**
Ideal, No 452, hand-engraved vine on sterling, lever filler, 1925, EX **$795.00**
Ideal, No 51½V, black chased hard rubber, nickel-plated trim, lever filler, 1925, EX.......................................**$45.00**
Ideal, 16 PSF, black chased hard rubber, gold-filled trim, lever filler, 1916, EX..**$400.00**
Mont Blanc, Masterpiece 12, black, gold-filled trim, initialed, twist filler, 1960, G...............................**$225.00**
Mont Blanc, 2-42G, black, gold-filled trim, twist filler, 1952, EX **$170.00**
Parker, Blue Diamond Vacumatic, gold pearl, gold-filled trim, vacumatic filler, 1939, EX **$180.00**
Parker, Blue diamond 51, black w/gold-filled metal cap, gold-filled trim, vacumatic filler, 1945, EX **$95.00**
Parker, Blue Diamond 51, blue w/aluminum cap, gold-filled trim, vacumatic filler, 1943, G **$50.00**
Parker, Blue Diamond 51, gray w/Lustraloy cap, gold-filled trim, vacumatic filler, 1946, EX **$52.00**
Parker, Canadian Vacumatic, blue pearl, gold-filled trim, vacumatic filler, 1944, EX......................................**$80.00**
Parker, Danish Duofold, black, gold-filled trim, button filler, 1946, EX **$100.00**

Parker, Deluxe Challenger, burgundy marbleized, button filler, 1937, EX...**$170.00**
Parker, Duofold Jr, black, gold-filled trim, 1930, EX.**$120.00**

Parker, Duofold Jr, green jade, gold-filled trim, button filler, 1930s **$135.00**
Parker, Duofold Jr, red, gold-filled trim, button filler, 1925, EX...**$130.00**
Parker, Duofold Sr, Mandarin yellow, gold-filled trim, 1927, EX **$400.00**
Parker, Duofold Sr, red, gold-filled trim, button filler, 1925, EX...**$400.00**
Parker, Jack Knife Safety No 14, sterling filigree, eye-drop filler, 1912, EX...**$995.00**
Parker, Parkette Deluxe, red pearl, gold-filled trim, 1936, EX...**$90.00**
Parker, Popular (Danish), black, gold-filled trim, button filler, 1949, EX...**$90.00**
Parker, Slender Maxima Vacumatic, blue pearl, gold-filled trim, vacumatic-filler, 1941, EX **$245.00**
Parker, Student (Danish), black, gold-filled trim, button filler, 1939, M...**$85.00**
Parker, True Blue, gold-filled trim, button filler, 1932, EX **$125.00**
Parker, Vacumatic, gold pearl, gold-filled trim, vacumatic filler, 1935, EX..**$170.00**
Parker, Vacuum Filler, burgundy pearl stripes, gold-filled trim, earliest vacumatic filler, 1933, EX **$495.00**
Parker, 21 Custom, blue w/gold-filled metal cap, gold-filled trim, aerometric filler, 1950, M **$60.00**
Parker, 51, green w/Lustraloy cap, chrome-plated trim, aerometric filler, 1950, EX....................................**$55.00**
Parker, 51 Flighter, stainless, gold-filled trim, aerometric filler, 1951, EX...**$225.00**
Parker, 51 Signet, gold-filled metal, gold-filled trim, aerometric filler, 1954, G **$150.00**
Parker, 51 Signet, gold-filled metal & trim, initialed, aerometric filler, 1957, G **$130.00**
Parker, 61, black w/Lustraloy cap, chrome-plated trim, capillary filler, 1960, NM......................................**$85.00**
Parker, 61, turquoise w/Lustraloy cap, chrome-plated trim, capillary filler, 1960, EX..................................**$80.00**
Redipoint, rolled gold, gold-filled trim, insignia on cap top, lever filler, 1926, EX....................................**$130.00**
Shaeffer, No 2 Self-Filling, black chased hard rubber, gold-filled trim, lever filler, EX **$125.00**
Sheaffer, #3, silver-red streaked pearl, chrome-plated trim, 1935, EX..**$70.00**
Sheaffer, Imperial III, black, gold-filled trim, touchdown filler, EX...**$60.00**
Sheaffer, Lifetime, black, gold-filled trim, lever filler, 1932, EX...**$90.00**
Sheaffer, Lifetime, black, gold-filled trim, lever filler, 1932, G..**$60.00**
Sheaffer, Lifetime Crest Triumph, black w/gold-filled metal cap, gold-filled trim, lever filler, 1945, EX..........**$160.00**

Sheaffer, Lifetime Feathertouch 1000, black, 1939, EX..**$250.00**

Sheaffer, No 3-25, black, gold-filled trim, lever filler, 1924, EX **$80.00**

Sheaffer, White Dot Crest Snorkel Triumph, coral w/gold-filled metal cap, gold-filled trim, touchdown filler, 1953, M...**$150.00**

Sheaffer, White Dot Sentinel TM Triumph, maroon w/chrome-gold banded cap, gold-filled trim, touchdown filler, M...**$80.00**

Sheaffer, White Dot Snorkel Triumph, black, gold-filled trim, touchdown filler, 1953, M **$85.00**

Wahl, Gold Seal, jade green marbleized, gold-filled trim, lever filler, 1928, EX **$295.00**

Wahl, Signature, wood-grain hard rubber, gold-filled trim, lever filler, desk type, 1927, EX **$130.00**

Wahl-Eversharp, Gold Seal, green & bronze marbleized, gold-filled trim, lever filler, 1929, G **$170.00**

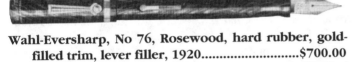

Wahl-Eversharp, No 76, Rosewood, hard rubber, gold-filled trim, lever filler, 1920............................$700.00

Wahl-Eversharp, Skyline (presentation), black w/gold-filled metal cap, gold-filled trim, lever filler, 1944, EX ..**$160.00**

Wahl-Oxford, black, gold-filled trim, initialed, lever filler, 1932, NM **$90.00**

Waterman, CF, black w/gold-filled metal cap, gold-filled trim, cartridge filler, 1955, M...............................**$100.00**

Waterman, Lady Stateleigh Taperite, black w/gold-filled metal cap, gold-filled trim, lever filler, 1949, EX...**$70.00**

Waterman, No 42½V Safety, black chased hard rubber, gold-filled trim, eyedrop filler, 1925, NM...................**$140.00**

Waterman, pearl, gold-filled trim, lever filler, 1944, EX .**$50.00**

Waterman, red w/red transparent ends, gold-filled trim, lever filler, 1941, EX **$180.00**

Waterman, 100 Year Teperite, solid 14k gold, 14k trim, lever filler, 1945, EX...**$1,500.00**

Waterman-Ideal, No 54, red ripple hard rubber, gold-filled trim, initialed, lever filler, 1927, NM **$395.00**

Fourth of July Collectibles

Mementos of any holiday celebration are always popular with collectors, but this is probably one that tends to be overlooked. Perhaps because most 4th of July memorabilia is generally blown up! But there is a collector market for any old firecrackers that somehow survived to the present still intact in their wrapping, or for the wrapping itself, for that matter. Fireworks catalogs, sparkler boxes, salesmen's display boards and samples, and anything else related to old-time fireworks manufacturers are included in this field.

Book, w/pyrotechnics as subject, minimum value **$10.00**

Broadside, American, minimum value.........................**$25.00**

Cannon (toy, cap, carbide, cartridge or black powder), minimum value...**$25.00**

Cap bomb, minimum value..**$50.00**

Cap cane, minimum value..**$15.00**

Catalog, manufacturer or distributor, minimum value.**$50.00**

Fireworks, Blarney Castle Irish Whiskey................**$4.00**

Firecrackers, Dixie Boy, Made in China, per pack **$20.00**

Firecrackers, Halco Brand, all sizes, minimum value.**$100.00**

Firecrackers, Home Run Brand, all sizes, per pack, minimum value **$100.00**

Firecrackers, Merry-Go-Round Brand, all sizes, minimum value **$100.00**

Firecrackers, Octopus Brand, all sizes, minimum value..**$100.00**

Firecrackers, Santa Claus Brand, all sizes, per pack, minimum value **$100.00**

Firecrackers, Tank Brand, all sizes, minimum value .**$100.00**

Firecrackers, Touch Down Brand, all sizes, per pack, minimum value **$100.00**

Firecrackers, Zebra Brand Made in China by To Yiu, all sizes **$25.00**

Label, Chinese foil, minimum value **$10.00**

Post card, minimum value...**$2.00**

Poster, Dixie Boy, shows firecrackers in boy's pocket, original, maximum value **$100.00**

Poster, Dixie Boy, shows handkerchief in boy's pocket, reprint **$10.00**

Poster, marked Made in Macau or China, minimum value..**$10.00**

Python Snakes, black, 20 boxes, in original display box..$75.00

Sparkler box, old, minimum value.................................**$5.00**

Frames

There always seems to be a market for antique picture frames. Some that seem to sell especially well are the tiny ones that decorators like to group together (these may be made of silver, chrome, glass-bead mosaics, etc.), the large oak frames that are often decorated with gilded gesso reliefs, and the crossed-corner Victorians with applied leaves.

Brass, 3½x2¾", plain border, metal back **$12.00**
Brass, 6x4½", flowers & leaves, oval shape, French origin, 1860s, EX...**$60.00**
Brass & copper, 6¼" dia, rope edge, easel back..........**$60.00**

Gold-washed metal, 8", Nouveau styling, Patented 1897 ....**$65.00**
Laminated mahogany & pine, 9x13", shaped perimeter w/applied bosses **$38.00**
Mission oak, 21x19", brass buttons at cross-points......**$30.00**
Pine, 10x8", 2½" wide, walnut inlaid heart, geometrics & diamonds...**$150.00**
Pine, 17x12", brown sponging w/fingerprint border.**$180.00**
Pine, 22x27", 2¾" wide, beveled w/burl grainpaint..**$200.00**
Silver, 9", bird on branch, engraving & embossing, shaped top, English origin **$825.00**
Walnut, 11", carved foliage & gadrooning, hexagonal shape, made from one piece of wood **$75.00**
Walnut, 8x10", carved criss-cross style w/hearts in corners, Pennsylvania, 1860s...**$165.00**

Franciscan Dinnerware

Franciscan is a tradename of Gladding McBean, used on their dinnerware lines from the mid-thirties until it closed its Los Angeles-based plant in 1984. They were the first to market 'starter sets' (four place settings), a practice that today is commonplace.

Two of their earliest lines were El Patio (simply styled, made in bright solid colors) and Coronado (with swirled borders and pastel glazes). In the late thirties, they made the first of many hand-painted dinnerware lines. Some of the best known are Apple, Desert Rose, and Ivy. From 1941 to 1977, 'Masterpiece' (true porcelain) china was produced in more than 170 patterns.

Many marks were used, most included the Franciscan name. An 'F' in a square with 'Made in U.S.A.' below it dates from 1938, and a double-line script F was used in more recent years.

For further information, we recommend *The Collector's Encyclopedia of California Pottery* by Jack Chipman.

Apple, ashtray, individual size **$12.00**
Apple, bowl, soup; flat..**$16.00**
Apple, bowl, 8¼"..**$40.00**
Apple, coffeepot **$72.50**
Apple, mug, large **$20.00**
Apple, pitcher, water size...**$57.50**
Apple, plate, 10½"..**$18.00**
Apple, platter, 12½"...**$35.00**

Apple, platter, 19½"...**$100.00**
Apple, salt & pepper shakers, tall, pr.........................**$35.00**
Apple, sugar bowl, large, w/lid **$35.00**
Apple, tumbler, 5⅛"...**$18.00**
Coronado, bowl, vegetable; serving, oval...................**$28.00**
Coronado, cigarette box **$40.00**
Coronado, coffeepot, w/lid..**$45.00**
Coronado, cup & saucer..**$12.50**
Coronado, gravy boat, w/attached underplate **$20.00**
Coronado, pitcher **$40.00**
Coronado, plate, 6½" **$8.00**
Coronado, plate, 8½" **$12.00**
Coronado, platter, 15½"..**$35.00**
Coronado, salt & pepper shakers, pr..........................**$17.50**
Coronado, sugar bowl, w/lid **$17.50**
Coronado, teapot **$40.00**

Desert Rose, bowl, batter $50.00
Desert Rose, bowl, small, lug handle $16.00
Desert Rose, bowl, 7½" $27.50
Desert Rose, coaster, 3¾" $17.50
Desert Rose, creamer, large......................................$16.00

Desert Rose, cup & saucer....................................$25.00
Desert Rose, cup & saucer, demitasse..........................$22.00
Desert Rose, goblet..$25.00
Desert Rose, plate, 10½"...$18.00
Desert Rose, plate, 8½"...$14.00
Desert Rose, relish, 11", 3-part..................................$35.00
Desert Rose, tray, 3-tier...$40.00
El patio, butter dish $32.50
El Patio, cup & saucer $12.50

El Patio, gravy boat w/ attached underplate.........$27.50
El Patio, sherbet..$10.00
El Patio, teapot, 6-cup $40.00
Fine china, bowl, vegetable; serving, oval $50.00
Fine china, cup $17.00
Fine china, plate, bread & butter $17.00
Fine china, plate, dinner..$28.00
Fine china, plate, salad...$20.00
Fine china, saucer...$12.00
Ivy, bowl, soup; flat...$16.00
Ivy, bowl, 8¼"..$40.00
Ivy, coffeepot...$72.50
Ivy, mug, large $20.00
Ivy, pickle dish, 10¼" $32.00
Ivy, pitcher, 1-pt...$25.00
Ivy, plate, 6½" $7.50

Ivy, plate, 9½" $16.00
Ivy, platter, 19½"...$110.00
Ivy, shakers, Rosebud, pr...$24.00
Ivy, sugar bowl, small, open.....................................$30.00
Ivy, tumbler, 5⅛"...$18.00
Metropolitan, cup & saucer, demitasse; solid color cup
    w/cream interior, cream saucer $25.00
Metropolitan, plate, dinner; 10", square w/rounded corners,
    solid color...$15.00
Tiempo, tumbler, squared cylindrical form, solid color...$12.00
Trio, coffeepot, variation of Metropolitan design w/stylized
    floral on solid color, 1954-57, w/lid.......................$30.00
Trio, plate, dinner; square form w/rounded corners, four
    stylized florals on solid color $12.00

Frankoma Pottery

This pottery has operated in Oklahoma since 1933, turning out dinnerware, figurines, novelties, vases, bicentennial plates and plaques, and political mugs in various lovely colors.

Their earliest mark was 'Frankoma' in small block letters; but when fire destroyed the pottery in 1938, all of the early seals were destroyed, so new ones had to be made. The new mark was similar, but slightly larger, and the 'O' (rather than being perfectly round) was elongated. Some of their early wares (1936-38) were marked with a 'pacing leopard'; these are treasured by collectors today. By the mid-1950s the mark was no longer impressed by hand but became instead part of the mold. Paper labels have been used since the late forties, and since 1942 nearly every item has had an impressed mold number.

In 1954, Frankoma began digging their clay from another area of the neighboring countryside. The early clay had been a light golden brown color; it was mined near the town of Ada, and collectors refer to this type of clay as 'Ada' to distinguish it from the red-firing Sapula clay that has been used since 1954.

Their glazes have varied over the years due in part to the change in the color of the clay, so with a knowledge of the marks and color variances, you can usually date a piece with a fair amount of accuracy. If you'd like to learn more, we recommend *Frankoma Treasures* by Phyllis and Tom Bess.

Bank, 7½", dog figural..$40.00

Billiken, 7", Prairie Green $75.00

Bookends, 5½", seated draped nude figural, #425, 1934-38, pr $700.00

Bookends, 5⅜", weeping lady, #427, green, pr..........$275.00

Bookends, 6", Charger, #420, pr $65.00

Bookend, 7¼", ocelot figural, Ada clay, #422, 1934-38, pr $400.00

Bookends, 8½", rearing clydesdale, ca 1942, pr.........$250.00

Candle holder, Oral Roberts, Christ, Light of the World, oval, bowl form w/tab handle, 1971 ....$10.00

Christmas card, 1955-56, each............................$70.00

Christmas card, 1967-68, each............................$40.00

Mug, donkey figural, Autumn Yellow, 1975 ....$25.00

Mug, donkey figural, Centennial Red, 1976................$25.00

Mug, donkey figural, Woodland Moss, 1978................$25.00

Mug, elephant figural, Prairie Green, 1972 ....$40.00

Pitcher, 2-qt, Wagon Wheel, #94-D $25.00

Plate, 9", Wagon Wheel......................................$8.00

Sculpture, 1¾", walking elephant, #169 ....$75.00

Sculpture, 13½", fan dancer, Ada clay, #113..............$225.00

Sculpture, 4½", circus horse, Cherokee Red, #138 ....$150.00

Sculpture, 6¼x8", Amazon Woman, marked Frankoma Potteries, #101 ....$350.00

Sculpture, 7½", seated puma, Prairie Green, pacing leopard mark...$200.00

Sugar bowl, Mayan, white, Ada clay $10.00

Teapot, 4¼", Mayan, white, Ada Clay (illustrated) ...$22.50

Vase, 5x8", cockatoo figural, pacing leopard mark ...$110.00

Wall pocket, 6½", boot figural, Robin Egg Blue, #133...$7.00

Wall pocket, 7", Wagon Wheel, #94-Y, 1949-53 ....$35.00

Fruit Jars

Did you know that we have Napoleon to thank for the invention of the fruit jar? History has it that it was because of a reward he offered to anyone who could come up with a palatable way of preserving food for him and his army during wartime. The money was claimed by a fellow by the name of Appert in 1812, whose winning ideas have been altered or copied more than 4,000 times since.

One of the more successful adaptations ever conceived was patented by John Mason on November 30, 1858. His jar wasn't perfect, but many years and several improvements later (after he'd sold the rights to a company who subsequently let them expire), the Ball Brothers picked it up and began to market them nationwide. They were made by the thousands and are very common today. Just remember that most of them date to the twentieth century (not to 1858, which is simply the patent date), and unless they're made in an uncommon color, they're worth very little. Most fruit jars are clear or aqua blue; other colors, for instance emerald green, amber, cobalt, milk glass, or black, are unusual. Values are based on condition, age, rarity, color, and special features.

AGWL Pitts PA (on base), aqua, wax sealer, small lip chip, 1-qt...$28.00

American (eagle & flag) Fruit Jar, light green, ½-gal.$138.00

Anchor Hocking (H in anchor) Mason, H over Anchor Mason on reverse, clear, 1-pt $1.00

Atlas Good Luck, clear, full wire bail, ½-pt.................$18.00

Atlas Junior Mason, clear, correct lid, ½-pt $9.00

Atlas Mason (serifs on letters), aqua, 1-qt $12.00

Ball Perfect Mason, clear, ribbed, ½-pt........................$3.00

Ball Refrigerator & Freezer Jar, clear, 16-oz $2.00

Ball Sure Seal, blue, ½-pt $48.00

Brockway Sur-Grip Mason, clear, ½-gal $8.00

Buckeye 3, aqua, light lid stain, 1-qt.......................$200.00

Clarke Fruit Jar Co Cleveland O, aqua, glass lid, metal cam lever closure, 1½-pt, rare size $160.00

Clark's Peerless, aqua, 1-qt..$6.00
Clark's Peerless (in circle), aqua, 1-qt.........................$7.00
Conserve Jar, clear, 1-pt...$5.00
Crown Cordial & Extract Co New York, aqua, ½-gal ..$10.00
Cunningham & Co Pittsburgh PA (on base), aqua, 1-qt..$33.00
DOC (on base), aqua, wax sealer, ½-gal.....................$23.00
Doolittle (in block letters), clear, 1-qt.......................$38.00
Doolittle Patented Dec 3 1901 (on lid), clear, 1-qt......$23.00
Double Safety, clear, narrow mouth, 1-pt....................$2.00
Double Safety, clear, ½-pt...$8.00
Eclipse Jar, aqua, ½-gal...$525.00
Empire, clear, ½-pt..$28.00
F&S (in circle), aqua, 1-qt..$18.00
FCGCo (on base), aqua, 1-qt....................................$23.00
Franklin No 1 Fruit Jar, aqua, no lid, 1-qt..................$55.00

Fruit Keeper GCCo (monogram), aqua, glass insert, metal clamp, ½-gal...$40.00

Glassboro Trade Mark Improved, aqua, 1-pt..............$33.00
Glassboro Trade Mark Improved, aqua, 1-qt...............$18.00
Globe, aqua, 1-qt...$20.00
Green Mountain C A Co (in frame), clear, 1-qt...........$10.00
H&C (in circle), aqua, 1-pt.......................................$23.00
Hamilton, clear, 1-qt..$85.00
Hansee's Place Home Jar, clear, 1-qt.........................$90.00
Harvest Time Mason, clear, 1-qt $10.00
Hazel Atlas E-Z Seal, aqua, 1-qt...............................$9.00
Hero Improved, aqua, 1-qt..$22.00
Johnson & Johnson New Brunswick NJ, amber, ½-pt..$12.00
Kerr 'Self Sealing' Mason, amber, 1-qt.......................$150.00
King (on banner crown & flags), clear, ½-pt $38.00
Klines Patent Oct 27 63 (on stopper), aqua, 1-qt..........$125.00
Knowlton Vacuum (star) Fruit Jar, aqua, 1-qt.............$23.00
KYGW (on base), aqua, wax sealer, 1-qt.....................$23.00
Lynchburg Standard Mason, aqua, 1-qt......................$18.00
Made in Canada (crown) Crown, clear, 1-qt.................$2.00
Mason Fruit Jar (three lines), aqua, 1-pt....................$10.00
Mason's (cross) Patent Nov 30th 1858, amber, 1-qt...$148.00

Mason's (keystone) Patent Nov 30th 1858, aqua, fair lid, midget..$25.00
Mason's CFJo Improved (Clyde NY on reverse), clear, midget..$48.00
Mason's Improved (hourglass on reverse), aqua, midget..$75.00
Mason's KBGCo Patent Nov 30th 1858, aqua, ½-gal ...$28.00
Mason's Patent Nov 30th 1858, aqua, midget $20.00
Mason's Patent Nov 30th 1858 (H&Co on base), aqua, 1-qt..$22.00
Mason's Patent Nov 30th 1858 (hourglass on reverse), aqua, midget..$85.00
Mason's 22 (underlined) Patent Nov 30th 1858, aqua, 1-qt..$26.00
Mason's 4 Patent Nov 30th 1858, aqua, 1-qt $8.00
Mellin's Infant Food Doliver-Goodale Co Boston, clear, no stopper, ⅓-pt..$3.00
Millville Atmospheric Fruit Jar, aqua, 48-oz $48.00
Moore's Patent Dec 3d 1861, aqua, 1-qt.....................$80.00
Mountain Mason, clear, round, 1-qt...........................$25.00
Pacific Mason, clear, 1-pt...$25.00
Patent Sept 18 1860, aqua, 1-qt...............................$100.00
Patented Oct 29 1858 (on lid), aqua, 1-qt $43.00
Preserves (fancy Letters), aqua, no lid, small lip crack on reverse, rare, 1-qt..$100.00
Protector (arched), aqua, 1-qt $50.00
Putnam Glass Works Zanesville O (on base), aqua, 1-qt..$33.00
Quick Seal (in circle), Pat'd July 14, 1908, blue, 1-qt $3.00
Safety Wide Mouth Mason Salem Glass Works NJ, aqua, original lid, 1-qt..$18.00
Schram Automatic Sealer (in script), clear, no lid, 1-qt ..$12.00
Security Seal (in triangles), clear, 1-pt $5.00
Simplex Mason, clear, 1-pt.......................................$90.00
Sko Queen Trademark, clear, ½-pt.............................$12.00
Sko Queen Trademark Wide Mouth Adjustable, clear, twin side clamps, ½-pt..$15.00
Sko TM Widemouth Adjustable Tall, clear, ½-pt..........$38.00
Standard (over shepherd's crook), aqua, wax sealer, 1-qt..$23.00
Star (below stippled star), light aqua, 1-qt..................$48.00
Sun (in circle w/radiating rays), aqua, 1-pt...............$100.00
Swasey Double Safety (in frame), clear, 1-pt $9.00
Thatchers Sugar & Milk Baking Powder, clear, w/label, ½-pt $12.00
The Automatic Sealer, aqua, thin lip chip, 1-qt $100.00
The Champion Pat Aug 31 1869, aqua, 1-qt $190.00
The King Pat Nov 2, 1869, aqua, 1-qt $220.00
The Magic (star) Fruit Jar, aqua, no closure, 1-qt $75.00
Trade Mark Lightning (on base), aqua, 1½-pt.............$38.00
Trade Mark Lightning (Putnam on base), aqua, 1-pt.....$2.00
Trade Mark Mason's CFJ Improved, aqua, midget.......$20.00
Trade Mark the Dandy, clear, 1-pt.............................$58.00
Trade Mark the Dandy, clear, 1-qt.............................$35.00
Trademark Keystone Registered, clear, 1-pt.................$7.00
Tropical TF (in diamond) Canners, Florida on reverse, clear, 1-qt..$12.00
Trues Imperial Brand DW True Portland ME, clear, 1-pt ..$14.00

Veteran (bust of veteran), clear, 1-pt............................$18.00
Victory (in shield), The Victory Jar (on lid), clear, ½-pt ..$12.00
Victory (in shield), The Victory Jar (on lid), clear, 1-pt.$4.00
Wears (on banner below crown), clear, twin side clamps, 1-qt $14.00
White Crown Mason (in frame), clear, 1-pt....................$8.00
Whitney's, clear, 1-qt $6.00
Woodbury, aqua, 1-qt...$38.00

Fry Oven Glassware

First developed in 1920, Ovenglass was a breakthrough in cooking methods, allowing the housewife to cook and serve in the same dish. The glassware was advertised as 'iridescent pearl' in color; today we would call it opalescent. Some pieces were decorated with engraved designs, and these are more valuable. It carried one of several marks; most contained the 'Fry' name, and some included a patent number as well as a mold number. (Though these might be mistaken for the date of manufacture, they're not!)

A matching line of kitchenware was also made — platters, sundae dishes, reamers, etc. — but these were usually marked 'Not Heat Resistant Glass' in block letters.

The company was sold in 1934, but the glassware they made is being discovered by collectors who will cherish it and preserve it for years to come.

To learn more about this subject, we recommend *The Collector's Encyclopedia of Fry Glassware* by the H.C. Fry Glass Society and *Kitchen Glassware of the Depression Years* by Gene Florence.

Bean pot, 1-qt, #1924 ....$55.00
Brown Betty, 9", #1930..$20.00
Cake pan, 6" dia, #1941..$35.00
Casserole, child's; 4" dia, #1938 ....$80.00
Casserole, 7" dia, #1938, engraved side & lid, in 8" metal holder $25.00
Chicken roaster, 14", #1946...$75.00
Cup & saucer, #1969..$35.00
Custard cup, 6", #1936...$8.00
Grill plate, 10½", #1957, 3-compartment, pearl w/blue trim...$25.00
Measuring cup, ½-cup size, #1933½, 3-spout $50.00
Meat platter, 13", #1918..$20.00
Meatloaf pan, 9", lid embossed w/grapes $30.00

Muffin pan, 9", six compartment, #1956 ....$55.00

Percolator top, 2½", #1929, pearl w/green finial..........$35.00
Perculator top, 2½", #1929..$15.00
Pie plate, child's; 5", #1916..$20.00

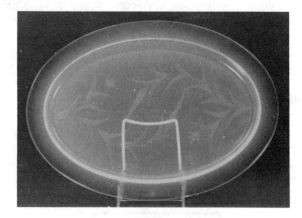

Platter, 10½x14½", w/etching.................................$35.00
Platter, 11", #1958, for fish, engraved $30.00
Shirred egg, 5" or 6", #1925, each................................$30.00
Snack plate, 6x9", #1968, w/cup...................................$30.00
Tray, 9" dia, #1959 ....$25.00

Furniture

A piece of furniture can often be difficult to date, since many 17th- and 18th-century styles have been reproduced. Even a piece made early in the 20th century now has enough age on it that it may be impossible for a novice to tell it apart from the antique. Even cabinetmakers have trouble identifying specific types of wood, since so much variation can occur within the same species; so although it is usually helpful to try to determine what kind of wood a piece has been made of, results are sometimes inconclusive. Construction methods are usually the best clues, so watch for evidence of 20th-century tools — automatic routers, lathes, carvers, and spray guns.

To learn about furniture and accessories from the twenties, thirties, and forties, we recommend *Furniture of the Depression Era* by Robert and Harriett Swedberg.

Armchair, golden oak, reclining Morris style, iron rods & flat-sawn boards, replaced cushion, 38x27x28" ..$550.00
Armchair, ladderback, cleaned down to old red, sausage turnings, repairs $550.00
Armchair, ladderback, 3-slat, turned finials, flat whittled arms, early..$700.00
Armchair, Louis XV, upholstered cartouch back, serpentine seat, 36", pr $1,900.00
Armchair, oak, back is adjustable, 5-slat sides, Harden label, EX $850.00
Armchair, oak, Colonial Revival style, carved finials, rolled handrest, scrolled back crest, ca 1900 ....$525.00
Armchair, Savanarola type, oak w/Baroque carvings of cherubs & foliage, paw feet $275.00
Armchair, Sheraton, red & black grainpaint & striping, EX details, repairs & replacements $375.00

Armchair, Windsor bow-back style, bamboo turnings, saddle seat, refinished & repaired $550.00

Armchair, Windsor bow-back style, saddle seat, turned supports & legs, replacements $750.00

Armchair, Windsor fan-back style, saddle seat, bulbous turnings, refinished, repaired, & restored $1,150.00

Armchair, Windsor writing style, shaped seat, low comb rest, repainted, replacements $450.00

Bed, baby's, brass, circular patterning at head & foot, low sides, 1800s, 38x54"...$1,800.00

Bed, canopy; birch & pine, Sheraton style, tall posts, reproduction, single size $450.00

Bed, canopy; mahogany, turned & carved foot posts, tapered head posts, 66" $650.00

Bed, cherry, rope style, EX turned posts w/acorn finials & scroll headboard $1,850.00

Bed, curly maple & poplar, rope type w/turned posts & paneled headboard, refinished $300.00

Bed, day; curly maple & cherry, scrolled posts w/turned spindles $975.00

Bed, day; Mission oak, worn leather pad, stepped finial on posts $500.00

Bed, Mission oak w/original finish, three wide slats in head- & footboards $175.00

Bed, oak, blanket roll at top of headboard & footboard, paneled trim, applied factory carvings, 73½x57x57"...$475.00

Bed, pine & maple, rope type, 72" simple turned posts, 88x64"...$2,200.00

Bed, trundle; hardwood w/pine headboard, rope style, round posts, old paint, 60".............................$350.00

Bed, 3-part headboard w/rows of daffodils, footboard the same, Majorelle, 56"......................................$1,000.00

Bed steps, pine & poplar w/worn grainpaint, turned & square legs, 22" $600.00

Bench, kneeling; pine w/worn original gray paint, primitive, 4x40" $175.00

Bench, pine, primitive style w/weathered brown finish, cutout legs, 61"...$150.00

Bench, pine, shaped sides, allover red, Pennsylvania, 1820s, 62" back, 58"...$1,600.00

Bench, settle; arrow-back, repaint w/gold striping, 72" ...$400.00

Bench, settle; nine back slats, three each side, upholstered, Limbert #558, 85" $3,500.00

Bench, settle; poplar, turned legs, plank seat, spindle back, refinished, 121" $320.00

Bench, walnut, Victorian style, cartouch-carved headboard, urn finials, 83"...$1,200.00

Bench, water; oak, Country style, bootjack feet, gallery top over shelf, repainted, 29x43".......................$400.00

Bench, Windsor, bulbous turnings, scroll arms, low back, repairs & replacements, 48" $2,100.00

Blanket chest, curly maple & poplar, Country style, raised panels, turned feet, replaced lid, 40"..................$550.00

Blanket chest, pine w/flame red grainpaint, dovetailed bracket feet & case, till, 40" $1,000.00

Blanket chest, pine w/red grainpainting & black feet, Country Chippendale, two drawers, till, EX $3,850.00

Bookcase, oak, four stepback stacking shelves, wood-framed glass doors raise & slide back on rails, 1900s, 66½x34"...$950.00

Bookcase, oak, sectional, 4-unit, restored & refinished, 1920s...$500.00

Bookcase, rosewood, classical style, two glass doors w/urn-form overlay over desk base, 90"...................$14,000.00

Bookcase-desk, walnut & burl, Eastlake style, box-type top, drop front, brass ring rails, 1870s, 79x38"........$1,200.00

Buffet, tiger-striped oak veneer, square wood pulls, year 1916 stamped on mirror, 52x46x20"...................$595.00

Cabinet, baker's; pine, top drawers w/porcelain knobs, brass handles below, top door storage, 1900s, 60x48"...$1,200.00

Cabinet, china; oak, leaded glass sides & door, mirror back, 1900s...$900.00

Cabinet, china; plain & quartered oak, three adjustable glass shelves, mirrored back, dog's feet, 87x43".......$1,250.00

Cabinet, china; quarter-sawn oak, Empire influence, three convex glass panels, casters, 1920s, 60x42x15"...$875.00

Cabinet, china; tiger & quarter-sawn oak, convex sides, four shelves, beveled gallery mirror, cabriole legs, 72x45"...$2,250.00

Cabinet, console; Victorian style, painted florals, shaped D-form marble top, 61" $3,000.00

Cabinet, kitchen, pine, two shelves, top w/two glass doors lifts off, two flat-panel doors in base, 1800s, 37x37½x12"...$1,200.00

Cabinet, kitchen; oak, two glass doors over step-back shelf, two drawers over two doors in base, 1920s $500.00

Cabinet, oak, Hoosier style, pull-out metal flour bin, roll-up door hides shelves, glass panels, porcelain top, 69"...$925.00

Candlestand, birch, Hepplewhite, spider legs, spade feet, oval 22" top (replaced), EX $475.00

Candlestand, birch, Hepplewhite style, turned pedestal, spider legs, refinished $900.00

Candlestand, cherry, Country Hepplewhite style, turned column, tripod, 1-board tilt top $525.00

Candlestand, cherry, Country style, tripod w/turned column, dished 1-board 19" dia top...........................$400.00

Candlestand, maple w/red stain, Pilgrim style, shoe feet, octagonal top $800.00

Candlestand, poplar, Windsor, turned & splayed legs, turned column, 14" 1-board top..................................$350.00

Chair, child's training; oak, jigsaw cut-out splat, aproned to conceal chamberpot, lift-lid in seat, 35x35x19" ..$225.00

Chair, corner; Country style, turned legs & posts, curved rail, rush seat, VG...$400.00

Chair, corner; hardwood, Country style, splint seat, black repaint $450.00

Chair, desk; walnut & burl, rocks & revolves, carved splat in bowed back, graduated arms, caned seat, 42x25x24"...$600.00

Chair, folding; pine, slat back, iron bolted, stamped Parks Mfg Co South Paris Maine USA, late 1800s-early 1900s...$50.00

Chair, kitchen; pine, 2-slat back w/shaped crest, low stretchers, ca 1800s, 32"...**$60.00**

Chair, parlor; burl walnut, Victorian style, turned legs, upholstered back & seat, 1800s, pr.........................**$250.00**

Chair, quarter-sawn oak, revolving desk type, new leather seat, height adjusts, casters, 36½x19¼x18".........**$195.00**

Chair, side; banister back, EX turned detail, replaced rush seat..**$425.00**

Chair, side; curly maple, three horizontal slats, worn rush seat, set of four **$750.00**

Chair, side; curly maple, turned & grooved balusters & stretchers, continuous scroll-cut crown, cane seat, low arms....**$220.00**

Chair, side; half-spindle back, stenciled fruit & foliage on brown, EX **$150.00**

Chair, side; mahogany, Country Chippendale style, molded crest w/scrolled ears **$750.00**

Chair, side; mahogany, Queen Anne style, reupholstered slip seat, ca 1900, set of eight **$800.00**

Chair, side; maple, Country style, shaped crest & slat, turned legs, replaced seat...**$300.00**

Chair, side; maple (some w/light curl), Country Chippendale, ornate slat, replaced rush seat **$500.00**

Chair, side; oak, 8-spindle w/deeply molded crest, tall finials w/fluted turnings, 36x16x16" **$225.00**

Chair, side; red & black grainpaint w/eagle & crest on two back slats, EX, set of six..............................**$4,200.00**

Chair, side; walnut, English Queen Anne style, EX detail, turned H-stretcher, VG **$1,850.00**

Chair, side; Windsor bow-back style, 9-spindle, turned legs, saddle seat, refinished **$600.00**

Chair, side; Windsor brace-back style, 7-spindle, saddle seat, refinished, EX...**$400.00**

Chair, side; Windsor style, bamboo turnings, medallion back, refinished...**$225.00**

Chest, bachelor's; mahogany, pull-out shelf, four drawers, repairs & replacements, 33x36" **$1,000.00**

Chest, blanket; cherry, square posts, turned feet, till w/secret compartment, 20x32"..............................**$725.00**

Chest, blanket; pine & poplar, brown grainpaint on yellow w/stenciled initials, turned feet, 49" **$950.00**

Chest, butternut, Country style, two step-back drawers over three, bracket feet, repairs, refinished, 38x40".**$2,200.00**

Chest, cherry, Chippendale style, claw & ball feet, fluted & chamfered corners, seven drawers, 45"............**$1,650.00**

Chest, cherry, Country Chippendale style, six dovetailed cockbeaded drawers, replaced hardware, 58x36" **$3,500.00**

Chest, cherry, Hepplewhite style, cove mold, French feet, three small drawers over five larger drawers, 63x43", EX..**$7,000.00**

Chest, cherry w/curly maple drawer front, County Sheraton style, bow front, 40"...**$900.00**

Chest, chestnut, elaborate brass pulls, two small dovetailed drawers over three larger drawers, 1930s, 36x38x14"...**$295.00**

Chest, crotch walnut, Victorian style, pink marble top, leaf pulls, five drawers...**$400.00**

Chest, curly maple, Empire style, scroll feet & pilasters, four drawers w/wooden pulls, EX.............................**$650.00**

Chest, lingerie; oak, two small drawers & door over three drawers, applied carvings, brass fixtures, skirted, 56x27x17"..**$850.00**

Chest, mahogany, Chippendale style, bow front, claw & ball feet, replaced hardware & feet, 35x40" **$800.00**

Chest, mahogany, Chippendale style, four dovetailed drawers, bracket feet, repairs, replacements, rare size, 30"..**$1,800.00**

Chest, mahogany w/inlay, Hepplewhite style, applied beading, replaced brasses, 46x44"..........................**$1,700.00**

Chest, maple, Queen Anne style, ink grainpaint (old but not original), original eagle hardware, 44x38".........**$700.00**

Chest, maple w/some curl & other woods, Country Empire, turned feet, pilasters, EX **$700.00**

Chest, mule; pine, original brown vinegar grainpaint, two drawers, EX detail, 40x43" **$2,400.00**

Chest, mule; pine w/red flame grainpaint, lift lid w/till, two drawers, 43x44" **$2,250.00**

Chest, pine, Country style, red stain, three dovetail drawers, simple, replaced pulls, 36x38" **$200.00**

Chest, pine, English Country style, worn red flame grainpaint, one drawer, 38" **$250.00**

Chest, pine, two small drawers over three drawers (all dovetailed), short ball-turned feet, 1800s, 48x46x20" ..**$495.00**

Chest, spice; mahogany; Chippendale style, fretwork spandrels in paneled door, 34x24"...........................**$1,900.00**

Chest, tiger maple, Chippendale, high ogee bracket base, refinished, replacements, 36x39" **$9,750.00**

Chest, walnut w/inlay, Hepplewhite style, French feet, scrolled apron, as found, EX............................**$3,000.00**

Chiffonier, oak veneer, wishbone style, five serpentine drawers, brass hardware, factory carved, beveled mirror, 69x33"..**$395.00**

Commode, mahogany w/ormolu mounts, Empire style, canister feet, four drawers, replaced top, 50"........**$2,200.00**

Commode, walnut, Italian neoclassic style, inlaid ivory maids & flowers, 52" **$7,500.00**

Cupboard, cherry, dovetailed construction, base & cornice moldings, hanging type, replacements, 30", EX..**$375.00**

Cupboard, corner; butternut, Country style, panel door w/beaded edge, 1856, 79x41".....................**$1,200.00**

Cupboard, corner; curly maple, Country style, two panel doors over three smaller over two, cove mold, 80"..**$2,700.00**

Cupboard, corner; pine, English Country style, four panel doors w/molding, 80", EX...........................**$3,000.00**

Cupboard, corner; pine, four shelves, original paint traces, natural refinish, ca 1820s, 61½x37½" front..........**$750.00**

Cupboard, corner; walnut, raised panel door, EX cornice, replacements, repairs, 990" **$4,000.00**

Cupboard, hanging; pine, original red flame paint, scrolled crest, 38"..**$600.00**

Cupboard, jelly; poplar, red repaint, simple cut-out feet, panel door, 40" **$485.00**

Cupboard, oak w/curly maple grainpaint, carved arch in door, hanging type, replacements, 38x28".........**$575.00**

Cupboard, pine, stepback style, four shelves, two chamfered panels in each of four doors, refinished, 79x21x62"..**$2,200.00**

Cupboard, pine w/red stain, two glazed doors, wide cornice, hanging type, 36x27"..................$325.00

Cupboard, walnut, Country style, mortised, square post feet, paneled ends, four doors, 1-pc, 77"..................$950.00

Cupboard, walnut, Country style, red traces, scalloped apron, 1-board door at top & base..................$1,950.00

Cupboard, walnut, Hepplewhite style, arched glazed door, ogee feet, 96", EX..................$6,250.00

Desk, birch, Country Queen Anne style, slant front, replaced brasses, repairs, refinished, 45x41"..................$2,000.00

Desk, cherry, Chippendale style, slant lid, fitted interior, one foot replaced, 39"..................$3,500.00

Desk, cherry, Hepplewhite style, slant front, fitted, restorations, replacements, refinished, 44x36"..................$1,400.00

Desk, golden oak, drop-front bookcase style, plain & quartered wood, brass fittings, 58½x33½x12"..................$875.00

Desk, lady's, oak, drop-front style, round beveled gallery mirror, bow-front drawer, brass hardware, 44x24½x14½"..................$395.00

Desk, mahogany, Regency style, tilt-up top over three small drawers, turned legs, 42"..................$1,050.00

Desk, mahogany veneer, 68x30x16" deep, hardwood base, drop lid, 1920s..................$385.00

Desk, plantation; pine, two doors on top, shelves & divided sections inside, drop front, 1800s, 34½x33x29"..**$595.00**

Desk, S-roll top; oak, vertical base panels, four drawers, 1910s, smaller size, 47x42x30"..................$1,750.00

Desk, S-roll top; walnut w/leather writing surface, concave bracket drawer stiles, metal pulls, 50x48x28"..**$2,650.00**

Desk, schoolmaster's, cherry w/inlaid escutcheons, Hepplewhite style, three drawers..................$675.00

Desk, schoolmaster's, pine, lift top, tapered legs, 1800s..................$250.00

Dresser, mahogany, Victorian style, serpentine, easel mirror, carvings, Henderon, 72"..................$800.00

Dresser, oak, curved facade, swivel mirror, pressed & carved decoration..................$450.00

Dry sink, baker's; oak, dough board raises, forms door for shelves, cutting board, pull-down flour bin, drawers, & doors..................$900.00

Dry sink, pine, Country style, 1-board door w/battens, cast iron thumbpiece, refinished, 30x38", EX..........$350.00

Dry sink, pine, original dark brick-red paint, porcelain knobs, two shelves inside wide doors, 1830s, 39x50x18"..................$425.00

Dry sink, pine w/red paint, dovetail drawer over two base drawers..................$650.00

Dry sink, poplar, Country style, light blue paint, simple well, two panel doors, 54"..................$975.00

Etagere, mahogany, Victorian style, turned & beaded gallery, four shelves, 41x18"..................$300.00

Footstool, carved mahogany, classical style, scroll ends w/turned balusters..................$500.00

Footstool, pine, Windsor style, black paint & striping, repainted top, signed..................$225.00

Footstool, walnut, Victorian style, upholstered top, 18x17"..................$1,300.00

Highboy, mahogany, Philadelphia Chippendale-style reproduction, Northern Co, 82"..................$1,500.00

Highboy, maple, Country Queen Anne style, nine drawers, scrolled apron, married, replacements, refinished, 70x40"..................$6,000.00

Highchair, oak, for older child (no tray), 5-spindle pressed back, rolled arms, 42"..................$225.00

Icebox, chestnut & oak, zinc lined, pull-out panel in base, tongue-&-groove wainscotting paneled back, old, 42x35x18"..................$525.00

Icebox, oak, front-top iron lift handle, ornate hinges, Gibson Cambria, 43x25x18"..................$595.00

Icebox, oak, pull-out bottom panel, 'Windsor' on brass plate, refinished, 49x25½x17½"..................$595.00

Icebox, oak, top lift handle center of door, brass fixtures, 'White Mountain' on brass plate, reproduction, 39x21x18"..................$350.00

Lowboy, cherry, Queen Anne style, cabriole legs, duck feet, original hardware, minor repaint, replacements..................$5,000.00

Lowboy, figured walnut veneer w/inlay, Queen Anne style, oval pad feet, repairs, refinished..................$2,200.00

Pie safe, butternut & poplar, six star-punched tin panels, 60", EX..................$700.00

Pie safe, oak, punched tin panels in doors & ends, two shelves, dovetailed drawer, 49x33x15"..................$750.00

Pie safe, pine, punched tin panels in doors over drawer, three shelves, porcelain knobs, 1800s, 59x38x15".........$275.00

Pie safe, pine & poplar, blue on gray paint, twelve tin panels, 58"..................$950.00

Rack, baker's; hardwood, English style, mortised, dowel shelves, 44x30"..................................**$175.00**

Rack, drying; pine, ten 19" slats, folding, 22x5", EX....**$50.00**

Rack, drying; pine & poplar, three mortised bars, primitive, 32x40", VG..................................**$95.00**

Rack, drying; pine w/gray repaint, folding, each part: 27x32"..................................**$300.00**

Rocker, figured maple, tall 4-slat ladderback.............**$550.00**

Rocker, oak, Mission type, original leather, dark stained, 32½x26"..................................**$250.00**

Rocker, oak, 7-spindle pressed back (pineapple centers), three spindles in sides of curved arms, 42x18½x17½"..................................**$295.00**

Rocker, pine & maple, Shaker style, restored splint seat, shaped stay rail & two plain slats, 1800s, 34½" ..**$225.00**

Rocker, worn red & black grainpaint, gold & yellow striping, turned legs **$150.00**

Secretary, cherry, Country style, slant lid, bookcase top, 2-pc, 80", EX..................................**$3,950.00**

Secretary, mahogany, Federal style, 2-part: bookcase w/Gothic-glazed door over four drawers, 86" .**$5,500.00**

Secretary, mahogany w/inlay, Hepplewhite style, bookcase w/geometric mullions, 88" **$3,100.00**

Secretary, poplar, Country style, refinished to yellow grainpaint, two glazed doors over pigeonholes over two doors, EX..................................**$550.00**

Secretary-bookcase, oak, French Revival influence, double mirror, dovetailed drawer, ca 1800, 66x50".........**$850.00**

Settee, mahogany, Georgian style, carved cabriole legs w/hoof feet, 1900, 6"..................................**$350.00**

Settee, rosewood, Victorian style, 3-shield back, fruit crest, open arms, 60"..................................**$1,800.00**

Settee, Windsor style, plank seat, spindle back, refinished, 40"..................................**$800.00**

Shelf, corner; painted pine, three shaped panels, wall mount, Zoar Ohio, 47" **$1,100.00**

Shelf, pine, black & red grainpaint & floral, whale ends, 4-tier, 38x26"..................................**$1,150.00**

Shelf, poplar w/old red stain, truncated sides, molded edges, 26x26"..................................**$1,050.00**

Sideboard, cherry, Country Sheraton style, bird's-eye veneer drawer fronts, 35x35" **$1,600.00**

Sideboard, mahogany, Federal style, marble top, ring-turned feet, acanthus capitals, 74"..................................**$1,200.00**

Sideboard, mahogany w/inlay, Federal style, serpentine front, bottle drawer, repairs, 72"..................................**$1,000.00**

Sideboard, mahogany w/inlay, Hepplewhite style, bow front, four doors (two curved), much restoration........**$1,000.00**

Sideboard, mahogany w/inlay, Hepplewhite-style Centennial, well made, 66"..................................**$3,200.00**

Sofa, mahogany frame, Classical style, scrolled arms, crest, elaborate feet, 88"..................................**$1,100.00**

Sofa, mahogany frame, Sheraton style, turned & reeded legs, open arms, 78", VG **$1,250.00**

Stand, ash, Country style, turned legs, two dovetailed drawers, loose 2-board 22x24" top, repainted **$350.00**

Stand, cherry, turned legs, dovetailed drawer, 1-board 18x18" top, refinished..................................**$350.00**

Stand, cherry & curly maple, Country style, turned legs, bow-front drawer, replaced 26" top **$275.00**

Stand, cherry & poplar w/red finish, EX turnings, drawer, 1-board 20" top..................................**$350.00**

Stand, cherry w/curly maple & burl veneer, turned legs, 3-board replaced top..................................**$275.00**

Stand, corner; Adirondack, black, red & gold paint, 4-tier, 63"..................................**$210.00**

Stand, curly maple, Country Sheraton style, bow front, dovetailed drawer, replaced 2-board top **$350.00**

Stand, drop leaf; birch, Country Sheraton style, two drawers, EX turnings, 17x22" top..................................**$375.00**

Stand, maple, Country Sheraton style, some curl, two dovetailed drawers, 1-board 17x19" top.....................**$500.00**

Stand, pine, Country Hepplewhite style, pencil legs, nailed drawer, 2-board top, VG **$350.00**

Stand, pine w/red traces, Country Hepplewhite style, square legs, dovetailed drawer, 2-board top..................**$275.00**

Stand, plant; rosewood w/marble top, three large scrolls on base w/three feet..................................**$1,600.00**

Stand, poplar w/original red flame grainpaint, compass stars, some wear **$1,100.00**

Stand, work; walnut & cherry, Country Sheraton style, single drawer, 21" lift lid (replaced)..................................**$400.00**

Stool, oak, worn finish, primitive, 9" dia top, 28"........**$75.00**

Stool, piano; walnut, Aesthetic style, carved pedestal w/two scrolled feet..................................**$375.00**

Stool, pine, four turned & splayed legs w/two stretchers for each side, 11½" dia seat, 21¼" H **$50.00**

Table, banquet; cherry w/pine inlay, Hepplewhite style, 17" square leaves (replaced)..................................**$900.00**

Table, card; curly maple, Hepplewhite style, drawer, replaced 34" square top..................................**$900.00**

Table, card; mahogany w/inlay, Sheraton style, reeded legs, wheat carving, signed..................................**$2,000.00**

Table, cherry, Country style, cut-out curved legs, cracked 1-board 20x34" top **$350.00**

Table, console; burlwood, French style, 3-volute support on stepped base, 43"..................................**$900.00**

Table, console; rosewood w/gilt, Baroque style, EX carving on apron & four legs..................................**$1,550.00**

Table, dining; pine, 6" aprons, 4-board top, small drawer on side w/porcelain knob, turned legs, 1800s, 77" long **$1,800.00**

Table, dressing; mahogany, English Hepplewhite style, square tapered legs, three drawers..................................**$350.00**

Table, drop leaf, rosewood veneer, Regency style, bronze feet, 34"..................................**$700.00**

Table, drop leaf; birch w/curly maple top, Country Sheraton style, 13" leaves..................................**$750.00**

Table, drop leaf; cherry w/inlay, Hepplewhite style, six legs, replaced 47" top..................................**$600.00**

Table, game; pine & maple, Country Chippendale style, drawer, 36x16" shaped top, refinished................**$600.00**

Table, hardwood & pine, Country Queen Anne style, turned legs & button feet, replaced 23x31" top..........**$2,400.00**

Table, hutch; hardwood & pine, worn red on base, square legs, 47" dia..................................**$3,000.00**

Table, library; Limbert #165, corbels support top, marked, refinished, 44" **$900.00**

Table, occasional; imitation bamboo curly maple, medial shelf, 28x23" **$1,000.00**

Table, pembroke; birch, Country Hepplewhite style, mortised & pinned, 44x14" leaves **$400.00**

Table, pembroke; mahogany w/inlay, Hepplewhite style, square legs, dovetailed drawer, replaced hardware **$700.00**

Table, pine sawbuck, 1-board edge-beaded 20x30" top, refinished..**$450.00**

Table, sewing; mahogany, Federal style, fold-over top, three drawers, carved knees, paw feet **$3,750.00**

Table, sewing; maple & curly maple, Sheraton style, splayed legs, drop leaves **$400.00**

Table, side; English pine, kitchen table type, three self-knob drawers w/dovetailed corners, wide apron, 72" long **$1,200.00**

Table, tavern; maple w/curl, Country Queen Anne style, scalloped apron, VG 22" top...........................**$750.00**

Table, tea; birch, Chippendale style, turned column, replaced birdcage, 36" tilt top **$600.00**

Table, tea; maple, Queen Anne, 32" tray top, small duck feet, much restoration & repairs **$1,900.00**

Table, work; mahogany, classical style, turned & reeded legs, replaced bag, 18x10".............................**$500.00**

Table, work; mahogany veneer, top drawer fitted w/writing surface & compartments, ca 1820s, 30x18x19" $750.00

Table, work; walnut, Country Queen Anne style, three drawers, original hardware, 3-board 33" top ...**$8,300.00**

Table, writing; figured walnut, Louis XVI style, ormolu mounts, 42" **$5,000.00**

Wardrobe, oak, applied flower top front corners, two flat panel doors over drawer, paneled sides, horizontal reeds, 72"..**$475.00**

Washstand, birch & pine, Country Sheraton style, red traces, shelf w/scalloped sides **$300.00**

Washstand, cherry, Country Sheraton style, gallery, base shelf, 4-board replaced top **$325.00**

Washstand, oak, hotel type, towel bar, tilting mirror, applied machine carvings, 72½x40x19" **$650.00**

Washstand, poplar, Country style, square posts, solid scalloped top & gallery..**$150.00**

Washstand, tiger maple, back splash, drawer, replaced lower shelf, EX...**$500.00**

Washstand, walnut, Victorian style, marble top, worn original finish, 31½"...**$550.00**

Games

Games from the 1870s to the 1970s and beyond are fun to collect. The early games are beautifully lithographed. Some of their boxes were designed by well-known artists and illustrators of the time. Many times these old games are appreciated more for their artwork than for their entertainment value. Some represent a historical event or a specific era in the social development of our country. Characters from the early days of radio, television, and movies have been featured in hundreds of games designed for children and adults alike.

If you're going to collect games, be sure that they're reasonably clean, free of water damage, and complete. Most have playing instructions printed inside the lid or on a separate piece of paper that include an inventory list. Check the contents, and remember that the condition of the box is very important, too.

If you'd like to learn more about games, we recommend *Toys, Antique and Collectible,* by David Longest and *Toys of the Sixties* by Bill Bruegman.

The sizes listed with board game descriptions indicate the dimensions of the boxes. See also TV Characters.

All American Football, Cadaco, 1969, EX **$8.00**

Around the World in 80 Days, Transogram, 1957, in original box, NM..**$30.00**

Assembly Line, Selchow & Righter, dated 1953, VG ...**$20.00**

Bas-Ket, Cadaco, 1969, EX **$8.00**

Bash, 8x10", Ideal, strike out sections of comical man to score points, 1967, M...**$20.00**

Bats in the Belfry, Mattel, 1963, EX **$70.00**

Battleship, 10x19", Milton Bradley, sink opponent's ships to win points, 1965..**$20.00**

Big Sneeze, 10x14", Ideal, build house of cards before plastic air-blowing figure blows it down, 1968 ....**$15.00**

Bird Brain, Milton Bradley, 1966, in original box, EX ...**$8.00**

Block the Clock, Ideal, 1981, M...................................**$14.00**

Booby Trap, 10x18", Parker Bros, remove pieces from board without releasing spring-activated bar, 1965, in original box, EX..**$20.00**

Camp Granada, 15x18", Milton Bradley, based on Allen Sherman's comical song, 1968 ....**$20.00**

Campaign! Civil War Game, Saalfield, capture the enemy capital, 1961, M...**$50.00**

Careers, Parker Brothers, in original box, EX................**$8.00**

Chaseback, Milton Bradley, 1962, in original box, EX...**$6.00**

Chutes Away Air Rescue, Gabriel, ca 1970s, EX..........**$15.00**

Dominoes, ivory celluloid w/red dots, set of 28..........**$45.00**

Dominoes, ivory or black Catalin, in original box......**$25.00**

Donkey Party, 1941, in original box, EX.....................**$12.00**

Double Master Set Hi-Q, Tyrne Sales Inc, ca 1960s.......**$8.50**

Dynamite Shack, Milton Bradley, 1968, EX..................**$15.00**

Evonne Goolagon's Execution Tennis, Tennis Luv, 1973, in original box, NM..**$10.00**

Fascination, 10x20", Remco, two electronic light mazes make marble race to light tower, 1962, in original box, NM..**$35.00**

Finance, Parker Brothers, 1958, in original box, NM...**$10.00**

Fortune Teller, Milton Bradley, in original box, VG....**$55.00**

Game of US Geography, Parker Bros, 1963, in original box, NM..**$20.00**

Great American Flag Game, Parker Bros, 1940, NM....**$40.00**

Hands Down, Ideal, try to be the last player holding cards, 1965...**$20.00**

How To Succeed in Business Without Really Trying, Milton Bradley, 1963, in original box, NM.....................**$37.50**

Hungry Henry, Ideal, 1969, EX..................................**$10.00**

Intellivision, Mattel, Model #2609, without tapes........**$18.00**

Jimmy the Greek Odds Maker Basketball, Aurora, 1974, in original box, NM...**$15.00**

Kentucky Derby Racing Game, spinner type, 1960s, in original box...**$20.00**

Kerplunk, Ideal, 1967, in original box, M....................**$18.00**

Korg: 70,000 BC; Milton Bradley, 1974, M..................**$25.00**

Kreskin's ESP, 10x19", Milton Bradley, test opponents' ESP skills on various topics, 1966, EX...........................**$20.00**

Marble Drag Track, Ohio Art, ca 1960s, M..................**$15.00**

Miss America Pageant Game, Parker Brothers, 1974, in original box, EX..**$12.00**

Monster Old Maid, 8x6", Milton Bradley, oversized photo cards of Universal Studio monsters, 1963, M........**$50.00**

Mouse Trap, 15x22", Ideal, chain reaction leads to trapping mouse, 1963...**$45.00**

Mystery Date, 15x20", Milton Bradley, player tries to be correctly dressed for mystery date, 1966....................**$45.00**

Name That Tune, Milton Bradley, 1957, VG.................**$30.00**

National Hockey League Strategy, Tudor, NM.............**$15.00**

NBC TV News w/Chet Huntley, Dadan, 1962, VG.......**$50.00**

Nevada 15 Gin Rummy, ES Lowe, 1975, NM...............**$10.00**

Operation, 10x20", Milton Bradley, patient buzzes if surgery unsuccessful, 1965, currently being re-issued, EX..**$15.00**

Pit, Parker Brothers, 1950s, in original box, VG..........**$15.00**

Police Surgeon, American Publishing, 1972, VG.........**$12.00**

Pollyanna, Parker Brothers, 1952, in original box, EX..**$15.00**

Roll-O-Fax, Dr G Crane, 1940s, in original box, EX....**$80.00**

Rook, Parker Brothers, 1943, in original box, VG.......**$15.00**

Rummy Royal, Whitman, 1965, in original box, M......**$10.00**

Run Mousey Run, Marx, 1979, in original box, M.......**$18.00**

Silly Safari, 10x22", Topper, catch wild animals w/crazy trapping techniques, 1966...**$75.00**

Snoop, The Marked Card Game; Ideal, 1965, in original box, VG...**$10.00**

Spingo & Whirlette, Transogram, MIB.................**$30.00**

Stock Market, Whitman, 1963, in original box, EX......**$18.00**

Stratego, 10x20", Milton Bradley, capture enemy flag, 1961, in original box, EX..**$25.00**

The Great Escape, Ideal, 1957, in original box, EX.....**$20.00**

Time Machine, 22x18", American Toy, travel through time reliving historical events to win race, 1961, M....**$125.00**

Tip-It, Ideal, 1965, in original box, EX.......................**$10.00**

Touring, Parker Bros, 1937, in original box, EX.........**$15.00**

Twister, 15x14", Milton Bradley, try to remain balanced on 72x60" vinyl sheet w/24 colored dots, 1966.........**$20.00**

Walt Disney Sleeping Beauty, 8x15", Parker Brothers 1958, complete in VG box................................**$25.00**

Whirl Out, Milton Bradley, 1971, EX............................**$8.00**

Wow! Pillow Fight for Girls, 10x20", Milton Bradley, plastic beds shoot small pillows to knock over opposing team, 1964..**$25.00**

Yahtzee, 10x15", Lowe, dice to make poker hand combinations, 1961...**$15.00**

Yankee Trader, 1941, in original box, EX....................**$35.00**

Gas Globes and Collectibles

As late as the 1950s, gas globes were a common sight. They were used to advertise special brands of gasoline being sold by each gas station. Some were simply lettered on each side with the brand name, but others carried logos and pictures such as birds, Indians, old cars, flowers, etc. as well.

There were four basic types: 1) one-piece milk glass globes with advertising on both sides (1914-1931), 2) metal-rimmed globes with glass lens inserts held in place with metal snap rings (1915-1930s), 3) glass-bodied globes with two glass advertising lenses held on by two or three tiny bolts on each lens (1926-1940s), and 4) the more common plastic globe bodies with two glass lenses (1931-1950s). Standard Crown one-piece globes were made again in the fifties, but because their letters are not raised as they were on those from the twenties, you'll be able to spot them immediately.

Gasoline-related items represent a special area of the advertising field that has recently been the focus of a good deal of collector attention. There have been several cataloged auctions in the East that have dealt exclusively with high quality oil- and gasoline-related material, much of which brought very respectable selling prices.

If you're interested in learning more about gas globes and related items, we recommend *Huxford's Collectible Advertising* by Sharon and Bob Huxford.

Can, Atlantic Motor Oil, 4" dia, 1-qt, tin, red airplane on blue arrow, embossed ribbing, 1935-45, EX **$85.00**

Can, Duplex Outboard Motor Oil, tin, two fishermen in red & blue boat, 1940-50, NM **$850.00**

Can, Pennelene Auto Oil, 6", ½-gal, tin, green w/black-shadowed gold letters, Penn Soo Oil Co, 1950s, EX **$60.00**

Can, Pennsylvania Motor Oil, 1-qt, tin, map of five states & oil fields on yellow, logo below, 1935-45, EX **$150.00**

Can, Pep Boys Western Motor Oil, 12x9", 2-gal, tin, Pep Boys on bucking horse, 1925-45, EX....................**$210.00**

Can, Quaker City Motor Oil, 1-qt, tin, city skyline on blue, '100% Pure PA' on orange, 1945-50, EX **$75.00**

Can, Renown Motor oil, 11x7", 2-gal, tin, cream w/green & blue letters, Standard Oil Co, 1925-45, EX **$80.00**

Can, Road Runner Motor Oil, 1-qt, waxed cardboard, yellow, road runner in white circle, 1975-85, NM **$30.00**

Can, Sterling Motor Oil, 1-qt, tin, green & black lettering & logo, 1935-45, M..**$40.00**

Can, Tankar Motor Oil, 12x9", 2-gal, tin, tank car on red background, beige letters, 1933-39, EX **$45.00**

Can, Thorobred Motor Oil, 9x8", 2-gal, tin, blue horse on red circle, red & cream letters, 1925-45, EX..........**$60.00**

Can, Welch Motor Oil, 1-qt, waxed cardboard, speeding car on yellow background, 'Welch Guaranteed,' 1962-65, EX..**$45.00**

Can, 20-W Motor Oil, 1-qt, tin, snow graphics on blue background, 'For Winters Driving,' 1935-45, NM..........**$50.00**

Globe, Ashland Flying Octanes, 16" dia, white w/red, green, yellow, & gold lettering, 1930s, EX....................**$375.00**

Globe, Atlantic Ethyl, 16½", metal frame w/glass insert, 1915-30s..**$350.00**

Globe, Atlantic White Flash, 17" dia, milk glass, white letters on red & blue, 1930-40, M **$300.00**

Globe, Diesel, 17x17", milk glass, crown shape w/blue letters, metal base, 1940-50, EX **$600.00**

Globe, Pennzoil, 17", milk glass, 'Pennzoil Gasoline' encircling Ethyl logo w/text, 1926-30, EX **$450.00**

Globe, Shamrock, plastic oval body, glass insert **$150.00**

Globe, Shell, milk glass, clam shape, glass frame & insert, 1926-40s..**$350.00**

Globe, Shell (etched), 1-piece glass, round, w/no insert, 1914-31..**$450.00**

Globe, Signal Gasoline, 19", 3-piece w/restored metal frame, stoplight signaling 'Go,' EX................................**$400.00**

Globe, Sinclair Diesel, 17" dia, milk glass w/plastic casing, white letters on green background, 1959-70, M .**$185.00**

Globe, Trophy, 'Our Premium Gasoline,' glass frame w/glass insert **$300.00**

Globe, Tydol, 16½", metal frame w/glass insert **$350.00**

Globe, 16½" dia, Atlantic White Flash, lens & outer casing of milk glass are held together by a metal ring, ca 1930-40...$300.00

Pump sign, Blue Sunoco 200 X, 21x15", die-cut porcelain, diamond & arrow on elongated yellow diamond, 1957-61, EX **$130.00**

Pump sign, BP Gas, porcelain, EX..............................**$45.00**

Pump sign, Cities Service Oils, 10" dia, porcelain, 'Once-Always' above logo, 1927-36, EX........................**$175.00**

Pump sign, Ethyl Gasoline, porcelain, Ethyl Anti Knock Compound logo on sunrays, 1940, EX..................**$45.00**

Pump sign, Polarine Motor Oil, 7" dia, porcelain, lettering on large triangle, text both sides, 1926-50, EX....**$350.00**

Pump sign, Sinclair Oils, 12" dia, porcelain, striped logo, 1920-30, NM **$325.00**

Pump sign, 5x9", Atlantic, porcelain, 'Atlantic' in blue on white band, red background, 1966-69, M..............**$35.00**

Salt & pepper shakers, Philgas, 2", light green plastic, in original box, pr **$20.00**

Sign, Atlantic White Flash, 42x15", porcelain on metal, 'Atlantic' & lettered circle above line, 1940s, EX...**$45.00**

Sign, Pennzoil, 9x30", double-sided porcelain, red arrow & 'Expert Lubrication' on white, 1930-40, EX.........**$160.00**

Sign, Texaco, 4x23", porcelain, 'No Smoking' flanked w/star logo, 1940s, EX **$110.00**

Sign, Texaco Sky Chief Gasoline, 18x12", porcelain, star logo w/winged device in background, EX............**$50.00**

Sign, Wolf's Head Motor Oil, 22x17", double-sided tin (w/ flange), red, white, & green, 1960s, EX................**$65.00**

Geisha Girl China

During the decade before the turn of the century, Western interest in Oriental and Japanese artwork, home furnishings, and accessories had increased to the point that imports were unable to keep pace with demand. In the country of Japan, years of internal strife and the power struggle that resulted had diverted the interests of the feudal lords away from the fine porcelains that had been made there for centuries, and many of the great kilns had closed down. As a result, many tiny household kilns sprang up around the country, worked by both skilled artisans and common laborers, all trying to survive in a depressed economy.

The porcelain they designed to fill the needs of this market was decorated with scenes portraying the day-to-day life of the Japanese people. There were hundreds of different patterns, some simple and others very detailed, but common to each were the geishas. So popular was the ware with the American market that its import continued uninterrupted until WWII. Even after the war, some of the kilns were rebuilt, and a few pieces were manufactured during the Occupied Japan period.

Each piece of this porcelain has a border of a particular color. Some colors are connected with certain time periods, and collectors often use this as a method of dating their pieces. For instance, reds, maroon, cobalt blue, and light and nile green borders were early. Pine green, blue-green, and turquoise were used after about 1917 or so, and in the late 1920s and '30s, a light cobalt was popular. Some pieces from the Occupied era have a black border. Border colors are given directly after pattern names in our descriptions.

Even if you're not sure of the name of your pattern, you can use the following listings as a general guide. If you'd like to learn more about this porcelain and its many variations, we recommend *The Collector's Encyclopedia of Geisha Girl Porcelain* by Elyce Litts.

Bowl, 8", Boat Festival, light cobalt.............................**$25.00**

Bowl, 8", fluted rim..$25.00

Bowl, 9", Flower Gathering, pine green, Japan mark..**$30.00**

Box, 4½x3¾x3½", Parasol D, egg form, red-orange, Made in Japan mark **$28.00**

Compote, 3½x7½", Child Reaching for Butterfly, handled, Made in Japan mark...**$30.00**

Creamer, 2½", Pointing A, red, Made in Japan mark...**$14.00**

Creamer, 4", Garden Bench G, multicolor border, Ozan mark..**$28.00**

Cup & saucer, bouillon; Garden Bench J, all hand-painted w/multicolor border, marked w/TN in wreath, w/lid..$45.00

Jug, 6", Drum A in floral reserve, blue & green with gold...$85.00

Mug, 4x3", Bamboo Trellis, red w/gold buds, Japan...**$26.00**

Mustard jar, Lesson, red w/gold, Yachi mark **$15.00**

Nut dish, Shell Game, footed, red w/gold & tan, Yasutera mark..**$7.00**

Plate, 7", Gardening, blue w/gold, Torii mark.............**$20.00**

Plate, 8", Dragonboat, cobalt w/gold, Kutani mark.....**$45.00**

Pot, cocoa; Parasol B, cobalt w/gold, SNB mark.........**$55.00**

Tea set, Cloud B, melon ribbed, red-orange w/yellow, 13-pc, Tashiro mark **$95.00**

Teapot, Geisha in Sampan A, gold, decal, Made in Japan mark..**$15.00**

Glass Animals and Figurines

Nearly every glasshouse in America has produced beautiful models of animals and birds — many are still being made today. Heisey was one of the largest manufacturers, and some of their more expensive figures are valued today at $2,000.00 and higher. As these companies closed, the molds were often bought by others who used them to press their own lines. Although some are marked so that you can identify the maker, many are not, and even advanced collectors are sometimes unable to make a positive identification.

Unless you're sure of what you're buying, we recommend you read *Glass Animals of the Depression Era* by Lee Garmon and Dick Spencer. If no other color is given, our prices are for animals in clear glass.

Cambridge, Blue Jay, flower holder $125.00
Cambridge, Heron, 12", large.................................$125.00
Cambridge, Lion, bookend, each............................$110.00

Cambridge, Sea Gull, flower frog............................$50.00
Cambridge, Swan, 4½", candlestick, milk glass $175.00
Cambridge, Swan, 8½", ebony....................................$125.00
Cambridge, Swan, 8½", emerald $125.00
Cambridge, Turkey, pink, w/lid....................................$400.00
Duncan & Miller, Duck, ashtray, 8" $20.00
Duncan & Miller, Goose, 6x6" $245.00
Duncan & Miller, Heron, 7"..$95.00
Duncan & Miller, Leaf Swan, 6½", blue or pink $125.00
Duncan & Miller, Ruffled Grouse $1,750.00
Duncan & Miller, Swan, ashtray, 4", crystal & black....$35.00
Duncan & Miller, Swan, 7", solid $45.00
Duncan & Miller, Swordfish, blue opalescent, rare ...$500.00
Fostoria, Chanticleer, 10¾"..$200.00
Fostoria, Chinese Lotus, 12¼", Silver Mist $225.00
Fostoria, Colts, blue, standing....................................$40.00

Fostoria, Horse, bookend..$65.00
Fostoria, Mermaid, 10"..$115.00
Fostoria, Owl, bookend, ebony $225.00
Fostoria, Polar Bear, amber.......................................$125.00
Fostoria, Sea Horse, bookend $100.00
Fostoria, Squirrel, amber $35.00
Fostoria, St Francis, 13½", Silver Mist, original issue .$325.00
Heisey, Cygnet, baby swan, 2½"...............................$185.00
Heisey, Duck, ashtray...$75.00
Heisey, Elephant, large..$350.00
Heisey, Fish, bowl, 9½"...$425.00
Heisey, Frog, cheese plate, marigold $285.00
Heisey, Ringneck Pheasant, 11¾"..............................$125.00

Heisey, Rooster, vase, 6½" $85.00
Heisey, Swan, 7"...$700.00
Imperial, Asiatic Pheasant, amber..............................$325.00
Imperial, Champ Terrier, 5¾", caramel slag................$95.00
Imperial, Clydesdale, salmon $325.00
Imperial, Donkey, caramel slag $55.00
Imperial, Donkey, Meadow Green Carnival................$95.00
Imperial, Filly, satin, head forward.............................$75.00
Imperial, Horse Head, bookend, pink, rare..............$300.00
Imperial, Sow, amber $325.00
Imperial, Tiger, paperweight, jade..............................$85.00
Paden City, American Eagle head, bookend, 7½" $125.00
Paden City, Bunny, cotton-ball dispenser, blue frosted, ears
    back $60.00
Paden City, Goose, 5", blue $100.00
Paden City, Pheasant, 12" long, head turned..............$90.00
Paden City, Pony, 12"...$90.00
Paden City, Pouter Pigeon, bookends, 6½", pr..........$150.00
Paden City, Rooster, 8¾", head down $75.00
Paden City, Squirrel, 5¾", on curved log....................$65.00

Glass Shoes

Little shoes of glass were made as early as 1800. In 1886 a patent was issued to John E. Miller for his method of pressing a glass slipper; George Duncan pressed a shoe in the Daisy and Button pattern, and soon every glasshouse in the country was following in their 'footsteps.' Even today, contemporary glass artists like Boyd and Mosser are making shoes very much like the older ones. You'll find shoes of every color and design imaginable. Some have been used to convey an advertising message. There are ladies' slippers and men's house shoes, high-top shoes and roller skates, babies' booties, 'wooden' shoes, shoes with lids, and shoes that are bottles.

To learn more about them all, we recommend *Shoes of Glass* by Libby Yalom.

Baccarat, 3½x10", Dutch type, crystal, 1956-75 ....**$125.00**
Bouquet holder, 4⅜x5½", amethyst, Pat Applied For..**$48.00**
Boyd, Cat Slipper, 3x6", Pippin Green Slag, 1982 ....**$16.00**
Central Glass, hanging match holder, 6¼", vaseline....**$70.00**
Degenhart, High Boot, 4⅛x4⅝", amberina..................**$15.00**
Degenhart, Roller Skate, 3¼x4¼", cobalt.....................**$35.00**
English, thimble holder, 1½x2⅜", green.....................**$110.00**
English, 3x5¾", cased multicolor spatter..................**$110.00**

Fenton, Daisy & Button boot, 4½", amber............$25.00
Fenton, Kitten Slipper, 3⅞x5⅝", Daisy & Button, blue
    opalescent **$25.00**
Gillinder, 2⅝x5½", centennial, frosted crystal.............**$35.00**
King Glass, knitted bootie, 2⅝x3⅝", blue **$48.00**
Waterford, bootee paperweight, 2x4", crystal, 1987....**$50.00**

Goebel

The Hummelwork Porcelain Manufactory (the same company that produces Hummel figures) has been located in Rodental, in the area formerly referred to as West Germany since 1871. In addition to the Hummels, they're also famous for their Disney characters, Art Deco pieces, bird and animal figures, and two types of novelty kitchenware

lines designed as Friar Tuck (brown-robed) monks and Cardinal (red-robed) monks.

The Goebel marks are indicative of particular time periods; see the section on Hummels for information concerning marks.

Bank, 4", Friar Tuck (brown monk), SD29, stylized bee
    mark...**$40.00**
Creamer, child's; yellow chick, 1950 mark..................**$30.00**
Creamer & sugar bowl, Friar Tuck (brown monk), S141/0 &
    Z 37, full bee mark **$60.00**
Decanter, 10", Friar Tuck (brown monk), KL95, stylized bee
    mark...**$60.00**

Decanter, Friar Tuck, w/six shot glasses $160.00
Egg timer, single; Friar Tuck (brown monk), E104, 3-line
    mark...**$45.00**

Figurine, Evening Prayer, 6", ca 1959...................$55.00

Figurine, 10", Colonial couple, crown mark $275.00
Figurine, 3½", cat, white w/brown spots.....................$35.00
Mug, 1½x1", Great Dane head figural, brown w/black trim, marked...$45.00
Mug, 5", Friar Tuck (brown), T74/1, full bee mark $40.00
Pitcher, 2½", Cardinal Tuck (red monk), S141 2/0, stylized bee mark...$50.00
Pitcher, 2½", Friar Tuck (brown monk), S141 2/0, full bee mark...$25.00
Pitcher, 4", Santa Claus, full bee mark.........................$75.00
Pitcher, 5", Friar Tuck (brown monk), S141/1, stylized bee mark...$35.00
Salt & pepper shakers, Friar Tuck (brown monk), P153, full bee mark, pr...$30.00
Salt & pepper shakers, Santa Claus, full bee mark, pr ..$50.00
Sugar bowl, Cardinal Tuck (red monk), Z37, stylized bee mark...$75.00
Sugar bowl, 4½", Santa Claus, full bee mark...............$75.00
Toby pitcher, 4", S129 3/0, crown mark.....................$45.00

Gone with the Wind

Very few of us have never read the book or seen the movie. We've gotten to know Scarlett and Rhet as well as we did last fall's presidential candidates. Margaret Mitchell's book was the second-best seller ever written and has been continually reprinted and reissued. The movie (recognized as the #1 movie of all time) was originally released in 1931. It was re-released in 1942, 1943, 1947, 1954, 1961, 1968, 1974, 1980, and again in 1989 when it was shown in Atlanta in celebration of its 50th anniversary.

So *Gone with the Wind* fans have a wealth of memorabilia available to them today. If you could find a rare copy of the May 1936 first edition with its original dust jacket, you'd probably have to pay at least $1,500.00 for it. A 1-sheet movie poster from January 1941 with a note at the bottom 'And presenting Vivien Leigh as Scarlett O'Hara' is valued at $5,000.00. But there are many other less-expensive items you can collect — souvenirs, lobby cards, programs, newspaper clippings, movie magazines, sheet music, and records, for instance — most for less than $100.00.

For enjoyable reading and lots of information, we recommend the *Gone with the Wind Collector's Guide* by Patrick McCarver.

Autograph, Butterfly McQueen on photo as Prissy $15.00
Calendar, cloth, 1977, in original box...........................$20.00
Coin purse, shows Scarlett, 1939, M $45.00
Figurine, Tara, Avon, 1985 ....$35.00
Hankerchief, child's, shows Bonnie, dated 1939, M....$30.00
Lobby card, title, 1961 ....$90.00
Magazine, 'Ladies' Home Journal,' Scarlett pictured on cover, 1939 ....$45.00
Magazine ad, Macmillan promotes book, December 1936, EX color..$25.00
Paint book, Merrill Publishing, ca 1940, 30-page $125.00

Paper dolls, Merrill, dated 1940, M......................$150.00
Paperback book, 'Gone with the Wind,' Perma Books, 4th printing, February 1961 ....$10.00
Plate, 10", Rhett portrait, Collectors Originals $45.00
Plate, 8", Mammy Laces Scarlett, Knowles $30.00
Plate, 8", Scarlett & Her Suiters, Knowles.....................$35.00
Poster, 1-sheet, Academy of Motion Pictures' Arts & Sciences, 1983...$25.00
Poster, 22x28", 1961 re-release, pastel colors $150.00
Press book, 1954..$75.00
Record, 'Gone Like the Wind,' sung by Connie Francis, 45 rpm, MGM label $7.50
Record, 'My Own True Love,' sung by Joe Marine, 45 rpm, Bell label..$25.00
Record, 'Tara Theme,' Buddy Morrow & Orchestra, 45 rpm, MGM label...$25.00
Still, 8x10", color from 1961, set of twelve, VG $37.50
Window card, 14x22", 1968...$60.00

Graniteware

Though it really wasn't as durable as its name suggests, there's still lots of graniteware around today, though much of it is now in collections. You may even be able to find a bargain. The popularity of the 'country' look in home decorating and the exposure it's had in some of the leading decorating magazines has caused graniteware prices, especially on rare items, to soar in recent years.

It's made from a variety of metals coated with enameling of various colors, some solid, others swirled. It's the color, the form, and of course the condition that dictates value. Swirls of cobalt and white, purple and white, green and white, and brown and white are unusual, but even solid gray items such as a hanging salt box or a chamberstick can be expensive, because pieces like those are rare. Decorated examples are uncommon — so are children's pieces and salesman's samples.

For further information, we recommend *The Collector's Encyclopedia of Granite Ware, Colors, Shapes, and Values*, by Helen Greguire.

Bowl, 8", green & white swirl, Emerald Ware, EX $185.00
Bread box, white w/blue lines, round, hinged, NM....$98.00

Bread box, 11½", green & white speckled, EX............**$55.00**

Cake pan, 10", blue & white swirl, EX **$55.00**

Canister, 'Meal' in white on blue, white interior, EX.**$110.00**

Chamber pot, child's size, gray & white mottle, EX **$20.00**

Churn, green to white shaded, floor-model, EX........**$765.00**

Coffee biggin, red & white mottle, 4-pc, NM.............**$575.00**

Coffee boiler, 2-gal, cobalt & white speckled, VG **$65.00**

Coffeepot, gray w/pewter trim, brass ring on base, NM..**$295.00**

Coffeepot, 10", blue & white large swirl, EX **$125.00**

Coffeepot, 10", blue & white swirl, NM.....................**$188.00**

Coffeepot, 11", gray mottle w/pewter trim.........$300.00

Coffeepot, 11½", roses on white, porcelain handle, pewter trim, EX...**$245.00**

Colander, green & ivory shaded w/black trim, Old Ivory Ware, NM **$145.00**

Colander, robin's-egg blue large swirl, EX.................**$150.00**

Colander, 10" dia, gray mottle, worn, VG $30.00

Cream can, blue & white large swirl w/black trim, wire bail handle, NM..**$178.00**

Creamer, cobalt solid, squat, NM...............................**$140.00**

Cup, 2x4½", medium teal blue, NM............................**$100.00**

Custard cup, white w/cobalt trim, Sweden, VG..........**$17.50**

Dipper, blue & white large mottle interior & exterior w/blue trim, flared, M...**$115.00**

Double boiler, cream & green, EX...............................**$98.00**

Dust pan, gray mottle, VG **$365.00**

Fry pan, lavender & white large swirl w/black rim & handle, white interior, EX..**$170.00**

Frying pan, small, blue & white large swirl, black rim & handle, EX..**$175.00**

Funnel, large, gray, elliptical, M.................................**$55.00**

Grater, large, cobalt solid, NM...................................**$20.00**

Kettle, blue & white large swirl, Lava Ware, EX........**$175.00**

Kettle, large, cream & green, bail handle, w/lid.........**$32.00**

Kettle, preserve; 13x6", light gray, side handles, NM ..**$32.00**

Ladle, soup; gray medium mottle, black turned wood handle, NM...**$98.00**

Lunch pail, cobalt solid, 4-pc, EX.............................**$125.00**

Mold, shell, brown to tan shaded, white interior, ring for hanging, M...**$145.00**

Mold, strawberry, gray solid, NM..............................**$350.00**

Muffin pan, 12-cup, gray large mottle, deep, NM........**$57.50**

Mug, mush; blue & white swirl w/black trim, M.......**$190.00**

Mug, royal blue w/white band & gold trim, EX **$32.00**

Pan, 5¾" dia, light blue & white swirl w/black trim, NM **$42.50**

Pie pan, 10", gray mottle, EX **$40.00**

Pie pan, 4¾", light gray w/blue rim, miniature, VG **$45.00**

Pitcher, molasses; white w/cobalt trim, flared cylinder, M **$150.00**

Pitcher, water; gray medium mottle, riveted handle, footed, EX **$160.00**

Plate, large, gray large mottle, M **$42.50**

Plate, reddish-brown & white fine mottle, white interior, 12-sided, EX...**$48.00**

Platter, 16x12½", blue-gray w/black rim, EX..............**$58.00**

Refrigerator dish, 5x8", blue & white swirl, ca 1950s, EX **$110.00**

Roasting pan, 1x4½x3", light green w/blue rim, miniature, EX **$60.00**

Sauce pan, blue & white large swirl, VG **$65.00**

Sink strainer, gray, triangular, EX..............................**$68.00**

Skimmer, white, pierced center, NM **$125.00**

Soap dish, aqua & white large swirl, pierced for hanging, NM **$135.00**

Spatula, small, gray medium mottle, NM....................**$68.00**

Spoon, basting, white w/cobalt handle, EX................**$48.00**

Tea strainer, gray mottle, VG **$48.00**

Teapot, green & white mottle w/green trim, NM **$235.00**

Teapot, red & white medium mottle, gooseneck spout, old, NM...**$500.00**

Teapot, red & white swirl, curving gooseneck spout, ca 1960, EX...**$130.00**

Teapot, small, blue & white mottle, curving gooseneck spout, VG **$195.00**

Teapot, white w/green veins, medium swirl 'snow on mountain,' Elite, EX **$415.00**

Wash pitcher & bowl, red w/black trim & handle, squat, M **$110.00**

Washboard, cobalt solid, no advertising, EX...............**$50.00**

Water pail, small, blue & white large swirl w/black trim, wooden bail handle, M **$150.00**

Griswold Cast Iron Cooking Ware

Late in the 1800s, the Griswold company introduced a line of cast iron cooking ware that was eventually distributed on a large scale nationwide. Today's collectors appreciate the variety of skillets, cornstick pans, Dutch ovens, and griddles available to them, and many still enjoy using them.

Several marks have been used, most contain the Griswold name, though some were marked simply 'Erie.'

If you intend to use your cast iron, you can clean it safely by using any commercial oven cleaner. (Be sure to re-season it before you cook in it.) A badly pitted, rusy piece may leave you with no other recourse than to remove what rust you can with a wire brush, paint the surface black, and find an alternate use for it around the house. For instance, you might use a kettle to hold a large floor plant or some magazines. A small griddle or skillet would be attractive as part of a wall display in a country kitchen.

For more information, we recommend *Griswold Cast Collectibles* by Bill and Denise Harned.

Bowl, Scotch; #3, 4-qt.......................................$60.00
Broiler & gridiron, 10½"...................................$115.00
Brownie pan, #9..$75.00
Bundt pan, #965, for Frank Hay $400.00
Cake mold, lamb...$125.00
Candy mold, 7¾", #100, star & hearts...........$145.00
Casserole, 9⅜x7⅜", large emblem, w/lid..........$40.00
Cornstick pan, #262, miniature, M.....................$95.00
Cornstick pan, 1¼x14¼x7½", twenty-two half-sticks.$125.00

Cornstick pan, 1x14x8", #283.....................$150.00
Cornstick pan, 13¼", #273...............................$115.00
Danish cake pan, #31, rimless, early $125.00
Danish cake pan, #32 ....$75.00
Deep fat fryer, #1003, 2½-qt............................$60.00
Deep fryer, 2½-qt..$60.00
Dutch oven, #10, w/trivet, Tite Top $90.00
Dutch oven, #10 Chuck Wagon, w/lid, 8-qt $145.00
Dutch oven, #12, 15-qt, Tite Top.......................$95.00
Dutch oven, #6, w/trivet $160.00
Dutch oven, #9, deep, Erie................................$95.00
Dutch oven, #9, 6-qt, large emblem, Tite-Top.............$55.00
French roll pan, #11...$55.00
French roll pan, 7½x6", #17, Erie.......................$68.00

Gem pan, 12¾x6¾", #8, large emblem.................$75.00
Griddle, #8, rectangular.....................................$50.00
Griddle, #9, round $100.00
Griddle, 10½" dia, #609A, large emblem.............$65.00
Griddle, 16¾x10", #18, small emblem, Erie..........$50.00
Griddle, 19x9⅛", #8, bail handle, diamond mark $88.00
Griddle, 20½x10¼", #9, oval..............................$60.00
Griddle, 22¼x10¼", #10, oval.............................$75.00
Griddle, 7¼" dia, #6, Erie.................................$50.00
Grill, barbeque; 12¼", #10, large emblem.............$100.00
Hibachi grill, 30x18x12", #903, mark..................$95.00
Kettle, #8, 6-qt, Maslin shape, Erie.....................$65.00
Kettle, #8, 7-qt, large emblem, flat bottom, Erie $60.00
Kettle, service; #000, small emblem, chrome finish.....$40.00
Kettle, 3", #0..$50.00
Kettle, 4½x8", #3, large emblem $58.00
Kettle, 7½x12⅜", #12, Erie.............................$100.00
Meat loaf pan, 2¾x10⅛x5½", #877, Erie............$85.00
Patty mold, M in box.......................................$55.00
Platter, 14½x8½", oval, 'tree style'.....................$45.00
Popover pan, 1⅝x9½x5½", #18, Erie.................$100.00
Popover pan, 10½x7½", #10, Erie.......................$60.00
Pot warmer & grill, 8" dia, #803, Erie.................$115.00
Roaster, #5, 6½-qt, oval..................................$55.00
Roaster, #95, small..$125.00
Roaster, 12¾", #3, large emblem, w/trivet, Erie.........$125.00
Sauce pan, 2-qt, Erie.......................................$50.00
Skillet, #11, large emblem, w/smoke ring.............$110.00
Skillet, #14, large emblem $125.00
Skillet, #34, 7-egg...$60.00
Skillet, #5, large emblem, no smoke ring...............$42.50
Skillet, #5, small emblem, no smoke ring $24.00
Skillet, #6, Erie..$45.00
Skillet, #7, w/smoke ring, Erie...........................$55.00
Skillet, #9, w/smoke ring, Erie...........................$60.00
Skillet, fish; 15" long, #15, Erie PA emblem, w/lid....$165.00
Skillet, Odorless; #8..$110.00
Skillet, snack; 1⅛x7½", #42, Erie.......................$85.00
Skillet, 13¼", #12, w/smoke ring, Erie................$150.00
Skillet, 3x12¼", #10, w/smoke ring, Erie..............$100.00
Skillet, ⅞x4⅛", #0 Toy $75.00
Skillet griddle, 12¾", #110, large emblem, Erie.........$115.00
Swedish pancake pan, #34, small emblem..................$50.00
Teakettle, #6, 4-qt, Erie...................................$80.00
Teakettle, #7 Safety Fill, 5-qt, Erie $55.00
Vienna roll pan, #6, Erie PA.............................$95.00
Waffle iron, #6...$185.00
Waffle iron, #8, later version, w/stand, American $115.00
Waffle iron, French; #7, wood handles $150.00
Waffle iron, 8½" pans, #19 Heart & Star..............$165.00
Waffle iron, 9⅜x4", #12, Erie...........................$115.00
Waffle iron, 9⅜x4" pans, #12, Erie.....................$130.00
Wheat stick pan, 13½x7", #28, seven sticks, Erie.......$150.00

Haeger Pottery

Many generations of the Haeger family have been associated with the ceramic industry. Starting out as a brickyard in 1871, the Haeger Company (Dundee, Illinois) progressed to include artware in their production line as early as 1914. That was only the beginning. In the thirties they began to make a line of commercial artware so successful that as a result a plant was built in Macomb, Illinois, devoted exclusively to its production.

Royal Haeger was their premium line, whose chief designer was Royal Arden Hickman. He was talented artist who worked in mediums other than just pottery. For Haeger he designed a line of wonderfully stylized animals and birds, high-style vases, and human figures and masks with extremely fine details.

Paper labels were used extensively before the mid-thirties. Royal Haeger ware has an in-mold script mark, and their Flower Ware line (1954-1963) is marked 'RG' (Royal Garden).

For those wanting to learn more about this pottery, we recommend *Collecting Royal Haeger* by Lee Garmon and Doris Frizell.

Bookends, 5½", ram's head figural, #R-718, green, pr...$28.00
Bookends, 6", calla lilies, #R-475, yellow & green, pr...$26.00
Bowl, console; 11" high, swan figural w/open back, #R-955, yellow...$26.00
Bowl, 5" dia, indents around sides, scalloped top, #345S, mottled colors $12.00
Candy box, 8" dia, applied Hawaiian-style flower on lid, #R-590 ....$26.00
Cigarette box, 7" long, #R-560, green, rectangular shape, w/lid $12.00
Cigarette box, 9¼" long, turtle figural, snail on back (finial), #R-684, green $22.00
Dish, 13" long, swan figural, pink & blue, open back...$18.00
Figurine, panther, 13" long, #R-733 ....$22.00
Flower block, #R-363, nude astride large fish, #R-299, white...$12.00
Flower holder, 12½", stylized colt figural, #R-235, mauve agate (mauve, blue, & green mottle).....................$28.00
Lamp, TV; 13½" long, scottie figural, #R-780, black $35.00
Lamp, TV; 9", Comedy & Tragedy masks, black..........$35.00
Lamp, 24", two applied cabbage roses, #7174, flower finial, pink..$40.00
Lamp, 27", flying fish figural, #5351, dark green, w/original shade..$58.00
Planter, 10" long, pig figural, #454N, white w/gold $24.00
Planter, 11" long, turtle figural, #R-834, open back, dark green mottle $24.00
Planter, 17" long, fawn w/wide-stretched front & back legs, #R-1351 ....$22.00
Planter, 4½", cow figural, creamy white $12.00
Planter, 6" long, scottie dog figural, #3377, white $10.00
Planter, 8½", fish figural, #R-752, light green $15.00
Vase, cornucopia; 13", #R-228, dark green....................$22.00
Vase, fan form, #R-523 ....$25.00

Vase, 11½", 'Pegasus,' horse head form, #R-393, blue..$40.00
Vase, 12", gazelle head figural, #R-857, brown...........$22.00
Vase, 12", laurel wreath w/bow, #R-303, pink & blue ..$22.00
Vase, 12" long, flower basket, #R-386, pink & blue $22.00
Vase, 12½", leaf figural, #R-138, dark green................$15.00
Vase, 14", lily form, #R-446, blue-gray w/green interior glaze..$28.00
Vase, 15", peacock (head turned) figural, #R-31, pink & blue, open tail $55.00
Vase, 7", snail shell figural, #R-299, white..................$15.00
Vase, 8", conch shell figural, #R-321, pink & blue......$12.00
Vase, 8", kneeling nude beside cornucopia form, #R-426, pink & blue $22.00
Vase, 8", swan figural, #R-713, pink & blue................$15.00
Vase, 9", sailfish figural, #R-271, pink & blue $28.00

Hall China Company

Hall China is still in production in East Liverpool, Ohio, where they have been located since around the turn of the century. They have produced literally hundreds of lines of kitchen and dinnerware items, for both home and commercial use. Several of these in particular have become very collectible.

They're especially famous for their teapots, some of which were shaped like automobiles, basketballs, donuts, and footballs. Each teapot was made in an assortment of colors, often trimmed in gold. Many were decaled to match their dinnerware lines. Some are quite rare, and collecting them all would be a real challenge.

During the 1950s, Eva Zeisel designed dinnerware shapes with a streamlined, ultra modern look. Her lines, Classic and Century, were used with various decals as the basis for several of Hall's dinnerware patterns. She also designed kitchenware lines with the same modern styling; they were called Casual Living and Tri-Tone. All her designs are popular with today's collectors.

Although some of the old kitchenware shapes and teapots are being produced today, you'll be able to tell them from the old pieces by the backstamp. To identify these new issues, Hall marks them with the shaped rectangular 'Hall' trademark they've used since the early 1970s.

For more information, we recommend *The Collector's Encyclopedia of Hall China* by Margaret and Kenn Whitmyer.

Acacia, bowl, 6", Radiance $8.50
Acacia, casserole, Medallion...$35.00
Acacia, teapot, Radiance..$90.00
Arizona, ash tray, Tomorrow's Classic...........................$4.00
Arizona, casserole, 1¼-qt, Tomorrow's Classic $12.00
Arizona, plate, 11"...$5.00
Arizona, platter, 15", Tomorrow's Classic....................$12.00
Arizona, teapot, 6-cup, Tomorrow's Classic.................$24.00
Autumn Leaf, bowl, 9" dia...$55.00
Autumn Leaf, coaster, 3⅛"..$4.00
Bean pot, Pert, Chinese red, no decals, tab handle.....$34.00
Blue Blossom, batter jug, Sundial.................................$100.00
Blue Blossom, bowl, 7½", Thick Rim $25.00
Blue Blossom, casserole, Five Band.............................$40.00
Blue Blossom, jug, 2-qt, Five Band..............................$45.00
Blue Bouquet, bowl, cereal; 6", D-style........................$6.00
Blue Bouquet, bowl, 7¾", flared..................................$16.00
Blue Bouquet, bowl, 9", Radiance................................$18.00
Blue Bouquet, casserole, Thick Rim............................$25.00
Blue Bouquet, coffeepot, Terrace................................$45.00
Blue Bouquet, French baker, fluted.............................$16.00
Blue Bouquet, gravy boat, D-style...............................$20.00
Blue Bouquet, jug, Medallion #3..................................$14.00
Blue Bouquet, plate, 9" dia, D-style..............................$8.50
Blue Bouquet, platter, 13¼", oval, D-style.................$18.00
Blue Bouquet, pretzel jar..$65.00
Blue Bouquet, teapot, Aladdin, round lid w/infusor...$50.00
Blue Garden, bowl, 8½", Thick Rim $25.00
Blue Garden, canister, Radiance...................................$95.00
Blue Garden, teapot, Aladdin $100.00
Bouquet, bowl, cereal; 6", Classic..................................$4.00
Bouquet, butter dish, Classic..$25.00
Bouquet, candlestick, 8", Classic.................................$14.00
Bouquet, egg cup, Classic...$18.00
Bouquet, gravy boat, Classic..$12.00
Bouquet, plate, 6", Classic..$2.00
Bouquet, platter, 15", Classic.......................................$14.00
Cactus, bowl, 7¼", Five Band......................................$14.00
Cactus, jug, 1½-pt, Five Band......................................$40.00
Cactus, sugar bowl, w/lid, Viking...............................$14.00
Cameo Rose, bowl, cereal; 6¼", tab handle.................$4.50
Cameo Rose, bowl, 10½", oval....................................$12.50
Cameo Rose, gravy boat & underplate.........................$20.00
Cameo Rose, plate, 8"..$5.00
Cameo Rose, platter, 13¼", oval $14.00
Cameo Rose, teapot, 8-cup $38.00

Canister, 2-qt, Radiance, cobalt, plain $60.00
Canister, 2-qt, Radiance, ivory, plain..........................$20.00

Caprice, plate, 10", small serving bowl, cup & saucer set, each..$6.00
Caprice, ashtray, Tomorrow's Classic $3.50
Caprice, casserole, 2-qt, Tomorrow's Classic $15.00
Caprice, jug, 3-qt, Tomorrow's Classic........................$15.00
Caprice, platter, 15", Tomorrow's Classic....................$14.00
Caprice, teapot, 6-cup, Tomorrow's Classic $25.00
Crocus, bowl, cereal; 6", D-style $7.50
Crocus, bowl, 7½", Radiance..$12.00
Crocus, coffeepot, Five Band..$35.00
Crocus, creamer, Medallion...$12.00
Crocus, French baker, fluted...$20.00
Crocus, gravy boat, D-style...$20.00
Crocus, mug, tankard style..$28.00
Crocus, plate, 8¼", D-style...$8.00
Crocus, platter, 11¼", oval, D-style.............................$16.00
Crocus, soup tureen, clover lid.....................................$90.00
Crocus, sugar bowl, w/lid, Medallion...........................$14.00
Crocus, teapot, 2-cup, Terrace $60.00
Crocus, tidbit, 3-tier, D-style...$40.00

Dripolator, Poppy & Wheat................................$125.00

Fantasy, bowl, fruit; 5¾", Tomorrow's Classic...............$3.00
Fantasy, bowl, 8½", Thick Rim..............................$16.00
Fantasy, butter dish, Tomorrow's Classic $18.00
Fantasy, casserole, Sundial...............................$30.00
Fantasy, casserole, 2-qt, Tomorrow's Classic $14.00
Fantasy, drip jar, w/lid, Thick Rim..........................$25.00
Fantasy, jug, 3-qt, Tomorrow's Classic $12.50
Fantasy, teapot, 6-cup, Tomorrow's Classic $20.00
Five Band, batter bowl, cobalt.............................$45.00
Five Band, bowl, 6", ivory....................................$5.00
Five Band, casserole, 8", cobalt $30.00
Five Band, casserole, 8", ivory $20.00
Five Band, jug, 5", cobalt $15.00
Five Band, jug, 6¼", red $20.00
Flamingo, batter bowl, Five Band.........................$35.00
Flamingo, creamer, Viking $15.00
Floral Lattice, bowl, 8¾", Five Band $12.50
Floral Lattice, salt & pepper shakers, canister style, pr..$36.00
Frost Flowers, ash tray, Tomorrow's Classic $4.00
Frost Flowers, candlestick, 8", Tomorrow's Classic $14.00
Frost Flowers, casserole, 2-qt, Tomorrow's Classic......$15.00
Frost Flowers, platter, 15", Tomorrow's Classic $14.00
Golden Clover, batter bowl, Five Band....................$35.00
Golden Clover, bowl, 7½", Thick Rim $14.00
Golden Clover, casserole, Radiance.......................$25.00
Golden Glo, ashtray, shell shape $3.00
Golden Glo, casserole, duck knob $12.50
Golden Glo, teapot, Aladdin $30.00
Harlequin, bowl, cereal; 6"..................................$4.00
Harlequin, candlestick, 8"..................................$10.50
Harlequin, gravy boat......................................$12.00
Harlequin, teapot, 6-cup...................................$25.00
Heather Rose, bowl, fruit; 5¼", E-style $3.00
Heather Rose, bowl, 8¾", Flare-style $10.00
Heather Rose, coffeepot, Terrace..........................$30.00
Heather Rose, gravy boat & underplate, E-style $14.00
Heather Rose, jug, Rayed $12.00
Heather Rose, plate, 7¼", E-style $3.50
Heather Rose, platter, 15½", oval, E-shape................$15.00
Heather Rose, teapot, Flare-style..........................$25.00
Holiday, bowl, salad; 14½".................................$10.00
Holiday, casserole, 2-qt $14.00
Holiday, platter, 15".......................................$14.00
Meadow Flower, bowl, 6", Thick Rim $12.00
Meadow Flower, casserole, Radiance $25.00
Morning Glory, bowl, 9", straight-sided...................$15.00
Morning Glory, casserole, Thick Rim $20.00
Morning Glory, teapot, Aladdin $40.00
Mulberry, bowl, cereal; 6" $3.00
Mulberry, butter dish $24.00
Mulberry, jug, 3-qt $10.00
Mulberry, platter, 17" $14.00
Mulberry, vase...$12.00
Mums, bowl, fruit; 5½", D-style.............................$4.00
Mums, bowl, 9½", Medallion, ruffled, tab handle........$40.00
Mums, creamer, Art Deco..................................$12.00
Mums, jug, Medallion #3 ....$25.00
Mums, plate, 8¼", D-style..................................$5.00

Mums, platter, 13¼", oval, D-style $15.00
Mums, stack set, Radiance.................................$50.00
Mums, teapot, Rutherford..................................$55.00
No 488, bowl, 7½", Radiance $12.00
No 488, casserole, Sundial.................................$35.00
No 488, coffeepot, Meltdown...............................$50.00
No 488, cookie jar, Five Band..............................$60.00
No 488, jug, Medallion, ice lip $35.00
No 488, plate, 9", D-style....................................$8.00
No 488, platter, 13¼", oval, D-style $18.00
No 488, salt & pepper shakers, Novelty Radiance, pr.$30.00
No 488, teapot, Radiance..................................$95.00
Orange Poppy, bowl, cereal; 6", C-style.....................$7.00
Orange Poppy, bowl, 10", Radiance $25.00
Orange Poppy, canister set, 4-pc, metal...................$40.00
Orange Poppy, casserole, 8", oval $25.00
Orange Poppy, creamer, Great American $10.00
Orange Poppy, plate, 9", C-style............................$8.00
Orange Poppy, platter, 13¼", oval, C-style................$16.50
Orange Poppy, teapot, Donut.............................$120.00
Orange Poppy, tray, oval, metal $20.00
Pastel Morning Glory, bowl, cereal; 6", D-style $6.00
Pastel Morning Glory, bowl, soup; 8½", flat, D-style...$10.00
Pastel Morning Glory, bowl, 7½", Radiance...............$10.00
Pastel Morning Glory, coffeepot, Terrace...................$45.00
Pastel Morning Glory, plate, 8¼", D-style...................$6.00
Pastel Morning Glory, platter, 13¼", D-style $18.00
Pastel Morning Glory, salt & pepper shakers, Novelty Radi-
    ance, pr..$30.00
Pastel Morning Glory, sugar bowl, w/lid, Art Deco $14.00
Pastel Morning Glory, teapot, Aladdin $50.00
Peach Blossom, bowl, oval, E-style $14.00
Peach Blossom, coffeepot, 6-cup..........................$30.00
Peach Blossom, plate, 8" $3.50
Peach Blossom, salt & pepper shakers, pr.................$12.00
Pine Cone, bowl, salad; 14½", Tomorrow's Classic $12.00
Pine cone, butter dish, Tomorrow's Classic $25.00
Pine Cone, casserole, 2-qt, Tomorrow's Classic..........$16.00
Pine Cone, gravy boat, Tomorrow's Classic...............$10.00
Pine Cone, ladle, Tomorrow's Classic.......................$6.00
Pine Cone, plate, 9¼", E-style..............................$4.00
Pine Cone, platter, 15", Tomorrow's Classic...............$14.00
Primrose, bowl, soup; 8", flat, E-style $6.00
Primrose, cake plate, E-style $12.00
Primrose, creamer, E-style..................................$5.00
Primrose, jug, Rayed $10.00
Primrose, plate, 10", E-style................................$5.00
Primrose, platter, 13¼", oval, E-style $12.00
Primrose, saucer, E-style....................................$1.50
Radiance, covered jug, red-orange $40.00
Red Poppy, bowl, cereal; 6", D-style $6.50
Red Poppy, bowl, 10¼", oval, D-style $15.00
Red Poppy, bowl, 7½", Radiance $8.50
Red Poppy, canister set, 4-pc, square, metal $35.00
Red Poppy, creamer, Daniel.................................$8.00
Red Poppy, gravy boat, D-style $20.00
Red Poppy, jug, 4", Daniel $25.00
Red Poppy, match safe, metal..............................$30.00

Red Poppy, plate, 9", D-style $7.50
Red Poppy, platter, 13¼", oval, D-style....................$18.00
Red Poppy, recipe box, metal.................................$20.00
Red Poppy, salt & pepper shakers, teardrop, pr.........$16.00
Red Poppy, tablecloth, cotton................................$50.00
Red Poppy, teapot, Aladdin, oval infusor & lid..........$50.00
Red Poppy, toaster cover, plastic...........................$14.00
Red Poppy, tray, rectangular, metal.........................$20.00
Red Poppy, tumbler, clear glass.............................$18.00
Red Poppy, waste can, 12½", oval, metal...................$25.00
Rose Parade, bean pot, tab handle..........................$35.00
Rose Parade, bowl, 9", straight-sided.......................$15.00
Rose Parade, jug, 5", Pert...................................$18.00
Rose White, bowl, 6", Medallion.............................$10.00
Rose White, casserole, tab handle...........................$16.50
Royal Rose, bowl, 6", straight-sided..........................$8.00
Royal Rose, bowl, 8½", Thick Rim...........................$15.00
Royal Rose, custard, straight-sided...........................$7.50
Sears' Arlington, bowl, cereal; 6¼", E-style................$3.50
Sears' Arlington, pickle dish, 9", E-style...................$5.00
Sears' Arlington, plate, 10", E-style........................$4.50
Sears' Arlington, platter, 15½", oval, E-style..............$14.00
Sears' Richmond, bowl, soup; 8", flat.......................$5.50
Sears' Richmond, plate, 6½"..................................$2.50
Sears' Richmond, platter, 15½", oval........................$15.00
Seranade, platter, 13¼", D-style............................$14.00
Serenade, bowl, cereal; 6", D-style..........................$5.00
Serenade, bowl, 9", Radiance...............................$10.00
Serenade, coffeepot, Terrace................................$25.00
Serenade, creamer, Art Deco.................................$10.00
Serenade, drip jar, w/lid, Radiance..........................$14.00
Serenade, French baker, fluted..............................$12.00
Serenade, gravy boat, D-style...............................$16.50
Serenade, platter, 13¼", oval, D-style......................$16.00
Serenade, pretzel jar...$50.00
Silhouette, bowl, soup; 8½", flat, D-style..................$12.00
Silhouette, bowl, 7¾", flared................................$20.00
Silhouette, bowl, 8½", Medallion............................$15.00
Silhouette, canister set, 4-pc, metal........................$35.00
Silhouette, coffeepot, Five Band.............................$35.00
Silhouette, gravy boat, D-style..............................$20.00
Silhouette, jug, Simplicity...................................$60.00
Silhouette, pitcher, crystal, MacBeth-Evans style.......$100.00
Silhouette, plate, 8¼", D-style...............................$7.00
Silhouette, salt & pepper shakers, Medallion, pr.........$30.00
Silhouette, tea tile, 6".......................................$80.00
Silhouette, teapot, Streamline...............................$80.00
Silhouette, tray, oval, metal.................................$25.00
Silhouette, tumbler, 10-oz, crystal..........................$16.00
Spring, ashtray, Tomorrow's Classic..........................$4.00
Spring, bowl, fruit; footed, Tomorrow's Classic...........$15.00
Spring, casserole, 2-qt, Tomorrow's Classic...............$15.00
Spring, plate, 8", Tomorrow's Classic.........................$3.50
Spring, vase, Tomorrow's Classic............................$14.00
Springtime, bowl, soup; 8½", flat, D-style...................$8.00
Springtime, bowl, 7½", Thick Rim............................$10.00
Springtime, casserole, Thick Rim............................$20.00
Springtime, creamer, modern..................................$6.00

Springtime, plate, 9", D-style................................$5.50
Springtime, platter, 15", oval, D-style......................$18.00
Sunglow, butter dish...$25.00
Sunglow, platter, 13¾".......................................$10.00
Sunglow, relish, 4-part.......................................$12.00

Teapot, football, emerald green w/gold trim $375.00
Teapot, 2-cup, New York, Cadet blue w/gold.............$30.00
Teapot, 2-cup, New York, delphinium blue w/gold...$22.00
Teapot, 3-cup, Pert, Chinese red, no decals...............$16.00
Teapot, 4-cup, Hollywood, daffodil, gold net.............$28.00
Teapot, 6-cup, Aladdin, Marine blue w/gold..............$40.00
Teapot, 6-cup, Automobile, cobalt w/platinum.........$400.00
Teapot, 6-cup, Damascus, turquoise....................$100.00
Teapot, 6-cup, Football, Chinese red.....................$400.00
Teapot, 6-cup, Melody, canary w/white & gold.........$175.00
Teapot, 6-cup, Modern, turquoise w/gold.................$42.00
Teapot, 6-cup, New York, red...............................$55.00
Teapot, 6-cup, Philadelphia, turquoise w/gold...........$45.00
Teapot, 6-cup, Radiance, cobalt, plain.....................$65.00
Teapot, 6-cup, Rhythm, cobalt.............................$150.00
Teapot, 6-cup, Star, turquoise w/gold & stars.............$35.00
Teapot, 6-cup, Sundial, red, plain.........................$60.00
Teapot, 6-cup, Windshield, maroon w/roses & gold...$35.00
Tulip, bowl, cereal; 6", D-style..............................$7.00
Tulip, bowl, 7½", Thick Rim.................................$14.00
Tulip, casserole, Radiance..................................$25.00
Tulip, gravy boat, D-style...................................$20.00
Tulip, plate, 10", D-style.....................................$8.00
Tulip, platter, 13¼", D-style................................$16.00
Tulip, sugar bowl, w/lid, modern...........................$12.00

Westinghouse, water jug, cobalt...........................$75.00

211

Wild Poppy, bowl, 9", Radiance $18.00
Wild Poppy, casserole, Thick Rim $30.00
Wild Poppy, drip jar, Radiance $22.00
Wild Poppy, salt & pepper shakers, Radiance, pr $25.00
Wildfire, bowl, fruit; 5½", D-style...................$3.50
Wildfire, bowl, 7½", Thick Rim $14.00
Wildfire, bowl, 9", straight-sided...................$12.00
Wildfire, casserole, tab handle $20.00
Wildfire, coffeepot, S-lid...................$35.00
Wildfire, drip jar, tab handle $12.50
Wildfire, egg cup $35.00
Wildfire, plate, 10", D-style...................$8.00
Wildfire, platter, 11¼", D-style...................$12.00
Wildfire, teapot, 6-cup, Pert $60.00
Wildfire, tidbit, 3-tier, D-style...................$30.00
Yellow Rose, bowl, soup; 8½", flat...................$8.00
Yellow Rose, bowl, 7½", Radiance $10.00
Yellow Rose, casserole, Radiance $25.00
Yellow Rose, coffeepot, Waverly $25.00
Yellow Rose, creamer, Norse $10.00
Yellow Rose, gravy boat, D-style...................$20.00
Yellow Rose, plate, 9", D-style...................$6.00
Yellow Rose, platter, 13¼", oval, D-style...................$14.00
Yellow Rose, saucer, D-style...................$2.00
Yellow Rose, sugar bowl, w/lid, Norse $12.00

Hallmark Ornaments

Some of the Hallmark Christmas ornaments that have been made since they were first introduced in 1973 are worth many times their original price. This is especially true of the first one issued in a particular series. For instance, Cardinals, first in the Holiday Wildlife series issued in 1982 has a value today of $400.00 (MIB).

If you'd like to learn more about them, we recommend *The Secondary Price Guide to Hallmark Ornaments* by Rosie Wells.

Our values are for ornaments that are mint and in their original boxes.

1973, Betsey Clark Series, #XHD 106-2, little girl feeds a deer on white glass ball, first in series, 3¼" dia..$125.00
1973, Christmas Is Love, #XHD 106-2, two flying angels playing mandolins on white glass ball, 3¼" dia....$52.00
1973, Manger Scene, #XHD 102-2, nativity scene on dark red ground on white glass ball, 3¼" dia................$65.00
1974, Angel, #QX 110-1, realistic bust portrait on white glass ball, 3¼" dia.................$65.00
1974, Norman Rockwell, #QX 111-1, working elves & napping Santa wearing tool apron on white glass ball, 3¼" dia...$60.00
1975, Adorable Adornments Drummer Boy, #QX 161-1, figural, $2.50 original price, 3½" $240.00
1975, Little Miracles, #QX 140-1, cherub & forest friends on white glass ball, 1¾" dia, set of 4.................$42.50
1976, Currier & Ives, #QX 209-1, 'To Commemorate Christmas 1976' under winter farm scene on white glass ball, 3" dia.................$45.00

1976, Raggedy Ann, #QX 212-1, Ann near stocking-trimmed fireplace on white satin ball, dated 1976, 2½" dia.................$55.00
1977, Baby's First Christmas, #QX 131-5, infant w/teddy bear on white satin ball, dated 1977, 3¼" dia.......$50.00
1977, Beauty of America Collection Desert, #QX 159-5, desert mission w/'Ring Out Christmas Bells,' 2⅝" dia.................$28.00
1977, Twirl-About Collection: Della Robia Wreath, #QX 193-5, kneeling & praying girl twirls in center of wreath, 3¼" $120.00
1978, Colors of Christmas Angel, 'stained-glass' acrylic angel in red dress w/gold wings & halo, 3⅝".................$45.00
1978, Holly & Poinsettia Ball, #QX 147-6, intricate carved detailing, 3½" dia $75.00
1979, A Christmas Treat, #QX 134-7, teddy bear wearing red cap & coat holds a giant candy cane, 4¾" $65.00
1979, Friendship, #QX 203-9, ice skating & sleigh riding scene on white glass ball, 3¼" dia.................$20.00
1979, Holiday Highlights Love, #QX 304-7, 'Time of Memories & Dreams' on silvered-foil acrylic heart, 3½".$90.00
1979, Holiday Highlights Snowflake, #QX 301-9, acrylic snowflake dated 1979 in center, 3½".................$60.00
1979, Thimble-A Christmas Salute, #QX 131-9, soldier dressed in red & blue wears thimble hat, 2nd in series, 2¼" $125.00
1980, A Spot of Christmas Cheer, #QX 153-4, figural teapot cottage w/chipmunk & tree inside, dated, 2¾"...$135.00
1980, Black Baby's First Christmas, #QX 229-4, baby sits in decorated tree w/birds on white satin ball, 3¼"...$20.00
1980, Dad, #QX 214-1, 'Dad' on red & green plaid ground w/'Dad Is Always Caring' on gold glass ball, 3¼" ..$16.00
1981, Christmas in the Forest, #QX 813-5, animals & 'Christmas Arrives in the Heart' on white glass ball, 3¼" ..$65.00
1981, Drummer Boy, #QX 148-1, jointed hand-painted wood figure, 3½" $38.00
1981, Little Trimmers Jolly Snowman, hand-crafted figure wearing top hat & scarf, 2¼".................$40.00
1982, The Spirit of Christmas, #QX 452-6, Santa in biplane, dated 1982, 1¾".................$115.00
1982, Twelve Days of Christmas, #QX 203-6, scenes from Christmas carol on white pebbled-glass ball, 3¼" ..$25.00
1983, Angel Messenger, #QX 408-7, angel in blue carries brass date (1983), 2".................$85.00
1983, Betsey Clark, #QX 440-1, painted porcelain angel on cloud w/star, 3½".................$22.50
1983, First Christmas Together, #QX 432-9, polished brass heart-form locket w/space for two photos, 2⅝" ..$35.00
1984, Bell Ringer Squirrel, #QX 443-1, squirrel & acorn form clapper in clear glass bell, 4" $20.00
1984, Cuckoo Clock, #QX 455-1, finely detailed figural clock w/'Merry Christmas' on brass face, 3¼".................$45.00
1984, Grandchild's First Christmas, #QX 460-1, lamb pull toy, dated 1984, 3⅜".................$20.00
1985, Art Masterpiece, #QX 377-2, 'Madonna of the Pomegranate' on bezeled satin, 2nd in series, 2¾" dia.................$14.00
1985, Fraggle Rock Holiday, #QX 265-5, Fraggle Rock gang w/'Happy Holidays' on blue glass teardrop, 3" $15.00

1985, Nostalgic Houses Toy Shop, #QX 497-5, 2-story house w/detailed interior, 2nd in series, 2½"....................**$55.00**

1985, Thimble Series Santa, #QX 472-5, Santa w/thimble backpack, 8th in series, 2⅜".................................**$27.50**

1986, Holiday Wildlife Cedar Waxwing, #QX 321-6, painted wood w/'Cedar Waxwing...,' 5th in series, 2½" **$18.00**

1986, Mr & Mrs Claus Merry Mistletoe Time, #QX 402-6, couple under mistletoe, 1st in series, 3½"............**$65.00**

1986, Rah Rah Rabbit, #QX 421-6, figural cheerleader rabbit w/megaphone & pompom, dated 1986, 2½"........**$22.50**

1987, Daughter, #QX 463-7, sleigh pulled by two reindeer, dated 1987, 1¼"..**$17.50**

1987, Jack Frosting, #QX 449-9, kneeling figure paints leaf w/large brush, 2½"...**$30.00**

1987, Porcelain Bear, #QX 442-7, hand-painted Cinnamon Bear w/large stocking, 5th in series, 2⅛" **$18.00**

1987, Wood Childhood Horse, hand-painted wood horse pull toy w/plush mane & yarn tail, 4th in series, dated 1987, 2¼"...**$15.00**

1988, Baby's First Christmas, #QLX 718-4, carousel w/horses under blue & white canopy, dated 1988, 4"..........**$35.00**

1988, Chris Mouse Star, #QLX 715-4, mouse in red nightcap & blue nightshirt cleans star, 4th in series, 2½" **$32.50**

1988, Country Express, #QLX 721-1, light & motion ball w/train going over trestle & through tunnel, 3½".**$40.00**

1988, Kitty Capers, #QLX 716-4, kitten tangled in box of blinking lights, clips to tree, 1½"...........................**$30.00**

1988, Noah's Ark, #QX 490-4, pressed tin toy w/movable wheels & pull cord, 2⅛" **$21.00**

1988, Sister, QX 499-4, porcelain bell w/scene of girl placing star on top of tree, dated 1988, 3" **$17.00**

1989, Cactus Cowboy, #QX 411-2, cactus dressed as cowboy & wrapped in red lights, dated 1989, 3½".............**$25.00**

1989, Cranberry Bunny, #QX 426-2, white-flocked bunny in stocking hat strings cranberries, 2⅝" **$14.00**

1989, Friendship Time, #QX 413-2, modeled as two mice in teacup, dated 1989, 2½"......................................**$24.00**

1989, Gentle Fawn, #QX 548-5, flocked fawn w/ribbon & holly at neck, 2¼" **$17.00**

1989, Paddington Bear, #QX 429-2, bear w/'Please Look After This Bear' on gift tag, 4¼"............................**$16.00**

1989, Rocking Horse, #QX 462-2, rocking horse w/brass stirrups & red yarn reins, 9th in series, 4" wide........**$26.00**

1989, Spirit of St Nick, #QLX 728-5, shows light & motion w/Santa barnstorming farm, 4"..............................**$44.00**

1989, Sweet Memories Photo Holder, #QX 438-5, peppermint wreath w/photo in center, dated, 3" **$12.00**

1989, Thimble Puppy, #QX 455-2, puppy sits in thimble, 12th & final in series, 1¾".......................................**$12.50**

1990, Baby's First Christmas, #QLX 724-6, shows light & motion w/stork flying over snowy village, 3¾" **$45.00**

1990, Blessings of Love, #QLX 736-3, nativity w/animals in lighted panorama ball, 4¾"................................**$25.00**

1990, From Our Home to Yours, #QX 216-6, needlepoint design of two homes joined by fence on blue glass ball, 2⅞" dia...**$7.00**

1990, Hark! It's Herald, #QX 446-3, elf w/bass drum, 2nd in series, 2⅛"..**$12.50**

1990, Lovable Dears, #QX 547-6, girl hugs neck of fawn, 2½"...**$15.00**

1990, Reindeer Champs Comet, #QX 443-3, reindeer in soccer uniform kicking ball, 5th in series, 3¼"..........**$14.50**

1990, Starlight Angel, #QLX 730-6, angel w/lighted bag of stars, 2¾"...**$26.50**

Halloween

Next to Christmas, you probably have more happy childhood recollections of Halloween than any other holiday of the year. If somehow you've managed to hang onto some old party decorations or one of the jack-o'-lanterns that we used to collect candy in, you already have a good start on a collection that you'll really enjoy.

Candy container, 6", nodder head on pumpkin body, marked w/purple stamp Made in Germany, M..**$245.00**

Decoration, girl clown, 11", celluloid w/crepe paper body, EX...**$75.00**

Decoration, large diecut of black cat w/arched back, Germany **$65.00**

Decoration, owl, pressed paper, Germany, 1930, EX..**$85.00**

Fan, cat face, 12½", paper w/crepe paper trim...........**$85.00**

Jack-o'-lantern, tin & glass, battery operated, M..........**$65.00**

Jack-o'-lantern, 4", papier-mache, w/insert, Germany.**$68.00**

Lantern, owl, pressed cardboard, black w/orange & gold .**$150.00**

Lantern, 5x6", owl, moon, & bat lithograph on tin, 1930 .**$95.00**

Mask, skeleton, gauze type, EX **$10.00**

Noisemaker, Black musicians lithographed on tin, wooden handle, EX **$15.00**

Noisemaker, clown playing drums lithographed on tin, wood handle, USA **$20.00**

Noisemaker, girls in costumes, tin & wood, Barone Toy Mfg Co...**$17.50**

Noisemaker, witch & pumpkin emblem on wood, 1920, EX $45.00
Noisemaker, 5", black devil lithograph on tin, wood handle, EX..$45.00
Nut cup, with diecut on black & orange paper $25.00
Rattle, 6x4" dia, witches & cats design lithographed on tin, Gotham $45.00
Roly poly, 3½", scarecrow, celluloid, NM..................$120.00
Tambourine, witches, cats, & goblins, plain top, EX...$65.00
Tambourine, 6½" dia, people dancing about pumpkin face $85.00

Halloween Costumes

If you can find one of these still in the original box and the price is right, buy it! During the fifties and sixties, Collegeville and Ben Cooper made these costumes to represent popular TV and movie characters of the day. Unless noted otherwise our values are for costumes that are absolutely mint and in their original boxes. If your costume or the box shows even a minimum amount of wear or damage, deduct at least 35%.

Aquaman, Ben Cooper, 1967, in original box, EX.......$50.00
Aquaman, Ben Cooper, 1967, in original box, M $100.00
Atom Ant, Ben Cooper, in original 10x12" box, M......$50.00
Batfink, Collegeville, 1965, 1-pc suit w/mask, in original box, M..$65.00
Batman, Ben Cooper, 1966, in original 8x10" box.......$35.00
Beatnik, Collegeville, 1961, mask & 1-pc suit, EX.......$35.00
Bewitched (Samantha), Ben Cooper, 1965, black & yellow dress w/plastic mask, in original 10x12" box, M ..$75.00
Birdman, Ben Cooper, 1967, original 10x12" box, M ..$35.00
Bride of Frankenstein, Collegeville, 1980, mask & 1-pc suit, EX..$30.00
Captain Action, Ben Cooper, 1966, original box, M..$200.00
Daredevil, Ben Cooper, 1967, in original box, M $125.00
Doctor Doom, Ben Cooper, 1967, in original 10x12" box, M $150.00
Flash Gordon, Collegeville, 1978, in original box, M ..$30.00
Frankenstein, Ben Cooper, 1963, 1-pc suit w/mask, in original box, M $60.00
Green Hornet, Ben Cooper, 1966, in original 12x14" box, M $200.00
Green Lantern, Ben Cooper, 1967, in original box, M ...$80.00
Herman Munster, Ben Cooper, 1964, 1-pc suit w/plastic mask, in original 12x14" box, M $225.00
Iron Man, Ben Cooper, 1967, original 10x12" box, M.$75.00
Land of the Giants, Ben Cooper, 1968, in original 10x12" box, M $125.00
Lurch, Ben Cooper, 1965, in original box, M............$200.00
Mad's Alfred E Neuman, Collegeville, 1959-60, 1-pc w/mask, in original box, M $175.00
Mandrake, Collegeville, 1978, in original box, M $30.00
Morticia, Ben Cooper, 1965, 1-pc suit w/painted plastic face, in original box, M $150.00
Mouseketeer, Ben Cooper, 1960s, original box, EX $25.00

Mr Spock, Collegeville, 1967, in original box, M.......$125.00
Napoleon Solo, Halso, 1965, 1-pc suit w/transparent mask, in original box, M $125.00
Olive Oyl, Collegeville, ca 1958, in original 3x9x11" box, NM..$30.00
Outer Limits, Collegeville, 1964, 1-pc suit shows monster on front, w/plastic monster mask, in original 10x12" box, M $200.00
Rat Fink, Ben Cooper, 1963, in original box, M $150.00
Rat Patrol, Ben Cooper, 1967, 1-pc w/mask wearing bush hat, in original box, M $50.00
Rin Tin Tin, Ben Cooper, 1956, in original box, EX....$57.50

Superman, Ben Cooper, 1950s, EX in box $50.00

Harker Pottery

Harker was one of the oldest potteries in the country; their history could be traced back to the 1840s. In the thirties, a new plant was built in Chester, West Virginia, and the company began manufacturing kitchen and dinnerware lines, eventually employing as many as three hundred workers.

Several of these lines are popular with collectors today. One of the most easily recognized is Cameoware. It is usually found in pink or blue and is decorated with white silhouettes of flowers, though other designs were made as well. Colonial Lady, Red Apple, Amy, Mallow, and Pansy are some of their other lines that are fairly easy to find and reassemble into sets.

If you'd like to learn more about Harker, we recommend *The Collector's Encyclopedia of American Dinnerware* by Jo Cunningham and *The Collector's Guide to Harker Pottery* by Neva W. Colbert.

Amy, bowl, soup; tab handles.......................................$6.00
Amy, sugar bowl $8.00
Basket, creamer $8.00
Birds & Flowers, plate, utility; 12" $17.00
Blue Blossoms, pitcher, sm $18.00
Boyce, pitcher, w/gold trim handle, lg.......................$35.00

Cameo Rose, cup & saucer	**$10.00**
Cameo Rose, salt & pepper shakers, pr	**$16.00**
Cherry Blossom, platter	**$8.00**
Cherry Trim, saucer	**$3.00**
Colonial Lady, bowl, mixing; 3-pc set	**$37.00**
Cottage, casserole, w/lid	**$28.00**
Countryside, rolling pin	**$125.00**
Deco Dahlia, ash tray, 5¼"	**$8.00**

Deco Dahlia, platter, 9½"	**$15.00**
English Countryside, custard, individual	**$4.00**
Fruits, pitcher, lg	**$32.50**
Heritage, sugar bowl, w/lid	**$10.00**
Ivy Vine, pitcher, 7"	**$30.00**
Ivy Vine, platter, 8"	**$18.00**
Jessica, bowl, utility; lg	**$27.50**
Leaf Swirl, coffeepot, w/lid	**$35.00**
Mallow, bowl, 7½"	**$8.00**
Old Vintage, bowl, soup; 8", flat	**$8.00**
Old Vintage, cup & saucer	**$10.00**
Pansy, bowl, 6"	**$6.00**
Pastel Tulip, pie plate, 10"	**$20.00**
Pastel Tulip, plate, 9"	**$6.00**

Pate sur Pate, Gravy boat, w/underplate	**$12.00**
Petit Point Rose, bowl, utility; 6x11½"	**$25.00**
Petit Point Rose, cake server	**$20.00**
Red Apple, bowl, utility; 10" dia	**$30.00**

Red Apple, bowl, 9"	**$30.00**
Rose Spray, bowl, cream soup; tab handles	**$10.00**
Rose Spray, cup & saucer	**$10.00**
Rose Spray, plate, dinner; 10x10"	**$10.00**
Rose Spray, plate, 6" dia	**$4.00**
Royal Rose, cake plate	**$15.00**
Ruffled Tulip, bowl, w/lid	**$18.00**
Slender Leaf, plate, 8"	**$6.00**
Springtime, plate, 10"	**$6.00**

Harlequin Dinnerware

This is another line of solid-color dinnerware made by the Fiesta people, Homer Laughlin. Harlequin was less-expensive, designed to cater to the dimestore trade. In fact, it was sold exclusively through the F.W. Woolworth Company. It was introduced to the public in the late 1930s, and records indicate that production continued until near the middle of the 1960s.

Like Fiesta, Harlequin is very Deco in appearance. But in contrast to Fiesta's ring handles, Harlequin's are angular, as are many of its shapes. The band of rings, similar to Fiesta's, is set farther away from its rims. Harlequin isn't nearly as heavy as Fiesta, and it was never marked.

Some of its colors are more desirable to collectors than others, so they're worth more. Two values are given for each item we've listed. The higher values apply to these colors: maroon, gray, medium green, spruce green, chartreuse, dark green, rose, mauve blue, red, and light green. Lower values are for items in turquoise and yellow.

Harlequin animals were made during the forties. There were six: a cat, a fish, a penguin, a duck, a lamb, and a donkey. They were made in maroon, spruce green, mauve blue, and yellow. These were reproduced by other companies; if you find one trimmed in gold, you've probably got a 'maverick.' If you find one in a color not listed, you're very lucky — these are worth twice as much as one in a standard color.

In 1979, complying with a request from the Woolworth company, HLC reissued a line of new Harlequin. It was made in original yellow and turquoise, medium green (slightly different than the original shade), and coral (an altogether new color). Some pieces were restyled, and the line was very limited. If you find a piece with a trademark, you'll know its new.

If you'd like to know more about Harlequin, it's included in _The Collector's Encyclopedia of Fiesta_ by Sharon and Bob Huxford.

Animals, mavericks, each	**$30.00**
Animals, non-standard colors, each	**$140.00**
Animals, standard colors, each	**$65.00**
Ashtray, basketweave, high	**$42.00**
Ashtray, basketweave, low	**$30.00**
Ashtray, regular, high	**$45.00**
Ashtray, regular, low	**$40.00**
Bowl, '36s oatmeal; high	**$16.00**

Bowl, '36s oatmeal; low $10.00
Bowl, '36s; high $22.00
Bowl, '36s; low $15.00
Bowl, cream soup; high $16.00
Bowl, cream soup; low..$12.00
Bowl, fruit; 5½", high..$8.00
Bowl, fruit; 5½", low $5.00
Bowl, individual salad; high..$20.00
Bowl, individual salad; low $15.00
Bowl, mixing; 10", yellow, Kitchen Kraft $110.00
Bowl, mixing; 6", red or spruce green, Kitchen Kraft .$70.00
Bowl, mixing; 8", mauve blue, Kitchen Kraft............$110.00
Bowl, nappy; 9", high...$22.00
Bowl, nappy; 9", low $15.00
Bowl, oval baker, high $22.00
Bowl, oval baker, low $16.00
Butter dish, ½-lb, high..$82.00
Butter dish, ½-lb, low...$70.00
Candle holders, high, pr..$180.00
Candle holders, low, pr...$150.00
Casserole, w/lid, high...$80.00
Casserole, w/lid, low $50.00
Creamer, any color, high lip $70.00
Creamer, individual; high $16.00
Creamer, individual; low $12.00
Creamer, novelty, high $20.00
Creamer, novelty, low $14.00
Creamer, regular, high..$12.00
Creamer, regular, low $8.00
Cup, demitasse; high $40.00
Cup, demitasse; low..$25.00
Cup, large, any color...$88.00
Cup, tea; high $9.00
Cup, tea; low $7.50
Egg cup, double, high $18.00
Egg cup, double, low $12.00
Egg cup, single, high...$20.00
Egg cup, single, low $16.00
Gravy boat, high $20.00
Gravy boat, low $15.00
Marmalade, any color..$100.00
Nut dish, basketweave, original color $7.50
Perfume bottle, any color..$65.00
Pitcher, service water; high $45.00
Pitcher, service water; low $35.00
Pitcher, 22-oz jug, high...$42.00
Pitcher, 22-oz jug, low..$24.00
Plate, deep; high $18.00
Plate, deep; low...$12.00
Plate, 10", high..$22.00
Plate, 10", low $13.00
Plate, 6", high...$4.50
Plate, 6", low $3.50
Plate, 7", high...$6.50
Plate, 7", low $4.50
Plate, 9", high..$12.00
Plate, 9", low $7.00
Platter, 11", high..$16.00

Platter, 11", low..$10.00
Platter, 13", high..$22.00
Platter, 13", low $15.00

Relish tray, mixed colors, w/four inserts $180.00
Salt & pepper shakers, high, pr $15.00
Salt & pepper shakers, low, pr....................................$12.00
Saucer, demitasse; high $10.00
Saucer, demitasse; low...$6.00
Saucer, high $3.50
Saucer, low $2.00
Saucer/ash tray, high $42.00
Saucer/ash tray, ivory..$60.00
Saucer/ash tray, low $40.00
Sugar bowl, w/lid, high..$16.00
Sugar bowl, w/lid, low...$12.00
Syrup, any color...$160.00
Teapot, high...$80.00
Teapot, low..$55.00
Tray, relish; mixed colors...$180.00
Tumbler, high...$40.00
Tumbler, low..$30.00

Hartland Plastics, Inc.

The Hartland company was located in Hartland, Wisconsin, where during the fifties and sixties they made several lines of plastic figures: Western and Historic Horsemen, Miniature Western Series, and the Hartland Sport Series of Famous Baseball Stars. Football and bowling figures and religious statues were made as well. The plastic, virgin acetate, was very durable, and the figures were hand painted with careful attention to detail. They're often marked.

Annie Oakley & horse, full-size, pink outfit w/ivory trim, matching hat, rearing palomino horse, VG........$125.00
Bat Masterson, 7½", in original 2x3½x9½" box, Famous Western Gunfighter series, w/cane, hat, gun, & catalog, M...$250.00
Bret Maverick, 7¾", black jacket w/frilled white shirt & olive vest, jointed arms, in original box $125.00

Bullet (Roy & Dale's dog), 6" long, VG........................$35.00
Cleveland Brown running back, NM.........................$275.00
Dale Evans & Buttermilk, full-size, olive green outfit &
    white hat, horse is cream w/brown accents, original
    guns, EX...**$175.00**
Dallas Cowboy lineman, EX......................................$275.00
Don Drysdale, near-white, M.....................................$850.00
Green Bay Packer lineman, EX..................................$185.00
Hank Aaron, creamy white, EX $250.00

Horse, 8", brown w/white stockings **$18.00**
Jim Hardie & horse, small-size, orange outfit & black hat,
    brown horse, EX....................................**$45.00**
Little Leaguer, near-white, NM...................................$300.00
Lone Ranger & Silver, full-size, 1st issue, light blue outfit &
    white hat, white horse, original guns, EX **$85.00**
Minnesota Viking running back, NM......................$215.00
New York Giant running back, EX............................$175.00
Palladin & horse, small-size, dark blue outfit & brown hat,
    horse is white w/black markings & saddle, VG....**$65.00**
Rifleman & Horse, full-size, light blue shirt w/yellow pants
    & white hat, brown horse, original rifle, EX **$125.00**
Roger Maris, near-white, NM $485.00
Roy Rogers & Trigger, full-size, blue outfit w/dark red shirt
    & white hat, palomino horse, original guns, EX.**$175.00**
Ted Williams, near-white, NM $400.00
Willy Mays, creamy white, EX $200.00
Wyatt Earp, full-size, white shirt w/khaki vest & green
    pants, brown hat, w/original guns, EX...............**$125.00**
Wyatt Earp, on 7x11½" card w/unopened plastic, from the
    Miniature Western Series, 5½" assembled, M......**$125.00**

Head Vases

These are fun to collect, and prices are still reasonable.
You've seen them at flea markets — heads of ladies, children, clowns, even some men and a religious figure now
and then. A few look very much like famous people —
there's a Jackie Onassis vase by Inarco that leaves no doubt
as to who it's supposed to represent!

They were mainly imported from Japan, although a few
were made by American companies and sold to florist shops
to be filled with flower arrangements. So if there's an old
flower shop in your neighborhood, you might start your
search with their storerooms.

If you'd like to learn more about them, we recommend
Head Vases, Identification and Values, by Kathleen Cole.

**Blond, 7¼" wearing pearl necklace & leaf pin, marked
Napcoware** **$27.50**
Child, 5½", Relpo #K1096, bonnet w/applied flowers, large
    bow at neck, applied flowers at collar **$25.00**
Child, 6", Enesco (paper label), small-brimmed cap, winking
    eye, turtleneck sweater..**$20.00**
Child, 6", Inarco #E1579, small girl praying, red gown
    w/long sleeves, 1964 ....**$20.00**
Child, 7", Inarco #E2965, scarf w/large bow at chin, long
    brown braids, large painted eyes...........................**$30.00**
Clown, 4½", Inarco #E5071, classic white face w/red nose &
    face, tiny black hat at side of bald head **$15.00**
Clown, 5½", Inarco #E6730, bouffant red curls, red nose &
    cheeks, blue & yellow hat & ruffled collar...........**$15.00**
Clown, 7", Inarco (no number), red nose & cheeks, tall red
    hat w/pom-pom, red & white ruffled collar.........**$20.00**
Infant, 5½", Inarco #E3156, girl w/pink bow in hair, ruffled
    collar..**$25.00**
Infant, 5½", no mark, girl w/kitten in hands, bow in blond
    hair..**$20.00**
Infant, 6", Inarco (paper label) #E4392, boy w/blue tele-
    phone to ear, 'Hello Gran'pa!' on bib...................**$20.00**
Infant, 6", no mark, girl w/bonnet, applied flowers at rim,
    small pink bow at neck...**$20.00**
Infant, 7½", Samson Import #5359, blond curls, pink & blue
    blanket draped around head, hands to chin........**$25.00**

Lady, 4½", Napco #C3342C, pearl earrings, white pointed collar, bow at side of flat-rimmed hat $20.00

Lady, 4½", Rozart (paper label), bonnet w/applied flowers, closed eyes, simple gold line forms neckline $20.00

Lady, 5", Inarco #E1610, heavy black lashes, long blond curls, pearl earrings & gloves w/closed fan, 1964 ....$25.00

Lady, 5", Lee Wards (paper label), geisha w/ornate hairdo, much gold trim...$25.00

Lady, 5", no mark, pearl earrings & necklace, heavy black lashes, gold band on hat, flowers at neckline.......$20.00

Lady, 5½", Inarco #3-91/M/c, pearl earrings & necklace, white collar, feather drapes from side of hat $25.00

Lady, 5½", Japan, heavy black lashes, pale blond hair w/long curls, hand to face $25.00

Lady, 5½", Japan, heavy black lashes, yellow hat w/white bow, white pointed collar on green bodice..........$20.00

Lady, 5½", Napco (paper label) #S126B, applied flower on flat hat & bodice, heavy black lashes $25.00

Lady, 5½", Napcoware #C5677, heavy black lashes, flat wide-brimmed hat, hand to face, ruffles at wrist & bodice $25.00

Lady, 5½", no mark, heavy black lashes, ruffled bonnet w/bow tied at side, curly hair, ruffled neckline....$25.00

Lady, 5¾", Rubens #495, pearl earrings & necklace, wide-rimmed hat, gloved hands cross at chin, black & white bodice $25.00

Lady, 6", Lefton's (paper label) #2900, heavy dark lashes, large hat, hands to face, strapless bodice..............$32.50

Lady, 6", no mark, upswept hair w/applied flower, scalloped Elizabethan-style collar, painted jewelry, porcelain $35.00

Lady, 6½", Glamour Girl, ivory w/gold-painted features & details at hair & bodice...$17.50

Lady, 6½", Rubens #483, side-swept blond hair, heavy brown lashes, pearl earrings & necklace, one hand to face $25.00

Lady, 7", Florence Ceramics, winter coat & bonnet w/gold trim, delicate painted features..............................$35.00

Lady, 7", green lustre hat, gold trim....................$22.50

Lady, 7", Inarco #3190/L, hand to face, pearl earrings & necklace, black hat, bodice & lashes, 1961..........$32.50

Lady, 7", no mark, brown side-swept hair w/roses at part, pearl earrings & necklace, gloved hand to face....$32.50

Lady, 8", no mark, South American features, turban around her head, low-cut bodice, wide smile, long painted earrings $40.00

Lady, 9", Napcoware #6986, pearl earrings & necklace, upswept brown & blond streaked hair w/bow, small ruffled collar...$45.00

Madonna & Child, 5½", no mark, hand supports baby enfolded in loosely-draped scarf that surrounds mother's head..$15.00

Teen girl, Sampson Import #5543B, smooth brown hair w/side bang, hand to face, ruffled collar, 1964 ....$27.50

Teen girl, 5", Inarco #E6211, windswept long blond hair, turtleneck sweater..$25.00

Teen girl, 5", Lark (paper label), blond hair flips to side, one pearl earring, pearl necklace, bows at shoulders .$20.00

Teen girl, 5½", Inarco #E3548, telephone to ear, ruffled collar...$20.00

Teen girl, 6", Inarco #E2782, light brown hair in flip style, red bodice w/white collar $25.00

Teen girl, 6", Rubens #4121, braid across top of head w/pink bow at each side, pearl necklace, cold paint, NM $17.50

Teen girl, 7", Inarco #E3523, fancy curls, wide-open painted eyes, ruffled collar w/gold trim.............................$30.00

Teen girl, 7", Napcoware (paper label) #C8494, long hair w/bow at top, one pearl earring, white collar......$30.00

Teen girl, 7½", Caffco (paper label) #3283, curls peek from green tam, scarf at neck, open coat collar $35.00

Teen girl, 7½", no mark, 2 long ponytails (low style), glasses at top of head...$35.00

Teen girl, 9", Napcoware #C7314, blond bouffant hair, pearl earrings & necklace, simple black bodice............$50.00

Toddler, 7", Relpo #2010, boy w/small-rimmed hat, short blond hair, small blue bow at white collar $35.00

Heisey Glass

From just before the turn of the century until 1957, the Heisey Glass Company of Newark, Ohio, was one of the largest, most successful manufacturers of quality tableware in the world. Though the market is well established, many pieces are still reasonably priced; and if you're drawn to the lovely patterns and colors that Heisey made, you're investment should be sound.

After 1901, their glassware was marked with their familiar trademark, the 'Diamond H' (an H in a diamond), or a paper label. Blown pieces are often marked on the stem instead of the bowl or foot.

Numbers in the listing are catalog reference numbers assigned by the company to indicate variations in shape or stem style. Collectors use them, especially when they buy and sell by mail, for the same purpose. Many catalog pages (showing these numbers) are contained in *The Collector's Encyclopedia of Heisey Glass* by Neila Bredehoft. This book and *Elegant Glassware of the Depression Era* by Gene Florence are both excellent references for further study.

Chintz, crystal, bowl, jelly; 6", 2-handled, footed **$15.00**
Chintz, crystal, finger bowl, #4107 ....**$8.00**
Chintz, crystal, ice bucket, footed.............................**$75.00**
Chintz, crystal, platter, 14", oval...............................**$30.00**
Chintz, crystal, stem, water; #3389, 9-oz **$15.00**
Chintz, crystal, tray, sandwich; 12" sq, center handle .**$35.00**
Chintz, crystal, tumbler, juice; #3389, 5-oz, footed......**$11.00**
Chintz, yellow, bowl, mint; 6", footed......................**$30.00**
Chintz, yellow, bowl, pickle & olive; 13", 2-part **$35.00**
Chintz, yellow, plate, bread; 6" sq **$15.00**
Chintz, yellow, plate, dinner; 10½" sq **$85.00**
Chintz, yellow, stem, cocktail; #3389, 3-oz **$35.00**
Chintz, yellow, sugar bowl, 3-dolphin foot.................**$42.50**
Chintz, yellow, tumbler, iced tea; #3389, 12-oz **$30.00**
Chintz, yellow, tumbler, juice; #3389, 5-oz, footed **$22.00**
Crystolite, crystal, bonbon, 7½", 2-handled................**$15.00**
Crystolite, crystal, bottle, bitters; 4-oz, w/short tube .**$175.00**
Crystolite, crystal, bottle, syrup..............................**$85.00**
Crystolite, crystal, bowl, dessert; 5½" **$12.00**
Crystolite, crystal, bowl, salad; 10" **$47.50**
Crystolite, crystal, cake salver, 11", footed................**$250.00**
Crystolite, crystal, candle block, 1-light, square..........**$15.00**
Crystolite, crystal, candlestick, 2-light.......................**$25.00**
Crystolite, crystal, candy box, 5½", w/lid...................**$50.00**
Crystolite, crystal, cigarette box, 4½", w/lid................**$20.00**
Crystolite, crystal, cigarette holder, round..................**$17.50**
Crystolite, crystal, coaster, 4".....................................**$6.00**
Crystolite, crystal, creamer & sugar bowl w/tray, oval..**$47.50**
Crystolite, crystal, cup...**$20.00**
Crystolite, crystal, ice tub, w/silverplated handle **$75.00**
Crystolite, crystal, jam jar, w/lid...............................**$50.00**
Crystolite, crystal, oil bottle, 2-oz, w/stopper **$30.00**
Crystolite, crystal, plate, dinner; 10½".......................**$60.00**
Crystolite, crystal, plate, salad; 7"...............................**$9.00**
Crystolite, crystal, salad dressing set, 3-pc **$38.00**
Crystolite, crystal, salt & pepper shakers, pr...............**$30.00**
Crystolite, crystal, stem, cocktail; #5003, blown..........**$20.00**
Crystolite, crystal, stem, water; #1503, 10-oz **$480.00**
Crystolite, crystal, tray, relish; 12", 3-part **$35.00**
Crystolite, crystal, vase, 3", short stem.......................**$20.00**
Crystolite, crystal, 10-oz, pressed.............................**$70.00**
Empress, alexandrite, bowl, cream soup; w/liner **$165.00**
Empress, alexandrite, cup **$100.00**
Empress, alexandrite, plate, 10½" sq **$175.00**
Empress, alexandrite, plate, 6" sq **$30.00**
Empress, cobalt, candy dish, 6", w/lid, dolphin foot...**$360.00**
Empress, cobalt, plate, 7" sq **$55.00**
Empress, green, bowl, preserve; 5", 2-handled...........**$27.50**
Empress, green, candlestick, 6", dolphin foot...........**$125.00**
Empress, green, jug, 3-pt, footed..............................**$225.00**
Empress, green, plate, 9"...**$40.00**
Empress, green, salt & pepper shakers, pr **$135.00**
Empress, green, tumbler, 8-oz, dolphin foot **$195.00**
Empress, pink, bowl, lemon; 6½", w/lid, oval............**$65.00**
Empress, pink, comport, 6" sq....................................**$70.00**
Empress, pink, cup, after dinner................................**$40.00**

Empress, pink, oil bottle, 4-oz **$80.00**
Empress, pink, plate, muffin; 12", sides up................**$50.00**
Empress, pink, tray, celery; 10"................................**$16.00**
Empress, yellow, bowl, frappe; w/center....................**$60.00**
Empress, yellow, bowl, pickle or olive; 13", 2-part **$30.00**
Empress, yellow, creamer, dolphin foot......................**$30.00**
Empress, yellow, ice tub, w/metal handles.................**$100.00**
Empress, yellow, plate, sandwich; 2-handled **$40.00**
Empress, yellow, plate, 4½"...**$6.00**
Empress, yellow, stem, oyster cocktail; 2½-oz.............**$25.00**
Empress, yellow, tray, buffet relish; 10", 4-part **$75.00**
Greek Key, crystal, bowl, almond; 5", w/lid, footed ...**$90.00**
Greek Key, crystal, bowl, jelly; w/lid, handles, footed..**$145.00**
Greek Key, crystal, bowl, jelly; 4", low foot, shallow..**$20.00**
Greek Key, crystal, bowl, nappy; 8", scalloped **$42.00**
Greek Key, crystal, bowl, orange; 14½", flared rim.....**$76.50**
Greek Key, crystal, bowl, 9", low foot, straight side ...**$45.00**
Greek Key, crystal, candy dish, 1-lb, w/lid...............**$140.00**
Greek Key, crystal, cheese & cracker set, 10" **$80.00**
Greek Key, crystal, creamer **$25.00**
Greek Key, crystal, egg cup, 5-oz..............................**$60.00**
Greek Key, crystal, jar, horseradish; large, w/lid.........**$75.00**
Greek Key, crystal, jar, pickle; w/knob lid **$125.00**
Greek Key, crystal, oil bottle, 4-oz, w/#8 stopper.......**$80.00**
Greek Key, crystal, pitcher, 1-qt................................**$85.00**
Greek Key, crystal, plate, 10"....................................**$60.00**
Greek Key, crystal, plate, 5"......................................**$11.00**
Greek Key, crystal, plate, 7"......................................**$17.00**
Greek Key, crystal, salt & pepper shakers, pr.............**$90.00**
Greek Key, crystal, sherbet, 4½-oz, footed, flared rim..**$12.50**
Greek Key, crystal, stem, claret; 4½-oz **$120.00**
Greek Key, crystal, stem, 9-oz, low foot **$85.00**
Greek Key, crystal, straw jar, w/lid...........................**$300.00**
Greek Key, crystal, tray, 15", oblong.........................**$120.00**
Greek Key, crystal, tumbler, water; 5½"......................**$20.00**
Greek Key, crystal, tumbler, 12-oz **$40.00**
Ipswich, alexandrite, stem, goblet; 10-oz..................**$750.00**
Ipswich, crystal, bowl, flower; 11", footed.................**$45.00**
Ipswich, crystal, pitcher, ½-gal................................**$150.00**
Ipswich, crystal, stem, oyster cocktail; 4-oz **$20.00**
Ipswich, crystal, tumbler, 10-oz **$30.00**
Ipswich, green, creamer...**$42.50**
Ipswich, green, pitcher, ½-gal..................................**$750.00**
Ipswich, green, sugar bowl..**$42.50**
Ipswich, pink or yellow, plate, 7" sq..........................**$25.00**
Ipswich, pink or yellow, tumbler, 8-oz, footed **$40.00**

**Ipswich, Sahara yellow, candy dish, ½-lb, w/
lid $250.00**

Ipswich, yellow, cocktail shaker, 1-qt, w/stopper.....**$700.00**
Lariat, crystal, basket, 10", footed **$195.00**
Lariat, crystal, bottle, oil; 6-oz, oval **$65.00**
Lariat, crystal, bowl, fruit; 12"....................................**$20.00**
Lariat, crystal, candlestick, 3-light **$35.00**
Lariat, crystal, candy dish, 7", w/lid **$50.00**
Lariat, crystal, cigarette box **$42.00**
Lariat, crystal, creamer **$15.00**
Lariat, crystal, cup **$12.00**
Lariat, crystal, plate, buffet; 21" **$90.00**
Lariat, crystal, plate, salad; 7" **$7.00**
Lariat, crystal, plate, sandwich; 14", 2-handled **$35.00**
Lariat, crystal, relish, 2-part (illustrated).............**$30.00**
Lariat, crystal, salt & pepper shakers, pr **$200.00**
Lariat, crystal, stem, oyster cocktail or fruit; 4¼-oz......**$15.00**
Lariat, crystal, stem, wine; 2½", blown **$25.00**
Lariat, crystal, stem, wine; 3½-oz, pressed **$20.00**
Lariat, crystal, stem, 9-oz, pressed **$20.00**
Lariat, crystal, sugar bowl **$15.00**
Lariat, crystal, tumbler, iced tea; 12-oz, footed, blown..**$18.00**
Lariat, crystal, tumbler, juice; 5-oz, footed **$15.00**

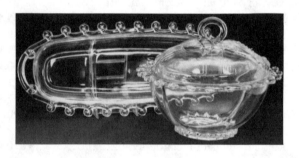

Lariat, 7", candy bowl w/lid **$50.00**
Lodestar, dawn, ash tray...**$70.00**
Lodestar, dawn, bowl, mayonnaise, 5" **$55.00**
Lodestar, dawn, bowl, 11", crimped **$95.00**
Lodestar, dawn, candlestick, 5¾", 2-light, pr **$600.00**
Lodestar, dawn, creamer **$50.00**
Lodestar, dawn, pitcher, #1626, 1-qt..........................**$150.00**
Lodestar, dawn, salt & pepper shakers, #1485, pr.....**$250.00**
Lodestar, dawn, sugar bowl, handled...........................**$85.00**
Lodestar, dawn, tumbler, juice; 6-oz............................**$35.00**
Lodestar, dawn, vase, 8", crimped **$175.00**
Minuet, crystal, bowl, pickle & olive; 13".....................**$30.00**
Minuet, crystal, bowl, salad dressing; 6½"...................**$25.00**
Minuet, crystal, bowl, sauce; 7½", footed....................**$30.00**
Minuet, crystal, creamer, dolphin foot..........................**$40.00**
Minuet, crystal, cup..**$35.00**
Minuet, crystal, dinner bell, #3408.............................**$60.00**
Minuet, crystal, mayonnaise, 5½", dolphin foot..........**$40.00**
Minuet, crystal, plate, salad; 7"..................................**$10.00**
Minuet, crystal, plate, sandwich; 12", 2-handled..........**$40.00**
Minuet, crystal, salt & pepper shakers, #10, pr...........**$50.00**
Minuet, crystal, stem, oyster cocktail; #5010, 4½-oz....**$15.00**
Minuet, crystal, stem, water; #5010, 9-oz....................**$30.00**
Minuet, crystal, stem, wine; #5010, 2½-oz..................**$65.00**
Minuet, crystal, tumbler, iced tea; #2351, 12-oz...........**$30.00**
Minuet, crystal, tumbler, juice; #5010, 5-oz.................**$30.00**

Minuet, crystal, vase, #5013, 5" **$40.00**
Octagon, amber, bowl, frozen dessert; #500...............**$15.00**
Octagon, amber, ice tub, #500...................................**$135.00**
Octagon, crystal, basket, #500, 5".............................**$60.00**
Octagon, crystal, cheese dish, #1229, 6", 2-handled......**$7.00**
Octagon, crystal, plate, bread; 7" **$5.00**
Octagon, crystal, tray, #500, 12", 4-part....................**$25.00**
Octagon, dawn, tray, #500, 12", 4-part.....................**$300.00**
Octagon, green, sugar bowl, #500.............................**$35.00**
Octagon, orchid, bowl, soup; 9", flat..........................**$50.00**
Octagon, orchid, tray, celery; 9" **$25.00**
Octagon, pink, bowl, cream soup; 2-handled...............**$20.00**
Octagon, pink, creamer, #500....................................**$20.00**
Octagon, pink, plate, muffin; #1229, 10", sides up......**$25.00**
Octagon, yellow, bowl, grapefruit; 6½".......................**$22.00**
Octagon, yellow, plate, sandwich; center handle........**$40.00**
Old Colony, amber, comport, 7", footed, oval...........**$95.00**
Old Colony, amber, finger bowl, #4075.....................**$18.00**
Old Colony, amber, grapefruit, #3380, footed...........**$30.00**
Old Colony, amber, stem, sherbet; #3380, 6-oz.........**$25.00**
Old Colony, crystal, decanter, 1-pt...........................**$150.00**
Old Colony, crystal, salt & pepper shakers, pr...........**$52.50**
Old Colony, crystal, stem, water; #3390, 11-oz, low......**$8.00**
Old Colony, green, creamer, dolphin foot...................**$50.00**
Old Colony, green, plate, 10½" sq.............................**$70.00**
Old Colony, green, stem, claret; #3380, 4-oz.............**$55.00**
Old Colony, green, tumbler, soda; 8-oz, footed..........**$25.00**
Old Colony, pink, bowl, dessert; 10", 2-handled.........**$40.00**
Old Colony, pink, plate, 6"..**$12.00**
Old Colony, pink, stem, cordial; #3380, 1-oz.............**$135.00**
Old Colony, pink, stem, water; #3390, 11-oz..............**$22.00**
Old Colony, yellow, comport, #3368, 7", footed **$62.50**
Old Colony, yellow, plate, 10½"................................**$70.00**
Old Colony, yellow, stem, wine; #3380, 2½-oz **$35.00**
Old Colony, yellow, sugar bowl, footed......................**$45.00**
Old Colony, yellow, tumbler, iced tea; #3390, 12-oz ..**$27.00**
Orchid, crystal, ashtray, 3"..**$27.50**
Orchid, crystal, bowl, gardenia; 13"...........................**$85.00**
Orchid, crystal, bowl, relish; 11", 3-part....................**$67.50**
Orchid, crystal, bowl, relish; 8", divided....................**$57.50**
Orchid, crystal, bowl, salad; 7".................................**$45.00**
Orchid, crystal, bowl, 10", crimped...........................**$65.00**
Orchid, crystal, cake plate or salver, 14", footed.......**$265.00**
Orchid, crystal, candy box, 6", w/lid, low-footed......**$150.00**
Orchid, crystal, cigarette holder, w/lid.....................**$125.00**
Orchid, crystal, comport, 5½", blown.......................**$87.50**
Orchid, crystal, creamer, footed...............................**$25.00**
Orchid, crystal, marmalade, w/lid **$200.00**
Orchid, crystal, mayonnaise, 5½", footed.................**$40.00**
Orchid, crystal, plate, cheese & cracker; 14".............**$130.00**
Orchid, crystal, plate, dinner; 10½"..........................**$130.00**
Orchid, crystal, plate, salad; 7".................................**$18.00**
Orchid, crystal, plate, sandwich; 11" **$50.00**
Orchid, crystal, salt & pepper shakers, pr..................**$60.00**
Orchid, crystal, stem, cocktail; #5025, 4-oz...............**$40.00**
Orchid, crystal, stem, water goblet; #5022, 10-oz........**$42.50**
Orchid, crystal, sugar bowl, footed...........................**$25.00**
Orchid, crystal, tray, celery; 13" **$47.50**

Orchid, crystal, tumbler, iced tea; #5022, 12-oz...........$60.00
Plantation, crystal, ashtray, 3½".................................$30.00
Plantation, crystal, bottle, syrup.................................$75.00
Plantation, crystal, bowl, honey; 6½", footed, cupped ..$45.00
Plantation, crystal, bowl, relish; 13", 5-part, oval.........$65.00
Plantation, crystal, bowl, salad; 9" $85.00
Plantation, crystal, butter dish, ¼-lb, w/lid, oval $85.00
Plantation, crystal, candlestick, 2-light.......................$50.00
Plantation, crystal, cup...$15.00
Plantation, crystal, marmalade, w/lid $100.00
Plantation, crystal, plate, demi-torte; 10½" $40.00
Plantation, crystal, plate, salad; 7"............................$15.00
Plantation, crystal, salt & pepper shakers, pr..............$45.00
Plantation, crystal, stem, cordial; 1-oz......................$100.00
Plantation, crystal, stem, fruit or oyster cocktail; 4-oz.$20.00
Plantation, crystal, tumbler, iced tea; 12-oz, footed, pressed or blown $45.00
Plantation, crystal, tumbler, juice; 5-oz, footed, pressed or blown..$35.00
Plantation, crystal, vase, 9", footed, flared..................$65.00
Pleat & Panel, crystal, bowl, nappy; 4½".......................$5.00
Pleat & Panel, crystal, pitcher, 3-pt.............................$45.00
Pleat & Panel, crystal, tumbler, 8-oz, ground bottom....$5.00
Pleat & Panel, green, cup...$17.50
Pleat & Panel, green, stem, 8-oz.................................$25.00
Pleat & Panel, green, vase, 8"....................................$55.00
Pleat & Panel, pink, bowl, vegetable; 9", oval.............$30.00
Pleat & Panel, pink, plate, dinner; 10¾".......................$40.00
Pleat & Panel, pink, sherbet, 5-oz, footed.....................$8.00
Provincial, crystal, butter dish, w/lid..........................$85.00
Provincial, crystal, candle holder, 3-light....................$50.00
Provincial, crystal, salt & pepper shakers, pr..............$25.00
Provincial, crystal, tumbler, 8-oz...............................$15.00
Provincial, limelight green, bowl, nappy; 5½" $40.00
Provincial, limelight green, creamer, footed $95.00
Provincial, limelight green, plate, luncheon; 8" $50.00
Provincial, limelight green, sugar, footed....................$95.00
Provincial, limelight green, tumbler, 9-oz, footed........$65.00
Queen Ann, crystal, bottle, oil; 4-oz...........................$35.00
Queen Ann, crystal, bowl, cream soup; w/liner...........$20.00
Queen Ann, crystal, bowl, vegetable; 10", oval $27.00
Queen Ann, crystal, creamer, dolphin foot..................$15.00
Queen Ann, crystal, cup, after dinner.........................$15.00
Queen Ann, crystal, marmalade, w/lid, dolphin foot..$50.00
Queen Ann, crystal, plate, 10½", round or square.......$40.00
Queen Ann, crystal, salt & pepper shakers, pr............$50.00
Queen Ann, crystal, tray, relish; 10", 3-part...............$18.00
Queen Ann, crystal, tumbler, 8-oz, ground bottom.....$15.00
Ridgeleigh, crystal, basket, bonbon............................$11.00
Ridgeleigh, crystal, bottle, bitters; 5-oz, w/tube..........$65.00
Ridgeleigh, crystal, bowl, centerpiece; 11".................$35.00
Ridgeleigh, crystal, bowl, jelly; 6", divided, handles....$12.75
Ridgeleigh, crystal, candle block, 3"...........................$18.00
Ridgeleigh, crystal, cigarette box, w/lid, oval..............$55.00
Ridgeleigh, crystal, cocktail shaker, 1-qt, w/strainer & stopper..$195.00
Ridgeleigh, crystal, comport, 6", w/lid, low foot.........$30.00
Ridgeleigh, crystal, creamer......................................$20.00

Ridgeleigh, crystal, cup..$8.00
Ridgeleigh, crystal, marmalade, w/lid.........................$50.00
Ridgeleigh, crystal, pitcher, ½-gal.............................$175.00
Ridgeleigh, crystal, plate, 8" dia................................$12.00
Ridgeleigh, crystal, plate, 8" sq.................................$22.00
Ridgeleigh, crystal, salt & pepper shakers, pr.............$30.00
Ridgeleigh, crystal, stem, claret; pressed...................$32.00
Ridgeleigh, crystal, sugar bowl..................................$20.00
Ridgeleigh, crystal, tray, relish; 11", 3-part................$40.00
Ridgeleigh, crystal, tumbler, soda; 8-oz, blown..........$21.00
Ridgeleigh, crystal, vase, 8".......................................$55.00
Rose, crystal, bowl, flower; Waverly, 12"....................$65.00
Rose, crystal, bowl, fruit or salad; Waverly, 9" $145.00
Rose, crystal, cake plate, Waverly, 15", footed..........$300.00
Rose, crystal, candlestick, #142, Waverly, 3-light........$78.00
Rose, crystal, candy dish, 6¼", w/lid........................$145.00
Rose, crystal, comport, Waverly, 7", footed, oval......$130.00
Rose, crystal, creamer, Waverly, footed......................$27.50
Rose, crystal, dinner bell, #5072..............................$145.00
Rose, crystal, mayonnaise, Waverly, 5½", footed.........$60.00
Rose, crystal, plate, dinner; 10½".............................$155.00
Rose, crystal, plate, salad; Waverly, 8" $30.00
Rose, crystal, salt & pepper shakers, Waverly pr.........$65.00
Rose, crystal, stem, cordial; #5072, 1-oz...................$145.00
Rose, crystal, stem, water; #5072, 9-oz.......................$45.00
Rose, crystal, sugar bowl, Waverly, footed..................$25.00
Rose, crystal, tumbler, iced tea; #5072, 12-oz, footed .$50.00
Saturn, crystal, bowl, relish; 9", 3-part......................$17.50
Saturn, crystal, candle block, 3", 1-light, footed..........$95.00
Saturn, crystal, salt & pepper shakers, pr...................$45.00
Saturn, crystal, stem, 10-oz.......................................$12.00
Saturn, crystal, tumbler, juice; 5-oz.............................$7.00
Saturn, crystal, tumbler, 10-oz...................................$18.00
Saturn, zircon/limelight green, bowl, baked apple......$65.00
Saturn, zircon/limelight green, candle block, 3", 1-light, footed $325.00
Saturn, zircon/limelight green, marmalade, w/lid $500.00
Saturn, zircon/limelight green, tumbler, juice; 5-oz...$120.00
Saturn, zircon/limelight green, tumbler, 10-oz.............$70.00

Stanhope, crystal, creamer & sugar bowl $30.00
Stanhope, crystal, cup & saucer (illustrated)........$16.00
Stanhope, crystal, plate, 7" (illustrated).................$7.00

Twist, amber or yellow, cup, zigzag handles..............$35.00
Twist, amber or yellow, salt & pepper shakers, pr ...$125.00
Twist, amber or yellow, tumbler, iced tea; 12-oz $45.00
Twist, crystal, bowl, baker; 9", oval............................$10.00
Twist, crystal, pitcher, 3-pt......................................$50.00
Twist, crystal, sugar bowl, footed.................................$20.00
Twist, green, candlestick, 2", 1-light...........................$25.00
Twist, green, plate, 8", ground bottom......................$15.00
Twist, green, tumbler, 8-oz, ground bottom, flat.........$21.00
Twist, pink, bowl, jelly; 6", 2-handled......................$15.00
Twist, pink, mustard, w/spoon & lid...........................$70.00
Twist, pink, tray, celery; 10"......................................$20.00
Waverly, crystal, bowl, salad; 7"................................$17.00
Waverly, crystal, bowl, vegetable; 9"..........................$20.00
Waverly, crystal, butter dish, 6" sq, w/lid....................$65.00
Waverly, crystal, candle holder, 3-light......................$65.00
Waverly, crystal, cheese dish, 5½", footed..................$20.00
Waverly, crystal, creamer, footed.............................$20.00
Waverly, crystal, plate, dinner; 10½"........................$45.00
Waverly, crystal, plate, luncheon; 8"...........................$8.00
Waverly, crystal, salt & pepper shakers, pr.................$50.00
Waverly, crystal, stem, cocktail; 3½-oz......................$25.00
Waverly, crystal, sugar bowl, footed..........................$20.00
Waverly, crystal, tumbler, iced tea; 13-oz, footed........$20.00
Yeoman, amber, bowl, baker; 9"................................$55.00
Yeoman, amber, plate, 6"...$15.00
Yeoman, amber, saucer, after dinner..........................$10.00
Yeoman, crystal, bowl, cream soup; 2-handled..........$10.00
Yeoman, crystal, comport; 5", high foot, shallow........$15.00
Yeoman, crystal, plate, 10½".....................................$20.00
Yeoman, crystal, stem, cocktail; 3-oz.........................$10.00
Yeoman, green, bowl, vegetable; 6½", handled.........$16.00
Yeoman, green, cup, after dinner...............................$35.00
Yeoman, green, salver, 12", low foot.........................$32.00
Yeoman, green, tumbler, 8-oz...................................$20.00
Yeoman, orchid, bowl, berry; 8½", 2-handled............$35.00
Yeoman, orchid, marmalade jar, w/lid.......................$55.00
Yeoman, orchid, saucer...$10.00
Yeoman, orchid, stem, oyster cocktail; 2¾-oz, footed.$14.00
Yeoman, orchid, sugar bowl, w/lid............................$40.00
Yeoman, pink, bowl, nappy; 4½".................................$8.00
Yeoman, pink, creamer..$20.00
Yeoman, pink, plate, relish; 11", 4-part.....................$27.00
Yeoman, pink, stem, champagne; 6-oz......................$16.00
Yeoman, yellow, bowl, lemon; 5", w/lid......................$25.00
Yeoman, yellow, cruet, oil; 4-oz...............................$50.00
Yeoman, yellow, platter, 12", oval............................$19.00
Yeoman, yellow, tray, celery; 13"..............................$32.00

Homer Laughlin China Co.

Since well before the turn of the century, the Homer Laughlin China Company of Newell, West Virginia, has been turning out dinnerware and kitchenware lines in hundreds of styles and patterns. Most of their pieces are marked either 'HLC' or 'Homer Laughlin.' As styles changed over the years, they designed several basic dinnerware shapes that they used as a basis for literally hundreds of different patterns simply by applying various decals and glaze treatments. If you find pieces stamped with a name like Virginia Rose, Rhythm, or Nautilus, don't assume it to be the pattern name; it's the shape name. Virginia Rose, for instance, was decorated with many different decals. If you have some you're trying to sell through a mail or a phone contact, it would be a good idea to send the prospective buyer a photocopy of the pattern.

For more information, we recommend *Homer Laughlin China, An Identification Guide,* by Darlene Nossman and *The Collector's Encyclopedia of Homer Laughlin China* by Joanne Jasper.

See also Fiesta, Harlequin.

Cavalier with Decals

Bowl, fruit; 5"..$4.00
Bowl, soup; 8"...$6.00
Casserole, w/lid...$22.50
Cup, demitasse...$7.00
Cup, tea...$4.00
Plate, luncheon; 9"...$6.00
Plate, 7"...$4.00
Platter, 15", oval..$12.50
Salt & pepper shakers, pr......................................$8.50
Sauce boat...$7.00
Sugar bowl, w/lid...$7.00
Teapot, w/lid..$32.50

Georgian Eggshell with Decals

Bowl, lug soup..$10.00
Bowl, vegetable; oval...$12.50
Chop plate, 14"..$18.00
Creamer...$10.00
Cup, tea...$7.00
Plate, bread & butter; 6".......................................$5.00
Plate, dinner; 10"...$8.00
Plate, luncheon; 8" sq..$7.00
Plate, luncheon; 9"...$8.50
Platter, 11", oval..$17.50
Platter, 15", oval..$22.50
Salt & pepper shakers, pr......................................$17.50
Sauce boat...$12.50
Sauce boat w/stand..$27.50
Saucer...$4.00
Teapot, w/lid..$37.50

Rhythm with Decals

Bowl, cereal; 5½"...$4.00
Bowl, coupe soup; 8"...$5.00
Bowl, vegetable; 8¼" dia.......................................$8.00
Casserole, w/lid...$22.50
Creamer...$7.50
Cup...$4.00

Plate, bread & butter; 6" $3.50
Plate, dinner; 10"...$5.00
Plate, 7"...$3.50
Platter, 11½", oval $8.00
Platter, 15½", oval $12.50
Salt & pepper shakers, pr...............................$8.50
Sauce boat $7.50
Teapot, w/lid..$27.50
Tidbit, 3-tier..$17.50

Swing with Decals

Butter dish, round..$22.50
Casserole, w/lid $27.50
Cream soup $10.00
Creamer $6.00
Cup $4.50
Cup, demitasse..$6.00
Egg cup $10.00
Pie plate, 7"...$5.00
Plate, bread & butter; 6" $5.00

Plate, dinner; 10"...$7.50
Platter, 11" $12.50
Salt & pepper shakers, pr..............................$15.00
Saucer $2.50
Saucer, demitasse..$4.00
Teapot, w/lid..$30.00

Virginia Rose with Decals

Bowl, fruit..$5.00
Bowl, soup $8.50
Butter dish, oblong..$60.00
Casserole, w/lid...$32.50
Cup, demitasse $8.50
Cup, tea $6.00
Egg cup..$12.50
Plate, bread & butter; 6" $5.00
Plate, dinner; 10"...$9.00
Plate, luncheon; 9"...$7.00

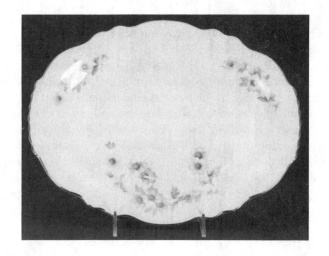

Platter, 13½"..$17.50
Salt & pepper shakers, pr..............................$25.00
Sauce boat w/stand..$22.50
Sugar bowl, w/lid...$12.50

Yellowstone with Decals

Bowl, baker; 7"..$7.00
Bowl, vegetable; 9".......................................$12.00
Casserole, w/lid...$27.50
Cup, coffee $3.50
Cup, demitasse $7.00
Cup, tea $3.50
Jug, syrup $22.50
Pickle dish $10.00
Plate, dinner; 10"...$7.00
Plate, 7"...$4.00
Platter, 11½"..$10.00
Saucer $2.50
Sugar bowl, w/lid..$7.00
Teapot..$37.50

Hull Pottery

Hull has a look of its own. Many of their lines are glazed in soft, pastel matt glazes and modeled with flowers and ribbons, resulting in a very feminine appeal.

The company operated in Crooksville (near Zanesville), Ohio, from just after the turn of the century until they closed in 1985. From the thirties until the plant was destroyed by fire in 1950, they preferred the soft matt glazes so popular with today's collectors, though a few high gloss lines were made as well. When the plant was rebuilt, modern equipment was installed which they soon found did not lend itself to the duplication of the matt glazes, so they began to concentrate on the production of glossy wares, novelties, and figurines.

During the forties and fifties, they produced a line of kitchenware items modeled after Little Red Riding Hood. Some of this line was sent to Regal China, who decorated Hull's whiteware. (See also Little Red Riding Hood.) All of these pieces are very expensive today.

Hull's Mirror Brown dinnerware line made from about 1960 until they closed in 1985 was very successful for them and was made in large quantities. Its glossy brown glaze was enhanced with a band of ivory foam, and today's collectors are finding its rich colors and basic, strong shapes just as attractive now as it was then. In addition to table service, there are novelty trays shaped like gingerbread men and fish, canisters and cookie jars, covered casseroles with ducks and hens as lids, vases, ashtrays, and mixing bowls. It's easy to find, and though you may have to pay 'near book' prices at co-ops and antique malls, because it's just now 'catching on,' the bargains are out there. It may be marked Hull, Crooksville, O; HPCo; or Crestone.

If you'd like to learn more about this subject, we recommend *The Collector's Encyclopedia of Hull Pottery* by Brenda Roberts.

Ashtray, 10¼", Continental, Evergeen w/white stripes, glossy, #52, incised mark..........................$30.00

Bank, 5", Corky Pig, Tawny Ridge (tan color), marked Corky Pig c 57..$22.50

Basket, 10½", Bow-Knot, floral decoration on blended pastels, bow at foot, #8-12, incised mark.................$525.00

Basket, 16½", Ebb Tide, seashell form, chartreuse & wine, glossy, #E-11, incised mark....................................$175.00

Basket, 6", Tulip, flower decoration on pink to blue shaded, matt, #102-33...$195.00

Basket, 8", Butterfly, butterfly & floral decoration on white, blue interior, matt, #B13, incised mark...............$100.00

Basket, 8", Tuscany, green grape cluster decoration on milk white, twig handle, glossy, #6, incised mark........$65.00

Bell, 6¼", Sun Glow, pink embossed floral decoration on yellow, rope handle, unmarked.............................$88.00

Bonbon, 7", Wild Flower, floral decoration on blended pastels, basket form w/handle, matt, #69.................$225.00

Bowl, batter; 9", yellowware w/embossed decoration, incised Pat Apl For, USA...$85.00

Bowl, console; 13", New Magnolia, floral decoration on ivory, glossy, H-23, embossed mark, foil label.....$75.00

Bowl, console; 13", Orchid, floral decoration on pink to blue, ruffled rim, handle, matt, #314, label.........$265.00

Bowl, mixing; 9½", Gun-Glow, pink floral decoration on yellow, embossed rope decoration at rim, glossy, unmarked..$35.00

Bowl, 6", semi-porcelain, yellow w/embossed band decoration, H-in-circle mark...$22.50

Bowl, 7", stoneware, green, glossy, #421.....................$35.00

Bowl, 9", stoneware, embossed/painted band decoration, #428...$32.00

Bowl, 9½", yellowware w/blue underglaze banding, square shoulder, USA..$50.00

Candle holder, 5", Iris, floral decoration on rose to blue, handles, #411, foil label...$55.00

Candle holders, 3½", Woodland, floral decoration on 2-toned pastels, twig handle, matt, #W30, pr...........$60.00

Candle holders, 3¼", Mardi Gras/Granada (shared mold), white, matt, unmarked, pr.....................................$55.00

Candle holders, 3¾", Dogwood, floral decoration on cream, cornucopia form, matt, #512, pr.........................$135.00

Candle holders, 4", Bow-Knot, floral decoration on blended pastels, cornucopia form, matt, #B-17, pr...........$135.00

Candle holders, 5", Parchment & Pine, pine cone sprays on pearl gray, glossy, #S-10", pr.................................$45.00

Candle holders, 6½", Serenade, chickadees on floral branch on pastel, matt, #S16, impressed mark, pr............$90.00

Casserole, 7½", Diamond Quilt, turquoise, glossy, w/lid, #D-13...$47.50

Casserole, 7½", Sun-Glow, floral decoration on pink, w/lid, glossy, #51..$42.50

Casserole, 9", Serenade, chickadees on floral branch decoration on yellow, w/lid, matt, #S20, incised mark...$75.00

Cookie jar, 10½", multicolor floral decoration on yellow to white shaded, cylindrical, ball finial...................$100.00

Cookie jar, 11", mixed fruit over-the-glaze decoration on white, glossy, unmarked.......................................$75.00

Cookie jar, 8", 2-qt, Fish Scale, peach, small handles, glossy, #C-20..$80.00

Cornucopia, 11", Royal Woodland, white spatter decoration on blue, glossy, #W10......................................$50.00

Cornucopia, 11", Tokay, pink grape cluster decoration on pink to green shaded pastels, glossy, #10............$50.00

Cornucopia, 8½", Magnolia, floral decoration on yellow to dusty rose, matt, #19, embossed mark, foil label..$80.00

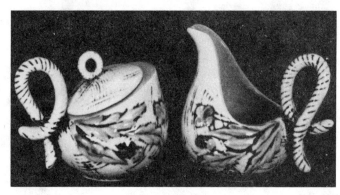

Creamer & sugar bowl, Blossom Flight.................$80.00

Creamer, 3¼", Tokay, pink grape cluster decoration on shaded pastels, twig handle, glossy, #17...............$35.00

Creamer, 5", Water Lily, floral decoration on 2-tone apricot, matt, #L-18, embossed or incised mark.................$42.50

Doorstop, 7¼", cat figural, ivory w/painted details, glossy or matt, unmarked...$215.00

Ewer, 10", Calla Lily, floral decoration on pink to blue shaded, matt, #506, foil label.............................$275.00

Ewer, 11", Imperial, Golden Mist, gurgling fish figural, #F482, incised mark 1949.....................................$75.00

Ewer, 12", Tuscany, green grape cluster decoration on milk white, twig handle, glossy, #13, incised mark....$175.00

Ewer, 12½", persimmon w/yellow vertical stripes on modernistic shape, angle handle, glossy, #56...........$145.00

Ewer, 13", Tulip, floral decoration on cream to blue shaded, matt, #109-33...$325.00

Ewer, 13½", Blossom Flite, floral & basketweave decoration on pink, rope handle, glossy, #T13.....................$125.00

Ewer, 13½", Royal Woodland, white spatter decoration on pink, twig handle, #W24 ....**$135.00**

Ewer, 4¾", Dogwood, floral decoration on rose to blue shaded, matt, #520, impressed mark **$75.00**

Ewer, 5½", Woodland, floral decoration on Dawn Rose duo-tone shaded pastel, twig handle, glossy, #W3, embossed mark...**$60.00**

Ewer, 6½", Serenade, chickadees on floral branch decoration on pastel, matt, #S6, incised mark..................**$65.00**

Figurine, Cactus Cat, 2¾", ivory, #964 ....**$25.00**

Figurine, rabbit, 6", green, glossy, #968 ....**$25.00**

Figurine, swan, 8½", Capri, coral shaded pastel, #23, incised mark...**$37.50**

Figurine, 6", Swing Band Accordionist, ivory matt w/gold trim & hand-painted features, unmarked **$70.00**

Flower bowl, 15½" long, Caribbean figure on white, boat shape, glossy, #T51, incised mark **$250.00**

Flowerpot, 4¼", Tulip, flower decoration on yellow to blue shaded, attached saucer, matt, #116-33, foil label ..**$75.00**

Honey pot, 6", Blossom Flite, floral & basketweave decoration on pink, glossy, #T1, incised mark **$55.00**

Jardiniere, 5½", Water Lily, floral decoration on walnut to apricot shaded, small handles, #L-23, marked **$85.00**

Jardiniere, 6", blue w/embossed flower & band decoration, matt, stoneware, H-in-circle mark...................**$50.00**

Jardiniere, 6", Butterfly, butterfly & flowers on white, turquoise interior, matt, #B22, incised mark **$50.00**

Jardiniere, 7", blended colors, turquoise interior, glossy, #551, H-in-circle mark **$80.00**

Jardiniere, 7", green w/embossed leaf band, matt.......**$65.00**

Jardiniere, 7½", Lovebirds, brown w/embossed bird decoration, glossy, unmarked **$85.00**

Jardiniere, 7½", Mardi Gras, blue w/horizontal ribs, glossy, semi-porcelain, unmarked.....................................**$35.00**

Lamp base, 13", embossed & painted florals in reserve on blue, #L-1, unmarked...**$135.00**

Lamp base, 6¾", Rosella, floral decoration on ivory, gold-tone metal foot, unmarked....................................**$180.00**

Leaf dish, 14", Tuscany, green grape cluster decoration on pink, glossy, #19, incised mark.............................**$40.00**

Mug, 3½", Fish Scale, turquoise, glossy, #C-25 ....**$30.00**

Pitcher, batter; 7", Orange Tree, embossed tree decoration on blue, w/lid, H-in-circle mark **$235.00**

Pitcher, 3¾", stoneware, green w/embossed vertical 'stripes' on lower body, #107-42...**$35.00**

Pitcher, 32-oz, Bouquet, multicolor floral decoration on white, yellow rim, glossy, #29, foil label..............**$45.00**

Pitcher, 4¾", yellowware w/brown band, #107-36......**$25.00**

Pitcher, 8½", Diamond Quilt, w/ice lip, peach, glossy, C-29 ....**$85.00**

Planter, 5½", pup w/yarn figural, brown & yellow, glossy, #88, marked or unmarked......................................**$27.50**

Planter, 7½", kitten beside bowl figural, pink & ivory w/under-glaze detailing, glossy, #61 ....**$37.50**

Planter, 8", giraffe among tall leaves figural, wine & dark green, glossy, #115, incised mark **$40.00**

Sugar bowl, 3¼", Tokay, pink grape-cluster decoration on shaded pastels, w/lid, glossy, #18, incised mark ..**$35.00**

Sugar bowl, 4", Bow-Knot, floral decoration on blended pastels, bow finial, matt, #B-22, incised mark.......**$90.00**

Teapot, 42-oz, Blossom, 6-petal flower decoration on white, glossy, #26, incised mark, foil label.....................**$95.00**

Teapot, 5½", Diamond Quilt, blue, glossy, #B-5.........**$85.00**

Teapot, 5½", Mardi Gras/Granada (shared mold), ivory to pink w/embossed floral, matt, #33, label............**$200.00**

Teapot, 6½", seashell figural, chartreuse & wine shaded, glossy, #E-14, incised mark **$150.00**

Teapot, 6½", Woodland, floral decoration on blended pastels, twig handle & finial, #W26.........................**$285.00**

Tile, 2¾x6", boat decoration on matt blues.................**$92.50**

Tile, 4¼x4½", hand-painted flowers on green satin, #360, incised Hull Faience, Cushion............................**$22.00**

Tile, 4¼x4¼", stippled beige, matt, incised Hull Faience, Cushion...**$17.50**

Tray, 11½", Butterfly, butterfly & floral decoration on white w/gold trim, 3-lobed, center handle, matt, #B23 ..**$80.00**

Vase, bud; 9½", Continental, Mountain Blue w/white vertical stripes, glossy, #66, incised mark..........................**$30.00**

Vase, 10", Mardi Gras, brown mottled w/embossed horizontal ribs, unmarked **$35.00**

Vase, 10¾", Royal Ebb Tide, white spatter on blue w/black trim on shell form, unmarked **$75.00**

Vase, 11", Magnolia, floral decoration on shaded pastels, handles, matt, #11, embossed mark, foil label......**$42.50**

Vase, 4¾", Camellia, floral decoration on blended pastels, #130 ....**$55.00**

Vase, 4¾", Iris, floral decoration on rose to blue, handles, petal-shaped rim, #407, foil label..........................**$55.00**

Vase, 6", Calla Lily, floral on blue to pink shaded, angle handles, matt, #503-33..**$80.00**

Vase, 6", Parchment & Pine, pine sprays on pine green w/black trim & interior, #S-1, incised mark **$47.50**

Vase, 6½", Dogwood, floral decoration on blended pastels, handles, #509, incised mark **$85.00**

Vase, 6½", Pine Cone, pine cone spray on pink pastel, handles, matt, #55 ....**$75.00**

Vase, 6½", Poppy, floral decoration on pink to blue shaded, matt, #607, embossed mark................................**$110.00**

Vase, 6½", Thistle, floral decoration on blue, handles, matt, #53, foil label..**$50.00**

Vase, 6½", Tulip, embossed floral decoration on pink to blue, handles, flared foot, #100-33, label **$80.00**

Vase, 6½", Woodland, glossy glaze, #W-4, post-1950.$75.00

Vase, 7", multicolor vertical stripes, glossy, #40..........$70.00

Vase, 7¾", Pagoda, white w/embossed oriental-style decoration, gray trim at rim, glossy, #P3, incised mark...$15.00

Vase, 8", blended colors on body w/solid-colored rim, matt, #32 ....$70.00

Vase, 8½", Iris, floral decoration on peach to rose shaded, handles, matt, #407, foil label $120.00

Vase, 8½", New Magnolia, floral decoration on ivory, gold handles, glossy, H-8.........$60.00

Vase, 8½", Wild Flower, floral decoration on blended pastels, ornate handles, ruffled rim, matt, #76, embossed mark.....................$160.00

Vase, 8½", floral decoration on shaded pastels, hand holding fan form, #126, foil label $215.00

Vase, 9", Crab Apple, embossed & painted flowering branches on ivory, #65/33 ink mark.....................$85.00

Vase, 9¼", Ebb Tide, fish figural, shrimp & turquoise, glossy, #E-6, incised mark $110.00

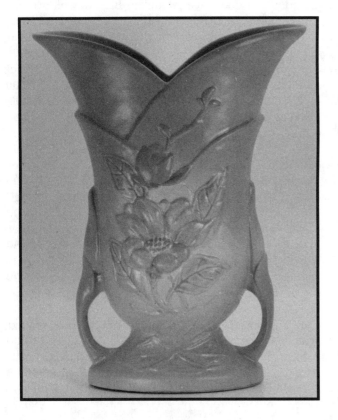

Vase, 10½", Magnolia, matt finish........................$140.00

Wall pocket, 6", Sun-Glow, floral decoration on yellow iron shape, unmarked $60.00

Wall pocket, 6½", Rosella, floral decoration on coral, heart shape, #R-10, foil label $85.00

Wall pocket, 9", Poppy, floral decoration on cream to pink shaded, #609, embossed mark...........$215.00

Window box, 12½" long, Royal Imperial, white spatter decoration on pink, glossy, #82.....................$25.00

Mirror Brown

Baker, 9½" sq $7.00

Bean pot, 6½".....................................$20.00

Bowl, batter; 10½", unmarked..................$14.00

Bowl, mixing; 8", unmarked.......................$4.00

Bowl, salad; 5½", incised rooster on oval shape $12.50

Bowl, 6", marked Crestone....................$2.50

Bowl, 6¾" $2.50

Canister, 9", 8", 7", 6", complete 4-pc set $130.00

Casserole, French; individual size, 5"....................$4.50

Cheese shaker, 6½".............................$12.50

Coffee server, 11"............................$25.00

Cookie jar, 8"................................$27.50

Cruet, vinegar or oil; 6½".....................$12.50

Leaf chip 'n dip, 15"........................$30.00

Leaf dish, 7½".................................$15.00

Pie plate, 9¼".................................$5.00

Pitcher, 7½", ice lip.........................$20.00

Planter, 5", unmarked $5.00

Plate, 10½"...................................$5.00

Plate, 9½", Crestone shape but no Crestone mark........$4.50

Salt & pepper shakers, 3¾", pr................$5.00

Soup & sandwich set, 5" mug, 9½" tray $17.50

Steak plate, 12", oval........................$7.50

Tea set, 3-pc $40.00

Vase, 9", cylindrical....................................$18.00

Hummels

Hummels have been made in Rodental, (West) Germany, since 1935. All have been inspired by the drawings of a Franciscan nun, Sister M. Innocentia. They're commonplace today, both on the retail level and the secondary market. You'll find them in any fine gift shop. In addition to the figurines, a line of collector plates and bells have been made as well.

The figurines have been in demand by collectors for many years, and some are very valuable. It's sometimes difficult to determine what prices you should be paying. Even if the figure is currently in production, the law of supply and demand may cause retail prices to fluctuate as much as 50% in different parts of the country. Several marks have been used over the years, and generally speaking, the older the mark, the more valuable the piece. But if a particular piece happens to be hard to find, scarcity may override the age factor.

Here are some of the marks you'll find: 1) Crown WG — a two-lobed crown over the letters 'W and G,' one super-imposed over the other, 1934-1950; 2) full bee — a realistically styled bee within a large 'V,' with variations, 1940-56; 3) stylized bee — bee (represented by a solid circle having triangular wings) within a large 'V,' with variations, mid-1950s until around 1965; 4) 3-line mark — same stylized bee plus three lines of words to the right: c by/W. Goebel/W. Germany; 5) Goebel bee or last bee — stylized bee in 'V' above and toward the right end of 'Goebel/W. Germany,' 1970-80; 6) missing bee — simple 'Goebel/W. Germany' (no bee), mid-eighties to present.

For further information we recommend _Hummel Figurines and Plates, A Collector's Identification and Value Guide,_ by Carl Luckey.

#III/38, Playmates, stylized bee, candy box, 5¼" **$295.00**
#III/53, Joyful, full bee, candy box, 6¼" **$350.00**
#10/I, Flower Madonna, last bee, color, 8¼" **$195.00**
#10/I, Flower Madonna, stylized bee, color, 8¼" **$220.00**
#11/2/0, Merry Wanderer, full bee, 4¼" **$130.00**
#112/3/0, Just Resting, full bee, 3¾" **$140.00**
#118, Little Thrifty, stylized bee, 5" **$175.00**
#119, Postman, 3-line mark, 5¼" **$145.00**
#125, Vacation Time, 3-line mark, plaque, 4x4¾" **$175.00**

#178, The Photographer, 3-line mark, 4¾" **$180.00**
#180, Tuneful Goodnight, stylized bee, 4¾x4" **$265.00**
#180, Tuneful Goodnight, 3-line mark, plaque, 4" **$250.00**
#183, Forest Shrine, stylized bee, 7x9" **$550.00**
#184, Latest News, stylized bee, 5¼" **$145.00**
#185, Accordion Boy, 3-line mark, 5¼" **$125.00**
#188, Celestial Musician, stylized bee, 7" **$195.00**
#195/I, Barnyard Hero, stylized bee, 5¾" **$225.00**
#196/0, Telling Her Secret, last bee, 5¼" **$185.00**
#2, Little Fiddler, stylized bee, 7½" **$300.00**
#20, Prayer Before Battle, last bee, 4¼" **$110.00**
#21/0, Heavenly Angel, last bee, 4¼" **$65.00**
#217, Boy w/Toothache, 3-line mark, 5½" **$130.00**
#24/III, Lullaby, stylized bee, candle holder, 6x8" **$400.00**
#25, Angelic Sleep, stylized bee, candle holder **$150.00**
#3/III, Bookworm, stylized bee, 9½" **$1,200.00**
#30/0A&B, Ba-Bee Rings, last bee, plaques, 5", pr **$150.00**
#32/1, Little Gabriel, full bee, 5" **$175.00**
#36/I, Child w/Flowers, full bee, 4½x3½" **$265.00**
#47/III, Goose Girl, 3-line mark, 7½" **$335.00**
#5, Strolling Along, last bee, 4¾" **$100.00**
#52/0, Going to Grandma's, stylized bee, 4¾" **$185.00**
#6/II, Sensitive Hunter, last bee, 7½" **$220.00**
#71, Stormy Weather, last bee, 6¼" **$275.00**
#73, Little Helper, stylized bee, 4¼" **$110.00**
#9, Begging His Share, stylized bee, w/hole, 5½" **$235.00**

#130, Duet, full bee, 5¼" $295.00
#131, Street Singer, last bee, 5" $110.00
#139, Flitting Butterfly, last bee, 2½x2½" $55.00
#140, Mail Coach, full bee, plaque, 4½x6¾" $325.00
#141/3/0, Apple Tree Girl, last bee, 4" $80.00
#142/3/0, Apple Tree Boy, 3-line mark, 4" $95.00
#152/A, Umbrella Boy, last bee, 5" $450.00
#153/0, Auf Widersehen, 3-line mark, 5¼" $160.00
#16/I, Little Hiker, full bee, 5½" $195.00
#165, Swaying Lullaby, stylized bee, plaque, 5¼" $140.00
#166, Boy w/Bird, last bee, ash tray, 3¼x6¼" $110.00
#174, She Loves Me, She Loves Me Not; 3-line mark, 4¼" $125.00

#87, For Father (Father's Joy), 3-line mark, 5½" .$165.00
#97, Trumpet Boy, stylized bee, 4¾" $75.00

Ice Cream Molds

Normally made of pewter (though you might find an aluminum example now and then), these were used on special occasions and holidays to mold ice cream (usually single servings) into a shape that was related somehow to the celebration — bells and snowmen at Christmas time, eggs and flowers at Easter, and cupids and rings for Valentine's Day or weddings, for instance. They were designed with two or three hinged sections, so that the ice cream could be removed with ease.

American standard, swords, cannon, flags, E-1200......**$55.00**
Apple, E-240...**$25.00**
Auto, #1080 ....**$65.00**
Basket, E-1013, octagon **$35.00**
Beehive, #302, 3", old dome style **$37.50**
Bonnet w/face, E-968 ....**$125.00**
Cabbage w/bunny, 3⅝" **$24.00**
Calla lily, #210, 3-part **$35.00**
Cat w/arched back, E-644 ....**$35.00**
Cherries, E-240, four in mold.......................................**$30.00**
Chick in egg, #600, 4", vertical.....................................**$35.00**
Chinaman, Palmer Cox Brownie, S-388.......................**$70.00**
Chrysanthemum, E-344...**$30.00**
Crab apple, CC-0001 ....**$25.00**
Cucumber, E-226..**$25.00**
Dahlia, #299, 3"...**$18.00**
Dove, S-347 ....**$50.00**
Dude in tuxedo, Palmer Cox Brownie, S-406 ....**$70.00**
Ear of corn, 5" **$10.00**
Egg, #906, 3" **$25.00**
Engagement ring, #376...**$30.00**
Goose egg, #298 ....**$25.00**
Gourd, 4"...**$18.00**

High-heeled slipper, #570, 3-part **$35.00**
Horse, E-639..**$45.00**
Kewpie, E-1115 ....**$80.00**
Log, #987 ....**$25.00**
Masonic emblem, #323..**$35.00**
Melon, E-204 ....**$18.00**
'Mother' scroll, E-1193 ....**$44.00**
Orange, #307, 3" **$27.50**
Peach, #152 ....**$22.50**
Pears, #942, 4", three in mold **$25.00**
Petunia, 3" **$22.00**
Pie slice, E-1097 ....**$30.00**
Pork chop, 5" **$45.00**

Potato, #245, sm..**$25.00**
Pumpkin, E-309...**$25.00**
Rose bud, 3", two in mold...**$22.00**
Rotary Club emblem, E-1110.......................................**$27.50**
Santa Claus, E-991 ....**$48.00**

Shield, #281, stars & stripes **$60.00**
Slipper, E-899A, 3-part..**$38.00**
Stork, #1151, 5" **$110.00**
Strawberry, E-1021 ....**$30.00**
Tomato medallion, #326, 3" **$25.00**
Turkey, E-650 ....**$38.00**
Uncle Sam, standing, #1073, 6" **$75.00**
Washington bust, #1084, 4"...**$60.00**
Wedding bell w/Cupid, E-1019....................................**$38.00**

Imperial Glass

Organized in 1901 in Bellaire, Ohio, the Imperial Glass Company made carnival glass, stretch glass, a line called NuCut (made in imitation of cut glass), and a limited amount of art glass within the first decade of the century. In the mid-thirties, they designed one of their most famous patterns (and one of their most popular with today's collectors), Candlewick. Within a few years, milk glass had become their leading product.

During the fifties, they reintroduced their NuCut line in crystal as well as colors, marketing it as 'Collector's Crystal.' In the late fifties they bought molds from both Heisey and Cambridge. The glassware they reissued from these old molds was marked 'IG', one letter superimposed over the other. When Imperial was bought by Lenox in 1973, an 'L' was added to the mark. The company changed hands twice more before closing altogether in 1984.

In addition to tableware, they made a line of animal figures, some of which were made from Heisey's molds. *Glass Animals of the Depression Years* by Lee Garmon and Dick Spencer is an wonderful source of information and can help you determine the value and the manufacturer of your figures.

Numbers in the listings were assigned by the company and appeared on their catalog pages. They were used to indicate differences in shapes and stems, for instance. Collectors still use them. For more information on Imperial in general, we recommend *Imperial Glass* by Margaret and Douglas Archer and *Elegant Glassware of the Depression Era* by Gene Florence.

See also Carnival Glass, Candlewick, Glass Animals.

Ashtray, Cathay Crystal, #5006, butterfly shape **$25.00**
Basket, caramel slag satin..**$35.00**
Basket, Monticello...**$25.00**
Basket, 9", Cape Cod, #160/221/0, crystal, crimped, handled **$160.00**
Bottle, decanter; 26-oz, Cape Cod, #160/244, crystal ..**$95.00**
Bowl, baked apple; Tradition **$10.00**
Bowl, banana; 12", footed, milk glass, glossy.............**$30.00**
Bowl, console; 15", Cape Cod, #16010L, crystal **$60.00**
Bowl, dessert; 5", Cape Cod, #160/49H, crystal, heart shape **$15.00**
Bowl, fruit; 6", Cape Cod, #160/3F, crystal **$10.00**
Bowl, gravy; 18-oz, Cape Cod, #160/202, crystal.........**$55.00**
Bowl, jelly; 3", #160/33, crystal **$10.00**
Bowl, nappy; 7", Cape Cod, #160/5F, crystal..............**$20.00**
Bowl, salad; 11", Cape Cod, #160/8B, crystal **$38.00**
Bowl, 10", Cape Cod, #160/8A, crystal **$35.00**
Butter dish, 5", Cape Cod, #160/144, crystal, w/lid **$25.00**
Cake plate, Tradition, crystal, 72-candle......................**$75.00**
Cake plate, 10½", Cape Cod, #160/67D, crystal, footed .**$38.00**
Cake stand, Vintage Grape, milk glass, glossy.............**$40.00**
Candle holder, centerpiece; 6", Cape Cod, #160/48B, crystal **$65.00**
Candle servants, Cathay Crystal, #5033/34, pr **$350.00**
Candy dish, Cape Cod, #160/110, crystal, w/lid **$60.00**
Candy jar, owl shape, purple slag satin.......................**$55.00**
Coaster, Cape Cod, #160/76, crystal, w/spoon rest **$10.00**
Comport, 6", Cape Cod, #160/140, crystal, w/lid, footed...**$55.00**
Creamer, Cape Cod, #160/190, crystal.........................**$15.00**
Creamer & sugar bowl, Crochet Crystal **$20.00**
Creamer & sugar bowl, owl shape, jade slag, glossy, pr **$35.00**
Cruet, 4-oz, Cape Cod, #160/119, w/stopper **$20.00**
Cup, bouillon; Cape Cod, #160/250, crystal................**$25.00**
Cup, coffee; Cape Cod, #160/37, crystal......................**$7.00**
Decanter, 30-oz, Cape Cod, #160/163, crystal, w/stopper **$53.00**
Egg cup, Cape Cod, #160/225, crystal **$33.00**
Epergne, Crochet Crystal **$28.00**
Flower bowl, Cathay Crystal, #5010, Chinese junk shape...**$250.00**
Ice bucket, 6½", Cape Cod, #160/63, crystal.............**$100.00**
Lamp, Dew Drop, opal...**$90.00**
Marmalade, Cape Cod, #160/89/3, crystal, 3-pc...........**$30.00**
Martini mixer, Big Shot Series, red **$100.00**
Mayonnaise, Cape Cod, #160/52H, crystal, 3-pc.........**$35.00**
Mustard, Cape Cod, #160/156, crystal, w/spoon & lid ..**$20.00**
Pagoda, Cathay Crystal, #5001 ....**$550.00**

Pitcher, Cape Cod, w/ice lip, crystal **$60.00**
Pitcher, milk; 1-pt, Cape Cod, #160/240, crystal..........**$40.00**
Pitcher, water; Tradition, crystal **$35.00**
Plate, bread & butter; 6½", Cape Cod, crystal **$4.00**
Plate, dinner; 10", Cape Cod, #160/10D, crystal **$33.00**
Plate, salad; 8", Cape Cod, #160/5D, crystal..................**$8.00**
Plate, 12" sq, Monticello **$10.00**
Plate, 14", Cape Cod, #160/75D, crystal **$33.00**
Plate, 16", Cape Cod, #160/20V, cupped, crystal.........**$50.00**
Plate, 8", Tradition, B1...**$10.00**
Plate, 9½", Vintage Grape, milk glass **$15.00**
Platter, 13½", Cape Cod, #160/124D, crystal, oval......**$45.00**
Relish dish, 8", Cape Cod, #160/223, crystal, divided..**$35.00**
Salt & pepper shakers, Cape Cod, #160/243, crystal, stemmed, footed, pr..**$28.00**
Salt & pepper shakers, Salz & Pfeffer, Carnival, pr......**$42.00**
Spoon, Cape Cod, #160/701, crystal **$8.00**
Stem, cordial; 3½", Cape Cod, #1602, crystal **$7.00**
Stem, oyster cocktail; Cape Cod, #1602, crystal **$8.00**
Stem, water; 9-oz, Cape Cod, #1602, crystal **$10.00**
Sugar bowl, Cape Cod, #160/30, crystal **$7.00**
Sweetmeat box, Cathay Crystal, #5022, fan shape.....**$175.00**
Tray, pastry; 11", Cape Cod, #160/68D, crystal, center handle **$50.00**
Tumbler, iced tea; 12-oz, Cape Cod, #1602, crystal, footed **$12.00**
Tumbler, 12-oz, Big Shot Series, red **$13.00**
Tumbler, 16-oz, Big Shot Series, red **$15.00**
Tumbler, 2½-oz, Little Shot, red...................................**$13.00**
Vase, Crochet Crystal **$25.00**
Vase, 5", Genie, footed, blue opal................................**$25.00**
Vase, 8", Cape Cod, #160/22, crystal, fan shape..........**$75.00**
Vase, 8", Peachblow satin **$175.00**

Imperial Porcelain

Figurines representing Paul Webb's Blue Ridge Mountain Boys were made by the Imperial Porcelain Corporation of Zanesville, Ohio, from the late 1940s until they closed in 1960. You'll see some knocking on outhouse doors by ashtrays, drinking from a jug of 'moonshine' as they sit by washtub planters, or embossed in scenes of mountain-life activity on mugs and pitchers. Imperial also made the Al Capp Dogpatch series and a line of twenty-three miniature animals, 2" tall and under, that they called American Folklore miniatures.

Ashtray, #103, hillbilly & skunk $75.00
Ashtray, #106, 'Barrel of Wishes,' w/hound $75.00
Box, cigarette; #98, dog atop, baby at door, sq.........$115.00
Decanter, #100, outhouse, man, & bird........................$75.00
Figurine, #101, man leans against tree trunk, 5"..........$90.00
Jug, #101, Willie & snake $75.00
Miniature, cat, 1½" $40.00
Miniature, hound dogs $35.00
Miniature, sow..$30.00

Mug, 6", 'Mountain Rug Cutting' $95.00
Mug, #94, 'Bearing Down,' 6" $95.00
Mug, #94, Ma handle, 4¼"..$95.00
Mug, #94, man w/blue pants forms handle, 4¼".........$95.00
Pitcher, lemonade...$200.00
Planter, #100, outhouse, man, & bird........................$75.00
Planter, #105, dog sitting by tub, IP mark...................$75.00
Planter, #110, man, w/jug & snake, 4½" $65.00
Planter, #81, man drinking from jug, sitting by washtub..$75.00
Salt & pepper shakers, pigs, 5", pr $95.00

Indiana Glass Carnival Ware

In the mid-1980s, the Indiana Glass Company produced a line of iridescent 'new carnival' glass, much of which was embossed with grape clusters and detailed leaves reminescent of the old Northwood carnival. It was made in blue, marigold, and green and was evidently a good seller for them, judging from the amount around today. Collectors always seem to gravitate toward lustre-coated glassware, whether it's old or recently made, and last summer we noticed a significant amount of interest in this line.

It's a little difficult to evaluate, since you see it in malls and at flea markets with such a wide range of 'asking' prices. On one hand, you'll have sellers who themselves are not exactly sure what it is they have, but since it's 'carnival' assume it should be fairly pricey. On the other hand, you have those who've just 'cleaned house' and want to get rid of it. They may have bought it new themselves and know it's not very old and wasn't expensive to start with. This is what you'll be up against if you decide you want to collect it.

As I mentioned up front, the collectibles market has changed. Nowadays, some shows' criteria regarding the merchandise they allow to be displayed is 'if it's no longer available on the retail market, it's OK.' I suspect that this attitude will become more and more widespread. At any rate, this is one of the newest interests at the flea market/antique mall level, and if you can buy it right (and like its looks), now is the time!

Bowl, fruit; large, embossed grapes & vines, wide oval
    shape $20.00
Candy dish, small, ribbed, open lace rim, w/lid............$8.00
Candy dish, 7½x5", embossed grapes & vines, cylindrical, w/lid $12.00
Compote, covered; 8" dia, embossed grapes & leaves,
    w/lid..$28.00
Compote, jelly; thumbprint band....................................$8.00

Compote, 10x8½", embossed grapes & vines $22.00
Covered dish, hen on nest $18.00
Creamer & sugar bowl on tray, embossed grapes &
    vines $15.00
Goblet, embossed grapes & vines.................................$8.00
Pitcher, 10", embossed grapes & vines, pedestal foot.$25.00

Tumbler, 5½", embossed grapes & vines, scarce.........**$10.00**

Jadite Glassware

For the past few years, jadite has been one of the fastest-moving types of collectible glassware on the market. It was produced by several companies from the 1940s through 1965. Many of Anchor Hocking's Fire-King lines were available in the soft opaque green jadite, and Jeannette Glass as well as McKee produced their own versions.

It was always very inexpensive glass, and it was made in abundance. Dinnerware for the home as well as restaurants and a vast array of kitchenware items literally flooded the country for many years. Though a few rare pieces have become fairly expensive, most are still reasonably priced, and there are still bargains to be had.

For more information we recommend *Kitchen Glassware of the Depression Years* and *Collectible Glassware of the 40s, 50s, and 60s*, both by Gene Florence.

Alice, cup, embossed florals at rim, Fire-King, early 1940s.................**$2.50**

Alice, plate, 9½", embossed florals at rim, Fire-King, early 1940s.................**$12.50**

Alice, saucer, embossed florals at rim, Fire-King, early 1940s.................**$1.00**

Charm, bowl, dessert; 4¾", square form, Fire-King, 1950-54.................**$4.00**

Charm, creamer, square form w/side handles, Fire-King, 1950-54.................**$5.50**

Charm, sugar bowl, square, Fire-King, 1950-54.........**$5.50**

Jane Ray, bowl, oatmeal; 5⅞", very fine ribs around sides & slightly flared top, Fire-King, 1945-63.................**$4.00**

Jane Ray, bowl, vegetable; 8¼", very fine ribs around sides & slightly flared top, Fire-King, 1945-63.................**$8.00**

Jane Ray, cup, demitasse; very fine ribbed design, w/demitasse saucer, Fire-King, 1945-63.................**$20.00**

Jane Ray, sugar bowl, very fine ribbed design w/tab handles at top, Fire-King, 1945-63.................**$4.00**

Leaf & Blossom, dessert set, 4½" bowl, 8" plate, Fire-King.................$8.00

Restaurant Ware, bowl, fruit; 4¾", plain w/lightly rolled rim, Fire-King, 1950-53.................**$3.00**

Restaurant Ware, cup, 7-oz, extra heavy, Fire-King, 1950-53.................**$5.00**

Restaurant Ware, plate, 9⅝", oval, 5-compartment, Fire-King, 1950-53.................**$12.50**

Restaurant Ware, platter, 11½", oval, Fire-King, 1950-53.**$7.50**

Restuarant Ware, mug, 7-oz, thick walled & heavy, Fire-King, 1950-53.................**$5.00**

Shell, bowl, cereal; 6⅜", swirl design, 1964-late 1970s..**$3.25**

Shell, creamer, swirl design w/foot, Fire-King, 1964-late 1970s.................**$5.00**

Shell, plate, dinner; 10", swirl design, Fire-King, 1964-late 1970s.................**$4.00**

Shell, platter, 9½x13", swirl design, oval, Fire-King, 1964-late 1970s.................**$9.00**

Shell, sugar bowl, swirl design w/lid, Fire-King, 1964-late 1970s.................**$8.00**

Miscellaneous

Batter bowl, 9" (across spout & handle).................$12.00

Bowl, mixing; 8", swirled rib design, 1940s-60s.............**$6.00**

Bowl, 9¾", vertical ribbed design, Jeannette Glass......**$18.00**

Butter dish, 1-lb, embossed 'Butter' in top, Jeannette Glass Co, 2-pc.................**$35.00**

Canister, 28-oz, square-sided w/'Sugar' in black letters, metal screw-on lid, McKee Glass Co.................**$40.00**

Canister, 29-oz, square-sided w/'Sugar' in black letters, flat lid, Jeannette Glass Co.................**$40.00**

Canister, 40-oz, cylindrical w/horizontal ribbed design & 'Coffee' in black letters, Jeannette Glass Co.........**$60.00**

Crock, 40-oz, round, w/flat lid, Jeannette Glass Co **$40.00**

Decanter, pinched sides w/'doorknob' stopper.........**$115.00**

Doorknob set, hexagonal form.................**$45.00**

Furniture coaster, sold through Montgomery Ward catalog, ca 1920s.................**$5.00**

Ice bucket, paneled sides, marked w/Fenton logo, w/rattan handle.................**$50.00**

Ladle, rounded bowl, minimum value.................**$20.00**

Measure, 1-cup, w/tab handle, for dry ingredients, minimum value.................**$15.00**

Measure, ¼-cup, minimum value.................**$8.00**

Mug, 'Bottoms Down,' marked McKee.................**$150.00**

Mug, 'Tom & Jerry' in black letters, angle handle, McKee Glass Co.................**$12.00**

Napkin holder, rectangular form w/'Serv-All' embossed on side.................**$150.00**

Pie plate, 10¾", juice saver, embossed floral design on bottom & embossed band around side, late 1940s-60s........**$70.00**

Pitcher, measuring; 2-cup, dark green, sunflower in bottom, Jeannette Glass Co **$45.00**

Pitcher, measuring; 2-cup, light green, sunflower design in bottom, Jeannette Glass Co **$15.00**

Pitcher, measuring; 2-cup; marked McKee, minimum value **$15.00**

Pitcher, measuring; 4-cup, paneled sides w/pour spout, McKee Glass Co **$225.00**

Reamer, large, dark green **$25.00**

Reamer, large, light green **$20.00**

Reamer, marked Sunkist....................................**$20.00**

Reamer, small, horizontal ribbed design, light green, Jeannette Glass Co **$22.00**

Refrigerator dish, pie-wedge form, w/flat lid **$20.00**

Refrigerator dish, 10x5", w/flat floral-embossed lid.....**$30.00**

Refrigerator jar, 4¼x4¾", w/flat lid **$22.50**

Rolling pin, metal screw-on end, marked McKee......**$325.00**

Salt & pepper shakers, 5", horizontal ribs, pr $30.00

Salt box, square-sided w/'Salt' in black letters, wooden lid, Jeannette Glass Co...**$225.00**

Sugar shaker, dark green, tapered paneled sides, metal screw-on lid..**$60.00**

Towel bar holders, pr...**$25.00**

Tumbler, 12-oz, horizontal ribbed design, Jeannette Glass Co...**$12.00**

Wall tumbler holder (for bathroom)............................**$10.00**

Whipped cream pail, paneled sides, w/metal handle .**$35.00**

Jewelry

Though the collectible jewelry frenzy of a few years ago seems to have subsided a bit, better costume jewelry remains a strong area of interest on today's market. Signed pieces are especially good. Check for marks on metal mounts. Some of the better designers are Hobé, Haskell, Monet, Trifari, Weiss, and Eisenberg.

Early plastic pieces (Lucite, Bakelite, and celluloid, for example) are very collectible; some Lucite is used in combination with wood, and the figural designs are especially

desirable. The better rhinestone jewelry, especially when it's signed, is a good investment as well.

There are several excellent reference books available, if you'd like more information. Lilian Baker has written several: *Art Nouveau and Art Deco Jewelry, An Identification and Value Guide; Twentieth Century Fashionable Plastic Jewelry;* and *50 Years of Collectible Fashion Jewelry.* Other books: *Collecting Rhinestone Colored Jewelry* by Maryanne Dolan and *The Art and Mystique of Shell Cameos* by Ed Aswad and Michael Weinstein.

Bracelet, bangle; Catalin, deeply carved, w/set-in rhinestones **$80.00**

Bracelet, bangle; Catalin, striped in three colors **$90.00**

Bracelet, bangle; Catalin w/no decoration or carving, narrow..**$6.00**

Bracelet, bangle; Catalin w/ornate floral carvings, wide style **$65.00**

Bracelet, bangle; Catalin w/scratch carvings, narrow style **$18.00**

Bracelet, bangle; plastic, butterscotch w/deeply carved floral motif, wide band...**$120.00**

Bracelet, bangle; Whiting & Davis, diagonal stripes, hinged **$40.00**

Bracelet, Charel, avocado green thermoset plastic ovals set in gold-toned links, 1960s-1970 ....**$50.00**

Bracelet, Coro, rhinestones on gilt metal, 1½" wide, 1940s **$130.00**

Bracelet, Florenza, gold-tone diamind-in-ring links, small pearls & turquoise...**$18.00**

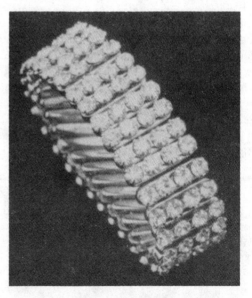

Bracelet, rhinestones, flexible, 4-row, 1950s........$85.00

Bracelet, seven copper 3-leaf components, 1½" wide.**$18.00**

Bracelet, stretch; Catalin & metal, original elastic........**$48.00**

Bracelet, Trifari, gold-plated w/large marquise rhinestone center, ½" wide **$38.00**

Bracelet, wrap-around bangle; plastic w/rhinestones, hinged, 1935-50..**$110.00**

Brooch, carved wood bird w/clear Lucite feathers & tail, brass beading, 1930s..**$110.00**

Brooch, Coro, brass, thin free-form w/large rhinestones in center, 2½" long **$45.00**

Brooch, Jomage, gold-filled leaf form w/rhinestones & imitation pearl **$50.00**

Brooch, unmarked, pink stones in wreath form, 1950s, 4¼" **$30.00**

Buckle, Catalin latch type, multicolored, novelty or figural applique..**$40.00**

Buckle, Catalin latch type, single color w/stylized floral or geometric decoration **$10.00**

Buckle, Catalin slide type, multicolored, no carving ...**$12.50**

Buckle, clear plastic w/twenty-five rhinestones, circular shape, 3" dia...**$27.50**

Buckle, large rhinestones pasted in base metal w/silver finish, rectangular form, brass hasp, 1930s................**$65.00**

Dress clip, 'apple-juice clear' & red Catalin carved into stylized floral shape, 1930s **$45.00**

Earrings, Bogoff, rhinestones, clip type, 1" long.........**$45.00**

Earrings, Emmons, starburst design, 1960s, pr....$40.00

Earrings, Kenneth Lane, starfish w/pearl & two rows of rhinestones, 1½"...**$125.00**

Earrings, Kramer, large rhinestones, 2" long dangle style .**$60.00**

Earrings, Kramer, rhinestones w/large red stones, arrow-shaped drop style, 2½" **$75.00**

Earrings, laminated wood & red Bakelite, long slim Deco design, ca 1930...**$40.00**

Earrings, Miriam Haskell, imitation pearl w/pronged rhinestones in sunrise pattern, gilt filigree, 1½x1½"......**$80.00**

Earrings, rhinestones set in red plastic, button shape, clip type, ca 1935 ....**$40.00**

Earrings, Weiss, rhinestone flowers w/imitation emerald, clip type, ⅞" **$25.00**

Fur clip, Eisenberg, rhinestones, teardrop form, 1940s .**$175.00**

Fur clip, Monet, gold-toned plumes, 1¼", pr **$24.00**

Fur clip, rhinestones & green stones on butterfly form, wings have tiny springs, 1930s **$90.00**

Necklace, cultured pearls, one strand of ninety-four, 7mm to 7.5mm..**$700.00**

Necklace, Miriam Haskell, chain w/gold-toned disks & oval stones, w/matching earrings **$45.00**

Necklace, Miriam Haskell, pearl choker w/butterfly pendant...**$150.00**

Necklace, molded plastic 'stones' on gold-toned chain, varied styles & shapes, 1955, from $25.00 up to........**$35.00**

Necklace, Peking glass, light green rondells & green tube beads, 39" **$35.00**

Necklace, Sara Coventry, leaf drop w/five green stones on gold-toned chain **$8.00**

Necklace, unmarked, gold-plated chain w/five metal flowers, rhinestone in center of each, short style, 1940s.....**$50.00**

Pendant, sterling, cloisonne rose under glass **$24.00**

Pendant/brooch, cameo, Three Graces in 14k yellow gold frame, Victorian age to modern, from 1¼" to 1⅞" long, each **$650.00**

Pin, amber Catalin & rosewood, duck in flight form, laminated before carving, glass eye, 1930s **$180.00**

Pin, banana figural, carved yellow Catalin w/hand-painted details, 1930s **$110.00**

Pin, cameo, Gay 90s lady on oval, detailed hair, high relief carving, ca 1920s, 2x1½" **$200.00**

Pin, cameo, Mediterranean woman in gold-filled metal twisted-ribbon frame, 1¾x1½" **$300.00**

Pin, Capri, gold-toned crescent w/large & small green stone cabochons, 1¾" **$15.00**

Pin, Coro, flower form w/five faceted red stones, w/drop earrings **$22.00**

Pin, Coro, pink stones on stem held by bow **$20.00**

Pin, Coro, three large amethysts on sterling spray, 5"...**$80.00**

Pin, Coro (marked Pat Pend), rhinestones on crown form, designed by Katz..**$50.00**

Pin, Coro Sterlingcraft, pelican, gold on sterling, 1⅝" .**$45.00**

Pin, Eisenberg, emerald green stone flower w/rhinestone accents **$90.00**

Pin, Eisenberg, mushroom w/blue & green enamel, 2"..**$38.00**

Pin, green Bakelite, carved Scottie dog figural, 1930s.**$80.00**

Pin, Hattie Carnegie, Bakelite w/rhinestones & gold overlay, ram's head form, 1950s, w/matching earrings **$150.00**

Pin, Hattie Carnegie, red, black, & yellow Bakelite, rooster figural, 1950s **$75.00**

Pin, Lang, sterling lamppost, 2¼"...............................**$22.00**

Pin, Lea Stein Paris, celluloid, found in green, yellow, black, white, red or violet, each **$125.00**

Pin, Lea Stein Paris, celluloid, lady w/broad shoulders (reminescent of Joan Crawford), 1950.......................**$55.00**

Pin, Lea Stein Paris, laminated plastic, bellhop figural, 1960s **$150.00**

Pin, Miriam Haskell, brass, ring of cloverleaves w/baroque pearls **$45.00**

Pin, Occupied Japan, plastic group w/girl & two elves $40.00

Pin, tortoise-color Bakelite & yellow metal, sword figural, 1930s **$65.00**

Pin, Trifari, blue enamel rhinestone-tip leaf w/lady bug, w/earrings...**$36.00**

Pin, Trifari, silver-finished seated Sheltie dog, 1½".........**$8.00**
Pin, Weiss, leaf form w/marquise rhinestones.............**$30.00**
Ring, George Jensen, sterling w/three moonstones, beading, 1910s...**$200.00**
Ring, sterling, aquamarine w/sixteen marcasites, man's size, 1920s...**$75.00**
Ring, Vendome, baroque pearls, chunky 'gold' & tiny rhinestones, 1¼" dia **$65.00**
Ring, 10k yellow gold filigree w/small ruby **$125.00**
Ring, 14k white gold, large oval peridot...................**$450.00**
Ring, 14k white gold filigree w/small diamond.........**$125.00**
Ring, 14k yellow gold, black onyx in white gold filigree, Eastern Star emblem **$110.00**
Ring, 14k yellow gold, tiger's eye & six small diamonds **$200.00**
Ring, 14k yellow gold, fire opal in flower setting **$125.00**
Ring, 18k yellow gold, four rubies (total weight 1.10 carat) in zigzag w/three diamonds (total weight .6 carat) .**$375.00**
Scarf slide, molded celluloid, lady's hand w/hand-painted red nails, 1938 Patent **$135.00**

Jukeboxes

Because so many suppliers are now going to CD players, right now the market is full of jukeboxes from the past twenty-five years that you can usually buy very inexpensively. One in good working order should cost you no more than $500.00. Look for one that has a little personality (some from the early seventies are fairly 'funky'), and if you're buying it for your own use and particularly enjoy hearing the 'oldies,' you'll find it to be one of the best investments you've ever made. Look in the Yellow Pages under 'Amusements' or 'Arcade Machines' to locate a supplier in your area.

The older models are another story. They've been appreciated by collectors for a long time, as their prices indicate. The forties was an era of stiff competition among jukebox manufactuers, and as a result many beautiful models were produced. Wurlitzer's 1015 with the bubble tubes (see our listings) is one of the most famous and desirable models ever made. It's being made again today as the 'One More Time.'

There are several books on the market that offer more information; two that we'd recommend are: *A Blast from the Past!, Jukeboxes,* by Scott Wood and *An American Premium Guide to Jukeboxes and Slot Machines* by Jerry Ayliffe.

Packard Manhattan, 1946, twenty selections, EX....**$5,000.00**
Rockola, #1422, 1946, revolving color cylinder w/fully visible record changer, 20-selection multi-selector, EX...**$6,500.00**
Rockola, #1434, 1951, 45 rpm model w/one hundred twenty selections, EX..**$3,500.00**
Rockola, #39A, 1939, counter model, no internal speaker, twelve selections, EX...**$3,000.00**
Scopitone, 1962, 25¢ for one play & a film of the recording artist synchronized to music, very rare, EX......**$4,000.00**

Seeburg, #KD 200, 1957 ....**$4,000.00**
Seeburg, #M100C, 1952, moving color cylinders inside the light-up plastics, EX..**$4,500.00**
Seeburg, #100B, 1950, first 45 rpm model on the market, 100 selections, EX...**$4,000.00**
Seeburg, #220, 1958, Seeburg's first stereophonic model, one hundred selections, channels labeled w/large '1' & '2', EX..**$3,300.00**
Wurlitzer, #1050, 1946, color wheels & bubble tubes, NM...**$13,000.00**
Wurlitzer, #1080, 1947, mirrored graphics, EX **$10,000.00**
Wurlitzer, #1800, 1956, one hundred four selections, EX..**$3,500.00**
Wurlitzer, #24, 1937, twenty-four selections w/rotary multi-selector, EX...**$4,500.00**
Wurlitzer, #2800, 1964, two hundred selections, features a mini LP w/three cuts on each side of the record, EX..**$1,700.00**
Wurlitzer, #600, 1938, twenty selections, w/rotary or keyboard selector, EX **$5,000.00**
Wurlitzer, #780, 1941, better known as the 'Colonial,' EX..**$7,000.00**
Wurlitzer, #800, 1940, 20-selection multi-selector w/visible turntable, EX..**$8,500.00**
Wurlitzer, #1900, NM...**$3,500.00**

Keen Kutter

The E.C. Simmons Company used 'Keen Kutter' as a tradename on an extensive line of tools, knives, and other hardware items made by them from about 1870 until the mid-'30s. The older items are especially collectible, so is advertising material such as catalogs, calendars, and wooden packing boxes.

For more information, we recommend *Keen Kutter Collectibles, An Illustrated Price Guide* by Elaine and Jerry Heuring.

Awl, scratch; KK #100, VG **$12.50**
Axe, #KMA1, octagon handle & round head **$25.00**
Axe, box; sliding top, word w/large EC Simmons & Keen Kutter logos **$35.00**
Axe, broad; Keen Kutter written out, no logo **$100.00**
Bar, carpenter's wrecking; 18", gooseneck.................**$20.00**
Bevel, sliding T; KK #12510, 10", EX **$22.50**
Bit, countersink; KK #120, EX **$12.50**
Bit brace, KK #16, 6", VG **$35.00**
Bits, auger; KK #9, in original box **$105.00**

Butcher saw blades, 25 ft continuous coil, KF #3/4 ...$35.00
Calipers, inside; KK #28, EX.....................................**$38.00**
Chisel, firmer; KK #8, set of eight, EX......................**$145.00**
Chisel, 1½"...**$12.00**
Clippers, hair; K #543, w/original box **$35.00**
Clippers, horse; KK #920, EX.....................................**$18.00**
Clippers, horse; KK #940 ....**$20.00**
Dividers, KK #110, EX **$42.50**
Drill, breast; KK #600, 16", EX **$65.00**
Grinder, hand; 7" wheel..**$125.00**
Grinder, tool; hand powered **$75.00**
Hammer, bill poster; K #55, 5-oz................................**$25.00**
Hammer, brick; KK #15, 24-oz, EX..............................**$42.50**
Hammer, saw setting; 7-oz, EX....................................**$42.50**
Hatchet, guage; S20 ....**$20.00**
Hatchet, lathing; KK #401, EX....................................**$27.50**
Hatchet, shingling; KK #1, EX....................................**$27.50**
Hoe, mortar; KK #10, EX..**$25.00**
Knife, butcher; K #160, 6", in original box, M **$20.00**
Knife, draw; K #8, 8" **$20.00**
Knife, grapefruit; 3¼", serrated double-edge curved blade..**$12.00**
Knife, linoleum; K #64...**$18.00**
Knife, office; 3¾", two large blades, w/etching on white celluloid handle **$95.00**
Knife, pruning; KK #105, 4⅜", cocobolo handle, EX...**$30.00**
Knife, scout; #843 ....**$85.00**

Knife steel, KK #540, 8"..**$20.00**
Level, KK #104, 12", non-adjustable w/brass plate **$45.00**
Level, KK #50, 26", adjustable....................................**$125.00**
Level, KK #612, 12", iron, EX **$80.00**
Level, KK #69, 9", cast iron **$100.00**
Level, 24", aluminum **$35.00**
Mallet, KK #306, VG..**$20.00**
Mitre box, KK #528, EX..**$125.00**
Nail apron..**$75.00**
Nail puller, 18"..**$40.00**
Plane, bottom; KK #28, 18", wood bottom...................**$45.00**
Plane, bull nose rabbet; KK #75, 4", not adjustable ..**$125.00**
Plane, circular, KK #115, 10", will cut concave or convex...**$225.00**
Plane, scrub; KK #240, 9½" **$85.00**
Plane, smooth; KK #35, 9", wood bottom & handle....**$45.00**
Pliers, channel lock; KK #507, 6½", EX **$22.50**
Pliers, combination; K #180 ....**$20.00**
Pliers, diagonal cutting; K #47-7 ....**$25.00**
Pliers, slim nose; KK #25, EX **$22.50**
Pocketknife, KK #1787, 3½", embossed iron handle ...**$90.00**
Pocketknife, KK #2884, 3¼", white celluloid handle, NM **$58.00**
Punch, revolving; KK #44, EX......................................**$22.50**
Razor, straight; KK #16, blue steel w/logo in center of handle & blade...**$35.00**
Razor, straight; KK #7423, white celluloid handle, EX ..**$35.00**
Razor strop, Automatic Safety; KK #600, w/original box, M **$45.00**
Reamer, KK #126, for reaming pipe & counter sinking .**$15.00**
Rule, zigzag; KK #506, 72", M **$27.50**
Rule, 8-fold; KK #504, 48", yellow enamel.................**$100.00**
Saw, butcher; KK #15, 20" blade.................................**$40.00**
Saw, compass; 14"...**$20.00**
Saw, hack; KK #188, not adjustable............................**$45.00**
Saw, hand; KK #18, 26" **$55.00**
Saw, keyhole; EC Simmons, 10" **$20.00**
Saw, kitchen; KK #2, 14" blade **$40.00**
Saw, metal cutting; KK #106, fifteen teeth per inch **$85.00**
Saw, stair builder; KK #6, applewood handle, M **$70.00**
Scraper, cabinet; KK #6, M **$65.00**
Screwdriver, KK #50, 8" blade, EX..............................**$17.50**
Shears, hedge; KK #8½, EX **$17.50**
Shears, mule; 10½" **$15.00**
Shears, roaching; 9¼"...**$15.00**
Spatula, metal **$15.00**
Square, combination; KK #60, 6", EX **$85.00**
Square, KK #3, Blue Brand **$25.00**
Square, try; KK #1226, 6", EX **$22.50**
Square, try; 4½", wooden handle w/logo on blade.....**$25.00**
Staple puller, 2⅝"..**$25.00**
Tack claws, KK #5...**$15.00**
Tap & die set, KK #30, EX...**$52.00**
Tin snips, KK #6, EX...**$22.50**
Vise, bench; KK #500, VG **$45.00**
Wagon, KK #98, 15½x34", EX......................................**$195.00**
Wrench, adjustable; S-shaped, logo stamped in jaw, Keen Kutter written on handle **$100.00**

Wrench, alligator; adjustable **$125.00**
Wrench, angle; #10, adjustable **$20.00**
Wrench, automobile; KK #96, EX **$37.50**
Wrench, monkey; KK #18, EX **$45.00**

Kentucky Derby Glasses

Since the 1940s, every running of the Kentucky Derby has been commemorated with a drinking glass. There were two in 1958. Race fans have begun to collect them, and now some of the earlier glasses are worth several hundred dollars.

1940s, aluminum **$165.00**
1940s, plastic Beetleware **$300.00**
1945, short **$400.00**
1945, tall **$175.00**
1948 .... **$65.00**
1949, He Has Seen Them All **$65.00**
1950 .... **$175.00**
1951 .... **$150.00**
1952, Gold Cup **$65.00**
1953 .... **$50.00**
1954 .... **$45.00**
1955 .... **$40.00**
1956 .... **$40.00**
1957 .... **$35.00**
1958, Gold Bar **$45.00**
1958, Iron Liege **$50.00**
1959-1960, each **$30.00**
1961 .... **$25.00**
1962-1965, each **$22.00**
1966 .... **$18.00**
1967-1968, each **$16.00**
1969 .... **$15.00**
1970 .... **$14.00**
1971-1972, each **$12.00**
1973 .... **$10.00**
1974 .... **$8.00**

1975 .... **$7.00**
1976 .... **$6.00**
1977-1980, each **$5.00**
1981-1983, each **$4.00**

1984-1988, each **$3.00**

Kitchen Appliances

If you've never paid much attention to old kitchen appliances, now is the time to do just that. Check in Grandma's basement—or your mother's kitchen cabinets, for that matter.

As styles in home decorating changed, so did the styles of appliances. Some have wonderful Art Deco lines, while others border on the primitive.

Most of those you'll find will still work, and with a thorough cleaning you'll be able to restore them to their original 'like-new' appearance. Missing parts may be impossible to replace, but if it's just the cord that's gone, you can usually find what you need at any hardware store.

Even larger appliances are collectible and are often used to add the finishing touch to a period kitchen.

Casserole, NESCO Thrifty Cook #B40, chrome & enamel, Bakelite handles & lid knob, National Enamel & Stamping, ca 1940s **$65.00**
Coffeepot, Labelle Silver Co, chrome ball form, spigot spout, strap handle, glass knob at top, ca 1950s **$60.00**
Coffeepot, Tricolor Co, Norfolk, 9-cup, decorated china base w/metal filter, ca 1933 .... **$25.00**
Corn popper, Dominion Electric Co, metal, straight sided w/handles, short legs, w/lid, Minneapolis, MN, 1930s **$40.00**
Doughnut maker, Wallace Ray Co, 2-pc oval w/seven convex rings, ca 1968 .... **$22.50**
Drink mixer, Hamilton Beach, enameled metal, 1926. **$55.00**
Egg cooker, Hankscraft Co, Fiesta, #599, red ceramic bottom w/chrome lid, 4-egg metal poaching rack, 1936... **$40.00**
Fan, oscillating; Diehl Mfg Co, cage w/cast iron base, 1930s **$40.00**
Food warmer, Chase Brass & Copper, copper w/Bakelite handles, 3-compartment, 1940s **$47.50**
Hot dog steamer, Sunbeam, enameled metal doghouse w/red plastic roof, 1980s, 7x7¾" **$25.00**
Mixer, FA Smith Mfg, Mixette, green cast iron w/wood handle, Jadite bowl, ca 1930s **$67.50**
Mixer, Knapp-Monarch Co, milk glass beater jar w/stainless steel blade, red wood knob, ca 1940s, 9½" **$40.00**
Mixer/food processor, Hobart Mfg, Kitchen Aid, enameled cast iron base & motor housing, 3-speed, w/attachments, ca 1930 .... **$90.00**
Potato baker, Knapp-Monarch Co, casserole w/bottom heating element, three metal legs, Bakelite handles & lid knob, 1930s **$40.00**
Shaker, milk glass, 'Sugar' & 'Electrochef' in black letters on square form w/metal screw-on lid **$8.00**
Teakettle, Electric Cooking, Simplex, ball form w/collar base, Art Nouveau-styled standing holder, 1914... **$60.00**
Teakettle, Electric Home, Speedmaster, cord plugs into handle, 1936 .... **$35.00**
Teapot, American Electric Heater Co, Detroit, MI, 1904.. **$30.00**

Toaster, Bersted Mfg, Victorian, Model #A65, 4-slice, chrome w/black-painted metal, flip-down doors, ca 1940s..**$35.00**
Toaster, Birtman Electric, Model #T-14, EX..................**$45.00**
Toaster, Chicago Mfg, Handy Hot, green-painted sheet metal, ca 1930s...**$22.50**
Toaster, Dominion, Model #1109, flip-down doors, w/cord, EX..**$35.00**
Toaster, Faultless Appliances, Model #1249, chrome w/Bakelite handles, 1930s-40s **$32.50**
Toaster, Manning Bowman, Model #1227, EX............**$85.00**
Toaster, Proctor Electric Co, Model #148C, rectangular chrome w/Bakelite handles & base, 2-slice, EX ...**$55.00**
Toaster, Son Chief Electric Co, Speed Master, Art Deco design, 1930s, w/original box...............................**$28.00**
Toaster, Sunbeam, flat half-round, chrome, 2-slice, Bakelite handles & base, red signal light, hinged crumb tray, 1940 ....**$35.00**
Toaster, Sunbeam, Model #T-9, EX.............................**$85.00**

Toaster, Universal, Model #33-2249......................$50.00
Toaster, Universal, Model #79312, EX **$50.00**
Waffle iron, 7¼" dia, Handy Hot #4704-H, square overflow tray, Chicago Electric Mfg Co, 1938....................**$100.00**

Kitchen Gadgets

Whether you're buying them to use or to decorate with, you'll find good examples just about anywhere you go at prices that won't wreck your buying budget. From the 19th century, cast iron apple peelers, cherry pitters, and food choppers were patented by the hundreds, and because they're practically indestructible, they're still around today. Unless parts are missing, they're still usable and most are very efficient at the task they were designed to perform.

A collection of egg beaters can be very interesting, and you'll find specialized gadgets for chores no one today would even dream of doing. Some will probably leave you in doubt as to their intended use.

If this area of collecting interests you, you'll enjoy *300 Years of Kitchen Collectibles* by Linda Campbell and *Kitchen Antiques, 1790-1940*, by Kathryn McNerney.

Apple peeler, Little Star, EX **$85.00**
Apple peeler, Mt Goodell, white, 1940s, M in box......**$25.00**
Batter beater, tinned iron wire forms five 'fingers,' green wooden handle, 1930s, EX.....................................**$6.00**

Beater jar, 10", Patented October 9, 1923..............$22.00
Biscuit cutter, tin w/scalloped edge, green wooden handle, 1930s **$6.00**
Biscuit cutter, 1" to 3" dia, crinkle-edged nesting set of nine, in box marked Veritas...for Thurnauer, NM **$30.00**
Biscuit cutter, 4x2" dia, Rumford Yeast Powder, tin w/fat cylindrical handle, EX..**$20.00**
Bread maker, Universal, tin, bucket type, embossed directions **$45.00**
Bread maker, Universal #4, pail type, w/instructions..**$40.00**
Can opener, A&J, nickeled steel shaft, tempered steel blade, turned wooden handle, 1940 ....**$14.00**
Can opener, Baumgarten, cast iron, adjustable blade in sliding frame, ear-shaped tabs on disk, ca 1900.........**$75.00**
Can opener, Champion Pat'd 1873, cast iron ring, ratchet clamp holds can, loop handles **$85.00**
Can opener, Clean Cut, iron w/wooden handle..........**$10.00**
Can opener, crowing rooster shape, cast iron, American, 1900s...**$17.50**
Can opener, Dazey, cast iron, wall mounted, 1900s ...**$10.00**
Can opener, Enbay, cast iron w/gears, 1900s, EX **$12.00**
Can opener, Vaughn's Open-All, cast iron, 1900s **$10.00**
Can opener, Wynn & Timmins, bulbous head, brass ferrule, wooden handle **$17.50**
Can opener, Yankee, cast iron....................................**$12.50**
Can opener, 6" long, bull's head & partial body formed in cast iron, spike & blade screwed into head, late 1800s...**$45.00**

Can opener, 6⅛", Midget, steel blade, flat sided, shaped wooden handle, 1904 ....$12.50

Can opener, 7½", Sterling, steel w/long black painted wooden handle, 1902 ....$15.00

Can opener & jar wrench combination, 7" long, Forster & Son, 4-in-1 tool, 1910......................$17.50

Candy dipper, 10" dia bowl, copper w/riveted handle, ca 1900 ....$50.00

Cheese slicer, 5½x5½", Handi-Kraft, green painted metal......................$18.00

Chopping knife, double heavy steel rocker-type blades, ca 1900, EX $35.00

Churn, Premier Two Minute Butter Machine, square glass jar, original label, wooden paddle, cast iron frame & gears $65.00

Churn, 1-qt, Dazey #10, high top, M......................$950.00

Churn, 1-qt, unmarked, embossed jar......................$150.00

Churn, 4-quart, Dazey #40 ....$95.00

Colander, Androck, wire mesh in tin & wire frame, wooden ear handles, 1936, EX............................$12.50

Colander, 14", sheet iron, soldered foot ring, primitive style, ca 1880s to 1900, EX............................$35.00

Cork puller, Yankee, Gilchrist Co Newark NJ, nickeled cast iron, lever action......................$30.00

Cracker pricker, 4¼x2" dia, fat wooden knob w/twelve iron pins, late 1800s............................$50.00

Crimper, 6" long, Dandy, cast aluminum w/wooden handle, 1925 ....$15.00

Crimper & trimmer, brass wheel, steel shaft w/molded black plastic handle, American, 1900s......................$22.50

Crimper & trimmer, 4¾", cast aluminum, trims as it crimps pie edge, unmarked, 1920s-30s $10.00

Doughnut cutter, Saturn, stainless steel w/wooden T-shaped handle, 1930s, EX............................$10.00

Doughnut cutter, 3", Fries, tin w/strap handle, three struts hold center hole maker, 1900s............................$17.50

Egg beater, bent & twisted wire, push-down drill action, American made, ca 1900, EX, minimum value......$18.00

Egg beater, Biltrite, Stuber & Kuck Co Peoria IL, tinned steel, center drive wheel, ca 1920..........................$35.00

Egg beater, tinned steel, turbine type w/green wooden handle, ca 1930s, EX............................$20.00

Egg beater, 11¼x3¾x3¾", New Keystone Beater, cast iron gear wheel & crank w/wooden knob, EX............$85.00

Egg beater, 12½", Eagle Precision Mfg, chrome & red plastic, EX............................$20.00

Egg beater, 12½", Taplin's Dover Pattern Improved, Pat 1903 ....$30.00

Egg separator, white enamelware, single thumb grip tab handle, hanging hole, 1900s $15.00

Egg separator, 6¾" long, aluminum w/ear handles, two slots in shallow 3¾" dia cup, ca 1915............................$7.00

Egg slicer & opener, GM Thurnauer NYC, scissors action, 1904 ....$22.00

Egg timer, hourglass type, plaid-painted frame, Mauchlin ware, 1880s............................$30.00

Egg timer, turned wood w/portholes for viewing sand bulbs, ca 1920s............................$25.00

Egg whip, coiled wire w/wire lacing holding springs in place around rim, wooden handle, EX.................$12.00

Egg whip, diamond-patterned wire over spoon shape, wooden handle $10.00

Egg whip, twisted wire, spoon-like shape w/crisscross wires, springs & wires around 'bowl,' American made, 1900s............................$12.50

Flour sifter, Savory #500, maple handle, turned knob, EX.$8.00

Flour sifter, 6½x6", tin, mug style, side crank w/green wooden handle, ca 1900, EX............................$12.00

Fork, 14½", stainless steel, green painted handle w/white stripe, 1930s............................$8.00

Fruit dryer, 9x14x10½", Arlington Oven Dryer on brass plate, tin frame w/wire screen & three shelves, 1890s............................$125.00

Fruit jar lifter, E-Z Lift, cast iron $4.00

Fruit jar opener, Cunnard Co, metal w/rubber grips, works like pliers, 1936 ....$8.00

Fruit jar wrench, CA Powell, cast iron, mechanical $6.00

Fruit jar wrench, Daisy Jar Opener, red rubber over heavy wire, 1900s............................$6.00

Fruit jar wrench, Wilson's, cast iron, 1900s.................$12.50

Fruit press, 4-qt, Griswold, cast iron............................$85.00

Funnel, 7x4" dia, w/filter & brass thumbpiece, American made, late 1800s, EX............................$30.00

Ice chipper, Briddell #60, cast iron w/brass ferrule, late 1800s or early 1900s............................$7.50

Ice chisel, Crown Ice Chipper, steel w/turned wooden handle, 1884 ....$12.50

Ice cream freezer, galvanized tin, blue painted lid, crank type w/Kwik Freeze on paper label, 1900s..........$50.00

Ice cream scoop, red Catalin handle $15.00

Ice crusher, Jiffy Ice Crax Deluxe, spring action $10.00

Ice cube tray, 10½" long, FlexoTray, green rubber w/metal wire puller $5.00

Ice grinder, Dazey, cast metal alloy, 1940s $25.00

Ice pick, nickeled steel w/wooden handle, advertising.$10.00

Ice shaver, Gem, nickeled cast iron, hinged hopper, removable blade $17.50

Ice shaver, Griswold, cast iron, EX............................$35.00

Ice tongs, 14", Butler Ice Co, iron............................$17.50

Ice tongs, 21", cast & forged iron, American.................$20.00

Juicer, Griswold #9 ....$135.00

Kraut cutter, 5¾x15", two blades in scalloped pine board............................$180.00

Lemon squeezer, Berger Bros Philadelphia 1895, cast iron w/porcelain-lined cup, EX............................$25.00

Lemon squeezer, wood w/tinned male & female inserts, lever action, 1850s, EX............................$175.00

Measure, 1½-gal, tin, reinforced handle, EX $27.00

Measure, 1-cup, tin $10.00

Measuring spoon, A&P advertising, tin, 1900s $6.50

Meat tenderizer, Yale Meat Scorer, cast iron w/wooden rod axle, set w/steel blades, EX............................$40.00

Meat tenderizer, yellow stoneware, Pat Dec 25, 1877.$85.00

Nutmeg grater, Everett, EX............................$75.00

Pastry blender, 5¾", Androck, wire & steel w/painted wood handle............................$8.00

Pie crimper, 8", Vaughn's, green Catalin handle..........**$85.00**

Potato masher, bent, woven, coiled or braided wire w/turned wooden handle, EX original paint.........................**$7.50**

Potato masher, plunger-type w/perforated tin cylinder & wooden plunger, wrought iron stand, ca 1900, minimum value...**$20.00**

Raisin seeder, Enterprise No 36, cast iron, screws to table, EX...**$40.00**

Rice baller, aluminum..**$10.00**

Rolling pin, crockery, advertising, ca 1900 ....**$125.00**

Rolling pin, ironstone, long turned wooden handles, late 1800s...**$140.00**

Rolling pin, Mil-Bar Co Canton OH, aluminum, 1900s..**$25.00**

Rolling pin, milk glass, wooden handles, advertising, late 1800s...**$130.00**

Rolling pin, solid brass **$85.00**

Rolling pin, 10¾", grooved iron w/maple handles **$50.00**

Rolling pin, 11¼", yellowware, oak handles, English or American, late 1800s...**$225.00**

Rolling pin, 14", free-blown bottle green glass, tapers to small knobs, English or American, 1800s...........**$115.00**

Rolling pin, 18", turned maple w/nylon ball bearings, Rowoco Inc, 1980s, M.......................................**$25.00**

Rolling pin, 19½", clear glass w/metal axle & turned wood handles, marked Gem, 1900s **$80.00**

Rolling pin, 24", cast iron w/wooden handles, American, ca 1900, EX...**$40.00**

Spice mill, Enterprise #0, painted cast iron, screws to table, ca 1900, EX...**$50.00**

Spoon, slotted w/wire handle, bottle-opener end.......**$12.50**

Spoon, 10", tinned sheet iron w/painted wooden handle, American maker's mark, ca 1920s-40s, EX, minimum value **$7.50**

Spoon, 10¾", Rumford Baking Powder, stamped & slotted nickeled metal w/green wooden handle, EX........**$15.00**

Strainer, 10¾", tin w/brass mesh, fits into milk can top, American made, ca 1900, EX...........................**$17.50**

Strawberry huller, Nip-It, Pat'd 12/18/1906, nickeled spring steel, EX...**$5.00**

Tea strainer, Tetley Tea advertising on silverplate, side handle **$20.00**

Teakettle, green & tan enamelware, gooseneck spout, 1930s **$35.00**

Teakettle, large size, Gilchrist, nickeled brass & copper, gooseneck style, 1903...**$35.00**

Teakettle, 10" dia base, Wagner, cast aluminum, side-swiveling lid, V-neck lip on spout, straight sides, ca 1910 ....**$37.50**

Teakettle, 2-cup, Kreamer, black paint on tin, 1900s..**$27.50**

Teakettle, 7" dia base, red enameled metal, aluminum snap-on whistle w/turned wooden knob, 1930s **$12.50**

Teakettle, 7¾", aluminum w/molded black chef's-head whistle stopper, copper bottom, 1900s **$15.00**

Teakettle, 8" dia base, blue enameling on cast iron, low squat type, fixed handle w/wooden grip, late 1800s **$65.00**

Teapot, tin, brass, & copper, brass finial on lid, footed, graceful style, 1800s, EX....................................**$90.00**

Thermometer, candy; Moeller Instrument Co Brooklyn NY, copper...**$55.00**

Thermometer, candy; Taylor Instrument Co Rochester NY, pallet-knife shape w/wooden handle, hanging loop, mid-1930s..**$7.00**

Vegetable slicer, Enterprise No 49, 16x11", cast iron w/revolving cylinder, ca 1900, EX.....................**$125.00**

Wax ladle, 8", Griswold, Erie, cast iron......................**$30.00**

Whisk, 9", wire in flat snowshoe shape, wire-wrapped handle, 1900s, EX...**$10.00**

Kitchen Glassware

Though there's still lots of this type of glassware around, some harder-to-find items and pieces in the more desirable colors and types of glass often bring unbelievably high prices. We've listed a cross section of values here, but you'll really need to study a good book before you decide to invest. One of the best is *Kitchen Glassware of the Depression Years* by authority Gene Florence.

See also Fry, Jadite Glassware, Fire King Ovenware, McKee, Reamers, Peach Lustre Glassware.

Apothecary jar, transparent green, fruit-jar form..........**$30.00**

Batter bowl, clear, ribbed design, Anchor Hocking **$10.00**

Batter bowl, milk glass w/painted peaches & grape design, marked Fire-King **$15.00**

Batter bowl, transparent green, swirled design, Anchor Hocking **$18.00**

Batter bowl, transparent green, vertical-rib design w/angle handle..**$30.00**

Batter bowl, transparent yellow, 2-spout, stick handle, US Glass **$35.00**

Batter jug, clear w/cobalt lid, Paden City.....................**$45.00**

Beater bowl w/hand mixer, transparent green base, Jeannette Glass Co **$20.00**

Bowl, batter; turquoise blue, w/spout, Fire-King, 1957-58, minimum value **$42.50**

Bowl, mixing; transparent green w/spout & small ring base **$22.50**

Bowl, mixing; 1-pt, turquoise blue, teardrop form, Fire-King, 1957-58, minimum value **$9.00**

Bowl, mixing; 11½", transparent green, paneled at square base, round top w/rolled rim, marked Hocking...**$20.00**

Bowl, mixing; 3-qt, turquoise blue, teardrop form, Fire-King, 1957-58, minimum value **$18.00**

Bowl, mixing; 4-qt, turquoise blue, round, Fire-King, 1957-58, minimum value **$12.50**

Bowl, mixing; 5½", delphite blue, horizontal rib design, Jeannette Glass Co, late 1930s..............................**$30.00**

Bowl, mixing; 5¼", fired-on blue, Crisscross pattern.....**$8.50**

Bowl, mixing; 6", cobalt, plain w/rolled rim, Hazel Atlas **$17.50**

Bowl, mixing; 7¼", fired-on yellow w/black trim at top edge, marked Fire-King **$5.00**

Bowl, mixing; 8", amber, plain w/rolled rim, US Glass Co **$25.00**

Bowl, mixing; 8", pink, concentric ring design............**$12.00**

Bowl, mixing; 8¾", transparent yellow, Hazel Atlas, marked Rest-Well **$25.00**

Bowl, mixing; 8⅜" dia, fired-on blue w/black trim at rim, marked Fire-King **$6.50**

Bowl, mixing; 9", delphite blue, vertical rib design, Jeannette Glass Co, late 1930s....................................**$35.00**

Butter dish, ultramarine, marked Jennyware **$125.00**

Butter dish, 1-lb, amber, Federal Glass Co..................**$30.00**

Butter dish, 1-lb, transparent green, Hex Optic pattern.**$65.00**

Butter dish, 1-lb, transparent green, low ribbed base w/'Butter' embossed on top of plain lid, Jeannette Glass Co **$35.00**

Butter dish, ¼-lb, amber, Federal Glass Co................**$25.00**

Butter dish, ¼-lb, cobalt, Crisscross design $100.00

Butter dish, ¼-lb, frosted clear, Federal Glass Co........**$15.00**

Butter dish, 2-lb, pink, embossed 'B' on top **$125.00**

Cake plate, cobalt, plain w/three feet, Fry Glass Co ...**$95.00**

Cake server, clear w/streamline amber handle............**$45.00**

Canister, custard, square sided w/'Coffee' in black letters, metal lid...**$50.00**

Canister, embossed dot design on clear w/metal lid, remnant of silver sticker on front.................................**$12.50**

Canister, green, fine vertical-rib design on ovoid form, 'Coffee' in vertical decal on front w/metal lid............**$65.00**

Canister, large, clear w/green decal of interior tavern scene, green metal lid, unmarked **$25.00**

Canister, large, colorful Dutch boy decal on clear, w/metal lid **$20.00**

Canister, tall, embossed zipper-type vertical stripes on clear, 'Coffee' embossed on front, w/metal lid...............**$20.00**

Canister, 128-oz, clear, melon-ribbed sides w/'Flour' embossed on front, w/metal lid..........................**$35.00**

Canister, 16-oz, embossed checkerboard design in clear glass w/'Coffee' in center of floral decal, red metal lid...**$7.50**

Canister, 20-oz, delphite blue, horizontal rib design, Jeannette Glass Co, late 1930s....................................**$125.00**

Coffee maker, 1-cup, crystal, w/filter, marked Jiffy, fits over cup or mug to brew individual serving................**$10.00**

Cruet, frosted w/clear stopper, shows black & red rooster w/'Oil' at base **$12.00**

Curtain ring, forest green, w/metal hanger, pr............**$20.00**

Funnel, transparent yellow, marked CW Hart..............**$45.00**

Gravy boat, amber, plain, 2-spout, Cambridge............**$20.00**

Jar, white with red tulips & lid **$18.00**

Jar, 8-oz, clear w/'Kroger Embassy Peanut Butter' paper label **$10.00**

Ladle, amethyst, rounded bowl...................................**$22.50**

Ladle, blue, wedge-shaped handle **$12.00**

Ladle, clear w/side spout **$12.00**

Ladle, punch; transparent green, 2-spout....................**$35.00**

Match holder, delphite blue, custard-cup form w/rolled rim & foot, 'Matches' in black on front, Jeannette Glass Co, '30s...**$75.00**

Measure, 1-cup, fired-on green, Hazel Atlas **$35.00**

Measure, 1-cup, fired-on red, Hazel Atlas **$40.00**

Measure, 1-cup, fired-on red, marked Glasbake.........**$30.00**

Measure, 1-cup, transparent green, w/tab handle **$28.00**

Mold, pink, Turk's head type, marked Tufglas **$25.00**

Napkin holder, milk glass, rectangular form, marked Nar-O-Fold...**$35.00**

Napkin holder, transparent green, marked Fan Fold ..**$95.00**

Pickle ladle, milk glass, drain hole in bowl **$15.00**

Pitcher, milk; cobalt, paneled sides, Hazel Atlas **$60.00**

Refrigerator dish, 4½x5", cobalt, w/lid, Hazel Atlas.....**$45.00**

Refrigerator dish, 4½x5", transparent green, Hex Optic pattern, Jeannette Glass Co **$22.00**

Refrigerator dish, 4½x5", transparent yellow, w/flat lid..**$35.00**

Refrigerator dish, 4x4" sq, transparent green, vertical-rib design, lid w/indent handle, marked Hocking **$15.00**

Refrigerator dish, 5¾" dia, cobalt, w/lid, Hazel Atlas ..**$60.00**

Refrigerator dish, 5⅞" sq, transparent green, marked Tufglas, w/flat lid **$25.00**

Refrigerator dish, 8-oz, pink, quilted design, lid w/indented handle **$20.00**

Rolling pin, clear w/cobalt handles............................**$200.00**

Rolling pin, cobalt w/wood handles **$400.00**

Rolling pin, forest green, 1-pc **$150.00**

Rolling pin, transparent green w/wood handles, unmarked...**$400.00**

Salad set, clear, w/Cambridge label, 2-pc **$40.00**

Salad set, clear tines or bowl w/cobalt prism-form handle, 2-pc **$70.00**

Salt box, transparent green, round, zipper-striped sides, wood lid **$150.00**

Shaker, delphite blue, horizontal rib design, 'Salt' in black on front, metal lid, Jeannette Glass Co, 1930s **$35.00**

Shaker, delphite blue, square sides w/metal lid, 'Pepper' in black letters on front, Jeannette Glass Co, late 1930s...**$65.00**

Shaker, fired-on red, 'Salt' in black letters on Roman Arch-style base **$10.00**

Shaker, spice; transparent green, tall w/fine vertical-ribbed design & metal screw-on lid, marked Sneath........**$40.00**

Shaker, ultramarine, melon-rib design w/foot, w/paper label & metal screw-on lid.....................................**$22.00**

Spoon holder, clear, paneled sides w/scalloped top, marked Pat Feb 11 1913.......................................**$18.00**

Sugar shaker, fired-on red w/metal screw-on lid, marked Gemco **$22.50**

Sundae dish, transparent green, fluted sides w/scalloped rim & footed base **$18.00**

Tumbler, pink, flared form, marked Mission Juice **$25.00**

Water bottle, 32-oz, transparent green, raised panel design w/metal lid **$18.00**

Knives

Knives have been widely collected since the 1960s. The most desirable are those from before WWII, but even some made since then have value. Don't try to clean or sharpen an old knife; collectors want them as found. Of course, mint unused knives are prefered, and any apparent use or damage greatly reduces their value. Our prices are for those in mint condition.

For more information we recommend *Sargent's American Premium Guide to Knives and Razors, Identification and Values,* by Jim Sargent.

Browning, #2118F20, brass & wood handle, 2-blade, marked USA, ca 1970s.......................................**$35.00**

Browning, #2418F2, wood handle, 2-blade, marked Japan, ca 1970s **$30.00**

Case, #A6250, Museum Founders, 4½", appaloosa bone handle, 2-blade, 1980..............................**$125.00**

Case, #R1212½, 4", candy stripe handle, switchblade, 1920-40 ....**$800.00**

Case, #11011, Hawkbill, 4", walnut handle, 1-blade, marked USA, 1940-64 ....**$35.00**

Case, #2202½, 3⅜", slick black handle, 2-blade, tested XX, 1920-40 ....**$135.00**

Case, #31095, 5", yellow composition handle, 1-blade, tested XX, 1920-40 ....**$250.00**

Case, #5172, 5½", stag handle, 1-blade, marked USA, 1965-69 ....**$165.00**

Case, #5265SAB, Folding Hunter, 5¼", stag handle, 2-blade, tested XX, 1920-40 ....**$325.00**

Case, #53047, 3⅞", stag handle, 3-blade, marked USA, 1965-69 ....**$70.00**

Case, #61011, 4", Rogers bone handle, 1-blade, tested XX, 1920-40 ....**$210.00**

Case, #6109B, 3¼", bone handle, 1-blade, tested XX, 1920-40 ....**$260.00**

Case, #6116, green bone handle, 3½", tested XX ..$175.00

Case, #6143, Daddy Barlow, 5", bone handle, 1-blade, marked USA, 1965-69 ....**$40.00**

Case, #62009, 3", red bone handle, 2-blade, XX, 1940-64 ....**$50.00**

Case, #6207, 3½", bone handle, 2-blade, marked USA, 1965-69 ....**$35.00**

Case, #6225½, Coke Bottle, 3", green bone handle, 2-blade, tested XX **$225.00**

Case, #6244, 3¼", bone stag handle, 2-blade, 10 Dot, 1970 ....**$35.00**

Case, #6250, Sunfish, 4⅜", laminated wood handle, 2-blade, 10-Dot, 1970 ....**$55.00**

Case, #6252, knife-fork combination, 3¾", green bone handle, tested XX, 1920-40......................**$450.00**

Case, #6308, 3¼", bone handle, 3-blade, XX, 1940-64.**$65.00**

Case, #64052, 3½", bone handle, 4-blade, marked USA, 1965-69 ....**$65.00**

Case, #92058, Birdseye, 3¼", French pearl handle, 2-blade, tested XX, 1920-40..............................**$125.00**

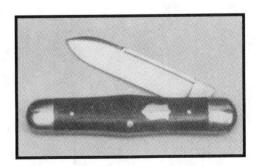

Keen Kutter, Swell Center Jack, 3⅜", 1-blade, walnut $30.00**

Primble, #5514, Belknap, 3¾", brown bone handle, 4-blade...**$60.00**

Primble, #7022, Belknap, 2⅝", bone handle, 2-blade..**$25.00**

Primble, #903, Belknap, 2⅞", imitation peachseed bone handle, 2-blade **$25.00**
Queen, #15, Congress, 3½", Rogers bone handle, 2-blade **$40.00**
Queen, #22, Barlow, 3½", brown bone handle, 2-blade . **$45.00**
Queen, #36, Lockback, 4½", Rogers bone handle, 1-blade **$75.00**
Queen, #4, Sleeveboard, 3⅜", pearl handle, Stainless stamp, 2-blade **$35.00**
Queen, #57, 3⅜", pearl handle, 3-blade **$30.00**
Queen Stainless, #35, Serpentine, 2⅝", rough black handle, 3-blade **$30.00**
Queen Steel, #16, 3¼", winterbottom bone handle, 3-blade **$30.00**
Queen Steel, #19, Trapper, 4⅛", winterbottom bone handle, 2-blade **$85.00**
Queen Steel, #20, Texas Toothpick, 5", winterbottom bone handle, 1-blade **$85.00**
Queen Steel, #25, 3½", brown bone handle, 2-blade .. **$60.00**
Queen Steel, #26, Serpentine, 3¼", winterbottom bone handle, 3-blade **$35.00**
Queen Steel, #5, Senator, 2½", winterbottom bone handle, 2-blade **$20.00**
Queen Steel, #61, Stockman, 3⅝", winterbottom bone handle, 3-blade **$50.00**
Remington, #R1240, Barlow, 5", brown bone handle, 1-blade **$300.00**
Remington, #R125, 3½", pyremite handle, 3-blade **$140.00**
Remington, #R3064, 4", pearl handle, 3-blade **$400.00**
Remington, #R3115G, Stockman, 3⅞", pyremite handle, 3-blade **$150.00**
Remington, #R3243W, 3¾", pyremite handle, 3-blade .. **$240.00**
Remington, #R3335, Scout Knife, 3¾", red, white, & blue handle, 4-blade **$325.00**
Remington, #R3643, 4", bone handle, 3-blade **$400.00**
Remington, #R3700BU, 4", buffalo horn handle, 3-blade **$230.00**
Remington, #R3855, Pruner, 4", imitation ivory handle, 2-blade **$250.00**
Remington, #R4133, Stockman, 3⅜", bone handle, 3-blade **$175.00**
Remington, #R4405, 3⅜", Christmas tree handle, 3-blade **$250.00**
Remington, #R4843, 3¼", imitation bone handle, 3-blade **$90.00**
Remington, #R51, Barlow, 3⅜", redwood handle, 2-blade **$90.00**

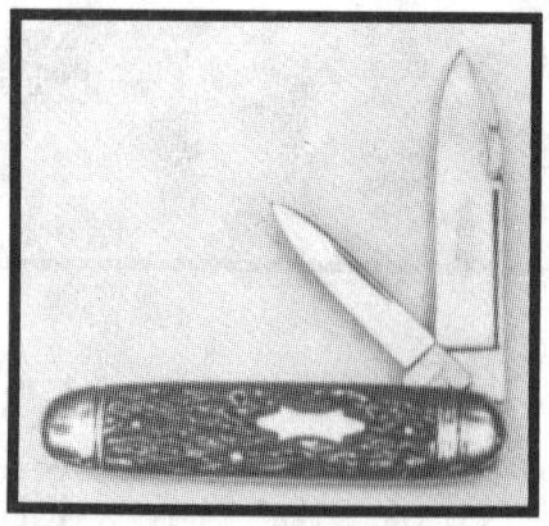

Remington, #R553, Equal-End-Jack, 3¼", brown bone handle, 2-blade, grooved bolster $150.00

Remington, #R6033, Congress, 3½", brown bone handle, 4-blade, extended grooved bolsters **$300.00**
Remington, #R6104, Congress, 3⅛", pearl handle, 2-blade **$150.00**
Remington, #R6400, 3⅜", buffalo horn handle, 3-blade . **$130.00**
Remington, #R6533, Whittler, 3", brown bone handle, 3-blade **$225.00**
Remington, #R708, Hawkbill, 3⅝", cocobolo handle, 1-blade **$125.00**
Schrade Cutlery, #151, 4", mottled celluloid handle, switch-blade **$100.00**
Schrade Cutlery, #2064W, 3⅝", ivory celluloid handle, 2-blade **$85.00**
Schrade Cutlery, #242, 3⅛", black peachseed bone handle, 2-blade **$30.00**
Schrade Cutlery, #8963, 3½", bone handle, 3-blade **$80.00**
Western States, #13208, 3⅜", brown & black swirl composition handle, 2-blade **$25.00**
Western States, #2100BH, 5¼", pearl overlay composition handle, 1-blade **$100.00**
Western States, #5206, 5⅛", genuine stag handle, buffalo skull etching, 2-blade **$75.00**
Western States, #5227, 5¼", genuine buckhorn handle, buffalo skull etching, 2-blade **$125.00**
Western States, #6344C, 2⅞", Rogers bone handle, 3-blade **$40.00**
Winchester, #1608, 3⅜", cocobolo handle, 1-blade **$70.00**
Winchester, #1922, 3⅜", stag handle, 1-blade **$120.00**
Winchester, #1936, Toothpick, 5", brown bone handle, 1-blade **$350.00**
Winchester, #2306, Senator, 2⅝", pearl handle, 2-blade.. **$110.00**
Winchester, #2312, Wharncliffe, 2⅞", pearl handle, 2-blade **$150.00**
Winchester, #2386, Sleeveboard, 3", pearl handle, 2-blade **$95.00**
Winchester, #2608, Stabber, 3⅝", cocobolo handle, 2-blade **$125.00**
Winchester, #2613, Sleeveboard, 3⅜", ebony handle, 2-blade **$110.00**
Winchester, #2640, Coke Bottle, 3¾", ebony handle, 2-blade **$250.00**
Winchester, #2853, Gunstock, 3½", brown bone handle, 2-blade **$400.00**
Winchester, #3018, Stockman, 4", candy-stripe handle, 3-blade **$400.00**
Winchester, #3022, Whittler, 3¼", imitation tortoise shell handle, 3-blade **$250.00**
Winchester, #4961, Premium Stockman, 4", bone handle, 4-blade **$400.00**

Edwin M. Knowles

This was one of the major chinaware manufacturers that operated in the Newell, West Virginia, area during the first half of the century. You'll find their marks on a variety of wares.

One of their most popular and collectible lines is

'Fruits,' marketed under the tradename of Sequoia Oven-ware through Montgomery Ward's in the 1930s. Its shapes are quaintly styled and decorated with decals of a red apple, a yellow pear, and some purple grapes. They made at least three of their own versions of the Mexican-style decaled ware that is so popular today and in the late thirties produced some dinnerware that is distinctly Art Deco.

For more information, we recommend *The Collector's Encyclopedia of American Dinnerware* by Jo Cunningham.

Daisies, platter, oval..**$8.00**
Deanna, bowl, lug soup; yellow..................................**$6.00**
Deanna, plate, dinner; dark blue.................................**$8.00**
Fruits, pie server **$20.00**
Fruits, pitcher, batter; w/lid...................................**$30.00**
Fruits, salt & pepper shakers, pr...............................**$20.00**
Mini Flowers, salt & pepper shakers, pr.....................**$15.00**
Penthouse, casserole, w/lid....................................**$30.00**
Picket Fence, cup...**$8.00**
Pink Pastel, sugar bowl, w/lid **$4.00**
Poppy, plate, 7"...**$4.00**
Rose, plate, 9"..**$6.00**
Tia Juana, bowl, mixing; medium.............................**$30.00**
Tia Juana, bowl, small, stacking set of three...............**$15.00**
Tia Juana, bowl, soup; 8", flat................................**$15.00**
Tia Juana, plate, utility; tab handles **$20.00**
Tia Juana, salt & pepper shaker, pr..........................**$20.00**
Tia Juana, saucer...**$3.00**
Tia Juana, syrup, w/lid..**$25.00**

Tulip, cookie jar **$35.00**
Tulip, pie plate (illustration)..............................**$15.00**
Tulip Time, saucer **$3.00**
Wildflower, saucer **$3.00**
Yellow Trim Poppy, plate, 8"....................................**$4.00**
Yorktown, teapot, Mango Red, w/lid.........................**$45.00**

L. E. Smith Glass

Originating just after the turn of the century, the L.E. Smith company continues to operate in Mt. Pleasant, Penn-sylvania, at the present time. In the 1920s they introduced a line of black glass that they are famous for today. Some pieces were decorated with silver overlay or enameling. Using their own original molds, they made a line of bird and animal figures in crystal as well as in colors. The com-pany is currently producing these figures, many in two sizes. They're one of the main producers of the popular Moon and Star pattern which has been featured in their cat-alogs since the 1960s in a variety of shapes and colors. (See also Moon and Star, Glass Animals.)

If you'd like to learn more about their bird and animal figures, *Glass Animals of the Depression Era* by Lee Garmon and Dick Spencer has a chapter devoted to those made by L.E. Smith.

Aquarium, Queen Fish, 15" **$225.00**
Bonbon, 3", #2400, black, handled, footed.................**$25.00**
Bowl, ¾", #50, black, bulbous **$10.00**
Bowl, 7", #515, black, footed **$20.00**
Cookie jar, green transparent.................................**$65.00**
Cup, aqua, Romanesque...**$9.00**
Fern bowl, cobalt, Greek Key decoration, 3-footed **$15.00**
Jardiniere, #23, black, Greek Key, 3-footed **$28.00**
Tray, cordial; green or pink **$10.00**
Vase, 5¾", cobalt, Stippled Thumbprint **$7.50**
Vase, 6", silver leaf band on black.............................**$15.00**
Vase, 6½", black, Mt Pleasant...................................**$9.00**
Vase, 7¼", #1900, black **$20.00**
Vase, 7¾", black, urn form.....................................**$22.50**
Window box, 6¼", milk glass, Pan & dancing girls.....**$15.00**

Labels

Each one a work of art in miniature, labels of all types appeal to collectors through their colorful lithography and imaginative choice of graphics representative of the product or the producer. Before cardboard boxes became so com-monplace, wooden crates were used to transport everything from asparagus to yams. Cigar boxes were labeled both out-side and in the lid. Tin cans had wonderful labels with Black children, lucious fruits and vegetables, animals, and birds. Some of the better examples are listed here. Many can be bought at much lower prices.

Can, Ace High beets, eagle in flight $1.50
Can, Au Gourmet, bowl of cherries............................$1.50
Can, Bert Marshalls grapefruit, grapefruit half $2.50
Can, Best Reserve succotash, ear of corn & lima bean pods..$12.50
Can, Delicious Pie Fruits, fox jumping over stream.......$4.50
Can, Pastore Olive Oil, Indian portrait $1.50
Can, Sea King clams, bowl of clams............................$15.00
Can, Yankee Brand squash, smiling Uncle Sam sitting on a stool $30.00

Crate, Buena Vista grapes, orchard & mountains, 1950s $2.00

Crate, Old Mission oranges, three Padres at mission ..$6.00
Cigar box, end; Grand Council, 4x4", three men in front of lake smoking cigars $4.00
Cigar box, end; Lucky Bill, 4x4", boy in knickers..........$2.00
Cigar box, inner lid; Alcazar, 6x9", race horse & logo, M.$8.50
Cigar box, inner lid; America's Pride, 6x9", Washington crossing the Delaware, M $8.00
Cigar box, inner lid; Baffin, 6x9", bust of Arctic explorer & ship, EX $15.00
Cigar box, inner lid; Bank Note, 6x9", large brown note resembling currency..$6.50
Cigar box, inner lid; Blue Ribbon, 6x9", blue ribbon design $2.00
Cigar box, inner lid; Daily Habit, 6x9", parrot on perch .$12.00
Cigar box, inner lid; Sun Maid, 6x9", lady holding box of cigars...$4.00
Cigar box, outer; Abraham Lincoln, 5x5", bust portrait of Abraham Lincoln...$20.00
Cigar box, outer; Belle Rose, 5x5", woman w/autumn leaves in the background, EX...$10.00
Cigar box, outer; Calvano, 5x5", Spanish man smoking a cigar, M...$4.00

Cigar box, outer; Chief, 5x5", portrait of an Indian chief, 1935 ....$35.00
Cigar box, outer; La Boda, 5x5", bride & groom at wedding reception, 1924..$3.50
Cigar box, top sheet; Sheik, 5x8", Arab scene $1.50
Crate, America's Delight for Washington apples, 9x11", apple over orchard & mountains, 1920s.................$5.00
Crate, Arboleda for California lemons, 9x13", valley & stream in oval inset, 1930s.....................................$4.00
Crate, Blue Goose for California oranges, 10x11¾", large blue goose, 1940 ....$3.50
Crate, Buffalo apples, 10x11¾", buffalo w/horns, 1930.$8.00
Crate, Butte pears, 10x11¾", mountain view, red lettering, 1930...$7.50
Crate, Cal-Crest lemons, 10x11¾", large lemon & lemon blossoms, 1940 ....$2.50
Crate, Challenger vegetables, 9x6", red silhouette of cowboy on horseback, 1940....................................$2.00
Crate, Dixie Delight, Florida citrus, 10x11¾", hearts & couple dancing..$5.00
Crate, Flavor for California oranges, 10x11¾", view of an orchard-filled valley, 1940 ....$2.00
Crate, High-Goal asparagus, 9x10½", polo player about to hit a ball, 1940..$6.00
Crate, Jack Rabbit yams, 9x9", large rabbit in triangle, 1923 ....$3.50
Crate, Justice, Florida citrus, 10x11¾", statue of Lady Justice, 1940...$4.00
Crate, Lucky Strike apples, 10x11¾", mountain scene w/hunter shooting a buck, 1920s...........................$8.50
Crate, Minots Light Brand cranberries, 7x10", black & white image of the White House......................................$6.50
Crate, San Marcus lemons, 10x11¾", orchard & mountain view, 1930..$2.00
Crate, Smoky Jim's yams, 9x9", Black man holding crate of yams...$4.00
Crate, Star Brand peaches, 10x11¾", large peach & small Indian head $15.00
Crate, Woodlake Gold for California oranges, 10x11¾", landscape w/mountains & lake, 1930 ....$4.00
Soda bottle, Pine Mountain, pictures lady, springs, & mountains...$1.50
Soda bottle, Yankee Doodle, colonist playing flute $1.00

Lenox China

Located in Trenton, New Jersey, the Lenox Company has produced dinnerware of the highest quality since the early 1900s. Since 1917, they have been the designers for the official White House china.

In addition to their dinnerware lines, they have also made some beautiful vases and decorative items, many similar to their current wares often seen displayed at fine gift and department stores.

Ashtray, 5½", gold ship, American Export 1960..........$40.00
Bouillon set, Empress $45.00

Bowl, fruit; small, Empress...............................$30.00
Bowl, soup; 9", Lenox Rose, rimmed $50.00
Bowl, vegetable; Lace Point, oval...................$50.00
Bowl, vegetable; 9½" long, Lenox Rose $95.00
Bowl, 13" dia, white ware, dragon handles, Belleek mark $160.00
Bowl, 5" sq, purple clematis w/gold, Belleek mark $65.00
Cake plate, Lenox Rose, low pedestal.............$135.00
Cake stand, Ming, low pedestal.......................$75.00
Chocolate pot, 5¼", silver overlay, Belleek mark $195.00
Coffeepot, 11", floral gardens, silver overlay, Belleek mark $660.00
Compote, 4x9", Lenox Rose $135.00
Cream & sugar bowl, Colonial, gold trim.......$95.00
Cup, Ming, black mark $40.00
Cup & saucer, Biltmore $40.00
Cup & saucer, Blue Ridge $40.00
Cup & saucer, demitasse; Lenox Rose...........$38.00
Cup & saucer, demitasse; Trent......................$45.00
Cup & saucer, Flirtation..................................$40.00
Cup & saucer, Montclair, old style.................$30.00
Cup & saucer, Springdale................................$40.00
Cup & saucer, Wyndcrest.................................$35.00
Figurine, First Waltz, limited edition, 1984.......$125.00
Figurine, Floradora $265.00
Figurine, 13", ivory, semi-nude lady w/greyhound..$190.00
Figurine, 6x4", seal on ledge, ivory..............$150.00
Mug, monk scene on brown..............................$90.00
Mug, 4½", hand-painted berries & leaves, Belleek mark $110.00
Mug, 5¼", Harvard College, green mark, 1910.........$125.00
Pitcher, 6½x7", cherries on green & blue Belleek.....$175.00
Pitcher, 8", silver overlay w/floral cameo, palette mark.$500.00
Plate, bread & butter; Flirtation......................$20.00
Plate, dinner; Blue Ridge.................................$38.00
Plate, dinner; Country Garden $35.00
Plate, dinner; Meadow Song $38.00
Plate, dinner; Tuxedo $30.00
Plate, salad; Flirtation......................................$25.00
Plate, 10", mallard duck among rushes, gold trim, signed Nosek..............................$175.00
Platter, 17", Kingsley.......................................$145.00
Platter, 19", Empress.......................................$150.00
Salt cellar, swan figural, 24k gold palette mark..........$45.00
Shell, 9", gold rim, blue mark $40.00
Swan, 2", gold mark...$25.00
Swan, 8½", blue mark.......................................$75.00

Tankard, 7", silver overlay $250.00

Teapot, Waldorf Astoria, pink w/silver bands, silver top, 1937 ....$95.00
Teapot, 2x3", gold bands, 1930s $85.00
Toby, William Penn, Indian handle.................$225.00
Vase, 10½", swan handles, green mark, 1930.............$85.00
Vase, 12", peacocks on blue Belleek, signed Hipple..$600.00
Vase, 16", poppies, baluster, signed Wilcox, Belleek mark $440.00
Vase, 8¼", shepherdess & sheep, classic form, Belleek mark $550.00
Vase, 9⅜", white, urn form, claw feet, green wreath mark $250.00

Letter Openers

Interesting together or singularly as a decorative accent, old letter openers are easy to find and affordable. They've been made in just about any material you can think of — some very fancy, others almost primitive. If you like advertising, you'll want to add those with product or company names to your collection.

Abalone, 5¼" $5.00
Bone, 5¼", red & black stain, scrimshaw leaves, cut-out hearts $78.00

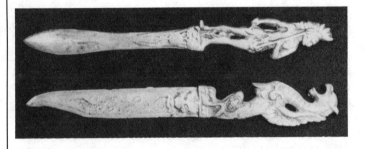

Brass, Indian, 8¾", Gargoyle, 9", each $25.00
Brass, lion handle, Victorian $45.00
Brass, w/ruler, Grammes, Allentown PA.....................$10.00
Brass, 6¾", Napoleon figural...............................$36.00
Brass, 7", small oriental idol on handle stamped Siam, w/box $8.00

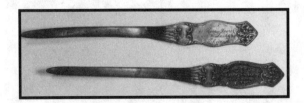

Brass, 9", advertising message, either $20.00
Brass dagger, 9½", in red leather scabbard.................$15.00
Celluloid, Capitol National Bank, Indianapolis $6.00
Celluloid, 10", relief violets & leaves w/some color....$15.00
Chromed steel, auger handle, Irwin Auger Bit, Wilmington..............................$25.00
Ebony wood, 12", tribal chieftain in headdress figural..$7.50

Ivory, 12", carved to represent a dagger, oriental........$35.00

Metal, arrowhead figural, Anaconda Copper +& Brass, EX $15.00

Metal, Nabisco Uneeda Biscuits $80.00

Metal, Prudential Life Insurance...............................$14.00

Metal, w/ruler, Cyprus Novelty, Brooklyn NY $13.50

Plastic, pink, Fuller Brush man figural.........................$8.00

Pot metal w/brass blade, 8", cowboy on rearing horse, black enamel $10.00

Silverplated, figural horse head handle, Reed & Barton..$85.00

Stanhope, ivory $60.00

Sterling, 7", floral relief, Jacobi & Jenkins $125.00

Whalebone, 4¼", sword form, EX................................$50.00

Whalebone, 7", w/rosewood handle, EX $75.00

License Plates

Some of the early porcelain license plates are valued at more than $500.00. First-year plates (the date varies from state to state, of course) are especially desirable. Steel plates with the aluminum 'state seal' attached range in value from $150.00 (for those from 1915-20) to $20.00 (for those from the early forties to 1950). Even some modern plates are desirable to collectors who like those with special graphics and messages.

1935, Georgia $20.00

1935, Idaho...$15.50

1937, South Dakota...$9.50

1938, North Dakota...$10.50

1941, Delaware $25.00

1945, Illinois $10.50

1949, Virginia...$9.00

1951, Florida...$10.50

1951, Vermont $6.50

1952, District of Columbia $28.00

1953, Utah...$20.00

1955, Rhode Island, Senate $25.00

1955, Wyoming $8.50

1956, Indiana...$4.50

1958, Texas...$6.50

1962, Arizona..$8.50

1964, Ohio..$2.75

1965, Arkansas $10.50

1965, Virginia..$4.50

1966, Alaska, shows totem pole.................................$25.00

1968, Connecticut..$9.00

1969, California $7.50

1969, New York $5.50

1970, Pennsylvania..$3.50

1971, Tennessee $5.50

1973, Oregon..$3.00

1976, New Jersey, Bicentennial front plate, NM $25.00

1976, West Virginia $6.00

1976-77, Minnesota, Red Lake Chippewa....................$50.00

1977, Indiana, Disabled Veteran $5.50

1978, South Carolina, National Guard $5.50

1979, Colorado, National Sports Festival....................$30.00

1979, Indiana..$4.50

1981, Wisconsin, Minominee Nation $10.50

1982, Hawaii...$9.50

1984, Oklahoma..$5.50

1985, Alabama, National Guard $4.50

1986, Alabama..$3.50

1986, Michigan $3.50

1987, Arizona, shows cactus..$2.00

1987, North Carolina, reads 'First in Flight' $3.50

1988, Alaska...$9.50

1989, South Carolina, taxi..$5.50

Liddle Kiddles

These tiny little dolls ranging from ¾" to 4" tall were made by Mattel from 1966 until 1979. They all had posable bodies and rooted hair that could be restyled, and they came with accessories of many types. Some represented storybook characters, some were flowers in perfume bottles, some were made to be worn as jewelry, and there were even spacemen 'Kiddles.' Our prices are for dolls still mint and in their original packaging. If only the package is missing, deduct 25%; if the doll is dressed but has none of the original accessories, deduct 75%.

Alice in Wonderliddle case, M in box $75.00

Beat-A-Diddle, 3½", for Sears, 1967, M on card..........$75.00

Calamity Jiddle, 2⅞", #3506, blond hair & blue eyes, large felt cowboy hat, M on card $25.00

Cinderiddle, 3½", #3528, white ballgown w/lace & silver trim, 1968, M on card..$45.00

Cookin' Kiddle, M on card $40.00

Freezy Sliddle, 3½", #3516, auburn hair, blue eyes, 1967, M on card...$25.00

Funny Bunny Kiddle, 2", #3532, 1968, M on card $12.00

Goodnight Kiddle, 3½", #3848, doll w/snap-together bedroom furniture, 1970, M in box..........................$75.00

Greta Griddle, 3½", #3508, 1966, M on card $30.00

Kampy Kiddle, 3½", #3753, freckles on face, fishing gear, 1968, M on card $35.00

Kiddles Collector's case, #3569, pink, 8 compartments inside, 1968, M $8.00

Kleo Kola, 2", gold metallic headband, fits in bottle w/brown cap & base, 1968, M in box..................**$12.00**

Lady Lace, 3½", #A-3840, long curls, w/large cup & saucer, 1970-1971, M in box.....................................**$30.00**

Lickety Spliddle & Her Traveldiddles, 4", doll w/4 vehicles, 1968, M in box.....................................**$30.00**

Liddle Diddle, M.....................................**$20.00**

Liddle Kiddle Town, NM.....................................**$40.00**

Liddle Middle Muffet, 3½", #3545, auburn hair, blue eyes, 1967-1968, M on card.....................................**$45.00**

Liddle Red Riding Hiddle, 3½", #3546, w/gray fuzzy wolf & storybook, 1967-1968, M on card.....................**$45.00**

Lorna Locket, 2", #3535, fits inside gold locket w/red stones & dark blue top, 1967, M on card.....................**$15.00**

Paper dolls, 13x10" booklet, Whitman #1981:59, 9 dolls, 44 outfits, 10 accessories, M.....................**$10.00**

Pop-Up Soda Parlor w/Kutie, ¾" mini Kiddle w/pink hair, book opens to form 3-D ice cream parlor, 1968, M on card.....................................**$15.00**

Robin Hood & Maid Marian Storybook Sweethearts, 2", #3785, 1959, M in box.....................................**$50.00**

Romeo & Juliet Storybook Sweethearts, 2", #3782, 1969, M in box.....................................**$50.00**

Shirley Skediddle, 4", #3766, pink flower in hair, pink vinyl dress w/lace skirt, 1958-1969, M in box..............**$15.00**

Sleeping Biddle & castle, NM.....................................**$42.00**

Sleeping Biddle's Castle, 1968, M in box..............$65.00

Storybook Kiddle Sweethearts paper dolls, 12x9¼" booklet, Whitman #1956, 8 dolls, 36 outfits, 26 accessories, M.....................................**$10.00**

Suke Skediddle, M.....................................**$20.00**

Surfy Skiddle, 3", #3517, pink vinyl 2-pc bikini, sunglasses & surf board, 1967, M on card.....................**$25.00**

Teeter Time Baby, 2", eyelet dress, hat w/pink ribbon, yellow plastic rocker, 1970, M on card.....................**$20.00**

Tricky Triddle, 2⅞", #2515, M on card.....................**$30.00**

Limited Editions

If you're going to buy any of these items, pick those that you will personally enjoy, because contrary to what you may have heard, investment potential is poor. Values we've listed are retail, but if you sell to a dealer, don't expect to get much more than 20% to 30%.

Bells

Bing & Grondahl, 1981, Christmas Peace.....................**$40.00**

Bing & Grondahl, 1988, Christmas Eve in Williamsburg.**$95.00**

Danbury Mint, 1975, Doctor & Doll, Norman Rockwell.**$50.00**

Danbury Mint, 1977, The Remedy, Norman Rockwell.**$38.00**

Gorham, 1976, Flowers in Tender Bloom, Norman Rockwell.....................................**$38.00**

Gorham, 1977, Chilling Chore, Norman Rockwell......**$36.00**

Gorham, 1984, Hitching Up, Currier & Ives, miniature..**$18.00**

Juan Ferrandiz, 1980, Spreading the Word, musical....**$60.00**

River Shore, 1977, Flowers for Mother, Norman Rockwell.....................................**$62.00**

River Shore, 1977, School Play, Norman Rockwell......**$72.50**

River Shore, 1978, Five Cents a Glass, Norman Rockwell 2nd series.....................................**$40.00**

Dolls

Edwin M Knowles, 1985, Jason, Yolanda Bello.........**$995.00**

Edwin M Knowles, 1987, Mary Had a Little Lamb, Yolanda Bello.....................................**$245.00**

Gorham, 1981, Christopher, 19".....................................**$800.00**

Gorham, 1982, Baby in Blue Dress, 12".....................**$365.00**

Gorham, 1983, Christmas Morning Holly Hobbie, 14".**$250.00**

Gorham, 1984, Faith, 18".....................................**$170.00**

Gorham, 1984, Summer Holly (Holly Hobby), 12"....**$180.00**

Gorham, 1985, Linda, 19".....................................**$465.00**

Gorham, 1987, Rebecca, Victorian Ladies series........**$300.00**

Lenox, 1984, Abigail, J Grammer, 20".....................**$1,650.00**

Lenox, 1985, Jennifer, J Grammer, cloth body, china face & limbs, 14".....................................**$1,000.00**

Figurines

Anri, 1969, Angel Sugar Heart, Juan Ferrandiz, 6"..**$2,300.00**

Anri, 1975, Inspector, Juan Ferrandiz, 6".....................**$365.00**

Anri, 1977, Tracker, Juan Ferrandiz, 6".....................**$365.00**

Anri, 1978, Spreading the Word, Juan Ferrandiz, 6"..**$500.00**

Anri, 1979, First Blossom, Juan Ferrandiz, 6"............**$365.00**

Anri, 1983, Admiration, Juan Ferrandiz, 6".....................**$245.00**

Anri, 1983, Sweeping, Sarah Kay, 6".....................**$425.00**

Anri, 1986, Finishing Touch, Sarah Kay, 6"..............**$315.00**

Anri, 1988, Penny for Your Thoughts, Sarah Kay, 4"..**$220.00**

Boehm, 1957, California Quail, pr.....................**$2,500.00**

Boehm, 1958, American Redstarts.....................**$1,850.00**

Boehm, 1961, Goldfinches.....................................**$4,000.00**

Boehm, 1961, Sugarbirds.....................................**$1,275.00**

Boehm, 1962, Ptarmigan, pr.....................................**$3,450.00**

Boehm, 1964, Bobolink.....................................**$1,400.00**

Boehm, 1965, Catbird..$2,000.00
Boehm, 1968, Roadrunner $3,500.00
Boehm, 1969, Western Bluebirds $6,200.00
Boehm, 1970, Oven-bird..$1,600.00
Boehm, 1971, Nuthatch $975.00
Boehm, 1971, Winter Robin.................................$1,275.00
Boehm, 1972, Barn Owl..$5,200.00
Boehm, 1973, Horned Larks $2,800.00
Boehm, 1974, Crested Tit.......................................$1,000.00
Boehm, 1974, Myrtle Warblers.............................$1,950.00
Boehm, 1975, Puma $6,500.00
Boehm, 1977, American Mustangs $5,250.00
Boehm, 1979, Cactus Dahlia $900.00
Boehm, 1979, Least Tern..$2,950.00
Boehm, 1979, Spanish Iris.......................................$600.00
Goebel, 1963, Home Cure, Norman Rockwell..........$385.00
Goebel, 1963, Little Veterinarian, Norman Rockwell.$385.00
Gorham, 1974, At the Vets, Norman Rockwell $62.50
Gorham, 1976, Independence.................................$135.00
Gorham, 1980, Jolly Coachman, Norman Rockwell ..$115.00
Ispanky, 1957, Pilgrim Family, decorated $700.00
Ispanky, 1967, Ballerina $875.00
Ispanky, 1973, Maid of the Mist............................$795.00
Ispanky, 1973, Texas Rangers.............................$1,500.00
Ispanky, 1976, Piano Girl $675.00
Royal Worcester, #3224, Bridesmaid $275.00
Royal Worcester, 1950, Magnolia Warbler, Dorothy
    Doughty $3,000.00
Royal Worcester, 1952, Yellow-Headed Blackbirds, Dorothy
    Doughty $2,000.00
Royal Worcester, 1959, Highland Bull, Doris Lindner..$685.00
Royal Worcester, 1961, Passionflower, Ronald Van Ruyck-
    evelt $385.00
Royal Worcester, 1964, Shire Stallion, Doris Lindner .$1,325.00
Royal Worcester, 1966, Swordfish, Ronald Van Ruyck-
    evelt...$615.00

Ornaments

American Greetings, 1981, disk, acrylic, Holly Hobbie .$5.50
American Greetings, 1983, disk, acrylic, 1st Christmas
    Together...$6.75
American Greetings, 1986, unicorn, clear acrylic...........$4.25
Reed & Barton, 1972, Christmas Cross, sterling........$120.00
Reed & Barton, 1979, Christmas Cross, 14k gold over ster-
    ling..$50.00
Reed & Barton, 1984, French Horns, from Twelve Days of
    Christmas series...$22.00
Wallace Silversmiths, 1980, Tree...................................$16.00
Wallace Silversmiths, 1982, Wintergreen candy cane..$62.50
Wallace Silversmiths, 1983, Husky................................$18.50
Wallace Silversmiths, 1988, Dragon..............................$10.00

Plates

Bing & Grondahl, 1896, New Moon......................$1,800.00
Bing & Grondahl, 1900, Christmas Bells Chiming $975.00
Bing & Grondahl, 1905, Christmas Night $165.00

Bing & Grondahl, 1912, Going to Church.................$125.00
Bing & Grondahl, 1918, Fishing Boat.......................$100.00
Bing & Grondahl, 1928, Eskimos..............................$90.00
Bing & Grondahl, 1937, Arrival of Christmas Guests ..$120.00
Bing & Grondahl, 1948, Watchman..........................$150.00
Bing & Grondahl, 1959, Christmas Eve $155.00
Bing & Grondahl, 1962, Winter Night $60.00
Bing & Grondahl, 1966, Home for Christmas $35.00
Edwin M Knowles, 1978, Scarlett, R Kursar $275.00
Edwin M Knowles, 1980, Easter, Spaulding $45.00
Edwin M Knowles, 1984, Office Hours, Friends I Remember
    series...$37.50
Edwin M Knowles, 1985, Fascination, Frances Hook..$22.00
Edwin M Knowles, 1988, Weathered Barn, Jerner.......$48.00
MI Hummel, 1971, Heavenly Angel...........................$525.00
MI Hummel, 1972, Hear Ye, Hear Ye........................$50.00
MI Hummel, 1974, Goose Girl $50.00
MI Hummel, 1977, Apple Tree Boy $60.00
MI Hummel, 1979, Singing Lesson.............................$30.00
Rockwell Society, 1974, Scotty Gets His Tree...........$105.00
Rockwell Society, 1977, Faith.....................................$52.50
Rockwell Society, 1978, Christmas Dream...................$32.50
Rockwell Society, 1979, Lighthouse Keeper's Daughter.$55.00
Rockwell Society, 1984, Grandpa's Treasure Chest $32.50
Rockwell Society, 1984, Reminiscing in the Quiet.......$37.50
Rockwell Society, 1984, Waiting on the Shore............$24.00
Rockwell Society, 1986, Musician's Magic...................$30.00
Rockwell Society, 1987, Grandpa's Gift......................$42.50
Rockwell Society, 1987, Serious Business $32.00
Rockwell Society, 1988, Banjo Player.........................$50.00
Rockwell Society, 1988, My Mother...........................$44.00
Rockwell Society, 1988, Sign of the Times..................$48.00
Rosenthal, 1934, Christmas Peace.............................$185.00
Rosenthal, 1945, Christmas in an Alpine Valley........$225.00
Rosenthal, 1961, Solitary Christmas $215.00
Rosenthal, 1972, Christmas in Franconia $90.00
Rosenthal, 1974, Memorial Church in Berlin.............$185.00
Rosenthal, 1977, Caspar..$395.00
Royal Copenhagen, 1909, Danish Landscape $165.00
Royal Copenhagen, 1914, Holy Spirit Church...........$200.00
Royal Copenhagen, 1922, Three Singing Angels $80.00
Royal Copenhagen, 1932, Frederiksberg Gardens.....$115.00
Royal Copenhagen, 1939, Greenland Pack Ice $375.00
Royal Copenhagen, 1945, Peaceful Scene..................$325.00
Royal Copenhagen, 1950, Boeslunde Church............$200.00
Royal Copenhagen, 1956, Rosenborg Castle.............$125.00
Royal Copenhagen, 1962, Little Mermaid..................$150.00
Royal Copenhagen, 1969, Old Farmyard....................$25.00
Royal Worcester, 1972, Boston Tea Party, PW Baston.$300.00
Royal Worcester, 1975, Old Grist Mill, PW Baston....$110.00
Royal Worcester, 1977, Washington's Inauguration, PW Bas-
    ton..$285.00
Royal Worcester, 1980, Shannon & Chesapeake $135.00

Little Golden Books

Everyone has had a few of these books in their lifetime,

some we've read to our own children so many times that we still know them word for word. Today they're appearing in antique malls and shops everywhere, and when they're found in good condition, dust jacket intact, first editions from the 1940s may go as high as $30.00.

The first were printed in 1942; these are recognizable by their blue paper spines (later ones had gold foil). Until the early 1970s, they were numbered consecutively; after that they were unnumbered.

First editions of the titles having a 25¢ or 29¢ cover price can be identified by either a notation on the first or second pages, or a letter on the bottom right corner of the last page (A for 1, B for 2, etc.). If these are absent, you probably have a first edition.

Condition is extremely important. Our prices are for books that are in mint condition — just as they looked the day they were purchased. Obviously, you won't find many in this shape. If your book is just lightly soiled, the cover has no tears or scrapes, the inside pages have only small creases or folded corners, and the spine is still strong (though the cover may be missing), it will be worth about half of its suggested value. Additional damage would of course lessen the value even more.

For more information, we recommend *Collecting Little Golden Books* by Steve Santi.

A Child's Garden of Verse, Simon & Schuster, 1957, #289, 1st edition, 24 pages, M............................**$7.00**

Bambi, Simon & Schuster, 1948, #D7, 7th edition, 28 pages, M............................**$12.00**

Boats, Simon & Schuster, 1951, #125, 1st edition, 28 pages, M............................**$6.00**

Buffalo Bill Jr, Simon & Schuster, 1956, #254, 1st edition, 24 pages, M............................**$15.00**

Christmas Story, Simon & Schuster, 1952, #158, 1st edition, 28 pages, M............................**$8.00**

Counting Rhymes, Simon & Schuster, 1947, #257, 1st edition, 24 pages, M............................**$6.00**

Daniel Boone, Simon & Schuster, 1956, #256, 1st edition, 24 pages, M............................**$8.00**

Davy Crockett, 'King of the Wild Frontier,' Simon & Schuster, 1955, #D45, 1st edition, 28 pages, M............**$12.00**

Dennis the Menace & Ruff, Golden Press, 1959, #386, 1st edition, 24 pages, M............................**$10.00**

Donald Duck & Santa Claus, Simon & Schuster, 1952, #D27, 3rd edition, Mickey Mouse Club Book, 28 pages, M............................**$12.00**

Donald Duck's Safety Book, Simon & Schuster, 1954, #D41, 2nd edition, Mickey Mouse Club Book, 24 pages, M............................**$15.00**

First Little Golden Book of Fairy Tales, Simon & Schuster, 1948, #9, illustrated by Gertrude Elliot, 42 pages, M. **$12.00**

Fuzzy Duckling, Simon & Schuster, 1949, #78, 1st edition, 28 pages, M............................**$10.00**

Golden Egg Book, Golden Press, 1962, #456, 1st edition, 29¢ original price, 24 pages, M............................**$7.00**

Hiawatha, Simon & Schuster, 1953, #D31, 1st edition, 28 pages, M............................**$12.00**

How To Tell Time, Simon & Schuster, 1957, #285, 1st edition, Gruen Precision on clock face, 24 pages, M...........**$15.00**

Howdy Doody's Circus, Simon & Schuster, 1950, #99, 2nd edition, 28 pages, VG............................**$12.00**

Johnny's Machines, Simon & Schuster, 1949, #71, 3rd edition, 42 pages, M............................**$10.00**

Jolly Barnyard, Simon & Schuster, 1950, #67P, 1st edition, puzzle edition, 42 pages, M............................**$30.00**

Life & Legend of Wyatt Earp, Simon & Schuster, 1958, #315, 1st edition, 25¢ original price, 24 pages, M...........**$15.00**

Little Golden Book of Hymns, Simon & Schuster, 1947, #34, 1st edition, 42 pages, M............................**$10.00**

Little Red Hen, Simon & Schuster, 1942, #6, 1st edition, illustrated by Rudolf Freund, 42 pages, M..................**$20.00**

Little Trapper, Simon & Schuster, 1949, #79, 1st edition, 28 pages, M............................**$10.00**

Magilla Gorilla, Golden Press, 1964, #547, 1st edition, 24 pages, M............................**$12.00**

Maverick, Simon & Schuster, 1959, #354, 1st edition, 25¢ original price, 24 pages, M............................**$15.00**

Night Before Christmas, Simon & Schuster, 1949, #20, 1st edition, illustrated by Cornelius DeWitt, 42 pages, M............................**$20.00**

Perri & Her Friends, Simon & Schuster, 1956, #D54, 1st edition, illustrated by Disney Studios, 24 pages, M ...**$12.00**

Puss in Boots, 1959, #359, 2nd edition, EX.............**$4.50**

Rin Tin Tin & the Outlaw, Simon & Schuster, 1957, #304, 1st edition, 24 pages, M............................**$8.50**

Roy Rogers & Cowboy Toby, Simon & Schuster, 1954, #195, 1st edition, 25¢ original price, 28 pages, M...........**$18.00**

Snow White & the Seven Dwarfs, Simon & Schuster, 1948, #D4, 1st edition, 42 pages, M............................**$15.00**

Tonka, Golden Press, 1959, #D80, 1st edition, illustrated by Disney Studios, 25¢ original price, 24 pages, M ...**$12.00**

Tootle, Simon & Schuster, 1946, #21, 1st edition, illustrated by Tibor Gergely, 42 pages, M............................**$18.00**

White Bunny & His Magic Nose, Simon & Schuster, 1957, #305, 1st edition, 25¢ original price, 24 pages, M.**$10.00**

Woodsy Owl & the Trail Bikers, Golden Press, 1974, #107, 1st edition, 24 pages, M.............................**$4.00**

Little Red Riding Hood

This line of novelty cookie jars, canisters, mugs, teapots, and other kitchenware items was made by both Regal China and Hull. Any piece today is expensive. There are several variations on the cookie jars. The Regal jar with the open basket marked 'Little Red Riding Hood Pat. Design 135889' is worth about $250.00. The same with the closed basket goes for about $25.00 more. An unmarked Regal variation with a closed basket, full skirt, and no apron books at $600.00. The Hull jars are valued higher, about $350.00 unless they're heavily decorated with decals and gold trim, which can add as much as $250.00 to the basic value.

A companion piece, the wolf on the basketweave jar, is valued at $950.00; it was also made by Regal.

The complete line is covered in *The Collector's Encyclopedia of Cookie Jars* by Joyce and Fred Roerig.

Butter dish..**$350.00**
Canister, salt..**$1,000.00**
Canister, spice..**$625.00**

Cookie jar, w/decals Hull **$350.00**
Creamer & sugar bowl, head pour, w/lid **$700.00**
Creamer & sugar bowl, side pour..............................**$250.00**
Jar, cracker; 8½", skirt held wide..............................**$500.00**
Jar, wolf on basketweave base, no mark **$600.00**
Match holder, Regal.....................................**$800.00**
Mug, white, no decoration, minimum value...........**$1,000.00**
Pitcher, milk; 8", standing **$235.00**
Pitcher, milk; 8½", ruffled skirt, w/apron, rare **$1,500.00**
Planter, standing, wall hanging.............................**$475.00**
Salt & pepper shakers, 3¼", standing, pr **$50.00**
Salt & pepper shakers, 4½", standing, rare, pr...........**$85.00**
Salt & pepper shakers, 5¼", standing, pr **$150.00**

Sugar bowl, crawling...**$225.00**
Teapot **$350.00**

Wall pocket...**$475.00**

Lladro Porcelains

Lladro porcelains have a unique style all their own, and their glazes are fairly standard, making them easy to identify. Their limited edition and retired figurines have become collectible, in fact there is a Lladro Collectors Club. Beware of imitations.

Arabian knight w/peacock, #1310, 14".......................**$265.00**
Ballerina, #68-3, 8", seated **$135.00**

Balloon girl, #5141, 11" **$195.00**

Bullfighter, #5115..**$130.00**
Couple w/dog, #4563, 19"..**$165.00**
Courting shepherd & shepherdess w/sheep, #4903, 15".**$265.00**
Flamenco dancers, 19"...**$325.00**
German shepherd & pup, 8x8½"................................**$185.00**
Girl selling vegetables, #1087, 5½".........................**$375.00**
Girl w/deer, 9"...**$175.00**
Goose, #4553, 6"...**$45.00**
Lady from Majorca, w/jug, #5240, 12"....................**$135.00**
Lady reclining against rock, #1217, 12x12"...............**$265.00**
Lady wearing shawl & holding parasol, #4914, 17"...**$250.00**
Man playing mandolin, #1247, 14", Gres glaze..........**$325.00**
Man w/wine bottle, #5165..**$150.00**
Old Cellist, #4651, 12½"..**$950.00**
Old man & troubador w/mandolin, #4652, 14".........**$185.00**
Peddler, #4864, 10", man w/burro..............................**$175.00**
Pekingese dog, 6x7"...**$65.00**
Poet, #5397, 12", man beside terrace wall...................**$265.00**
Soccer player, #4809...**$124.00**
Spring Breeze, #4936, 14", lady w/wide-brimmed hat.**$145.00**
Swan, #4829, 6"...**$55.00**
Traveling artist w/case, 14"..**$135.00**
Unicorn, 9"...**$65.00**

Lu Ray Pastels

This was one of Taylor, Smith, and Taylor's most popular lines of dinnerware. It was made from the late 1930s until sometime in the early '50s in five pastel colors: Windsor Blue, Persian Cream, Sharon Pink, Surf Green, and Chatham Gray.

If you'd like more information, we recommend *The Collector's Encyclopedia of American Dinnerware* by Jo Cunningham.

Bowl, berry; small..**$6.00**
Bowl, fruit; 5½"...**$4.50**
Bowl, vegetable; 9"..**$10.00**
Casserole, w/lid..**$60.00**
Egg cup, Chatham gray, rare color..............................**$15.00**

Mixing bowl set, 4-pc..$150.00

Muffin cover, w/8" underplate....................................**$65.00**
Nut dish...**$22.50**
Pitcher, bulbous w/flat bottom....................................**$40.00**
Plate, chop; 14"...**$18.00**
Plate, serving; tab handle..**$25.00**
Plate, 10"..**$10.00**
Plate, 7", Chatham gray, rare color.............................**$6.00**
Platter, oval, 13"...**$10.00**
Relish, 4-part...**$60.00**
Sauce pitcher...**$18.00**
Sugar bowl, w/lid...**$9.00**
Tidbit, 2-tier..**$18.00**
Tumbler, water..**$37.50**

Lunch Boxes

Character lunch boxes and thermoses have been very collectible for the past few years. Metal lunch boxes are preferred over vinyl, and the dome tops over the rectangular ones.

The first one ever produced featured Hopalong Cassidy. Made by the Aladdin company, it was constructed of steel and decorated with decals. But the first fully lithographed steel lunch box and matching thermos bottle was made a few years later (in 1953) by American Thermos. Roy Rogers was its featured character.

Hundreds have been made, and just as is true in other areas of character-related collectibles, the more desirable lunch boxes are those with easily recognizable, well-known subjects — western heroes; TV, Disney, and cartoon characters; and famous entertainers.

Watch for these at garage sales. They're still easy to find, and they're usually priced very low.

If you'd like to learn more about them, we recommend *A Pictorial Price Guide to Metal Lunch Boxes and Thermoses* by Larry Aikins.

A-Team, w/plastic thermos, King Seeley, 1985, M.......**$35.00**
Alice in Wonderland, white vinyl, w/thermos, 1974, EX..**$90.00**
America on Parade, w/plastic thermos, Aladdin, 1976, M..**$60.00**
Annie, w/plastic thermos, Aladdin, 1982, M................**$30.00**
Annie Oakley & Tagg, w/steel thermos, Aladdin, EX.**$300.00**
Astronauts, dome top, 1960, M......................................**$300.00**
Atom Ant, King Seeley, 1966, NM.................................**$90.00**
Batman, w/steel thermos, Aladdin, 1966, EX.............**$175.00**
Bedknobs & Broomsticks, Walt Disney, 1972, EX.......**$32.00**
Bernstein Bears, w/plastic thermos, American Thermos, 1983, EX...**$65.00**
Betsey Clark, w/thermos, 1977, EX...............................**$30.00**
Bionic Woman, w/thermos, 1977, EX............................**$35.00**
Black Hole, King Seeley, 1969, M.................................**$90.00**
Blondie, 1969, EX..**$75.00**
Bozo, dome top, Aladdin, 1963, NM.............................**$275.00**
Brady Bunch, King Seeley, 1970, NM...........................**$100.00**
Brave Eagle, American Thermos, 1957, EX...............**$190.00**
Buccaneer, dome top, 1957, NM....................................**$235.00**

Bugaloos, w/plastic thermos, Aladdin, 1971, EX **$85.00**

Care Bear Cousins, w/plastic thermos, Aladdin, NM..**$15.00**

Central Station, dome-top fire station, 1955, VG..........**$50.00**

Charlie's Angels, w/plastic thermos, Aladdin, M..........**$60.00**

Chitty Chitty Bang Bang, w/steel thermos, King Seeley, 1969, M **$85.00**

Chuck Wagon, dome top, w/thermos, 1958, EX **$250.00**

Circus Wagon, dome top, EX.......................................**$165.00**

Colonial Bread Van, w/plastic thermos, 1984, NM......**$90.00**

Corsage, w/steel thermos, American Thermos, 1963, EX..**$80.00**

Curiosity Shop, w/steel thermos, King Seeley, 1972, NM **$75.00**

Daniel Boone, Aladdin, 1955, VG...........................**$325.00**

Dark Crystal, w/plastic thermos, King Seeley, 1982, M ..**$35.00**

Davy Crockett & Kit Carson, w/steel thermos, Adco Liberty, 1955, EX **$250.00**

Davy Crockett Indian Fighter, 1955, EX **$140.00**

Disney School Bus, orange, dome top, w/steel thermos, Aladdin, 1961, NM **$85.00**

Disney School Bus, yellow, dome top, w/thermos, EX .**$55.00**

Disney World 50th Anniversary, w/plastic thermos, Aladdin, 1976, M **$35.00**

Disneyland (Castle), w/steel thermos, Aladdin, 1957, EX **$200.00**

Doctor Dolittle, w/steel thermos, Aladdin, 1968, M ..**$125.00**

Dr Seuss, w/plastic thermos, Aladdin, 1970, M.........**$150.00**

Dudley Do-Right, Universal, 1962, EX........................**$385.00**

Dukes of Hazzard, w/plastic thermos, Aladdin, 1980, NM **$12.50**

Early West, Ohio Art, 1982, NM **$55.00**

Emergency, dome top, w/thermos, 1977, VG.............**$75.00**

ET, w/plastic thermos, Aladdin, 1982, EX **$20.00**

Evel Knievel, w/thermos, 1974, EX............................**$35.00**

Family Affair, w/plastic thermos, King Seeley, 1969, EX **$85.00**

Fat Albert, w/steel thermos, King Seeley, 1965, NM .**$225.00**

Flintstones, Aladdin, 1971, M....................................**$150.00**

Flipper, w/steel thermos, King Seeley, 1966, NM......**$190.00**

Fox & the Hound, w/plastic thermos, Aladdin, 1981, M...**$25.00**

Frontier Days, Ohio Art, 1957, NM............................**$250.00**

Gentle Ben, Aladdin, 1968, M....................................**$80.00**

Get Smart, w/thermos, 1966, VG...............................**$70.00**

GI Joe, w/steel thermos, King Seeley, 1967, M..........**$150.00**

Gomer Pyle, Aladdin, 1966, NM **$125.00**

Gremlins, w/plastic thermos, Aladdin, 1984, NM **$17.50**

Gunsmoke, Aladdin, 1959, EX...................................**$125.00**

Hansel & Gretel, Ohio Art, 1982, NM........................**$90.00**

He-Man & Masters of the Universe, w/plastic thermos, Aladdin, 1984, M **$10.00**

Heathcliff, w/plastic thermos, Aladdin, 1982, M..........**$30.00**

Hector Heathcote, NM..**$120.00**

Hogan's Heroes, dome top, Aladdin, 1966, M...........**$250.00**

Holly Hobbie, w/plastic thermos, Aladdin, 1973, M....**$25.00**

Holly Hobbie, w/plastic thermos, Aladdin, 1968, M....**$10.00**

Hong Kong Phooey, w/plastic thermos, King Seeley, 1975, M...**$65.00**

Hopalong Cassidy, red tin, 1951, EX **$100.00**

Hot Wheels, w/thermos, 1970, EX..............................**$40.00**

Howdy Doody, Adco Liberty, 1954, NM **$300.00**

Incredible Hulk, w/plastic thermos, Aladdin, 1978, M...**$30.00**

Indiana Jones, w/plastic thermos, King Seeley, 1984, M.**$25.00**

It's a Small World, white vinyl, w/thermos, 1969, VG.**$95.00**

James Bond, Aladdin, 1966, EX **$150.00**

Julia, w/steel thermos, King Seeley, 1969, EX **$100.00**

Kid Power, w/plastic thermos, American Thermos, 1974, M...**$65.00**

King Kong, w/plastic thermos, American Thermos, 1977, NM **$65.00**

Land of the Giants, w/plastic thermos, King Seeley, 1968, M...**$180.00**

Laugh In, riding tricycle, w/plastic thermos, Aladdin, 1979, NM **$165.00**

Little House on the Prairie, w/plastic thermos, King Seeley, 1978, NM **$110.00**

Little Red Riding Hood, Ohio Art, 1982, M **$60.00**

Ludwig Von Drake, w/steel thermos, Aladdin, 1962, NM **$175.00**

Magic Kingdom, w/plastic thermos, Aladdin, 1980, M..**$12.00**

Man from UNCLE, w/steel thermos, King Seeley, 1966, NM **$140.00**

Flying Nun, EX **$185.00**

Masters of the Universe, EX **$8.00**

Mork & Mindy, w/thermos, 1979, VG $30.00

Muppet Babies, w/plastic thermos, King Seeley, 1985, NM $15.00

Muppet Show, w/plastic thermos, King Seeley, 1978, M ..$30.00

Nancy Drew Mysteries, King Seeley, 1977, M.............$35.00

Osmonds, Aladdin, 1973, EX....................................$50.00

Partridge Family, King Seeley, 1971, NM....................$42.50

Peter Pan, w/plastic thermos, Aladdin, 1969, NM $130.00

Peter Pan Sandwich, maker unknown, 1974, NM $180.00

Pigs in Space, w/plastic thermos, King Seeley, 1977, M.$40.00

Plaid Scotch, Ohio Art, 1962, M $60.00

Popples, w/plastic thermos, Aladdin, 1986, M............$30.00

Porky's Lunch Wagon, dome top, American Thermos, 1959, EX $225.00

Rambo, w/plastic thermos, King Seeley, 1985, NM $12.50

Rat Patrol, w/steel thermos, Aladdin, 1967, NM $140.00

Return of the Jedi, w/plastic thermos, King Seeley, 1983, M...$15.00

Robin Hood, Aladdin, 1965, NM................................$50.00

Rocky & Bullwinkle, w/thermos, 1962, EX...............$300.00

Roy Rogers & Dale Evans, w/thermos, 1954.......$175.00

Sesame Street, w/plastic thermos, Aladdin, 1979, EX..$10.00

Sigmond & Sea Monsters, Aladdin, 1974, NM...........$130.00

Six Million Dollar Man, w/thermos, 1978, EX.............$35.00

Smokey Bear, metal, Okay Industries, 1975, EX........$250.00

Smokey the Bear, black vinyl, w/thermos, 1965, VG.$160.00

Snow White, metal, Ohio Art, M................................$45.00

Space: 1999, 1976..$55.00

Spiderman & Hulk, w/plastic thermos, Aladdin, 1980, NM $35.00

Sports Afield, Ohio Art, 1957, NM $200.00

Steve Canyon, Aladdin, 1959, NM $200.00

Street Hawk, Aladdin, 1985, NM..............................$120.00

Super Powers, w/plastic thermos, Aladdin, 1983, NM.$80.00

Superman, 1954, EX..$175.00

Transformers, w/plastic thermos, Aladdin, 1986, NM..$17.50

Underdog, Okay Industries, 1974, EX $500.00

US Mail, dome top, w/plastic thermos, Aladdin, 1969, NM..$80.00

US Mail, dome top, w/thermos, EX $60.00

US Mail, w/plastic thermos, Aladdin, 1969, NM...........$80.00

Wagon Train, King Seeley, 1964, NM.......................$135.00

Waltons, 1974, VG..$30.00

Welcome Back Kotter, w/thermos, 1977, EX...............$85.00

Winnie the Pooh, w/steel thermos, Aladdin, 1967, M..$180.00

Wonder Woman, blue vinyl, w/thermos, 1978, EX $70.00

Woody Woodpecker, 1972, EX.................................$100.00

Yankee Doodles, King Seeley, 1975, M.......................$55.00

Maddux of California

Founded in Los Angeles in 1938, Maddux not only produced ceramics but imported and distributed them as well. They supplied chain stores nationwide with well-designed figural planters, TV lamps, novelty and giftware items, and during the mid-1960s their merchandise was listed in every major stamp catalog. Because of an increasing amount of foreign imports and an economic slowdown in our own country, the company was forced to sell out in 1976. Under the new management, manufacturing was abandoned, and the company was converted solely to distribution. Collectors have only recently discovered this line, and prices right now are affordable though increasing.

Figurine, elongated rooster, #932 ....$28.00

Figurine, flamingo, #400 & #401, pr $47.50

Figurine, stylized geese w/very long necks, #968, pr..$35.00

Figurine, 11", cockatoo on floral-trimmed branch, ca 1947, in-mold Wm Maddux mark $40.00

Figurine, 12", stylized & elongated deer, pr................$40.00

Lamp, TV; basset hound, #896 ....$50.00

Lamp, TV; 10", Malibu shell figural, Pearltone.............**$30.00**

Lamp, TV; 11", mare & colt figural, Porcelain white glaze **$47.50**

Lamp, TV; 11½", flying mallard figural, #839 ....**$45.00**

Planter, 6", flamingo figural against willow reeds, early 1950s, in-mold mark **$40.00**

Planter, 11", two cockatoos, #515 ....$40.00

Vase, 12", horse's head figural at top, straight-sided body, #225, aqua **$25.00**

Vase, 5", twin flamingos w/spread wings figural, early 1950s, in-mold mark **$40.00**

Magazines

There are lots of magazines around today, but unless they're in fine condition (clean, no missing or clipped pages, and very little other damage); have interesting features (cover illustrations, good advertising, or special-interest stories); or deal with sports greats, famous entertainers, or world-reknowned personalities, they're worth very little, no matter how old they are.

Adventure, 1935, October 15, VG.................................**$12.50**

Alfred Hitchcock, 1960, May, VG....................................**$7.50**

Alfred Hitchcock, 1972, January, EX............................**$13.50**

Amazing Stories, 1930, May, VG **$35.00**

Amazing Stories, 1942, June, VG **$12.50**

Amazing Stories, 1959, May, VG **$7.50**

American Cookery Magazine, 1943, May-June, G..........**$2.00**

American Home, 1937, April, VG.....................................**$2.50**

American Needlewoman, 1926, May **$3.00**

Aviation Week & Space Technology, 1959, June, 'Next Decade in Space,' EX...**$18.00**

Cavalier, 1960, July, features Mickey Spillane article, VG.**$12.00**

Child Life, 1937, December, VG.....................................**$4.00**

Collier's, 1955, November 11, features an Agatha Christie short story, VG...**$10.50**

Collier's, 1956, August 31, VG.....................................**$10.50**

Coronet, 1960, March, VG...**$15.00**

Cosmopolitan, 1939, May, G...**$15.50**

Country Gentleman, 1928, December, Santa cover by Sundblom, VG...**$6.00**

Dare-Devil Aces, 1935, April, NM **$12.50**

Dime Mystery Magazine, 1949, October, NM..............**$12.50**

Escapade, 1961, February, VG **$8.50**

Esquire, 1937, May, M...**$20.00**

Esquire, 1966, April, 'Problems for Frank Sinatra,' EX.**$12.50**

Etude, 1932, April, VG **$3.00**

Good Housekeeping, 1945, August, VG........................**$2.50**

Herald of Osteopathy, 1928, July, NM..........................**$3.00**

International Star Trek, 1975 convention program included, VG...**$10.00**

Isaac Asimov's, 1979, December, VG **$2.50**

Ladies' Home Journal, 1981, October, features Stephen King article, VG...**$10.50**

Laugh Book, 1962, February, VG **$4.50**

Life, 1937, Harpo Marx cover, NM...............................**$50.00**

Life, 1937, May 3, Jean Harlow cover, VG **$15.00**

Life, 1937, September 27, Nelson Eddy cover, G...........**$8.00**

Life, 1938, Carole Lombard cover, NM **$35.00**

Life, 1938, Fred Astaire & Ginger Rogers cover, NM ...**$50.00**

Life, 1938, Rudolph Valentino cover, EX......................**$20.00**

Life, 1939, December 11, Betty Grable cover, G............**$8.00**

Life, 1942, March 30, Shirley Temple cover, VG.........**$12.00**

Life, 1944, Judy Garland cover, NM..............................**$50.00**

Life, 1945, May 21, Winston Churchill cover, G............**$4.00**

Life, 1953, Marlon Brando cover, EX............................**$75.00**

Life, 1956, Julie Andrews cover, EX.............................**$20.00**

Life, 1960, Doris Day cover, EX **$7.50**

Life, 1960, October 24, Nancy Kwan cover, EX.............**$7.50**

Life, 1961, May 17, Alan B Shepard cover....................**$10.00**

Life, 1963, June 28, Claire Booth Luce cover, EX **$10.00**

Life, 1964, August 28,1964, Beatles cover, VG $25.00

Life, 1965, April 2, Gus Grissom & John Young cover, VG...**$15.00**

Life, 1966, August 5..**$8.00**
Life, 1968, October 25...**$8.00**
Life, 1969, August 8...**$7.00**
Life, 1969, Barbara Streisand cover, EX.....................**$7.50**
Life, 1969, November 7, Paul McCartney & family cover,
EX **$10.00**
Life, 1969, September 12, Coretta King cover, VG.......**$12.00**
Life, 1972, January 28, John Wayne cover, EX.............**$15.00**
Life, 1980, Miss Piggy cover, VG................................**$7.50**
Life, 1981, June, EX **$4.00**
Life, 1985, December, EX **$4.00**
Literary Digest, 1923, December 22, Rockwell cover, M..**$42.50**
Literary Digest, 1931, February 14, VG **$5.00**
Look, 1938, February 1, Sonja Henie on cover, NM....**$20.00**
Look, 1938, July 19, Marlene Dietrich cover, VG.........**$25.00**

Look, 1953, February 24, 'Nixon Fit To Be President?,'
VG $12.00

Look, 1970, January 27, Steve McQueen cover, NM....**$10.00**
Mammoth Detective, 1946, July, VG..........................**$12.50**
Marvel, 1939, August, VG.......................................**$20.00**
Marvel, 1951, February, VG.....................................**$10.50**
Modern Photography, 1954, Marilyn Monroe cover, 1954,
EX...**$35.00**
National Geographic, 1932, March, Morocco, EX..........**$4.00**
National Geographic, 1940, July, 'Old Masters in a New
National Gallery,' EX...**$5.00**
National Geographic, 1940, March, 'Classical Lands of the
Mediterranean,' EX..**$4.00**
National Lampoon, 1972, March, VG...........................**$4.00**

Newsweek, 1972, October 16, Marilyn Monroe cover,
NM **$25.00**
Omni, 1980, August, Stephen King article, VG.............**$6.50**
Paris Art, ca 1930s, D&S Publishing Co, New York, VG ...**$9.50**
Penthouse, 1982, April, features Stephen King interview,
VG..**$10.50**
Planet Stories, Spring 1949, G **$15.00**
Playboy, 1961, December, VG **$12.50**
Playboy, 1981, January, features Stephen King article,
VG **$6.50**
Psycho, 1971, November, VG....................................**$4.00**
Radio Guide, 1934, October 13, Dorothy Lamour cover,
EX **$27.50**
Ranch Romances, 1938, March 2, Canadian, VG **$12.50**
Redbook, 1984, May, Stephen King article, VG............**$10.50**
Satellite, 1959, February, VG...................................**$10.00**
Saturday Evening Post, 1936, July 4, Captain America cover,
NM **$15.00**
Saturday Evening Post, 1941, April 12, 'Spirit of Spring Cry-
ing' by Hunter, EX...**$5.00**
Saturday Evening Post, 1945, August 11, 'Swimming Hole'
cover by Rockwell, NM **$25.00**
Saturday Evening Post, 1953, April 4, Rockwell cover ..**$10.00**
Saturday Evening Post, 1961, April 1, Rockwell cover,
NM **$10.00**
Saturday Evening Post, 1963, December 14, John F Kennedy
cover by Rockwell, EX..**$9.00**
Saturday Evening Post, 1964, February 15, Sophia Loren
cover, EX **$10.00**
Saturday Evening Post, 1965, November 20, Hell's Angels
cover, EX **$8.00**
Saturday Evening Post, 1980, March, VG.....................**$4.00**
Science Fiction Adventures, 1957, December, VG.........**$4.50**
Short Stories, 1950, October, VG **$10.50**
Space Science Fiction, 1957, August, G **$8.50**
Spinning Wheel, 1949, November, G **$3.00**
Sports Illustrated, 1955, August 15, 1st Anniversary issue,
M **$10.00**
Sports Illustrated, 1967, December, 18, NM **$6.00**
Sports Illustrated, 1968, September 23rd, Denny McLain on
cover, EX **$16.50**
Sports Illustrated, 1971, January 18, Super Bowl, M......**$7.50**
Starship, Summer 1980, VG....................................**$12.00**
Startling Stories, 1953, April, VG **$7.50**
Super Detective, 1941, January, VG...........................**$15.00**
Ten Detective Aces, 1935, March, EX.........................**$15.00**
Thrilling Wonder, 1950, October, VG..........................**$6.50**
Time, 1941, November 10, Rita Hayworth cover, VG..**$10.00**
Time, 1944, July 17, Ernie Pyle cover, EX.....................**$6.00**
Time, 1944, June 19, Eisenhower cover, EX **$10.00**
Twilight Zone, 1984, December, VG **$7.50**
Venture, 1969, August, VG......................................**$10.00**
Vogue, 1944, January 15th, VG................................**$12.50**
Weird Tales, 1935, August, G...................................**$20.00**
Western Story, 1942, November 21, VG **$12.50**
Wild West Weekly, 1942, October 17, VG **$12.50**
Woman's Day, 1940, August.......................................**$2.00**
Women's Day, 1946, November.................................**$2.00**

Wonder Stories, 1935, April, VG $22.50
Yank, 1945, June 8, 'How Long Will We Have To Fight the Jap War?' $5.00

Majolica

Vast amounts of majolica were made by potters both here and abroad from the Victorian era until the early 1900s, so it has roots in a much earlier time period than we generally deal with in this publication, but there are many examples of it still around today, and because it is such an interesting field, we want to at least touch on it.

Broadly defined, majolica is a lead-glazed pottery with relief designs taken from nature. Colors are nearly always vivid. Figural pieces are common. Much of it is unmarked, but items that are will be stamped with names like Winton, George Jones, Sarreguemines, Griffin Smith and Hill (Etruscan), Wedgwood, and Fielding.

It's rather expensive but very beautiful. You'll have no trouble finding wonderful examples. The hard part will be deciding what direction to take with your collection. Plates? Figural humidors? Pitchers? I personally love them all, but until I can decide how to begin, I'll just 'window shop.'

For more information, we recommend *The Collector's Encyclopedia of Majolica* by Mariann Katz-Marks.

Basket, 8¾x11¼", floral on basketweave w/double handles, George Jones $700.00
Bowl, Picket Fence, 9", turquoise, brown & white mottling inside, handles $185.00
Bowl, Strawberry Blossom, 5", cobalt ground, unmarked $115.00
Bowl, 10½", Sunflower on light blue, lavender interior, Wardle, 1882 ....$265.00
Bowl, 10½", vining leaves border, twig footed, Holdcroft $300.00
Bowl, 15" long, turquoise basketweave & pink prunus, 6-sided shape on four feet, lavender interior $350.00
Bowl, 8", pond lily figural, brown, green & white, Holdcroft $185.00
Box, 6½", trunk form w/sailor applied to lid, Continental $550.00
Bread tray, 13" long, Bamboo & Fern, cobalt center, Wardle $150.00
Butter dish, 7½", floral on cobalt ground, frog finial.$255.00
Butter pat, 3", Shell & Seaweed, Wedgwood copy $22.50
Butter pat, 3¾", begonia leaf figural, Etruscan $20.00
Cake stand, 2x9", asters on white, attributed to James Scollay Taft of Hampshire Pottery $145.00
Cake stand, 9", Cauliflower, Etruscan, Griffin, Smith, & Hill $350.00
Cheese dish, 11", lilies of the valley w/rope frame, Stilton, 1880s $1,400.00
Cheese keeper, 10" high, dogwood on blue, twig handle, George Jones $2,250.00
Cheese keeper, 9" high, Pond Lily, lily bud finial, Holdcroft $425.00

Colander, 2½x11½", sixteen holes, three feet, ca 1890s $400.00
Creamer, 4½", Wild Rose, Etruscan $125.00

Creamer & sugar bowl, 3", 4", figural cottages ...$285.00
Creamer & sugar bowl, 4", 3", floral branch on light blue, branch finial & handles, light blue interior $120.00
Cup & saucer, 6" saucer, Bamboo & Basketweave, red blossoms on tan bamboo w/green accents $215.00
Cuspidor, 5½", floral on basketweave, lavender interior, canted corners $275.00
Cuspidor, 7", Sunflower, Etruscan $600.00
Figurine, Bacchus w/staff, 16", Wedgwood, 1860s.$1,500.00
Figurine, magpie, 22", tail up, trunk base, Minton .$1,200.00
Humidor, pipe finial, Germany $110.00
Inkwell, 9" long, bird rests at each end of leaf form, head removes to reveal well, Minton $800.00
Jardiniere, 11", blackberries on bark, Wedgwood, 1882 ....$800.00
Match holder, 7¾", monkey in loincloth by holder $300.00
Mug, 4", trailing ivy on cobalt, lavender interior, bamboo handle $135.00
Mustache cup & saucer, 8", Shell & Seaweed, Etruscan $600.00
Oyster plate, 9", Basketweave & Seaweed, four large blue shells on yellow basketweave, square shape, Minton $285.00
Oyster plate, 9", five green & brown mottled shells surround central blue well, small nautilus shells between $125.00
Oyster plate, 9⅛", five green shells on multicolor frame, Minton, 1874 ....$400.00
Pitcher, 11½", double fish form, Brownfield & Son, 1879 ....$1,100.00
Pitcher, 12", rooster form, bright colors, France $150.00
Pitcher, 3½", coral, Etruscan, Giffin, Smith, & Hill.....$235.00
Pitcher, 5¾", red flowers on brown ground w/embossed yellow geometrics at rim & base $115.00
Pitcher, 6", ear of corn figural, stalk forms handle, Etruscan, lavender interior, Griffin, Smith, & Hill $350.00
Pitcher, 6¼", brown banana leaves form sides, embossed florals at blue rim, lavender interior, green handle $90.00
Pitcher, 6¼", hummingbird & flower on stippled off-white, bamboo handle $135.00

Pitcher, 7", birds & nest of newly hatched young on turquoise, twig handle, lavender interior **$215.00**

Pitcher, 7", chickens w/sheaf of wheat figural, lavender interior, unmarked English.....................**$300.00**

Pitcher, 7", fish jumps from water on cobalt ground, JRL mark..**$295.00**

Pitcher, 7", wheat & leaves, rope trim, George Jones, 1870s..**$650.00**

Pitcher, 8", blackberry vines & blossoms on turquoise, twig handle, lavender interior **$200.00**

Pitcher, 8", dogwood on bark, lavender interior, oval shape, unmarked but colors imitate Wedgwood...........**$175.00**

Pitcher, 8", gulls on blue band over varied seascape on body, cylindrical shape, George Jones................**$400.00**

Pitcher, 8", ivy embossed on brown & green mottle, marked Brownfield...**$135.00**

Pitcher, 8", shell figural, ocean waves at base, lavender interior, Fielding.................................**$350.00**

Pitcher, 9", monkey w/shell on back figural, lavender interior **$375.00**

Pitcher, 9", two pelicans standing beside rushes figural, neck & head forms handle, lavender interior, unmarked...**$475.00**

Pitcher, 9½", ear of corn figural, stalk forms handle, pewter lid, English Registry mark....................**$265.00**

Pitcher, 9¾", bird & squirrel cartouches, Fielding, 1880s..**$700.00**

Planter, 8", Picket Fence & Raspberry, lavender interior......................................**$400.00**

Plate, 8", Dogwood, simple branches at rim, Holdcroft.**$175.00**

Plate, 8", Water Lily, large leaf form w/small embossed flower & bud figural, George Jones.....................**$125.00**

Plate, 8½", shell figural, green, brown & yellow mottle, Wedgwood..**$75.00**

Plate, 9", apples & strawberries on white w/blue at rim, Etruscan...**$225.00**

Plate, 9", chrysanthemums in six triangular sections on gray mottled, Wedgwood **$185.00**

Plate, 9", Morning Glory & Picket Fence, deep, brown, green, & white **$120.00**

Plate, 9", portrait, floral swags on 8-sided rim, Wedgwood **$300.00**

Plate, 9", Shell & Seaweed, Etruscan **$235.00**

Platter, 11", cherries & butterflies on blue, Germany **$85.00**

Platter, 13", multicolor stripes w/embossed vining geometrics, 6-sided, embossed daisy handles.................**$185.00**

Platter, 14", Bird & Fan on white, oval, small handles.**$235.00**

Platter, 14", Picket Fence, floral vines along rim, cobalt center.......................................**$200.00**

Salt dip, 5", child holding wicker basket figural, Wedgwood **$400.00**

Sardine box, 6" long, sardines on lid, Etruscan............**$675.00**

Sardine box, 8" long, fish in relief on lid, rope edge at lid & base, rustic style, unmarked................**$300.00**

Sardine box, 8" long, Sardinia, boat form, green stripes, Wedgwood...............................**$800.00**

Spoon, 5", leaf forms bowl, brown twig handle, Holdcroft **$300.00**

Strawberry dish, 8½", berries & flowers, Minton, 1868 ....**$1,000.00**

Syrup pitcher, 6", floral decoration on white, twig handle, pewter lid **$165.00**

Tazza, 9½", leaves on trunk base, Griffin, Smith, & Hill, 1885 ....**$400.00**

Teapot, strawberries & bows on blue basketweave, vine handle w/strawberry, strawberry finial...............**$400.00**

Teapot, 5", flowering branch on light blue basketweave, flower finial **$235.00**

Teapot, 6", holly & berries, bark handle............$200.00

Teapot, 6", Sunflower & Classical Urn, lavender rim, flower finial, Samuel Lear...............................**$275.00**

Teapot, 7", Chinaman on coconut figural, Holdcroft.**$650.00**

Teapot, 7", monkey holding coconut figural, tail forms handle, Minton **$965.00**

Teapot, 7¼", floral, branch handle, acorn finial, England, 1860s **$300.00**

Teapot, 8", 3-legged man figural, marked W Broughton So Duke St Douglas......................................**$1,750.00**

Tile, 7¼", birds beside nest on brass frame, Minton, Hillins, & Co...**$300.00**

Tray, fruit; 12", acorns & oak leaves, Etruscan **$400.00**

Tray, 14", basketweave w/strawberries...............$300.00

Vase, 19¼", pond lilies on shell shape, Continental, 1880s **$600.00**

Vase, 5", songbird beside trumpet flower form, pr ...**$800.00**

Vase, 7¼", pineapple & hand figural, cuff w/tassel at base **$235.00**

Wine cooler, 10", Bacchus scene on white, turquoise interior, Wedgwood.....................................**$650.00**

Male Action Figures and Accessories

Just as the generations before them enjoyed playing with lead soldiers and munitions of war, since the sixties, boys have engaged in 'battle' with combat-ready warriors dressed in camouflage fatigues, trained with would-be pilots in orange jumpsuits, and explored the universe with spacemen in suits made of the same silver fabric used to clothe real US Astronauts.

GI Joe is the most famous of these action figures. He has been made in hundreds of variations by Hasbro from 1964 to the present. They also made vehicles for all types of terrains and situations, accessories such as bunk beds and footlockers, and even buildings. Action figures were so successful here that companies overseas obtained the rights and became licensed to produce their own versions. Eventually they were made in Japan, England, Australia, Spain, Brazil, and Germany.

If you'd like to learn more about them, we recommend *Collectible Male Action Figures* by Susan and Paris Manos.

Our listings are for figures in mint condition and in their original boxes. 'Played-with' figures in excellent condition may be worth from 60% to 75% less.

Action Man, basic figure, Palitoy of England, M in box, minimum value.................................**$75.00**

Action Man, Indian Brave, Palitoy of England, M in package, miminum value **$75.00**

Action Man, SAS Airstrike helicopter, Palitoy of England, M in box, minimum value **$150.00**

Action Man, Space Ranger Captain, Palitoy of England, M in box, minimum value $100.00

Action Man, Space Ranger Talking Commander, Palitoy of England, M in box, minimum value **$100.00**

Action Man, Talking Commander, Palitoy of England, M in box, minimum value.....................**$100.00**

Action Team, Hard Rock figure, Schildkrot of Germany, M in box, minimum value **$100.00**

Action Team, Polar Adventure set, Schildkrot of Germany, M in package, minimum value **$60.00**

Captain Action, Aquaman disguise (alone), Ideal, M, minimum value **$100.00**

Captain Action, Aquaman disguise (w/figure), Ideal, M, minimum value **$200.00**

Captain Action, basic figure, Ideal, 11½", M in box, minimum value................................$200.00

Captain Action, Batman disguise (w/figure), Ideal, M, minimum value **$225.00**

Captain Action, Lone Ranger disguise (no figure), Ideal, M in package, minimum value **$100.00**

Captain Action, Superman disguise & accessories, Ideal, M in package, minimum value **$100.00**

Combat Joe, accessory pack, Takara of Japan, assorted packs, each, minimum value.............................**$25.00**

Combat Joe, American Soldier, Takara of Japan, M in box, minimum value **$100.00**

Combat Joe, SWAT Team Member, Takara of Japan, M in box, minimum value.............................**$100.00**

GI Joe, Action Marine #770, Hasbro, camouflage clothes, brown jump boots, dog tag, manual & insignias, M in box...**$175.00**

GI Joe, Action Marine Dress Parade set #7710, Hasbro, M in box...**$150.00**

GI Joe, Action Pilot set #7823 (w/figure), Hasbro, complete, M in box...**$200.00**

GI Joe, Action Sailor #7600, Hasbro, denim shirt & pants, Navy cap, dog tag, manual & insignias, M in box **$175.00**

GI Joe, Action Sailor Pack, Hasbro, various sailor accessories, M in package, each pack from $40.00 up to..**$50.00**

GI Joe, Action Soldier, Hasbro of Canada, marked Made in Canada, M in box, minimum value **$200.00**

GI Joe, Action Soldier #7500, Hasbro, realistic fatigues, dog tag & insignias, M in box $175.00

GI Joe, Action Soldier Pack, Hasbro, various packs of different accessories, M in package, each, from $30.00 up to....................$50.00

GI Joe, Adventure Team outfit, Hasbro, various articles of clothing, each, M in package $7.00

GI Joe, Adventure Team Vehicle, Hasbro, M, minimum value $175.00

GI Joe, Air Adventure Fantastic Freefall set, M in box .$175.00

GI Joe, Adventure Team Vehicle, from the 'Recovery of the Lost Mummy Set,' vehicle only, minimum value $175.00

GI Joe, Air Adventurer, Hasbro, bearded figure, complete, M in box $125.00

GI Joe, America's Movable Fighting Man, Hasbro, talking figure alone, 1967, NM $200.00

GI Joe, Annapolis Cadet set #7624 (no figure), M in open-front box, minimum value....................$150.00

GI Joe, Annapolis Cadet set #7624 (w/figure), M in box, minimum value $275.00

GI Joe, armored car, Hasbro, plastic, friction powered, 20" long, M, minimum value $100.00

GI Joe, Australian Jungle Fighter, Hasbro, dressed figure, no accessories, 1966, NM....................$300.00

GI Joe, Black Action Soldier #7500, Hasbro, redressed in Marine camouflage fatigues, brown boots, w/dog tag & hat, NM....................$400.00

GI Joe, Black Adventurer w/Kung-Fu Grip, Hasbro, dressed in camouflage shorts, M in package....................$100.00

GI Joe, bunk bed, Hasbro, M, minimum value............$40.00

GI Joe, Combat Construction set #7572 (w/figure), Hasbro, M, minimum value....................$150.00

GI Joe, Combat Field Pack #7502 (no figure), Hasbro, M in open-front box $50.00

GI Joe, Commando outfit (w/figure), M, minimum value $225.00

GI Joe, Crash Crew Fire Truck, Hasbro, M, minimum value....................$200.00

GI Joe, Deck Commander set #76219, Hasbro, M in package $75.00

GI Joe, Deep Freeze set (w/figure), Hasbro, parka, ski pants, boots, sled w/rope, flare gun & ice pick, M, minimum value $200.00

GI Joe, Electric Drawing Set, Hasbro, complete w/40-pc artist's kit, M in box, minimum value $25.00

GI Joe, French Resistance Fighter, Hasbro, black turtleneck sweater, denim pants, black beret, 1966, M in box $300.00

GI Joe, German Soldier, Hasbro, dressed figure w/complete acessories (nine pieces), 1966, M in box $400.00

GI Joe, German Soldier, Hasbro, dressed figure w/no fighting accessories (came separately), 1966, M in box $300.00

GI Joe, Green Beret, Hasbro, complete original clothes & bazooka accessory pack, M in box....................$260.00

GI Joe, Green Beret, Hasbro, green uniform, gun & holster, dog tag, green beret, black boots, M in box.......$225.00

GI Joe, Heavy Weapons set #7538 (w/figure), Hasbro, M in box, minimum value....................$225.00

GI Joe, Hidden Missile Discovery play set, Hasbro, M in box $175.00

GI Joe, Imperial Soldier, Hasbro, brown uniform, w/rifle, gun & holster, dagger & backpack, complete, 1966, M in box....................$450.00

GI Joe, Land Adventures White Tiger Hunt set, Hasbro, M in package $150.00

GI Joe, Marine Jungle Fighter Set #7732, Hasbro, M in box, minimum value $250.00

GI Joe, Military Police set #7521 (no figure), M in open-front box $150.00

GI Joe, Military Police set #7539 (w/figure), Hasbro, complete, green or beige uniform, M....................$275.00

GI Joe, motorcycle & side car, Hasbro, red plastic, M, minimum value $100.00

GI Joe, Parachute Pack #7811, Hasbro, M....................$25.00

GI Joe, Sailor, Hasbro, dress uniform, (1st style, zipper from waist to sleeve cuff), w/dog tag, M, minimum value....................$125.00

GI Joe, Talking Action Marine, Hasbro, figure alone, 1967, M....................$250.00

GI Joe, Talking Adventurer Team Commander, Hasbro, bearded figure, complete, M....................$150.00

GI Joe, Talking Astronaut, Hasbro, dressed figure only, 1969, M....................$225.00

GI Joe, Talking Man of Action, Hasbro, fatigues, hat, boots & dog tag, M in box $150.00

GI Joe, Tank Commander set #7732 (w/figure), Hasbro, M in box, minimum value $200.00

GI Joe, Underwater Diver play set, Hasbro, M in box .$175.00

GI Joe, Walkie Talkie set, Hasbro, child size, M, minimum value $20.00

Mar-Crest Dinnerware

This is a line of brown-glazed stoneware made by the

Western Stoneware Company of Monmouth, Illinois, and its old-fashioned charm is beginning to make collectors notice it more and more. It's heavy and sturdy, obviously serviceable, but made more attractive by the little 5-petal flowers and scalloped lines of its pattern. You'll find a good variety of interesting shapes, and for now, at least, it can be purchased at very reasonable prices.

Bean pot, individual	$4.50
Bean pot, lg	$28.00
Bowl, cereal	$7.50
Bowl, divided vegetable; oval	$15.00
Bowl, mixing; size #1, 5"	$6.50
Bowl, mixing; size #2, 6"	$6.50
Bowl, mixing; size #3, 7"	$7.50
Bowl, mixing; size #4, 8¼"	$10.00
Bowl, mixing; size #5, 9½"	$12.50
Carafe	$17.50
Casserole, 8½", w/lid	$17.50

Casserole, 9" dia, w/lid & warming stand	**$28.00.**
Casserole warmer	$10.00
Cookie jar	$22.00
Creamer	$9.00
Cup & saucer	$8.00
French soup, open, individual	$10.00
Mug	$4.50
Pitcher, 6"	$12.00
Pitcher, 8"	$15.00
Plate, dinner	$9.00
Salt & pepper shakers, pr	$12.00
Sugar bowl	$12.00

Marbles

Antique marbles can be very expensive (some are worth more than $1,500.00) and variations are endless. In his books *Antique and Collectible Marbles* and *Machine-Made and Contemporary Marbles*, author Everett Grist thoroughly describes and pictures each type. These books are a must, if you plan on doing much in the way of buying or selling marbles.

Mr. Grist divides antique marbles into several classes: 1) Transparent Swirls, of which he lists six types (Solid Core, Latticinio Core, Divided Core, Ribbon Core, Lobed Core, and Coreless); 2) Lutz or Lutz-type, having bands containing copper flecks which alternate with colored or clear bands; 3) Peppermint Swirl, made with red, white, and blue opaque glass; 4) Indian Swirl, made of black glass with multicolored surface swirls; 5) Banded Swirl, opaque or transparent, having wide swirling bands; 6) Onionskin, given an overall mottled appearance by its spotted, swirling lines or lobes; 7) End of Day, single pontil, allover spots, 2-colored or multicolored; 8) Clambroth, evenly spaced swirled lines on opaque glass; 9) Mica, transparent color with mica flakes added; 10) Sulphide, usually made of clear glass (though colored examples may be found) containing figures.

In addition to the glass marbles, there were those made of clay, pottery, china, steel, and various types of semiprecious stones.

Then come the machine-made marbles! Most of these defy description. Many are worth no more than 50¢, but some of the harder-to-find colors and those with well-defined color placement may run from $10.00 up to $20.00. Guineas (Christensen agates with small multicolored specks instead of swirls) go for as much as $200.00, and the comic character marbles made by Peltier range from $60.00 to $80.00, except for Betty Boop and Kayo which are worth $100.00 to $150.00 each.

As for condition, it is all-important. An absolutely mint marble is very rare and may be worth as much as three to five times more than one in near-mint condition. Marbles in only 'good' condition, having large chips and cracks, may be worth half (or less) of near-mint values. The same is true of one that has been polished, regardless of the improvement the polishing makes.

Agate, 1¾", contemporary, carnelian	**$175.00**

Banded Opaque, ¾"	**$50.00**

Banded Opaque, 2", green & white $375.00
Banded Transparent Swirl, 1¾", light green..............$300.00
Banded Transparent Swirl, ¾", blue $40.00
Bennington, 1¾", fancy $20.00
China, 1¾", decorated, glazed, apple decoration $350.00
Clambroth, ¾", opaque, blue & white........................$150.00
Clear Swirl Lutz-type, 1¾", clear w/white & gold
     swirls $375.00
Cloud, 1¼", w/mica, red & white $450.00
End of Day, 1¾", blue & white..................................$400.00
Indian Swirl, 1¾"...$700.00
Indian Swirl Lutz-type, ¾", gold flakes.....................$300.00
Onionskin, 1¼", 4-lobe..$175.00
Onionskin, 2", 16-lobe, unusual $700.00
Onionskin, ¾", w/mica..$75.00
Opaque Swirl, ¾", green...$35.00
Peppermint Swirl, ¾", opaque, red, white, & blue $85.00
Pottery, 1¾", tan w/purple lines $35.00
Slag, 1½", machine-made..$85.00
Solid Opaque, ¾", green $75.00
Sulfide, alligator, 1¾"...$160.00
Sulfide, baboon, 2⅛", NM...$230.00
Sulfide, bear, 1⅝", sitting, EX..................................$80.00
Sulfide, bear, 2¼", standing......................................$250.00
Sulfide, bird, 1¼", flying, surface wear, two interior bub-
     bles...$80.00
Sulfide, bust of George Washington, 2⅜", NM $650.00
Sulfide, camel, 2" $250.00
Sulfide, cat, 1¼"..$75.00
Sulfide, child w/ball & mallet, 1¼" $250.00
Sulfide, coin w/number seven, 2"..............................$350.00
Sulfide, cow, 1⅛" $100.00
Sulfide, cow grazing, 2⅛", NM..................................$225.00
Sulfide, dog begging, 2", NM $160.00
Sulfide, dog w/bird in mouth, 2"................................$600.00
Sulfide, donkey, 1⅝", M $125.00
Sulfide, double eagle, 1¾", very rare.........................$675.00
Sulfide, dove, 1⅝", M $160.00
Sulfide, eagle, 1⅝" $185.00
Sulfide, elephant, 1⅝", M..$160.00
Sulfide, fish, 2⅛", M $200.00
Sulfide, fox, 1½", EX...$130.00
Sulfide, goat, 1¾", M...$150.00
Sulfide, hen, 1⅛"..$100.00
Sulfide, jackal, 1", EX..$150.00
Sulfide, lady in dress, 1¼", M....................................$700.00
Sulfide, lamb, 1¼", EX..$100.00
Sulfide, lion, 1⅝", NM..$85.00
Sulfide, man & lady, 2⅜", NM..................................$1,500.00
Sulfide, monkey, 1⅛"..$95.00
Sulfide, otter, 1½"...$135.00
Sulfide, papoose, 1⅝"...$300.00
Sulfide, pelican, 1¼" $275.00
Sulfide, pig, 1¼" $90.00
Sulfide, rabbit running, 2" $180.00
Sulfide, raccoon, 2"...$200.00
Sulfide, Santa Claus, 2"...$350.00
Sulfide, squirrel w/nut, 2", EX...................................$200.00

Transparent Swirl, ribbon core, ¾" $50.00

Match Covers

Only two or three match covers out of a hundred have any value to a collector. Of that small percentage, most will be worth considerably less than $10.00. What makes a match cover collectible? First of all it must be in mint condition. Collectors prefer to remove the staples and the matchsticks and to store them in special albums for protection. Secondly, those with the striker on the front are preferred. These predate the mid-1970s, when new laws were passed that resulted in the striker being moved to the back cover.

General categories include restaurants, hotels and motels, political, girlies, and sports stars and events.

The American Match Cover Association publishes a book with information on both pricing and identification.

A few of the following values are for groups of match covers; we'll indicate those within the descriptions. Otherwise values are for single items.

Al Hirt 'Live at Carnegie Hall,' 30-stick size, color photo of
     record album on back...$4.00
Best Western (hotel), group of 14 assorted non-stock, mixed
     strikers...$5.00
Bond Bread, 20-stick size, WWII Navy Plane Kingfisher, one
     of series of six $5.00
Buckeye Beer, 20-stick size, brewing ad for Buckeye Brew-
     ing Co, Toledo OH $5.00
California Western Railroad, 20-stick size, Ft Bragg & skunk
     trains on front & back..$3.00
Champion Spark Plug, 20-stick size, Indy 500 driver Dick
     Rathman & car, 1956...$5.00
Chicago Great Western Railway, 20-stick size, logo on front
     & route map on back...$4.00
Chicken Ranch Brothel, 20-stick size, nude drawing, striker
     on back $3.00
Chinese restaurants (assorted), group of 25 covers, 20-stick
     size, all front strikers..$5.00
Delicious Tootsie Rolls 1¢ & 5¢, 20-stick size, full-length ad,
     colorful graphics...$6.00
Democratic National Convention, 1940s.....................$6.00
Diamond Movie Star series, 20-stick size, Dorothy Lamour,
     1934..$4.00

Dog racing from Palm Beach, Hollywood & Daytona; group of 3 covers, 20-stick size..$4.00

Dukakis for President, 30-stick size, black & white photo on front, striker on back, dated 'Nov 1988'.................$2.00

Festival of Britain, 20-stick size, marked Bryant & May Ltd, dated 1951...$5.00

Hanley's Ale, 20-stick size, James Hanley Co, full-length ad w/bulldog on back...$6.00

Jack Dempsey's Restaurant, 30-stick size, color photo of restaurant on cover...$7.50

JLT College Football Schedule, group of 25 from 1970s-80s, mixed strikers...$20.00

Katy Lines South-Western Railroad, 20-stick size, shows orange logo on purple background on front & train on back .$4.00

Kennedy Space Center, 30-stick size, shows colorful photo of blast-off on back & seal on front..........................$5.00

Larkspur Rose Bowl, 20-stick size, dated April 13, 1940 inside...$4.00

Lion Match Co Knotholes, group of 3 assorted covers, 30-stick size $7.00

Military bases & officers' messes, group of 25 assorted covers, 20 stick size, all front strikers............................$8.00

Miller High Life, 20-stick size, shows ad w/girl on moon & 'Hotel Miller, Milwaukee'......................................$8.00

NY State Transist Authority, 20-stick size, shows sea gull & 'Times Savers, Free Maps'......................................$12.00

Olympics, 20-stick size, ad for Hotel Alameda, marked 'Visit Mexico Site of Olympics 1968'..............................$3.00

Rival Dog Food, 20-stick size, shows dog steering ship's wheel on back...$4.00

Thompson Girlie Set #3, group of 5 covers, 20-stick size, dated 1955, all w/same ad.......................................$6.00

Universal Studios, 20-stick size, personalized for Don Ameche, no photo, only imprinted name on front.$5.00

US Navy ship USS Cavallaro, 20-stick size, ca 1946.......$3.00

US Navy ship USS Hazelwood, 20-stick size, ca 1946 ...$2.50

Voice of America, 30-stick size, shows logo on front, marked 'International Broadcasting,' striker on back, 1941..$4.00

Wilkie for President, 'No Third Term,' shows black & white photo on front..$8.00

World's Fair, 20-stick size, NY Silver Set, shows Hall of Marine Transportation, 1939.............................$5.00

World's Fair, 20-stick size, shows ad for Hungarian Pavillion on front...$8.00

World's Fair, 20-stick size, shows full-length ad for Golden Gate Expo, Towers of East at Night, 1939, 1 of set..$12.00

Wrigley's Spearmint, 20-stick size, full-length ad in yellow & brown w/green arrow..$5.00

1 Pull Quick, Diamond Match Co, no ad, shows two Scottie dogs on front...$8.00

McCoy Pottery

This is probably the best-known of all American potteries, due to the wide variety of manufactured goods they produced from 1910 until the pottery finally closed only a few years ago.

They were located in Roseville, Ohio, the pottery center of the United States during the first half of the century. They're most famous for their cookie jars, of which were made several hundred styles and variations. Some of the rarer, more desirable jars are 'Mammy with Cauliflowers,' 'Leprechaun,' and 'Hillbilly Bear,' any one of which is worth at least $1,000.00. Many are in the $200.00 to $400.00 range, and even the most common jars generally bring $30.00 to $40.00. Condition is important, not only in regard to hairlines and chips, but paint as well. Many of the early jars were painted over the glaze with 'cold' (unfired) paint which over the years tends to wear off. Be sure to evaluate the amount of remaining 'cold' paint when you buy or sell.

In addition to the cookie jars, McCoy is well-known for their figural planters, novelty kitchenware, and dinnerware. A line introduced in the late 1970s is beginning to attract collectors — a glossy brown stoneware-type dinnerware with frothy white decoration around the rims. Similar lines of brown stoneware was made by many other companies, Hull and Pfaltzgraff among them. See Hull and/or Pfaltzgraff for values that will also apply to McCoy's line.

They used a variety of marks over the years, but with little consistency, since it was a common practice to discontinue an item for awhile and then bring it out again decorated in a manner that would be compatible with current tastes. All of McCoy's marks were 'in the mold.' None were ink stamped, so very often the in-mold mark remained as it was when the mold was originally created. Most marks contain the McCoy name, though some of the early pieces were simply signed 'NM' for Nelson McCoy (Sanitary and Stoneware Company, the company's original title). Early stoneware pieces were sometimes impressed with a shield containing a number. If you have a piece with the Lancaster Colony Company mark (three curved lines — the left one beginning as a vertical and terminating as a horizontal, the other two formed as 'C's contained in the curve of the first), you'll know that your piece was made after the mid-70s when McCoy was owned by that group. Today, even these later pieces are becoming collectible.

If you'd like to learn more about this company, we recommend *The Collector's Encyclopedia of McCoy Pottery* by Sharon and Bob Huxford.

Basket, oak leaves & acorns embossed, twig handle, marked...$32.50

Bean pot, yellow w/three small feet & ring handles, w/lid, marked...$16.00

Bean pot, 2-qt, Suburbia Ware, marked........................$28.00

Bookends, lilies figural, marked, pr.............................$50.00

Bookends, rearing white horse, marked, pr.................$35.00

Bowl, centerpiece; leaf figural, small feet $12.00

Bowl, 5½", nesting shoulder type, shield w/in circle mark, 1935 ....$12.00

Canning jar, Albany slip on stoneware........................$20.00

Casserole, 1-qt, blue mottled glaze, molded handles, w/lid, marked...$26.00

Cookie jar, American Eagle, eagle embossed on side of woven basket shape, no mark..............................$35.00

Cookie jar, Animal Crackers, multicolor embossed animal cracker figures on side, clown head finial, marked..$85.00

Cookie jar, Apple, marked $45.00

Cookie jar, Apple on Basketweave, marked.................$45.00

Cookie jar, Bananas, yellow, marked.........................$85.00

Cookie jar, Barnum's Animals (also known as Nabisco Wagon), clown head finial..............................$275.00

Cookie jar, Bear, no 'Cookies' on front, marked $50.00

Cookie jar, Black Kettle, painted flowers on side, immovable bail, marked $30.00

Cookie jar, Brown Milk Can, marked.........................$22.50

Cookie jar, Caboose, 'Cookie Special' on side $150.00

Cookie jar, Cat on Coal Scuttle, 1983...................$190.00

Cookie jar, Chef, head figural, red at neck, hat forms lid, marked...$100.00

Cookie jar, Chipmunk, figure eating nut, marked $90.00

Cookie jar, Christmas Tree, star finial, marked, minimum value $550.00

Cookie jar, Circus Horse, marked............................$165.00

Cookie jar, Clown, bust figural, marked....................$65.00

Cookie jar, Clown in Barrel, marked.........................$110.00

Cookie jar, Coalby Cat, black w/pink mouth, head & shoulders form lid, marked.......................................$325.00

Cookie jar, Coffee Grinder, marked...........................$30.00

Cookie jar, Colonial Fireplace, hearth scene embossed on front, clock finial, marked USA............................$80.00

Cookie jar, Cookie Boy, tan, marked $150.00

Cookie jar, Cookie Cabin, 'Cookie Cabin' on side, roof forms lid, marked..$70.00

Cookie jar, Cookie Jug, marked...............................$25.00

Cookie jar, Cookie Safe, marked USA on leg..............$55.00

Cookie jar, Cookstove, black w/red & white details, marked...$35.00

Cookie jar, Corn, marked $115.00

Cookie jar, Country Stove (also known as Potbellied Stove), black w/gold & red details, marked $30.00

Cookie jar, Covered Wagon, marked..........................$90.00

Cookie jar, Dalmations in Rocking Chair, marked, minimum value $350.00

Cookie jar, Drum, red, small drum finial, marked.......$55.00

Cookie jar, Duck on Basketweave, marked.................$50.00

Cookie jar, Dutch boy, multicolored figure on white, pink at rim & base, marked $32.50

Cookie jar, Dutch Treat Barn, brown w/yellow details, no mark...$55.00

Cookie jar, Early American, Frontier Family, embossed scene, no mark...$45.00

Cookie jar, Early American Chest (also known as Chiffonier), marked $70.00

Cookie jar, Elephant, EX paint, 1943......................$125.00

Cookie jar, Engine, black train engine w/red & yellow details, marked..$130.00

Cookie jar, Fortune Cookie, Chinese Lantern $55.00

Cookie jar, Freddy Gleep, comic figure w/egg-shaped body, oversized feet, light green w/black details, minimum value $450.00

Cookie jar, Gingerbread Boy, embossed figure in reserve w/multicolored cookie shapes, marked $45.00

Cookie jar, Grandfather Clock, brown, marked USA...$75.00

Cookie jar, Granny, hair up in bun (bun forms lid), round glasses, red skirt & white apron, marked USA......$75.00

Cookie jar, hand-painted leaves on round shape, marked $45.00

Cookie jar, Have a Happy Day, round smiling face, yellow w/black details...$35.00

Cookie jar, Hen on Nest, 'Cookies' on side, marked USA...$75.00

Cookie jar, Hexagon, pink flowers, square handles, 'W' finial, marked $40.00

Cookie jar, Hillbilly Bear, marked, minimum value ..$900.00

Cookie jar, Hobby Horse, marked............................$110.00

Cookie jar, Honey Bear, marked $70.00

Cookie jar, Honeycomb, overall pattern on ball shape, no mark...$22.50

Cookie jar, House, half of roof forms lid, marked......$95.00

Cookie jar, Indian, head figural, feathers form finial, marked $285.00

Cookie jar, Jack-o'-Lantern, minimum value.............$500.00

Cookie jar, Jug, brown over cream (resembling Albany slip & salt glaze), marked...$20.00

Cookie jar, Kettle, jumbo size, movable bail, marked.$35.00

Cookie jar, Kitten on Basketweave, marked $50.00

Cookie jar, Kittens on Ball of Yarn, 'Three Little Kittens' on lid, marked $95.00

Cookie jar, Kookie Kettle, black w/gold letters, movable bail handle, marked...$22.50

Cookie jar, Liberty Bell, bronze color, marked...........$35.00

Cookie jar, Little Clown, full figure, marked...............$60.00

Cookie jar, Lollipop, multicolored lollipops on sides, lollipops form finial, marked.......................................$50.00

Cookie jar, Lovebirds (also known as Kissing Penguins), marked...$75.00

Cookie jar, Mac Dog, paw up, head & shoulders form lid, marked USA $75.00

Cookie jar, Mammy, 'Cookies' embossed on skirt, marked...$175.00

Cookie jar, Mammy w/Cauliflowers, marked, minimum value..$1,100.00

Cookie jar, Modern, 'Cookies' in pink on white modernistic shape, marked...$35.00

Cookie jar, Monk, 'Thou Shalt Not Steal' on robe, no mark $35.00

Cookie jar, Mother Goose, worn paint, marked........$100.00

Cookie jar, Mr & Mrs Owl, comic figures joined at shoulders, each w/hat, marked...............................$85.00

Cookie jar, New Strawberry, stem finial, no mark......$32.00

Cookie jar, Oaken Bucket, rope loop forms handle, marked USA $22.50

Cookie jar, Old Churn, wood grain brown staves w/dark brown bands, unmarked $30.00

Cookie jar, Old Fashioned Auto (also known as Touring Car), marked...$75.00

Cookie jar, Pelican, marked $135.00

Cookie jar, Picnic Basket, 'Cookies' on side, marked USA $65.00

Cookie jar, Pineapple, leaves finial, marked...............$60.00

Cookie jar, Pirate's Chest, dark & light brown, no mark..$65.00

Cookie jar, Pitcher, couple at harvest time painted on side, marked...$42.50

Cookie jar, Pitcher, white 'ironstone' look w/ornate handle no mark..$22.50

Cookie jar, Quaker Oats, Quaker man in reserve, cylindrical, marked USA, minimum value $350.00

Cookie jar, Rooster, strutting, bright red comb & waddle, marked...$85.00

Cookie jar, Snoopy, dog resting on roof of dog house, marked USA $195.00

Cookie jar, Spaceship, 'Friendship' on side $150.00

Cookie jar, Strawberry, marked..................................$35.00

Cookie jar, tall shape w/molded handles, flower bouquet painted on front, marked USA $27.50

Cookie jar, Teapot, 'Cookies' embossed on side, marked..$40.00

Cookie jar, Tepee, straight top, marked.....................$215.00

Cookie jar, Tomato, stem finial, marked $30.00

Cookie jar, Tulip, flower painted on side of flowerpot shape, tulip in flowerpot finial, no mark $135.00

Cookie jar, Turkey, green (rare color), marked........$225.00

Cookie jar, Uncle Sam's hat, red & white stripes, blue band w/white stars, marked USA $200.00

Cookie jar, WC Fields, head figural, hat forms lid, marked USA $165.00

Cookie jar, Wedding Jar, gold decoration on white, marked...$80.00

Cookie jar, white ball shape w/gold band & rooster finial, marked...$70.00

Cookie jar, white cylinder w/pink flowers, block handles, half-ring finial, marked.....................................$22.50

Cookie jar, White Rooster, red comb & waddle, yellow beak...$50.00

Cookie jar, Windmill, marked $90.00

Cookie jar, Wishing Well, 'Wish I Had a Cookie' on front, marked...$35.00

Cookie jar, Woodsy Owl, owl playing guitar, title at base, green hat forms lid, marked USA.......................$185.00

Cookie jar, Wren House, bird finial, marked...........$100.00

Cookie jar, Yosemite Sam, cylindrical, no mark........$175.00

Creamer, dog figural, tail handle, marked..................$30.00

Creamer, individual size, ivory w/stick handle.............$7.50

Creamer, Sunburst Gold, marked................................$17.50

Cuspidor, grapes embossed on green or brown, no mark...$27.50

Figurine, black panther, no mark $27.50

Figurine, deer, standing w/head up, white, no mark..$12.00

Figurine, duck, white, head down, no mark...............$12.00

Figurine, Hillbilly, small, arms folded over knees, marked USA $20.00

Figurine, rabbit, yellow, marked USA.........................$12.00

Flower basket, pine cones embossed, rustic glaze, marked...$27.50

Flowerpot, lotus motif embossed on green, marked...$12.00

French casserole, 1-pt, pink w/black lid, marked $10.00

Grease jar, head of cabbage figural, marked $35.00

Jardiniere, 10½", fruit & foliage embossed at rim, basketweave all over body, marked...........................$50.00

Jardiniere, 7½", flying birds embossed on light green, no mark...$30.00

Jardiniere & pedestal, 13", flowers embossed on green, no mark...$90.00

Lamp base, boots, small size, marked..........................$55.00

Lamp base, horse, right foot raised $75.00

Lamp base, mermaid w/shell, white figure on black base w/large black shell at back $75.00

Lamp base, pitcher & bowl, white 'ironstone' look.....$35.00

Mug, buccaneer embossed on green, shield mark......$20.00

Mug, green, Willow Ware, basketweave ground........$20.00

Novelty, baseball glove, no mark $10.00

Pitcher, Antique Rose, pink roses decaled on white, gold trim, marked...**$17.50**
Pitcher, elephant figural, marked...............................**$40.00**
Pitcher, embossed cloverleaves on side, marked........**$20.00**
Pitcher, embossed water lilies, all white w/simple handle, no mark..**$17.50**
Pitcher, floral on brown, tilt style **$26.00**
Pitcher, green w/embossed water lilies, fish handle, no mark...**$40.00**
Planter, anvil figural w/applied chain & hammer, marked...**$12.00**
Planter, butterfly figural..**$22.50**
Planter, carriage figural, movable wheels, parasol, marked...**$75.00**
Planter, cowboy roping calf embossed on front............**$45.00**
Planter, cradle figural, marked...................................**$12.00**
Planter, dog w/cart figural, marked............................**$14.00**
Planter, dutch shoe figural, no mark.........................**$12.00**
Planter, flying ducks at rim of bowl w/embossed leaves along sides, marked................................**$27.50**
Planter, frog figural, marked **$12.50**
Planter, hand figural, opening in palm, marked USA..**$16.50**
Planter, hobby horse figural, marked.........................**$17.50**
Planter, kitten w/basket figural, yellow, marked USA.**$12.50**
Planter, lamb w/large blue bow at neck figural, marked...**$14.00**
Planter, Liberty Bell figural, marked...........................**$65.00**

Planter, Paddlewheeler 'Lorena,' made for the Zanesville Chamber of Commerce..................$40.00
Planter, pear figural, marked......................................**$17.50**
Planter, pheasant in tall grass figural, marked **$25.00**
Planter, poodle dog figural, marked **$12.50**
Planter, rocking chair figural, black, marked **$22.50**
Planter, stork perched on edge of basket figural, marked...**$14.00**
Planter, swan figural, ivory w/black details & yellow bill, marked...**$17.50**
Planter, turtle figural, open back, marked...................**$17.50**
Salt & pepper shakers, placed together form head of cabbage, pr **$25.00**
Sand jar, Sphinx head motif.......................................**$350.00**
Snack dish, three large leaves form separate compartments, Rustic glaze...**$12.00**
Spoon rest, penguin figural, marked **$40.00**
Sprinkler, turtle figural, green w/twig handle..............**$32.50**

Strawberry jar, exotic bird perched on rim $22.00
Tankard, banded barrel shape, brown or green, shield mark #4 ....**$37.50**
Tankard, Indian Peace sign, brown, no mark..............**$70.00**
Teapot, cat figural, paw spout, tail handle..................**$55.00**
Teapot, Pine Cone, marked, w/creamer & sugar bowl, 3-pc set...**$55.00**
Teapot, Sunburst Gold, marked..................................**$40.00**
Urn vase, blue onyx, large, no mark **$32.50**
Vase, Blossomtime, pink flowers & green leaves embossed on white, angle handles, marked.............**$17.50**
Vase, fish figural, large, marked.................................**$40.00**
Vase, green classic form, marked Made in USA............**$7.50**
Wall pocket, grapes figural **$38.00**
Wall pocket, lovebirds, marked **$37.50**
Wall Pocket, mail box, 'Letters' embossed across top, marked...**$40.00**
Wall pocket, orange figural...**$32.00**
Wall pocket, Sunburst Gold, fan figural, marked **$35.00**
Wall pocket, three bananas & leaves figural................**$37.50**
Wall pocket, umbrella figural, yellow w/green handle, marked...**$20.00**

McKee Glass

This company was organized in the early 1850s in Pittsburgh, Pennsylvania. Thirty years later they changed their location to better avail themselves of the natural resources their state afforded and, in so doing, founded the city of Jeanette. They underwent a series of name and management changes, eventually becoming part of the Jeannette Glass Company in the 1960s.

Among collectors today, they're best known for their kitchen glassware, Jadite, and Rock Crystal. (The latter, though actually introduced in the twenties, is today regarded as as Depression Glass. It's a beautiful line with a deeply 'carved' floral pattern and was made in both crystal and ruby red.)

See also Depression Glass, Jadite Glassware, Kitchen Glassware, Reamers, Ruby Glass.

Baking dish, 7" long, Seville yellow, marked McK....$12.00

Batter jug, black w/bulbous body & spout, metal frame w/handle & lid **$65.00**

Bottoms Up, caramel w/crystal....................................**$70.00**

Bottoms Up, clear frost w/black **$95.00**

Bottoms Up, jade w/crystal...**$60.00**

Bottoms Up, jade w/green frost....................................**$60.00**

Bottoms Up, jadite, w/coaster.......................................**$95.00**

Bowl, mixing; 9¼", yellow opaque, plain w/rolled rim .**$22.50**

Bowl, 8", custard, plain w/rolled rim **$18.00**

Butter dish, yellow opaque, 2-pc..................................**$65.00**

Canister, 40-oz, caramel, cylindrical form w/flat lid **$80.00**

Canister, 48-oz, caramel, square w/rounded corners, 'Sugar' in black letters on front, painted metal screw-on lid..**$100.00**

Canister, 48-oz, milk glass, 'Cereal' in black letters on square form w/metal screw-on lid..................................**$45.00**

Canister, 48-oz, milk glass, black dots & 'Tea' on side panel...**$40.00**

Clock, Tambour Art, amber.................................$300.00

Measure, 1-cup, fired-on red, w/handle & spout, marked Glasbake..**$12.00**

Measure, 1-cup, green, 3-spout, no handle..................**$20.00**

Measure, 1-cup, milk glass, marked Glasbake.............**$45.00**

Measure, 2-cup, milk glass w/stylized floral decal **$22.50**

Measure, 4-cup, yellow opaque, footed, w/handle.....**$70.00**

Measure, 1-cup, marked McKee Glasbake Scientific Measuring...**$20.00**

Pitcher, measuring; 2-cup, custard..............................**$18.00**

Pitcher, measuring; 2-cup, fired-on green...................**$12.00**

Pitcher, measuring; 2-cup, milk glass, diamond check pattern...**$25.00**

Pitcher, measuring; 2-cup, milk glass w/red & white checked bow decal...**$25.00**

Pitcher, measuring; 4-cup, custard, w/footed base......**$30.00**

Pitcher & reamer set, 2-cup, milk glass, marked US Glass...**$150.00**

Reamer, custard, marked Sunkist.................................**$30.00**

Reamer, milk glass, marked Sunkist **$10.00**

Reamer, milk glass, w/tab handle, marked US Glass ..**$30.00**

Reamer, opaque yellow, marked Sunkist.....................**$40.00**

Reamer, 6", custard, w/ring handle, embossed McK mark **$35.00**

Rolling pin, crystal, w/screw-on cobalt handles........**$200.00**

Rolling pin, custard, w/metal screw-on lid **$200.00**

Salt shaker, custard, decal of lady wearing apron, red metal screw-on lid..**$20.00**

Salt shaker, milk glass, Roman-arch style w/'Pepper' in black script letters **$12.00**

Shaker, milk glass, Roman-arch style w/'Flour' in black script letters **$15.00**

Skillet, clear, w/rolled rim & handle, marked Range Tec.**$10.00**

Tumbler, custard, footed base......................................**$10.00**

Water dispenser, milk glass, rectangular form w/flat lid & metal spigot...**$110.00**

Metlox Pottery

Founded in the late 1920s in Manhattan Beach, California, this company initially produced tile and commercial advertising signs. By the early thirties, their business in these areas had dwindled, and they began to concentrate their efforts on the manufacture of dinnerware, figurines, and kitchenware.

Carl Romanelli was the designer responsible for modeling many of the figural pieces they made during the late thirties and early forties. These items are usually imprinted with his signature and are very collectible today.

Poppytrail was the tradename for their kitchen and dinnerware lines. Among their more popular patterns were California Ivy, Red Rooster, Homestead Provincial, and the later embossed patterns, Sculptured Grape, Sculptured Zinnia, and Sculptured Daisy.

If you'd like to learn more about this pottery, we recommend *The Collector's Encyclopedia of California Pottery* by Jack Chipman.

Ashtray, Homestead Provincial **$15.00**

Bowl, berry; 5¼", California Ivy **$6.00**

Bowl, soup; Homestead Provincial, flat **$10.00**

Bowl, vegetable; 9", California Ivy...............................**$18.00**

Bowl, 5", Provincial Fruit, one tab handle.....................**$6.00**

Bowl, 6", Sculptured Daisy..............................$4.00
Bowl, 7", Sculptured Zinnia..............................$3.00
Bowl, 9½", Antique Grape, divided.............$15.00
Butter dish, Sculptured Zinnia $15.00
Chop plate, 13", California Ivy $25.00

Coffee server, Red Rooster......................$38.00
Coffeepot, California Provincial $40.00
Compote, 4½x12", Ceramic Art Traditions, speckled matt glaze, ca 1956..$45.00
Cookie jar, Brownie Scout, two paper labels: Metlox Mfg Co Made in CA & Poppytrail Pottery by Metlox.......$350.00
Cookie jar, clown, black & pink details on white glaze, marked Made in Poppytrail, Calif.....................$125.00
Cookie jar, Dino (dinosaur figural), blue glaze, Metlox Calif USA copyright '87 by Vincent..............................$105.00
Cookie jar, downy woodpecker on large acorn, Made in Poppytrail, Calif USA $85.00
Cookie jar, gray squirrel w/acorn on pine cone, Made in USA $55.00
Cookie jar, green frog w/yellow tie, unmarked..........$75.00
Cookie jar, pelican w/'US Diving Team' across front at bottom, marked Metlox Calif USA..............................$75.00
Cookie jar, rabbit on cabbage, unmarked.....................$65.00
Cookie jar, Sculptured Daisy.........................$45.00
Cookie jar, seated Raggedy Ann, marked Made in Poppytrail, Calif $150.00
Cookie jar, Slenderella (pig figural on weight scales), blue & brown trim on white, marked Metlox Calif USA...$75.00
Creamer, California Provincial..............................$7.00
Creamer, Delphinium..............................$7.00
Creamer, Homestead Provincial $8.00
Creamer, Red Rooster.....................$10.00
Cup & saucer, California Ivy $8.00
Cup & saucer, Delphinium......................$10.00

Cup & saucer, Golden Blossom, yellow florals, branch handle, early 1960s, stamped mark..............................$12.00
Cup & saucer, Homestead Provincial $10.00
Cup & saucer, Red Rooster $10.00
Cup & saucer, Sculptured Zinnia $6.50
Ewer, 15", California Contemporary, hourglass form, Poppytrail Artware, ca 1957..............................$30.00
Figurine, reclining bear, Metlox Miniatures series, late 1930s..$45.00
Figurine, standing elephant, Metlox Miniature series, late 1930s..$65.00
Figurine, 4½", monkey on all fours, Metlox Miniatures series, turquoise glaze w/rust shading, ca 1939 ....$65.00
Figurine, 4½", sea horse, Metlox Miniature series, satin white glaze..$45.00
Figurine, 8¼", rooster, satin white glaze.....................$55.00
Figurine, 9", alligator, Metlox Miniature series, satin blue glaze..$65.00
Figurine, 9", Indian Brave, Modern Masterpieces series, late 1930s-early 1940s, in-mold mark $125.00
Figurine, 9½", cowgirl, multicolored hand-painted details, #1819..$195.00
Figurine, 9½", water bird, Romanelli, satin white........$75.00
Gravy boat, Sculptured Daisy.........................$20.00
Jug, Poppytrail, w/ice lip, peach satin, ca 1939...........$35.00
Miniature, 4½", monkey on all fours, Romanelli, turquoise & brown $65.00
Miniature, 4½", sea horse, Romanelli, satin white $45.00
Miniature, 9", alligator, Romanelli, satin blue..............$65.00
Pepper mill, Homestead Provincial $18.00
Pitcher, Provincial Fruit, w/ice lip $25.00
Plate, 10", Homestead Provincial $6.00
Plate, 10", Peach Blossom $10.00
Plate, 10", Red Rooster.....................$15.00
Plate, 10½", Antique Grape $8.50
Plate, 6", Homestead Provincial $4.00
Plate, 6", Peach Blossom $4.00
Plate, 7½", Red Rooster.....................$6.00
Platter, 13", Homestead Provincial.....................$20.00
Platter, 14½", Sculptured Daisy $22.00
Platter, 9½", Fruit Basket.....................$8.50
Relish dish, California Aztec, jawbone shape, stamped mark..$30.00
Relish tray, 14" dia, modeled as a straw hat................$30.00
Salt & pepper shakers, Fruit Basket, pr $8.50
Salt & pepper shakers, Homestead Provincial, 1-handle, pr..$8.00
Salt & pepper shakers, Red Rooster (illustrated), pr.....................$35.00
Sugar bowl & creamer, Red Rooster.....................$18.00
Teapot, Homestead Provincial $40.00
Teapot, Sculptured Zinnia.....................$35.00
Tumbler, California Contemporary, colorful abstract design on white, stamped mark.....................$15.00
Tumbler, 6", California Ivy $18.00
Vase, angel fish, signed Romanelli, white matt, ca 1940s $75.00
Vase, 8", Leo (lion), Zodiac series, ca 1939................$85.00

Vase, 8½", Tina, Poppets by Poppytrail, partially glazed stoneware, ca 1970 ....$20.00
Vase, 9½", water-bearer woman figural, satin white glaze, #1816...$95.00
Vase, 9¼", sea horse figural, satin blue.......................$125.00

Moon and Star

Moon and Star (originally called Palace) was first produced in the 1880s by John Adams & Company of Pittsburgh. But because the glassware was so heavy to transport, it was made for only a few years. In the 1960s, Joseph Weishar of Wheeling, West Virgina, owner of Island Mould & Machine Company, reproduced a few of the original molds and incorporated the pattern into approximately forty new and different items. Two of the largest distributors of this line were L.E. Smith of Mt. Pleasant, Pennsylvania, who pressed their own glass, and L.G. Wright, of New Martinsville, West Virginia, who had theirs pressed by Fostoria, Fenton, and Westmoreland. Both companies carried a large and varied assortment of shapes and colors. Several other companies were involved in its manufacture as well, especially of the smaller items.

The glassware is beautiful and is being actively collected today, even though it is still being made on a limited basis. Colors you'll see most often are amberina (yellow shading to orange-red), green, amber, crystal, light blue, and ruby. Pieces in ruby and light blue are most collectible and harder to find than the other colors, which seem to be abundant. Purple, pink, cobalt, amethyst, tan slag, and light green and blue opalescent were made, too, but on a lesser scale.

Current L.W. Smith catalogs contain a dozen or so pieces that are still available in crystal, pink, cobalt (lighter than the old shade), and these colors with an iridized finish. A new color was introduced in 1992, teal green.

Our values are given for ruby and light blue. For amberina, green, and amber, deduct 30%. This is a very new area of collecting, and values are not well established for the other colors.

Ashtray, 5½", patterned 'moons' at rim, 'star' in base, 6-sided shape $12.00

Butter dish, 6x5½" dia, allover pattern, scalloped foot, patterned lid & finial....................................$45.00

Cake salver, 5x12", allover pattern w/scalloped rim, raised foot w/scalloped edge...$45.00
Candle holders, 6", allover pattern, flared foot w/scalloped edge, pr $30.00
Compote, 10x8", allover pattern, raised foot on stem, w/patterned lid & finial..$45.00
Compote, 12x8", allover pattern, raised foot on stem, w/patterned lid & finial..$65.00
Compote, 5½x8", allover pattern, footed, scalloped rim .$30.00
Compote, 5x6½", allover pattern, footed, scalloped rim...$15.00
Compote, 7½x6", allover pattern, raised foot, w/patterned lid & finial...$35.00
Compote, 7x10", allover pattern, footed, scalloped rim ..$40.00
Compote, 8x4" dia, allover pattern, scalloped foot on stem, w/patterned lid & finial $30.00
Console bowl, 8" dia, allover pattern, scalloped rim, flared foot w/flat (not scalloped) edge $25.00
Creamer, 5¾x3", allover pattern, raised foot w/scalloped edge $30.00
Creamer & sugar bowl, small, open, disk foot $20.00
Decanter, 32-oz, 12", bulbous body w/allover pattern, plain neck, disk foot, original patterned stopper...........$45.00
Goblet, wine; 4½", no pattern at rim or foot..................$9.00
Jelly dish, 10½", allover pattern, stemmed foot, w/patterned lid & finial...$45.00
Jelly dish, 6¾x3½" dia, patterned body w/plain flat rim & disk foot, w/patterned lid & finial $30.00
Jelly dish, 8½", allover pattern, stem foot, w/patterned lid & finial...$35.00
Nappy, 2¾x6" dia, allover pattern, crimped rim..........$18.00
Pitcher, water; 1-qt, 7½", patterned body, straight sides, smooth rim, plain disk foot...................................$60.00
Relish bowl, 1½x8" dia, 6 large scallops form allover pattern $12.00
Relish dish, 2x8" dia, allover pattern, one plain handle .$18.00
Relish tray, 8" long, patterned 'moons' form scalloped rim, 'star' in base, rectangular.......................................$18.00
Salt & pepper shakers, 4x2" dia, allover pattern, metal tops, pr..$25.00
Salt cellar, allover pattern, scalloped rim, small flat foot .$7.00
Sherbet, 4¼x3¾", patterned body & foot w/plain rim & stem $12.00
Soap dish, 2x6", allover pattern, oval shape $12.00
Spooner, 5¼x4" dia, allover pattern, scalloped rim, straight sides, raised foot (illustrated)............$30.00
Sugar bowl, 5¼x4" dia, allover pattern, small flat foot, patterned lid & finial..$30.00
Sugar bowl, 8x4½", allover pattern, straight sides, scalloped foot, w/patterned lid & finial $35.00
Sugar shaker, 4½x3½" dia, allover pattern, metal top $25.00
Syrup, 4½x3½" dia, allover pattern, metal top.............$25.00
Toothpick holder, allover pattern, scalloped rim, small flat foot...$9.00
Tumbler, iced tea; 11-oz, 5½", no pattern at flat rim or on disk foot...$14.00
Tumbler, juice; 5-oz, 3½", no pattern at rim or on disk foot $10.00

Tumbler, water; 7-oz, 4¼", no pattern at flat rim or on disk foot......................................$12.00

Mortens Studio

During the 1940s, a Swedish sculpturer by the name of Oscar Mortens left his native country and moved to the United States, settling in Arizona. Along with his partner, Gunnar Thelin, they founded the Mortens Studios, a firm that specialized in the manufacture of animal figurines. Though he preferred dogs of all breeds, horses, cats, and wild animals were made, too, but on a much smaller scale.

The material he used was a plaster-like composition molded over a wire framework for support and reinforcement. Crazing is common, and our values reflect pieces with a moderate amount, but be sure to check for more serious damage before you buy. Most pieces are marked with either an ink stamp or a paper label.

Afghan, 7x7", tan w/charcoal face................................$90.00
Beagle pup, #555 ....$38.00
Boston Terrier, 6", ivory markings on black, standing ..$75.00
Boxer, 5½x5½", ivory & black details on medium brown, standing $75.00

Cat, 4¼x4", seated $50.00
Chow pup, 3x3", tan & brown.....................$50.00
Cocker Spaniel, #763D $55.00
Collie, 6x7", tan & ivory, standing $75.00

Collie, 6½", seated $75.00

Dalmation, small, #812 ....$45.00
Doberman Pinscher, 7½x8", black & tan, standing......$80.00
English Setter, 6x7", ivory & charcoal, standing..........$75.00
French Poodle, 5x5", ivory, black details, standing $70.00
German Shepherd, 7", standing $85.00
Great Dane, 7½x6½", tan w/black details, recumbent .$75.00
Mexican Chihuahua, 3x3½", tan black, sitting.............$55.00
Pekingese, 3½x4½", black details on tan, standing $80.00
Pomeranian, 4½", standing (illustrated) $70.00
Samoyed, 4x4½", ivory w/black details, sitting...........$65.00
Scottie, 4½", black, sitting.................................$55.00
Spaniel pup, 3¼x3½", ivory & tan, recumbent $40.00
St Bernard, 6½x8½"...$95.00

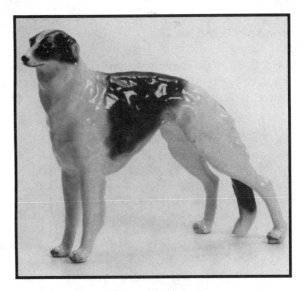

Whippet, 6½", standing............................$90.00
Wire-Haired Terrier pup, 3x3¼", recumbent...............$40.00

Morton Pottery

Morton, Illinois, was the location for six potteries that operated there at various times over the course of nearly one hundred years. The first was established in 1877; the last one closed in 1976. Each was founded by one of six brothers by the name of Rapp, who immigrated to America from Germany. Various types of pottery was made by each — Rockingham and yellowware in the early years, novelties and giftware from the 1920s on.

To learn more about these companies, we recommend _Morton's Potteries: 99 Years,_ by Doris and Burdell Hall.

American Art Potteries

Creamer, 4", bird figural, tail handle, spray glaze..........$7.00
Figurine, hen & rooster, 8", gray & white spray, pr.....$30.00
Flower bowl, 2x10", yellow & green spray, octagonal, elongated $8.00
Flower bowl, 2x10", yellow & white, S-shape $10.00
Flower frog, 2½", frog form, green & yellow spray.....$12.00
Flower frog, 3¾", turtle form, green & yellow spray...$14.00

Flower frog, 8", titmouse on raised dish form, mauve & yellow spray **$16.00**

Lamp, TV; 12", cardinals on planter form, mauve & gray spray **$25.00**

Lamp, TV; 15", two Afghan hounds, black..................**$57.50**

Lamp, 12", gnarled tree form, green & black spray........**$20.00**

Lamp, 15", begging poodle, black & pink **$25.00**

Planter, 4", fish figural, mauve & pink spray **$14.00**

Vase, 10", 6-sided, pink w/blue interior......................**$20.00**

Vase, 10½", double cornucopia, blue & rose spray.....**$20.00**

Vase, 4", blue & lavender spray, miniature **$8.00**

Vase, 7", pitcher form, blue & gray spray w/gold **$18.00**

Wall pocket, 5", tree trunk w/applied bird, brown & gray spray **$14.00**

Cliftwood Art Potteries, Inc.

Ashtray, 2½" dia, jade green, individual......................**$10.00**

Bookends, 3¼", elephant, blue & mulberry, pr **$92.50**

Bowl, sweetmeat; 2x5x5", yellow & green drip, w/lid.....**$30.00**

Clock, 7", drip glaze..**$75.00**

Dresser set, apple green, tray, jar, powder box, two candle holders..**$72.50**

Figurine, 13" long, panther............................**$75.00**

Flower bowl insert, 2x6", water lily pad #2, medium blue **$20.00**

Lamp, 10⅝", fluted pillar, bulbous, handles, blue & mulberry **$52.50**

Lamp, 20", bulb shape w/embossed lovebirds, jade green, w/harp **$57.50**

Planter, 5", German shepherd, white matt **$20.00**

Planter, 6½", crane, turquoise matt, open back **$18.00**

Planter, 7x5", elephant, brown chocolate drip, open back **$40.00**

Vase, 14", rectangular w/simulated palm fronds, turquoise matt **$35.00**

Vase, 18", brown chocolate drip, cone shape.............**$75.00**

Vase, 6½", dark blue & dark yellow drip, bulbous......**$45.00**

Vase, 9", turquoise & pink drip, fan form, handles **$35.00**

Vase, 9", white matt & old rose spray, dolphin base...**$50.00**

Midwest Potteries, Inc.

Bookends, bald eagle, brown & white, pr **$30.00**

Bowl, flower; 2½x11", deep turquoise matt................**$18.00**

Candle holder, 7", Jack-be-nimble type, handle, lime green..**$17.50**

Cookie jar, cylindrical, yellow & orange, circus animals ..**$35.00**

Ewer, 8", white w/pink interior **$18.00**

Figurine, bird of paradise, 12", blue & brown spray ...**$25.00**

Figurine, gull in flight, 12", white w/gold **$35.00**

Figurine, squirrel, 7½", brown drip.............................**$35.00**

Figurine, 4", canaries, two on stump, yellow w/gold..**$25.00**

Figurine, 4½", Irish setter, brown drip, green base......**$40.00**

Flower bowl, 6½", nest w/attached bird form, blue spray..**$15.00**

Pitcher, 4½", cow figural, tail handle, white w/gold ...**$22.50**

Pitcher, 9½", fish form, jade green..............................**$38.00**

Planter, broken egg, 6", green, tripod base.................**$10.00**

Planter, 4", kingfisher on stump, blue matt.................**$8.00**

Planter, 4", elephant, blue & yellow drip **$8.00**

Planter, 6", clown holding pants legs out, white w/cold paint..**$14.00**

Plaque, African native, 8", black, glossy, female.........**$30.00**

Plaque, African native, 9", black, glossy, male............**$30.00**

Morton Pottery Works - Morton Earthenware Co.

Ashtray, Meuhlebach Hotel, Kansas City, burgundy....**$14.00**

Bank, acorn, 2½", brown Rockingham w/Acorn stove advertising **$70.00**

Bank, 7", scottie dog form, black..................................**$25.00**

Bowl, mixing; yellowware, white slip bands, Hohullin..., Ill..**$55.00**

Bowl, 15½", yellowware, four narrow white slip bands, waffled bottom..**$95.00**

Easter item, 5", rabbit, creeping, brown spray............**$15.00**

Easter item, 9½", rabbit in top hat, yellow egg at side.**$17.50**

Figurine, 7", Colonials, he w/bouquet, she w/two baskets, pr..**$40.00**

Honey jug, Herm's Honey, underglaze flowers & bee..**$17.50**

Jug, ice box; 4", Woodland glaze, w/lid....................**$110.00**

Lamp, TV; 18", horse's head form, brown...................$40.00

Lapel stud, 1", brown Rockingham, 'We Want...,' donkey handle...$50.00

Mug, coffee; 3½", brown Rockingham $50.00

Paperweight, buffalo, 2½", brown, advertising Rock Sand Co $50.00

Planter, covered wagon form, 'Compliments of Weidman's Store' $22.50

Planters, hen & rooster figurals, pr......................$35.00

Rice nappy, 11", yellowware, fluted...........................$75.00

Stein, barrel form, 'Blatz' embossed on side, brown Rockingham...$20.00

Stein, barrel form, 'Goldenglow' embossed on side, brown Rockingham...$20.00

Stein, cylindrical, 'Old Heidelberg' embossed on side, brown Rockingham...$22.50

Wall pocket, harp, white w/underglaze florals...........$17.50

Wall pocket, lady gardener w/watering can, ringed pot.$12.00

Movie Stars

Americans have been fans of the silver screen stars since the early days of movies. Cashing in on their popularity, manufacturers took full advantage of the moment by filling stores with merchandise of all types — coloring books, paper dolls, games, and toys for the children; calendars, books, magazines, and pin-up posters for more mature fans. The movies themselves generated lobby cards, presskits, trailers, and posters, all of which are very collectible today.

See also Paper Dolls, Magazines.

Abbott & Costello, press book, 'Abbott & Costello Meet the Killer,' 1949, EX...$27.50

Abbott & Costello, sheet music, 'Abbott & Costello in Jack & the Beanstalk,' dated 1952, M $30.00

Abbott & Costello, sheet music, 'My Dreams Are Getting Better All the Time,' 1944, EX $20.00

Abbott & Costello, window card, 14x22", 'Abbott & Costello Meet the Keystone Cops,' 1955, VG $55.00

Alan Ladd, lobby card, 11x14", 'One Foot in Hell,' 1960, EX $20.00

Alan Ladd, Modern Screen magazine, 1943, December, NM $35.00

Andy Griffith & Don Knotts, lobby card, 14x11", 'No Time for Sergeants,' 1958.....................................$30.00

Anthony Perkins & Janet Leigh, poster, 1-sheet, 'Psycho,' 1960 ....$15.00

Arnold Swartzenaeger & Danny Devito, press kit, 'Twins,' 3 stills, 30 pages, NM $8.00

Ava Gardner, Hit Parader magazine, 1949, Nov $12.50

Barbara Stanwyk, lobby card, 11x14", 'Cattle Queen of Montana,' 1954, VG $7.00

Barbara Streisand, lobby card, 11x14", 'Hello Dolly,' 1970 ....$3.00

Barbara Streisand, poster, 1-sheet, 'Hello Dolly,' 1969, EX $20.00

Bette Midler & Lily Tomlin, trailer, 'Big Business,' 35mm.$5.00

Bette Davis, Bright Lights magazine, #9, article w/many photos, 1980, EX...$20.00

Bette Davis, poster, 14x34", 'Pocket Full of Miracles,' 1962, VG $15.00

Betty Grable, coloring book, 1951, NM......................$30.00

Betty Grable, Movie Classic magazine, Dec 1973 ....$7.00

Bill Murray, press kit, 'Caddyshack,' 9 stills, 50 pages..$20.00

Bing Crosby, coloring book, Saalfield, 1954 ....$20.00

Bing Crosby, record duster, 1950s.............................$20.00

Bing Crosby, sheet music, 'Swinging on a Star,' from the movie 'Going My Way,' 1944 ....$10.00

Bing Crosby, sheet music, 9x12", 'White Christmas,' cast photo cover, 1954, M...$12.50

Bing Crosby & Bob Hope, still photo, 'Road to Hong Kong,' 1962, EX...$7.50

Bob Hope, coloring book, Saalfield, 1954, NM $35.00

Bob Hope, still photo, 8x10", 'I'll Take Sweden,' 1965, NM $4.50

Boris Karloff, lobby card, 11x14", 'The Haunted Strangler,' 1958, VG..$32.50

Bowery Boys, still photo, 8x10", 'Spooks Run Wild,' 1950s, set of 5, VG $32.50

Brigitte Bardot, lobby card, 11x14", 'Agent 38-24-36,' 1965, EX...**$15.00**

Broderick Crawford, lobby card, 11x14", 'Big House USA,' 1955, EX...**$5.00**

Burt Reynolds, lobby card, 11x14", 'Smokey & the Bandit,' set of 4 ....**$40.00**

Burt Reynolds, poster, 22x28", 'White Lightning,' 1973, EX **$10.00**

Buster Crabbe, lobby card, 11x14", 'Bad Men of Arizona,' ca 1951, VG **$5.00**

Carmen Miranda, doll, 8½", plastic, ca 1940 ....**$75.00**

Carol Lombard, Movie Life magazine, 1930s, Carol w/Charlie McCarthy on cover...**$20.00**

Cary Grant, poster, 22x28", 'That Touch of Mink,' 1962, NM **$27.50**

Charlie Chan, candy container, 4", painted glass, EX..**$95.00**

Charlie Chan, game, 'The Great Charlie Chan Detective Game,' Milton Bradley, 1937, NM **$85.00**

Charlie Chaplin, coloring book, 'Charlie Chaplin in the Great Dictator Coloring Book,' Saalfield, 1941, M **$55.00**

Charlie Chaplin, figurine, 2½", lead, 1930s, M **$35.00**

Charlie Chaplin, pencil box, lithograph on tin, 1930s.**$40.00**

Charlie Chaplin, wind-up toy, marked Made in Spain, ca 1960s, M...**$65.00**

Charlie McCarthy, birthday card, 4x5½", 1938, EX......**$40.00**

Charlie McCarthy, game, 'Edgar Bergen's Charlie McCarthy Put & Take Bingo,' 1938, NM.................................**$70.00**

Charlie McCarthy, game, 'Rummy,' 1939, original box....**$50.00**

Charlie McCarthy, get well card, 1930s, EX.................**$20.00**

Charlie McCarthy, paint book, Whitman, 1938..............**$60.00**

Charlie McCarthy, spoon, silverplate, ca 1930 ....**$20.00**

Charlton Heston, photo, 8x10", 'Planet of the Apes,' color **$7.50**

Cher, poster, 1-sheet, 'Moonstruck,' 1988...................**$15.00**

Chevy Chase, press kit, 'Fletch Lives,' 10 stills, 30 pages..**$20.00**

Clark Gable, lobby card, 11x14", 'Across the Wide Missouri,' 1951, EX...**$35.00**

Clark Gable, lobby card, 11x14", 'It Started in Naples,' 1960, set of 8, EX...**$75.00**

Clark Gable, pin-back button, 1", celluloid w/photo in center, 1930s **$50.00**

Clint Eastwood, poster, 27x41", 'The Eiger Sanction,' 1975, EX...**$17.50**

Clint Eastwood, press book, 'The Enforcer,' 1976, EX ..**$10.00**

Clint Eastwood, trailer, 16mm, 'Magnum Force,' 30-second spot **$3.00**

Cornell Wilde, tray, 12½x17½", lithograph on tin, marked Nesco, 1952 ....**$50.00**

Dan Aykroyd, poster, 'Doctor Detroit,' 1983.................**$7.50**

Danny Kaye, lobby card, 11x14", 'Knock on Wood,' 1954, EX...**$8.00**

Deanna Durbin, doll, 24", marked Novelty Ideal, 1939, VG..**$200.00**

Debbie Reynolds, coloring book, 1953, EX **$25.00**

Debbie Reynolds & Eddie Fisher, Motion Picture magazine, 1955, May, VG..**$12.50**

Debby Reynolds, press book, 'Tammy & the Doctor,' 1963 ....**$5.00**

Dennis Morgan, lobby card, 11x14", 'Cattletown,' 1952, EX...**$7.50**

Dennis O'Keefe, lobby card, 11x14", 'Getting Gertie's Garter,' 1943, set of 8, NM...................................**$45.00**

Dick Van Dyke, poster, 27x41", 'Chitty Chitty Bang Bang,' 1969, EX...**$15.00**

Dolly Parton, doll, in original box, M...........................**$52.50**

Dolly Parton, stand-up figure, 44", cardboard, 1970s, M.**$28.00**

Dolores Del Rio, Modern Screen magazine, 1934, September, VG...**$22.50**

Doris Day, coloring book, dated 1958.........................**$20.00**

Doris Day, poster, 1-sheet, 'Pajama Game,' 1957 ....**$50.00**

Dustin Hoffman, poster, 1-sheet, 'Rain Man,' 1988......**$12.50**

Eddie Cantor, puzzle, Einson-Freeman, jigsaw type, 1933 ....**$40.00**

Elizabeth Taylor, coloring book, Whitman, 1950, EX..**$27.50**

Elizabeth Taylor, Photoplay magazine, 1954, Feb, EX ..**$17.50**

Esther Williams, coloring book, 1950 ....**$30.00**

Eve Arden, coloring book, dated 1953, EX **$28.00**

Farrah Fawcett, doll, 12", in original box **$48.00**

Forrest Tucker, lobby card, 11x14", 'Gunsmoke in Tucson,' 1958, EX...**$5.00**

Frank Sinatra, insert card, 14x36", 'Joker Is Wild,' 1957, VG...**$25.00**

Frank Sinatra, trailer, 16mm, 'Dirty Dingus Magee,' 60-second spot, ca 1970, EX...**$5.00**

Frankie Avalon, poster, 1-sheet, 'Operation Bikini,' 1963, EX **$15.00**

Fred Astair, dance studio trophy, 1960........................**$38.00**

Gene Tierney, lobby card, 11x14", 'Way of the Gaucho,' 1952, EX.....**$10.00**

George Maharis, lobby card, 11x14", 'Sylvia,' 1965, EX.**$5.00**

Ginger Rogers, lobby card, 11x14", 'Forever Female,' 1953, set of 8, NM.....**$50.00**

Gloria Stuart, Screen Book magazine, 1933, w/articles on Gable, Crawford, & Laughton, NM.....**$40.00**

Grace Kelly, coloring book, 1956, EX.....**$38.00**

Gregory Peck, lobby card, 11x14", 'Captain Newman MD,' black & white, NM.....**$5.00**

Greta Garbo, lobby card, 11x14", 'Two-Faced Woman,' 1941, VG.....**$310.00**

Groucho Marx, window card, 14x22", 'A Girl in Every Port,' 1952, VG.....**$65.00**

Harold Lloyd, mask, 9", paper, 1930s.....**$35.00**

Harrison Ford, poster, 1-sheet, 'Indiana Jones & the Temple of Doom,' 1984.....**$30.00**

Ingrid Bergman, lobby card, 11x14", full color scene from 'Stromboli,' late 1940s, EX.....**$50.00**

Jack Lemmon, poster, 1-sheet, 'How to Murder Your Wife,' 1966, EX.....**$15.00**

Jack Palance, press book, 'Big Knife,' 1955, EX.....**$5.00**

Jackie Coogan, pencil box, lithograph on tin, M.....**$40.00**

James Cagney, press kit, 'Yankee Doodle Dandy,' VG..**$25.00**

James Cagney, tobacco card, 1⅜x2⅝", 'Angels w/Dirty Faces,' black & white scene.....**$3.50**

James Dean, book, 'James Dean A Short Life,' by Venable Herdon, paperback, 1975, EX.....**$30.00**

James Dean, lobby card, 11x14", 'Giant,' 1956, VG.....**$45.00**

James Stewart, serving tray, 17x13", lithograph of cast of 'Greatest Show on Earth' on tin, marked Nesco, 1952, NM.....**$45.00**

Jane Fonda, trailer, 16mm, 'Cat Ballou,' 60-second spot, EX.....**$6.00**

Jane Fonda & Donald Sutherland, poster, 27x41", 'Klute,' EX.....**$12.00**

Jane Russell, lobby card, 11x14", 'Montana Belle,' 1952, VG.....**$12.50**

Jane Wyman, pencil tablet, 1942, EX.....**$25.00**

Jayne Mansfield, hot water bottle, modeled as Jayne wearing bikini.....**$68.00**

Jean Harlow, card game, 'Lucky Strike Bridge,' 1930s, NM.....**$32.50**

Jeannette MacDonald, lobby card, 11x14", 'Three Darling Daughters,' 1948, VG.....**$25.00**

Jerry Lewis, poster, 27x41", 'The Nutty Professor,' 1963, VG.....**$22.50**

Joan Carroll, coloring book, Saalfield, 1942, NM.....**$25.00**

Joel McCrea, lobby card, 11x14", 'Ramrod,' 1947, set of 8, M.....**$100.00**

John Ford, Film Culture magazine #25, 1962, Ford on cover directing 'Liberty Valance,' VG.....**$25.00**

John Gavin, insert card, 14x36", 'A Time To Love,' 1958, EX.....**$12.50**

John Payne, lobby card, 11x14", 'Silver Lode,' 1954, VG.**$4.00**

John Travolta, lobby card, 11x14", 'American Grafitti,' 1973.....**$5.00**

John Wayne, poster, 27x41", 'Big Jake,' 1971, VG.....**$30.00**

John Wayne, press book, 'Circus World,' 1964, EX.....**$15.00**

John Wayne, 1-sheet, 28x41", 'The Barbarian & the Geisha,' 1958, VG.....**$27.50**

Johnny Mack Brown, lobby card, 11x14", 'Dead Man's Trail,' 1952, VG.....**$10.00**

Judy Canova, lobby card, 11x14", 'Carolina Cannonball,' 1955, VG.....**$10.00**

Judy Garland, coloring book, dated 1941.....**$50.00**

Judy Garland, lobby card, 14x22", 'Easter Parade,' 1948, NM.....**$80.00**

June Allyson, coloring book, dated 1952, M.....**$35.00**

June Allyson, Movie Life magazine, 1952, August, M..**$22.50**

Kim Basinger, photo, 8x10", semi-nude pose, color...**$12.50**

Kurt Russell, still photo, 'The Barefoot Executive,' 1971, EX.....**$5.00**

Lana Turner, paint book, Whitman, 1947, EX.....**$28.00**

Leslie Caron, poster, 27x41", 'Gigi,' 1958, NM.....**$25.00**

Lucille Ball, lobby card, 11x14", 'Sorrowful Jones,' 1949, color.....**$30.00**

Lucille Ball & Desi Arnaz, coloring book, 1950s, EX...**$28.00**

Margaret O'Brien, coloring book, ca 1930, M.....**$30.00**

Marilyn Monroe, calendar, 10x17", 'Golden Dreams' pose, 1955, EX.....**$42.50**

Marilyn Monroe, Films in Review magazine, 1975, June-July, features 15-page article w/photos, EX.....**$25.00**

Marilyn Monroe, lobby card, 14x11", 'Asphalt Jungle,' 1950, G.....**$130.00**

Marilyn Monroe, Screen Annual Magazine, photo cover, swimsuit pin-ups of other stars on back, 1955, EX.....**$40.00**

Marilyn Monroe, window card, 14x22", 'Clash by Night,' 1952, VG.....**$65.00**

Marlene Dietrich, Modern Screen magazine, 1932, November, VG.....**$35.00**

Marlon Brando, press book, 'Mutiny on the Bounty,' 1962, EX.....**$15.00**

Marlon Brando, press book, 'Wild One,' 1953, EX.....**$20.00**

Michael Keaton, trailer, 'Beetlejuice,' 35mm.....**$5.00**

Mickey Rooney, ashtray, 7" dia, marked Sascha B (Brastoff) **$30.00**

Mickey Rooney, paint book, dated 1940, M..................$40.00

Monte Hale, lobby card, 11x14", 'Outcasts of the Trail,' 1949, EX....................$5.00

Myrna Loy, lobby card, 11x14", 'Cheaper by the Dozen,' 1950, VG....................$12.50

Olivia de Haviland, Hollywood magazine, 1941, February, VG....................$20.00

Our Gang, coloring book, Saalfield, 1938, M..............$40.00

Our Gang, pencil box, ca 1930s, M......................$35.00

Peggy Shannon, Hollywood magazine, 1933, February, w/King Kong movie ad, VG....................$25.00

Peter Lorre, mask, 9½x12", cardboard, 1930s, EX........$20.00

Peter Sellers, poster, 27x41", 'After the Fox,' 1966, EX..$15.00

Peter Sellers, poster, 27x41", 'Return of the Pink Panther,' 1975, VG....................$7.50

Piper Laurie, coloring book, dated 1953, M................$30.00

Planet of the Apes, wall plaque kit, 11x20x1½", Milton Bradley, 1967, M....................$32.50

Ray Milland, lobby card, 11x14", 'The River's Edge,' 1957, EX....................$15.00

Red Skelton, mask, 1950s, set of 3, M....................$55.00

Richard Burton, still photo, 'Alexander the Great,' 1956, EX....................$5.00

Richard Chamberlain, photo, 8x10", black & white, 1963..$7.50

Richard Harris & Vanessa Redgrave, record, 33⅓ rpm, 'Camelot'....................$5.00

Robert Stack, lobby card, 11x14", 'War Paint,' 1953, EX..$5.00

Robert Taylor, Motion Picture magazine, 1943, November, NM....................$35.00

Robert Young, lobby card, 11x14", 'The Half Breed,' 1952, VG....................$5.00

Rock Hudson, lobby card, 11x14", 'Bengal Brigade,' 1954, NM....................$27.50

Roger Moore, lobby card, 11x14", 'Moonraker,' set of 8..$125.00

Ronald Colman, souvenir program, 'Beau Geste,' 1926, 20-pages, VG....................$65.00

Ronald Reagan, lobby card, 11x14", 'Hong Kong,' 1951, VG....................$20.00

Rory Calhoun, lobby card, 11x14", 'Four Guns to the Border,' 1954, NM....................$10.00

Rudy Vallee, valentine, 6", ABC on front, 1920s, M.....$30.00

Sal Mineo, lobby card, 11x14", 'Dino,' 1957, EX..........$15.00

Sean Connery, poster, 27x41", 'Diamonds Are Forever,' 1971, VG....................$75.00

Spencer Tracy, still photo, 'Boom Town,' 1946, EX.......$8.00

Stan Laurel, bank, vinyl, marked Transogram, ca 1966, M on original card....................$65.00

Superman, poster, 11x14", 3-dimensional, full color, 1978....................$4.00

Sylvester Stallone, poster, 1-sheet, 'Rocky III,' 1982, EX...$10.00

Tab Hunter, lobby card, 11x14", 'Burning Hills,' 1956, EX....................$5.00

Tab Hunter, Movieland magazine, 1957, Dec, VG.........$7.50

Tim Holt, lobby card, 11x14", 'Saddle Legion,' 1951, EX...$7.50

Tim McIntire, press book, 'American Hot Wax,' 1978, EX.$6.50

Tommy Kelly, game, 'Peck's Bad Boy w/the Circus,' Milton Bradley, 1939, M....................$45.00

Tuesday Weld, Photoplay magazine, 1961, EX...........$10.00

Vincent Price, poster, 27x41", 'Return of the Fly,' 1959, G..$40.00

WC Fields, lobby card, 11x14", 'My Little Chickens,' 1940, G....................$260.00

WC Fields, figurine, 6½", cast aluminum, M...............$60.00

WC Fields, Stage magazine, 10x14", color photo cover, NM....................$25.00

Whoopie Goldberg, poster, 18x24", 'Color Purple'........$2.50

Will Rogers, press book, 'Ambassador Bill,' 1931, VG .$37.50

William Holden, lobby card, 11x14", 'Bridge Over the River Kwai,' 1958, VG....................$50.00

Woody Allen, poster, 27x41", 'Bananas,' 1971, NM.....$10.00

New Martinsville Glass

Located in a West Virginia town by the same name, the New Martinsville Glass Company was founded in 1901 and until it was purchased by Viking in 1944 produced quality tableware in various patterns and colors that collectors admire today. They also made a line of glass animals which Viking continued to produce until they closed in 1986. In 1987 the factory was bought by Mr. Kenneth Dalzell who reopened the company under the title Dalzell-Viking. He used the old molds to reissue his own line of animals, which he marked 'Dalzell' with an acid stamp. These are usually priced in the $50.00 to $60.00 range. Examples marked 'V' were made by Viking for another company, Mirror Images. They're valued at $15.00 to $35.00.

See also Glass Animals.

Basket, 8¼", Janice, cobalt or ruby..........................$110.00

Basket, 8¼", Janice, crystal..............................$55.00

Bonbon, Janice, crystal, handles, #4524................$11.00

Bookends, lady's head, crystal, pr.......................$195.00

Bookends, ship, crystal, pr...............................$125.00

Bottle, scent; Geneva, crystal, w/black stopper..........$30.00

Bowl, bonbon; 6", Radiance, ice blue or red............$15.00

Bowl, console; Prelude, crystal..........................$23.00

Bowl, relish; 7", Radiance, amber, divided................$12.00

Bowl, 10", Radiance, ice blue or red, crimped or flared .$32.50

Bowl, 6", Prelude, crystal, 3-footed....................$10.00

Butter dish, Radiance, amber............................$175.00

Butter dish, Radiance, ice blue or red....................$395.00

Cake salver, 10", Mardi Gras, crystal....................$65.00

Candlestick, 5", Prelude, crystal.......................$24.00

Candlesticks, 8", Radiance, amber, pr....................$35.00

Candy dish, Florentine, crystal, 3-part, #44/29..........$23.00

Comport, 6", Radiance, ice blue or red....................$27.50

Cordial, Moondrops, red....................................$15.00

Creamer, Radiance, amber..................................$12.00

Cruet, 4-oz, Prelude, crystal, w/stopper....................$38.00

Cup & saucer, Janice, light blue.........................$12.50

Cup & saucer, Prelude, crystal...........................$15.00

Dresser set, 5" bottle, triangular box with 5" long sides, triangular tray, jadite & black, 4-pc set..................$165.00

Goblet, cordial; 1-oz, Radiance, ice blue or red.........$35.00

Goblet, 4", ruby w/platinum trim, #1000....................$5.00

Goblet, 6", Mt Vernon, crystal, ruby golf ball stem........$7.50

Mayonnaise, Prelude, crystal, 3-pc..............$35.00

Mayonnaise, Radiance, crystal, 3-pc set..............**$35.00**
Mayonnaise, Radiance, ice blue or red, 3-pc **$50.00**
Old fashioned, 3¼", Prelude, crystal..............**$25.00**
Pitcher, 64-oz, Radiance, amber..............**$135.00**
Pitcher, 64-oz, Radiance, cobalt..............**$350.00**
Plate, sandwich; 14", Prelude, crystal **$42.00**
Plate, torte; Prelude, crystal..............**$55.00**
Plate, 8½", Janice, ruby..............**$20.00**
Punch cup, Radiance, ice blue..............**$12.00**
Relish, Flower Basket, crystal..............**$12.00**
Relish, 6", Janice, crystal, silver overlay, divided **$18.00**
Sherbet, Mt Vernon, ruby, golf ball stem..............**$8.00**
Sugar bowl, Radiance, ice blue or red..............**$19.00**
Tumbler, 4½", Oscar, red, footed..............**$10.00**
Tumbler, 4¾", Addie, black, footed..............**$10.00**
Tumbler, 9-oz, cobalt..............**$28.00**
Vanity set, two bottles, puff box & triangular tray, blue..**$115.00**

Newspapers

Papers that cover specific events, whether historical, regarding well-known political or entertainment figures, natural disasters of unusually large proportions, or catastropic events of any nature, are just the type that people tend to keep, and they're also the most collectible. Those that carry first-report accounts are more valuable than those with subsequent reporting. Other factors that bear on value are where the article appears (front page is best), how visual it is (are there photographs or a large headline), and whether it is from a small town or city paper.

An authentic copy of The New York Herald's April 15, 1865, 10 AM edition, reporting the assassination of Lincoln is rare and expensive, valued at about $2,000.00. There are thousands of reprints around today, so beware!

1927, June 13, 'Spirit of St Louis Crippled, Welcome Lindy' headline, EX color and graphics, New York Journal, complete, EX..............**$100.00**
1932, Dec 22, prohibition ends, many beer ads, Wisconsin News, complete, EX..............**$16.00**
1932, Mar 2, 'Lindbergh Baby Kidnapped From Bed' headline, large photo of parents on front page, complete, VG..**$10.00**

1932, May 3, Supreme Court turns down Capone's appeal, Los Angeles Times, VG..............**$5.00**
1932, Nov 7, Roosevelt battles for votes, Los Angeles Herald Express, complete, VG..............**$6.00**
1934, Oct 9, 'Fans Riot Wildly as Cards Win' headline, Wisconsin News, complete, EX..............**$20.00**
1935, Sept 10, Hewey Long killed, large photo of Long, Wisconsin News, complete, EX..............**$20.00**
1936, Dec 8, King & Mrs Simpson headline, Los Angeles Times, complete, EX..............**$5.00**
1937, May 7, Hindenburg explodes, photo of Hindenburg in flames, Wisconsin News, complete, EX..............**$40.00**
1938, July 18, story of Wrong Way Corrigan, Queen of Rumania dies, Los Angeles Evening News, incomplete, EX..............**$12.50**
1938, Oct 16, 'Link US Arms Recovery Plan' headline, Dionne quints story inside, Chicago Sunday Times, small folio, EX..............**$5.00**
1939, May 23, US submarine sinks off coast, Indianapolis News, complete, EX..............**$12.50**
1939, Sept 5, French attack Hitler WASS, British bomb Nazi warships, Boston Globe, complete, EX..............**$15.00**
1941, Dec 12, Japanese battleship being bombed, Russian & Nazi relations, Nashville Tennessean, front page only, EX..............**$3.00**
1941, Dec 18, 'Japs Hurled Back on Luzon' headline, map of war in Pacific, Nashville Banner, front page only, EX..............**$4.00**
1941, Dec 8, 'US Declares War; Manila Bombed; 1500 Dead at Oahu' headlines, Pasadena Star-News, complete, EX..............**$25.00**
1942, Aug 22, Brazil declares war on Axis, US sinks four Japanese vessels, Nashville Banner, front page only, VG..............**$3.50**
1942, Feb 28, sea battle w/Japanese, British raid on France, large headlines, Herald Express Extra, first section, EX..............**$5.00**
1942, July 14, 'Roosevelt Hints British May Sink Vichy's Fleet' headline, NY World Telegram, front page only, EX..............**$3.00**
1944, June 7, Allied forces show success at beginning of invasion, Los Angeles Times Extra, front page only, VG..............**$4.50**
1945, Apr 14, 'Truman, Military Chiefs Confer; All of US in Mourning Today' headline, San Francisco Examiner, 3-page, EX..............**$4.00**
1945, April 13, 'Pres Roosevelt Dies; Truman Sworn in as Chief' headline, San Jose Mercury Herald, front page only, EX..............**$6.00**
1945, Jan 30, news of Russian troops nearing Berlin, Call Bulletin, front page only, VG **$3.50**
1945, July 26, 'British Vote Churchill Out' headline, Churchill, Atlee, & Eden photos, Forfolk Ledger Dispatch, EX..............**$6.00**
1945, June 26, crowds cheer Truman, full-page photo, President's address, San Francisco Examiner, front page only, EX..............**$4.00**

1952, Feb 7, 'Queen Nears Home' headline, millions mourn King George VI, Los Angeles Examiner, complete, EX...$12.00

1952, July 26, 'Stevenson Accepts Nomination Draft' headline, Los Angeles Times, front page only, EX..........$5.00

1952, Nov 5, Eisenhower & Nixon election news, large Eisenhower photo on front page, Clarion Ledger, complete, EX $8.00

1953, Feb 3, 'Ike Ends Formosa Blockage, Asks To Scrap Secret Pacts' headline, Los Angeles Examiner, complete, VG...$4.50

1953, Jan 2, Rose Bowl parade & game news, Los Angeles Mirror, small folio, complete, EX $4.50

1953, Mar 6, 'Stalin Dies; Mystery Veils Successor' headline, Stalin photo, Los Angeles Times, complete, VG $7.00

1961, Jan 20, 'Kennedy 35th President' headline, Los Angeles Herald Express, front page only, EX.................$5.00

1962, Aug 6, 'Marilyn Monroe Dies' headline, large photo on front page, Los Angeles Times, 1st section, EX.....$25.00

1962, Feb 20, John Glenn makes first orbits around world, photos on front page, Roanoke World News, complete, EX...$12.00

1963, June 3, death of Pope John XXIII, large photo of Pope, Los Angeles Herald Examiner, front page only, EX...$5.00

1963, Nov 21, 'U-2 Spy Plane Crashes After Flight over Cuba' headline, Washington DC Evening Star, complete, EX $4.00

1963, Nov 23, 'Kennedy Assassinated' headline, motorcade pictured, Los Angeles Times, complete, EX $3.00

1963, Nov 25, 'Taps for a Martyr' headline, world leaders in Kennedy funeral procession photo, Herald Examiner, EX...$10.00

1963, Nov 26, 'Johnson Pushing Kennedy Program' headline, Washington Post, complete, EX.......................$4.00

1964, Apr 6, 'Gen MacArthur Succumbs at 84' headline, large photo, Washington Daily Chronicle, 10 pages, EX...$8.00

1964, Nov 4, 'LBJ Landslide!' headline, photo of LBJ w/Lady Bird, Los Angeles Times election extra, first section, NM...$8.00

1964, Oct 16, 'China Explodes A-Bomb' headline, Russian power change, British election, Tucson Citizen, complete, EX $6.50

1965, Jan 25, 'World Weeps for Churchill' headline, large Churchill photo, Tucson Citizen, complete, EX $7.50

1967, May 20, 'MIG Force Blasted & Syria Waits Signal To Attack Israel' headlines, Los Angeles Herald, front page, EX ..$3.00

1968, Apr 1, Johnson refuses renomination, front page picture of LBJ, Los Angeles Times, complete, EX........$7.00

1968, June 5, Robert Kennedy critically wounded, Herald Examiner, complete, EX $15.00

1968, Nov 4, Humphrey closing gap in election, Fullerton News Tribune, 2 sections, EX................................$4.00

1969, July 20, news of moon landing of Apollo 11 mission, Denver Post, full Sunday paper, EX $15.00

1969, Nov 15, 'On the Way to the Moon' headline, Apollo XII news, Los Angeles Times, EX $10.00

1971, June 1, 'Audie Murphy Dead in Crash' headline, The Register, complete, EX.................................$6.00

1971, Mar 5, Nixon requests support for Vietnam policies, Los Angeles Times, complete, EX $3.00

1972, May 22, 'Nixon in Moscow' headline, Los Angeles Examiner, complete, EX $6.00

1973, Jan 27, 'Peace Accord Signed' headline, Vietnam cease-fire begins, Long Beach Press Telegram, complete, EX $8.00

1974, Aug 9, 'It's President Ford' headline, Ford taking oath photo, Los Angeles Herald Examiner, complete, EX...$6.00

1974, Aug 9, 'Nixon Resigns' headline, large photo of Nixon & Ford, Orange County Register, 3 sections, EX ..$12.00

1979, June 12, death of John Wayne, many photos on front page, Los Angeles Times, complete, EX.................$8.00

1986, Jan 29, 'Shuttle Explodes' headline, Pasadena Star News, complete, EX.................................$8.00

1989, Aug 24, expulsion of Pete Rose from baseball, Giamatti photo on front page, Cincinnati Post, complete, M $8.00

Niloak Pottery

This company operated in the Little Rock area of Arkansas from the turn of the century until 1947 (when it was converted to a tile company which is still in existence). It was founded by Charles Hyten, whose partner was a former Rookwood potter, Arthur Dovey. It was originally known as the Hyten Pottery, renamed Eagle Pottery soon after that, and finally was incorporated in 1911 as the Niloak Pottery Company. Niloak (the backwards spelling of kaolin, a type of clay) is best known today for their Mission Ware line, characterized by swirled colors of natural and artificially dyed clay. Though other companies made swirled pottery, none were as successful as Hyten, who received a patent for his process in 1928. Except for a few rare examples, Mission Ware was glazed only on the inside.

Facing financial difficulties at the onset of the Depression, the company changed ownership and began to manufacture a more extensive line of molded wares, including figural planters, vases, jardineres, clocks, and some tile.

Several marks were used, all of which include the company name, and paper labels were used as well.

Bowl, 2½x7½", blue, scalloped rim $32.00
Bowl, 3½", Mission Ware, swirled colors, paper label .$50.00

Candlesticks, 8", Mission Ware, swirled colors, pr .$300.00

Creamer, 3½", light blue w/stylized flowers in relief...**$12.50**
Ewer, 10", pink & green, embossed wing & star decor .**$16.00**
Ewer, 7", rose, matt...**$20.00**
Ewer, 8¼", maroon w/green tint overglaze.................**$20.00**
Figurine, razorback hog, maroon, Arkansas emblem ..**$75.00**
Figurine, 2½", piglet, barrel shape **$21.00**
Flower frog, 1½x3½", Mission Ware, swirled colors, overall
    glaze...**$50.00**
Jug, 7", blue, glossy **$35.00**
Mug, 3½", pink, glossy...**$8.00**
Pitcher, 5", tan to ivory, bulbous **$10.00**
Pitcher, 7½", embossed flowers, pink, glossy **$32.00**
Pitcher, 8", Mission Ware, swirled colors, bulbous....**$155.00**

Planter, bear figure by open tub............................**$35.00**
Planter, camel figural...**$45.00**
Planter, swan figural **$18.00**
Planter, 3¾", white bunny figural **$35.00**
Planter, 5", white & orange pelican **$35.00**
Planter, 5½", kangaroo w/boxing gloves at front **$20.00**

Planter, 9" long, fish figural, blue...........................**$45.00**
Salt & pepper shakers, penguin form, original labels, pr ..**$35.00**
Tumbler, 4½", Mission Ware, swirled colors, slightly flared
    rim..**$40.00**
Vase, pink to blue flower & leaf, multiple openings...**$25.00**
Vase, 3½", Mission Ware, swirled colors, bulbous.......**$54.00**
Vase, 4½", Mission Ware, swirled dark brown & deep reds,
    barrel shape..**$65.00**
Vase, 5½", Mission Ware, swirled colors, pear
    shape..**$65.00**

Vase, 6½", chartreuse, ringed neck w/handles & melon
    base...**$24.00**

Nippon

In 1890, the McKinley Tariff Act was passed by congress, requiring that all items of foreign manufacture be marked in 'legible English' with the name of the country of origin. In compliance, items imported from Japan were marked 'Nippon,' the Japanese word for their homeland. For many years, this was acceptable. In 1921, however, the United States government reversed its position and instructed their custom agents to deny entry to imported items bearing only the Nippon mark, and in so doing forced the Japanese to add or substitute the English word 'Japan' in their trademarks.

This was an era of prosperity in our country, a time when even laboring families had money to spend on little niceties. The import business was booming. Japanese-made porcelains were much more inexpensive than similar items from Germany and Austria, and as a result, it was imported in vast quantities. It was sold at fairs, through gift stores, five and ten cent stores, Sears and Roebuck, and Montgomery Wards.

Today Nippon is an active area of buying and selling among collectors. Quality varies from piece to piece. The more desirable pieces are those with fine art work and lavish gold overlay. The term moriage used in the descriptions that follow refers to a decorating method where soft clay is piped on with a squeeze bag, similar to decorating a cake with icing. Items with animals in relief, children's dinnerware, unusual forms (such as hanging hatpin holders, for instance), and those with out-of-the-ordinary decorative themes are good to invest in.

If you'd like to learn more about this subject, we recommend *The Collector's Encyclopedia of Nippon Porcelain* (there are three volumes) by Joan Van Patten.

Ashtray, 5½", moriage dragon on tricornered shape, M-in-
    wreath mark..**$125.00**
Ashtray, 8", Indian chief in relief, w/match holder, M-in-
    Wreath mark...**$800.00**
Bowl, 7", pink flowers on green-shaded background, three
    ring handles, M-in-wreath mark.........................**$75.00**
Bowl, 7½", floral medallions, 8-scallop rim, blue Maple Leaf
    mark...**$85.00**
Bowl, 9¾", pink & yellow roses w/cobalt & gold scalloped
    rim, Maple Leaf mark..**$200.00**
Bowl, 11", reticulated rim, heavy gold trim, green
    mark...**$225.00**
Box, powder; 5¼", portrait on lid, gold overlay, Maple Leaf
    mark...**$200.00**
Box, trinket; 4", stork w/baby decoration, gold trim, green
    M-in-wreath mark **$150.00**
Candlestick, 8¼", moriage landscape, triangular shape, M-in-
    wreath mark..**$275.00**

Cheese & cracker dish, 8½", sampan scene in earth tones, Maple Leaf mark **$135.00**

Chocolate pot, 10½", moriage dragon, hand-painted mark, w/four cups & saucers...**$400.00**

Cookie jar, 7", moriage dragon on brown, footed, M-in-wreath mark **$325.00**

Cookie jar, 9½" dia, flowers on tan, cobalt rim & foot, unmarked **$200.00**

Cup, bouillon; 3¾", roses & gold swags on white, footed, marked **$20.00**

Cup & saucer, 2⅛", 5", child's size, doll face, Rising Sun mark **$65.00**

Egg cup, 2½", sampan scene in earth tones, marked....**$55.00**

Ewer, 10", multicolored flowers on black w/cobalt top, angle handle, Royal Kinran mark **$250.00**

Hair receiver, 4¾", flowers on white w/gold trim & feet, square shape, M-in-wreath mark **$75.00**

Humidor, 6", devil & cards on brown, M-in-wreath mark **$2,000.00**

Humidor, 6½", Egyptian figures & writing in relief, M-in-wreath mark **$1,300.00**

Humidor, 6½", sampan scenic in earth tones, M-in-wreath mark **$350.00**

Humidor, 8", gold pine cones, gold squirrel finial, Maple Leaf mark **$600.00**

Incense burner, 8", East Indian lady figural, marked **$300.00**

Mug, 5", Egyptian figures w/geometric border, gold M-in-wreath mark **$250.00**

Pitcher, 7¾", cobalt w/flowers & gold trim 435.00

Pitcher, 13¾", rose medallion on black w/gold beads, Maple Leaf mark...**$450.00**

Plaque, 10", portrait reserve w/much gold overlay, Maple Leaf mark...**$350.00**

Plaque, 11", Indian fishing from canoe, green M-in-wreath mark...**$400.00**

Punch bowl, 13", multicolored grapes on brown background w/much gold trim, footed, handles, M-in-wreath mark...**$900.00**

Snack set, cup on 8½" tray, white floral on light blue w/gold, marked **$60.00**

Tea set, child's size, blue & yellow butterflies on white, Rising Sun mark, 15-pc set.......................................**$250.00**

Teapot, 5¼", gold overlay swags on white, blue M-in-wreath mark, with matching creamer & sugar bowl.......**$150.00**

Vase, 13", ostrich reserve w/gold overlay on cobalt background, handles, M-in-wreath mark **$500.00**

Vase, 14", exotic bird reserves, geometric decoration, handles, M-in-wreath mark.......................................**$475.00**

Vase, 5½", windmill scene in earth tones on loving cup form, M-in-wreath mark **$100.00**

Vase, 6", camel rider in desert scene on urn form, angle handles, M-in-wreath mark **$850.00**

Vase, 6", grapes tapestry, bulbous form, blue Maple Leaf mark...**$550.00**

Vase, 6¾", pink roses on blue, classic form, gold handles, Maple Leaf mark **$65.00**

Vase, 7½", floral reserve band on cobalt w/gold overlay, M-in-wreath mark...**$475.00**

Vase, 8", man on camel w/much gold trim, integral handles, Maple Leaf mark **$400.00**

Vase, 9", Wedgwood-type bird on floral branch, handles, M-in-wreath mark...**$350.00**

Wine jug, 9½", English coaching scene reserve on green, Maple Leaf mark **$650.00**

Noritake

Before the government restricted the use of the Nippon mark in 1921, all porcelain exported from Japan (even that made by the Noritake Company) carried the Nippon mark. The company that became Noritake had its beginning in 1904, and over the years experienced several changes in name and organization. Until 1941 (at the onset of WWII) they continued to import large amounts of their products to America. (During the occupation, when chinaware production was resumed, all imports were marked 'Occupied Japan.')

Many variations will be found in their marks, but nearly all contain the Noritake name. If you'd like to learn more about this subject, we recommend *The Collector's Encyclopedia of Noritake* by Joan Van Patten.

Basket, 5½", red w/flower-decorated interior, gold handle, M-in-wreath mark **$125.00**

Basket, 5¾", two birds on perch on yellow, tan interior, gold handle & trim, M-in-wreath mark.................**$80.00**

Basket, 7½" dia, nuts molded in relief, silver handle, green mark...$150.00

Bowl, 6½", house in snow scene, five lobes, three handles, red M-in-wreath mark **$50.00**

Box, powder; 3¾", river scene on lid, Komaru mark ..**$50.00**

Cake plate, 11", multicolored flowers in center medallion & along rim, gold handles, red M-in-wreath mark ...**$40.00**

Chamberstick, 4¾" underplate, pink rose in blue band on white, gold trim, green M-in-wreath mark **$125.00**

Chamberstick, 6½", Egyptian band on orange lustre, green M-in-wreath mark, pr...**$155.00**

Chocolate set, 8¾" pot, 2¾" cups, exotic bird on silver lustre, orange lustre interior, M-in-wreath mark, 13-pc..**$250.00**

Compote, 7x10", gold rose panels & multicolored flowers on blue, marked **$225.00**

Creamer, 5¾", exotic flowers on white, orange lustre at rim & foot, gold handle, red M-in-wreath mark **$35.00**

Demitasse set, 12" tray, 7" pot, large flowers on white, orange lustre at top & along rims, M-in-wreath mark, 16-pc...**$285.00**

Egg cup, 3½", river scene w/small windmill in earth tones, green M-in-wreath mark.....................................**$30.00**

Flower holder, 4¾", tropical bird figural on base, green M-in-wreath mark...**$195.00**

Humidor, 6¾", silhouette-style figures, green M-in-wreath mark..**$375.00**

Lemon dish, 6½" long, flowering branch on tan lustre, red M-in-wreath mark **$30.00**

Match holder, 3½", horses on tan background, bell form, M-in-wreath mark..**$110.00**

Mustard jar, 2½", river scenic in earth tones, green M-in-wreath mark **$35.00**

Nut cup, individual size, pastel flower on white, 3-footed, green M-in-wreath mark......................................**$12.00**

Plaque, 10½" dia, embossed scene of forest w/elk, green mark...$500.00

Plate, luncheon; 7½", exotic flowers on dark blue, green M-in-wreath mark...**$22.50**

Punch bowl, 13", flowers inside & on rim, turquoise w/gold, M-in-wreath mark, plus eight cups.....................**$800.00**

Tea caddy, 3¾", oriental scene on orange lustre, red M-in-wreath mark **$220.00**

Teapot, 6", exotic flowers on cobalt w/gold, M-in-wreath mark, plus creamer & sugar bowl **$125.00**

Tray, 11" long, Deco-style fruit band, rectangular shape w/gold handles, red M-in-wreath mark................**$90.00**

Vase, 6½", wide floral band on green, footed fan form, M-in-wreath mark **$90.00**

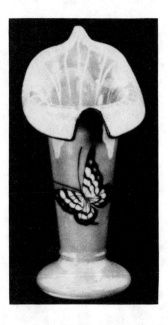

Vase, 6¾", jack-in-the-pulpit shape w/butterfly on front, red mark w/M in center $125.00

Vase, 7¼", Deco-style flowers in four reserves, small gold integral handles, green M-in-wreath mark **$265.00**

Vase, 8¾", pastoral scene w/bridge in earth tones, gourd shape, green M-in-wreath mark **$90.00**

Vase, 9½", blue & white jasper, angle handles, Komaru mark..**$350.00**

North Dakota School of Mines

The University of North Dakota's School of Mines' professor Earle J. Babcock had an interest in the state's natural resources. Before the turn of the century, he had discovered clay deposits suitable for pottery production. He shipped some of this clay to a company in the east who used it to make vases for him. At first they decorated the vases as well, but eventually some were shipped back to the University to be decorated by the students. By 1909 the work had progressed to where the students themselves were making tile, brick, and other utilitarian items. Then in 1901, a ceramic department was established under the direction of Margaret Kelly Cable. Under her supervision, the students learned to produce fine art ware, usually decorated with animals, birds, flowers, and other subjects representative of North Dakota. Until she retired in 1949, the pottery the students made was distributed throughout the state in fine gift stores and souvenir shops. Much of the ware was marked with their official seal — 'Made at School of Mines, N.D. Clay, University of North Dakota, Grand Forks, N.D.,' and most are signed by the artist. Though some pieces are simply thrown and glazed, the more desirable examples are hand decorated.

Ashtray, Flossie the Fish, signed M Cable **$165.00**
Bowl, 4½x5½", Indian decoration, signed by artist ...**$395.00**
Bowl, 4x7", green w/brown band, carved leaf frieze, signed Tobiason **$300.00**
Bowl, 5½", brown gloss, signed Julia Mattson **$70.00**
Bowl, 7", sky blue, signed Julia Mattson **$115.00**
Bowl base, 2x4", blue gloss w/vertical ribs, signed by artist **$150.00**
Coaster, 3½" dia, fawn outlined in buff clay on light blue **$95.00**
Paperweight, Rebecca, green gloss, signed EL Harriman.**$70.00**
Pitcher, 6", florals, signed Huck **$195.00**

Trivet, 5½", stylized flower, green & blue, signed Julia Mattson $350.00
Trivet, 6½", 3-color w/embossed flowers **$225.00**
Vase, 3½", green matt, signed Huck **$100.00**
Vase, 4", green to ivory, signed Hall, 1942 ....**$125.00**
Vase, 4", Pasque Flower, carved & titled on red-brown, signed C Huck/#53 ....**$225.00**
Vase, 4½", crazed chrome yellow, signed FLH-463 ...**$140.00**
Vase, 4¼x5", teal gloss, pear shape **$195.00**
Vase, 5", green, ribbed, hand thrown **$98.00**
Vase, 5x4", turquoise to aqua flambe, signed Fretz...**$165.00**
Vase, 7", cobalt, signed Julia Mattson **$99.00**

Novelty Clocks

The largest producers of these small clocks were Lux, Keebler, Westclox, and Columbia Time. Some had moving

parts, others a small pendulette. They were made of wood, china, Syroco (a pressed wood product), and eventually plastic. Until the late 1940s when electric-powered novelties were made by the Mastercrofter Company, they were all wind-up. The last Lux clocks were made in the mid-1950s.

Beer barrel drinker, non-animated, pendulette **$225.00**
Bell, mechanical w/digital readout, marked Lux, VG..**$50.00**
Black shoeshine boy, marked Lux.............................**$250.00**
Bluebird, animated, pendulette...................................**$30.00**
Boy & girl on swing, animated, Mastercrofter..............**$50.00**
Boy Scout, non-animated, pendulette **$300.00**
Dog w/ball on nose, ball rolls to top of nose, marked General Electric...**$160.00**
Enchanted Forest, animated, pendulette **$125.00**
Hunting Scene, non-animated, pendulette **$85.00**
Lovebirds, animated, pendulette...............................**$125.00**
Rudolph, animated, pendulette.................................**$115.00**
Sailor, animated, pendulette.....................................**$125.00**

Schmoo, pendulette, marked Lux......................$150.00
Small Dove, non-animated, pendulette **$35.00**
US Capitol, non-animated, pendulette.......................**$300.00**
Waterfall, animated, marked Mastercrofter.................**$35.00**
Woody Woodpecker, animated, pendulette **$225.00**

Occupied Japan Collectibles

Some items produced in Japan during the period from the end of WWII until the occupation ended in 1952 were marked Occupied Japan. No doubt much of the ware from this era was marked simply Japan, since obviously the 'Occupied' term caused considerable resentment among the Japanese people, and they were understandably reluctant to use the mark. So even though you may find identical items marked simply Japan or Made in Japan, only those with the more limited Occupied Japan mark are evaluated here.

Assume that the items described below are ceramic unless another material is mentioned. For more information, we recommend *The Collector's Encyclopedia of Occupied Japan* (there are three in the series) by Gene Florence.

Ash tray, metal w/emblem & Statue of Liberty, NY City souvenir..$10.00
Ash tray, 2½", nude Black baby by clothesline...........$26.00
Ash tray, 2⅝", Wedgwood type, white Indian on blue..$8.00
Atomizer, blue glass, embossed diamond pattern.......$20.00
Bookends, Dutch boy & girl, bright paint, red mark, pr..$35.00
Bookends, 4", penguins, black, blue, & orange on white, pr..$35.00
Bottle, scent; 3½", embossed pressed glass.................$20.00
Bowl, 8⅞", Livonia (Dogwood), Mieto Norleans China.$8.00
Box, 9x6", floral medallion on lacquerware, Maruni...$60.00
Bracelet, gold expansion style w/blue stones, emblem mark..$20.00
Brooch & earrings, carved florals, celluloid.....................$25.00
Candle holder, 4", Colonial lady between two holders.$20.00
Candy dish, 5½x5½", floral handle, square w/round corners..$10.00
Cigarette lighter, elephant w/howdah, gold-painted metal, emblem mark..$17.00
Cigarette lighter, 1¼x¾", alligator on metal.................$13.00

Covered jar, 7", silvered metal w/glass liner........$22.50
Cup & saucer, demitasse; tulips on red.......................$12.50
Cup & saucer, floral, pink on black, scalloped rim.....$15.00
Cup & saucer, floral decoration on white w/gold trim, ornate handle, red mark.......................................$15.00
Cup & saucer, floral medallions on blue, yellow interior, Saji China..$17.50
Cup & saucer, green w/ornate gold rim.......................$10.00
Cup & saucer, pink roses on white, scalloped rim, Ucagco..$12.00
Doll, 2¾", Kewpie, celluloid.......................................$20.00
Doll, 4½", feather dancer, celluloid, emblem mark.....$15.00
Doll, 7", baby boy, celluloid, crochet clothes.............$35.00
Doll, 8⅝", Dutch girl w/instrument, celluloid.............$45.00

Egg cup, 3¾x2½", Blue Willow...................................$15.00
Fan, 8¾" wooden spine, floral decoration on blue paper..$15.00
Figurine, 10", lady wears aqua hat & scarf.................$20.00
Figurine, 10½", lady, feathers in hair, fancy gown, red mark..$45.00
Figurine, 2½", man w/hands in pockets, bisque...........$7.00
Figurine, 2¼", lady bug w/bat.....................................$8.00
Figurine, 2¾", boy seated on stump playing horn, chick on ground..$7.00
Figurine, 3", angel w/horn sits by vase.......................$10.00
Figurine, 3", pups in basket.......................................$10.00
Figurine, 3½", dog w/hat & pipe, red mark.................$12.50
Figurine, 3½", pixie playing drum & cymbals.............$12.00
Figurine, 3¼", baseball player w/catcher's mitt...........$17.00
Figurine, 3¼", dancing lady in orange gown.................$8.00
Figurine, 3¼", Dutch girl, blue & white.......................$8.00
Figurine, 4", accordion player, red hat, blue pants, blue mark..$12.50
Figurine, 4", boy & girl on fence, pr.........................$20.00
Figurine, 4", bride & groom, bisque...........................$20.00
Figurine, 4", couple at piano, red mark.......................$12.50
Figurine, 4", Oriental coolie, red hat, shoulder yoke..$12.00
Figurine, 4", Oriental girl kneels in green kimono, holds fan..$12.00
Figurine, 4", Oriental religious symbol, brown & ivory.$6.50
Figurine, 4½", Dutch girl, Delft style.........................$20.00
Figurine, 4½x4", elf on snail.....................................$25.00
Figurine, 4½x5½", spaniel, sitting, black & white........$15.00
Figurine, 4⅛", girl w/dog, red mark...........................$10.00
Figurine, 4¾", Aborigine man & lady, comic, red mark, pr..$45.00
Figurine, 4⅝", boy w/saxophone, blue pants & red hair.$10.00
Figurine, 5", Art Nouveau-style lady holds dress wide, red mark..$17.50
Figurine, 5", cowboy w/gun belt, shotgun at side.......$15.00

Figurine, 5", dancing girl...................................$14.00

Figurine, 5", Oriental lady w/fan, green trousers.........**$15.00**
Figurine, 5", seaman, Delft style **$20.00**
Figurine, 5½", girl hiker, backpack & umbrella **$18.00**
Figurine, 5⅜", dancer, ruffled dress, Delft style **$20.00**
Figurine, 6", Black fiddler, blue hat & red pants **$50.00**
Figurine, 6", lady w/lute, seated, bisque **$22.00**
Figurine, 6½", cowboy & cowgirl, bisque, pr..............**$36.00**
Figurine, 6¼", Oriental lady dressed in white..............**$15.00**
Figurine, 7", lady playing violin, applied flower on base.**$25.00**
Figurine, 7", Mexican w/guitar, red & white sombrero ..**$25.00**
Figurine, 7½", Balinese boy & girl dancers, blue mark,
  pr **$70.00**
Figurine, 7½", Oriental figure w/hands folded & head
  bowed, Moriyama **$15.00**
Figurine, 8", Colonial farmer, arms full of grapes........**$25.00**
Figurine, 8", Colonial lady, brown & white, red mark ..**$37.50**
Fishbowl decoration, 4⅜", mermaid reclining, green tail,
  bisque **$20.00**
Incense burner, elephant, howdah on back forms lid, gold
  trim, Ucagco **$32.00**
Jar, powder; 2¾", windmill scene on heart form.........**$15.00**
Lamp, 10" (to socket top), Colonial couple figural, pink &
  purple shade **$30.00**
Lamp, 10" (to socket top), lady's head figural, 4-footed.**$50.00**
Lamp, 7⅛" (to socket top), Colonial man & lady in blue &
  yellow, pr **$70.00**
Leaf dish, 2½", floral decoration on white w/gold trim, blue
  mark **$4.00**
Match holder, 3⅜", bald fat man w/fly on upper lip...**$25.00**
Miniature, 1¾", water can, hand-painted floral decora-
  tion **$3.00**
Miniature, 2", coffeepot, hand-painted floral decoration on
  white w/gold trim **$5.00**

Mug, barrel form w/comical boy as handle..........$22.50
Mug, Santa figural, cap forms handle, red mark..........**$32.00**
Pin, bird in flight, blue wings & tail, celluloid, incised
  mark...**$12.50**
Planter, 2½x5¼", kitten on slipper................................**$12.50**
Planter, 3½", wheelbarrow filled w/flowers.................**$10.00**
Planter, 3½x3½", bird at birdhouse, thatched roof **$12.00**
Planter, 4", dog figural, blue...**$5.00**
Planter, 4¼", Mexican w/guitar beside basket vase.....**$16.00**
Planter, 4⅜x5", shoe-shaped house, bird on toe **$10.00**
Planter, 4x2½x3", clown couple, log fence **$14.00**
Planter, 5¼", baby buggy...**$15.00**

Planter, 5¼x7½", couple w/rabbits, bisque, Paulux ..**$150.00**
Planter, 5⅛", Oriental man w/big hat & white suit........**$8.00**
Planter, 6¾x5", duck w/top hat **$15.00**
Plaque, 7½", Dutch boy figural, chalkware, Yomake..**$22.00**
Plate, banana & plums center, signed Parry **$20.00**
Plate, 5", ladies, lacy rim **$20.00**
Plate, 8¼", Hibiscus, Rosetti, Chicago USA.................**$20.00**
Powder box, w/gold emblem, Ucagco China **$90.00**
Salt & pepper shakers, bride & groom, pr **$20.00**
Salt & pepper shakers, metal w/embossed florals, pr.**$15.00**
Salt & pepper shakers, penguin, shiny metal, embossed
  mark, pr **$20.00**
Salt & pepper shakers, pig, black & gray spotted, pr..**$15.00**
Salt & pepper shakers, 2⅝x4", apples in basket, pr **$15.00**
Salt & pepper shakers, 3", Indian head bust, pr **$16.00**
Salt cellar, 1¾x1¾", swan figural..................................**$7.00**
Shelf, corner; 13¾", black lacquerware, 2-tier, folds flat.**$50.00**
Shelf, corner; 9¼", lacquerware, folds flat.................**$40.00**
Shelf sitter, 4½", musician girl, unglazed pottery, pr...**$20.00**
Shelf sitter, 5", ballerina, net tutu...............................**$24.00**
Shelf sitter, 6⅛", ballerina, pink costume, right hand on
  head..**$25.00**

Shelf sitters, Oriental boy & girl, pr $25.00
Sugar bowl, corn figural, yellow & green, w/lid **$12.50**
Sugar bowl, 4½", cottage form, w/lid...........................**$16.00**
Tea set, floral on white w/orange lustre, 15-pc...........**$95.00**
Tea set, floral pattern, 11-pc, miniature......................**$40.00**
Toby mug, 2", devil bust **$25.00**
Toy, dog, celluloid, w/squeaker **$20.00**
Tray, 6x2⅛", multicolor plaid **$5.00**
Tumbler, 3", tomato figural, Maruhon Ware **$10.00**
Vase, cornucopia; 2½", tea roses, red on white w/gold.**$7.00**
Vase, 2½", clown child beside egg figural...................**$10.00**
Vase, 2¾", florals on green, maroon trim **$7.00**
Vase, 3¾", floral on brown, ewer form.........................**$7.50**
Wall pocket, iris figural, blue, green, & white **$12.50**
Water lily, celluloid, M in box....................................**$15.00**

Old MacDonald's Farm

This is a wonderful line of novelty kitchenware items
fashioned as the family and the animals that live on Old
MacDonald's Farm. It's been popular with collectors for

quite some time, and over the past year or so, prices have become astronomical. But I've found shakers at a garage sale and spice jars that were way underpriced at a small flea market, and at these prices, just one good find can make your day.

These things were made by the Regal China Company, who also made some of the Little Red Riding Hood items that are so collectible, as well as figural cookie jars, 'hugger' salt and pepper shakers, and decanters. The Roerig's devote a chapter to Regal in their book _The Collector's Encyclopedia of Cookie Jars_ and, in fact, show the entire Old MacDonald's Farm line.

Butter dish, cow, marked Pat Pending 388...............**$200.00**
Canister, 'Coffee' on barrel shape w/farmer boy in yellow hat figural lid, marked Pat Pending 389, small ...**$225.00**
Canister, 'Cookie' on barrel shape w/Mrs MacDonald figural lid, marked Pat Pending 387, large.....................**$275.00**
Canister, 'Flour' on barrel shape w/horse figural lid, marked Pat Pending 389, small **$225.00**
Canister, 'Peanuts' on barrel shape, Old MacDonald in yellow hat figural lid, marked Pat Pending 387, large **$275.00**
Canister, 'Popcorn' on barrel shape, Old MacDonald figural lid, marked Pat Pending 387, large.....................**$275.00**
Canister, 'Salt' on barrel shape w/Old MacDonald figural lid, marked Pat Pending 389, small............................**$225.00**
Canister, 'Sugar' on barrel shape, girl w/braided hair lid, marked Pat Pending 389, small............................**$225.00**
Canister, 'Tea' on barrel shape, farmer boy in straw hat figural lid, marked Pat Pending 389, small................**$225.00**
Canister, 'Tid-Bit' on barrel shape w/Mrs MacDonald figural lid, marked Pat Pending 387, large.....................**$275.00**
Canister, Cereal, barrel shape w/turkey wearing top hat figural lid, marked Pat Pending 389, small..............**$225.00**
Cookie jar, barn figural, marked Pat Pending 381.....**$250.00**

Creamer, rooster figural, Pat Pending 383.............$100.00
Grease jar, barrel shape, pig figural lid, marked Pat Pending 386 ....**$180.00**
Jar, 'Allspice' on barrel shape, turkey figural lid, marked Pat Pending 390 ....**$100.00**
Jar, 'Cinnamon' on barrel shape, Mrs MacDonald figural lid, marked Pat Pending 390 ....**$100.00**
Jar, 'Cloves' on barrel shape, farmer boy figural lid, marked Pat Pending 390 ....**$100.00**

Jar, 'Nutmeg' on barrel shape, Old MacDonald figural lid, marked Pat Pending 390 ....**$100.00**
Jar, 'Pepper' on barrel shape, horse figural lid, marked Pat Pending 390 ....**$100.00**
Jar, 'Spice' on barrel shape, farmer girl figural lid, marked Pat Pending 390 ....**$100.00**
Pitcher, milk; cream w/embossed cow, red handle & spout, marked Pat Pending 380 ....**$350.00**
Salt & pepper shakers, churn shape w/gold tops, marked Pat Pending 385, pr...**$55.00**
Salt & pepper shakers, feed sack shape w/sheep on front, marked Pat Pending 384, pr...............................**$165.00**
Sugar bowl, hen on nest figural, handled, marked Pat Pending 382 (illustrated) $100.00

Teapot, duck figural, marked Pat Pending 391...$250.00

Olympic Memorabilia

The 1874 Los Angeles Olympiad had a very positive effect on collectors of Olympic material. Many corporate sponsors issued commemorative pins, singly and in sets, causing a renewed interest in the older pins as well as all other types of official souvenirs that have been issued through the years since the 1896 games.

Autograph, Jim Thorpe or Jesse Owens, minimum value, each **$100.00**
Doll, Dorothy Hamill, w/skating rink, Ideal, 1977, in original box, NM...**$75.00**
Official program, opening or closing ceremony, Los Angeles, 1984, each..**$5.00**
Pin-back button, 2" dia, 'Mockba 80' w/logo, Russian, 1980, NM..**$5.00**
Pin-back button, 2" dia, 1984 Olympics, M on card **$1.50**

Pin-back button, , 2" dia, 3rd Pan American Games, torch on gold metallic **$2.50**

Playing cards, Bicycle, red, white, & blue symbols for 23rd Olympiad in Los Angeles, 1984, M in box **$15.00**

Souvenir, Los Angeles, not official issue, minimum value.**$5.00**

Telephone, 9" sq, desk top style w/Los Angeles logo & Olympic intersecting circles on top **$40.00**

Ticket stub, 2x3", Los Angeles, Xth Olympiad, Track & Field event, 1932 ....**$22.50**

Toy, Olympic Eagle, stuffed plush, Applause, 1980, M.**$25.00**

Trade card, M&Ms, Los Angeles, 1984, minimum value..**$10.00**

Tumbler, 5⅜", 'The Taste of Victory' w/Coca-Cola logo & 'Copyright 1980 LA Olympics Commission' on clear glass, 1981 ....**$6.00**

Wristwatch, official symbols for 1984 Los Angeles games, digital w/stop watch feature, M on marked card..**$25.00**

Opalescent Glass

Opalescent glass is press molded in many patterns and colors, but the characteristic common to all of it is its white (or opalescent) rims and patterns, developed through the application of a strong acid to those areas. It was made early in the century by many American glasshouses, and it isn't at all uncommon to find a piece from time to time at estate sales, flea markets, or even garage sales, for that matter. Colors are more valuable than clear, and examples of major patterns are usually worth more than those with few or no matching pieces.

If you'd like to learn more about the subject, we recommend *The Standard Opalescent Glass Price Guide* by Bill Edwards.

Alaska, bowl, master; blue **$160.00**

Alaska, pitcher, blue **$385.00**

Alaska, tumbler, emerald...**$70.00**

Arabian Nights, tumbler, vaseline **$67.00**

Argonaut, salt & pepper shakers, white, pr **$70.00**

Argonaut Shell, butter dish, white **$235.00**

Ascot (English), bowl, blue **$50.00**

Astro, bowl, 8", green..**$45.00**

Autumn Leaves, bowl, banana; white..........................**$30.00**

Autumn Leaves, bowl, blue..**$40.00**

Barbells, bowl, white...**$26.00**

Beaded Cable, bowl, vaseline, footed **$35.00**

Beaded Drapes, bowl, banana; white, footed............**$34.00**

Beaded Fan, bowl, blue, footed...................................**$37.00**

Beaded Fleur-de-lis, compote, blue or green, various tops **$45.00**

Beaded Ovals in Sand, creamer, green **$70.00**

Beaded Ovals in Sand, toothpick holder, blue..........**$185.00**

Beaded Ovals in Sand, tumbler, blue..........................**$80.00**

Beads & Bark, vase, green, footed...............................**$55.00**

Beatty Rib, bowl, master; blue **$40.00**

Beatty Rib, butter dish, blue......................................**$180.00**

Beatty Rib, match holder, white...................................**$30.00**

Beatty Rib, mustard jar, white....................................**$100.00**

Beatty Rib, pitcher, white...**$125.00**

Beatty Swirl, celery vase, blue **$75.00**

Beatty Swirl, spooner, white **$50.00**

Beatty Swirl, tumbler, blue or white **$30.00**

Berry Patch, nappy, green, dome base **$40.00**

Blown Drape, bottle, barber; blue..............................**$110.00**

Blown Drape, pitcher, white.......................................**$200.00**

Blown Twist, sugar shaker, vaseline............................**$80.00**

Brideshead (English), butter dish, blue **$75.00**

Brideshead (English), creamer, blue............................**$57.00**

Bullseye, bowl, cranberry...**$45.00**

Button Panels, bowl, vaseline **$45.00**

Buttons & Braids, bowl, white **$35.00**

Calyx, vase, blue..**$55.00**

Carousel, green, bowl...**$45.00**

Cashews, bowl, blue or green **$40.00**

Chippendale (English), compote, canary **$60.00**

Christmas Pearls, cruet, green....................................**$250.00**

Christmas Snowflake, tumbler, cranberry...................**$100.00**

Chrysanthemum Base Swirl, butter dish, white **$270.00**

Chrysanthemum Base Swirl, creamer, blue..................**$80.00**

Chrysanthemum Base Swirl, toothpick holder, white..**$65.00**

Circle Scroll, compote, jelly; green **$135.00**

Circle Scroll, creamer, blue **$65.00**

Circle Scroll, creamer, white **$25.00**

Circle Scroll, tumbler, green **$85.00**

Coin Spot, bowl, master; green....................................**$40.00**

Coin Spot, compote, white **$35.00**

Coin Spot, toothpick holder, canary..........................**$225.00**

Coin Spot, tumbler, rubena **$60.00**

Colonial Stairsteps, creamer, blue...............................**$90.00**

Colonial Stairsteps, sugar bowl, blue..........................**$90.00**

Consolidated Crisscross, bowl, sauce; cranberry **$55.00**

Consolidated Crisscross, finger bowl, white...............**$80.00**

Consolidated Crisscross, tumbler, white......................**$90.00**

Contessa (English), basket, amber, handled **$65.00**

Coral, bowl, vaseline or canary...................................**$35.00**

Cornucopia, basket, blue, handled..............................**$50.00**

Daffodils, pitcher, cranberry......................................**$280.00**

Dahlia Twist, vase, green **$40.00**

Daisy & Fern, bowl, sauce; green.................................**$35.00**

Daisy & Fern, mustard pot, blue..................................**$85.00**

Daisy & Fern, spooner, green **$70.00**

Daisy & Fern, sugar bowl, white **$65.00**

Daisy in Crisscross, tumbler, blue................................**$55.00**

Daisy May (Leaf Rays), bonbon, blue or green **$30.00**

Desert Garden, bowl, green..**$30.00**

Diamond Spearhead, compote, jelly; blue **$95.00**

Diamond Spearhead, goblet, cobalt **$110.00**

Diamond Spearhead, sugar bowl, white **$110.00**

Diamond Weave, tumbler, cranberry **$30.00**

Diamonds, vase, 6", white, decorated **$25.00**

Dolly Madison, bowl, master; white.............................**$40.00**

Dolly Madison, creamer, green **$90.00**

Dolly Madison, tumbler, blue.......................................**$75.00**

Dolphins, bowl, footed, blue..**$75.00**

Double Greek Key, creamer, blue.................................**$70.00**

Double Greek Key, salt & pepper shakers, white, pr.**$150.00**

Double Greek Key, sugar bowl, white.........................**$130.00**

Double Greek Key, tumbler, white.................$40.00
Drapery, bowl, sauce; white $25.00
Drapery, creamer, blue................................$65.00
Drapery, tumbler, blue................................$35.00
Drapery, tumbler, white...............................$18.00
Duchess (English), butter dish, white...........$130.00
Duchess (English), cruet, blue $180.00
Duchess (English), pitcher, vaseline or canary..........$150.00
Everglades, salt & pepper shakers, blue, pr.............$230.00
Everglades, sugar bowl, white $100.00
Everglades, tumbler, vaseline, canary, or blue............$70.00
Fan, bowl, master; white $38.00
Fan, gravy boat, blue.................................$40.00
Fan, tumbler, green...................................$27.00
Fern, pitcher, white, various styles $160.00
Fern, spooner, cranberry..........................$125.00
Fern, sugar bowl, cranberry........................$195.00
Fern, vase, celery; blue..............................$100.00
Flora, bowl, sauce; vaseline or canary $35.00
Flora, pitcher, vaseline or canary..................$460.00
Flora, sugar bowl, blue.............................$120.00
Flora, toothpick holder, white $240.00
Fluted Scrolls, creamer, vaseline, canary, or blue........$60.00
Fluted Scrolls, puff box, blue.......................$55.00
Fluted Scrolls, sugar bowl, white...................$80.00
Frosted Leaf & Basket Weave, spooner, blue $130.00
Hobnail (Hobbs), creamer, blue or white.................$100.00
Hobnail (Hobbs), finger bowl, cranberry...............$90.00
Hobnail (Hobbs), tumbler, vaseline, canary, or blue ..$70.00
Hobnail (Northwood), bowl, master; white................$50.00
Hobnail (Northwood), pitcher, white.................$90.00
Hobnail (Northwood), sugar bowl, white................$95.00
Hobnail in Square (Vesta), salt & pepper shakers, white, pr................$85.00
Hobnail in Square (Vesta), sugar bowl, white..........$120.00
Hobnail in Square (Vesta), tumbler, white.............$30.00
Honeycomb & Clover, bowl, master; white................$40.00
Honeycomb & Clover, butter dish, green $180.00
Honeycomb & Clover, tumbler, green $75.00
Idyll, creamer, white.................................$38.00
Idyll, pitcher, blue $150.00
Idyll, sugar bowl, green $160.00
Idyll, tray, green....................................$85.00
Inside Ribbing, bowl, master; white $35.00
Inside Ribbing, spooner, blue......................$50.00
Inside Ribbing, tray, vaseline, canary, or blue.............$45.00
Intaglio, creamer, blue...............................$60.00
Intaglio, cruet, vaseline or canary..................$285.00
Intaglio, cruet, white................................$125.00
Intaglio, tumbler, blue..............................$100.00
Intaglio, tumbler, white..............................$50.00
Inverted Fan & Feather, bowl, sauce; blue $45.00
Inverted Fan & Feather, tumbler, blue $85.00
Iris w/Meander, pickle dish, vaseline, or blue.............$75.00
Iris w/Meander, sugar bowl, green..................$125.00
Iris w/Meander, toothpick holder, vaseline or canary.$80.00
Jackson, bowl, 7x7½", vaseline, footed $40.00
Jackson, creamer, blue $70.00

Jackson, epergne, small, white $82.00
Jackson, powder jar, vaseline or canary................$50.00
Jackson, tumbler, white..............................$60.00
Jewel & Fan, bowl, banana; green $110.00
Jewel & Flower, creamer, vaseline or canary............$150.00
Jewel & Flower, novelty bowl, vaseline, canary, or blue...............$35.00
Jewel & Flower, sugar bowl, blue $190.00
Jewelled Heart, compote, green $120.00
Jewelled Heart, creamer, blue or green $110.00

Jewelled Heart, novelty bowl, green $30.00
Jewelled Heart, plate, small, green $45.00
Jewelled Heart, tumbler, green $55.00
Leaf Mold, bowl, master; cranberry $120.00
Leaf Mold, bowl, sauce; cranberry..................$40.00
Leaf Mold, creamer, cranberry $110.00
Leaf Mold, pitcher, cranberry......................$495.00
Lustre Flute, creamer, white........................$55.00
Lustre Flute, custard cup, white....................$16.00
Lustre Flute, tumbler, blue..........................$65.00
Northern Star, bowl, green..........................$55.00
Northwood Block, vase, celery; blue or green $50.00
Open O's, novelty bowl, vaseline or canary................$38.00
Over-All Hob, creamer, white........................$40.00
Over-All Hob, finger bowl, vaseline or canary $40.00
Over-All Hob, tumbler, blue.........................$50.00
Palm Beach, bowl, master; blue $70.00
Palm Beach, creamer, vaseline or canary................$120.00
Palm Beach, pitcher, blue $385.00
Palm Beach, plate, 8", vaseline or canary, rare.........$375.00
Panelled Holly, novelty bowl, blue $45.00
Panelled Holly, salt & pepper shakers, white, pr $80.00
Panelled Holly, spooner, blue $125.00
Panelled Holly, tumbler, white $45.00
Panelled Sprig, toothpick holder, white $70.00
Picadilly (English), basket, small, green $60.00
Plain Jane, nappy, blue, footed....................$38.00
Poinsettia, bowl, fruit; green $65.00
Poinsettia, pitcher, white...........................$120.00

Polka Dot, salt & pepper shakers, blue, pr $60.00
Polka Dot, syrup, white $95.00
Prince William (English), sugar bowl, blue, open $55.00
Prince William (English), tumbler, vaseline or canary. $28.00
Princess Diana (English), bowl, salad; blue $40.00
Princess Diana (English), butter dish, vaseline or canary $85.00
Princess Diana (English), plate, blue, crimped $40.00
Princess Diana (English), water tray, vaseline, canary, or blue. $40.00
Regal, cruet, white $295.00
Regal, pitcher, green $285.00
Regal, vase, celery; blue $165.00
Reverse Drapery, plate, green $36.00
Reverse Swirl, bowl, master; cranberry $75.00
Reverse Swirl, custard cup, white $28.00
Reverse Swirl, finger bowl, cranberry $95.00
Reverse Swirl, mustard, blue $70.00
Reverse Swirl, toothpick holder, vaseline or canary.. $120.00
Ribbed Spiral, compote, jelly; white $25.00
Ribbed Spiral, cup & saucer, vaseline or canary $80.00
Ribbed Spiral, plate, blue $35.00
Ribbed Spiral, sugar bowl, white $125.00
Richelieu (English), basket, vaseline or canary, handled.. $65.00
Richelieu (English), creamer, blue $58.00
Scroll w/Acanthus, bowl, sauce; blue or green $20.00
Scroll w/Acanthus, salt & pepper shakers, vaseline or canary, pr. $85.00
Scroll w/Acanthus, sugar bowl, blue $150.00
Seaweed, pitcher, blue $310.00
Seaweed, pitcher, cranberry $40.00
Seaweed, spooner, white $70.00
Seaweed, sugar shaker, white $160.00
Shell, bowl, master; blue $60.00
Shell, creamer, white $60.00
Shell, tumbler, green $85.00
Spanish Lace, bowl, sauce; cranberry $35.00
Spanish Lace, bride's basket, blue $105.00
Spanish Lace, cruet, vaseline or cranberry $240.00
Spanish Lace, jam jar, blue $260.00
Spanish Lace, pitcher, white $125.00

Stripe, condiment set, cranberry $400.00
Stripe, tumbler, white $28.00
Stripe (Wide), cruet, blue $160.00
Stripe (Wide), tumbler, cranberry $80.00
Sunburst on Shield, bowl, master; blue $60.00
Sunburst on Shield, nappy, blue, rare $120.00
Sunburst on Shield, spooner, vaseline or canary $90.00
Swag w/Brackets, compote, jelly; vaseline or canary.. $45.00
Swag w/Brackets, creamer, blue $75.00
Swag w/Brackets, pitcher, green $260.00
Swirl, bowl, master; green $45.00
Swirl, custard cup, green $45.00
Swirl, sugar bowl, cranberry $160.00
Swirl, sugar shaker, white $57.00
Thousand Eye, butter dish, white $115.00
Thousand Eye, pitcher, white $80.00
Thousand Eye, vase, celery; white $120.00
Tokyo, bowl, sauce; green $14.00
Tokyo, creamer, green $60.00
Tokyo, syrup, white $65.00
Tokyo, tumbler, blue $70.00
Waterlily & Cattails, bonbon, blue $58.00
Waterlily & Cattails, breakfast set, green, 2-pc $110.00
Waterlily & Cattails, plate, white $46.00
Waterlily & Cattails, spooner, amethyst $65.00
Wild Bouquet, tumbler, blue $100.00
Windows (Plain), finger bowl, blue $45.00
Windows (Plain), tumbler, cranberry $90.00
Windows (Plain), tumbler, white $28.00
Windows (Swirled), bowl, master; cranberry $70.00
Windows (Swirled), creamer, white $50.00
Windows (Swirled), tumbler, blue $75.00
Wreath & Shell, creamer, vaseline or canary $80.00
Wreath & Shell, pitcher, white $170.00
Wreath & Shell, salt cellar, white $60.00
Wreath & Shell, sugar bowl, blue $180.00

Pacific Clay Products

This company was formed by the consolidation of several small California potteries. In the early twenties, they produced stoneware staples from local clay taken from their own mines. Their business, along with many others, suffered at the onset of the Depression, and taking note of Bauer's success, they initiated the production of earthenware dishes which they marketed under the tradename Hostess Ware. During the next decade they developed several dinnerware lines in both vivid colors and pastel glazes as well as artware such as vases, figurines, flowerpots, and large architectural sand jars and bird baths. 1942 saw the end of all pottery manufacture, due to the company's committment to full-time defense work. Today they are located in Corona, California, where they specialize in the production of roof tile.

If you're interested in learning more about this company, we recommend *The Collector's Encyclopedia of California Pottery* by Jack Chipman.

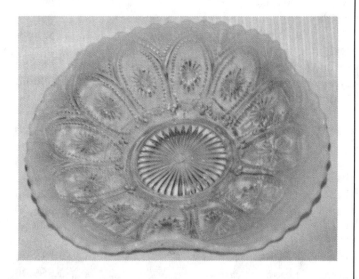

Spokes & Wheels, novelty plate, blue, rare $50.00

Baby plate, 9", divided, w/bunny border, 1934 ....$60.00

Baking dish, 6¼", jade green, early in-mold Pacific mark, w/clip-on wood handle..$50.00

Coaster, 4", Ring-style, Hostess Ware, turquoise...........**$6.00**

Coffeepot, demitasse; slim body w/angular handle, Sierra White $65.00

Cup & saucer, Ring-style, Hostess Ware **$15.00**

Egg cup, double; 4", Ring-style, Pacific Blue, in-mold mark **$25.00**

Figurine, 12", Mexican dancers, 'Valencia' across front at base, early 1930s, Apache Red............................**$175.00**

Figurine, 8¼", hand-painted stylized bird, ca 1939, stamped mark...**$35.00**

Jug, ball form, orange, early $50.00

Pie plate, 11", Pacific Blue, early in-mold mark, w/clip-on wood handles..**$55.00**

Pitcher, 2-qt, Ring-style, Hostess Ware, Pacific Blue ...**$50.00**

Plate, baby's; 9" dia, divided, orange w/embossed bunny design border, ca 1934 ....**$60.00**

Plate, dinner; Plaid, blue & brown tones **$25.00**

Plate, salad; Spiral, orange & earth tones, ca 1935......**$15.00**

Teapot, individual; Apache Red, in-mold mark...........**$50.00**

Teapot, Ring-style, footed, w/long spout, yellow........**$85.00**

Tumbler, matches ball-type jug pitcher, early (illustrated) $15.00

Tumbler, 4", Ring-style, flared top, orange **$15.00**

Vase, 5", Floral Artware line, low style, handled, solid matt glaze, early 1930s...**$55.00**

Vase, 7¾", bust figural, Pacific Artware, white matt glaze **$30.00**

Paden City Glass

Operating in this West Virginia City from 1916 until 1951, this company is best known to collectors for their many handmade lines of colored dinnerware such as we have listed here. They almost never marked their glass, making it very difficult to identify.

A line of glass animals and birds was also made here; see also Glass Animals.

Ardith, cake plate, 11½", yellow w/cherry etching, footed **$60.00**

Ardith, compote, yellow w/cherry etching, high standard **$55.00**

Ardith, tumbler, 5⅛", amber, flat................................**$25.00**

Bees Knees, cup & saucer, crystal **$8.00**

Bees Knees, plate, 7½", crystal....................................**$5.00**

Bees Knees, plate, 9", crystal **$10.00**

Black Forest, batter jug, crystal................................**$125.00**

Black Forest, bowl, console; 11", amber **$50.00**

Black Forest, bowl, console; 13", black.......................**$65.00**

Black Forest, bowl, finger; 4½", crystal **$125.00**

Black Forest, cake plate, green, 2" pedestal................**$40.00**

Black Forest, candy dish, pink, w/lid **$75.00**

Black Forest, creamer, red..**$65.00**

Black Forest, ice pail, 3x6", amber **$75.00**

Black Forest, pitcher, 8", crystal..............................**$165.00**

Black Forest, plate, bread & butter; 6½", black...........**$22.00**

Black Forest, plate, 8", black $30.00

Black Forest, salt & pepper shakers, pink, pr............$125.00
Black Forest, sugar bowl, red $65.00
Black Forest, tumbler, iced tea; 5½", green.................$40.00
Crow's Foot, bowl, 12", red, footed..............................$55.00
Crow's Foot, compote, red...$25.00
Crow's Foot, cup & saucer, amber.................................$10.00
Crow's Foot, plate, 6" sq, red $4.00
Crow's Foot, plate, 9", amber.......................................$10.00
Crow's Foot, sugar bowl, red...$13.00
Cupid, bowl, 10½", green or pink, rolled edge $95.00
Cupid, bowl, 8½", green or pink, footed, oval $125.00
Cupid, cake plate, 11¾", green or pink.....................$125.00
Cupid, candlesticks, 5" wide, green or pink, pr $125.00
Cupid, comport, 6¼", green or pink.............................$65.00
Cupid, creamer, 4½", green or pink, footed.................$75.00
Cupid, ice bucket, 6", green or pink $125.00
Cupid, plate, 10½", green or pink.................................$75.00
Cupid, sugar bowl, 4¼", green or pink, footed $75.00
Cupid, tray, 10¾", green or pink, center handle.........$80.00
Cupid, vase, 8¼", green or pink, elliptical $250.00
Gazebo, server, light blue, center handle $35.00
Gothic Garden, bowl, yellow, square...........................$38.00
Gothic Garden, cake stand, 9¼", pink..........................$55.00
Lucy, cup & saucer, red..$20.00
Nora Bird, candlesticks, green or pink, pr $65.00
Nora Bird, candy dish, 6½", green or pink, w/lid, 3-part...$85.00
Nora Bird, cup, green or pink.......................................$47.00
Nora Bird, mayonnaise, green or pink, w/liner..........$75.00
Nora Bird, plate, 8", green or pink $20.00
Nora Bird, sugar bowl, 5", green or pink, pointed handle..$38.00
Nora Bird, tumbler, 4¾", green or pink, footed..........$50.00
Orchid, bowl, 11" sq, yellow, green, amber, or pink..$45.00
Orchid, bowl, 4⅞" sq, black, cobalt, or red $30.00
Orchid, bowl, 8½", red or blue, handled $75.00
Orchid, bowl, 8" sq, yellow, green, amber, or pink....$30.00
Orchid, candlesticks, 5¾", black, cobalt, or red.........$100.00
Orchid, creamer, black, cobalt, or red..........................$45.00
Orchid, creamer, yellow or green..................................$25.00
Orchid, ice bucket, 6", red or blue $100.00
Orchid, ice bucket, 6", yellow, green, or pink.............$55.00
Orchid, mayonnaise, yellow, green, amber, or pink, 3-pc..$50.00
Orchid, sandwich server, black, cobalt, or red, center handle...$65.00
Orchid, vase, 10", yellow, green, amber, or pink........$45.00
Party Line, ice tub, pink $22.00
Party Line, salt & pepper shakers, amber, pr.................$9.00
Party Line, salt & pepper shakers, ruby, pr.................$45.00
Peacock & Wild Rose, bowl, console; 11", all colors ..$65.00
Peacock & Wild Rose, bowl, 8½", all colors, flat.........$50.00
Peacock & Wild Rose, bowl, 8¾", all colors, footed....$65.00
Peacock & Wild Rose, cake plate, all colors, low foot..$75.00
Peacock & Wild Rose, candy dish, 7", all colors, w/lid.$125.00
Peacock & Wild Rose, ice bucket, 6", all colors $110.00
Peacock & Wild Rose, relish, all colors, 3-part...........$50.00
Peacock & Wild Rose, vase, 12", all colors $100.00

Peacock Reverse, bowl, 4⅞" sq, all colors $30.00
Peacock Reverse, candlesticks, 5¾", all colors, square base, pr $110.00
Peacock Reverse, plate, sherbet; 5¾", all colors $20.00
Peacock Reverse, plate, 10⅜", all colors, 2-handled....$45.00
Peacock Reverse, sugar bowl, 2¾", all colors, flat.......$75.00
Peacock Reverse, tumbler, 4", all colors, flat $55.00

Peacock Reverse, vase, 8½", green.....................$125.00
Penny Line, cup & saucer, ruby.....................................$10.00
Penny Line, goblet, green..$12.00
Penny Line, goblet, 6", ruby...$20.00
Popeye & Olive, plate, 8", red $12.00
Popeye & Olive, sherbet, 3¼", red.................................$12.00
Popeye & Olive, vase, 7", red, ruffled $40.00
Utopia, vase, 10½", black...$175.00
Vermillion, bowl, 9", crystal $15.00
Vermillion, mayonnaise, w/undertray & spoon, crystal..$25.00
Watta Line, creamer, crystal..$5.00
Watta Line, plate, 9½", crystal $8.00
Watta Line, saucer, crystal $3.00

Paden City Pottery Company

Founded in 1907, this company produced many dinnerware and kitchenware lines until they closed in the 1950s. Many were decaled, in fact this company is credited with originating the underglaze decal process.

One of their most collectible lines is called Caliente. It was Paden City's version of the solid-color dinnerware lines that became so popular in the thirties and forties. Caliente's shapes were simple and round, but its shell-like finials, handles, and feet did little to accentuate its Art Deco possibilities, which the public seemed to prefer at that time. As a result, it never sold in volume comparable to Fiesta or Bauer's Ring, but you should be able to rebuild a set eventually, and your efforts would be well worthwhile. If you'd like to see photographs of this line and many others produced by Paden City, see *The Collector's Encyclopedia of American Dinnerware* by Jo Cunningham.

Acacia Flowers, creamer, Shellcrest shape, footed **$10.00**
Acacia Flowers, sugar bowl, Shellcrest shape, footed.**$10.00**
Blossoms, platter, Shellcrest shape, oval **$6.00**
Caliente, candle holder...**$15.00**
Caliente, casserole, w/lid...**$30.00**
Caliente, cream soup **$14.00**
Caliente, creamer **$14.00**
Caliente, cup & saucer...**$15.00**
Caliente, plate, dessert..**$7.50**
Caliente, plate, dinner...**$10.00**
Caliente, salt & pepper shakers, pr.............................**$15.00**
Caliente, sugar bowl, w/lid **$18.00**

Caliente, teapot **$45.00**
Corn Is Green, utility plate, large.................................**$18.00**
Duchess, plate, dinner; round..**$6.00**
Duchess, plate, salad; Regina shape..............................**$4.00**
Far East, creamer, Shellcrest shape, footed **$10.00**
Far East, plate or bowl, 6", Shellcrest shape **$3.00**
Far East, sugar bowl, Shellcrest shape, footed............**$12.00**
Far East plate, 9", Shellcrest shape................................**$6.00**
Jonquil, creamer, floral pattern on ivory **$5.00**
Jonquil, sugar bowl, floral pattern on ivory, handled ...**$5.00**
Modern Orchid, bowl, sauce; round..............................**$3.00**
Modern Orchid, plate, small, round...............................**$3.00**
Nasturtium, plate, dinner; Shellcrest shape **$5.00**
Paden Rose, cup & saucer..**$8.00**
Paden Rose, plate, bread & butter; 6" dia **$2.00**
Paden Rose, plate, salad; 7" sq......................................**$3.00**
Paden Rose, platter...**$12.00**
Posies, cup & saucer...**$6.00**
Posies, plate or bowl, small...**$3.00**
Rust Tulip, plate, dinner; Shellcrest shape **$5.00**
Yellow Rose, creamer..**$8.00**
Yellow Rose, cup & saucer, Minion shape...................**$10.00**
Yellow Rose, plate, dinner; Minion shape.....................**$8.00**
Yellow Rose, plate, salad; Minion shape........................**$6.00**
Yellow Rose, sugar bowl...**$8.00**

Paper Dolls

One of the earliest producers of paper dolls was Raphael Tuck of England, who distributed many of their dolls in the United States in the late 1800s. Advertising companies used them to promote their products, and some were often included in the pages of leading ladies' magazines.

But over the years, the most common paper dolls were those printed on the cover of a book that contains their clothes on the inside pages. These were initiated during the 1920s and, because they were inexpensive, retained their popularity even during the Depression years. They peaked in the 1940s, but with the advent of television in the fifties, children began to loose interest.

Be sure to check old boxes and trunks in your attic, you may find some waiting for you. Even dolls from more recent years are collectible, for instance celebrity dolls from television shows like 'The Brady Bunch' or 'The Waltons.' Cut sets are worth only about half the price of dolls in mint, uncut, origininal condition, if all dolls and outfits are still present.

If you'd like to learn more about them, we recommend *Collector's Guide to Paper Dolls* (there are two in the series) and *Collector's Guide to Magazine Paper Dolls,* all by Mary Young.

Ann & Joe, MA Donohue & Co, #80, EX.....................**$20.00**
Annette Funicello, Whitman, 1958, EX.......................**$30.00**
Arlene Dahl, Saalfield #158710, 1953, uncut...............**$65.00**
Baby Sparkle Plenty, Saalfield #1510, 1948, uncut **$85.00**
Bedknobs & Broomsticks, uncut, M **$25.00**
Bette Davis, Merrill, 1942, EX.....................................**$45.00**
Betty & Dick Tour the USA, Standard Toykraft, 1940,
    NM **$22.00**
Birthday Party Cutouts, Whitman #2084, 5" child figures,
    eight pages of clothes, 1961, uncut, NM **$25.00**
Black Lydia, uncut, 1970s, NM.....................................**$7.50**
Carol Lynley, Whitman, uncut, 1950, NM...................**$22.50**

Children of America, Saalfield, 1941, EX **$25.00**
Claudette Colbert, Saalfield, 1943, EX.........................**$40.00**
Daisy & Donald Duck, uncut, 1970s, NM.....................**$6.50**
Debbie Reynolds, Whitman, 1955, partially cut clothes,
    EX **$45.00**

Dennis the Menace, Whitman #1991, uncut, 1960, NM..**$35.00**
Dolly Dingle Gives a Thanksgiving Dinner, uncut, EX..**$27.50**
Doris Day, Whitman #1952, 1955, uncut, NM..............**$55.00**
Dotty & Danny on Parade, Burton #875, 1935, EX......**$25.00**
Elly May of Beverly Hillbillies, uncut, M.....................**$35.00**
Gloria Jean, Saalfield, 1940, NM...............................**$50.00**
Gone with the Wind, Merrill, 1940............................**$150.00**
Gulliver's Travels, uncut, 1930, NM...........................**$35.00**
Hello I'm Adeline, Animated Book Co, 1944, EX........**$18.00**
I Love Lucy, Whitman #2101, 1953, EX.......................**$65.00**
Jane Fonda, Saalfield #1369, 1965, M **$30.00**

Jane Powell, Whitman, 1952, NM...........................$60.00
Janet Lennon, Whitman 1964, 9" figure w/uncut clothes, M
  in NM 10¼x12" cardboard album **$45.00**
Jeanette MacDonald, Merrill #3460, 1941, EX **$45.00**
Josie & the Pussy Cats, uncut, book type, M...............**$45.00**
Magic Doll, Parker Bros, ca 1948, EX..........................**$12.00**
Mary Frances Housekeeper, JC Winston, ca 1914, EX .**$135.00**

Munsters, Whitman #1959, 1966, NM....................$35.00
My Dolly Sister Nan, Sam Gabriel Sons #D-90, EX......**$27.50**
My Farm, Whitman #1942, farmer & family w/animals &
  vehicles, 1955, uncut, NM **$25.00**
Paper Doll Family & Their House, cut, #2094, 39-pc,
  EX **$60.00**

Pollykins Pudge, by Barbara Hale, uncut sheet, NM....**$12.50**
Ricky Nelson, Whitman #2081, uncut, 1959, M..........**$125.00**
Rita Hayworth, Saalfield, 1948, NM **$65.00**

**Rock Hudson Universal International Star, Whitman
  #2087, 1957, EX...$60.00**
Roy Rogers & Dale Evans, Whitman #1950, 1954, uncut,
  NM **$120.00**
Roy Rogers & Dale Evans, 1947, EX............................**$95.00**
Shirley Temple, uncut, 18", NM **$95.00**
Susan Dey of Partridge Family, M...............................**$35.00**
That Girl (TV show), Saalfield #1379, 1967, uncut, NM .**$35.00**
Twiggy, 9½" figure, Whitman, w/six pages of clothes, 1967,
  M in 10x13" folder...**$60.00**

Magazine Sheets

Betsy McCall, from 'McCall's,' 1958...............................**$5.00**
Betsy McCall, from 'McCalls,' 'Betsy McCall Meets Captain
  Kangaroo,' 1957..**$6.00**
Betty Bonnetts, from 'Ladies' Home Journal,' 1917 .....**$25.00**
Bobbie, from 'Pictorial Review,' December 1934, M ...**$15.00**
Caroline, from 'Good Housekeeping,' 1923, NM.........**$12.50**
Caroline Goes to China, from 'Good Housekeeping,'
  1924 ....**$12.00**
Children's Happy Hour Story of Little Queen of May, from
  'Comfort,' 1916 ....**$7.00**
Dotty Daisy & Her Spring Clothes, from 'Junior Home Maga-
  zine,' 1923..**$7.00**
Dress Up Teddy Bear, from 'Comfort,' 1915 ....**$7.00**
Hildegarde Lives in Holland, from 'Good Housekeeping,'
  1925 ....**$12.00**
Joan & Billy's Easter Party, from 'Canadian Home Journal,'
  1933 ....**$12.00**
Joan & Bobby Go to a Halloween Party, from 'Canadian
  Home Journal,' 1934 ....**$12.00**
Little Lord Fauntleroy, from 'The American Woman,'
  1922 ....**$12.00**
Mary Lou & Bobby Go to Dancing School, from 'Canadian
  Home Journal,' 1933 ....**$12.00**
Mary Louise & Pussykins, from 'Canadian Home Journal,'
  1928 ....**$14.00**

Nippers, from 'McCalls,' 1924.....................$12.00

Polly & Peter Perkins, from 'Pictorial Review,' M....$12.00

The Christmas Skating Girl, from 'Canadian Home Journal,' 1928 ....$14.00

The Christmas Sunbonnet Babies, from 'The Housekeeper,' 1909 ....$18.00

The Princess & the Goblin, from 'The American Woman,' 1922 ....$12.00

Topsy, from 'Canadian Home Journal,' 1934 ....$14.00

Paperback Books

Here is a field that you can really have some fun with. These are easy to find, but you may have to spend some time going through many to find some really good ones. Most collectors prefer those that were printed from around 1940 until the late 1950s. Obviously you could buy thousands, so you may prefer to limit your collection to a particular author, genre, publisher, or illustrator. Be particular about the condition of the books you buy.

American Gothic, Robert Bloch, Crest #P-2391, 1975, VG.........................$11.50

Bachelor's Guide to the Opposite Sex, Avon #815, 1958, 1st edition, M $25.00

Baseball Stars of 1955, Bruce Jacobs, Lion Library #LL-12, 1955, paperback original, VG.........................$20.00

Battle of the Sexes, anthology, Avon #617, 1955, cartoon illustrated, VG.........................$7.00

Black Horse Canyon, Les Savage Jr, Gold Medal #411, 1954, 2nd printing, Joel McCrea cover, VG.........................$22.00

Black Opium, Claude Farrere, Berkeley #G-120, 1958, cover art by Maguire, VG.........................$40.00

Blood Alley, AS Fleischman, Gold Medal #499, 1955, John Wayne & Lauren Bacall cover, NM.........................$16.00

Brass Cupcake, John D MacDonald, Gold Medal #124, 1950, paperback original, VG.........................$57.50

Broken Lands, Saberhagen, Ace #G-740, 1968, VG $3.00

Campus Town, Hart Stilwell, Popular Library #331, 1951, cover art by Bergey, EX.........................$44.00

Close to Critical, Hal Clement, Ballantine #U-2215, 1964, paperback original, cover art by Lehr, VG..............$2.50

Community of Women, Sheldon Lord, Beacon #446, 1961, EX.........................$20.00

Creation of the Universe, George Gamow, Mentor #MD-214, 1957, EX.........................$3.50

Cry Plague/Judas Goat, Brachman/Edgley, Ace #D-13, 1953, VG.........................$26.50

Currents of Space, Isaac Asimov, Crest #T-1541, 1971, VG.........................$2.50

Dead or Alive, Patricia Wentworth, Dell #2, 1943, VG..$40.00

Deadline at Dawn, William Irish, Bestseller Mystery #90, no date, digest, EX $30.00

Digits & Dastards, Frederik Pohl, Ballantine #U-2178, 1966, paperback original, VG.........................$3.00

Doctor Barbara, Elizabeth Wesley, Bantam #A-1962, 1960, VG.........................$2.50

Dope Doll/Bigamy Kiss, Steve Harragan, Universal Giant #4, no date, VG.........................$65.00

Dwellers in the Mirage, Merritt, Avon #413, NM.........$22.00

Enjoying Modern Art, Sarah Newmeyer, Mentor #MD-211, 1957, VG.........................$2.50

Eye in the Sky, Philip K Dick, Ace #H-39, 1967, cover art by Freas, G.........................$5.00

Far-Out Worlds of AE Van Vogt, Ace #H-92, paperback original, cover art by Jones, VG $3.00

Fighting Man of Mars, Edgar Rice Burroughs, Ballantine #U-2037, 1964, cover art by Abbett, NM.........................$5.00

Fire in the Flesh, David Goodis, Gold Medal #691, 1957, cover art by Barye, VG $37.50

First Men in the Moon, HG Wells, Ballantine #U-2232, 1964, 3rd printing, VG $2.50

Flame of Sunset, LP Holmes, Pocket #514, 1948, cover art by Wolsky, VG.........................$4.00

Fortunes of Captain Blood, Rafael Sabatini, Popular Library #241, 1950, cover art by Belarski, EX $12.00

Foxes of Harrow, Frank Yerby, Pocket #577, 1949, cover art by Ward, VG.........................$4.00

Gentlemen Prefer Blonds, Anita Loos, Popular Library #221, 1950, cover art by Bergey, VG $15.00

Girl in the Cockpit, Michael Avallone, Curtis #07261, VG.........................$3.50

Golden Apples of the Sun, Ray Bradbury, Bantam #J-2306, 1961, illustrated by Mugnaini, NM $5.00

Golden Spike, Ellson, Ballantine #2, NM.........................$24.00

Guns on the Cimarron, Allan V Elston, Pocket #530, 1948, cover art by Clark, EX.........................$5.00

Gunsmoke, Chris Stratton, Popular Library #08146, 1970, James Arness cover, M.........................$10.00

Halo For Satan, John Evans, Bantam #800, 1st paperback edition, 1950, EX.....................................**$24.00**

Hazard, Chanslor, Bantam #474, NM.............................**$7.00**

History of Western Art, Erwin O Christensen, Mentor #MT-262, 1959, VG...**$3.00**

I Wouldn't Be in Your Shoes, William Irish, Mercury Mystery #82, no date, cover art by Salter, NM....................**$28.50**

In Pursuit of Death, Roger Hart Davis, Micron W-3, 1961, NM...**$12.00**

Jealous & the Free, March Hastings, Midwood #80, 1961, paperback original, cover art by Rader, VG..........**$22.00**

Killer's Town, Falk, Avon #17731, 1973, 1st edition, NM....**$8.00**

King, Queen, Knave; Vladimir Nabokov, Crest #T-1287, 1969, VG...**$3.00**

Laughing Buddha Murders, Richard Foster, Vulcan #3, 1944, paperback original, cover art by Hoffman, NM....**$30.00**

Lila My Lovely, Dean Dudley, Gold Medal #1014, 1960, paperback original, VG...**$4.50**

Listerdale Mystery, Christie, Fontana #493, 1961..........**$32.50**

Lone Star, Borden Chase, Gold Medal #236, 1952, NM..**$14.00**

Lustful Ape, Bruno Fischer, Gold Medal #901, 1959, VG...**$10.00**

Mad Max 2, P Manoeuvre, J'Ai Lu #1533, 1983, French edition, illustrated w/movie photos, NM....................**$26.00**

Man Who Murdered Himself, Geoffrey Homes, Century #10, 1945, digest, NM...**$40.00**

Man with the Golden Arm, Nelson Algren, Cardinal #C-31, 1951, w/dust jacket, VG.......................................**$24.00**

Master Mind of Mars, Edgar Rice Burroughs, Ballantine #U-2036, 1963, VG...**$3.00**

Meaning in Star Trek, Karin Blair, Warner #92-095, 1979, EX...**$10.00**

Message from the Eocene, Margaret St Clair, Ace #M-105, 1964, paperback original, VG.................................**$4.00**

Modern Casanova's Handbook, HT Elmo, Ace #S-93, 1955, VG...**$8.50**

Myopic Mermaid, Carter Brown, Signet #1924, 1961, 1st edition, NM...**$12.50**

No Way Back, Karl Zeigfried, SA (British), Fox cover, 1967, NM...**$55.00**

Not So Funny, Charlene White, After Hours #145, 1966, paperback original, NM...**$18.00**

On Wheels, John Jakes, Warner #75-123, 1973, paperback original, cover art by Punchatz, VG.....................**$3.50**

Only the Valiant, Charles Marquis Warren, Bantam #F-2068, 1960, VG...**$2.50**

Outlaw Valley, Cody, Harlequin #153, VG...................**$15.00**

Paingod & Other Delusions, Harlan Ellison, Jove #3646, 1978, signed, NM...**$10.00**

Partridge Family Two: The Haunted Hall; Michael Avallone, Curtis #05004, VG...**$3.00**

Perversity, Francis Carco, Avon #401, 1950, NM..........**$35.00**

Plunderers, LP Holmes, Bantam #1822, 1958, VG.........**$2.50**

Poorhouse Fair, John Updike, Crest #D-677, 1964, NM.**$3.50**

Rainbow, Lawrence, Avon #G-1038, 1959, 1st paperback edition, M...**$5.00**

Rare Breed, Theodore Sturgeon, Gold Medal #1626, 1966, paperback original, small remainder stamp, NM..**$15.50**

Rascals in Paradise, JA Michener, Bantam #F-1844, 1958, cover art by Hooks, VG...**$2.50**

Red Brain, Dashiell Hammett, Belmont #239, 1951, NM.**$5.50**

Red Moon, Robeson, Warner #75-610, 1974, 1st edition, Avenger #26, M...**$7.00**

Regan's Planet, Silverberg, Pyramid #F-986, 1964, 1st edition, NM...**$8.00**

Renegade Ranch, Roy Manning, Pocket #663, 1950, cover art by Lupo, VG...**$4.00**

Return to Vikki, John Tomerlin, Gold Medal #900, 1959, paperback original, VG...**$5.50**

Revolt of the Triffids, John Wyndham, Popular Library #411, 1952, VG...**$10.00**

Rio Bravo, Leigh Brackett, Bantam #1893, 1959, movie tie-in cover, EX...**$20.00**

Rivals, Sheldon Lord, Beacon #680, 1963, EX.............**$14.00**

Run Thief Run, Frank Gruber, Crest #115, 1955, VG...**$12.50**

Satan's Mate, George H Smith, Newsstand Library #507, 1960, VG...**$6.00**

Science Fiction Terror Tales, Groff Conklin, Pocket Book #1045, 1955, paperback original, NM **$14.00**

Scout, Robert Turner, Pocket Book #1216, 1958, paperback original, TV tie-in, NM **$7.50**

Shrinking Man, Richard Matheson, Gold Medal #1203, 1962, 2nd printing, signed, VG **$11.00**

Shroud for Jesso, Peter Rabe, Gold Medal #528, VG...**$50.00**

Sin Street, Dorine Manners, Pyramid #21, 1950, VG....**$20.00**

Slam the Big Door, John D MacDonald, Gold Medal #S-961, 1960, paperback original, G **$12.50**

Spies for the Blue & the Gray, Harnett T Kane, Ace #K-132, VG **$3.50**

Stepford Wives, Ira Levin, Crest #P-1876, 1973, NM......**$3.00**

Strumpet Sea, Ben Ames Williams, Popular #371, 1951, cover art by Belarski, VG.............................**$7.00**

Sun in Their Eyes, Monte Barrett, Popular Library #224, 1950, cover art by Belarski, EX **$10.00**

Take a Step to Murder, Day Keene, Gold Medal #874, 1959, VG..**$15.00**

The Real Jack Paar, George Johnson, Gold Medal #S-1263, 1962, paperback original, w/photo cover, VG........**$5.00**

Toffee Takes a Trip, Imaginative Tales #2, 35¢ original price, VG..**$18.00**

Too Hot To Hold, Day Keene, Gold Medal #931, paperback original, EX..**$17.00**

True Grit, Charles Portis, Signet #3761, 1969, movie tie-in cover, VG...**$6.50**

Tuned for Murder, Kenneth Robeson, Warner #74-025, 1973, Avenger Series #9, VG **$3.00**

Turning On, Knight, Ace #G-677, VG......................**$4.00**

Twenty-Three Women, anonymous, Pyramid #46, 1952.**$8.50**

Undefeated, Jim Thompson, Popular Library #60-8104, 1969, movie tie-in cover, NM **$32.50**

War of the Worlds/Time Machine, HG Wells, Dolphin #C-304, 1961, NM.......................................**$4.00**

War Wagon, Clair Huffaker, Gold Medal #1807, 1967, John Wayne & Kirk Douglas cover, NM.......................**$22.00**

Werewolf Versus the Vampire Woman, Arthur N Scarm, Guild-Hartford #200, 1972, movie tie-in cover, VG............**$30.00**

Westport Landing, Homer Hatten, Red Seal #79, same cover as Gold Medal #157, VG **$8.00**

What Mad Universe, Frederic Brown, Boardman #154, 1954, VG..**$30.00**

While the Wind Howled, Audrey Gaines, Dell #51, 1944, EX...**$35.00**

White Fawn, Olive H Prouty, Dell #167, 1947, EX **$24.00**

Wild Blood, AC Abbott, Gold Medal #208, 1951, EX...**$20.00**

Willie Mays, Say-Hey Kid; Arnold Hano, Sports Magazine Library #6, 1961, 1st edition, M **$20.00**

Paperweights

The most collectible weights on the market today are the antique weights, those made from 1845 to 1870, and those made by contemporary artists like Rick Ayotte and Paul Ysart. There are many types — millefiori, sulphides, and those that contain fruit and animals. These are usually very expensive. Among the lower priced weights are those that were sold through gift stores, made in American glasshouses and studios, China, Murano, Italy, and Scotland.

Ayotte, Rick; 1⅞", robin on flowering dogwood **$225.00**

Ayotte, Rick; 3¾", cedar waxwings on fall foliage.....**$800.00**

Ayotte, Rick; 3¾", ducks on pond **$1,450.00**

Baccarat (antique), 2½", garlanded red & white primrose, pink & white star center......................$935.00

Baccarat (modern), Queen Elizabeth II, 3¼", sulfide, outer cane garland, faceted, 1977....................**$275.00**

Baccarat (modern), 2¾", three strawberries & blossom on dark blue ground, 1974 cane **$400.00**

Baccarat (modern), 2⅞", frog & white flower on dark green-pebbly ground, signed, 1974....................**$450.00**

Baccarat (modern), 3", Abe Lincoln, double-overlay sulfide, faceted, signed GP, 1953 ....**$400.00**

Baccarat (modern), 3", salamander on pebbly yellow, three silvery rocks, 1973 cane **$550.00**

Banford, Bob; 3", striped snake on pebbly ground w/branch, 'B' cane...................................**$600.00**

Banford, Bob; 3", triple pansy bouquet.....................**$800.00**

Banford, Bob; 3½" (approximate), five multicolored flowers surround pansy in French-style bouquet, diamond-cut base **$2,000.00**

Banford, Bob; 3¼", blue morning-glories on white trellis, pink ground **$750.00**

Banford, Bobby; 3", yellow flower w/purple buds ...**$450.00**

Banford, Bobby; 3½" (approximate), pink foxgloves on cobalt ground, honeycomb facets......................**$600.00**

Banford, Bobby; 3½" (approximate), three butterfly fish w/coral & shell...**$600.00**

Banford, Bobby; 3¼", compound buckeyes **$600.00**

Banford, Ray; 2½", two roses on purple aventurine, two gold bees, faceted, 1976...............................**$300.00**

Banford, Ray; 2⅞", pink & white iris on purple aventurine, signed **$400.00**

Banford, Ray; 3", iris & roses in cut-out basket, diamond-cut base, cane signed **$1,000.00**

Banford, Ray; 3", triple rose bouquet on blue ground ..**$800.00**

Banford, Ray; 3½" (approximate), five pink & white roses on cobalt ground **$850.00**

Grubb, Randy; 3", branch of white plum blossoms...**$425.00**

Grubb, Randy; 3", compound triple clusters of green grapes **$375.00**

Grubb, Randy; 3", rose over white double overlay enhances mauve plum blossoms...**$800.00**

Hansen, Ron; 1⅞", large pink rose & four leaves in clear, signed in cane **$140.00**

Harker, Harold; 2¼", black snake on spatter ground, signed **$325.00**

Kaziun, Charles, 2¼", pink crimped rose, yellow over white overlay, faceted...**$1,760.00**

Kaziun, Charles, 3½", pink shaded tulip, upright type w/pedestal...**$1,100.00**

Kaziun, Charles; 1½", 6-petal yellow flower w/three leaves, blue & white 'K' cane, faceted top, six on sides.**$600.00**

Kaziun, Charles; 1¼", red rose, gold bee, three pastel canes on white latticinio on blue, pedestal base **$550.00**

Kaziun, Charles; 2¼", pansy set on purple ground.**$1,045.00**

Lundberg Studios, James Lundberg, pink chrysanthemum, 1990 ....**$290.00**

Lundberg Studios, James Lundberg, pink jonquils, 1990...**$260.00**

Lundburg Studios, Daniel Salazar, pink & blue hydrangias, 1990 ....**$225.00**

New England, 2½", three florettes, four green leaves in cane garland on latticinio cushion..............................**$500.00**

New England Glass, 2½", five pears & four cherries on white latticinio ground **$650.00**

New England Glass, 2¾", close concentric millefiori w/central cane in pastel colors **$400.00**

New England Glass, 3¼", apple, orange-red to yellow, lying on round pad base **$800.00**

Perthshire, 1⅝", concentric millefiori on black **$45.00**

Perthshire, 2½", five pink millefiori loops tied at center on blue, w/label **$30.00**

Perthshire, 2⅞", pattern millefiori, cluster of five+one w/in garland on dark green, 1975 ....**$65.00**

Perthshire, 3", carpet ground w/central blue flower, 1983 ....**$300.00**

Perthshire, 3", pattern millefiori w/center cane, ribbon twist & garland of canes.....................................**$95.00**

Perthshire, 3", 5-flower bouquet, white cushion ground, black cut overlay, signed w/'P' cane **$400.00**

Perthshire, 3½", sea horse & two fish among pink seaweed, crab & shell, faceted, signed w/'P'cane, 1981 .....**$300.00**

Perthshire, 3¼", setup canes w/latticinio twists in square on cobalt, faceted, 1979 ....**$150.00**

Rosenfeld, Ken; 3", six orange orchids, blue ground **$500.00**

Rosenfeld, Ken; 3", yellow daffodils, lilacs & wild rose spring bouquet...**$450.00**

Rosenfeld, Ken; 3½", fall bouquet on orange ground.**$600.00**

Smith, Gordon; 3", snake w/rocks, flowers, & buds on sand ground **$650.00**

Smith, Gordon; 3", three strawberries, white blossoms, & bud...**$650.00**

St Louis (modern), 2½", sulfide, King St Louis w/in cane garland, faceted top, five on sides, 1967 ....**$130.00**

St Louis (modern), 2¾", camomile w/fifty-two blue petals, cane center, latticinio ground, 1975...................**$400.00**

St Louis (modern), 2¾", handcooler, eight twisted red & blue ribbons, white latticinio, St Louis 1976 ....**$300.00**

St Louis (modern), 3", carpet ground (purple, green, white & red), w/six millefiori clusters, 1972.................**$300.00**

St Louis (modern), 3", general De Gaulle in 1940, faceted sulfide, latticinio base, 1977 ....**$750.00**

Stankard, Paul; 2¾", Field Pansy, 3-flower, dark blue over white ground, signed 'S,' 1978.....................**$850.00**

Stankard, Paul; 2¾", Meadowreath, 5-petal yellow flower, buds, etc, on clear, signed in cane, 2¾"............**$800.00**

Stankard, Paul; 2⅝", three tiger orchids, floating seed pods, & roots, limited edition, 1978..............................**$950.00**

Stankard, Paul; 3", oriental floral, curved tan floral branch on clear, signed 'S,' 1978.................................**$950.00**

Stankard, Paul; 3⅛", multi-layered bouquet, signed, H-153, dated 1982..**$1,900.00**

Tarsitano, Debbie; 2¼", 10-petal pink flower w/bee inside **$500.00**

Tarsitano, Debbie; 2¾", four flowers form yellow & orange bouquet, signed **$475.00**

Tarsitano, Debbie; 3", bee w/in 10-petal pink flower, blue buds, star base, signed **$750.00**

Tarsitano, Debbie; 3¼", three multicolored flowers in white-handled yellow basket, star base, signed...........**$550.00**

Tarsitano, Delmo; 2¾", 2-berry sprig w/blooms on clear, signed w/cane...**$550.00**

Tarsitano, Delmo; 3", large peach on brown branch w/eight leaves, signed...**$750.00**

Tarsitano, Delmo; 3", two peaches on branch, star base, signed w/cane...**$800.00**

Tarsitano, Delmo; 3⅜", Earth Life, spider & flowers on sand ground, cane signed **$875.00**

Trabucco, David & Jon; 3", bouquet of red blossoms, red berries, white buds **$300.00**

Trabucco, David & Jon; 3½", acorns & berries on branch, frosted surface w/clear leaves.............................**$450.00**

Trabucco, Victor; 3¼", magnum strawberries w/foliage & stem **$950.00**

Trabucco; Victor; 3⅛", large pink & white citron flower w/two pink buds & three smaller brown buds...**$600.00**

Whitefriars, 3", concentric millefiori w/butterfly silhouette in center, faceted, 1977.............................**$350.00**

Whitefriars, 3½", concentric millefiori, 8-pointed star center, footed **$150.00**

Whitefriars, 3⅛", pattern millefiori w/Three Wisemen in center, faceted top, five on sides, signed, 1976........**$300.00**

Whitefriars, 3⅛", patterned millefiori, American flag in center, faceted top, five on sides, signed, 1976........**$235.00**

Whittemore, Francis D; 2⅛", two yellow pears on pink jasper, two green leaves & stems, signed in cane...........**$250.00**

Whittemore, Francis D; 2⅜", bleeding heart & two buds w/four leaves on green flashed ground **$350.00**

Ysart, Paul; 2¾", fish over sandy ground w/shells & rocks..**$850.00**

Ysart, Paul; 2⅞", pattern millefiori, large central setup, multi-colored perimeter on pink, signed **$275.00**

Ysart, Paul; 3", blue fish w/gold & orange fins on tan & pink w/two shells...**$500.00**

Ysart, Paul; 3", double pink clematis in white latticinio basket, signed in cane...**$550.00**

Ysart, Paul; 3", green aventurine fish & pink fish on pastel sea bed w/shells **$375.00**

Ysart, Paul; 3", parrot on branch w/leaves on blue jasper ground **$900.00**

Peach Lustre Glassware

Fire-King made several lines of peach lustre glassware that have been causing lots of excitement among today's collectors. Peach lustre was their white glassware with a fired-on iridescent gold finish (called 'copper-tint' when applied to their ovenware line).

Their first pattern, introduced in 1952 was ('laurel leaf') Peach Lustre. It consisted of a cup and saucer, creamer, sugar bowl, vegetable bowl, dessert bowl, soup bowl, dinner and salad plates, and an 11" serving plate. It was made until about 1965.

Lustre Shell was introduced in the late 1960s. By this time, Peach Lustre was used to describe the finish of the glassware rather than a particular pattern. Lustre Shell, as the name suggests, was a swirled design. In addition to the pieces mentioned above, a 13" platter and a demitasse cup and saucer were added to the assortment. A set of nested mixing bowls were also avilable.

You'll find baking dishes, bowls and mugs in other styles, vases, and miscellaneous items in this glassware, too; all are collectible and at this point, at least, none are very expensive. If you'd like to learn more about Peach Lustre, we recommend *Collectible Glassware from the 40s, 50s, and 60s* by Gene Florence.

Leaf & Blossom, dessert set, 5" bowl, 6¾" plate, Fire-King, 1952 ....**$7.00**

Lustre Shell, bowl, soup; 7⅝", swirl design, Fire-King, 1966-late 1970s **$4.00**

Lustre Shell, bowl, vegetable; 8½", swirl design, Fire-King, 1966-late 1970s **$6.50**

Lustre Shell, cup, demitasse; 3¼-oz, swirl design, Fire-King, 1966-late 1970s **$6.00**

Lustre Shell, plate, dinner; 10", swirl design, Fire-King, 1960s-late 1970s...**$5.00**

Lustre Shell, sugar bowl, swirl design, w/foot, Fire-King, 1966-late 1970s...**$5.00**

Novelty, dessert bowl, 4¾", Leaf & Blossom design, w/8" underplate, 1940-76, 2-pc set **$10.00**

Novelty, dish, 7", maple leaf form, 1940-76 ....**$3.00**

Novelty, dish, 7", seashell form, 1940-76.....................**$4.00**

Novelty, vase, 7¼", vertical ribs w/flared top, 1940-76..**$6.50**

Ovenware, cake pan, 8" dia, w/'Fire-King Copper Tint Ovenware' label, 1958-71 ....**$6.50**

Ovenware, casserole, 1-qt, w/clear lid, 1958-71 ....**$5.50**

Ovenware, dessert, 6-oz, plain, flared & cupped..............**$2.50**

Ovenware, French casserole, 12-oz, vertically ribbed sides, 1958-76...**$4.00**

Ovenware, loaf pan, 5x9", lustre finish on white glass, 1958-71 ....**$5.00**

Ovenware, pie pan, 9" dia, plain, slightly flared **$4.50**

Peach Lustre, bowl, soup; 7⅝", embossed leaf design at rim, Fire-King, 1952-63 ....**$3.00**

Peach Lustre, cup, 8-oz, embossed leaf design around sides, Fire-King, 1952-63 ....**$3.00**

Peach Lustre, plate, dinner; 9⅛", embossed leaf design at rim, Fire-King, 1952-63 ....**$2.50**

Peach Lustre, plate, serving; 11", embossed leaf design at rim, Fire-King, 1952-63 ....**$7.50**

Peach Lustre, sugar bowl & creamer, embossed leaf design around sides, footed, Fire-King, 1952-63..$8.00

Royal Lustre, cup, demitasse; 3¼-oz, ribbed design at base w/plain band at top, ca 1976 ....**$3.50**

Royal Lustre, cup, 8-oz, ribbed design at base, w/angle handle, 1976 ....**$2.50**

Royal Lustre, plate, dinner; 10", ribbed band at scolloped rim, 1976...**$4.50**

Royal Lustre, platter, oval, ribbed band at scalloped rim, 1976...**$6.50**

Royal Lustre, sugar bowl, ribbed band at base, w/plain band at top, 1976...**$4.50**

Three Bands, cup, wavy band around sides, w/curved handle, Fire-King, 1950s **$3.00**

Three Bands, plate, dinner; 9", wavy band at rim, Fire-King, 1950s...**$4.50**

Peanuts Collectibles

Charles M. Schultz first introduced the world to the

Peanuts cartoon strip in 1950. Today it appears in more than 2,000 newspapers across the United States. Its popularity naturally resulted in the manufacture of hundreds of items, each a potential collectible. Books, toys, movies, and theme parks have been devoted to entertaining children and adults alike through the characters of this cartoon — Linus, Snoopy, Lucy, and Charlie Brown.

If you're going to collect *Peanuts* items, be sure to look for the United Features Syndicate logo and copyright date. Only these are authentic. The copyright date (in most cases) relates not to when an item was made but to when the character and the pose in which he is depicted first appeared in the strip.

If you'd like to learn more about this subject, we recommend *The Official Price Guide to Peanuts Collectibles* by Freddi Margolin and Andrea Podey.

Album, photograph; 11¼x9", Lucy & Linus & 'Snaps, Scraps & Souvenirs' on cover, Hallmark, early 1970s, NM **$28.00**

Bank, 11", Happy Snoopy, dog figural, ceramic, Determined, #1557, ca 1975...**$85.00**

Bell, Clown Capers, Snoopy w/whip & chair taming lion, Snoopy figural handle, Schmid, 1985 ....**$30.00**

Bookends, sitting Snoopy hugs Woodstock, heart-shaped red rubber base & back, Butterfly, 1981, pr, in original box, M...**$22.00**

Cake decorating set, Snoopy as Flying Ace in center w/ten candle holders & six Woodstocks, Hallmark, ca 1975, M **$15.00**

Candle, 5¾", Charlie Brown sitting w/hand to each cheek, Ambassador, late 1970s, M **$25.00**

Candle, 7", Charlie Brown standing figural, Hallmark, late 1970s, M..**$15.00**

Centerpiece, Snoopy lying on house holds 'Happy Birthday' pennant, Hallmark, late 1960s, in original package **$20.00**

Charm bracelet, Snoopy charms (five poses), cloisonne on gold-tone metal, Aviva, 1969, M **$35.00**

Christmas cards, Lucy, Snoopy, Linus, or Charlie Brown in Christmas-related activities, Hallmark, late '60s, M in box...**$15.00**

Cookie jar, Snoopy on the Doghouse, McCoy Pottery Co...**$200.00**

Dinnerware set, cup w/7" bowl & 7¾" plate, cartoon graphics on china, Iroquois, Determined, ca 1972, in original box..**$70.00**

Doll, Dress Me Belle, pink dress w/blue dots & blue hair ribbon, Knickerbocker, 1983, in original box **$35.00**

Doll, 12", Snoopy, stuffed plush, felt eyes, eyebrows & nose, sitting position, Determined, #835, 1971, in original box **$20.00**

Doll, 14", Snoopy as magician in cape, high hat, formal wear & long mustache, Ideal, 1977, M in original box **$125.00**

Doll, 7", Linus w/blanket, painted plastic, Hungerford Plastics, EX...**$60.00**

Doll, 8", Belle, red jacket & blue pants, carries walkman radio, Determined, 1982 ....**$35.00**

Egg cup, 4½", Snoopy as chef figural, egg sits in depression in top of hat, Determined, 1979, M.....................**$20.00**

Figurine, Snoopy & Woodstock w/typewriter, 'My Secretary Isn't Worth Anything Before Coffee Break,' in original box, M...**$35.00**

Figurine, 4½", Snoopy lying on tummy on house roof, 'I'm Allergic to Morning,' Determined, ca 1972, in original box..**$15.00**

Figurine, 5½", Snoopy dancing on spring, Sparkies series, plastic, mounted on teakwood base, Aviva, 1971-72, EX...**$22.50**

Figurine, 8½", Snoopy, vinyl, 1960s..............................**$30.00**

Gift box, 4½x3½", Snoopy w/Woodstock figural on looped blue ribbon, ceramic, Determined, mid-1970s, M.**$40.00**

Ice bucket, Snoopy & Woodstock in formal attire on black vinyl, Shelton ware, 1979, M..............................**$100.00**

Invitation packet, Halloween, Linus & Snoopy w/sign 'Join Us at the Pumpkin Patch,' Hallmark, 1970s, in original package...**$6.00**

Latch hook kit, Snoopy hugging Woodstock, entitled 'Buddies,' Malina, #26/13, mid-1970s, in original box..**$40.00**

Magazine, Christian Herald, September 1967, 'A Visit With Charles Schultz,' NM...**$10.00**

Money clip, Schroeder at piano, cloisonne on gold-tone metal, Aviva, 1969, NM..**$22.50**

Mug, 3⅜", Snoopy sitting next to piece of cherry pie, stoneware, Taylor International, late 1970s, M........**$8.00**

Music box, 2x6½x4½", Linus in pumpkin patch on lid, 'Who Can I Turn To,' wood, Anri, #33905/1, M **$110.00**

Music box, 6", Snoopy in nightcap on half moon figural, 'Impossible Dream,' stars at base, ceramic, Aviva, 1974, M **$75.00**

Mustard jar, 3", Woodstock figure on lift-off lid, ceramic w/plastic spoon, Determined, 1977.......................**$15.00**

Nodder, 5½", Linus, plastic w/head on spring, Lego, 1959, NM **$58.00**

Pajama bag, Sally, felt details on printed cotton, Simon Simple, 1971 ....**$30.00**

Paperweight, 3x2½", Snoopy sitting w/Woodstock & 'Friends' are etched inside heart-shaped glass, Butterfly, 1979, EX..**$35.00**

Patch, Lucy w/'Kiss Me,', machine-embroidered cotton, oval, Interstate Brands premium, early 1970s.................**$5.00**

Picture frame, 3x4½", Snoopy & Woodstock wear party hats & hold three cut-out balloons, enameled, Butterfly, 1979 ....**$20.00**

Pin, Snoopy lying atop jack-o'-lantern, cloisonne on gold-tone metal, Aviva, 1973, NM **$17.50**

Plate, Snoopy & Woodstock w/'Happy Birthday' balloons in center, Determined for Dupont Collection Ltd, mid-1970s **$30.00**

Poster, 'Snoopy Come Home' movie promotion, Snoopy carrying hobo sack w/food dish on head, 1972, EX .**$12.00**

Poster, Snoopy in the ocean on surfboard w/thought balloon 'Cowabunga,' Springbok, 1972 ....**$20.00**

Poster, 17x22", To Each Member of the Apollo Team, Snoopy as astronaut, signed by Wally Schirra, 1969, M **$100.00**

Silverplate set, baby's, Snoopy-handled fork, spoon & knife, w/spillproof plastic cup, Leonard Silver, 1979, M.**$40.00**

Snoopy in the Music Box, 5x5x5½", metal litho box, plastic head, cloth body, Mattel.......................$15.00

Stein, Snoopy sitting in red sleigh w/'Merry Christmas 1976,' ceramic, Determined, EX...**$28.00**

Switchplate, Snoopy on his house as Flying Ace & 'Contact,' Hallmark, ca 1975, M in original package **$8.00**

Toothbrush holder, Snoopy figure lying atop large toothbrush designed to hold four brushes, Determined, 1979, EX ..**$18.00**

Trophy, 2", Snoopy in disco jacket w/'Saturday Night Beagle,' ceramic, Aviva, 1974, EX **$3.00**

Waste basket, 13", shows Snoopy as Flying Ace & 'Curse You Red Baron,' Chein, early 1970s **$25.00**

Wristwatch, 1" dia on red band, Snoopy dancing w/Woodstock as the second hand on red dial, Timex, 1977, w/box, M **$40.00**

Pennsbury Pottery

From the 1950s throughout the '60s, this pottery was sold in gift stores and souvenir shops up and down the Pennsylvania Turnpike. It was produced in Morrisville, Pennsylvania, by Henry and Lee Below. Much of the ware was hand painted in multicolor on caramel backgrounds, though some pieces were made in blue and white. Most of the time, themes centered around Amish people, barber shop singers, roosters, hex signs, and folky mottos.

Much of the ware is marked, and if you're in the Pennsylvania/New Jersey area, you'll find lots of it. It's prevalent in the Mid-West as well and can still sometimes be found at bargain prices. If you'd like to learn more about this pottery, we recommend *Pennsbury Pottery Video Book* by Shirley Graff and BA Wellman.

Ashtray, 3¼x5", pink tulip, octagonal **$12.00**
Ashtray, 5", 'It Wonders Me' **$20.00**
Ashtray, 5", round, Hex **$15.00**
Bird, 3¼x3", Nuthatch...**$125.00**
Bird, 6x4½", Barn Swallow...**$125.00**
Bowl, cereal; 5½", Hex..**$12.00**
Bowl, soup; deep, Folkart..**$25.00**
Bowl, 11", round, Folkart...**$30.00**
Bowl, 11¼", Dutch figures & sayings..............................**$40.00**
Bowl, 7", footed, Revere **$25.00**
Bowl, 7", gray, 'Fidelity Mutual' **$40.00**
Bowl, 9", footed, Revere **$30.00**
Bread plate, Wheat **$30.00**
Butter dish, Lovebirds...**$25.00**
Candlesticks, 2x5", Tulip, pr...**$40.00**
Candlesticks, 5", hummingbird on flower, pr **$145.00**
Candy dish, heart form, Bird Over Heart **$18.00**
Canister, 6½", wood lid, Hex **$60.00**
Casserole, 7" dia, w/lid, Black Rooster.........................**$35.00**
Casserole, 9", w/lid, Hex..**$35.00**
Cheese & cracker set, 3½x11", Hex...............................**$60.00**
Cheese & cracker set, 3½x11", Red or Black Rooster..**$45.00**
Cigarette box, 2½x4¼", Red Rooster..............................**$25.00**
Coffeepot, 6½", 2-cup, Red Rooster................................**$50.00**
Coffeepot, 8½", 6-cup, Folkart **$45.00**
Compote, 5", footed, Hex..**$18.00**
Creamer, 5", Black Rooster...**$25.00**
Creamer & sugar bowl, 4", Folkart..................................**$30.00**
Cup & saucer, Rooster...**$22.00**
Desk basket, 5x5¼x3¼", Red Rooster.............................**$30.00**
Figurine, 3½", Liberty Bell **$25.00**
Figurine, 3x3½", Sparrow **$45.00**
Gravy boat, Black Rooster...**$25.00**
Hot plate, 6x6", tile in metal frame, electric, Red Rooster **$75.00**
Mug, beer; 4½", Eagle or Fisherman...............................**$20.00**
Mug, coffee; 3¼", Eagle, Folkart, Gay Nineties or Hex .**$15.00**
Mug, pretzel; 5", Amish **$22.00**
Pitcher, Red Rooster, 5" **$30.00**
Pitcher, 2", Amish man **$20.00**
Pitcher, 5", 1-pt, Folkart...**$25.00**

Pitcher, 9¾", Red Rooster $55.00

Plaque, 'Pennsylvania RR, 1856, Tiger' $40.00
Plaque, 5" dia, 'Solebury, New Hope' $25.00
Plaque, 7x5", Amish Sayings $25.00
Plate, 10", Black Rooster..$40.00
Plate, 10", Folkart or Hex $25.00
Plate, 8", Courting Buggy $20.00
Platter, 11x14", oval, Folkart or Hex...........................$25.00
Platter, 11x8", Red Rooster $25.00
Tile, 6" dia, 'Come in Without Knocking'....................$20.00
Tile, 6" sq, Eagle $30.00
Tray, 5x3", horse $25.00
Wall pocket, 6½", 'God Bless Our Mortgaged Home' $40.00
Wall pocket, 6½x6½", sailboat $45.00

Perfume Bottles

Here's an area of bottle collecting that is right now coming into its own. Commercial bottles, as you can see from our listings, are very popular. Their values are based on condition: is it sealed or full, does it have its original label, and is the original package or box present.

Figural bottles are interesting, especially the ceramic ones with tiny regal crowns as their stoppers.

Blown, 2⅜", purse type, yellow heart shape, gold mercury glass stopper w/long dauber..................................$80.00
Blown, 3½", blue opaque umbrella (closed) form, handle forms stopper w/long dauber $175.00
Blown, 3¼", gold, green & orange swirls on white w/gold mercury glass base & stopper $65.00
Commercial, Adele Simpson, Collage, 6", clear urn shape w/pedestal base, gold lettering, stopper w/plastic tip, M in box $50.00
Commercial, Aubusson, Caravan de France, 2⅞", clear flat oval form, black enameled streetlamp & lettering, M in box.$35.00
Commercial, Bourjois, Evening in Paris, 2", cobalt w/atomizer attachment, silver cap & label, in blue & silver box...$100.00

Commercial, Breyenne, Chu Chin Chow, 2⅜", cobalt Oriental figure w/fan, white opalescent head-form overcap, empty..$600.00
Commercial, Caron, Muguet du Bonheur, 5½", clear urn shape w/long tapered neck, attached flower sprig, M in box..$130.00
Commercial, Caron, Nuit de Noel, 3", black w/gold label, glass stopper...$37.50
Commercial, Caron, Royal Bain de Champagne, 5", clear bottle form w/champagne labels, white screw cap, near full...$35.00
Commercial, Chu Chin Chon, Bryenne, 2⅜", cobalt w/white opalescent glass overcap....................................$600.00
Commercial, Ciro, Danger, 3⅛", alternating stacked rectangles, gold enameling, black Bakelite overcap.......$60.00
Commercial, Ciro, Le Chavelier de la Nuit, 3¾", stylized knight form, frosted glass w/gray patina highlights $200.00
Commercial, Ciro, New Horizons, 2¾", clear w/stylized eagle stopper, blue enamel lettering $45.00
Commercial, Ciro, New Horizons, 2⅞", clear, curved shape w/Art Deco-style T-bird stopper.........................$50.00
Commercial, Ciro, Oh La La, 4½", clear waisted form w/frosted fan-like stopper, black enamel lettering.$60.00

Commercial, Ciro, Reflexions, 4", clear w/gold names, faceted w/pyramid stopper, marked Baccarat, empty..$90.00
Commercial, Ciro, Surrender, 3½", clear faceted diamond form, labels on side, matching stopper, M in beige & gold box $72.50
Commercial, Ciro, Surrender, 4", clear w/gold labels at neck & shoulders, clear faceted gemstone-like stopper ..$75.00
Commercial, Conde, Jasmin, 5¾", clear rectangular form w/gold labels at base & upper corner, blue glass stopper...$110.00
Commercial, Coty, Emeraude, 2½", clear w/glass stopper, gold label on bottom $22.00
Commercial, Coty, Imprevu, 2⅝", clear w/gold lettering, glass stopper...$20.00
Commercial, Coty, L'Aimant, 4⅛", clear flask shape w/gold label, green plastic cap, M in flower-decorated box $22.50

Commercial, Coty, Le Vertige, 3", clear w/red enameling, gold label tied at neck, clear stopper, M in gold & white box....**$135.00**

Commercial, Coty, Styx, 3¼", clear modified rectangular shape, gold cuff at neck, gold label, NM in original box....**$80.00**

Commercial, D'Orsay, Intoxication, 6", clear w/pleated star-like shape, label on cord at neck, M in box....**$135.00**

Commercial, Dana, Ambush, 2", clear w/paper label, embossed mark on base, glass stopper....**$22.50**

Commercial, Dana, Tabu, 6¾", clear rectangular form w/gold label, frosted glass stopper, sealed....**$55.00**

Commercial, Dana, 20 Carats, 3", clear w/gold screw cap, gold paper label....**$15.00**

Commercial, De Richmond, France, clear round form w/front label, teardrop stopper w/plastic tip, M in satin-lined box....**$35.00**

Commercial, Dior, Miss Dior, 3", clear flask w/paper label, ground glass stopper....**$25.00**

Commercial, Dior, Miss Dior, 5¼", clear w/black & white herringbone label, screw cap....**$17.50**

Commercial, Dorothy Gray, Wedgwood, 3", glass w/'Wedgwood' painted decoration on urn form, M in Wedgwood-style box....**$80.00**

Commercial, Evyan, Golden Shadows, 3¼", clear bell shape, molded vertical lines, gold label, handle-form stopper....**$55.00**

Commercial, Evyan, White Shoulders, 2", clear w/gold label & cap....**$20.00**

Commercial, Faberge, Straw Hat, 3", clear w/screw cap covered in woven straw & red fabric, red enamel letters, M in box....**$72.50**

Commercial, Faberge, Straw Hat II, 3¼", clear caterpillar shape w/green plastic screw cap, M in box....**$16.50**

Commercial, Fragonard, Gamin, 2⅜", gold urn shape w/gold stopper, label missing....**$90.00**

Commercial, Goubaud, Blue Smoke, 5⅛", light blue crystal, modernistic faceted shape, gold label, velvet bow, M in box....**$50.00**

Commercial, Goubaud, Habibi, 2¾", clear & frosted w/gold label, M in box....**$35.00**

Commercial, Gucci, Parfum 1, 3½", clear w/red & green stripes on cap & bottle, black lettering....**$20.00**

Commercial, Guerlain, Shalimar, 3⅞", signed Baccarat, paper label, blue glass stopper, M in box....**$65.00**

Commercial, Helena Rubenstein, Apple Blossom, 2⅞", clear 3-sectioned cylinder, worn label....**$48.00**

Commercial, Houbigant, Bois Dormant, 3¾", clear w/triangular label & lines enameled in gold, brass overcap, M in box....**$100.00**

Commercial, Houbigant, Essence Rare, 3⅞", clear polyhedron shape w/intersecting triangles, gold overcap....**$120.00**

Commercial, Houbigant, Quelques Fleurs, clear round shape w/label on front, M in original lavender box....**$55.00**

Commercial, Jean Patou, Moment Supreme, 5¾", clear rectangular form w/large gold label, ball stopper, sealed....**$80.00**

Commercial, Kathryn, Forever Amber, 9¼", clear lady's torso form, label around bottom, abstract vegetal motif stopper....**$95.00**

Commercial, Lancome, Envol, 3½", frosted teardrop shape, lay-down type, brass screw-on cap & red ribbon.**$70.00**

Commercial, Lander, Gardenia, 4⅝", clear w/gold label, jewel-like green plastic cap....**$22.50**

Commercial, Lanvin, Arpege, 6¼", clear w/black label, rectangular, black glass stopper....**$80.00**

Commercial, Lucien Lelong, Impromptu, 6½", clear & frosted futuristic shape, no label....**$145.00**

Commercial, Lucien Lelong, Les Plumes, 2¾", clear feather forms (3) w/round gold caps set in original holder....**$155.00**

Commercial, Lucien Lelong, Taglio, 2⅜", clear rectangular form w/molded logo medallion on front, M in Lucite box....**$110.00**

Commercial, Lucien Lelong, Tailspin, 5", large red & gold neck label, metal screw cap w/embossed logo....**$15.00**

Commercial, Lucien Lelong, Tempest, 3¾", clear, prismatic, gold label....**$90.00**

Commercial, Machiabelli, Aviance, 2⅜", label on bottom, glass stopper....**$22.00**

Commercial, Machiabelli, Cachet, 7⅜", no label, glass stopper....**$16.00**

Commercial, Machiabelli, Stradivari, 4⅝", sceptre form w/cross stopper, paper label on base....**$22.50**

Commercial, Merle Norman, Vivons, 4⅛", clear w/rectangular stopper, M in velvet-trimmed box....**$45.00**

Commercial, Monico, 2¾", clear w/white enamel lettering, frosted glass stopper w/cork tip, empty, w/original box....**$60.00**

Commercial, Raphael, Réplique, 3", clear w/gold cord & paper label, glass stopper, M (sealed) in box....**$27.50**

Commercial, Renaud, Sweet Pea, 4", green flask form w/gold label, green stopper, empty, original gold-foil box....**$200.00**

Commercial, Renoir, Chi-Chi, 4", clear & frosted w/amber Bakelite cap in form of heart pierced by arrow, w/label....**$150.00**

Commercial, Renoir, Futur, 3⅛", clear w/gold stripes, label on bottom....**$26.00**

Commercial, Revillon, Detchema, 2", clear inverted brandy snifter form, label on stopper, M in box....**$90.00**

Commercial, Revillon, Tornade, 2¾", clear rectangular form w/scalloped left side, gold label, M in box....**$45.00**

Commercial, Richard Hudnut, Narcisse, 3", clear w/frosted & moulded design, gold embossed paper label, dauber....**$27.50**

Commercial, Schiaparelli, Shocking, 2⅞", clear, rectangular, paper label, frosted glass ball stopper, M....**$35.00**

Commercial, Shulton Cosmetics, Cie, clear w/large 'gemstone' stopper w/plastic top, empty, in gold & ecru box....**$75.00**

Commercial, Studio Girl, Always Yours, 2¼", clear moulded rose form, paper label, black plastic cap....**$14.00**

Commercial, Sulton Cosmetics, Natif de France, 2¾", clear rectangular form w/label, frosted stopper, M in box....**$30.00**

Commercial, Vigny, Heure Intime, 4", clear w/embossed squares, triangular silver label, faceted stopper....**$50.00**

Commercial, Vigny, Le Golliwogg, 3", frosted glass, black glass stopper, sealskin hair **$220.00**

Commercial, Weil, Cassandra, 3⅝", clear classical column form, small tied-on gold label, wax sealed **$90.00**

Commercial, Worth, Je Reviens, 1¾", cobalt, column-like w/silver base & cap (each engraved) **$17.50**

Commercial, Yardley, English Lavender, 4¼", clear, angular shape, brass screw-on cap embossed Yardley........**$6.00**

Figural, 2¼", head of googly-eyed parrot, white glass, multicolored paint, bottom stamped Germany..............**$72.50**

Figural, 2¾", clown w/hands in pockets, ceramic, yellow cap & suit, red & black details, unmarked Germany **$135.00**

Figural, 2½", baby sitting in highchair, ceramic, multicolor paint, unmarked, EX....................................**$275.00**

Figural, 2⅜", frog, ceramic w/metal crown stopper, green & yellow paint, marked Germany #3759................**$165.00**

Figural, 2⅜", old man slumped in chair, ceramic, all painted bluish-gray, crown stopper, unmarked Germany..**$150.00**

Figural, 3", Oriental court figure seated on cushion, ceramic, multicolor paint, unmarked France, small chip ..**$145.00**

Figural, 3½", Pierrette w/ruffled collar & bouquet, ceramic, multicolor paint, unmarked Germany **$120.00**

Figural, 3½", 18th-century man w/roses, ceramic w/metal crown stopper, multicolor paint, marked Germany **$120.00**

Figural, 3¼", flapper's head, ceramic, multicolor paint, laydown type, gold mercury glass stopper, unmarked Germany..**$200.00**

Figural, 3⅛", Dutch boy puckered for kiss, ceramic, multicolor paint, crown stopper, unmarked Germany **$120.00**

Figural, 3⅛", lady w/large vase, ceramic, red, yellow & black paint, crown stopper, marked #5625 (from Germany)..**$110.00**

Figural, 4", basket of forget-me-nots, ceramic w/blue, green & yellow paint, metal crown stopper, marked Germany #1489..**$90.00**

Figural, 4¼", baby in striped dress, ceramic, multicolor paint, crown stopper, Goebel Co emblem, stamped Germany..**$310.00**

Figural, 5½", nude holding cornucopia, ceramic, multicolor paint, Germany **$125.00**

Figural, 6", lady holding urn, ceramic, multicolor paint, crown stopper, signed Limoges, minor restoration at base..**$120.00**

Porcelain, 3¾", hand-painted blue forget-me-nots, gold lip & stopper, marked Germany....................................**$50.00**

Porcelain, 4", crown form, white w/gold & light blue trim, signed RPM w/eagle emblem...............................**$80.00**

Porcelain, 5", hand-painted daisies on white, gold ball stopper, signed Vienna Austria **$120.00**

Pez Candy Containers

Though Pez candy has been around since the late 1920s, the dispensers that we all remember as children weren't introduced until the 1950s. Each had the head of a certain character — a Mexican, a doctor, Santa Claus, an animal, or perhaps a comic book hero. It's hard to determine the age of some of these, but if yours have tabs or 'feet' on the bottom so they can stand up, they were made in the last ten years. As a general rule, collectors prefer them with no feet, but since some were only made in the footed versions, no collection would be complete without a few. It's scarcity and desirability that bears heaviest on value, though, not age. Some are already being seen with price tags that exceed $100.00, for instance, Alpine Man, Wolfman, Cowboy, Indian Brave, and bride and groom.

Angel, w/cast eyes..$15.00
Baseball glove...$120.00
Batgirl..$40.00
Betsy Ross...$40.00
Casper...$65.00
Cat, black derby, orange face $25.00
Cockatoo, w/blue face...$20.00
Crockodile, dark green $65.00
Dopey...$150.00
Garfield, VG $3.50
Home plate..$35.00
Lamb, w/yellow face $10.00
Little Bad Wolf..$9.00
Mexican $30.00
Pilgrim...$75.00
Ringmaster..$50.00
Rudolph...$10.00
Santa, full body...$85.00
Skull..$10.00
Smurf, EX..$5.00
Sylvester Cat $5.00
Tinkerbell..$75.00
Wolfman...$185.00
Wonder Woman, soft head $35.00

Pfaltzgraff Pottery

Pfaltzgraff has operated in Pennsylvania since the early 1800s making redware at first, then stoneware crocks and jugs, yellowware and spongeware in the twenties, artware and kitchenware in the thirties, and stoneware kitchen items through the hard years of the forties. In 1950 they developed their first line of dinnerware, called Gourmet Royal (known in later years as simply Gourmet). It was a high-gloss line of solid color accented at the rims with a band of frothy white, similar to lines made later by McCoy, Hull, Harker and many other companies. Although it also came in pink, it was the dark brown that became so popular. Today these brown stoneware lines are one of the newest interests of young collectors.

The success of Gourmet was the inspiration the company needed to initiate the production of the many dinnerware lines that have become the backbone of the Pfaltzgraff company.

A giftware line called Muggsy was designed in the late 1940s. It consisted of comic character mugs, ashtrays, bottle stoppers, children's dishes, a pretzel jar, and a cookie jar. All of the characters were given names. It was very successful and continued in production until 1960.

For further information, we recommend *Pfaltzgraff, America's Potter,* by David A. Walsh and Polly Stetler, published in conjunction with the Historical Society of York County, York, Pennsylvania.

Gourmet Royale, bowl, cereal; 5½" $2.00
Gourmet Royale, bowl, vegetable; divided................$14.00
Gourmet Royale, bowl, 7x10", #241, oval $12.00

Gourmet Royale, butter dish, ¼-lb, w/lid...................$12.00
Gourmet Royale, casserole, round, w/lid...................$16.00
Gourmet Royale, creamer, #24...................................$4.00
Gourmet Royale, cup..$2.00
Gourmet Royale, gravy boat, large, #426, w/two spout.$12.00
Gourmet Royale, mug, #91..$3.00
Gourmet Royale, pitcher, #415, w/ice lip..................$16.00
Gourmet Royale, plate, dinner; 10".............................$4.00
Gourmet Royale, plate, salad; 6¾"..............................$1.50
Gourmet Royale, salt & pepper shakers, pr $4.50
Gourmet Royale, saucer...$1.50
Gourmet Royale, sugar bowl, #22, w/lid......................$5.00
Village, bowl, cereal; 6¼"...$2.00
Village, butter dish, ¼-lb, w/lid $12.00
Village, canister, w/lid, set of 4.................................$70.00
Village, coffeepot, 10", #550......................................$20.00
Village, creamer...$3.50
Village, cup..$2.00
Village, cup & saucer, set..$3.00
Village, custard cup...$1.50
Village, mug, 4", #289...$2.00
Village, mug, 5¼", w/foot..$3.00
Village, mustard jar...$8.00
Village, pitcher, water; 2-qt, #416.............................$16.00
Village, plate, dinner; 10½"..$4.00
Village, plate, salad; 7"..$1.50
Village, platter, 14", oval...$7.00
Village, salt & pepper shakers, pr...............................$4.00
Village, sugar bowl w/lid...$4.00

Phoenix Bird Pottery

This is a type of blue and white porcelain dinnerware that has been imported from Japan since the early 1900s. It is decorated with the bird of paradise and stylized sprigs of Chinese grass. You'll find several marks on the older pieces. The newer ones, if marked at all, carry a paper label; backgrounds are whiter and the blue more harsh.

For more information, we recommend *Phoenix Bird China* by Joan Collett Oates.

Bowl, bouillon; w/underplate.....................................$20.00
Bowl, cereal; 6"..$11.50
Bowl, 5½", scalloped rim..$20.00
Butter pat, old..$9.00
Butter tub & drain, 2¾x5", w/handles $65.00
Cake tray, round $70.00
Candy & nut tub, 2", handles.....................................$25.00
Chamberstick, old...$135.00
Condensed milk container, w/underplate.................$125.00
Cracker jar, 5½"...$50.00
Creamer, bell form...$20.00
Creamer & sugar bowl, w/lid.....................................$45.00
Cup, bouillon; inside border, w/handles & underplate..$22.00
Cup & saucer, demitasse; Occupied Japan.................$18.00
Custard cup, inside border...$15.00
Egg cup, 2¼", single $10.00

Egg cup, 3¼", double $16.50
Gravy boat, 7", w/attached underplate.......................$70.00

Jar, 5½"...$45.00
Ladle, gravy; 6"...$45.00
Plate, dinner; 9¾"..$48.00
Plate, 7¼", hand painted, scalloped rim......................$35.00
Plate, 7¼", transfer print, plain edge...........................$9.00
Salt & pepper shakers, mushroom form, pr................$20.00
Salt & pepper shakers, 2", globular, pr.......................$30.00
Sugar bowl, w/lid, Nippon..$22.00
Teapot, 8¼" wide, loop handle.....................................$50.00
Tureen, vegetable; oval, w/lid.....................................$135.00

Phoenix Glass

Though this company has operated in Monaca, Pennsylvania, from 1880 until the present (it's now a division of the Newell Group), collectors are primarily interested in the sculptured glassware lines they made during the thirties and forties. These quality artware items were usually made in milk glass or crystal with various color treatments or with a satin finish. Most of the time, the backgrounds were colored and the relief designs left plain. The glassware was never signed, instead the company used paper labels in the shape of a phoenix bird.

Ashtray, 3" long, mother-of-pearl flowers on milk glass, slate
   gray background $40.00
Bowl, 8" sq, Lace Dew Drop, pink on milk glass........$40.00
Bowl, 9", Ivy & Snow, crystal, oval..............................$15.00
Candle holders, 4", Strawberry, blue on milk glass, pr .$135.00
Candle holders, 4", Strawberry, tan on milk glass, pr ..$130.00
Candle holders, 4¾", Water Lily, green on clear, pr..$115.00
Candlesticks, Sawtooth, dark blue on milk glass, pr.$135.00
Cigarette box, blue flowers & green leaves, white satin
   background, w/lid $100.00
Comport, 8" dia, Moon & Star, pearl on milk glass.........$45.00

Goblet, Blackberry, caramel lustre on milk glass $25.00
Jam jar, 4½", Lace Dewdrop, caramel lustre on milk glass,
   w/lid $20.00
Jell-O mold, Queen Anne, star-shape, crystal $4.00
Shade, 5" w/2" fitter, crystal w/acid-etched design $18.00
Sugar bowl, Catalonian, triangular, dark blue on crystal.$30.00
Sugar bowl, Lace Dewdrop, blue wash, w/lid.............$60.00
Vase, Bicentennial, crystal w/red, white, & blue design .$50.00
Vase, fan; 7", Catalonian, dark blue on crystal $50.00
Vase, Philodendron, amber, 1960s.............................$40.00
Vase, Wild Geese, pearlized white on white $175.00
Vase, 10½", Wild Rose, shaded pattern, tan background on
   milk glass..$165.00
Vase, 10½", Wild Rose, white on light blue $110.00
Vase, 11", Philodendron, amber...................................$45.00
Vase, 5", Jewel, mother-of-pearl pattern on milk glass, light
   blue background...$65.00
Vase, 7", Bluebell, taupe background on satin milk
   glass $115.00
Vase, 7½", Cosmos, white flowers on crystal, aqua back-
   ground..$150.00
Vase, 8", Freesia, wine background on milk glass $150.00
Vase, 8", Lily, frosted pattern, aqua on crystal, 3-crimp
   rim $250.00

Vase, 10", Sunflowers, clear-cased white.............$225.00
Vase, 10¼", Madonna, burgundy background on milk glass
   w/mother-of-pearl design....................................$175.00

Pie Birds

Popular since Victorian times, a pie bird is a hollow figure used in the middle of the pie to allow steam to vent through the top crust. They're glazed inside and out and were made as various types of birds, as elephants, and sometimes as chefs and bakers. Be aware that reproductions are commonplace.

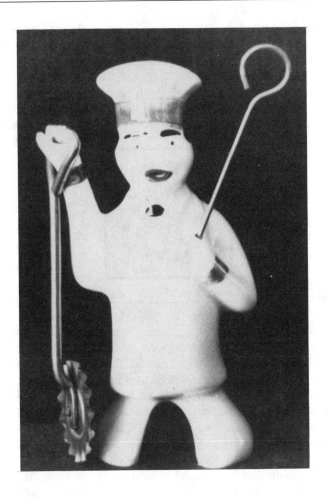

Benny the Baker, Cardinal China, marked Pat Pending **$68.00**
Bird, big mouth, white, ceramic $30.00
Bird, Morton Pottery $20.00
Bird baby, 3½", multicolor, marked Yellowstone Park.. $25.00
Black Chef, 4½", black skin tone w/white hat & yellow outfit, pottery, M.. **$100.00**
Black Chef, 4½", James Barry Products, blue or yellow clothes $50.00
Black Chef holding rolling pin, ceramic...................... $55.00
Black circus clown, vents from pointed hat................. $35.00
Black monk, praying, vents from bald pate................. $35.00
Bluebird, 4½", black wings... $20.00
Chick, 5", long neck, Pillsbury premium, common $15.00
Dragon's head, vents from between horns $35.00
Duckling, 5", long neck, blue, pink, yellow, or multicolor, 1950 .... $18.00
Elephant, brown, ceramic... $55.00
Elephant on stand, vents from mouth $35.00
Humpty Dumpty, marked England.............................. $52.00
Irish funnel, mythological figure emblem on side....... $35.00
Owl, stylized, pottery... $45.00
Pelican, perched on rock $35.00
Rooster, Blue Willow.. $17.50

Howard Pierce

Mr. Pierce is a potter who has had his own studio in Claremont, California, since the 1940s. His distinctively styled sculptures of animals, birds, and human figures have been sold in gift shops and department stores nationwide. Many of his animal 'families' were sold in pairs or three-piece sets.

You may also find examples of vases and lamps with openings containing small animals or plant forms. Most of his work, except for some of the smaller animals, was marked.

If you'd like to learn more about Howard Pierce and his work, *The Collector's Encyclopedia of California Pottery* by Jack Chipman contains a chapter devoted to him.

African head, 1950s.. **$45.00**
Ash tray, light gray lava w/glossy cobalt interior......... $40.00
Bear, 6", blue speckled, 1950s $30.00
Bowl, 5x9½", brown on white, gondola shape............ $20.00
Bull, large, brown, 1950s... $25.00
Bulldog, small, brown, recent, marked USMC $20.00

Cat, 8", black matt **$40.00**
Cat, 14", sandstone.. $45.00
Duck decoy, gray & white $25.00
Elephant, pink, recent $18.00
Eskimos, 7", brown, pr $40.00
Female bust, 10½", brown agate, ca 1956, limited production.. **$125.00**
Giraffes, 10½", brown agate, mid-1950s, in-mold marks, pr ..$50.00
Heron, white $25.00
Hippo, 6", stamped Howard Pierce $30.00
Monkey, 6", stamped Howard Pierce $30.00
Partridge, large, brown, 1950s................................... $25.00
Penguin, 7", black on white, ca 1953, stamped Howard Pierce $35.00
Pigeon, 7½", 1950s, stamped marks............................ $20.00
Polar bear, 4½", brown on white, 1950s $30.00
Quail family, large quail 5½", 1950s, stamped Howard Pierce, 3-pc set... $60.00

Raccoon, brown & white, pr $32.00
Roadrunner, large, black, recent $22.00
Roadrunner, large, brown & white $24.00
Robin, 3", black & green $20.00
Squirrel, gray, 4" $12.00
Turtle, 5", speckled brown on white, 1950s................$25.00
Unicorn, small, recent...$18.00
Vase, green, Art Deco-style girl w/in circular cutout, creche style, square $45.00
Vase, 7¼", green mottle, glossy, in-mold mark............$30.00
Vase, 8", green w/white deer & tree at side, creche style, Claremont $35.00
Water bird, 14", 1950s, stamped marks $40.00

Pin-Back Buttons

Literally hundreds of thousands of pin-back buttons are available; pick a category and have fun! Most fall into one of three fields — advertising, political, and personality related, but within these three broad areas are many more specialized groups. Just make sure you buy only those that are undamaged, are still bright and unfaded, and have well-centered designs and properly aligned printing. The older buttons (those from before the 1920s) may be made of celluloid and the cardboard backing printed with the name of a company or a product.

All Star Dairies, 1⅜", shield in center, red, white & blue, 1950s, NM $12.50
American League Champions NY Yankees, 1¼", blue on white, 1932, NM $22.00
Batman & Robin, 1", 1966 ....$4.00
Batman Crime Fighter, 1½"...$6.00
Big Boy Club, 1⅛", smiling boy, multicolor, 1960s, small scratches, EX $10.00
Buy American, eagle on shield, red, white & blue, 1930s, NM $8.00

C & O For Progress, 1½", yellow lettering on navy ..$6.00
CBS TV logo, 1¼"..$3.00
Dairyland Heart, 1", red heart on white, Sandman Soldiers along bottom, 1930s, EX..$10.00
Disney World Silver 20th Birthday, 3" $4.00
Duck Tales, 3", 1987 ....$4.00
Famous Monsters Fan Club, 2½"................................$12.50
Flipper, ⅞", multicolored, M.......................................$15.00
General MacArthur, 2¼", portrait between flags forming V, red, white & blue, EX $55.00
Green Hornet Agent, 4", EX $20.00
Green Lantern Superheroes Club, 3½", 1966...............$25.00
Hamm's Beer, 1⅝", bear lithograph on tin, 1970s, M $2.00
Jerry Brown & Linda Ronstadt (1980 photos) for President, 2½" $18.00

John Wayne, 1¼" $20.00
Kellogg's Early Bird Breakfast Club, 1⅛", comic bird, multicolored, 1950s, EX $12.00
Kick 'Em in the Axis, cartoon, multicolor, 1940s, 1¼", EX $15.00
Let's Be Friends Sunbeam Bread, girl w/slice of bread on blue background, 1930s, M $4.00
Mickey Mouse Club, 3½" $10.00
Pepsi, Take the Challenge, 4"..$4.00
Pepsi Light, Lemony Taste, 3" $4.50
Peter Pan, 3½", Walt Disney Productions......................$7.00
Reddy Kilowatt, 1", multicolored early version, 1930s, EX $28.00
Remember Pearl Harbor, 1¼", white on red, EX $18.00
Riddler, 1", multicolored, 1960s, NM $15.00
Soupy Sales Society, 3½" $15.00
Southern Bread & Cake, ⅞", Baker & cartoon-style child, blue & white w/yellow rim, 1930s, EX.................$14.00
Support Black Liberation, John Brown portrait on green, 1950s, M...$2.50
The Fonz for President, 1976 ....$4.00
Vote Yes for Sunday Movies, blue & white, 1930s, EX .$7.00
Winnie the Pooh, 3½", Pooh's face, Walt Disney Productions $7.00
Witches of Eastwick, 2"..$3.00
Vote Dry, ⅞", promoting prohibition..........................$15.00
7-Up Uncola, 2¼", 'Follow the Un' in center, multicolored, late 1960s, NM $15.00

Pin-Up Art

Some of the more well-known artists in this field are Vargas, Petty, Ballantyne, Armstrong, and Phillips, and some pin-up art enthusiasts pick a favorite and concentrate their collections on just his work. From the mid-thirties until well into the fifties, pin-up art was extremely popular. Female movie stars from this era were ultra-glamorous, voluptous, and very sensual creatures, and this type of media influence naturally impacted the social and cultural attitudes of the period. As the adage goes, 'Sex sells.' And well it did. You'll find calendars, playing cards, magazines, advertising, and merchandise of all types that depict these unrealistically perfect ladies. Though not all will be signed, most of these artists have a distinctive, easily identifiable style that you'll soon be able to recognize.

Advertisement for Community Plate & Silver Co, Coles Phillips, lady reclines on ledge, Ladies' Home Journal, 1923, M **$12.50**

Advertisement for Community Silver, Rolf Armstrong, Ladies' Home Journal, June 1924, M **$7.50**

Advertisement for Esquire calendar, Vargas, nine sepia pin-ups, 1946, M **$5.00**

Advertisement for Janzen Bathing Suits, 'One of Us Must Flag that Ship with Our Janzen,' George Petty, June, 1936 ....**$15.00**

Advertisement for Old Gold, 'Bothered by a Beach Bore,' man & pretty girl, George Petty, M.........................**$12.00**

Advertisement for Old Gold, 'Smacked by a Sappy Santa,' lady in black, George Petty, December 1935, M...**$15.00**

Ash tray, nude blond by coffee table painted on metal, late 1950s, M..**$15.00**

Ash tray, 4x4", Playmate holding key painted on glass, 1960s, M..**$25.00**

Blotter, 3⅜x6½", 'Call Anytime,' blond in tight dress, holds fan, sits (half-turned) in chair, Vargas, M **$18.00**

Book, 'Esquire's Handbook for Hosts,' 10x6", many cartoon illustrations, recipes & games, Grosset & Dunlap, 1949, EX...**$50.00**

Calendar, 12½x8¼", 'Playboy's Playmate,' Jayne Mansfield as January Playmate, 1960, NM **$110.00**

Calendar, 12x8½", Glamour Gallery, twelve pin-ups, TN Thompson for Esquire, 1950s, EX.........................**$20.00**

Calendar, 12x8½", twelve pin-ups, Smith for Esquire, spiral bound, 1944, EX **$100.00**

Calendar, 12x8½", Vargas for Esquire, spiral bound, 1946, EX...**$80.00**

Calendar, 13x8½", 'Glamour Gal Proverbs,' Jayne Mansfield on January & April pages, 1957, EX **$110.00**

Calendar, 14½x8½", 'Girls of 1951,' twelve pin-ups, Moran, spiral bound, 1951, EX **$120.00**

Calendar, 14x8¼", twelve pin-ups, Vargas for Esquire, 1942, complete, EX **$40.00**

Calendar, 22½x29", 'The Right Touch,' cowgirl using paints, Rolf Armstrong for B&B Jumbo Calendars, late 1940s, EX...**$75.00**

Calendar, 22x28", 'Good News,' cowgirl reading letter at mailbox, Zoe Mozert, late 1940s, NM **$85.00**

Calendar, 4x5", twelve pin-ups, Lenlee Arts Corp, 1951, unused, NM **$25.00**

Calendar, 9x12", twelve sketches, TN Thompson for Esquire, 1957, in original mailing envelope, M **$22.50**

Calendar print, 15x17", 'Sheer Delight,' Elvgren, late 1940s, NM **$17.50**

Card, 5x6", Jayne Mansfield, full color, 1950s **$3.00**

Foldout, 'Red Means Go,' Vargas for Esquire, 1940, M ..**$20.00**

Gatefold, 'From Bill w/Love,' blond in white hat w/blue feather, blue gloves, Vargas for Esquire, December, 1941, M...**$30.00**

Gatefold, 'Torch Singer,' blond in long black gown clapping hands, Vargas for Esquire, February, 1945, EX.....**$28.00**

Key chain telescope viewer, extends to 1¼", view of pin-up when held to light, 1950s, M..................................**$10.00**

Label, 3x12", 'Sweet Patootie,' 1940s **$2.00**

Letter opener, 8½", plastic nude diecut, in 8½" slotted folder w/painted dress, 'Designed by Elvgren,' 1950s, NM ..**$32.00**

Magazine, 'Europe's Top Pin-Ups,' 1956, Gina Lollobrigida on cover, VG **$22.50**

Magazine, Avant Garde, 11x11", Marilyn Monroe cover, psychedelic colors, 1968, EX..................................**$28.00**

Magazine, Esquire, 'Will You Surely Help,' George Petty, August 1936, M...**$20.00**

Magazine, Jayne Mansfield Pin-Up Book, Standard Magazines, color cover & center, many black & white photos, 1957, NM **$45.00**

Magazine, Modern Man, 8½x11", Jayne Mansfield cover, many photos inside, 1958, EX................................**$24.00**

Magazine, Modern Photography, Marilyn Monroe cover, 1954, EX...**$35.00**

Magazine, True, 'Autumn Rise,' Vargas, Jan 1952, EX......**$17.50**

Magazine page (Esquire), 'I've Been Frightfully Restless,' redhead on bed, Vargas, March 1936, EX **$12.50**

Paper doll, 3x5", Cherie, pull tab to remove clothes, 1940s, NM...**$3.50**

Playing card, Vargas, blond in white bathing suit & large white hat tied at neck, red background, 1945, single, EX..**$3.00**

Playing cards, artist unknown, Duratone, baton twirler & pin-up fishergirl, double deck, in original box, 1950s, EX..**$20.00**

Print, 12x17", 'Danger!,' cowgirl by split-rail fence, D'Amaro, early 1950s, NM **$22.50**

Sheet music, 'I Am Forever Thinking of You,' Rolf Armstrong cover, 1920, M **$17.50**

Shot glass, 3", Playboy Playmate w/key painted on glass, 1960s, M..**$40.00**

Steering knob, 1¾" dia, nude w/dog in her lap contained w/in clear plastic disk, ca 1950, EX......................**$20.00**

Tie holder, 2¾" wide, brass w/peep hole to hold toward light, shows nude image, 1930s, NM on card **$40.00**

Planters Peanuts

The personification of the Planters Company, Mr. Peanut has been around since 1916, adding a bit of class and dash to all their advertising efforts. Until the company was sold in 1961, he was a common sight on their product containers and at special promotional events. He was modeled as salt and pepper shakers, mugs, whistles, and paperweights. His image decorated neckties, playing cards, beach towels, and T-shirts. Today he has his own fan club, a collectors' organization for those who especially enjoy this area of advertising memorabilia.

Just about everyone remembers the Planters Peanut jars, though they're becoming very scarce today. There are more than fifteen different styles and shapes, and some have been reproduced. The earliest, introduced in 1926, was the 'pennant' jar. It was octagonal, and the back panel was embossed with this message: 'Sold Only in Printed Planters Red Pennant Bags.' A second octagonal style carried a paper label instead. Pennant jars marked 'Made in Italy' are reproductions, beware!

Bag, 6x2¾", textured wax paper, holds 1¼-oz, 1930s, M $20.00
Beach towel, shows Mr Peanut on white terry cloth, M ..$35.00
Beer mug, ceramic, 1950s, M $50.00
Bookmark, 7¾x3", Mr Peanut figural, cardboard...........$8.00
Charm, Mr Peanut figural, glows in the dark $6.00
Cigarette lighter, Mr Peanut, marked Bic, EX..............$20.00
Coloring book, American Ecology & Mr Peanut, 1972, NM $12.50

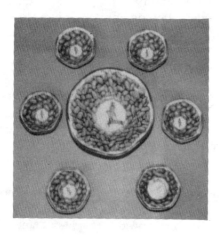

Dishes, six small, one large, VG.............................$25.00
Doll, Mr Peanut, jointed wood, EX..............................$75.00
Golf cap, Mr Peanut on bill, M $15.00
Ice bucket, 16x12", wood, w/logo on lid.....................$28.00
Jar, barrel form w/nut finial on lid, clear glass, reproduction..$32.50
Jar, football form w/peanut finial on lid $300.00
Jar, octagon shaped w/seven embossed sides & 'Pennant 5¢', clear glass, w/lid $250.00
Jar, peanut butter, clear glass, shows early Mr Peanut on tin lid, scarce...$25.00
Jar, square w/'Planters' embossed on each side, clear glass, peanut finial..$150.00
Knife, red plastic $5.00
Mug, 4x2½" dia, Mr Peanut figural, arm forms handle, ceramic, hand painted, 1950s, NM........................$68.00
Necktie, Mr Peanut on maroon, M in original box......$35.00
Nut set, New York World's Fair, dated 1940...............$35.00
Paint book, 'Seeing the USA,' dated 1950 ....$35.00
Pencil, lead-filled w/figural top, 1950s, M.....................$7.50
Plate, 6", pewter, M..$35.00
Playing cards, in original box, M $18.00
Radio, 10", Mr Peanut figural $75.00
Salt & pepper shakers, Mr Peanut figural w/rhinestone eyes, ceramic, pr, rare...$125.00

Salt & pepper shakers, Mr Peanut figural, plastic, EX, pr $25.00
Salt & pepper shakers, 3", Mr Peanut figural, silvered plastic, EX, pr...$17.50
Sign, 11¾", Mr Peanut figural, cardboard....................$12.50
T-shirt, 'Planters Potato Chips,' cotton blend, M..........$15.00
Thimble, light yellow plastic $4.50
Toothbrush, Mr Peanut figural handle, blue, M...........$10.00
Whistle, orange plastic..$8.00
Whistle, 3½", green & red plastic................................$12.00

Plastics

Early plastics such as Bakelite, Catalin, gutta percha, and celluloid are not new to collectors, and most of us realize the value of the wonderful radios and jewelry items, but did you know that even plastics from after WWII are becoming collectible as well? The market is not yet well established, and here's an area where you will be able to make some good buys well before the public in general. Prices are still low, and besides, it's fun.

Because plastic was such an inexpensive material, manufacturers produced literally thousands of household items with the intent of very short-term appeal. Their theory was simple: replace existing models with those that varied just enough to promote sales. Buyers would be willing to throw out the old and replace with the new, since most items were very cheap. As a result, new colors, new styles, new looks epitomized the public's fascinations and fads. Pop beads, flying saucer lamps, and kitchenware items in streamlined shapes all had their time in the spotlight.

Items that you may want to buy are interesting pieces of jewelry, well-designed kitchenware and appliances, and things that relate to celebrities, Disney characters, advertising, or special holidays. Whatever aspect of plastic collecting you personally enjoy should afford you good shopping and lots of satisfaction.

Bottle opener, chrome plate w/red, green or amber Catalin handle...$8.00
Buttons, ¾" dia, ivoroid or pearlescent celluloid, six on card...$8.00

Carving set, Catalin, three pieces w/wooden wall rack .**$40.00**

Checkers, red & black Catalin, full set, in box............**$32.00**

Chopsticks, ivory Catalin, pr **$3.00**

Cigarette box, dark brown Bakelite, half-cylinder, rotates open..**$40.00**

Cigarette box, 5½x3¾", light green Catalin w/wooden bottom, rectangular shape **$30.00**

Cigarette case, Bakelite & pigskin, clear w/streaks of brown, marked A Rolinx, Made in England...$85.00

Cigarette lighter, red or black Catalin, Arco-Lite devil's head **$150.00**

Clock, ivoroid celluloid, Greek temple facade, wind-up alarm **$45.00**

Clock, mantel, dark brown Bakelite, Art Deco design w/wind-up alarm **$50.00**

Clock, Seth Thomas, 3½", maroon Catalin case, wind-up alarm **$42.00**

Corkscrew, chrome w/red, green, or amber Catalin handle..**$12.50**

Crib toy, Tykie Toy, Clown w/Laolin head & Catalin body **$60.00**

Crib toy, Tykie Toy, eleven Catalin multicolor spools on string, 1940s..**$50.00**

Crib toy, Tykie Toy, kitten...............................$100.00

Dice, ¾", ivory or red Catalin, pr **$2.00**

Dominoes, red or green Catalin, full set, w/wood box....**$40.00**

Dresser set, amberoid & green marbleized celluloid, 7-pc set...**$70.00**

Flatware, chrome plate w/single-color Catalin handle, each piece **$1.50**

Flatware, green pearl on black celluloid handle, 3-pc set **$9.00**

Flatware, ivoroid celluloid handle, each piece **$1.00**

Flatware, stainless, 1-color Catalin handle, 36-pc set in leatherette box **$180.00**

Flatware, stainless, 2-color Catalin handle, 3-pc matched place setting **$12.00**

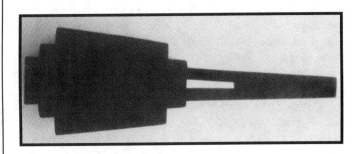

Hairbrush, brown, stepped Art Deco shape $8.00

Ice cream scoop, stainless w/red Catalin handle.........**$19.00**

Lamp base, 10", brass & amber Catalin, Art Deco............**$30.00**

Letter opener, chrome w/Catalin handle, Art Deco design...**$14.00**

Letter opener, marbleized green Catalin, dagger shape .**$20.00**

Manicure set, four celluloid miniature tools on tube holder w/painted flowers...**$35.00**

Manicure set, ivoroid celluloid, 18-pc in roll-up leather case **$25.00**

Memo pad, amber Catalin, Carvacraft Great Britain **$35.00**

Mirror, dresser; 13", ivoroid celluloid, oval beveled glass **$28.00**

Nail brush, 3½", dark amber Catalin, turtle shape **$16.00**

Pencil sharpener, yellow Catalin, scotty dog silhouette shape **$20.00**

Pencil sharpener, ¾x1", red Catalin w/Mickey Mouse decal...**$30.00**

Penholder, red Catalin, black base, scotty dog form...**$45.00**

Picture frame, 2" dia, ivoroid celluloid, easel back......**$12.00**

Picture frame, 6", clear Lucite, Art Deco style.............**$14.00**

Pipe, amber & green Catalin, clay-lined bowl **$28.00**

Powder box, ivoroid, pearlescent, or amber celluloid **$10.00**

Powder box, 4", amber & green Catalin, fluted cylinder **$56.00**

Purse, amber & brown w/tortoise shell rope handle **$65.00**

Ring case, amber or maroon Catalin, hinged lid **$100.00**

Salad servers, Chase chrome, ivory, black, or brown Catalin handles, pr...**$30.00**

Salt & pepper shakers, glass, in 3" Catalin holder, pr ..**$19.00**

Salt & pepper shakers, 3½", Catalin, stepped cylinder shape, pr...**$25.00**

Salt & pepper shakers, 4", translucent red Lucite, pr...**$12.00**
Shaving brush, red, green, or amber Catalin...............**$18.00**
Spatula, stainless, red, green, or amber Catalin handle.**$4.50**
Strainer, 2¾" dia, red, green, or amber Catalin handle..**$4.00**
Swizzle stick, amber or red Catalin, baseball-bat shape.**$4.00**

Playing Cards

Here is another collectible that is inexpensive, easy to display (especially single cards), and very diversified. The backs are printed with reproductions of famous paintings and pin-up art, carry advertising of all types, and picture tourist attractions and world's fair scenes. Early decks are scarce, but those from the forties on are usually more attractive anyway, so pick an area that interests you most and have fun! Though they're usually not dated, you may find some clues that will assist you in determining an approximate date. Telephone numbers, zip codes, advertising slogans, and patriotic messages are always helpful.

Everett Grist has written an informative book, *Advertising Playing Cards*, which we highly recommend to anyone interested in playing cards with any type of advertising.

Advertising

Booth, double deck, Fletcher Class Trawler backs, 104+4 Jokers, each deck NM in box...................**$10.00**
Corby's Canadian Whiskey, wide, 'A Little Touch' (painting) on back, ca 1900, 52+advertising card, VG in taped & broken box..**$130.00**
Das Pfungstadter Glucksblatt, horseshoe-shaped cards, 32 complete, NM in torn box......................**$25.00**
EB Co Submarines, double deck, diamonds & hearts have black border, 104+2 Jokers, one deck EX in box/one VG in box...**$165.00**
Guston-Bacon Mfg, special Aces, 1940s, 52+special Joker+score card+2 advertising cards, M in wrapper w/tax stamp..**$35.00**
Honda, non-standard, 52 different motorcycle pictures, 52 complete, NM in worn box....................**$6.00**
Jack Daniel's, wide, non-standard, portrait on black background backs, M in box, sealed............................**$6.00**

Lubaid Company, red & black lettering on white, complete in original box............................$7.50

Molson Ale, wide, Goodall Ace of Spades, 1900s, 52, G in partial box **$18.00**
Phillips 66, green & gold bands top & bottom, red lettering, complete in original box **$6.50**
Saint Mary of the Woods Alumnae, blue & gold backs, special Ace of Spades, 52+special Joker+score card, VG, no box..**$35.00**
Sam Thompson Whiskey, wide, special Ace of Spades, 1900, 52+Joker+advertising card, fair condition in torn box **$66.00**
Sony Rock 'n Pop, non-standard, 8 British illustrators portray rock stars on Courts, Aces & Jokers, M in box, sealed..**$25.00**
Stroh Light, can shaped, 1979, 52+2 Jokers+advertising card, M in box **$12.00**
Year of the Child, Belgium, non-standard, gold border on backs, 1979, 52+2 different special Jokers+fact card, M in box **$16.50**

Games, Tarot, Magic and Miscellaneous

Baseball, Whitman #3923, 44 cards, EX w/instructions on original box **$35.00**
Chess 'O' 64, chess pieces on each card, 64 complete+2 Jokers, M in box **$17.50**

Dick Tracy, characters from the strip on each card, copyrighted Chester Gould, 1937, Whitman Publishing, EX in original box................................$25.00
ESP Cards, Rhine, Duke University, 1935, 25 complete+2 instruction cards, EX in box **$6.00**
Esso Baseball Challenge, Canada, 1988, M in box **$4.00**
Golf, Warren #494, plays 18 holes of golf, 40 complete, +3 instruction cards, EX in box **$27.50**
Jacob's Ladder, Mental Diversion Dream Picture Card Game, 1936, 54 complete+instructions, VG in box.............**$9.00**
Kam-Ra, 5 suits (star, circle, square, dollar sign, triangle), 1928, 50 complete+rules, M in box......................**$32.50**
Madame Signa, fortune telling, early 1900s, 36 complete+booklet, G in box **$42.50**
Mahjong Playing Cards, M in box, sealed **$8.00**

Pecos Bill, foreign, special Aces, 40 complete+instructions, NM in box **$12.50**

Singer Domino Cards, Domino faces, Singer Sewing Machine advertising backs, 28 complete, VG in box **$15.00**

Modern Decks

Classique, Draeger Freres, specially designed Courts, 1950, 52+2 special Jacks, M in box................................**$35.00**

Dallas Cowboy Cheerleaders, wide, photo on each card, 1979, 52+2 Jokers, M in box...................................**$7.50**

Elvgren, double deck, lady on red couch or lady on suitcase, each deck M in plastic box, sealed **$45.00**

Esquire, double deck, girls on animal skins, special Ace of Spades, each 52+special Joker, EX/VG in original boxes.........**$82.50**

Far East, plastic, non-standard, 52+2 deer Jokers, M, no box...**$10.00**

Glamour, non-standard, glamour tips on backs, miniature size, 52 complete, NM in handmade original box.**$35.00**

Historic Denmark, historic Courts, gold trim, pantographs on Pips, 53+3 special Jokers, M, no box **$15.00**

Las Rosas/Argentina, wide, Vigor, standard faces, 52+2 special Jokers, NM in box **$17.50**

Models of All Nations, nudes w/'accessories' from other nations, 52 photos, 1950s, 52+wolf Joker, EX in torn box..**$27.50**

Sheba, wide, non-standard Courts of African Heroes, 1972, 52+2 Jokers, M in box, sealed..............................**$20.00**

Smiling Brand, nudes, color photos, 52+pin-up Joker, 1960s, M in box **$8.00**

Tally-Ho #43, pinochle deck, Dougherty, 1960s tax stamp, M in box, sealed **$6.00**

Torpedo, Russell Ace of Spade, US Playing Cards, 1942, 52+cowboy Joker+2 advertising cards+score card, M in box, sealed **$16.50**

Vargas, 52 pin-ups on faces, 1953, 52+special Joker+biographical card, EX in torn box **$100.00**

Older Decks, Narrow, Odd Sizes and Shapes

Bijou #1, US Playing Cards, plaid back w/coat of arms center, 52+cherub Joker, VG in box............................**$35.00**

Brazil-Cartas Para Jogar, red pattern backs, French-type Courts, ca 1940, 52+Joker+score card, EX in partial box..**$37.50**

Buster Brown, 53 color cartoons, 1905, 52+Joker, miniature size, EX in torn box **$60.00**

Chitrashala, foreign, 1940s, 52+2 Jokers, NM in box....**$45.00**

Congress #606, double deck, Pirate Girl or Masqueraders backs, US Playing Cards, 52 in each, M in box **$8.00**

Elf #93, NY Cards Co, ca 1900, miniature, 52 complete, G, no box...**$8.00**

Hausedmann, aluminum, red back w/beige coating, Austria, 1932, 52 complete, VG, no box **$55.00**

India, lacquered circular cards, for game of Mogul Ganjifa, 96 complete, in carved wooden box....................**$77.00**

Little Duke #24, US Playing Cards, ca 1900, small size, 52+Joker+blank card, VG in box **$10.00**

Red Seal #016, A Dougherty, pinochle deck, 48 complete, NM in box, rare...**$72.50**

Victory Playing Cards, non-standard, issued after VE Day, Hitler & Mussolini Jokers, M in box, sealed........**$100.00**

Older Decks, Wide

#500, blue dragon backs, US Playing Cards, 52+'500' Joker, VG in box...**$10.00**

Congress, geometrical backs, US Playing Cards, 52+Dundreary Joker, fair in slipcase................................**$45.00**

Court of Music, non-standard, Presser, music symbol suits, musician Courts, 1900s, 52+Caruso Joker+fact card, EX in box..**$330.00**

Dondorf #324, 2-way Courts, 52+Joker, G in torn box ..**$16.50**

Foster's Self Playing 2nd Series, A Dougherty, 128 deals shown on backs, 1891, 52+patent/fact card+booklet, EX in box..**$55.00**

Goodall-Bezique Set, 2-way Courts, ca 1871, 4 packs of 32 cards each+4 leather registers+instructions, EX in case..**$82.50**

Hunt & Sons, plain backs, square corners, 1-way stencil-colored Courts, Frizzle Ace of Spades, 52 complete, NM, no box..**$160.00**

Mystic #888, Knights of Pythias logo backs, US Playing Cards, special Ace of Spades, 52+special Joker, VG in broken box...**$170.00**

Sheldon's Fortune Telling, readings at top & bottom, gold edges, 1921, NM in oversized slipcase.................**$75.00**

Success #28, Russell, Kalamazoo, red diamond-patterned backs, 52+Success #28 Joker, VG in slipcase........**$40.00**

Souvenir

Alaska-Yukon Pacific Expo, Eskimo, Alaska & Fair scene photos, 1909, 50 of 52, no Joker, VG in box........**$95.00**

Basque Spain, wide, 54 color photos, suits are coins, cups, etc, 52+2 Jokers, NM, no box................................**$10.00**

California, Rieder, 52 photos, 1911, 52+Joker+booklet, VG in box...**$22.00**

Great Southwest, Fred Harvey, Indian & train photos, dancers on Ace of Spades, 52+Joker+map card+booklet, EX in box..**$90.00**

Hawaii, wide, color photos repeat each suit, 1980, 52+2 Jokers, M in box **$8.00**

Hawaii State, wide, color views, 1961, 52+Menuhune Joker, M in box **$30.00**

Joyaux de Belgique, wide, personalities & monuments, 54 black & white photos, 52+2 Jokers, EX in box **$20.00**

New York City, River Bank backs, Standard Playing Cards, ca 1890-1905, 52+Central Park Joker, NM in broken box..**$180.00**

New York World's Fair, color drawings on each card, gold edges, 1964-65, 52+2 Jokers, M, no box...............**$10.00**

National Air & Space Museum, Smithsonian Insitiution, complete in original box **$10.00**

Portland by the Sea, photos of Portland, Chisolm Bros, 1910, 52+Joker+score card+fact card, M in box.............**$98.00**

Regional Costumes of Spain, wide, 54 costumes, 1968, 52+2 Jokers+extra card+map card, M in torn box **$50.00**

Rock City, Lookout Mountain, Tennessee, complete in original box **$6.50**

Rocky Mountains, late 1800s photos, Tom Jones, 1899, 52+special Joker+fact card, EX/VG, no box..........**$27.50**

San Diego, narrow, 52 photos, 1950s, 52+city seal Joker, M in box **$12.50**

Vistas de Lima Peru, 52 photos, Sablich, ca 1910-15, 52+San Martin Joker, VG in worn/broken box **$45.00**

XIII Commonwealth Games, standard faces, special Ace of Spades, 1986, 52+Joker+advertising card, M in box..**$12.50**

Transportation

Air India, First Class in red on white background, M in box, sealed...**$15.00**

American Airlines, light blue background, special Aces, 52+2 Jokers, 1959, NM in original box **$15.00**

CB&Q, double deck, green & white logo, special Aces & Jokers, each deck M in wrapper...........................**$10.00**

Delta, 3rd City series, Impressionistic paintings on back, 4 decks w/plane Aces & 2 w/regular Aces, 6 decks, M in boxes **$16.50**

EJ&E, double deck, triangle logo, special Aces, each deck 52+2 Jokers, M in boxes..**$24.00**

Gulf Air, plastic, Gold Horizon bands, 52+2 Jokers, NM in broken paper box...**$10.00**

Milwaukee Railroad, logo & 3 Lines on blue, 52+special Joker, M in box...**$6.00**

Monarch Charter Airlines, B-757 plane backs, M in box ..**$8.00**

New York Central, Morning on the Mohawk backs, special Ace of Spades & Joker, 52+Joker+score card, VG in taped box **$20.00**

Pullman, wide, green & gold logo backs, special Ace of Spades & Joker, 52+Joker, ca 1925, VG in G box.**$10.00**

Southern Pacific, wide scenic souvenir, Mt Shasta backs, 52+Golden West Joker+map card+booklet, 1915, EX in broken box...**$33.00**

SS Emerald Seas, wide, Supercruise colorful backs, 52+2 Jokers, NM in torn box **$5.00**

Union Pacific, Jackson Lake backs, 52+advertising card+map card, ca 1950, M in box **$15.00**

Political Memorabilia

From 1840 until 1896 when celluloid (cellos) buttons appeared, American voters showed support for presidential candidates and their platforms by wearing sulphide brooches, ferrotype pins, mechanical badges, silk ribbons and other lapel devices. Today some of these are valued at thousands of dollars. Celluloid pin-backs were made until the 1920s; many are attractively and colorfully designed, and their values hinge on scarcity, historical significance, and of course condition. Most (but not all) buttons since then have been produced by lithography directly on metal disks (lithos). Jugates are those that feature both the presidential and the vice-presidential candidates and are generally preferred by collectors, but there are several specialty areas that are also desirable such as state and local, third party, and 'cause' types.

Many buttons have been reproduced, but because of a bill passed by Nixon called 'The Hobby Protection Act,' they are all marked. A set distributed by the American Oil company in 1972 can be confusing, however; look on the edge of the button for this mark: 'A-O-1972.' Don't buy buttons that have been tampered with, because unscrupulous dealers sometimes try to scratch off or paint over the 'Reproduction' mark. When these marks are on the paper backing, they may paint that too, so beware.

Besides buttons, look for pamphlets, leaflets, flyers, tickets, electoral ballots, and hand cards used to promote candidates to the presidency. Even memorabilia from the past few decades is something you'll want to hang on to, especially items dealing with Kennedy, Nixon (Watergate) — and, who knows, maybe even Perot.

Bank, 11x4½" dia, hand-painted peanut w/Jimmy Carter's caricature smile, 1970s, EX **$20.00**

Bracelet, Nixon & Lodge, brass w/double brass links that hold elephant charm w/jugate flasher, EX...........**$35.00**

Brooch, 'Nixon' spelled out in rhinestones..........**$65.00**

Bumper sticker, 4x18", 'Kennedy for President,' black & white photo on red, white, & blue background, EX **$20.00**

Cigar box, 2½x9½x8½", Campaign De Luxe 1940, Roosevelt or Willkie for President w/photos, EX..................$37.50

Cigarettes, 3x2x1" package, 'I Like Ike' slogan on red, white & blue package, EX $30.00

Clicker, Richard Nixon, tin, pear shape, M $20.00

Convention booklet, Republican National Convention, San Francisco, 1964, 160 pages, EX............................$25.00

Cuff links, Nixon & Agnew jugate, 1973 Inagural ball, M in box..$32.00

Earrings, 'Ike' formed in light blue rhinestones set in silver metal w/bow design at top, EX $30.00

Election card, 2½x4½", 'Vote for Candidates of Roosevelt Democracy in PA,' candidates listed, 1934, EX.....$20.00

Figure, 2½", rubber Spiro Agnew caricature, ca 1973, EX..$15.00

Figurine, 4½", Richard Nixon, EX $35.00

Figurine, 6", Barry Goldwater, Remco, 1964, in original box, NM $75.00

Flyer, contrasts Kennedy & McCarthy on domestic issues, 1968 ....$10.00

Game, 'Exciting Game of the Kennedys,' Harrison-Winter, 1962, M in original box...$65.00

Hat, 'I Like Ike,' paper, 1956, EX...............................$22.50

Key fob, Harry S Truman, brass w/raised loop on top, 'Souvenir...Inauguration Jan 20 1949,' NM luster........$22.00

License plate, 5x6", diecut w/embossed figure of elephant, '1948' on its blanket, 'Let's GOP Places' slogan, EX..$50.00

License plate, 6x12", 1968 National Republican Convention, metal, red & blue on cream background, NM $20.00

Magazine, Ramparts, October 1973, 'Impeach Nixon, Impeach Agnew' w/caricatures on cover, Watergate articles, M..$15.00

Medal, 2¾", John F Kennedy inaugural, bronze, few scratches, EX $65.00

Membership certificate, 6½x9", 'Roosevelt (Theodore) Memorial Association,' EX..................................$10.00

Model, John F Kennedy, Aurora, sitting in rocking chair, all plastic, 1963, in original 10x11" box.....................$75.00

Necklace, Jimmy Carter, peanut figural dangles on chain, ca 1978, M..$22.50

Newspaper, 'Roosevelt (Theodore) Elected President' headline, 1932, complete, EX.......................................$15.00

Pendant, 2¼x3", 'I'm for Nixon' flasher on white metal w/gold finish, 1960, NM $25.00

Pin-back button, 'Americans for Bush in '88,' black & white on blue, EX..$7.50

Pin-back button, 'Dole for Vice-President,' tan on yellow w/red letters, EX $12.50

Pin-back button, 'Friends of Franklin Roosevelt,' celluloid, EX..$12.50

Pin-back button, 'Keep Americans Working Buy American,' red & blue slogans on white, 1950s, EX $15.00

Pin-back button, 'March on Washington To Bring All the GIs Home, GIs & Vets for Peace in Vietnam,' 1969, EX..$20.00

Pin-back button, 'Nixon's Still the One in '72,' cartoon of pregnant lady pushing baby carriage, M..............$15.00

Pin-back button, 'Re-Elect Jimmy,' black & white on light blue, EX..$12.50

Pin-back button, 'Women for Humphrey,' black & white photo on white w/red-circled blue rim, EX..........$12.00

Pin-back button, Democratic 1936 emblem, white donkey on dark blue ground w/silvered rim, EX..............$35.00

Pin-back button, 1½", 'Democrat A Clean Sweep in '58,' red on white w/lettering forming broom handle, EX..$12.50

Pin-back button, 1½", 'Goldwater in 1964' in dark blue letters on gold background, EX $25.00

Pin-back button, 1⅜", 'Peace Jobs McGovern '72,' red, white & blue lithograph, EX...$12.50

Pin-back button, 3½", 'Goldwater, The Best Man for the Job,' EX $10.00

Pin-back button, 3½", 'JF Kennedy, Our 35th President' $25.00

Pin-back button, 3½", 'Kennedy for US Senator' w/Robert Kennedy photo, 1964 campaign, EX $22.50

Pin-back button, ⅝", 'Ford,' red, white & blue, EX......**$10.00**

Pin-back button, ⅞", 'I'll Bet My (kicking ass) on Willkie,' black on light blue, EX...........................**$20.00**

Play set, 'Amy Carter at the White House,' ca 1978, NM in original box........................**$150.00**

Post card, 'Vote for JFK,' color print, M.......................**$20.00**

Post card, Eisenhower birthplace, Denison TX, M.........**$3.50**

Poster, 11x14", Dewey & Bricker jugate, cardboard w/black & white photos on flag background, VG **$40.00**

Poster, 11x15", FD Roosevelt black & white photo, name in bright red, dated 1944, EX.......................**$25.00**

Poster, 16x20", Carter & Mondale jugate, portraits in brown & white on red, 1976, M............................**$15.00**

Poster, 17x22", Reagan portrait, 'He'll Provide the Strong New Leadership American Needs' slogan, EX **$22.50**

Poster, 20x28", 'Nixon's the One, National Youth for Nixon & Agnew,' NM.......................**$25.00**

Poster, 24x24", 'Mondale & Ferraro: For the Family of America,' cardboard, NM.................**$15.00**

Poster, 38x27", Ronald Reagan, paper, EX...................**$10.00**

Radio, 7½x3" dia, Jimmy Carter caricature head atop peanut shell, marked copyright Kong Wah Instrument Co, 1977.................**$50.00**

Record, John F Kennedy speeches, 12" square color cover, 1963, M **$4.00**

Sheet music, 'Grover Cleveland's Grand March,' by Louis List, 1892 ....**$40.00**

Sheet Music, Jimmy Carter, 'Jimmy Who?,' Bards Music Co, 1975, M.......................**$17.50**

Stickpin, 1½", John F Kennedy profile at top, die-cut brass w/black details on face, hair & jacket, European made.......................**$20.00**

Ticket, 3x5", 1940 Republican National Convention, NM, light wear on original envelope............................**$12.00**

Tie bar, 'Vote Adlai,' silvered brass w/flasher that has portrait & slogan, EX.......................**$25.00**

Tie clip, 2", 'First for Ike' on shaft of gold-toned metal Yale key shape, 1952, NM **$80.00**

Tumbler, 5⅝", John Kennedy, 'Ask Not What Your Country...' painted on clear glass, portrait w/1917-63 on front, 1964.......................**$6.00**

Post Cards

Post cards are generally inexpensive, historically interesting, graphically pleasing, simple to store, and very easy to find. They were first printed in Austria in 1886, where they were very well accepted. In this country, souvenir cards were printed for the Columbian Exposition in 1892, and post cards became the rage.

Until WWI, they remained very collectible, with many being preserved in special post card albums. Even today post cards rank near the top of paper collectibles, second only to stamps.

Today's collectors often specialize in certain types of post cards. Advertising, holiday, Black themes, and patriotic cards are just a few of the more popular. Other's prefer the work of a particular artist. Some of the better-known post card illustrators are Ellen Clapsaddle, Frances Brundage, Rose O'Neill, Raphael Tuck, Charles Dana Gibson, and Philip Boileau. Don't forget how important condition is with any type of paper collectible. Even though many of these cards are sixty to ninety years old, they must be in excellent shape to have value, whether used or unused.

There are several books available for further study, we recommend *The Collector's Guide to Post Cards* by Jane Wood and *Post Cards, Mail Memories,* by John M. Kaduck.

Advertising, Acme Boots, 1950s, EX **$3.50**

Advertising, Boston Rubber Shoes, pictures company mill, EX.......................**$1.50**

Advertising, boy ironing his trousers, 'Why Were Sunday Togs Ever Invented?,' multicolor, EX.....................**$15.00**

Advertising, Buster Brown Cider Days, Buster Brown, Mary Jane, & Tige, October 1907, G **$12.00**

Advertising, Coen Bros, w/July 1911 calender $10.00

Advertising, Dr Pepper, 10¢ coupon, M **$5.00**

Advertising, Fab, little girl ironing, 'To Be Thought Fab Is the Thing I S'pose but Oh Dear...,' EX.................**$10.00**

Advertising, General Electric, astronomical background w/blue-tinted irons, EX.......................**$10.00**

Advertising, Hood's Sarsaparilla, 'Born Tired,' puppy, EX **$2.00**

Advertising, Kellogg's, Tony the Tiger, chromo............**$2.00**

Advertising, Lash's Bitters, two drunks, 'For Constipation,' EX.......................**$10.00**

Animal, 'Twice One Are Two,' owl, frog, & mouse, #4615, Salmon publisher **$8.00**

Animal, chimney sweep w/shamrocks & four pigs, #2619, 1930 .... **$14.00**

Buchanan, Red Riding Hood, #874, w/six inserts, Knight publisher, VG **$15.00**

Canada, Cartier & His Two Daughters, 1863, VG **$10.00**

Hold-to-light/cutout, King's Chapel, Boston, MA, VG. **$28.00**

Holiday, A Merry Halloween, girl & black cat on black background, signed Clapsaddle, VG **$28.00**

Holiday, All Hallow's Eve, Series #30, girl bobbing for apples, signed Nash **$15.00**

Holiday, Erin Go Bragh, Ellen Clapsaddle, VG $10.00

Holiday, Halloween Greetings, witch & jack-o'-lantern, signed Gibson, VG **$8.00**

Holiday, Happy Halloween, couple w/jack-o'-lantern, signed Woehler, EX **$20.00**

Holiday, Happy Thanksgiving, lady in plaid, Wolf, signed Clapsaddle, VG **$7.50**

Holiday, Love's Message to My Valentine, boy & heart, signed Clapsaddle, VG **$12.00**

Holiday, Santa w/real hair, whiskers & eyebrows, scarce, VG **$75.00**

Langsdorf, A Cotton Picker, #S640, alligator border, VG. **$32.00**

Langsdorf, Harvard University Girl in red dress, VG ... **$14.00**

Map, State of Texas, Flying Eagle publisher, VG **$8.00**

Mechanical, Happy Hooligan's Hard Luck, squeeze to move **$15.00**

Mechanical, Mischievous Katzenjammer, kids hit collie, EX **$15.00**

Mechanical, Winsch, Valentine Thoughts, 1912, VG ... **$12.00**

Noury, Gaston; nude w/raised arm & butterfly wings, VG **$50.00**

Novelty, cut-out paper dolls, Letty & Betty, signed Hayes, EX **$90.00**

Novelty, Spanish dancers, the lady w/real ribbon skirt, Made in Spain **$25.00**

Photo, Harley-Davidson motorcycle racing team, VG. **$20.00**

Photo, Mexican border, pup tents in field w/troops dressing **$6.00**

Political, 'He's Good Enough for Me,' Uncle Sam & Roosevelt **$30.00**

Russell, Scattering the Riders, Glacier publisher, EX ... **$22.00**

Souvenir, Comiskey Park Chicago, plastichrome interior, EX **$4.00**

Souvenir, Municipal Stadium Cleveland, aerial view, EX. **$3.50**

Sports, Hit Hard but Play Fair, boys play hockey, VG **$15.00**

Stamp, Austria, #5, 17 stamps, Ottmar-Zieher publisher, VG **$12.00**

Tuck, Acaquot-Type Kite Balloon, army balloon, EX.. **$17.00**

Tuck, Ever Welcome, girl in brown & green dress, signed Tuck, EX **$25.00**

Tuck, Little Boy Blue, #9301, signed Barnes, VG **$10.00**

Tuck, Mary Mary Quite Contrary, #3328, Mary in garden, VG **$15.00**

Tuck, Monte Carlo, #7053, set of six w/original envelope, EX **$25.00**

Tuck, Old Mother Hubbard, cat holding puppy, signed Barnes, VG **$10.00**

Tuck, Spherical Balloons, #3246, signed Clarkson, VG. **$20.00**

Wain, 'Din Din Please,' three cats at table, #874, Salmon publisher, VG **$33.00**

Wain, 'Run a Muck,' German cat soldier w/sword, VG . **$42.00**

Wall, 'Ain't Man Generous? Everything but the Vote,' #6342 .... **$18.00**

Woven-in-silk, steamship, RMS Cedric, signed Stevens, VG **$55.00**

Posters

Over the past ten years, the poster market has been booming. They are popular among many collectors not only as an alternative to more expensive art forms, but because of the very good likelihood that they will very quickly appreciate in value based on the evidence of past performance.

Though you may not find a Cheret or a Lautrec, there are many kinds of contemporary posters that will well be worth your attention. Travel posters, rock posters, and movie posters may still be found at affordable prices. Look for good color and interesting subject matter, and of course, watch for condition.

See also Movie Stars.

Banyuls-Trilles, Quinquina, 52x36", printed in color by Vercasson, Paris **$450.00**

Budweiser Beer, 7x11", bottle & eagle on cardboard, 1940s, EX **$5.00**

Cavalier King-Size Cigarettes, 20x28", paper, cavalier & large package of cigarettes, EX **$25.00**

David Bowie, life size, paper, EX **$15.00**

Del Monte, 35x24", paper, EX **$100.00**

Dr Meyer's Foot Soap, 38x25", paper litho, pictures variety of people & package of soap, NM **$150.00**

Dunlap's Seeds, paper litho, girl seated among variety of vegetables, 'Good Harvest from Good Seed,' framed, EX. **$160.00**

Eastern Airlines, Mickey Mouse, framed, 1983, NM.... **$40.00**

Griffith & Boyd Fertilizers, 20x24", paper, stock image of Asti girl in profile, matted & framed, EX **$150.00**

Hires Root Beer, 39x24", cardboard, woman holding glass w/1930s-style graphics, framed, EX.................$500.00

Jenkins & Armstrong, 20x30", 'Greatest Bout of All Time,' July 17, 1940, matted & framed.........$750.00

Kissel's Garage, 22x17", paper, pictures tow truck on circular background, EX.................$25.00

Lighthouse Footwear, 45x30", Andy Warhol, 1979, EX.**$100.00**

Missouri Pacific Railway, 20x26", sepia photo of US Grant's cabin on advertising mat, EX.................$60.00

Nehi-Royal Crown, 9x18", color, 1940s, EX.................**$4.50**

Plaza de Toros de Madrid, bullfighting scene, ca 1968, EX.................**$45.00**

Sorcar, World's Greatest Magician, 29x18½", 1952, EX.**$200.00**

White Mule Soda, 12x17", kicking mule on bottle, 1962, M.................**$4.00**

WWII, 'Buy a Share in America,' 40x28", Billings, EX.**$80.00**

WWII, 'For Peace & Security Buy Bonds,' paper, 26x18½", EX.................**$15.00**

WWII, 'Plan Today, Build Tomorrow with War Bonds Through Pay Roll Savings,' 28x22", EX.................**$20.00**

WWII, 'The Marines Have Landed,' 40x30", JM Flagg, EX.................**$200.00**

WWII, 'Till We Meet Again,' 28x22", soldier at ship's porthole, EX.................**$100.00**

WWII, 'We French Workers Warn You...Defeat Means Slavery, Starvation...,' 29x40", lithograph on paper, EX......**$550.00**

Precious Moments

These modern collectibles are designed by Samuel J. Butcher and produced in the orient by the Enesco company. You'll see them in gift stores and card shops all across the nation. They were introduced less than fifteen years ago, and already some are selling on the secondary market for as much as five or six times their original retail price. Each piece is marked, and like the Hummel figures to which they're sometimes compared, the older retired items are the most valuable. Their figurines, bells, ornaments, and plates all portray children actively engaged in a particular pursuit, and many have an inspirational message.

If you'd like to learn more, we recommend *Precious Moments Secondary Market Price Guide* by Rosie Wells.

Bell, Jesus Loves Me, boy w/teddy, E-5208, Dove mark, 1985.................**$35.00**

Figurine, Christmastime Is for Sharing, boy giving teddy to poor boy, E-0504, Dove mark, 1985.................**$70.00**

Figurine, Eggs Over Easy, girl & frying pan, E-3318, Hourglass mark, 1982.................**$70.00**

Figurine, God Is Love, girl w/goose in lap, E-5213, Olive Branch mark, 1986.................**$40.00**

Figurine, God Loveth a Cheerful Giver, E-1378, retired, 1981.................$550.00

Figurine, God Sent His Son, girl looking into manger, E-0507, Cedar Tree mark, 1987.................**$55.00**

Figurine, Love Cannot Break a True Friendship, girl & piggy bank, E-4722, Flower mark, 1988.................**$75.00**

Figurine, May Your Christmas Be Warm, boy next to potbelly stove, E-2348, Hourglass mark, 1982.................**$90.00**

Figurine, Sharing Our Season Together, boy pushing girl on sled, E-0501, Olive Branch mark, 1986.................**$100.00**

Figurine, Thank You for Coming to My Ade, lemonade stand, E-5202, Cross mark, 1984.................**$65.00**

Figurine, The First Noel, angel w/candle, E-2365, Flower mark, 1988.................**$35.00**

Figurine, The Lord Bless You & Keep You, bride & groom, E-3314, Bow 'N Arrow mark, 1989 ....**$37.50**

Figurine, Thee I Love, boy carving tree, E-3316, Flower mark, 1988...**$37.50**

Figurine, Tubby's First Christmas, rooster & bird on pig, E-0511, Vessel mark, 1991 ....**$16.50**

Figurine, You Can't Run Away from God, boy & dog running away, E-0525, Flower mark, 1988..................**$60.00**

Frame, Blessed Are the Pure in Heart, baby in cradle, E-0521, Olive Branch mark, 1986.............................**$30.00**

Musical, Wee Three Kings, three kings, E-0520, Dove mark, 1985 ....**$75.00**

Night light, My Guardian Angel, boy & girl angels on cloud, E-05207, Flower mark, 1988.........................**$75.00**

Ornament, Baby's First Christmas, boy in stocking, E-2362, Cedar Tree mark, 1987 ....**$25.00**

Ornament, Dropping in for Christmas, boy ice skating, E-2369, Hourglass mark, 1982 ....**$35.00**

Ornament, Mother Sew Dear, mother in chair sewing, E-0514, G-Clef mark, 1992 ....**$15.00**

Ornament, The Perfect Grandpa, grandpa w/newspaper, E-0517, Cross mark, 1984.....................................**$25.00**

Ornament, The Purr-fect Grandma, grandma in rocking chair, E-0516, Flame mark, 1990 ....**$25.00**

Ornament, To a Special Dad, boy in Dad's duds, E-0515, Flower mark, 1988 ....**$20.00**

Ornament, Wishing You a Merry Christmas, choir girl, E-5387, Cross mark, 1984.......................................**$27.50**

Plate, Christmastime Is for Sharing, boy w/teddy, E-0505, Fish mark, 1983 ....**$65.00**

Plate, I'll Play My Drum for Him, drummer boy & manger, E-2356, Dove mark, 1985 ....**$60.00**

Plate, Let Heaven & Nature Sing, angel w/friends, E-2347, Cross mark, 1984.....................................**$45.00**

Plate, Love Is Kind, boy & girl on swing, E-2847, Cross mark, 1984..**$45.00**

Plate, Love One Another, boy & girl on stump, E-5215, Flower mark, 1988 ....**$30.00**

Plate, The Lord Bless You & Keep You, bride & groom, E-5216, Flower mark, 1988 ....**$30.00**

Purinton Pottery

The Purington Pottery Company moved from Ohio to Shippenville, Pennsylvania, in 1941 and began producing several lines of dinnerware and kitchen items hand painted with fruits, ivy vines, and trees in bold brush strokes of color on a background reminiscent of old yellowware pieces. The company closed in 1959 due to economic reasons.

Purington has a style that's popular today with collectors who like the country look. It isn't always marked, but you'll soon recognize its distinct appearance. Some of the rarer designs are Palm Tree and Pheasant Lady, and examples of these lines are considerably higher than the more common ones. You'll see more Apple and Apple and Pear pieces than any, and in more diversified shapes.

Apple, coffeepot, 3-cup...**$30.00**

Apple, cup & saucer **$10.00**

Apple, 'Oil' & 'Vinegar' cruets, pr **$25.00**

Apple, salt & pepper shakers, large, pr.....................**$22.50**

Apple & Pear, canisters, 4-pc set **$125.00**

Apple & Pear, creamer & sugar bowl, w/lid.............**$25.00**

Apple & Pear, salt & pepper shakers, small, pr..........**$10.00**

Apple & Pear, tumbler, 4¾"...**$10.00**

Chartreuse, bowl, vegetable; 8" **$12.00**

Chartreuse, butter dish, ¼-lb.....................................**$35.00**

Intaglio, bowl, spaghetti; 14½".................................**$60.00**

Intaglio, jug, 5-pt...**$32.00**

Intaglio, pickle dish, 6"..**$10.00**

Intaglio, teapot, 6-cup...**$25.00**

Ivy, range set, grease jar along w/salt & pepper shakers, 3-pc **$40.00**

Ivy, tumbler, 10-oz..**$12.00**

Palm Tree, honey jug..**$25.00**

Palm Tree, salt & pepper shakers, pr **$35.00**

Pennsylvania Dutch, plate, dinner size.......................**$25.00**

Plaid, bowl, salad; 11" **$30.00**

Plaid, chop plate, 12"..**$30.00**

Plaid, creamer & sugar bowl......................................**$15.00**

Plaid, cup & saucer..**$10.00**

Plaid, plate, 9¾" **$12.50**

Plaid, platter, 11"...**$16.00**

Rose, mug, juice; 6-oz **$12.00**

Puzzles

The first children's puzzle was actually developed as a learning aid by an English map maker, trying to encourage the study of geography. Most 19th-century puzzles were made of wood, rather boring, and very expensive. But by the Victorian era, nursery rhymes and other light-hearted themes became popular. The industrial revolution and the inception of color lithography combined to produce a stunning variety of themes ranging from technical advancements, historical scenarios, and fairy tales. Power saws made production more cost effective, and wood was replaced with less expensive cardboard.

As early as the twenties and thirties, American manufacturers began to favor character-related puzzles, the market already influenced by radio and the movies. Some of these were advertising premiums. Die-cutters had replaced jigsaws, cardboard became thinner, and now everyone could afford puzzles. During the Depression they were a cheap form of entertainment, and no family get-together was complete without a puzzle spread out on the card table for all to enjoy.

Television and movies caused a lull in puzzle making during the fifties, but advancements in printing and improvements in quality brought them back strongly in the sixties. Unusual shapes, the use of fine art prints, and more challenging designs caused sales to increase.

If you're going to collect puzzles, you'll need to remember that unless all the pieces are there, they're not of much value, especially those from the 20th century. The condition of the box is important as well.

To learn more about the subject, we recommend *Character Toys and Collectibles* and *Toys, Antique and Collectible,* both by David Longest; and *Toys of the Sixties, A Pictorial Guide,* by Bill Bruegman.

Addams Family, Milton Bradley, 1965, jigsaw type, 'Cleopatra's Plight,' in original 8x10" box **$50.00**
Alice in Wonderland, 10¼x11½", unmarked (not Disney), 1950s, jigsaw type, EX **$17.50**

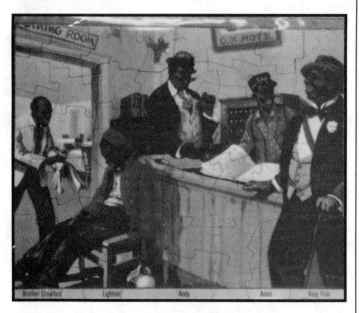

Amos & Andy, copright 1932, Pepsodent Co, EX .$35.00
Aquaman, 100-pc, Whitman, 1967, shows Aquaman & Mera fighting giant squid, in original box **$30.00**
Banana Splits, Whitman, 1970, jigsaw type..................**$45.00**
Batman, Watkins Strathmore, 1966, tray type, shows Batman & Robin w/flaming monster **$20.00**
Batman, 100-pc, Whitman, 1966, in original 8x12" box ..**$30.00**

Beverly Hillbillies, Jaymar, 1963, Granny & Elly May, in original box...**$35.00**
Captain Marvel, Reed & Associates, jigsaw type, in original envelope **$25.00**
Charlie's Angels, 14x10", 150-pc, #435-02, HG Toys, 1977, NM **$48.00**
Cinderella, Jaymar, ca 1950s, marked Disney **$10.00**
Combat, 125-pc, Milton Bradley, 1964, in original box.**$25.00**
Donald Duck, Parker Brothers, 1950s **$25.00**
Dukes of Hazzard, 11x17", 100-pc, 1981, jigsaw type, in original box, M..**$40.00**
Eddie Cantor, Einson Freeman, 1933, jigsaw type.......**$40.00**
Flash Gordon, 9x12", Milton Bradley, jigsaw type, M..**$35.00**
Flintstones, Whitman, 1966, 'A Man Called Flintstone,' framed-tray type, M..**$35.00**
Flipper, Whitman #4526, 1965, framed-tray type, M....**$20.00**
Frankenstein, Jaymar, 1963, framed-tray type, Frankenstein fighting Wolfman in dungeon laboratory **$50.00**
Frankenstein, 8x12", Jaymar, 1963, jigsaw type, in original large blue box, M..**$150.00**
Happy the Hopper, Whitman, 1966, framed-tray type, M..**$55.00**
Huckleberry Hound, Whitman, 1962, jigsaw type.......**$25.00**
Jetsons, Whitman #4423, 1962, framed-tray type, M....**$50.00**
Jetsons, 11x14", Whitman, 1963, framed-tray type, George & Elroy..**$25.00**
Linus the Lionhearted, 11x14", Whitman, 1965, framed-tray type **$20.00**
Little Lulu, Whitman, 1950s, jigsaw type **$35.00**
Little Orphan Annie, Jaymar, 1940s, jigsaw type **$30.00**
Little Orphan Annie No 1, Novelty Distributing Co, jigsaw type, made by Stephens & Kindred Co of New York, in box **$35.00**
Lost in Space, Milton Bradley, 1965, framed-tray type, battle w/cyclops monster, M **$75.00**
Man from UNCLE, Jaymar, 1965, M in original box.....**$35.00**
Marvel Super Heroes, 100-pc, Milton Bradley, 1966, in original 8x12" box **$65.00**

Movieland Cut-Ups, Wilder Manufacturing Company, marked AJ Saxe, copyright 1930, in 8x9" box, EX $60.00

Munsters, 100-pc, Whitman, 1964, in original box **$35.00**

Munsters, Whitman, 1964, framed-tray type **$35.00**

Our Beloved Skippy, jigsaw type, shows whistling Skippy walking through grass on box lid, 3-puzzle set **$60.00**

Outer Limits, 100-pc, Milton Bradley, 1964, in original 8x13" box **$150.00**

Roger Ramjet, Whitman, 1966, framed-tray type, EX ...**$35.00**

Six Million Dollar Man, 224-pc, Whitman, 1966, in original illustrated box, M **$37.50**

Skippy, walking along old wooden fence, jigsaw type, marked ca 1933 Skippy Inc, EX **$25.00**

Sleeping Beauty, Whitman, 1959, framed-tray type **$10.00**

Snow White & the Seven Dwarfs, 11x14", Jaymar, no date, framed-tray style, 11x14", originally sold for 29¢, M **$30.00**

Space Kidettes, Whitman, 1968, framed-tray type, M ..**$40.00**

Space Kidettes, Whitman, 1968, jigsaw type, NM **$30.00**

Starsky & Hutch, 150-pc, #5, HG Toys, 1976, M in original illustrated box **$37.50**

Stingray, Whitman, 1966, framed-tray type, M **$50.00**

Superman, Whitman, 1966, Superman Versus Brainstorm, jigsaw type, EX **$30.00**

Top Cat, Whitman, 1961, Top Cat & Officer Dibbles, framed-tray type, EX **$25.00**

Twelve O'Clock High, 100-pc, Milton Bradley, 1965, in original box **$20.00**

Underdog, 11x14", Whitman, 1965, framed-tray type, Underdog saving Polly Purebread from Simon Bar Sinister **$20.00**

Voyage to the Bottom of the Sea, 19x10", Milton Bradley, 1965, jigsaw type, in original box **$35.00**

Wagon Train, Whitman, 1960, framed-tray type, Major Seth Adams & Flint McCullough on covered wagon **$15.00**

Weird-Ohs Davy, 100-pc, Hawk, 1963, in original box ..**$50.00**

Wild & Weird, 100-pc, Jaymar, 1963, in original 2x8x10" box **$40.00**

Yogi Bear, Whitman #4435, 1963, framed-tray type, EX ..**$20.00**

Quilts

Early quilts were considered basic homemaking necessities. They were used not only on the bed for warmth but also to hang over the windows and walls for extra insulation from gusty winter winds and on the floor as mattresses for overnight guests. Even into the thirties and forties they were made primarily to be used. But most of the contemporary quilts (though they may be displayed with care as a bed covering), are designed and made as show pieces, some of them requiring several months of steady work to complete. Quilts from any circa are collectible and should be judged on condition, craftsmanship, intricacy of design, and color composition.

Though modern quilt artists sometimes devise some very unique methods of dying, printing, and construction, basically there are four types of quilts: 1) crazy — made up of scraps and pieces of various types of materials and sometimes ribbons sewn together in no specific design; 2) pieced — having intricate patterns put together with pieces that have been cut into specific shapes; 3) appliqued — made by applying a cut-out design (sometimes of one piece, sometimes pieced) to background material that is basically the size of the finished quilt; 4) trapunto — having a one-piece top lined with a second layer of loosely woven fabric through which padding is inserted to enhance the stitched pattern.

If you like quilts, you'll want to get these books: *Collecting Quilts* by Cathy Gaines Florence and *Gallery of American Quilts, 1849-1988,* and *Arkansas Quilts*, each published by The American Quilter's Society.

Appliqued, Alphabet, 39½x49½", green & yellow, hand sewn, machine washable, 1985, M **$175.00**

Appliqued, Bouquets of Roses, 82x97", pink, green, & yellow cotton, hand sewn, 1985, M **$345.00**

Appliqued, Butterflies, 111x110", red & black on white w/red & black borders, hand sewn, 1986, M **$525.00**

Appliqued, Butterflies in Squares, 96x78", multicolor w/black quilting, 1930s, NM **$450.00**

Appliqued, English Flowerpot, 74x76", yellow, pink, & green on white background, lightweight, EX **$375.00**

Appliqued, Flowerpot & Blue Birds, 108x84", multicolor on yellow, 1930s, EX **$450.00**

Appliqued, Flowers, 68x81", pastel on white blocks w/orange gridwork, machine pieced, hand quilted, light wear, 1920s **$140.00**

Appliqued, Poppies, 72x88", multicolored flowers w/black embroidered details on white, 1950s, EX **$350.00**

Appliqued, Rose of Sharon, 92x104", green intersecting bands, bow knot swag border, 1870s, stained, wear **$650.00**

Appliqued, Snowflake Medallions, 72x74", red on white, nine repeats, EX **$365.00**

Appliqued, Sunbonnet Girl, 72x84", multicolor on white w/lime green border, hand appliqued, machine quilted, 1986, M **$150.00**

Appliqued, Sunflower, 78x94", yellow, green, & brown solids on white background, machine pieced, hand quilted, 1945, M **$495.00**

Appliqued, Tulip Basket, 65x83", blue, red, pink & green on white cotton, hand sewn, 1930s, M **$385.00**

Appliqued, Tulips, full size, cotton sateens on cream, 1930s, NM **$450.00**

Appliqued, Tulips, 74x80", multicolored flowers w/long green stems & leaves, green border, 1940s, EX..**$400.00**

Appliqued & pieced, Dresden Plate, 74x84", blue & white cotton, machine pieced, hand appliqued & quilted, 1940s, M **$700.00**

Appliqued & pieced, Poinsettia or Rose of Sharon, 80x93", red, & green on white, hand sewn, 1930s, M **$525.00**

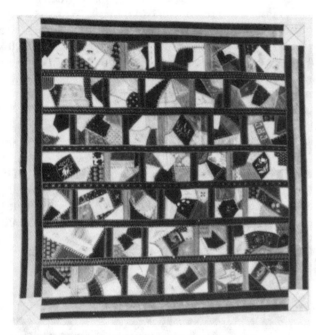

Crazy, 64x64", embroidered & hand-painted satin & velvet with ribbon borders, unbacked, 1800s, EX **$600.00**

Pieced, Attic Windows, 75x92", multicolor w/black & gray, machine pieced, hand tied, washable, 1987, M..**$235.00**

Pieced, Basket, 66x72", multicolor feedsack prints & periwinkle cotton, 1930s, VG **$300.00**

Pieced, Bear Paw, 70x86", multicolor prints w/red binding & sawtooth border, EX................................**$350.00**

Pieced, Bear's Paw, 76x91", red, blue & off-white pre-washed cotton, machine pieced, hand quilted, 1986, M......**$345.00**

Pieced, Bow Ties, 85x90", green prints & white, EX quilting, 1930s, EX...**$325.00**

Pieced, Broken Star, 72x85", mixed cotton solids & prints, hand sewn, 1945, EX................................**$300.00**

Pieced, Carpenter's Wheel or Eccentric Star, 82x108", earth tones of percale & muslin, hand sewn, 1987, M.**$345.00**

Pieced, Cathedral Window, 86x104", multicolor polyester, cotton, & blends, hand sewn, 1985, M...............**$575.00**

Pieced, Checkerboard, 60x80", Kelly green & white cotton & cotton blend, machine pieced, hand quilted, 1986, M...**$185.00**

Pieced, Clarke's Favorite, 77x95", apricot & cream cotton, hand pieced, Amish hand quilted, 1972, M **$400.00**

Pieced, Concentric Triangles, 45x56", beige & tan cottons & blends, machine pieced, hand quilted, 1986, M.**$200.00**

Pieced, Corn & Beans, 70x82", indigo prints on white w/red print in alternating blocks, 1930s, EX.................**$350.00**

Pieced, Country Patchwork, 86x92", multicolored prints on white, scalloped sides, hand sewn, reversible, 1986, M **$200.00**

Pieced, Crotch Patch, 72x82" red, white & blue calicos, paisley back, EX quiltings, 1900s, EX.....................**$325.00**

Pieced, Crown of Thorns, 92x84", navy calico & ecru muslin, diamond quiltied border, muslin back, NM.........**$500.00**

Pieced, Dahlia, 96x110", forest green on off-white, machine pieced, hand quilted, signed & dated 1987, M ...**$400.00**

Pieced, Double Irish Chain, full size, light blue on white, NM **$400.00**

Pieced, Double Wedding Ring, full size, pink on white, 1900s, EX...**$400.00**

Pieced, Double Wedding Ring, 86x72", pastel prints w/solid green & pink, scalloped edge, 1930s, EX............**$400.00**

Pieced, Dresden Plate, 71x85", multicolor calicos on rose background, machine pieced, hand appliqued & quilted, 1930s, M..**$275.00**

Pieced, Dresden Plate, 76x66", multicolored percale on white, hand sewn, 1930s, NM....................**$450.00**

Pieced, Drunkard's Path, 70x78", pink & white w/pink sawtooth border, 1930s, VG **$200.00**

Pieced, Evening Star, 64x81", multicolored prints on white ground, hand sewn, 1930s, G **$275.00**

Pieced, Fan, 100x100", light & dark blue on white, machine pieced, hand quilted, 1986, M..............................**$255.00**

Pieced, Feathered Star, red on white, quilted w/diamond & feather roundels, ca 1890................**$495.00**

Pieced, Feathered Star, 78x90", turkey red & yellow on white ground, 1930s, EX **$545.00**

Pieced, Flower Garden, 102x104", multicolored flowers, green leaves, ecru ground, machine pieced, hand quilted, 1986, M $275.00

Pieced, Flower Garden, 74x84", multicolor prints & yellow, wide scalloped border, hand sewn, 1930s, EX ...$325.00

Pieced, Flying Geese, 54x79", beige & purple cotton & cotton blends, machine pieced, hand quilted, 1986, M $400.00

Pieced, Flying Swallows, 89x99", dark blues, royals & light blue on white, machine pieced, hand quilted, 1987, M $345.00

Pieced, Four Leaf Clover, 88x80", multicolored prints w/orange border, VG $245.00

Pieced, Garden Wedding, 95x106", multicolor on white background, machine pieced, hand quilted, 1986, M $345.00

Pieced, Giant Dahlia, 80x95", rust & cream, machine pieced, hand quilted, double bound, reversible, 1980s, M $500.00

Pieced, Golden Double Wedding Ring, 91x76", multicolor prints on white w/gold areas between rings & border, 1930s, EX $265.00

Pieced, Grandmother's Choice, 74x87", blue, multicolored, & white, machine pieced, hand tied, 1987, M $375.00

Pieced, Grandmother's Fan, 70x80", mixed prints w/black & white, hand sewn, 1985, M $225.00

Pieced, Hexagon Star, 84x118", navy & red on white, hand & machine sewn, hand quilted, 1986, M............$235.00

Pieced, Hidden Star, 92x97", blues & white cotton & polyester, hand & machine pieced, hand quilted, 1987, M $400.00

Pieced, Improved Nine Patch, 71x82", blue & red cotton, unbleached muslin back, hand sewn, 1930, EX .$200.00

Pieced, Indian Wedding Ring, 58x77", multicolor prints, 1940s, EX $450.00

Pieced, Irish Chain, 45x57", rust & gray on beige, machine sewn, 1986, M $75.00

Pieced, Jackson Star, full size, fuchsia on white, 1930s, EX $425.00

Pieced, Jacob's Ladder, 68x80", blue prints & mixed calico blocks, ca 1930, NM........................$300.00

Pieced, Kansas Dugout, 70x78", multicolor calicos (mostly blue), no fading, unused, ca 1900 ....$300.00

Pieced, Kansas Dust Storm, full size, multicolor, fine piecing & quilting, 1930s, M........................$265.00

Pieced, Kansas Sunflower, 78x94", large flowers in gold tones w/green leaves, flower quilting throughout, 1930s $450.00

Pieced, LeMoyne Star, 70x82", cotton pastel prints on white calico, 4½" white border w/blue binding, 1930s, EX $285.00

Pieced, Log Cabin, 100x100", green & yellows, cotton & polyester-cotton blends, machine pieced, hand quilted, 1985, M........................$400.00

Pieced, Log Cabin, 75x96", blue w/rust, cotton & polyester, machine pieced, hand quilted, 1986, M $375.00

Pieced, Log Cabin, 76x94", browns & blues (cotton), hand sewn & quilted, 1982, M........................$400.00

Pieced, Lone Star, 72x80", pink, rose, blue & green prints on pale pink ground, diamond quilting, 1930s, EX .$365.00

Pieced, Lone Star, 83x103", burgundy & rose on pink, machine pieced, hand quilted, 1986, M $650.00

Pieced, Lover's Knot, 70x70", pumpkin & white cotton, machine pieced, hand quilted, lightweight, 1940s, EX $150.00

Pieced, Martha Washington Flower Garden, 77x80", multicolored flowers on white, hand pieced & quilted, 1945, EX $350.00

Pieced, Martha's Star, 91x108", brown, rust, navy, & ivory, cotton blend, machine pieced, hand quilted, 1984, M $475.00

Pieced, May Basket, 80x90", gold & green print w/white, machine pieced, hand quilted, 1986, M $325.00

Pieced, Monkey Wrench, 63x76", dominating brown tones, old pieces, newly assembled, M........................$375.00

Pieced, Mosaic, 70x94", multicolor pastels, lightweight, NM $325.00

Pieced, Ocean Waves, 68x82", cherry, red & white prints, wide border, medallion quilting, 1900s, EX........$500.00

Pieced, Ohio Star, 78x86", scrap w/pink & white settings, hand sewn, 1962, M........................$300.00

Pieced, Patchwork, 72x78", multicolor prints form circle-in-square design, EX $215.00

Pieced, Philadelphia Pavement, 73x97", blues, greens & rose w/white, machine pieced, detailed hand quilting, 1987, M $465.00

Pieced, Pine Tree, full size, green on white, 1900s, EX..$215.00

Pieced, Pineapple, 76x78", blue & white calico, machine quilted........................$495.00

Pieced, Prairie Flower, 85x100", burgundy & pink cotton prints, machine pieced, hand quilted, 1985, M...$300.00

Pieced, Rail Fence, 80x96", browns, hand pieced, Amish hand quilted, 1984, M........................$400.00

Pieced, Red Tulip, 66x79", red, blue, & green on muslin background, hand pieced & quilted, 1950, unused, M........................$265.00

Pieced, Richmond, 73x92", multicolored cotton prints on white, machine pieced, hand quilted, 1930s, G..$225.00

Pieced, Seven Sisters, 81x93", red, blue & light green cotton, machine pieced, hand quilted, 1984, M $345.00

Pieced, Seven Sisters, 91x100", light to dark prints, cotton & polyester, machine pieced, hand quilted, 1980, M $300.00

Pieced, Square in Square, 67x84", multicolor scraps, machine pieced, hand quilted, 1977, M $230.00

Pieced, Square in Square, 70x80", multicolor w/black, VG $250.00

Pieced, Star of Bethlehem, 66x76", calicos & burgundy, diamond border, EX fine quilting, 1920s, EX..........$165.00

Pieced, Star of Many Points, queen size, calicos & white, green sashing & border, heart quilting, 1930s, M............$335.00

Pieced, Stars & Squares, 85x97", multicolor stars on white w/green squares, muslin back, hand sewn, 1986, M $545.00

Pieced, Stepping Stones, 72x80", multiple calicos, white, red, & navy print, ca 1900, NM $225.00

Pieced, Sunflower, full size, bright colors, hand sewn, 1938, EX $425.00

Pieced, Triangles, full size, prints on white on goldenrod, feather-stitch quilting, M......................................$365.00

Pieced, Trip Around the World, 80x92", red & white cotton & polyester blends, hand pieced, machine quilted, 1986, M...$325.00

Pieced, Triple Irish Chain, 75x101", green & white broadcloth, machine pieced, hand quilted, 1986, M....$345.00

Pieced, Tumblin' Star, 100x102", blue on blue cotton, machine pieced, detailed hand quilting, 1986, M.$565.00

Pieced, Turkey Tracks, 68x80", gold & green on white ground, close quilting, 1930s, EX $375.00

Pieced, Wandering Diamond, 83x99", multicolored prints w/blue & white, solid black border, spider web quilting, M..$575.00

Pieced, Wedding, 70x82", multicolored calicos, wide yellow border, diamond quilting, EX..............................$375.00

Pieced, Wheel of Fortune, 106x106", blue prints w/unbleached muslin, machine pieced, hand quilted, 1986, M..$465.00

Pieced, Wheel of Fortune, 84x98", muslin, polyester & cotton print, machine pieced, hand quilted, washable, 1986, M..$235.00

Pieced, Whirligig, 74x80", green, red, white, & blue print, hand sewn, recent, M $340.00

Pieced, Wild Goose Chase, twin size, gold & lavender, 1930s, VG $425.00

Pieced, 9-Patch, 82x70", blue, gray & white prints, EX.$395.00

Quimper

This is a type of enamel-glazed earthenware made in Quimper, France, since the 1600s. They still operate there today, so some of their production falls into the time period we're interested in. Since its inception, the company has undergone several management and name changes, and since 1983 it has been owned by Americans.

Most of the ware you'll see is decorated by hand with colorful depictions of peasant men and women on a yellowware background. Besides dinnerware, they also made vases, figurines, tiles, and bookends.

If you'd like to learn more about the subject, we recommend *Quimper Pottery: A French folk Art Faience* by Sandra V. Bondhus.

Bell, 5", peasant figure, 1930s $60.00

Bookends, 7¼", goose girl & biniou player, HBQF, pr..$350.00

Bowl, 7½", peasant man, 6-sided, HB Quimper $85.00

Butter pat, Eskimos, green background w/scalloped rim, HenRiot..$15.00

Candle holder, 8¾", Deco figure w/polka dots & stripes, HBQF $90.00

Candy dish, 7x5¼", man & lady, inverted Celtic heart handle, HBQ $100.00

Cup & saucer, 2¾", 7½", Breton broderie variant $70.00

Figurine, 11½", biniou players, Micheau-Vernez, HQ .$100.00

Figurine, 9x3x4¼", Saint Anne La Palud w/child, HQ.$50.00

Inkwell, 3¼x5x5", heart shape, HBQ.................$150.00
Pitcher, 5", broderie sprays on paneled body, HBQ $60.00

Pitcher, 6", coats of arms & flowers, marked 'Chocolate de Royale' $500.00

Pitcher, 7x7½", flowers & sponging, ca 1980, HQ.......$30.00

Pitcher, 8x7", Art Deco-style lady's portrait, HBQ $55.00

Plate, 10", floral sprays w/croisille, canted corners, HBQF $75.00

Plate, 11⅛", Breton man, La Touche border, HQF $90.00

Plate, 9¾", 2-tone blue decorated riche border w/gold, ca 1940s..$45.00

Salt & pepper shakers, 3½", man & lady, 1930s, HBQF, pr.$85.00

Salt cellar, 2½x4", Breton man & lady on barrel shape, 1920s, HBQF $80.00

Tile, 4¾", lady, blue border..$60.00

Vase, 4½", ivoire corbeille decoration, squat ewer form, HQ $30.00

Vase, 6½x6", Art Deco-style lady, jug shape, HBQ ...$100.00

Wall pocket, 5½", peasant, cone shape, 1960s, HB Quimper..$80.00

Wall pocket, 7¾x2¾", Breton lady, slipper shape, HB..$325.00

Radios

Vintage radios are those made from 1920 through the

fifties. The most desirable and those whose values have been increasing the most consistently are the streamlined Deco styles, novelties, and of course the harder-to-find sets. But experts tell us that as the older sets become more scarce and expensive, even some transistors are beginning to attract radio collectors.

There are several basic types: 1) breadboard — having exposed tubes and other components that are simply attached to a rectangular board; 2) cathedral — vertical shape with a rounded or peaked top; 3) console — floor model consisting of a cabinet on legs or a tall rectangular case; 4) portable — smaller set made to be used at any location; 5) table — general term referring to sets of all shapes and sizes designed to be used atop a table; 6) novelty — having an unusual case such as a bottle or a camera, or one depicting a character such as Mickey Mouse.

The primary factor to consider when evaluating a radio is condition. Whether or not it plays, be sure that all parts are present. Cabinet condition is important as well, and even though it is unrealistic not to expect a few nicks and scratches, be sure there are no cracks, chips, or other highly visible damage. These are the criteria our evaluations are based on.

If you'd like to learn more, we recommend *The Collector's Guide to Antique Radios,* by Sue and Marty Bunis and *Collecting Transistor Novelty Radios, A Value Guide,* by Robert F. Breed.

Admiral, #Y-2127, Imperial 8, portable, leather case, transistor, right round dial, left lattice grill w/knob, 1959...**$35.00**
Admiral, #159-5L, table model w/phonograph, wood case, outer right front dial, left wraparound louvers, 1939...**$40.00**
Admiral, #47-J55, table model, walnut case, 3-knob dial, horizontal louvers, two bands, AC/DC, 1940........**$35.00**
Admiral, #5F11, portable, plastic, inner right dial, lattice grill, flip-up front handle, AC/DC or battery, 1949........**$35.00**
Admiral, #6C22, table model, plastic, large center metal dial over cloth grill, footed, center knob, AC/DC, 1954...**$45.00**
Admiral, #6RT44A-7B1, table model, wooden case, slide rule 4-knob dial, horizontal louvers, lift top, AC, 1947...**$35.00**
Admiral, #7T01C-N, table model, plastic, slide rule 2-knob dial, upper horizontal louvers, broadcast, 1948....**$35.00**
Admiral, #811B, Super 8, table model w/clock, transistor, right front dial, horizontal bars, footed, 1960........**$25.00**
Air Castle, #102B, portable, plastic case, slide-rule dial, horizontal louvers, handle, 2-knob front, 1950...........**$30.00**
Air Castle, #611-1, Tombstone, wooden case, cylindrical dial, upper grill cloth, six push buttons, four knobs...**$85.00**
Air Castle, #7B, console model w/phonograph, wooden case, inner right slide rule dial, four knobs, AC, 1948...**$80.00**
Air Castle, #935, table model w/clock, plastic case, round dial, horizontal center bars, four knobs, 1951.......**$30.00**

Air Castle, #1200, 2-tone wood, right dial, four push buttons, left grill w/cutouts, five knobs, battery...$50.00
Air King, #A-511, table model, plastic case, right front dial, left lattice grill, two knobs, AC/DC, 1947..............**$45.00**
Airline, #04WG-754C, table model, wood case, cylindrical dial, six push buttons, upper grill w/cutouts, battery.......**$50.00**
Airline, #14BR-514B, table model, Deco-styled painted plastic case, slide rule dial, push buttons, louvers, 1946...**$100.00**
Airline, #15BR-1535B, table model, plastic case, front slide rule dial, quarter-moon louvers, four knobs...........**$50.00**
Airline, #25BR-154A, table model, plastic case, slide rule dial, upper lattice grill, four knobs, AC/DC, 1953.**$45.00**
Airline, #62-84, console model, wooden case, lowboy, half-moon dial, lower cloth grill w/cutouts, six legs, three knobs...**$150.00**
Airline, #63-131, Tombstone, wood case, shouldered, airplane dial, upper grill w/three vertical bars, four knobs, 1935........**$85.00**
Airline, #74BR-1501B, table model, walnut-color plastic case slide rule dial, upper horizontal louvers, metal back, 1946...**$80.00**
Airline, #94HA-1562, table model, plastic case, round metal dial over large plastic woven grill, two knobs, 1945.......**$25.00**
American Bosch, #10, Tombstone, small 2-toned wooden case, lower round dial, cloth grill w/cutouts, three knobs, ca 1935...**$70.00**
American Bosch, #660T, table model, wood case, round dial, two grills w/horizontal bars, four knobs, short wave, 1936...**$55.00**
Arvin, #350P, portable, plastic case, dial part of circular grill bars, handle, two knobs, AC/DC or battery, 1949..**$40.00**
Arvin, #358T, table model, plastic case, left half-moon dial, right & left wraparound louvers, two bullet knobs, 1948...**$45.00**
Arvin, #444, table model, midget, metal case, right front dial, horizontal louvers, two knobs, AC/DC, 1946........**$80.00**
Arvin, #850T, table model, plastic case, large right round dial over oval metal perforated grill, AC/DC, 1955...**$35.00**

Arvin, #950T2, table model, rectangular plastic case, upper right front round dial over checkered grill, AC/DC, 1958...$30.00

Atwater Kent, #627, Cathedral, wood, center half-round dial, upper grill w/cutouts, front columns, three knobs, AC, 1932 ....$400.00

Atwater Kent, #465Q, Tombstone, wood case w/rounded top, lower airplane dial, upper grill cutouts, four knobs, 1934 ....$235.00

Atwater Kent, #711, console model, wood case, lowboy, quarter-round dial, double doors, five knobs, short wave, 1933 ....$260.00

Automatic, #C-65, portable, leatherette case, right front dial, left horizontal louvers, handle, AC/DC or battery, 1942 ....$35.00

Bendix, #PAR-80, portable, luggage-style case, slide rule dial, fold-down front, handle, AC/DC or battery, 1948 ....$35.00

Bendix, #115, table model, 2-tone plastic case, slide rule dial, wraparound grill bars, two knobs, AC/DC, 1948...$275.00

Coronado, #15RA1-43-7902A, console model w/phonograph, wood case, inner right slide rule dial, four knobs, 1951 ....$70.00

Coronado, #35RA37-43-8355, table model, plastic case, recessed slide rule dial & lattice grill, three knobs, AC/DC, 1953...$35.00

Crosley, #E15TN, table model, plastic case, upper front dial, grill w/horizontal bar, two knobs, AC/DC, 1953 ...$75.00

Crosley, #F-110BK, Skyrocket, portable, plastic case, right front round dial over lattice grill w/crest, handle, 1953 ....$35.00

Crosley, #11-109U, table model, plastic case, center front dial, inner checkered grill & crest, two knobs, AC/DC, 1952 ....$60.00

Crosley, #14AG, table model, wood case, right front square dial, grill w/horizontal bars, handle, three knobs, AC/DC..$55.00

Crosley, #35AK, table model w/phonograph, wood case, right front square dial, left grill, three knobs, AC, 1941 ....$30.00

Crosley, #56TX, table model, plastic case, right front square dial, horizontal wraparound grill bars, three knobs, 1946 ....$50.00

Crosley, #62-148, Tombstone, wood case, flower front round airplane dial, upper grill w/cutouts, inlay design, two knobs $130.00

Crown, #TR-875, portable, transistor, slide rule dial, perforated grill, telescoping antenna, battery, 1960 ......$25.00

Dalbar, #400, table model, wood case, right square dial, left diamond-shaped grill, two knobs, AC, 1946.........$35.00

Dewald, #F-404, table model, plastic case, right round dial knob, left horizontal wraparound louvers, AC/DC, 1952 ....$45.00

Dewald, #L-546, portable, leather case, transistor, right front dial, left lattice cutouts, handle, battery, 1959.......$30.00

Dumont, #1210, leather case, transistor, right round dial, crisscross grill, strap handle, BC, battery, 1957 ....$40.00

Echophone, #EC-600, table model, wood case, slide rule dial, cloth grill, round corners, four knobs, battery, 1946 ....$40.00

Emerson, #AX-211, Little Miracle, table model, midget, plastic case, horizontal grill bars, two knobs, 1938.....$65.00

Emerson, #CU-265, table model, plastic case, square dial over horizontal front bars, five tubes, two knobs, AC/DC, 1939...$45.00

Emerson, #414, table model, ornate pressed wood case w/fleur-de-lis designs, lower right dial, two knobs, 1933...$135.00

Emerson, #510, table model, wood case, right round dial, plastic grill panel w/circular cutouts, two knobs, AC/DC, 1946...$60.00

Emerson, #520, table model, 2-tone Catalin case, round dial, white panel w/checkered grill, two knobs, AC/DC, 1946...$175.00

Emerson, #522, table model, plastic case, black dial, Deco-styled grill, two knobs, four feet, handle, AC/DC, 1946...$50.00

Emerson, #570, Memento, table model, jewelry-box style w/photo frame in lid, slide rule dial, two knobs, battery, 1949 ....$135.00

Emerson, #706-B, table model, small plastic case, lower half-round dial over checkered grill w/logo, 1952.......**$50.00**

Emerson, #811, table model, small plastic case, half-round dial over horizontal grill bars, slide knob, four feet, 1955 ....**$40.00**

Emerson, #888, Vanguard, portable, plastic case, transistor, random-patterned grill, swing handle, battery, 1958 ....**$55.00**

Fada, #1452A, Tombstone, walnut case, round airplane dial, upper cloth grill w/Deco-styled cutouts, four knobs, 1934 ....**$120.00**

Fada, #263W, table model, plastic case, small right front dial, left Deco-styled grill, plastic back, three knobs, 1936 ....**$85.00**

Farnsworth, #ET-067, table model, wood case w/vertical fluting, upper slide rule dial, lower grill, two knobs, AC, 1946 ....**$45.00**

Firestone, #4-A-163, table model, plastic case, right dial over random-patterned panel, checkered grill, AC/DC, 1957 ....**$20.00**

Firestone, #4-A-26, Newscaster, table model, plastic case, slide rule dial, lower horizontal louvers, two knobs, 1948 ....**$45.00**

General Electric, #C-415C, table model w/clock, plastic case, slide rule dial, right & left vertical grill bars, 1958 ..**$30.00**

General Electric, #H-610, table model, plastic, right front square dial, four push buttons, left lattice grill, two knobs, AC, 1939................................$65.00

General Electric, #J-80, Cathedral, wood case, window dial, cloth grill w/cutouts, fluted columns, three knobs, 1932 ....**$295.00**

General Electric, #L-630, table model, 2-toned wood case, slide dial, cloth grill w/horizontal bar, four knobs, 1940 ....**$45.00**

General Electric, #P-746A, portable, 2-tone plastic case, transistor, right round dial, left vertical grill bars, 1958......................**$30.00**

General Electric, #P-796A, portable, blue leatherette case, transistor, right side dial knob, front lattice grill, 1958......................**$35.00**

General Electric, #T-128C, table model, yellow plastic case, round dial, lattice grill, left knob, four feet, 1959 .**$25.00**

General Electric, #428, table model, plastic case, raised center w/half-moon dial, vertical bars, two knobs, 1955 ....**$30.00**

General Electric, #50, table model w/clock, plastic case, right front dial, upper checkered grill, square clock, 1946 ....**$45.00**

General Electric, #517F, table model, plastic case, thumb-wheel dial, left alarm clock, right vertical grill bars, 1951 ....**$45.00**

Hallicrafters, #5R60, table model, mahogany-colored plastic case, round dial, checkered grill, two center knobs, 1955 ....**$35.00**

Howard, #906, table model, wood case, slide rule dial, upper crisscross grill w/center bar, AC, 1947........**$45.00**

Knight, #5F-525, table model, plastic case, round dial, checkerboard grill, ridged base, two knobs, AC/DC, 1949 ....**$40.00**

Knight, #68B-151K, table model, wood case, black dial, cloth grill w/cutouts, tuning eye, four knobs, battery **$60.00**

Majestic, #259-EB, table model, walnut case, slide rule dial, push buttons, curved grill w/cutouts, AC, 1939......**$85.00**

Majestic, #6FM714, table model, plastic case, slide rule dial, horizontal wraparound louvers, two knobs, AC/DC, 1948 ....**$60.00**

Majestic, #921, Melody Cruiser, table model, wooden sailing ship form w/chrome sails, horizontal louvers, 1946......................**$375.00**

Mantola, #R-78162, console model w/phonograph, wood case, inner right slide rule dial, four knobs, FM, 1948 ....**$75.00**

Meck, #DA-601, table model, plastic case, right front dial, vertical wrap-over grill bars, two knobs, AC/DC, 1950 ....**$55.00**

Motorola, #X11B, portable, transistor, upper dial, perforated grill w/'M' logo, rear swing-out stand, battery, 1960......................**$30.00**

Motorola, #45P2, Pixie, portable, plastic case, metal dial plate, vertical grill bars, two thumbwheel knobs, 1956 ....**$40.00**

Motorola, #5A1, portable, inner right round dial, set plays when flip-up lid opens, handle, battery, 1946......**$40.00**

Motorola, #5T, Tombstone, wood case, lower dial w/escutcheon, grill w/bars, five tubes, four knobs, short wave, 1937 ....**$100.00**

Motorola, #5T11M, table model, plastic case, right front round dial, left lattice grill, two knobs, AC/DC, 1959......................**$20.00**

Motorola, #56CJ, table model, plastic, left front dial, right alarm clock, center panel w/'M' logo, five knobs, AC $25.00

Motorola, #57X11, table model, plastic case, slide rule dial, horizontal louvers, slanted sides, two knobs, AC/DC, 1947 ....**$45.00**

Motorola, #76F31, console model w/phonograph, wood case, inner-right slide rule dial & knobs, FM, AC, 1948 ....**$75.00**

Olympic, #6-502P, table model, wood case, slanted round black dial, vertical grill bars, two knobs, AC/DC, 1946..**$60.00**

Olympic, #7-537, table model, plastic case, slanted right round dial, wraparound louvers, three knobs, AC/DC, 1948 ....**$65.00**

Packard-Bell, #551, table model, plastic case, upper curved slide rule dial, lower vertical grill bars, handle, AC, 1946..**$65.00**

Packard-Bell, #892, console model w/phonograph, wood case, slide rule dial, crisscross grill, four knobs, 1949..**$55.00**

Philco, #B570, Transitone, table model, plastic case, round dial, horizontal grill bars, arched base, two knobs, 1954..**$30.00**

Philco, #F-673-124, portable, leather case, right half-moon dial, metal perforated grill, handle, left side knob, 1957 ....**$25.00**

Philco, #T-65, portable, plastic case, transistor, round dial, left horizontal louvers, handle, AM, battery, 1959 ....**$25.00**

Philco, #37-84, Cathedral, wood case, lower round dial, upper grill w/vertical cutouts, four tubes, two knobs, AC, 1937 ....**$145.00**

Philco, #38-10, table model, wood case, round dial, rounded left side, cloth grill w/Deco cutouts, four knobs, 1938..**$100.00**

Philco, #38-4, console model, wood case, automatic tuning dial, lower vertical grill bars, eight tubes, AC, 1938 ....**$150.00**

Philco, #41-231, table model, Deco-style wood case, right dial, horizontal louvers, push buttons, AC/DC, 1941 ....**$75.00**

Philco, #42-1-T-96, Transitone, table model, wood case, right dial w/red pointer, square cloth grill, two knobs, 1942 ....**$45.00**

Philco, #46-420-I, table, plastic case, curved dial, two knobs on top, horizontal louvers, AC/DC, 1946 ....**$60.00**

Philco, #49-601, portable, plastic case, lower slide rule dial, horizontal grill bars, two knobs, handle, battery, 1949 ....**$35.00**

Philco, #52-540, Transitone, table model, plastic case, slide rule dial, upper horizontal grill bars, two knobs, 1952 ....**$25.00**

Philco, #71H, console model, wood case, lowboy, window dial, lower grill w/cutouts, seven tubes, six legs, AC, 1932 ....**$140.00**

Phillips 66, #3-12A, portable, upper slanted slide rule dial, lower horizontal louvers, handle, two knobs, battery, 1948 ....**$35.00**

RCA, #BX-57, portable, plastic case, simulated alligator skin panels, horizontal louvers, two side knobs, handle, 1950 ....**$40.00**

RCA, #2-C-521, table model, plastic case, right round dial, left alarm clock, center horizontal bars, five knobs, 1953..**$20.00**

RCA, #3-RF-91, table model, plastic case, large center round dial over horizontal front lines, side knobs, AM/FM, 1952 ....**$45.00**

RCA, #40X53, La Siesta, table model, painted Mexican scene on wood, left cloth grill, handle, two knobs, AC, 1939 ....**$300.00**

RCA, #66X12, table model, ivory plastic case, slide rule dial, rectangular grill cutouts, three knobs, AC/DC, 1947 ....**$50.00**

RCA, #8R71, table model, plastic case, recessed dial on top, large front cloth grill, four knobs, FM, AC, 1949 ..**$45.00**

RCA, #8X521, table model, maroon plastic case w/round dial on top horizontal louvers, right side knob, AC/DC, 1948 ....**$55.00**

RCA, #45X16, table model, 2-tone wood, right front dial, left horizontal louvers, two knobs, BC, AC/DC, 1940 ....$50.00

RCA, #96-X-1, table model, Deco-style plastic case, right dial, left w/wraparound louvers, raised top, three knobs, 1939..**$175.00**

RCA, 79-10, Tombstone, wood case, lower front dial, tuning eye, upper cloth grill w/vertical bars, five knobs..**$145.00**

Regal, #205, table model, plastic case, slanted slide rule dial, lower horizontal louvers, two knobs, AC/DC, 1947.**$45.00**

Roland, #4C2, table model, plastic case, side dial knob, left front alarm clock, right lattice grill, 1957...............**$20.00**

Roland, #51-481, portable, plastic case, transistor, step-back top, thumbwheel dial, horizontal grill bars, handle, 1960 ....**$25.00**

Sentinel, #205BL, portable, cloth-covered case, slide rule dial, upper grill, handle, two knobs, battery, 1940........**$25.00**

Sentinel, #286PR, portable, plastic case, inner thumbwheel dial, center metal grill, flip-up lid, AC/DC or battery, 1947 ....**$45.00**

Silvertone, #1745, Tombstone, wood case, double step-down top, round dial, grill cutouts, six tubes, five knobs..**$150.00**

Silvertone, #2, table model, metal case, right round dial, horizontal grill bars, two contrasting knobs, AC/DC, 1950 ....**$75.00**

Silvertone, #2002, table model, ivory metal case, round dial knob over crisscross grill, lower left knob, AC, 1950 ....**$50.00**

Silvertone, #213, portable, blue plastic case, transistor, wedge-shape dial, perforated grill, battery, 1960..**$25.00**

Silvertone, #4206, table model, ivory plastic case, recessed front w/right dial & left grill cloth, three knobs, AM/FM **$35.00**

Silvertone, #7206, table model, ivory plastic case, two slide rule dials, cloth grill, Hi-Fi, three knobs, AM/FM, 1957 ....**$25.00**

Silvertone, #9204, portable, plastic case, transistor, triangle dial, lower perforated grill, stand, AM, battery, 1959 ....**$25.00**

Sonora, #LD-93, table model, walnut case, right front square dial, left horizontal louvers, three knobs, AC/DC, 1941 ....**$40.00**

Sparton, #132, table model, plastic oval case, half-moon dial, metal perforated grill, two knobs, AC/DC, 1950 ....**$60.00**

Sparton, #4AW17-A, table model, plastic case, slide rule dial, vertical grill bars, raised top, two knobs, battery, 1948 ....**$30.00**

Stewart-Warner, #07-51H, table model, streamlined plastic case, right front dial, wraparound louvers, 1940 ..**$85.00**

Toshiba, #6TP-304, portable, transistor, left vertical slide rule dial, lower right perforated grill, AM, battery, 1960...**$35.00**

Toshiba, #6TR-186, portable, transistor, right thumbwheel dial, left patterned grill, AM, battery, 1959 ....**$45.00**

Toshiba, #7TP-352S, portable, transistor, upper slide rule dial, lower grill, telescoping antenna, battery, 1960 ....**$45.00**

Trav-Ler, #5010, table model, wood case, upper front dial, lower cloth grill, four knobs, AC/DC, 1946...........**$40.00**

Truetone, #D-2020, table model, plastic case, slide rule dial, grill bars w/center strip, two knobs, AM/FM, AC/DC, 1950 ....**$40.00**

Truetone, #D117, table model, wood case, slide rule dial, grill w/cutouts, decorative molding, side handles, three knobs **$60.00**

Westinghouse, #H-188, table model, plastic case w/oriental design dial, left grill w/cutouts, two knobs, AC/DC, 1948.......**$80.00**

Westinghouse, #H-356T5, table model, ivory plastic, right thumbwheel dial, left clock, center grill w/horizontal bar, BC, AC, 1952 ....$50.00

Westinghouse, #H-417T5, table model, maroon plastic case, round dial over large front lattice grill, wire stand, 1954 ....**$35.00**

Westinghouse, #H-503T5A, table model, gray plastic case, dial knob over plaid metal perforated grill, AC/DC, 1955 ....**$30.00**

Zenith, #B-600, Transoceanic, portable, leatherette case, multi-band slide rule dial, fold-up front, antenna, handle **$80.00**

Zenith, #Royal 500D, portable, transistor, plastic case, upper 'owl eye' knobs, lower round grill, swing handle, 1959 ....**$60.00**

Zenith, #R511F, table model, plastic case, half-moon dial, checkered grill w/crest, four feet, handle, AC/DC, 1955 ....**$50.00**

Zenith, #Y-723, table model, plastic case, round dial over checkered grill w/crest, side knob, handle, AM/FM, 1956 ....**$35.00**

Zenith, #5-D-027, Consoltone, table model, 2-toned wood case, black dial, left cloth grill, fluted sides, AC/DC, 1946 ....**$50.00**

Zenith, #5-G-03, table model w/clock, plastic oblong case, right dial, left clock, center perforated grill w/crest, 1950 ....**$40.00**

Zenith, #6-D-311, table model, Deco-styled Bakelite case, half-moon dial, left wraparound louvers, 'Z' knob, 1938..**$150.00**

Zenith, #6-D-516, table model, plastic case, black dial, horizontal wraparound grill bars, handle, two knobs, 1940 ....**$45.00**

Zenith, #6-S-511, table model, brown plastic case, right dial, horizontal wraparound grill bars, push buttons, 1941 ....**$55.00**

Novelty

Abon, Zany, 4¾x5", red & white perfume bottle, marked Made in Hong Kong..**$45.00**

Aimor Corp of Los Angeles California, Life Preserver, #BCR 1300, 10½" dia, radio & clock combination, Made in Japan..**$30.00**

Amico, Hot Dog w/Mustard, 2½x8¼" long, Made in Hong Kong **$35.00**

Amico, Oreo Cookie, 6" dia, black & white w/bite out, Made in Hong Kong, 1977 ....**$30.00**

Borden Inc, Cracker Jack, 2¾x5" long horizontal box shape, marked copyright 1968 & 1974, Made in Hong Kong **$35.00**

Cal Fax, Robot Starroid IR12 (I Are One Too), 8", yellow & black plastic w/controls on chest, Made in Hong Kong, 1977 ....**$60.00**

Coca-Cola, Coke Bottle, actual size, volume control in top section, tuning in movable base plate, Hong Kong .**$25.00**

Columbia Telecommunications, Lady's High-Heel Shoe, #SH920, 5¼", red, marked 1987 Wonder Tooling .**$30.00**

Concept 2000, #GB 1085, Marshmallow Man (from Ghost Busters), 7½", thumbwheel dials in base, marked Made in China **$25.00**

Concept 2000, Mork from Ork Eggship Radio, #4461, 7x4½" dia, 1979, Paramount Pictures Hong Kong **$35.00**

Corgi, Radio Tele Luxembourg Sound Truck, #RTL 208, 5x2⅜", diecast metal, controls behind rear doors, Made in England **$45.00**

Durham Industries, My Little Pony, 3½x4", 2-dimensional w/thumbwheel dials, marked 1973 Hasbro Hong Kong **$16.00**

Durhan Industries, Garfield w/Odie Charm, 3¾x4", Garfield face w/thumbwheel dials on side, Odie charm on strap handle **$45.00**

Emerson, embossed Mickey Mouse w/various instruments on wood composition cube, two knobs, 1934, EX... **$700.00**

Ertl, Big Foot 4X4, 9⅜x6½", dial & control knobs on side between tires, marked Made in Korea **$35.00**

Franklin, Grandfather Clock, #LF 210, 13¼", white w/gold trim, made in Japan **$45.00**

Franklin, Harp, #3170119, 11½x4¾", black & white, Japan **$50.00**

Gabriel, Mickey Mouse, 6½x6½", two transistors, controls & marks on large ears, marked Disney Japan **$60.00**

General Electric, Alligator, 11½x4", eyes display settings on controls, thumbwheel dials under eyes **$35.00**

General Electric, Big Mac Box, #2789, 2¾x4x4", red & white w/Golden Arches on sides, Made in Hong Kong... **$25.00**

General Electric, The General (locomotive), 7x9¼", blue & orange plastic w/gold trim, Made in Japan **$35.00**

General Mills, Hamburger Helper Helping Hand, 6½", volume-control nose, Made in Hong Kong **$45.00**

H Fishlove & Co, Country Music, 5½", outhouse w/crescent moon in door, thumbwheel dials, Made in Japan, 1971 .... **$25.00**

Heinz, Tomato Ketchup Bottle, actual bottle size, volume control in top, tuning in movable base section, Hong Kong **$50.00**

Heritage, #6801, Ancient Castle, 5¾x10" wide, wooden, controls on roof, Made in Japan **$35.00**

Hong Kong, Roller Skate, 6x5", UK Registration #3442752, distributed by Prime Designs $30.00

Hyman Products Inc, Golf Ball, 4½" dia, black base w/logo, Made in Hong Kong, 1987 .... **$25.00**

Japan, 1917 Touring Car, 4½x6½", brass-plated metal, thumbwheel controls above running boards **$50.00**

Kraft, Parkay Margarine, 1-lb stick-sized box, 4½", w/strap handle, thumbwheel dials, Made in Hong Kong .. **$35.00**

Kraft Foods, Miracle Whip The Bread Spread, 5x3" dia can w/thumbwheels at sides, Made in Hong Kong..... **$30.00**

Leadworks Inc, Microphone 'On-The-Air,' 12½", 1930s-style microphone, AM/FM, Made in Taiwan, 1987 .... **$50.00**

Lewco, Gumby & Pokey, #7012, shown on rectangular 6x3" AM/FM unit, Made in China **$20.00**

Luxtone, Panda Bear, 6x4⅞", yellow & black, eye control knobs, Made in Hong Kong **$20.00**

Markatron Inc, Coke Vending Machine, #2002, 7½x3¼", marked 'Enjoy Coke' & 'Coke Is It' on front, AM/FM **$50.00**

Matrix, Opticurl Variable Action Acid Wave, 4½" box shape, thumbwheel dial, marked Made in Hong Kong ... **$35.00**

Nasta, Raisin Man, 7x6¾", posable arms, marked 1988 CalRab & Applause, Made in China **$35.00**

Nasta, Smurf Head, 4x4", 2-dimensional, copyright Peyo 1982, Made in Hong Kong **$20.00**

Nasta, Wuzzle (Butter Bear), 7¼x5", strap handle, marked Walt Disney, Made in Hong Kong **$45.00**

Panasonic, Wrist Style, 7" dia, large plastic ring **$16.00**

Philco, #P22, Ford Mustang Fastback, 7½x2¾", 1966 .... **$50.00**

Philgee International, Donald Duck, 7½x5", 2-dimensional w/strap handle, marked Disney & Made in Hong Kong **$40.00**

Philgee International, Raggedy Ann & Andy, 4x4¾", decal on 2-dimensional heart form, marked 1974 Bobbs Merrill **$25.00**

Picker International, Nashville Picker, 12½x4¼" amplified guitar form, marked Made in Hong Kong **$35.00**

Pillsbury Co, Little Sprout, 6¼x4⅜", 2-dimensional, marked Made in Hong Kong **$45.00**

Pillsbury Co, Pillsbury Doughboy, 6½", plastic, walkman type, marked Made in Hong Kong, 1985 .... **$25.00**

Planter Peanut Co, Mr Peanut, 10¼", plastic, 2-dimensional, thumbwheel dial controls, marked Made in Hong Kong **$45.00**

Playtime Products, Cabbage Patch Girl, 6½x6¼", reclining on rectangular radio base w/thumbwheel controls, 1985 .... **$25.00**

Playtime Products, Care Bear Cousins, 5x3", 2-dimensional unit w/slider controls, copyright American Greetings, 1985 .... **$18.00**

Playtime Products, Radio Gobot, 2⅜x8" transformer car converts to robot, marked Tonka Toy Made in Hong Kong, 1985 .... **$20.00**

Premium Resources, Mobil Premier Battery, 3⅞x4", red, yellow & black plastic, Made in Hong Kong **$25.00**

Prestige, Fleischmann's Distilled Dry Gin Bottle, 11x3¾", unusual clear plastic showing radio **$60.00**

Pro Sports Marketing, Football Helmet w/Los Angeles Rams insignia, 6½x7", marked Made in USA **$25.00**

Radio Ceramics of California, Lady in Hoop Skirt, 10½x9" seated figure, ceramic, marked Made in USA **$150.00**

Radio Shack, D Cell Battery, 4¾x2¼" dia, red, white & gold, marked Made in Korea **$25.00**

Radio Shack, Football Helmet, 5⅛x5⅜", marked TC (Tandy Corp) w/controls on sides, Made in Korea **$20.00**

Radio Shack, Pepsi Bottle, actual bottle size, 9⅝", controls in top & base, marked Made in Hong Kong **$20.00**

Radio Shack, Pound Puppy, 7¼x5½", reclining on molded plastic radio base w/thumbwheel dials, 1987 ....**$16.00**

Radio Shack, Radiobot, 8" plastic robot w/black strap handle, marked Made in Hong Kong **$16.00**

Radio Shack, Space Shuttle Columbia, 6½", plastic, realistic, marked Made in Hong Kong...............................**$25.00**

Radio Shack, Speedway Special #3, 3x9¾x5", controls under driver's seat & behind front wheel.........................**$35.00**

Radio Shack, Statue of Liberty, 11¾", cast metal on plastic radio base, Made in Korea, 1986 ....**$40.00**

Radio Shack, World Globe, 5" globe on oval stand containing radio, 8" total height..................................**$25.00**

Raleigh Electronics, Piper Brut Champagne Bottle, 10½", controls in split cap, marked Piper-Heidsieck & Japan **$50.00**

RJ Reynolds Tobacco Co, Punchy (logo of Hawaiian Punch), 6x7" 2-dimensional figure.................................**$40.00**

Ross Co, Bookcase, 4⅛x7¼" long, low wooden cased unit, top opens to hold jewelry, Made in Japan...........**$25.00**

Sanyo, Dice, #RP 1711, red & white dice, 3¼" sq, controls on back..**$20.00**

SC Johnson & Son Inc, Raid clock & radio combination, 7x7", bug leaning on large round dial on rectangular base..**$75.00**

Starkist Foods, Charlie the Tuna, 5½", colorful plastic, marked Made in Hong Kong, 1970...................**$60.00**

Stewart, Owl, 4½x3", stylized form, plastic w/black control eyes & black strap handle, marked Made in Hong Kong **$20.00**

Sutton Associates, Bozo the Clown, 5¾x6¾", Made in Hong Kong, Larry Harmon Pictures $50.00

Sutton Associates, Love Is...For Us, 4⅝x7½", 2-dimensional cartoon variation of Adam & Eve, 1973.................**$25.00**

Synanon, Gas Pump, 9½x3⅛" dia, 1930s style, marked Made in China **$25.00**

Tokai, Piano, 6¼x8", wood-cased baby grand, Made in Japan..**$80.00**

Trico, Mercedes Benz Sedan, 2½x8½", plastic, marked Made in Hong Kong..**$30.00**

Waco, Knight Helmet, 8¼", pewter-plated bust showing knight's face behind face plate, Made in Japan **$75.00**

Windsor, Jukebox, #380, 7x4", resembles Wurlitzer #1015, Made in China **$30.00**

Windsor, Rest Room Radio, solid-color plastic holds toilet tissue, marked Solid State Hi-Fi Deluxe **$20.00**

Windsor, TWA Transworld 747 Jet, 13" long, 12½" wingspan, Made in Hong Kong **$45.00**

Railroad Collectibles

Prices continue to rise as this hobby gains in popularity. It is estimated that almost two hundred different railway companies once operated in this country, so to try to collect just one item representative of each would be a real challenge. Supply and demand is the rule governing all pricing, so naturally an item with a marking from a long-defunct, less-prominent railroad generally carries the higher price tag.

Railroadiana is basically divided into two main categories, paper and hardware, with both having many subdivisions. Some collectors tend to specialize in only one area — locks, lanterns, ticket punches, dinnerware, or timetables, for example. Many times estate sales and garage sales are good sources for finding these items, since retired railroad employees often kept such memorabilia as keepsakes. Because many of these items are very unique, you need to get to know as much as possible about railroad artifacts in order to be able to recognize and evaluate a good piece. For more information, we recommend *Railroad Collectibles, 4th Edition*, by Stanley L. Baker.

Apron, 11x15", Union Pacific, bartender's, Overland logo in waist, EX...**$17.50**

Ashtray, 3½", Chesapeake & Ohio Railway, Chessie, chinaware **$65.00**

Ashtray, 3½" dia, McCloud Railroad, logo in red on glass **$16.00**

Ashtray, 3½" sq, Erie, 100th anniversary commemorative, glass **$25.00**

Ashtray, 3¾", Missouri Pacific, red buzz saw logo on 6-sided glass shape **$17.50**

Ashtray, 4", Atchison Topeka & Santa Fe, Santa Fe in script on glass, oval...**$35.00**

Ashtray, 4½", Great Northern, Mountains & Flowers, chinaware **$75.00**

Ashtray, 4¼", Union Pacific, amber glass **$12.50**

Ashtray, 5" dia, Baltimore & Ohio Credit Union, gold-toned metal, NM **$8.50**

Ashtray, 5", clear glass w/bias corners.........................**$5.00**

Badge, Chicago, Milwaukee, St Paul & Pacific, waiter's, metal, M..**$15.00**

Badge, hat; Norfolk & Western, brakeman, silver skeleton letters, M...**$58.00**

Badge, hat; 3½" long, Atlantic Coast Line, fireman's, nickel plated, EX...**$42.50**

Badge, hat; 3½x1½", Santa Fe, porter's, blue logo on silver, M...**$55.00**

Blanket, Canadian National, maple leaf logo, Pendleton wool, EX..**$40.00**

Blanket, Northern Pacific, light tan w/brown letters, North Star wool, EX...**$150.00**

Blanket, Pullman, pink wool w/dark pink logo in center, EX..**$70.00**

Book, promotional; 11x13", Georgetown Loop, pictures, 1910, 22 pages, EX...**$45.00**

Book, telegraph code, embossing on leatherette cover, 1928, 73 pages, M...**$5.00**

Book, 6x9", Western Union, telegraph blanks, unused, NM...**$7.50**

Bottle, milk; ½-pt, Missouri Pacific, buzz saw logo on glass, NM...**$15.00**

Bowl, bouillon; Atchison Topeka & Santa Fe, chinaware, double handle..**$50.00**

Bowl, bouillon; Reading, Stotesbury, chinaware, back stamped...**$75.00**

Bowl, bouillon; Southern, Peach Blossom, chinaware..**$25.00**

Bowl, cereal; 6", Atchison Topeka & Santa Fe, Adobe, chinaware, top marked..................................**$45.00**

Bowl, cereal; 6", Pennsylvania Railroad, Mountain Laurel, chinaware..**$20.00**

Bowl, cereal; 6½", Great Northern, Glacier, chinaware, back stamped...**$100.00**

Bowl, cereal; 6½", Great Northern, Glory of the West, chinaware...**$35.00**

Bowl, cereal; 6½", Union Pacific, Blue & Gold, chinaware...**$18.00**

Bowl, cereal; 6½", Union Pacific, Desert Flower, bottom stamped...**$38.00**

Bowl, grapefruit; 2½x6½", Pullman, silverplate, 1925.**$88.00**

Bowl, soup; 8½", New York Central, DeWitt Clinton, chinaware, top marked..................................**$42.00**

Bowl, soup; 9", Baltimore & Ohio, Centenary, chinaware, bottom stamped...**$80.00**

Bowl, soup; 9", Chicago Burlington & Quincy, Violets & Daisies, chinaware, bottom stamped.................**$125.00**

Bowl, soup; 9", Union Pacific, Harriman Blue, chinaware, bottom stamped...**$45.00**

Brochure, 4x6", Southern Pacific, Great Salt Lake Cutoff, 1920, 29 pages, EX...**$17.50**

Brochure, 4x9", Hotels & Resorts of Union Pacific, red cover, 1911, EX...**$17.50**

Butter pat, Atchison Topeka & Santa Fe, Mimbreno, chinaware..**$45.00**

Butter pat, Atlantic Coast Line, Flora of the South, chinaware, bottom stamped..............................**$95.00**

Butter pat, Chicago & Northwestern, Depot Ornaments, chinaware..**$45.00**

Butter pat, Delaware & Hudson, Canterbury, chinaware..**$28.00**

Butter pat, Louisville & Nashville, Green Leaf, chinaware..**$45.00**

Butter pat, Southern Pacific, Prairie-Mountain Wildflowers, chinaware, bottom stamped................**$87.50**

Butter pat, Southern Pacific, Sunset, chinaware..........**$85.00**

Butter pat, Union Pacific, Union Streamliner, chinaware..**$26.00**

Butter pat, 2⅝" sq, Santa Fe, International silverplate, rounded corners..**$55.00**

Button, uniform; large, Atchison Topeka & Santa Fe, chrome or brass, M, each..**$1.00**

Button, uniform; large, Chicago & Northwestern, brass, flat shape..**$1.00**

Calendar, pocket size, Atchison Topeka & Santa Fe, 1964, M **$275.00**

Cap, Northern Pacific, conductor's, black grosgrain w/yellow cord, gold letters on black badge, Carlson & Co **$85.00**

Cap, Pullman, conductor's, gold badge & braid, NM..**$125.00**

Coat, Union Pacific, waiter's, collarless style, pearl buttons, EX...**$15.00**

Cocktail set, pitcher & 2½" roly-polys, Union Pacific, logo on glass..**$38.00**

Coffeepot, 14-oz, California Zephyr, worn silverplate, bottom marked...**$95.00**

Coffeepot, 14-oz, Great Northern, silverplate, intertwined logo, side marked, dated 1946, EX.....................**$55.00**

Coffeepot, 8-oz, Union Pacific, International silverplate, back stamped, VG..**$85.00**

Corn cob skewers, Great Northern, silverplate, light wear, pr..**$42.50**

Cover, hot food; 6", Great Northern, silverplate, intertwined logo, bottom stamped................................**$32.00**

Creamer, individual size, Kansas City Southern, Roxbury, chinaware..**$35.00**

Creamer, individual size, Union Pacific, Harriman Blue, chinaware..**$55.00**

Creamer, 2¼", Pennsylvania Railroad, Keystone, chinaware, side logo..**$67.50**

Cruet, Southern Pacific, Daylight w/ball & wing logo on glass...**$175.00**

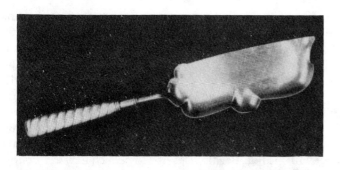

Crumber, 12" long, Northern Pacific (script), 1847 Rogers Brothers silverplate, spiral pattern handle **$125.00**

Cup, bouillon; Atlantic Coast Line, Flora of the South, chinaware, bottom stamped.............................**$145.00**

Cup, 2½x3½", Pennsylvania Railroad, Keystone logo embossed on tin, EX.................................**$65.00**

Cup & saucer, Baltimore & Ohio, Centenary, chinaware, bottom stamped **$95.00**

Cup & saucer, Chicago Burlington & Quincy, Violets & Daisies, chinaware **$55.00**

Cup & saucer, demitasse; Chesapeake & Ohio, Centenary, chinaware, bottom stamped......................**$75.00**

Cup & saucer, demitasse; Chicago Milwaukee St Paul & Pacific, Traveler, chinaware..................**$75.00**

Cup & saucer, demitasse; Southern Pacific, Sunset, chinaware, side logo, bottom stamped **$275.00**

Cup & saucer, Fred Harvey, Webster, chinaware.......**$18.00**

Cup & saucer, Missouri Pacific, The Eagle, chinaware, top marked, side logo **$35.00**

Cup & saucer, Norfolk & Western, Dogwood, chinaware **$45.00**

Cup & saucer, Pullman, Indian Tree, chinaware, top marked...**$225.00**

Cup & saucer, Spokane Portland & Seattle Railway, Red Leaves, chinaware...............................**$22.50**

Cup & saucer, Union Pacific, Challenger, chinaware ..**$45.00**

Cuspidor, 7x3", Pullman, nickel-plated brass, bottom stamped, EX **$75.00**

Egg cup, double; Great Northern, Oriental, chinaware..**$75.00**

Egg cup, large, Missouri Pacific, Eagle, chinaware, side logo **$67.50**

Egg cup, small, Union Pacific, Streamliner, chinaware .**$42.00**

Finger bowl, 3", Rio Grande, silverplate w/'speed' letters, bottom marked, 1941..............................**$32.00**

Gauge, 7⅜", Ashton Standard Test, nickel-plated brass, EX **$35.00**

Gravy boat, large, Union Pacific, Streamliner, chinaware **$80.00**

Gravy boat, New York Central, Platinum Blue, chinaware, bottom stamped.................................**$100.00**

Gravy boat, small, Kansas City Southern, Roxbury, chinaware **$28.00**

Gravy boat, Southern Pacific, Reed & Barton silverplate, winged ball, side logo, bottom stamped, EX **$35.00**

Headrest cover, Union Pacific, yellow w/red Streamliner logo, button-down style, EX.....................**$17.50**

Ice cream shell, Canadian National, Bonaventure, chinaware, top marked...............................**$35.00**

Key chain, Penn Central, cast metal, Credit Union logo...**$8.00**

Knife, steak; Atchison Topeka & Santa Fe, Cromwell silverplate, 1912 ....**$17.50**

Knife, Union Pacific, 3-bladed type w/cuticle pusher, bottle opener & screwdriver, NM.............................**$7.50**

Lamp, berth; Pullman, steel & porcelain, egg shape, NM, pr..**$45.00**

Lamp, caboose bunk; Union Pacific, pebbled top globe, brass & steel, hanging type **$40.00**

Lamp, inspector's, Star Headlight & Lantern Co, ornate style, NM **$65.00**

Lamp, semaphore; Great Northern, Adlake, oil burning, clear lens, complete w/fuel pot, EX **$135.00**

Lamp, semaphore; Union Pacific, Adlake, electric, double bull's eye lens, NM..........................**$85.00**

Lantern, Columbus & Greenville Railway, Armspear, pot insert, clear unmarked globe, Patent 1913, NM **$95.00**

Lantern, Delaware Lackawanna & Western, Dietz Vesta 1951, unmarked red globe, EX.......................**$45.00**

Lantern, Louisville & Nashville, Armspear, tall clear marked globe, top marked, dated 1895, complete..........**$145.00**

Lantern, Missouri Pacific, Handlan-Buck, bell-bottom style w/clear globe, M.......................................**$175.00**

Lantern, New York New Haven & Hartford, Adlake 1913 Reliable, red Dietz unmarked globe, EX **$65.00**

Lantern, Pennsylvania Railroad, Adams, amber marked globe, Patent 1897, EX..............................**$165.00**

Laundry bag, 30x28", Union Pacific, canvas w/brass grommets at top, EX....................................**$15.00**

Lighter, Soo Line, Warco slimline, white logo on red ground, M...**$22.50**

Lighter, Union Pacific, 'We Can Handle It' & shield logo, Zippo type, EX.....................................**$17.50**

Lock, Chicago, St Paul, Minneapolis, & Omaha (stamped on shackle), ET Fraim Lock Co stamped on drop, general use, chain attached.............$25.00

Map, 11x14", Atlantic & East Carolina Railway, color, system, 1940s...**$17.50**

Matchbook, Texas & Pacific, Fast Freight, diesel logo on blue, M, unused **$2.00**

Menu, Baltimore & Ohio, opens to 4x18", child's, train form, EX.................................**$15.00**

Menu, 5x8", Chicago & Northwestern, single card, 1942, EX **$5.00**

Menu, 8x11", Fred Harvey, Los Angeles Union Station, 1955, EX.................................**$12.00**

Menu, 9¼x6", Chicago Democratic Convention, logo of three railroads on back, scarce $25.00

Menu card, Rock Island Line, breakfast, 1975.................**$2.50**

Napkin, Rio Grande, white w/white embroidered script logo, EX.................................**$6.00**

Napkin, 16x18", Union Pacific, yellow w/interwoven winged streamliner logo, EX.................................**$7.50**

Napkin, 21x16", California Zephyr, logo interwoven in center, M.................................**$12.00**

Oiler, 31", long spout, missing spring, Patent 1896, EX .**$32.00**

Patch, shoulder; Amtrak, policeman's, G.................**$9.50**

Patch, shoulder; Conrail, policeman's, M **$12.50**

Patch, 3x4", Burlington Northern Explorer, green & white, M **$7.00**

Patch, 6" dia, Boston & Maine, logo **$7.50**

Pen, Atchison Topeka & Santa Fe, ballpoint, blue plastic w/gold-toned metal, 'The Complete Transportation Co' & logo, NM.................................**$4.50**

Pen, British Columbia Railway, ballpoint, blue & white plastic, M.................................**$2.50**

Pen, Chicago & Northwestern, ballpoint, chrome metal, 'Safety First a Pointed Reminder' on side, M.........**$6.50**

Pen, Soo Line, ballpoint, green plastic w/gold-toned metal top, logo in black, early thin style, EX **$6.00**

Pen, Wabash, ballpoint, 'Serving the Heart of America' on side, NM.................................**$6.50**

Pencil, mechanical; Chicago & Northwestern, Redipoint, green & yellow, EX.................................**$8.00**

Pencil, mechanical; Chicago & Northwestern, yellow & chrome, 'Stay Alert, Stay Alive' on side, NM **$25.00**

Pencil, mechanical; 5½", Missouri Pacific, 'The Eagle' w/buzz saw & eagle logos on plastic, NM.................**$30.00**

Pillowcase, California Zephyr, over-stamp on Pullman logo on pink, EX **$15.00**

Pin, lapel; Amtrack, gold, half-round w/logo, EX.......**$32.00**

Plate, 10", Union Pacific, Desert Flower, chinaware, bottom stamped **$85.00**

Plate, 5½", Southern Pacific, Prairie-Mountain Wildflowers, chinaware, bottom stamped.................................**$35.00**

Plate, 7", Northern Pacific, Monad, chinaware, top logo..**$70.00**

Plate, 7½", Pullman, Indian Tree, chinaware **$80.00**

Plate, 7¼", Southern Pacific, Sunset, chinaware, bottom stamped **$110.00**

Plate, 8", Great Northern, Oriental, chinaware.............**$85.00**

Plate, 8", Pennsylvania Railroad, Broadway, chinaware, top marked.................................**$45.00**

Plate, 8", Union Pacific, Zion, chinaware **$190.00**

Plate, 8½", Southern Pacific, Harriman Blue, chinaware, bottom stamped.................................**$95.00**

Plate, 9", New York Central, Mercury, chinaware, bottom stamped **$35.00**

Plate, 9½", Atchison Topeka & Santa Fe, California Poppy, chinaware **$35.00**

Plate, 9½", Western Pacific, Feather River, chinaware, top marked.................................**$225.00**

Platter, 12", Union Pacific, International silverplate, Overland shield, 1914 ....**$88.00**

Platter, 5½x8", Baltimore & Ohio, Centenary, chinaware, bottom stamped.................................**$110.00**

Platter, 5½x8½", Chicago, Rock Island, & Pacific, Golden State, chinaware, top marked.................................**$185.00**

Platter, 5½x8½", Delaware & Hudson, Canterbury, chinaware.................................**$145.00**

Platter, 6x8½", Missouri Kansas Texas, Katy Ornaments, chinaware.................................**$125.00**

Platter, 6x9", Chesapeake & Ohio, George Washington, chinaware, top logo.................................**$185.00**

Platter, 7x9", Union Pacific, Harriman Blue, chinaware, bottom stamped.................................**$50.00**

Platter, 7x9½", Southern Pacific, Sunset, chinaware, top marked.................................**$125.00**

Platter, 9x11", Union Pacific, Desert Flower, chinaware, bottom stamped.................................**$75.00**

Post card, Monon's Lew Wallace, M **$6.50**

Post card, Northern Pacific, black & white picture of Minnetonka at 1949 Chicago World's Fair, M.................**$2.00**

Relish, 3½x7½", Chicago Burlington & Quincy, Violets & Daisies, chinaware **$55.00**

Relish, 5½x11½", Baltimore & Ohio, Centenary, chinaware, bottom stamped.................................**$185.00**

Relish, 5x10½", Union Pacific, Blue & Gold, chinaware.**$28.00**

Ruler, 12", Chicago, Burlington & Quincy, tin, EX.........**$8.00**

Ruler, 6", table determines train speeds, w/original leather case **$20.00**

Ruler, 7", Burlington Northern, plastic, 'Trains Can't Stop Quickly, You Can,' M.................$3.50

Sheet, twin size, Burlington Route, stamped logo, NM .$8.00

Sheet, twin size, Denver & Rio Grand, sleeping car, w/logo, EX.................$15.00

Sheet music, 'I've Been Working on the Railroad,' Calumet Music, 1935, EX.................$10.00

Sherbet, Louisville & Nashville, Regent, chinaware.....$85.00

Sherbet, 3¼", Great Northern, silverplate, intertwined logo, bottom stamped & side marked, ca 1946.............$36.00

Shot glass, 2¾", Delaware & Hudson logo in shield on glass $11.00

Sign, 4x12", Amtrak, 'Tickets & Tours Sold Here,' stand-up type, VG $45.00

Signal lock, Atlantic Coast Line, brass, w/chain, NM...$16.00

Signal lock, Baltimore & Ohio, Fraim, brass, double stamp, no post, VG $35.00

Signal lock, Norfolk & Western, Yale, brass, no chain, EX $15.00

Spoon, iced tea; Century, International silverplate $17.50

Stationery, Northern Pacific, North Coast Limited, Yellowstone, one sheet w/envelope $3.50

Stationery, 4x6", California Zephyr, 'Aboard the Vista Dome,' w/envelope, M $2.50

Step stool, 7x13", Cincinnati & Ohio, embossed letters, yellow paint, safety top, EX.................$165.00

Stool, 16x14", Wabash, metal w/rubber feet, Morton nameplate, EX.................$185.00

Sugar tongs, New York Central, Commonwealth, Reed & Barton silverplate $60.00

Switch key, Burlington Route, Adams & Westlake, steel, EX $24.00

Switch key, Chicago & Northwestern, 'S' on reverse...$22.50

Switch key, Cincinnati Indiana & Western Railway, Adams & Westlake, EX $85.00

Switch key, New York New Haven & Hartford, steel, EX $10.00

Switch lamp, Cincinnati & Ohio, Handlan, snow hoods, glass lenses, restored $125.00

Switch lock, Atchison Topeka & Santa Fe, Slaymaker, iron w/brass rivets, 1967, EX $15.00

Switch lock, Denver & Rio Grand Western, steel, w/marked brass key, EX.................$27.50

Switch lock, New York Central System, Fraim, steel, 1968, unmarked brass key w/chain.................$225.50

Swizzle stick, Chicago & Northwestern, logo w/in circle ..$1.00

Swizzle stick, Fred Harvey, black, M $2.50

Tablecloth, 44" sq, Great Northern, white-on-white leaf design, green script letters, EX.................$32.50

Tablecloth, 48x33", Missouri Pacific Line, linen, white on white, EX.................$45.00

Tablecloth, 50x36", Chicago Burlington & Quincy Railroad, Burlington Route square logo, EX $20.00

Tablespoon, Fred Harvey, Cromwell, International silverplate, 1912 ....$15.00

Tablespoon, Union Pacific, Zephyr, International silverplate, back marked, M $12.50

Tag, 1½x3", Chicago & Eastern Illinois, cast brass, NM.$17.50

Teapot, Baltimore & Ohio, Centenary, chinaware, bottom stamped $195.00

Teapot, Chicago Rock Island & Pacific, LaSalle, chinaware, bottom stamped $235.00

Teapot, 8-oz, Chicago & Northwestern, International silverplate, pagoda style, bottom stamped, 1925.........$75.00

Teaspoon, New York Central, Century, International silverplate, bottom marked $17.50

Telephone, Western Electric 1915P model, scissors style, EX.................$165.00

Timetable, employee; Kansas City System, Northern Terminal Division, 1945, EX.................$15.00

Timetable, public; Atlantic Coast Line, full system, 1932, EX $22.00

Timetable, public; Great Northern System, Empire Builder, 1939, EX.................$18.00

Toothpick holder, Boston & Albany, Aroostook, chinaware.................$45.00

Towel, 15x20", Pennsylvania Railroad, Cannon, red stripe on white, EX $5.00

Tray, 9x5¾", Missouri Pacific, silverplate, fancy applied edge, bottom marked, 1930s.................$88.00

Tumbler, juice; 3" New York Central, white enameling on glass $28.00

Tumbler, 4½", Atchison Topeka & Santa Fe, 'Santa Fe' in white script on glass $12.50

Tumbler, 4¼", Missouri Pacific, eagle logo on glass......$8.00

Tumbler, 6", Atchison Topeka & Santa Fe, 'Sante Fe' in white script on glass $14.00

Tureen, soup; 3-pc, Santa Fe, Reed & Barton silverplate, #3400 series.................$125.00

Wax sealer, American Express, Rossville IN, brass w/oval head, EX $25.00

Wax sealer, Wells Fargo Express, Saxman KS, brass w/round head, EX $135.00

Wine, 4½", Canadian National Railway, etched logo on glass $27.00

Wrench, double end; Southern Railway, heavy steel, strong mark.................$12.00

Reamers

Reamers have been around since the mid-1700s. They've been made in silver, fine china, wood, pottery, and glass, in plain basic styles, patented models with hand-cranks; and as unusual figurals. Before soda pop became such a convenience, fruit juices were routinely served at social gatherings. Sunkist reamers were introduced around 1915 and until the sixties were cranked out in hundreds of styles and color variations. Many other companies followed suit, and novelty reamers were imported from Japan and Germany as well. Then came the age of convenience foods and the demise of the reamer.

Today some of the rarer reamers are worth hundreds of dollars. We've listed some of those you're more apt to find here; but if you'd like to know more about them, we recommend that you read *Kitchen Glassware of the Depression Years* by Gene Florence.

Anchor Hocking, fired-on black, tab handle...............**$12.50**
Anchor Hocking, green, loop handle..........................**$15.00**
Cambridge, crystal, small tab handle.........................**$14.50**
Cambridge, Jadite, flat, loop handle..........................**$125.00**
Cambridge, light pink, loop handle...........................**$175.00**
Federal Glass Company, green, pointed cone, tab handle **$14.50**
Federal Glass Company, green, ribbed, tab handle.....**$14.50**
Fenton, clear w/elephant on base, loop handles **$70.00**
Fleur-de-Lis, white, embossed emblem on side, loop handle **$80.00**
Fleur-de-Lis, white opalescent, embossed emblem on side, loop handle **$55.00**
Foreign, crystal, 'Tcheco-Scovaquie' embossed on tab handle..**$45.00**
Foreign, crystal w/embossed fruit, loop handle **$55.00**
Foreign, green or pink, embossed lettering, loop handle..**$45.00**
Fry, light green, straight-sided, tab handle..................**$20.00**
Hazel Atlas, cobalt blue, tab handle, large................**$250.00**
Hazel Atlas, Crisscross, crystal, tab handle...................**$5.00**
Hazel Atlas, crystal, pointed cone, loop handle............**$8.00**
Hazel Atlas, fired-on red, loop handle **$45.00**
Hazel Atlas, green, tab handle, large...........................**$15.00**
Hazel Atlas, pink, tab handle, small **$35.00**
Hazel Atlas, white w/red trim, loop handle...........**$24.00**

Hocking, green, vertically ribbed sides, orange reamer..**$15.00**

Indiana Glass Company, crystal, horizontal handle.....**$12.50**
Jeannette Glass Company, crystal, loop handle, large .**$10.00**
Jeannette Glass Company, dark Jadite, loop handle, large.**$22.00**
Jeannette Glass Company, Delphite, loop handle, small .**$60.00**
McKee, custard w/red trim, footed, loop handle........**$35.00**
McKee, Jadite, footed, loop handle **$20.00**
McKee, opalescent, embossed 'Sunkist,' Made in USA .**$90.00**
McKee, pink, embossed 'Sunkist,' loop handle **$45.00**
McKee, Seville yellow, embossed 'Sunkist,' loop handle .**$40.00**
US Glass Company, crystal, graduated measurements on side, slick handle **$20.00**
US Glass Company, dark pink, slick handle................**$95.00**
US Glass Company, green frost w/decoration, slick handle.**$25.00**
US Glass Company, frosted pink w/decoration, slick handle **$30.00**

US Glass Company, green, graduated measurements on side, slick handle **$35.00**
US Glass Company, green, vertical ribs, slick handle........**$45.00**
US Glass Company, turquoise, graduated measurements on side, slick handle **$90.00**
Westmoreland, crystal w/lemon decoration, flat loop handle...**$80.00**
Westmoreland, frosted blue, bottom only...................**$40.00**
Westmoreland, light or dark green, flat loop handle ..**$90.00**
Westmoreland, sun-colored amethyst, flat loop handle.**$85.00**

Records

Records are still plentiful at flea markets and some antique malls, though not to the degree they were a year or so ago. Garage sales are sometimes a great place to buy old records, since most of what you'll find there have been stored more carefully by their originial owners.

There are two schools of thought concerning what is a collectible record. While some collectors prefer the rarities — those made in limited quantities, by an unknown who later became famous, or those aimed at a specific market — others like the vintage Top-10 recordings. Now that they're so often being replaced with CDs, we realize that even though we take them for granted, the possibilty of their becoming a thing of the past may be reality tomorrow.

Whatever the slant your collection takes, learn to visually inspect records before you buy them. Condition is one of the most important factors to consider when assessing value. To be judged as mint, a record may have been played but must have no visual or audible deterioration — no loss of gloss to the finish, no stickers or writing on the label, no holes, no skips when it is played. If any of these are apparent, at best it is considered to be excellent, and its value is at least 50% lower. Many of the records you'll find that seem to you to be in wonderful shape would be judged only very good, excellent at the most, by a knowledgeable dealer. Sleeves with no tape, stickers, tears, or obvious damage at best would be excellent; mint condition sleeves are impossible to find unless you've found old store stock.

It's not too uncommon to find old radio station discards. These records will say either 'Not for Sale' or 'Audition Copy' and may be worth more than their commercial counterparts.

If you'd like more information, we recommend *American Premium Record Guide* by L.R. Docks.

Aaronson, Irving; An Evening in June, Columbia 3037-D, 78 rpm **$12.50**
Adams, Faith; Johnny Lee, Imperial 5456, 45 rpm.......**$30.00**
Adams, Jo Jo; Call My Baby, Parrot 788, 45 rpm **$45.00**
Admarils, Oh Yes, King 4772, 45 rpm......................**$75.00**
Alabama Slim, Boar Hog Blues, Savoy 5553, 78 rpm **$8.00**
Alimo, Steve; I Want You To Love Me, Marlin 6064, 45 rpm **$12.00**
Allen, Henry Jr; Lost in My Dreams, Vocalion 3340, 78 rpm **$8.00**

Alpert, Herb; Spanish Flea, A&M 792, 45 rpm, VG........**$2.50**

Amy Curtis; Sleepin' Blues, Gold Star 618, 78 rpm......**$25.00**

Anderson, John; Swingin', Warner Brothers 0446, 45 rpm, reissue.................**$3.50**

Anderson, Lynn; It Wasn't God Who Made Honky Tonk Angels, Chart 5113, 45 rpm, VG.............................**$3.00**

Archies, Sugar Sugar, Calendar 1008, 45 rpm, VG.........**$4.50**

Arnold, Eddy; Make the World Go Away, RCA 8679, 45 rpm, VG.................**$3.50**

Arnold, Kokomo; Bad Luck Blues, Decca 7540, 78 rpm..**$20.00**

Autry, Gene; Wild Cat Mama, Victor 23642, 78 rpm....**$75.00**

Avalon, Frankie; Venus, Chancellor 1031, 45 rpm, VG .**$6.50**

Badgers, It All Depends on You, Broadway 1058, 78 rpm **$7.50**

Bailey, Pearl; Zing Went the Strings of My Heart, Sunset 2018, 45 rpm, VG.................**$9.00**

Barbecue Bob, Brown-Skin Gal, Columbia 14257-D, 78 rpm.................**$30.00**

Bare, Bobby; Detroit City, RCA 8183, 45 rpm, G...........**$2.00**

Bartholemew, Dave; The Monkey, Imperial 5438, 45 rpm.................**$50.00**

Beach Boys, Barbara Ann, Capitol 5561, 45 rpm, VG ...**$7.50**

Beatles, Help!, Capitol 5476, 45 rpm, VG.................**$11.00**

Beatles, Lady Madonna, Capitol 2138, 45 rpm, VG **$4.00**

Bennett, Tony; I Left My Heart in San Francisco, Columbia 33062, 45 rpm, VG.................**$2.50**

Berry, Chuck; Maybellene, Chess 1604 (second press), 45 rpm, VG **$2.00**

Big Bill, Little City Woman, Chess 1546, 45 rpm **$100.00**

Big Bopper, Chantilly Lace, D 1006, 45 rpm.................**$50.00**

Big Richard, Pig Meat Mama, Varsity 6063, 78 rpm.....**$10.00**

Bill & Slim, Papa's Gettin' Hot, Champion 16015, 78 rpm **$75.00**

Blake, Charley; Daddy & Home, Supertone 9476, 78 rpm **$10.00**

Bland, Bobby; IOU Blues, Duke 105, 45 rpm.............**$50.00**

Bo, Eddie; If It's Good to You, Scram 119, 45 rpm.....**$20.00**

Bonds, Gary 'US'; New Orleans, Legrand 1003, 45 rpm, G **$2.50**

Boone, Pat; Beach Girl, Dot 16658, 45 rpm **$5.00**

Boone, Pat; Love Letters in the Sand/Bernadine, Dot 15570, 45 rpm, VG.................**$3.50**

Bowers, Earl; The Contented Hobo, Superior 2607, 78 rpm **$15.00**

Bradley, Marie; Down Home Moan, Paramount 12456, 78 rpm **$100.00**

Bread, Hooked on You, Electra 45390, 45 rpm, VG......**$3.00**

Brewer, Teresa; Mutual Admiration Society, Coral 61737, 45 rpm, EX.................**$2.50**

Brooks, Dusty; Heaven of Fire, Sun 183, 45 rpm **$130.00**

Brostic, Earl; I Got Loaded, King 4491, 45 rpm **$25.00**

Brown, Ruth; Teardrops, Atlantic 919, 45 rpm **$200.00**

Bryant, Anita; Paper Roses, Carlton 528, 45 rpm, VG....**$2.50**

Bucktown Five, Mobile Blues, Gennett 5405, 78 rpm.**$80.00**

Cameos, He, Gigi 100, 45 rpm.................**$25.00**

Campbell, Gene; Western Plain Blues, Brunswick 7154, 78 rpm **$80.00**

Campbell, Glen; Galveston, Capitol 2428, 45 rpm, VG .**$2.50**

Cardinals, The; You Are My Only Love, Atlantic 995, 45 rpm.................**$30.00**

Carlisle, Clifford; Crazy Blues, Champion 16140, 78 rpm..**$20.00**

Carpenters, We've Only Just Begun, A&M 1217, 45 rpm, VG.................**$3.50**

Carr, Vikki; It Must Be Him, Liberty 55986, 45 rpm, VG .**$2.00**

Carter Family, Coal Miner's Blues, Decca 5596, 78 rpm **$10.00**

Cash, Johnny; Boy Named Sue, Columbia 4494, 45 rpm, VG.................**$4.00**

Cavaliers, Charm Bracelet, NRC 28, 45 rpm.................**$30.00**

Charles, Ray; Born To Lose, ABC-Paramount 10330, 45 rpm, VG.................**$6.00**

Checker, Chubby; Slow Twistin', Parkway 835, 45 rpm, VG.................**$5.50**

Chicago Footwarmers, Ballin' the Jack, Okeh 8533, 78 rpm **$60.00**

Clark, Petula; I Know a Place, Warner Brothers 5612, 45 rpm, VG.................**$6.00**

Cline, Patsy; Walkin' After Midnight, Decca 30221, 45 rpm, VG.................**$7.50**

Cobras, Cindy, Modern 964, 45 rpm.................**$150.00**

CoCoas, Flip Your Daddy, Chesterfield 364, 45 rpm.**$200.00**

Cole, Kid; Sixth Street Moon, Vocalion 1186, 78 rpm..**$50.00**

Collins, Judy; Send in the Clowns, Elektra 45253, 45 rpm, VG.................**$4.50**

Como, Perry; Hot Diggity, RCA 6427, 45 rpm, VG **$4.00**

Cotton Pickers, Rampart Street Blues, Brunswick 4325, 78 rpm.................**$10.00**

Cowsills, Indian Lake, MGM 13944, 45 rpm, VG...........**$2.00**

Craddock, Billy 'Crash'; Rub It In, ABC 11437, 45 rpm, VG.................**$2.50**

Crosby, Bing; White Christmas, Decca 23778, 45 rpm, VG.................**$3.00**

Daniels, Charlie; Heaven Can Be Anywhere, Epic 50456, 45 rpm, VG.................**$3.00**

Darin, Bobby; Dream Lover, ATCo 6140, 45 rpm, G.....**$2.00**

Dave Clark Five, Glad All Over, Epic 9656, 45 rpm, VG..**$7.50**

Davis, Mac; One Hell of a Woman, Columbia 46004, 45 rpm, VG.................**$2.50**

Davis, Sammy Jr; Dangerous, Decca 30158, 45 rpm, NM.................**$6.00**

Davis, Walter; Santa Claus, Bluebird 6125, 78 rpm......**$30.00**

Day, Doris; Whatever Will Be Will Be, Columbia 40704, 45 rpm, VG.................**$3.00**

Dee, Ronnie; Action Packed, Backbeat 522, 45 rpm...**$70.00**

Def Leppard, Armageddon It, Mercury 870 692, 45 rpm, VG.................**$3.00**

Delmore Brothers, Alabama Lullaby, Bluebird 6034, 78 rpm **$10.00**

Denver, John; Sunshine on My Shoulder, RCA 0213, 45 rpm, VG.................**$3.00**

Diamond, Neil; September Morn, Columbia 11175, 45 rpm, VG.................**$3.50**

Dion, Lonely Teenager, Laurie 3070, 45 rpm, VG.........**$6.50**

Doctor Ross, Juke Box Boogie, Sun 212, 45 rpm **$175.00**

Domino, Fats; Walking to New Orleans, Imperial 5675, 45 rpm.................**$8.00**

Donovan, Mellow Yellow, Epic 10098, 45 rpm, VG **$4.00**

Doors, Hello I Love You, Elektra 45635, 45 rpm, VG ...**$6.00**

Downbeats, Midnight Express, Amp 792, 45 rpm........**$25.00**

Dr Hook, When You're in Love w/a Beautiful Woman, Capitol 4705, 45 rpm, VG................**$3.00**

Duerson, Herve; Avenue Strut, Gennett 7009, 78 rpm..**$150.00**

Dylan, Bob; Knockin' on Heaven's Door, Columbia 45913, 45 rpm, VG................**$3.50**

Eagles, Lyin' Eyes, Asylum 45279, 45 rpm, VG.............**$4.00**

Easton, Sheena; Jimmy Mack, EMI 8309, 45 rpm, VG ...**$2.50**

El Dorados, My Loving Baby, red plastic, Vee Jay 115, 45 rpm................**$200.00**

El Rays, The; Darling I Know, Checker 794, 45 rpm.**$100.00**

Erby, John; Lonesome Jimmy Blues, Columbia 14151-D, 78 rpm **$20.00**

Eurythmics, Sweet Dreams, RCA 13533, 45 rpm, VG **$3.00**

Exile, Woke Up in Love, Epic 04247, 45 rpm, VG........**$2.50**

Fenton, Carl; Delirium, Brunswick 3519, 78 rpm...........**$7.50**

Fifth Dimension, Aquarius, Flashback 9489, 45 rpm, M..**$3.50**

Five Keys, Deep in My Heart, Aladdin 3245, 45 rpm.**$200.00**

Five Royales, With All Your Heart, Apollo 467, 45 rpm.**$20.00**

Fleetwood Mac, Hold Me, Warner Brothers 29966, 45 rpm, VG................**$2.50**

Fleming & Townsend, Ramblin' Boy, Victor 23557, 78 rpm **$30.00**

Four Aces, Yes Sir That's My Baby, Decca 30348, 45 rpm, G **$2.00**

Four Buddies, Delores, Club 51105, 45 rpm.............**$400.00**

Four Tops, Could It Be You, Chess 1623, 45 rpm.......**$25.00**

Four Tops, If I Were a Carpenter, Motown 1124, 45 rpm, VG................**$4.00**

Franklin, Aretha; Since You've Been Gone, Atlantic 13058, 45 rpm, M **$3.50**

Franklin, Buck; Crooked World Blues, Victor 23310, 78 rpm, EX **$175.00**

Franklin; Aretha; Respect, Atlantic 2403, 45 rpm, VG....**$2.00**

Gayle, Crystal; Don't It Make My Brown Eyes Blue, United Artists 1016, 45 rpm, VG................**$3.00**

Gentry, Bobbie; Fancy, Capitol 2675, 45 rpm, VG.........**$2.50**

Georgia Pot Lickers, Up Jumped the Rabbit, Brunswick 595 78 rpm **$15.00**

Gibbons, Irene; Longing, Columbia 14296-D, 78 rpm.**$25.00**

Goodman, Benny; A Jazz Holiday, Vocalion 15656, 78 rpm **$150.00**

Gordon, Big Mike; Walkin', Slippin', & Slidin', Baton 219, 45 rpm **$15.00**

Gordon, Roscoe; Weeping Blues, Flip 227, 78 rpm.....**$12.50**

Gore, Leslie; It's My Party, Mercury 72119, 45 rpm, VG..**$7.50**

Goulet, Robert; My Woman My Woman My Wife, Columbia 45165, 45 rpm, NM................**$4.00**

Grass Roots, Temptation Eyes, Dunhill 4263, 45 rpm, VG................**$4.00**

Greer, Big John; Bottle It Up & Go, Groove 0002, 45 rpm.**$25.00**

Gregory, Bobby; Runaway Boys, Okeh 45350, 78 rpm.**$15.00**

Griffin Brothers, Weepin' & Cryin', Dot 1071, 45 rpm.**$100.00**

Guess Who, These Eyes, RCA 0102, 45 rpm, EX...........**$5.00**

Haggard, Merle, Ramblin' Fever, MCA 40743, 45 rpm, VG................**$2.50**

Hall, Getri; Mr Blues, RAI 101, 45 rpm.......................**$40.00**

Hanson, William; Stop & Listen Blues, Okeh 45506, 78 rpm................**$35.00**

Harlem Stars, All Right Baby, E&W 100, 78 rpm.........**$15.00**

Harptones, Shrine of St Cecelis, Rama 221, 45 rpm.....**$75.00**

Harris, Emmylou; Tennessee Rose, Warner Brothers 49892, 45 rpm, VG................**$3.00**

Harris, Mary; Happy New Year Blues, Champion 50045, 78 rpm................**$25.00**

Hawkins, Jay; When I Tried, Wing 90005, 45 rpm.....**$40.00**

Heatwave, Boogie Nights, Epic 50370, 45 rpm, NM......**$3.50**

Helton, Ernest; Royal Clog, Okeh 45010, 78 rpm........**$20.00**

Henderson, Bertha; Jamboree Blues, Okeh 8265, 78 rpm................**$60.00**

Henley, Don; All She Wants To Do Is Dance, Geffen 29065, 45 rpm, VG................**$2.50**

Hill, Alex; Southbound, Vocalion 1465, 78 rpm **$150.00**

Hollies, Carrie-Anne, Epic 10180, 45 rpm, VG..............**$4.00**

Holly, Buddy; Blue Days, Black Nights, Decca 29854, 45 rpm................**$60.00**

Hooker, John Lee; High Priced Woman, Chess 1505, 45 rpm................**$100.00**

Hopkins, Lightning; Santa Fe Blues, RPM 398, 45 rpm.**$75.00**

Horton, Johnny; Happy Millionaire, Abbott 101, 78 rpm................**$10.00**

Hot Dogs, Carolina Shuffle, Silvertone 3572, 78 rpm..**$100.00**

Houston, David; Sugar Sweet, RCA Victor 6611, 45 rpm.**$15.00**

Houston, Whitney; Greatest Love of All, Arista 9466, 45 rpm, VG................**$2.50**

Howlin' Wolf, My Last Affair, Chess 1528 ....**$75.00**

Humperdinck, Engelbert; Last Waltz, Parrot 40019, 45 rpm................**$3.50**

Hunter's Serenaders, Sensational Mood, Vocalion 1621, 78 rpm................**$175.00**

Huskey, Ferlin; Sweet Misery, Capitol 2999, 45 rpm, EX.**$7.50**

Impressions, This Time, Cotillion 44211, 45 rpm, EX....**$5.00**

Jackson, George; Uh Huh, Atlantic 1024, 45 rpm........**$15.00**

Jackson, Janet; Rhythm Nation, A&M 1455, 45 rpm, NM..**$3.50**

Jackson, Lillian; Cow Cow Blues, Supertone 9294, 78 rpm................**$60.00**

Jackson, Michael; Billie Jean, Epic 03509, 45 rpm, VG..**$2.50**

Jackson 5, I'll Be There, Motown 1171, 45 rpm **$2.00**

James, Elmore; Can't Stop Lovin', Flair 1014, 45 rpm..**$50.00**

James, Tommy & the Shondells; Hanky Panky, Roulette 4686, 45 rpm, VG................**$2.00**

Jammin' Jim, Shake Boogie, Savoy 1106, 78 rpm **$10.00**

Joel, Billy; An Innocent Man, Columbia 04259, 45 rpm, EX................**$3.50**

John, Elton; I Guess That's Why They Call It the Blues, Geffen 29460, 45 rpm, VG................**$2.50**

Johnson, Earl; Shortenin' Bread, Okey 45112, 78 rpm.**$20.00**

Johnson, James P; Go Harlem, Columbia 2248-D, 78 rpm................**$25.00**

Johnson, Margaret; Absent Minded Blues, Okeh 8162, 78 rpm................**$75.00**

Johnson, Rev A; God Don't Like It, Glory 4011, 45 rpm.**$25.00**

Johnson, Stan; Baby Baby Doll, Ruby 550, 45 rpm...**$100.00**

Judds, Love Can Build a Bridge, RCA 2708, 45 rpm......**$3.50**

Jungle Kings, Friars Point Shuffle, Paramount 12654 78 rpm **$250.00**

Kansas City Kitty, Scrochin', Vocalion 1632, 78 rpm ...**$80.00**

Kansas Katie, Deep Sea Diver, Bluebird 8944, 78 rpm .**$12.00**

KC & the Sunshine Band, Please Don't Go, TK 1035, 45 rpm, VG **$2.50**

King, Charles; Bop Cat, Folk Star 1131, 45 rpm.........**$100.00**

Kirby Fred; My Heavenly Sweetheart, Bluebird 6597, 78 rpm **$8.00**

Kirk, Andy; Casey Jones Special, Brunswick 4653, 78 rpm **$30.00**

Kittrell, Christine; Evil-Eyed Woman, Republic 7055, 45 rpm..**$60.00**

Knight, Curtis; Hornet's Nest, RSVP 1124, 45 rpm **$50.00**

Knight, Gladys & the Pips; Midnight Train to Georgia, Buddah 383, 45 rpm, EX **$3.50**

Lanin, Sam; My Pet, Perfect 14978, 78 rpm **$7.50**

Lauper, Cyndi; Time After Time, Portrait 04432, 45 rpm, VG **$2.50**

Leaders, Bennie; Naggin' Woman, Freedom 5029, 78 rpm **$8.00**

Lee, Brenda; I'm Sorry, Decca 31093, 45 rpm, VG **$2.50**

Lee, Peggy; Bewitched, Capitol 5404, 45 rpm, EX.........**$9.50**

Lewis, Jerry Lee; Whole Lot of Shakin' Going On, Sun 267, 45 rpm, G **$4.00**

Lewis, Smiley; Come On, Imperial 5372, 45 rpm.........**$40.00**

Liggins, Jimmy; I Ain't Drunk, Aladdin 3250, 45 rpm.**$100.00**

Lillie Mae, Mama Don't Want It, Okeh 8920, 78 rpm ..**$40.00**

Limelighters, My Sweet Norma, Joz 795, 45 rpm **$75.00**

Liston, Virginia; Bed Time Blues, Okeh 8092, 78 rpm...**$15.00**

Little Anthony & the Imperials, Hold On, Avco 4651, 45 rpm, EX...**$5.00**

Little Esther, Stop Cryin', Decca 48305, 45 rpm **$50.00**

Loggins, Kenny; Heart to Heart, Columbia 03377, 45 rpm, EX **$3.50**

Lulu, To Sir w/Love, Epic 10187, 45 rpm, VG................**$2.00**

Luther, Frank; Memphis Yodel, Broadway 8102, 78 rpm..**$8.00**

Lynn, Barbara; Oh Baby, Jamie 1277, 45 rpm.............**$10.00**

Lynn, Loretta; I Can't Feel You Anymore, MCA 41021, 45 rpm, EX **$3.50**

Mack, Bill; Cat Just Got in Town, Saturday 252 ....**$35.00**

Mae, Lonnie; Record Hop Dream, Fine 601120, 45 rpm.**$55.00**

Mainer, JE; Great Reaping Day, Bluebird 7965, 78 rpm .**$8.00**

Mancini, Henry; Windmills of Your Mind, RCA 0131, 45 rpm, VG **$4.00**

Manilow, Barry; Could It Be Magic, Arista 0126, 45 rpm, EX **$3.50**

Mannone, Joe; Cat's Head, Columbia 14282-D, 78 rpm..**$80.00**

Martin, Billy; If It's Lovin' That You Want, Lucky 0009, 45 rpm **$20.00**

Martin, Dean; Send Me the Pillow You Dream On, Reprise 0344, 45 rpm, VG **$4.50**

Martino, Al; Love Is Blue, Capitol 2102, 45 rpm, VG.....**$3.00**

McClennan, Tommy; My Little Girl, Bluebird 8605, 78 rpm **$12.50**

McCoy, Clyde; Nobody's Sweetheart, Columbia 2808-D, 78 rpm **$15.00**

McEntire, Reba; Little Rock, MCA 52848, 45 rpm, VG ...**$2.50**

McGuire Sisters, Something's Gotta Give, Coral 61423, 45 rpm, VG **$4.50**

Meters, Chican Strut, Josie 1018 ....**$4.00**

Miami Sound Machine, Rhythm Is Gonna Get You, Epic 07059, 45 rpm, VG **$2.50**

Michall, Ernest; Sidewalk Blues, Black Patti 8046, 78 rpm **$250.00**

Miles, Josie; Sweet Man Joe, Edison 51476, 78 rpm **$50.00**

Milsap, Ronnie; Any Day Now, RCA 13216, 45 rpm, VG.**$3.00**

Mississippi Sheiks, I Am the Devil, Bluebird 5516, 78 rpm **$40.00**

Monroe Brothers, The Old Crossroad, Bluebird 6676, 78 rpm **$10.00**

Moonlight Revelers, Memphis Stomp, Gray Gull 1786, 78 rpm **$35.00**

Morgan, Lorrie; Picture of Me (Without You), RCA 62014, 45 rpm, M **$3.50**

Muddy Waters, She's All Right, Chess 1537, 45 rpm .**$100.00**

Murray, Ann; Shadows in the Moonlight, Capitol 4716, 45 rpm, VG **$2.50**

Nappi, William; I'll Dream of You, Columbia 1042-D, 78 rpm **$12.50**

Nelson, Red; Gambling Man, Decca 7256, 78 rpm **$15.00**

Nelson, Red; Sweetest Thing Born, Decca 7155, 78 rpm ..**$30.00**

Nelson, Willie; Blue Eyes Crying in the Rain, Columbia 10176, 45 rpm, VG **$2.50**

New Kids on the Block, Cover Girl, Columbia 63088, 45 rpm, VG **$2.50**

Newton-John, Olivia; Physical, MCA 51182, 45 rpm, EX.**$3.50**

Nichols, Red; Mean Dog Blues, Brunswick 3597, 78 rpm **$10.00**

Noble, Georgia; New Milk Cow Blues, Vocalion 02905, 78 rpm **$150.00**

Noland, Terry; Hypnotized, Brunswick 55017, 45 rpm.**$15.00**

Noles, Flora; Little Mohee, Okeh 45037, 78 rpm............**$8.00**

Oakdale, Slim; Cowboy's Heaven, Crown 3503, 78 rpm .**$10.00**

Olsen, George; Bless Your Heart, Columbia 2803-D, 78 rpm **$10.00**

Orlando, Tony & Dawn; Tie a Yellow Ribbon Round the Ole Oak Tree, Bell 318, 45 rpm, NM **$4.00**

Osmond, Donny; Lonely Boy, MGM 14424, 45 rpm, VG.**$2.00**

Owens Brothers, Harvest Field, Victor V-40309, 78 rpm **$15.00**

Page, Patti; Doggie in the Window, Mercury 1, yellow label, 45 rpm, G **$2.50**

Parton, Dolly; 9 to 5, RCA 12133, 45 rpm, VG.............**$2.50**

Paycheck, Johnny; Fifteen Beers, Epic 50863, 45 rpm, VG...**$2.50**

Pendergrass, Teddy; I Want My Baby Back, PI 04302, 45 rpm, VG **$2.50**

Perkins, Carl; Gone Gone Gone, Sun 224, 45 rpm......**$75.00**

Peterson, Walter; Over the Waves, Superior 349, 78 rpm **$8.00**

Pettis, Jack; Ain't She Sweet?, Banner 1942, 78 rpm **$8.00**

Pierce, Webb; In the Jailhouse, Pacemaker 1015, 78 rpm **$10.00**

Pitney, Gene; Liberty Valance, Musicor 1020, 45 rpm, VG...**$4.00**

Platters, Twilight Time, Mercury 71289, 45 rpm, VG.....**$6.50**

Poor Bill, A Hundred Women, Varsity 6020, 78 rpm...**$15.00**

Poor Boy Lofton, Poor Boy Blues, Decca 7010, 78 rpm.................**$75.00**

Powell, Tommy; That Cat Is High, Decca 7231, 78 rpm.................**$10.00**

Presley, Elvis; Don't Be Cruel/Hound Dog, RCA 47-6604, 45 rpm, VG.................**$16.50**

Presley, Elvis; Jailhouse Rock, RCA 47-7035, 45 rpm, VG.................**$6.00**

Presley, Elvis; Love Me Tender, RCA 47-6643, 45 rpm, VG.................**$23.00**

Presley, Elvis; Milkcow Blue's Boogie, Sun 215, 45 rpm, NM **$350.00**

Presley, Elvis; Suspicious Minds, RCA 47-9764, 45 rpm, VG.................**$4.00**

Presley, Elvis; Wear Your Ring Around My Neck, RCA 47-7240, 45 rpm, M **$12.00**

Prisonaires, Softly & Tenderly, Sun 189, 45 rpm **$100.00**

Queen, Crazy Little Thing Called Love, Elektra 46579, 45 rpm, VG.................**$2.00**

Quillan, Rufus & Ben; Keep It Clean, Columbia 14560-D, 78 rpm **$25.00**

Ray Brothers, Jake Legg Wobble, Victor V-40291, 78 rpm.**$40.00**

Reddy, Helen; I Am Woman, Capitol 3350, 45 rpm, EX..**$3.00**

Reeves, Jim; Anna Marie, RCA 7070, 45 rpm, VG **$4.00**

Reneau, George; Red Wing, Vocalion 5049, 78 rpm ...**$10.00**

Rich, Charlie; Most Beautiful Girl, Epic 11040, 45 rpm, VG.................**$2.50**

Rich, Fred; Piccolo Pete, Banner 6508, 78 rpm.............**$7.50**

Righteous Brothers, You've Lost That Lovin' Feelin', Philles 124, 45 rpm, VG.................**$3.00**

Riley, Bill; Red Hot, Sun 277, 45 rpm **$25.00**

Rivers, Johnny; Poor Side of Town, Imperial 66205, 45 rpm, VG.................**$3.50**

Robbins, Marty; Return to Me; Columbia 10673, 45 rpm, VG.................**$4.00**

Robinson, Elzadie; Houston Bound, Paramount 12420, 78 rpm **$125.00**

Rodgers, Jimmie; Old Love Letters, Bluebird 6198, 78 rpm **$20.00**

Rolling Stones, Satisfaction, London 9766, 45 rpm, VG.**$4.00**

Ronstadt, Linda; Blue Bayou, Asylum 45431, 45 rpm, VG.................**$2.50**

Rose, Lucy; Papa You're Too Slow, Champion 15471, 78 rpm.................**$50.00**

Royal, Billy Joe; Tulsa, Columbia 45289, 45 rpm, EX....**$7.00**

Sam the Sham & the Pharoahs, Ring Dang Doo, MGM 13397, 45 rpm, VG.................**$3.50**

Savoy Bearcats, Senegalese Stomp, Victor 20182, 78 rpm.................**$25.00**

Scott, Jack; Flakey John, Groove 0049, 45 rpm...........**$15.00**

Shelor Family, Big Bend Gal, Victor 20865, 78 rpm **$15.00**

Shirelles, Foolish Little Girl, Scepter 1248, 45 rpm, VG.**$3.50**

Simms, Howard; Pensacola Joe, Harmograph 841, 78 rpm.................**$35.00**

Simon & Garfunkle, I Am a Rock, Columbia 53617, 45 rpm, VG.................**$4.00**

Sinatra, Frank; High Hopes, Capitol 4214, 45 rpm, VG.**$9.00**

Sinatra, Frank; That's Life, Reprise 0531, 45 rpm, VG....**$4.50**

Skelton, Eddie; That's Love, Saturday 315, 45 rpm......**$15.00**

Sloan, Earl; Bullfrog Boogie, Ring 1219, 45 rpm **$125.00**

Sly & the Family Stone, Hot Fun in the Summertime, Epic 10497, 45 rpm, VG **$4.00**

Smith, LC; Let the Big Times Roll, Wango 202, 45 rpm..**$75.00**

Smith, Ruby; Back Water Blues, Vocalion 04903, 78 rpm..**$15.00**

Smith, Trixie's Blues, Black Swan 2039, 78 rpm **$25.00**

Snow, Hank; Ramblin' Rose, RCA 11377, 45 rpm, VG...**$2.50**

Spaniels, Let's Make Up, red plastic, Vee Jay 116, 45 rpm **$200.00**

Specht, Paul; Roll Up the Carpets, Columbia 1186-D, 78 rpm.................**$10.00**

Springfield, Dusty; Son-of-a-Preacher Man, Atlantic 2580, 45 rpm, VG.................**$3.00**

Springsteen, Bruce; Born in the USA, Columbia 04680, 45 rpm, VG.................**$2.50**

Starlighters, Hotlicks, Wheel 1004, 45 rpm.................**$40.00**

Steppenwolf, Rock Me, Dunhill 4182, 45 rpm, EX........**$4.50**

Stewart, Rod; Tonight's the Night, Warner Brothers 8262, 45 rpm, EX.................**$3.00**

Stowers, Freeman; Railroad Blues, Gennett 6814, 78 rpm.................**$75.00**

Streisand, Barbra; Kiss Me in the Rain, Columbia 11179, 45 rpm, VG.................**$2.50**

Streisand, Barbra; The Way We Were, Columbia 45944, 45 rpm, VG.................**$3.00**

Summer, Donna; Last Dance, Casablanca 814 298, 45 rpm, VG.................**$2.50**

Tanner, Arthur; Two Little Children, Columbia 15180-D, 78 rpm.................**$12.00**

Tarpley, Slim; Alabama Hustler, Paramount 13062....**$175.00**

Tate Rose; My Man Left Me Blues, Champion 15302, 78 rpm.................**$80.00**

Taylor, James; Your Smiling Face, Columbia 10602, 45 rpm, VG.................**$2.50**

Taylor, Jasper; Stomp Time Blues, Paramount 12409, 78 rpm.................**$300.00**

Temptations, Treat Her Like a Lady, Gordy 1765, 45 rpm, VG.................**$3.50**

Thomas, BJ; It's Only Love, Scepter 12244, 45 rpm, VG.**$3.00**

Thomas, BJ; Raindrops Keep Fallin' on My Head, Scepter 12265, 45 rpm, VG.................**$3.00**

Thompkins, Jed; Mississippi Sawyer, Harmony 5099-H, 78 rpm.................**$6.00**

Three Dog Night, Mama Told Me, Dunhill 4239, 45 rpm, VG.................**$3.00**

Tillotson, Johnny; Talk Back Trembling Lips, MGM 13181, 45 rpm, EX.................**$2.50**

Tin Pan Paraders, Clowning, Gennett 7012, 78 rpm....**$12.50**

Tom, Georgia; Levee Bound Love, Decca 7362, 78 rpm.................**$8.00**

Tommie & Willie, By the Old Oak Tree, Champion 16034, 78 rpm **$10.00**

Townsend, Jesse; No Home Blues, Victor 23322, 78 rpm.**$200.00**

Tubb, Ernest; My Mother Is Lonely, Bluebird 8966, 78 rpm **$75.00**

Tucker, Tanya; Delta Dawn, Columbia, 45588, 45 rpm, VG..**$2.00**

Twitty, Conway; Slow Hand, Elektra 47443, 45 rpm, VG..**$2.50**

Tyler, Bonnie; It's a Heartache; RCA 11249, 45 rpm, VG .**$2.50**

University Orchestra, Lady Luck, Gennett 7042, 78 rpm.**$10.00**

Van Halen, Feels So Good, Warner Brothers 27565, 45 rpm, VG..**$2.50**

Vaughn, Billy; He'll Have To Go, Dot 16106, 45 rpm, VG..**$3.50**

Venuti, Joe; There's No Other Girl, Columbia 2535-D, 78 rpm **$12.50**

Vernon, Ray; I'm Counting on You, Cameo 115, 45 rpm **$75.00**

Vigal, John; Fowler Twist, Black Swan 14115, 78 rpm.**$20.00**

Vinton, Bobby; I Love How You Love Me, Epic 10397, 45 rpm..**$3.50**

Vinton, Bobby; Roses Are Red, Epic 9509, 45 rpm, VG ..**$3.00**

Waldman, Herman; Cocktails for Two, Bluebird 5437, 78 rpm..**$7.50**

Walker's Corbin Ramblers, I Had a Dream, Vocalion 02719, 78 rpm **$15.00**

Washington, Louis; Standin' on a Rock, Vocalion 02658, 78 rpm **$80.00**

Wells, Junior; Tomorrow Night, States 143, 45 rpm ..**$300.00**

West, Dottie; Country Sunshine, RCA 0072, 45 rpm, VG..**$2.50**

Whitter, Henry; Poor Lost Boy, Victor V-40061, 78 rpm **$15.00**

Williams, Clarence; Slow River, Brunswick 3580, 78 rpm **$15.00**

Williams, Don; That's the Thing About Love, MCA 52389, 45 rpm, EX..**$3.50**

Williams, Roger; More Than a Miracle, Kapp 843, 45 rpm, VG..**$3.00**

Williamson, Sonny Boy; Sunny Land, Bluebird 7500, 78 rpm..**$20.00**

Wilson, Nancy; Can't Take My Eyes Off You, Capitol 2644, 45 rpm, VG..**$2.50**

Wonder, Stevie; Blowin' in the Wind, Tamla 54136, 45 rpm, M **$5.00**

Wood, Tommy; Can't Play Hookey, D1000, 45 rpm .**$200.00**

Yale Collegians, You'll Do It Someday, Edison 52018 ..**$20.00**

Yas Yas Girl, Worried Heat Blues, Okeh 05870, 78 rpm **$8.00**

Yellow Jackets, Medley, Gennett 7262, 78 rpm **$12.50**

Young, Faron; World's Greatest Love, Mercury 72313, 45 rpm, VG..**$3.00**

Young Brothers, Are You from Dixie?, Columbia 15219-D, 78 rpm **$12.50**

Zenith Knights, Congratulations, QRS 1021 ....**$12.50**

ZZ Top, Sleeping Bag, Warner Brothers 28884, 45 rpm, VG..**$3.00**

Red Wing Potteries, Inc.

For almost a century, Red Wing, Minnesota, was the center of a great pottery industry. In the early 1900s, several local companies merged to form the Red Wing Stoneware Company. Until they introduced their dinnerware lines in 1935, most of their production centered around stoneware jugs, crocks, flowerpots, and other utilitarian items. To reflect the changes made in '35, the name was changed to Red Wing Potteries, Inc. In addition to scores of lovely dinnerware lines, they also made vases, planters, flowerpots, etc., some with exceptional shapes and decoration.

Some of their more recognizable lines of dinnerware and those you'll most often find are Bob White (decorated in blue and brown brush strokes with quail), Tampico (featuring a collage of fruit including watermelon), Random Harvest (simple pink and brown leaves and flowers), and Village Green (or Brown, solid color pieces introduced in the fifties). Often you'll find complete or nearly complete sets, and when you do, the lot price is usually a real bargain.

If you'd like to learn more about the subject, we recommend _Red Wing Stoneware, An Identification and Value Guide,_ and _Red Wing Collectibles,_ both by Dan and Gail DePasquale and Larry Peterson.

Art Ware

Ashtray, #1019, magnolia..**$10.00**

Ashtray, 7", maroon & green, scalloped shell shape, 3-footed **$6.00**

Bowl, #866, 6¾", leaves, berries, & bows relief on white **$7.50**

Bowl, 13½", floral relief on gun-metal brown, lime interior **$25.00**

Bowl, 5½", oak leaves & acorns on green & tan, dark green interior **$9.50**

Candlesticks, #1226, white, magnolia, pr **$28.00**

Cornucopia, #1356, 5½x7½", green & yellow interior w/leaf base..**$10.00**

Jardiniere, 6½", Brushware, green-washed...........$75.00

Planter, #1561, 12", speckled gold, glossy, fluted........$12.00
Planter, #670, blue, hat form $6.00
Reamer/juice pitcher, #256, yellow $125.00
Urn, #159, 9", Grecian motif..$45.00
Vase, #1082, 9", white w/turquoise interior, leaf relief on pitcher form...$15.00
Vase, #879, blue, fish figural w/open mouth..............$38.00
Vase, 12½", copper-oxide green, gourd shape w/tall slim neck $14.00

Vase, 13", King or Queen Chess piece, oatmeal w/lavender interior, pr.....................................$200.00
Wall pocket, #1004, tan, marked Red Wing Potteries .$18.00

Cookie Jars

Bob White, unmarked $65.00
Bunch of Bananas, blue or pink.................................$40.00
Crock, white...$25.00
Dutch girl, yellow w/brown trim.................................$60.00
French Baker, tan & brown, marked...........................$65.00
Grapes $65.00
Jack Frost on Pumpkin, short $395.00
Jack Frost on Pumpkin, tall.......................................$395.00
King of Tarts, unmarked $250.00
Monk, yellow w/brown trim.......................................$65.00
Pineapple, yellow $40.00

Dinnerware

Bob White, bowl, salad; large......................................$30.00
Bob White, casserole, 4-qt, w/lid & stand..................$65.00
Bob White, cup & saucer...$18.00
Bob White, pitcher, 60-oz $35.00
Bob White, plate, 10"..$10.00

Bob White, plate, 6½"...$6.00
Bob White, platter, 13"...$20.00
Bob White, salt & pepper shakers, bird form, pr $35.00
Brittany, bowl, buffet...$13.00
Brittany, plate, dinner...$8.00
Brittany, salt & pepper shakers, pr $10.00
Capistrano, bowl, vegetable; divided $15.00
Capistrano, plate, dinner; 10".....................................$10.00
Capistrano, platter, 15"..$15.00
Driftwood, bowl, vegetable; divided $12.00
Driftwood, butter dish...$25.00
Driftwood, creamer..$10.00
Driftwood, plate, bread & butter...................................$5.00
Driftwood, platter, 13"...$15.00
Frontenac, bowl, cereal $5.00
Frontenac, plate, dinner...$8.00
Hearthside, plate, 10"...$10.00
Hearthside, salt & pepper shakers, tall, pr $15.00
Lanterns, bowl, fruit; 5¼"..$4.00
Lanterns, plate, 10½"..$8.00
Lotus, bowl, vegetable; divided $18.00
Lotus, plate, grill...$20.00
Lotus, platter, 13"...$18.00
Lotus, relish, 3-part..$18.00
Lotus, teacup $7.00
Lupine, plate, bread & butter $4.00
Lute song, bowl, cereal; 6¾"..$8.00
Lute Song, cup & saucer..$9.00
Lute Song, plate, dinner; 10½".......................................$9.00
Morning-Glory, creamer & sugar bowl..........................$8.00
Morning-Glory, gravy boat, w/attached underplate $10.00
Morning-Glory, plate, 10¼"..$8.00
Pepe, cup & saucer..$10.00
Pepe, plate, 6½"..$3.00
Provincial Oomphware, bowl, 11½"............................$45.00
Random Harvest, casserole, w/lid...............................$25.00
Random House, coffeepot, tall.....................................$25.00
Random House, plate, 10"...$8.00
Random House, relish, 13¼"...$15.00
Round-Up, gravy boat $95.00
Round-Up, platter, 13"..$125.00
Smart Set, beverage server $45.00
Smart Set, bowl, vegetable; divided............................$20.00
Tampico, bowl, cereal $12.00
Tampico, plate, 10½"..$10.00
Tampico, sugar bowl, w/lid $15.00

Tampico, water pitcher, 13"....................................$40.00

Tip Toe, bowl, fruit..$3.00
Two Step, creamer $3.00
Two Step, plate, 10"..$6.00
Zinnia, chop plate, 12½x11"..............................$8.00

Stoneware

Bowl, 11", red & blue sponging, paneled body $110.00
Chamber pot, blue bands on salt glaze, marked MN ..$65.00
Churn, 3-gal, red wing & the number three on salt glaze, marked RWUS $140.00

Cooler, 5-gal, crock shape, 'drop 8' cobalt design, no mark $250.00
Cooler, 25-gal, birch leaves, the number twenty-five, & 'Ice Water' on white, marked RWUS $220.00
Crock, butter; 1-lb, Albany slip, low style, marked RW .$75.00
Crock, butter; 10-lb, salt glaze, low style, marked RW..$65.00
Crock, 12", red wing & the number twelve on white, marked RWUS $65.00
Crock, 6-gal, two elephant-ear leaves & the number six on white, marked MN $50.00
Cuspidor, brown & salt glaze, mold seam, unmarked ..$95.00
Custard cup, blue to white shaded, unmarked............$48.00
Jug, beehive; 4-gal, red wing & number four on white, marked RWUS $265.00
Jug, shoulder; 1-gal, brown & salt glaze, pear top, marked NS $145.00
Jug, syrup; ½-gal, white, cone top w/pour spout, marked, MN $70.00
Jug, wide mouth; ½-gal, Albany slip, marked MN.......$50.00
Jug, 1-qt, Albany slip, cone top, common, marked MN.$68.00
Jug, ½-gal, white, bail handle, molded seam, marked RW $95.00
Pan, milk; 7", salt glaze, marked MN..........................$65.00
Pitcher, milk; ½-gal, Albany slip, Russian style...........$60.00
Pitcher, small, Spongeband & Saffron, marked RWUS ..$95.00

Wax sealer, 1-qt, Albany slip, straight sides, marked RW $165.00

Riviera Dinnerware

A sister to the Fiesta line, Riviera was made by The Homer Laughlin China Company from 1938 until just before 1950. It was a thinner line, unmarked, and inexpensive. Their major marketing outlet was the Murphy Company chain of dime stores. Its pieces are squared with shaped, rounded corners. Colors are mauve blue, red, yellow, light green, and ivory.

If you'd like to learn more about Riviera, we recommend *The Collector's Encyclopedia of Fiesta* by Sharon and Bob Huxford.

Bowl, baker; 9" $16.00
Bowl, cream soup; w/liner, in ivory...........................$45.00
Bowl, fruit; 5½" $8.00
Bowl, nappy; 9¼"..$15.00
Bowl, oatmeal; 6"...$18.00
Bowl, utility; ivory $45.00
Butter dish, ½-lb..$75.00
Butter dish, ¼-lb...$85.00
Casserole $65.00
Creamer $7.50
Cup & saucer, demitasse; ivory................................$45.00

Jug, covered..$85.00
Pitcher, juice; mauve blue....................................$125.00
Plate, deep..$14.00
Plate, 10"..$20.00
Plate, 6"..$5.50
Plate, 7"..$7.50
Plate, 9"...$12.00
Platter, 11½"...$12.00
Platter, 11¼", closed handles................................$15.00

Platter, 12", cobalt $28.00
Salt & pepper shakers, pr $12.00
Sauce boat $15.00
Saucer $3.00
Sugar bowl, w/lid $12.00
Syrup, w/lid $85.00
Teacup $8.50
Teapot $75.00
Tidbit, 2-tier, ivory $65.00
Tumbler, handled $50.00
Tumbler, juice $32.00

Road Maps

Thousands of these maps have been printed since the early part of the century. More than seventy oil companies published them, and they were distributed by gas stations, state highway departments, and tourist information centers free of charge. Those that are still in excellent condition are becoming collectible today.

American, 1961, New York $2.00
American, 1968, Georgia $2.00
Amoco, 1935, reprint of 25th-Anniversary $5.00
Amoco, 1946, Ohio $4.00
Amoco, 1956, New York $3.00
Amoco, 1960, Pennsylvania $2.00
Amoco, 1977, Texas $2.00
Apco, 1968, Oklahoma $2.00
Arco, 1969, Texas & Oklahoma $2.00
Atlantic, 1938, Philadelphia $5.00
Boron, 1969, Pennsylvania $2.00
Brandall, 1934, Illinois $5.00
Brandall, 1942, Nebraska $4.00
British American, 1949, Ontario $4.00
British American, 1960, Ontario $2.00
British Petroleum, 1980, Europe $1.00
Carter, 1951, Idaho $3.00
Champlin, 1935, Minnesota $5.00
Champlin, 1973, Kansas & Nebraska $2.00
Chevron, 1946, Los Angeles $4.00
Chevron, 1957, California $3.00
Chevron, 1961, New Mexico $2.00
Chevron, 1971, Georgia & Alabama $2.00
Citgo, 1965, Michigan $2.00
Citgo, 1970, New Jersey $2.00
Citgo, 1973, Quebec $2.00
Cities Service, 1934, Iowa $5.00
Cities Service, 1947, Wisconsin $4.00
Cities Service, 1952, New Jersey $3.00
Cities Service, 1964, Missouri $2.00
Clark, 1966, Milwaukee $2.00
Co-Op, 1960, Kansas $2.00
Conoco, 1934, Kansas $5.00
Conoco, 1946, California & Nevada $4.00
Conoco, 1959, Colorado $3.00

Conoco, 1967, Montana $2.00
Conoco, 1978, Yellowstone National Park $2.00
Deep Rock, 1948, Texas $4.00
Deep Rock, 1972, Central & Western United States $2.00
Derby, 1950, Texas $3.00
Diamond/D-X, 1934, Colorado $5.00
Diamond/D-X, 1942, Oklahoma $4.00
Diamond/D-X, 1963, Central United States $2.00
Dixie, 1950, Nebraska $3.00
El Paso, 1961, Arizona $2.00
En-Ar-Co, ca 1930s, Arkansas $5.00
Enco, 1961, South Dakota $2.00
Enco, 1968, Los Angeles $2.00
Enco, 1971, Sacramento $2.00
Esso, 1934, Washington, DC $5.00
Esso, 1940, New York $4.00
Esso, 1951, New England $3.00
Esso, 1963, Tennessee & Kentucky $2.00
Exxon, 1973, New Jersey $2.00
Fina, 1972, Colorado $2.00
Flying A, 1953, California $3.00
Flying A, 1963, New Jersey $2.00
Getty, 1974, New Jersey $2.00
Giant, 1988, Arizona & New Mexico $1.00
Globe, 1936, Illinois $5.00
Globe, 1941, Colorado $4.00
Gulf, 1939, New Jersey $5.00
Gulf, 1949, Pittsburgh $4.00
Gulf, 1958, New York & New Jersey $3.00
Gulf, 1967, Eastern United States $2.00
Gulf, 1974, California $2.00
Humble, 1952, Texas $3.00
Humble, 1971, Ohio $2.00
Imperial, 1950, Indiana $3.00
Imperial Esso, 1939, Central Canada $5.00
Imperial Esso, 1967, Montreal Expo $2.00
Knight, 1959, Missouri $3.00
Marathon, 1967, Indiana $2.00
Marathon, 1987, Tennessee $1.00
Mobil, 1932, New York $5.00
Mobil, 1947, New Jersey & Delaware $4.00
Mobil, 1953, Wyoming $3.00
Mobil, 1963, Wisconsin $2.00
Mobil, 1971, Illinois $2.00
Pan-Am, 1952, Alabama $3.00
Pate, 1960, Wisconsin $2.00
Pennzip, 1955, New York $3.00
Phillips 66, 1936, Texas $5.00
Phillips 66, 1948, Texas $4.00
Phillips 66, 1950, Central United States $3.00
Phillips 66, 1961, Georgia $2.00
Phillips 66, 1969, Arkansas $2.00
Phillips 66, 1972, Wisconsin $2.00
Phillips 66, 1978, Minnesota $2.00
Phillips 66, 1982, Alabama $1.00
Pure, 1936, New York $5.00
Pure, 1952, Illinois $3.00
Quaker State, 1970, Pennsylvania $2.00

Richfield, 1959, California $3.00
Richfield, 1964, California $2.00
Shamrock, 1963, Central & Western United States........$2.00
Shamrock, 1981, South-Eastern & South-Western United States $1.00
Shell, 1935, Utah $5.00
Shell, 1940, Kentucky & Tennessee $4.00
Shell, 1941, South Dakota $4.00
Shell, 1957, Ohio $3.00
Shell, 1963, New Hampshire & Vermont $2.00
Shell, 1972, Washington, DC $2.00
Sinclair, 1933, Chicago $5.00
Sinclair, 1946, Colorado, Utah & Wyoming $4.00
Sinclair, 1954, Central United States.....................$3.00
Sinclair, 1968, Eastern United States $2.00
Skelly, 1939, Arkansas..$5.00
Skelly, 1948, Wyoming $4.00
Skelly, 1956, Illinois $3.00
Skelly, 1965, Kansas $2.00
Skelly, 1976, Wisconsin $2.00
Sohio, 1947, Indiana $4.00
Sohio, 1965, Ohio $2.00
Sovereign, 1936, Wyoming...................................$5.00
Sovereign, 1952, Missouri $3.00
Spur, 1964, Wisconsin...$2.00
Standard Oil, 1936, Iowa $5.00
Standard Oil, 1949, North Dakota $4.00
Standard Oil, 1956, Western United States $3.00
Standard Oil, 1963, Eastern United States.................$2.00
Standard Oil, 1972, Montana $2.00
Sunoco, 1962, Eastern United States $2.00
Tenneco, 1965, Texas $2.00
Texaco, 1930, Arizona & New Mexico......................$5.00
Texaco, 1947, Illinois, Iowa & Missouri....................$4.00
Texaco, 1947, Western Canada $4.00
Texaco, 1957, Texas...$3.00
Texaco, 1964, Kentucky.......................................$2.00
Texaco, 1969, New York $2.00
Texaco, 1973, New Jersey $2.00
Union 76, 1945, Washington & Oregon.....................$4.00
Union 76, 1953, Western United States.....................$3.00
Union 76, 1978, Alabama......................................$2.00
Utoco, 1955, Western United States $3.00
Vickers, 1972, Illinois..$2.00
White Rose, 1939, Colorado $5.00
White Rose, 1941, Missouri....................................$4.00
Wilshire, 1963, Los Angeles $2.00

Rock 'n Roll Memorabilia

Buy these items with an eye to the future! Already some of the large auction houses in the East have had rock 'n roll celebrity auctions, and some of the one-of-a-kind examples they've sold have brought high dollar results.

See also Beatles Collectibles, Elvis Presley Memorabilia.

Alice Cooper, banner, Hey Stoopid $15.00

Bee Gees, radio w/sing-along microphone, 7½x8", shows group on paper decal on purple rectangular form, ca 1977 ....$30.00
Bee Gees, tour book, 24-page 1989..............................$5.00

Bill Haley & His Comets, glass tumbler, 4½", souvenir of Monroe College concert, 1948 ....$25.00
Bruce Springsteen, photo, 8x10", color $5.00
Buckinghams, song sheet, 'Don't You Care'................$25.00
Canned Heat, song sheet, 'Let's Work Together' $15.00
Captain Beefheart, concert poster, 20x14", Griffin art, red & blue shading on black, 1972, NM $65.00
Card set, Rock 'n Roll Stars, complete set of 3¼x5¼" cards (64 total), Nu Trading Cards, ca 1958, M..............$90.00
Cheap Trick, concert poster, 16x23", Robert Plant, New York City, 1988..$12.00
Chubby Checker, game, 'Twister,' Empire, object is to be team to 'Twist' the best, 1961, in original 12x8" box, M $75.00
Chubby Checker, limbo set, M................................$65.00
Dave Clark Five, souvenir booklet, 9x12½", 1960s, 28 pages, M $25.00
David Bowie, concert poster, German Sounds & Visions Tour, 1990 ....$25.00
David Cassidy, concert poster, 22x15", black & white photo, 1971, NM $32.00
David Cassidy, photo, 8x10", color............................$12.50
David Lee Roth, scarf, Skyscraper Tour, 1988, M..........$6.00
Deep Purple, tour book, Japan, 1972..........................$60.00
Diana Ross, poster, 36x36", 'Why Do Fools Fall in Love,' RCA $12.00
Dick Clark, book, 'Twenty Years of Rock 'n Roll,' Buddha Records Inc, 1953-1973, 24 pages, EX $48.00
Dick Clark, pin-back button, 1¾x1¾", Dick Clark's American Bandstand brass diecut, ca 1960, EX $22.00
Doors, poster, 22½x13½", orange & green w/black lettering, 1967, M $75.00
Duran Duran, tour book, 'Strange Behavior,' 38-page 1987 ....$12.00

Eric Clapton, poster, 38x27", heavy paper, EX $10.00

Fabian, Tender Teen Lotion, 3½" plastic bottle, M on 6" display card w/Fabian picture, 1950s........................$32.00

Family Dog, concert poster, 20x14", R Fried art, 1957, NM..$65.00

Fleetwood Mac, T-shirt, Tusk Tour, 1979-80, EX...........$5.00

Frank Zappa, tape, Waka Jawaka Reel to Reel, NM in original box...$60.00

Freddy & the Dreamers, pin-back button, 3½", 'I Love Freddy & the Dreamers' & group photo, 1960s, EX..$38.00

Herman's Hermits, pin-back button, Herman's Hermits Official Fan Club, 1950s, fan club issue, M.................$25.00

Herman's Hermits, souvenir booklet, 10x13", 1960s, 20 pages, M..$25.00

Jackson Five, pennant, 11x29", 'We Love the Jacksons' w/black & white photo of group, felt, 1970s, EX .$50.00

James Brown, concert poster, 22x14", black & white photo, 1960s, EX...$275.00

Kiss, backpack, 13x16", Kiss photo on red canvas, 1977, NM..$35.00

Kiss, belt buckle, 2x4", bronzed metal, late 1970s, EX.$30.00

Kiss, board game, 'On Tour,' M..................................$50.00

Kiss, Dynasty Tour program, 10x14", 16 pages of glossy paper w/color photos, 1979, NM.........................$40.00

Kiss, eraser, in original package, M............................$10.00

Kiss, gum cards, 38 w/picture pieces on back & 6 w/information, 1981, EX..$12.00

Kiss, model, van, in original package.........................$72.00

Kiss, Paul doll, Mego, plastic & vinyl, rooted hair, 'AUCOIN/ M G M T INC' on head, 1976 ....$50.00

Kiss, pin-back button...$8.00

Led Zepplin, figural blow-up zeppelin, 36x18", promotional item...$100.00

Madonna, photo, 8x10", color................................$12.00

Madonna, tour book, 'Blond Ambitions,' 1990 ....$12.00

Magazine, 'Bandstand Blast,' 8x11", Trend Books, 1950, EX...$22.50

Michael Jackson, radio, 5¾x2¾", paper photo decal on rectangular form, slider controls, 1984 MJ products ...$20.00

Mick Jagger, poster, life-size, EX.............................$15.00

Monkees, book, 'Who's Got the Button,' 1968, EX.......$8.00

Monkees, bubble gum wrapper, 5x6", waxed paper, from 1967 gum pac..$25.00

Monkees, doll, Mike Nesmith, on original card...........$12.50

Monkees, fan club kit, 8½x11½", multicolored folder w/applications, photos, etc, Royburt Productions, 1957, EX...$100.00

Monkees, flasher ring, silver plastic w/flashing portraits & 'I Love Monkees,' M..$27.50

Monkees, model, Monkee-Mobile, MPC, ⅕ scale, 1967, in original 9x6" box..$40.00

Monkees, model kit, Mustang GT Convertible, Monogram, 1987, M in original box $100.00

Monkees, program, 20th Anniversary World Tour, 1986, 20 pages, M..$27.50

Monkees, scarf, 22x22", color picture of group, dated 1967 ....$12.50

Monkees, ukulele, 12", Mattel, 1966, NM $75.00

New Kids on the Block, concert poster, Live in Germany, 1990 ....$15.00

New Kids on the Block, photo, 7x9", cast of animated show $4.50

Robin Gibb of the Bee Gees, lunch box, plastic thermos, EX..$70.00

Rolling Stones, American Tour poster, 22½x36", heavy poster paper, Jovan, 1981, NM..............................$45.00

Rolling Stones, fan club kit................................$8.00

Rolling Stones, poster, 38x27", EX................................$10.00

Rolling Stones, promotion kit, 39x32", 7-11 Convenience Store promotion of Bud beer & tour, complete....$50.00

Rolling Stones, tour book, Tour of Americas, 1975, 28-page..$18.00

Scorpions, concert program $2.50

Sheet music, 9x12", 'Paper Boy,' Bill Haley & His Comets photo cover, 1956, two pages, EX........................$25.00

Stevie Ray Vaughn, concert poster, 18x12", Austin, 1984..$75.00

Strawberry Alarm Clock, song sheet, 'Incense & Peppermints' $30.00

Three Dog Night, concert poster, Stage Shot, 1973 tour..$25.00

Uriah Heap, tour book, Japan, 1973.............................**$60.00**
Young Rascals, song sheet, 'A Girl Like You' **$20.00**

Rookwood

Although this company was established in 1879, it continued to produce commercial artware until it closed in 1967. Located in Cincinnati, Ohio, Rookwood is recognized today as the largest producer of high-quality art pottery ever to operate in the United States.

Most of the pieces listed here are from the later years of production, but we've included a few early pieces as well. With few exceptions, all of these early art pottery companies produced an artist decorated brown-glaze line — Rookwood's was called Standard. Other early lines were Sea Green, Iris, Jewel Porcelain, Wax Matt, and Vellum.

Virtually all of Rookwood's pieces are marked. The most familiar is the 'reverse R'-P monogram. It was first used in 1886, and until 1900 a flame point was added above it to represent each passing year. After the turn of the century, a Roman numeral below the monogram indicated the current year. In addition to the dating mark, a die-stamped number was used to identify the shape.

The Cincinnati Art Galleries held two large and important cataloged auctions in 1991. The full-color catalogs contain a comprehensive history of the company, list known artists and designers with their monograms (as well as company codes and trademarks), and describe each lot thoroughly. Collectors now regard them as an excellent source for information and study.

Ashtray, 6" dia, #2647, fox sitting on rim, cream gloss, advertising **$70.00**
Ashtray, 6" dia, #744, purple & blue glossy, made for Elk's Club of Cincinnati, BPOE, rhinestone inset, 1904.**$30.00**
Bookends, 6", #2275, three rooks, caramel gloss, signed W McD, 1954, pr...**$325.00**
Bowl, 3x7", #2760, blue matt w/dark blue matt interior, three handles, 1925..**$160.00**
Bowl, 3x8", berry & leaf decoration on green & brown matt, 1922 ....**$180.00**
Bowl, 4x10", #2713E, light & dark brown matt w/green matt interior, shell shape, 1925....................................**$70.00**
Bowl, 4x6", #1807, incised geometric designs on powder blue matt w/touches of rose, handles, 1924, M..**$100.00**
Bowl, 5x12", #6051, seashell shape, green matt w/pink interior, 1928..**$240.00**
Bowl, 5x8", #7071, handkerchief type w/thick brown & white drip, 1958..**$100.00**
Bowl, 7½" dia, incised & painted leaves & berries on green matt, signed Cecil Duell, 1907 ....**$275.00**
Candlestick, 6½", #8220, yellow matt **$50.00**
Ewer, 10", #611, standard glaze w/oak leaf & acorn decoration, signed ABS, 1893, hairline **$210.00**
Inkwell, 3x4", #4418C, green matt w/incised geometric decoration, small lid (chipped) w/applied frog, 1904...**$150.00**

Jardiniere, 6x7", #484E, orange & green w/floral decoration on green, orange & dark brown ground, signed CA Baker, 1890 ....**$300.00**
Leaf dish, 7" dia, #1691, molded grapes on green & blue wax matt, 1910...**$350.00**
Leaf dish, 8x12", #4020, brown-gray & white high-gloss, 1958 ....**$50.00**
Mug, 5", #587, rabbit in grass, yellows, browns & green on brown to green shaded, 1890, small hairline in base **$250.00**
Mug, 5", green matt w/molded moon & star decoration, Alpha Delta Phi, 1905, EX.......................................**$65.00**
Paperweight, #2797, elephant, 3", signed WC McDonald, green matt, 1931 ....**$145.00**
Paperweight, #6065, cat, 2x4", signed CK, white high-gloss w/blue flowers around neck, pink details, 1946..**$375.00**
Pitcher, 9", #1014C, rook (w/black drip) on branch, pine cones & needles embossed on reverse on green matt, Toohey, 1905...**$900.00**
Rookwood, 5", #110, pink matt w/Arts & Crafts-style floral decoration, 1920...**$130.00**

Tile, 5½" sq, windmill scene, 3-color, 1920, edge crack...$125.00
Tile, 5½" sq, parrot in exotic foliage, 1930 (illustrated)..$275.00
Tile, 6" sq, #1631, light green matt w/yellow tulips on dark blue ground, heavy peppering, 1922 ....**$120.00**
Tile, 6" sq, #1977Y, faience, brown & green w/lavender highlights, framed..**$140.00**
Tile, 6" sq, #3077Y, multicolored parrot on pale pink .**$280.00**
Tile, 6" sq, faience, basket of flowers w/butterflies, framed **$170.00**
Tile, 6" sq, green & brown leaves on dark blue-green, framed **$115.00**
Vase, 7¾", #295E, wax matt w/flowers, signed Katherine Jones, 1926...**$365.00**
Vase, 10", #2377, molded florals at top & shoulder on blue crystalline, 1923...**$280.00**
Vase, 10", #833, orange berries & leaves on brown to orange to yellow shaded, signed S Toohey, 1898...........**$150.00**
Vase, 11", #S1770, standard glaze w/blue irises, signed Rose Fecheimer, 1904...**$600.00**
Vase, 11", #1358C, green matt w/carved & raised decoration of sea grasses, signed Albert Pons, 1908............**$425.00**

Vase, 12", #693, rose matt multiple-ribbed flared form, 1923, M...........$250.00

Vase, 14", wax matt, red, orange & green floral & leaf design outlined in black on orange to blue-green, Coyne, 1924...........$950.00

Vase, 5", #2122, fruit & flower decoration at neck on blue & green crystalline, 1926...........$110.00

Vase, 5", #2284, pink matt over geometric banded design, 1926...........$70.00

Vase, 5", #2592, light pink & green matt over banded cattail decoration, 1922...........$120.00

Vase, 5", #6255, green crystalline over classical line decoration, 1932...........$70.00

Vase, 5", #6459, bird & flower on brown high gloss...$60.00

Vase, 5½", #6632, pink high-gloss over leaf & berry design, 1946...........$90.00

Vase, 6", #1311, dark green feathered matt w/raised carved design, tiny chip, 1907...........$200.00

Vase, 6", #1890, medium blue matt, molded design at bottom, 1923...........$140.00

Vase, 6", #2111, pink matt w/flower band, 1929...........$120.00

Vase, 6", #2135, pink matt on Greek Key design, 1940...$80.00

Vase, 6", #2312, pink matt w/geometric band at shoulder, 1929...........$130.00

Vase, 6", #2853, orange & tan high-gloss on molded design, 1936...........$80.00

Vase, 6½", #2374, dark blue matt w/incised panels, 1920...........$170.00

Vase, 7", #1912, pink & green wax matt w/molded panels, 1925...........$140.00

Vase, 7", #1930, brown & red wax matt, incised line decoration, 1912...........$180.00

Vase, 7", #2018, dark blue matt, handles, 1914...........$150.00

Vase, 7", #2141, molded florals between broad leaves on blue matt, 1920, M...........$140.00

Vase, 7", #2814, florals molded between five panels on pink matt w/green at top, 1926, M...........$90.00

Vase, 7", #6830, daffodil & leaf design on brown high-gloss leaves, flake on bottom, 1944...........$60.00

Vase, 7", blue & green matt over molded floral decoration, 1914...........$200.00

Vase, 7½", #2323, blue & red wax matt w/molded fish decoration around base, 1916...........$190.00

Vase, 7½", green crystalline, footed, 1926...........$70.00

Vase, 8", #2062, wax matt w/red & blue roses w/yellow centers & yellow leaves, signed Sally Coyne, 1927..$400.00

Vase, 8", #927E, light greenish-yellow w/orange matt, raised & beaded leaves w/dark brown drip, signed E Barrett, 1929...........$350.00

Vase, 9", #1919, white mums & green leaves & branches on green to yellow to pink, signed Ed Diers, 1912..$850.00

Vase, 9", #2393, light blue & green matt w/molded geometric decoration, 1927...........$200.00

Vase, 9", #2431, green matt w/molded stylized floral decoration, 1923...........$200.00

Vase, 9", #271, molded florals on dark blue matt, signed ET Hurley, 1914, chip on base...........$100.00

Vase, 9", #30E, hand thrown, 2-tone brown, 1924....$130.00

Vase, 9", #419, blue & green wax matt w/molded decoration, signed CS Todd, 1918...........$300.00

Roselane Sparklers

Beginning as a husband and wife operation in the late 1930s, the Roselane Pottery Company of Pasadena, California, expanded their inventory from the figurines they originally sold to local florists to include a complete line of decorative items that eventually were shipped to Alaska, South American, and all parts of the United States.

One of their lines was the Roselane Sparklers. Popular in the fifties, these small animal and bird figures were airbrush decorated and had rhinestone eyes. They're fun to look for and not at all expensive.

If you'd like to learn more, there's a chapter on Roselane in *The Collector's Encyclopedia of California Pottery* by Jack Chipman.

Dealer sign, 3x12½", deep aqua gloss...........$150.00

Figurine, 11", Bali dancer, gray gloss, in-mold mark...$35.00

Figurine, 5½", boy w/dog, neutral colors, in-mold mark.$10.00

Figurine, 5½", giraffe, light gray gloss, ca 1960...........$20.00

Figurine, 6", Oriental man, Chinese Modern line, late 1940s...........$10.00

Figurine, 7¾" or smaller, stylized pheasant, brown on white, ceramic seed pearl eyes, pr...........$45.00

Figurine, 11", Bali dancer, gray gloss, in-mold mark..$35.00

Sculpture, 8", stylized elephant, brown lustre, on wooden base, early 1950s, wood-burned logo on base...$100.00

Sparkler, 1¾", sitting kitten, aqua jeweled eyes...........$2.00

Sparkler, 2¼", baby owl, black w/gold trim, plastic eyes, 1960s-1970s...........$6.00

Sparkler, 4½", angelfish, pink jeweled eyes, marked California USA...........$7.00

Sparkler, 4½", deer, jeweled eyes & collar...........$10.00

Sparkler, 4½", sitting cat, slanted aqua jeweled eyes, marked C in circle USA **$4.00**

Sparkler, 4½", spaniel dog, blue jeweled eyes, marked Roseland C in circle USA **$5.00**

Sparkler, 4½", standing deer w/antlers, jeweled eyes & collar, no mark **$6.00**

Sparkler, 4x3½", deer w/upturned head, satin-matt brown on white glaze, plastic eyes, ca 1965 ....**$12.00**

Sparkler, 5½", standing deer, pink jeweled eyes, no mark **$5.00**

Sparkler, 5¼", modern owl, black w/gold trim, large plastic eyes, 1960s-1970s **$10.00**

Sparkler, 6", elephant, jeweled eyes & headpiece **$12.00**

Sparkler, 7", sitting Siamese cat, jeweled eyes & collar, no mark **$10.00**

Vase, 9¾", raised oriental design, footed, pastel exterior w/dark-colored interior **$25.00**

Rosemeade

The Wahpeton Pottery Company of Wahpeton, North Dakota, chose the tradename Rosemeade for a line of bird and animal figurines, novelty salt and pepper shakers, bells, and miscellaneous items which were sold from the 1940s to the '60s through gift stores and souvenir shops in that part of the country. They were marked with either a paper label or an ink stamp; the name Prairie Rose was also used.

Ashtray, deer figural..**$75.00**
Bell, peacock..**$150.00**
Creamer & sugar bowl, ear of corn mold....................**$35.00**
Creamer & sugar bowl, free-form **$30.00**
Figurine, bear, large..**$275.00**
Figurine, bear, miniature, walking...............................**$50.00**

Figurine, buffalo, 4" long $100.00
Figurine, goat, 5" long (illustrated) $85.00
Figurine, pheasant, miniature.....................................**$50.00**
Figurine, pheasant hen, 11½".....................................**$260.00**
Figurine, seals, miniature, set of 3 ....**$50.00**
Figurine, striped gopher, 4"...**$85.00**

Flower frog, bird..**$35.00**
Flower frog, fish...**$55.00**
Flower frog, pheasant..**$65.00**
Incense burner, elephant...**$20.00**
Lamp, TV; cock pheasant, 14¾" long **$425.00**
Pin tray, International Peace Gardens, w/dove figurine.**$75.00**
Pitcher, Minnesota Centennial....................................**$95.00**
Planter, bird on log..**$50.00**
Planter, boot, 4" **$30.00**
Planter, dove **$125.00**
Planter, lamb **$45.00**
Planter, pony...**$75.00**
Planter, squirrel on log...**$40.00**
Salt & pepper shakers, black bear, pr **$50.00**
Salt & pepper shakers, bloodhound head, pr.............**$30.00**
Salt & pepper shakers, buffalo, pr.............................**$75.00**
Salt & pepper shakers, bulldog head, pr....................**$40.00**
Salt & pepper shakers, cock, fighting, pr...................**$100.00**
Salt & pepper shakers, elephant, pr **$65.00**
Salt & pepper shakers, fox, pr **$175.00**
Salt & pepper shakers, fox terrier head, pr................**$40.00**
Salt & pepper shakers, horse head, pr **$55.00**
Salt & pepper shakers, leaping deer, pr.....................**$60.00**
Salt & pepper shakers, pelican, large, pr **$65.00**
Salt & pepper shakers, pelican, small, pr...................**$50.00**
Salt & pepper shakers, pheasant (hen & cock), tail up, pr **$30.00**
Salt & pepper shakers, quail, pr.................................**$40.00**
Salt & pepper shakers, rooster, strutting, pr..............**$70.00**
Salt & pepper shakers, swan, pr **$50.00**
Salt & pepper shakers, tulip, pr **$35.00**
Salt cellar, dove..**$100.00**
Spoon rest, cactus **$75.00**
Spoon rest, pheasant **$65.00**
Vase, dusty pink matt, flared, ruffled rim, 7½" **$60.00**
Vase, flower arranger, rolled edge..............................**$40.00**
Vase, turquoise matt, flared top, bulbous, 5½"...........**$50.00**

Roseville Pottery

This company took its name from the city in Ohio where they operated for a few years before moving to Zanesville in the late 1890s. They're recognized as one of the giants in the industry, having produced many lines of the finest in art pottery from the beginning to the end of their production days. Even when machinery took over many of the procedures once carefully done by hand, the pottery they produced continued to reflect the artistic merit and high standards of quality the company had always insisted upon.

Several marks were used over the years as well as some paper labels. The very early art lines often carried an applied ceramic seal with the name of the line (Royal, Egypto, Mongol, Mara, or Woodland) under a circle containing the words Rozane Ware. From 1910 until 1928 an Rv mark was used, the 'v' being contained in the upper loop of the 'R.' Paper labels were common from 1914 until 1937.

From 1932 until they closed in 1952, the mark was Roseville in script, or R USA. Pieces marked RRP Co Roseville, Ohio, were not made by the Roseville Pottery but by Robinson Ransbotton of Roseville, Ohio. Don't be confused. There are many jardiniers and pedestals in a brown and green blended glaze that are being sold at flea markets and antique malls as Roseville that were actually made by Robinson Ransbottom as late as the 1970s and '80s. That isn't to say they don't have some worth of their own, but don't buy them for old Roseville.

Most of the listings here are for items produced from the 1930s on — things you'll be more likely to encounter today. If you'd like to learn more about the subject, we recommend *The Collector's Encyclopedia of Roseville Pottery, Vols 1 and 2,* and *The Catalog of Early Roseville,* all by Sharon and Bob Huxford.

Apple Blossom, basket, 10", floral on green, twig handle, shape #310, embossed mark **$135.00**

Apple Blossom, basket, 12", floral on light to dark blue shaded, twig handle, embossed mark **$140.00**

Apple Blossom, bowl, 2½x6½", floral on pink, embossed mark **$55.00**

Apple Blossom, cornucopia, 6", floral on green, embossed mark **$45.00**

Apple Blossom, vase, 15", floral on pink, branch handles, embossed mark **$300.00**

Artwood, planter set, 6" center section, two 4" side sections, yellow to brown shaded, embossed mark **$75.00**

Baneda, bowl, 3½x10", wide floral band on rose, handles, no mark **$175.00**

Baneda, candle holder, 5½", wide floral band on rose, silver paper label **$135.00**

Baneda, candle holders, 4½", wide floral band on rose, paper label, pr..**$225.00**

Baneda, urn, 5", wide floral band on rose, silver paper label..**$225.00**

Baneda, vase, 12", wide floral band on rose, low handles, silver label **$525.00**

Baneda, vase, 4", wide floral band on rose **$115.00**

Baneda, vase, 8", wide floral band on rose, curved low handles, black paper label **$250.00**

Bittersweet, basket, 8½", berries & leaves on pastel shaded, branch handle, embossed mark **$65.00**

Bittersweet, bowl, console; 12½", berries & leaves on pastel, embossed mark **$90.00**

Bittersweet, cornucopia, 8", berries & leaves on golden yellow, shape #882, embossed mark **$50.00**

Bittersweet, planter, 10½", berries & leaves on green, embossed mark **$60.00**

Bittersweet, planter, 11½" long, berries & leaves on green, angle handles, embossed mark **$65.00**

Bittersweet, vase, 10", berries & leaves on green, embossed mark **$100.00**

Bittersweet, vase, 5", berries & leaves on pastel ground, small twig handles, shape #972, embossed mark .**$40.00**

Blackberry, bowl, 8" dia, berries & leaves on green, small handles, black paper label **$175.00**

Blackberry, candle holders, 4½", berries & vines on green, flared base, black paper label, pr **$300.00**

Blackberry, jardiniere, 4", berries & vines on green, small silver label..**$150.00**

Blackberry, jardiniere, 7", berries & vines on green, no mark..**$345.00**

Blackberry, vase, 6", berries & vines on green, small ring handles, silver label **$235.00**

Blackberry, vase, 12½", berries & leaves on green, w/handles $900.00

Blackberry, wall pocket, 8½", berries /vines on green..**$400.00**

Bleeding heart, candlestick, 5", floral on pink, silver label...**$55.00**

Bleeding Heart, ewer, 10", floral on tan, shape #972, embossed mark..**$115.00**

Bleeding Heart, hanging basket, 8" wide, floral on pink, embossed mark..**$150.00**

Bleeding Heart, pitcher, floral on blue-green, shape #1323, embossed mark..**$150.00**

Bleeding Heart, vase, 15", floral on blue, handles, embossed mark..**$185.00**

Bleeding heart, vase, 6½", floral on blue, low handles, embossed mark..**$85.00**

Burmese, candle holder-bookends, Eastern head form, white or black, pr **$250.00**

Bushberry, bowl, console; 13", leaves & berries on brown, twig handles, embossed mark...........................**$135.00**

Bushberry, bowl, 4", leaves & berries on green, twig handles, embossed mark **$55.00**

Bushberry, cider pitcher, 8½", leaves & berries on green, twig handle, embossed mark **$250.00**

Bushberry, cornucopia vase, 8", leaves & berries on brown, embossed mark..**$45.00**

Bushberry, double cornucopia, 6", leaves & berries on blue, embossed mark..**$100.00**

Bushberry, ewer, 6", leaves & berries on brown, slim neck w/widely flared base, green handle, embossed mark **$55.00**

Bushberry, vase, 14½", leaves & berries on brown, twig handles, embossed mark **$250.00**

Bushberry, vase, 4", leaves & berries on brown, small handles, no mark **$50.00**

Capri, ash tray, 9", green shell form, embossed mark.**$30.00**

Capri, leaf dish, 16", tan, embossed veins inside, embossed mark..**$30.00**

Cherry Blossom, bowl, 6", floral on brown, fluted decoration at base, small handles, paper label **$225.00**

Cherry Blossom, jardiniere, 10", floral on brown, fluted decoration at base, small handles, paper label..........**$300.00**

Cherry Blossom, jardiniere & pedestal, 25½", floral on brown, no mark **$1,750.00**

Clemana, bowl, 4½x6½", floral on blue, footed, small angle handles, impressed mark......................................**$85.00**

Clemana, candle holders, 4½", floral on green, wide flared base, unmarked, pr...**$125.00**

Clemana, flower frog, 4", floral on brown, impressed mark **$65.00**

Clemana, vase, 12½", floral on brown, small angle handles, flared rim, impressed mark **$250.00**

Clemana, vase, 7", floral, footed, small handles, unmarked..**$115.00**

Clemana, vase, 9½", floral on green, gourd shape, impressed mark..**$200.00**

Clematis, basket, 8", flower on blue-green, shape #388, embossed mark...**$85.00**

Clematis, bowl, console; 14", floral on green shaded, handles, embossed mark **$85.00**

Clematis, double bud vase, 5", flower serves to connect two slim vases, shape #194, embossed mark **$45.00**

Clematis, flowerpot, 5½", floral on brown shaded, embossed mark..**$70.00**

Clematis, tea set (pot, creamer & sugar bowl), flower on brown to green shaded, shape #5, embossed mark **$225.00**

Clematis, vase, 6½", floral on brown to green shaded, embossed mark **$45.00**

Columbine, bookend planter, 5", floral on blue, embossed mark..**$150.00**

Columbine, cornucopia, 5½", floral on brown to green shaded, embossed mark **$50.00**

Columbine, ewer, 7", floral on blue, shape #18, embossed mark..**$70.00**

Columbine, hanging basket, 8½", floral on blue, embossed mark..**$150.00**

Columbine, vase, 8", floral on brown to green shaded, angle handles, shape #20, embossed mark **$60.00**

Cosmos, candle holders, 2½", floral, impressed or embossed mark, pr...**$100.00**

Cosmos, flower frog, 3½", floral, no mark **$45.00**

Cosmos, urn, 4", floral, embossed mark....................**$80.00**

Cosmos, vase, 4", floral, shape #954, handles on gourd shape, impressed or embossed mark **$45.00**

Cosmos, vase, 8", floral, impressed mark..................**$115.00**

Dawn, bowl, 16" long, floral on yellow, tab handles, impressed mark..**$125.00**

Dawn, ewer, 16", floral on pale green, impressed mark **$300.00**

Dawn, vase, 12", floral on pale green, tab handles, square foot, impressed mark..**$135.00**

Falline, vase, 6", brown & green, ear-shaped handles, footed, no mark **$250.00**

Falline, vase, 6", brown & green, small round handles, marked w/silver paper label **$215.00**

Falline, vase, 7½", cream & brown, small ear handles on bulbous form, small silver label..........................**$225.00**

Falline, vase, 8", brown & green, urn form w/small ring handles marked w/silver paper label **$235.00**

Ferella, candlestick, 4½", red w/reticulated decoration, no mark..**$185.00**

Ferella, lamp base, 10½", blended blue & green w/reticulated decoration at rim & base, no mark............**$450.00**

Ferella, urn, 6", brown w/reticulated decoration at rim & foot, no mark **$225.00**

Ferella, vase, 4", brown w/reticulated decoration at rim & foot, small handles, no mark..............................**$135.00**

Florentine, vase, 10¼", textured panels alternate w/leaf devices..**$145.00**

Foxglove, cornucopia, 6", floral on blue, embossed mark **$60.00**

Foxglove, ewer, 10", floral on dark green, shape #5, embossed mark...**$150.00**

Foxglove, flower frog, 4", floral on blue, embossed mark **$35.00**

Foxglove, jardiniere & pedestal, 30½", floral on green shaded, embossed mark...................................**$850.00**

Foxglove, tray, 11", floral on blue, impressed mark....**$85.00**

Foxglove, tray, 8½", floral on blue, impressed mark...**$65.00**

Foxglove, vase, 12½", floral on brown, ring handles, embossed mark...**$225.00**

Foxglove, vase, 14", floral on blue, embossed mark.**$260.00**

Foxglove, vase, 3", floral on blue, handles, #659, embossed mark..**$27.50**

Freesia, basket, 8", floral on brown to green shaded, shape #391, embossed mark...................................**$115.00**

Freesia, bowl, console; 16½", floral on blue, handles, embossed mark...**$115.00**

Freesia, bowl, 4", floral on blue, small handles, embossed mark...**$55.00**

Freesia, bowl, 8½", floral on blue, handles, embossed mark...**$50.00**

Freesia, cookie jar, 10", floral on dark to light green shaded, angle handles, shape #4, embossed mark...........**$225.00**

Freesia, flowerpot, 5", floral on brown to green shaded, shape #670, embossed mark.................................**$65.00**

Freesia, vase, 10½", floral on brown shaded, low handles, embossed mark...**$115.00**

Freesia, window box, 10½", floral on green, rectangular shape w/handles, embossed mark.........................**$75.00**

Fuchsia, bowl, console; 3½x12½", floral on brown, impressed mark...**$135.00**

Fuchsia, candlestick, 2", floral on green, impressed mark...**$55.00**

Fuchsia, pitcher, 8", floral on tan & green shaded, shape #1322, impressed mark.................................**$250.00**

Fuchsia, vase, 6", floral on brown, handles, impressed mark...**$135.00**

Fuchsia, vase, 7", floral on cream & blue shaded, round handles, shape #895, impressed mark................**$125.00**

Fuchsia, vase, 8", floral on blue, handles, impressed mark...**$185.00**

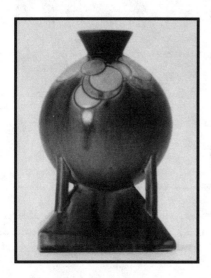

Futura, vase, 8", ball form w/'balloons,' pyramidal base, four upright posts..............................**$1,000.00**

Gardenia, basket, 8", floral on green, integral circle handle, shape #609, embossed mark.................**$115.00**

Gardenia, bowl, 5", floral on pastel shaded, embossed mark...**$50.00**

Gardenia, cornucopia, 6", floral on brown, shape #621, embossed mark...**$40.00**

Gardenia, vase, 10", floral on green, ruffled rim, flared foot, low handles, embossed mark.................**$90.00**

Gardenia, vase, 14½", floral on green, 'petal-like' rim, flared foot, handles, embossed mark...............**$175.00**

Gardenia, window box, 3x8½", floral on pastel shaded, embossed mark...**$50.00**

Iris, basket, 9½", floral on shaded background, impressed mark...**$225.00**

Iris, bowl vase, 4", floral, shape #2117, impressed mark...**$45.00**

Iris, ewer, 10", flower on tan to green shaded, shape #926, impressed mark.................................**$175.00**

Iris, vase, 8½", floral on shaded background, pillow shape w/handles, impressed mark.........................**$135.00**

Iris, vase, 10", floral on blue shaded, handles, impressed mark...**$165.00**

Ivory II, bowl vase, 5", white, Russco shape (#259), impressed mark or silver paper label...................**$50.00**

Ivory II, candlestick, 2½", white, impressed mark.......**$30.00**

Ivory II, hanging basket, 7", soft white, hangs from three handles...**$85.00**

Ivory II, nude figurine, 9", soft white, no mark.........**$350.00**

Ivory II, vase, 10", white, Carnelian shape w/handles, impressed mark or silver paper label...................**$55.00**

Ixia, basket, 10", floral, shape #346.........................**$135.00**

Ixia, bowl, console; 3½x10½", floral on green shaded, impressed mark...**$45.00**

Ixia, bowl, 6", floral on yellow, shape #387................**$55.00**

Ixia, candlestick, double; 3", floral on yellow, impressed mark...**$55.00**

Ixia, vase, 8½", floral on pink to cream shaded, gourd shape w/handles, impressed mark.....................**$65.00**

Jonquil, bowl, 5½", white flowers w/green leaves on brown, handles...**$200.00**

Jonquil, bud vase, 7", white flowers w/green leaves on brown, slim form w/low handles.........................**$57.50**

Laurel, bowl, 7", floral, silver paper sticker.................**$90.00**

Lotus, planter, 3½x4", cream-colored embossed leaves w/green at rim & base, square shape, embossed mark...**$55.00**

Lotus, vase, 10½", cream-colored embossed leaves, blue at rim & base, square pillow form, embossed mark...**$125.00**

Luffa, jardiniere, 5½" dia base, floral w/large leaves on brown, small angle handles, silver paper label ..**$300.00**

Luffa, lamp, 9½", floral w/large leaves on green to blue shaded, small angle handles, no mark...............**$400.00**

Luffa, vase, 15½", floral w/large leaves on green, footed, small angle handles, silver paper label...............**$465.00**

Luffa, vase, 7", floral w/large leaves on brown w/irregular band decoration, small angle handles....................**$115.00**

Luffa, vase, 9", florals & large leaves on green..........**$150.00**

Luffa, wall pocket, 8½", florals & large leaves on brown to green shaded, no mark.................................**$425.00**

Magnolia, candle holder, 2½", floral branch on shaded ground, wide angle handles, embossed mark......**$35.00**

Magnolia, cider pitcher, 7", floral branch on blue, tilt style, shape #132, embossed mark.......................**$200.00**

Magnolia, cookie jar, 10", floral branch on blue, angle handles, shape #2, embossed mark.........................**$225.00**

Magnolia, cornucopia, 6", floral on blue, embossed mark...**$50.00**

Magnolia, ewer, 10", floral branch on brown to green shaded, embossed mark.................................**$125.00**

Magnolia, planter, 8", floral branch on blue, angle handles, #389, embossed handle $90.00

Magnolia, planter, 8½", floral branch on blue, twig handles, embossed mark...$60.00

Mayfair, bowl, 4", large embossed leaves & small blossoms embossed on ivory, embossed mark $22.50

Mayfair, bowl, 7", yellow shell form, impressed mark ..$25.00

Mayfair, vase, 12½", simple brown cylinder w/small indents along sides, yellow interior, embossed mark........$65.00

Ming Tree, ashtray, 6", oriental tree decoration on green, embossed mark $40.00

Ming Tree, basket, 13", oriental tree decoration on blue, twig handle, embossed mark $175.00

Ming Tree, basket, 8", oriental tree decoration on white, twig handle...$85.00

Ming Tree, bowl, 4x11½", oriental tree decoration on green, twig handles, embossed mark......................$50.00

Ming Tree, candle holders, short, oriental decoration, twig handles, pr..$50.00

Ming Tree, ewer, 10", oriental tree decoration on turquoise, twig handle, slim form.................................$80.00

Ming Tree, floor vase, 15½", oriental tree decoration on green, twig handles, embossed mark.................$550.00

Ming Tree, vase, 10½", oriental tree decoration on blue, twig handles, embossed mark.................................$115.00

Ming Tree, wall pocket, 8½", oriental tree decoration on blue, embossed mark $165.00

Ming Tree, window box, 4x11", oriental tree decoration on blue, rectangular, embossed mark.......................$70.00

Mock Orange, basket, 6", floral on green shaded, embossed mark $90.00

Mock Orange, bowl, 4", floral decoration, embossed mark $30.00

Mock Orange, planter, tall, floral on green shaded, square shape, embossed mark...$50.00

Mock Orange, vase, 13", floral on green, flared rim, low handles on gourd shape, embossed mark or label $125.00

Mock Orange, window box, 4½x8½", floral on green shaded, embossed mark or foil label.................$45.00

Moderne, vase, 6½", stylized embossed floral on urn shape, impressed mark..$85.00

Moderne, vase, 8½", stylized embossed florals, impressed mark, small silver label.....................................$135.00

Monticello, basket, 6½", stylized band decoration, integral handle...$215.00

Monticello, urn, 9", stylized band decoration on brown, small round handles $200.00

Monticello, vase, 5", stylized band decoration on brown, handles, no mark..$100.00

Morning Glory, bowl, console; 4½x11½", allover floral decoration on blue & green, handles, no mark.........$275.00

Morning Glory, bowl vase, 4", allover floral decoration on white, angle handles, gold paper label $175.00

Morning Glory, candlestick, 5", allover floral decoration on blue & green, no mark $145.00

Morning Glory, vase, 12", allover flower decoration on blue & green, angle handles, flared foot, gold paper label...$400.00

Morning Glory, vase, 7", allover floral decoration on ivory, pillow form w/low handles, small silver label....$235.00

Moss, console bowl, 13" long, irregular 'moss-like' decoration on sides, small angle handles, impressed mark...$150.00

Moss, urn, 6", irregular 'moss-like' decoration on pink to green shaded, low handles on ball form, impressed mark...$110.00

Moss, vase, 8", irregular 'moss-like' decoration on pink to green shaded, pillow form w/small handles, impressed mark...$135.00

Orian, console bowl, 5", green w/pink interior, square foot, no mark..$115.00

Orian, vase, 12", cream w/blue accents at handles, gold paper label..$135.00

Orian, vase, 9", blue w/beige accents, low handles, small silver label..$85.00

Pasadena, bowl, 3", light pink drip effect over darker pink, embossed mark..$35.00

Pasadena, flowerpot, 4", light pink drip effect over darker pink, embossed mark...$34.00

Pasadena, planter, 3½x9" sq, light pink drip effect over darker pink, embossed mark $25.00

Peony, bookends, 5½", floral on tan, pr $125.00

Peony, bowl, 4", floral w/green leaves on brown, small angle handles, shape #427, embossed mark........$40.00

Peony, ewer, 10", floral on tan, shape #8, embossed mark $125.00

Peony, planter, 10", floral on green, embossed mark .$65.00

Peony, tray, 8", floral on tan, embossed mark............$40.00

Peony, vase, 8", floral on tan, urn form w/angle handles, embossed mark..$85.00

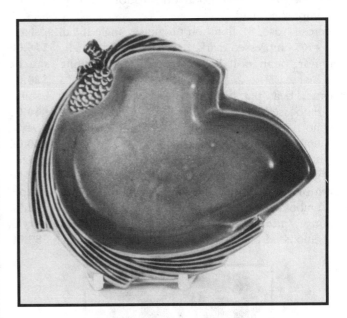

Pine Cone, ashtray, 7" wide, pine cone decoration on brown **$135.00**

Pine Cone, basket, 10", pine cone decoration on brown to green, twig handle, shape #338, impressed or embossed mark...$275.00

Pine Cone, bowl, console; 11", pine cone decoration on blue, twig handles, silver paper label..................$250.00

Pine Cone, bowl, 3", pine cone decoration on brown, small twig handles, shape #632, impressed or embossed mark..$55.00

Pine Cone, candle holder, 2½", pine cone decoration on brown, impressed mark..$65.00

Pine Cone, pitcher, 10½", pine cone decoration on blue, embossed mark..$235.00

Pine Cone, planter, 5", pine cone decoration on blue, embossed mark..$85.00

Pine Cone, vase, 7", pine cone decoration on green to ivory shaded, footed, twig handles, impressed mark.....$85.00

Pine Cone, vase, 8", pine cone decoration on blue, pillow form, impressed mark..$235.00

Pine Cone, vase, 8", pine cone decoration on blue, urn form, twig handles, impressed mark..................$175.00

Pine Cone, wall pocket, 9", pine cones on blue, impressed mark..$225.00

Pine Cone, window box, 3½x15½", pine cone decoration on brown, impressed mark..$350.00

Poppy, basket, 8", floral, shape #354, impressed mark.$175.00

Poppy, bowl, 12", floral on cream to green shaded, green handles, impressed mark..$120.00

Poppy, ewer, 18½", floral, impressed mark...............$300.00

Poppy, jardiniere, 6½", floral, ring handles, impressed mark $115.00

Poppy, vase, 7½", floral, handles, impressed mark...$115.00

Poppy, wall pocket w/candle holder attached each side, 9", floral, shape #1281, impressed mark..................$200.00

Primrose, bowl, 4", floral on brown, angle handles, impressed mark..$65.00

Primrose, vase, 6½", floral on turquoise, angle handles, impressed mark..$85.00

Primrose, vase, 8", floral on turquoise, angle handles, shape #767, impressed mark..$115.00

Raymor, bean pot, brown cup shape w/white 'saucer' rest..$25.00

Raymor, bean pot, brown w/stick handle, white lid & stand, embossed mark..$40.00

Raymor, casserole, 13½", brown, simple modernistic style, embossed mark..$50.00

Raymor, corn server, 12½" long (individual serving size), green mottled, embossed mark..$17.50

Raymor, gravy boat, 9½", brown, modernistic shape, embossed mark..$12.50

Raymor, pitcher, 10", creamy white, modernistic style, embossed mark..$85.00

Raymor Modern Art Ware, bowl, 8" long, charcoal gray..$85.00

Silhouette, cornucopia vase, 8", embossed flower on white, embossed mark..$30.00

Silhouette, ewer, 6", embossed flower reserve on turquoise, embossed mark..$45.00

Silhouette, ewer, 6½", embossed leaves, creamy white, angle handle, embossed mark..$40.00

Silhouette, planter, 14" long, embossed leaf on white, embossed mark..$55.00

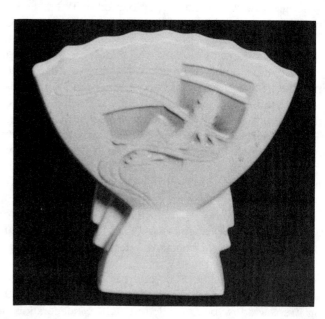

Silhouette, vase, 7", #783, nude reclining on fan form..$235.00

Silhouette, vase, 14", embossed leaves in reserve on tan, gourd shape w/irregular-shaped rim, embossed mark $175.00

Silhouette, wall pocket, 8", embossed leaves on rose, embossed mark..$125.00

Snowberry, ashtray, white berries on leafy branch on brown shaded, embossed mark..$40.00

Snowberry, basket, 8", white berries on leafy branch on green shaded, embossed mark..$90.00

Snowberry, bowl, console; 11", white berries on leafy branch on blue shaded, embossed mark..............$60.00

Snowberry, candle holders, short, white berries on leafy branch on blue shaded, angle handles, embossed mark, pr..$40.00

Snowberry, ewer, 16", white berries on leafy branch on green, embossed mark..$200.00

Snowberry, vase, 6½", white berries on leafy branch on blue, pillow form, embossed mark..$50.00

Snowberry, vase, 8½", white berries on leafy branch on blue, flared foot & rim, angle handles, embossed mark $95.00

Sunflower, bowl, 4", yellow sunflowers on green, no mark..$220.00

Sunflower, jardiniere & pedestal, 29", yellow sunflowers on green, no mark $2,500.00

Sunflower, urn, 5½", yellow sunflowers on green, black paper label $275.00

Sunflower, vase, 10", yellow sunflowers on green, small handles on gourd shape.................**$500.00**

Sunflower, vase, 10", yellow sunflowers on green, small handles, no mark.................**$500.00**

Sunflower, vase, 5", yellow sunflowers on green, handles, no mark.................**$200.00**

Sunflower, wall pocket, 7½", yellow sunflowers on green, no mark.................**$350.00**

Sunflower, window box, 3½x11", yellow sunflowers on green, no mark.................**$350.00**

Teasel, vase, 10", embossed thistle decoration, impressed mark.................**$135.00**

Teasel, vase, 12", embossed thistle decoration, impressed mark.................**$160.00**

Teasel, vase, 6", embossed thistle decoration, impressed mark.................**$50.00**

Thornapple, vase, double bud; 5½", floral, impressed mark.................**$65.00**

Thornapple, vase, 9½", floral on brown shaded, footed, small angle handles, impressed mark.................**$135.00**

Topeo, vase, 15", four tapering beaded buttresses, red, no mark.................**$350.00**

Topeo, vase, 7", four tapering beaded buttresses, red, silver paper label.................**$135.00**

Tourmaline, bowl vase, 5", blue, marked w/silver or gold paper label.................**$55.00**

Tourmaline, candlesticks, 5", blue, wide flared base, marked w/silver paper label, pr.................**$45.00**

Tourmaline, vase, 10", green, 6-sided shape.................**$70.00**

Tourmaline, vase, 7½", blue ball form w/small foot, ring decoration at top, no mark.................**$55.00**

Velmoss, vase, 14½", berries & leaves on blue, footed, angle handles, no mark.................**$135.00**

Velmoss, vase, 7", floral on blue-green, angle handles midway on body, gold paper label.................**$55.00**

Velmoss, vase, 8", berries & leaves on blue, angle handles, no mark.................**$60.00**

Water Lily, bowl, 3", large flower & leaves on burnt orange, angle handles, shape #663, embossed mark.................**$35.00**

Water Lily, hanging basket, 9", large flower & leaves, embossed mark.................**$145.00**

Water Lily, vase, 12", large flower & leaves on blue, gourd form w/handles, shape #81, embossed mark.................**$115.00**

Water Lily, vase, 9", large flower & leaves on tan to brown, handles, embossed mark.................**$115.00**

White Rose, basket, 7½", floral on shaded ground, green handle, embossed mark.................**$135.00**

White Rose, bowl, 4", floral on tan to green shaded, handles, shape #387, embossed mark.................**$45.00**

White Rose, candlestick, 4½", floral on tan to green shaded, embossed mark.................**$50.00**

White Rose, ewer, 15", floral on turquoise, shape #993, embossed mark.................**$165.00**

White Rose, vase, 12½", floral on turquoise, angle handles, embossed mark.................**$200.00**

White Rose, vase, 4", floral on tan to green shaded, embossed mark.................**$35.00**

White Rose, wall pocket, 6½", floral on blue, embossed mark.................**$115.00**

Wincraft, basket, 12", floral on brown, embossed mark .**$85.00**

Wincraft, cornucopia, 5x9", floral on tan, embossed mark.................**$40.00**

Wincraft, mug, 4½", apricot shaded w/no floral decoration, no mark.................**$55.00**

Wincraft, planter, 10", floral on turquoise, boat shape, embossed mark.................**$55.00**

Wincraft, vase, 10", floral on turquoise, cylindrical, embossed mark.................**$80.00**

Wincraft, vase, 7", floral on chartreuse, embossed mark.................**$65.00**

Windsor, bowl, 3½x10½", brown & green mottle, angular rim-to-base handles, no mark.................**$125.00**

Windsor, vase, 7", green & brown mottle, bulbous, handles, small black paper label.................**$265.00**

Wisteria, vase, 10", floral, cylindrical, small angle handles, silver sticker.................**$400.00**

Wisteria, vase, 7", floral, small angle handles, silver sticker.................**$275.00**

Zephyr Lily, basket, lily on dark to light green background, ruffled rim, shape #395, embossed mark.................**$125.00**

Zephyr Lily, candlestick, 2", lily on brown, embossed mark.................**$35.00**

Zephyr Lily, console boat, 10", lily on brown to green shaded, shape #475, embossed mark.................**$85.00**

Zephyr Lily, vase, 12", lily on brown shaded, low handles, embossed mark.................**$125.00**

Zephyr Lily, vase, 6½", lily on green shaded, fan form w/low handles, embossed mark.................**$60.00**

Zephyr Lily, vase, 8½", lily on brown shaded, urn form, embossed mark.................**$90.00**

Zephyr Lily, vase, 8½", lily on green, footed, low handles, embossed mark.................**$60.00**

Royal Copenhagen Figurines

The Royal Copenhagen Manufactory was established in Denmark in the late 1800s and since that time has produced quality china dinnerware, vases, collector plates, and the figurines such as we've listed here. They're very appealing, high in quality, and very collectible.

Airdale Terrier, #11079, 6½".................**$195.00**

Barn owl, #273, 8½".................**$390.00**

Bear, brown, #21433.................**$85.00**

Bedlington Terrier, standing, #11075, 5".................**$195.00**

Boy in carnival attire, #4794.................**$155.00**

Boy on rock w/book, #1096, 6½".................**$265.00**

Calf, #1072, 4x7".................**$225.00**

Desert fox, recumbent, #1236, 5".................**$245.00**

Fox, #1475, 5½".................**$235.00**

French Bulldog, recumbent, #11038, 6½".................**$250.00**

Geese, 9", #2068.................**$300.00**

German Shepherd, recumbent, #11084, 10¼".................**$445.00**

Girl in long dress, #5605, 8".................**$145.00**

Girl w/doll, #1938, 5¼".....................................$285.00
Great Dane, recumbent, #11679, 4½"........................$240.00
Lovebirds, #402, 5¼"......................................$175.00
Owl, #1741, 3½"...$85.00
Pan on goat, #1228...$175.00
Pan on goat, #737, 8"......................................$575.00

Pan w/pipes, 5½", #1736............................**$350.00**
Pekingese, #11337, 5".....................................$185.00
Penguin, #3003, 3"...$65.00
Pointer puppies, #453, 2".................................$135.00
Poodle, #4368...$195.00
Robin, #2238, 1½"..$75.00
Scottie, sitting, #3162, 3¼"..............................$165.00
Seal, #1441...$135.00
Turkey, white, #04784, 3".................................$115.00
Wirehaired Fox Terrier, #11001, 7½".......................$285.00
Wolf howling, #1258, 9"...................................$280.00
Young girl carries lunch to field, #815, 8½".............$135.00

Royal Copley

This is a line of planters, wall pockets, vases, and other novelty items, most of which are modeled as appealing animals, birds, or human figures. They were made by the Spaulding China Company of Sebring, Ohio, from 1942 until 1957. The decoration is underglazed and airbrushed, and some pieces are trimmed in gold (which can add 25% to 50% to their values). Not every piece is marked, but they have a style that is distinctive. Some items are ink stamped; others have (or have had) labels.

Examples are readily found, and prices are still low. Unmarked items may often be found at a bargain. Some people choose a particular animal to collect. For instance, if you're a cat lover, they were made in an extensive assortment of styles and sizes. Teddy bears are also popular; you'll find them licking a lollipop, playing a mandolin, or modeled as a bank. Wildlife lovers can collect deer, pheasants, fish, and gazelles, and there's a wide array of songbirds to be had as well.

If you'd like more information, we recommend *Royal Copley* written by Leslie Wolfe, edited by Joe Devine.

Bank, 6½", pig w/bow tie, any color variation, paper label only...$21.50
Bank, 7½", pig in striped shirt, any color variation, paper label or green stamp on base................$30.00
Bank, 7½", rooster figural, coin slot at top of tail, 'Chicken Feed' embossed at feet, paper label only.............$38.00
Bank, 7½", teddy bear figural, paper label only, scarce...$42.50
Creamer, 3", leaves form body, yellow to pink shaded, green stamp on base.................................$12.00
Figurine, 4½", nuthatch, full bodied, any color variation, paper label.................................$12.50
Figurine, 4½", vireo, full bodied, any color variation, paper label only, easily found.................$12.00
Figurine, 5", bluebird, blue w/pink at throat, paper label only.......................................$20.00
Figurine, 5", doves (two on stump), full bodied, any color variation, paper label only................$13.50
Figurine, 5", kingfisher, any color variation, paper label only.......................................$20.00
Figurine, 5", kinglet, full bodied, any color variation, paper label only, easily found...............$12.50
Figurine, 5", lark (or skylark), full bodied, any color variation, easily found.......................$10.00
Figurine, 6½", thrush, full bodied, any color variation, paper label only.............................$14.00
Figurine, 6¼", wren, full bodied, any color variation, paper label only, easily found.................$14.00
Figurine, 7", hen, feet hidden, paper label only, easily found.......................................$20.00
Figurine, 7", swallow w/extended wings, full bodied, any color variation, paper label only............$32.00
Figurine, 7½", oriental boy & girl, any color variation, paper label only, each........................$14.00
Figurine, 7¼", cockatoo, full bodied, any color variation, paper label only, scarce...................$26.00
Figurine, 7¼", swallow on heavy double stump, full bodied, any color variation, paper label only......$22.50
Figurine, 8", parrot, full bodied, any color combination, paper label..................................$25.00
Figurine, 8", titmouse, full bodied, any color variation, paper label only............................$18.00
Figurine, 8¼", cockatoo, full bodied, any color variation, raised letters on base, easily found.......$25.00
Figurine, 9¼", mallard duck, erect head, paper label only, easily found...............................$22.50
Lamp, dancing girl figural mounted on metal base, any color variation, scarce.........................$45.00
Pitcher, 6¼", large rose decal on creamy white, embossed beads at neck, gold stamp on base.............$9.00
Pitcher, 8", blue flowers embossed across center of pink body, green stamp or embossed letters on base ..$24.00
Pitcher, 8", daffodils & stems form body, yellow flowers w/pink leaves, pink handle, green stamp on bottom..........$24.00

Pitcher, 8", Pome Fruit, fruit in relief on blue background, green stamp on base...**$24.00**

Planter, 2½x6¼", 3-sectioned, various colors, each **$9.00**

Planter, 3" high, large embossed flower on front & back, blue & pink, green stamp on base...........................**$9.00**

Planter, 3½", boat shaped, turquoise w/brown specks, paper label only...**$9.00**

Planter, 3¼x6", coach form, beige or blue, green stamp on base, each..**$12.00**

Planter, 3¾", duck & wheelbarrow figural, paper label only...**$12.50**

Planter, 4", green ivy on ivory background, footed, paper label only...**$6.00**

Planter, 4¾", grazing horse in deep relief before trough-like planter, paper label only, scarce...........................**$24.50**

Planter, 4¾", oriental child w/big vase, paper label only ..**$9.00**

Planter, 5", cocker spaniel's head figural, raised letters on back, easily found...**$10.00**

Planter, 5", duck eating grass figural, open back, paper label only, easily found **$10.00**

Planter, 5", running gazelles embossed on square shape, yellow on green, paper label only, scarce **$10.00**

Planter, 5", sitting mallard, paper label only, easily found...**$18.00**

Planter, 5½", Copley's Big Apple, made to hang or rest on table, raised letters on back, easily found.............**$10.00**

Planter, 5½", hat w/flowers along band, any color variation, hangs or rests on table, raised letters on back......**$17.50**

Planter, 5½", salt box figural, 'Salt' in reserve on front, raised letters on back, scarce **$18.00**

Planter, 5½", teddy bear beside open tree stump figural, paper label only, scarce...**$18.00**

Planter, 5½", walking rooster embossed on side, made to hang or rest on table, raised letters on back.........**$15.00**

Planter, 5¼", hummingbird on flower figural, paper label only, scarce..**$16.00**

Planter, 6", Dutch boy or girl w/bucket, paper label only, each **$14.00**

Planter, 6", lady w/bare shoulders figural, any color variation, paper label only, easily found......................**$18.00**

Planter, 6", Teddy bear figural, hard to find.........$25.00

Planter, 6½", Indian boy w/drum figural, paper label only, easily found..**$12.50**

Planter, 6½x11½", three jumping salmon among foaming waves, paper label only, scarce **$42.00**

Planter, 6¼", girl leaning on barrel figural, dark green & rose clothes, paper label only, easily found..................**$13.50**

Planter, 6¼", tanager beside open stump, any color variation, green stamp or raised letters on base **$13.50**

Planter, 6¼", woodpecker beside open stump, any color variation, green stamp or raised letters on base ...**$14.00**

Planter, 6¼", wren on tree stump figural, paper label only, scarce..**$16.00**

Planter, 7", girl & wheelbarrow figural, red hat, light green dress, dark green wheelbarrow, paper label only...**$16.00**

Planter, 7", hat w/flowers along band, bow at back, any color, hangs or rests on table, easily found.....................**$17.50**

Planter, 7", pup w/suitcase figural, name tag on pup reads 'Skip,' paper label only, scarce............................**$22.50**

Planter, 7", resting deer figural, paper label only, scarce .**$18.00**

Planter, 7", white poodle stands erect beside shiny black planter, scarce...**$18.00**

Planter, 7½", barefooted boy or girl figural, any color variation, paper label only, each **$18.00**

Planter, 7½", dog figural, raised right foot, paper label only, scarce...**$27.50**

Planter, 7½", elephant w/yellow ball figural, trunk up, paper label only, easily found **$22.50**

Planter, 7½", playful kitten & boot figural, paper label only, scarce...**$27.50**

Planter, 7½", teddy bear w/concertina figural, paper label only, scarce..**$44.00**

Planter, 7¾", mallard duck figural, paper label only, easily found **$12.50**

Planter, 8", angel figural, kneeling, hands as in prayer, blue or pink robe, paper label only, scarce **$22.50**

Planter, 8", birdhouse w/bird perched at roof, paper label only, rare **$45.00**

Planter, 8", black cat w/pink bow figural, paper label only..**$18.00**

Planter, 8", Colonial old man, raised letters on back (Japanese reproduction can easily be spotted).....**$27.50**

Planter, 8", deer stands beside open stump, paper label only, easily found **$18.00**

Planter, 8", kitten in picnic basket figural, paper label only, rare..**$47.50**

Planter, 8", pirate's head, pink head covering, hangs or rests on table, raised letters on back...........................**$30.00**

Planter, 8", rooster & wheelbarrow figural, rare **$48.00**

Planter, 8", rooster figural, paper label only, scarce...**$18.00**

Planter, 8¼", bear cub clinging to open stump figural, paper label only..**$24.00**

Planter, 8¼", kitten w/red ball of yarn figural, paper label only..**$27.50**

Planter/wall pocket, girl in wide-brimmed hat, puckered mouth, hand to cheek, raised letters on back.......**$26.00**

Planter/wall pocket, 7½", Chinese girl or boy w/wide-brimmed hat, puckered lips, raised letters on back, each **$20.00**

Plaque/planter, 6¾", fruit in relief on white w/scalloped border, hangs or rests on table, raised letters on back **$12.50**

Plaque/planter, 8", The Mill, scene signed by Jacob van Ruysdael, hangs or rests on table **$30.00**

Vase, bud; 5", warbler perched on open stump, any color variation, green stamp or raised letters on base ... **$12.00**

Vase, 5½", dragon embossed on side, footed, paper label only, easily found **$9.00**

Vase, 5½", stylized leaves embossed on yellow ground, paper label only, easily found **$7.50**

Vase, 6", fish form, paper label only, scarce **$27.50**

Vase, 6¼", blue w/gold rim, gourd shape w/embossed flowers at handles, gold stamp on base **$10.00**

Vase, 6¼", green ivy on ivory background, pillow form, footed, paper label only **$10.00**

Vase, 6¼", rose decals on creamy white, two small upturned handles, gold stamp on base **$9.00**

Vase, 7", Carol's Corsage, blue flowers in deep relief on pink classic form, green stamp on base **$12.00**

Vase, 7", green ivy on ivory background, footed, paper label only **$9.00**

Vase, 7", rose decal on white, pink at rim & base, classic form w/handles **$12.50**

Vase, 7½", green philodendron on ivory, footed, paper label only, scarce **$10.00**

Vase, 8", bamboo w/green leaves forms cylinder, paper label only, scarce size **$12.00**

Vase, 8", embossed deer head by oval center opening $14.00

Vase, 8", fish swim on cylindrical form, gold trim, raised letters on base, easily found **$16.00**

Vase, 8", horse's head w/flying mane form, brown w/black mane, paper label only **$26.00**

Vase, 8", rose decal on creamy white, handles, gold stamp on base **$14.00**

Vase, 8¼", dogwood blossoms in diagonal band across body, paper label only **$17.00**

Vase, 8¼", roses decal on creamy white w/gold trim, cornucopia form, raised letters on base **$18.00**

Vase/planter, 7¼", bird in flight embossed on side, paper label only, scarce **$18.00**

Vase/planter, 9", gazelle's head form, gold details (many found w/no gold), raised letters on base, easily found **$22.00**

Royal Doulton

Probably the best-known producers of figurines, character jugs, and series ware ever to exist, the Royal Doulton Company was established in 1815 and continues today to make quality items that are sold through fine gift stores and distributors worldwide.

Kingsware (1899-1946) was a brown-glazed line decorated with drinking scenes. A popular line of collector plates, twenty-four in all, was called the Gibson Girl series. Made from 1901 until sometime in the forties, it was decorated in blue and white with scenes that portrayed a day in the life of 'The Widow and Her Friends.' From 1908 until the early 1940s, they produced Dickensware, decorated with illustrations from Charles Dickens. Robin Hood and Shakespeare were both introduced around 1914, and their Bunnykin series has been made since 1933.

The first character figures were made in 1913 and have remained very popular with collectors ever since. They are not only marked, but each character (and variation) is assigned an identifying number which is printed on the base following the prefix letters 'HN.' Factors that bear on the value of a figurine are age, detail, color, and availability. The presence of an artist's signature or a 'Potted' (pre-1939) mark adds to it as well.

Many collectors favor the bird and animal figures. They were made in a full-size line (having 'HN' prefixes) as well as miniatures (which have a 'K' prefix). Popular domestic breeds are usually valued higher than the more generic animals.

Toby and character jugs were introduced in the 1930s. Both styles are marked with numbers in a 'D' series; the character jugs are made in three sizes (large, small, and miniature). Occasionally you may find a jug with an 'A' mark which, though apparently used for only factory identification purposes, usually boosts its value to some extent. Dates found on the bottom of some jugs are merely copyright dates, not necessarily production dates.

Animal, Airdale, K5 .... **$175.00**
Animal, Boxer dog, medium, #2643 .... **$145.00**
Animal, Bull Terrier, medium, #1132 .... **$650.00**
Animal, Bulldog, small, brown & white, #1047 .... **$150.00**
Animal, Bulldog, small, white, #1074 .... **$150.00**
Animal, Bulldog pup, 1¾", K2 .... **$70.00**
Animal, Collie, Ashstead Applause, #1058 .... **$165.00**
Animal, Cocker Spaniel, medium, blue roan, #1020 . **$125.00**
Animal, Dachshund, 4", #1128 .... **$145.00**
Animal, Dalmation, 5¾", #1113 .... **$125.00**

Animal, Doberman Pinscher, medium, #2645............**$185.00**
Animal, Elephant, 5½", #2644.............................**$95.00**
Animal, Foxhound, 2½", K7 ....**$50.00**
Animal, Hare, recumbent, K-37.........................**$95.00**
Animal, Irish Setter, medium, #1055....................**$150.00**
Animal, Lamb, #2505 ....**$200.00**
Animal, Persian cat, black & white, #999 ....**$145.00**
Animal, Piglet, #2653 ....**$225.00**
Animal, Polar Bear, #119.................................**$145.00**
Animal, Siamese cat, Chatcull, #2655 ....**$115.00**
Animal, Terrier pup in basket, 3", #2587................**$45.00**
Ash pot, Sairey Gamp, D6009 ....**$95.00**
Ash tray, Dickensware, 4" **$35.00**
Ash tray, Gnomes, blue underglaze......................**$75.00**
Ash tray, Welsh Ladies, 2⅝" dia, signed Noke, marked .**$40.00**
Beaker, stoneware, hunt scene, brass rim................**$60.00**
Beaker, Wedding, A Princess for Wales, 1981 ....**$35.00**
Bird, Kingfisher, #858 ....**$165.00**
Bird, Robin, #2617 ....**$175.00**
Bird, Sea Gull, small, #2574 ....**$135.00**
Bird, Wren, #144 ....**$110.00**
Biscuit jar, Royal Mail Coach, 8" **$160.00**
Bowl, cereal; Shakespeare, Romeo, 7½", marked......**$125.00**
Bowl, Gaffers, 11", oval..................................**$150.00**
Bowl, Gypsies, 6"...**$150.00**
Bowl, Under the Greenwood Tree, Robin Hood/Friar Tuck,
7¾" **$125.00**
Box, Nursery Series, girl by shore **$50.00**
Bust, Mr Pickwick, D6049 ....**$65.00**
Bust, Sam Weller, D6052 ....**$65.00**
Candlestick, Dutch People, D1881, pr.....................**$195.00**
Character jug, Apothecary, small, D6574..................**$65.00**
Character jug, Aramis, miniature, D6508 ....**$45.00**
Character jug, Arriet, miniature, D6250 ....**$85.00**
Character jug, Artful Dodger, miniature **$40.00**
Character jug, Auld Mac, large, D5823 ....**$85.00**
Character jug, Bacchus, miniature, D6521................**$45.00**
Character jug, Blacksmith, small, D6578 ....**$65.00**
Character jug, Bootmaker, miniature **$50.00**
Character jug, Cap'n Cuttle, small, D5842 ....**$95.00**
Character jug, Captain Ahab, large, D6500, 1958 ......**$110.00**
Character jug, Captain Hook, small, D6601 ....**$350.00**
Character jug, Cardinal, small, D6033....................**$75.00**
Character jug, Cavalier, large, D6614.....................**$160.00**
Character jug, Dick Turpin, small, gun handle, D5618 ..**$70.00**
Character jug, Drake, large, D6115........................**$145.00**
Character jug, Falstaff, large, D6287 ....**$100.00**
Character jug, Farmer John, small, D5789.................**$85.00**
Character jug, Fat Boy, miniature, D6139.................**$75.00**
Character jug, Fortune Teller, small, D6503..............**$295.00**
Character jug, Gaoler, large, D6570.......................**$95.00**
Character jug, Gardener, small, D6634....................**$60.00**
Character jug, George Washington, large, D6669........**$95.00**
Character jug, Gladiator, small, D6553...................**$350.00**
Character jug, Gone Away, large, D6531 ....**$650.00**
Character jug, Granny, large, w/tooth, D5521 ....**$95.00**
Character jug, Grant & Lee, large, D6698.................**$275.00**
Character jug, Gulliver, small, D6563 ....**$335.00**

Character jug, Henry Morgan, small, D6469.................**$50.00**
Character jug, Jane Seymour, large, D6646 ....**$95.00**
Character jug, John Peel, small, D5731......................**$65.00**
Character jug, Lumber Jack, large, D6610 ....**$110.00**
Character jug, Mad Hatter, small, D6602 ....**$75.00**
Character jug, Mikado, miniature, D6525.................**$325.00**
Character jug, Mine Host, small, D6470 ....**$55.00**

Character jug, Mr Pickwick, large, D6060 ....$150.00
Character jug, Night Watchman, miniature, D6583......**$55.00**
Character jug, Old Charley, miniature, D6046 ....**$45.00**
Character jug, Paddy, small, D5768 ....**$65.00**
Character jug, Parson Brown, large, D5486 ....**$135.00**
Character jug, Porthos, large, D6440 ....**$95.00**
Character jug, Punch & Judy, miniature, D6596 ....**$355.00**
Character jug, Regency Beau, miniature, D6565........**$650.00**
Character jug, Robin Hood, small, D6234.................**$60.00**
Character jug, Robinson Crusoe, small, D6539 ....**$50.00**
Character jug, Sairey Gamp, miniature, D6045 ....**$45.00**
Character jug, Sam Weller, miniature, D6140..............**$45.00**
Character jug, Sancho Panza, miniature, D6518 ....**$50.00**
Character jug, Santa Claus, large, doll handle, D6675.**$150.00**
Character jug, Scrooge, tiny **$40.00**

Character jug, Smuggler, large, D6616 ....$120.00
Character jug, Tam O'Shanter, miniature, D6640.........**$45.00**

Character jug, Toby Philpots, miniature, D6043 ....**$50.00**
Character jug, Tony Weller, large, D5531 ....**$145.00**
Character jug, Tony Weller, miniature, D6044 ....**$45.00**
Character jug, Town Crier, small, D6537....................**$95.00**
Character jug, Trapper, small, D6612 ....**$50.00**
Character jug, Ugly Duchess, miniature, D6607 ....**$285.00**
Character jug, Viking, large, D6496 ....**$185.00**
Character jug, Viking, small, D6502..........................**$95.00**
Character jug, Walrus & Carpenter, small, D6604.......**$65.00**
Character jug, Yachtsman, large, D6622.....................**$115.00**
Cigarette lighter, Long John Silver, table type.............**$95.00**
Coffeepot, Moorish Gate, merchants, 7x3¾".............**$145.00**
Cup & saucer, demitasse; Dickensware, 2¼", marked.**$75.00**
Cup & saucer, Don Quixote.......................................**$50.00**
Cup & saucer, Nursery Rhymes, Mother Goose...........**$65.00**
Decanter, Uncle Sam, Dewars Whiskey, eagle handle.**$185.00**
Figurine, Adrienne, HN2152......................................**$145.00**
Figurine, Alice, HN2158..**$130.00**
Figurine, All Aboard, HN2940...................................**$150.00**
Figurine, Amy, HN2958...**$120.00**
Figurine, Angela, white dress & tiara, HN2389 ....**$95.00**
Figurine, Antoinette, HN2326....................................**$125.00**
Figurine, At Ease, HN2473 ....**$185.00**
Figurine, Autumn Breezes, red dress, HN1934..........**$175.00**
Figurine, Bachelor, HN2319 ....**$225.00**
Figurine, Ballerina, HN2116......................................**$295.00**
Figurine, Beachcomber, HN2487...............................**$180.00**
Figurine, Bedtime, HN1978 ....**$95.00**
Figurine, Biddy, red dress, HN1513...........................**$165.00**
Figurine, Blithe Morning, HN2021 ....**$195.00**
Figurine, Bonnie Lassie, HN1626...............................**$275.00**
Figurine, Bridesmaid, HN2196 ....**$110.00**
Figurine, Bridesmaid, HN2874 ....**$75.00**
Figurine, Buddies, HN2546 ....**$185.00**
Figurine, Buttercup, HN2309.....................................**$175.00**
Figurine, Captain, 9½", HN2260 ....**$250.00**
Figurine, Captain Cook, 8", HN2889......................**$225.00**
Figurine, Carpet Seller, hand closed, HN1464 ....**$275.00**
Figurine, Charlotte, HN2421.....................................**$150.00**
Figurine, China Repairer, HN2943.............................**$140.00**
Figurine, Choir Boy, HN2141....................................**$125.00**
Figurine, Christmas Time, HN2110 ....**$350.00**
Figurine, Clare, HN2793 ....**$150.00**
Figurine, Clarissa, HN2345.......................................**$150.00**
Figurine, Cookie, HN2218...**$145.00**
Figurine, Country Lass, HN1991A **$115.00**
Figurine, Cup of Tea, HN2322 ....**$165.00**
Figurine, Debby, HN2400...**$70.00**
Figurine, Diana, red dress, HN1986...........................**$125.00**
Figurine, Dimity, HN2169...**$350.00**
Figurine, Doctor, HN2858 ....**$350.00**
Figurine, Dreamweaver, HN2283...............................**$175.00**
Figurine, Enchantment, HN2178................................**$150.00**
Figurine, Fair Lady, HN2193.....................................**$250.00**
Figurine, Farmer's Wife, HN2069...............................**$475.00**
Figurine, Favourite, HN2249.....................................**$150.00**
Figurine, First Dance, HN2803 ....**$175.00**
Figurine, Foaming Quart, HN2162.............................**$280.00**

Figurine, Francine, HN2422.......................................**$95.00**
Figurine, Gay Morning, HN2135................................**$250.00**
Figurine, Genie, HN2989..**$150.00**
Figurine, Georgina, HN2377 ....**$120.00**
Figurine, Gollum, HN2913..**$95.00**
Figurine, Goody Two Shoes, HN2037.......................**$125.00**
Figurine, Grace, HN2318...**$150.00**
Figurine, Gypsy Dance, 2nd version, HN2230...........**$250.00**
Figurine, Hilary, HN2335...**$150.00**
Figurine, Huckleberry Finn, HN2927...........................**$95.00**
Figurine, Innocence, HN2842 ....**$150.00**
Figurine, Ivy, HN1768..**$95.00**
Figurine, Jane, HN2806...**$150.00**
Figurine, Jill, HN2061 ....**$145.00**
Figurine, Julia, HN2705...**$150.00**
Figurine, Kate, HN2789 ....**$150.00**

Figurine, Lady Charmain, green shawl, HN1948 ..$300.00
Figurine, Lady Pamela, HN2718................................**$150.00**
Figurine, Laurianne, HN2719 ....**$165.00**
Figurine, Lavinia, HN1955 ....**$95.00**
Figurine, Linda, HN2106..**$145.00**
Figurine, Lisa, matt, HN2310.....................................**$150.00**
Figurine, Little Nell, M-51 ....**$55.00**
Figurine, Lorna, HN2311 ....**$150.00**
Figurine, Lunchtime, HN2485 ....**$150.00**
Figurine, Make Believe, HN2225 ....**$150.00**
Figurine, Marguerite, HN1928 ....**$295.00**
Figurine, Mary Mary, HN2044 ....**$165.00**
Figurine, Master, HN2325 ....**$200.00**
Figurine, Meditation, HN2330 ....**$295.00**
Figurine, Melanie, HN2271 ....**$150.00**
Figurine, Milkmaid, HN2057A...................................**$145.00**
Figurine, Minuet, HN2019 ....**$275.00**
Figurine, Miss Demure, HN1402 ....**$195.00**
Figurine, Monte Carlo, HN2332 ....**$225.00**
Figurine, Musicale, HN2756.......................................**$75.00**
Figurine, My Pet, HN2238 ....**$135.00**

Figurine, Nicola, blue, HN2839................................$250.00
Figurine, Nina, HN2347 ....$175.00
Figurine, Old Meg, HN2494 ....$195.00
Figurine, Olga, HN2463......................................$175.00
Figurine, Paisley Shawl, HN1988 ....$165.00
Figurine, Parisian, HN2445 ....$165.00
Figurine, Pearly Boy, HN2035..............................$175.00
Figurine, Peggy, HN2038.....................................$110.00
Figurine, Pied Piper, HN2102..............................$225.00
Figurine, Polka, HN2156 ....$250.00
Figurine, Pollyanna, HN2965...............................$95.00
Figurine, Pretty Polly, HN2768............................$150.00
Figurine, Professor, HN2281 ....$150.00
Figurine, Rag Doll, HN2142.................................$95.00
Figurine, Rest Awhile, HN2728 ....$175.00
Figurine, River Boy, HN2128................................$150.00
Figurine, Rose, HN1368 ....$95.00
Figurine, Roseanna, HN1926...............................$325.00
Figurine, School Marm, HN2223 ....$225.00
Figurine, Shore Leave, HN2254............................$175.00
Figurine, Simone, HN2378 ....$140.00
Figurine, Soiree, HN2312.....................................$145.00
Figurine, Sonata, Enchantment series, HN2438...........$85.00
Figurine, Sophie, HN2833 ....$125.00
Figurine, Spring Morning, HN1923 ....$195.00
Figurine, Stitch in Time, HN2352.........................$150.00
Figurine, Suitor, HN2132 ....$350.00
Figurine, Sweet Dreams, HN2380 ....$135.00
Figurine, Taking Things Easy, HN2677 ....$175.00
Figurine, Thank You, HN2732 ....$150.00
Figurine, This Little Pig, HN1793 ....$125.00
Figurine, Tinkle Bell, HN1677..............................$95.00
Figurine, To Bed, HN1805....................................$145.00
Figurine, Tom, HN2864 ....$125.00
Figurine, Top o' the Hill, HN1833 ....$195.00
Figurine, Treasure Island, HN2243 ....$135.00
Figurine, Twilight, HN2256 ....$175.00
Figurine, Uriah Heep, HN1892.............................$295.00
Figurine, Valerie, HN2107 ....$170.00
Figurine, Veneta, HN2722 ....$125.00
Figurine, Votes for Women, HN2816.....................$195.00
Figurine, Wayfarer, HN2362.................................$175.00
Figurine, Winsome, HN2220 ....$155.00
Figurine, Young Master, HN2872..........................$225.00
Flask, Kingsware, Dewars, Bonnie Prince Charlie.....$200.00
Flower bowl, Isaac Walton....................................$150.00
Humidor, stoneware, 5x4¼", brown to tan, figures in relief,
    marked...$165.00
Jug, Pickwick Papers, embossed figures, D5756 ....$180.00
Jug, stoneware, Sea Shanty, 6⅝x4¾", sailor & girl,
    marked $80.00
Jug, stoneware, 7¼", embossed Cupids & vintage, Lambeth $175.00
Match holder, Mr Squeers, 2"...............................$95.00
Mug, Kingsware, Drink Wisely $195.00
Mug, Minstrels, 3¼x3½", marked.........................$65.00
Mug, Sir Andrew Aguecheek series, 5⅝", tankard form,
    marked...$75.00

Pitcher, Dickensware, Curiosity Shop, square top.....$165.00
Pitcher, dog, signed Cecil Alden............................$125.00
Pitcher, Egyptian, 6⅜", geometric border, marked $95.00
Pitcher, Fox Hunting, 4" $85.00
Pitcher, Medieval Minstrels, 7½x4½", marked...........$125.00
Pitcher, Old Sea Dogs, Jack's the Boy for Play, 6" $125.00
Pitcher, Oliver Twist, embossed figures, tankard form,
    D6286 ....$165.00
Pitcher, Polar Bear, D3128 ....$95.00
Pitcher, Shakespeare, Romeo, 4½"........................$70.00
Pitcher, Sporting Squire, Dewars Whiskey, 8¼"........$275.00
Pitcher, stoneware, 3⅜", tan tapestry w/red, gold, & white
    trim...$45.00
Plate, Airships, 10½", men in varied craft, signed.....$195.00
Plate, American Views, Pikes Peak, 10½".................$60.00
Plate, Autumn Glory, landscape, square $75.00
Plate, child's; Shakespeare, Shylock, 8¼", marked $80.00
Plate, Fairy Tales, Pied Piper................................$75.00
Plate, Gibson Girl, She Goes into Colors $125.00
Plate, Greenaway Almanack, Gemini, May $30.00
Plate, Hiawatha, Wampum Belt, 10" $95.00
Plate, Old English Inns, Australia, D6072 ....$35.00
Plate, Old English Proverbs, Fine Feather.................$75.00
Plate, Proverbs, 10", vintage border.......................$55.00
Plate, Souter's Cats, 6" $65.00
Plate, Windsor Castle, 10½"..................................$50.00

Plate, 10¼", The Gypsies, figures & campfire in landscape...$100.00

Soap dish, Shakespeare, Shylock, 3¾x5¼", 3-part,
    marked $100.00
Tankard, 6", Oliver Twist, Old Curiosity Shop...........$135.00
Teapot, Dutch People, D1884................................$115.00
Teapot, stoneware, 5x4½", floral tapestry, marked....$145.00
Tile, Canterbury Pilgrims $65.00
Tile, Coaching Days, 6½" sq..................................$50.00
Toby jug, Cap'n Cuttle, 4½", D6266........................$185.00
Toby jug, Charrington, One Toby Leads to Another.$345.00
Toby jug, Falstaff, D6020......................................$135.00
Toby jug, Happy John, D6070 ....$85.00

Toby jug, Honest Measure, D6108................................**$85.00**
Toby jug, Huntsman, 7½", D6320 ....**$135.00**
Toby jug, Jolly Toby, D6109 ....**$85.00**
Toby jug, Mr Furrow, 4", D6701 ....**$45.00**
Toby jug, Old Charley, D6030 ....**$185.00**
Toby jug, Reverend Cassock, D6702 ....**$45.00**
Toby jug, Sir Francis Drake, 9", D6660.....................**$135.00**
Toby jug, Sir Winston Churchill, 5½", D6172.............**$70.00**
Toothpick holder, sunset scene, two handles..............**$85.00**
Tray, sandwich; Zunday Zmocks, 11x5", signed Noke,
    marked..**$85.00**
Vase, Dickensware, Cap'n Cuttle, 4⅝", early mark......**$85.00**
Vase, Dickensware, Mr Micawber, 5", two handles.....**$95.00**
Vase, stoneware, miniature, hunting scene, Coleman.**$35.00**
Vase, stoneware, 5⅞", gray mottle, cobalt leaf decoration,
    marked..**$135.00**
Vase, stoneware, 6½", embossed flowers, blue on blue-
    green mottle, Lambeth..**$80.00**
Vase, Welsh Ladies, 3⅜", two ladies beside fence,
    marked..**$110.00**
Vase, 4⅝", cows in pastoral scene, marked **$100.00**

Ruby Glass

Red glassware has always appealed to the buying public, and today there are lots of collectors who look for it. It has been made for more than one hundred years by literally every glasshouse in the country, but most of what's out there today was made during the Depression era through the decade of the seventies. Anchor Hocking made lots of it; they called their line 'Royal Ruby.'

If you like this type of glassware, we recommend you read *Ruby Glass of the 20th Century* by Naomi Over.

See also Moon and Star.

Batter pitcher, bulbous body on saucer-form tray w/screw-on
    metal lid & slide-open pour spout, unmarked **$150.00**
Batter pitcher, glass body, w/metal handle, lid & base,
    marked McKee **$85.00**
Bell, 3¾", Viking Glass, 1984-85 ....**$15.00**
Bell, 5", Viking Glass, 1984-85 ....**$20.00**
Bell, 6½", floral decoration, Westmoreland, 1977........**$20.00**
Bonbon, 7", Viking Glass, 1984-85 ....**$17.50**
Bowl, 10½", Maple Leaf pattern, Westmoreland, 1982..**$35.00**
Bowl, 7¼", Sheffield, Fenton, 1930s **$20.00**
Butter dish, ¼-lb, w/crystal top **$100.00**
Butter dish, 6½", Hobnail, distributed by LeVay only, made
    by Westmoreland, 1980s......................................**$45.00**
Candy box, square shape, Westmoreland, 1980-83 .....**$35.00**
Candy dish, 3¾", Sweetheart, fluted, LG Wright, 1976.....**$20.00**
Cocktail shaker w/chrome lid **$35.00**
Creamer & sugar bowl, 5¼", Strutting Peacock, Westmore-
    land limited edition, 1980s **$65.00**
Fairy lamp, 4¼", Sweetheart, LG Wright, 1974-81........**$15.00**
Figurine, apple, 3¾", Viking Glass.............................**$15.00**
Figurine, Buddha, 6½", marked Gillinder on base.......**$85.00**
Mug, Tally-Ho pattern, Cambridge **$25.00**

Nut dish, 3" dia, enameled floral design **$15.00**
Percolator top, w/knob finial **$17.50**
Planter basket, 5½", handles **$50.00**
Plate, 9¼", divided into four sections, handles............**$45.00**
Relish, 3-compartment, crystal handle.........................**$25.00**
Salt & pepper shakers, 3¼", Mirror & Rose, LG Wright, 1974-
    81, pr...**$20.00**
Shot glass, rings at base...**$4.00**
Tumble-up set, unmarked, 2-pc.................................**$175.00**
Vase, 10", Rachel, Anchor Hocking, 1940s..................**$40.00**

Russel Wright Designs

One of the country's foremost industrial designers, Russel Wright, was also responsible for several dinnerware lines, glassware, and aluminum that have become very collectible. American Modern, produced by the Steubenville Pottery Company (1939-1959) is his best known and most popular today. It had simple, sweeping lines that appealed to tastes of that period, and it was made in a variety of solid colors.

Iroquois China made his Casual line, and because it was so serviceable, it's relatively easy to find today. It will be marked with both Wright's signature and 'China by Iroquois.' (To price Brick Red and Aqua Casual, double our values; for Avocado Yellow, reduce them by half.)

Wright's aluminum ware is highly valued by today's collectors, even though it wasn't so well accepted in its day, due to the fact that it was so easily damaged.

If you'd like to learn more about the subject, we recommend *The Collector's Encyclopedia of Russel Wright Designs* by Ann Kerr.

American Modern

Bowl, divided vegetable; Cedar, Coral, Gray, Black Chutney
    or Seafoam..**$60.00**
Bowl, divided vegetable; Chartreuse **$55.00**
Bowl, vegetable; Cedar, Coral, Gray, Black Chutney or
    Seafoam **$17.00**
Bowl, vegetable; Chartreuse.......................................**$15.00**

Bowl, vegetable; 12", Cedar, Coral, Gray, Black Chutney
or Seafoam, w/lid $40.00
Bowl, vegetable; 12", Chartreuse, w/lid **$35.00**

Carafe, Canteloupe, Glacier Blue, Bean Brown or White, w/stopper **$240.00**
Carafe, Cedar, Coral, Gray, Black Chutney or Seafoam, w/stopper **$120.00**
Carafe, Chartreuse **$85.00**
Celery dish, Canteloupe, Glacier Blue, Bean Brown or White **$48.00**
Celery dish, Chartreuse **$22.00**
Chop plate, Cedar, Coral, Gray, Black Chutney or Seafoam **$25.00**
Chop plate, Chartreuse **$22.00**
Coffeepot, 8x8½", Cedar, Coral, Gray, Black Chutney or Seafoam **$80.00**
Coffeepot, 8x8½", Chartreuse **$70.00**
Creamer, Canteloupe, Glacier Blue, Bean Brown or White **$9.00**
Cup & saucer, Cedar, Coral, Gray, Black Chutney or Seafoam **$10.00**
Cup & saucer, Chartreuse **$9.00**
Gravy boat, 10½", Canteloupe, Glacier Blue, Bean Brown or White **$18.00**
Gravy boat, 10½", Chartreuse **$16.00**
Lug soup, Canteloupe, Glacier Blue, Bean Brown or White **$24.00**
Lug soup, Cedar, Coral, Gray, Black Chutney or Seafoam **$12.00**
Plate, 10", Chartreuse **$6.50**
Plate, 10", Glacier Blue, Bean Brown or White **$15.00**
Plate, 6¼", Cantelope, Glacier Blue, Bean Brown or White **$8.00**
Plate, 8", Cedar, Coral, Gray, Black Chutney or Seafoam..**$10.00**
Platter, 13¼", Cantelope, Glacier Blue, Bean Brown or White **$40.00**
Platter, 13¼", Cedar, Coral, Gray, Black Chutney or Seafoam **$20.00**
Salad fork & spoon, Cedar, Coral, Gray, Black Chutney or Seafoam **$170.00**
Salad fork & spoon, Chartreuse **$75.00**
Salt & pepper shakers, Cedar, Coral, Gray, Black Chutney or Seafoam, pr **$14.00**
Salt & pepper shakers, Chartreuse, pr **$12.00**
Sauce boat, 8¾", Canteloupe, Glacier Blue, Bean Brown or White **$36.00**
Sauce boat, 8¾", Chartreuse **$15.00**
Sugar bowl, Cedar, Coral, Gray, Black Chutney or Seafoam, w/lid **$12.00**
Sugar bowl, Chartreuse **$10.00**
Teapot, 6x10", Canteloupe, Glacier Blue, Bean Brown or white **$110.00**
Teapot, 6x10", Chartreuse **$50.00**

Casual

Bowl, cereal; 5" **$7.00**
Bowl, fruit; 5¾", restyled **$6.00**
Bowl, soup; 18-oz, restyled...................................**$10.00**
Bowl, vegetable; 8⅛" **$18.00**
Butter dish, half pound...**$50.00**

Casserole, 10", open **$20.00**
Casserole, 8", 4-qt **$50.00**

Coffeepot, original **$70.00**

Creamer & sugar bowl, stacking type **$20.00**
Creamer, restyled **$12.00**
Creamer, stacking type **$10.00**
Cup & saucer, restyled...**$10.00**
Gravy bowl, 5¼", 12-oz **$9.00**
Gravy stand, 7½" **$7.50**
Gumbo (flat soup), 21-oz **$20.00**
Plate, 10" **$8.00**
Plate, 13⅞" **$25.00**
Plate, 7½" **$6.00**
Platter, 14½", oval **$25.00**
Salt & pepper shakers, stacking, pr **$12.00**
Sugar bowl, 4", stacking **$10.00**
Teacup & saucer **$10.00**

Glassware

American Modern, bowl, dessert; Smoke..................**$30.00**
American Modern, chilling bowl **$100.00**

American Modern, cocktail, Chartreuse or Gray..........**$22.00**
American Modern, cordial...**$40.00**
American Modern, goblet, Chartreuse.........................**$15.00**
American Modern, goblet, Smoke..................................**$20.00**
American Modern, tumbler, 13-oz, Coral **$25.00**
American Modern, wine, Chartreuse **$17.00**
Eclipse, old fashioned..**$15.00**
Eclipse, shot glass...**$10.00**
Flair, tumbler, iced tea; 14-oz.......................................**$30.00**
Flair, tumbler, 11-oz...**$50.00**
Flair, tumbler, 6-oz...**$28.00**
Snow Glass, candle holders, pr **$150.00**
Snow Glass, tumbler, 10-oz...**$90.00**
Snow Glass, tumbler, 5-oz..**$90.00**
Snow Glass tumbler, 14-oz...**$90.00**

Highlight

Bowl, vegetable; White, Pepper, or Blueberry, oval ...**$40.00**
Cover for soup, Citron or Nutmeg................................**$16.00**
Cup, Citron or Nutmeg..**$14.00**
Mug, White, Pepper or Blueberry...................................**$35.00**
Plate, bread & butter; Citron or Nutmeg.......................**$8.00**
Platter, large or small, Citron or Nutmeg, oval, each...**$35.00**
Platter, large or small, White, Pepper, or Blueberry, oval,
      each **$40.00**
Salt & pepper shakers (either of two sizes), Citron or Nut-
      meg, pr **$30.00**
Sugar bowl, Citron or Nutmeg.......................................**$16.00**
Sugar bowl, White, Pepper or Blueberry **$20.00**

Knowles

Bowl, divided vegetable..**$48.00**
Bowl, 6¼"...**$7.00**
Plate, 10¾"..**$9.00**
Platter, 13", Grass...**$25.00**
Platter, 14¼"..**$17.50**
Salt & pepper shakers, Mayfair, pr................................**$20.00**
Teapot, Fontaine **$80.00**

Plastic

Flair, bowl, vegetable; oval, deep.................................**$12.00**
Flair, cup & saucer..**$9.00**
Flair, lug soup...**$10.00**
Flair, plate, salad...**$5.00**
Flair, tumbler..**$15.00**
Home Decorator, cup & saucer **$9.00**
Home Decorator, plate, dinner...**$5.00**
Home Decorator, platter...**$15.00**
Home Decorator, tumbler...**$15.00**
Ideal Ware, beverage set, 6-pc, in original carton **$195.00**
Meladur, bowl, cereal; 9-oz..**$8.00**
Meladur, bowl, soup; 12-oz...**$8.00**
Meladur, cup, 7-oz..**$7.00**
Meladur, plate, 6¼"..**$5.00**
Meladur, plate, 9"...**$8.00**

Meladur, plate, 9½", compartments...............................**$7.00**
Meladur, saucer..**$3.00**
Residential, bowl, vegetable; oval, shallow.............**$10.00**
Residential, creamer & sugar bowl, w/lid **$20.00**
Residential, lug soup...**$10.00**
Residential, plate, dinner **$5.00**

Spun Aluminum

Bain marie server...**$400.00**
Bowl..**$50.00**
Candelabra **$175.00**
Casserole, each...**$50.00**
Cheese board, from $35.00 up to **$50.00**
Cooking items of various types, each.........................**$75.00**
Flower ring..**$75.00**
Gravy boat..**$125.00**
Hot relish server...**$175.00**
Ice bucket...**$50.00**
Relish rosette...**$75.00**
Sandwich humidor..**$150.00**
Sherry pitcher..**$225.00**
Smoking stand..**$300.00**
Spaghetti set...**$325.00**
Tidbit tray...**$50.00**
Vase, 12"..**$65.00**
Vase or flowerpot, sm **$50.00**
Waste basket..**$100.00**

Sterling

Ashtray...**$60.00**
Bouillon, 7-oz...**$10.00**
Bowl, 5"..**$7.00**
Bowl, 7½"..**$12.00**
Creamer, 1-oz...**$8.00**
Creamer, 3-oz...**$10.00**
Cup, demitasse; 3½-oz...**$25.00**
Cup, 7-oz...**$10.00**
Pitcher, 2-qt..**$40.00**
Pitcher, 2-qt, restyled...**$45.00**
Plate, 10¼"...**$8.00**
Plate, 6¼"..**$4.00**
Plate, 7½"..**$5.00**
Platter, 10½", oval **$15.00**
Sauce boat, 9-oz..**$16.00**
Saucer, 6¼"..**$3.50**
Sugar bowl, 10-oz, w/lid **$14.00**
Teapot, 10-oz...**$45.00**

White Clover (for Harker)

Ashtray, 2-qt, clover decoration **$45.00**
Bowl, divided vegetable; clover decoration.................**$30.00**
Bowl, vegetable; 8¼", w/lid **$30.00**
Clock, General Electric **$50.00**
Creamer, clover decoration **$12.00**
Gravy boat, clover decoration...**$18.00**

Plate, barbecue; 11", color only $15.00
Plate, chop; 11", clover decoration $18.00
Plate, 10", clover decoration.........................$12.00
Plate, 9¼", clover decoration........................$10.00
Salt & pepper shakers (either of two sizes), pr...........$20.00
Sugar bowl, w/lid $16.00

Sabino

Ernest Sabino produced glassware in France as early as the 1920s. It was made various colors and was decidedly Art Deco in style. But it's the opalescent glass figurines designed in the sixties that are most familiar to collectors today. They're marked either in the mold or with an etched signature. Once you've see an example, though, you'll quickly learn to recognize Sabino glass simply by its unique appearance — it has an intense golden opalescence that radiates a strong bluish fire.

Sabino died in the seventies, but the business was continued by the family.

Bottle, scent; Frivolites, women & swans, 6¼", opalescent...$70.00
Bowl, shell w/star center, large $195.00
Box, powder; Petalia, medium......................$95.00
Figurine, bird, perched.................................$58.00
Figurine, butterfly, wings open, small $32.00
Figurine, chick, jumping...............................$55.00
Figurine, dove, head up, small $24.00
Figurine, fish, 2x2"......................................$23.00
Figurine, mockingbird, large $90.00

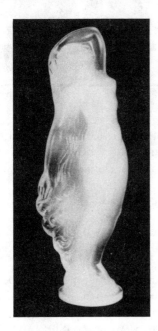

Figurine, nude w/long hair, 6¾", embossed & incised marks..$195.00
Figurine, Venus de Milo, large $50.00
Knife rest, bee form or fish form $25.00
Tray, shell, small $35.00

Vase, Colombes, opalescent.......................$500.00
Vase, Ovals & Pearls.................................$235.00

Salem China

This company operated in Salem, Ohio, from 1920 until the fifties, producing various lines of dinnerware, most of it marked with some form of the company name and various logos. The pattern name was often included in the mark. Styles naturally changed from decade to decade and ranged from very formal lines heavily encrusted with gold to very simple geometric shapes glazed in solid colors.

For more information, we recommend *The Collector's Encyclopedia of American Dinnerware* by Jo Cunningham.

Basket, dessert plate, 8", octagon shape.........................$4.00
Basket, saucer, 6", w/cup ring, octagon shape $3.00
Bluebird, plate, 6", round...............................$6.00
Colonial, ash tray w/Farberware frame $15.00
Goldtrim, butter pat $5.00
June, plate, 9", Briar Rose shape...................$4.00
Maple Leaf, plate, 9" $3.00

Sailing, plate, on Tricorne shape...........................$7.00
Yellowridge, plate, 9", octagon shape $4.00

Salt Shakers

Probably the most common type of souvenir shop merchandise from the twenties through the sixties, salt and pepper shaker sets can be spotted at any antique mall or flea market today by the dozens. Most were made in Japan and imported by various companies, though American manufacturers made their fair share as well. There is a states series called 'America,' made in the U.S. by Parkcraft. Each set is made up of one shaker in the shape of a state with the other modeled as an object that represents it — an ear of corn for Iowa or a cactus for Arizona, for instance.

'Miniature shakers' are hard to find and their prices have risen faster than any others. They were made by Arcadia Ceramics (probably an American company). They're under 1½" tall, some so small they had no space to accommodate a cork. Instead they came with instructions to 'use

Scotch tape to cover the hole.'

Advertising sets and premiums are always good, since they appeal to a cross section of collectors. If you have a chance to buy them on the primary market, do so. The F&F Mold & Die Works of Dayton, Ohio, made plastic shakers (as well as other kitchenware items) with painted details for such companies as Quaker Oats, Kools Cigarettes, and Ken-L Ration Pet Food. You'll find Aunt Jemima and Uncle Mose, Willie and Millie Penguin, and Fido and Fifi with the F&F mark. The Black couples (there are two sizes) will range in value from $40.00 to $50.00, the others are about $12.00 per pair. F&F also made Luzianne Mammy shakers (so marked) for the tea company — they're worth about $135.00 — and a set representing the Campbell Kids that usually goes for about $45.00.

There are several good books on the market. We recommend *Salt and Pepper Shakers, Identification and Values, Vols I, II, and III,* by Helene Guarnaccia; and *The Collector's Encyclopedia of Salt and Pepper Shakers, Figural and Novelty, First and Second Series,* by Melva Davern.

Advertising

Amoco gas pumps, plastic, one yellow & one green w/logoed labels, ca 1940s-50s, pr............**$25.00**
Ball Mason jars, miniature, glass, pr............**$28.00**
Borden's Elsie & Elmer, ceramic, half-length figurals w/'Elmer' & 'Elsie' lettered at bottom, 1940, pr **$70.00**

Bud Man, ceramic, Busch Gardens, 1970s, pr.......$50.00
Campbell Kids, plastic, yellow-haired kids in white chef's hats, F&F plastics imprinted on bottom, pr...........**$40.00**
Chicken of the Sea, fish figurals, ceramic, one light blue & one yellow, pr........................**$18.00**
Dairy Queen ice cream cones, ceramic, one vanilla curly top & one chocolate-dipped curly top, pr **$10.00**
Falstaff Beer bottles, miniature, amber glass, pr..........**$30.00**
Fido & Fifi for Ken-L Ration Pet Food, F&F plastic, yellow dog & black cat sitting on back legs, 1950s, pr **$12.00**
Firestone tires, ceramic, black around tires' edges, white walls w/'Firestone,' center holes, pr......................**$15.00**
General Electric coil-top refrigerators, milk glass, GE labels on front, ca late 1920s, pr........................**$40.00**

Handy Flame, blue gas flame forms w/animated faces, ceramic, 1940s promotion for a gas company, pr.**$22.00**
Hershey Kisses, ceramic, brown w/embossed 'S' & 'P,' pr..................................**$8.00**
Luzianne Mammies, F&F plastic, figures in yellow tops & green skirts, holding trays w/teapots & cups of tea, pr **$135.00**
Mr Peanut (for Planters), plastic, gold peanut figures in black top hats, black arms & pants legs, round bases, pr..................................**$15.00**
Mr Peanut (for Planters), plastic, large gold half-length figures w/handles, pr................................**$15.00**
Pepsi bottles, 'full' or clear, glass, pr **$5.00**
Phillips 66 gas pumps, plastic, red w/black bases, reads '13 gallons $3.54,' pr..........................**$18.00**
Pillsbury's Poppin' & Poppie Fresh, ceramic, white figures w/blue details, 1974, pr........................**$18.00**
Sealtest dairy bottles, miniature, clear glass w/red & white labels, pr..................................**$18.00**

Squirt, plastic, green w/yellow tops, pr................$10.00
Willie & Millie Penguin for Kool cigarettes, F&F plastic, Millie has red beads, bow on head, ca early 1940s, pr **$12.00**

Amimals, Birds, and Fish

Bear hanger, ceramic, two playful brown bears hang from tree trunk w/three acorns stacked around base, Japan..................................**$7.00**
Bear nester, ceramic, cute 2-tone brown bear holding smiling yellow beehive, Japan........................**$10.00**
Bears, American Pottery, cute, sitting upright, wearing jackets & pants, white w/blue bow ties & red ears, pr **$10.00**
Bears, ceramic, natural looking, appear to be dancing, dark brown, glossy, Japan, pr........................**$10.00**
Bears, chalkware, whimsical, black, attacking silver beehives w/yellow & black bee on hives, pr **$9.00**

Birds, ceramic, Sherlock & Dr Watson character birds, one w/red hat & black pipe, one w/black hat & coat, Japan, 50s, pr **$8.00**

Birds, ceramic, stylized, dark pink birds w/tails wrapped around T-shaped tree trunk w/white flowers & grassy base, pr..**$10.00**

Birds, ceramic, two in a brown nest, red on tops of heads, black under yellow beaks, Japan, pr....................**$10.00**

Cat hugger, ceramic, yellow cat w/big round blue eyes hugs white & brown trash can, Japan, pr........................**$7.00**

Cat's heads, ceramic, in metal frame w/napkin holder in center, marked Holt Howard, 1950s, pr.....$14.00

Cats, ceramic, whimsical Siamese, yellow w/brown tails, paws, & noses, Japan, pr..**$6.00**

Cats, red clay, stylized, upright seated position, glossy black w/gold collars & red ears, Japan, pr......................**$10.00**

Cats, wood, stylized, tall cone shapes w/gold 'S' & 'P,' jeweled eyes & nose w/whiskers, pr............................**$7.00**

Chickens, ceramic, sitting hen & standing rooster w/white & black feathers, red breasts & tops, Japan, pre-1960, pr..**$10.00**

Chickens, ceramic, 1-pc, black w/red & gold details, chickens' necks are crisscrossed, Japan **$12.00**

Chickens, chalkware, natural looking, one crowing & one nesting, reddish-brown w/red tops & yellow beaks, pr...**$8.00**

Chickens, red clay, stylized hens, black w/red tops & gold beaks, glossy, pr..**$5.00**

Chickens in a basket, ceramic, yellow, nesting in blue baskets connected by a center handle, Occupied Japan, pr **$18.00**

Chimps, ceramic, lovable looking, sitting w/legs crossed, hands on tummies, 2-tone brown (airbrushed), Japan, pr...**$8.00**

Chipmunks, ceramic, whimsical fireman & doctor on call, light brown & white fireman, gray doctor w/black bag, pr...**$10.00**

Cow carrier, ceramic, black & white cow carrying white milk cans lettered 'P' & 'S,' Japan, ca 1940s-early 50s..**$8.00**

Cow carrier, ceramic, comical purple cow sitting w/calf, salt & pepper hanging from horns, Japan, ca 1940s-early 50s..**$12.00**

Cow nester, ceramic, happy green cow sitting on haunches is holding smiling white milk can, pr **$10.00**

Cows, ceramic, naturalistic, white w/rusty brown spots, marked PY Japan, pr............................$20.00

Cows, ceramic, stylized, white w/blue floral design on sides & top of heads, Japan, pr..**$8.00**

Dachshund, ceramic, 1-pc, white & black dachshund wearing white & yellow plaid shirt & lime-green pants, Japan...**$15.00**

Dachshund, red clay, animated style, split in half, brown w/ball-shaped nose, blue & black eyes, glossy, Japan **$10.00**

Dachshunds, ceramic, realistic style, warm brown, glossy, one looking ahead, one looking upward, Japan, pr...**$10.00**

Deer, ceramic, stylized w/the 'Bambi' look, one sitting on haunches & one lying down, brown (airbrushed), Japan, pr...**$9.00**

Dog & slipper, ceramic, whimsical puppy, 2-tone brown w/big black eyes, brown slipper, Japan, pre-1960, pr **$10.00**

Dog nester, ceramic, happy white dog w/blue spots & yellow collar sits on plaid pillow, separates at neck, Japan...**$15.00**

Dogs, ceramic, comic, honey-colored, one sits w/spoon & bone, one balances cup & saucer on nose, Japan, pr **$40.00**

Dogs, ceramic, stylized, white w/black spots & red bows around necks, Japan, pre-1960, pr........................**$6.00**

Donkey carrier, ceramic, black & white donkey pulling Conestoga wagon which is salt, pepper, & mustard, Japan, 1950s..**$15.00**

Donkeys, ceramic, comical, sitting upright w/happy expressions, both brown, one in yellow hat & one in gray hat, pr...**$10.00**

Donkeys, wood, cutout, wood stain w/incised eyes & marks around ears, mouth, neck, & legs, pr **$5.00**

Ducks, ceramic, natural looking w/white undersides, standing on round grassy base, Occupied Japan, pr.....**$12.00**

Ducks, Czech ceramic, whimsical white ducks w/orange beaks, black details, on round bases, pr.................**$7.00**

Elephants, ceramic, natural looking in antique finish, one standing w/feet apart, one rearing back, Japan, pr...**$10.00**

Elephants, ceramic, whimsical looking, sitting w/trunks held high in the air, Japan, pr...**$8.00**

Fish, ceramic, animated looking, light blue w/big round eyes closed & mouths open, large fin on top, pr ...**$8.00**

Fish, silverplated cast metal, upright, w/mouths open, painted in realistic metallic tones, pr.....................**$15.00**

Flamingos, ceramic, stately looking, standing straight on grassy bases, Japan, pr **$18.00**

Foxes, ceramic, natural looking, reddish-brown w/white chest & dark brown legs, glossy, Japan, pr...........**$10.00**

Giraffes, ceramic, whimsical looking, necks entwined, yellow w/black spots & streaks down backs, Japan, pr **$12.00**

Goats, ceramic, natural looking, posed in wide stance, white w/black & brown spots, Japan, pr.........................**$12.00**

Gorillas, ceramic, fearsome looking, sitting, warm brown w/dark brown faces, Japan, pr...........................**$8.00**

Hippos, ceramic, realistic looking, 2-tone gray w/red mouths & nostrils, Japan, pr..............................**$10.00**

Horses, ceramic, in full stride, light honey color w/white manes, tails & socks, Japan, pr **$12.00**

Hound dogs, porcelain, natural looking, white w/brown & black markings, one standing & one sitting, Japan, pre-1960, pr...**$10.00**

Kittens, ceramic, playful tiger kittens w/red bows around their necks, Japan, pr...**$8.00**

Lambs, American Pottery, eyes closed, sitting upright, wearing shirts & pants, white w/blue, black, & red details, pr...**$10.00**

Lambs, chalkware, cute little white lambs w/embossed coats, black eyes, pr...**$9.00**

Lobsters, ceramic, standing upright on tails, orange-red w/black eyes, pr **$12.00**

Mice, ceramic, kissing couple, gray w/black tails, he in glasses, she w/white bow on top of head, Japan, 1950s, pr...**$7.00**

Mice, ceramic, modeled w/very large ears, pr $12.00

Mice, porcelain, gray, bursting through ears of yellow corn w/green husks, Japan, pr **$10.00**

Monkey & palm tree, ceramic, half-length brown & white monkey swinging from palm tree w/dark brown base, Japan, pr..**$15.00**

Monkey nester, ceramic, seated brown & tan monkey has arms wrapped around two bunches of bananas, Japan **$10.00**

Mouse nester, ceramic, whimsical, yellow w/big round eyes, sitting up & holding two pieces of green cheese, Japan..**$10.00**

Owls, chalkware, stylized, short embossed bodies w/large red & black decorated eyes, red beak, black toes, pr..**$8.00**

Owls, wood, white w/gold & red accents on red base, one lettered 'Salty', one lettered 'Peppy', pr.................**$5.00**

Pandas, ceramic, large, stylized, glossy black & white, Japan, pr...**$8.00**

Pelicans, ceramic, stylized, light blue w/black details, Occupied Japan, pr...**$12.00**

Pelicans, chalkware, stylized bust length, one in yellow & one in orange, both w/black eyes, pr **$8.00**

Penguins, ceramic, stylized urn-shaped bodies, white w/black heads & feathers, tan beaks & eyes, pr.....**$8.00**

Pigs, American Pottery, whimsical, sitting upright, dressed in pants & shirts w/red & blue details, pr **$10.00**

Pigs, ceramic, natural looking, black w/white, front shoulders & legs, Japan, pre-1960, pr...........................**$12.00**

Pigs, ceramic, sitting, wearing chefs' hats, one holds plate & one holds fork, white w/blue & pink details, pr **$8.00**

Pigs, silverplated cast metal, natural looking, standing on hind legs on round bases, pr **$18.00**

Pigs, wood, cutout, in wood stain w/incised eyes & marks around legs & ears, pr **$5.00**

Poodle carrier, ceramic, black poodle in wide stance, salt & pepper shakers carried on sides, Japan, 1940s-early 50s..**$10.00**

Poodles, bone china, natural looking, heads cocked, white w/red bows & eyes, paws, & nose, pr **$9.00**

Rabbits, porcelain, cross-eyed, sitting w/one ear up & one ear down, gold lustre, 1940s, pr...........................**$9.00**

Raccoons, ceramic, natural looking, brown & tan, one sitting & one standing, Japan, pr.....................................**$10.00**

Redbirds, ceramic, natural looking, perched on 3-limbed tree branch w/lightly shaded leaves, Japan, pr.....**$15.00**

Scottie dogs, ceramic, stylized, sitting upright, cream w/brown & black details, Occupied Japan, pr......**$12.00**

Scottie dogs, ceramic, 1-pc, two cute Scotty dogs joined at the side & ear, one black & white, one gray & white..**$12.00**

Sharks, ceramic, natural looking, resting on bottom fins, dark brown, honey, & tan, Japan, pr....................**$10.00**

Siamese cats, bone china, stylized, sitting upright, white w/brown details, pr **$15.00**

Squirrel hugger, ceramic, cute reddish-brown squirrel sits upright & hugs large brown & cream-colored acorn, Japan, pr...**$10.00**

Squirrels, ceramic, happy looking, upright, brown & white (airbrushed) w/large green acorns, Japan, pr **$8.00**

Squirrels, chalkware, natural looking, reddish-brown, hugging tree trunks w/green grassy base, pr **$9.00**

Swans, bone china, natural looking, white w/blue & white embossed flowers on wings, black bills, pr **$15.00**

Tigers, ceramic, natural looking, one prancing & one lying down, glossy, Japan, pr..................................**$18.00**

Turkeys, ceramic, gray & blue shaded w/dark pink waddles, standing on round bases, Japan, pr.....................**$12.00**

Walruses, ceramic, dapper looking, gold top hats & white shirts, black tuxedos & white tusks, pr.................**$12.00**

Zebras, ceramic, stylized, one sitting upright w/front legs in the air, one standing, glossy, Japan, pr **$10.00**

Fruit, Vegetables, and Other Food

Apples, ceramic, red shading to yellow, each w/green leaf, Occupied Japan, pr..**$12.00**

Apples, porcelain, light red shading to white w/a touch of yellow, white leaves w/green details, Japan, pr **$7.00**

Artichoke & cauliflower, porcelain, upright, green-shaded artichoke, white cauliflower head w/green leafy base, pr..**$6.00**

Asparagus, porcelain, white w/purple tops standing upright in bundles, pr..**$6.00**

Baked potatoes, ceramic, sliced open w/pats of butter melting on top, 1940s-50s, Japan, pr **$7.00**

Banana hanger, ceramic, two banana stalks hang from T-shaped tree on brown base w/bunch of bananas resting on top, Japan...**$10.00**

Bananas, ceramic, resting on sides, warm yellow w/brown details, 1940s-50s, Japan, pr **$5.00**

Cabbage, porcelain, upright w/bottom leaves flared out around heads, medium green, pr.............................**$7.00**

Chili peppers, ceramic, one in green & one in red, 1940s-50s, Japan, pr...**$5.00**

Corn, ceramic, light brown tassels & green husks, Occupied Japan, pr...**$12.00**

Corn, ceramic, slanted ears as heads w/bodies, sitting & wearing blue shirts & brown pants, pr..................**$15.00**

Corn, porcelain, standing upright, yellow w/green husks, pr..**$6.00**

Cucumbers, ceramic, 1-pc, one cucumber lying across the other, dark green w/shades of yellow, Japan **$8.00**

Cucumbers, porcelain, green w/yellow details, pr........**$6.00**

Cupcakes, ceramic, white pleated cups w/chocolate & yellow icing, 1040s-50s, Japan, pr.................................**$7.00**

Deviled eggs, ceramic, white w/yellow centers piled high, 1940s-50s, Japan, pr...**$6.00**

Egg figurals, ceramic, egg couple on round bases, she w/bow on top of head & he wearing top hat, 1940s-50s, Japan...**$8.00**

French bread, ceramic, browned tops w/white bottoms, 1940s-50s, Japan, pr...**$7.00**

Fruit forms, ceramic, marked Japan, pr, from $6.00 to...$12.00

Grapes, porcelain, rounded bunches of purple grapes w/green leaves & brown stems, Japan, pr **$6.00**

Grapes, porcelain, two bunches of purple grapes, upright on green grape leaf, Japan, 3-pc set.......................**$8.00**

Green peppers, porcelain, upright, dark green, pr........**$5.00**

Ice cream cones, glass w/metal tops, in metal stand, pr...$10.00

Hamburger & hot dog, ceramic, hot dog w/mustard, 1940s-50s, Japan, pr...**$8.00**

Mushrooms, porcelain, off-white to light brown w/smaller mushrooms growing out of stems, pr.....................**$7.00**

Onions, wood, 'Peppery' & 'Salty' lettered above painted faces, one w/black topknot & one w/red, pr..........**$4.00**

Oranges, porcelain, upright, on green bases, pr **$10.00**

Peanuts, ceramic, in-the-shell peanut couple w/surprised looks, she in green hat, he in black hat & glasses, pr..**$15.00**

Pears, porcelain, upright, yellow w/red blush & green leaves, Japan, pr...**$7.00**

Peas, ceramic, 1-pc, two pods full of peas side by side, Japan...**$8.00**

Pineapples, ceramic, pineapples as cocked heads w/bodies in sitting position, wearing red bow ties, pr **$15.00**

Pineapples, porcelain, yellow w/green tops & bottoms, sitting on large green leaf (tray), Japan, 3-pc set........**$8.00**

Potatoes, porcelain, light reddish-brown, pr **$5.00**

Radishes, ceramic, perky faces, sitting & wearing blue jackets & brown pants, pr...**$15.00**

Radishes, porcelain, red w/short green tops, pr **$6.00**

Red peppers, ceramic, glossy, 1940s-50s, Japan, pr.......**$5.00**

Red peppers, ceramic, resting on sides, Occupied Japan, pr **$12.00**

Strawberries on the vine, porcelain, red w/brownish-green leaves, Japan, pr...**$8.00**

Tomatoes, ceramic, two red tomatoes in green double basket (holder) w/center handle, Occupied Japan, 3-pc set...**$15.00**

Tomatoes, porcelain, upright, red w/dark green leaves around bottom, pr.....................................$6.00

Watermelons, porcelain, oblong w/green & yellow stripes, Japan, pr $7.00

Household Items

Binoculars & case, ceramic, gold trim, pr.............$15.00

Clocks, ceramic, round white faces w/facial features, yellow legs, red numbers, black ringers on top, Japan, pr .$8.00

Coffeepots, ceramic, urn shapes on round bases, gold handles & blue decoration, Occupied Japan, pr.........$25.00

Coffeepots, red clay, cylindrical, black w/'Salt' & 'Pepper' surrounded by floral decoration, 1940s-50s, Japan, pr..$10.00

Faucets, ceramic, white w/colored buttons, pr $10.00

Frying pans, plastic, aluminum-looking, black handles & knobs, 1950s, pr..$6.00

Hand sweepers, metal, one white w/red decoration & one black w/gold decoration, Japan, pr......................$10.00

Hat & coat stand, plastic, yellow hat w/black band & black derby on green pole w/black footed base, 1950s......$10.00

Irons, metal, one black & one white, resting upright, decoration on handles, Japan, pr...................................$8.00

Lamps, metal, black urn shapes w/silver-looking shades & bases, Occupied Japan, pr...................................$15.00

Mixer, plastic, white & black mixer on base w/mixing bowl under beaters, 1950s.................................$15.00

Phonographs, ceramic, pink tops shading into white on brown bases, 1940s-50s, Japan, pr.........................$7.00

Potbellied stoves, ceramic, white w/light brown footed bases, gold trim & floral decoration, 1940s-50s, Japan, pr..$6.00

Potbellied stoves, metal, one white & one black, both w/gold details, pr...$8.00

Refrigerator & stove, ceramic, both white w/red handles, knobs, & hinges, 1940s-50s, Japan, pr...................$10.00

Rocker & fireplace, ceramic, black rocker, silver pot hanging from yellow fireplace, 'God Bless Our Home' on mantle, pr..$7.00

Rocking chairs, metal, bow-backed, one white & one black w/floral decoration, pr....................................$10.00

Rolling pins, wood, w/lettering, pr.......................$5.00

Sewing machines, ceramic, white w/floral decoration & gold trim, 1940s-50s, Japan, pr $7.00

Spinning wheels, ceramic, brown wheels w/blue centers on white 3-legged bases, flowers on sides, 1940s-50s, Japan, pr..$6.00

Teakettles, porcelain, white w/black handles, berries & green leaves on sides, 1940s-50s, Japan, pr $8.00

Telephones, ceramic, early desk-tops w/large rotary disks, one red-orange & one lime green, Japan, pr........$12.00

Telephones, metal, early wall type, one white & one black, Japan, pr..$10.00

Umbrella stand, plastic, two red umbrellas hang from hooks w/pr of black boots & shoes on round red base, 1950s, pr..$12.00

Washing machines, metal, early spin-dry style on three legs, white w/blue & black details, pr $18.00

Washing machines, plastic, 3-footed wringer style, 1950s, pr..$15.00

Miniatures

Baby shoes & bottle, ceramic, light blue shoes & white bottle w/gold nipple, pr................................$30.00

Bee & flower, ceramic, yellow bee w/gold stripes, white flower w/green stem & leaves & gold details, pr .$30.00

Bowling ball & pin, ceramic, black ball & white pin w/red top & gold band around neck of pin, pr..............$30.00

Bride's cookbooks, ceramic, pr $20.00

Camera & photo album, ceramic, camera in white w/brown antiquing, album in black & white edged in gold, pr...**$35.00**

Chair & grandfather clock, ceramic, white chair w/dark brown legs, light brown clock w/white face & gold pendulum, pr...**$35.00**

Coat rack & umbrella stand, ceramic, coat rack w/hat, coat & red scarf, yellow umbrella stand w/gold trim, pr...**$40.00**

Coffeepot & coffee grinder, ceramic, gray graniteware-type coffeepot & honey-colored grinder w/gold-toned top, pr...**$25.00**

Donkey & grape cart, ceramic, gray donkey sitting upright w/green cart full of purple grapes, pr...................**$35.00**

Forge & anvil, ceramic, silver-toned anvil on tree stump & dark gray forge w/burning coals, pr.....................**$40.00**

Genie & lamp, ceramic, cream-colored genie on flying carpet & purple lamp, pr...**$40.00**

Ice cream soda & canister of straws, ceramic, white soda sits in silver base, silver canister w/yellow straws, pr.**$40.00**

Lighthouse & sailboat, white lighthouse w/brown wash & white sailboat w/gold trim, pr.............................**$35.00**

Loaf of bread & dish of butter, ceramic, silver knife slicing through loaf of bread, yellow butter on silver dish, pr...**$30.00**

Office desk & chair, ceramic, light honey-colored desk w/drawers down one side & chair on pedestal legs, pr...**$40.00**

Picnic basket & beverage cooler, ceramic, light yellow picnic basket & cobalt blue cooler w/silver lid & spigot, pr...**$40.00**

Pie a la mode & cup of coffee, ceramic, white cup & saucer w/gold spoon, brown & white pie on white plate, pr...**$25.00**

Rainbow & pot of gold, ceramic, brown pot w/pale yellow, white, & pink rainbow, pr.......................................**$35.00**

Ring & marriage license, ceramic, gold ring in black & white box, license in white w/black print, pr.................**$30.00**

Roaster & turkey on platter, ceramic, gray graniteware roaster & browned turkey on silver platter, pr.....**$35.00**

Rocking horse & drum, ceramic, light blue w/gold mane, saddle, tail, & hooves, blue & gold drum, pr........**$35.00**

Snake charmer, ceramic, cream-colored figure blowing gold-toned horn & snake in honey-colored round basket w/lid, pr...**$40.00**

Stagecoach & saloon, ceramic, brown stagecoach & white saloon w/black shingled roof, pr...........................**$35.00**

Stove & icebox, ceramic, black cookstove on legs w/gold details, light brown icebox w/gold details, pr......**$40.00**

Train engine & coal car, ceramic, light brown w/gold details & black coal, pr..**$30.00**

Trash can & mailbox, ceramic, silver-toned mailbox on light brown base & silver-tone trash can w/lid, pr.......**$30.00**

Waffle iron & stack of waffles on plate w/knife & fork, ceramic, silver waffle iron w/black handle & lid up, pr...**$35.00**

Water pump & bucket, ceramic, brown 3-legged pump & green wood-look bucket, pr.............................**$35.00**

Whisk broom & dustpan, ceramic, pale yellow broom & lime green dustpan, pr...**$30.00**

People

Babies, ceramic, Kewpie-like seated nude figures, 1940s-50s, Japan, pr...**$12.00**

Boxers, ceramic, fighters in action, one in black shorts, one in yellow, both w/gray gloves, 1940s-50s, Japan, pr...**$15.00**

Boy & girl, ceramic, Hummel-type figures seated on grassy bases, he w/violin & she w/basket, 1940s-50s, Japan, pr...**$10.00**

Chefs, porcelain, bust-length, mustaches, white hats & collars, black ties, one marked 'Salt,' one marked 'Pepper,' pr...**$8.00**

Clown & drum, ceramic, clown in white w/red dots & green hat & collar frolics on brown drum, Japan, pr......**$28.00**

Clown acrobats, ceramic, feet in the air, orange suits, blue hats, black shoes, 1940s-50s, Japan, pr.................**$25.00**

Clown teapots, ceramic, 3-footed pots w/embossed smiling hobo faces, red noses, black spout & bail handles, Japan, pr...**$25.00**

Clowns, metal, standing on round bases, one black w/red & gold details, one white w/red & green details, Japan, pr...**$22.00**

Clowns, porcelain, boy & girl in white w/cone-shaped hats, red & blue details, 1940s-50s, Japan, pr...............**$15.00**

Couple, ceramic, turn-abouts, young couple on reverse, pr..**$22.00**

Cowboy & cowgirl, ceramic, boy w/red tie in black hat & pants, girl w/blue tie in red hat & pants, 1940s-50s, Japan, pr...**$8.00**

Dutch kissing couple, ceramic, red, white & blue clothes, he holds a boat & she holds flowers (behind their backs), pr...**$10.00**

Genies, ceramic, seated, white turbans, gold jackets, oversized white balloon pants, & black shoes, Japan, pr **$12.00**

Indian beating drums, ceramic, Indian in full headdress behind two drums on oval base, 3-pc set.............**$20.00**

Indian boy & girl, ceramic, he in buckskins & full headdress, holding tomahawk, she in buckskin pants & red top, pr..**$15.00**

Indian chief & brave, ceramic, natural looking, each stands on base, brave in blue, chief in yellow, hand painted, pr..**$20.00**

Indian chief & brave, dark-skinned busts on round pedestals w/orange, blue, green, & orange details, pr........**$12.00**

Indian couple, ceramic, comical, dark skin & hair, she in green dress, he w/potbelly, white pants, & eye patch, pr..**$18.00**

Indian couple in canoe, ceramic, both in yellow, he in full headdress & she holding baby, 3-pc set **$20.00**

Mr & Mrs Snowman, ceramic, she in yellow hat & scarf w/black muff, he in black top hat & yellow scarf waving, pr **$12.00**

Oriental boy & pagoda in boat, ceramic $12.00

Old Salty & Cap'n Pepper, ceramic, 'Salty' in yellow slicker, 'Cap'n' in black & white w/pipe, hand painted, matt, pr **$10.00**

Oriental boy & girl, ceramic, white & light blue Oriental attire, he holds basket & she holds fan, Japan, pr..**$7.00**

Oriental couple, ceramic, seated, both in red, black, & gold, she is reading & he is playing an instrument, pr..**$10.00**

Praying boy & girl, ceramic, both on knees, boy in blue, girl in dark pink, both w/yellow hair, 1940s-50s, Japan, pr...**$10.00**

Santa & Christmas tree, ceramic, green tree w/red & yellow decorations, smiling Santa w/hands crossed, pr...**$10.00**

Santa & Mrs Claus, ceramic, waving & seated in white rocking chairs w/gold trim, pr......................................**$18.00**

Scottish couple, ceramic, realistic looking, Scottish attire, she holds a purse & he plays the bagpipes, pr **$10.00**

Sled & snowman, ceramic, red sled, snowman w/black hat & features, yellow & black broom, pr $20.00

Wedding couple kissing, ceramic, she in white wedding dress & he in black jacket & black & white striped pants, pr...**$12.00**

Hedi Schoop

One of the most successful California ceramic studios was founded in Hollywood by Hedi Schoop, who had been educated in the arts in Berlin and Germany. She had studied not only painting but sculpture, architecture, and fashion design as well. Fleeing Nazi Germany with her husband, the famous composer Frederick Holander, Hedi settled in California in 1933 and only a few years later became involved in producing a line of novelty giftware items so popular that it was soon widely copied by other California companies. She designed many animated human figures, some in matched pairs, some that doubled as flower containers. All were hand painted and many were decorated with applied ribbons, sgraffito work, and gold trim. To a lesser extent, she modeled animal figures as well. Until fire leveled the plant in 1958, the business was very productive. Nearly everything she made was marked.

If you'd like to learn more about her work, we recommend *The Collector's Encyclopedia of California Pottery* by Jack Chipman.

Bowl, 13" dia, lady's figure at side, bowl formed from her skirt, #418 ....**$65.00**

Candle holder, 13½", mermaid w/raised arms holds two shell holders, ca 1950, stamped mark **$150.00**

Cookie jar, Queen, rare..**$175.00**

Figurine, Chinese male & female heads, high-gloss glaze, 1950s, pr **$65.00**

Figurine, Dutch boy & girl, 10½", pr $75.00

Figurine, girls dancing, 11", 12", rose to charcoal dresses w/black hand-painted lace, applied ribbons in their hair, pr..................................$90.00

Figurine, 12½", clown playing cello, overglaze platinum trim, ca 1943, stamped mark $65.00

Figurine, 13", Josephine, girl in sarong holds bowl, high-gloss glaze w/gold trim, ca 1943, stamped mark..$55.00

Figurine, 14", Siamese lady dancer, tinted bisque w/high-gloss glaze & overglaze gold trim, 1947, stamped mark..$55.00

Flower holder, 12", peasant woman figural $35.00

Lamp base, 11½", Colbert (modeled after Claudette Colbert), holds twin basket pots, ca 1940, underglaze painted mark..$45.00

Tray, King of Diamonds, multicolored incised suit card design, in-mold mark...$35.00

Vase, 10", fan form w/gold trim...................................$25.00

Vase, 12", crowing rooster figural, tinted clay body w/transparent high-gloss glaze & gold trim, ca 1949.......$40.00

Scottie Dog Collectibles

Collectors of Scottie dog memorabilia have banded together to form a club called Wee Scots, who hold regional and national shows each year. There's also a quarterly newsletter called the *Scottie Sampler* that includes historical data, current market prices, photographs, ads, and feature articles. They're interested in anything showing Scottie dogs — advertising items, magazine covers, post cards, glassware, ceramic figures, and household items.

Bank, 3½x4½", puppies in basket, marked Vanio Inc.**$50.00**

Book, 'Dogs by Zito,' illustrated, dated 1937, EX........**$30.00**

Bookends, 6½", figurals, bronze, marked McClelland Barclay, pr..**$75.00**

Christmas ornament, 3", begging Scottie on hand-painted glass, marked Germany **$45.00**

Door knocker, 4x2", dog figural, brass........................**$15.00**

Doorstop, 6x8¾", pair of white Scotties on black base, EX...$100.00

Doorstop, 8x8", sitting on his haunches, EX (illustrated)..$175.00

Doorstop, 9x11", #302, standing, Hubley Mfg **$160.00**

Figurine, #K10, begging, Royal Doulton **$85.00**

Hooked rug, 21x32", Scottie w/red bow & holly leaves.**$200.00**

Inkwell, 3", head figural w/glass eyes & hinged lid, glass **$150.00**

Mold, chocolate; #28842, standing full-body shape, Anton Reiche...**$150.00**

Pin-back button, lithographed tin w/Scottie & 'Ford V-8'..**$25.00**

Planter, 4x3½", marked Niloak....................................**$15.00**

Plate, 10", Scottie in mountainous background, marked Royal Doulton **$155.00**

Powder jar, 6", Scottie on lid, more embossed around base, blue, Akro Agate **$65.00**

Print, 'Check & Double Check,' by Gracy Drayton, ca 1930 ....**$30.00**

Tea set, child's, decal of girl & dog on ceramic, 13-piece set in original box..**$25.00**

Wall pocket, 7", Scottie head form, marked Japan **$25.00**

Wind-up toy, 4½", Tippy, marked US Zone Germany, Schuco **$100.00**

Sebastians

These tiny figures were first made in 1938 by Preston W. Baston and sold through gift stores, primarily in the New England area. When he retired in 1976, the Lance Corporation chose one hundred designs which they continued to produce under Baston's supervision. Since then, the discontinued figures have become very collectible.

Baston died in 1984, but his son, P.W. Baston, Jr., continues the tradition.

The figures are marked with an imprinted signature and a paper label. Early labels (before 1977) were green and silver foil shaped like an artist's palette; these are referred to as 'Marblehead' labels (Marblehead, Massachusetts, being the location of the factory), and figures that carry one of these are becoming hard to find and are highly valued by collectors.

Abe Lincoln, Marblehead label $85.00
Betsy Ross $85.00
Chiquita Banana..$375.00
Cow Hand, Marblehead label......................................$80.00
Evangeline...$125.00

George & Martha Washington, Marblehead label, 1939, pr $150.00
Giraffe, Jell-O, 1955 ....$300.00
Girl on Diving Board...$400.00
Great Stone Face, 1951...$700.00
Henry Hudson, 1959...$130.00
Indian Warrior...$145.00
Jean LaFitte...$90.00
Joan of Arc, 1952..$320.00
John Adams, pewter $75.00
Old Salt, Marblehead label $85.00
Oliver Twist & the Beadle, 1949 ....$45.00
Our Lady of Good Voyage...$250.00
Patrick Henry $125.00
Pocahontas...$125.00
Princess Elizabeth $235.00

Priscilla Fortescue, w/base, 1939..............................$275.00
Romeo & Juliet, 1948..$385.00
Sam Houston..$100.00
Santa, Jell-O, 1955..$500.00
Town Crier, Marblehead label....................................$85.00

Sewing Collectibles

Once regarded simply as a necessary day-to-day chore, sewing evolved into an art form that the ladies of the 1800s took much pride in. Sewing circles and quilting bees became popular social functions, and it was a common practice to take sewing projects along when paying a visit. As this evolution took place, sewing tools became more decorative and were often counted among a lady's most prized possessions.

Of course, 19th-century notions have long been collectible, but there are lots of interesting items from this century as well. When machine-made clothing became more readily available after the 1920s, ladies began to loose interest in home sewing, and the market for sewing tools began to drop off. As a result, manufacturers tried to boost lagging sales with novelty tape measures, figural pincushions, and a variety of other tools that you may find hard to resist.

Retail companies often distributed sewing notions with imprinted advertising messages; these appeal to collectors of advertising memorabilia as well. You'll see ads for household appliances, remedies for ladies' ills, grocery stores, and even John Deere tractors.

Bodkin, ¾" wide, sterling, Art Deco-style embossed decoration, flat, VG $40.00
Book, Singer Sewing Library, 4-volume set, 1930, EX.$40.00
Buttonhole cutter, 4" long, wrought steel $35.00
Crochet hook, brass, sliding retract mechanism $45.00
Crochet hook, carved bone, EX...................................$35.00
Darner, ceramic girl, Darn-It $20.00
Darner, milk glass, 6", blown w/ridged handle $70.00
Darner, mold-blown glass, dark blue, foot form $32.00
Emery, strawberry, 2", red satin w/sterling cap $65.00
Knitting gauge, 6½", celluloid, advertising.................$15.00
Measure, apple, plastic, M..$50.00
Measure, barrel, 1", vegetable ivory, stanhope in handle..$100.00
Measure, bear, celluloid, Japan....................................$65.00
Measure, British Queen Alexandria portrait, 1½" dia, advertising on back, dated 'Xmas 1901'.........................$95.00
Measure, chicken, 1½", ceramic, multicolored............$35.00
Measure, clock w/moving hands, 1¼", tin $95.00
Measure, dog w/ball, 2½", celluloid $75.00
Measure, duck, celluloid, VG $45.00
Measure, emossed owl face w/glass eyes, 1½", marked Germany $25.00
Measure, fish, 4½", gray-shaded plastic, EX details $40.00
Measure, gingham dog, ceramic, 1950s......................$25.00
Measure, girl w/dog, celluloid $65.00
Measure, house, gray w/red roof, plastic....................$40.00
Measure, Indian boy's head, celluloid, Germany $125.00

Measure, John Deere, celluloid, M..........................$25.00
Measure, Liberty Bell, plastic..............................$55.00
Measure, man in tux on red, celluloid.................$10.00
Measure, sewing machine, china, 1970s................$20.00
Needle book, Century of Progress, cardboard............$12.50
Needle book, Piccadilly, airplane, cardboard.............$12.50
Needle case, Bakelite doll unscrews at shoulders, NM.$45.00
Needle case, Lydia Pinkham, circular.....................$45.00
Needle case, 1½x2", Tunbridge, mosaic book form....$85.00
Needle case, 2¾", vegetable ivory, acorn ends..........$75.00
Needle case, 3½", wood, Shaker............................$30.00
Needle case, 4" umbrella form, ivory & black celluloid $75.00
Needle guard, metal & brass, USA........................$4.00
Pincushion, cat, Deco-style lustreware, Japan $15.00
Pincushion, cat, sterling, Jennings Bros.................$40.00
Pincushion, dog in man's shoe, bisque w/cushion, Japan $32.00

Pincushion, dog, pull out tongue for measure.....$10.00
Pincushion, fabric shoe w/cushion in heel, 1920s.......$45.00
Pincushion, man's shoe, 3½", spelter.....................$25.00
Pincushion, swan, silverplate, padded top...............$35.00
Scissors, embroidery; sterling, engraved $65.00
Scissors, embroidery; 4", sterling w/repousse finger loops...$75.00
Scissors, pinking; chrome, lever action, 1939, EX.......$18.00
Scissors, 2", celluloid handles & shanks, folding, EX ..$55.00
Sewing kit, Bakelite w/rhinestone chips on lid $20.00
Sewing kit, metal tube, Lydia Pinkham $25.00
Sewing kit, red Bakelite w/thimble cap, M................$45.00
Tatting shuttle, Bakelite, 1920s, VG $20.00
Tatting shuttle, sterling, in original floral box..........$100.00
Tatting shuttle, Tartanware, minor wear $165.00
Thimble case, sweet grass, w/lid & loop, EX.............$22.00
Thimble case, transfer ware, resort scene, casket shape $165.00

Thread winder & brush, celluloid, EX.....................$4.50
Threader, brass, Threadmaster Automatic, M in package...$18.00
Threader, sterling, double engraved lines, F&B mark, pr $40.00

Shawnee Pottery

In 1937, a company was formed in Zanesville, Ohio, on the suspected site of a Shawnee Indian village. They took the tribe's name to represent their company, recognizing the Indians to be the first to use the rich clay from the banks of the Muskingum River to make pottery there. Their venture was very successful, and until they closed in 1961, they produced many lines of kitchenware, planters, vases, lamps, and cookie jars that are very collectible today.

They specialized in figural items. There were 'Winnie' and 'Smiley' pig cookie jars and salt and pepper shakers; 'Bo Peep,' 'Puss 'n Boots,' 'Boy Blue,' and 'Charlie Chicken' pitchers; Dutch children; lobsters; and two lines of dinnerware modeled as ears of corn.

Values sometimes hinge on the extent of an item's decoration. For instance, a 'Smiley' pig cookie jar with no decoration is valued at $50.00, while one with a painted neckerchief and a few scattered flowers or cloverleaves may be worth $150.00. Add brown trousers and gold trim and the value zooms to $300.00. And while a 'Bo Peep' pitcher is basically worth $90.00, the addition of some decals and gold adds about 75% more. Most items will increase by 50% to 200% when heavily decorated and gold trimmed.

Not all of their ware was marked Shawnee; many pieces were simply marked USA with a three- or four-digit mold number. If you'd like to learn more about this subject, we recommend _The Collector's Guide to Shawnee Pottery_ by Duane and Janice Vanderbilt, and _Collecting Shawnee Pottery_ by Mark E. Supnick.

Bank, bulldog..$90.00
Bank, Howdy Doody riding a pig, marked USA Bob Smith $300.00
Bank, Smiley the Pig, brown pants, gold trim, marked Shawnee Smiley 60, minimum value.................$300.00
Bank, tumbling bear $85.00
Bowl, cereal; Corn Line $32.50
Bowl, fruit; Corn Line $27.50
Bowl, mixing; embossed snowflake decoration, nesting set of 5", 6", & 7" bowls $42.50
Bowl, mixing; 5", Corn Line $22.50
Bowl, mixing; 6", Corn Line $27.50
Bowl, mixing; 8", Corn Line $32.50
Bowl, vegetable; Corn Line $35.00
Butter dish, Corn Line..$47.50
Casserole, fruit lid on basketweave bowl form, marked Shawnee 83 ....$50.00
Casserole, 1½-qt, Corn Line, w/lid..........................$35.00
Cigarette box, embossed trademark on lid, marked USA..$50.00

Cookie jar, Bean Pot Snowflake, bean pot shape w/embossed snowflakes, marked USA, minimum value **$50.00**

Cookie jar, Corn Line, marked 66 ....**$145.00**

Cookie jar, Cottage, marked USA 6, minimum value .**$400.00**

Cookie jar, Drum Major, marked USA 10, minimum value **$150.00**

Cookie jar, Dutch Boy, cold paint, marked USA, minimum value **$50.00**

Cookie jar, Dutch Boy, double stripes on pants, marked USA, minimum value **$125.00**

Cookie jar, Dutch Boy, patches on pants, gold trim, marked USA, minimum value **$225.00**

Cookie jar, Dutch Girl, cold paint, marked USA, minimum value **$50.00**

Cookie jar, Dutch Girl, gold decals, marked USA, minimum value **$200.00**

Cookie jar, Dutch Girl, paint under glaze, marked USA, minimum value **$75.00**

Cookie jar, Dutch Girl, tulip on skirt, w/decals & gold trim, marked USA, minimum value **$225.00**

Cookie jar, Fruit Basket, marked Shawnee 84, minimum value **$125.00**

Cookie jar, Hexagon Basketweave, 6-sided shape w/embossed basketweave, w/decals & gold trim, marked USA, minimum value **$100.00**

Cookie jar, Jo Jo the Clown, gold trim, marked Shawnee 12, minimum value **$300.00**

Cookie jar, Jug, blue w/cold-painted flowers, marked USA, minimum value **$75.00**

Cookie jar, Jug, green, marked USA, minimum value .**$75.00**

Cookie jar, Little Chef, green, marked USA, minimum value **$75.00**

Cookie jar, Little Chef, white w/gold trim, marked USA, minimum value **$150.00**

Cookie jar, Muggsy, green scarf, w/decals & gold trim, marked Pat Muggsy USA, minimum value **$700.00**

Cookie jar, Muggsy, w/decals & gold trim, marked Pat Muggsy USA, minimum value **$450.00**

Cookie jar, Owl, marked USA, minimum value.........**$125.00**

Cookie jar, Pink Elephant, marked Shawnee 60, minimum value **$80.00**

Cookie jar, Puss 'n Boots, tail behind foot, minimum value **$150.00**

Cookie jar, Puss 'n Boots, tail over foot, w/decals & gold trim, marked Pat Puss 'n Boots, minimum value.**$275.00**

Cookie jar, Puss 'n Boots, w/decals & gold trim, Marked Pat Puss 'n Boots, minimum value **$250.00**

Cookie jar, Sailor Boy, blond hair, gold trim, marked USA, minimum value **$400.00**

Cookie jar, Sitting Elephant, cold paint, marked USA, minimum value **$75.00**

Cookie jar, Sitting Elephant, w/decals & gold trim, marked USA, minimum value (illustrated)...$200.00

Cookie jar, Smiley the Pig, blue bib, marked USA, minimum value **$150.00**

Cookie jar, Smiley the Pig, chrysanthemums on pants, marked USA, minimum value **$150.00**

Cookie jar, Smiley the Pig, cold painted or plain, minimum value **$50.00**

Cookie jar, Smiley the Pig, gold w/decals, marked USA **$225.00**

Cookie jar, Smiley the Pig, tulips on pants, marked USA, minimum value **$150.00**

Cookie jar, Winnie the Pig, blue collar, gold trim, marked USA, minimum value **$250.00**

Cookie jar, Winnie the Pig, clover buds on coat, marked Pat Winnie USA, minimum value **$200.00**

Cookie jar, Winnie the Pig, red collar, gold trim, marked USA, minimum value **$250.00**

Cookie jar, Owl, gold trim, marked USA, minimum value $225.00

Creamer, Corn Line $22.50

Creamer, Elephant, gold trim, marked Pat USA, minimum value **$80.00**

Creamer, Elephant, w/decals & gold trim, marked Pat USA, minimum value **$140.00**

Creamer, embossed snowflakes, marked USA, minimum value **$15.00**

Creamer, Puss 'n Boots, green & yellow, marked Shawnee 85, minimum value **$40.00**

Creamer, Puss 'n Boots, pink & white w/gold trim, marked 85, minimum value **$45.00**

Creamer, Smiley the Pig, blue & yellow, marked Shawnee 86, minimum value **$45.00**

Creamer, Smiley the Pig, peach flower on pants, gold trim, marked Pat Smiley, minimum value **$85.00**

Creamer, Tulip Ball Jug, tulip painted on ball-jug shape, marked USA, minimum value **$50.00**

Cup, Corn Line **$27.50**

Figurine, deer **$65.00**

Figurine, Orientals playing mandolin, pr **$37.00**

Figurine, pekingese **$37.50**

Figurine, pekingese, w/decals, gold trim **$75.00**

Figurine, puppy dog **$37.50**

Figurine, rabbit, w/decals, gold trim **$75.00**

Figurine, raccoon **$37.50**

Figurine, squirrel **$37.50**

Figurine, squirrel, w/decals, gold trim **$75.00**

Figurine, tumbling bear **$37.50**

Figurine, tumbling bear, w/decals, gold trim **$75.00**

Hors d'oeuvre holder, red lobster shape w/twenty-five holes for toothpicks **$75.00**

Lamp base, Champ the Dog **$17.50**

Mug, Corn Line **$45.00**

Mug, white w/red lobster handle, marked 911 ....**$37.50**

Pie bird **$27.50**

Pitcher, Bo Peep, blue bonnet, market Pat Bo Peep, minimum value **$85.00**

Pitcher, Bo Peep, smaller size, marked Shawnee 47, minimum value **$75.00**

Pitcher, Bo Peep, w/decals & gold trim, marked Pat Bo Peep, minimum value **$150.00**

Pitcher, Boy Blue, marked Shawnee 46, minimum value **$85.00**

Pitcher, Charlie Chicken, marked Pat Chanticleer, minimum value **$65.00**

Pitcher, Charlie Chicken, w/decals & gold trim, marked Chanticleer, minimum value **$145.00**

Pitcher, Corn Line **$60.00**

Pitcher, Corn Line, gold trim, marked USA **$95.00**

Pitcher, Octagon Jug, jug form w/eight embossed ferns, marked USA, minimum value **$45.00**

Pitcher, Pennsylvania Dutch-style flowers on ball form, marked USA 64, minimum value **$90.00**

Pitcher, Smiley the Pig, flowers on pants, marked Pat Smiley or Pat Smiley USA, minimum value **$85.00**

Pitcher, Smiley the Pig, neckerchief & apple, marked Pat Smiley USA, minimum value **$95.00**

Pitcher, Sunflower, ball shape w/painted sunflowers, marked USA, minimum value **$75.00**

Planter, boy at stump, marked USA 533 ....**$7.50**

Planter, boy w/wheelbarrow, marked USA 750 ....**$15.00**

Planter, Buddha, marked USA 524 ....**$17.50**

Planter, butterfly, marked Shawnee USA 524 ....**$6.50**

Planter, Children Who Lived in a Shoe, marked USA 525 ....**$15.00**

Planter, clown, marked USA 607 ....**$18.00**

Planter, cockatiel, marked Shawnee 523 ....**$7.50**

Planter, coolie w/rickshaw, marked USA 539 ....**$7.50**

Planter, donkey w/basket, marked Shawnee 722 ....**$17.50**

Planter, dove, marked Shawnee 2025 ....**$24.00**

Planter, elephant, small, marked USA 759 ....**$12.50**

Planter, flying goose, marked USA 707 ....**$17.50**

Planter, gazelle, gold trim, marked USA 613 ....**$25.00**

Planter, girl playing mandolin, marked USA 576 ....**$17.50**

Planter, globe, marked Shawnee USA **$15.00**

Planter, highchair, marked USA 727 ....**$45.00**

Planter, hound, marked USA **$7.50**

Planter, large watering can, embossed flower decoration, marked USA **$12.50**

Planter, man w/push cart, marked USA **$20.00**

Planter, mountain sheep, marked USA #515 ....**$20.00**

Planter, mouse w/cheese, marked USA 705................$22.50

Planter, open car, 4-spoke wheels, marked USA 506..$17.50

Planter, pig w/wheelbarrow, embossed flower, marked USA................$12.50

Planter, squirrel, marked Shawnee 664 ....$6.00

Planter, squirrel pulling acorn, marked Shawnee 713.$32.50

Plate, 8", Corn Line................$17.50

Platter, 10", Corn line................$27.50

Platter, 12", Corn line................$42.50

Relish tray, Corn Line $15.00

Salt & pepper shakers, large, band decoration embossed on blue, pr, minimum value................$27.50

Salt & pepper shakers, large, blue jug, pr, minimum value................$27.50

Salt & pepper shakers, large, Charlie Chicken, pr, minimum value................$27.00

Salt & pepper shakers, large, Dutch Boy & Girl, pr, minimum value................$42.00

Salt & pepper shakers, large, Dutch Boy & Girl, w/decals & gold trim, pr, minimum value................$80.00

Salt & pepper shakers, large, fruit (grapes, peach, & pear), gold trim, marked USA 8, pr $50.00

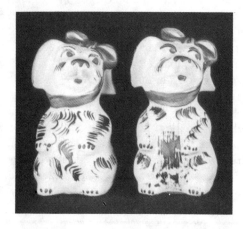

Salt & pepper shakers, large, Muggsy, gold trim, pr..$95.00

Salt & pepper shakers, large, Muggsy, pr, minimum value................$50.00

Salt & pepper shakers, large, Smiley the Pig, blue bib, w/decals & gold trim, pr, minimum value $95.00

Salt & pepper shakers, large, Smiley the Pig, green bib, pr, minimum value................$55.00

Salt & pepper shakers, large, Smiley the Pig, green bib, w/decals & gold trim, pr, minimum value $85.00

Salt & pepper shakers, large, Winnie & Smiley, clover bud decoration, pr, minimum value................$80.00

Salt & pepper shakers, small, Charlie Chicken, gold trim, pr................$37.50

Salt & pepper shakers, small, Charlie Chicken, pr.......$17.50

Salt & pepper shakers, small, Chef 'S' & 'P' shapes, pr.$12.50

Salt & pepper shakers, small, cottage, marked USA 9, pr................$80.00

Salt & pepper shakers, small, ducks, pr................$32.50

Salt & pepper shakers, small, Farmer Pig, pr.............$45.00

Salt & pepper shakers, small, flowerpot, gold trim, pr..$27.50

Salt & pepper shakers, small, flowerpot, pr................$12.50

Salt & pepper shakers, small, fruit, pr $12.50

Salt & pepper shakers, small, milk can, pr................$12.50

Salt & pepper shakers, small, milk can, w/decals & gold trim, pr................$37.50

Salt & pepper shakers, small, Muggsy, pr................$37.50

Salt & pepper shakers, small, owl, gold trim, pr $37.50

Salt & pepper shakers, small, owl, green eyes, pr.......$25.00

Salt & pepper shakers, small, Puss 'n Boots, gold trim, pr................$55.00

Salt & pepper shakers, small, watering can, gold trim, pr................$37.50

Salt & pepper shakers, small, watering can, pr............$12.50

Salt & pepper shakers, small, wheelbarrow, gold trim, pr................$32.50

Salt & pepper shakers, small, Winnie & Smiley, clover bud decoration, pr................$47.50

Salt & pepper shakers, small, Winnie & Smiley, gold trim, pr................$55.00

Salt & pepper shakers, small, Winnie & Smiley, pr $35.00

Salt & pepper shakers, 3½", Corn Line, pr $17.00

Salt & pepper shakers, 5½", Corn Line, pr $25.00

Saucer, Corn Line................$12.00

Sock darner, lady figural, marked USA................$27.50

Spoon holder, red lobster shape................$75.00

Sugar bowl, bucket form, w/decals & gold trim, w/lid, marked USA $55.00

Sugar bowl, bucket form, w/lid, marked USA $27.50

Sugar bowl, Corn Line, w/lid, marked USA $27.50

Sugar bowl, cottage shape, roof lid, marked USA 8..$125.00

Sugar bowl, flower & fern decoration embossed on yellow, w/lid, marked USA................$17.50

Sugar bowl, fruit lid on bowl base, marked Shawnee 83 ....$32.50

Sugar bowl, Pennsylvania Dutch-style flowers on jug form, w/lid, marked USA................$55.00

Sugar bowl, Sunflower, w/lid, marked USA................$27.50

Sugar shaker, Corn Line $55.00

Sugar shaker, Corn Line, gold trim $85.00

Teapot, blue leaves on white, fluted lid & bottom half, marked USA $42.00

Teapot, blue leaves on white, gold trim, w/decals, fluted lid & bottom half, marked USA $65.00

Teapot, clover bud decoration, marked USA $65.00

Teapot, elephant figural, gold trim, marked USA $130.00

Teapot, elephant figural, marked USA $100.00

Teapot, Granny Ann, matt finish w/gold trim, marked Pat Granny Ann USA..$175.00

Teapot, Granny Ann, w/decals & gold trim, marked Pat Granny Ann..$135.00

Teapot, heart-shaped flower on white, fluted spout, marked USA $27.50

Teapot, Pennsylvania Dutch-style flower decoration, marked USA (no number)..$80.00

Teapot, red flower on white, round body, fancy handle, marked USA $27.50

Teapot, snowflake decoration embossed on blue, bulbous w/horizontal ridges, marked USA........................$22.50

Teapot, Sunflower, gold spout, finial, & handle, marked USA $125.00

Teapot, Tom Tom, gold trim, marked Tom the Piper's Son Pat USA..$130.00

Teapot, Tom Tom, marked Tom the Piper's Son Pat USA...$65.00

Teapot, yellow tulip on white, fluted collar around top, bulbous, marked USA $35.00

Teapot, 10-oz, Corn Line $115.00

Teapot, 18-oz, Pennsylvania Dutch decoration, marked USA 18 ....$70.00

Teapot, 30-oz, Corn Line $57.50

Utility jar, white basketweave w/green rope trim, marked USA $55.00

Vase, Bow Knot, marked USA 819 ....$17.50

Vase, bud; embossed flowers, marked USA 875............$5.00

Vase, bud; handles, marked USA 1178.........................$12.50

Vase, bud; leaf form, gold trim, marked 1125..............$12.50

Vase, cornucopia form, marked USA 835.......................$6.00

Vase, large, embossed flowers, marked Shawnee 827 ..$25.00

Vase, swan, marked USA 806...$15.00

Wall pocket, birds at birdhouse, gold trim, marked USA 830 ....$27.50

Wall pocket, birds at birdhouse, marked USA 830 ......$20.00

Sheet Music

Flea markets are a good source for buying old sheet music, and prices are usually very reasonable. Most examples can be bought for less than $5.00. More often than not, it is collected for reasons other than its contents. Some of the cover art was done by well-known illustrators like Rockwell, Christy, Barbelle, and Starmer, and some collectors like to zero in on their particular favorite, often framing some of the more attractive examples. Black Americana collectors can find many good examples with Black entertainers being featured on the covers or with the music revolving around an ethnic theme.

You may want to concentrate on music by a particularly renowned composer, for instance George M. Cohan or Irving Berlin. Or you may find you enjoy covers featuring famous entertainers and movie stars from the forties through the sixties. At any rate, be critical of condition when you buy or sell sheet music. As is true with any item of paper, tears, dog ears, or soil will greatly reduce its value.

If you'd like a more thorough listing of sheet music and prices, we recommend *The Sheet Music Reference and Price Guide* by Anna Marie Guiheen and Marie-Reine A. Pafik and *The Collector's Guide to Sheet Music* by Debbie Dillon.

A Boy Named Sue, Shel Silverstein, Johnny Cash photo cover, 1969, M...$5.00

A Broken Promise, from movie 'Jamboree,' James Goldsborough, The Four Coins photo cover, 1957, M $5.00

A Bushel & a Peck, from musical 'Guys & Dolls,' Jo Swerling, Abe Burrows, & Frank Loesser, 1950, M.........$5.00

After All the Good Is Gone, Conway Twitty photo cover, 1975, M $5.00

All in a Golden Afternoon, from movie 'Alice in Wonderland,' Bob Hilliard & Sammy Fain, 1951, M $15.00

Allegheny Moon, Al Hoffman & Dick Mannery, Patti Page photo cover, 1956, M..$5.00

Alleluia, Anthony Garlick, 1967, M $2.00

Am I That Easy To Forget?, Carl Belew & WS Stevenson, 1958, M $5.00

America, from movie 'West Side Story,' Stephen Sondheim & Leonard Bernstein, 1957, M.....................................$5.00

America Beauty Rose, Hal David, Redd Evans & Arthur Altman, 1950, M...$5.00

And So To Sleep Again, Joe Marsala & Sunny Skylar, Patti Page photo cover, 1951, M.......................................$5.00

And Then I Remember, Janis Moss Rosenburg, 1956....$5.00

And This Is My Beloved, from musical 'Kismet,' Robert Wright & Chet Forrest, 1953, M..............................$5.00

Anywhere I Wander, from movie 'Hans Christian Anderson,' Frank Loesser, Danny Kaye photo cover, 1951, M .$5.00

Applause, from musical 'Applause,' Lee Adams & Charles Strouse, 1970, M..$5.00

April in Portugal, Jimmy Kennedy & Raul Ferras, Vic Damone photo cover, 1953, M..................................$3.00

April Love, from movie 'April Love,' Paul Webster & Sammy Fain, 1957, M **$5.00**

Around the World in 80 Days, from movie 'Around the World in 80 Days,' Harold Adamson & Victor Young, 1956, M **$5.00**

Auf Wiederseh'n Sweetheart, John Sexton, John Turner & Eberhard Storch, Vera Lynn photo cover, 1951, M .**$5.00**

Baby Don't Get Hooked on Me, Mac Davis, Mac Davis photo cover, 1972, M **$5.00**

Baby Me, Carroll & Dick Manning, Eileen Barton photo cover, 1950, M **$3.00**

Baby Talk to Me, from movie 'Bye Bye Birdie,' Lee Adams & Charles Strause, 1960, M **$5.00**

Backward, Turn Backward, Dave Coleman, 1954, M **$5.00**

Ballin' the Jack, from movie 'That's My Boy,' Jim Burris & Chris Smith, Pete Fountain photo cover, 1951, M ...**$3.00**

Ballin' the Jack, from movie 'That's My Boy,' Jim Burris & Chris Smith, Dean Martin & Jerry Lewis photo cover, 1951, M **$5.00**

Ballin' the Jack, by Jim Burris & Chris Smith, Gene Hodgkins & Irene Hammond on cover, 1951, EX.$15.00

Bam It's Going, Going, Gone, Cincinnati Reds photo cover, 1939 ....**$60.00**

Banana Boat Song, Erik Darling, Bob Carey & Alan Arkin, The Tarriers photo cover, 1956, M **$3.00**

Be Anything, Irving Gordon, Helen O'Connell photo cover, 1952, M **$5.00**

Be My Life's Companion, Bob Hilliard & Milton DeLugg, 1951, M **$5.00**

Bean Song, Ray Stanley, Eileen Burton photo cover, 1956, M **$5.00**

Because You're Mine, from movie 'Because You're Mine,' Sammy Cahn & Nicholas Brodsky, 1952, M **$5.00**

Believe in Me, from movie 'Believe in Me,' Michael Sarrazin & Jacqueline Bisset photo cover, 1972, M **$5.00**

Bernadine, from movie 'Bernadine,' Johnny Mercer, Pat Boone & Terry Moore photo cover, 1957, M **$5.00**

Best Thing for You, from musical 'Call Me Madam,' Irving Berlin, caricature of Ethel Merman on cover, 1950, M **$10.00**

Better Not Roll Those Blue, Blue Eyes, Jack Jureens, Kay Twomey & Al Goodhart photo cover, 1952, M.......**$3.00**

Bible Tells Me So, Roy Rogers & Dale Evans photo cover, 1940, VG **$4.00**

Big Spender, from movie 'Sweet Charity,' Cy Coleman & Dorothy Fields, Shirley Maclaine photo cover, 1969, M **$3.00**

Blacksmith Blues, Jack Holmes, Ella Mae Morse photo cover, 1952, M **$3.00**

Blue Mirage, Sam Coslow & Lotar Olias, 1954, M.........**$5.00**

Blue Star, Medic Theme, Edward Heyman & Victor Young, Felicia Sanders photo cover, 1955, M **$5.00**

Blue Tango, Leroy Anderson, Leroy Anderson photo cover, 1951, M **$5.00**

Boomp! Pa-Deedle Doodle, Phalen & Todd, Arthur Murray photo cover, 1951, M **$5.00**

Born Free, Don Clark & John Barry, Roger Williams photo cover, 1966, M **$5.00**

Breakfast at Tiffany's, from movie 'Breakfast at Tiffany's,' Henry Mancini, Audrey Hepburn on photo cover, 1961, M **$5.00**

Bring Back the Thrill, Ruth Poll & Peter Rugolo, Eddie Fisher photo cover, 1950, M **$3.00**

Broken-Down Merry-Go-Round, Arthur Herbert & Fred Stryker, Margaret Whiting & Jimmy Wakely photo cover, 1950, M **$3.00**

Bundle of Southern Sunshine, Sunny Clapp, Eddy Arnold photo cover, 1951, M **$3.00**

Busybody, Sid Tepper & Roy Brodsky, Pee Wee King photo cover, 1952, M **$3.00**

By the Time I Get to Phoenix, Jim Webb, Glen Campbell photo cover, 1967, M **$3.00**

C'est Si Bon, Jerry Seelen & Henri Betti, 1950, M.........**$2.00**

Cabaret, from musical 'Cabaret,' Fred Ebb & John Lander, 1966, M **$3.00**

Calypso, John Denver, John Denver photo cover, 1975, M **$3.00**

Can Anyone Explain?, Bennie Benjamin & George Weiss, Dinah Shore photo cover, 1950, M **$3.00**

Can't Take My Eyes Off You, Bob Crewe & Bob Gaudio, 1967, M **$3.00**

Canadian Sunset, Norman Gimbel & Eddie Heywood, 1956, M **$2.00**

Candy Doll, Jessie L Gaynor, 1959, M **$3.00**

Dog Barking, Al Stillman, Crew Cuts photo cover, 1954, M **$5.00**

Doncha' Think It's Time?, Elvis photo cover, EX.........**$30.00**

Gentlemen Prefer Blondes, Marilyn Monroe photo cover, NM **$30.00**

Here Comes Santa Claus, Gene Autry photo cover, 1948 ....**$8.00**

I Wonder What's Become of Sally, Al Johnson cover, copyright 1924, EX **$10.00**

If I Was What I Ain't Instead of What I Is, Black photo cover, 1922 ....**$5.00**

My Blossom Bride, Hopi Indian photo, 1928, EX **$35.00**

On The Atchison, Topeka & Santa Fe, Judy Garland photo cover, 1945 ....**$22.50**

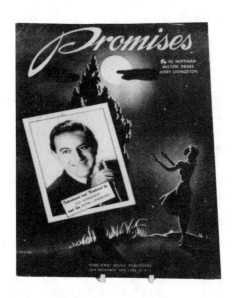

Promises, by Al Hoffman, Milton Drake, & Harry Livingston, Guy Lombardo on cover, 1945, EX.....$5.00

Santa Baby, Eartha Kitt photo cover, 1953.....................**$5.00**

Three Little Words, Amos & Andy photo cover, 1930, NM...**$22.50**

Why Can't You?, Al Jolson photo cover, EX...................**$5.00**

Shirley Temple

Born April 23, 1928, Shirley Jane Temple danced and smiled her way into the hearts of America in the movie *Stand Up and Cheer.* Many, many successful roles followed and by the time Shirley was eight years old, she was #1 at the box offices around the country. Her picture appeared in publications almost daily, and any news about her was news indeed. Mothers dressed their little daughters in clothing copied after hers and coifed them with Shirley hairdos.

The extent of her success was mirrored in the unbelievable assortment of merchandise that saturated the retail market. Dolls, coloring books, children's clothing and jewelry, fountain pens, paper dolls, stationery, and playing cards are just a few examples of the hundreds of items that were available. Shirley's face was a common sight on the covers of magazines as well as in the advertisements they contained, and she was featured in hundreds of articles.

Though she had been retired from the movies for nearly a decade, she had two successful TV series in the late fifties, *The Shirley Temple Story-Book* and *The Shirley Temple Show.* Her reappearance caused new interest in some of the items that had been so popular during her childhood, and many were reissued.

Always interested in charity and community service, Shirley became actively involved in a political career in the late sixties, serving at both the state and national level.

If you're interested in learning more about her, we recommend *Shirley Temple Dolls and Collectibles* by Patricia R. Smith.

Album, 'Shirley Temple 21st Birthday,' Dell, April 1949, 15¢ original price **$20.00**

Barrette & bow set, 1930s, M.....................................**$50.00**

Book, 'Heidi,' Saalfield, 1937, M................................**$35.00**

Book, 'Little Princess,' #1783, 1939, M.....................**$20.00**

Book, 'Now I Am Eight,' Saalfield, 1937, M **$35.00**

Book, 'Shirley Temple at Play,' Saalfield, 1930s...........**$35.00**

Book, 'Shirley Temple Christmas Book,' Saalfield #1770, 1937, M **$40.00**

Book, 'Shirley Temple Christmas Book,' Saalfield #1770, 1937, VG $18.00

Book, 'Shirley Temple in Stowaway,' Saalfield, 1937, M...**$40.00**

Book, 'Shirley Temple in the Little Princess Movie,' Saalfield, ca 1939, EX...**$40.00**

Book, 'Shirley Temple Starring Roles,' paperback, Saalfield, 1930s, M..**$40.00**

Book, 'Shirley Temple's Book of Fairy Tales,' Saalfield, 1936, has pictures of Shirley w/animals **$25.00**

Bowl, cereal; cobalt blue glass, 1930s, VG..................**$35.00**

Box, 'Shirley Temple Slippers,' Restful, 1930s, shows Shirley kneeling at bed **$20.00**

Box, cereal; 1930s, EX..**$225.00**

Buggy, buttons on the hood & hubcaps all say 'Shirley Temple,' her photo is on the sides, minimum value...**$400.00**

Christmas card, Hallmark, dated 1935, EX **$25.00**

Coloring book, 'Shirley Temple Crossing the Country,' M **$25.00**

Coloring book, 'This Is My Crayon Book,' Saalfield, 1935, M **$40.00**

Coloring set, Saalfield, 1930s, in original box, M.......**$100.00**

Doll, 12", 'Rebecca of Sunnybrook Farm,' vinyl, original outfit w/straw hat, marked Ideal, 1958, M................**$165.00**

Doll, 12", vinyl, dressed as 'Heidi,' Ideal, 1982, M in box **$200.00**

Doll, 12", vinyl, green & white dress, original slip, marked Ideal, complete, M in box **$200.00**

Doll, 13", 'Little Miss Marker,' all composition, original dimity dress, marked, in original box, NM................**$700.00**

Doll, 13", composition, tagged blue & white dress w/pin, 1930s, all original **$665.00**

Doll, 15", 'Heidi,' vinyl, original costume w/tag, marked Ideal, ca 1960 ....$265.00

Doll, 15", vinyl, Ideal, redressed, EX **$245.00**

Doll, 15", vinyl, white dress w/red bodice, Montgomery Ward, 1972, in original box, M **$200.00**

Doll, 16", composition, open/close eyes, open mouth, handmade clothes, 1936, EX **$350.00**

Doll, 16", vinyl, 'Stand Up & Cheer' dress, 1973, M in box **$200.00**

Doll, 20", 'Littlest Rebel,' all composition, original clothes, marked Ideal N & T Co, 1935, M........................**$975.00**

Doll, 8", vinyl, 'Littlest Stowaway,' Ideal, 1982, M **$50.00**

Dress, child's, red w/short sleeves, white cuffs & Peter Pan collar, white smocking on front, Nanette Mfg, ca 1960s, NM **$70.00**

Dress, doll's, Premier, for 12" doll, gingham check w/white trim, late 1950s, in original package, minimum value...**$10.00**

Embroidery set, Gabriel #310, 1959, in original package, minimum value **$30.00**

Fan, hand type, premium for Royal Crown Cola, 1930s, M **$20.00**

Figurine, 12", 'Stand Up & Cheer,' painted chalkware, 1930s...**$200.00**

Figurine, 4½", salt type, ca 1935, minimum value **$175.00**

Flower seeds, Shirley Temple Sweet Peas, Mandeville & King Co, ca 1936, 25¢ original price on packet....**$30.00**

Fountain pen, pink w/gold trim & 'Shirley Temple' on barrel, Eversharp, 1930s...**$45.00**

Gloves, blue leather, Nolan Glove Co, 1930s in original box, M **$45.00**

Greeting card, Christmas, 1935, Hallmark, EX **$25.00**

Handkerchief, Shirley as 'The Little Colonel' **$30.00**

Hanger, doll's dress, Ideal Novelty, 'Shirley Temple Doll Outfit' w/portrait on blue cardboard, 1930s, minimum value **$10.00**

Magazine, 'Parents,' October 1938.............................**$15.00**

Magazine, 'Photoplay,' January 1935 (Shirley's 1st Photoplay cover)..**$30.00**

Magic slate, 'Shirley Temple Treasure Board,' Saalfield #8806, 1959..**$20.00**

Mug, cobalt glass, M **$35.00**

Paper dolls, 'Shirley Temple Dolls & Dresses,' Saalfield #1761, 1937, complete & uncut..............................**$75.00**

Paper dolls, Saalfield #2112, 1934, complete & uncut.**$70.00**

Pattern, #418, McCall's, copyright 1938, 25¢ original price, VG **$15.00**

Pin, 1¾", enameled metal figural in sailor dress, 1930s, minimum value..**$60.00**

Pin-back button, 'The World's Darling Genuine Shirley Temple, an Ideal Doll' w/photo center, 1930s, EX......**$60.00**

Playing cards, 'Shirley Temple Bridge Cards,' US Playing Card Co, in original photo-cover box, EX.............**$45.00**

Purse, dated 1934, EX...**$70.00**

School tablet, 6x9", 1930s, M...................................**$35.00**

Scrapbook, 12x13", Saalfield, 1935, M **$85.00**

Sewing cards, Saalfield #1721, 1936, complete w/crayons, yarn, & needle, in original box **$50.00**

Sheet music, 'Polly-Wolly-Doodle,' Sam Fox Pub Co, 1935, Shirley w/banjo on cover **$15.00**

Soap figural, Kirk Guild, 1930s, in original box, NM.**$135.00**

Socks, child's, Trimfit, 1958, in original package.........**$25.00**

Stationery, ca 1930, in original box, M **$65.00**

Tea set, pink plastic w/script monogram 'ST' in center, Ideal, dated 1959, in original box, NM..................**$70.00**

Tobacco card, 4x2¾", cast scene from 'The Blue Bird,' full color, EX **$12.50**

Shot Glasses

The more desirable shot glasses are those that were distributed from 1890 until 1918, before Prohibition. Their values are calculated by the type of their decoration as well as the name of the distiller who's product is being advertised. Shot glasses with hand-painted labels, under-glass labels, those etched with calligraphy or detailed graphics are rare and expensive.

What you're most apt to find, though, are those with graphics and lettering in fired-on enamel, from more recent vintage. These can generally be purchased for under $5.00.

If you'd like to learn more about the subject, we recommend _Shot Glasses: An American Tradition_ by Mark Pickvet.

Aluminum **$3.00**
Glass, barrel form...**$6.00**
Glass, clear w/advertising.......................................**$2.00**
Glass, clear w/shield-shaped pewter trim **$10.00**
Glass, clear w/soda advertising.................................**$10.00**
Glass, coated inside & out w/black enamel to look like
    porcelain...**$4.00**
Glass, colors, 1930s-40s **$6.00**

Glass, fired-on advertisement **$4.00**
Glass, large, round, clear w/pewter trim.....................**$10.00**
Glass, marked Culver, w/22k gold trim........................**$7.50**
Glass, plain...**$3.00**
Glass, plain w/etching...**$7.50**
Glass, plain w/frosted & gold design **$6.00**
Glass, plain w/frosted design......................................**$3.00**
Glass, plain w/gold trim **$4.50**
Glass, small, cylindrical w/gold trim, European origin..**$3.00**
Glass, square, clear w/etching **$10.00**
Glass, square, clear w/2-tone pewter trim **$12.50**
Glass, tall, clear, tourist souvenir, ca 1930s-40s **$4.00**
Glass, tourist souvenir, marked Taiwan **$3.00**
Glass, tourist souvenir, turquoise & gold trim..............**$4.00**
Porcelain, tourist souvenir..**$4.00**

Silhouette Pictures

These novelty pictures are familiar to everyone. Even today a good number of them are still around, and you'll often see them at flea markets and co-ops. They were very popular in their day and never expensive, and because they were made for so many years (the twenties through the fifties) many variations are available. Though the glasses in some are flat, others were made with curved glass. Back-grounds may be foil, a scenic print, hand tinted, or plain. Sometimes dried flowers were added as accents. But the characteristic common to them all is the subject matter reverse painted on the glass. People (even complicated groups), scenes, ships, and animals were popular themes. Though quite often the silhouette was done in solid black to create a look similar to the 19th-century cut silhouettes, colors were sometimes used as well.

In the twenties, making tinsel art pictures became a popular pastime. Ladies would paint the outline of their subjects on the back of the glass and use crumpled tinfoil as a background. Sometimes they would tint certain areas of the glass, making the foil appear to be colored. This type is popular with today's collectors.

If you'd like to learn more about this subject, we recommend _The Encyclopedia of Silhouette Collectibles on Glass_ by Shirley Mace.

Convex Glass

Couple at fence, black on colorful scenic background, Benton, late 1930s, 5x4"..**$20.00**
Couple in flower garden, black on white, Benton, 5x4"..**$20.00**
Courting couple, black on colorful mountainous back-ground, Benton, 7x5"..**$35.00**
Courting couple beneath tree, black on white background w/colored flower border, Benton, 8x6".................**$35.00**
Courting couple in garden in colored background, bird-bath, birds, etc on glass, Morris & Bendien NY, Benton, 8x6" **$20.00**
Courting couple in parlor, black on white background, Benton, 8x6"...**$36.00**
Fox hunter jumping fence, black, red, & white on woodgrained background, Peter Watson's Studio, 5" dia..**$12.50**

Gentleman pushing lady in swing, scenic background, 5x4"..**$30.00**

Indian chief on horse, black on colorful Western landscape background, Benton, 5x4".................**$20.00**

Ladies in outdoor scene w/flowers & birds, red on white, Benton, 4x5"...................................**$35.00**

Lady on stairs w/parasol & scottie dog, black on white background, unknown manufacturer, marked Hand Painted, 4" dia **$15.00**

Lady w/parasol, black on white, Bilderback's, 9" dia......**$32.00**

Little Thank You, boy beside two birds on branch, advertising, CE Erickson, late 1930s-early 40s, 7" dia........**$17.50**

Man & boy looking out to sea, black on realistic sunset scene background, Benton, 5x4" **$20.00**

Man sitting in overstuffed chair & smoking pipe, black on white background, Benton, 5x4" **$15.00**

Man stands behind lady archer, black on colorful scenic background, Benton, 5x4"....................................**$20.00**

Man w/bouquet & top hat, black on 'mother-of-pearl' background, Peter Watson's Studio, 5" dia **$17.50**

Sailing ship, black on white, Benton, 5x4".................**$17.50**

Sailing ship, white on rose background, Benton, ca 1940, 8x6"..**$48.00**

Scottie dog chasing butterfly, black on white background, Benton, 5x4"...**$22.50**

This Little Piggy, black curtain & lamb on glass, baby examining toes fills background, signed C Becker, Benton, 8x6"..**$28.00**

Flat Glass

At the Gate, couple at gate, black on foil background, Deltex, 1930s, 5x4"...**$17.50**

Baggage car, coach & engine, crossing river in multicolored scenic background, Newton Manufacturing Company...$20.00

Child chasing dog, dried flowers in background, Fisher, 4x4"..**$15.00**

Country scene, hand painted to resemble butterfly-wing colors, Reliance, 7x11"....................................**$32.00**

Courting couple, black on silver tinsel background, 10x8"...**$27.50**

Courtship, man w/flowers, lady w/parasol, black on white background, Reliance, 4x4" **$15.00**

Dancing sprites along seashore, black on white background, signed Ellery Friend, Volland, 9x6½"......................**$42.50**

Days of Yore, ladies knit & spin thread beside fireplace, black on white background, thermometer at side, Newton, 6x8"...**$17.50**

Dutch boy stands amid tulips, black outlines & background w/tinted glass on tinsel, 10x8" **$27.50**

Elfin Music, elf-like figure playing violin, black on white background, CA Richards, Boston MA, 7x5".........**$38.00**

Florals, hand-colored bouquet, CA Richards Boston MA, 5x4" oval..**$10.00**

Flower bouquet, hand painted to resemble butterfly-wing colors, Reliance, 5x3½"..**$12.50**

Flowers & butterfly in oval, Art Publishing Co, 1930s, 12x8"..**$12.50**

Goodnight, couple kissing at gate, black on white background, Buckbee-Brehm, 1930s, 6x4" **$22.00**

Happy in Her Garden, lady watering flowers, black on white background, Plaquette Art Co, West Coast Picture Co, 8x5½" **$20.00**

Hearts, couple at tree, man carving hearts, black on silver foil, Deltex, 1930s, 10x8" **$37.50**

Lady at spinning wheel, black & color on foil background, Newton, 8x6"..**$17.50**

Lady w/whippet, black on foil background, Deltex, 10x8"...**$37.50**

Lady w/whippet, full color scene, Art Publishing Company, 7x10"..**$15.00**

Lady's portrait in profile to shoulders, Buckbee-Brehm, ca 1930, 5½x4½" **$12.50**

Man & two ladies, butterfly wings provide color to figures, unknown manufacturer, 7x5"...............................**$80.00**

Out Where the West Begins, cowboys at campfire, black on colored mountain background, Newton, 8x10" **$15.00**

The Dance, couple dancing as musicians play, black on gold background, Buckbee-Brehm, ca 1930, 10x28"..**$27.50**

Vanity Fair, lady sits at vanity, hand painted to resemble butterfly-wing colors, Reliance, NRA stamp, 9x12".....**$35.00**

Silver Flatware

You may have inherited a set of silver flatware with a few pieces missing, or you may become interested in collecting a pattern simply because you find yourself drawn to its elegance and the quality of its workmanship. Whatever the reason, if you decide to collect silver flatware, many matching services advertise in the trade papers listed in the back of this book.

Popular patterns are the most expensive, regardless of their age, due simply to collector demand. Monogrammed pieces are hard to sell and are worth only about half price.

American Beauty, dessert spoon, Shiebler $45.00	Cupid, youth knife, Dominick & Haff $30.00
American Beauty, preserve spoon, Shiebler $110.00	Damask Rose, cream soup, Heirloom $16.00
Baltimore Rose, demitasse spoon $24.00	Damask Rose, knife, 8¾", Heirloom $17.00
Baltimore Rose, dinner knife................................$30.00	Della Robbia, bouillon, Alvin................................$11.00
Baltimore Rose, gumbo $60.00	Della Robbia, iced teaspoon, Alvin...........................$17.00
Baltimore Rose, tablespoon $95.00	Della Robbia, salad fork, Alvin $16.00
Blossomtime, butter spreader, flat handle, International.$12.00	Della Robbia, tablespoon, Alvin $28.00
Blossomtime, cream soup, International $16.00	Dunstan, cold meat fork.....................................$150.00
Bridal Bouquet, bouillon, Alvin $15.00	Dunstan, serving spoon.....................................$165.00
Bridal Bouquet, cocktail fork, Alvin $13.00	Etruscan, baby fork, Gorham $10.00
Bridal Bouquet, fruit spoon, Alvin $18.00	Etruscan, iced teaspoon, Gorham $18.00
Bridal Bouquet, iced teaspoon, Alvin........................$20.00	Etruscan, luncheon knife, Gorham $12.00
Bridal Bouquet, teaspoon, Alvin.............................$11.00	Etruscan, oyster fork, Gorham $16.00
Bridal Rose, butter pick, Alvin $110.00	Fairfax, cold meat fork, Gorham............................$40.00
Bridal Rose, cold meat fork, large, Alvin.................$295.00	Fairfax, demitasse spoon, Gorham $11.00
Bridal Rose, preserve spoon, Alvin..........................$110.00	Fairfax, luncheon knife, Gorham $18.00
Bridal Rose, sauce ladle, Alvin................................$85.00	Fairfax, salad fork, Gorham....................................$29.00
Burgundy, place fork, Reed & Barton $28.00	Flemish, cold meat fork, Tiffany $135.00
Burgundy, salad serving spoon, Reed & Barton........$130.00	Flemish, preserve spoon, Tiffany............................$80.00
Burgundy, tablespoon, Reed & Barton......................$60.00	French Renaissance, cocktail fork, Reed & Barton $14.00
Burgundy, teaspoon, Reed & Barton........................$17.00	French Renaissance, iced teaspoon, Reed & Barton....$18.00
Buttercup, dinner fork, Gorham $35.00	French Renaissance, salad fork, Reed & Barton $28.00
Buttercup, dinner knife, Gorham.............................$45.00	French Renaissance, teaspoon, Reed & Barton..........$14.00
Buttercup, round soup, Gorham..............................$45.00	Frontenac, cocktail fork, International.....................$25.00
Buttercup, salad fork, Gorham................................$35.00	Frontenac, cold meat fork, large, International...........$95.00
Buttercup, sugar spoon, Gorham.............................$35.00	Frontenac, dessert spoon, International $38.00
Buttercup, teaspoon, Gorham................................$20.00	Frontenac, long pickle fork, International.................$100.00
Cambridge, cracker scoop, pierced, Gorham $325.00	Frontenac, tablespoon, International $42.00
Cambridge, ice tongs, Gorham $295.00	Frontenac, teaspoon, International $25.00
Cambridge, medium cold meat fork, Gorham $85.00	Grande Baroque, dinner fork, Wallace......................$48.00
Cambridge, sardine fork, Gorham $60.00	Grande Baroque, luncheon fork, Wallace...................$30.00
Cambridge, sugar shell, Gorham.............................$32.00	Grande Baroque, strawberry fork, Wallace.................$17.00
Candlelight, butter spreader, flat handle, Towle.........$11.00	Grande Baroque, teaspoon, Wallace $20.00
Candlelight, fork, 7¼", Towle.................................$16.00	Greenbrier, butter knife, flat handle, Gorham $11.00
Candlelight, iced teaspoon, Towle $17.00	Greenbrier, teaspoon, Gorham $12.00
Candlelight, knife, 8¾", Towle................................$15.00	Hunt Club, salad fork, Gorham................................$19.00
Candlelight, pickle fork, Towle................................$14.00	Hunt Club, teaspoon, Gorham................................$11.00
Candlelight, place fork, Towle $14.00	Kings, gumbo, Wallace $25.00
Candlelight, salad fork, Towle $16.00	Kings, luncheon fork, Wallace................................$22.00
Candlelight, teaspoon, Towle.................................$8.00	Kings, luncheon knife, Wallace $20.00
Castle Rose, butter spreader, flat handle, Royal Crest .$10.00	Kings, teaspoon, Wallace $14.00
Castle Rose, cream soup, Royal Crest....................$14.00	Lady Constance, bouillon, Towle.............................$10.00
Castle Rose, iced teaspoon, Royal Crest....................$14.00	Lady Constance, butter spreader, flat handle, Towle.....$9.00
Castle Rose, teaspoon, Royal Crest $8.00	Lady Constance, lemon fork, Towle $10.00
Chantilly, butter spreader, flat handle $14.00	Lady Constance, tablespoon, Towle $24.00
Chantilly, dinner fork, Gorham................................$28.00	Lady Constance, teaspoon, Towle $10.00
Chantilly, iced teaspoon $22.00	Lancaster, berry fork, Gorham $39.00
Chantilly, luncheon fork, Gorham $16.00	Lancaster, butter fork, Gorham $95.00
Chantilly, pie fork, Gorham....................................$55.00	Lancaster, chocolate spoon, Gorham........................$42.00
Chantilly, ramekin fork, Gorham $70.00	Lancaster, olive spoon, large, Gorham $52.00
Chantilly, table service, Gorham. 138 pieces...........$3000.00	Lancaster, salad fork, Gorham................................$55.00
Chantilly, teaspoon, Gorham..................................$13.00	Lancaster, salt spoon, Gorham................................$23.00
Chateau Rose, cream soup, Alvin $22.00	Legato, cold meat fork, Towle $45.00
Chateau Rose, luncheon fork, Alvin $20.00	Legato, cream soup, Towle $22.00
Chateau Rose, sugar spoon, Alvin $21.00	Legato, iced teaspoon, Towle $20.00
Chateau Rose, tablespoon, Alvin $38.00	Legato, lemon fork, Towle $14.00
Chateau Rose, teaspoon, Alvin................................$12.00	Legato, master butter spreader, hollow handle, Towle.$20.00
Cluny, teaspoon, Gorham $30.00	Legato, place fork, Towle......................................$23.00

Legato, place knife, Towle $16.00
Legato, salad fork, Towle $19.00
Legato, sugar spoon, Towle $20.00
Legato, tablespoon, Towle $45.00
Legato, teaspoon, Towle $12.00
Lily, dinner fork, Whiting $75.00
Lily, fruit knife, Whiting $55.00
Lily, grapefruit, square tip, Whiting $60.00
Louis XV, toast fork, Whiting $295.00
Louix XV, butter fork, Whiting......................$65.00
Louix XV, mustard, Whiting $85.00
Madame Jumel, cake knife, Whiting...............$140.00
Madame Jumel, dessert spoon, Whiting $35.00
Madame Jumel, luncheon fork, Whiting..........$24.00
Madame Jumel, luncheon knife, Whiting $20.00
Madame Jumel, master butter knife, Whiting....$25.00
Madame Jumel, orange spoon, Whiting $20.00
Madame Jumel, pastry fork, Whiting $40.00
Madame Jumel, pickle fork, long handle, Whiting.....$45.00
Madame Jumel, sugar spoon, Whiting.............$20.00
Mademoiselle, butter spreader, International.............$12.00
Mademoiselle, dessert spoon, International $19.00
Mademoiselle, luncheon fork, International................$17.00
Mademoiselle, tablespoon, International......................$36.00
Majestic, butter pick, Alvin $88.00
Majestic, dessert spoon, Alvin $28.00
Majestic, salt spoon, Alvin $45.00
Majestic, tablespoon, Alvin $38.00
Majestic, teaspoon, Alvin $11.00
Marachal Niel, ice cream fork, gold washed, Durgin ..$45.00
Marlborough, butter spreader, flat handle, Reed & Barton..$16.00
Marlborough, fork, 7¼", Reed & Barton.......$22.00
Marlborough, teaspoon, Reed & Barton........$12.00
Milburn Rose, luncheon fork, Gorham..........$16.00
Milburn Rose, luncheon knife, Gorham $13.00
Milburn Rose, tablespoon, Gorham...............$32.00
Milburn Rose, teaspoon, Gorham $10.00
Mille Fleurs, luncheon fork, International $28.00
Mille Fleurs, teaspoon, International $13.00
Moonbeam, butter spreader, flat handle, Rogers........$11.00
Moonbeam, cream soup, Rogers....................$15.00
Moonbeam, iced teaspoon, Rogers................$15.00
Moonbeam, salad fork, Rogers......................$15.00
Moonbeam, teaspoon, Rogers $10.00
Old English, bonbon spoon, Towle................$35.00
Old English, horseradish spoon, Towle $45.00
Old English, lettuce fork, Towle $45.00
Old English, toast fork, 7", Towle.................$100.00
Old Master, butter spreader, flat handle, Towle.........$12.00
Old Master, demitasse spoon, Towle.............$10.00
Old Master, iced teaspoon, Towle.................$16.00
Old Master, pickle fork, Towle $14.00
Old Master, place fork, Towle.......................$22.00
Old Master, salad fork, Towle.......................$18.00
Old Master, tablespoon, Towle......................$40.00
Old Master, teaspoon, Towle.........................$12.00
Old Mirror, cold meat fork, Towle.................$50.00

Old Mirror, place fork, Towle.......................$24.00
Old Mirror, teaspoon, Towle........................$11.00
Old Orange Blossom, ice cream spoon, Alvin...........$75.00
Old Orange Blossom, luncheon fork, Alvin................$55.00
Old Orange Blossom, teaspoon, Alvin.......................$30.00
Palm, luncheon fork, Tiffany.......................$45.00
Palm, pickle fork, Tiffany $60.00
Palm, sauce ladle, Tiffany $110.00
Palm, tablespoon, Tiffany $60.00
Pansy, butter spreader, flat handle, International........$16.00
Pansy, dinner fork, International $30.00
Pansy, teaspoon, International $15.00
Poppy, berry fork, Gorham...........................$44.00
Poppy, pickle fork, Gorham..........................$39.00
Poppy, salt spoon, Gorham...........................$38.00
Prelude, baby fork, International $17.00
Prelude, butter spreader, flat handle, International $10.00
Prelude, luncheon fork, International..........................$16.00
Prelude, tablespoon, International...............................$35.00
Prelude, teaspoon, International...................................$9.00
Processional, butter spreader, flat handle, International.$11.00
Processional, cream soup, International........................$15.00

Queen's, table service (partial set), Angell & Hyams, 1862, 39 pieces................................$1200.00
Rapallo, butter spreader, hollow handle, Lunt............$12.00
Rapallo, cake server, Lunt $25.00
Rapallo, dinner knife, Lunt..........................$14.00
Rapallo, sugar spoon, Lunt..........................$15.00
Rapallo, teaspoon, Lunt $10.00
Renaissance, butter spreader, flat handle, Wallace......$13.00
Renaissance, cream soup, Wallace $18.00

Renaissance, demitasse spoon, Durgin.........................$25.00
Renaissance, dinner fork, Wallace $26.00
Renaissance, gravy ladle, Wallace..............................$38.00
Renaissance, sardine fork, Durgin $75.00
Renaissance, tablespoon, Wallace...............................$38.00
Renaissance Scroll, butter spreader, individual, Reed & Barton..$12.00
Renaissance Scroll, gravy ladle, Reed & Barton...........$42.00
Renaissance Scroll, salad fork, Reed & Barton.............$22.00
Rose, cake serving fork, Wallace $150.00
Rose, olive fork, large, Wallace $45.00
Rose, salad fork, Wallace..$50.00
Rose Tiara, cold meat fork, Gorham............................$35.00
Rose Tiara, place fork, Gorham $18.00
Rose Tiara, place knife, Gorham $16.00
Rose Tiara, teaspoon, Gorham.....................................$10.00
Royal Danish, butter spreader, hollow handle, International..$14.00
Royal Danish, cocktail fork, International $15.00
Royal Danish, demitasse spoon, International $14.00
Royal Danish, iced teaspoon, International..................$20.00
Royal Danish, luncheon fork, International $21.00
Royal Danish, salad fork, International $27.00
Royal Danish, steak knife, International.......................$23.00

Royal Danish, table service, International, 86 pieces...$1700.00

San Lorenzo, cream soup, Tiffany $36.00
San Lorenzo, dessert spoon, Tiffany............................$40.00
San Lorenzo, teaspoon, Tiffany....................................$26.00
Southern Charm, cream soup, Alvin............................$18.00
Southern Charm, dinner fork, Alvin.............................$24.00
Southern Charm, teaspoon, Alvin $10.00
Southwind, gravy ladle, Towle $42.00
Southwind, salad fork, Towle $24.00
Southwind, sugar spoon, Towle $18.00
Southwind, teaspoon, Towle...$15.00
Spanish Lace, butter spreader, hollow handle, Wallace.$12.00
Spanish Lace, cocktail fork, Wallace............................$14.00
Spanish Lace, master butter spreader, Wallace $15.00

Spanish Lace, teaspoon, Wallace $14.00
Stately, place fork, State House....................................$15.00
Stately, place knife, State House...................................$14.00
Stately, salad fork, State House....................................$13.00
Stately, teaspoon, State House......................................$10.00
Swan Lake, iced teaspoon, International.....................$16.00
Swan Lake, jelly spoon, International..........................$15.00
Swan Lake, place knife, International...........................$15.00
Swan Lake, tablespoon, International...........................$35.00
Tulip, pastry fork, gold washed, Alvin $55.00
Versailles, cake knife, hollow handle, Imperial.........$395.00
Versailles, dinner fork, International............................$50.00
Versailles, fish fork, Imperial......................................$65.00

Versailles, table service (partial set), 56 pieces...$1750.00

Versailles, teaspoon, Imperial $25.00
Vine, coffee spoon, Tiffany...$35.00
Violet, berry spoon, large, Wallace..............................$95.00
Violet, bouillon, Wallace $19.00
Violet, butter pick, Wallace $110.00
Violet, cocktail fork, Wallace.......................................$21.00
Violet, pastry server, Wallace.....................................$125.00
Violet, sauce ladle, Wallace...$36.00
Violet, tongs, 4½", Wallace..$40.00
Wave Edge, dessert spoon, Tiffany..............................$65.00
Wave Edge, dinner fork, Tiffany..................................$75.00
Wave Edge, ice cream fork, Tiffany..............................$65.00
Wave Edge, luncheon fork, Tiffany..............................$55.00
Wave Edge, tablespoon, Tiffany...................................$75.00
Wave Edge, teaspoon, Tiffany $35.00
Waverly, beef fork, Wallace..$45.00
Waverly, ice cream knife, Wallace..............................$165.00
Waverly, sardine tongs, Wallace.................................$120.00
Waverly, sauce ladle, Wallace......................................$50.00
Wedgwood, cake server, International..........................$42.00
Wedgwood, gravy ladle, International $40.00
Wedgwood, luncheon fork, International $24.00
Wedgwood, tablespoon, Wedgwood $45.00
Wedgwood, teaspoon, International..............................$14.00
Wild Rose, master butter spreader, flat handle, International $15.00
Wild Rose, pickle fork, International............................$14.00
Wild Rose, place fork, International $18.00
Wild Rose, place knife, International............................$15.00
Wild Rose, teaspoon, International...............................$12.00

William & Mary, cake server, L unt.................................$19.00
William & Mary, cocktail fork, Lunt.............................$12.00
William & Mary, gravy ladle, Lunt $28.00
William & Mary, iced teaspoon, Lunt $14.00
William & Mary, jelly spoon, Lunt $14.00
William & Mary, sugar spoon, Lunt $14.00

Silverplated Flatware

When buying silverplated flatware, avoid pieces that are worn or have been monogrammed. Replating can be very expensive. Matching services often advertise in certain trade papers and can be very helpful in helping you locate the items you're looking for. One of the best sources we are aware of is *The Antique Trader*, listed with the trade papers in the back of this book. If you'd like to learn more about the subject, we recommend *Silverplated Flatware, Revised Fourth Edition*, by Tere Hagan.

Adam, butter spreader, individual................................$6.00
Adam, dinner fork, hollow handle $12.00
Adam, soup ladle $40.00
Adam, tablespoon $6.00
Adoration, luncheon fork $5.00
Adoration, salad fork $7.00
Adoration, tablespoon $6.00
Affection, salad fork $6.00
Affection, sugar spoon $4.00
Alhambra, bouillon $6.00
Alhambra, cocktail fork $6.00
Alhambra, cold meat fork..$25.00
Alhambra, dinner fork $8.00
Alhambra, dinner knife, hollow handle...........................$14.00
Alhambra, fruit spoon...$10.00
Alhambra, grapefruit..$6.00
Alhambra, iced teaspoon $7.00

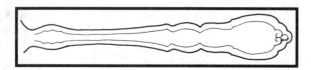

Alouette, dinner knife, hollow handle...................$7.00
Alouette, tablespoon..$9.00
Ambassador, cake knife..$30.00
Ambassador, cold meat fork $15.00
Ambassador, demitasse spoon $5.00
Ambassador, dinner fork $6.00
Ambassador, master butter spreader..............................$5.00
Ambassador, meat fork...$18.00
Ambassador, tablespoon..$6.00
Ambassador, teaspoon..$3.00
Ancestral, gravy ladle..$15.00
Ancestral, sugar spoon..$4.00
Ancestral, tablespoon...$6.00
Anniversary, dinner fork..$6.00
Anniversary, dinner knife $6.00

Anniversary, salad fork $6.00
Anniversary, teaspoon $3.00
Arbutus, gravy ladle, gold wash.................................$22.00
Arbutus, sugar tongs..$15.00
Arcadian, cheese scoop..$95.00
Arcadian, pie knife...$65.00
Ashford, butter spreader, individual $6.00
Ashford, dinner fork $7.00
Ashford, gumbo $8.00
Ashford, iced teaspoon..$7.00
Ashford, place spoon $6.00
Assyrian Head, crumber $95.00
Assyrian Head, fish set, 2-pc...................................$150.00
Assyrian Head, nut pick $20.00
Assyrian Head, sugar sifter ladle, pierced......................$135.00
Bird of Paradise, carving fork $17.00
Bird of Paradise, dinner fork...................................$5.00
Bird of Paradise, dinner knife, hollow handle...................$6.00
Bordeaux, butter spreader, individual...........................$6.00
Bordeaux, teaspoon..$4.00
Bride's Bouquet, chipped beef fork..............................$45.00
Bride's Bouquet, jelly knife $45.00
Bride's Bouquet, sardine fork $65.00
Camille, pie server $30.00
Camille, salad fork $6.00
Camille, table serving spoon $8.00
Caprice, dinner fork $8.00
Caprice, sugar spoon $4.00
Carnation, berry fork $30.00
Carnation, bouillon $25.00
Carnation, butter spreader, individual $20.00
Carnation, cold meat fork.......................................$22.50
Carnation, ice cream spoon......................................$35.00
Carnation, meat fork..$38.00
Carnation, pie fork...$30.00
Carnation, salad fork $9.00
Carnation, seafood fork $15.00
Coronation, cream soup ladle $6.00
Coronation, sugar spoon $5.00
Crown, fish server, embossed blade..............................$35.00
Daffodil, cold meat fork $16.00
Daffodil, iced teaspoon $10.00
Danish Princess, gravy ladle....................................$17.50
Danish Princess, tablespoon, pierced............................$15.00
Duchess, gumbo $8.00
Duchess, iced teaspoon $7.00
Emperor, dinner knife, hollow handle $8.00
Emperor, teaspoon...$5.00
Eternally Yours, cocktail spoon.................................$6.00
Eternally Yours, dinner knife $6.00
Eternally Yours, fruit spoon $10.00
Eternally Yours, iced teaspoon..................................$7.00
Eternally Yours, teaspoon.......................................$4.00
Evening Star, baby fork & spoon.................................$12.00
Evening Star, cold meat fork $16.00
Evening Star, pickle fork $8.00
First Love, dinner knife, hollow handle.........................$8.00
First Love, relish spoon..$9.00

Flair, baby fork & spoon $10.00
Flair, cold meat fork $16.00
Flair, gravy ladle.......................................$16.00
Flair, iced teaspoon....................................$10.00
Flair, tablespoon, pierced $10.00
Flower, sugar spoon $10.00
Flower, tablespoon $8.00
Flower, teaspoon..$5.00
Friendship, gravy ladle $25.00
Friendship, place spoon $6.00
Friendship, salad fork $6.00
Friendship, tomato server $30.00
Grape, dessert spoon, Williams $10.00
Grape, dinner fork, Williams..........................$12.00
Grape, dinner knife, hollow handle, Williams............$20.00
Grape, tablespoon, Williams $12.00
Grape, teaspoon, Williams $6.00
Grosvenor, bouillon spoon $10.00
Grosvenor, demitasse spoon $12.00
Grosvenor, dinner fork $5.00
Grosvenor, fruit knife $10.00
Grosvenor, luncheon fork $5.00
Grosvenor, luncheon knife................................$5.00
Grosvenor, master butter spreader $7.00
Grosvenor, oval soup spoon $6.00
Grosvenor, punch ladle..................................$65.00
Grosvenor, sugar spoon $7.00
Grosvenor, tablespoon, pierced.........................$15.00
Heritage, iced teaspoon................................$15.00
Heritage, round soup spoon $12.50
Joan, fish serving fork.................................$20.00
Joan, preserve spoon $15.00

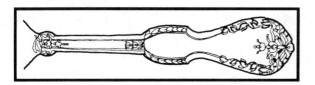

Louis XVI, dinner knife, hollow handle................$12.00
Louis XVI, tablespoon $9.00
Louis XVI, dinner fork, hollow handle $8.00
Marquise, dinner fork $6.00
Marquise, gravy ladle...................................$15.00
Marquise, salad fork.....................................$7.00
Nenuphar, dinner knife, hollow handle $25.00
Nenuphar, luncheon fork, hollow handle..................$25.00
Newport, berry spoon, gold washed $65.00
Newport, cake saw $100.00
Newport, fish slice $40.00
Newport, oyster ladle $40.00
Newport, salt spoon......................................$9.00
Old Colony, cheese spreader, hollow handle.............$35.00
Old Colony, cold meat fork $26.00
Old Colony, dinner fork $10.00
Old Colony, knife, flat handle...........................$8.00
Old Colony, knife, hollow handle $15.00

Old Colony, luncheon fork $7.00
Old Colony, master butter spreader......................$9.00
Old Colony, sugar spoon $18.00
Old Colony, sugar tongs................................$27.50
Orange Blossom, demitasse spoon $15.00
Orange Blossom, dessert spoon $12.00
Orange Blossom, grapefruit spoon......................$10.00
Orange Blossom, ice cream fork........................$16.00
Orange Blossom, salad fork $22.00
Orange Blossom, sugar spoon $15.00
Orange Blossom, teaspoon $6.00
Patrician, cake server.................................$15.00
Patrician, pickle fork.................................$12.00
Peerless, soup ladle $38.00
Raphael, cocktail fork $25.00
Raphael, cucumber server...............................$85.00
Raphael, fish knife $35.00
Remembrance, baby fork $6.00
Remembrance, dinner knife, hollow handle $7.00
Remembrance, gravy ladle..............................$17.50
St James, crumber, etched w/birds & flowers............$30.00
St James, teaspoon $6.00
Starlight, dinner fork $5.00
Starlight, dinner knife, hollow handle $6.00
Vintage, baby spoon, curved $32.00
Vintage, cake lifter...................................$60.00
Vintage, dinner fork...................................$12.00
Vintage, ice cream fork................................$65.00
Vintage, iced teaspoon $65.00
Vintage, soup ladle $120.00
Vintage, tablespoon $15.00
Vintage, tablespoon, pierced...........................$17.50
Vintage, teaspoon $6.00

Slot Machines

Coin-operated gambling machines have been around since before the turn of the century. There are many types. One-arm bandits, 3-reelers, uprights, trade stimulators, and bell machines are some of the descriptive terms used to describe them. Until the Johnson Act was signed by Harry Truman in 1951, the slot machine industry was thriving. This bill prohibited the shipment of slots into states where they were illegal and banned them from all military installations in the United States. One by one nearly every state in the union outlawed gambling devices, and soon the industry was practically non-existent.

Today, it is legal to own an 'antique' slot machine in all but eight states: Alabama, Connecticut, Hawaii, Indiana, South Carolina, Tennessee, and Nebraska and Rhode Island (whose views are uncertain.) Check your state's laws before you buy; the age of allowable machines varies from fifteen to thirty years.

Values of slots range from several hundred to thousands of dollars. If you decide to invest in this hobby, you'll need to study a good book on the subject. One we would recommend is *An American Premium Guide to Jukeboxes and Slot Machines* by Jerry Ayliffe.

Bally 25¢ Reliance Dice, green finish, 16x18x11", EX..**$3,400.00**

Buckley Bones, ca 1936, countertop model, EX original condition...$5,000.00
Buckley Long-Shot Horse Race, EX original condition .**$600.00**
Buckley 5¢ Criss Cross Bell, ca 1947, EX original condition **$1,250.00**
Caille Big Six, ca 1940, VG **$8,500.00**
Caille Commander-Streamline, ca 1930s, yellow, EX original condition **$700.00**
Caille 5¢ Cadet Bell, ca 1936, EX original condition .**$1,200.00**

Caille Superior Jackpot, ca 1928, EX condition.$2,700.00
Jennings Victoria JP, 1932, EX original condition...**$1,500.00**
Jennings 25¢ Standard Chief, restored **$1,550.00**

Jennings 5¢ Dixie Bell, console model, EX original condition **$1,575.00**
Jennings 5¢ Lite-Up Sun Chief, ca 1940s, EX restored condition **$1,800.00**
Jennings 5¢ New Victoria, ca 1931, EX original condition **$1,500.00**
Jennings 5¢ Silver Moon, ca 1940, console model, EX original condition..**$1,150.00**
Jennings 5¢ Sportsman Bell, ca 1938, VG original condition **$1,400.00**
Jennings 50¢ Greyhound, ca 1930s, EX original condition **$1,500.00**
Keeney Track Time, ca 1937, console model, NM.**$1,650.00**
Keeney 5¢ Super Bell, VG original condition.........**$1,250.00**
Mills Skyscraper, EX original condition...................**$1,200.00**
Mills 1¢ Mystery Bell Castle Front, ca 1933, VG original condition **$2,000.00**
Mills 1¢ QT Diamond Front, 19x12½x13½", VG original condition **$950.00**
Mills 1¢ QT Firebird Bell, ca 1934, EX original condition **$1,850.00**
Mills 25¢ Anniversary, ca 1936, oak case, VG original condition **$2,200.00**
Mills 25¢ Bursting Cherry, ca 1941, VG original condition **$2,000.00**
Mills 25¢ Extra Bell, ca 1946, EX original condition.**$1,600.00**
Mills 25¢ Golden Falls, EX original condition.........**$1,800.00**
Mills 25¢ Gooseneck Silent Bell, ca 1930s, skyscraper front, VG original condition......................................**$1,700.00**
Mills 25¢ War Eagle, ca 1931, NM **$3,200.00**
Mills 5¢ Bonus Horse Head, ca 1939, EX original condition **$2,500.00**
Mills 5¢ Bursting Cherry, ca 1940s, EX original condition **$1,600.00**
Mills 5¢ QT Smoker, ca 1930s, EX original condition, rare **$1,200.00**
Mills 5¢ Vest Pocket, ca 1935, metal case, 7x9x8", EX original condition **$425.00**
Pace 5¢ Chrome Comet Deluxe, ca 1939, VG original condition **$1,300.00**
Rockola 5¢ War Eagle, NM original condition........**$2,000.00**
Watling 10¢ Rol-A-Top, ca 1935, bird & coin cast front, EX original condition **$4,000.00**
Watling 25¢ Blue Seal, EX original condition.........**$1,850.00**
Watling 25¢ Rol-A-Top, NM restored condition **$3,000.00**
Watling 5¢ Lincoln Deluxe, EX original condition .**$1,700.00**

Snowdomes

Snowdome collectors buy them all, old and new. The older ones (from the thirties and forties) are made in two pieces, the round glass globe that sits on a separate base. They were made here as well as in Italy, and today this type is being imported from Austria and the Orient.

During the fifties, plastic snowdomes made in West Germany were popular as souvenirs and Christmas toys. Some were half-domes with blue backs; others were made in bottle shapes or simple geometric forms.

There were two styles produced in the seventies. Both were made of plastic. The first were designed as large domes with a plastic figure of an animal, a mermaid, or some other character draped over the top. In the other style, the snowdome itself was made in an unusual shape.

Snowdomes have become a popular fun-type collectible, and Nancy McMichael has written an illustrated book called *Snowdomes*, which we recommend if you'd like to read more about the subject.

Advertising, shows scene of truck or building in 2¾" glass globe w/company name on black flat-sided base, 1950s..**$50.00**
Christmas scene, in plastic half-moon dome, marked Marx, 1960s...**$10.00**
Figural, 'Best Paperboy' in 2¾" glass globe w/oily liquid on flat-sided brown base, 1950s.................................**$60.00**
Figural, animal draped over large plastic dome...........**$10.00**
Figural, bear w/water ball in tummy, 1970s.................**$12.00**
Figural, Disney character in plastic dome, marked Monogram, 1960s **$30.00**
Figural, lion draped over top of large plastic dome....**$10.00**
Figural, owl w/water ball in tummy **$12.00**
Figural, Popeye in plastic dome, 1970s **$50.00**
Flintstones, Hanna Barbera, 1975, M **$40.00**
Lone Ranger, lassoing calf, M..**$95.00**
Moon Landing Commemorative, in plastic bottle **$15.00**
Order of Moose, fraternal theme in glass globe w/oily liquid on flat-sided black base, 1950s **$60.00**
Roly-poly, Santa or snowman on top half of water compartment, plastic, 1970s...**$14.00**
Rudolph the Red-Nosed Reindeer, 1950s, M................**$45.00**
Snoopy ice skating w/trees in scene, Simple Simon, early 1970s, in original box **$30.00**
Snowman, bisque figure in glass globe on brown ceramic base, 1940s **$30.00**
Souvenir, bisque figurine in glass globe on brown ceramic base w/place decal, 1940s...................................**$40.00**
Souvenir, flat panel scene in glass globe on black Bakelite base...**$30.00**
Souvenir scene, in glass globe on shell-covered scalloped base, marked Italy, 1940s **$12.00**
Souvenir scene, in glass-globed water paperweight set on black Bakelite ash tray base w/decal on front, 1930s **$55.00**
Souvenir scene, in plastic salt & pepper shakers, 1960s, pr.**$15.00**
Souvenir scene, inside large round plastic ball, coin slit on back of square-sided base **$8.00**
World War II general in glass globe on brown ceramic base **$50.00**
World's Fair, scene in plastic half-moon form **$15.00**
World's Fair, shows bisque figural Trylon & Perisphere in glass ball, 1939 ....**$75.00**

Soda Bottles

The earliest type of soda bottles were made by soda producers and sold in the immediate vicinity of the bottling company. Many had pontil scars, left by a rod that was used to manipulate the bottle as it was blown. They had a flat bottom rather than a 'kick-up,' so for transport, they were laid on their side and arranged in layers. This served to keep the cork moist, which kept it expanded, tight, and in place. Upright the cork would dry out, shrink, and expel itself with a 'pop,' hence the name 'soda pop.'

Until the twenties, the name of the product or the bottler was embossed in the glass. Nearly all bottles produced after that time had painted-on (pyro-glazed) lettering, and logos and pictures were often added. This is the type you'll encounter most often today, and collector interest is on the increase. If you'd like to learn more about them, we recommend *The Official Guide to Collecting Applied Color Label Soda Bottles* by Thomas E. Marsh.

Paper labels were used to some extent from the thirties into the sixties, sometimes pasted over reused returnable bottles.

Embossed Soda Bottles

Bacon's Soda Works Sonora Cal, 7", light green glass w/blob top..**$10.00**
Bee Candy Mfg Co San Antonio TX; 8", rectangular base w/wide shoulder, amethyst glass w/applied top **$8.00**
Bryant's Root Beer, 4½", 'This Bottle Makes Five Gallons,' on bowling pin form, amber glass w/applied top ..**$3.00**
Clarke & Co New York, 8", cylindrical, blue glass **$40.00**
Clarke & Co New York, 8", cylindrical, dark green glass..**$14.00**
Clinquist Club, 9½", 'Trade Mark Registered,' bright green glass w/crown top, w/bail & rubber stopper........**$20.00**
Congress & Empire Spring Co, 8", green glass w/applied top..**$30.00**
Cripple Creek Bottling Works, 7", cylindrical w/name embossed in circle, aqua glass **$8.00**
Crystal Soda Water Co, 7¾", cylindrical, blue glass w/applied top..**$8.00**

Dudenhofer Bottling Company Danville IL, 7¾", aqua glass **$12.00**

Eagle Soda, 7", cylindrical, green glass w/applied top.$10.00

Gettysburgh Katalysine Water, 9½", cylindrical w/name around circle on front, olive-green glass...............**$10.00**

Hawaiian Soda Works, 7½", name & place on front, aqua glass **$10.00**

Henry Kuck Savannah GA, 7¼", green glass w/blob top & iron pontil..**$20.00**

James Ray Savannah GA, 7½", green glass w/blob top..**$25.00**

John Ryan 1866, 'Excelsior Soda Works Savannah Geo' on back, 7½", cobalt glass w/blob top & iron pontil.**$50.00**

Lewis Soda Bottles Sacramento, 8½", slender form, clear glass **$8.00**

Samuel Soda Bottling Works St Helena Calif, 9", aqua glass w/applied top..**$4.00**

SAW (Savannah Aerated Water), 10", amber glass.........**$6.00**

Sun-Rise Soda Works Sacramento Cal, 7½", aqua glass.**$4.00**

Wilson's Soda Works Eureka Calif, 8", aqua glass **$4.00**

Painted-Label Soda Bottles

ABC, 1-qt, ABC blocks & 'Sparkling Beverages Cleveland Ohio' on clear glass **$10.00**

Arctic Beverages, 10-oz, polar bears on clear glass.....**$20.00**

August, 7-oz, 'August Full-Flavored Beverages' on green glass **$8.00**

Berkey's, 7-oz, 'Drink Berkey's Beverages, Quality Has No Substitutes' on clear glass **$6.00**

Berry's Big Time, 10-oz, 'It's Always Time for Big Time Beverages' on clear glass **$8.00**

Big Boy, 12-oz, 'Big Boy Quality Beverages Serve-Cold, Cleveland Ohio' on green glass **$10.00**

Black Kow, 12-oz, cow's head & 'Black Kow, Just a Swell Drink' on amber glass..**$25.00**

Black Rock, 7-oz, large black rock & 'Black Rock Pale Dry Ginger Ale, Buffalo NY' on green glass...................**$8.00**

Canada Dry, 7-oz, 'Canada Dry Sparkling Bitter Lemon' on green glass...**$6.00**

Catawissa, 7-oz, 'Catawissa Sparkling Beverages Delicious Healthful Refreshing, Every Bottle Sterilized' on green glass **$6.00**

Chief Muskogee, 9½-oz, Indian chief's profile & 'Fine Flavors' on clear glass...**$40.00**

College Club, 1-qt, mortarboard hat, diploma & 'Windsor Pennsylvania' on green glass.................................**$8.00**

Dixieland, 7-oz, factory on clear glass........................**$8.00**

Dodge City, 12-oz, saloon interior scene & 'Dodge City Sarsaparilla' on base w/cowboy hat at neck on green glass **$10.00**

Dr Swett's Root Beer, 7-oz, head silhouette on clear glass..**$6.00**

Durham's, 8-oz, clipper ship & 'Durham's Beverages' on clear glass **$8.00**

Fruit Bowl, 7-oz, 'Fruit Bowl Beverage' & quality seal on rectangular label on clear glass **$8.00**

Gator, 10-oz, alligator w/bottle in his mouth & 'Gator Beverages' on clear glass **$60.00**

Harmony Club, 1-qt, stage dancer in top hat w/piano in the background on green glass **$20.00**

Hermann, 10-oz, clown's face & 'Top Quality Hermann' in circle on clear glass..**$10.00**

Hornet Brand, 10-oz, hornet caricature in top hat & 'Hornet Brand Beverages' in circle on clear glass **$25.00**

Husker, 7-oz, running football player & 'Husker' on clear glass **$15.00**

Kick, 10-oz, kicking mule & 'Kick Like a Mule, Just Ain't None Better' on green glass **$10.00**

Kleer Kool, 12-oz, pouring bottle & hand-held glass w/icicles on clear glass..**$12.00**

Liberty, 12-oz, Statue of Liberty's bust portrait w/'Liberty' on banner below on clear glass **$20.00**

Lindy, 10-oz, airplane in cloud & 'Lindy Beverages' on clear glass **$50.00**

Little Egypt, 10-oz, outline of state of Illinois & 'Wolf's King Size' at neck on clear glass..................................**$8.00**

Mahaska, Indian chief portrait in oval w/'Mahaska' at base on clear glass..**$40.00**

Mason's, 1-qt, 'Drink Mason's Root Beer' on amber glass.**$15.00**

Moran, 1-qt, bellboy & 'Always Call for Moran Beverages' on clear glass..**$20.00**

Natural Set Up, 12-oz, pair of dice showing '4' & '3' on green glass **$20.00**

Nemo, 7-oz, circus elephant on one foot & 'Nemo Beverages' on clear glass **$20.00**

Peter Pan, 7-oz, head portrait & 'Peter Pan' in medallion w/'Delicious Refreshing' on bar on clear glass **$25.00**

Polly's, 12-oz, large parrot in ring swing on clear glass.**$20.00**

Royal Palm, 10-oz, calligraphy-type letters w/palm trees at sides & bottom on clear glass **$10.00**

Sanders, 7-oz, 'Famous over a Half Century' $2.00

Saturn, 1-qt, planet & 'Saturn Club Soda' on rectangular label w/'Saturn' at neck on clear glass **$20.00**

Tiny Tim, 7-oz, bellboy w/bottle & 'Pale Dry Ginger Ale' on green glass..**$20.00**

Universe, 7-oz, two ringed planets on clear glass.......**$20.00**

Vienna, 1-qt, street scene & 'Vienna, Double Eagle Bottling, Cleveland Ohio' on green glass **$25.00**

Wolf's, 12-oz, wolf heads around bottle w/'Beverages of Mt Carmel' on clear glass..**$10.00**

Jet Up, 7-oz, rocket in space w/ringed planet & 'Jet Up Space Age Beverages' on green glass....................**$15.00**

Paper-Labeled Soda Bottles

Abilena, 10", 'The Ideal Cathartic Water,' amber glass w/applied top...**$4.00**

Bethesda Water, 12", round bottle w/pear-shaped label, light green glass **$4.00**

Cascade Ginger Ale, 8", cylindrical, light green glass....**$6.00**

Moxie, 28-oz, orange shield w/red letters on red background $18.00

Pepsi-Cola, 28-oz, ca 1940s...**$135.00**

Ross's Royal Belfast Ginger Ale Ireland, 10", cylindrical w/diamond-shaped label, medium green glass w/applied top...**$4.00**

Shasta Cream Soda, 8", cylindrical w/crown cap & diamond-shaped label, light green glass **$4.00**

Whistle, 11½", cylindrical, 'Whistle a Liquid Food' on front, clear glass **$4.00**

Soda Fountain Collectibles

This is an area of collecting related to the advertising field, but of course zeroing in on items such as glassware once used to serve ice cream sundaes and malts, soda dispensers, ice cream dippers, straw holders, and signs that display products that were sold at ice cream parlors and soda fountains.

While some items such as the dispensers, the straw holders, and many of the dippers have become very expensive, you'll be able to find other interesting items at low prices, so whether you're wanting to recreate a vintage soda fountain in your family room or simply buying to resell, you should be able to do very well.

If you want more pricing information, we recommend *Huxford's Collectible Advertising* by Sharon and Bob Huxford.

Bottle, syrup; Cherry Smash, w/lid.............................**$135.00**

Bottle, syrup; vanilla, w/lid..**$35.00**

Carton, ½-pt, Peerless Ice Cream Co, EX......................**$8.00**

Container, Borden's Malted Milk, aluminum.................**$50.00**

Cup, Armour's Bouillon Cubes, chinaware **$25.00**

Cup, Armour's Vigoral **$25.00**

Dipper, Gem Trojan..**$40.00**

Dipper, Icy-Pi, Automatic Cone Co, VG.....................**$175.00**

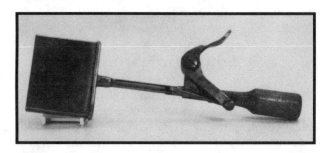

Dipper, Mayer, for ice cream sandwiches, sixteen to twenty per quart $300.00

Dipper, tin, cone shape, key release **$15.00**

Dipper, 1¾", Benedict, EX in original box..................**$45.00**

Dipper, 10", Hamilton Beach, chrome plated, M.........**$35.00**

Dish, banana split; amber glass, flat **$10.00**

Dish, banana split; clear glass, footed **$15.00**

Dish, banana split; clear glass w/fluted sides & holding tab..**$10.00**

Dish, banana split; green glass, boat type...................**$12.50**

Dish, banana split; Heisey, clear glass, flat **$20.00**

Dish, banana split; pink glass, footed.........................**$60.00**

Dish, ice cream sundae; clear glass, tulip form............**$2.50**

Dish, ice cream sundae; Dixie Vortex, metal **$3.50**

Dish, ice cream sundae; Lilly, metal **$3.00**

Dish, ice cream sundae; pink glass.............................**$25.00**

Fountain glass, Bush (ginger ale) etched on clear.......**$20.00**

Fountain glass, Fanta, clear glass **$15.00**

Fountain glass, Green River, syrup line.......................**$20.00**

Fountain glass, ice cream soda; 7", clear glass.............**$7.50**

Fountain glass, ice cream soda; Tea Room, green Depression glass **$60.00**

Fountain glass, Julep, yellow glass w/syrup line.........**$15.00**

Fountain glass, Lucky Mondae, clear glass..................**$30.00**

Fountain glass, Nesbitt's, frosted glass, tall $10.00
Fountain glass, Royal Purple grape juice,.....................$15.00
Fountain glass, Seven-Up, green glass.........................$15.00
Fountain glass, Zipp's Orangeade, clear glass $25.00
Fountain glass, 7-Up in script, clear glass $5.50
Holder, sundae cup; Vortex, metal...............................$6.00
Juicer, Arnold Electric, EX $55.00
Milk shake mixer, Gilchrist #22, as found...................$50.00
Milk shake mixer, Hamilton Beach #10.......................$50.00
Mug, Hires Root Beer, plastic, early $16.00
Mug, Lash's Root Beer, clear glass..............................$50.00
Mug, Rochester Root Beer, clear glass.........................$50.00
Photograph, interior view, front counter service, after
    1905..$10.00
Plate, ice cream; product name on chinaware.............$35.00
Plate, ice cream; product name on waxed cardboard.$15.00
Rack, potato chip; black metal, EX.............................$17.50
Receipt holder, metal $3.50
Sign, ice cream flavors, cardboard.............................$25.00
Sign, ice cream flavors, tin $50.00
Straw holder, 10", common type, w/lid & insert $100.00
Straw holder, 11", wide mouth, lift lid & straws rise,
    NM $200.00
Trade card, ice cream freezer.....................................$10.00
Trade card, ice cream related.......................................$5.00

Souvenir Spoons

Before the turn of the century, collecting silver spoons commemorating towns, states, fairs, holidays, and famous people became popular. Huge quantities were produced, and many are now found on the antiques and collectibles circuit, still interesting to collectors. There are many types of spoons; some are gold-washed, some enameled. Handles may be figural, representing something especially noteworthy about a particular area or state (for instance, a gold miner from Nevada or a salmon from Washington), or they may have a cut-out design. Indians and nudes are unusual, and along with the more interesting designs — past presidents, war memorials, or fraternal emblems, for instance — usually carry the higher price tags.

Atlantic City NJ, 'Atlantic City' etched in bowl, twisted han-
    dle $12.50
Bar Harbor ME, 'Bar Harbor' etched in bowl, loggers & pine
    cones on handle..$17.50
Bermuda, embossed onion in bowl, 'Bermuda' on back of
    handle, Shiebler $32.00

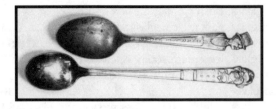

Charlie McCarthy, figural handle $10.00

Chicago IL, gold & silver 'Chicago' in bowl, floral decoration
    on handle, Reed & Barton.....................................$35.00
Colorado, emossed state seal on handle, American flag in
    enameled bowl, sterling, 1908........................... $145.00
Colorado, 'Garden of Gods' embossed in bowl, 'Colorado'
    on front & cowboy scene on back of handle $60.00
Concord MA, plain bowl, minuteman cutout on handle..$7.50
Crater Lake OR, plain bowl, Crater Lake cutout on han-
    dle..$7.50
Denver CO, plain bowl, cutout of state capitol on han-
    dle..$12.50
Hampton VA, 'Hampton VA' engraved in bowl, applied crab
    on handle $20.00
Hotel Alvarado, 'Albuquerque NM' embossed in bowl, floral
    decoration on handle...$12.50
Howdy Doody, figural handle (illustrated)...........$10.00
Kalamazoo IL, celery stalks etched in bowl, ears of corn on
    front & corn & leaves on back of handle..............$15.00
Knights of Columbus, plain bowl, enameled cross on han-
    dle, Watson...$32.00
Lenape-Penn Treaty, Indian scene embossed in bowl,
    'Lenape-Penn Treaty' on handle, Simons $40.00
Los Angeles CA, 'Los Angeles' etched in bowl, etched flow-
    ers w/enameling on handle $16.50
Los Angeles CA, 'Los Angeles' in gold-washed bowl, 'Cali-
    fornia' & floral decoration embossed on handle,
    Gorham..$32.00
Los Angeles CA, etched poinsettia in bowl, Indian
    head w/corn on front & embossed 'M' on back of
    handle..$27.50
Los Gatos CA, two cats etched in bowl, floral decoration on
    handle..$12.50
Mansfield IL, 'Mansfield' etched in bowl, floral decoration
    on front & back of handle....................................$12.50
Marinette WI, Queen Marinette etched in bowl, cut-out
    flower on front & leaves on back of handle $16.50
Mt Pleasant IA, 'Mt Pleasant IA' etched in bowl, poppy on
    front & 'M' embossed on back of handle..............$15.00
Nashville TN, Jackson's birthplace in bowl, state seal on
    handle..$11.00
New York NY, plain bowl, Empire State Building on han-
    dle $7.50
Niagara Falls, view of Niagara Falls embossed in bowl, scroll
    decoration on handle...$17.50
Palm Springs CA, plain bowl, small 'Palm Springs' enameled
    on handle...$6.00
Portland OR, engraving of Mount Hood in bowl, Indian face
    & papoose on front & Indian shooting bow on back of
    handle..$28.00
Portland OR, plain bowl, 'Portland' embossed in large letters
    on handle $35.00
San Bernardino CA, etched arrowhead in bowl, scroll design
    on front & scroll design (at edge only) on back of han-
    dle..$15.00
Santa Barbara CA, courthouse tower etched in bowl, state
    seal, flag, & gold miner on handle $15.00
St Augustine FL, plain bowl, cutout of Lightner Museum on
    handle...$7.50

St Louis MO, plain bowl, 'St Louis' & Indian head embossed on handle, Watson.....................$22.50

St Paul MN, state capitol etched in bowl, simple design on each side of handle.......................$11.50

Sterling IL, plain bowl, 'Sterling IL' enameled on front & scroll design on back of handle........................$15.00

Syracuse NY, 'Syracuse' etched in bowl, raised flowers on handle.................................$12.50

Utah, Mormon Temple engraved in bowl, 'Utah' embossed on handle $25.00

Yellowstone, plain bowl, embossed bear on handle, Watson.$27.50

Yosemite CA, plain bowl, mountains on handle $8.00

Space Collectibles

Even before the first man landed on the moon, the idea of space travel had always intrigued us. This is an area of collecting that is right now attracting lots of interest and includes not only serious documentary material, but games, toys, puzzles, and models as well.

Book, 'Liftoff: Story of America's Adventure in Space,' Michael Collins, Grove Press, 1st edition, w/dust jacket, M $22.00

Book, 'Mariner 6 & 7 Pictures of Mars,' NASA #SP-263, hardcover edition, red cloth binding, 1971, 159 pages, VG.................................$38.00

Book, 'Space-Age Photographic Atlas,' by Kevin Fitzgerald, Crown Publishing, 1970, 1st edition, w/dust jacket, EX $15.00

Booklet, 'Earth Orbital Science in the '70s,' NASA #EP-83, 28 pages.................................$4.00

Coloring book, 'Man on the Moon,' Artcraft, 1969, NM ..$4.00

Costume, US astronaut, Ben Cooper, 1-piece suit & plastic mask, 1961, in original 8x10" box, M $30.00

Figure, 4½", 'Billy Blast-Off,' Eldon, bendable plastic, 1968, in original 8x14x6" box w/accessories, M $75.00

Figurine, 9", Neil Armstrong landing on moon, metal w/wooden base, NM $95.00

Flashlight, 7" long, tin & plastic w/Space Boy illustrations, ca 1950s, VG.......................................$40.00

Game, 'Blast-Off,' 20x22", Waddington, board shows planets, 1969, M $40.00

Game, 'Countdown,' Lowell, 2-piece capsule w/color photo cards of US astronauts in stages of their mission, 1966, M $40.00

Game, 'Moon Shot,' Cadaco, 1967 ....$10.00

Game, 'Space Station Darts,' Amsco, 1950s, 15" square target w/rocket-like darts, EX $50.00

Globe, 9", moon, tin lithograph showing 1969 landing site & other proposed sites, tin lithograph base, M.........$55.00

Goblet, Apollo Moon Landing, red, white & blue on clear glass $20.00

Gum cards, 'Man on the Moon,' photos from space program, 1960s, 20-card set, NM $7.50

Helmet & record set, 'Blast Off to the Moon,' RCA Victor, built-in speaker phones & plastic visor, 1960, in original box...$65.00

Juice carafe, 7¾", patriotic graphics for Apollo missions on clear glass w/white plastic cap, Libbey Glass Co .$25.00

Kite, 28x22", Alox Manufacturing Co, colorful space graphics on paper w/wooden supports, 1950s, M..............$25.00

Lunch box, satellite, American Thermos, 1959-62, w/original thermos, M.......................................$95.00

Model, 'Apollo Lunar Module,' Revell, 1969, in original box.......................................$65.00

Model, astronaut, Revell, all plastic, 1966, in original 7x12" box.......................................$25.00

Model, capsule, 38", Perry, cardboard w/cut-away windows, 1966, in original 36x14x4" box, M $50.00

Paint set, 'Rocket Patrol,' 1½x18½x9" box, Hassenfield Bros, complete contents, 1950s, NM $65.00

Pencil set, 'Mars Invades Earth,' Crafthouse, 12 pre-numbered sketches w/12 color pencils, 1963, in original box $150.00

Pin-back button, 2", 'Well Done Colonel Glenn, First American in Orbit,' 1962, NM $20.00

Pin-back button, 2½", Space Shuttle, color picture from past flight, each.......................................$1.50

Pin-back button, 6", Apollo XI, three astronauts, M $5.00

Play set, 'Astro Base,' Ideal, space station w/remote-control scout car, in original 24x12x10" box, M.............$165.00

Play set, 'Cape Canaveral Missile,' Marx, in original box, NM.......................................$125.00

Play set, 'Cape Kennedy,' Remco, replica launching center & accessories, 1966, in original box, M...................$175.00

Play set, 'Zeroid Commander Action Station,' Ideal, complete w/accessories, in original 17x14x5" box, M.........$150.00

Post card, 5x6½", moon landing scene in three dimensions, 1965, unused, M.......................................$30.00

Puzzle, Apollo Moon Mission 11 crew, jigsaw, 1969, EX .$5.00

Toy, 'Apollo Moon Exploring Series' set #J, Imperial Toys, plastic astronaut & two vehicles, 1970, M on 5x7" card.......................................$15.00

Toy, 'Apollo Moon Trek' flying rocket, 6½", plastic, battery operated, late 1960s, M in box.............................$28.00

Toy, 'Apollo Space Station,' 8½x11", Marx, seven 3" figures w/accessories on 8½x11" card, 1970, M...............$90.00

Toy, 'Bionic Mission Vehicle,' 20" long, plastic, transparent shield not shown, 1977.....................$15.00

Toy, 'Cape Canaveral Rocketship,' 10½", Hong Kong, spring-loaded launcher & two rockets, 1970s, M in display bag.......................................$48.00

Toy, 'Friendship-7' ship, 3x4x6½", Japan, tin friction capsule w/astronaut inside, 1960s, EX **$95.00**

Toy, 'Moon Scout' helicopter, 5x14x15", Marx, plastic & metal, battery operated, Nasa logos, flags, etc on sides, EX **$165.00**

Toy, 'Nasa Astronaut,' 6x2x2", lithograph on tin w/plastic arms & base, wind-up, NM..................**$85.00**

Toy, 'Nasa Daiya Spaceship,' 12", battery operated, Made in Japan, NM..................**$100.00**

Toy, 'Nasa Technical Services' vehicle, 5", Japan, lithograph on tin, 1960s, light wear **$60.00**

Toy, 'Nasa 905 Space Shuttle Challenger,' 12" plane & 7" shuttle, Taiwan, plastic & metal, M in EX box....**$185.00**

Toy, 'Space Robot-Rocket 7,' 5x3x6", Japan, tin friction rocket ship w/3-dimensional robot on top, 1960s, EX **$200.00**

Toy, 'Space Shuttle Flying Saucer,' Formis Mfg Chattanooga, w/instruction sheet, 1950s, EX **$20.00**

Toy, 'Spacecraft Apollo 11 Lunar Module,' battery operated, Made in Japan, M..................**$150.00**

Toy, 'UFO #X05,' 7" dia, tin & plastic saucer form, in original box, M **$75.00**

Toy, 'USA Nasa Gemini' spacecraft, 9", colorful lithograph on tin, battery operated, Japan, in original box, NM **$175.00**

Toy, flying saucer, 7" dia, Marx, ca 1958-62, saucer form w/gyroscope mechanism & accessories, in original box, M..................**$100.00**

Toy, rocket launcher, 2-stage, battery operated, marked Japan, in original box, NM **$250.00**

Toy, satellite, 8", 2-stage, marked LineMar & Japan, 1950s, NM **$140.00**

Toy, satellite, 9" dia, lithograph on tin, battery operated, Cragstan, NM..................**$80.00**

Toy, space capsule, 10", #7, battery operated w/space-walking astronaut, marked TM Co & Japan, M..........**$100.00**

Toy, spaceship, 8" dia, Marx, hand crank operates gyroscope inside plastic saucer shape, 1960-61, in original box, M **$150.00**

Toy, UFO, 7" dia, #8, tin friction type, marked Maji & Japan, 1950s, NM..................**$80.00**

Tumbler, 4", 'Apollo 12' & 'Return to the Moon' in red, white & blue on clear glass, Libbey Glass Co, dated 1969..................**$7.50**

Sports Collectibles

When the baseball card craze began sweeping the country a decade ago, memorabilia relating to many types of sports began to interest sports fans. Ticket stubs, uniforms, autographed baseballs, sports magazines, and game-used bats are prized by baseball fans, and some items, depending on their age or the notoriety of the player or team they represent, may be very valuable. Baseball and golfing seem to be the two sports most collectors are involved with, and there are several books on the market you'll want to read if you're personally interested in either:

Value Guide to Baseball Collectibles by Donald Raycraft and Craig Raycraft, *Collector's Guide to Baseball Memorabilia* by Don Raycraft and Stew Salowitz, and *The Encyclopedia of Golf Collectibles* by John M. Olman and Morton W. Olman. See also Baseball Cards.

Badminton, instruction handbook, published by Athletic Institute, ca 1940s, set of four, in original box, EX **$15.00**

Baseball, ad, 11x14", from 'Life', 1953, Phil Rizutto (New York Yankees) in batting pose, framed, EX..........**$27.50**

Baseball, autograph, signed ball, Henry Aaron, EX.......**$35.00**

Baseball, autograph, 3x5" card, Lou Brock, EX.............**$8.00**

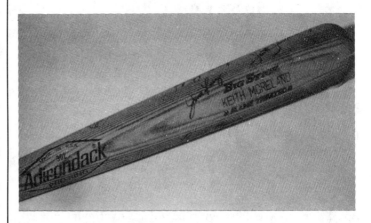

Baseball, bat, Adirondak, game-used by Keith Moreland..................**$28.00**

Baseball, bat, Adirondak, #459B, used by Tony Fernandez, cracked **$65.00**

Baseball, bat, Hillerich & Bradsby, #L1864, used by US Grant, cracked..................**$15.00**

Baseball, bat, Louisville Slugger, #C217, used by Dave Magadan, uncracked..................**$65.00**

Baseball, bat, Louisville Slugger, #R161, used by Luis Aquino, uncracked..................**$40.00**

Baseball, book, 'Baseball Guide & Record Book 1952,' 601 pages, EX..................**$15.00**

Baseball, book, 'Big Baseball Book for Boys,' 1931....**$45.00**

Baseball, book, 'Nice Guys Finish Last,' by Leo Durocher, 1975, EX..................**$25.00**

Baseball, exercise kit, 'Isometric Minute a Day Gym,' Mickey Mantle & Bonnie Prudden, Beacon, 1960s, EX..........**$80.00**

Baseball, figurine, full-figure Yogi Berra w/catcher's mitt & face mask, Hartland, EX..................**$170.00**

Baseball, figurine, 4", Fernando Valenzuela, Kenner starting lineup series, in original box, 1988, EX................**$12.50**

Baseball, figurine, 4", Jack Morris, Kenner starting lineup series, 1988, in original box, NM..................**$15.00**

Baseball, guide book, 5x7", 'Official Major & Minor League,' 1944, VG..................**$10.00**

Baseball, key chain, given to fans who saw Willie May's 600th career home run in San Francisco, EX........**$25.00**

Baseball, magazine, 'Baseball Digest,' World Series Highlights cover & article, 1979 ....**$4.00**

Baseball, magazine, 'Collier's,' Babe Ruth article & photo, VG $10.00

Baseball, magazine, 'Life,' September 1962, Don Drysdale & Dodgers article, EX $20.00

Baseball, magazine, 'Newsweek,' Nolan Ryan cover, 1975, June 16, NM..$10.00

Baseball, magazine, 'Sports Illustrated,' preview issue w/Willie Mays cover, 1957, NM $25.00

Baseball, newspaper, New York Times w/'Second MVP Award Bolsters Gehrig's All-Time Star Rating' headline, 1936, NM $125.00

Baseball, nodder, Cleveland Indians, w/bobber head, EX $18.00

Baseball, nodder, 7x3½", Cincinnati Reds player, w/bobber head, ca 1962, NM $55.00

Baseball, patch, 'San Francisco Giants 25 Years, 1958-82,' EX..$15.00

Baseball, patch, '100th Anniversary of Philadelphia' franchise, worn by Phillies during 1983 season, EX......$8.00

Baseball, pennant, 30", 1963 World's Series, Dodgers versus Yankees, M $17.50

Baseball, photo, 8x10", Stan Musial, EX $35.00

Baseball, photo, 8x6", shows lady batter & catcher, dated 1930, VG $15.00

Baseball, pin-back button w/ribbon, 'Souvenir SF Giants versus NY Yankees World Series 1962,' EX $20.00

Baseball, poker chip, 1½", Jackie Jensen of Red Sox on red plastic, 1950s, EX..$4.50

Baseball, poster, 22x14", advertising Superior Malts versus Sheller's, ca 1930, VG $25.00

Baseball, press pin, 'All-Star Game, Houston, 1968' ..$100.00

Baseball, press pin, 'World Series, Los Angeles Dodgers, 1959' $300.00

Baseball, program, 'Candlestick Park on Willie Mays Day,' EX...$10.00

Baseball, program, Coperstown, commemorates Jackie Robinson stamp, 1982, August 2, EX $45.00

Baseball, program, Milwaukee Braves versus New York Yankees, 1975, unscored, EX $75.00

Baseball, program, St Louis Cardinals versus Philadelphia, World Series, 1931 ....$150.00

Baseball, schedule card, Los Angeles Dodgers, 1971, Maury Wills on front, M $20.00

Baseball, score book, Cleveland Indians versus Boston Red Sox, 1948, VG $12.50

Baseball, score card, Cleveland Indians, 1936, G $15.00

Baseball, score card, Comiskey Park, Chicago White Sox, unscored, 1958 ....$15.00

Baseball, silk, 3½x5", shows pitcher & 'University of Chicago,' Murad Cigarette Co premium, EX.........$17.50

Baseball, silk, 3½x5", University of Pennsylvania, ca 1920s, EX...$20.00

Baseball, sticker, advertising 'Ted's (Ted Williams) Creamy Root Beer,' 1950s $20.00

Baseball, ticket stub, for game when Pete Rose broke Ty Cobb's record, 1985 ....$8.00

Baseball, ticket stub, World Series, 1949 at New York, Game 2 ....$40.00

Baseball, ticket stub, World Series, 1972 at Cincinnati, Game 1 ....$20.00

Baseball, vegetable crate label, 4x7", 'Safe Hit Brand' above ballpark scene, 1930s-40s, EX $3.00

Baseball, whistle, lithographed tin figural player in hand-sewn case marked 'Home Run Whistle,' ca 1930s, EX $30.00

Baseball, yearbook, Blue Jays, 1979 ....$15.00

Baseball, yearbook, Boston Braves, 1950 ....$150.00

Baseball, yearbook, Milwaukee Braves, 1964.............$30.00

Basketball, paperback, 'Official Basketball Guide for Women for 1930-31,' published by Spalding, 90 pages, VG ..$7.50

Basketball, photo, 6x8", lady college player, ca 1930, EX $17.50

Bowling, photo, 5x3½", shows men's team, ca 1910, VG $12.50

Bowling, ticket, 5x3", for international bowling, dated 1932, EX..$7.50

Boxing, magazine, 'Boxing Illustrated,' Cassius Clay cover, 1965, EX...$4.50

Boxing, magazine, 'Ramparts,' June 1967, Muhammad Ali cover w/stories of draft & name change, NM $32.50

Boxing, pin-back button, 3½", Sugar Ray Robinson photo & 'The Greatest of the Champs 1921-89,' EX $7.50

Car racing, ticket, 'Third Annual Pebble Beach Sports Road Races,' April 1952, EX......................................$12.50

Football, photo, 6½x9", Captain Tardy of Stanford, ca 1930, EX $7.50

Football, program, Army-Michigan game, October 8, 1949, NM $12.50

Football, program, college match, dated 1941, EX......$10.00

Golf, ad, 6x9", shows Hornet brand golf balls in box w/original price of $8 for three dozen, ca 1920, VG $7.50

Golf, book, 'The Secret of Par Golf,' 10x13", 1935, hardcover w/original dust jacket, EX $12.50

Golf, handbook, 3x4", instructional techniques, ca 1940s, set of four, in original box, NM $22.50

Golf, photo, for NBC Special, 'Arnold Palmer, an American Legend,' 1973, EX..$22.50

Golf, photo, 5x7", full-length view of lady swinging club, ca 1920, EX..$17.50

Golf, photo, 9x7", Women's Golf Championship, shows players, dated 1938, EX $10.00

Golf, poster sticker, 1½", PGA Championship, Pinehurst NC, 1935, golfer on gold foil, EX $5.00

Golf, silk, 3½x4¾", golfer w/club & 'Annapolis,' Murad Cigarette Co, ca 1915, NM $17.50

Hockey, photo, 6½x8½", shows college lady player, ca 1925, EX $17.50

Horse racing, manual, 'The American Racing Manual,' hardcover, w/diagrams & photos, dated 1947, 978 pages, EX $17.50

Horse racing, program, Delaware Park, 1945, VG.........$2.00

Ice skating, ribbon award, gold on silk, ca 1920s, EX...$7.50

Skiing, poster sticker, 'Enjoy Winter Sports in New Hampshire,' shows skier, ca 1930 ....$5.00

Tennis, booklet, 7x5", 'Want To Be a Tennis Champion?,' photos, 29 pages, VG $10.00

Tennis, photo, 6x8", National Tennis Tournament, full-length view of lady w/racket, 1931, EX..................**$7.50**
Tennis, photo, 8x10", shows winners of National Doubles, dated 1946, EX..**$12.50**

World of Sports, thermos bottle............................**$25.00**

Stanford Corn

Teapots, cookie jars, salt and pepper shakers, and other kitchen and dinnerware items modeled as ears of yellow corn with green shucks were made by the Stanford company, who marked most of their ware. The Shawnee company made two very similar corn lines; just check the marks to verify the manufacturer.

Butter dish...**$45.00**

Cookie jar **$80.00**

Corn tray, individual..**$20.00**
Creamer & sugar bowl......................................**$45.00**

Pitcher, 7½"..**$55.00**
Relish tray..**$35.00**
Salt & pepper shakers.......................................**$25.00**
Teapot..**$60.00**

Stangl Birds

The Stangl Pottery Company of Flemington and Trenton, New Jersey, made a line of ceramic birds which they introduced in 1940 to fullfill the needs of a market no longer able to access foreign imports, due to the onset of WWII. These bird figures immediately attracted a great deal of attention, and at the height of their production, sixty decorators were employed to hand paint the birds at the plant, and the overflow was contracted out and decorated in private homes. After WWII, inexpensive imported figurines once again saturated the market, and for the most part, Stangl curtailed their own production, though the birds were made on a very limited basis until as late as 1977.

For the most part, all the birds were marked. A four-digit number was used to identify the species, and some pieces were signed by the decorator. An 'F' indicates a bird that was decorated at the Flemington plant.

Detailed information and a complete listing is available in *The Collectors Handbook of Stangl Pottery* by Norma Rehl.

Bird of Paradise, 5½", #3408 ....**$115.00**
Black Poll Warbler, #3810 ....**$150.00**
Blue Headed Vireo, 4¼", #3448 ....**$85.00**
Bluebirds, 8½", #3276D **$150.00**
Bobolink, 4¾", #3595..**$125.00**
Broadbill Hummingbird, #3629...................................**$135.00**
Broadtail Hummingbird, #3626 ....**$175.00**
Cardinal, 6½", red matt, #3444 ....**$85.00**

Cerulean Warbler, 4¼", #3456....................$100.00
Cock Pheasant, 6¼x11", #3492.....................$250.00
Duck, Flying, 9", gray, #3443 ....$320.00
Evening Grosbeak, #3813...............................$140.00
Golden Crown Kinglet, 4", #3848 ....$125.00
Goldfinches, #3635 ....$235.00

Gray Cardinal, 5", #3596.............................$60.00
Hen Pheasant, #3491 ....$235.00
Indigo Bunting, #3589 ....$70.00
Kentucky Warbler, 3", #3598...........................$55.00
Key West Quail Dove, 9", #3454.....................$255.00
Kingfisher, 3½", #3406 ....$85.00
Lovebird, 4", #3400 ....$65.00
Lovebirds, 5½", #3404D $95.00
Oriole, 3¼", #3402 ....$65.00
Painted Bunting, #3452 ....$125.00
Parula Warbler, 4¾", #3583 ....$65.00
Red-Faced Warbler, 3", #3594 ....$85.00
Rufous Hummingbird, 3", #3585 ....$65.00
Titmouse, 2½", #3592.......................................$60.00

Western Tanagers, 8", #3750D $400.00

Wilson Warbler, 3½", yellow, #3597 ....**$50.00**
Yellow Warbler, #3447 ....**$85.00**

Stangl Dinnerware

The Stangl Company of Trenton, New Jersey, grew out of the Fulper company that had been established in Flemington early in the 1800s. Martin Stangl, president of the company, introduced a line of dinnerware in the 1920s. By 1954, 90% of their production centered around their dinnerware lines. Until 1942, the clay they used was white firing, and decoration was minimal, usually simple one-color glazes. In 1942, however, the first of the red-clay lines that have become synonomous with the Stangl name was created. Designs were hand carved into the greenware, then hand painted. More than one hundred different patterns have been cataloged. From 1974 until 1978, a few lines previously discontinued on the red clay were reintroduced with a white clay body. Soon after '78, the factory closed.

If you'd like more information on the subject, read _The Collector's Handbook of Stangl Pottery_ by Norma Rehl and _The Collector's Encyclopedia of American Dinnerware_ by Jo Cunningham.

Amberglo, bowl, 8"......................................**$20.00**
Amberglo, cruet, w/stopper **$25.00**
Amberglo, gravy boat **$10.00**
Antique Gold, pitcher, 12"...........................**$20.00**
Antique Gold, server, center handle **$15.00**
Blueberry, bowl, 10".....................................**$40.00**
Blueberry, bowl, 12".....................................**$50.00**
Blueberry, cup..**$10.00**
Blueberry, plate, dinner size, 10".................**$12.00**
Country Garden, bowl, divided vegetable **$35.00**
Country Garden, bowl, 8" **$30.00**
Country Garden, coaster................................**$7.00**
Country Garden, cup **$12.00**
Country Garden, plate, dinner size, 10" **$15.00**
Dahlia, plate, 6"...**$4.50**
Fruits, bowl, soup **$18.00**
Fruits, pitcher, ½-pt......................................**$15.00**
Fruits, plate, dinner size, 10".......................**$15.00**
Fruits, plate, 8" **$12.00**
Fruits, sugar bowl, w/lid **$18.00**
Golden Harvest, coffeepot **$30.00**
Golden Harvest, cup......................................**$5.00**
Golden Harvest, pitcher, 2-qt.......................**$35.00**
Golden Harvest, plate, dinner size, 10" **$7.50**
Little Bo Peep, bowl, Kiddieware **$40.00**
Little Bo Peep, cup, Kiddieware **$35.00**
Magnolia, butter dish....................................**$35.00**
Magnolia, casserole, 4¼", w/lid....................**$12.00**
Magnolia, chop plate, 12½".........................**$20.00**
Magnolia, cup & saucer................................**$12.00**
Magnolia, plate, dinner size, 10" **$10.00**
Magnolia, relish tray **$16.00**
Magnolia, salt & pepper shakers, pr............**$15.00**

Maple Whirl, plate, dinner size, 10".............................$10.00
Orchard Song, coaster $5.00
Orchard Song, plate, dinner size, 10" $10.00
Orchard Song, plate, 5"..$5.00
Orchard Song, server, center handle $12.00
Prelude, plate, 8"...$8.00
Terra Rose, egg cup, yellow Tulip...............................$10.00
Terra Rose, sherbet, high standard $25.00
Thistle, bowl, divided vegetable..................................$16.00
Thistle, bowl, 8"..$25.00
Thistle, coaster $5.00
Thistle, creamer & sugar bowl, w/lid $20.00
Thistle, cup & saucer $12.00
Thistle, plate, 5"...$3.00
Thistle, platter $30.00
Town & Country, bowl, cereal; 5½", yellow, deep......$10.00
Town & Country, casserole, large, blue, w/lid $85.00
Town & Country, cup, green $12.00
Town & Country, mug, large, brown $25.00
Town & Country, plate, dinner size, blue, 10"............$20.00
Town & Country, salt & pepper shakers, green, handles,
  pr $20.00

Star Trek Memorabilia

Trekkies, as fans are often referred to, number nearly 40,000 today, hold national conventions, and compete with each other for choice items of Star Trek memorabilia, some of which may go for hundreds of dollars.

The Star Trek concept was introduced to the public in the mid-1960s through a TV series which continued for many years in syndication. An animated cartoon series (1977), the release of six major motion pictures (1979 through 1989), and the success of 'Star Trek, The Next Generation' television show (Fox network, 1987) all served as a bridge to join two generations of loyal fans.

Its success has resulted in the sale of vast amounts of merchandise, both licensed and unlicensed, such as clothing, promotional items of many sorts, books and comics, toys and games, records and tapes, school supplies, and party goods. Many of these are still available at flea markets around the country. An item that is 'mint in box' is worth at least twice as much as one in excellent condition but without its original packaging.

Bank, Captain Kirk figural, Play Pal, 1975....................$40.00
Calendar, Ballantine Books, 1976 ....$35.00
Communicators, Remco, 1967, pr..............................$125.00
Costume, Mr Spock, cloth w/plastic face mask, 1975, in
  original 8x11x3½" box $30.00
Decanter, bust of Mr Spock, in original box...............$72.00
Doll, Mego, 1974, 1st series, any crew member, each.$30.00
Doll, Mego, 1975, 2nd series, aliens, each $75.00
Figure, 'Q' from 'Next Generation,' on original card...$42.00
Frisbee, Remco, 1967...$30.00
Game, 'Super Phaser Target,' Mego, in original box...$60.00
Game, 10x20", Ideal, complete mission & return to earth,
  1967, in original box, M..$50.00

Gun, 'Star Trek Pocket Pistol,' Remco, photo of Mr Spock
  firing gun on 14x10" box, 1968, M $120.00
Gun, phaser, w/photo of Kirk & Mr Spock, Remco, in origi-
  nal box, NM..$85.00
Gun, 10", 'Astro Buzz-Ray' Remco, three turrets project
  colored light when switch is on, 1968, in original
  box $120.00
Liquor decanter, Mr Spock figural, Grenadier, 1979....$75.00
Model, 'K-7 Space Station,' Ertl, 1976 ....$75.00
Oil paint set, 28x20", Hasbro, pre-numbered sketched
  canvas w/eight vials of oil paints & plastic frame,
  1967, M $200.00
Photo, 8x10", entire cast of 'Next Generation,' color, M...$12.50
Photo, 8x10", Marina Sirtis of 'Next Generation' in character,
  signed, EX...$45.00
Plate, 8½", 'City on the Edge of Forever,' gold-trimmed
  rim $200.00
Plate, 8½", Data portrait, 'New Generation' $250.00
Play set, 'Mission to Gamma VI,' Mego, 1976...........$500.00
Post card, 3½x5½", full-color scenes, Paramount Pictures,
  1977, set of 48, EX...$25.00
Punch-out book, 'Star Trek Action Toy Book,' Random
  House, 1976, complete, EX $30.00
Ring, Star Trek series, Spock, w/secret compartment .$12.00
Ring, Star Trek series, Star Trek logo, yellow w/secret com-
  partment, 1979 ....$12.00
Shuttlecraft, 'Galileo,' in original box $48.00
Spoon, 'Scotty' figural handle.......................................$20.00

**Tumbler, 6", Mr Spock shown, indented base, Dr
  Pepper 1976..$30.00**
TV tray, Mr Spock lithograph, 1979............................$20.00
Walkie-talkies, Remco, yellow & red plastic, hand-held
  w/twenty feet of hollow plastic line, 1968, on original
  card, pr $50.00

Water pistol, Aviva, 1979................................$25.00

Star Wars Trilogy

In the late seventies, the movie 'Star Wars' became a box office hit, most notably for its fantastic special effects and its ever-popular theme of space adventure. Two more movies followed, 'The Empire Strikes Back' in 1980 and 'Return of the Jedi' in 1983. After the first movie, an enormous amount of related merchandise was released. A large percentage of these items was action figures, made by the Kenner company who included the logo of the 20th Century Fox studios (under whom they were licensed) on everything they made until 1980. Just before the second movie, Star Wars creator, George Lucas, regained control of the merchandise rights, and items inspired by the last two films can be identified by his own Lucasfilm logo. Since 1987, Lucasfilm, Ltd., has operated shops in conjunction with the Star Tours at Disneyland theme parks.

Action set, 'Star Wars Play-Doh,' three hinged molds, knife, three cans of Play-Doh, Kenner, 1978-79, complete in box, M.................$10.00

Bop bag, 33", R2D2, inflatable vinyl bag w/weight in the bottom, Kenner, 1978-79, M.................$15.00

Collector case, 16x15", Darth Vader bust figural in molded plastic w/hinge, Kenner, 1980-present, EX...........$15.00

Costume, Chewbacca, in original box.................$20.00

Costume, Darth Vader, Ben Cooper, 1980, in original box.................$25.00

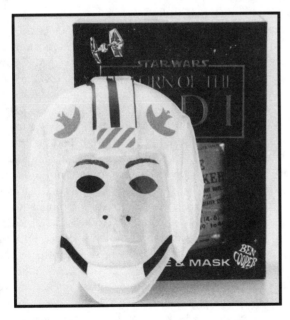

Costume, Luke Sky Walker, w/mask $15.00

Figurine, 11½", Princess Leia Organa, jointed vinyl w/bendable knees, Kenner, 1978-80, w/original clothing, MIB....$150.00

Figurine, 12", Ben Kenobi, jointed vinyl w/bendable knees, original outfit w/yellow light saber, Kenner, in original box.................$150.00

Figurine, 12", C3PO, metallic molded plastic, jointed at hips, shoulders & neck, Kenner, 1979-80, in original box, M $60.00

Figurine, 12", Hans Solo, jointed vinyl, bendable knees, complete outfit w/accessories, Kenner, 1978-80, in original box $225.00

Figurine, 12", Luke Skywalker, jointed vinyl w/bendable knees, Kenner, 1978-80, in original box, M $150.00

Figurine, 15", Chewbacca, molded plastic jointed at hips & shoulders, Kenner, 1978-80, in original box, M..$135.00

Figurine, 6", Tauntaun, molded plastic w/removable vinyl saddle & bridle, Kenner, 1980-81, M $10.00

Figurine, 8¾", Jawa, molded plastic in suede cloak, flexible hands turn 360 degrees, Kenner, 1979-80, in original box.................$150.00

Game, 'Destroy Death Star,' board w/spinner & X-Wing fighters play pieces, Kenner, 1979-80, in original box, M......$12.00

Game, 'Electronic Battle Command Game,' 8x6¼x4½", computer styled, uses six AA batteries, Kenner, M......$45.00

Game, 'Escape from Death Star,' includes cards & spinner, Kenner, 1978-79, M.................$15.00

Game, 'X-Wing Aces Target Game,' 23x14¾x1½", molded gray plastic body w/black & blue plastic gun, Kenner, 1978, M $60.00

Lamp, large, Darth Vader bust figural, ceramic $90.00

Laser pistol, plastic replica of Han Solo's gun w/logo on side, Kenner, 1978-83, M.................$25.00

Light saber, 35", inflatable vinyl tube fits on flashlight-type handle w/'Star Wars' emblem around outside, Kenner, M.................$20.00

Model, 'The Fighter,' MIB $25.00

Movie viewer, 6¾x6¾", molded plastic w/logo on one side, takes snap-in cartridge of scenes from movie, Kenner, M.................$20.00

Paperback, 'Return of the Jedi,' Del Rey, illustrated, EX...$7.00

Paperback, 'Star Wars Album,' Ballentine, VG $6.00

Plane, 'Twin Ion Engine Fighter,' 10½x9x7", molded plastic w/pop-off solar panels, battery operated, Kenner, M.................$45.00

Plane, 'X-Wing Fighter' (wings open), 4¾x4x1½", painted die-cast metal body w/plastic wings, Kenner, 1978-81, M..**$30.00**

Play set, 'Creature Cantina,' 14x8", molded plastic base w/action lever controls, cardboard background, Kenner, 1978, M..**$25.00**

Play set, 'Death Star Space Station,' 22½x16", molded plastic & cardboard, Kenner, 1978-80, in original box, EX..**$45.00**

Play set, 'Droid Factory,' 13x10¾", molded plastic, movable crane & interchangeable pieces to build droids, Kenner, M..**$35.00**

Play set, 'Hoth Ice Planet Adventure,' 12x17", molded plastic foreground w/printed cardboard background, Kenner, 1980, M..**$20.00**

Play set, 'Imperial Attack Base,' 17x9½x3", molded plastic w/collapsing bridge & movable gun, Kenner, 1980-81, M..**$25.00**

Play set, 'Land of the Jawas,' 18½x10x11", molded plastic base w/action lever, Kenner, 1979-80, in original box, M..**$25.00**

Puzzle, 'Luke Skywalker & Princess Leia Leap for Their Lives!,' 500-pc, Kenner, 1979, M.............................**$8.00**

Puzzle, 'Millenium Falcon in Hyper Space,' 1500-pc, Kenner, 1979, M..**$10.00**

Puzzle, R2D2 & C3PO pictured, 140-pc, Kenner, 1978, M.**$7.00**

Robot, 8", R2D2, battery operated, red 'eye' lights up, electronic sounds, head turns 360 degrees, Kenner, 1978-80, M.**$60.00**

Telephone, Darth Vader figural, M.............................**$65.00**

Van, 7¼x3x3", all plastic, makes 'Sonic Sound' & 'Blazin' Sparks,' characters on sides, Kenner, 1978-79, M..$25.00

Vehicle, 'Jawa Sandcrawler,' 16½x5½x8", molded plastic, radio controlled, Kenner, 1979-80, M **$85.00**

Vehicle, 'Land Speeder,' 4¾x3x1⅜", painted die-cast metal w/figures, Kenner, 1978-81, M.............................**$20.00**

Vehicle, 'Land Speeder,' 9½x6x2¾", molded orange plastic w/clear windshield, Kenner, 1978-80, NM............**$40.00**

Steiff Animals

These stuffed animals originated in Germany around the turn of the century. They were created by Margarete Steiff, whose company continues to operate to the present day. They are identified by the button inside the ear and the identification tag (which often carries the name of the animal) on their chest. Over the years, variations in the tags and buttons help collectors determine approximate dates of manufacture.

Teddy bear collectors regard Steiff bears as some of the most valuable on the market. When assessing the worth of a bear, they use some general guidelines as a starting basis, though other features can come into play as well. For instance, bears made prior to 1912 that have long gold mohair fur start at a minimum of $75.00 per inch. If the bear has dark brown or curly white mohair fur instead, the price may go as high as $135.00. From the 1920 to 1930 era, the price would be about $50.00 minimum per inch. A bear (or any other animal) on cast iron or wooden wheels starts at $75.00 per inch; but if the tires are hard rubber, the value is much lower, at $27.00 per inch.

It's a fascinating study which is well-covered in *Teddy Bears and Steiff Animals, First and Second Series,* by Margaret Fox Mandel.

Alligator puppet, incised button, split chest tag, M **$70.00**

Bear, 10", #0202/26, caramel mohair w/attached tag, 'Original Teddy,' Trevira velvet pads, ca 1960s.............**$75.00**

Bear, 10", #5325, gold mohair, non-working squeaker, glass eyes, black floss nose, original ribbon, ca 1950s-60s **$325.00**

Bear, 11", gold mohair, fully jointed, glass eyes, yellowish felt pads on long feet, brown floss nose & mouth, ca 1950 ....**$350.00**

Bear, 13", gold mohair, fully jointed, squeaker, glass eyes, black twisted floss nose & mouth, ca 1950s-60s.**$375.00**

Bear, 16", gold mohair, fully jointed, loud squeaker, glass eyes, floss nose, script button, 1950s-1960s, NM..**$550.00**

Bear, 20", mohair, hump, growler, glass eyes, EX.....**$500.00**

Bear, 3½", #5310, gold mohair, glass eyes, black floss nose, ca 1950s-60s **$200.00**

Bear, 3½", white mohair, fully jointed, glass bead eyes, no pads, w/attached tag: 'Original Teddy,' rare, ca 1950s **$325.00**

Bear, 6", mohair, fully jointed, straw stuffed, no pads, 1950s to mid-1960s, M **$250.00**

Bear, 7", #5318, caramel mohair, non-working squeaker, glass eyes, brown floss nose, ca 1950s-60s........**$225.00**

Bear, 8", 'Yorkie,' gold mohair, fully jointed, squeaker, shoe-button eyes, black floss nose, mouth, & claws, pre-1910 ....**$350.00**

Bear, 8½", gold mohair, fully jointed, glass eyes, non-working squeaker, 1950s to mid-1960s, NM................**$275.00**

Bear, 8½", 'Orsi,' caramel-colored mohair, jointed head & arms, amber glass eyes, open felt mouth, four claws, 1956 (Orsis made since 1956 are much less collectible), rare.........**$550.00**

Bear, 9", tan mohair, glass eyes, tags & button, recent, EX **$45.00**

Bear cub, 12", brown, original collar & bell, US Zone tag, M **$965.00**

Bear cub on all fours, chest tag, no button, 1970s, NM .**$90.00**
Bear on wheels, 19x26", brown mohair, glass eyes, beige floss claws, metal rod w/disk wheels & rubber tires, 1950s, M **$650.00**
Boar, 5", incised button, EX **$85.00**
Clown, roly poly, new limited edition.............**$160.00**
Cocker Spaniel, 9", incised button, old chest tag, EX..**$65.00**
Collie, 8", sitting, open mouth, red felt tongue, no identification, EX **$165.00**
Deer, 9", 'Bocky,' incised button, split tag, M.............**$75.00**
Dog puppet, 'Mopsy,' incised button, EX.............**$65.00**

Dog, 12", 'Maidy,' curly Persian wool plush, unjointed, glass eyes, no pads, 1959 only.............$350.00
Elephant, 12", 'Burri,' #6210/30, split tag, EX.............**$60.00**
Elephant, 4", standing, red felt bib, raised script button, EX **$55.00**
Elephant, 8", 'Floppy,' red bib, incised button, EX....**$135.00**
Elephant on wheels, 12x11", gray mohair w/felt tusks, original red circus blanket, spoked cast iron wheels, 1925 ....**$900.00**
Fish, 11", 'Flossy,' blue & purple, incised button, old tag, EX **$75.00**
Frog, 11", lying down, incised button, EX.............**$65.00**
Frog, 5", green velvet, incised button, EX.............**$75.00**
Giraffe, 13½", spotted mohair, squeaker, plastic eyes, airbrushed facial features, raised script button, 1965-67 ....**$125.00**
Hamster, 5", old chest tag, EX.............**$60.00**
Horse, 7", 'Ferdy,' gold button, split tag, M.............**$55.00**
Kangaroo juggler, new limited edition.............**$140.00**
Koala, 8½", light gold long-pile mohair, jointed head, glass eyes, gray felt nose, sheared mohair paws, ca late 1950s **$450.00**
Lion, 4", sitting, old chest tag, EX **$75.00**
Llama, 6", raised script button, old chest tag, EX **$125.00**
Mole, 7", plush, no identification, EX.............**$35.00**

Okapi, 10", velvet, old chest tag, EX.............**$225.00**
Owl puppet, split chest tag, EX.............**$70.00**
Panda, 6", #5315, mohair, fully jointed, glass eyes, black twisted floss nose, gray suede-like pads, 1950s-60s.............**$400.00**
Panda, 6", felt pads, chest tag, original ribbon, 1948, EX **$800.00**
Penguin, 4", black velvet wings, red beak & feet, no identification, EX **$95.00**
Polar bear, #0090/11, Museum series, M.............**$165.00**
Polar bear, 5", standing, blue eyes, no identification, EX **$175.00**
Pony, 19x25", white mohair w/brown spots, glass eyes, horsehair mane & tail, original trappings.........**$1,200.00**
Rabbit, 14", 'Manni,' open mouth, jointed head, incised button, EX.............**$425.00**
Rabbit, 3", old chest tag, EX.............**$55.00**
Rabbit Hide-a-Gift, orange dress, old chest tag, EX ..**$120.00**
Rabbit puppet, #6600/17, incised button, split tag, M.**$75.00**
Rooster, 10", no identification, EX.............**$150.00**
Spider set, new limited edition **$240.00**
Tiger jumping through hoop, new limited edition....**$145.00**
Tiger puppet, split chest tag, EX.............**$75.00**

Tiger, 6½", 'Ponx,' Dralon, unjointed, green plastic eyes, no claws or pads, originally made in 1971.............$85.00
Weasel, 8", white, no identification, EX.............**$135.00**

String Holders

Before Scotch tape made string obsolete, every household and business had a string holder of sorts. Some were made of cast iron, for heavy duty office work or for use in general stores and groceries. Others were frivolous and decorative, perhaps modeled as a human face or a big red apple, and made of various materials such as plaster or ceramic.

Apple, 4x4", 2-part, lithograph on tin figural, EX	**$75.00**
Apple w/worm, plaster	**$30.00**
Bird, yellow on green string nest, ceramic	**$30.00**
Black porter, 6½", Fredericksburg Art Pottery, M	**$135.00**
Chef's face, ceramic	**$35.00**
Court jester, plastic	**$40.00**
Indian man's head, plaster	**$70.00**

Mexican man's head, 8", chalkware $35.00
Old lady in rocker, chalkware $32.00
Pear, ceramic...$26.00
Pull w/Me, heart shape, ceramic, Clemenson.........$30.00
Pumpkin face, ceramic $48.00
Sailor, eyes to side, w/pipe, chalkware..............$35.00

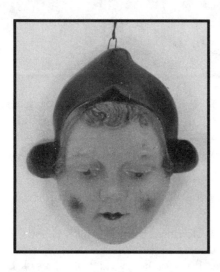

Girl w/hat, chalkware, EX paint $45.00

Swanky Swigs

These glass tumblers ranging in size from 3¼" to 4¾" were originally distributed by the Kraft company who filled them with their cheese spread. They were primarily used from the 1930s until the fifties and were decorated with fired-on designs of flowers, 'Bustling Betty' scenes (assorted chores being done by a Gibson-type Betty), 'Antique' patterns (clocks, coal scuttles, lamps, kettles, coffee grinders, spinning wheels, etc.), animals (in their 'Kiddie Cup' line), or solid colors of red, yellow, green, and blue (Fiesta ware look-alikes).

Even the lids are collectible and are valued at a minimum of $3.00, depending on condition and the advertising message they convey.

For more information, we recommend *Collectible Glassware of the 40s, 50s, and 60s* and *The Collector's Encyclopedia of Depression Glass, Revised Tenth Edition,* both by Gene Florence.

Antique pattern, churn & cradle, orange, 3¼"...............**$8.50**
Antique pattern, spinning wheel & bellows, red, 3¼"...**$8.50**
Bird & elephant, w/label, 3¾".........................**$8.50**
Bustling Betsy, all colors, 3¼" **$8.50**

Cornflowers #1, light blue, 3½"	**$15.00**
Cornflowers #2, dark blue, 3½"	**$3.50**
Cornflowers #2, light blue, 3½" (illustrated)	**$3.50**
Cornflowers #2, red, 3½"	**$3.50**
Daisy, red, white, & green, 4½"	**$14.50**
Daisy, red & white, 3¾"	**$20.00**
Dog & rooster w/cheese, 3¾"	**$25.00**
Duck & horse, black, 3¾"	**$3.50**
Forget-Me-Nots, red, 3½"	**$3.50**
Forget-Me-Nots, yellow w/label, 3½"	**$8.50**
Squirrel & deer, 3½" (illustrated)	**$10.00**
Violets, purple, 4½"	**$14.50**

Syracuse Dinnerware

Until 1970, the Onandaga Pottery Company produced

many lines of beautiful china dinnerware for home use. Located in Syracuse, New York, they are still in business, but the tablewares they make today are for commercial use only (hotels, restaurants, airlines, etc.). They marked their china with the trade name 'Syracuse,' and in 1966 they adopted that name in order to more easily identify with the fine chinaware lines for which they had become famous.

Each piece is marked with a dating code that will help you determine just when your pattern was produced. In her book *Lehner's Encyclopedia of U.S. Marks on Pottery, Porcelain, & Clay*, Lois Lehner gives the details of this code. Nine columns of information and mark facsimiles are given as well, and if you're interested in learning more about Syracuse china, this is probably the best source available for study.

Apple Blossom, cup & saucer	$40.00
Apple Blossom, salad plate	$20.00
Arcadia, cream soup, w/underplate	$30.00
Arcadia, cup & saucer	$28.00
Arcadia, plate, 9¾"	$25.00
Arcadia, platter, 14"	$55.00
Arcadia, salad plate	$20.00
Avalon, cup & saucer, gold trim	$27.50
Avalon, plate, 10"	$25.00
Baroque Gray, dinner plate	$28.00
Baroque Gray, vegetable bowl, w/lid, small	$40.00
Bombay, chop plate, ivory w/gold trim	$85.00
Bombay, cup & saucer	$35.00
Bombay, gravy boat, ivory w/gold trim	$65.00
Bombay, platter, ivory w/gold trim, 14"	$40.00
Bracelet, dinner plate	$38.00
Bracelet, platter, 12"	$50.00
Briarcliff, dinner plate	$26.00
Briarcliff, fruit bowl, small	$20.00
Briarcliff, plate, 10"	$25.00
Carvel, dinner plate, 10"	$30.00
Coralbel, cup & saucer, Winchester shape	$40.00
Coralbel, gravy boat	$60.00
Coronet, cup & saucer	$30.00
Coronet, salad plate	$20.00
Countess, platter, large	$60.00
Countess, vegetable bowl, round	$45.00
Coventry, bowl, 6¼"	$12.50
Coventry, cup & saucer	$20.00
Coventry, dinner plate	$25.00
Coventry, salad plate	$12.50
Indian Tree, cereal bowl	$20.00
Jefferson, cup & saucer	$30.00
Jefferson, plate, 10"	$28.00
Jefferson, platter, 12"	$70.00
Lady Mary, plate, 9¾"	$20.00
Lady Mary, platter, 12"	$55.00
Lady Mary, platter, 8"	$30.00
Lyric, cup & saucer	$30.00
Lyric, fruit bowl, small	$20.00
Meadow Breeze, bread & butter plate	$20.00
Meadow Breeze, cup & saucer	$38.00

Meadow Breeze, sugar bowl, w/lid	$55.00
Monticello, cake plate	$50.00
Monticello, cup & saucer	$40.00
Romance Maroon, bread & butter plate	$16.00
Rose Marie, dinner plate	$25.00
Rose Marie, salad bowl	$20.00
Selma, cup & saucer	$35.00
Selma, salad plate	$20.00
Stansbury, cream soup, w/underplate	$30.00
Stansbury, cup & saucer	$35.00
Stansbury, gravy boat	$65.00
Stansbury, vegetable bowl, w/lid	$125.00
Suzanne, bread & butter plate	$20.00
Suzanne, dessert bowl, 7"	$18.00
Suzanne, fruit bowl, small	$22.00
Woodbine, bowl, 6½"	$18.00
Woodbine, plate, 8"	$12.00
Woodbine, salt & pepper shakers, pr	$20.00

Teapots

Have you ever noticed the assortment of teapots being shown at antique malls and flea markets? Or had the opportunity to view a collection? Aren't they wonderful! There is such a variety of figural pots, and they're not only fascinating to look at, but functional as well. Imagine pouring tea for a friend out of an elephant's trunk or a cat's paw. Lovely teapots of any sort are collectible right now, especially the more innovative or imaginative ones.

Autumn Leaf, 7", long spout	$45.00
Black boy on elephant, 3¾", pottery w/bamboo handle, EX	$50.00

Black cat, 6¼" tall, white clay, no mark $45.00

Ellgreave, Wood & Sons England, floral decoration on iron-stone $35.00

Japan, 7½x9½", elephant figural, brown w/orange & turquoise flowers & gold trim $45.00

Japan, 9", rooster w/specks, w/head creamer & neck sugar bowl, three stacking units $28.00

Lenox, 2x3", gold bands, 1930s $85.00

Made in Japan, 5½", small painted floral decoration at rim on glossy brown $20.00

Maruhon Ware HP Japan, 6¾", embossed & painted floral on cream, flower finial, on original hot plate $50.00

McCoy, cat, begging, gray w/black airbrushed head, tail & haunches, pink bow at neck, unmarked...............$45.00

Ming Tea Co, Made in Japan, 1½-cup, w/label............$18.00

Pyrex mark, 6-cup, blown glass w/etched flowers......$45.00

Red roses on white w/gold trim, 6", embossed floral band, bud finial $25.00

Royal Canadian Art Pottery, 6½", multicolor floral cold paint on glossy black $15.00

Sadler, 6-cup, small flower decoration on pink, oval..$35.00

Toby, 3", child's size, marked Allertons, Made in England, ca 1929-42 ....$75.00

Wales CM, 2½", Charles & Diana, brown pottery........$78.00

WS George, 6-cup, yellow w/gold, round, EX $20.00

Telephones

Where better can the advancement of technology be portrayed than by comparing the large wood and metal wall phones of the late 1870s to the very small plastic portables of today. We've listed a few of the older styles, but remember the values we give you are retail. If you're buying to sell, you'll want to examine them and try to determine how much refurbishing you'll need to do. Many times dealers who specialize in old telephones will pay only 25% to 35% of retail.

Novelty phones have been popular for the past fifteen years or so, and many of them are now being seen on the secondary market. Especially good are character- and advertising-related models.

American Electric, oak, wall style, mouthpiece swivels, beveled glass at top door, VG........................$500.00

American Telecom, 1972, EX $35.00

Automatic Electric, #40, Bakelite, desk style, ca 1940s, EX..$80.00

Kellogg, metal, wall type w/dial.................................$95.00

Kellogg, red-bar desk style..$95.00

National Cash Register, EX...$125.00

Stromberg-Carlson, Bakelite, cradle style, 1920s $125.00

Utica Fire Alarm, nickeled brass, candlestick form....$195.00

Western Electric, brass, candlestick form w/dial $350.00

Western Electric, oval base, non-dial cradle style......$225.00

Western Electric, Spacesaver, w/dial $125.00

Novelty

AC Spark Plug, push buttons in base, 10½", EX $75.00

Apple, 4", red plastic figural w/hinged top, push-button pad inside, marked Apple Phone & Touchtone...........$35.00

Cigarette pack, opened 'Salem' package figural, 5½"..$60.00

Crayon, 9", standing figural w/'Crayon Communicator' on label, marked Made by Tote, 1983 ....$40.00

Football, figural, Frito Lay premium, NM $50.00

Garfield, reclining figural, EX.....................................$59.00

Gas Pump, 1930s style, push buttons under base $65.00

Ghostbusters, in original box $55.00

Heinz Ketchup, 8½", in original box, M.......................$90.00

Keebler Elf, figural, 1980s, NM...................................$75.00

Kermit the Frog, 11½", reclining in chair w/foot cradle, marked Henson Assn, 1983.................................$275.00

Little Sprout, 12", standing figural, 1984 ....**$75.00**

Mickey Mouse, 14½", standing, w/hand cradle, marked Disney & American Telecommunications.................**$275.00**

Piano, 3x7¼", baby grand, push-button dial keyboard, marked Columbia Telecommunications **$59.00**

Pizza Baker, full-figured moustached man in white apron on round base w/'Pizza Inn,' in original box.............**$85.00**

Popeye, seated vinyl figural on duffle bag w/keg of spinach on shoulder, 1982, EX **$75.00**

Punchy, 11", mascot of Hawaiian Punch, outstretched hand is cradle, dial on base, 11"....................................**$75.00**

Raid Bug, 9", push-button keys in base, NM **$95.00**

Shoe Fashion Fone, 5¾", lady's high-heel shoe, marked Columbia Telecommunications,1987 ....**$75.00**

Snoopy & Woodstock, 14", figural, marked American Telecommunications...**$275.00**

Stars & Stripes, candlestick type, EX $38.00

Superblocks Telephone, 8x4x7", arrangement of Lego blocks w/push-button pad in center, marked Tyco **$55.00**

TV Guide, 8½", numeral 1 w/'TV Guide' logo, NM.....**$60.00**

7-Up Can, 6¼", push-button pad in bottom of can, made by Enterprex **$35.00**

Televisions

If you're too young to remember what the very early TV

sets looked like, screens were very small. Some measured only 7" — a few even less. In 1938 a miniature unit designed to be held in the hand was on display in London. It had an earphone to amplify the sound, and the screen was a tiny 2" square. By the late forties, luxurious home entertainment consoles were available, complete with glide-out turntables, hidden radios mounted on fold-out doors, and a big 10" 'direct view' screen, all for only $499.95.

Today pre-WWII TVs sometimes sell for as much as $4,000.00. Unusual cabinet models from the forties may go as high as $300.00. Generally, any kind of vintage TV with a screen less than 14" is very collectible. Supply, demand, and of course, condition are the most important price-assessing factors. Our values are given for sets in fine condition and in working order.

If you'd like to see photos of these and many more fascinating early TVs (and learn what they're worth as well), we recommend *Classic TVs, Pre-War Through 1950s,* by Scott Wood.

Admiral, 10", 1949 console...**$75.00**

Admiral, 7", #19A15, 1947, wood table top model....**$175.00**

Airline 84GSE-3011A, 7" screen, leatherette portable..$150.00

Andrea 1-F-5, 5" screen, console, 1939, minimum **$4,000.00**

Arvin, 8", #4080T, 1950, metal w/mahogany front **$155.00**

CBS Columbia, 15", #RX90, 1954, color console model **$1,500.00**

Crosley, 7", #9-425, 1949, portable **$175.00**

Fada, 10", #799, 1948, table top model **$125.00**

General Electric, 10", #806, 1949 ....**$100.00**

General Electric, 17", #17T027, 1956, metal cabinet **$75.00**

Motorola VT-71, ca 1947 ....**$175.00**

Motorola, 17", 1951, Bakelite **$50.00**

Motorola, 8", #9VT1, wood table top model.............**$100.00**

Motorola, 8", 1949, plastic grill cloth **$100.00**
Philco, 10", #48-1001, 1948, walnut **$125.00**
Philco, 7", #50-701, 1950, black Bakelite..................**$250.00**
RCA, 12", #2T51, 1950, metal cabinet........................**$100.00**
RCA, 7", #621 TS, 1946, walnut.................................**$400.00**
Sentinel, 7", #405TV, 1949...**$150.00**
Silvertone, 8", #9115, upright portable w/leatherette
    case..**$150.00**
Truetone, 7", 1949...**$200.00**
Zenith, 1949, porthole console model.......................**$150.00**

Thimbles

Collectors relate several reasons for their fascination with these small basic tools of needlework. First, many are beautiful — tiny works of art in their own right. Enameling, engraving, and embossing are seen on thimbles made of metals such as gold, silver, brass, and pewter; and there are china thimbles that have been hand painted. Many were made as souvenirs or as keepsake gifts to mark a special occasion. In the 19th century when social functions for ladies often revolved around their needlework projects, a fine, fancy thimble was a status symbol.

Some collectors are intrigued by the inscriptions they find. Many suggest a glimpse into a thimble's history. For instance, 'Mother, 12-25-01' inside a lovely gold thimble conveys a scene around a turn-of-the-century Christmas tree and a loving child presenting a special gift to a cherished parent.

Others simply like the older thimbles because to them they evoke a bit of nostalgia for a bygone era. But new thimbles are collectible as well. Bone china thimbles from England commemorating Charles' and Diana's marriage, Olympiad XXIII done in blue and white Jasperware by Wedgwood, hand-decorated examples with a 'Christmas 1982' message, and Norman Rockwell thimbles by Gorham are just a few examples of those that are 'new' yet very collectible.

If you'd like to read more about them and see hundreds shown in large, full-color photographs, we recommend *Antique and Collectible Thimbles and Accessories* by Averil Mathis.

Brass, souvenir of 1982 World's Fair, unmarked...........**$8.00**
Brass, unmarked, from $6.00 up to **$10.00**
Carol Bradley, gold-plated finger guard, embossed rose dec-
    oration, 1975...**$22.00**
Cloisonne, no mark...**$6.00**
Goldsmith-Stern, sterling silver w/wide gold band, marked
    USA **$110.00**
Gorham, china, marked USA......................................**$15.00**
Ketchum & McDougall, sterling silver, palmated design,
    marked KMD **$25.00**
Leather, marked USA **$3.00**
Prudential advertising, aluminum **$12.50**
Simons, sterling silver w/gold decorated band, marked
    USA..**$45.00**

Simons Brothers, alloy w/engraved leaf & berry band, SBC logo **$8.00**
Simons Brothers, child's size, sterling silver w/engraved ani-
    mal band..**$38.00**
Simons Brothers, sterling silver, Quaker type, Simons shield,
    marked USA **$22.00**
Stern Brothers, gold filled, double anchors, marked USA ..**$35.00**

Vegetable ivory, acorn-shape thimble holder $85.00

Three Stooges Memorabilia

The ever-popular comedy trio, Curly, Larry, and Moe (known as the Three Stooges) continues today to dazzle their fans, who find lots of enjoyment searching the secondary market for merchandise that was made in their honor. One of the first items to hit the stores in 1935 was a set of hand puppets. Through the fifties and sixties, coloring books, children's costumes, and comic books were produced, evidence of their continuing fame; and only a few years ago, you could buy a set of 'Three Stooges' Christmas ornaments!

Cane, 36", Empire Plastic Corp, 1959, plastic trick type, com-
    plete w/original display card, EX...........................**$80.00**
Colorforms set, 1959...**$25.00**
Comic book, Dell, 1962...**$5.00**
Doll, ventriloquist; Moe, Horsman, 1981.....................**$20.00**
Fan club kit, Norman Maurer Products, in original 6x9"
    envelope, NM..**$90.00**
Gum card display box, Fleer, 1966, EX.......................**$85.00**

Halloween costume, Moe, Ben Cooper Inc, 1961, in original package **$30.00**
Photo, 8x10", full color, promotional giveaway, 1960....**$10.00**
Poster, 11x14", General Foods cereal promotion, 1977.**$2.00**
Puppet, finger; plastic, Wilkening Mfg, 1959, set of three, in original package..**$50.00**
Puppet, hand; vinyl head & cloth body, Curly, 1959, in original package **$50.00**
Puppet, hand; vinyl head & cloth body, Larry, 1959, in original package **$35.00**
Record, 33rpm, 'Wreck the Halls w/Boughs of Holly,' in original sleeve, M..**$37.50**
Ring, Vari-View w/flicker action, Moe..........................**$5.00**
School bag, Carry-Case Mfg **$15.00**

Tiffin Glass

This company was originally founded in 1887 in Tiffin, Ohio, and later became one of several that was known as the U.S. Glass Company. U.S. Glass closed in the early sixties, and the plant reopened in 1963 under the title of the Tiffin Art Glass Company.

They have made many lovely lines of tableware and decorative items, but they are probably most famous for their black satin glass which was produced in the twenties.

Beaumont, goblet, water size...**$12.50**
Byzantine, cordial **$35.00**
Byzantine, tumbler, iced tea...**$22.00**
Cadena, champagne, yellow **$30.00**
Cadena, goblet, water size, 5¼", pink or yellow **$27.50**
Cadena, pickle bowl, 10", pink or yellow **$25.00**
Cadena, pitcher, footed, w/lid **$200.00**
Cadena, tumbler, juice; 4½", footed............................**$15.00**
Cadena, vase, 9", pink or yellow **$55.00**
Cadena, wine, 6", pink or yellow **$35.00**
Camelot, sherbet **$7.50**

Cerice, cocktail...**$18.50**
Cherokee Rose, bowl, centerpiece; 13" **$65.00**
Cherokee Rose, bud vase, 6".......................................**$22.00**
Cherokee Rose, creamer..**$28.00**
Cherokee Rose, finger bowl, 5" **$18.00**
Cherokee Rose, plate, sandwich; 14"...........................**$45.00**
Elyse, wine **$35.00**
Empire, champagne **$20.00**
Empress, vase, 11¾", smoke & crystal.........................**$150.00**
Flanders, claret, pink **$75.00**
Flanders, cordial, yellow **$55.00**
Flanders, goblet, water size...**$25.00**
Flanders, parfait, yellow **$75.00**
Flanders, relish, 3-part **$25.00**
Flanders, salt & pepper shakers, yellow, pr...............**$100.00**
Flanders, wine...**$25.00**
Fuchsia, celery, 11" **$35.00**
Fuchsia, creamer, footed **$28.00**
Fuchsia, cup **$37.50**
Fuchsia, goblet, water size, tall....................................**$25.00**
Fuchsia, mayonnaise, w/liner..**$75.00**
Fuchsia, plate, 8½" **$15.00**
Fuchsia, relish, 5-part...**$35.00**
Fuchsia, sherbet **$12.00**
Fuchsia, tumbler, iced tea **$30.00**
Fuchsia, vase, urn form, handles **$95.00**
Huntington, goblet, water size......................................**$15.00**
Huntington, sherbet, tall standard................................**$12.00**
June Night, bud vase, 8"...**$30.00**
June Night, wine **$27.00**
Montclair, sherbet **$10.00**
Nouvelle, goblet, water size..**$24.00**
Paulina, cocktail, topaz...**$11.00**
Paulina, cordial, topaz **$28.00**
Persian Pheasant, champagne...**$22.50**
Persian Pheasant, wine, 6"...**$35.00**
Riviera, goblet, water size **$20.00**
Tiffin Rose, goblet, water size, cut decoration.............**$15.00**
Twilight, vase, 8½", teardrop form................................**$95.00**

Candlestick, 8½", black satin w/hand-painted bird .$60.00

Wall pocket, 9", crystal frost w/jeweling & hand painting..**$200.00**

Willow, goblet, water size $20.00
Wisteria, champagne $15.00
Wisteria, tumbler, juice $25.00

Toothpick Holders

One reason these are so popular with collectors is their small size — and it's one of the reasons that so many have survived to the present day. Once a common accessory on any dining table, around the turn of the century, many were relegated to the back of the china cupboard and eventually became family heirlooms. Because they're so highly collected, many have been reproduced, so be sure of what you're buying. Knowing your dealer can be very helpful. Many that look 'old' have been made recently by several small glass studios such as Degenhart, Boyd, St. Clair, and Mosser.

Besides glass, toothpick holders have been made in china, some to match dinnerware patterns, some modeled as figures of animals or people, and some simply as novelties. Silverplated styles were made during Victorian times, and other materials have been used as well.

Amberina, Diamond Quilt, square top $220.00
Atlas, etched leaf & berry design $30.00
Beggar's Hand $17.50
Box-in-Box, green w/gold trim $30.00
Bristol, hat-shape w/turned-over brim, blue w/gold floral decoration $125.00
Bulging Loops, green opaque $55.00
Chrysanthemum Leaf Swirl, clear w/gold trim $95.00
Chute & Ladders $22.00
Cornell, green $45.00
Cranberry, multicolored forget-me-nots w/gold, ruffled $175.00
Croesus, emerald green, 3-footed $85.00
Cut crystal, black enamel Deco-style bands, 2¼x2" $65.00
Daisy & Button with Variant, amber $25.00
Delaware, clear w/gold trim $65.00
Dolphin, amber $60.00
Double Ring Panel, apple green, rare $45.00
Falcon Strawberry $30.00
Flower & Pleat, amber stained $110.00
Gaelic, clear w/gold trim $32.00
Horseshoe & Clover, milk glass $20.00
Iris with Meander, green opalescent $45.00
Jefferson Optic, blue, souvenir $55.00

Manhattan, clear w/gold trim $32.00

Michigan, yellow stained w/rose carnations $65.00
Minnesota, clear w/gold trim, 3-handled (illustrated) $30.00
New Jersey $45.00
Palm Leaf, green opaque $95.00
Pansy, blue $45.00
Pleating, ruby stained $30.00
Ribbed Spiral, clear opalescent $45.00
Rising Sun $35.00
Royal Ivy, rubena, glossy $75.00
Scalloped Panel, green $35.00
Shoshone, clear w/gold trim $20.00
Star in Bull's Eye, gold trim $30.00
Stippled Sand Burr $50.00

Swag Bracket, amethyst w/gold trim $65.00
Swirl & Leaf $65.00
Texas, clear w/gold trim $25.00
US Regal $24.00
Ward's Regal, green $25.00
Wheeling Block $45.00
Wisconsin, pink opalescent $55.00
X-Ray, green w/gold trim $45.00

Toys

Toy collecting has long been an area of very strong activity, but over the past decade it has really expanded. Many of the larger auction galleries have cataloged toy auctions, and it isn't uncommon for scarce 19th-century toys in good condition to go for $5,000.00 to $10,000.00 and up. Toy shows are common, and there are clubs, newsletters, and magazines that cater only to the needs and wants of toy collectors. Though once buyers ignored toys less than thirty years old, in more recent years, even some toys from the eighties are sought after.

Condition has more bearing on the value of a toy than any other factor. A used toy in excellent condition with no major flaws will still be worth about half (in some cases much less) than one in mint (like new) condition. Those mint and in their original boxes will be worth much more than the same toy without its box.

There are many good toy guides on the market today including: *Teddy Bears and Steiff Animals* by Margaret Fox Mandel; *Toys, Antique and Collectible,* and *Character Toys and Collectibles,* both by David Longest; *Modern Toys, American Toys 1930 to 1980,* by Linda Baker; *Collecting Toys* and *Collecting Toy Soldiers,* both by Richard O'Brien; and *Collector's Guide to Tootsietoys* by David E. Richter.

See also Barbie Collectibles, Breyer Horses, Bubble Bath Containers, Cracker Jack Collectibles, Disney Collectibles, Fast Food Toys and Figurines, Halloween Costumes, Liddle Kiddles, Paper Dolls, Star Trek Memorabilia, and Star Wars Trilogy.

Airplanes

Alps, Amphibian Navy Patrol Plane, 15" wingspan, battery, 1950s, EX **$675.00**
Cragstan, Biplane 7518, 14½" wingspan, battery, 1950s, M.**$240.00**
HTC, UN Hospital Plane, 12" wingspan, tin, friction, EX **$120.00**
Ingap, Fiat CR-41, 10" wingspan, tin, wind-up, EX..**$400.00**
Linemar, American Airlines Electra, 19½" wingspan, 1950s, M..**$320.00**
Linemar, Disney Comic Plane, 10" wingspan, tin, friction, EX **$100.00**
M-T Co, Boeing 727 Jet Plane, 10⅜" wingspan, three actions, 1960s, M **$200.00**
Marx, Fighter Jet, 7" wingspan, battery, 1960s, M........**$80.00**
Rico, De Havilland Comet, 13" wingspan, tin, wind-up, M.**$200.00**
S&E, Bluebird, 13" wingspan, tin, friction, M.............**$125.00**
S&E, Bristol bulldog, 14" wingspan, tin, friction, M ..**$175.00**
Spain, WW II Tri-Motor, 9" wingspan, tin, wind-up, EX ..**$75.00**
TN, Cessna, 25" wingspan, tin, friction, EX................**$125.00**
TN, Ford, 15" wingspan, tin, friction, EX.....................**$90.00**
Waco Co, 4-Prop Airliner American Airlines, 16½" wingspan, four actions, 1960s, M...**$160.00**

Aurora Model Kits

The Aurora Plastics Corporation began on a very small scale in the early 1950s and immediately found a ready market for the model airplanes and ships which they sold through hobby stores and retail chains. But the company soon expanded and during the fifties and sixties went on to become the world's leading manufacturer of quality figure model kits, producing kits for assembling figures of TV heroes, presidents, sports legends, and movie monsters. If this is an area you find yourself interested in, you'll want a copy of the book *Aurora, History and Price Guide,* by Bill Bruegman. (Note: Models mint in box are worth approximately twice as much as one 'built up' or already assembled. If the original box is present, add about 50% to the value of the assembled model.)

Armored Dinosaur, 1974, kit #744, burnt-orange plastic, assembled, well made, from $25.00 up to.............**$30.00**

Batmobile, 1966, kit #486, black w/clear window pieces, assembled, well made, from $75.00 up to **$100.00**
Black Knight, 1963-1968 (re-issue), kit #473, black plastic, unassembled, M in box, from $20.00 up to **$25.00**
Blackbeard, 1965-1966, kit #463, flesh plastic, unassembled, M in box, from #50.00 up to **$75.00**
Bride of Frankenstein, 1965-1966 (original issue), light gray plastic, assembled, well made, from $200.00 up to **$300.00**
Captain Action, 1966-67, kit #480, dark metallic blue plastic, unassembled, M in box, from $250.00 up to **$350.00**
Chitty Chitty Bang Bang, 1968, kit #828, dark brown, orange, & chrome plastic, unassembled, M in box, from $50.00 up to **$100.00**
Creature, 1969-1975, Glow-in-the-Dark series kit #483, green plastic, unassembled, M in box, from $300.00 up to **$400.00**
Creature from the Black Lagoon, 1975, kit #653, metallic green plastic, unassembled, M in box, from $100.00 up to...**$140.00**
Cro-Magnon Woman, 1971, kit #731, tan plastic, unassembled, M in box, from $20.00 up to.........................**$25.00**
George Washington, 1965, kit #852, ivory plastic, unassembled, M in box, from $40.00 up to.........................**$75.00**
Gigantic Frankenstein, 1964-1965, kit #470, four colors of plastic, unassembled, M in box, from $300.00 up to...**$350.00**
Green Beret, 1966-1967, kit #413, green plastic, unassembled, M in box, from $50.00 up to......................**$100.00**
Hercules & the Lion, 1966, kit #481, light tan plastic, assembled, well made, from $100.00 up to **$125.00**
Incredible Hulk, 1966-1968, kit #421, metallic green plastic, unassembled, M in box, from $200.00 up to **$300.00**

Indian Chief, 1957, kit #417, ivory plastic, assembled, well made **$35.00**
John F Kennedy, 1965, kit #851, flesh plastic, assembled, well made, from $25.00 up to **$40.00**

King Arthur of Camelot, 1968, kit #825, gold plastic w/green & gray base, unassembled, M in box, from $40.00 up to...**$50.00**

King Kong, 1964-1968 (original issue), kit #468, black & tan plastic, unassembled, M in box, from $450.00 up to...**$600.00**

Lone Ranger, 1967-1968, kit #808, flat blue & white plastic, unassembled, M in box, from $100.00 up to **$150.00**

Moon Bus, 1968, kit #828, white & light green plastic, unassembled, M in box, from $150.00 up to **$250.00**

Mummy, 1969, Frightening Lightning Series kit #452, light gray plastic, unassembled, M in box, from $250.00 up to **$350.00**

Pain Parlor, 1971, kit #635, dark brown plastic, unassembled, M in box, from $40.00 up to..........................**$45.00**

Pendulum, 1971, kit #636, dark brown plastic, assembled, well made, from $20.00 up to **$25.00**

Phantom of the Opera, 1963-1968 (original issue), kit #428, black plastic, unassembled, M in box, from $250.00 up to...**$300.00**

Rodan, 1975, kit #657, dark brown & tan plastic, assembled, well made, from $100.00 up to............................**$175.00**

Saber Tooth Tiger, 1971, kit #733, yellow plastic, unassembled, M in box, from $25.00 up to..........................**$35.00**

Scotch Lad, 1956, kit #419, ivory plastic, unassembled, M in box, from $25.00 up to...**$30.00**

Silver Knight, 1963-68 re-issue, kit #471, silver plastic, unassembled, M in box, from $20.00 up to **$25.00**

Spartacus, 1965 (re-issue of Roman Gladiator), kit #405, ivory plastic, unassembled, M in box, from $100.00 up to..**$175.00**

Tarzan, kit #820, M in box.......................................$70.00

Tyrannosaurus Rex, 1975, kit #746, orange plastic w/glow eyes, nails & teeth, unassembled, M in box, from $35.00 up to **$50.00**

Vampirella, 1971, kit #638, flesh plastic, assembled, well made, from $40.00 up to **$50.00**

Wolfman, 1962-1968, kit #425, dark gray plastic, unassembled, M in box, from $300.00 up to....................**$350.00**

Wolfman, 1975-1977, kit #652, dark gray plastic, unassembled, M in box, from $100.00 up to....................**$140.00**

Wonder Woman, 1965-1966, kit #479, flesh & tan plastic, unassembled, M in box, from $400.00 up to **$500.00**

Battery Operated

It is estimated that approximately 95% of the battery-operated toys that were so popular from the forties through the sixties came from Japan. The remaining 5% were made in the United States by other companies. To market these toys in America, many distributorships were organized. Some of the largest were Cragstan, Linemar, and Rosko. But even American toy makers such as Marx, Ideal, Hubley, and Daisy sold them under their own names, so the trademarks you'll find on Japanese battery-operated toys are not necessarily that of the manufacturer, and it's sometimes just about impossible to determine the specific company that actually made them. After peaking in the sixites, the Japanese toy industry began a decline, bowing out to competition from the cheaper die-cast and plastic toy makers.

Remember that it is rare to find one of these complex toys that have survived in good, collectible condition. Batteries caused corrosion, lubricants dried out, cycles were interrupted and mechanisms ruined, rubber hoses and bellows aged and cracked, so the mortality rate was extremely high. A toy rated excellent, that is showing signs of wear but well taken care of, is generally worth about twice the same toy in mint (like new) condition. Besides condition, battery-operated toys are rated on scarcity, desirability, and the number of 'actions' they preform. A 'major' toy is one that has three or more actions, while one that does only one or two is considered 'minor.' These, of course, are worth much less.

Alps Co, Balloon Blowing Teddy Bear, 11", five actions w/balloon, 1950s, EX...**$75.00**

Alps Co, Accordion Player Bunny, 12x9", six actions 1950s, M...**$200.00**

Alps Co, Arthur A-Go-Go, 10", six actions, w/cymbals & drum set, 1960s, EX...**$120.00**

A-1 Co, Blacksmith Bear, 9½", six actions, 1950, EX...**$150.00**

Alps Co, Big John, 12", three actions, 1960s, EX **$75.00**

Alps Co, Bobby the Drumming Bear, 10", four actions 1950s, M..**$260.00**

Alps Co, Bongo Player, 10", four actions, 1960s, EX...**$75.00**

Alps Co, Bunny the Magician, 14½", five actions, w/card-ribbon apparatus for card trick, 1950s, EX **$165.00**

Alps Co, Cappy the Baggage Porter Dog, 11", four actions, 1960s, EX **$105.00**

Alps Co, Charlie the Drumming Clown, six actions, w/drum & cymbals, 1950s, EX $135.00

Alps Co, Dalmation 1-Man Band #90262, 9", six actions, w/cymbals & stand, 1950s, M $180.00

Alps Co, Dog Family, 11", four actions, 1960s, M........$60.00

Alps Co, Drumming Clown Charlie, 9½", six actions, w/drums & cymbals, 1950s, M...........................$200.00

Alps Co, Drumming Polar Bear, 12", three actions, 1960s, EX $90.00

Alps Co, Frankie the Rollerskating Monkey, 12", 1950s, M...$160.00

Alps Co, Fred Flintstone Bedrock Band, 9½", four actions, 1962, M...$400.00

Alps Co, Grandpa Bear, 9", in rocking chair, five actions, 1950s, M $200.00

Alps Co, Hooty the Happy Owl, 9", six actions, 1960s, M..$100.00

Alps Co, Indian Joe, 12", four actions, 1960s, EX $60.00

Alps Co, Jolly Drummer Chimpy, 9", six actions, w/cymbals & stand, 1950s, M $100.00

Alps Co, Major Tooty, 14", three actions, w/drum & hat, 1960s, M $140.00

Alps Co, Mexicali Pete Drum Player, 10½", three actions, 1960s, M $100.00

Alps Co, Monkey Artist, 8", five actions, 1950s, EX...$180.00

Alps Co, Mumbo Jumbo Hawaiian Drummer, 9¾", three actions, 1960s, EX $90.00

Alps Co, Pet Turtle, 7", four actions, two cycles, 1960s, M..$120.00

Alps Co, Picnic Bunny, 10", four actions, 1950s, EX .$105.00

Alps Co, Reading Bear, 9", five actions, 1950s, EX....$105.00

Alps Co, Rocking Santa, 10", four actions, 1950s, M .$300.00

Alps So, Saxophone Playing Monkey, 9½", four actions, 1950s, M $160.00

Bandai, Happy Miner, 11", three actions, 1960s, M...$160.00

BC Co, Jungle Jumbo, 9", five actions, 1950s, M $140.00

Cragstan, Crapshooting Monkey, 9", three actions, w/pair of small dice, 1950s, M..$120.00

Cragstan, Marching Drummer Bear, made in Japan, Mint in box...$125.00

Cragstan, Playboy, 13", five actions, 1960s, EX.........$105.00

Cragstan, Satellite, 5½x8" dia, 1950s, M....................$140.00

Cragston, Tootin'-Chuggin' Locomotive, 24", three actions, 1950s, M...$60.00

Daiya, Josie the Walking Cow, 8½x14", seven actions, two cycles, 1950s, EX..$105.00

Eldon Co, Billy Blastoff Space Scout, 16", four actions, 1960s, M...$100.00

Haji Co, Air Taxi Helicopter, three actions, 1960s, M..$60.00

Haji Co, Dapper Jigger Dancer, 12", 1950s, M...........$140.00

HTC Co, Animated Santa on Rotating Globe, 14", five actions, 1950s, EX...$195.00

Ideal, Electronic Countdown, 24", six actions, 1959, M...$60.00

Japan, Charlie Chimp, Hula Expert, M in box....$125.00

K Co, Fruit Juice Counter, 8x8", three actions, w/plastic barrel, lid, glasses, & tin tray, 1960s, M $160.00

K Co, Mighty Mike the Barbell Lifter, 10½", four actions, 1950s, EX...$150.00

K Co, Zoom Motorboat, 12", three actions, 1950s, M..$60.00

Linemar, Ball Playing Dog, 9", three actions, 1950s, M .$100.00

Linemar, Betty Bruin, Cashier, 9", six actions, 1950s, EX..$300.00

Linemar, Bubble Blowing Popeye, 12", five actions, 1950s, M...$1,000.00

Linemar, Bubbling Bull, 8x6½", five actions (plastic bowl), 1950s, M $100.00

Linemar, Busy Secretary, 7½x7", seven actions, 1950s, M..$200.00

Linemar, Calypso Joe, 11", four actions, 1950s, EX ...$150.00

Linemar, Crawling Baby, 8½x11", 1940s, M $80.00

Linemar, Donald Duck, 8", four actions, 1960s, EX..$225.00

Linemar, Drill, 6", w/attachments, 1950s, M................$40.00

Linemar, Jocko the Drinking Monkey, 11", four actions, w/top hat, 1950s, M..$120.00

Linemar, Sleeping Baby Bear, 9", six actions, w/detachable alarm clock, 1950s, EX...$165.00

Linemar, Snake Charmer (& Casey the Trained Cobra), 8", four actions, 1950s, EX....................................$2,250.00

Linemar, Susie the Cashier Bear, 9", six actions, 1950s, EX.................$375.00

M-T Co, B-Z Rabbit, 7", four actions, 1950s, EX..........$45.00

M-T Co, Bear, The Cashier, 7½", five actions, 1950s, M.$300.00

M-T Co, Bubble Blowing Lion, 7½", four actions, 1950s, M................$120.00

M-T Co, Busy Bizzy Friendly Bug, 6", three actions, 1950s, M................$80.00

M-T Co, Cyclist Clown, 6½", six actions, 1950s, EX...$120.00

M-T Co, Good Time Charlie, 12", seven actions, 1960s, M................$140.00

M-T Co, Papa Bear, Reading & Drinking in His Old Rocking Chair, 10", four actions, 1950s, EX.................$135.00

M-T Co, Pinkee the Farmer, 9½", seven actions, 1950s, M................$140.00

M-T Co, Rocking Chair Bear, 10", five actions, 1950s, M................$140.00

M-T Co, Santa Claus on Scooter, 10", four actions, 1960s, EX.................$90.00

M-T Co, Sparky the Seal, 6x7", four actions, two cycles, w/celluloid ball, 1950s, M.................$120.00

Marusan, Jolly Pianist, 8", five actions, 1950s, EX......$135.00

Marusan, Pistol Pete, 10", w/tin hat, 1950s, M...........$240.00

Marusan, Smokey Bear, 9½", five actions, 1950s, M..$280.00

Marx, Alley, The Exciting New Roaring Stalking Alligator, 17½", five actions, 1960s, EX.................$180.00

Marx, Barking Spaniel Dog, 7", 1950s, M....................$20.00

Marx, Brewster the Rooster, 9½", five actions, 1950s, EX.................$135.00

Marx, Buttons, Puppy w/a Brain, 12", eight actions, 1960s, M................$250.00

Marx, Dino the Dinosaur & Fred Flintstone, 22", eight actions, 1961, EX.................$300.00

Marx, Electric Powered TV & Radio Station, 20", three actions, 1950s, M.................$120.00

Marx, Nutty Mad Indian, 12", four actions, 1960s, M.$120.00

Marx, Roarin' Jungle Lion, 16", four actions, two cycles, 1960s, EX.................$180.00

Marx, Walking 'Esso' Tiger, 11½", four actions, 1950s, EX.................$300.00

Mego, Chee Chee Chihuahua, 8", five actions, 1960s, EX.................$30.00

Mikuni Co, Cock-A-Doodle-Doo Rooster, 8", four actions, 1950s, M.................$100.00

Murusan Co, Christmas Time, 10x7", three actions, 1950s, EX.................$50.00

Plaything Toy Co, Sam the Shaving Man, 11½", seven actions, w/metal mirror, 1960s, EX.................$150.00

Remco Co, Coney Island Penny Machine, 13", w/plastic prizes, 1950s, EX.................$135.00

S&E Co, Drinking Captain, 12", six actions, 1960, M..$140.00

S&E Co, VIP the Busy Boss, 8", six actions, 1950s, EX.$195.00

S-H Co, Mr Zerox, 9½", four actions, 1960s, M..........$260.00

Santa Creations Co, Automated Santa, 10¼", three actions, 1960s, EX.................$90.00

Saunders, Marvelous Mike, 17", four actions, 1950s, M.$180.00

Sonsco, Funland Cup Ride, 7x6", three actions, w/6" umbrella, 1960s, EX.................$105.00

STS Co, Barking Dog, 7x7", four actions, two cycles, 1950s, EX.................$45.00

T-N Co, Ball Blowing Clown, 11", three actions w/ball, 1950s, M.................$200.00

T-N Co, Barber Bear, 9½", five actions, 1950s, M......$300.00

T-N Co, Brave Eagle, 11", five actions, 1950s, M.......$120.00

T-N Co, Charlie Weaver, 12", six actions, 1962, M......$60.00

T-N Co, Clown w/Lion, 12", four actions, w/spiral apparatus, 1950s, M.................$220.00

T-N Co, Cowboy Riding Horse, 7", three actions, 1950s, M.................$80.00

T-N Co, Dancing Sweethearts, 7", 1950s, EX.............$105.00

T-N Co, Drinking Licking Cat, 10", six actions, 1950s, EX.................$75.00

T-N Co, Electric Vibraphone, 5½x7½", three actions, 1950s, M.................$100.00

T-N Co, Girl w/Baby Carriage, 8", three actions, 1960s, M.................$120.00

T-N Co, Holiday Sink-Stove Combination, 9", w/3-piece pan set, M.................$60.00

T-N Co, Knitting Grandma, 8½", three actions, 1950s, EX.................$120.00

T-N Co, Linda Lee Laundromat, 6½", 1940s, EX..........$30.00

T-N Co, Mimi Poodle w/Bone, 10x11", five actions, w/plastic bone, 1950s, M.................$60.00

T-N Co, Miss Friday the Typist, 8", six actions, removable head, 1950s, EX.................$135.00

T-N Co, Mr Baseball Junior, 7", three actions, 1950s, EX.................$195.00

T-N Co, Penguin on Tricycle, 6½", three actions, 1950s, M.................$120.00

T-N Co, Pretty Peggy Parrot, 12", four actions, 1950s, EX.................$300.00

T-N Co, Shoe Maker Bear, 8½", three actions, 1960s, EX.................$105.00

T-N Co, Shoe Shine Monkey, 9", five actions, 1950s, EX.................$120.00

T-N Co, Shutterbug Photographer, 9", five actions, 1950s, M.................$400.00

T-N Co, Singing Bird in Cage, 9", four actions, 1950s, EX.................$90.00

TPS Co, Climbing Fireman, 24" (assembled), five actions, 1950s, EX.................$165.00

Y Co, Accordion Bear, 10½", six actions, 1950s, M...$400.00

Y Co, Astro Dog, 11", two cycles, five actions (looks like Snoopy, 1960s, M.................$140.00

Y Co, Bear Chef (Cuty Cook), 9½", five actions, w/chef hat & tin litho egg, 1960s, EX.................$120.00

Y Co, Billy the Kid Sheriff, 10½", four actions, two cycles, 1950s, EX.................$120.00

Y Co, Blushing Willie, 10", four actions, 1960s, EX.....$60.00

Y Co, Bruno the Accordion Bear, 10½", five actions, 1950s, EX.................$150.00

Y Co, Bubble Blowing Boy, 7", four actions, 1950s, EX ..$90.00

Y Co, Burger Chef, 9", eight actions, w/chef's hat & tin litho hamburger, 1950s, EX.................$120.00

Y Co, Chimp w/Xylophone, 8x12", w/four records & hammer, 1970s, M.................$100.00

Y Co, Happy 'n Sad Magic Face Clown, 10", five actions, 1960s, M **$160.00**

Y Co, Hasty Chimp, 9", four actions, 1960s, M **$60.00**

Y Co, Hippo Chef (Cuty Cook), 10", five actions, w/chef hat & tin litho egg, 1960s, EX....................................**$120.00**

Y Co, Hungry Baby Bear, 9½", six actions, 1950s, M..**$180.00**

Y Co, Mac the Turtle, 8", five actions, 1960s, EX.......**$120.00**

Y Co, Marshall Wild Bill, 10½", two cycles, four actions, w/tin cowboy hat, 1950s, EX **$180.00**

Y Co, Ol' Sleepy Head Rip, 9", seven actions, rare, 1950s, EX **$165.00**

Y Co, Playful Pup in Shoe, 10", three actions, 1960s, M..**$60.00**

Y Co, Puffy Morris, 10", five actions, uses real cigarettes, 1960s, EX..**$120.00**

Y-M Co, Acro Chimp Porter, 8½", 1960s, EX.............**$45.00**

Y-M Co, Champion Weight Lifter, 10", five actions, 1960s, EX **$90.00**

Yada Co, Drum Monkey, 8", three actions, 1970s, M ..**$60.00**

Z Co, Jig-Saw-Matic, 7¼", 1950s, M......................**$60.00**

Dakin Figures

About all we can determine is that Dakin produced both plush and vinyl toys from the sixties to the seventies, and then in the eighties they issued a line of Warner Brother's characters made of plush. Toy dealers tell us that unless the character is a rare one, most will sell for about $40.00 to $50.00 mint in original packaging.

Baby Puss, complete w/paper tag, rare, M **$175.00**

Bamm-Bamm, removable clothing, NM **$40.00**

Barney Rubble, removable clothing, NM **$40.00**

Bear, Misha 1980 Olympic mascot, 12", plush w/printed-on Olympic belt, M **$35.00**

Bozo the Clown, 7", removable arms, both paper cuffs in place, complete, EX **$50.00**

Bugs Bunny, large, holding carrot, M w/carrying bag ..**$50.00**

Bugs Bunny, 12½" bank, on basket of fruit, EX.............**$45.00**

Bugs Bunny, 9", Bicentennial issue, jointed w/soft vinyl head, minor wear, EX...**$75.00**

Cool Cat, ears & tail pop up, removable beret, M in carrying bag...**$150.00**

Daffy Duck, M in box..**$40.00**

Deputy Dawg, w/removable hat, M in carrying bag ...**$45.00**

Deputy Dawg, w/removable hat, NM..........................**$38.00**

Eagle w/aviator gear, 7", 1976 bank promotional figure, M..**$33.00**

Elmer Fudd, in street clothes, M in cellophane bag **$40.00**

Hobo Joe, 11", advertising bank, stands w/dog on large base, missing coin trap, scarce, NM......................**$80.00**

Hoppy Hoparoo, 8¾", w/paper tag, rare, M.............**$175.00**

Li'l Miss Just Rite, 7½", advertising figure w/movable limbs, blond version, w/shoes, EX **$150.00**

Merlin Mouse, yellow shirt, NM................................**$30.00**

Oliver Hardy, w/removable jacket, M in bag.............**$70.00**

Pebbles, 8", removable clothing, Hanna Barbera trademark, 1970s, NM...**$40.00**

Pepe Le Pew, stands on 4" dia base w/Goofygram: You're a Real Stinker, scarce, NM **$98.00**

Pink Panther, not faded, M in colorful box.................**$45.00**

Pink Panther, not faded, NM....................................**$32.50**

Pinocchio, jointed, removable clothing & shoes, NM..**$45.00**

Road Runner, EX..**$30.00**

Scooby Doo, 7", sitting, scarce, NM..........................**$90.00**

Smokey the Bear, M in colorful box............................**$50.00**

Snagglepuss, not faded, removable tail, collar & tie, NM w/paper tag...**$120.00**

Snagglepuss, slightly faded, complete, EX **$85.00**

Speedy Gonzalez, 14" bank, stands on wedge of cheese, removable cloth clothing, NM.................................**$45.00**

Stan Laurel, NM..**$50.00**

Sylvester the Cat, 6¼" bank, stands on his flat feet, head swivels, left arm moves, VG **$30.00**

Sylvester the Cat, 8¾", M in carrying bag.................**$45.00**

Tweety Bird, non-movable arms, NM..........................**$37.50**

Tweety Bird, 10½" bank, movable arms, removable sprout of hair on head, missing trap, EX **$40.00**

WC Fields Mouse, stands on 4" dia base w/Goofygram: I'll Drink to That, M **$50.00**

Yogi Bear, 5" bank, 1980, NM................................**$40.00**

Yogi Bear, 7", 1980, NM **$40.00**

Yosemite Sam, M in cellophane bag **$40.00**

Erector Sets

These were made by the A.C. Gilbert Company which was located on 'Erector Square,' in New Haven, Connecticut. They were very popular during the twenties through the forties, and over the past few years, collectors have taken a strong interest in them. Prices are escalating.

#1, complete, M **$40.00**

#1, Patented Jan 16th 1917, 1919, M in box...............**$80.00**

#10053, rocket launcher, instructions, complete, EX.**$150.00**

#10062, steam engine, EX..**$30.00**

#2, Junior, copyright 1949, complete, M **$40.00**

#2½, instructions, complete, EX................................**$30.00**

#3, M..**$40.00**

#4, instructions, complete, 1919, EX, original box.......**$45.00**

#4, instructions, 1930, complete, M in box **$260.00**

#4, instructions, 1940, EX in box **$250.00**

#4½, copyright 1938, M in box **$60.00**

#6½, electric engine, M in box................................**$30.00**

#7, builds steam shovel, complete in wood box, EX..**$250.00**

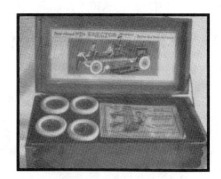

#7½, makes truck, complete, M............................$200.00

411

#8½, instructions, complete, M $80.00
#9, instructions, complete in wood box, EX.............$120.00

Farm Toys

Since the decade of the twenties, farm machinery manufacturers have contracted with many of the leading toy companies to produce scale models of their machines. Most were made on a 1/16 scale, but other sizes have been made as well.

Combine, John Deere Turbo, 11x14", Ertl, EX.............$20.00
Corn planter, Arcade, cast iron w/rubber wheels, EX original paint $70.00
Corn planter, Arcade, rubber wheels............................$27.50
Cub Cadet mower, International Harvester, Ertl #473, plastic, radiator frame, NM paint, EX $30.00
Disk, Ertl #1862, wing type, M on card $5.00
Disk, 6½x8x1½", Carter True Scale, 4-gang, twenty-eight blue blades, light wear on paint, EX $35.00
Disk harrow, Arcade, cast iron, paint traces $42.50
Gravity feed wagon, Ertl #1864, 1982, M on card..........$5.00
Lumber wagon, 4x7", Carter True Scale, red w/four yellow wheels, rubber tires, NM $22.00
Manure spreader, International Harvester, 2½x6", Ertl, red paint, two wheels, VG $7.50
Manure spreader, Massey Ferguson, Ertl, diecast, red paint, rubber tires, EX $12.00
Mower, Arcade, sickle bar style, EX original paint....$145.00
Pickup truck, International, 9", Arcade, worn paint, rubber wheels, 1939, VG $255.00
Pickup truck, International Harvester, plastic & metal .$100.00
Pickup truck, Jeep, Matchbox #71, 1964, light wear ...$15.00
Pickup truck, Tonka, w/livestock rails, 1960s, NM....$115.00
Pickup truck, Tonka #580, newer style w/rounded fenders, EX original paint, very little rust $75.00
Planter, Oliver, 2-row style, 1950s, EX $75.00
Plow, Arcade, 2-gang, worn paint, VG......................$200.00
Plow, International Harvester, Ertl, 4-bottom w/disk, EX $16.00
Plow, Oliver, 2-bottom, ca 1950, EX $70.00
Stake truck, 12", Tonka, #991, 1956, EX....................$100.00
Stake truck, 15", Nylint, metal w/worn white & green paint, marked Nylint Farms, w/9" stock trailer, VG $27.50
Thresher, John Deere, Vindex, 1935, M.................$1,150.00
Thresher, McCormick-Deering, 10", Arcade, painted cast iron, G $200.00
Thresher, McCormick-Deering, 9½", Arcade #450x, 1932, EX original paint..$160.00
Tractor, Allis-Chalmers, 9½", Arcade, painted cast iron w/white rubber tires, heavy wear, VG $55.00
Tractor, Allis-Chalmers AC-20, Ertl, plastic wheels, console control, orange paint, EX $145.00
Tractor, Allis-Chalmers type, 5", Japan, friction, VG........$22.00
Tractor, Allis-Chalmers 4-U Standard, red paint on cast iron, EX $195.00
Tractor, Avery, 4¾", Arcade, painted cast iron, 1920s, EX $125.00

Tractor, Deutz-Allis 6260, Ertl #1241, M on card............$7.50
Tractor, Farmall Model B, Arcade, painted cast iron, EX original paint $325.00
Tractor, Ford, Matchbox #46, NM $3.50
Tractor, Ford, 3½", Auburn Rubber, blue w/yellow tires, 1950, EX..$40.00
Tractor, Ford, 3½", Auburn Rubber, original plack tires, w/driver, NM...$60.00
Tractor, Ford, 4", Arcade, painted cast iron, NM $150.00
Tractor, Ford TW 35, 3", Ertl, blue & white, EX............$6.00
Tractor, Ford 6000, Hubley, EX original paint $32.00
Tractor, Fordson, Matchbox #72, 1959, NM $37.50
Tractor, Fordson, 5¾", Firestone, cast iron, w/driver, EX original paint $215.00
Tractor, Graham-Bradley, 4¼", Auburn Rubber $24.50
Tractor, International Harvester type, Japan, red & yellow lithograph on tin, friction motor, 4½" rubber tires, EX $25.00
Tractor, International Harvester 24 Farmall, 6½", Lincoln Toys, green paint, rubber wheels, EX $125.00
Tractor, John Deere, 4", cast metal w/cast lug wheels, green & yellow paint, light rust spots, G $12.50
Tractor, John Deere A, 5", Auburn Rubber, NM $24.00
Tractor, Massey Ferguson, Corgi #73, w/saw, M in box .$110.00
Tractor, Massey Harris #44, w/driver, EX....................$35.00
Tractor, McCormick-Deering, Arcade, replaced driver, solid red wheels, black tires, EX paint, ca 1922..........$495.00
Tractor, Minneapolis-Moline, cast driver, ca 1956, EX.$22.50
Tractor, Minneapolis-Moline, SLIK, cast-in man & steering wheel, 1956, EX $22.00
Tractor, Minneapolis-Moline A, 4", Auburn Rubber, EX..$18.00
Tractor, Monarch, 5½", Hubley $125.00

Tractor (9") & mowing machine (4"), Oliver, marked SLIK, 1952..$750.00
Tractor, 10", diesel, Marx, plastic w/large lithograph on metal wheels, man in seat, battery operated, EX..$95.00
Tractor, 3", Arcade, orange paint on cast iron, bright steel wheels, VG $60.00
Tractor, 4", Art Plastic, 2" back tires, decals worn, EX.....$12.00
Tractor, 4", Auburn Rubber, aqua w/black wheels, molded-in driver, EX...$50.00
Tractor, 4", Tonka Tiny #685, red & white, EX $4.00
Tractor, 5", Buddy L, metal front loader, green paint, blade missing, G $5.00
Tractor, 6", Buddy L, metal, EX green paint, front loader (no blade), G $5.00

Tractor/trailor, Allis-Chalmers, 12", Arcade, 1927, G ...**$65.00**

Wagon, International Harvester, 2½x4x2", red paint, rubber wheels, tailgate opens, NM.........................**$6.00**

Wagon, International Harvester, 8", Ertl #0393, flared top, rubber wheels, NM **$10.00**

Wagon, John Deere, plastic, automatic steering, yellow wheels, swinging gate, NM paint, tongue gone....**$16.00**

Wagon, McCormick-Deering, Arcade, EX **$175.00**

Wagon, 2⅜x5½x2½", Carter True Scale, flared top, black rubber wheels, red paint, NM **$13.00**

Fisher-Price

Since the thirties, Fisher-Price has been one of the best-known manufacturers of toys in this country. If your toy has any plastic parts at all, you can be certain that it was made after 1949. Toys made before 1962 carry the black and white rectangular logo.

Allie Gator, 4¼x10⅛", green plastic feet on red wheels, vinyl hat brim, 1960-62, EX **$45.00**

Bucky Burro, pull toy, 1955, EX **$50.00**

Bunnies, pulling egg cart, 1940, NM **$120.00**

Buzzy Bee, 5½x6", plastic wheels & spring antennae w/plastic tips, 1950-56, EX **$18.00**

Cash Register, 7½x10x9", paper lithographs on plastic, w/six coins, 1974-present, EX..............................**$6.00**

Chatter Monkey, pull toy, 1957, EX.............................**$25.00**

Chatter Telephone, dial rotates, eyes move up & down when pulled, spiral cord on receiver, 1970s, common, EX..**$2.00**

Choo-Choo, 3¼x17", engine & four cars connected by steel rods, wooden wheels, 1955-57, EX.....................**$50.00**

Cracklin' Hen, 10x6½", pull toy w/clucking mechanism, vinyl comb & tail feathers, 1958-66, EX.............**$35.00**

Ding Dong Ducky, pull toy, 1949, NM.........................**$55.00**

Dinkey Engine, 6", blue vinyl cab & cowcatcher, connecting rods on wheels, w/clicking sound, 1959, EX........**$45.00**

Ducky Cart, 5x8¼", cardboard figural pulling 2¾" dia cylindrical cart w/metal bottom, 1940-42, EX **$50.00**

Elsie's Dairy Truck, 1948, M.........................**$135.00**

Freddy Bear, 12", foam-stuffed plush w/vinyl eyes & inside squeaker, 1975-80, EX...............................**$5.00**

Fuzzy the Dog, pull toy, 1940, NM.............................**$55.00**

Goldilocks & the Three Bears Playhouse, 7x6½x7", plastic on wooden base, w/figures, 1967-70, complete, EX ...**$20.00**

Huckleberry Hound Xylophone Player, 1961, EX **$32.00**

Husky Dump Truck, 12", plastic cab & grill w/balloon wheels, driver bobs up & down, bed dumps, 1961-63, EX...**$15.00**

Jingle Giraffe, pull toy, 1956, EX.................................**$22.50**

Ladybug, 4½x8", plastic-domed shell revolves & chimes, spring antennae w/wood knobs, 1961-63, EX **$20.00**

Looky Fire Truck, 1950s, NM **$30.00**

Merry Mutt, 7½x8", dog plays 2-key metal xylophone when pulled, 1949, EX..**$100.00**

Music Box Pocket Radio, plays 'Yankee Doodle,' 1975, EX..**$3.00**

Music Box Record Player, 4½x9x8½", all plastic w/wind-up knob & on-off switch, five records, 1971-present, VG...**$8.00**

Musical Push Chime, metal bracket holds chiming cylinder, wooden handle, paper logos on wheels, 1950s, EX..**$20.00**

Musical Sweeper, 3x8½x7", 'Whistle While You Work' lithographed on metal, wood wheels & handle, 1950-52, EX..**$75.00**

Nosey Pup, 4x6", black felt ears & 3½" long black vinyl tail, 1956-59, EX...**$20.00**

Patch Pony, 7x8", vinyl ears & balloon wheels, wooden bead on spring tail, w/clicker, 1961-65, EX **$15.00**

Play Family A-Frame, set w/cabin & deck loungers, furniture & five family figures included, 1975-76, EX **$25.00**

Play Family Camper, includes: trunk, camper, boat, camping supplies & figures, paper & painted plastic, 1972, EX..**$25.00**

Play Family Castle, 13¼x17x12¾", complete with furniture, figures & carriage, 1975-77, EX............................**$35.00**

Play Family Houseboat, includes: boat, life preservers, five figures, table, two chairs & loungers, BBQ grill, & speedboat, 1972-present, NM.......................$15.00

Puffy Train Engine, pull toy, 1950, NM **$30.00**

Rocka-Bye Bunny Pushing Cart, pull toy, 1940, EX **$80.00**

Snap Quack Duck, pull toy, 1947, EX.........................**$55.00**

Snoopy Sniffer, 14", dog w/brown felt ears, pin-jointed plastic feet & beaded spring tail, 1961-80, EX **$22.50**

Snoopy Sniffer, 5¼x16½", dog w/black felt ears, rubber feet & spring tail, ca 1940s, EX....................................**$60.00**

Teddy Tooter, 9½x6¾x4¾", plastic horn & inner 'blowing' mechanism, head & hands move when pulled, 1957, VG...**$80.00**

Teddy Zilo, 11x9x4¾", bear plays 5-key metal xylophone when pulled, 1946-50, NM **$45.00**

This Little Pig, 3x13x3", string of five pink plastic pigs w/wheels, each 'oinks' when squeezed, 1959-62, VG...**$10.00**

Timmy Turtle, pull toy, hard plastic shell, 1950s, NM. **$30.00**

Tool Box Workbench, 8¾x13x6", molded plastic hinged lid holds tools, w/plastic tools & accessories, 1969-70, EX........**$18.00**

Whistling Engine, pull toy, 1957, EX...........................**$20.00**

Wobbles, 9x14x8½", dog on large plastic wheels w/spring tail & red vinyl tongue, 1964-67, VG **$15.00**

Guns

One of the best-selling kinds of toys every made, toy guns were first patented in the late 1850s. Until WWII, most were made of cast iron, though other materials were used on a lesser scale. After the war, cast iron became cost prohibitive, and steel and die-cast zinc were used. By 1950, most were made either of die-cast material or plastic. Hundreds of names can be found embossed on these little guns, a custom which continues to the present time. Because of their tremendous popularity and durability, today's collectors can find a diversity of models and styles, and prices are still fairly affordable.

Bang-O, 7", cast iron top-loading cap pistol w/plastic grips, NM silvering, unused **$65.00**

Colt Dakota, 9", metal cap pistol w/plastic inset grips & cylinder, EX in box..**$150.00**

Daisy, #195 Buzz Barton Special, 34" long, BB air rifle, blued steel barrel w/wood stock, late 1940s or early 1950s, EX **$95.00**

Daisy, 'Lectric Revolver, 11½", lithograph on tin w/plastic cylinder, battery operated, 1960s, NM in box.....**$100.00**

Daisy, Model 1894 Classic, 38" long, black metal & wood-grain plastic, pump-action BB air rifle, 1960s, EX **$40.00**

Daisy, Squirt-o-Matic, #72, VG **$95.00**

Gang Busters, gun & target set, NM in box **$175.00**

Gray Iron Casting Co, Anti-Aircraft Rapid Fire machine gun, 7", cast iron cap shooter, EX paint, 1930s...........**$145.00**

Hubley, Dagger Derringer, 7", white metal w/black plastic grips, M on card...**$45.00**

Hubley, Deputy, 10", metal, highly scrolled barrel, cowboy on horseback embossed on grips, w/original badge, NM in box **$120.00**

Hubley, Dick, 4¼", die-cast cap pistol, nickel finish, M in red, white & blue box **$65.00**

Hubley, Flintlock Jr, 7½", die-cast single-shot cap pistol, brown plastic stock, 1950s, M in box **$35.00**

Hubley, Rodeo, cap pistol, M in box.........................**$125.00**

Hubley, Texan, 9½", silvered cast iron cap pistol w/plastic grips (each w/embossed steer head), VG **$35.00**

Hubley, Texan 38, 10½", silvered white metal cap pistol w/plastic grips, 1950s, NM **$70.00**

Hubley, Tommy Gun, 10", VG $25.00

Ideal, Trick Shot, 26½", red plastic dart-shooting rifle, complete w/target & four rubber-tipped darts, M in EX box..**$70.00**

Japan, X-Ray Space Gun, 17", tin, battery-operated gun mounts on stand, lights flash when fired, NM in box **$165.00**

Kilgore, Big Bill, cast iron, VG..**$75.00**

Kilgore, Big Horn Six-Shooter, 7", metal w/embossed sheep horn on handle, uses disk caps, EX......................**$50.00**

Kilgore, Clip 50, Bakelite pistol, EX in box..............**$110.00**

Kilgore, Eagle, cap pistol, M in box **$110.00**

Kilgore, Grizzly, 10", die-cast pistol, revolving cylinder fires disk caps, black grips w/embossed bear, 1950s, M in box...**$230.00**

Kilgore, Laredo, 9", silvered metal cap pistol w/ivory grips, 1970, M on 10½" card..**$50.00**

Kilgore, Presto, nickeled cast iron, pop-up cap magazine, brown plastic grips, 1940, NM in box **$175.00**

Kilgore, Private Eye, pistol, M in box.........................**$80.00**

Kilgore, Ranger, 8½", silvered cast iron pistol w/maroon plastic grips, uses roll caps, EX..............................**$65.00**

Kilgore, Self Timer, cap pistol, original belt & holster....**$95.00**

Kilgore, Six-Shooter, cast iron, NM.........................**$100.00**

Marx, Gung Ho Commando Outfit, 32x24x12", 28" plastic .50 caliber machine gun w/accessories, 1963 .....**$150.00**

Marx, Jet Shot Repeater, airplane-shaped water pistol, 1950s, EX in original box..**$40.00**

Mattel, Colt Shooting Shell Six Shooter, rifle, complete w/target & papers, M in box..............................**$650.00**

Mattel, Fanner 50, 10½", silvered white metal cap pistol w/plastic grips, EX **$50.00**

Mattel, M-16 Marauder, automatic rifle, EX..............**$225.00**

Mattel, Shootin' Shell, 25½", metal & plastic Winchester replica, metal & plastic cap shooter, VG **$65.00**

Mattel, Shootin' Shell 45, 11", metal cap pistol w/plastic grips, holds six bullets & has bullet ejector, EX..**$325.00**

Nichols, Dyna-Mite derringer, 1950s, M in box **$95.00**

Nichols, Mustang 500, 12½", silvered metal revolver w/grained plastic grips, 1950s, M in box **$165.00**

Nichols, Spitfire, 8½", metal snub-nosed rifle w/tan plastic stock, lever-cocking action for disk caps, M in G box...**$65.00**

Payton, US Army Bazooka Tank Destroyer, 35" long, plastic & cardboard, shoots plastic bullets, 1960s, NM in box...**$60.00**

Rangeland, single gun & holster set, M in box...........**$75.00**

Redondo, Revolver Mauser, 6¼", die-cast, automatic style w/pop-up cap magazine, 1960s, M in box...........**$10.00**

Remington 36, cap pistol, EX......................................**$20.00**

Smoky Joe, 9", white metal cap pistol, glossy black plastic grips, 1950s, EX..**$65.00**

Stevens, Big Scout, 7½", nickel-plated cast iron cap pistol w/plastic grips, 1930s, NM in box **$98.00**

Strato Gun, 9", heavy metal, cap pistol, futuristic appearance, M in box...**$150.00**

Topper, Johnny Eagle Lieutenant Pistol, 10" plastic pistol w/6-round clip, in original 12x8" display case......**$65.00**

Western, 7", w/red 'jewel,' VG...............................$35.00

Monsters

TV shows like Land of the Giants, Lost in Space, Munsters, Addams Family, Twilight Zone, and Outer Limits have spawned some great monster toys that collectors are zeroing in on today. Universal Studios are responsible for some as well, and it's not just the monster figures that are collectible but board games, puzzles, Halloween costumes, coloring books, and gum cards, too.

Dracula, 12", Bendee, soft rubber w/wire inserts for posing, 1974, EX...$50.00
Dracula, 3¾", Remco glow-in-the-dark figure, M on original card $10.00
Dracula, 6", World Toy House, soft rubber, painted clothes & features, 1960s, M on card.................................$40.00
Frankenstein, 11", Bendee, soft rubber w/wire inserts for posing, 1974, EX $55.00
Frankenstein, 3¾", Remco glow-in-the-dark figure, M on card $12.00
Frankenstein, 7½", Azrak-Hamway, hard plastic w/jointed arms & legs, 1973, NM...$48.00
Frankenstein bank, vinyl head form, M in box...........$20.00
Freddie Krueger doll, Max FX, M in box.....................$25.00
King Kong, 16", Samet & Wells (on original tag), stuffed plush figure w/vinyl face, 1975, EX.....................$45.00
Monster case, Remco, fits 3¾" figure, M in package $20.00
Monster Machine, Gabriel, makes different plaster monster heads, NM in box..$40.00
Wolfman, 3¾", Remco glow-in-the-dark figure, M on card..$40.00

Premiums

From the early thirties until the advent of TV, kids hurried home to tune in their favorite radio show. They were glued to the set for the thirty-minute program, and these bigger-and-better-than-life heroes were a very real part of their lives. They agonized over cliff-hanger episodes and were always vastly relieved when Tom Mix (or whoever) was rescued from the 'bad guys' the very next day. These radio superstars were made even more real to the children through the premiums they could obtain for nothing more than a box top or an inner label and a few pennies for postage. Secret manuals, signet rings, decoders, compasses, flashlights, pocketknives, and badges were just a few of the items available. Who could have known that by the nineties, some of these would be worth hundreds of dollars! See also Character Collectibles.

Amos & Andy, puzzle, M....................................$25.00
Bobby Benson, Code Rule 1935 cardboard decoder, Hecker H-O, EX $45.00
Buck Jones, club ring, M $35.00
Buck Jones Jr, Sheriff Badge, EX $20.00
Buck Rogers, Birthstone & Initial Ring, EX $75.00
Buck Rogers, Flight Commander Whistle Badge, M....$70.00
Buck Rogers, helmet, EX......................................$85.00
Buck Rogers, Lite Blaster Flashlight, EX....................$10.00
Buck Rogers, Repeller Ray (seal) Ring, M.................$160.00
Buck Rogers, telescope, M...................................$75.00
Buffalo Bill Jr, brass ring, buffalo in relief on top, TV premium, EX $20.00
Captain Franks, Air Hawks Ring, M........................$45.00
Captain Gallant, medal, shaped as a cross w/'GRI' on it, 1950s, EX...$15.00
Captain Marvel, Magic Whistle, American Seed Co, portrait on each side, 1943, M...................................$25.00
Captain Midnight, American Flag Loyalty Badge, 1940, EX $40.00
Captain Midnight, Code-O-Graph, works as a whistle, 1947, M...$45.00

Captain Midnight, Code-O-Graph Badge, w/picture of Captain Midnight, 1942, M............................$110.00
Captain Midnight, Code-O-Graph Decoder Pin, eagle on top, 1941, M $100.00
Captain Midnight, Code-O-Graph Magnifier, 1945, M..$100.00
Captain Midnight, Detect-O-Scope, 1941, M $60.00
Captain Midnight, Flight Commander Ring, 1941, EX..$115.00
Captain Midnight, MJC-10 Plane Detector, distance finder, 1942, M $90.00
Captain Midnight, Mystic Eye Detector Ring, 1942, M .$125.00
Captain Midnight, Secret Squadron Decoder Badge, 1956, M $95.00

Captain Midnight, Surprise Package, 1942, EX............**$30.00**

Captain Midnight, Weather Wings, predicts weather, 1940, EX..**$35.00**

Captain Midnight, 1942 Manual for Decoder, EX **$150.00**

Captain Midnight, 1947 Manual for Code-O-Graph, M .**$85.00**

Captain Video, Flying Saucer Ring, M **$75.00**

Captain Video, Secret Seal Ring, 1950s, EX................**$75.00**

Captain Video, X-9 Rocket Balloon, 1950s, M............**$45.00**

Cisco Kid, badge, Western hat on chain, 1950s, M......**$20.00**

Cisco Kid, face mask, 1953, M **$20.00**

Cisco Kid, Picture Ring, 1950s, M.........................**$65.00**

Dick Tracy, Air Detective Ring, M **$65.00**

Dick Tracy, Badge, Crime Stoppers, M.....................**$12.00**

Dick Tracy, Decoder, green, 1948, EX **$25.00**

Dick Tracy, Detective Club Badge, w/secret money pouch in rear, M..**$45.00**

Flash Gordon, ring, Post Toasties Corn Flakes, 1949, M..**$30.00**

Hopalong Cassidy, Bar 20 Compass Ring, M............**$25.00**

Hopalong Cassidy, Face Ring, M **$25.00**

Howdy Doody, climber, cardboard w/string, Welch's premium, 1950s, EX **$20.00**

Howdy Doody, Flicker Ring, flicks from Howdy to Poll, Poll Parrot premium, M......................................**$15.00**

Howdy Doody, puppet, 15", cardboard, Mars Candy, 1950s, EX..**$35.00**

Jack Armstrong, Explorer's Telescope, EX **$20.00**

Jack Armstrong, flashlight, M **$25.00**

Jack Armstrong, Magic Answer Box, M......................**$55.00**

Jack Armstrong, Ped-O-Meter (blue or silver), M **$35.00**

Jack Armstrong, Secret Whistle Code Card, for Secret Egyptian Coder Siren Ring, M.............................**$25.00**

Jack Armstrong, 3-D viewer, filmstrip, M **$35.00**

Jimmie Allen, High-Speed Gasoline Flying Cadet Wings, bronze, 1930s, EX **$15.00**

Jimmie Allen, Richfield Hi-Octane Pilot's ID Bracelet, all metal, 1930s, EX......................................**$28.00**

Jimmie Allen, Skelly Oil Flying Cadet Wings, bronze, late 1930s, M..**$20.00**

Lone Ranger, A Republic Serial, brass star badge, M...**$75.00**

Lone Ranger, Atom Bomb Ring, common, M **$55.00**

Lone Ranger, Bond Bread Safety Club Badge, 1938, EX..**$20.00**

Lone Ranger, Deputy Shield, brass w/secret compartment, M..**$45.00**

Lone Ranger, Glow-In-the-Dark Belt, 1941, EX **$60.00**

Lone Ranger, Movie Film Ring, Cherrios premium, 1940s, M..**$75.00**

Lone Ranger, Safety Scout Badge, Silvercup Bread, 1935, EX..**$20.00**

Lone Ranger, Secret Compartment Ring, w/picture of Lone Ranger & Silver, M................................**$75.00**

Lone Ranger, Silver Bullet, secret compartment compass, M..**$45.00**

Lone Ranger, Victory Corps Badge, Kix Cereal, 1942, EX..**$30.00**

Melvin Purvis, Law & Order Patrol Secret Operator Badge, late 1930s, EX **$20.00**

Melvin Purvis, Law & Order Ring, M.........................**$45.00**

Melvin Purvis, Secret Operator, Girl's Division, EX **$30.00**

Mickey Mouse, Globe Trotters Map, 28x20", NBC Bread, 1937, M..**$350.00**

Mickey Mouse, Playboard, 9", comics giveaway, 1946, EX..**$15.00**

Radio Orphan Annie, Annie & Joe Corntassel Button, 1931, M..**$20.00**

Radio Orphan Annie, Birthstone Ring, 1935, EX **$30.00**

Radio Orphan Annie, Circus Cutouts, 1935, EX..........**$75.00**

Radio Orphan Annie, Code Captain Pin, 1939, M **$45.00**

Radio Orphan Annie, Decoder Badge, 1936, M.....$25.00

Radio Orphan Annie, Decoder Badge, 1940, M..........**$25.00**

Radio Orphan Annie, ID Bracelet, 1935, EX **$28.00**

Radio Orphan Annie, Magic Transfer Picture, 1937, EX..**$25.00**

Radio Orphan Annie, pin, 1937, M...........................**$20.00**

Radio Orphan Annie, Punchouts, 1942, EX **$150.00**

Radio Orphan Annie, ring, 1935, M...........................**$45.00**

Radio Orphan Annie, Secret Society Pin, 1934, M.......**$30.00**

Radio Orphan Annie, Shake-Up Game, 1931, EX......**$15.00**

Radio Orphan Annie, Silver Star Pin, 1934, M............**$30.00**

Radio Orphan Annie, Silver Star Ring, 1938, M **$25.00**

Radio Orphan Annie, Treasure Hunt Game, 1940, M..**$45.00**

Radio Orphan Annie, 1936 Decoder Manual, M..........**$65.00**

Red Ryder, Lucky Coin, M......................................**$8.00**

Roy Rogers, Branding Iron Ring, M..........................**$65.00**

Roy Rogers, Paint Set, 1950s, EX.............................**$12.00**

Roy Rogers, Silver Hat Ring, M **$30.00**

Roy Rogers, Tuck-A-Way Gun, M.............................**$10.00**

Sgt Preston, Klondike Land Pouch, M **$20.00**

Sgt Preston, Pedometer, M......................................**$30.00**

Sgt Preston, Skinning Knife, M................................**$45.00**

Sgt Preston, Yukon Village, EX................................**$275.00**

Sky King, Aztec Indian Ring, M **$95.00**

Sky King, Detecto Writer, M....................................**$65.00**

Sky King, Magni-Glo Ring, M...................................**$45.00**

Sky King, Navajo Indian Ring, EX............................**$75.00**

Sky King, Stamp Kit, M...**$35.00**

Space Patrol, Jet Glow Code Belt, 1951, EX................**$75.00**

Space Patrol, Smoke Gun, 1950s, M **$90.00**

Space Patrol, Space-O-Phone, 1952, M **$100.00**

Straight Arrow, Picture Ring, early 1950s, M **$65.00**

Straight Arrow, Tom-Tom, early 1950s, M...................**$25.00**

Superman, Crusader Ring, M...................................**$150.00**

Superman, Kellogg's Silver Jet Airplane Ring, plane flies off, M..**$40.00**

Superman, planes from Pep cereal, set of eight, 1948, EX $35.00

Tom Mix, Airplane & Parachute, M $125.00

Tom Mix, bandana, w/TM Brand, M $75.00

Tom Mix, baseball, M $35.00

Tom Mix, Blowdart Game, M $95.00

Tom Mix, Bullet Flashlight, EX.............$50.00

Tom Mix, Bullet Telescope, 4", bird call device included, EX $30.00

Tom Mix, Charm Bracelet, w/charm steer head, gun, horseman, TM brand, M $60.00

Tom Mix, cowboy shirt, EX.............$75.00

Tom Mix, Decoder Buttons Instruction Sheet, Ralston, 1946, EX.............$15.00

Tom Mix, Deputy Ring, chewing gum premium, 1934, EX $55.00

Tom Mix, Gold Ore Badge, M $35.00

Tom Mix, Good Luck Spinner, M $30.00

Tom Mix, ID Bracelet, M.............$45.00

Tom Mix, Magnifying Glass Compass, brass, 1939, M.$65.00

Tom Mix, Ralston Straight Shooters Pocket Knife, 1940, EX $50.00

Tom Mix, Ranch Box Badge, M $55.00

Tom Mix, Secret Code Manual, M.............$55.00

Tom Mix, Signal Flashlight, M.............$65.00

Tom Mix, Six Shooter, wooden, barrel spins, 1936, EX .$75.00

Tom Mix, Six Shooter, wooden, no moving parts, 1939, M ..$75.00

Tom Mix, Straight Shooters Campaign Medal, silver, M.$45.00

Tom Mix, Telephone Set, M.............$65.00

Tom Mix, Tiger Eye Ring, Ralston, 1945, M.............$125.00

Tom Mix, Wrangler Badge, Ralston, 1936, EX $45.00

Tom Mix, 1941 Manual, EX.............$45.00

Tom Mix, 1946 Manual, M.............$55.00

Ramp Walkers

Though ramp-walking figures were made as early as the 1870s, ours date from about 1935 on. They were made in Czechoslovakia from the twenties through the forties and in this country during the fifties and sixties by Marx, who made theirs of plastic. John Wilson of Watsontown, Pennsylvania, sold his worldwide. They were known as 'Wilson Walkies' and stood about 4½" high. But the majority has been imported from Hong Kong.

Barney Rubble & Fred Flintstone, walking single file, NM $95.00

Bear, orange-brown w/black spotting, walks on all fours, EX.............$60.00

Black Mammy, 1940s, EX $48.00

Boxer dog, lime green or pink $18.00

Bull, orange-brown, horns point straight ahead, realistic appearance, NM $55.00

Camel, 1¼x2", Hong Kong, yellow, M.............$20.00

Choo Choo Cherry, Pillsbury's Funny Face drink premium, 1971, very scarce, EX.............$98.00

Circus horse, red w/yellow legs, has slot on saddle for removable rider (missing), standard size, M $28.50

Cow, tan w/brown spots, pink udder & ears, white face & horns, comic appearance, NM $48.00

Cowboy on horseback, 2x2", 1950s.............$35.00

Dachshund dog, brown w/beige tummy, NM $45.00

Donald Duck pulling wagon filled w/three nephews, Disney copyright, EX.............$48.50

Donald Duck pushing wheelbarrow, Disney copyright, EX.............$44.00

Duckling, ivory w/black details, orange bill, comic character eyes, M.............$30.00

Elephant, 1¼x2", Hong Kong, pink, M.............$15.00

Elephant w/trunk up, red blanket w/gold trim on head, larger blanket on back, EX.............$32.00

Figaro the Cat, black w/blue & white ribbon, white paws, flesh-toned face, NM.............$50.00

Horse w/rider, 4½x5", rider w/red tails & black top hat, 1960s, M in Marx display box $95.00

Jiminy Cricket pushing a bass fiddle, Disney copyright, M.............$60.00

Jumbo the Elephant, 1960.............$20.00

Kangaroo, yellow body w/red feet, fragile upturned ears, M.............$30.00

Kangaroo w/baby in pouch, M in unopened wrap.....$60.00

Man pushing wheelbarrow, blue hat & overalls, red feet, blue & white wheelbarrow, NM.............$55.00

Minnie Mouse pushing baby carriage, Disney copyright, EX $45.00

Mother Goose w/three baby geese behind her, blue apron & hat, red feet, EX.............$45.00

Parrot, green body, yellow feet & bill, red head, 1980s premium, scarce, M.............$50.00

Penguin pulling sled w/seated baby penguin, M in unopened wrap.............$55.00

Pluto, 2x4½", Disney copyright, bright yellow, EX......$55.00

Popeye, 5½", celluloid, ca 1930s, EX.............$150.00

Popeye pushing spinach barrel, 1960.............$35.00

Rabbit pushing cart, ivory w/red coveralls, green eyes, fragile ears, EX.............$65.00

Rhinoceros, 1¼x2", Hong Kong, yellow or pink, ea ...$20.00

Rootin' Tootin' Raspberry, Pillsbury's Funny Face drink premium, 1971, M.............$120.00

Wimpy, 5½", composition w/wooden feet, EX paint, ca 1935, scarce.............$185.00

Yogi Bear w/Huckleberry Hound, walking single file, EX $95.00

Robots

As early as 1948, Japanese toy manufacturers introduced their toy robots. Some of the best examples were made in the fifties, during the 'golden age' of battery-operated toys. They became increasingly complex, and today some of these in excellent condition may bring well over $1,000.00. By the sixties, more and more plastic was used in their production, and the toys became inferior.

#2007, 4", Hong Kong, white plastic w/metallic green limbs, wind-up w/key, ca 1970s, EX $18.00

Atomic Robot Man, 5", Japan, tin lithograph, wind-up, 1950s, EX **$880.00**

Big Max Conveyor Robot, Remco, battery operated, 1950s, VG in box **$185.00**

Cosmic Fighter Robot, NM **$85.00**

Dino the Robot, 11", Japan, lithograph on tin, battery operated, robot head splits open, lights go on, NM in box **$875.00**

Fireman Ding-A-Ling Robot, M in box **$25.00**

Flying Saucer Ding-A-Ling Robot, M in box **$25.00**

Godaiken Guardian Robot, Bandai, M in box **$50.00**

Japan, 5", tin, green w/red tin earmuffs, wind-up walker, EX **$120.00**

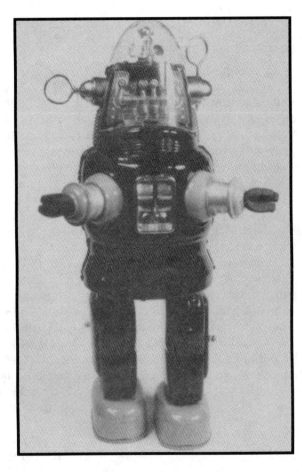

Japan, 13", metal & plastic, early look, NM $225.00

Jetto the Air-Powered Robot, 5x4", Tri-Play Toys Chicago, blue & orange plastic, balloon-powered, M in NM box **$15.00**

Jupiter Robot, M in box **$175.00**

Marx, 12", metal & plastic w/battery-operated box, Japan **$275.00**

Mighty Robot, blue & green, red sparking chest, NM ..**$165.00**

Mirror Man, M in box **$245.00**

Mister Robot, 11", Cragston, hard plastic, battery operated, 1950s, NM in box **$200.00**

Mr Rembrant, 7", Ideal, multicolored plastic, complete w/six plastic cams & colored pens, 1970s, EX in box **$60.00**

Planet Robot, 12¾", tin, rubber & plastic, battery operated, M in box **$800.00**

Robert the Robot, 15", Ideal, plastic w/remote-control steering, 1950s, M in box **$225.00**

Robot Bulldozer, 8", United Pioneer, tin bulldozer w/robot driver, battery operated, 1950s, EX **$895.00**

Rom, 13", Parker Brothers, hard plastic, three plug-in attachments, 1979, M in box **$110.00**

Sparky Robot, 8", Japan, tin, wind-up toy, sparks seen through eyes, EX **$325.00**

Star Strider Robot, red, M in box **$95.00**

Super Explorer, 11½", Japan, black plastic w/some red, battery operated, 1970s, M in worn box....................**$18.00**

Tinka-a-Tron, 11½x5x16", Hasbro, gray, blue & white plastic, battery-operated, 1960s, NM in worn box.......**$35.00**

X-70 (Tulip Robot), 12", Japan, lithograph on tin, 1960s, NM...**$1,250.00**

Slot Car Racers

When no condition code is listed, values are for slot cars that are in mint (not mint in box) condition.

HO Scale, Aurora AFX, #1753 Dodge Charger Daytona, M...**$25.00**

HO Scale, Aurora AFX, #1782 Peace Tank, M **$40.00**

HO Scale, Aurora AFX Magna Traction, Porsche, rally striped in orange & blue w/black roof, 1981, M in blister pack...**$27.00**

HO Scale, Aurora AFX Ultra T, Mercury Stocker, type 'B' car, M in box **$18.00**

HO Scale, Aurora Hop-up Kit, Boxed Hop-up Kit, M.**$10.00**

HO Scale, Aurora Thunderjet, #1368 Ferrari, M...........**$40.00**

HO Scale, Aurora Thunderjet, #1372 Mustang Hardtop, white, M..**$60.00**

HO Scale, Aurora Thunderjet, #1374 Ford GT, M........**$30.00**

HO Scale, Aurora Thunderjet, #1375 Cobra GT, white **$30.00**

HO Scale, Aurora Thunderjet, #1381 Dino Ferrari, red **$30.00**

HO Scale, Aurora Thunderjet, #1384 Green Hornet.....**$150.00**

HO Scale, Aurora Thunderjet, #1385 Batmobile, M...**$150.00**

HO Scale, Aurora Truck, #8001 Ryder Rental, yellow, M...**$20.00**

HO Scale, Aurora Vibrator, #1541 Jaguar Convertible, white, M...**$50.00**

HO Scale, Aurora Vibrator, #1542 Mercedes Benz Convertible, gray, M...**$50.00**

HO Scale, Aurora Vibrator, #1554 Hot Rod Coupe, M ..**$50.00**

HO Scale, Aurora Xcellerator, #2746 Vega #3, M **$40.00**

HO Scale, Ideal, Dodge Charger General Lee, #4661, M on card..**$33.00**

HO Scale, Ideal Total Control Racing, Ferry, #3272, red, M on card..**$20.00**

HO Scale, Tyco, Buick Riviera, #S624, beige, M in box.**$75.00**

1/24 Scale, Authentic Model Turnpike (AMT), most cars, M...**$40.00**

1/32 Scale, Cox, McLaren, white...................................**$40.00**

1/32 Scale, Eldon, Indy Formula Car, open wheeled, w/driver, yellow, EX..**$35.00**

1/32 Scale, Eldon, Mustang Fastback, M **$30.00**

1/32 Scale, Eldon, Snowmobile, #3765, blue w/#2 on front, M on card..**$135.00**

1/32 Scale, Eldon, Station Wagon, M..........................$35.00
1/32 Scale, Eldon, 1964 T-Bird, blue, EX.....................$45.00
1/32 Scale, Gilbert Auto-Rama Over & Under Figure '8'
Corvette Race #19080, 1983, NM in box.............$250.00
1/32 Scale, Marx, Ferry GT-250, #2278, green, w/motor
noise, M in box..$95.00
1/32 Scale, Strombecker, Cheetah, M.........................$35.00
1/32 Scale, Strombecker, Ford GT, M..........................$30.00
1/32 scale, Strombecker, Pontiac, #9535, light blue w/black
roof, 1960s, M in box..$100.00

Squeeze Toys

Most of these soft rubber or vinyl toys were made from the forties through the sixties, and especially those modeled after Disney or other comic characters are becoming quite collectible. Condition is very important; watch for cracking and paint loss which can sometimes devaluate one of these toys to nearly nothing. The earlier examples are the most expensive; some of the better ones were made by Sun Rubber who did several Disneys.

Bradford House Restaurants, Bucky Bradford, 9", 1-pc vinyl
pilgrim boy...$6.00
Dell, Donald Duck, 10½", standing w/binoculars in hand,
blue jacket, red bow tie, NM...............................$70.00
Dell, Donald Duck, 8", hand to bow tie, other pointing
down, blue clothes, red buttons, NM...................$60.00
Dell, Shaggy Dog, 5¼", Disney character sitting up
w/tongue out, NM...$65.00
Disney, Dumbo, 5½", trunk up, left ear cocked to side,
clown hat, red collar, NM.....................................$55.00
Disney, Lucky Pup, 7", from 101 Dalmations, red collar
w/name tag, NM..$62.50
Disney, Mickey Mouse, 5¼", flower in hands behind back,
red bow tie & shorts, NM.....................................$45.00
Disney, Pinocchio, 7½", apple & schoolbooks, all vinyl,
NM..$48.00
Disney, Sleeping Beauty, 5½", rabbit in hands, blue crown &
dress, NM...$75.00
Eastern Moulded Products, Barney Rubble, 6", red shirt, yellow hat, 1967, M in package.................................$40.00
Eastern Moulded Products, Dino Dinosaur, 7", front legs
up, blue paint, large squeaker in base, 1967, M in
package...$48.50
Edward Moberly Co, Cindy, 8", vinyl, girl holds baby,
molded-on clothes, no paint, 1963.........................$4.00
Harvey, Baby Hewie, 10", vinyl.....................................$4.00
Holland Hall Products, Eeyore, 1966, missing squeaker,
EX...$10.00
Holland Hall Products, Winnie the Poo, 13", copyright
1960s, EX paint..$65.00
Ideal, boy w/daisies behind back, 6", all vinyl, molded
orange hair, oversize feet, 1966............................$3.00
Irwin, nude girl holding doll, 5½", 1-pc vinyl, molded-on
booties...$4.00
Japan, Kewpie-like figure w/baseball & mitt, 4", vinyl,
molded-on underwear, painted eyes.......................$3.00

JE McConnell, frog, 5", vinyl, molded-on clothes & shoes,
wide smile...$3.00
King Features, 6½", vinyl, molded-on clothes & hat....$20.00
Larry Harmon copyright, Oliver Hardy, 7½", gray suit, black
hat, 1962, NM..$175.00
Larry Harmon copyright, Stan Laurel, 8", blue-green suit &
black hat, 1962, NM..$175.00
Oak Manufacturing, Bozo the Clown, 8½", yellow clothes
w/red trim, brown shoes, late 1940s, M in box..$135.00
Oak Manufacturing, Snuffles the Mouse, 5½", hands behind
back, red jacket, late 1940s, M in box................$135.00
Oak Manufacturing, Sylvester Cat, 6½", red bow tie, right
hand raised, early pose, late 1940s, M in box.....$135.00
Oak Manufacturing, Tweetie Pie, 5½", blue bow at neck,
diapers w/safety pin, early version, M in box....$135.00
Parkersmith Corporation, Googly, 6", all vinyl, rooted hair,
googly-eyed boy w/bow tie, 1969.........................$4.00

Rempel, Collie, large, EX..$10.00
Rempel, Hobo, 6¾", EX (illustrated).........................$15.00
Rempel, Puppy in a Barrel, EX (illustrated)............$5.00

Rempel, Santa Claus, 10½", latex rubber, ca 1950s,
EX...$18.00

Stahlwood Toy Mfg, Buck, 8", vinyl, molded-on clothes, hat, guns & holster, painted features, 1955 ....**$4.00**

Sun Rubber, Donald Duck, 10½", hands at sides, red hat, sailor suit, late 1940s, EX..**$50.00**

Sun Rubber, Donald Duck, 5½x6", red clothes w/yellow bow tie, EX...**$65.00**

Sun Rubber, Mickey Mouse, 10½", standing, arms at sides, yellow gloves, shoes & shorts, EX........................**$58.00**

Sun Rubber, Mickey Mouse, 7¾", standing, arms away from sides of body, head swivels, squeaker in back of head, EX **$48.00**

Sun Rubber, Peter Pan, 10", arms away from body, paint wear **$15.00**

Sun Rubber, Peter Pan, 9½", green clothes & red shoes, ca 1953, VG..**$42.50**

Sun Rubber, Pluto, ca 1940, EX **$20.00**

Sun Rubber, Thumper the Rabbit, 7", thin latex, 1940s, M in NM box...**$125.00**

Teddy Bears

Though the top-of-the-line collectible bears are those made by Steiff, there have been several other companies whose teddies are just about as high on many collectors' want lists. Hermann, Ideal, and Schuco are just a few, and even high-quality bears produced during the past ten years have collector potential; so with that in mind, hang on to more modern bears as well.

American, 15", jointed, mohair, button eyes, felt pads, G..$300.00

American, 20", jointed, mohair, straw stuffed, 1920s, VG **$300.00**

American, 32", jointed, mohair, straw stuffed, ca 1910, VG...**$600.00**

Animal Toys Plus, Banker Bear, 16", unjointed, brown plush, plastic eyes, removable vest/jacket, 1979, M..**$18.00**

Anker-Munich, 12", brown mohair, velveteen snout, hands, feet & ears, glass eyes, ca 1940-50, hard to find, EX...$175.00

Bruin, 15", gold mohair, pull toy w/bell, VG.............**$225.00**

Clemens, 18", fully jointed, tan mohair, glass eyes, EX..**$325.00**

Gund, 8", jointed, brown mohair, 85th Anniversary, tags, M **$125.00**

Hermann, 16", fully jointed, swivel head, long tan mohair, 1950s, M **$400.00**

Ideal, 12", fully jointed, strawberry blond mohair w/white mohair snout, glass eyes, molded plastic nose, 1950s, NM **$75.00**

Ideal, 18½", unjointed, white cotton plush, glass eyes, open mouth w/rubber teeth, ca 1950s, tagged, NM.....**$250.00**

Ideal, 19", fully jointed, gold mohair, glass eyes, 1920s, VG...**$350.00**

Japan, 15", jointed, mohair, flannel paws, glass eyes, 1920s, G **$135.00**

Knickerbocker, 15", unjointed, painted vinyl face w/brown plush body, ca 1955, NM......................................**$25.00**

Merrythought, 20", jointed, gold mohair, glass eyes, 1950, NM **$300.00**

Schuco, 10", long pile mohair tipped w/brown, straw stuffed, glass eyes, long snout, mohair pads, EX.............**$425.00**

Schuco, 2½", caramel mohair, West Germany tag, M **$250.00**

Schuco, 5", yes/no, fully jointed, gold mohair over metal form, glass eyes, 1920s, EX **$500.00**

Sebastian, 24", designed by Robert Raikes for Applause, wooden face & paws, limited edition from 1985 when retail was $90.00, M..**$250.00**

Smokey the Bear, original hat, belt & badge, 1940s, EX ..**$65.00**

Unknown manufacturer, 14", fully jointed, gold mohair, swivel head, 1920s, VG **$135.00**

Unknown manufacturer, 14", fully jointed, wool, hump, straw stuffed, VG **$250.00**

Unknown manufacturer, 18", brown mohair, swivel head, original pads, soft stuffed, VG **$65.00**

Unknown manufacturer, 19", tan mohair, glass eyes, swivel head, 1920s, VG **$195.00**

Unknown manufacturer, 22", fully jointed, wool, glass eyes, straw stuffed, 1930s, VG **$195.00**

Unknown manufacturer, 24", fully jointed, yellow mohair, hump, button eyes, ca 1900, VG **$500.00**

Unknown manufacturer, 25", gold mohair, straw stuffed, glass eyes, 1920s, EX **$375.00**

Toy Soldiers

For a thoroughly definitive book on this subject, you must get a copy of Richard O'Brien's book, *Collecting Toy Soldiers*. It covers them all, from plastic dimestore soldiers to those he calls 'connisseur category.' All our listings are for figures in mint condition. A soldier in only 'very good' shape is one that has obviously seen use, has signs of wear and aging, but retains most of its paint and has a generally good appearance. In this condition, it would be worth only half of mint value. Of course, there are grades in between, and they would be evaluated accordingly.

All-Nu, 100, officer marching w/sabre, paper **$6.00**

All-Nu, 109, charging w/rifle, port arms, WWI helmet ..**$6.00**

Auburn, A002, US Infantry Private **$11.00**

Auburn, A007, Ethiopian w/shield & rifle **$120.00**

Auburn, A009, officer marching **$14.00**

Auburn, A014, doctor **$27.00**

Auburn, A016, stretcher bearer **$30.00**

Auburn, A018, kneeling w/binoculars **$15.00**

Auburn, A019, signalman **$55.00**

Auburn, A020, sniper, crawling, rifle over shoulder **$72.00**

Auburn, A024, motorcycle w/sidecar **$50.00**

Auburn, A028, firing soldier **$44.00**

Auburn, A034, running w/ammo box **$35.00**

Auburn, Infantry Set #231, 1939, M in EX box **$100.00**

Authenticast, foot soldiers, each (average) **$8.00**

Authenticast, mounted figures, each (average) **$30.00**

Barclay, B007, flagbearer w/cast helmet **$18.00**

Barclay, B058, marine in dress uniform **$25.00**

Barclay, B077, soldier bomb thrower, rifle off ground, cast hemet **$21.00**

Barclay, B079a, machine gunner, seated, cast helmet, bandage-type puttees....................**$27.00**

Barclay, B084, sharpshooter, prone position **$20.00**

Barclay, B089, running, w/rifle, tin helmet **$16.00**

Barclay, B092, gas mask, charging w/rifle, cast helmet..**$26.00**

Barclay, B093, Army motorcyclist **$40.00**

Barclay, B094, cowboy w/tin hat brim **$11.00**

Barclay, B095, cowboy w/lasso **$14.00**

Barclay, B097, Indian chief, tomahawk & shield **$10.00**

Barclay, B101, camera man, kneeling, tin helmet........**$30.00**

Barclay, B103, surgeon, w/stethoscope....................**$21.00**

Barclay, B105, raiding, in crouch, tin helmet..............**$16.00**

Barclay, B107a, bayoneting (no bayonet, thrusting w/gun muzzle), cast helmet............................$160.00

Barclay, B107, bayoneting (no bayonet, thrusting w/gun muzzle), tin helmet....................**$40.00**

Barclay, B109, clubbing w/rifle, cast helmet (illustrated) $90.00

Barclay, B112, standing at searchlight, smooth base connected to searchlight, no elevation wheel............**$32.00**

Barclay, B114, w/short binoculars **$80.00**

Barclay, B117, anti-aircraft gunner, tin helmet............**$18.00**

Barclay, B125, standing at searchlight, high seat, no rivets in front of left leg **$28.00**

Barclay, B128, officer w/gas mask, cast helmet...........**$20.00**

Barclay, B129, standing, firing behind wall................**$50.00**

Barclay, B132, leaning out, w/field phone, antenna, cast helmet....................**$62.00**

Barclay, B136, skier in white, no skis.........................**$18.00**

Barclay, B140, marching w/gun on back, cast helmet ..**$14.00**

Barclay, B144, mechanic w/airplane engine, prop spins, brace on back of engine bulges...........................**$34.00**

Barclay, B146, surgeon & soldier.......................**$100.00**

Barclay, B151, w/typewriter & table...........................**$60.00**

Barclay, B153, machine gunner & driver....................**$42.00**

Barclay, B157, woman passenger, w/dog **$12.00**

Barclay, B161, conductor....................**$13.00**

Barclay, B164, girl **$10.00**

Barclay, B167, minister, walking...............................**$50.00**

Barclay, B171, detective w/pistol, blue or gray suit, each....................**$125.00**

Barclay, B175, girl in rocker...................**$16.00**

Barclay, B180, man speed skater **$13.00**

Barclay, B183, Boy Scout, hiking...............................**$36.00**

Barclay, B186a, policeman, figure-8 base....................**$16.00**

Barclay, B192, man on sled...................**$15.00**

Barclay, B197, Santa Claus, seated, bag of toys at side, made to ride in sleigh....................**$200.00**

Barclay, B201, flagbearer, pot helmet........................**$22.00**

Barclay, B203, port arms $25.00

Barclay, B207, Tommy gunner...............................$18.00

Barclay, B212, AA gunner $20.00

Barclay, B213, drum major, WWII helmet...................$55.00

Barclay, B218a, blue sailor $35.00

Barclay, B221, 2-soldier crew at searchlight, pod foot series $20.00

Barclay, B226, Indian on horse, pod foot series..........$21.00

Barclay, B230, knight w/orange & black shield & sword, pod foot series $14.00

Barclay, B235, soldier officer, pod foot series $10.00

Barclay, B240, machine gunner, lying flat, pod foot series $10.00

Barclay, B241, w/pistol, crawling, pod foot series $28.00

Barclay, B253, Indian w/knife & spear, pod foot series.$10.00

Barclay, B256, wounded head & arm, pod foot series..$18.00

Barclay, B257, nurse, pod foot series $34.00

Barclay, B260, marching w/gun on back, pod foot series $10.00

Barclay, B262, flame thrower, pod foot series............$11.00

Barclay, B264, bugler, midi size.............................$60.00

Barclay, B271, cowboy w/rifle, midi size...................$12.00

Beton, BT105, Indian warrior, lasso, plastic, 4" $8.00

Beton, BT108, Infantry w/walkie-talkie, plastic, July 16, 1951 ....$5.00

Beton, BT113, Infantry saluting, WWII helmet, plastic, October 1, 1949 ....$5.00

Beton, BT118, machine gunner, kneeling, plastic, October 1, 1949 ....$5.00

Beton, BT124, machine gunner in prone shooting position, WWII helmet, plastic, October 1, 1949 ....$5.00

Beton, BT135, rider, Cavalry officer, plastic, February 1, 1951 ....$10.00

Beton, BT141, rifleman, marching position, WWII helmet, plastic, October 1, 1949 ....$5.00

Beton, BT151, signaller, WWII helmet, plastic, October 1, 1949 ....$5.00

Britains, lead, assorted styles, each......................$15.00

Comet, soldier, each $9.00

Grey Iron, G001, Colonial soldier............................$23.00

Grey Iron, G004, Colonial mounted officer.................$40.00

Grey Iron, G010, shoulder arms $14.00

Grey Iron, G011, US Infantry, port arms $21.00

Grey Iron, G021, carrying ammo boxes....................$90.00

Grey Iron, G024, US Infantry, charging, early............$15.00

Grey Iron, G029, US Doughboy, charging $14.00

Grey Iron, G034, Cavalryman, small..........................$30.00

Grey Iron, G035, US Cavalryman............................$30.00

Grey Iron, G042, Royal Canadian Police....................$32.00

Grey Iron, G048, chief attacking, upraised tomahawk..$100.00

Grey Iron, G050, Indian mounted, lying on horse $75.00

Grey Iron, G062, US machine gunner $17.00

Grey Iron, G063, US sailor, blue, early.......................$17.00

Grey Iron, G073, Boy Scout, walking, early................$17.00

Grey Iron, G077, pirate w/hook $20.00

Grey Iron, G085, Legion color bearer.......................$15.00

Grey Iron, G095, litter bearer.................................$28.00

Jones, J004, observer w/binoculars & rifle $75.00

Jones, J013, officer pointing...................................$225.00

Jones, J010, firing machine gun on stump $80.00

Jones, J014, prone w/rifle, trunk upraised $150.00

Jones, J016, kneeling, firing anti-tank gun $80.00

Jones, J016, sitting w/anti-tank gun $85.00

Jones, J019, motorcycle rider $100.00

Jones, J021, kneeling w/searchlight $75.00

Jones, J026, bugler..$165.00

Jones, J031, cowboy on rearing horse, firing backward $260.00

Jones, J036, tramp...$15.00

Manoil, M003, flag bearer......................................$22.00

Manoil, M006, campaign cap straight on head $40.00

Manoil, M011, bugler, hollow base version $60.00

Manoil, M014, drummer, stocky version $25.00

Manoil, M021, cadet, hollow base, no buckle on belt.$44.00

Manoil, M030, cowboy, hollow base version...............$40.00

Manoil, M033, cowboy w/hands up $20.00

Manoil, M035, doctor, khaki...................................$32.00

Manoil, M040, machine gunner sitting, marking under base $23.00

Manoil, M048, sniper $20.00

Manoil, M049, Tommy gunner, bloated version $30.00

Manoil, M056, bomb thrower, two grenades in pouch..$18.00

Manoil, M059, sitting..$40.00

Manoil, M062, soldier w/bayonet charging.................$35.00

Manoil, M066, kneeling w/bayonet $62.00

Manoil, M069, officer, lying down, shooting revolver.$54.00

Manoil, M074, anti-aircraft gunner, barrel of gun ends at arm..$21.00

Manoil, M077, policeman $17.00

Manoil, M086, paymaster.......................................$185.00

Manoil, M088, parachute jumper $20.00

Manoil, M089, soldier writing letter $65.00

Manoil, M092, soldier w/camera.............................$62.00

Manoil, M101, lineman & telephone pole $86.00

Manoil, M104, anti-tank gun, wooden wheels.............$60.00

Manoil, M105, marching w/gun slung at angle..........$175.00

Manoil, M112, aviator holding bomb........................$26.00

Manoil, M116, radio operator, standing....................$55.00

Manoil, M124, running w/cannon, wood wheels, thin face $50.00

Manoil, M128, jumping w/machine gun.....................$66.00

Manoil, M170, flagbearer, thin, ca 1945....................$26.00

Manoil, M182, tommy gunner, WWII, regular size **$30.00**

Manoil, M184, w/shell for bazooka (some marked 46/14)..**$30.00**

Manoil, M190, combat **$31.00**

Manoil, M197, machine gunner, sitting.......................**$30.00**

Manoil, M206, wounded, lying down.........................**$115.00**

Manoil, M210, mounted cowboy, shooting.................**$48.00**

Manoil, M214, bull, head turned................................**$15.00**

Manoil, M81, motorcycle rider, number over rear wheel, grass base **$30.00**

Marx, Battleground figures, each **$10.00**

Marx, Gallant Men character figures, each.................**$35.00**

Marx, Germans, each **$1.00**

Marx, Indians, 3", soft plastic, each **$5.00**

Marx, Marines, 6", USMC on shirt, each **$15.00**

Marx, Union Arm, 60mm, soft plastic, each **$6.00**

Marx, United Nations, 60mm soft plastic, each...........**$20.00**

Marx, US Army, 40mm, common, each **$1.00**

Marx, West Point cadets, 60mm, soft plastic, no overcoat, each...**$2.50**

Marx, WWI Doughboys, 60mm, soft plastic, each.........**$8.00**

Marx, 15Ma, seaman, 3½", equipped for landing force, tin lithographed **$8.00**

Marx, 26Ma, Infantry First Lieutenant, 3½", tin lithographed, flat **$11.00**

Marx, 4Ma, Infantry Private, 3½", lying prone, fixing bayonet, tin lithographed, flat **$9.00**

Marx, 42Ma, wounded, 3½", tin lithograhed, flat...........**$8.00**

Marx, 7th Cavalry figures from carryall set, 54mm, mounted, rare, each...**$7.00**

Marx, 7th Cavalry from Fort Apache sets, 60mm, each..**$10.00**

Metal Cast, 22, American Infantry Private, marching in helmet, rifle at slope, 2½" **$25.00**

Metal Cast, 23a, pilot w/bomb, 3⅛".........................**$200.00**

Metal Cast, 24a, Suicide Squad, w/gas mask & pistol, 3" ..**$70.00**

Metal Cast, 30a, motorcycle officer on motorcycle, peaked cap **$70.00**

Miller, ML001, stretcher bearer, plaster.....................**$13.00**

Miller, ML004, General MacArthur, plaster **$40.00**

Miller, Ml010, soldier prone w/rifle, plaster **$17.00**

Miller, ML013, soldier advancing w/rifle, plaster **$15.00**

Miller, ML019, kneeling w/sub-machine gun **$20.00**

Tommy Toy, TT003, soldier marching **$160.00**

Tommy Toy, TT013, doctor, white uniform..............**$200.00**

Trains

Lionel is a name that is almost synonymous with toy trains. The Lionel company was the one that introduced the O guage to the public in 1915, and it became the industry's standard for years to come. Some of their best toys came from the period of 1923 to 1940, when in addition to their trains they also brought out an extensive line of special sets. They bought out their competitors, the Ives corporation, in 1928, and except for the years from 1929 until 1934 when the nation was crippled by financial collapse and during WWII, they remained a giant industry. Sales began to decline in the fiftes, but even today, Lionel trains are being

made in limited numbers.

Some of the other toys companies whose trains you may encounter are American Flyer, Marx, Buddy L, Tootsie-toy, Unique, and Manoil. All these companies are included in *American Premium Guide to Electric Trains* by Richard O'Brien.

American Flyer, S gauge Franklin locomotive & tender, VG...**$155.00**

American Flyer L2002, steam locomotive, Erie, 1963, EX..**$225.00**

American Flyer 1106, 0 gauge Dominion Flyer coach, brown & black, EX..**$55.00**

American Flyer 1107, 0 gauge passenger car, gray, red & green, VG..**$225.00**

American Flyer 1218, 0 gauge locomotive, red, black & yellow, EX...**$265.00**

American Flyer 3001, 0 gauge Illini pullman car, EX ..**$65.00**

American Flyer 3018, 0 gauge tank car, eight wheels, EX **$35.00**

American Flyer 316, steam locomotive, PRR (Pennsylvania Railroad), 1952, VG.............................**$65.00**

American Flyer 910, tank car, Gilbert Chemical, green, 1954, NM **$85.00**

American Flyer 97, station, G....................................**$150.00**

American Flyer 9910, 0 gauge locomotive, Burlington Zephyr w/9912 baggage & 9900 observation cars, EX.....**$625.00**

Lionel 1002, 027 gauge gondola car, black (unpainted) plastic w/white lettering, 1948, EX.....................**$6.50**

Lionel 1019, 027 gauge remote control track set, 1946, NM **$7.50**

Lionel 1032, transformer, 75 watts, 1948 through mid-50s, EX...**$15.00**

Lionel 1050, 027 gauge steam locomotive w/1050 tender, 1959, NM **$42.50**

Lionel 1110, 027 gauge steam locomotive, Scout, 1950, NM **$32.00**

Lionel 1615, 027 gauge steam locomotive, w/1615T tender, 1955, NM **$145.00**

Lionel 1631, 027 gauge observation car, blue sides, aluminum roof, 1938, EX..**$45.00**

Lionel 1865, 027 gauge coach car, Western & Atlantic, 1959, EX...**$32.50**

Lionel 202, 027 gauge diesel engine, UP (Union Pacific) Alco A, orange w/black lettering, 1957, EX **$70.00**

Lionel 208, 027 gauge diesel locomotive, ATSF (Atchison Topeka & Santa Fe), Alco, 1958, EX....................**$135.00**

Lionel 2242, 027 gauge diesel locomotive, New Haven, AB units, silver & black checkerboard, single motor, 1958, EX **$825.00**

Lionel 2353, 0 gauge diesel locomotive, Santa Fe, AA units, silver w/red nose, double motor, 1953, EX........**$575.00**

Lionel 238, 027 gauge steam locomotive, w/tender, 1963-64, EX..**$45.00**

Lionel 2401, 027 gauge observation car, Hillside, green, 1948, EX **$125.00**

Lionel 243, 027 gauge steam locomotive, w/tender, 1960, EX..**$45.00**

Lionel 2465, 027 gauge tank car, Sunoco, double dome, 1946, EX..$12.50

Lionel 249, 027 gauge steam locomotive, PRR (Pennsylvania Railroad), w/#250T tender, 1958, EX...............$40.00

Lionel 2554, Super 0 gauge pullman car, Craig Manor, 1957, EX...$300.00

Lionel 2615, 0 gauge baggage car, Blue Comet, 2-tone blue, 1938, EX.............................$235.00

Lionel 2855, 0 gauge tank car, single dome, SUNX on black, 1946, EX.............................$165.00

Lionel 3535, 0 gauge AEC security car, red shell w/white letters, gray gun & searchlight, 1960, EX.............$85.00

Lionel 365, 0 gauge dispatching station, 1958-59, EX..$72.50

Lionel 3820, 0 gauge operating submarine car, USMC, 1960, EX...$175.00

Lionel 419, Heliport control tower, 1962, NM...........$265.00

Lionel 4457, 0 gauge electronic caboose, 1946, EX..$130.00

Lionel 6015, 027 gauge tank car, one dome, Sunoco, silver, 1954, EX...$30.00

Lionel 6037, 027 gauge caboose, Lionel Lines, 1962, EX..$5.00

Lionel 637, 0 gauge steam locomotive, w/2046W tender, 1959, EX...$87.50

Lionel 6428, 0 gauge boxcar, US Mail, red, white, & blue, 1960, EX...$32.50

Lionel 6467, 0 gauge bulkhead car, red frame w/two black bulkheads, 1956, EX.............................$55.00

Lionel 671, 0 gauge steam locomotive, w/671W tender, 1946, EX...$140.00

Lionel 6822, 0 gauge searchlight car, red w/black housing and blue man, gray searchlight, 1961, EX.............$45.00

Lionel 773, 0 gauge steam locomotive, Hudson, w/773W tender, 1964, EX.............................$750.00

Transformers

Autobot, Defense Base Omega Supreme, M...............$40.00
Autobot, Hoist, M in box.....................................$25.00
Autobot, Red Alert, M in box..................................$25.00
Autobot, Skids, M in box.....................................$30.00
Autobot, Tracks, M in box....................................$25.00
Autobot, Trailbreaker, M in box..............................$25.00
Beachcomber, NM...$25.00
Blitzwing, NM..$45.00
Decepticon, Dirge, NM in box.................................$30.00
Decepticon, Ramjet, M in box.................................$40.00
Decepticon, Scourge, M in box................................$20.00
Decepticon, Trypticaon, M....................................$40.00
Dinobot, Commander Grimlock..................................$15.00
Dive Bomb, NM..$35.00
Double Cross, NM...$20.00
Fly Wheels, NM...$25.00
Headstrong, NM...$35.00
Joyride, NM..$25.00
Jumpstarter, Twin Twist, M in box............................$20.00
Optimus Prime, M in box......................................$50.00
Pretenders, Autobot Landmine.................................$15.00
Rampage, NM..$35.00
Rollbar, NM..$25.00

Sharkticon, Gnaw...$15.00
Skullgrin, NM..$30.00
Snaptrap, NM...$30.00
Soundwave, NM..$50.00
Splashdown, NM...$50.00
Submarauder, NM..$30.00
Wideload, NM...$25.00

Vehicles

These are the types of toys that are intensely dear to the heart of many a collector. Having a beautiful car is part of the American dream, and over the past eighty years, just about as many models, makes, and variations have been made as toys for children as the real vehicles for adults. Novices and advanced collectors alike are easily able to find something to suit their tastes as well as their budgets.

One area that is right now especially volatile covers those fifties and sixties tin scale-model autos by foreign manufacturers — Japan, U.S. Zone Germany, and English toy makers. Since these are relatively modern, you'll still be able to find some at yard sales and flea markets at reasonable prices.

Alps, Happy Car, 9", lithograph on tin, Buick style friction car, EX...$175.00

Arco, Wrecker Truck, 7", plastic, w/crane, worn paint.$5.00

Bandai, Mercedes Benz 220, 10½", tin w/plastic steering wheel & windshield, sliding sunroof, friction type, NM....$270.00

Bandai, Porsche, 10", tin w/plastic steering wheel & windshields, friction type, EX.........................$175.00

Bandai, 1959 Cadillac, 11½", bench seats, EX...........$450.00

Buddy L, Amazing Spider Van, 5", red & black metal, EX...$7.50

Buddy L, Big Wheel Pickup, 5", 1984 (red) decals, EX.$6.50

Buddy L, Dodge Custom Van, 5", brown, orange & red, EX...$7.50

Buddy L, Ice Delivery Truck, 25", sheet metal, restored...$700.00

Buddy L, School Bus, 6½", orange w/decals, 1980, EX..$10.00

Buddy L, Zoo Pickup, 13", heavy metal, red paint, light rust on wheels, G...$22.00

Corgi, 'Man From UNCLE' Car w/'Waverly Ring,' #497, M in torn box................$125.00

Corgi, Avengers, #40, M in box $650.00

Corgi, Chevrolet Impala, #220, flamingo pink, M in box ..$100.00

Corgi, Chitty Chitty Bang Bang, #266, M in box........$350.00

Corgi, Chrysler Ghia, #241, metallic copper, M in box ..$60.00

Corgi, Fiat 1800, #217, blue, M in box.....................$75.00

Corgi, Ford Tractor-Conveyor on trailer, #6547, M in box $150.00

Corgi, Green Hornet 'Black Beauty,' #268, M in box ..$350.00

Corgi, Hillman Husky, #206, brown, M in box..........$110.00

Corgi, Holmes Wrecker Recovery Vehicle, #1142, M in box $175.00

Corgi, Jaguar XJ12C, #286, black & yellow, M in box.$30.00

Corgi, Jaguar XK120, #804, cream, M $15.00

Corgi, James Bond Toyota 2000GT, M $350.00

Corgi, Lamborghini, #342, yellow, M in box............$60.00

Corgi, Landover Tow Truck, 4½", Whizz Wheels, red & yellow, 1969, EX $16.00

Corgi, Lincoln Continental Executive Limousine, #262, M in EX box................$150.00

Corgi, Lunar Bug, #806, M in box.....................$160.00

Corgi, Mazda maintenance truck, #413, M in box $50.00

Corgi, Mercedes 'Michelin', #1112, M in box $15.00

Corgi, Oldsmobile Super 88, #235, blue & white, M in box.....................$80.00

Corgi, Raygo Rascal, #459, yellow $40.00

Corgi, Renault 5 TS, #293, golden orange, M in box...$15.00

Corgi, Rover 2000, #252, metallic blue, M in box........$70.00

Corgi, Simon Snorkel Fire Engine, #1127, M in box..$350.00

Corgi, State Landau, Queen's Jubilee, #41, M in box ..$35.00

Corgi, VW Delivery Van, #433, red & white, M in box..$80.00

Corgi, 1927 Bently, #9001, green, M in box $65.00

Dinky, Airport Fire Rescue Tender, #264, red, M in box.$95.00

Dinky, Coast Guard Missile Launch, #672, M in box...$27.00

Dinky, Demotaso-Mangusta, #187, red & white, M in box $50.00

Dinky, Ferrari 312, #226, metallic red, M in box $35.00

Dinky, Ford Corsair, #130, blue, M in box.................$90.00

Dinky, Ford Cortina Rally Car, #212, white, M in box ..$125.00

Dinky, Ford Zodiac, #164, silver, M in box.................$70.00

Dinky, Galactic War Chariot, #361, M in box $30.00

Dinky, Jaguar Police Car, #269, white, M in box.......$175.00

Dinky, Jaguar Racing Car, #238, turquoise, M in box .$150.00

Dinky, Johnston Road Sweeper, #449, green, M in box...$65.00

Dinky, Lamborghini Marzal, #189, green & white, M in box................$50.00

Dinky, Mercedes Benz 600, #128, blue, M in box $50.00

Dinky, Mini Blubman, #178, bronze, M in box...........$40.00

Dinky, Monte Verdi 375 L, #190, metallic red, M in box.$75.00

Dinky, Rolls Royce Phantom V, #124, metallic blue, M in box................$50.00

Dinky, Singer Gazelle, #168, green & gray, M in box.$140.00

Dinky, Telephone Service Van, #261, green, rare, M in box................$250.00

Dinky, Triumph 1300, #162, blue, M in box $90.00

Ertl, General Lee, 1981, M on card $8.00

Ertl, Gold Bonneville Police Car, #1728, Replica series.$8.00

Ertl, Smokey & the Bandit, #1790, Replica series $15.00

Ertl, Texaco Truck & Tanker, 1981, M in box............$30.00

Ertl, West Germany Mercedes-Benz C-111, #1605, Cars of the World series, 1979, M $7.50

Ertl, 1913 Ford Model-T Van, #1830, Street Rods series, 1981, M $7.50

Ertl, 1950 Mercury, #1629, Cars of the 50s series, 1981, M on card $7.50

Ertl, 1956 Ford Victoria, #1633, Cars of the 50s series, M on card $7.50

Ertl, 1957 T-Bird, #1615, Cars of the World series, 1978, M $7.50

Hess, B-Mack Truck, 1964, missing pieces, G $175.00

Hess, Box Truck, labeled barrels, 1976, M in box.....$225.00

Hess, Fire Truck, red, 1989, M in box $25.00

Hess, Fire Truck, white, 1989, M in box $20.00

Hess, Race Car Transporter Truck, 1988, M in box $40.00

Hess, Tanker Truck, 1977, M in box $125.00

Hess, Tanker Truck Bank, 1981, M in box.................$10.00

Hess, 18-Wheeler Truck, 1987, M in box $25.00

Hubley, Dump Trailer #508, 11", steel, no paint, G $35.00

Hubley, Dump Truck, green & red plastic, cab lifts to view motor, M in box................$37.50

Hubley, Hook & Ladder Truck #473, 10", cast metal w/nickel-plated ladder, driver, & dash, M in box................$225.00

Hubley, Kiddie Toy Racer #3, 6", silver & red, black rubber wheels, EX................$12.50

Hubley, School Bus #2, 9", heavy metal, yellow paint, EX................$32.00

Hubley, Station Wagon #476, 8½", cast steel, red paint, EX................$35.00

Hubley, Tow Truck, 6", plastic, red cab & beige back, green cranking mechanism, rubber wheels, 1950s, M $42.50

Hubley, Volkswagon Beetle #1480, 7", metal, white interior, sunroof & window cutouts, plastic bumpers, VG.$12.00

Ideal, Hertz Rental Truck, yellow & gray, rear door opens, VG................$5.00

Japan, Argo Chrysler, 4" rubber sheels, 4-door, streamline, red & cream, w/windshield wipers, EX................$12.50

Japan, Aston-Matrin DB5 (James Bond), 11½", 1960s, Gilbert, EX................$75.00

Japan, Buick Wildcat, 15", 1963, friction, EX $200.00

Japan, Cadillac Sedan, 12", friction, Bandai, EX..........$75.00

Japan, Cattle Trailer, 4", silver paint, rear door missing, VG................$6.50

Japan, Chevrolet Corvett, 9½", 1968, battery, Taiyo, EX.$50.00

Japan, Chevrolet Red Cross Ambulance, 8", 1958, friction, Bandai, M................$50.00

Japan, Chevrolet Secret Agent, 14", 1962, battery, EX.$75.00

Japan, Chrysler, 13", 1958, battery, EX $250.00

Japan, Circus Bus, 9", tin friction type, NM in box....$165.00

Japan, Circus U-Turn Motorcycle, 6", lithograph on tin, wind-up style, EX................$145.00

Japan, Daihatsu Midget, 5", 1950, friction, Kokyu Shokai, EX................$100.00

Japan, Edsel, 10½", 1958, friction, Yonezawa, EX $400.00

Japan, Ford Hard Top, 13", 1964, friction, Ichiko, M..$200.00

Japan, Ford Mustang, 13", 1967, battery, Bandai, EX ..$65.00

Japan, Mercedes Benz 219 Sedan, 8", 1960s, friction, Bandai, M **$75.00**

Japan, MP Motorcycle, 7", lithograph on tin, friction type w/'engine' noise, early colors, 1950s, NM **$265.00**

Japan, Nash, 8", 1950s, battery, MSK, M **$90.00**

Japan, Pierrot Monkey Cycle, 10", tin & vinyl clown w/tin monkey, battery operated, M in box **$525.00**

Japan, Rambler Rebel Station Wagon, 12", 1960s, friction, Bandai, M **$125.00**

Japan, Renault, 7½", 1960, friction, Bandai, EX **$150.00**

Japan, Volkswagen Pickup Truck, 8", 1960s, friction, Bandai, EX **$60.00**

Kidco, Tough Wheels, 1932 Ford Roadster, Cars of the 30s series, 1978, M on card **$5.00**

Kidco, Tough Wheels, 1937 Chevy Coupe, Cars of the 30s series, 1978, M on card **$7.50**

Lido, U-Haul, car & trailer, plastic, 1960s, M in package ..**$42.00**

Linemar, Mercedes, 1½x3½x1", tin friction, bright yellow paint, plastic windshield, EX **$17.50**

Linemar, XV-3 Bell Helicopter, lithograph (US Army) on tin, friction toy, props spin, EX **$225.00**

Marx, Amphibious Jeep, M in box **$85.00**

Marx, Climbing Bulldozer, 11", lithograph on tin, wind-up w/adjustable front-end shovel, EX in box **$275.00**

Marx, Dodge Cabover Cement Mixer, 3½", metal, yellow paint, minor rust, G **$6.50**

Marx, Electric Lighted Car, 10", plastic molded, friction motor, battery-operated headlights, 1950s, NM in box **$185.00**

Marx, Four-Motored Transport Plane, 18" wing span, lithograph on tin, friction toy w/spinning props, NM in box **$400.00**

Marx, Gold Star Moving Van truck, 21", lithograph on tin, opening rear doars, w/fourteen plastic animals, 1950s, NM **$225.00**

Marx, Marvel Superhero Train, wind-up, 1967, NM ..**$575.00**

Marx, PD Police Cycle, 3½", lithograph on tin, wind-up cycle w/attached sidecar & policeman driver, EX **$200.00**

Marx, Skyview Parking Playset, metal garage w/plastic cars, complete, 1954, NM **$75.00**

Marx, Toy Town Express Van Lines Truck, 12", multicolor lithograph on tin, VG **$120.00**

Marx, Wacky Taxi, 7½", lithograph on tin, friction toy (travels crazy path), EX **$260.00**

Matchbox, Ambulance, #41, 1978, EX **$4.00**

Matchbox, Austin Taxi, #17, 1960, EX **$32.50**

Matchbox, Big Banger, #26, 1972, MIB **$7.50**

Matchbox, Blaze Buster, #22, 1975, MIB **$5.00**

Matchbox, Cadillac Sedan, #27, 1960, EX **$24.00**

Matchbox, Camper, #38, 1981, M in box **$5.00**

Matchbox, Chevrolet Corvette, #61, 1979, M in box **$5.00**

Matchbox, Chevrolet Corvette, #62, 1980, EX **$4.00**

Matchbox, Chevrolet Impala, #57, 1955, EX **$22.50**

Matchbox, Citroen SM, #51, 1972, M in box **$9.00**

Matchbox, Esso Petrol Tanker, #11, 1955, NM **$40.00**

Matchbox, Fandango, #35, 1975, EX **$7.00**

Matchbox, Harley-Davidson Motorcycle, #50, 1981, M in box **$5.00**

Matchbox, Horse-Drawn Milk Cart, #7, 1955, EX **$48.00**

Matchbox, Hot Chocolate VW, #46, 1972, M in box......**$7.50**

Matchbox, Hovercraft, #2, 1976, NM **$10.00**

Matchbox, Jaguar SS 100, #47, 1982, M in box **$5.00**

Matchbox, Jeep Eagle 4x4, #5, 1981, M on card **$5.00**

Matchbox, Kingsize, Pickup Truck #611, blue, 1974, EX.**$10.00**

Matchbox, Kingsize, Super King Mercedes Truck #K8, orange paint, M **$6.50**

Matchbox, Kingsize, Transport Trailer, K-10, red, 1975, M **$10.00**

Matchbox, Land Rover, #12, M in box...................**$20.00**

Matchbox, Lotus Racing Car, #19, 1965, M.....................**$8.00**

Matchbox, Mercedes Tourer, #6, 1974, EX.....................**$5.00**

Matchbox, Mustang Piston Popper, #60, 1973, M on card .**$10.00**

Matchbox, Night Bird Glo-Racer, #1, 1982, M on card..**$6.00**

Matchbox, Prime Mover, #15, 1955, EX.....................**$32.00**

Matchbox, Revin Rebel Dodge Challenger, #1, 1975, M on card **$10.00**

Matchbox, Rolls Royce Silver Cloud, #39, 1978, M on card **$7.50**

Matchbox, Rolls Royce Silver Shadow, #24, 1967, NM..**$10.00**

Matchbox, Slingshot Dragster, #64, 1972, EX.....................**$5.00**

Matchbox, Turbo Flash Glo-Racer, #99, 1982, M on card ..**$6.00**

Matchbox, Vampire Chevy Van, #68, 1979, M in box ...**$7.50**

Matchbox, Volks Dragon, #31, 1971, EX **$7.50**

Matchbox, Wells Fargo Security, #69, 1978, EX.............**$3.50**

Matchbox, 1909 Opel Coupe, #4, Models of Yesteryear, 1966, NM in box.....................................**$20.00**

Matchbox, 1911 Maxwell Roadster, #14, Models of Yesteryear, 1965, EX.....................................**$15.00**

Matchbox, 1929 Woody Wagon, #21, Models of Yesteryear, 1981, EX.....................................**$7.00**

Mattel, Hot Wheels, Cadillac Seville, #1698, 1980, M on card **$5.00**

Mattel, Hot Wheels, Cement Mixer, #6452, 1970, EX ..**$25.00**

Mattel, Hot Wheels, Classic Nomad, M.....................**$65.00**

Mattel, Hot Wheels, Custom Camaro, M......................$65.00

Mattel, Hot Wheels, Custom Fleetside, M....................$65.00

Mattel, Hot Wheels, Custom Mustang, M $85.00

Mattel, Hot Wheels, Custom T-Bird, M.......................$45.00

Mattel, Hot Wheels, Mega Force Motorcycle, M $500.00

Mattel, Hot Wheels, Mercedes 280SL, red, 1969, M on card................$30.00

Mattel, Hot Wheels, Mighty Maveric, M in box...........$85.00

Mattel, Hot Wheels, Motorcross I, M $85.00

Mattel, Hot Wheels, Noodle Head, M...........................$75.00

Mattel, Hot Wheels, Paddy Wagon, #6402, blue, 1970, M................$30.00

Mattel, Hot Wheels, Pepsi Challenger, #2023, pop-up body, 1977, M on card......................$20.00

Mattel, Hot Wheels, Peterbilt Dump Truck, #9550, 1979, M on card................$5.00

Mattel, Hot Wheels, Porsche 917, #6416, 1970, NM.......$25.00

Mattel, Hot Wheels, Ramblin Wrecker, #7659, 1974, M on card $7.50

Mattel, Hot Wheels, Red Baron, 1973, M $125.00

Mattel, Hot Wheels, Rock Buster, M...........................$50.00

Mattel, Hot Wheels, Rolls Royce Silver Shadow, #6276, green, 1969, M on card................$40.00

Mattel, Hot Wheels, Snake Dragster, M......................$95.00

Mattel, Hot Wheels, Team Trailer, #6019, white, 1971, M on card $75.00

Mattel, Hot Wheels, VW Beach Bomb, M $65.00

Mattel, Hot Wheels, 1957 Chevy, #9638, red, 1976, NM..$25.00

Mattel, Street Eater Motorcycle, #7559, yellow, 1975, M..$40.00

Mattel, Vroom Guide Whip Racer, yellow version, M in box................$45.00

Mego, Force Commander, w/Magno-Power action firing fist & missiles................$65.00

Mego, Galactic Cruiser, M in box $55.00

Mego, Hydra, Multiple Action Vehicle, M in box $55.00

Mego, Ultronic Scooter, motorized vehicle, M in box.$65.00

Nylint, Brinks Truck, 16", red & white paint w/dial lock on back door, EX $37.50

Nylint, Heavy Equipment Trailer, 10", orange paint, two wheels, VG $10.00

Nylint, Hook & Ladder Fire Truck & Trailer, EX.........$35.00

Nylint, Napa Automotive Parts Trailor & Tractor, 27", worn paint & decals, G $25.00

Nylint, Towing Truck, 12", 24-Hour Service, white w/red trim, red blinker light, working cable, NM...........$40.00

Nylint, Vista Dome Horse Van & Trailer, 22", tan paint w/decals, minor rust spots, G $27.50

Red Convertible, 7", plastic windshield, 1950s, EX ..$125.00

Remco, Fighting Lady Battleship, VG in box.............$250.00

Remco, Firebird 99 Dash, battery operated, VG........$125.00

Remco, Swap Mobile, 3x9x3", plastic, can be assembled into four different models, battery operated, 1970s, EX $15.00

Remco, Tru Smoke Diesel Twin Wrecker, 1969, EX in box $35.00

Remco, Whirly Bird Helicopter, 1961, EX in box $95.00

Structo, City of Toyland #7 utility garbage truck, 21", red & orange hood w/gray body, EX $150.00

Structo, Dodge Ready Mix Concrete Truck, 12", 10-wheeler, green & yellow, scratches, light rust, G................$37.50

Structo, Highway Dump Truck, 12½", heavy metal, yellow w/side decals, 1966, VG $50.00

Structo, International Hydraulic Dump Truck, 13", orange & white, missing grill, horns & gas tanks, G.............$12.50

Structo, Ready Mix Concrete Truck, 12", 1955, unloading shoot missing, G $50.00

Structo, Refrigerated Express Van, 21", brown & yellow cabover, rust on wheels, light scratches, VG $95.00

Structo, Tractor Trailer Fire Truck Tractor, 'Fire Department' on side of hood, nickel wheels, 18" & 27" ladders, VG $150.00

Sun Rubber, Race Car, 2x4½x1", w/two passengers, EX paint $18.00

Tonka, Big Mike Dual Hydraulic Dump Truck, 14" long, 1957, EX $125.00

Tonka, Bulldozer, #2300, 3-position lever, missing a rubber track, VG $10.00

Tonka, Bulldozer, 4", yellow w/black blade, VG $6.00

Tonka, Bulldozer, 8⅞" long, #100, 1960, EX.............$80.00

Tonka, Bulldozer Loader, 11½", #402, 1962, NM.........$70.00

Tonka, Camper, 9½", #70, 1964, EX $55.00

Tonka, Cement Mixer, 8", #1240, yellow & white paint, VG................$12.50

Tonka, Cement Mixer, 9", #77, red & cream paint, 1965, EX................$35.00

Tonka, Cement Mixer Truck, 15½", #120, 1960, EX ..$190.00

Tonka, Crane, #3940, red repaint, ca 1972, G.............$15.00

Tonka, Crane Truck, 9", #1099, orange & black paint, light rust, VG................$8.00

Tonka, Deluxe Sportsman Next Generation Car w/boat trailer, 22¾" long, 1958, EX................$185.00

Tonka, Dump Truck, 9", #60, yellow & red, grill missing, 1963, G $22.50

Tonka, Dump Truck & Sand Loader, 23¼", #116, 1961, VG................$88.00

Tonka, Dune Buggy, 7", white w/black trim & blue decal, NM paint $8.50

Tonka, Explorer Jeep, 5", red & black, w/roll bars, EX.$7.50

Tonka, Fire Truck, 19½", w/36" extension ladder (working), painted steel w/red & white decals, EX $70.00

Tonka, Ford State Highway Department Dump Truck, 13", #975, orange paint, 1954, VG................$92.50

Tonka, Front-End Loader, 6x3½", green & yellow, four wheels, black scoop, M................$10.00

Tonka, Garbage Truck, 4", green & white paint on metal, EX................$6.50

Tonka, Grader, 17½" blade rotates, #2510, oversize tires, yellow paint, 1968, EX..**$48.00**

Tonka, Helicopter, #23, red & black paint, 1979, EX **$6.50**

Tonka, Jeep Pumper, 10¾", #425, EX.........................**$125.00**

Tonka, Jeep w/Box Trailer, 19⅜", #384, 1964, NM....**$100.00**

Tonka, Line Repair Bell Telephone Truck, 6", #55010, w/repair bucket, EX...**$16.50**

Tonka, Livestock Semi-Tractor, 16", #90, 1964, M.......**$50.00**

Tonka, Livestock Van, 24", #36, repainted but w/original decals, ca 1954, VG...**$88.00**

Tonka, Logger Semi-Tractor, 22¼", #575, 1953, NM..**$275.00**

Tonka, Lumber Truck, 18¾", #998, 1956, NM............**$225.00**

Tonka, Mini Cherokee Chief Jeep Wagon, 9", red & black paint, NM..**$12.50**

Tonka, Mini Pickup, #1050, white paint, w/trailer hitch, missing tailgate, G...**$7.50**

Tonka, Pickup Truck, #580, 1954, EX.........................**$80.00**

Tonka, Pickup Truck, #880, 1955, NM.......................**$185.00**

Tonka, Pickup Turck w/Box Trailer, 20½", 1957, NM ..**$185.00**

Tonka, Power Boom Loader, 18½", #115, 1960, VG .**$110.00**

Tonka, Road Builder Set, #775, 1954, 5-piece set, VG ..**$350.00**

Tonka, Sanitary Service Truck, 22¾", B-203, 1959, NM...**$275.00**

Tonka, Servi-Car, 9⅛", #201, 1962, EX.......................**$80.00**

Tonka, Snorkel Pumper, #2950, red & white, ladders & accessories missing, G **$16.00**

Tonka, Snorkel Pumper, 17½", #2950, heavy steel, red paint, white wheels, flotation tires, EX **$90.00**

Tonka, Star Kist Van, 14½", #725, 1954, EX..............**$315.00**

Tonka, Thunderbird Express Semi-Tractor, 24", 1957, EX **$275.00**

Tonka, Transport Van, 22¼", #140, VG.....................**$145.00**

Tonka, Trencher, 18¼", #534, 1963, EX.......................**$25.00**

Tonka, Utility Hauler, 12", #175, 1951, EX................**$200.00**

Tonka, Wrecker, 9½", #68, 1964, VG...........................**$18.00**

Tootsietoy, American LaFrance Pumper, 3", red paint, 1954, M...**$20.00**

Tootsietoy, Army Jeep CJ3, 4", olive drab paint, 1950, NM...**$10.00**

Tootsietoy, Buick Estate Wagon, 6", bright yellow paint, 1948, M...**$35.00**

Tootsietoy, Buick LaSabre, 6", worn red paint, 1951, EX....**$35.00**

Tootsietoy, Buick Roadmaster, 4-door, worn blue paint, 1949, VG...**$25.00**

Tootsietoy, Chevy Fastback, 3", blue paint, 1950, M...**$20.00**

Tootsietoy, Chevy Panel Truck, 4", green paint, 1950, NM...**$30.00**

Tootsietoy, Chrysler Convertible, 4", worn blue-green paint, 1960, EX...**$15.00**

Tootsietoy, Chrysler New Yorker, 6", blue paint, 1953, VG...**$20.00**

Tootsietoy, Chrysler Windsor Convertible, 4", green paint, 1941, EX...**$30.00**

Tootsietoy, Classic Series 1907 Stanley Steamer, 1960-1965, M...**$20.00**

Tootsietoy, Classic Series 1929 Ford Model A, 1960-1965, NM...**$15.00**

Tootsietoy, F-94 Starfire, green paint, 1970s, M in box **$10.00**

Tootsietoy, Ford B 1931 Hotrod, red paint, 1960, M...**$10.00**

Tootsietoy, Ford Convertible, 3", red paint, 1949, NM.**$15.00**

Tootsietoy, Ford C600 Oil Tanker, 3", yellow paint, NM..**$12.00**

Tootsietoy, Ford Falcon, 3", red paint, 1960, M...........**$12.00**

Tootsietoy, Ford F600 Army Stake Truck, 6", olive drab paint w/white US Army & star, 1955, M **$45.00**

Tootsietoy, Ford Ranch Wagon, 4", yellow & green paint, 1954, NM..**$20.00**

Tootsietoy, Ford Station Wagon, 3", blue paint, 1960, EX...**$35.00**

Tootsietoy, Greyhound Bus, #1045, blue & white paint, 1937-1941, EX...**$25.00**

Tootsietoy, HO Series Cadillac, 2", blue & white paint, 1960, NM...**$10.00**

Tootsietoy, International K5 Dump Truck, 6", green bed, yellow body, M..**$25.00**

Tootsietoy, International Metro Van, 5", blue paint, rare, NM...**$45.00**

Tootsietoy, Lincoln Capri, 6", red paint, tan top, 2-door, NM...**$27.50**

Tootsietoy, Mack L-Line Semi & Stake Trailer, red paint, M...**$21.00**

Tootsietoy, Mercedes 190 SL Coupe, 6", light blue paint, 6", NM...**$40.00**

Tootsietoy, Mercury Fire Chief Car, 4", red paint, 1949, EX...**$20.00**

Tootsietoy, Navy Jet, red paint, 1970s, M in box.........**$10.00**

Tootsietoy, Offenhauser Racer, 4", dark blue, 1947, M.**$10.00**

Tootsietoy, Oil Tanker, 3", four caps, post-war, 100% paint **$15.00**

Tootsietoy, Oldsmobile 88 Convertible, 4", yellow paint, 1949, NM..**$22.50**

Tootsietoy, Oldsmobile 98, 4", red paint, tan top, open fenders, 1955, NM...**$22.50**

Tootsietoy, Oldsmobile 98 Police Set, 4", 1955, M in package **$45.00**

Tootsietoy, Playtime Set, 10-pc, 1950s, M in open box **$130.00**

Tootsietoy, Plymouth, 3", blue paint, 2-door, 1957, M..**$16.00**

Tootsietoy, Porsche Roadster, 6", red paint, 1956, M ..**$40.00**

Tootsietoy, Racer, 3", orange paint, 1950s, NM **$12.00**

Tootsietoy, Studebaker Coupe, 3", green, 1947, EX........**$20.00**

Tootsietoy, Twin Coach Bus, 3", orange, 1950, NM........**$30.00**

Tootsietoy, Volks Wagon Bug, 3", green paint, 1960, M.**$9.00**

Wolverine, Dump Truck, 13" long, tin & pressed steel, lever activated dumping action w/swivel back, M in box..**$175.00**

Wyandotte, ambulance, 11", steel w/wood tires, 1930s, EX $40.00

Wyandotte, Cadillac Station Wagon, 21", tin, Woodie type, EX $100.00

Wyandotte, Convertible Woodie Car, 12", metal, 1940s, EX $110.00

Wyandotte, Mack Dump Truck, 13", orange, 1930s, VG.$50.00

Wyandotte, Stake Truck, 7", red, VG.........................$20.00

Yonezawa, Lincoln Retractible Convertible, 11", friction, M in EX box...$200.00

Wind-Ups

Wind-up toys, especially comic character or personality-related, are greatly in demand by collectors today. Though most were made through the years of the thirties through the fifties, they carry their own weight against much earlier toys and are considered very worthwhile investment items. Mechanisms vary, some are key wound while others depended on lever action to tighten the mainspring and release the action of the toy. Tin and celluloid were used in their manufacture, and although it is sometimes possible to repair a tin wind-up, experts advise against putting your money into a celluloid toy whose mechanism is not working, since the material is too fragile to tolerate the repair.

Chein, Dandee Oil Truck, 9", NM.......................$225.00

Chein, Hercules roller coaster, lithograph on tin, 1930s, NM in box $250.00

Eldon, Tic Toy Clock, working $45.00

Japan, cat w/tin ball, 5", lithograph on tin w/plastic head & tail, M in box..$45.00

Japan, crawling baby, 4½", celluloid, M in box $65.00

Japan, Mr Dan, Hot Dog Eating Man, 7", lithograph on tin, vinyl mouth, EX in box $125.00

Japan, Sammy the Life-Like Seal, 6x3x4", black rubber body w/fabric bow at neck, ball on nose, EX in box....$25.00

Japan, Uncle Sam plays drum, 7½", lithograph on tin, EX $85.00

Linemar, Popeye Turnover Tank, 4", lithograph on tin, NM $235.00

Marx, Barney Rubble Riding Dino, 8", lithograph on tin, 1960s, M $145.00

Marx, Donald Duck Duet, 10", 1946, EX..................$500.00

Marx, Ferdinand the Bull, 7", lithograph on tin, VG in box $325.00

Marx, Honeymoon Express, 9¼", lithograph on tin, EX in box..$375.00

Marx, Old Jalopy, 7", lithograph on tin, EX........$195.00

Marx, Popeye Express, Popeye pushing box w/parrot, 1935, EX...$675.00

Mattel, Cowboy Ge-Tar, 14", plastic, music box inside, 1952, EX..**$15.00**

Mattel, Jolly Jack-in-the-Music Box, clown lithograph on box, non-working in EX box **$45.00**

Schuco US Zone Germany, Clown Violinist, 4½", tin & cloth, NM **$180.00**

Strauss, Inter-State Bus, 10½", lithograph on tin, VG **$425.00**

TPS Co, Squirrel Barber, 5", tin, Japan, NM $50.00

Unique Art, Dogpatch Band, 8x9½", lithograph on tin, 1945, G **$110.00**

US Zone Germany, sport convertible, 9½", G............**$110.00**

Wyandotte, Army Truck, 10", steel w/wood wheels, M..**$50.00**

Wyandotte, Car Carrier, early 1930s, EX **$120.00**

Wyandotte, Convertible (open) Roadster, 10", 1930s, EX...**$135.00**

Wyandotte, Dump Truck, 7", steel, 1937, EX.............**$52.50**

Wyandotte, Dump Truck #122, M................................**$90.00**

Wyandotte, Fire Truck, 12", w/ladder, ringing bell, EX .**$38.00**

Wyandotte, Motor Express Trailer Truck, 1950s, EX.**$100.00**

Wyandotte, Pickup Truck, 6", late 1930s, EX..............**$40.00**

Wyandotte, Tow Truck, late, M **$70.00**

Wyandotte, Wrecker, 10", wooden wheels, 1930s, EX...**$35.00**

Trolls

The legend of the Troll originated in Scandinavia. Ancient folklore has it that they were giant, supernatural beings, but in more modern times, they're portrayed as dwarfs or imps who live in underground caverns. During the seventies there was a TV cartoon special called *The Hobbit* and a movie, *The Lord of the Rings*, that caused them to become popular; as a result, books, puzzles, posters, and dolls of all types were available on the retail market. In the early eighties, Broom Hilda and Irwin Troll were featured in a series of books as well as Saturday morning cartoons, and

today trolls are enjoying a strong comeback. They were among the most popular toys last year for Christmas; and stores were full of bed linens, houseshoes, pillows, coloring books, school pencils, earrings, and clothing for children, all decorated with colorful trolls with psychedelic hair.

The three main manufacturers of the 'vintage' trolls are Dam Things (Royalty Des. of Florida), Uneeda (Wishnicks), and A/S Nyform of Norway. Some were made in Hong Kong and Japan as well, but generally these were molded of inferior plastic.

The larger trolls (approximately 12") are rare and very desirable to collectors, and the troll animals, such as the giraffe, horse, cow, donkey, and lion made by Dam, are bringing premium prices. Today's renewed marketing push has resulted not only in heavy volumes of sales on the retail level but on the secondary market as well. Trolls that were selling for $20.00 last year now are being seen with $35.00 price tags, and some of the rarer examples in like-new condition may go for as much as $350.00.

Dam, Alligator, 5½", rare, minimum value **$350.00**

Dam, Elephant, 3", w/drum, dated 1964, NM **$45.00**

Dam, Eskimo, 13", green hair, pink & white clothes, dated 1964, EX, minimum value **$100.00**

Dam, Lion, 5x8" (approximate), minimum value **$100.00**

Dam, little girl, 5", original clothes, 1960s, M................**$30.00**

Dam, pirate bank, 6½", dressed, 1960s, M, minimum value **$40.00**

Dam, Santa Claus bank, 6½", 1960s, M, minimum value .**$65.00**

Dam, 11", 1960s, M, minimum value **$75.00**

Dam, 3", orange hair & eyes, white felt dress w/sequins, EX **$12.00**

Dam, 3", 1960s, EX..**$8.00**

Dam, 3", 1960s, M in package.......................................**$25.00**

Dam, 6½", orange hair, blue suit, dated 1977, EX, minimum value **$25.00**

Dam, 7", white hair, flushed face, violet eyes, circle mark **$30.00**

Dam, 8", dressed, dated 1961, M, minimum value **$50.00**

Dam, 12", felt clothes, either boy or girl, minimum value, each...$75.00

Reisler of Denmark, Little Devil, 1965, M....................**$45.00**

Royalty Designs, hobo bank, 10", all original, 1967, M, minimum value..$40.00

Uneeda, Wishnick, Sock-it-to-Me, 6", blue hair, googly eyes, EX..$45.00

Uneeda, Wishnick, 3", white hair, orange eyes, EX.......$8.00

Unmarked, 2-headed, 3", minimum value $45.00

Uneeda, 2-headed 2-year-old, 4", dated 1965, M, minimum value $55.00

Unmarked, 3", brown hair & eyes, brown print clothes, belt & shoes, EX $12.00

Unmarked, 3", sitting, purple hair, green eyes, gold outfit, EX..$35.00

TV and Movie Memorabilia

Since the early days of TV and the movies right up to the present time, hit shows have inspired numerous toys and memorabilia. If they were well established, manufacturers often cashed in on their popularity through the sale of more expensive items such as toys and dolls; but more often than not, those less established were promoted through paper goods such as books, games, and paper dolls, just in case their fame turned out to be short lived.

Already in some of the newsletters specializing in toys, you see dealers speculatively offering Roger Rabbit memorabilia for sale, and the same is true of Indiana Jones, The Equalizer, and Ninja Turtles. So with an eye to the future (possibly the *near* future), see if you can pick the shows that will generate the collectibles you need to be hanging on to.

See also Beatles Collectibles, Betty Boop Collectibles, Character and Promotional Drinking Glasses, Character Collectibles, Dionne Quintuplets, Elvis Presley Memorabilia, Movie Stars, Peanuts Collectibles, Shirley Temple, Star Trek Memorabilia, Star Wars Trilogy, Three Stooges Memorabilia, and Western Heroes.

A-Team, coloring book, 1938, M $37.50

A-Team, model, Pow-R-Pull van, Ertl, 1983, in original package, EX...$15.00

Addams Family, bank, 4½x4½x3½", Thing figural, Poynter Products Inc, 1964, EX in original box.................$85.00

Addams Family, bop-bag, 42", Lurch plastic figural weighted at bottom w/blinking eyes & beeping nose, 1965, M..$100.00

Addams Family, game, 10x20", Ideal, 1965, in original box...$35.00

Addams Family, mask, 6½x8", Morticia portrait, Ben Cooper, 1964, NM $50.00

Alfred Hitchcock, game, 'Alfred Hitchcock Presents Game,' Milton Bradley, 1958.....................................$30.00

Alice, script, December, 1983, cover signed by Linda Lavin $20.00

Art Linkletter's House Party, game, M $40.00

Batman, figurine, 8", Mego, on original card $72.00

Batman, lobby card, 1966, EX....................................$42.00

Batman, model, Aurora, all-plastic figural, 1964, in original 7x13" box, M $200.00

Batman, mug, red graphics on milk glass, Anchor Hocking .$25.00

Batman, puzzle, 11x14", Watkins Strathmore, self-framed tray, 1966, M...$20.00

Batman, slippers, child's, VG $22.50

Batman, toy, 11½", Batmobile, red lithographed tin, battery operated, 1970s.......................................$125.00

Batman & Robin, photo, signed by Adam West & Burt Ward, color..$55.00

Batman & Robin, post card, series #2, Dexter Press, 1966, color, set of eight, M................................$35.00

Beetlejuice, doll, talking, in original box.....................$45.00

Beverly Hillbillies, card game, 1963, NM....................$15.00

Bewitched, doll, 12", Ideal, posable in red dress w/broom, 1965, in original box................................$400.00

BJ & the Bear, script, April 3, 1979.............................$15.00

Bozo the Clown, game, 8x16", Transogram, 1960.......$25.00

Brady Bunch, puzzle, self-framed tray, Whitman, 1972, NM...$12.00

Bullwinkle, telescope, 1959, in original package.........$35.00

Captain Hook, doll, 10", Sears, 1989, in original box..$30.00

Captain Kangaroo, block set, Playschool, 1960s, in original box, VG $30.00

Casper the Friendly Ghost, coloring book, 'Casper & His Harvyland Friends,' Artcraft, 1959, M....................$35.00

Charles in Charge, paperback book, 1984, 142-pg........$3.50

Charlie's Angels, poster, 23x35", Bi-Rite, 1977, in mailer, NM ..$20.00

China Beach, photo, 8x10", cast shot, black & white..$12.50

Chitty-Chitty-Bang-Bang, car, 1969, Post premium, M.$20.00

Combat, game, 10x20", Ideal, capture enemy headquarters, 1963, in original box...$30.00

Combat, record, Columbia Records, 'Songs of the Combat Years,' premium of AC Sparkplug, 1963, w/photo cover, EX..$65.00

Crazy Like a Fox, photo, 5x7", Jack Warden & John Rubinstein, VG $2.50

Dark Shadows, game, Barnabas Collins, Milton Bradley, 1969, EX $35.00

Dark Shadows, game, 10x20x3", Milton Bradley, be first to build a skeleton, 1969, M $50.00

Dick Tracy, game, 'Master Detective,' 10x20", Selchow & Righter, 1961, EX $70.00

Dr Kildare, game, 10x20", Ideal, diagnose patient's illness, 1962, in original box $25.00

Dr Who, calendar, 1986, EX $10.00

Dragnet, game, 'Target Darts,' Knickerbocker, 1955, in original box, EX $95.00

Dynasty, post card, Joan Collins as Alexis, color, EX $4.00

Evel Knievel, colorforms $48.00

F-Troop, coloring book, 8x11", Saalfield, 70-pg, M $20.00

F-Troop, photo, 8x10", Melody Patterson, black & white..$5.00

Flintstones, ashtray, 5½x8", Arrow Houseware Products, 1961, Fred figural playing golf, M $65.00

Flintstones, bank, Pebbles figural, vinyl $25.00

Flintstones, bubble pipe, Bam Bam figural, 1963, in original package $22.00

Flintstones, coloring book, 8x11", Whitman, 1965, 192-pg, NM $30.00

Flintstones, game, 'Mechanical Shooting Gallery,' Marx, lithographed tin target w/plastic pistol, 1962, w/original box...$250.00

Flintstones, game, 'Stoneage,' Transogram, 1961, complete, in original box, M $40.00

Flintstones, kite, 1973, in original package $25.00

Full House, photo, 8x10", cast in front of Christmas tree, 1988, black & white, EX $4.00

George of the Jungle, game, 10x19", Parker Bros, 1968, EX $45.00

GI Joe, coloring book, M...............................$10.00

Godzilla, record, soundtrack for movie, made in Japan.$38.00

Goldfinger, game, Milton Bradley, 1966, M $45.00

Green Acres, game, 10x20", Standard Toykraft, 1965, M.$75.00

Green Acres, paper dolls, Whitman, 1967, EX.............$28.00

Green Acres, photo, signed by Pat Buttram, black & white...$22.50

Green Hornet, car, 5", Corgi, die-cast metal w/missle launcher in front grille, 1966, in original box w/display stand, M $400.00

Green Hornet, figurine, on original card.....................$78.00

Green Hornet, kite, Roalex, plastic, 1967, in original 34x6" package $125.00

Green Hornet, pin-back button, 3", flasher type, 1966, NM $25.00

Groovie Ghoulies, coloring book, Whitman, 1971, EX..$35.00

Groucho Marx, game, 'Television Quiz Game,' Pressman, 1950s...$30.00

Gumby, figure, 5", bendable rubber, Lakeside, 1965, on original card $30.00

Happy Days, game, 'Fonz Pinball,' 16x36", Coleco, electric, NM $160.00

Happy Days, paper dolls, Fonzie, uncut, in box $32.50

Happy Days, post card, Henry Winkler as Fonzie, EX..$5.00

Hector Heathcote, cartoon kit, 8x12", Colorforms, 1964, EX $35.00

Hoppity Hopper, coloring book, Whitman, 1966, NM..$45.00

Howdy Doody, coloring book, 8½x10½", Whitman, 1956, VG...$30.00

Howdy Doody, ice cream spoon, marked Kayran, M.$10.00

Howdy Doody, pin, full-figure plastic.........................$18.00

Howdy Doody, spoon, w/figural handle, 7".............$25.00

Howdy Doody, wall walker.....................................$35.00

Huckleberry Hound, bank, plastic, 1950s, NM $25.00

Huckleberry Hound, shooting gallery, 1959, EX.........$40.00

Hulk Hogan, doll, 16", in original box $95.00

Hunchback, 5", solid aqua-colored plastic, Marx, 1963, NM...$20.00

I Dream of Jeannie, doll, 18", Ideal, posable, dressed in genie outfit, 1966, in original box........................$250.00

I Dream of Jeannie, photo, 8x10", Barbara Eden as Jeannie, color...$12.50

Incredible Hulk, bank, 6x7x15", figural, green plastic w/stickers, 1978, EX......................................$30.00

Incredible Hulk, sweatshirt, Marvel Comics, 'Here Comes the Incredible Hulk' on white, long sleeves, 1966, EX $32.00

Jackie Gleason, coloring book, 1955, VG..................$65.00

James Bond, beach towel, 36x20", 1965, shows image of Sean Connery w/007 logo & facsimile signature, M $50.00

James Bond, doll, 12", Gilbert, plastic w/spring-activated hand to shoot gun, w/swim trunks, 1964, in original box...$125.00

James Bond, game, 'Secret Agent,' NM $30.00

Jeff Chamberlain, post card, as 'Capitol' star, color, EX...$3.50

Jem, doll, 10", in original box $38.00

Jetsons, Fun Pad, 12x12", Milton Bradley, 1963, NM...$50.00

Johnny Lightning, sticker book, Whitman, 1970, M.....$30.00

Johnny Quest, coloring book, Whitman, 1967, VG $45.00

Johnny Quest, crayon by number set, Transogram, 1965, EX $85.00

Knight Rider, post card, David Hasselhoff, M $7.50

Kukla & Ollie, game, Parker Brothers, 1962 ....$25.00

Land of the Giants, pencil coloring set, Hasbro, ten pre-numbered sketches w/twelve color pencils, 1968, M...$90.00

Laugh-In, notebook binder, illustrated w/characters of show on cover, 1968...$15.00

Laugh-In, wastebasket, 10x7½x13", color litho of cast on metal, Romart Inc, 1968, EX $25.00

Linus the Lionhearted, game, 'Uproarius,' Transogram, 1965, NM...$50.00

Lost in Space, game, 9x17", Milton Bradley, be the first to reach designated color space, 1965, M..................$45.00

Man from UNCLE, doll, 12", Gilbert, plastic w/spring-loaded arm to shoot gun, 1965, in original photo box, NM $85.00

Mary Hartman, Mary Hartman; post card, cast photo, EX..$5.00

Matt Houston, ID set, bracelet, key, fob & wallet, 1983, on original card $10.00

Mighty Mouse, coloring book, early 1950s, NM..........$25.00

Mission Impossible, game, 20x10", Ideal, 1968, M $50.00

Mister Magoo, car, 9" long, Hubley, lithographed tin w/cloth top, figure at wheel, battery operated, 1961, original box..$250.00

Mod Squad, game, Remco, solve the crime & catch the criminal, 1968, in original box.....................................$75.00

Moonlighting, photo, 8x10", Bruce Willis & Cybil Shepherd, color..$5.00

Mork & Mindy, Mork w/talking spacepack, 9", ca 1979, M $10.00

Mork, doll, 3¾", w/egg-shaped spaceship, on original card..$36.00

Mr Ed, coloring book, 8x11", Whitman, 1963, EX $32.00

Mr Ed, doll, talking $70.00

Mr T, doll, 12", in original box..$42.00

Munsters, board game, Hasbro, 1964, in original box, M..$55.00

Munsters, book, 'The Great Camera Caper,' Whitman, 1965, hardcover, EX..$12.00

Munsters, hand puppet, 10", Ideal, Lily, plastic head on cloth body, VG...$30.00

Munster, hand puppet, 10", Ideal, Lily, plastic head on cloth body, 1964, in original box, M............................$200.00

Munsters, kite, Pressman, shows Herman, 1964, in original 32x6" illustrated package......................................$50.00

Munsters, movie poster, 3-sheet, M...........................$145.00

Munsters, sticker book, 8x12", Whitman, 1964, M.......$60.00

Muttley, bank, ceramic, Hanna Barbera, VG...............$45.00

My Favorite Martian, coloring book, 8x11", Whitman, 1964, 65-pg, M..$25.00

My Three Sons, coloring book, Whitman, 1963, M $20.00

Orphan Annie, sheet music, 'Orphan Annie's Song,' 1931 ....$18.00

Our Gang, book, 'Story of Our Gang,' full color, 1939, EX $35.00

Our Gang, coloring book, Saalfield, 1938, EX $40.00

Our Gang, plate, Jean Darling portrait, ceramic, 1920s, M $50.00

Partridge Family, comic book, VG................................$12.50

Pee Wee Herman, doll, talking, in original box $50.00

Perfect Strangers, photo, 7x9", scene from show...........$4.00

Pinocchio, toy, Playing Xylophone, battery operated, 1961, in original box...$125.00

Planet of the Apes, doll, 8", Azak, posable plastic in cloth outfit, 1969, on original card $20.00

Planet of the Apes, wall plaque kit, 11x20x1½", Milton Bradley, 1967, M..$32.50

Popeye, book, 'House That Popeye Built,' Wonder Book, 1960, NM $10.00

Popeye, chalk, 1953, in original box $18.00

Popeye, charm bracelet, enameled metal, 1930s, EX ..$65.00

Popeye, figurine, 3", celluloid................................$225.00

Popeye, modeling clay, American Crayon Co, 1936, M..$65.00

Popeye, paint book, 10x13", McLoughlin Brothers, 1932 ....$35.00

Ramar of the Jungle, puzzle, 1955, set of four............$30.00

Rat Patrol, game, 10x17", Transogram, beat the German tanks, 1967, in original box....................................$30.00

Richard Dean Anderson, photo, 8x10", as MacGyver, color..$12.50

Ricochet Rabbit, change purse, 3" dia, Estelle, vinyl w/zipper, 1964, on original card $25.00

Ricochet Rabbit, coloring book, Whitman, 1965, EX...$30.00

Rin Tin Tin, puzzle, 14x19", Jaymar, 1957, EX.............$12.50

Rocky & Bullwinkle, sewing cards, Whitman, 1961, set of six illustrated punched cards w/colored yarn laces, NM $50.00

Roger Ramjet, coloring book, Whitman, 1966, M $40.00

Sanford & Son, script, May 16, 1975............................$12.50

Scarlett O'Hara, game, 'One of Her Problems,' NM.....$45.00

Sesame Street, plush figure of Big Bird, 18½", ca 1971, EX..$12.00

433

Sledge Hammer, photo, 8x10", David Rasche w/rocket launcher **$5.00**

Smurf, bank, house figural, porcelain.........................**$18.00**

Soupy Sales, pin-back button, 3½", portrait center w/'Soupy Sales Society,' color lithograph on metal, 1960, M ..**$15.00**

Starsky & Hutch, poster, 23x28", Bi-Rite, in tube mailer, NM **$27.50**

Stingray, coloring book, Whitman, 1965, EX **$35.00**

Street Hawk, photo, 7x9", Rex Smith as Jesse Mach, black & white, EX **$4.50**

Superboy, coloring book, Whitman, 1967, M **$18.00**

Superman, Colorforms, 1964, NM...........................**$36.00**

Superman, game, 'Speed,' 1940s, EX......................**$120.00**

Superman, puzzle, in self-framed tray, 1966.............**$12.50**

Superman, shoelaces, in original box.........................**$8.00**

Superman, utensil set, Imperial Knife Co, figural handles & word 'Superman' on fork & spoon, 1966, on original card **$35.00**

Sweet Pea, bank, figural, 1980, M...........................**$35.00**

Tennessee Tuxedo, magic slate, 8x11", Saalfield, cardboard back w/plastic draw sheet, 1963, M **$40.00**

Top Cat, game, 10x17", Transogram, 1962, NM..........**$70.00**

Trapper John, MD; post card, cast photo, EX **$4.50**

V, figure, Ljn, in uniform w/human mask, sunglasses & laser weapon, 1984, in original package........................**$30.00**

Wolfman, mask, Universal, 1990...........................**$45.00**

Wolfman, tumbler, 7", Anchor Hocking, colored wraparound scene on frosted clear glass, 1963 ....**$30.00**

Wonder Woman, valentine, 1940s...........................**$15.00**

Woody Woodpecker, game, 'Travel w/Woody Woodpecker,' 1956, EX..**$40.00**

Yogi Bear, coloring book, Whitman, 1963, NM..........**$25.00**

Yogi Bear, punch-out book, Whitman, 1961, M..........**$45.00**

TV Guides

Has it been ten years since M*A*S*H's final episode? Yes, it has, and it's documented on the cover of the February 12, 1983 edition of *TV Guide*. This publication goes back to the early 1950s, and granted, those early issues are very rare; but what an interesting, very visual way to chronicle the history of TV programing. For insight into *TV Guide* collecting, we recommend *The TV Guide Catalog* by Jeff Kadet, the *TV Guide* Specialist.

1953, December 18, Bob Hope cover, NM **$25.00**

1953, September 18, Fall Preview issue, NM **$150.00**

1954, August 14, Dean Martin & Jerry Lewis cover, NM ..**$35.00**

1954, July 17, Roy Rogers cover, EX...........................**$45.00**

1954, May 14, Frank Sinatra cover, EX **$20.00**

1955, December 10, Lucille Ball cover, NM **$30.00**

1955, January 22, Ed Sullivan cover, EX......................**$12.50**

1955, March 5, Liberace cover, NM...........................**$15.00**

1955, November 19, Jack Benny cover, EX...................**$12.50**

1956, April 14, Grace Kelly cover, EX **$20.00**

1956, July 7, Lassie cover, NM **$25.00**

1957, August 10, Bob Cummings cover, EX.................**$10.00**

1957, December 28, Ricky Nelson cover, EX.............**$20.00**

1958, January 18, John Payne of 'The Restless Gun' cover, NM **$12.00**

1958, May 10, Richard Boone of 'Have Gun, Will Travel' cover, NM **$22.50**

1959, May 16, Loretta Young cover, NM **$7.00**

1959, October 17, Ingrid Bergman cover, NM **$8.00**

1960, July 9, Chet Huntley & David Brinkley cover, M .**$7.00**

1960, March 5, Jay North as 'Dennis the Menace' cover, NM **$22.00**

1960, September 24, Special Fall Preview issue, NM...**$35.00**

1961, January 28, Ronnie Howard & Andy Griffith cover, NM **$15.00**

1961, July 22, George Maharis & Martin Milner of 'Route 66' cover, NM **$25.00**

1961, July 29, Captain Kangaroo cover, NM **$12.00**

1962, January 6, Vince Edwards as 'Ben Casey' cover, NM **$10.00**

1962, March 3, Raymond Burr as 'Perry Mason' cover, NM **$15.00**

1962, September 29, Lucille Ball cover, NM................**$27.00**

1963, August 17, Fred MacMurray cover, NM **$5.00**

1963, December 28, Patty Duke of 'Patty Duke Show' cover, NM **$25.00**

1963, March 30, 'Bonanza' cast cover, NM.................**$35.00**

1964, August 1, 'Today' cast cover, M **$5.00**

1964, March 7, Richard Chamberlain cover, M.............**$8.00**

1964, October 3, Mia Farrow of 'Peyton Place' cover, M .**$8.00**

1965, December 11, 'F Troop' cast cover, M **$15.00**

1965, January 2, 'The Munsters' cast cover, M **$40.00**

1965, July 31, 'My Three Sons' cast cover, M **$8.00**

1965, March 6, David Janssen as 'The Fugitive' cover, M..**$20.00**

1965, November 13, Joey Heatherton cover, M **$6.00**

1966, February 5, Larry Hagman & Barbara Eden of 'Jeannie' cover, M..**$42.00**

1966, July 9, Brian Kelly & Flipper cover, M................**$10.00**

1966, May 28, Sally Field as 'Gidget' cover, M............**$12.00**

1967, April 29, Lawrence Welk cover, NM **$10.00**

1967, April 8, Dick Van Dyke cover, M.......................**$5.00**

1967, December 23, 'Merry Christmas' issue, M............**$7.00**

1967, July 22, 'Bonanza' cast cover, M **$30.00**

1969, January 25, 'Land of the Giants' cast cover, M...**$20.00**

1969, May 31, 'Family Affair' cast cover, M **$6.00**

1969, October 4, Bill Cosby cover, M...........................**$6.00**

1970, April 4, 'The Brady Bunch' cast cover, M...........**$20.00**

1970, August 15, Johnny Carson by Norman Rockwell cover, M..**$8.00**

1970, January 17, 'Ironside' cast cover, M **$5.00**

1970, November 28, 'John Wayne's $2,000,000 Special' cover, M..**$22.00**

1971, January 23, Flip Wilson cover, M **$6.00**

1971, May 1, Mary Tyler Moore cover, NM **$6.00**

1971, November 13, 'The Partners' cast cover, NM **$5.00**

1972, December 9, Julie Andrews cover, M **$6.00**

1972, March 18, Sonny & Cher cover, M......................**$7.00**

1972, May 27, 'All in the Family' cast cover, M............**$5.00**

1972, November 4, John Wayne cover, M......................**$8.00**

1973, April 28, Peter Falk as 'Columbo' cover, M.........**$7.00**

1973, December 1, Bill Bixby, 'The Magician' cover, M...**$3.00**
1973, January 27, 'The Rookies' cast cover, M **$5.00**
1973, October 20, Telly Savalas as 'Kojak' cover, M......**$4.00**
1973, September 1, Miss America Contest cover, M **$4.00**
1974, August 3, 'Emergency' cast cover, M **$6.00**
1974, December 7, Michael Landon of 'Little House on the Prairie' cover, M..**$10.00**
1974, May 18, Lee Majors as 'The Six-Million Dollar Man' cover, M..**$6.00**
1974, October 26, 'The Waltons' cast cover, M **$4.00**
1975, August 9, Buddy Ebsen cover, M.........................**$3.00**
1975, January 11, David Janssen of 'Harry O' cover, M.**$8.00**
1975, May 17, Barry Newman of 'Petrocelli' cover, M...**$3.00**
1975, November 15, 'Starsky & Hutch' cover, M...........**$8.00**
1976, January 17, 'Police Woman' cast cover, M...........**$4.00**
1976, June 19, Louise Lasser as 'Mary Hartman' cover, M **$3.00**
1976, March 6, 'The Rockford Files' cast cover, M.........**$5.00**
1976, May 8, Lindsay Wagner as 'The Bionic Woman' cover, M...**$8.00**
1976, November 13, Dorothy Hamill cover, M **$4.00**
1977, August 6, 'The Muppets' cover, M **$5.00**
1977, December 17, 'One Day at a Time' cast cover, M...**$4.00**
1977, January 1, John Travolta cover, M.......................**$4.00**
1977, May 21, Farrah Fawcett of 'Charlie's Angels' cover, M...**$8.00**
1977, November 26, 'Soap' cast cover, M......................**$4.00**
1978, April 8, 'Alice' cast cover, M **$3.00**
1978, July 1, 'Fantasy Island' cast cover, M **$4.00**
1978, July 29, 'Saturday Night Live' cast cover, M..........**$5.00**
1978, November 25, Benji cover, M..............................**$3.00**
1979, April 28, Danny DeVito & Judd Hirsch of 'Taxi' cover, M...**$5.00**
1979, December 29, 'Charlie's Angels' cast cover, M.....**$8.00**
1979, January 27, Katherine Hepburn cover, M.............**$3.00**
1979, October 20, 'WKRP in Cincinnati' cast cover, M..**$6.00**
1979, September 29, Pope John Paul II cover, M **$3.00**
1980, December 27, Tom Selleck as 'Magnum PI' cover, M **$5.00**
1980, February 16, 'Barnaby Jones' cast cover, M..........**$3.00**
1980, July 5, 'Little House on the Prairie' cast cover, M...**$7.00**
1980, May 17, 'The Jeffersons' cast cover, M.................**$3.00**
1980, September 13, Special Fall Preview issue, M **$10.00**
1981, January 24, Super Bowl '81 cover, M...................**$3.00**
1981, May 30, Dan Rather cover, M..............................**$3.00**
1981, November 21, John Lennon cover, M...................**$5.00**
1982, February 27, 'Dynasty' cover, M..........................**$4.00**
1982, January 6, Michael Landon cover, M....................**$6.00**

1982, May 1, 'Dukes of Hazzard' cast cover, M $4.00

1982, September 18, Victoria Principal cover, NM.........**$3.00**
1983, April 25, Fred Dryer of 'Hunter' cover, M............**$4.00**
1983, December 24, 'The Love Boat' cast cover, M.......**$4.00**
1983, February 12, 'M*A*S*H' final episode cover, M **$6.00**
1983, July 23, 'Knot's Landing' cast cover, NM.............**$4.00**
1983, May 7, 'Silver Spoons' cast cover, NM.................**$4.00**
1983, October 29, 'Hotel' cast cover, M.........................**$3.00**
1984, December 22, 'Webster' cast cover, NM..............**$3.00**
1984, February 11, 'Scarecrow & Mrs King' cast cover, M..**$5.00**
1984, March 17, Priscilla Presley cover, M....................**$5.00**
1984, May 26, 'Hardcastle & McCormick' cast cover, M..**$5.00**
1985, April 13, 'Space' cast cover, M.............................**$3.00**
1985, December 7, Cybill Shepherd cover, M................**$5.00**
1985, October 19, 'Golden Girls' cast cover, M............**$4.00**
1986, April 26, 'Kate & Allie' cover, M..........................**$4.00**
1986, August 30, Patrick Duffy of 'Dallas' & 'Exploring the Mystery of Bobby's Return' cover, M......................**$3.00**
1986, July 19, 'Spencer for Hire' cast cover, M.............**$4.00**
1987, January 3, Angela Lansbury cover, M **$4.00**
1987, September 12, Special Fall Preview Issue, M **$8.00**
1988, January 2, 'Falcon Crest' cast cover, M **$3.00**
1988, July 2, 'Designing Women' cast cover, M.............**$5.00**
1988, October 1, Special Fall Preview Issue, M **$8.00**
1989, January 14, 'Moonlighting' cast cover, M.............**$4.00**
1989, June 10, Fred Savage of 'The Wonder Years' cover, M..**$4.00**
1989, May 27, Kristie Alley of 'Cheers' cover, M...........**$3.00**
1989, October 21, Jamie Lee Curtis of 'Anything but Love' cover, M...**$4.00**
1990, March 10, 'LA Law' cast cover, M........................**$4.00**
1990, May 12, 'Growing Pains' cast cover, M................**$3.00**
1990, November 24, Linda Evans cover, M **$3.00**
1991, April 20, Burt Reynolds & Marilu Henner of 'Evening Shade' cover, M...**$3.00**
1991, November 23, Madonna cover, M........................**$3.00**

Twin Winton

A California-based company founded by twins Ross and Don, the company called Twin Winton Ceramics had its beginnings in the mid-thirties. The men remained active in the ceramic industry until 1975, designing and producing animal figures, cookie jars and matching kitchenware items. One of their most successful lines was mugs, pitchers, bowls, lamps, ashtrays, and novelty items modeled after the mountain boys in Paul Webb's cartoon series.

If you'd like more information, read *The Collector's Encyclopedia of California Pottery* by Jack Chipman.

Bank, Friar, Thou Shalt Not Steal, 1960s-70s, in-mold mark **$25.00**
Cookie jar, Butler, woodtone finish, 1960s-70s, in-mold mark **85.00**
Cookie jar, Dobbin (seated hatted horse), woodtone finish w/painted details, #80, 1962, marked...................**$50.00**
Cookie jar, Duck w/Mixing Bowl, woodtone finish w/painted detail, marked **$65.00**

Cookie jar, Mother Goose, woodtone finish w/painted detail, 1962, marked..................$45.00

Decanter, Robin Hood, multicolor high-gloss glaze, modeled by Don Winton, manufactured by Winfield.........$20.00

Figurine, 3¼", bashful boy elf, underglaze Burke Winton mark..................................$15.00

Figurine, 4", large-eyed girl w/freckles & pigtails, painted underglaze Burke Winton mark............................$15.00

Mug, Open Range, full-figure cowboy handle on staved barrel form, longhorn head on side, late 1940s.........$25.00

Napkin holder, Ranger Bear, woodtone finish w/lightly painted detailing, unmarked......................$25.00

Pitcher, Open Range line, full-figure cowboy handle, bucking bronc on side, belt as band at top, late 1940s........$45.00

Salt & pepper shakers, hillbilly in barrel, 1940s, pr.....$12.00

Salt & pepper shakers, range size, cow figurals, woodtone finish, 1960s-70s, in-mold mark, pr.......................$25.00

Salt & pepper shakers, range size, lamb figurals, woodtone finish w/painted details, ca 1965, pr......................$25.00

Table lamp, hillbilly on moonshine barrel, ca 1949....$65.00

Tankard, tall, hillbilly figural handle on ringed barrel form, ca 1940s.......................$25.00

Typewriter Ribbon Tins

From about 1900 through the 1970s, typewriter ribbons were packaged in tin boxes. They're about 2½" in size, most were round, and some were decorated with colorful scenic or figural lithographs. These make for an interesting collection, and as you can see from our listings, they're not at all expensive (yet!). Value is based on age, condition (avoid those with rust, dents, or fading), rarity, and graphic appeal. The most desirable are the ones with perhaps an Indian, a Black subject, or a typewriter. Airplanes, ships, and birds are next on the one-to-ten scale, and those with only lettering are usually near the bottom.

Allied, sea gull...$5.00
Battleship...$7.00
Carter's Ideal, flowers..............................$5.00
Ditto, plain..$3.00
Herald Square, plain.................................$4.00
Panama..$6.00
Queen, plain..$3.00
Rainbow..$8.00
Silver Brand..$2.00
Type Bar...$3.00
Wonder, lady & mirror.............................$8.00

Universal Dinnerware

This pottery incorporated in Cambridge, Ohio, in 1934, the outgrowth of several smaller companies in the area. They produced many lines of dinnerware and kitchenware items, most of which were marked. They're best known for their Ballerina dinnerware (simple modern shapes in a variety of solid colors) and Cat-tail (See Cat-tail Dinnerware). The company closed in 1960.

Ballerina, bowl, mixing; 3-pc set...........................$55.00
Ballerina, plate, 6"...$2.00
Ballerina, salt & pepper shakers, pr.......................$8.00
Ballerina gravy boat, gray....................................$7.50
Calico Fruit, plate, 7"..$3.50
Calico Fruit, soup bowl, flat.................................$7.00
Canister set, floral, 1940s, 4-pc, +refrigerator jug.........$45.00

Fruit pattern, refrigerator jar, w/lid, 4".............$10.00.
Garden Gate, refrigerator jar, 4".....................$10.00
Iris, pitcher, w/reamer top................................$150.00
Iris, soup, tab handle..$4.00
Largo, bowl, 6"...$8.00
Poppy, fork..$12.00
Poppy, refrigerator jug......................................$18.00

Van Briggle

This pottery was founded in Colorado Springs around the turn of the century by Artus Van Briggle who had previously worked at Rookwood. After his death in 1904, his wife, Anna, took over the business which she controlled until it sold in 1913. The company has continued to operate up to the present time.

Because many of the original designs were repeated down through the years, it is often very difficult to determine when some pieces were produced. There are several factors to consider. Until late 1907, pieces were marked with the 'double A' logo, 'Van Briggle,' and the date. The 'double A' logo was in constant use until the mid-fifties, and a few marks still indicated the date; others contained a design number. Many times 'Colorado Springs' was included as well. Earlier pieces had glazed bottoms, but from 1921 until 1930, the bottoms were left unglazed. From 1922 until 1929, U.S.A. was added to the Colorado Springs designation. Pieces made from 1955 to 1968 were usually marked 'Anna Van Briggle' with no 'double A' logo, but it does appear again on those made after '68.

Colors are another good indicator of age. Until 1930,

colors were limited to turquoise, blue, maroon, brown, green, and yellow (in blended effects or in combination). In 1946, the mulberry was lightened, and the shade was named 'Persian Rose.' It was a popular until 1968. 'Mountain Craig Brown,' used from about 1915 until the mid-thirties, was one of their most famous glazes. It was a warm brown color with a green overspray. (This effect has been reproduced in recent years.) 'Moonglow' (white matt) has been in constant production since 1950, and their turquoise matt was made from the very early years on. High-gloss colors of brown, blue, black, and green were introduced in the mid-fifties, though matt colors were still favored. Other colors have been made in addition to those we've mentioned.

Still another factor that can be helpful is the type of clay that was used. Dark clays (including terra cotta) indicate a pre-1930 origin. After that time, the body of the ware was white.

If you'd like more information, we recommend *A Collector's Guide to Van Briggle Pottery* by Scott H. Nelson, Lois Crouch, Euphemia Demmin, and Robert Newton, and *Collector's Encyclopedia of Van Briggle Art Pottery* by Richard Sasicki & Josie Fania. *Lehner's Encyclopedia of U.S. Marks on Pottery, Porcelain, and Clay* by Lois Lehner is another good source.

Bookends, dog, Persian Rose, AA mark (after 1920) only, pr..**$145.00**
Bowl, 3½x3¾", pansies, turquoise, #19 ....**$65.00**
Bowl, 3½x5", copper clad, leaves & horizontal ridges ...**$14.00**
Bowl, 3x4½" dia, dragonflies, Persian Rose & blue, #837...**$65.00**
Bowl, 4½x7½", leaves extend to base, turquoise & blue, #510, marked USA **$95.00**
Bowl, 5½", stylized floral, blue & turquoise, crazed, post-1920 mark..**$210.00**
Creamer, 2", turquoise, hexagonal.............................**$15.00**
Figurine, 4½x8", elephant, white **$55.00**
Figurine, 7", nude seated w/legs crossed, holding large shell, light blue..**$15.00**

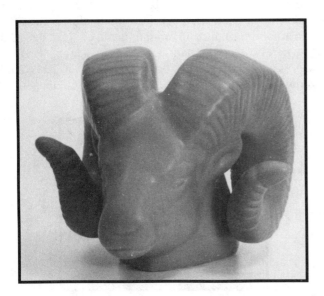

Head of a mountain goat, 6", blue w/turquoise overspray...**$75.00**

Lamp, 11½", Grecian urn, turquoise, original shade....**$55.00**
Lamp base, 17", Colonial lady figural, turquoise, 1940s ..**$210.00**
Paperweight, 2½x5¼x4⅜", sombrero form, turquoise.**$60.00**
Sugar bowl, 2x2¼", Persian Rose, hexagonal..............**$15.00**

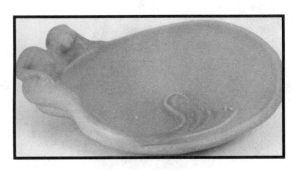

Tray, 10½" wide, Siren of the Sea, ca 1950s $240.00
Vase, 10", narcissi in high relief, green w/yellow, slim form, ca 1904 ....**$700.00**
Vase, 12", three Indian heads, green & brown, ca 1920 ..**$450.00**
Vase, 2¾", luna moths, Persian Rose & blue, #684......**$45.00**
Vase, 4", flowers on squatty base, Persian Rose & blue, flared..**$65.00**
Vase, 4", ochre, small mouth, bulbous shoulder, #349, dated 1907 ....**$350.00**
Vase, 4½", violets & leaves, dark turquoise, #645........**$80.00**
Vase, 4½x4¾", six leaves at rim, turquoise, #847.........**$55.00**
Vase, 5", dark blue w/green traces, #119, 1908-11 ....**$135.00**
Vase, 7", clover at rim, robin's egg blue, #821, ca 1910 ..**$475.00**
Vase, 8x4", robin's egg blue, classic form, #313, dated 1918..**$195.00**
Vase, 9", wide upright leaves, thick light green, #797, ca 1909 ....**$300.00**

Vending Machines

Coin-operated machines that were used to sell peanuts, gumballs, stamps, even sandwiches were already popular by the turn of the century. But they saw their heaviest use from the first decade of the 20th century until about 1940. Some of the better-known vending machine manufacturers were Ad-Lee, Columbus, Exhibit, Northwestern, and Victor.

Values are determined in part by condition. Original paint and decals are certainly desirable, but because these machines were often repainted by operators while they were still in use, collectors often allow a well-done restoration. There are variations that bear on value as well, such as color, special features and design.

Abbey 5¢, peanuts, 1930s, cash tray, EX......................**$70.00**
Acorn, gumball, ca late 1940s, oak w/embossed scrolls, EX **$65.00**
Adams Gum, hexagonal shape, six columns, Stewart & McGuire, 1930s, EX...**$165.00**
American Flags 1¢, gumball, ca 1930s, EX................**$195.00**
Baby Grand, gumball, golden oak, VG **$50.00**

Columbia Model A, peanuts, star globe, cast iron, ca 1920s, EX $350.00

Columbus #18, aluminum $275.00

Columbus M Bi-Mor, two machines in one, light green porcelain finish, ca 1930-late 40s, NM $300.00

Exhibit Esco 2¢, cards, EX..$150.00

Hershey 5¢, candy bars, tan, brown, white & silver, 28", EX $150.00

National Automatic Vending Machine Co Model S, chocolate, 1917, EX $250.00

Northwestern Jet, peanuts, ca 1950s, VG $40.00

Northwestern Model 33, peanuts, porcelain, 1933, EX ..$115.00

Silver King Deluxe, peanuts, ca late 1930s, EX............$85.00

Vendex, gumball, EX..$125.00

Victor Challenger, gum, cylindrical globe, cast iron base, 1940s, EX $335.00

Victor Vendorama, ca 1950s, VG $25.00

Victor 1¢ Basketball, gumball, ca 1950s, wood, EX $145.00

Victor 1¢ Model V, peanuts, ca 1940s, EX..................$65.00

Vernon Kilns

Founded in Vernon, California, in 1930, this company produced many lines of dinnerware, souvenir plates, decorative pottery, and figurines. They employed several well-known artists whose designs no doubt contributed substantially to their success. Among them were Rockwell Kent, Royal Hickman, and Don Blanding, all of whom were responsible for creating several of the lines most popular with collectors today.

In 1940, they signed a contract with Walt Disney to produce a line of figurines and several dinnerware patterns that were inspired by Disney's film *Fantasia*. The figurines were made for a short time only and are now expensive.

The company closed in 1958, but Metlox purchased the molds and continued to produce some of their best-selling dinnerware lines through a specially established 'Vernon Kiln' division.

Most of the ware is marked in some form or another with the company name and, in some cases, the name of the dinnerware pattern.

If you'd like to learn more, we recommend *The Collector's Encyclopedia of California Pottery* by Jack Chipman.

Bowl, mixing; Early California, assorted high-glaze colors, 5-pc set .:..$100.00

Calico, pitcher, syrup; pastel banded contemporary design on ivory, metal lid w/ivory handle $45.00

Chatelaine, plate, dinner; 10½" sq, Platinum, leaf spray in one corner, 1953 ....$15.00

Dewdrop Fairies, salt & pepper shakers, 1940, pr.......$35.00

Ecstasy, pitcher, 2-qt, florals on disk sides..................$40.00

Fantasia, bowl, 2½x12", Winged Nymph, Walt Disney, #122 ....$275.00

Fantasia, figurine, 10½", Centaur, Walt Disney.......$1,100.00

Fantasia, figurine, 4", stretching Satyr, Walt Disney, #4..$300.00

Fantasia, figurine, 5", Hippo Ballerina, Walt Disney, #33 ....$600.00

Fantasia, salt & pepper shakers, 3½", Mushroom, Walt Disney, pr $135.00

Hawaiian Flowers, tumbler, iced tea; enhanced transfer florals on cream, stamped Blanding mark................$20.00

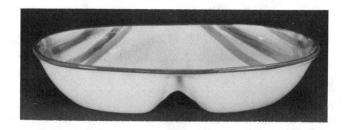

Homespun, divided vegetable bowl, 12" long.......$13.50

Homespun, tumbler..$17.50

Lei Lani, chop plate, 14", over-all multicolor floral center w/floral rim, stamped Blanding mark..................$45.00

Mayflower, bowl, soup; flat..$18.00

Modern California, egg cup, double; plain color........$20.00

Organdie, casserole, w/lid..$40.00

Planter, bird figural, 6x7"..$45.00

Plate, souvenir; 10½", Hollywood, blue on white, scenes of city, ca 1940..**$25.00**

Raffia, bowl, 6" **$2.50**
Raffia, plate, 10" (illustrated) **$5.00**
Raffia, platter, 9½" (illustrated).........................**$6.00**
Rhythmic, cup & saucer, ca 1935, stamped Hamilton mark **$30.00**
Rhythmic, plate, dinner; 10½", pastel color, ca 1935, stamped Hamilton..**$20.00**
Salamina, chop plate, 17", enhanced transfer portrait, stamped Kent mark **$200.00**
Salamina, cup & saucer **$50.00**
Salamina, plate, 14" **$150.00**
Salamina, plate, 9½"..**$95.00**
Salamina, sugar bowl, regular size, w/lid................**$35.00**
Salamina, tumbler **$32.00**
Tam O'Shanter, bowl, serving; divided **$20.00**
Ultra California, bowl, chowder; 6", Carnation...........**$15.00**
Ultra California, cup & saucer, Ice Green **$20.00**
Ultra California, plate, bread & butter; 6½", Gardenia...**$6.00**
Ultra California, plate, luncheon; 9½", Aster...............**$12.00**
Winchester 73, chop plate, 13", cowboy on bronc in center, spur & horse head rim band, ca 1950, stamped mark **$55.00**

View-Master Reels and Packets

William Gruber was the inventor who introduced the View-Master to the public at the New York World's Fair and the Golden Gate Exposition held in California in 1939. Thousands of reels and packets have been made since that time on every aspect of animal life, places of interest, and entertainment.

Over the years the company has changed ownership five times. It was originally Sawyer's View-Master, G.A.F. (in the mid-sixties), View-Master International (1981), Ideal Toy, and most recently Tyco Toy Company. The latter three companies produced it strictly as a toy and issued only cartoons, making the earlier non-cartoon reels and the 3-reel packets

very collectible.

Sawyer made two cameras so that the public could take their own photo reels in 3-D. They made a projector as well, so that the homemade reels could be viewed on a large screen. 'Personal' or 'Mark II' cameras with their cases usually range in value from $100.00 to $200.00; rare viewers such as the blue 'Model B' start at about $100.00, and the 'Stereo-Matic 500' projector is worth $175.00 to $200.00. Most single reels range from $1.00 to $5.00, but some early Sawyer's & G.A.F.'s may bring as much as $25.00 each.

Black Hills-Badlands, South Dakota; Sawyer, ca 1940s, 3-reel set w/booklet, in original photo envelope, NM....**$18.00**
Carlsbad Caverns National Park, Sawyer, ca 1940s, 3-reel set, in original photo envelope, NM............................**$16.00**
Conquest of Space, GAF, 1969, 3-reel set of moon landing w/booklet & color photo envelope......................**$15.00**
Dark Shadows, GAF, 1968, 3-reel set w/16-page booklet, in original photo envelope, M...................................**$40.00**
Deputy Dawg, Sawyer, 1962, 3-reel set w/16-page booklet, in original 5x5" illustrated envelope.....................**$30.00**
Egypt, Land of the Pharoahs, Sawyer, ca 1940s, 3-reel set w/guide book, NM..**$18.00**
Hawaii 5-O, #B590, 1973, 3-reel set w/16-page booklet, M..**$25.00**
Holland, Nations of the World Series, Sawyer, ca 1940s, 3-reel set w/16-page booklet, in original photo envelope, NM **$22.00**
Julia, #B572, 1969, 3-reel set w/16-page booklet, M ...**$30.00**
Land of the Giants, GAF, 1968, 3-reel set w/16-page booklet, in original envelope...**$35.00**
London, England; Sawyer, ca 1940s, 3-reel set, in original photo envelope, NM..**$16.00**
Marvel Super Heroes, Kenner, 1966, 5-card set, on original 7x5" display package...**$35.00**
Mod Squad, #B478, 1968, 3-reel set w/16-page booklet, M..**$30.00**
Modern Israel, Sawyer, ca 1940s, 3-reel set w/guide book, in original photo envelope, NM **$18.00**
See-a-Show, Kenner, 5 rectangular reels of Marvel Super Heroes, 1966, in original package, M....................**$35.00**
Time Tunnel, Sawyer, 1966, 3-reel set w/16-page booklet, in original photo envelope **$40.00**
Tron, gift set...**$42.00**

Viewer, Stereoscope, black plastic, reel inserts on top, original box **$7.50**

Vistosa Dinnerware

This was a solid color line of dinnerware made from 1938 until sometime in the middle forties in an effort to compete with the very successful Fiesta line by Homer Laughlin. Vistosa was produced by Taylor, Smith, and Taylor, who were also located in the famous East Liverpool/Newell, Ohio, pottery district. Though T.S. & T. duplicated several of Fiesta's popular early glazes (mango red, cobalt blue, light green, and deep yellow), they completely lost out on the design. Instead of the wonderful Art Deco shapes the public evidently favored in combination with the primary colors, Vistosa's evoked more country charm than sophistication because of the dainty 5-petal flower molded into the handles and lid finials.

Vistosa is relatively scarce, but collectors find the same features that spelled doom for the line in the early forties more appealing today, and its scarcity only adds fun to the hunt. Red is the most desirable color, and you may have to pay a little more to get it.

Bowl, salad..$95.00
Bowl, 5¾"...$10.00
Bowl, 6⅜"...$15.00
Chop plate, 11" $25.00
Creamer...$12.00
Cup & saucer...$15.00

Egg cup $22.50
Gravy boat..$78.00
Pitcher..$50.00
Plate, 6"..$4.00
Plate, 7"..$7.00
Plate, 9"..$1.00
Salt & pepper shakers, pr....................................$18.00
Sugar bowl, w/lid $15.00
Teapot...$75.00
Teapot, red...$80.00

W. S. George Dinnerware

From the turn of the century until the late 1950s, this East Palestine, Ohio, company produced many lines of dinnerware. Some were in solid colors, but the vast majority were decaled. Most of the lines were marked. If you'd like more information, we recommend *The Collector's Encyclopedia of American Dinnerware* by Jo Cunningham.

Bird, plate, 9", Derwood shape....................................$12.00
Blossoms, plate, dinner; 10", Lido shape.....................$10.00
Blossoms, salt & pepper shakers, Ranchero shape, pr..$17.50
Blossoms, sugar bowl, Lido shape, w/lid....................$12.50
Bluebird, plate, 6", Derwood shape $12.00
Floral, bowl, small, tab handled..................................$5.00
Flower Rim, plate, dinner; 10", Lido shape $5.00
Petalware, bowl, 5½", ivory..$5.00
Petalware, plate, 7½", pink...$6.50
Petalware, plate, 9", maroon $8.00
Petalware, sugar bowl, pink, w/lid..............................$12.00
Petit Point Rose, plate, dinner; 10", Fleurette shape......$8.00
Plain Jane, plate, dinner; 10", Lido shape....................$5.00
Poppy, platter, 11½", Rainbow shape..........................$12.00

Rainbow, bowl, 5½", pink $4.00
Rainbow, cup (illustrated)......................................$8.00
Rainbow, egg cup, blue (illustrated)......................$15.00
Roses, gravy boat w/attached liner, Bolero shape.......$10.00
Rosita, creamer, Ranchero shape $7.50
Rust Floral, cup, Lido shape..$5.00
Shortcake, coffeepot, Ranchero shape $45.00
Shortcake, salt & pepper shakers, Ranchero shape, pr $35.00
Tiny Roses, egg cup, Lido shape $12.00

Wade Porcelain

If you've attended many flea markets, you're already very familiar with the tiny Wade animals, most of which are 2" and under. Wade made several lines of animal figures, but the most common were made as premiums for the Red Rose Tea company; and though most sell for $3.50 to $7.00 or so, some (Colt and the Gingerbread Man, for instance) may bring $20.00 or so. A few larger animals were made as well, and these often sell for more than $100.00.

The Wade company dates to 1810. The original kiln was located near Chesterton in England. The tiny pottery merged with a second about 1900 and became known as the George Wade Pottery. They continued to grow and to absorb smaller nearby companies and eventually manufactured a wide range of products from industrial ceramics to Irish porcelain giftware. In 1990 Wade changed its name to Seagoe Ceramics Limited.

If you'd like to learn more, we recommend *The World of Wade* by Ian Warner and Mike Posgay.

Baa Baa Black Sheep, Red Rose Tea, 1971-79 .... **$10.00**
Bear Cub, Red Rose Tea, 1950s **$38.00**
Beefeater Gin, pitcher **$26.00**
Boy Blue, Red Rose Tea, 1971-79 .... **$5.00**

Buffalo, 1¾x2¼", Whoppas series $8.00
Colt, Red Rose Tea, 1950s **$40.00**
Doctor Foster, Red Rose Tea, 1971-79 .... **$7.00**
Gingerbread Man, Red Rose Tea, 1971-79 .... **$30.00**
Goosey Gander, Red Rose Tea, 1971-79 .... **$7.00**
Hickory Dickory Dock, Red Rose Tea, 1971-79 .... **$3.50**
Jack, Red Rose Tea, 1971-79 .... **$7.00**
Little Bo-Peep, Red Rose Tea, 1971-79 .... **$3.50**
Little Jack Horner, Red Rose Tea, 1971-79 .... **$3.50**
Little Miss Muffet, Red Rose Tea, 1971-79 .... **$7.00**
Little Red Riding Hood, Red Rose Tea, 1971-79 .... **$5.00**
Mary Mary, Red Rose Tea, 1971-79 .... **$25.00**
Mother Goose, Red Rose Tea, 1971-79 .... **$12.00**
Pied Piper, Red Rose Tea, 1971-79 .... **$4.00**
Puss 'n Boots, Red Rose Tea, 1971-79 .... **$6.50**
Pusser's Rum, decanter, full-size, w/stopper **$80.00**
Pusser's Rum, flagon, full-size, w/stopper **$50.00**
Pusser's Rum, flagon, miniature **$18.00**
Queen of Hearts, Red Rose Tea, 1971-79 .... **$12.00**
Shaving mug, multicolor decoration, 1960s-1980s **$25.00**
Shaving mug, single color decoration, 1960s-1980s **$20.00**
Souvenir dish, Veteran Car series, mid-1950s-1961 ..... **$15.00**
Squirrel, Red Rose Tea, 1950s **$32.50**
Tankard, Veteran Car series, 1950s-1980s **$18.00**
Teapot, bramble decoration **$60.00**
Teapot, copper lustre, early 1950s **$85.00**
Three Bears, Red Rose Tea, 1971-79 .... **$22.00**
Tom the Piper's Son, Red Rose Tea, 1971-79 .... **$7.00**
Wee Willie Winkie, Red Rose Tea, 1971-79 .... **$4.00**
Wild Boar, Red Rose Tea **$5.00**

Wallace China

Although they made decaled lines and airbrush-stencil patterns as well, this California pottery (1931-1964) is most famous for their 'Westward Ho' package of housewares. There were three designs, 'Rodeo,' 'Boots and Saddle,' and 'Pioneer Trails,' all created by western artist Till Goodan.

Today, anything related to the West is highly collectible, and as a result, values have drastically accelerated on many items that only a few months ago tended to be sometimes overlooked on the secondary market. Any dinnerware line with a Western or Southwestern motif has become extremely popular.

Jack Chipman's book, *The Collector's Encyclopedia of California Pottery*, has a chapter on Wallace China.

Ashtray, Christmas Greetings from Wallace China Co, round, ca 1950, stamped mark **$35.00**
Ashtray, commemorative of Los Angeles' Biltmore Hotel, dated 1949, stamped mark **$35.00**
Boots & Saddle, ashtray **$45.00**
Boots & Saddle, creamer **$35.00**
Chuck Wagon, bowl, 6¾", restaurant china, dated 1955 .. **$15.00**
Desert Ware, bowl, small, restaurant china, stamped mark **$15.00**
Hibiscus, plate, dinner **$10.00**
Mission Palm Tree, platter, 11½" **$45.00**
Rodeo, ash tray **$75.00**
Rodeo, bowl, cereal; 5¾" **$25.00**
Rodeo, cup, 7½-ounce **$45.00**

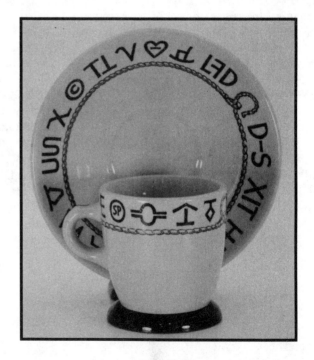

Rodeo, cup & saucer **$60.00**
Rodeo, pitcher **$125.00**
Rodeo, plate, bread & butter; 7¼" **$30.00**
Rodeo, plate, dinner; 10¾" **$45.00**
Rodeo, salt & pepper shakers, pr **$60.00**
Rodeo, saucer **$15.00**
Rodeo, shakers, range size, pr **$200.00**
Rodeo, sugar bowl & creamer **$150.00**

Watch Fobs

Strap-type watch fobs have been issued by the thousands by companies advertising farm machines, traps, guns, ammunition, heavy equipment, and products of many types. Some are relatively common and are worth only about $3.00 to $10.00, but others may go for $100.00 or more. To learn more about their values, we recommend *Collecting Watch Fobs* by John M. Kaduck.

Alaska Pacific Steamship Navigation Co, steamship....**$90.00**
Allis-Chalmers, harvester **$50.00**
American Accident Insurance Co, Indian bust............**$47.50**
American Auto Digest, Cincinnati, flying wheel & tire..**$75.00**
American Rose Society, red & green enamel on porcelain..**$38.00**
Avery Bulldog, brass, minor wear **$75.00**
Blue Brute Rock Drills, drill **$40.00**
BPOE, clock face, large elk...**$38.00**
Brotherhood Railroad Trainmen, enameled................**$42.50**
Bull Moose, EX **$20.00**
Case Centennial, tractor & plow **$80.00**
DeLaval, enamel...**$95.00**
Ford, celluloid center, 1960-70....................................**$10.00**
Ford, porcelain **$70.00**
Glass Bottle Blowers' Association, bottle form **$22.50**
Gold Bond Flour, sack shape, NM **$38.00**
Hamlight Lanterns..**$88.00**
Hercules Wheat Flakes, well-muscled man.................**$70.00**
Horse's head, carved mother-of-pearl **$30.00**
International Harvester, brass, w/strap, NM.................**$30.00**
Jamestown 1907 Expo, Connecticut House..................**$45.00**
Jersey Creme, The Perfect Drink...................................**$45.00**
Litchfield Bulldog Tractor, NM.....................................**$135.00**
Loom Lodge, enameled...**$20.00**
Moon Face Solarine, EX **$38.00**
National Woolen Mills, $15 Suit...................................**$37.50**
Old Dutch Cleanser, multicolor enameling on porcelain, EX..**$85.00**
Pabst Brewing, enameled...**$125.00**
Peter's Weatherbird Shoes, red, white & black, NM....**$75.00**
Pierce Arrow **$100.00**

Polarine, embossed w/polar bear..........................$50.00

Poll Parrot Shoes, celluloid, EX....................................**$75.00**
Pontiac, Chief of the Sixes..**$30.00**
Red Diamond Overalls & Shirts, celluloid, NM...........**$37.50**
Salvet Worm Destroyer...**$60.00**
Shapeleigh Hardware, brass, worn **$25.00**
Standard Horseshoe Co, Boston **$70.00**
Travelers Insurance, Ticket Dept, train, w/strap.........**$75.00**
US Master Brewer's Association **$55.00**
Wallis, tractor **$75.00**

Warren Paints, bronze w/red, paint can form, ca 1910 ....**$35.00**
William Jennings Bryan, leather & celluloid **$125.00**
1933 Century of Progress, aerial view **$40.00**

Watt Pottery

The Watt Pottery operated in Crooksville, Ohio, from 1922 until sometime in 1935. The ware they produced is easily recognized and widely available today. It appeals to collectors of country antiques, since the body is yellowware and its decoration simple. Several pieces of Watt pottery were featured in *Country Living* magazine a few years ago, and it was this exposure that seemed to catapult it onto the collectibles market.

Several patterns were made: Apple, Autumn Foliage, Cherry, Dutch Tulip, Morning-Glory, Pansy, Rooster, Tear Drop, Starflower, and Tulip among them. All were executed in bold brush strokes of primary colors. Some items you'll find will also carry a stenciled advertising message, made for retail companies as premiums for their customers.

For further study, we recommend *Watt Pottery, An Identification and Price Guide,* by Sue and Dave Morris.

Apple, baker, 5¾x8½" dia, small handle, w/lid, #96, USA mark..**$125.00**
Apple, bowl, mixing; 2¾x5", embossed ribs, #5, USA mark **$55.00**
Apple, bowl, mixing; 4½x8", #8, USA mark................**$45.00**
Apple, cookie jar, 7½x7", #21, USA mark **$300.00**
Apple, cookie jar, 8¼x8¼", #503, USA mark.............**$300.00**
Apple, creamer, 4¼x4½", #62..**$75.00**
Apple, Dutch oven casserole, 6x9½", 10¼" dia lid, #73, USA mark..**$200.00**

Apple, fondue, 3x9" long, marked Made in USA.......**$175.00**

Apple, grease jar, 5½x5¼", w/lid, #01, USA mark **$250.00**

Apple, mug, #121...**$175.00**

Apple, pie plate, 1½x9" dia, #33, marked **$150.00**

Apple, pitcher, 6½x6¾", #16, USA mark **$110.00**

Apple, pitcher, 8x8½", w/ice lip, #17, USA mark **$225.00**

Apple, plate, dinner size, 9½"...................................**$400.00**

Apple, spaghetti bowl, 1½x8", #44.......................$100.00

Autumn Foliage, bean pot, 6½x7½", handles, w/lid, #76, USA mark...**$90.00**

Autumn Foliage, bowl, 3x7¾", embossed ribs, #600, USA mark **$30.00**

Autumn Foliage, bowl, 4x9½", #73, USA mark **$45.00**

Autumn Foliage, fondue, 3x9", Made in USA mark **$90.00**

Autumn Foliage, oil & vinegar set, 7", #126, USA mark, pr **$550.00**

Autumn Foliage, pitcher, 5½x5¾", #15, USA mark **$35.00**

Autumn Foliage, platter, 15" dia, #31, USA mark **$110.00**

Autumn Foliage, salt & pepper shakers, 4¼x2½", hourglass shape, embossed letters on front, no marks, pr .**$155.00**

Autumn Foliage, sugar bowl, 4½x5", 3" dia at top, w/lid, 398, USA mark **$175.00**

Brown-Banded, mug, 3¾x3", #121, USA mark **$115.00**

Brown-Banded, plate, salad; 7½", #102, USA mark **$25.00**

Brown-Banded, sugar bowl, 4½x5", 3" dia at opening, w/lid, #98 ....**$150.00**

Cherry, bowl, cereal/salad; 2½x6½", #52, USA mark...**$25.00**

Cherry, bowl, mixing; 3x6", #6, USA mark..................**$35.00**

Cherry, cookie jar, 7½x7", #21, USA mark **$160.00**

Cherry, pitcher, 5½x5¾", #15, USA mark **$45.00**

Cherry, platter, 15" dia, #31, USA mark.....................**$145.00**

Cut-Leaf Pansy, creamer & sugar bowl, 2¾x6" (each), open, both pieces marked **$100.00**

Cut-Leaf Pansy, cup & saucer, 2¾"x4½", 6½" dia, marked **$75.00**

Cut-Leaf Pansy, platter, 15", marked.........................**$100.00**

Cut-Leaf Pansy, spaghetti bowl, 3x13", marked...........**$80.00**

Cut-Leaf Pansy w/Bullseye pattern, 7½" dia, marked..**$45.00**

Double Apple, boxl, mixing; 2x4", #04, USA mark ...**$110.00**

Double Apple, boxl, mixing; 3¾x7", #07, USA mark...**$75.00**

Dutch Tulip, bowl, 4x5", w/lid, #05 ....**$175.00**

Dutch Tulip, bowl, 6½x8½", w/lid, #67, USA mark...**$175.00**

Dutch Tulip, cheese crock, 8x8½", w/lid, #80, USA mark **$400.00**

Dutch Tulip, creamer, 4¼x4½", #62............................**$95.00**

Dutch Tulip, refrigerator pitcher, 8x8½", square shape, #69, USA mark **$325.00**

Eagle, bowl, cereal; 2x5½", #74, USA mark.................**$55.00**

Eagle, bowl, mixing; 4x7", #7, USA mark....................**$65.00**

Eagle, bowl, mixing; 6x12", #12, USA mark.................**$85.00**

Green & White Banded, bowl, 2¾x5", #5, USA mark .**$25.00**

Green-On-Brown Starflower, casserole, 4x5" dia, tab handles, w/lid, #18, USA mark.................................**$125.00**

Green-On-Brown Starflower, cookie jar, 7½x7", #21, USA mark..**$125.00**

Green-On-Brown Starflower, pitcher, 8x8½", #17, marked R-F USA..**$150.00**

Light Blue & White Banded, cookie jar, 7½x7", marked.**$65.00**

Light Blue & White Banded, pitcher, 7x7¾", marked..**$45.00**

Morning Glory, cookie jar, 10¾x7½", #95, USA mark .**$95.00**

Morning Glory, pitcher, 8x8½", w/ice lip, #96, USA mark **$300.00**

Old Pansy, casserole, 4¼x7½" dia, #2/48, w/lid, marked...**$55.00**

Old Pansy, platter, 15" dia, #31, USA mark................**$100.00**

Old Pansy, spaghetti bowl, 3x13", #39, USA mark **$70.00**

Open Apple, bowl, mixing; 2¾x5", #5, USA mark **$85.00**

Open Apple, bowl, mixing; 4½x8", #8, USA mark **$125.00**

Pink-On-Black Starflower, casserole, 3¾x7½" long, stick handle, USA mark **$150.00**

Pink-On-Black Starflower, cup & saucer, 2¾x4½", 6" dia, both pieces marked **$85.00**

Pink-On-Green Starflower, bread plate, 6½" dia, USA mark **$35.00**

Pink-On-Green Starflower, cup & saucer, 2¾x4½", 6" dia, both pieces marked **$65.00**

Pink-On-Green Starflower, platter, 15" dia, #31, USA mark **$110.00**

Raised Pansy, casserole, 3¾x7½" long, French handle, individual, marked **$175.00**

Rooster, bean pot, 6½x7½", handles, #76, USA **$175.00**

Rooster, bowl, 3¾x10½", #58, USA mark **$90.00**

Rooster, bowl, 4x9½", #73, USA mark **$75.00**

Rooster, bowl, 6½x8½", w/lid, #67, USA mark **$150.00**

Rooster, pitcher, 6½x6¾", #16, USA mark.................**$125.00**

Rooster, refrigerator pitcher, 8x8½", square shape, #69, USA mark..**$275.00**

Rooster, salt & pepper shakers, 4½x2½", hourglass shape, holes on top depict 'S' & 'P,' pr..........................**$175.00**

Starflower, bean pot, 6½x7½", handles, #76, USA mark..**$90.00**

Starflower, bowl, cereal/salad; 2½x6½", #52, USA mark ..**$25.00**

Starflower, bowl, mixing; 2½x5", #05, USA mark **$45.00**

Starflower, bowl, 3x7½", #64, USA mark....................**$45.00**

Starflower, casserole, 4x5", tab handles, w/lid, #18, USA mark **$150.00**

Starflower, cookie jar, 7½x7", #21, USA mark............$160.00

Starflower, ice bucket, 7¼x7½", w/lid, no mark........$185.00

Starflower, platter, 15" dia, #31, USA mark...............$140.00

Starflower, refrigerator pitcher, 8x8½", square shape, #69, USA mark $250.00

Starflower, salt & pepper shakers, 4½x2½", hourglass shape, embossed letters, pr..$175.00

Starflower, tumbler, 4½x4", #56, slant sides, USA mark ..$225.00

Tear Drop, bean pot, 6½x7½", handles, w/lid, #76, USA mark..$90.00

Tear Drop, bowl, mixing; 3¾x7", #07, USA mark........$40.00

Tear Drop, bowl, mixing; 5x7½", #64, USA mark........$40.00

Tear Drop, bowl, 3x7", #66, USA mark $45.00

Tear Drop, casserole, 4x8" long, French handle, #18, marked...$200.00

Tear Drop, casserole, 6x8x8", square shape, no mark .$275.00

Tear Drop, creamer, 4¼x4½", #62 ....$75.00

Tear Drop, refrigerator pitcher, 8x8½", square shape, #69, USA mark $250.00

Tulip, bowl, mixing; 5¾x8½", #65, USA mark $80.00

Tulip, bowl, 4x9½", #73, USA mark...........................$110.00

Tulip, boxl, mixing; 4x6½", #63, USA mark $60.00

Tulip, pitcher, 5½x5¾", #15, USA mark, rare.............$225.00

White Daisy, casserole, 5x8¾", w/lid, USA mark.......$165.00

White Daisy, cup & saucer, 2¾x4½", 6" dia, both pieces marked...$75.00

White Daisy, pitcher, 7x7¾", USA mark $125.00

Woodgrain, chip 'n dip bowl, 2¾x11¼", #611W, USA mark $75.00

Woodgrain, pitcher, 5¾"x4½", #613W, USA mark $75.00

Yellow Morning Glory, bowl, mixing; 3½x6", #6, USA mark $50.00

Weil Ware

Though the Weil company made dinnerware and some kitchenware, their figural pieces are attracting the most collector interest. They were in business from the 1940s until the mid-fifties, another of the small but very successful California companies whose work has become so popular today. They dressed their 'girls' in beautiful gowns of vivid rose, light dusty pink, turquoise blue and other lovely colors enhanced with enameled 'lacework' and flowers, sgraffito, sometimes even with tiny applied blossoms. Both paper labels and ink stamps were used to mark them, but as you study their features, you'll soon learn to recognize even those that have lost their labels over the years. Four-number codes and decorators' initials are also common.

If you want to learn more, we recommend *The Collector's Encyclopedia of California Pottery* by Jack Chipman.

Ashtray, 5", Bamboo $5.00

Bowl, vegetable, Rose $10.00

Bowl, 8¾" long, Blossom, rectangular.....................$15.00

Butter dish, ¼-lb, Blossom $25.00

Cup & saucer, Blossom...$8.00

Cup & saucer, Rose..$5.00

Figurine, 11", lady, rose-colored dress w/hand-painted floral decoration, pocket at back............................$35.00

Figurine, 7", Buddy, boy.......................................$15.00

Figurine, 7", Dee Lee, girl.....................................$15.00

Plate, dinner size, Bamboo....................................$5.00

Plate, 10", Rose $6.00

Platter, 10", Rose $10.00

Shelf sitter, Oriental boy, pr..................................$40.00

Vase, 10½", girl by square post $32.50

Vase, 11", girl w/two blue vases, one by her side, one on her shoulder..$35.00

Wall pocket, Oriental girl, #4046 ....**$22.50**

Weller Pottery

Though the Weller Pottery has been closed since 1948, they were so prolific that you'll be sure to see several pieces anytime you're 'antiquing.' They were one of the largest of the art pottery giants that located in the Zanesville, Ohio, area, using locally dug clays to produce their wares. In the early years, they made hand-decorated vases, jardinieres, lamps, and other decorative items for the home, many of which were signed by notable artists such as Fredrick Rhead, John Lessell, Virginia Adams, Anthony Dunlavy, Dorothy England, Albert Haubrich, Hester Pillsbury, E.L. Pickens, and Jacques Sicard, to name only a few. Some of their early lines were First and Second Dickens, Eocean, Sicardo, Etna, Louwelsa, Turada, and Aurelian. Portraits of Indians, animals of all types, lady golfers, nudes, and scenes of Dickens' stories were popular themes, and some items were overlaid with silver filigree. These lines are rather hard to find at this point in time, and prices are generally high; but there's plenty of their later production still around, and most pieces are relatively inexpensive.

If you'd like to learn more, we recommend _The Collector's Encyclopedia of Weller Pottery_ by Sharon and Bob Huxford.

Arcadia, vase, 5½", creamy beige, embossed leaves form body, #A-4, marked Weller Since 1872..................**$27.50**
Arcadia, vase, 8½", blue-green, small embossed leaves allover, scalloped top formed by leaf tips, marked **$45.00**
Atlas, bowl, 2" high, ivory, star shape, #C-2, in-mold script mark...**$40.00**
Atlas, covered dish, 3½" high, blue, star shape, #C-2, in-mold script mark...**$70.00**
Atlas, vase, 5½", blue, star-shaped rim, in-mold script mark **$30.00**
Blo' Red, vase, 3½", golden tan mottling on dark red, small handles, ink stamp mark **$45.00**
Blo' Red, vase, 9½", golden tan mottling on dark red, shouldered cylindrical shape, paper label...................**$125.00**
Blossom, cornucopia, 6", floral decoration on green, in-mold script mark..**$22.50**
Blossom, vase, 14", floral decoration on green, ornate handles, footed, shaped rim, in-mold script mark....**$120.00**
Blossom, vase, 9½", floral decoration on green, gourd shape, in-mold script mark...................................**$30.00**
Bonito, candle holder, 1½", floral decoration on cream, marked, pr..**$60.00**
Bonito, vase, 10", floral on cream, small handles, artist signed NC, small paper label **$215.00**
Bouquet, bowl vase, 9", white embossed floral decoration on medium green, #B-7, in-mold mark.................**$17.50**
Bouquet, vase, 12", white embossed florals on blue, shaped & folded rim, in-mold mark **$55.00**

Bouquet, vase, 5", white embossed floral decoration on creamy tan, small green handles, #B-15, in-mold script mark..**$17.50**
Cactus, figurine, camel, 3½", green, glossy, marked by hand **$80.00**
Cactus, figurine, camel, 4", brown, glossy, marked by hand **$70.00**
Cactus, figurine, duck, 4½", green, glossy, marked by hand **$75.00**
Cameo, planter, 4" high, white flower embossed on blue, rectangular, marked Weller Pottery Since 1872 ....**$27.50**
Cameo, vase, 5", white flower embossed on blue, ornate handles, no mark **$22.50**
Cameo vase, 8½", white flower embossed on green, square sides, in-mold script mark **$22.50**
Clarmont, bowl, 3" high, stylized florals on dark brown, handles, impressed mark......................................**$40.00**
Clarmont, candle holder, 8", stylized floral decoration on dark brown, shoulder-to-base handles, impressed mark **$165.00**
Classic, bowl, 8", white, reticulated design at flared rim, in-mold script mark..**$35.00**
Classic, window box, 4" high, rectangular, reticulated design at rim, paper label & in-mold script mark............**$65.00**
Coppertone, basket, 8½", brown & green 'bronze-like' appearance, no mark..**$175.00**
Coppertone, vase, 8", brown & green 'bronze-like' appearance, ring handles, ink stamp **$450.00**
Cornish, bowl, 4", leaves & berries on tan, small handles, in-mold script mark..**$30.00**
Cornish, jardiniere, 5", leaves & berries on blue, small handles, in-mold script mark.................................**$27.50**

Cornish, vase, 5½", leaves & berries on tan, small handles, in-mold script mark $40.00
Darsie, flowerpot, 5½", ivory w/embossed swags & tassels, lightly scalloped rim, in-mold script mark............**$25.00**
Darsie, vase, 7½", ivory w/embossed swags & tassels, lightly scalloped rim, cylindrical, in-mold script mark.....**$25.00**

Delsa, vase, pink floral decoration on medium green, scalloped rim, footed, in-mold script mark **$17.50**

Elberta, console bowl, 6x11½" long, peachy-tan to green shaded, handles, marked by hand.........................**$35.00**

Elberta, vase, 6", peachy-tan shaded to green, classic form, marked by hand...**$25.00**

Evergreen, pelican, 5½", green, open back, marked by hand...**$65.00**

Florenzo, basket, green to ivory shaded, embossed multicolor floral decoration along handle, impressed mark & ink stamp..**$52.50**

Florenzo, planter, ivory w/floral decoration at base, green along scalloped rim, square shape, ink stamp......**$30.00**

Gloria, bowl, 3½" high, embossed multicolor floral decoration on green, folded & shaped rim, #G-15, in-mold script **$22.50**

Gloria, ewer, 9", embossed multicolor floral branch on medium brown, #G-12, in-mold script mark.........**$35.00**

Goldenglow, bowl, 3½x16" long, dark golden tan w/embossed floral decoration, handles, no mark **$55.00**

Goldenglow, candle holder, triple; 3½", dark golden tan, in-mold script mark...**$35.00**

Goldenglow, candle holder, 4½", green & brown floral decoration on golden tan, 3-footed, no mark.............**$40.00**

Greenbriar, pitcher, 10", marble-like mottling, faint vertical ribbing, flat rim, no mark **$150.00**

Greenbriar, vase, 8½", marble-like mottling, classic form, no mark..**$140.00**

Lido, planter, 4½", green to blue shaded, triangular form designed w/leaf shapes, footed, marked...............**$40.00**

Lido, vase, 6", pink pastel on swirled shape w/ruffled foot & rim, ornate handles, in-mold script mark **$27.50**

Loru, bowl, 4" high, maroon shaded paneled shape w/embossed leaf decoration at base, in-mold script mark...**$30.00**

Loru, vase, 9½", green w/twelve panels on body, embossed brown leaves at base, marked Weller Pottery Since 1872 ....**$37.50**

Malverne, circle vase, 8", floral decoration on green to brown shaded, ink stamp....................................**$50.00**

Manhattan, pitcher, 10", dark green embossed flowers & leaves on medium green, cylindrical, marked by hand **$95.00**

Manhattan, vase, 8", dark green embossed leaves & flowers on medium green, handles, marked by hand.......**$65.00**

Novelty, ashtray, 4", three pigs sit on rim, no mark **$65.00**

Novelty, tray, 2x5½", seal figural, black, glossy, in-mold script mark...**$45.00**

Novelty, tray, 3x7", fox at side, marked by hand..........**$120.00**

Oak Leaf, basket, 7½", oak leaf decoration on medium brown, twig handle, #G-1, in-mold script mark....**$55.00**

Oak Leaf, ewer, 14", oak leaf decoration on medium green, shaped rim, angle handle, in-mold script mark...**$95.00**

Oak Leaf, vase, 6", oak leaf decoration on medium blue, in-mold script mark...**$17.50**

Panella, bowl, 3½", pansy decoration on peach shaded, three tab-shaped feet, in-mold script mark **$22.50**

Panella, vase, 6½", pansy decoration on blue shaded, gourd shape w/low handles, in-mold script mark..........**$17.50**

Pastel, planter, 4x7" long, blue pastel, organic form w/four small feet, #P-3, marked **$30.00**

Patra, basket, 5½", floral decoration on brown textured ground, marked by hand......................................**$85.00**

Patra, vase, 3½", stylized floral decoration on brown textured ground, green rim & angle handles, #1, marked by hand...**$27.50**

Patrician, bowl, 13" dia, ivory w/eight geese heads along rim, embossed foliage at base, in-mold script mark **$125.00**

Patrician, planter, 6½", ivory duck form, head & tail handles, open back, in-mold script mark.........................**$100.00**

Patrician, vase, 4", ivory w/goose-head handles, in-mold script mark...**$25.00**

Patrician, vase, 18", tan crystalline glaze w/embossed leaves, swan handles, signed DE, marked....$225.00

Pierre, cookie jar, 10", green basketweave, in-mold script mark...**$65.00**

Pierre, sugar bowl, 2", pink basketweave, small handles, in-mold script mark...**$12.50**

Raydence, vase, 7½", ivory w/embossed leafy decoration, small upturned handles, flared lightly scalloped rim, marked...**$30.00**

Reno, bowl, 3", brown band on tan, no mark............**$12.00**

Roba, ewer, 6", floral decoration on blue shaded, swirled body shape, twig handle, in-mold script mark **$40.00**

Roba, vase, 12", floral spray on medium tan, small handles, #R-20, marked Weller Pottery Since 1872 ....**$135.00**

Roba, vase, 9", blue shaded w/pink flower at one handle, #R-2, marked Weller Pottery Since 1872...............**$65.00**

Roba, vase, 13", stalk of white flowers on tan, curlique handles, marked R-20 ....$150.00

Rudlor, console bowl, 4½x17½" long, floral decoration on ivory, graduated 'beads' form handles, marked....**$45.00**

Rudlor, vase, 6", pink flower w/dark leaves on ivory, graduated 'beads' form handles, in-mold script mark....**$22.50**

Senic, vase, 5½", green embossed scene on blue, small angle handles, #S-4, in-mold script mark..............**$50.00**

Senic, vase, 6½", embossed palm scene, tan to medium brown shaded, ruffled rim, #S-2, in-mold script mark **$30.00**

Softone, vase, 10", blue w/embossed linear 'swag-like' decoration, bulbous, in-mold script mark.....................**$45.00**

Softone, vase, 5½", pastel pink w/embossed linear 'swag-like' decoration, in-mold script mark.....................**$17.50**

Stellar, vase, 5", white star decoration on black ball shape, in-mold script mark **$135.00**

Stellar, 6", white star decoration on blue, classic shape, in-mold script mark..**$135.00**

Sydonia, double candle holder w/bud vase, 11½", blue mottle **$120.00**

Sydonia, planter, 4", blue mottle on footed 'shell-like' form, marked by hand..**$30.00**

Sydonia, vase, double; 10½", blue mottle on two trumpet shapes sharing heavily mottled base **$75.00**

Teapot, 4", Gold-Green, ink stamp..............................**$45.00**

Teapot, 6", pink w/gold diamond shapes forming band & gold linear decoration, gold stamp.......................**$65.00**

Teapot, 7½", blue w/gold 'snowflake' & linear decoration, gold stamp..**$65.00**

Turkis, vase, 5", drip glaze on maroon, tub handles, marked by hand..**$40.00**

Turkis, vase, 5½", drip glaze on maroon, wide angle handles, marked by hand...**$85.00**

Turkis, vase, 8", drip glaze on maroon, ruffled rim, footed, marked by hand..**$75.00**

Utility ware, bean pot, 5½", brown, simple style w/flared rim, impressed mark **$25.00**

Utility ware, pitcher, 5½", brown, simple style w/square handle, flat rim, no mark......................................**$32.50**

Utility ware, pitcher, 7", blue band on cream, no mark ..**$42.50**

Utility ware, teapot, 6", pumpkin figural, green vine handle, stem finial, ink stamp **$100.00**

Utility ware, teapot, 6½", pineapple figural, light golden tan w/green lid, in-mold script mark.........................**$165.00**

Wildrose, vase, 6½", white open flower on medium green, stylized handles, in-mold script mark...................**$22.50**

Woodcraft, jardiniere, 8x9", woodpecker on side..**$500.00**

Woodrose, bowl, 2½x8½", two rose buds on 'wooden' tub form, upturned handles, no mark......................**$50.00**

Woodrose, wall vase, 5½", two rose buds on 'wooden' vase form, shape #348, impressed mark.......................**$85.00**

Zona, pitcher, 8", kingfisher in panel........................**$200.00**

Western Heroes

No friend was ever more true, no brother more faithful, no acquaintance more real to us than our favorite cowboys of radio, TV, and the silver screen. They were upright, strictly moral, extremely polite, and tireless in their pursuit of law and order in the American West. How unfortunate that such role models are practically extinct nowadays.

This is an area of strong collector interest right now, and prices are escalating. Some collectors prefer one cowboy hero over the others and concentrate their collections on that particular star. Some unlikely items are included in this specialized area — hair tonic bottles, cookie jars, wallets, and drinking mugs, for instance.

For more information and some wonderful pictures, we recommend *Character Toys and Collectibles, First* and *Second Series,* by David Longest.

See also Big Little Books, Paper Dolls, Character Watches, Pin-back Buttons, Toys (Premiums and Guns).

Allan 'Rocky' Lane & Black Jack, poster, 27x40", 'Bandits of the West,' 1953, EX $25.00
Bat Masterson, gun & holster set, 1950s, w/cane, EX .**$65.00**
Bobby Benson, book, 'The Lost Herd,' 1936, premium giveaway $25.00
Bobby Benson, bowl, cereal; 1930s, premium giveaway $25.00
Bobby Benson, coloring book, 'B-Bar-B Riders,' Whitman, 1950, M $20.00
Bonanza, coloring book, 8x11", Artcraft, Cartwright family on cover, 1965, 60-pg, M.....................................$20.00
Bonanza, game, 14½x14½x1¼", Parker Brothers, 1964, VG...$17.50
Bonanza, photo, 8x10", color cast shot $12.50
Bonanza, puzzle, 12x14", Milton Bradley, 125-pc, 1964, in original 10x12" box...$35.00
Buck Jones, membership card, 'Buck Jones Ranger Club' $15.00
Buck Jones, rifle, Daisy, w/compass, NM **$150.00**
Buffalo Bill, cap gun, cast iron, EX **$65.00**
Buffalo Bill, coloring book, 8½x10½", Whitman, 1957, NM **$27.50**
Cheyenne, photo, 8x10", Clint Walker in character.......**$6.00**
Cisco Kid, bread labels, from Tip Top Bread, set of three, NM **$7.50**
Cisco Kid, comic album, 1953, EX.............................$20.00
Cisco Kid, hobby horse $85.00
Cisco Kid & Pancho, cereal bowl, blue graphics on milk glass $20.00

Cisco Kid & Pancho, coloring book, Saalfield, no date, M $20.00

Cowboy, figurine, 7", celluloid w/jointed arms, Japan, 1930s **$90.00**
Dale Evans, book, 'Fun w/Cards,' 1943, hardcover, 118 pages w/dust jacket, EX **$17.50**
Dale Evans, wash mitt, cloth......................................$20.00
Daniel Boone, coonskin cap, ca 1950 ....$25.00
Daniel Boone, whistle, 6" long, brown & white plastic, marked 'Daniel Boon/Fess Parker Official Woodland,' M in box **$47.50**
Davy Crockett, bank, 5¼", metal, ca 1950.................$20.00
Davy Crockett, belt, 3½x2", embossed flintlock rifles on red-painted metal buckle, 30" long leather belt, EX....$20.00
Davy Crockett, card game, ca 1950, in original box....$15.00
Davy Crockett, knife, Imperial Knife Co, 1950s...........$40.00
Davy Crockett, lamp, chalkware figural, dated 1955, EX ..**$55.00**
Davy Crockett, leather belt w/cast metal buckle, NM.**$30.00**
Davy Crockett, mug, red graphics on milk glass, Fire-King..**$14.00**

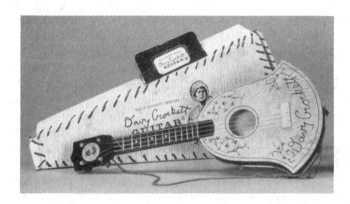

Davy Crockett, official wood guitar, 25", in original box, M...$300.00
Davy Crockett, party favor, 9x1½" dia, crepe paper popper type, 1950s, M $12.50
Davy Crockett, plaque, 5x8", painted profile in plaster, unmarked, EX..$20.00
Davy Crockett, powder horn, in original box.............$40.00
Davy Crockett, suspenders, 1950s, on original card....$27.50
Davy Crockett, tumbler, 5⅞", red graphics on clear glass .$15.00
Gene Autry, album, Columbia, 1947, set of four 78 rpm records $32.00

Gene Autry, bass drum, 24", from set, M (price is for complete drum and trap set)..........................$90.00

Gene Autry, bicycle horn, ca 1950, M **$50.00**

Gene Autry, book, 'Apache Country,' 1952, EX..........**$20.00**

Gene Autry, cap gun, 8", 50-shot, marked Leslie Henry, in original photo box, M......................................**$250.00**

Gene Autry, coloring book, 8½x11", Whitman, 1955, EX **$20.00**

Gene Autry, game, 1950s, 'Gene Autry Dude Ranch,' 1950s, in original box, EX...**$45.00**

Gene Autry, guitar, marked Emenee Professional, in original box...**$75.00**

Gene Autry, gun & holster set, Flying A, NM **$190.00**

Gene Autry, paint book, 10x15", Merrill Publishing, 1940, M...**$35.00**

Gene Autry, sheet music, 9x12", 'South of the Border,' 1941, EX **$17.50**

Gene Autry, song book, 9x12", 'Cowboy Songs & Mountain Ballads,' MM Cole Pub Co, 1934, 64-page, EX......**$25.00**

Gene Autry, song book, 9x12", 'Songs Gene Autry Sings' w/Gene on Champion on cover, Western Music Publishing, EX **$20.00**

Gene Autry, writing tablet, 1950s, M **$20.00**

High Chaparral, photo, 8x10", all cast pose, color **$15.00**

Hoot Gibson, circus program, Robbins Bros Circus, 1930s **$45.00**

Hopalong Cassidy, bicycle horn, 1950s, in original box, M **$95.00**

Hopalong Cassidy, binoculars, metal, NM....................**$42.00**

Hopalong Cassidy, book, 'Lends a Helping Hand'......**$35.00**

Hopalong Cassidy, cereal bowl, graphics on milk glass, 1950s, NM **$25.00**

Hopalong Cassidy, coin, 'Good Luck' **$10.00**

Hopalong Cassidy, coloring book, dated 1954, NM **$45.00**

Hopalong Cassidy, cowgirl costume, blouse & skirt w/fringe & border trim, 1950s, EX **$120.00**

Hopalong Cassidy, double gun & holster set............**$575.00**

Hopalong Cassidy, field glasses, 1950s in original box.**$75.00**

Hopalong Cassidy, game, 'Canasta' card set, in original box, M **$45.00**

Hopalong Cassidy, game, bean bag toss, 1950s, in original box..**$40.00**

Hopalong Cassidy, game, shooting gallery, in original box, NM **$300.00**

Hopalong Cassidy, gun, marked 'Zoomerang,' red, in original box **$125.00**

Hopalong Cassidy, hair trainer in bottle, Rubicon, 1950...**$20.00**

Hopalong Cassidy, hat, gray felt, EX **$175.00**

Hopalong Cassidy, ice cream container, 6½", 'Hopalong Cassidy's Favorite Ice Cream' on cylindrical paper form **$20.00**

Hopalong Cassidy, milk bottle, 1-qt, 1950s.................**$30.00**

Hopalong Cassidy, neckerchief, black satin, 1950s **$25.00**

Hopalong Cassidy, pin-back button, w/Topper..........**$15.00**

Hopalong Cassidy, pogo stick, 46", metal, 1950s, NM .**$100.00**

Hopalong Cassidy, puzzle, Milton Bradley, 1950s, NM.**$22.50**

Hopalong Cassidy, radio, Arvin #441-T, red metal table model, aluminum Hoppy & Topper cutout on front, right dial, 1950 ....**$425.00**

Hopalong Cassidy, record, 78 rpm, 'Hoppy's Good Luck Coin/Legend of Phantom Scout Pass,' Capitol, 1950s, NM **$18.00**

Hopalong Cassidy, rug, 24x28", EX **$125.00**

Hopalong Cassidy, scrapbook, 14", simulated leather cover, 1950s, EX **$60.00**

Hopalong Cassidy, song folio, Consolidated Music Publishers, EX...**$15.00**

Hopalong Cassidy, woodburning set, 'Bar 20,' 1950s, in original box...**$45.00**

Hopalong Cassidy, wristwatch, in original saddle-shaped box...**$200.00**

Hopalong Cassidy & Topper, plate, 9½" dia, w/facsimile signature near bottom **$40.00**

Jesse James, game, 20x10", Milton Bradley, object to get home safely, 1966, in original box........................**$50.00**

John Wayne, magazine, 'Time,' August 1969, 'True Grit' cover, EX **$15.00**

Kit Carson, photo, 8x10", sunset background, signed.**$50.00**

Lone Ranger, badge, w/secret compartment...............**$45.00**

Lone Ranger, binoculars, plastic w/decals, 1950, EX...**$45.00**

Lone Ranger, blotter, premium for Bond Bread, EX ...**$20.00**

Lone Ranger, brush, G...**$60.00**

Lone Ranger, cap pistol, cast iron, EX.......................**$250.00**

Lone Ranger, double gun & holster set, NM.............**$450.00**

Lone Ranger, first aid kit, 4x4", lithographed tin, marked American White Cross Labs 1938........................**$55.00**

Lone Ranger, game, 'Hi-Yo Silver!,' Parker Brothers, 1938 ....**$70.00**

Lone Ranger, game, 'Ride w/the Lone Ranger,' G.......**$65.00**

Lone Ranger, game, 'Ring Toss,' 1950s, in original box ..**$35.00**

Lone Ranger, game, 'Target Darts,' Marx, 1946...........**$60.00**

Lone Ranger, game, 'Target Game,' metal target, ca 1930s, M..$65.00

Lone Ranger, game, 'Target Practice,' hand-held bead game under glass **$35.00**

Lone Ranger, jail keys, on original card, rare **$125.00**
Lone Ranger, mug, Clayton Moore, 1961, M...............**$95.00**
Lone Ranger, overalls, child's, Levi...............................**$65.00**
Lone Ranger, paint book, Whitman, 1940, EX............**$40.00**
Lone Ranger, pedometer, metal, NM...........................**$45.00**
Lone Ranger, pencil, 'Silver Bullet,' on original card...**$45.00**
Lone Ranger, pencil case...**$75.00**
Lone Ranger, post card, General Mills premium, 1951, EX...**$25.00**
Lone Ranger, poster, 50th anniversary **$22.00**
Lone Ranger, record player, G.....................................**$375.00**
Lone Ranger, ring, 'Atom Bomb,' Kix cereal premium..**$45.00**
Lone Ranger, rocking horse, VG..................................**$225.00**
Lone Ranger, soap figural..**$75.00**
Lone Ranger, spoon, silverplate, ca 1930s, NM...........**$40.00**
Lone Ranger, sticker book, 10½x12", Whitman, 1952, EX...**$20.00**
Lone Ranger & Silver, toothbrush holder, 1938, NM...**$65.00**
Maverick, double gun & holster set, in original box.**$185.00**
Maverick (James Garner), photo, 8x10", color, M........**$10.00**
Paladin, gun & holster set **$45.00**
Pecos Bill, wind-up, 10", Marx, plastic figural twirls rope...**$150.00**
Range Rider, coloring book, Abbott, 1956, M.............**$40.00**
Range Rider, photo, 8x10", Jock Mahoney, black & white, EX...**$6.00**
Rawhide, canteen, in original package........................**$35.00**
Rawhide, photo, 8x10", cast photo, EX **$7.50**
Red Ryder, BB gun, w/plastic stock, Plymouth MI......**$70.00**
Red Ryder, book, 'Red Ryder & the Squaw Tooth Rustlers,' 1946, EX..**$25.00**
Red Ryder, coin, 1940s **$12.00**
Red Ryder, comic book, Dell, 1950, EX **$10.00**
Red Ryder, game, 'The Red Ryder Target Game,' Whitman, dated 1939, complete, in original box, M.............**$80.00**
Red Ryder, 1-sheet, 28x41", 'California Gold Rush,' 1946, VG...**$50.00**
Rex Allen, lobby card, 11x14", 'Under Mexicali Stars,' 1950, EX...**$7.50**
Rifleman, paint by number set, Standard Toykraft, die-cut canvas figures & town buildings, 1960, in original box, M...**$100.00**
Rifleman, photo, signed by Chuck Connors, black & white, EX...**$28.00**
Rifleman, rifle, in original box, M............................**$295.00**
Rin Tin Tin, scrapbook, Rusty or Rinty cover, NM **$10.00**
Roy Rogers, alarm clock, animated, working, EX......**$250.00**
Roy Rogers, annual book, 1954 ....**$40.00**
Roy Rogers, badge, 5-pointed star, EX........................**$25.00**
Roy Rogers, belt, child's, 1950s...................................**$35.00**
Roy Rogers, book, 'Favorite Western Stories,' Whitman, 252-pg..**$40.00**
Roy Rogers, book, 'Sure 'Nough Cowpoke'.................**$10.00**
Roy Rogers, book, 'Trigger to the Rescue' **$15.00**
Roy Rogers, calendar, 1959, EX **$80.00**
Roy Rogers, camera, box style, w/Trigger, EX............**$35.00**
Roy Rogers, chaps, child's size, graphics on cloth w/metal studs, 1950s, NM **$58.00**

Roy Rogers, coloring book, 1951, EX..........................**$25.00**
Roy Rogers, double gun & holster set.......................**$575.00**
Roy Rogers, guitar, Jefferson, in original box **$65.00**
Roy Rogers, horseshoe set, in original box.................**$85.00**
Roy Rogers, lamp, 24", painted plaster-cast base, electric w/original scenic shade, NM.............................**$170.00**
Roy Rogers, lantern, #90, battery operated, marked Ohio Art Co, in original box, M...**$75.00**
Roy Rogers, lobby card, 11x14", scene from 'Ridin' Down the Canyon,' 1942, VG...**$30.00**
Roy Rogers, lobby card, 14x11", 'Night Time in Nevada,' G...**$25.00**
Roy Rogers, mug, 4", painted plastic bust figural w/handle in back, M...**$22.00**
Roy Rogers, neckerchief...**$35.00**
Roy Rogers, notebook, w/portrait cover **$15.00**
Roy Rogers, plate, dinner; w/Trigger, ceramic, M **$38.00**
Roy Rogers, raincoat & hat, vinyl **$425.00**
Roy Rogers, saddle, EX tooled leather **$650.00**
Roy Rogers, single gun & holster set, NM.................**$165.00**
Roy Rogers, souvenir book, dated 1950, NM.............**$40.00**
Roy Rogers, toothbrush, in original package **$30.00**
Roy Rogers & Trigger, camera, 4", '620 Snapshot,' Herbert George Co **$45.00**
Roy Rogers & Trigger, post card, from Roy & Dale fan club, 1955, NM **$30.00**

Roy Rogers, rodeo set, plastic figures, jeep, cacti, flag, and corral by Marx, M in box........................$125.00
Sky King, ring, 'Magni-Glow' **$60.00**
Sky King, ring, 'Tele-blinker,' EX.................................**$90.00**
Sky King, ring, Aztec, rare...**$400.00**
Smiley Burnette, photo, 5x7", Alexander Pictures, 1940s, w/original mailing envelope, NM **$45.00**
Smoking Tex, cap pistol, 7½", Hubley, 1960s.............**$25.00**
Sunset Carson, poster, 40x80", 'Red River Renegades,' Republic Studios, EX..**$25.00**
Tom Corbett, binoculars, metal, in original box..........**$95.00**
Tom Mix, ad, Safety Story Radio Show **$45.00**
Tom Mix, badge, Deputy, EX.......................................**$45.00**
Tom Mix, badge, Dobie Country, radio premium **$20.00**
Tom Mix, bandana, promotional giveaway, EX..........**$45.00**
Tom Mix, belt buckle, w/secret compartment.............**$75.00**
Tom Mix, book, 'Tony & His Pals'................................**$75.00**

Tom Mix, bracelet, w/Indian design, ordered from comic book ad **$52.00**

Tom Mix, camera, ordered from comic book ad **$58.00**

Tom Mix, circus program, 'Life of Tom Mix,' 1929......**$50.00**

Tom Mix, coin, 'Lucky Pocket Piece,' rare **$125.00**

Tom Mix, comic book, #8, EX **$50.00**

Tom Mix, cowboy boots, in original box...................**$300.00**

Tom Mix, magnet, horseshoe figural, ordered from comic book ad **$27.50**

Tom Mix, manual, 1933, EX **$48.00**

Tom Mix, manual, 1941, EX **$45.00**

Tom Mix, manual, 1944, w/original mailer **$65.00**

Tom Mix, medal, glows in the dark, w/ribbon............**$85.00**

Tom Mix, patch, by Ralston Purina Co.........................**$65.00**

Tom Mix, photo, framed **$125.00**

Tom Mix, pistol, wood, w/moving chamber, 1939, NM...**$120.00**

Tom Mix, pocketknife, w/Tony **$250.00**

Tom Mix, poster, 17x22", 'Tom Mix Safety Story,' 1950s, NM..**$40.00**

Tom Mix, premium catalog, 5x7", Ralston Purina Co, 1933, 22-pg, EX **$42.00**

Tom Mix, ring, horseshoe nail **$22.00**

Tom Mix, ring, Look Around, in original mailer w/instructions **$125.00**

Tom Mix, ring, tiger eye, EX **$200.00**

Tom Mix, rocket parachute, 1936, in original box **$100.00**

Tom Mix, rocking horse, w/Tony, NM.......................**$250.00**

Tom Mix, rope, used for rodeo, in box, NM.............**$125.00**

Tom Mix, scarf, Ralston Purina Co premium **$125.00**

Tom Mix, telegraph, in original mailer **$75.00**

Tom Mix, walkie talkies, pr..**$125.00**

Tom Mix, watch fob, gold color **$55.00**

Tonto, coloring book, Whitman, 1957, NM.................**$15.00**

Tonto, doll, 18", wood & composition, in original costume, EX, rare..**$400.00**

Virginian, game, Transogram, 1962, in original 2x10x19½" box, EX **$40.00**

Wagon Train, puzzle, Whitman, self-framed tray, shows Major Seth Adams & Flint McCullough on covered wagon, 1960, M...**$15.00**

Wyatt Earp, book, picture story **$10.00**

Wyatt Earp, coloring book, 1950s...............................**$20.00**

Wyatt Earp, gun & holster set, without the box **$45.00**

Wyatt Earp, mug, red graphics on milk glass, M **$22.00**

Wyatt Earp, photo, 8x10", Hugh O'Brien, color............**$7.50**

Wyatt Earp, wallet, vinyl, w/Hugh O'Brien signature, EX **$28.00**

Westmoreland Glass

Before the turn of the century, this company was known as the Specialty Glass Works and was located in East Liverpool, Ohio, where they produced tableware as well as utilitarian items. They moved to Grapeville, Pennsylvania, in 1890 and added many more decorative glassware items to their inventory. Carnival glass was their mainstay before the years of the twenties, but they're most famous today for their milk glass, black glass, and colored glass tableware patterns.

Early pieces carried paper labels, but by the 1960s, the mark was embossed in the glass itself. The superimposed 'WG' mark was the first of the embossed marks; the last was a circle containing 'Westmoreland' around the outside with a large 'W' in the center.

For more information, we recommend *Westmoreland Glass* by Philip J. Rosso, Jr., and Phil Rosso.

See also Animal Dishes, Carnival Glass.

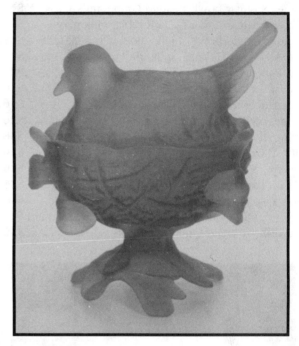

Animal dish, bird on nest, deep mist blue............$70.00

Ashtray, 4" dia, Beaded Grape, milk glass **$12.00**

Ashtray, 4" sq, Beaded Grape, milk glass....................**$15.00**

Basket, 6½", Panelled Grape, milk glass, oval **$25.00**

Bottle, scent; English Hobnail, milk glass, w/stopper.**$35.00**

Bowl, berry; 4½", Panelled Grape, mint green **$15.00**

Bowl, 11", Princess Feather, amber, oval **$35.00**

Bowl, 12", Panelled Grape, milk glass, lipped...........**$100.00**

Bowl, 4¼", English Hobnail, milk glass **$6.00**

Bowl, 6½", Panelled Grape, milk glass, oval................**$22.50**

Bowl, 7" sq, Beaded Grape, milk glass, high foot, square **$35.00**

Bowl, 8", Dolphin, footed shell shape, crystal mist.....**$32.00**

Butter dish, ¼-lb, Old Quilt, milk glass, w/lid **$25.00**

Butter dish, ¼-lb, Panelled Grape, milk glass **$30.00**

Cake salver, Ring & Petal, milk glass, low foot...........**$45.00**

Candlestick, Old Quilt, milk glass, pr.........................**$24.00**

Candlestick, 4", Beaded Grape, milk glass, pr **$22.00**

Candlestick, 4", Dolphin, milk glass **$22.00**

Candlestick, 4", Old Quilt, milk glass, pr **$20.00**

Candle holders, 4", Panelled Grape, milk glass, pr **$24.50**

Candy dish, Panelled Grape, milk glass, basket form .**$22.00**

Candy dish, 5", Beaded Grape, milk glass, footed, square, w/lid **$22.00**

Candy dish, 5", Old Quilt, milk glass, low foot, w/lid. **$18.00**
Champagne, English Hobnail, crystal **$7.00**
Cheese dish, American Hobnail, milk glass **$35.00**
Cheese dish, Panelled Grape, milk glass....................**$48.00**
Chocolate box, Panelled Grape, milk glass, w/lid.......**$45.00**
Cocktail, rooster, milk glass **$10.00**
Compote, 9", Panelled Grape, milk glass **$60.00**
Compote, 7", Panelled Grape, milk glass, w/lid **$35.00**
Cordial, Waterford/Wakefield, ruby stained................**$20.00**
Creamer, Beaded Grape, milk glass.............................**$10.00**
Creamer, 4¼", English Hobnail, milk glass..................**$12.00**
Creamer & sugar bowl, American Hobnail, milk glass..**$20.00**
Creamer & sugar bowl, Beaded Grape, milk glass......**$17.50**
Creamer & sugar bowl, Della Robbia, milk glass **$22.00**
Creamer & sugar bowl, small, Old Quilt, milk glass ...**$25.00**
Cruet, American Hobnail, milk glass **$22.00**
Cruet, Panelled Grape, milk glass................................**$24.00**
Cup & saucer, Beaded Edge, milk glass......................**$10.00**
Cup & saucer, Panelled Grape, milk glass **$16.00**
Figurine, owl, amber mist, rhinestone eyes **$20.00**
Figurine, rooster, milk glass **$38.00**
Goblet, 8-oz, Panelled Grape, milk glass **$16.00**
Jardiniere, 5", Panelled Grape, milk glass, footed........**$25.00**
Jug, 1-qt, Panelled Grape, milk glass..........................**$35.00**
Mayonnaise, 6", English Hobnail, milk glass...............**$10.00**
Nappy, 4", Old Quilt, milk glass, flat **$22.50**
Pickle dish, 10", Old Quilt, milk glass **$30.00**

Puff box, American Hobnail, milk glass, w/lid **$25.00**
Puff box, Panelled Grape, milk glass..........................**$28.00**
Punch cup, Three Fruits, milk glass............................**$10.00**
Punch set, Pineapple & Grape, milk glass, red hooks, w/14
punch cups...**$250.00**
Rose bowl, American Hobnail, milk glass, footed.......**$12.00**
Salt & pepper shakers, Beaded Grape, milk glass, pr.**$25.00**
Salt & pepper shakers, Panelled Grape, milk glass, footed,
pr...**$20.00**
Sherbet, English Hobnail, milk glass...........................**$7.00**
Sugar bowl, small, Panelled Grape, milk glass,
w/lid **$15.00**
Tidbit tray, 10½", Panelled Grape, milk glass **$45.00**
Toothpick holder, swan, milk glass..............................**$15.00**
Tumbler, iced tea; American Hobnail, milk glass,
footed..**$10.00**
Tumbler, 4½", Old Quilt, milk glass **$15.00**
Tumbler, 4¾", English Hobnail, milk glass, footed........**$8.00**
Tumbler, 8-oz, Beaded Edge, hand-painted fruit on milk
glass, footed **$15.00**
Urn, 13", Waterford/Wakefield, ruby stained, w/lid....**$45.00**
Vase, Old Quilt, milk glass, footed fan form...............**$18.00**
Vase, 9", Beaded Grape, milk glass, bell shape,
footed..**$26.00**
Vase, 9", Panelled Grape, milk glass, belled,
footed **$25.00**

Wheaton Bottles

Of interest to bottle collectors and political buffs as well, Wheaton bottles were first produced in the late 1960s. The first canteen-shaped presidential bottle commemorated J.F.K., and it was followed by a complete series, one for each of our country's former leaders. They were designed with a well-detailed relief portrait on one side and a famous quote or slogan on the back. Colors varied; some were iridescent. Production was turned over to the Wheaton Historical Association in 1974, who limited their bottles to about 5,000 each. Then in 1976, the molds went to the Millville Art Glass Company.

Other series were made as well and include: Great Americans, Astronauts, Christmas, Political Campaigns, American Patriots, and American Military Leaders. Most of these are worth under $15.00. In 1984, miniature bottles (3") called Mini-Presidentials were made, one for each president. Some Wheaton bottles have been reproduced by Viking and are so marked. The originals are marked 'Wheaton, NJ, First Edition,' or 'Wheaton Hand-Made, First Edition, Millville, NJ.'

Abraham Lincoln, from $20 up to................................**$25.00**
Andrew Jackson, from $30 up to.................................**$35.00**
Andrew Johnson, from $10 up to **$15.00**
Benjamin Harrison, from $20 up to **$25.00**
Calvin Coolidge, from $20 up to..................................**$25.00**
Chester A Arthur, from $30 up to **$35.00**
Eisenhower, from $15 up to..**$20.00**
FDR (Franklin Delano Roosevelt), from $20 up to......**$25.00**

Pitcher, water; Old Quilt, milk glass......................$30.00
Pitcher, 1-qt, Panelled Grape, milk glass....................**$25.00**
Pitcher, ½-gal, American Hobnail, milk glass...............**$50.00**
Plate, open heart, milk glass, #32 ....**$15.00**
Plate, 10½", Panelled Grape, mint green.....................**$22.00**
Plate, 7½", Beaded Edge, milk glass..........................**$18.00**

Franklin Pierce, from $30 up to **$35.00**
Franklin Pierce, second or corrected version, from $30 up
    to **$35.00**
George Bush, from $10 up to **$12.00**
George Washington, from $12 up to **$15.00**
Gerald R Ford, from $10 up to....................**$15.00**
Grover Cleveland, from $20 up to **$25.00**
Harry S Truman, ruby red, from $30 up to **$35.00**
Herbert Hoover, from $10 up to..................**$15.00**
Ike (General), from $15 up to.......................**$20.00**
James Buchanan, from $10 up to..................**$15.00**
James Garfield, from $30 up to.....................**$35.00**
James K Polk, from $30 up to........................**$35.00**
James Madison, from $30 up to.....................**$35.00**
James Monroe, from $50 up to.......................**$60.00**
Jimmy Carter, from $10 up to **$12.00**
John Adams, from $20 up to...........................**$25.00**
John F Kennedy, light blue, from $75 up to............**$100.00**
John Quincy Adams, from $35 up to............**$40.00**
John Tyler, from $15 up to.............................**$25.00**
John Tyler, second or corrected version, from $20 up
    to...**$25.00**
Lyndon Johnson, from $15 up to..................**$20.00**
Martin Van Buren, from $30 up to...............**$35.00**
Millard Fillmore, from $30 up to..................**$35.00**
Richard Nixon, $15 up to **$20.00**
Ronald Reagan, $10 up to **$15.00**
Rutherford B Hayes, from $35 up to **$40.00**
Rutherford B Hayes, second or corrected version, from $30
    up to **$35.00**
Teddy Roosevelt, royal blue, from $15 up to.............**$20.00**
Thomas Jefferson, from $20 up to **$25.00**
Ulysses S Grant, from $15 up to **$20.00**
Warren G Harding, from $20 up to **$25.00**
William H Harrison, from $10 up to.............**$15.00**
William McKinley, from $30 up to................**$35.00**
Wm Howard Taft, from $20 up to **$25.00**
Woodrow Wilson, from $10 up to **$15.00**
Zachary Taylor, from $30 up to.....................**$35.00**
Zachary Taylor, second or corrected version, from $30 up
    to **$35.00**

Wizard of Oz Collectibles

Inspired by the famous stories written by Frank L. Baum, 'The Wizard of Oz' became an award-winning movie in 1939 featuring Judy Garland and a cast of many well-known stars as supporting actors. The film's Golden Anniversary a few years ago sparked renewed interest, and as a result, more 'Wizard' items became available on the retail market, and some of the originals were reproduced.

Jay Scarfone and William Stillman have written _The Wizard of Oz Collector's Guide_, which we recommend for further study.

Ad, page from 'Collier's' magazine, full color, 1939,
    VG..**$12.50**

**Book, 'Story of the Wizard of Oz,' Whitman, 1939,
M...$35.00**
Coloring book, 'The Story of the Wizard of Oz,' Whitman,
    1939, M..**$35.00**
Comic book, 'Land of Oz,' Marvel Comics, marked 'Special
    Collector Issue,' 1975.............................**$25.00**
Game, 'Off To See the Wizard,' Milton Bradley, 1968, in
    original box, NM................................**$35.00**
Game, 12x15", Lowell, 1962, M......................**$50.00**
Magazine, 'Life,' July 1939........................**$30.00**
Magic kit, 1960s..**$30.00**
Mask, Dorothy, Einson-Freeman, paper, dated 1939...**$30.00**
Paint book, 10½x15", Whitman, #663, 1939, 40-pg **$35.00**
Paint-by-number set, Crafthouse, 1979, in original box .**$42.00**
Record, 33 rpm, MGM movie soundtrack, 1950s, in original
    sleeve, NM...**$50.00**
Sheet music, 'Over the Rainbow,' movie cast on cover, ca
    1939 ....**$18.00**
Soap figure, 4", Dorothy, M.........................**$30.00**
Soap figurine, 4", late 1930s, set of four, M **$75.00**
Tobacco card, 1⅜x2⅝", full-color scene w/five major cast
    members, EX.......................................**$20.00**
Tumbler, 5", 'Wizard of Oz, Wizard' written about top
    edge, white graphics on clear glass, marked 'Copyright
    Baum'...**$12.00**
Valentine, color photo of cast on stiff die-cut cardboard,
    1939-40, M...**$35.00**

World's Fair Collectibles

Souvenir items have been issued since the mid-1800s for every world's fair and exposition. Few fairgoers have left the grounds without purchasing at least one. Some of the older items were often manufactured right on the fairgrounds by glass or pottery companies who erected working kilns and furnaces just for the duration of the fair. Of course the older items are usually more valuable, but even souvenirs from the past fifty years are worth hanging onto.

Philadelphia, 1926

Booklet, 'The Sesqui-Centennial International Exposition,' soft cover, 40 pages, EX $12.50

Key, 2¼" long, metal, head of key in shape of Liberty Bell, marked 'Sesqui-Centennial 1776-1926 Phila PA,' EX $15.00

Medallion, 1¼" dia, brass, bust of Washington, Liberty Bell, etc, man w/torch on winged horse on reverse, EX $12.50

Paperweight, 1½x3x3", heavy metal, 3-D, Liberty Bell shape, EX $25.00

Pencil case, 3x8", leather, Liberty Bell on front, 1926 calendar shows through transparent pocket on side, EX $30.00

Spoon, 6" long, sterling silver, gold washed bowl, Independence Hall on handle, 'Declaration of...,' on reverse, EX..$20.00

Chicago, 1933

Ashtray, 6" dia, rubber tire w/amber glass insert marked 'Firestone, A Century of Progress,' EX...................$50.00

Bank, 3½"x2" dia, American Can Company, tin litho, multiple buildings in color, complete w/closure, EX....$25.00

Key, 4½", copper-coated metal, shows Hall of Science & '1933 Century of Progress,' NM..............................$12.50

Medal, 1¼" dia, brass, comet design, marked 'Good Luck' on reverse, EX...$12.50

Mug, stoneware w/brown glaze, 'Century of Progress' $20.00

Napkin ring, 1½" dia, metal, gold on red, comet logo designs of three fair buildings, EX.......................$15.00

Newspaper, 'Chicago World's Fair Big News,' w/headline 'Million's See Weird Sinclair Dinosaurs,' complete, EX $10.00

Piano scarf, 18x18", salmon-color w/fringe, shows pictures of nine buildings, EX...$48.00

Post card, Ripley's Official Post Card series, 'Paul Desmuke the Armless Wonder...,' EX......................................$15.00

Teapot, 1¼", metal, comet logo on medallion attached w/chain, EX...$18.50

Ticket, 2¼x4", 'Polish Week of Hospitality Spectacle,' EX $8.00

New York, 1939

Booklet, 'The Story of Lucky Strike,' by Roy Flannagan, 7¾x5", '1939 World's Fair' & logo on cover, 94 pages, EX...$12.00

Cane, 36", decal on black & brown wood w/rubber tip, EX..$65.00

Coaster, 4½" dia, design of Ballantine Inn, limerick & space for address & stamp on reverse, EX.......................$10.00

Folder, 'Ten Commandments of the Portuguese New State,' EX $2.50

Luggage tag, large, shows Trilon & Perisphere, VG $7.50

Magazine, 'Life,' August 7, New York World's Fair Special issue w/color pages & fair ads, EX.......................$37.50

Official Guide Book, 5x8", Exposition Publications Inc, 2nd edition, 256 pages, VG $30.00

Official Guide Book, 5x8", 1st edition, well illustrated & very detailed, 256 pages, EX $20.00

Polaroid lenses for viewing 3-D movie 'In Tune with Tomorrow,' die-cut car w/lenses for headlights, cardboard, NM $18.00

Post card, 3½x5½", 'Tower of Light' w/Reddy Kilowatt, M.$10.00

Radio, RCA, #40X56, table model, Trylon & Perisphere pressed into front wood, right dial, handle, two knobs, AC, 1939 ....$900.00

Salt & pepper shakers, pot metal Trylon & Perisphere, silvered finish, pr $15.00

Thermometer, Perisphere & Trylon figurals on 2¼x3¾" Bakelite base, EX...$35.00

San Francisco, 1939

Booklet, 'Treasure Island & the World's Greatest Spans of

Steel,' 32 pages, w/original envelope, NM............**$40.00**
Booklet, 9x12", 'Magic in the Night,' 20 pages, in original envelope, M..**$80.00**
Compact, 2¾" sq, Exposition Tower & Gateway in blue enamel border, in original box, M........................**$78.00**
Post card, 3¼x5", 'Bridge of Tomorrow,' M **$8.50**
Radio, RCA, #40X57, table model, Golden Gate bridge pressed in wood front, right dial, left grill, handle, AC, 1939 ....**$750.00**

Seattle, 1962

Cup & saucer, average size, saucer shows bird's-eye view of the fair in color, cup has fair logo in black, VG ...**$10.50**
Dish, 11" dia, white china, fairgrounds & space needle in center, marked 'Century 21 Seattle World's Fair 1962,' EX...**$20.00**
Dish, 4" dia, white china w/gold trim, space needle pictured in gold, EX.......................................**$7.50**
Lapel pin, less than 1" in size, 'Century 21 Exposition' in silver on blue enameled background, EX.................**$10.00**
Pin-back button, 2" dia, black on orange, design of Space Needle & Monorail, marked 'Seattle Center I Was There,' EX..**$7.50**
Tumbler, 6½x2¾" dia, frosted glass, United States Science Pavilion in blue w/information about pavilion, EX **$15.00**

New York, 1964

Booklet, 'Four Roses Trip Planner' **$3.00**
Coaster, chrome plated w/Unisphere on orange background **$3.50**

Paperweight, 2x3½", silverplated metal, shows Unisphere & New York City skyline, EX......................**$4.50**
Snowdome, Unisphere in clear plastic dome on 3x2" base, M **$25.00**
Tray, 3¾x4¾", black glass, shows Unisphere & New York City skyline in color................................**$4.50**

Knoxville, 1982

Pocket watch, official, w/fair logo, made by Wagner Time Inc, M in original box.................................**$30.00**

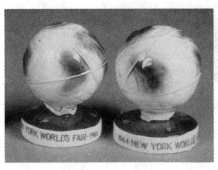

Salt & pepper shakers, globes on disk bases, blue & white plastic, pr.................................$8.00
Tumbler, 5½", 'Knoxville World's Fair' on clear glass, dated 1982, distributed by McDonald's.....................**$7.50**
Tumbler, 5½", shows family at fair w/'The 1982 World's Fair' & 'Energy Turns the World' on clear glass.............**$6.50**

Auction Houses

Many of the auction galleries we've listed here have appraisal services. Some, though not all, are free of charge. We suggest you contact them first by phone to discuss fees and requirements.

A-1 Auction Service
P.O. Box 540672, Orlando, FL 32854; 407-841-6681. Specializing in American antique sales

Alderfer Auction Company
501 Fairground Rd., Hatfield, PA 19440; 215-368-5477 or FAX: 215-368-9055

America West Archives
Warren Anderson
P.O. Box 100, Cedar City, UT 84721; 801-586-9497; quarterly 26-page illustrated catalog includes auction section of scarce and historical early western documents, letters, autographs, stock certificates, and other important ephemera. Subscription: $10 per year

Andre Ammelounx
The Stein Company
P.O. Box 136, Palatine, IL 60078; 708-991-5927 or FAX: 708-991-5947. Specializing in steins, catalogs available

Anthony J. Nard & Co.
US Rt. 220, Milan, PA 18831; 717-888-9404 or FAX: 717-888-7723

Arman Absentee Auctions
P.O. Box 174, Woodstock, CT 06281; 203-928-5838. Specializing in American glass, Historical Staffordshire, English soft paste, paperweights

Autographs of America
Tim Anderson
P.O. Box 461, Provo, UT 84603. Free sample catalog of hundreds of autographs for sale

Barrett Bertoia Auctions & Appraisals
1217 Glenwood Dr., Vineland, NJ 18630; 609-692-4092. Specializing in antique toys and collectibles

Berman's Auction Gallery
33 West Blackwell St., Dover, NJ 07081; 201-361-3110

Bider's
241 S. Union St., Lawrence, MA 01843; 508-688-4347 or 508-683-3944. Antiques appraised, purchased, and sold on consignment

Bob Koty Professional Auctioneers
Koty, Bob & Clara
P.O. Box 625, Freehold, NJ 07728; 908-780-1265

Brian Riba Auctions, Inc.
P.O. Box 53, Main St., S. Glastonbury, CT 06073; 203-633-3076

Butterfield & Butterfield
7601 Sunset Blvd., Los Angeles, CA 90046; 213-850-7500

Butterfield & Butterfield
220 San Bruno Ave., San Francisco, CA 94103; 415-861-7500

C.E. Guarino
Box 49, Denmark, ME 04022

Castner Auction & Appraisal Service
Leon Castner, President
6 Wantage Ave., Branchville, NJ 07826; 201-948-3868

Charles E. Kirtley
P.O. Box 2273, Elizabeth City, NC 27096; 919-335-1262. Specializing in World's Fair, Civil War, political, advertising, and other American collectibles

Chase Gilmore Art Galleries
724 W. Washington, Chicago, IL 60606; 312-648-1690

Christie's
502 Park Ave., New York, NY 10022; 212-546-1000

Cincinnati Art Gallery
635 Main St., Cincinnati, OH 45202; 513-381-2128. Specializing in American art pottery, American and European fine paintings, watercolors

Col. Doug Allard
P.O. Box 460, St. Ignatius, MT 59865

Collectors Auction Services
326 Seneca St., Oil City, PA 16301; 814-677-6070. Specializing in advertising, oil and gas, toys, rare museum and investment-quality antiques

David Rago
P.O. Box 3592, Station E, Trenton, NJ 08629; 609-397-9374. Gallery: 17 S. Main St., Lambertville, NJ 08530. Specializing in American art pottery and Arts & Crafts

Don Treadway Gallery
2128 Madison Rd., Cincinnati, OH 45208; 513-321-6742 or FAX: 513-871-7722. Member: National Antique Dealers Association, American Art Pottery Association, International Society of Appraisers, and American Ceramic Arts Society

Douglas Auctioneers
Douglas B. Bilodeau
R.R. 5, S. Deerfield, MA 01373; 413-665-3530 or FAX: 413-665-2877. Year-round sales, specializing in antiques, estates, fine art, appraising

Doyle, Auctioneers & Appraisers
R.D. 3, Box 137, Osborne Hill Road, Fishkill, NY 12524; 914-896-9492. Thousands of collectibles offered: call for free calendar of upcoming events

Duane Merrill
32 Beacon St., S. Burlington, VT 05403; 802-878-2625

Du Mouchelles
409 E. Jefferson Ave., Detroit, MI 48226; 313-963-6255 or FAX: 313-963-8199

Dunning's Auction Service, Inc.
755 Church Rd., Elgin, IL 60123; 312-741-3483 or FAX: 708-741-3589

Dynamite Auctions
Franklin Antique Mall & Auction Gallery, 1280 Franklin Ave., Franklin, PA 16323; 814-432-8577 or 814-786-9211

Early Auction Co.
123 Main St., Milford, OH 45150

F.B. Hubley & Co., Inc.
364 Broadway, Cambridge, MA 02139; 617-876-2030

Fredericktowne Auction Gallery
Thom Pattie
5305 Jefferson Pike, Frederick, MD 21701; 301-473-5566 or 800-962-1305

Freeman/Fine Arts of Philadelphia
Leslie Lynch, ASA
1808-10 Chestnut St., Philadelphia, PA 19103; 215-563-9275 or FAX: 215-563-8236

Garth's Auctions, Inc.
2690 Stratford Rd., Box 369, Delaware, OH 43015; 614-362-4771

Glass-Works Auctions
James Hagenbuch
102 Jefferson, East Greenville, PA 18041; 215-679-5849. America's leading auction company in early American bottles and glass

Greenberg Auctions
7566 Main St., Sykesville, MD 21784. Specializing in trains: Lionel, American Flyer, Ives, Marx, HO

Guernsey's
136 E. 73rd St., New York, NY 10021; 212-794-2280. Specializing in carousel figures

Gunther's International Auction Gallery
P.O. Box 235, 24 S. Virginia Ave., Brunswick, MD 21716; 301-834-7101 or 800-274-8779. Specializing in political, Oriental rugs, art, bronzes, antiques, the unusual

Gustave White Auctioneers
P.O. Box 59, Newport, RI 02840; 401-847-4250

Hake's Americana & Collectibles
Specializing in character and personality collectibles along with all artifacts of popular culture for over 20 years. To receive a catalog for their next 3,000-item mail/phone bid auction, send $5 to Hake's Americana, P.O. Box 1444M, York, PA 17405

Hanzel Galleries, Inc.
1120 S. Michigan Ave., Chicago, IL 60605; 312-922-6234

Harmer Rooke Galleries
3 East 57th St., New York, NY 10022; 212-751-1900 or FAX: 212-758-1713

Harris Auction Galleries
8783-875 N. Howard St., Baltimore, MD 21201; 301-728-7040

Iroquois Auction Gallery
Box 66, Port Henry, NY 12974; 518-546-7003

Jack Sellner
Sellner Marketing of California
P.O. Box 308, Fremont, CA 94536; 415-745-9463

James D. Julia
P.O. Box 210, Showhegan Rd., Fairfield, ME 04937

James R. Bakker
Antiques, Inc.
370 Broadway, Cambridge, MA 02139; 617-864-7067. Specializing in American paintings, prints, and decorative arts

Jim Depew Galleries
1860 Piedmont Rd., N.E., Atlanta, GA 30324; 404-874-2286

L.R. 'Les' Docks
Box 691035, San Antonio, TX 78269-1035. Providing occasional mail-order record auctions, rarely consigned; the only consignments considered are exceptionally scarce and unusual records

Leslie Hindman Auctions
215 W. Ohio St., Chicago, IL 60610; 312-670-0010 or FAX: 312-670-4248

Litchfield Auction Gallery
Clarence W. Pico
425 Bantam Rd., P.O. Box 1337, Litchfield, CT 06759; 203-567-3126 or FAX: 203-567-3266

Lloyd Ralston Toys
447 Stratford Rd., Fairfield, CT 06432
Lubin Galleries, Inc. Irwin Lubin 30 W. 26th St., New York, NY 10010; 212-924-3777 or FAX: 212-366-9190

Manion's International Auction House, Inc.
P.O. Box 12214, Kansas City, KS 66112

Mapes Auctioneers & Appraisers
David W. Mapes
1600 Vestal Parkway West, Vestal, NY 13850; 607-754-9193
or FAX: 607-786-3549

Maritime Auctions
R.R. 2, Box 45A, York, ME 03909; 207-363-4247

Marvin Cohen Auctions
Box 425, Routes 20 & 22, New Lebanon, NY 12125; 518-794-7477

Mid-Hudson Auction Galleries
One Idlewild Ave., Cornwall-on-Hudson, NY 12520; 914-534-7828 or FAX: 914-534-4802

Milwaukee Auction Galleries, Ltd.
4747 W. Bradley Rd., Milwaukee, WI 53223; 414-355-5054

Morton M. Goldberg Auction Galleries, Inc.
547 Baronne St., New Orleans, LA 70113; 504-592-2300 or
FAX: 504-592-2311

Noel Barrett Antiques & Auctions
P.O. Box 1001, Carversville, PA 18913; 215-297-5109

Northeast Auctions Ronald Bourgeault
694 Lafayette Rd., Hampton, NH 03842; 603-926-9800 or
FAX: 603-926-3545

Nostalgia Co.
21 S. Lake Dr., Hackensack, NJ 07601; 201-488-4536

Nostalgia Galleries
657 Meacham Ave., Elmont, NY 11003; 516-326-9595. Auctioning items from almost every area of the collectibles field, catalogs available

Parker's Knife Collector Service
P.O. Box 23522, 5950 'C' Shallowford Rd., Chattanooga, TN 37422; 615-892-0448 or 800-247-0599. FAX: 615-892-4165

Paul McInnis
356 Exeter Rd., Hampton Falls, NH 03844; 603-778-8989

Pennypacker Auction Center
1540 New Holland Rd., Reading, PA 19807

Phillips Fine Art & Auctioneers
406 E. 79th St., New York, NY 10021

Rex Stark Auctions
49 Wethersfield Rd., Bellingham, MA 02019

Richard A. Bourne Co., Inc.
Estate Auctioneers & Appraisers
Box 141, Hyannis Port, MA 02647; 617-775-0797

Richard Opfer Auctioneering, Inc.
1919 Greenspring Dr., Timonium, MD 21093; 301-252-5035

Richard W. Oliver, Inc.
Plaza One, Rt. 1, Kennebunk, ME 04043; 207-985-3600 or
FAX: 207-985-7734. Outside Maine: 800-992-0047

Richard W. Withington, Inc.
R.D. 2, Box 440, Hillsboro, NH 03244; 603-464-3232

Roan, Inc.
Box 118, R.D. 3, Cogan Station, PA 17728

Robert W. Skinner, Inc.
Auctioneers & Appraisers
Rt. 117, Bolton, MA 01740; 617-779-5528

Sanders & Mock Associates, Inc.
Mark Hanson
P.O. Box 37, Tamworth, NH 03886; 603-323-8749 or 603-323-8784

Sloan's
Ben Hastings
4920 Wyaconda Rd., Rockville, MD 20852; 301-468-4911

Smith House
P.O. Box 336, Eliot, ME, 03903; 207-439-4614 or FAX: 207-439-8554. Specializing in toys

Sotheby Parke Bernet, Inc.
980 Madison Ave., New York, NY 10021

Sotheby's Arcade Auction
1334 York Ave. at 72nd St., New York, NY 10021; 212-606-7409

South Bay Auctions, Inc.
485 Montauk Highway E. Moriches, NY 11940; 516-878-2909
or FAX: 516-878-1863

TSACO (The Stein Auction Company) East
Ron Fox
416 Throop St., N. Babylon, NY 11704. Telephone and FAX:
516-669-7232

Weschler's
Adam A. Weschler & Son
905 E. St. N.W., Washington, DC 20004

Willis Henry Auctions
22 Main St., Marshfield, MA 02050

Winter Associates, Inc.
Regina Madigan
P.O. Box 823, Plainville, CT 06062; 207-793-0288 or 800-962-2530

Wolf's Auctioneers
1239 W. 6th St., Cleveland, OH 44113; 216-575-9653 or 800-526-1991 FAX: 216-621-8011

Woody Auction Company
P.O. Box 618, Douglass, KS 67039; 316-746-2694

Newsletters, Catalogs, Magazines, and Other Publications

There are hundreds of newsletters available to collectors today, some are generalized and cover the entire realm of antiques and collectibles, while others are devoted to a specific interest such as toys, coin-operated machines, character collectibles, or railroadiana. Most of those we've listed will be happy to send you a sample copy. See the introduction for suggestions on how to compose an ad or carry on a successful mail bid.

AAA Newsletter
Antique Advertising Association
P.O. Box 1121, Morton Grove, IL 60053; 708-446-0904

AB Bookman's Weekly
P.O. Box AB, Clifton, NJ 07015; 201-772-0020 or FAX: 201-772-9281. $80 per year bulk mail U.S. ($75 per year Canada or Foreign). $125 per year 1st class mail (U.S., Canada, and Mexico). Foreign Air Mail: Inquire. Sample copies: $10. AB Bookman's Yearbook: $20. All advertising and subscriptions subject to acceptance

Abingdon Pottery Collectors Newsletter
Abingdon Pottery Club
Penny Vaughan, President
212 S. Fourth, Monmouth, IL 61462; 309-734-2337

Action Toys Newsletter
P.O. Box 31551, Billings, MT 59107; 406-248-4121

The Akro Agate Gem
Akro Agate Art Association
Joseph Bourque
P.O. Box 758, Salem, NH 03079

The Aluminist
Aluminum Collectors
Dannie Woodard
P.O. Box 1347, Weatherford, TX 76086; 817-594-4680

America West Archives
Warren Anderson
P.O. Box 100, Cedar City, UT 84721. 26-page illustrated catalogs issued quarterly. Has both fixed-price and auction sections offering early Western documents, letters, stock certificates, autographs, and other important ephemera. Subscription: $10 per year

American Barb Wire Collectors Society
John Mantz
1023 Baldwin Rd., Bakersfield, CA 93304; 805-397-9572

American Carnival Glass News
Dennis Runk, Secretary
P.O. Box 235, Littlestown, PA 17340; 717-359-7205

American Ceramic Circle Journal & Newsletter
American Ceramic Circle
Grand Central Station, P.O. Box 1495, New York, NY 10163

American Quilter magazine
American Quilter's Society
P.O. Box 3290, Paducah, KY 42002-3290. $15 annual membership includes 4 issues.

American Lock Collectors Association Newsletter
Charles Chandler
36076 Grennada, Livonia, MI 48154; 313-522-0920

The American STAR
American Scouting Traders Assoc., Inc.
Dave Minnihan, President
P.O. Box 92, Kentfield, CA 94914-0092; 415-665-2871

American Willow Report
Lisa Kay Henze, Editor
P.O. Box 900, Oakridge, OR 97463. Bimonthly newsletter, subscription: $15 per year, out of country add $5 per year

Antique & Collectible News
P.O. Box 529, Anna, IL 62906. Monthly newspaper for auctions, antique shows, collectibles and flea markets for the Midwest U.S. Subscription: $12 per year

Antique Gazette
6949 Charlotte Pk., #106, Nashville, TN 37209. Monthly publication covering the antique and collectibles market. Subscription: $16.95 per year

Antique Monthly magazine
Stephen C. Croft, Publisher
2100 Powers Ferry Rd., Atlanta, GA 30339; 404-955-5656 or FAX: 404-952-0669. Subscription: $19.95 per year (11 issues)

Antique Press of Florida
12403 N. Florida Ave., Tampa, FL 33612. Subscription: $12 (6 issues) per year

Antique Souvenir Collectors' News
Gary Leveille, Editor
P.O. Box 562, Great Barrington, MA 01230

The Antique Trader Weekly
P.O. Box 1050 CB, Dubuque, IA 52004. Subscription: $28 (52 issues) per year; sample: 50¢

Antique Week
P.O. Box 90, Knightstown, IN 46148. Weekly newspaper for auctions, antique shows, antiques, collectibles and flea markets. Eastern States' publication (states of ME, VT, NH, RI, MA, ME, NC, SC, WA, VA, etc.) is $20.95 for 51 weekly issues (no paper during Christmas week). Central States' publication (states of MI, WI, OH, PA, WV, KY, TN, OH, MO, IA, MN) is $24.95 for 51 weekly issues (no paper during Christmas week). Mastercard, VISA, or billing is accepted. These are rates for the year, but subscriptions of 3 months to 3 years are available. A free sample copy may be requested. Included in the subscription is an antique shop guide that is issued once a year giving reference for shops to be found in Eastern or Central states. If the guide is not wanted, you may deduct $1 from the yearly subscription.

Antiques & Collecting Hobbies
1006 S. Michigan Ave., Chicago, IL 60605. Monthly magazine with a wide variety of information and an extensive classified section. Subscription: $24 per year; sample: $2.95 (refundable with subscription order)

Antiques Americana
K.C. Owings, Jr.
P.O. Box 19, N. Abington, MA 02351; 617-857-1655. Specializing in paper collectibles

Appraisers Information Exchange
International Society of Appraisers
P.O. Box 726, Hoffman Estates, IL 60195; 708-882-0706

Art Deco Reflections
Chase Collectors Society
Barry L. Van Hook, Director
2149 W. Jibsail Loop, Mesa, AZ 85202; 5524; 602-838-6971

Arts & Crafts Quarterly
P.O. Box 3592, Station E Trenton, NJ 08629; 1-800-541-5787

Auction Block newspaper
P.O. Box 337, Iola, WI 54945; 715-445-5000. Subscription: $8 per year

Auction Opportunities, Inc.
Doyle Auctioneers & Appraisers
109 Osborne Hill Rd., Fishkill, NY 12524; 800-551-5161. Subscription: $25 per year

The Autograph Review, bimonthly newsletter
Jeffrey Morey
305 Carlton Rd., Syracuse, NY 13207; 315-474-3516

Automobile License Plate Collectors Newsletter
Gary Brent
Kincade P.O. Box 712, Weston, WV 26452; 304-842-3773

Avon Times newsletter
c/o Dwight or Vera Young
P.O. Box 9868, Dept. P., Kansas City, MO 64134. Inquires should be accompanied by LSASE

Barbie Talks Some More!
Jacqueline Horning
7501 School Rd., Cincinnati, OH 45249

The Baum Bugle
The International Wizard of Oz Club
Fred M. Meyer
220 N. 11th St., Escanaba, MI 49829

Beam Around the World
International Association of Jim Beam Bottle & Specialties Club
Shirley Sumbles, Secretary
5013 Chase Ave., Downers Grove, IL 60515; 708-963-8980

Beer Can Collectors News
Beer Can Collectors of America
Don Hicks, President
747 Merus Court, Fenton, MO 63026; 314-343-6486 or FAX: 314-343-6486

The Bell Tower
American Bell Association
Charles Blake
P.O. Box 172, Shoreham, VT 05770

Berry-Bits
Strawberry Shortcake Collectors' Club
Peggy Jimenez
1409 72nd St., N. Bergen, NJ 07047

Beyond the Rainbow Collector's Exchange
P.O. Box 31672, St. Louis, MO 63131

Big Little Times
Big Little Book Collectors Club of America, Larry Lowery
P.O. Box 1242, Danville, CA 94526; 415-837-2086

Blue & White Pottery Club Newsletter
224 12th St. NW, Cedar Rapids, IA 52405; 319-362-8116

Bookmark Collector
Joan L. Huegel
1002 W. 25th St., Erie, PA 16502. Quarterly newsletter: $5.50 per year ($6.50 in Canada); sample copy: $1 plus stamp or LSASE

Books Are Everything
302 Martin Dr., Richmond, KY 40475. Subscription: $25 (4 issues) per year in U.S.; $7.50 for sample

Bossons Briefs
International Bossons Collectors
Dr. Robert E. Davis, Executive Director
21 John Maddox Dr., Rome, GA 30161; 404-232-1266

Bridal Collector's Roster
Ann C. Bergin
P.O. Box 105, Amherst, NH 03031; 603-673-1885

Bulletin
Doll Collectors of America
14 Chestnut Rd., Westford, MA 01886; 617-692-8392

Bulletin of the NAWCC
National Assoc. of Watch & Clock Collectors, Inc.
Thomas J. Bartels, Executive Director
514 Poplar St., Columbia, PA 17512-2130; 717-684-8621 or
FAX: 717-684-0878

Butter Pat Collectors' Notebook
c/o 5955 S.W. 179th Ave., Beaverton, OR 97007. LSASE
required for information

The Cambridge Crystal Ball
National Cambridge Collectors, Inc.
P.O. Box 416, Cambridge, OH 43725-0416. Dues: $15 for
individual member and $3 for associate member of same
household

The Candlewick Collector Newsletter
Virginia R. Scott
275 Milledge Terrace, Athens, GA 30306; 404-548-5966

The Candy Gram
Candy Container Collectors of America
Douglas Dezso
864 Paterson, Ave., Maywood, NJ 07607; 201-845-7707

The Cane Collector's Chronicle
Linda Beeman
15 2nd St. N.E., Washington, D.C. 20002; $30 (4 issues) per
year

Captain's Log magazine
World Airline Historical Society
Paul F. Collins, President
3381 Apple Tree Lane, Erlanger, KY 41018; 606-342-9039

Cast Iron Seat Collectors Association Newsletter
RFD #2, Box 40, Le Center, MN 56057; 612-357-6142

Cat Collectors Club
33161 Wendy Dr., Sterling Heights, MI 48310. Subscription:
$18 per year (includes bimonthly newsletter & catalogs);
sample package: $4

Cat Talk
Marilyn Dipboye
31311 Blair Dr., Warren, MI 48092; 313-264-0285

Century Limited
Toy Train Collectors Society
160 Dexter Terrace, Tonawanda, NY 14150; 716-694-3771

Chicagoland Antique Advertizing
Slot Machine & Jukebox Gazette
Ken Durham, Editor
P.O. Box 2426, Rockville, MD 20852. 20-page newsletter
published twice a year. Subscription: 4 issues for $10; sam-
ple: $5

Classic Amusements
Wordmarque Design Associates
12644 Chapel Rd., Suite 204, Box 315, Clifton, VA 22024.
Subscription: $36 (6 issues) per year in USA; $42 in Canada

Clear the Decks
52 Plus Joker
Bill Coomer, Secretary
1024 S. Benton, Cape Girardeau, MO 63701. For collectors
of playing cards, unusual and antique decks

Coca-Cola Collectors News
Coca-Cola Collectors Club International
P.O. Box 546, Hamdel, NJ 07733

Coin Machine Trader
Ted & Betty Salveson
569 Kansas S.E., P.O. Box 602, Huron, SD 57350; 605-352-
3870

Coin-Op Newsletter
Ken Durham, Publisher
909 26th St., N.W., Washington, DC 20037. Subscription (10
issues): $24; sample: $5

The Collector
Box 158, Heyworth, IL 61745; 309-473-2466. Newspaper
published monthly

Collectors' Classified
William Margolin
P.O. Box 347, Hollbrook, MA 02343-0347; 617-961-1463.
Covers collectibles in general; 4 issues: $1

Collector's Digest
P.O. Box 23, Banning, CA 92220; 714-849-1064. Subscription: $11 (6 issues) per year

Collector's Mart magazine
P.O. Box 12830, Wichita, KS 67277. Subscription: $23.95 per
year; add $15 in Canada

Cookbook Gossip
Cookbook Collectors Club of America, Inc.
Bob & Jo Ellen Allen
231 E. James Blvd., P.O. Box 85, St. James, MO 65559; 314-
265-8296

Cookie Crumbs
Cookie Cutter Collectors Club
Ruth Capper
1167 Teal Rd. S.W., Dellroy, OH 44620; 216-735-2839 or
202-966-0869

Cookie Jarrin' with Joyce: The Cookie Jar Newsletter
R.R.2, Box 504, Walterboro, SC 29488

The Co-Op Connections
Sagebrush Treasures
963 Williams, Fallon, NV 89406. Subscription $15 per year
for 12 issues

Coors Pottery Newsletter
Robert Schneider
3808 Carr Pl. N., Seattle, WA 98103-8126

Costume Society of America Newsletter
55 Edgewater Dr., P.O. Box 73, Earleville, MD 21919; 301-
275-2329 or FAX: 301-275-8936

The Cutting Edge
Glass Knife Collectors' Club
Adrienne S. Escoe, Editor
P.O. Box 342, Los Alamitos, CA 90720. Subscription: $3 (4
issues) per year; sample: 50¢

Decoy Magazine
Joe Engers
P.O. Box 277, Burtonsville, MD 20866; 301-890-0262

Depression Glass Daze
Teri Steel, Editor/Publisher
Box 57, Otisville, MI 48463; 313-631-4593. The nation's mar-
ketplace for glass, china, and pottery

Dept. 56 Collectors: *The Village Press*
Roger & Khristine Bain, Publishers
1625 Myott Ave., Rockford, IL 61103. Subscription: $20 (8
issues) per year; free sample copy

DISCoveries Magazine
Mark Phillips, Associate Editor
P.O. Box 255, Port Townsend, WA 98368-0255. Specializing
in collectible records, international distribution

Doll Investment Newsletter
P.O. Box 1982, Centerville, MA 02632

Doll News
United Federation of Doll Clubs
P.O. Box 14146, Parkville, MO 64152

Ephemera News
The Ephemera Society of America, Inc.
P.O. Box 37, Schoharie, NY 12157; 518-295-7978

The Ertl Replica
Ertl Collectors Club
Mike Meyer, Editor
Highways 136 & 20, Dyersville, IA 52040; 319-875-2000

Fair News
World's Fair Collectors' Society, Inc.
Michael R. Pender, Editor
P.O. Box 20806, Sarasota, FL 34238. Dues: $12 (12 issues)
per year in U.S.A.; $13 in Canada; $20 for overseas members

The Federation Glass Works
Federation of Historical Bottle Clubs
Barbara A. Harms
14521 Atlantic, Riverdale, IL 60627; 312-841-4068

The Fenton Flyer
National Fenton Glass Society
P.O. Box 4008, Marietta, OH 45750

Fiesta Collector's Quarterly
China Specialties, Inc.
19238 Dorchester Circle, Strongsville, OH 44136. $12 (4
issues) per year

Fire Collectors Club Newsletter
David Cerull
P.O. Box 992, Milwaukee, WI 53201

FLAKE, The Breakfast Nostalgia Magazine
P.O. Box 481, Cambridge, MA 02140; 617-492-5004.
Bimonthly illustrated issue devoted to one hot collecting
area such as Disney, etc., with letters, discoveries, new
releases, and ads; single issue: $4 ($6 foreign); annual: $20
($28 foreign); free 25-word ad with new subscription

Flag Bulletin
Flag Research Center
P.O. Box 580, Winchester, MA 01890; 617-729-9410

Flashlight Collectors of America Newsletter
Bill Utley
P.O. Box 3572, Downey, CA 90242. $12 (4 issues) per year

Flea Marketeer
P.O. Box 686, Southfield, MI 48037; 313-351-9910 or FAX:
313-351-9037

Folk Art Messenger
P.O. Box 17041 Richmond, VA 23226

Fox Hunt Newsletter
R. Atkinson Fox Society
Sherri Fountain
1511 W. 4th Ave., Hutchinson, KS 67501; 316-663-4293

The Front Striker Bulletin
Bill Retskin
3417 Clayborne Ave., Alexandria, VA 22306-1410. Quarterly
newsletter for match cover collectors. $15 per year for 1st
class mailing

Game Times
American Game Collectors Association
Joe Angiolillo, President
4628 Barlow Dr., Bartlesville, OK 74006

George Kamm Paperweights
24 Townsend Court, Lancaster, PA 17603. Specializing in paperweights; color brochure published 4 to 5 times a year. $5 (1-time charge)

Ginny Doll Club News
Jeanne Niswonger
305 W. Beacon Rd., Lakeland, FL 33803; 813-687-8015

Glass Chatter
Midwest Antique Fruit Jar & Bottle Club
P.O. Box 38, Flat Rock, IN 47234

Glass Collector's Digest
P.O. Box 553, Marietta, OH 45750-9979; 800-533-3433. Subscription: $19 (6 issues) per year; Add $5 for Canada and Foreign

Glass Shards
The National Early American Glass Club
P.O. Box 8489, Silver Spring, MD 20907

Gonder Pottery Collectors' Newsletter
c/o John & Marilyn McCormick
P.O. Box 3174, Shawnee KS 66203

Gone with the Wind Collectors Club Newsletter
8105 Woodview Rd., Ellicot City, MD 21043; 301-465-4632

Headhunters Newsletter for head vase collectors
Maddy Gordon
P.O. Box 83H, Scarsdale, NY 10583; 914-472-0200. Subscription: $16 (4 issues) per year

The Heisey News
Heisey Collectors of America
169 W. Church St., Newark, OH 43055; 612-345-2932

Hobby News bimonthly newsletter
J.L.C. Publications
Box 258, Ozone Park, NY 11416

Hopalong Cassidy Newsletter
Hopalong Cassidy Fan Club
P.O. Box 1361, Boyes Hot Springs, CA 95416

Ice Screamer
c/o Ed Marks, Publisher
P.O. Box 5387, Lancaster, PA 17601. Published bimonthly, dues: $15 per year

Inside Antiques Monthly Newsletter
Antique & Collectible News Service
Robert Reed, Editor
P.O. Box 204, Knightstown, IN 46148; 317-345-7479

International Brick Collectors Association Journal
International Brick Collectors Association
8357 Somerset Dr., Prairie Village, KS 66207; 913-341-8842

The International Carnival Glass Association
LeRoy Mackley, Secretary
R.R. 1, Mentone, IN 46539 or R.R. 1, Wawaka, IN 46794. Publishes quarterly bulletin. $10 per family

International Pin Collectors Club Newsletter
P.O. Box 430, Marcy, NY 13403; 315-736-5651 or 315-736-4019

International Society of Antique Scale Collectors
Bob Stein, President
111 N. Canal St., Suite 380, Chicago, IL 60606. Publishes quarterly magazine

Just for Openers Newsletter
John Stanley
605 Windsong Lane, Durham, NC 27713. Quarterly newsletter covers all types of bottle openers and corkscrews

Lucy Collector's Gazette
Lucy Collector's Club
Jane Elliot, President
P.O. Box 851057, Mesquite, TX 75185-1057

Madame Alexander Fan Club Newsletter
Earl Meisinger
11 S. 767 Book Rd., Naperville, IL 60564

Maine Antique Digest monthly newspaper
Sam & Sally Pennington
P.O. Box 645, Waldoboro, ME 04572; 207-832-7534

Majolica International Society Newsletter
Michael G. Strawser, President
Suite 103, 1275 First Ave., New York, NY 10021

Marble Mania
Marble Collectors Society of America
Stanley Block
P.O. Box 222, Trumbull, CT 06611; 203-261-3223

Martha's Kidlit Newsletter
Box 1488A, Ames, IA 50010. A bimonthly publication for children's books collectors. Subscription: $25 per year

Matchbox U.S.A.
Charles Mack
62 Saw Mill Rd., Durham, CT 06422; 203-349-1655

McDonald's Collecting Tips
Meredith Williams
Box 633, Joplin, MO 64802. Send SASE for information

Medical Collectors Association Newsletter
Dr. M. Donald Blaufox, MD
1300 Morris Park Ave., Bronx, NY 10461

The Milk Route
National Association of Milk Bottle Collectors, Inc.
Thomas Gallagher
4 Ox Bow Rd., Westport CT 06880-2602; 203-277-5244

Mini Thistle
Pairpoint Cup Plate Collectors of America
Box 52, E. Weymouth, MA 02189

The Miniature Bottle Collector
Briscoe Publications
P.O. Box 2161, Palos Verdes Peninsula, CA 90274

Modern Doll Club Journal
Jeanne Niswonger
305 W. Beacon Rd., Lakeland, FL 33803

Morgantown Newscaster
Morgantown Collectors of America
Jerry Gallagher & Randy Supplee
420 1st Ave. N.W., Plainview, MN 55964. Subscription: $15 per year. SASE required for answers to queries

The Mouse Club East (Disney collectors)
P.O. Box 3195, Wakefield, MA 01880. Family membership: $25 (includes newsletters and 2 shows per year)

Movie Advertising Collector magazine
George Reed
P.O. Box 28587, Philadelphia, PA 19149

Mystic Lights of the Aladdin Knights
J.W. Courter
R.R. 1, Box 256, Simpson, IL 62985. Subscription: $20 (6 issues, postpaid 1st class) per year with current buy-sell-trade information

NAPAC Newsletter
National Association of Paper & Advertising Collectors
P.O. Box 500, Mount Joy, PA 17552; 717-653-9797

National Blue Ridge Newsletter
Norma Lilly
144 Highland Dr., Blountsville, TN 37617. Subscription: $12 (6 issues) per year

National Book Collector
National Book Collectors Society
65 High Ridge Rd., Suite 349, Stamford, CT 06095. Annual dues: $20 (includes 6 issues) per year in U.S.; $25 in Canada and foreign countries; sample copy: $2

National Button Bulletin
National Button Society
Lois Pool, Secretary
2733 Juno Place, Akron, OH 44333-4137; 216-864-3296

National Ezra Brooks Bottle & Specialty Club Newsletter
420 W. 1st St., Kewanee, IL 61443

National Fantasy Fan Club (for Disney collectors)
Dept. AC, Box 19212, Irvine, CA 92713. Membership: $20 per year, includes newsletters, free ads, chapters, conventions, etc.

National Fishing Lure Collectors Club
Rich Treml, Secretary
P.O. Box 1791, Dearborn, MI 48121; 313-842-2589

National Graniteware News
National Graniteware Society
P.O. Box 10013, Cedar Rapids, IA 52410-0013

National Greentown Glass Association Newsletter
LeAnne Miliser
19596 Glendale Ave., South Bend, IN 46637

National Imperial Glass Collectors' Society
P.O. Box 534, Bellaire, OH 43906. Dues: $12 per year (plus $1 for each additional member in the same household), quarterly newsletter, convention every June

National Milk Glass Collectors' Society & Quarterly Newsletter
c/o Arlene Johnson, Treasurer
1113 Birchwood Dr., Garland, TX 75043. Please include SASE

National Reamer Collectors Association Quarterly Review
R.R. 3, Box 67, Frederic, WI 54837; 715-327-4365

National Valentine Collectors Bulletin
Evalene Pulati
P.O. Box 1404, Santa Ana, CA 92702; 714-547-1355

News & Views
The National Depression Glass Association
Anita Wood
P.O. Box 69843, Odessa, TX 79769; 915-337-1297

Noritake News
David H. Spain
1237 Federal Ave. East, Seattle, WA 98102; 206-323-8102

North America Torquay Society
Jerry & Gerry Kline, members
604 Orchard View Dr., Maumee, OH 43537. Quarterly newsletter sent to members; information and membership form requires LSASE

Novelty Salt & Pepper Club
c/o Irene Thornburg, Membership Coordinator
581 Joy Rd., Battle Creek, MI 49017. Publishes quarterly
newsletter and annual roster. Annual dues: $20 in U.S.,
Canada, and Mexico; $25 for all other countries

Old Ivory Newsletter
Pat Fitzwater
P.O. Box 1004, Wilsonville, OR 97070. SASE for sample
copy

Old Morgantown Topics
Old Morgantown Glass Collectors' Guild
Jerry Gallagher, President
420 1st Ave. N.W., Plainview, MN 55964; 507-534-3511

The Olympic Collectors Newsletter
Bill Nelson
P.O. Box 41630, Tucson, AZ 85717-1630

Our McCoy Matters
Kathy Lynch, Editor
P.O. Box 14255,
Parkville, MO 64152; 816-587-9179

Paper Collectors' Marketplace
470 Main St., P.O. Box 128, Scandinavia, WI 54977; 715-467-
2379. Subcription: $17.95 (12 issues) per year in U.S.;
Canada and Mexico add $15 per year

Paper Doll News
Ema Terry
P.O. Box 807, Vivian, LA 71082

Paper Pile Quarterly
P.O. Box 337, San Anselmo, CA 94979-0337; 415-454-5552.
Subscription: $12.50 per year in U.S. and Canada

Paperback Parade
c/o Gryphon Publications
P.O. Box 209, Brooklyn, NY 11228-0209. Subscription: $20
(6 issues) per year; Sample: $6

Paperweight Collector's Bulletin
Paperweight Collector's Association, Inc.
150 Fulton Ave., Garden City Park, NY 11040; 516-741-3090
or FAX: 506-741-3985

Peanuts Collector Club Newsletter
Peanuts Collector Club
Andrea C. Podley
P.O. Box 94, N. Hollywood, CA 91603

The Pen & Quill
Universal Autograph Collectors Club
P.O. Box 6181, Washington, DC 20044-6181

Pen Fancier's Club
1169 Overcash Dr., Dunedin, FL 34698. Publishes monthly
magazine of pens and mechanical pencils; Subscription: $45
per year; sample: $4

The Pencil Collector
American Pencil Collectors Society
Robert J. Romey, President
2222 S. Millwood, Wichita, KS 67213; 316-263-8419

Pepsi-Cola Collectors Club Newsletter
Bob Stoddard
P.O. Box 1275, Covina, CA 91722; 714-593-8750

Perfume & Scent Bottle Collectors
Jeane Parris
2022 E. Charleston Blvd., Las Vegas, NV 89104. Membership: $15 U.S.A or $30 foreign (includes quarterly newsletter). Information requires SASE

Phoenix Bird Discoveries
Joan Oates
685 S. Washington, Constantine, MI 49042. Membership: $10
per year. Includes newsletter published 3 times a year

Pie Birds Unlimited
Lillian M. Cole
14 Harmony School Rd., Flemington, NJ 08822

Plantation Galleries International Newsletter
6400 Davison Rd., Burton, MI 48509; 313-743-5258 or FAX:
313-743-5791. Subscription: $24.95 per year

Plate-O-Holic
Plate Collector's Stock Exchange
478 Ward St. Extension, Wallingford, CT 06492; 203-265-
1711

Playing Card Collectors Association (PCCA) Bulletin
P.O. Box 783, Bristol, WI, 53014; 414-857-9334

Points newsletter and *Pictorial Journal*
International Club for Collectors of Hatpins & Hatpin Holders (ICC of H&HH)
Lillian Baker, Founder
15237 Chanera Ave., Gardena, CA 90249

Police Collector News
Mike Bondarenko, Publisher
R.R. 1, Box 14, Baldwin, WI 54002

Postcard History Society Bulletin
John H. McClintock, Director
P.O. Box 1765, Manassas, VA 22110; 703-368-2757

Pottery Lovers Newsletter
Pottery Lovers Reunion
Pat Sallaz
4969 Hudson Dr., Stow, OH 44224

Powder Puff
P.O. Box Letter S, Lynbrook, NY 11563. Subscription: $25 (4 issues, U.S. or Canada) per year

Precious Collectibles magazine for Precious Moments figurine Collectors, *The Ornament Collector* magazine for Hallmark ornaments and other ornaments, and the *Collectors' Bulletin* magazine for all Limited Edition collectibles
Rosie Wells Enterprises, Inc.
R.R. 1, Canton, IL 61520. Rosie also has informational secondary market price guides for Lowell Davis collectors, Hallmark Ornament collectors, and Precious Moments collectors

Quint News
Dionne Quint Collectors
P.O. Box 2527, Woburn, MA 01888; 617-933-2219

Red Wing Collectors Newsletter
Red Wing Collectors Society, Inc.
David Newkirk
R.R.3, Box 146, Monticello, MN 55362

Rinker's Antiques & Collectibles Market Report
Harry L. Rinker
P.O. Box 248, Zionsville, PA 18092; 215-965-1122 or FAX: 215-965-1124

Rockwell Society News
597 Saw Mill River Rd., Ardsley, NY 10502

Roseville's of the Past
Jack Bomm, Editor
P.O. Box 681117, Orlando, FL 32868-1117; Subscription: $19.95 per year for 6 to 12 newsletters

Royal Doulton International Collectors Club Newsletter
c/o Royal Doulton, Inc.
P.O. Box 1815, Somerset, NJ 08873; 908-356-7929 or 800-582-2102

Schoenhut Newsletter
Schoenhut Collectors Club
Robert Zimmerman
45 Louis Ave., W. Seneca, NY 14224

Scottie Sampler and fellowship group Wee Scotts
P.O. Box 1512, Columbus, IN 47202

Scouting Collectors Quarterly
National Scouting Collectors Society
806 E. Scott St., Tuscola, IL 61953

Sebastian Miniatures Collectors Society News
Cyndi Gavin McNally
c/o Lance Corp., 321 Central St., Hudson, MA 01749; 508-568-1401 or FAX: 508-568-8741

SFPCS Newsletter
Southern Folk Pottery Collectors Society
Roy Thompson
1224 Main St., Glastonbury, CT 06033; 203-633-3121 or 203-659-3695

Shawnee Pottery Collectors' Club
P.O. Box 713, New Smyrna Beach, FL 32170-0713. Monthly nationwide newsletter. SASE (c/o Pamela Curran) required when requesting information. Optional: $3 for sample of current newsletter

The Shirley Temple Collectors News
8811 Colonial Rd., Brooklyn, NY 11209; Dues: $20 per year; checks paybable to Rita Dubas

The Shot Glass Club of America
Mark Pickvet, Editor
P.O. Box 90404, Flint, MI 48509. Non-profit organization publishes 12 newsletters per year. Subscription: $6; Sample: $1

Singing Wires
Telephone Collectors International, Inc.
George W. Howard
19 N. Cherry Dr., Oswego, IL 60543; 708-554-8154

Smurf Collectors Club
24ACH, Cabot Rd. W., Massapequa, NY 11758. Membership includes newsletters. LSASE for information

Snow Biz
c/o Nancy McMichael
P.O. Box 53262, Washington, D.C. 20009. Quarterly newsletter (subscription: $10 per year) and collector's club

Spoutings
Watt Pottery Collectors
Box 26067, Fairview Park, OH 44126. Supscription (4 issues): $10 per year

The Spur
National Bit, Spur & Saddle Collectors Association
P.O. Box 3098, Colorado Springs, CO 80934

The Stained Finger
The Society of Inkwell Collectors
Vince McGraw
5136 Thomas Ave. S., Minneapolis, MN 55410; 612-922-2792

Steiff Life
Steiff Collectors Club
Beth Savino
c/o The Toy Store, 7856 Hill Ave., Holland, OH 43528; 419-865-3899 or 800-862-8697

Stein Line
Thomas A. Heiza, Publisher
P.O. Box 48716, Chicago, IL 60648-0716 or FAX: 708-673-2634. Bimonthly newsletter concerning stein sales, auctions, values, etc.

Stretch Glass Society
P.O. Box 770643, Lakewood, OH 44107. Membership: $8; quarterly newsletter, annual convention

Table Topics
Table Toppers Club
1340 West Irving Park Rd., P.O. Box 161, Chicago 60613; 312-769-3184. Membership: $18 (6 issues) per year. For those interested in table-top collectibles

Tea Leaf Reading
Tea Leaf Club International
P.O. Box 904, Mt. Prospect, IL 60056. Membership: $20 (single) or $25 (couple) per year

Tea Talk
Diana Rosen
419 N. Larchmont Blvd. #225, Los Angeles, CA 90004; 213-871-6901 or FAX: 213-828-2444

Thimble Guild
Wynneth Mullins
P.O. Box 381807, Duncansville, TX 75138-1807

Tin Type
Tin Container Collectors Association
P.O. Box 44010, Aurora, CO 80044

Toothpick Bulletin
National Toothpick Holder Collectors' Society
c/o Joyce Ender, Box 246, Sawyer, MI 49125. Dues: $10 (single) or $15 (couple) per year. Includes monthly issues; convention held in August

Torquay Pottery Collectors Society Newsletter
Torquay Pottery Collectors Society
Beth Pulsipher
Box 373, Schoolcraft, MI 49087; 616-679-4195

Toy Gun Collectors of America Newsletter
Jim Buskirk, Editor & Publisher
312 Starling Way, Anaheim, CA 92807. Published quarterly, covers both toy and BB guns. Dues: $15 per year

Toys & Prices magazine
700 E. State St., Iola, WI 54990-0001; 715-445-2214 or FAX: 715-445-4087. Subscription: $14.95 per year

The Trade Card Journal
Kit Barry
86 High St., Brattleboro, VT 05301. A quarterly publication on the social and historical use of trade cards

Trainmaster newsletter
P.O. Box 1499, Gainesville, FL 32602; 904-377-7439 or 904-373-4908. FAX: 904-374-6616

UHL Collectors' Society
Steve Brundage, President
80 Tidewater Rd., Hagerstown, IN 47346
Dale Blann, Vice President
R.R. 1, Box 136, Wheatland, IN 47597. For membership and newsletter information contact either of the above

The Upside Down World of an O.J.Collector
The Occupied Japan Club
c/o Florence Archambault
29 Freeborn St., Newport, RI 02840. Published bimonthly. Information requires SASE

Vernon Views
P.O. Box 945, Scottsdale, AZ 85252. Published quarterly beginning with the Spring issue, $6 per year

Vintage Clothing Newsletter
Terry McCormick
P.O. Box 1422, Corvallis, OR 97339; 503-752-7456

Walking Stick Notes
Cecil Curtis, Editor
4051 E. Olive Rd., Pensacola, FL 32514. Quarterly publication with limited distribution

Watt's News
c/o Susan Morris & Jan Seeck
P.O. Box 708, Mason City, IA 50401. Subscription: $10 per year

Wedgwood Collectors Society Newsletter
P.O. Box 14013, Newark, NJ 07198

The Wrapper
Bubble Gum & Candy Wrapper Collectors
P.O. Box 573, St. Charles, IL 60174; 708-377-7921

Zeppelin Collector
Zeppelin Collectors Club c/o Aerophilatelic Federation
P.O. Box 1239, Elgin, IL 60121-1239; 708-888-1907

Interested Buyers of Miscellaneous Items

In this section of the book we have listed hundreds of buyers who are actively looking to buy items from specific areas of interest. Don't expect a response from them unless you include an SASE (stamped self-addressed envelope) with your letter. If you'd rather they contact you by phone, give them your number and make sure you tell them to call collect. Describe your merchandise throughly and mention any marks; you can sometimes do a pencil rubbing to duplicate the mark exactly. Photographs are still worth a 'thousand words,' and photocopies are good, especially if you're selling paper goods, patterned dinnerware, or even smaller 3-dimensional items. Be sure to read the Introduction for more suggestions about how to carry on a successful transaction by mail.

Buyers are listed alphabetically under bold topics. A line in italics indicates only the specialized interests of the particular buyer whose name directly follows it. Recommended reference guides not found in the 1993 Nostaligia Publishing Catalog may be purchased directly from the authors whose addresses are contained in this section.

Abingdon
Vintage Charm
P.O. Box 26241
Austin, TX 78755

Advertising
Cream of Wheat ads from magazines
Antiques by the Beatties
3374 Ver Buker Ave.
Port Edwards, WI 54469

Trade cards
Bernie Berman
755 Isenberg St. #305
Honolulu, HI 96826

Porcelain signs
Michael Bruner
6980 Walnut Lake Rd.
W Bloomfield, MI 48323

Porcelain door push plates
Edward Foley
227 Union Ave.
Pittsburgh, PA 15202

Terri Mardis Ivers
1104 Shirlee
Ponca City, OK 74601

Robert S. Macdowall
106 Hathaway Circle
Arlington, MA 02174

John Deere and Caterpillar-related items
J. Schreier
Rte. 1, Box 1147
Norwalk, WI 54648

Connie Sword
P.O. Box 23
McCook, NE 69001

African Art
Scott Nelson
Box 6081
Santa Fe, NM 87502

Airline Memorabilia
Richard R. Wallin
Box 1784
Springfield, IL 62705

Animal Dishes
Robert and Sharon Thoerner
15549 Ryon Ave.
Bellflower, CA 90706

Art Deco
Greyhounds
Pamela Elkin
R.F.D. 1, Box 1
Strafford, NH 03884

Jean Griswold
1371 Merry Ln.
Atlanta, GA 30329

Figural lady flower frogs
William G. Sommer
9 W 10th St.
New York, NY 10011

Art Glass
Antique Silver House
8976 Seminole Blvd.
Seminole, FL 34642

Especially Boyd, Summit, and Mosser
Chip and Dale Collectibles
3500 S Cooper
Arlington, TX 76015

Scott Roland
P.O. Box 262
Schenevus, NY 12155

Art Pottery
Frank Bernhard
2791 Fiesta Dr.
Venice, FL 34293

Betty Bird
107 Ida St.
Mount Shasta, CA 96067

With pheasant decoration
Delores Saar
45 - 5th Ave. NW
Hutchinson, MN 55350

Autographs
Especially early businessmen and financiers
David M. Beach
Paper Americana
P.O. Box 2026
Goldenrod, FL 32733

Judith Katz-Schwartz
222 E 93rd St., 42D
New York, NY 10128

Gary Struncius
P.O. Box 1374
Lakewood, NJ 08701

Vintage Charm
P.O. Box 26241
Austin, TX 78755

Autumn Leaf
Completer pieces and tin items
Brent Dilworth
89 W Pacific
Blackfoot, ID 83221

Cookie jars
Shirley Aden
1400 4th St.
Fairbury, NE 68352

Avon Collectibles
Author of book
Bud Hastin
P.O. Box 43690
Sal Vegas, NE 89116

Tammy Rodrick
Stacey's Treasures
R.R. #2, Box 163
Sumner, IL 62466

Banks
Phil Helley
Old Kilbourn Antiques
629 Indiana Ave.
Wisconsin Dells, WI 53965

Marked Ertl
Homestead Collectibles
P.O. Box 173
Mill Hall, PA 17751

Mechanical
Darrell Bemis
Shady Lane Antique Mall
R.R. 23, Box 19
Terre Haute, IN 47802

Barbed Wire
John Mantz
American Barbed Wire Collectors Society
1023 Baldwin Rd.
Bakersvield, CA 93304

Baskets
Sharon Hamer
P.O. Box 246
Durango, CO 81302

Bathroom Porcelain and Related Items
Virgina S. Morgan
P.O. Box 5345
Chesapeake, VA 23324

Especially miniature items
Rosemarie Ovellette
3510 Stanton Rd.
Oxford, MI 48371

Bedroom Accessories and Glassware
K. Hartman
7459 Shawnee Rd.
N Tonawanda, NJ 14120

Beer Steins
Tammy Rodrick
Rt. 2, Box 163
Sumner, IL 62466

Betty Boop
Leo A. Mallette
2309 Santa Anita Ave.
Arcadia, CA 91006-5154

Judith Katz-Schwartz
222 E 93rd St., 42D
New York, NY 10128

Black Americana
Jean Griswold
1371 Merry Ln.
Atlanta, GA 30329

Irene M. Houdek
Rt. 2, Box 231
Cresco, IA 52136

Linda Rogers
4041 A N 11th St.
Milwaukee, WI 53209

Depicting popular dance forms
William G. Sommer
9 W 10th St.
New York, NY 10011

Black Glass
Joe Brell
607 Center Ave.
Pittsburgh, PA 15215

Author of book
Marlena Toohey
405 Beaconfield
Sherwood, AR 72116

Black Cats
Shafford only
Doug Dezo
864 Paterson Ave.
Maywood, NJ 07607

Blacksmith's Grindstone
Jack Zimmerly, Jr.
c/o 11711 Sharp Rd.
Waterford, PA 16441

Blue Moon Girl
Bill Sinesky
7228 McQuaid Rd.
Wooster, OH 44691

Blue Ridge
Christina Caldwell
Rt. 1, Box 336
Hawkins, TX 75765

G.D. Johnson
7565 Roosevelt Way NE
Seattle, WA 98115

Robert R. Sabo
2248 Lakeroad Blvd. NW
Canton, OH 44708

Blue Willow
The Antique Emporium
P.O. Box K
214 S State St.
Athens, WV 24712

Tammy Rodrick
Rt. 2, Box 163
Sumner, IL 62466

Bookmarks
Joan L. Huegel
1002 W 25th St.
Erie, PA 16502

Books
Children's illustrated
Noreen Abbott Books
2666 44th Ave.
San Francisco, CA 94116

Anthologies of cartoonists
Abalone Cove Rare Books
7 Fruit Tree Rd.
Portuguese Bend, CA 90274

Fine antiquarian
The Book Collector
2347 University Blvd.
Houston, TX 77005

Book Den South
2249 First St.
Ft. Myers, FL 33901

Children's illustrated
Arthur Bouiette
410 W Third St.
Suite 200
Little Rock, AR 72201

Western Americana
Carroll Burcham
5546 17th Pl.
Lubbock, TX 79416

By Marie Weatherman
Pat Jackson
2804 N. Monroe
Stillwater, OK 74075

Robert L. Merriam
Rare, Used and Old Books
Newhall Rd.
Conway, MA 01341

Charles Shaffer
321 Prospect St.
Willimantic, CT 06226

Norma Wadler
P.O. Box 418 - S 7th and Pacific
Long Beach, WA 98631

Modern first editions
Wellerdts
3700 S Osprey Ave., Ste. 214
Sarasota, FL 34239

Tooth Fairy and related items
Rosemary Wells
Tooth Fairy Consultant
1129 Cherry St.
Deerfield, IL 60015

Little Blue Books
Judy Wilson
10125 River Acres RD.
Scott, AR 72142

Bottles
Perfume
Betty Bird
107 Ida St.
Mt. Shasta, CA 90607

Commercial perfumes and samples
Luc A. De Broqueville
8650 S Western 2623
Dallas, TX 75206

Perfume
K. Hartman
7459 Shawnee Rd.
N Tonawanda, NJ 14120

Ed Keeler
8 Forest Rd.
Burnt Hills, NY 12027

Dairy and milk
O.B. Lund
13009 S 42nd St.
Phoenix, AZ 85044

Author of book, Soda Bottles
Thomas Marsh
914 Franklin Ave.
Youngstown, OH 44502

Dairy and milk
John Tutton
R.R. 4, Box 929
Front Royal, VA 22630

James P. Skinner
5209 W Hutchinson
Chicago, IL 60641

Bowie Knives
David L. Hartline
P.O. Box 775
Worthington, OH 43085

Boy Scout
Judith Katz-Schwartz
222 E 93rd St., 42D
New York, NY 10128

Brayton Laguna
Ray Vlach, Jr.
5364 N Magnet Ave.
Chicago, IL 60630-1216

Breyer Figures
Ellen Deen
34111 Ave. F, Sp. 24
Yucaipa, CA 92399-2648

Bette Robinson
Gretchen and Wildrose Playdolls
5816 Steeplewood Dr.
N Richland Hills, TX 76180-6418

Bride and Groom Figurines
For cakes, pre-1960
Jeannie Greenfield
310 Parker Rd.
Stoneboro, PA 16153

V. Schupbach
P.O. Box 64
Tuscarora, NV 89834

British Royal Commemoratives
Audrey Zeder
6755 Coralite St. S
Long Beach, CA 90808

Bronzes
Any made before 1940
Stephen R. Carter
2101 Sheffield Ct.
Mobile, AL 36693

Butter Pats
Marjorie Geddes
P.O. Box 5875
Aloha, OR 97007

Buttons
Gwen Daniel
18 Belleau Lake Ct.
O'Fallon, MO 63366

National Button Society
Miss Lois Pool, Secretary
2733 Juno Place
Akron, OH 44333-4317

P. Kay's Antiques and More
359 Scotland St.
Dunedin, FL 34698

Patricia Quink
Box 733
Big Piney, WY 83113

Judith Katz-Schwartz
222 E 93rd St., 42D
New York, NY 10128

Betty I. Yates
P.O. Box 759
Greeneville, TN 37744-0759

Shirley Yoder
4983 Oak St. SW
Kalona, IA 52247

Buzza Mottoes
Antiques by the Beatties
3374 Ver Bunker Ave.
Port Edwards, WI 54469

California Raisins
Larry De Angelo
516 King Arthur Dr.
Virginia Beach, VA 23464

Candy Containers
Doug Dezo
864 Paterson Ave.
Maywood, NJ 07607

Canes and Walking Sticks
Arthur Boutiette
410 W Third St.
Suite 200
Little Rock, AR 72201

Capo Di Monte
Val Arce
23029 Cerca Dr.
Valenca, CA 91354

Camark
Vintage Charm
P.O. Box 26241
Austin, TX 78755

Carnival Collectibles
Thomas W. Davis
147 Longleaf Dr.
Blackshear, GA 31516

Carnival Chalkware
Author of book
Thomas G. Morris
P.O. Box 8307
Medford, Oregon 97504

Carnival Glass
Antique Emporium
214 S State St., P.O. Box K
Athens, WV 24712

John and Sandra Stafford
125 E Oak St., Box 14
Dalton, WI 53926

Cast Iron Cookware
David G. Smith
11918 2nd St.
Perrysburg, NY 14129

Catalina Island Pottery
Patrice Berlin
9315 Burnet Ave.
N Hills, CA 91343

Shelby Good
4640 W Ave. L-2
Quartz Hill, CA 93536

Ray Vlach, Jr.
5364 N Magnet Ave.
Chicago, IL 60630-1216

Ceramic Arts Studio
Vera Skorupski
226 Deerfield Dr.
Berlin, CT 06037

Author of book
B.A. Wellman
#106 Cordaville Rd.
Ashland, MA 01721-1002

Cereal Boxes and Premiums
Scott Bruce, Mr. Cereal Box
P.O. Box 481
Cambridge, MA 02140

Tammy Rodrick
Rt. 2, Box 163
Sumner, IL 62466

Character Collectibles
Author of book
Bill Bruegman
Toy Scouts, Inc.
137 Casterton Ave.
Akron, OH 44303

Terri Mardis Ivers
1104 Shirlee
Ponca City, OK 74601

Michael Paquin
That Toy Guy
57 N Sycamore St.
Clifton Heights, PA 19018

Tammy Rodrick
Rt. 2, Box 163
Sumner, IL 62466

Chauffers' Badges
Dr. Edward H. Miles
888 - 8th Ave.
New York, NY 10019

Loren J. Snyder
6867 Navarre Rd. SW
Massillon, OH 44646

Children's Dishes
Majorie Geddes
P.O. Box 5875
Aloha, OR 97007

Gary Reed
P.O. Box 342
Fenton, MO 63026

Judith Katz-Schwartz
222 E 93rd St., 42D
New York, NY 10128

China
Minatures
Marjorie Geddes
P.O. Box 5875
Aloha, OR 97007

Hand-painted marked items
Rhonda Hallden
21958 Darvin Dr.
Saugus, CA 91350

Vintage Shoppe
24 Baytree Pl.
Remerton
Valdosta, GA 31601

Christmas
Pre-1950
Diane and Bob Kubicki
7636 Emerick Rd.
W Milton, OH 45383

Cigar Labels and Boxes
David M. Beach
Paper Americana
P.O. Box 2026
Goldenrod, FL 32733

Clocks
Comic character
Howard S. Brenner
106 Woodgate Terrace
Rochester, NY 14625

Novelty animated and non-animated
Carole S. Kaifer
P.O. Box 232
Bethania, NC 27010

Tammy Rodrick
Rt. 2, Box 163
Sumner, IL 62466

Norma Wadler
P.O. Box 418 - S 7th and Pacific
Long Beach, WA 98631

Cocktail Shakers
Arlene Lederman Antiques
150 Main St.
Nyack, NY 10960

Steven Visakay
P.O. Box 1517
W Caldwell, NJ 07007-1517

Coin-Operated Machines
Dembecks Keys and Locksmiths
24711 Harper
St. Clair Shores, MI 48080

Comic Books
Judith Katz-Schwartz
222 E 93rd St., 42D
New York, NY 10128

Shawn Vincent
Rt. 1, Box 327, Apt. B
Manton, CA 96059

Windmill Antiques
315 SW 77th Ave.
N Lauderdale, FL 33068

Comic Strip Art
David H. Begin
138 Lansberry Ct.
Los Gatos, CA 95032

Cookbooks
Cheryl Erling
37 Linden St.
New Britain, CT 06051

Judith Katz-Schwartz
222 E 93rd St., 42D
New York, NY 10128

Cookie Jars
James Goad
1152A S Eagle Cir.
Aurora, CO 80012

Debbie Yates
P.O. Box 1461
Decatur, GA 30031-1461

Gene A. Underwood
909 N Sierra Bonita, Apt. 9
Los Angeles, CA 90046-6562

Coors
Pat and Bill Ogden
3050 Colorado Ave.
Grand Junction, CO 81504

Corkscrews
Antique and unusual
Paul P. Luchsinger
104 Deer Run
Williamsville, NY 14221

Country Store Collectibles
William A. (Bill) Shaw
801 Duval Dr.
Opp, AL 36467

Cowan Pottery
Joe Brell
607 Center Ave.
Pittsburgh, PA 15215

Cranberry Glass
Christina Caldwell
Rt. 1, Box 336
Hawkins, TX 75765

Cracker Jack Items
Phil Helley
Old Kilbourn Antiques
629 Indiana Ave.
Wisconsin Dells, WI 53965

Wes Johnson
1725 Dixie Hwy.
Box 169001
Louisville, KY 40256-0001

Credit Cards and Related Items
Walt Thompson
Box 2541
Yakima, WA 98907-2541

Cupids
Especially prints and Black items
Antiques by the Beatties
3374 Ver Bunker Ave.
Port Edwards, WI 54469

Czechoslovakian Collectibles
Delores Saar
45 - 5th Ave. NW
Hutchinson, MN 55350

Danish Items
Lona Seigfried
P.O. Box 25
Carterville, IL 62918

Darners
Cheryl Erling
37 Linden St.
New Britain, CT 06051

Decanters
Homestead Collectibles
P.O. Box 173
Mill Hall, PA 17751

Dedham Pottery
Rose Blundell
1700 Macon St.
McLean, VA 22101

Depression Glass
Larry D. Cook
3401 SW 12th St.
Des Moines, IA 50315-7513

Judith French
1623 Troy Dr.
Madison, WI 53704

Rhonda Hasse
566 Oak Terrace Dr.
Farmington, MO 63640

Pat Jackson
2804 N. Monroe
Stillwater, OK 74075

Pat and Bill Ogden
3050 Colorado Ave.
Grand Junction, CO 81504

Vintage Charm
P.O. Box 26241
Austin, TX 78755

Pamela Wiggins
6025 Sunnycrest
Houston, TX 77087

Dick Tracy Collectibles
Larry Doucet
2351 Sultana Dr.
Yorktown Heights, NY 10598

Dinnerware
Especially Bauer, Blair, and Hull
Tori Adams
664 Jay St.
Gallup, NM 87301

Robert R. Sabo
2248 Lakeroad Blvd. NW
Canton, OH 44708

Ray Vlach, Jr.
5364 N Magnet Ave.
Chicago, IL 60630-1216

Disneyana
Paul J. Baxter
P.O. Box 176
Stronghurst, IL 61480

Cohen Books and Collectibles
Joel J. Cohen
P.O. Box 810310
Boca Raton, FL 33481

Judith Katz-Schwartz
222 E 93rd St., 42D
New York, NY 10128

Documents
David M. Beach
Paper Americana
P.O. Box 2026
Goldenrod, FL 32733

Dog Collectibles
Jan Ennis
1823 Breezewood Dr.
Akron, OH 44313

Especially books
Kathleen Rais
3901 Conshohocken Ave. #2310
Philadelphia, PA 19131

Dolls
Pincushion
Elizabeth Baer
P.O. Box 266
Perry, IA 50220

Shirley Bertrand
971 N Milwaukee Ave., Box 99A
Wheeling, IL 60090

From 1960s-70s
Jean Brown
824 N Main
Independence, MO 64050

Lulu and Tubby by Georgene
Gwen Daniel
18 Belleau Lake Ct.
O'Fallon, MO 63366

Barbie and related items
Denise Davidson
834 W Grand River Ave.
Williamston, MI 48895

Barbie and related items
Irene Davis
27036 Withams Rd.
Oak Hall, VA 23416

Shari M. Decker
289 Green St.
Martinsville, IN 46151

Dresser and pincushion
K. Hartman
7459 Shawnee Rd.
N Tonawanda, NJ 14120

Manufacturer catalogs
Judy Izen
208 Follen Rd.
Lexington, MA 02173

Ralonda Lindsay
2504 E Vancouver
Broken Arrow, OK 74014

Pat Lockerby
885 Beltrees St., Apt. 2
Dunedin, FL 34698

Captain Action
Michael Paquin
That Toy Guy
57 N Sycamore St.
Clifton Heights, PA 19018

P.J.'s Carousels and Collectibles
P.O. Box 65395
W Des Moines, IA 50265

Especially Barbie and modern collectibles
Bette Robinson
Gretchen and Wildrose Playdolls
5816 Steeplewood Dr.
N Richland Hills, TX 76180-6418

Dawn Rossi
Orphans of the Attic
P.O. Box 484
Canandaigua, NY 14424

Judith Katz-Schwartz
222 E 93rd St., 42D
New York, NY 10128

Noreen Stayton
P.O. Box 379
Doyle, CA 96109-0379

Sherry Thornhill
Rt. 1, Box 32
Hawk Point, MO 63349

Monica H. Tobin
7101 W Yale Ave., #1304
Denver, CO 80227

Sandi Waddell
2791 C.R. 302
Durango, CO 81301

Dollhouse Furniture and Accessories
Judith Katz-Schwartz
222 E 93rd St., 42D
New York, NY 10128

Doorstops
Rhonda Hallden
21958 Darvin Dr.
Saugus, CA 19350

Dragonware
Susie Hibbard
2570 Walnut Blvd. #20
Walnut Creek, CA 94596

Egg Cups
Majorie Geddes
P.O. Box 5875
Aloha, OR 97007

Egg Timers
Jeannie Greenfield
310 Parker Rd.
Stoneboro, PA 16153

Elsie the Cow
Marci Van Ausdall
666 - 840 Spring Creek Dr.
Westwood, CA 96137

Elvis Presley Memorabilia
Joan and Don Komlos
1502 Windriver Dr.
Arnold, MO 63010-4619

Enamelware
Linda Hicks
3055 E Lake
Gladwater, TX 75647

Ephemera
David M. Beach
Paper Americana
P.O. Box 2026
Goldenrod, FL 32733

All categories
Judith Katz-Schwartz
222 E 93rd St., 42D
New York, NY 10128

Fans
Judith Katz-Schwartz
222 E 93rd St., 42D
New York, NY 10128

Fast Food Glasses
Tammy Rodrick
Rt. 2, Box 163
Sumner, IL 62466

Fiesta
Kate's Collectibles
28-US 41 East
Negaunee, MI 49866

Pat and Bill Ogden
3050 Colorado Ave.
Grand Junction, CO 81504

M.C. Wills
103 Virginia St.
Dyess AFB, TX 79607

Figurines
James Goad
1152A S Eagle Cir.
Aurora, CO 80012

Firefighting Memorabilia
Richard Price
Box 219, 27 Pearl St.
Arendtsville, PA 17303

Fireworks and 4th of July
Dennis C. Manochio
4th of July Americana and Fireworks Museum
P.O. Box 2010
Saratoga, CA 95070

Fishing Lures
T.C. Wills
103 Virginia St.
Dyess AFB, TX 79607

Randy Hilst
1221 Florence #4
Pekin, IL 61554

Flashlights
Bill Utley
P.O. Box 3572
Downey, CA 90242

Flow Blue
Arthur Boutiette
410 W Third St.
Suite 200
Little Rock, AR 72201

Fountain Pens
Also mechanical pencils
Cliff and Judy Lawrence
1169 Overcash Dr.
Dunedin, FL 34698

Bill Majors
P.O. Box 9351
Boise, ID 83707

Judith Katz-Schwartz
222 E 93rd St., 42D
New York, NY 10128

Norma Wadler
P.O. Box 418 - S 7th and Pacific
Long Beach, WA 98631

Fostoria
Pat Jackson
2804 N.Monroe
Stillwater, OK 74075

Frames
K. Hartman
7459 Shawnee Rd.
N Tonawanda, NJ 14120

Frankoma
Authors of book
Phyllis and Tom Bess
14535 E 13th St.
Tulsa, OK 74108

Plates or political mugs
Joe Brell
607 Center Ave.
Pittsburgh, PA 15215

M.C. Wills
103 Virginia St.
Dyess AFB, TX 79607

Franciscan
Pat and Bill Ogden
3050 Colorado Ave.
Grand Junction, CO 81504

Fruit Jars
John Hathaway
Rt. 2, Box 220
Bryant Pond, ME 04219

Furniture
Oak
Shirley Aden
1400 4th St.
Fairbury, NE 68352

Antique Silver House
8976 Seminole Blvd.
Seminole, FL 34642

1950s designer
Ralph Frattaroli
2114 Manor Ave.
Poland, OH 44514

Mission style
Gary Struncius
P.O. Box 1374
Lakewood, NJ 08701

Gambling and Gambling-Related Items
Robert Eisenstadt
P.O. Box 020767
Brooklyn, NY 11202-0017

Games
Phil McEntee
Where the Toys Are
45 W Pike St.
Canonsburg, PA 15317

Judith Katz-Schwartz
222 E 93rd St., 42D
New York, NY 10128

Shawn Vincent
Rt. 1, Box 327, Apt. B
Manton, CA 96059

Garden Water Sprinklers
Tom Mattingly
P.O. Box 278
Churchton, MD 20733

Glass Animals
Lee Garmon
1529 Whittier St.
Springfield, IL 62704

Robert and Sharon Thoerner
15549 Ryon Ave.
Bellflower, CA 90706

Glass Hats
B. McCurry
c/o Terrye Stevens
Rt. 3, Box 97
Plainview, TX 79072

Glass Knives
Adrienne Esco
P.O. Box 342
Los Alamitos, CA 90720

Glass Scoops
Al Morin
668 Robbins Ave. #23
Dracut, MA 01826

Glass Shoes
All other types as well
Susan K. Holland
Springfield, OR 97478

Author of book
The Shoe Lady
Libby Yalom
P.O. Box 852
Adelphi, MD 20783

Glassware
Black amethyst, Mt. Pleasant pattern
Barbara Craft
202 Lincoln
Emporia, KS 66801

Black amethyst
Judy Polk Harding
604 Hwy. 1 West
Iowa City, IA 52246

Rhonda Hallden
21958 Darvin Dr.
Saugus, CA 91350

Author of book, Ruby glass
Naomi L. Over
8909 Sharon Lane
Arvada, CO 80002

Goebel
Cat figurines
Linda Nothnagel
Rt. 3, Box 30
Shelbina, MO 63468

Friar Tuck items
Pat and Bill Ogden
3050 Colorado Ave.
Grand Junction, CO 81504

Golf
Norm Boughton
1356 Buffalo Rd.
Rochester, NY 14624

Early prints
Antiques by the Beatties
3374 Ver Bunker Ave.
Port Edwards, WI 5449

Pat Romano
32 Sterling Dr.
Lake Grove, NY 11755

Virginia Young
P.O. Box 42
Amherst, NH 03031

Gone with the Wind Collectibles
Author of book
Patrick McCarver
5453 N Rolling Oaks Dr.
Memphis, TN 38119

Grapette
Hicker Nut Hill Antiques
Robert and Genie Prather
Rt. 2, Box 532-Y
Tyler, TX 75704

Connie Sword
P.O. Box 23
McCook, NE 69001

Graniteware
Daryl D. Alpers
P.O. Box 2621
Cedar Rapids, IA 52406

Betty Martin
Box 41B, RT 4
Eolia, MO 63344

Griswold
Author of book
Denise Harned
P.O. Box 330373
Elmwood, CT 06133-0373

Hall China
Red Poppy and Cameo Rose
Bonnie Neely
Rt. 1, Box 47A
Purdy, MO 65734

Pat and Bill Ogden
3050 Colorado Ave.
Grand Junction, CO 81504

Hallmark Ornaments
Susan K. Holland
6151 Main St.
Springfield, OR 97478

Author of book
Rosie Wells Enterprises, Inc.
R.R. #1
Canton, IL 61520

Halloween
Diane and Bob Kubicki
7636 Emerick Rd.
W Milton, OH 45383

Hartland Figures
Ellen Deen
34111 Ave. F, Sp. 24
Yucaipa, CA 92399-2648

Hatpins and Hatpin Holders
K. Hartman
7459 Shawnee Rd.
N Tonawanda, NJ 14120

Judith Katz-Schwartz
222 E 93rd St., 42D
New York, NY 10128

Haviland
Val Arce
23029 Cerca Dr.
Valencia, CA 91354

Head Vases
Jean Griswold
1371 Merry Ln.
Atlanta, GA 30329

Tammy Rodrick
Rt. 2, Box 163
Sumner, IL 62466

Heisey
Floyd F. Gilmer
P.O. Box 13983
Roanoke, VA 24038

Homer Laughlin China
Author of book
Darlene Nossaman
5419 Lake Charles
Waco, TX 76710

Ray Vlach, Jr.
5364 N Magnet Ave.
Chicago, IL 60630-1216

Hull
Antiquity Collectibles
3714 Lexington Rd.
Michigan City, IN 46360

Daryl D. Alpers
P.O. Box 2621
Cedar Rapids, IA 52406

Early stoneware
Joe Brell
607 Center Ave.
Pittsburgh, PA 15215

Pat and Bill Ogden
3050 Colorodo Ave.
Grand Junction, CO 81504

Especially baskets and vases
Beth Shank
956 E Riddle
Ravenna, OH 44266

Vintage Charm
P.O. Box 26241
Austin, TX 78755

Hummel Figurines
Linda Seboe
1242 Moorhead Rd.
Cloquet, MN 55720

Ice Cream Scoops
Lillian M. Cole
14 Harmony School Rd.
Flemington, NJ 08822

Illustrator Art
Antiques by the Beatties
3374 Ver Bunker Ave.
Port Edwards, WI 54469

Imperial Porcelain
Geneva D. Addy
P.O. Box 124
Winterset, IA 50273

Indian Art and Artifacts
Rose Blundell
1700 Macon St.
McLean, VA 22101

Carl Vincent
Rt. 1, Box 327
Manton, CA 96050

Len and Janie Weidner
13706 Robins Rd.
Westerville, OH 43081

Inkwells and Desk Items
Betty Bird
107 Ida St.
Mount Shasta, CA 96067

Jadite
Florence Hiojer
Star Rt., Box 8A
Stephenson, MI 49887

Jewelry
Angie's Attic
2562 S Halsted
Chicago, IL 60608

Antique Silver House
8976 Seminole Blvd.
Seminole, FL 34642

Rhinestone
Nancy Beall
1043 Greta
El Cajon, CA 92021

Mexican sterling
Jewell Evans
4215 Cork Ln.
Bakersfield, CA 93309

Designer copper
Ralph Frattaroli
2114 Manor Ave.
Poland, OH 44514

Judy Polk Harding
604 Hwy. 1 West
Iowa City, IA 52246

Vicki Harper
410 S First St.
Trenton, OH 45067

Pat Lockerby
885 Beltrees St., Apt. 2
Dunedin, FL 34698

Judith Katz-Schwartz
222 E 93rd St., 42D
New York, NY 10128

Stuart Nye, sterling silver
Paul L. Trentz
126 E McKinley
Stoughton, WI 53589

Costume
Pamela Wiggins
6025 Sunnycrest
Houston, TX 77087

Diane Wilson
P.O. Box 561
Wexford, PA 15090

Jukeboxes
Jim Dunham
4514 Maher Ave.
Madison, WI 53716-1725

Kaleidoscopes
Joan Walsh
520 Oak Run Dr. #9
Bourbonnais, IL 60914

Kansas Collectibles
Pottery, glass, and related items
Billy and Jeane Jones
P.O. Box 82
Dearing, KS 67340

Kentucky Derby and Horse Racing
B.L. Hornback
707 Sunrise Lane
Elizabethtown, KY 42701

Ron Kramer
P.O. Box 91431
Louisville, KY 91431

Jerry Newfield
1236 Wilbur Ave.
San Diego, CA 92109

Key Chains
Marked 'Return to Senders'
Kayla Conway
4500 Napal Ct.
Bakersfield, CA 93307

Knives
Author of book
Jim Sargent
Books Americana, Inc.
Florence, AL 35630

Ladies' Compacts
Elizabeth Baer
P.O. Box 266
Perry, IA 50220

Author of book
Roselyn Gerson
P.O. Box Letter S
Lynbrook, NY 11563

Lori Landgrebe
2331 E Main St.
Decatur, IL 62521

Lamps
Antique Silver House
8976 Seminole Blvd.
Seminole, FL 34642

Aladdin
Author of book
J.W. Courter
R.R. 1
Simpson, IL 62985

Figural dresser type
K. Hartman
7459 Shawnee Rd.
N Tonawanda, NJ 14120

Handel
Shady Lane Antique Mall
Darrell Bemis
R.R. 23, Box 19
Terre Haute, IN 47802

Aladdin Genie
Jerry Shover
P.O. Box 10744
Portland, OR 97210

Law Enforcement, Crime-Related Memorabilia
Antiques of Law and Order
Tony and Martha Perrin
H.C. 7, Box 53A
Mena, AR 71953

License Plate Attachments
Edward Foley
227 Union Ave.
Pittsburgh, PA 15202

License Plates
Veteran
Kayla Conway
4500 Napal Ct.
Bakersfield, CA 93307

Richard Diehl
5965 W Colgate Pl.
Denver, CO 80227

Lighters
Bill Majors
P.O. Box 9351
Boise, ID 83707

Lil' Abner
Kenn Norris
P.O. Box 4830
Sanderson, TX 79848-4830

Little Golden Books
Steve Santi
19626 Ricardo Ave.
Hayward, CA 94541

Lucy Collectibles
Lucy Collector's Club
Jane Elliott, President
P.O. Box 851057
Mesquite, TX 75185-1057

Magazines
Country Collectibles
P.O. Box 1147
Midland, MI 48640

George and Pamela Curran
P.O. Box 713
New Smyrna Beach, FL 32170-0713

Men's
James R. Kruczek
N 11584 Moore Rd.
Alma Center, WI 54611-8301

Diana McConnell
14 Sassafras Lane
Swedesboro, NJ 08085

Judith Katz-Schwartz
222 E 93rd St., 42D
New York, NY 10128

Shawn Vincent
Rt. 1, Box 327, Apt. B
Manton, CA 96059

Marbles
Judy Beal
908 E Maywood Ave.
Peoria, IL 61603

Andrew H. Dohan
49 E Lancaster Ave.
Frazer, PA 19355

Gram and Me, Marbles
908 E Maywood Ave.
Peoria, IL 61603

Anthony Niccoli
823 E 25th Ave.
N Kansas City, MO 64116

Judith Katz-Schwartz
222 E 93rd St., 42D
New York, NY 10128

David Smith
1142 S Spring St.
Springfield, IL 62704

Matchcovers
Bill Retskin
3417 Clayborne Ave.
Alexandria, VA 22306-1410

Match Safes
George Sparacio
R.D. #2, Box 139C
Newfield, NJ 08344

McDonald's ®

Authors of book
Joyce and Terry Losonsky
7506 Summer Leave Lane
Columbia, MD 21046-2455

Metlox

Aztec
Ray Vlach, Jr.
5364 N Magnet Ave.

Militaria

Antique Silver House
8976 Seminole Blvd.
Seminole, FL 34642

Especially German
David L. Hartline
P.O. Box 775
Worthington, OH 43085

Dora Lerch
P.O. Box 586
N White Plains, NY 10603

Thomas Winter
817 Patton
Springfield, IL 62702

Milk Glass

Pink, by Jeannette Glass
Janie Evitts
265 Colonial Oaks
Dayton, TX 77535

Linda Seboe
1242 Moorhead Rd.
Cloquet, MN 55720

Miniatures

Judith Katz-Schwartz
222 E 93rd St., 42D
New York, NY 10128

Model Kits

Author of book, Aurora
Bill Bruegman
137 Casterton Dr.
Akron, OH 44303

Other than Aurora
Gordy Dutt
Box 201
Sharon Center, OH 42274-0201

Moorcroft

John Harrigan
1900 Hennepin
Minneapolis, MN 55403

Motorcycles and Accessories

Virginia Young
P.O. Box 42
Amherst, NH 03031

Movie Memorabilia

George Reed
7216 Kindred St.
Philadelphia, PA 19149

Moxie

E. Sargent Legard
P.O. Box 262
Stratham, NH 03885

Music

American-made guitars
Brett Ivers
1104 Shirlee Ave.
Ponca City, OK 74601

Marsha Lambert
1200 W University
Lafayette, LA 70506

Fretted instruments
Jeff Soileau
155 N College St.
Auburn, AL 36830

Napkin Rings

Betty Bird
107 Ida St.
Mount Shasta, CA 96067

Judith Katz-Schwartz
222 E 93rd St., 42D
New York, NY 10128

Naval Academy Memorabilia

Walnut Leaf Antiques
Joel Litzky
50 Maryland Ave.
Annapolis, MD 21401

Nautical Instruments

Walnut Leaf Antiques
Joel Litzky
50 Maryland Ave.
Annapolis, MD 21401

Nippon

Robert R. Allen
P.O. Box 273
Manns Harbor, NC 27953

Val Arce
23029 Cerca Dr.
Valencia, CA 91354

Julius Calloway
884 Riverside Dr.
New York, NY 10032

Rhonda Hasse
566 Oak Terrace Dr.
Farmington, MO 63640

Non-Sports Cards
James R. Kruczek
N 11584 Moore Rd.
Alma Center, WI 54611-8301

Noritake
Val Arce
23029 Cerca Dr.
Valencia, CA 91354

Occupied Japan
Brent Dilworth
89 W Pacific
Blackfoot, ID 83221

Pat and Bill Ogden
3050 Colorado Ave.
Grand Junction, CO 81504

Mary Zuzan
Rt. 2, Box 65
Denton, MD 21629

Ocean Liner Memorabilia
Judith Katz-Schwartz
222 E 93rd St., 42D
New York, NY 10128

Oil Paintings
Antique Silver House
8976 Seminole Blvd.
Seminole, FL 34642

Olympic Memorabilia
Ray Smith
Sands Antiques
P.O. Box 254
Elizabeth, NJ 07207

Oriental Rugs
Julius Calloway
884 Riverside Dr.
New York, NY 10032

Mike Epple
260 Lakewive Dr.
Defiance, OH 43512

Orientalia
Susie Hibbard
2570 Walnut Blvd. #20
Walnut Creek, CA 94596

Carl Vincent
Rt. 1, Box 327
Manton, CA 96059

Oyster Cans
Memory Tree
P.O. Box 9462
Madison, WI 53715

Paper Dolls
Judith Katz-Schwartz
222 E 93rd St., 42D
New York, NY 10128

Paperweights
Betty Bird
107 Ida St.
Mount Shasta, CA 96067

Andrew H. Dohan
49 E Lancaster Ave.
Frazer, PA 19366

George Kamm
24 Townsend Ct.
Lancaster, PA 17603

Monica H. Tobin
7101 W Yale Ave. #1304
Denver, CO 80227

Parasols
Arthur Boutiette
410 W Third St.
Suite 200
Little Rock, AR 72201

Patriot China
All Disney items
Ray Vlach, Jr.
Chicago, IL 60630-1216

Pattern Glass Shakers
Authors of book
Mildred and Ralph Lechner
P.O. Box 554
Mechanicsville, VA 23111

Peanuts and Schultz Collectibles
Author of book
Freddi Margolin
P.O. Box 512P
Bay Shore, NY 11706

Pen Delfin Rabbit Figurines
George Sparacio
R.D. #2, Box 139C
Newfield, NJ 08344

Pencil Sharpeners
Martha Hughes
4128 Ingalls St.
San Diego, CA 92103

Pennsbury Pottery
Author of book
Shirley Graff
4515 Grafton Rd.
Brunswick, OH 44212

Author of book
BA Wellman
#106 Cordaville Rd.
Ashland, MA 01721-1002

Pez
Jill Russell
3103 Lincoln Ave.
Alameda, CA 94501

Beth Shank
956 E Riddle
Ravenna, OH 44266

Photographica
Rose Blundell
1700 Macon St.
McLean, VA 22101

David L. Hartline
P.O. Box 775
Worthington, OH 43085

Judith Katz-Schwartz
222 E 93rd St., 42D
New York, NY 10128

Pie Birds
Christina Caldwell
Rt. 1, Box 336
Hawkins, TX 75765

Also funnels
Lillian M. Cole
14 Harmony School Rd.
Flemington, NJ 08822

Pin-Up Art
Robert C. Vincent
Rt. 1, Box 327
Manton, CA 96059

Pipes
Briar, Dunhill, Meerschaum, etc.
Reader's and Smoker's Den
36-42 N 4th St.
P.O. Box 1162
Zanesville, OH 43702-1162

Political
Michael Engel
29 Groveland St.
Easthampton, MA 01027

James C. Gernard
1023 S Anderson St.
Elwood, IN 46036

Judith Katz-Schwartz
222 E 93rd St., 42D
New York, NY 10128

Popeye Collectibles
Official Popeye Fan Club
5995 Stage Rd., #151
Bartlett, TN 38134

Judith Katz-Schwartz
222 E 93rd St., 42D
New York, NY 10128

Post Cards
Bernie Berman
755 Isenberg St. #305
Honolulu, HI 96926

Antique to modern
S. Dobres Post Cards
Sheldon Dobres
P.O. Box 1855
Baltimore, MD 21203-1855

Author of book
Margaret Kaduck
P.O. Box 26076
Cleveland, OH 44126

Judith Katz-Schwartz
222 E 93rd St., 42D
New York, NY 10128

Debby Yates
P.O. Box 1461
Decatur, GA 30031-1461

Mary Zuzan
Rt. 2, Box 65
Denton, MD 21629

Pottery
James Goad
1152A S Eagle Cir.
Aurora, CO 80012

John Harrigan
1900 Hennepin
Minneapolis, MN 55403

Pat and Bill Ogden
3050 Colorado Ave.
Grand Junction, CO 81504

Precious Moments®
Author of book
Rosie Wells Enterprises, Inc.
R.R. #1
Canton, IL 61520

Prints
Antiques by the Beatties
3374 Ver Bunker Ave.
Port Edwards, WI 54469

Victorian type
Rhonda Hallden
21958 Darvin Dr.
Saugus, CA 91350

Tammy Rodrick
Rt. 2, Box 163
Sumner, IL 62466

Purses
Judy Beal
908 E Maywood Ave.
Peoria, IL 61603

Kayla Conway
4500 Napal Ct.
Bakersfield, CA 93307

Linda Fancher
1118 Park Ave.
Alameda, CA 94501

Beaded
Rhonda Hallden
21958 Darvin Dr.
Saugus, CA 91350

Veronica Trainer
P.O. Box 40443
Cleveland, OH 44140

Radio Premiums
Phil Helley
Old Kilbourn Antiques
629 Indiana Ave.
Wisconsin Dells, WI 53965

Radios
Gerald Schneider
3101 Blueford Rd.
Kensington, MD 20895-2726

Raggedy Anns and Andys
Also related items
Gwen Daniel
18 Belleau Lake Ct.
O'Fallon, MO 63366

Railroadiana
Dean D. Collins
P.O. Box 9623
Madison, WI 53715

William F. Hayley
3305 Chartwell Rd.
Birmingham, AL 35226-2603

Judith Katz-Schwartz
222 E 93rd St., 42D
New York, NY 10128

Loren J. Snyder
6867 Navarre Rd. SW
Massillon, OH 44646

David H. Ward
20406 Little Bear Cr. Rd. #25
Woodinville, WA 98072

Records
L.R. 'Les' Docks
Shellac Shack; Discollector
Box 691035
San Antionio, TX 78269-1035

45 rpm
Sunrise Records
Mark Phillips
2425 S 11th St.
Beaumont, TX 77701

Red Riding Hood by Hull
Antiquity Collectibles
3714 Lexington Rd.
Michigan City, IN 46360

Redwing Pottery
Juanita Lind
Box 464
Columbia Falls, MT 59912

Tom Tangen
2930 Hwy. 12
Wilson, WI 54027

Paul L. Trentz
126 E McKinley
Stoughton, WI 53589

Road Maps
Oil company or states
Noel Levy
P.O. Box 595699
Dallas, TX 75359-5699

Robinson Ransbottom
Tammy Rodrick
Rt. 2, Box 163
Sumner, IL 62466

Rolling Pins
Glass or ceramic
Christina Caldwell
Rt. 1, Box 336
Hawkins, TX 75765

Rookwood
Joe Brell
607 Center Ave.
Pittsburgh, PA 15215

Roselane Sparklers
Lee Garmon
1529 Whittier St.
Springfield, IL 62704

Rosemeade
Clayton Zeller
Rt. 2, Box 46
Grandforks, ND 58203

Roseville
James Goad
1152A S Eagle Cir.
Aurora, CO 80012

Zephyr Lily (brown)
Juanita Lind
Box 464
Columbia Falls, MT 59912

Pat and Bill Ogden
3050 Colorado Ave.
Grand Junction, CO 81504

Vintage Charm
P.O. Box 26241
Austin, TX 78755

Royal China
Currier and Ives; Colonial Homestead
Linda Flowers
1777 St. Rd. #14
Deerfield, OH 44411

Currier and Ives; Memory Lane
Pat and Bill Ogden
3050 Colorado Ave.
Grand Junction, CO 81504

Colonial Homestead
Tammy Rodrick
Rt. 2, Box 163
Sumner, IL 62466

Royal Copley
Joe Devine
D&D Antique Mall
1411 3rd St.
Council Bluffs, IA 51503

Royal Doulton
James Goad
1152A S Eagle Cir.
Aurora, CO 80012

E. Sargent Legard
P.O. Box 262
Stratham, NH 03885

Royal Haeger and Royal Hickman
Lee Garmon
1529 Whittier St.
Springfield, IL 62704

Russel Wright
Ray Vlach, Jr.
5346 N Magnet Ave.
Chicago, IL 60630-1216

Salt and Pepper Shakers
James Goad
1152A S Eagle Cir.
Aurora, CO 80012

James P. Skinner
5209 W Hutchinson
Chicago, IL 60641

Vera Skorupski
226 Deerfield Dr.
Berlin, CT 06037

G.A. Underwood
909 N Sierra Bonita Ave., Apt. 9
Los Angeles, CA 90046-6562

Salts, Open
Marjorie Geddes
P.O. Box 5875
Aloha, OR 97007

Schoolhouse Collectibles
Kenn Norris
P.O. Box 4830
Sanderson, TX 79848-4830

Scottie Dog Collectibles
Wee Scots, Inc.
Donna Newton
P.O. Box 1512
Columbus, IN 47202

Sewing Collectibles
Marjorie Geddes
P.O. Box 5875
Aloha, OR 97007

Dorothy Van Deest
494 Saint Nick Dr.
Memphis, TN 38117-4118

Sewing Machines
Jerry Propst
P.O. Box 45
Janesville, WI 53547-0045

Shawnee Pottery
John Hathaway
Rt. 2, Box 220
Bryant Pond, ME 04219

Linda Hicks
3055 E Lake
Gladwater, TX 75647

Pat and Bill Ogden
3050 Colorado Ave.
Grand Junction, CO 81504

Shawnee Pottery Collectors
Pamela D. Curran
P.O. Box 713
New Smyrna Beach, FL 32170-0713

Sheet Music
Relating to Black Americana
William G. Sommer
9 W 10th St.
New York, NY 10011

Shirley Temple
Gen Jones
294 Park St.
Medford, MA 02155

Sandi Waddell
2791 Country Rd. 302
Durango, CO 81301

Shot Glasses
Author of book
Mark Pickvet
P.O. Box 90404
Flint, MI 48509

Silhouettes
Rose Blundell
1700 Macon St.
McLean, VA 22101

Shirley Mace
Author of book, *Shadow Pictures*
Shadow Enterprises
P.O. Box 61
Cedar, MN 55011-066

Silverplate
Rhonda Hallden
21958 Darvin Dr.
Saugus, CA 91350

Slag Glass Animals
Especially Imperial or Westmoreland
Robert and Sharon Thoerner
15549 Ryon Ave.
Bellflower, CA 90706

Slot Machines and Games
Angie's Attic
2562 S Halsted
Chicago, IL 60608

Dembeck Keys and Locksmiths
24711 Harper
St. Clair, MI 48080

Snowdomes
Nancy McMichael, Editor
P.O. Box 53262
Washington, DC 20009

Souvenir Spoons
Sandi Waddell
2791 County Rd. 302
Durango, CO 81301

Space Collectibles
Judith Katz-Schwartz
222 E 93rd St., 42D
New York, NY 10128

Sports Collectibles
Sports Cards
Sally S. Carver
179 South St.
Chestnut Hill, MA 02167

Sports Pins
Tony George
22366 El Toro Rd. #242
Lake Forest, CA 92630

Ray Smith
SandS Antiques
P.O. Box 254
Elizabeth, NJ 07207

Any baseball collectible
Windmill Antiques
315 SW 77th Ave.
N Lauderdale, FL 33068

Liberty Bell
Pat and Bill Ogden
3050 Colorado Ave.
Grand Junction, CO 81504

Stangl
Birds
Joe Brell
607 Center Ave.
Pittsburgh, PA 15215

Birds
G.D. Johnson
7565 Roosevelt Way NE
Seattle, WA 98115

Birds
Pat and Bill Ogden
3050 Colorado Ave.
Grand Junction, CO 81504

Ranger and children's pieces
Ray Vlach, Jr.
5346 N Magnet Ave.
Chicago, IL 60630-1216

Statue of Liberty
Mike Brooks
7335 Skyline
Oakland, CA 94611

Peter B. Kaplan
7 E 20th St., Suite 4R
New York, NY 10003

Star Trek and Star Wars
George J. Seiger
Closet Collectibles
531 Hoyt St.
Pringle, PA 18704

Steamship
Great Lakes
Dean D. Collins
P.O. Box 9623
Madison, WI 53715

Sterling Silver
Antique Silver House
8976 Seminole Blvd.
St. Petersburg, FL 34642

Dressing table items
K. Hartman
7459 Shawnee Rd.
N Tonawanda, NJ 14120

Stocks and Bonds
David M. Beach
Paper Americana
P.O. Box 2026
Goldenrod, FL 32733

Stoneware (blue and white)
Ralonda Lindsay
2504 E Vancouver
Broken Arrow, OK 74014

Strawberry Shortcake
Geneva D. Addy
P.O. Box 124
Winterset, IA 50273

Surveying Equipment
Richard Price
Box 219, 27 Pearl St.
Arendtsville, PA 17303

Tea-Related Items
Betty Bird
107 Ida St.
Mount Shasta,CA 96067

Tina Carter
882 S Mollison
El Cajon, CA 92020

Teddy Bears
Shirley Bertrand
971 N Milwaukee Ave., Box 99A
Wheeling, IL 60090

Shelby Good
4640 W Ave. L-2
Quartz Hill, CA 93536

Mary Ellen Sparr
3213 Seventh St.
Cuyahoga Falls, OH 44221

Sherry Thornhill
Rt. 1, Box 32
Hawk Point, MO 63349

Telephones
Also telegraph memorabilia
Mike Bruner
6980 Walnut Lake Rd.
W Bloomfield, MI 48323

Antique to modern; also parts
Phoneco
207 E Mill Rd.
P.O. Box 70
Galesville, WI 54630

The Three Stooges
Soitenly Stooges Inc.
Harry S. Ross
P.O. Box 72
Skokie, IL 60076

Tobacco Tins
Clayton Zeller
Rt. 2, Box 46
Grandforks, ND 58203

Tools
Ed Keeler
8 Forest Rd.
Burnt Hills, NY 12027

Betty Martin
Box 41B Rt. 4
Eolia, MO 63344

Larry Smith
2432 S Park Rd.
Bethel Park, PA 15102

Machinist
John R. Treggiari
5 Pioneer Cir.
Salem, MA 01970-1225

Flat-belt powered for shop
Jack W. Zimmerly Jr.
c/o 11722 Sharp Rd.
Waterford, PA 16441

Toys
Toys of the Sixties
Author of book
Bill Bruegman
137 Casterton Ave.
Akron, OH 44303

Especially die-cast vehicles
Mark Giles
P.O. Box 821
Ogallala, NE 69153-0821

Wind-ups
Floyd F. Gilmer
P.O. Box 13983
Roanoke, VA 24038

Trains
William F. Hayley
3305 Chartwell Rd.
Birmingham, AL 35226-2603

Phil Helley
Old Kilbourn Antiques
629 Indiana Ave.
Wisconsin Dells, WI 53965

Terri Mardis Ivers
1104 Shirlee
Ponca City, OK 74601

Especially transformers and robots
David Kolodny-Nagy
3701 Connecticut Ave. NW #500
Washington, DC 20008; 202-364-8753

Items for consignment auctions
Dora Lerch
P.O. Box 586
N White Plains, NY 10603

Before 1960
Lor-Wal Antiques
P.O. Box 142
S Jamesport, NY 11970

Phil McEntee
Where the Toys Are
45 W Pike St.
Canonsburg, PA 15317

Slot race cars from 1960s-70s
Gary T. Pollastro
4156 Beach Dr. SW
Seattle, WA 98116

Relating to transportation
Gary Reed
P.O. Box 342
Fenton, MO 63026

Tammy Rodrick
Rt. 2, Box 163
Sumner, IL 62466

Especially from 1950s-60s
Rick Rowe, Jr.
Childhood, The Sequel
HC 1, Box 788
Saxon, WI 54559

Relating to John Deere or Caterpillar
J. Schreier
Rt. 1, Box 1147
Norwalk, WI 54648

Especially from 1870-1950
David A. Smith
1142 S Spring St.
Springfield, IL 62704

BB Guns
Loren J. Snyder
6867 Navarre Rd. SW
Massillon, OH 44646

Judith Katz-Schwartz
222 E 93rd St., 42D
New York, NY 10128

Farm-related from 1950-1980
Edward T. Wegman
3818 Mt. Read Blvd. 'Z'
Rochester, NY 14616

Walkers, ramp-walkers, and wind-ups
Randy Welch
1100 Hambrooks Blvd.
Cambridge, MD 21613

Tramp Art
Judith Katz-Schwartz
222 E 93rd St., 42D
New York, NY 10128

Trolls
Roger Inouye
2622 Valewood Ave.
Carlsbad, CA 92008-7925

Tammy Rodrick
Rt. 2, Box 163
Sumner, IL 62466

Trunks
Sharon Hamer
P.O. Box 246
Durango, CO 81302

Patricia Quink
Box 733
Big Piney, WY 83113

TV Guides
Author of book
TV Guide Specialists
Jeff Kadet
P.O. Box 20
Macomb, IL 61455

TV Lamps
Horse figurines
Trudy E. Jorde
P.O. Box 82
Devils Lake, ND 58301

Twin Winton/Winfield
Ray Vlach, Jr.
5346 N Magnet Ave.
Chicago, IL 60630-1216

Typewriter Ribbon Tins
Ken Stephens
12 Lloyd Ave.
Florence, KY 41042

Hobart D. Van Deusen
28 the Green
Watertown, CT 06795

Typewriters
Jerry Propst
P.O. Box 45
Janesville, WI 53547-0045

Van Briggle
James Goad
1152A S Eagle Cir.
Aurora, CO 80012

Author of book
Scott Nelson
Box 6081
Santa Fe, NM 87502

Pat and Bill Ogden
3050 Colorado Ave.
Grand Junction, CO 81504

Terre Sue Stevens
Rt. 3, Box 97
Plainview, TX 79072

Vernon Kilns
Ray Vlach, Jr.
5346 N Magnet Ave.
Chicago, IL 60630-1216

Vises
Small with patent mark
John R. Treggiari
5 Pioneer Cir.
Salem, MA 01970-1225

View Master Reels and Packets
Walter Sigg
3-D Entertainment
P.O Box 208
Smartswood, NJ 07877

Umbrellas and Umbrella Handles
Arthur Boutiette
410 W Third St.
Suite 200
Little Rock, AR 72201

Wade
Author of book
Ian Warner
P.O. Box 93022
Brampton, Ontario
Canada L6V 4V8

Shirley Yoder
4983 Oak St. SW
Kalona, IA 52247

Watch Fobs
Author of book
Margaret Kaduck
P.O. Box 260764
Cleveland, OH 44126

Watches
Comic character
Howard S. Brenner
106 Woodgate Terrace
Rochester, NY 14625

Vintage
Julius Calloway
884 Riverside Dr.
New York, NY 10032

All brands and character
James Lindon
5267 W Cholla St.
Glendale, AZ 85304

Swatch
Walt Thompson
Box 2541
Yakima, WA 98907-2541

Swatch
Timesavers
Box 400
Algonquin, IL 60102

Swatch
W.B.S. Marketing
P.O. Box 3280
Visalia, CA 93278

Watt Pottery
Lona Siegfried
P.O. Box 25
Carterville, IL 62918

Tom Tangen
2930 Hwy. 12
Wilson, WI 54027

Weller
Vintage Charm
P.O. Box 26241
Austin, TX 78755

Western Americana
Ephemera and unusual books
Carroll Burcham
5546 17th Place
Lubbock, TX 79416

Roland Folsom
Rt. 3, 10th St.
Waukon, IA 52172

Rusty and Iris Gilbert
P.O. Box 92
Adkins, TX 78101

Cowboy gear
James A. Lindsay
P.O. Box 562
Julliaetta, ID 83535

Wicker
Sharon Hamer
P.O. Box 246
Durango, CO 81302

Wizard of Oz
Lori Landgrebe
2331 E Main St.
Decatur, IL 62521

World's Fair
Judith Katz-Schwartz
222 E 93rd St., 42D
New York, NY 10128

Yo-Yos
Figural, advertising, etc.
Jim Marvey
5810 Salsbury Ave.
Minnetonka, MN 55345

Index

NOSTALGIA PUBLISHING COMPANY, INC. 1993 CATALOG

This catalog contains over 200 titles that we recommend on antiques & collectibles. These titles were chosen from several leading publishers in this field. These are the titles that we are currently stocking, and would be happy to fill your order within 24 hours of receipt. So please look over the next few pages and if there are titles that are of interest to you, simply fill out the order form on page 512 and send it to:

Nostalgia Publishing • P.O. Box 277 • La Center, KY 42056

General Antiques

Schroeder's Antiques Price Guide
Eleventh Edition
More than 45,000 items in almost 500 categories are listed along with hundreds of sharp original photos that illustrate not only the rare and unusual, but the common collectibles as well – not postage stamp photos, but large close-up shots that show important details clearly. Each subject is represented with histories and background information.
#3323, 8½ x 11, 608 Pgs., PB $12.95

Kovel's Antiques & Collectibles Price List
25th Edition • by Ralph & Terry Kovel
Included in this 25th Anniversary edition are up-to-date prices for virtually every category of antiques and collectibles. More than 50,000 current values, hundreds of factory marks and identifying logos, and more than 500 photos are included.
#2361, 5½ x 8½, 864 Pgs., PB $13.00

Flea Market Trader • 8th Edition
Edited by Bob & Sharon Huxford
The *Flea Market Trader* is one of the few guides that deal exclusively with all types of merchandise you'll be likely to encounter in the market-place. It contains not only reliable pricing information, but the *Flea Market Trader* will be the first to tune you in to the market's newest collectible interests.
#3316, 5½ x 8½, 336 Pgs., PB $9.95

Warman's 26th Antiques and Their Prices
1992 Edition
Included are over 1,000 photos, illustrations & factory marks which will help make identification of collectibles easier. Over 50,000 items are fully indexed from ABC Plates through Zsolnay Pottery in this revised edition. Also included is a section of pattern glass including over 120 pages of illustrations & current values.
#2395, 5½ x 6¾, 704 Pgs., PB $14.95

Glassware & Bottles

Avon Collectibles Price Guide
by Bud Hastin
This is THE guide to collectible Avon bottles and products. This new 1st edition features the most popular items for Avon bottle collectors. It contains over 250 pages with thousands of photographs and items with information, circa date and current values.
#2291, 7½ x 9, 272 Pgs., PB $14.95

Collecting Barber Bottles
by Richard Holiner
Until now, very little has been produced concerning the many varied and colorful patterns of barber bottles. This book fills that void. The color illustrations accurately portray the beauty of antique glass and the variety of shapes. Included are hundreds of full color photos with current values and informative text.
#1713, 8½ x 11, 128 Pgs., HB $24.95

Bottle Pricing Guide
3rd Edition • by Hugh Cleveland
This revised 3rd edition of Hugh Cleveland's popular bottle guide features over 4,000 bottles listed alphabetically. It contains hundreds of photos including Avons, medicine bottles, Jim Beam bottles, bitters, and a revised value guide.
#1128, 5½ x 8½, 251 Pgs., PB $7.95

Cambridge Glass, 1930-1934
We were excited when The Cambridge Collectors of America Inc. brought us four old Cambridge catalogs to be reprinted. These catalogs have over 3,400 etchings of Cambridge Glass and are combined and cased. Updated current values are included.
#1006, 11 x 8½, 254 Pgs., PB $14.95

Children's Glass Dishes, China & Furniture
by Doris Lechler
This large hardbound book has over 2,500 children's accessories illustrated. Includes Depression glass, pattern glass, Heisey & Imperial glass, miniature furniture and much more.
#2310, 8½ x 11, 240 Pgs., HB $19.95

Cambridge Glass 1949-1953
The Cambridge Collectors of America Inc. have once again compiled an edition of catalog reprints. This edition is a companion volume to the previous Cambridge guide. Thousands of pieces of the popular Cambridge Glass are illustrated and current values are included.
#1007, 8½ x 11, 304 Pgs., PB $14.95

Children's Glass Dishes, China & Furniture
2nd Series • by Doris Lechler
This 2nd series has no repeats of items in the first series and includes approximately 2,000 children's items and current values.
#1627, 8½ x 11, 208 Pgs., HB.................................$19.95

Collector's Encyclopedia of Akro Agate Glassware
by Gene Florence
This marbleized glass that was produced from 1911 to 1951 has now won the hearts of collectors. The many that have been searching for this book will be glad to know it's back in print and all values have been updated.
#2352, 8½ x 11, 80 Pgs., PB..................................$14.95

The Collector's Encyclopedia of American Art Glass
By John Shuman
This book combines beautiful full color photos with an extensive text. Complete descriptions, original catalog and advertising material make this book the most informative available.
#1810, 8½ x 11, 336 Pgs., HB..................................$29.95

Collector's Encyclopedia of Children's Dishes
by Margaret & Kenn Whitmyer
Featuring over 500 color photos, this hardbound edition includes recent & repros, & reissues, catalog reprints and current values for each piece.
#3312, 8½ x 11, 278 Pgs., HB................................$19.95

Collector's Encyclopedia of Fry Glass
by Fry Glass Society

Collectors of Depression-era glassware look for the opalescent reamers and opaque green kitchenware made during the early 30's. This encyclopedia has some of the most complete history and background information ever published on any glass subject. This book is produced with 80% of its photography in full color. Includes current prices.

#1961, 8½ x 11, 224 Pgs., HB..................$24.95

Cartoon & Promotional Drinking Glasses
by John Hervey

A fine quality book to help you price your collection of drinking glasses. Everything from McDonalds to Sports to Pepsi to Disney and much more. Includes 100's of photographs and 8 pages of full color. Current values are included for all photographs.

#2184, 8½ x 11, 176 Pgs., PB $17.95

Covered Animal Dishes
by Everett Grist

Included are over 200 beautiful, full color photos that include nearly 600 different dishes. Some very interesting text is provided and of course current values. Mr. Grist has spent a lifetime dealing in antiques and collectibles including covered animal dishes. Collectors and dealers alike will welcome this book.

#1843, 8½ x 11, 120 Pgs., PB $14.95

Electric Lighting of the 20's & 30's
Edited by James Edward Black

Lamps of Jeanette, Handel, Moe Bridges, Art Deco, wicker, floor, & table. Fine catalog reprints and photos with hundreds of lamps priced. Features black and white photographs with some color.

#1979, 8½ x 11, 124 Pgs., PB $12.95

The Collector's Encyclopedia of Pattern Glass
by Mollie Helen McCain

This author is one of the country's most recognized authorities on pattern glass. This comprehensive volume contains hundreds of illustrations of patterns and a complete pricing system for the glass.

#1380, 5½ x 8½, 541 Pgs., PB..................$12.95

Imperial Glass Identification & Value Guide

The popular glassware of the Imperial Glass Company has become a very collectible item in recent years. This guide combines several of the company's early catalogs and gives the glassware current market values. Glass dealers and collectors will love this large edition.

#1008, 8½ x 11, 212 Pgs., PB $14.95

The Opalescent Glass Price Guide
by Bill Edwards

This handy guide contains scores of color photos and is the 1st book on the subject to list prices for virtually every pattern, color and shape made from 1890-1940.

#2347, 8½ x 11, 64 Pgs., PB $9.95

The Standard Encyclopedia of Carnival Glass
3rd Edition • by Bill Edwards

This is the most comprehensive carnival glass book available today. This large format, deluxe hardbound edition features hundreds of full color photographs and lots of information on patterns, available colors, manufacturers, and much more. The value guide is now bound within this edition at no additional charge.

#2221, 8½ x 11, 288 Pgs., HB..................$24.95

Collector's Encyclopedia of Heisey Glass 1925-1938
by Neila Bredehoft

This encyclopedia has 32 pages of full color. Original sales catalogs #14B, 212, and 109 are reprinted featuring 1000's of pieces of glass plus current values.

#1664, 8½ x 11, 464 Pgs., HB..................$24.95

Colors in Cambridge
by National Cambridge Society

The National Cambridge Society has banded together to produce this beautiful book. They photographed more Cambridge Glass than has ever been put into one book. This full color book has many pieces illustrated with complete history of the company. Also included are current values.

#1523, 8½ x 11, 128 Pgs., HB..................$19.95

Czechoslovakian Glass & Collectibles
by Dale & Diane Barta & Helen M. Rose

This title not only includes the most beautiful glass but also includes purses, jewelry, pottery, porcelain, china, lamps and other collectibles made in Czechoslovakia. Full color photos, histories, descriptions, dates, and current values are also included. The authors have traveled and researched this collectible for several years.

#2275, 8½ x 11, 152 Pgs., PB..................$16.95

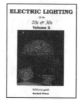

Electric Lighting of the 20's & 30's, Vol. 2
by James Edward Black

Volume 2 contains no repeats of the first volume and is produced to be a companion to Volume I. Lamps included are Handel, Jeanette, boudoir, floor, hanging, wall, and many more. This book also contains current values. Lamp collectors will want both editions of this popular series.

#2115, 8½ x 11, 110 Pgs., PB..................$12.95

400 Trademarks on Glass
by Arthur G. Peterson

This definitive text will be of lasting interest and value to collectors of glassware for years to come. This scholarly study of trademarks on glass has been summarized in concise and convenient form for excellent identification of glass.

#3471, 5½ x 8½, 54 Pgs., PB..................$9.95

1000 Fruit Jars Priced and Illustrated
by Bill Schroeder

This is the fifth edition of what is probably the best selling jar and bottle book ever published. This little book shows an illustration of each embossing on the front of the jar. Each jar has such information as size, color, closure and value.

#1782, 5½ x 8½, 76 Pgs., PB..................$5.95

Quality Electric Lamps, A Pictorial Price Guide
by Arthur G. Peterson

Hundreds of full color examples of quality electric lamps are featured in full color. This book will help you identify and price the lamps in your collection, or it might help you identify that lamp you have been looking for. Collectors will enjoy this release.

#3423, 8½ x 11, 188 Pgs., HB..................$39.95

Standard Carnival Glass Price Guide
8th Edition • by Bill Edwards

Hundreds of patterns and pieces of carnival glass are listed and priced in this value guide by popular glass author Bill Edwards. Many illustrations are provided for identification. This easy to use price guide to carnival glass is ideal for the advanced collector as well as the novice.

#2222, 8½ x 11, 64 Pgs., PB..................$7.95

The Standard Old Bottle Price Guide
by Carlo & Dorothy Sellari
The authors, well-known authorites on collectible bottles, produced this listing of thousands of old bottles with current values. They have included hundreds of excellent photographs for ease of identification.
#1922, 8½ x 11, 176 Pgs., PB..............$14.95

The World of Salt Shakers
2nd Edition • by Mildred & Ralph Lechner
Thousands of antique salt shakers are featured in beautiful full color. Comprehensive text includes factual descriptions, dates, current values, and much more.
#2224, 8½ x 11, 312 Pgs., HB..............$24.95

— Depression Era Glassware —

Bedroom & Bathroom Glassware of the Depression Years
by Kenn & Margaret Whitmyer
Collectors have now begun buying this glassware made during the mid 20's to mid 30's. Over 300 beautiful, full-color photographs containing 1,000's of items are included. Current values are given for each piece.
#2016, 8½ x 11, 256 Pgs., HB..............$19.95

Collectible Glassware of the 40's, 50's, 60's...
by Gene Florence
Produced in the same easy-to-use format as Florence's *Collector's Encyclopedia of Depression Glass,* with large full-color photos of 1000's of pieces with current values, descriptions and company histories.
#2270, 8½ x 11, 144 Pgs., HB..............$19.95

Collector's Encyclopedia of Depression Glass
10th Edition • by Gene Florence
Depression glass collectors have recently reported that glass collecting has never been better, and prices are still rising. This 10th Anniversary Edition has been completely revised and many new finds have been added. A special section is included to expose re-issues and fakes.
#2273, 8½ x 11, 224 Pgs., HB..............$19.95

Elegant Glassware of the Depression Era
5th Edition • by Gene Florence
Features the better glassware made during the Depression. Florence has added many new finds and re-photographed much of his 4th edition making this a totally new book. A large setting photograph is included for each pattern as well as a close-up of patterns to help the collector better identify the glass.
#3315, 8½ x 11, 224 Pgs., HB..............$19.95

Glass Animals of the Depression Era
by Lee Garmon & Dick Spencer
Probably the most popular items collected out of the Depression glass family are the many different glass animals. This book represents an in-depth look at the animal and figurine production during the Depression Era, and also features a section on reissues that have been produced.
#3318, 8½ x 11, 240 Pgs., HB..............$19.95

Very Rare Glassware of the Depression Years
by Gene Florence

Are you still wondering if that piece of Depression glass that you found is rare and possibly valuable? This set of 3 *Very Rare Glassware of the Depression Years* may be just what you need to identify and evaluate that glassware. These editions are just jam-packed with new finds presented in full color. Each is a companion volume to the other with all new photos and prices presented in each series.

Kitchen Glassware of the Depression Years
4th Edition • by Gene Florence
A revised 4th edition features all the new finds that have turned up since the 3rd edition. Gene Florence also added many new group shots as well as updated the values on all the popular pieces in each color. It features over 3,000 pieces of glass listing size, color, pattern description & current values.
#2024, 8½ x 11, 224 Pgs., HB..............$19.95

1st Series, #1848, 8½ x 11, 128 Pgs., HB $24.95

2nd Series, #2140, 8½ x 11, 144 Pgs., HB $24.95

3rd Series, #3326, 8½ x 11, 144 Pgs., HB $24.95

Pocket Guide To Depression Glass
8th Edition • by Gene Florence
This popular guide has been completely revised with all values being updated. Full color presentation and the same easy-to-use format with bold photographs make pattern identification simple. Also includes a section on re-issues and fakes.
#3322, 5½ x 8½, 160 Pgs., PB..............$9.95

— Pottery, Porcelain & China —

Blue & White Stoneware
by Kathryn McNerney
Blue & white pitchers, crocks and bowls have increased in popularity and price making this guide a must for collectors. This full-color guide has 100's of photos, descriptions and values.
#1312, 5½ x 8½, 160 Pgs., PB..............$9.95

Blue Ridge Dinnerware, Revised 3rd Edition
by Betty & Bill Newbound
Expanded to a larger format, this 3rd editon has 100's of color photos of new finds and known pieces. Includes updated values, a complete marks section and many old company catalogs.
#1958, 8½ x 11, 160 Pgs., PB..............$14.95

Blue Willow Revised 2nd edition
by Mary Frank Gaston
Completely rephotographed in full color, this revised edition has been expanded to include over 400 photos, complete descriptions, updated values and a special marks section.
#1959, 8½ x 11, 192 Pgs., PB..............$14.95

Collecting Yellowware
by Lisa McAllister & John Michel
Filled with over 300 color photos, the comprehensive chapters include molds, pitchers, miniatures, figural and more. Current values and a special marks section make this a great reference guide.
#3311, 8½ x 11, 128 Pgs., PB..............$16.95

Collector's Encyclopedia of American Dinnerware
by Jo Cunningham
This comprehensive dinnerware book featuring 100's of pieces in color and black & white. Includes backstamps, advertising, loads of company info, and current values.
#1373, 8½ x 11, 336 Pgs., HB....................................$24.95

Collector's Encyclopedia of Cookie Jars
by Fred & Joyce Roerig
The authors have brought to you what very well could be the last word on this subject. 1,000's of full-color examples are beautifully photographed in this 312 page encyclopedia. Each photograph includes complete descriptions, manufacturers, sizes, histories and, of course, current values.
#2133, 8½ x 11, 312 Pgs., HB....................................$24.95

Collector's Encyclopedia of Flow Blue China
by Mary Frank Gaston
This hardbound edition features 436 illustrations in full color and 168 different marks. An excellent background section is also included with this current value and identification guide.
#1439, 8½ x 11, 160 Pgs., HB....................................$19.95

Collector's Encyclopedia of Figural & Novelty Salt & Pepper Shakers
by Melva Davern

Thousands of figural and novelty shakers are photographed in color – animals, clowns, birds, children, and more. Each encyclopedia features large photos and an easy-to-use format to help aid in identification. Huggers, nesters, longfellows, turn-abouts, go-withs and one piece shakers are explored as well as the traditional two piece set. These two volumes will give you an extensive amount of reference material on ceramic, plastic, metal, chalkware, china, and glass salt & pepper shakers, both foreign and domestic. All with a current value guide.

Volume I, #1634, 8½ x 11, 160 Pgs., PB.................$19.95
Volume II, #2020, 8½ x 11, 216 Pgs., PB.................$19.95

Collector's Encyclopedia of Limoges Porcelain
2nd Edition • by Mary Frank Gaston
This revised edition features 100's of beautiful pieces in full color. All are described and valued in this beautiful hardbound volume.
#2210, 8½ x 11, 224 Pgs., HB....................................$24.95

Collector's Encyclopedia of Majolica
by Mariann Katz-Marks
Over the past 10 years Mariann Katz-Marks has authored two books on Majolica Pottery. Now in this third book we have included over 500 beautiful, full color photos & of course, all the values have been updated to reflect the latest trends of this collectible.
#2334, 8½ x 11, 192 Pgs., HB....................................$19.95

Collector's Encyclopedia of McCoy Pottery
by Sharon & Bob Huxford
The most popular pottery authors have written this informative resource. This guide has 121 color photos featuring 100's of pieces of McCoy pottery with current values.
#1358, 8½ x 11, 248 Pgs., HB....................................$19.95

Collector's Encyclopedia of California Pottery
by Jack Chipman
California Pottery has far too long been a missing chapter in the annals of collectible American ceramics. In fact, it has been one of the least documented of all collectibles. But not anymore. Over 26 different companies are represented, each containing company histories, background information and a marks section.
#2272, 8½ x 11, 168 Pgs., HB....................................$24.95

Collector's Encyclopedia of Fiesta
7th Edition • by Sharon & Bob Huxford
Revised and updated with several new finds being added, this expanded edition is in full color with over 1,000 pieces of Fiesta illustrated.
#2209, 8½ x 11, 190 Pgs., HB....................................$19.95

Collector's Encyclopedia of Gaudy Dutch & Welsh
by John Shuman
The author has written what could be the last word on Gaudy Dutch and Welsh earthenware. This book includes a complete marks section, color photos, comprehensive information and current values.
#2086, 8½ x 11, 176 Pgs., PB $16.95

Collector's Encyclopedia of Hall China
by Margaret & Kenn Whitmyer
This full color presentation features all the popular lines of Hall China and dinnerware and provides collectors with a general price guide with current values to the many pieces pictured.
#1915, 8½ x 11, 256 Pgs., HB....................................$19.95

Collector's Encyclopedia of Hull Pottery
by Brenda Roberts
Over 2,500 items are illustrated and described in this hardbound volume. Descriptions of 116 Hull lines with an in-depth history of the pottery as well as a current value guide make this an excellent resource.
#1276, 8½ x 11, 208 Pgs., HB....................................$19.95

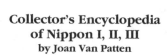

Collector's Encyclopedia of Nippon I, II, III
by Joan Van Patten

Joan Van Patten has compiled the most complete series ever published on Nippon porcelain. This porcelain is becoming more valuable each day and colletors will want to keep up with this ever changing market. With this series they will be able to do just that, because each volume contains useful information, photographs and current values. Each volume features over 700 illustrations that are not included in the other volumes. The complete set contains over 2,000 items illustrated in full color. The set has over 3,000 listings, most of them pictured, and all with current values.

Volume I, #1039, 8½ x 11, 238 Pgs., HB...............$19.95
Volume II, #2089, 8½ x 11, 256 Pgs., PB $24.95
Volume III, #1665, 8½ x 11, 336 Pgs., PB.............$24.95

Collector's Encyclopedia of Niloak Pottery
by David Edwin Gifford
This work corrects much misinformation about Niloak pottery and features over 750 pieces, many in full color. Also includes a complete marks section with dates. This is far more than just a value guide.
#3313, 8½ x 11, 255 Pgs., HB...................$19.95

Collector's Encyclopedia of Noritake
by Joan Van Patten
This Japanese china is becoming more and more popular with collectors. Prefaced by a short history of the company, this full color guide has over 450 photos and a large marks section. A current value guide is bound within the book.
#1447, 8½ x 11, 200 Pgs., HB $19.95

Collector's Encyclopedia of Occupied Japan
by Gene Florence

Gene Florence has been collecting & researching Occupied Japan collectibles about 20 years and is regarded as the foremost authority in this field. Each volume has 1000's of items with descriptions and current values. Complete this five volume set and have all the updated information available on this subject.

Volume I, #1037, 8½ x 11, 107 Pgs., PB $14.95
Volume II, #1038, 8½ x 11, 112 Pgs., PB................................$14.95
Volume III, #2088, 8½ x 11, 144 Pgs., PB................................$14.95
Volume IV, #2019, 8½ x 11, 128 Pgs., PB................................$14.95
Volume V, #2335, 8½ x 11, 128 Pgs., PB $14.95

Collector's Encyclopedia of RS Prussia
by Mary Frank Gaston
This volume contains 575 full-color photos of this porcelain. Complete descriptions and a large marks section are also included to help the collector in identification.
#1311, 8½ x 11, 216 Pgs., HB $24.95

Collector's Encyclopedia of RS Prussia
2nd Series • by Mary Frank Gaston
This 2nd series contains no repeats of the 1st book. Beautiful porcelain is once again featured in full color with well over 700 pictures.
#1715, 8½ x 11, 230 Pgs., HB $24.95

Collector's Encyclopedia of Russel Wright Designs
by Ann Kerr
Russel Wright designs, including dinnerware, furniture, housewares and accessories, are extremely collectible. This book includes 100's of photos in full color and black and white with a complete marks section and current value guide.
#2083, 8½ x 11, 192 Pgs., HB...................$19.95

Collector's Encyclopedia of Roseville Pottery I & II
by Sharon & Bob Huxford

This complete set has over 4,000 items illustrated in beautiful full color and a completely illustrated marks section. With this set, one will be able to learn about the history of Roseville as well as having a beautiful full-color identification and value guide.

Volume I, #1034, 8½ x 11, 192 Pgs., HB....$19.95
Volume II, #1035, 8½ x 11, 208 Pgs., HB ..$19.95

Collector's Encyclopedia of Van Briggle Art Pottery
by Richard Sasicki & Josie Fania
A comprehensive guide with over 400 color photos of more than 800 pieces, it includes info on the company history, production, identification and dating, and catalogs, all with current values.
#3314, 8½ x 11, 144 Pgs., HB...................$24.95

Collector's Guide to Weller Pottery
by Sharon & Bob Huxford
This reference work features 175 full-color photos, loads of information and current values. It's the most informative identification guide available on the subject.
#2111, 8½ x 11, 392 Pgs., HB $29.95

Collector's Guide to Country Stoneware & Pottery
by Don & Carol Raycraft
Featuring 182 beautiful, full-color photos. All types of jugs and crocks are identified, described and evaluated.
#3452, 5½ x 8½, 160 Pgs., PB...................$11.95

Collector's Guide to Country Stoneware & Pottery
2nd Series • by Don & Carol Raycraft
This makes a great companion to the first series. 100's of pieces in full color with current values, descriptions, dates, and sizes.
#2077, 8½ x 11, 120 Pgs., PB $14.95

Collector's Guide to Shawnee Pottery
by Don & Carol Raycraft
A refreshing book for the Shawnee collector. There are over 400 full color photos including 120 cookie jars. Many items in this book have never been pictured or listed in any other guides. Also includes catalog pages and current values. The cookie jar section alone will make this a highly sought after edition.
#2339, 8½ x 11, 160 Pgs., HB...................$19.95

Collector's Guide to Harker Pottery
by Neva W. Colbert
Complete histories, tips about collecting, displaying and caring for your collection are all included. With over 100 full color photographs and a current value for each piece, this is the most complete guide available on this popular pottery.
#3433, 8½ x 11, 128 Pgs., PB $17.95

An Illustrated Guide to Cookie Jars
by Ermagene Westfall
Cookie jars were made by many companies in many shapes, styles, and sizes. This full-color identification guide has 100's of jars with important info such as maker, marks, and current values.
#1425, 5½ x 8½, 160 Pgs., PB $9.95

Head Vases, Identification & Value Guide
by Kathleen Cole
This book has over 200 photographs in full-color. Each vase is identified by company, number, date and size. Also included is the current value for all vases listed. Collectors of pottery and porcelain will welcome this release.
#1917, 8½ x 11, 144 Pgs., PB $14.95

Red Wing Collectibles
by Dan & Gail DePasquale & Larry Peterson
This companion volume features 100's of items not featured in *Red Wing Stoneware*. Beautiful, full color examples fill this identification and value guide.
#1670, 5½ x 8½, 160 Pgs., PB $9.95

Red Wing Stoneware
by Dan & Gail DePasquale & Larry Peterson
Kitchen stoneware, crocks, jugs, churns and other items are presented in full-color. Includes special section on marks and 100's of photos help to identify pieces.
#1440, 5½ x 8½, 168 Pgs., PB $9.95

Watt Pottery – An Identification & Value Guide
by Sue & Dave Morris
This popular book contains a history of the pottery and includes over 350 full color photos with dimensions, marks, and current values. Also features unusual and one-of-a-kind pieces.
#3327, 8½ x 11, 160 Pgs., HB $19.95

An Illustrated Value Guide to Cookie Jars
Book II • by Ermagene Westfall
With the ever increasing popularity of cookie jars, Mrs. Westfall has authored an all-new book as a companion volume to her first. Book II contains so many photos and listings it was enlarged to a 8½ x 11 format. It contains over 650 full color photos of 1,000's of jars, each with complete descriptions and current values.
#3440, 8½ x 11, 240 Pgs., PB..............................$19.95

Luckey's Hummel Figurines & Plates
9th Edition • by Carl Luckey
This is the only guide which reflects the drastic price changes that occur annually. Many more rare pieces are included as well as illustrations and information on soon-to-be released pieces. Foremost authority Carl Luckey has made this guide the standard for the collector.
#3360, 5½ x 8½, 446 Pgs., PB $14.95

Lehner's Encyclopedia of U.S. Marks on Pottery, Porcelain & Clay
by Lois Lehner
This book represents about 15 years of intensive work on the part of the author. It contains over 1,900 companies with over 8,000 marks, logos, symbols, etc. divided about equally among the old folk potters, studio potters, dinnerware manufacturers, distributors and decoration companies.
#2379, 8½ x 11, 636 Pgs., HB...............................$24.95

Salt & Pepper Shakers Volumes I, II & III
by Helene Guarnaccia
Salt & Pepper shakers were made in every size and shape imaginable. These identification guides contain full color photos, complete descriptions, interesting facts, dates, plus current values. Virtually every type of shaker is included.

Volume I, #1632, 5½ x 8½, 160 Pgs., PB $9.95
Volume II, #1888, 8½ x 11, 192 Pgs., PB..................$14.95
Volume III, #2220, 8½ x 11, 152 Pgs., PB $14.95

Dolls & Toys

Advertising Dolls
by Joleen Robinson & Kay F. Sellers
Advertising dolls have gained popularity with doll lovers everywhere. This guide illustrates and gives current values for 100's of advertising dolls including Aunt Jemima, Campbell Kids, the Uneeda Biscuit Boy, Kellogg's dolls, plus much more! Over 300 pages packed with interesting information and values.
#2382, 5½ x 8½, 328 Pgs., PB $9.95

Antique & Collectible Marbles
by Everett Grist
This 3rd revised edition has been totally updated. There are 100's of full color examples with interesting comments and current values to virtually every type of marble ever produced. A listing of collectors, clubs, dealers, glass-grinders and marble restorers, plus a section on valuing marbles make this a must for the marble collecting enthusiasts!
#2333, 5½ x 8½, 96 Pgs., PB $9.95

Barbie Fashion, Volume I, 1959-1967
by Sara Sink Eames
This style book shows the clothes and accessories of these popular dolls. Included are complete histories of the wardrobes of Barbie doll, her friends and her family from 1959 to 1967. This deluxe, large format book features hundreds of full color illustrations, complete descriptions and current values.
#2079, 8½ x 11, 256 Pgs., PB..............................$24.95

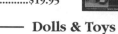

Antique Collector's Dolls I, II
by Patricia Smith
Another popular series by doll authority Patricia Smith features dolls made from 1870 through 1935. Each volume contains about 1,200 dolls with photographs and 2,000 current values. Patricia Smith is probably the most popular doll author and has many titles to her credit. There are no duplicates in either of the books.

I, #2300, 8½ x 11, 304 Pgs., PB.................$17.95
II, #2301, 8½ x 11, 248 Pgs., PB..................$17.95

Black Dolls 1820-1991
An Identification & Value Guide
by Myla Perkins
Myla Perkins' book contains over 1,400 dolls photographed, identified, documented and described. This book includes papier-maché dolls from the 1800's, china dolls from 1" to 20", bisque dolls, including Jumeaus, composition dolls, topsy-turvy dolls, cloth dolls, plastic and vinyl dolls.
#3310, 8½ x 11, 344 Pgs., PB..............................$17.95

Character Toys & Collectibles
by David Longest
This guide has over 400 full-color photos of toys and collectibles. Included in this deluxe edition are: Disney characters, radio characters, space and super heroes, western heroes, Popeye, Orphan Annie and other comic characters, puppets, windups, tin, plastic and rubber toys.
#1514, 8½ x 11, 184 Pgs., HB $19.95

Collectible Male Action Figures
by Paris & Susan Manos
Male action figures and dolls have become more collectible and the need for a good book on the subject increased until two of our popular doll authors filled that need with this informative book. Nearly 250 full color photographs of 100's of dolls with complete listings and values are included.
#2021, 8½ x 11, 112 Pgs., PB $14.95

Collector's Encyclopedia
of Madame Alexander Dolls 1965-1990
by Patricia Smith
Mrs. Smith has been an avid doll collector for many years and has authored over 30 different doll reference value guides. This particular encyclopedia has been in the works for a number of years. Loaded with a wealth of information, it could be the last word on the subject.
#2211, 8½ x 11, 264 Pgs., HB $24.95

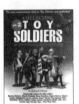

Collecting Toy Soldiers #2
An Identification & Value Guide
by Richard O' Brien
Many newly-discovered early American makers have been added, with their soldiers shown in depth. In the American dimestore area, many new finds are shown, as well as such "new" companies as Wilton, H.B. Toys and Paul Paragine.
#3386, 8½ x 11, 627 Pgs., PB $29.95

Collecting Toys #6
A Collector's Identification & Value Guide
by Richard O' Brien
This is the most comprehensive book on toys ever published. A complete revision and update of the fantastic 5th edition. Thousands of new listings and photos have been added to the existing information. 520 pages loaded with illustrations, many in full color.
#3446, 8½ x 11, 586 Pgs., PB $22.95

Collector's Guide to Tootsietoys
by David Richter
These toys have become hot items at the shows across the country. This book has over 300 pictures that are full size to the toy, wheel identification and separate chapters on each subject such as airplanes, trains, ships, cars, etc.
#2151, 8½ x 11, 152 Pgs., PB $16.95

Grist's Machine Made
& Contemporary Marbles
by Everett Grist
Machine made and contemporary marbles have really become a hot item at flea markets and antique shows in recent months. This book has over 100 full color photographs containing hundreds of marbles. Also included is a very interesting text with complete descriptions and values.
#2278, 5½ x 8½, 96 Pgs., PB $9.95

Madame Alexander Collector's Dolls
Price Guide #18
by Patricia Smith
This full color guide is anxiously awaited each year by collectors of America's most popular dolls. The values are revised annually to reflect today's market and can be used alone or as a companion volume to Smith's other Madame Alexander books.
#3441, 8½ x 11, 80 Pgs., PB $9.95

Character Toys & Collectibles
2nd Series • by David Longest
This series has over 600 full-color photos with no repeats of the first edition. It features a character toy hall of fame with such notables as: Felix, Barney Google, Mutt and Jeff, Uncle Wiggley, Betty Boop, Li'l Abner, and more. This series employs the same easy-to-use format as the first book and has current values plus updates of all the values in the first book.
#1750, 8½ x 11, 256 Pgs., HB $19.95

Collector's Encyclopedia of
Barbie Dolls and Collectibles
by Sibyl DeWein & Joan Ashabraner
Because of popular demand, we have reprinted this detailed and informative publication. With 100's of photos of Barbie doll and her family and friends, this comprehensive book contains information gained from years of intensive research.
#1529, 8½ x 11, 312 Pgs., HB $19.95

Encyclopedia of Toys & Banks
Edited by L-W Publishing
A very nice book on old toys and banks. Everything from Cast Iron to Tin to Wind Ups to Autos and more. Very large selection of cast iron and still banks.
#2046, 8 x 11, 208 Pgs., PB $14.95

Collecting Toy Trains #3
Identification and Value Guide
by Richard O' Brien
This new 3rd edition has added hundreds of new photos and listings. Lionel, Marx, American Flyer, Ives, Buddy L, plus others. This guide includes engines, cars and accessories with descriptions, prices and photos.
#2293, 8½ x 11, 224 Pgs., HB $22.95

The Collector's Encyclopedia of Disneyana
by David Longest & Michael Stern
This is the definitive guide to collecting the golden age of Disneyana, containing more than 860 full color photos of common, rare unusual and highly collectible items. Toys included represent items from the 1930's through the early 1960's with a heavy concentration on Micky Mouse items.
#2338, 8½ x 11, 224 Pgs., HB $24.95

A Historical, Rarity, Value Guide
Fisher-Price® 1931-1963
by John Murray & Bruce Fox
Two of the country's foremost collectors of antique Fisher-Price toys trace the history of Fisher-Price and its evolving toy lines from 1931 to date, concentrating on the 30's, 40's 50's and early 60's. Their book contains nearly 75 black and white and 150 color photographs.
#2358, 8½ x 11, 224 Pgs., PB $24.95

Madame Alexander Collector Dolls
by Patricia Smith
Madame Alexander Dolls are the most popular limited edition dolls manufactured today. A complete reference and value guide, this large, 8½ x 11 hardbound title now includes current values bound in the book. Included are over 600 photos and a wealth of information. After 16 years, it is still one of our bestselling doll books.
#1067, 8½ x 11, 328 Pgs., HB $19.95

Modern Collector's Dolls Update
1993 Edition • by Patricia Smith
Patricia Smith's *Modern Collector's Dolls Series I-IV* contains over 8,000 values & this book completely revises each of those values. This update can be used with any of the *Modern Collector's Dolls* books or it can be used independently, either way it's a bargain at $9.95. Each doll listed contains name, size, date and current values so one can quickly evaluate their dolls.
#3472, 8½ x 11, 96 Pgs., PB $9.95

Modern Collector's Dolls
I, II, III, IV, & V
by Patricia Smith

This series is considered to be the finest and most complete set of identification and value guides ever produced for modern dolls. Each book features 1,200 different photographs and up to 2,000 current values, making the five book series a must for the advanced doll collector and dealer. Dolls from 1935 through 1983 are included in this series with a total of 5,700+ photographs and 8,000+ values. There are no duplicates in any of the five volumes. This deluxe 8½ x 11, hardbound set has over 1,600 pages of modern dolls. Virtually every doll company is represented with photos and current values. Foreign dolls are covered extensively in addition to sections on trolls and puppets.

Volume I, #2185, 8½ x 11, PB.................................$17.95
Volume II, #2186, 8½ x 11, PB $17.95
Volume III, #2187, 8½ x 11, PB $17.95
Volume IV, #2188, 8½ x 11, PB $17.95
Volume V, #2189, 8½ x 11, PB $17.95

Stern's Guide to Disney Collectibles
by Michael Stern
Mickey Mouse and his friends are the most sought after Disney collectibles because everyone of every age identifies with them. Their popularity continues to grow among collectors. Our 8½ x 11, full-color edition is packed full of Disney memorabilia. This book will assist you in dating & pricing your various pieces.
#1886, 8½ x 11, 128 Pgs., PB.................................$14.95

Teddy Bears and Steiff Animals
by Margaret Fox Mandel
With teddy bears becoming more collectible each day, Mrs. Mandel filled the need for a good book on the entire field of Teddy Bears and Steiff Animals. Over 500 full color photographs of bears and animals from 1903-1980 are included in this complete identification and value guide.
#1513, 5½ x 8½, 288 Pgs., PB $9.95

Teddy Bears and Steiff Animals
2nd Series • by Margaret Fox Mandel
Hundreds of bears and animals are featured in full color in this 8½ x 11, hardbound book. Lots of information and a current value guide are included. There is no repeat material from the first book.
#1817, 8½ x 11, 200 Pgs., PB $19.95

Teddy Bears and Steiff Animals
3rd Series • by Margaret Fox Mandel
Each book in this series contains over 300 photos not repeated in any of the other books. This third series includes 100's of examples of teddy bears, Steiff animals & Annalee figures all photographed in color. Includes complete histories, interesting facts, dates, sizes & current values.
#2084, 8½ x 11, 224 Pgs., PB $19.95

Modern Toys 1930-1980
by Linda Baker
This full color guide has thousands of toys with full descriptions and wonderful photographs. Crammed full of toys made from 1930 to 1980 with current values. This deluxe edition contains all American toy manufacturers and their products from the Depression thru Star Wars era.
#1540, 8½ x 11, 267 Pgs., HB $19.95

Patricia Smith's Album of All Bisque Dolls
by Patricia Smith
This all new guide is produced in full color including over 200 dolls. Each color photograph includes size, description, histories, any important information and current values. Most doll collectors will enjoy finding the little dolls in this album. Hopefully going through this book will help each collector better appreciate their collection.
#2344, 8½ x 11, 104 Pgs., PB.................................$14.95

Patricia Smith's Doll Values
9th Series • by Patricia Smith
This new edition includes over 450 full color photos. Practically every doll manufacturer is represented. Over 6,000 dolls are featured and described with current values, histories, tips and a wealth of facts to help in identification.
#3442, 5½ x 8½, 320 Pgs., PB $12.95

Riding Toys

Many color photos of wagons, tricycles, scooters, sleds, irish mails, ride-ons, mobos, and rocking horses. Covering pre 1900's and later. Also included in this book are many catalog pages for reference and pricing. The price guide has current values.
#3448, 8½ x 11, 194 Pgs., PB.................................$29.95

Stern's Guide to Disney Collectibles
2nd Series • by Michael Stern
This second series contains no repeats of the first, hundreds of examples of Disney collectibles in full color and current values. Over 240 beautiful color photographs including virtually every type of Disney collectible from the Golden Age to modern merchandise.
#2139, 8½ x 11, 152 Pgs., PB.................................$14.95

Toys, Antique & Collectible
by David Longest
With over 10,000 listings and values this book is a must for both the new as well as the advanced collector. From the old cast iron toys of yesteryear to the newer modern toys of the 50's & 60's, this book has it all.
#2028, 8½ x 11, 240 Pgs., PB.................................$14.95

The Wonder of Barbie
by Paris and Susan Manos
This book, by the authors of World of Barbie, studies this collecting phenomenon and provides information, values, and photographs of dolls and accessories from 1976 to 1986.
#1808, 5½ x 8½, 134 Pgs., PB $9.95

The World of Barbie Dolls
by Paris and Susan Manos
This edition has 100's of dolls illustrated in full color. Containing Barbie, Ken, Skipper and other friends and family as well as cases, houses, furniture and accessories. This pocket size guide is perfect for the collector on the go! Over 140 pages of Barbies, related items and current values fill this book.
#1430, 5½ x 8½, 144 Pgs., PB $9.95

Antique & Collectible Thimbles
by Averil Mathis

Now with this complete book one will be able to identify and evaluate their collectible thimbles. Over 700 items are featured in full color in this beautiful value guide.

#1712, 8½ x 11, 184 Pgs., HB $19.95

Art Nouveau & Art Deco Jewelry
by Lillian Baker

This guide to Art Nouveau & Art Deco jewelry is by America's best known jewelry author. Hundreds of pieces are described and illustrated in color with values for each item. It is full of information about the Art Nouveau and Art Deco movement.

#1278, 5½ x 8½, 176 Pgs., PB. $9.95

Identification & Value Guide
Collecting Comic Character Clocks & Watches
by Howard Brenner

This is the first and only price guide to deal with those timepieces that we all treasured as youngsters. They are all illustrated with full descriptions, makers, dates and values. Many are in full color. Not only is it a great reference tool for the collector but it's also a trip down memory lane.

#1797, 8½ x 11, 136 Pgs., PB. $14.95

Fifty Years of Fashion Jewelry
by Lillian Baker

More than 75 individual designer-name examples with many full color photos are included in this exciting value guide. Over 400 individual pieces of jewelry are represented from over 25 different collections.

#1716, 8½ x 11, 192 Pgs., HB. $19.95

Answers To Questions About Old Jewelry
3rd Edition • by Jeanenne Bell

This popular book by Jeanenne Bell has been expanded in this new edition with approximately 1,500 photos, many in full color. Each photo is fully described and valued. It also includes information on how to determine whether it's authentic or synthetic. Each period includes information on what influenced the jewelry of that time.

#2390, 5½ x 8½, 445 Pgs., PB. $14.95

Identification & Value Guide To Cameos
by Ed Aswad & Michael Weinstein

For hundreds of years, cameos have been treated as decorations for clothing, fingers and necks with little thought as to the care that went into their making. This is the first reference guide to bring these beautifully handcarved pieces of art to the forefront with full descriptions and detailed photography of over 100 cameos.

#2195, 5½ x 8½, 184 Pgs., PB. $12.95

Antique Purses
Revised 2nd Edition • by Richard Holiner

Richard Holiner has included all the color photos that were in the first edition & added at least that many more to complete this revised second edition. This value guide features hundreds of purses in full color.

#1748, 8½ x 11, 208 Pgs, PB..................$19.95

Collecting Rhinestone Colored Jewelry
An Identification and Value Guide
2nd Edition • by Maryanne Dolan

Rhinestones are becoming more and more valuable! Several hundred pieces have been added to the existing photos with all new prices. This also includes colored stones. The "Designers' Marks" section has now been greatly expanded.

#1985, 5½ x 8½, 464 Pgs, PB.. ....$12.95

Complete Price Guide To Watches
13th Edition • by Shugart & Gilbert

This 13th edition has over 1,000 packed pages with over 7,400 illustrations, 35,000+ current values and 8 pages of full color. The wristwatch section alone has 6,320 illustrations with prices for each. It's professional standard for watch collectors and dealers.

#3456, 5½ x 8½, 1,024 Pgs, PB.. ....$19.95

Hatpins & Hatpin Holders
by Lillian Baker

This full color identification and value guide is filled with useful information. The beautiful photographs are accompanied by descriptions, sizes and circa dates. An easy-to-use value guide is included. This book is an excellent addition to any jewelry or antique collectors library.

#1424, 5½ x 8½, 160 Pgs, PB.. ....$9.95

100 Years of Collectible Jewelry
by Lillian Baker

In this comprehensive guide to collectible and antique jewelry, 100's of pieces of jewelry are photographed in beautiful full color and are presented with authoritative descriptions and current market values.

#1181, 5½ x 8½, 170 Pgs, PB $9.95

Twentieth Century Fashionable Plastic Jewelry
by Lillian Baker

This complete encyclopedia includes great photos, a glossary of terms and types of plastic jewelry, new conceptions and historical footnotes. Virtually every aspect of this prized plastic jewelry is covered in detail, including full descriptions with dates, nomenclature and current values.

#2348, 8½ x 11, 240 Pgs, HB $19.95

American Premium Guide
To Pocket Knives & Razors
3rd Edition • by Jim Sargent

Jim Sargent has added hundreds of photos of rare knives. The collector will also find additional sections on Pal and Browning knives with photos & full descriptions. All existing values have been updated. Other manufacturers include: Winchester, Queen, Western States and Keen Kutter.

#2368, 8½ x 11, 474 Pgs., PB. $22.95

Early Archaic Indian Points & Knives
by Robert Edler

Each of the over 40 types of archaic points are beautifully illustrated and include detailed histories. Also included is a complete section on how Indian points and tools were originally made.

#2015, 8½ x 11, 120 Pgs, PB, No Values. $14.95

Antique Tools: Our American Heritage
by Kathryn McNerney

A much needed reference, this guide to old tools is filled with information on both the common and unusual tools of the past. Fully illustrated, this quality paperback includes current values and descriptions.

#1868, 5½ x 8½, 156 Pgs.........................$9.95

Arrowheads & Projectile Points
by Lar Hothem

Projectile points of American Indians have long been objects of interest to students and historians. Recently they have come to be valuable to collectors as well. This book has 100's of photos of points, information about origin, methods of production, sizes, values and a section on detecting fakes.

#1426, 5½ x 8½, 224 Pgs., PB. $7.95

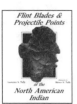

Flint Blades & Projectile Points of the North American Indian
by Lawrence Tully

Lawrence Tully has been studying Indian artifacts for over 40 years and he included all his knowledge into this book. Each artifact pictured is photographed to actual size and there are 100's of good sharp photos. This is without a doubt the last word to the many artifacts of the North American Indian.

#1668, 8½ x 11, 240 Pgs., HB, ...$24.95

Indian Axes & Related Stone Artifacts
by Lar Hothem

This value guide to these primitive axes and stone artifacts is filled with photos and explains the basics, the how-to's and the identification of axe collecting. Both history of Indian axes and the future of axe collecting are included.

#1964, 8½ x 11, 224 Pgs., HB $14.95

Modern Guns Identification & Values
by Russell & Steve Quertermous

This huge collection features 480 pages crammed full of valuable information and photographs that are indispensable to gun lovers. Over 2,250 models of rifles, handguns and shotguns from 1900 to the present are described and priced in excellent and very good condition with suggested retail prices for those models still in production.

#3320, 8½ x 11, 480 Pgs., PB $12.95

North American Indian Ornamental & Ceremonial Artifacts
by Lar Hothem

144 pages with over 400 photos, descriptions and values. Featured are: Effigy stones, Birdstones, Bannerstones, Gorgets, Pendants, Celts, Beadwork, Quiltwork, Trade Ornaments, Pipes plus much more.

#2192, 8½ x 11, 133 Pgs., PB $19.95

The Standard Knife Collector's Guide
2nd Edition • by Roy Ritchie & Ron Stewart

This complete revised 2nd edition includes virtually all knife manufacturers both old and new plus commemoratives, and serves as a general price guide to 1,000's of knives. Many photographs and line drawings are also included to aid the collector. The authors are the publishers of the monthly newsletter *The Whittler*.

#3325, 5½ x 8½, 608 Pgs., PB $12.95

Indian Artifacts of The Midwest
by Lar Hothem

This publication is loaded with all types of artifacts coming from the midwest. It includes a comprehensive text and is much more than just a value guide. Hundreds of photos are included to help in identification.

#2279, 8½ x 11, 208 Pgs., PB $14.95

Keen Kutter Collectibles
by Jerry & Elaine Heuring

Probably the most respected trade name from yesterday's hardware companies was Keen Kutter. Any item marked with this famous logo is sought by today's collector. From hammers & axes through razors, scissors & knives this book covers almost every item that was marked Keen Kutter. This book is well illustrated & contains current values.

#2023, 8½ x 11, 128 Pgs., PB $14.95

North American Indian Artifacts
4th Edition • by Lar Hothem

All values based on the 1991 Allard Auction. This is the guide for collectors and historians on all aspects of North American Indian artifacts. Over 2,300 items listed, described and valued, fully illustrated with many in color.

#2364, 5½ x 8½, 440 Pgs., PB $14.95

Primitives Our American Heritage
1st & 2nd Series • by Kathryn McNerney

Primitives are becoming more and more popular and demanding premium prices. These two books are a wonderful look at life in days gone by featuring identification and value guides on such primitive items as tools, furniture and household goods. Each guide includes hundreds of black & white photographs with no repeats, plus current values. Loaded with information, this set is a must for primitive collectors and dealers.

1st Series, #2164, 5½ x 8½, 190 Pgs., PB ..$9.95
2nd Series, #1759, 8½ x 11, 160 Pgs., PB.$14.95

Furniture

American Oak Furniture
by Kathryn McNerney

This book has over 440 photos with current values for each piece. Benches, stools, bookcases, desks, chairs, beds, dressers, store accessories and much more are featured in this informative and beautiful volume on American oak furniture.

#1457, 5½ x 8½, 176 Pgs., PB $9.95

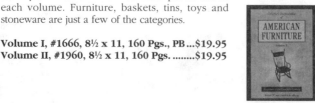

The Book of Country
Volume I & II • by Don & Carol Raycraft

The Raycrafts have loaded these books with wonderful country collectibles. Over 200 color photos are in each volume. Furniture, baskets, tins, toys and stoneware are just a few of the categories.

Volume I, #1666, 8½ x 11, 160 Pgs., PB ...$19.95
Volume II, #1960, 8½ x 11, 160 Pgs. $19.95

Antique Oak Furniture
by Conover Hill

Probably the most collectible furniture available today is oak. Quarter sawn golden oak was the furniture of the era from 1900 to 1930. *Antique Oak Furniture* is the first and foremost value guide on the market today. It contains over 900 pictures and current values.

#1118, 8½ x 11, 124 Pgs., PB $7.95

Collector's Encyclopedia of American Furniture
Volume I • by Robert & Harriet Swedberg

First in a series of furniture books, Volume I contains the dark woods of the nineteenth century including mahogany, cherry, rosewood, and walnut. This beautiful furniture has been photographed in full color with complete descriptions and current values.

#2132, 8½ x 11, 128 Pgs., HB $24.95

Collector's Encyclopedia of American Furniture
Volume II • by Robert & Harriet Swedberg

This volume contains oak, ash, and elm furniture of the Depression era, none of which is included in the first volume. Over 450 full color photos make this a very informative edition and companion to Volume I.

#2271, 8½ x 11, 144 Pgs., HB $24.95

Collector's Guide To Country Furniture
by Don & Carol Raycraft
This price guide features over 100 full-color illustrations with lots of information and values. This first volume contains furniture, baskets, folk art, small decorative items, furniture trends, and a special section on detecting authentic country furniture.
#1437, 5½ x 8½, 112 Pgs., PB $9.95

Collector's Guide To Country Furniture
Book II • by Don & Carol Raycraft
It has been four years since Don & Carol Raycraft wrote their first book on country furniture. After many hours of research they released Book II which has hundreds of full color photos. This companion volume includes the everyday fun-type of collectible, not museum-type funiture.
#1842, 8½ x 11, 112 Pgs., PB $14.95

Furniture of the Arts & Crafts Period
This book has all of the leading manufacturers of Arts & Crafts furniture of the early nineteenth-century. It will be THE book pricing Arts & Crafts furniture. All prices are actual auction prices that these items have sold for. A must for any Arts & Crafts furniture collector.
#3424, 8½ x 11, 160 Pgs., PB $19.95

Furniture of the Depression Era
by Robert & Harriett Swedberg
This is the first and only book to date that deals exclusively with furniture made during the 1920's, 30's & 40's. When one reads this book he will learn what type of furniture was made, why it was made, how it was made, the year it was made, the value today and much more.
#1755, 8½ x 11, 144 Pgs., HB $19.95

Pine Furniture, Our American Heritage
by Kathryn McNerney
Since colonial times, pine furniture has held its own distinctively respected place in our heritage. Kathryn McNerney presents excellent references to pine furniture. In an 8½ x 11, 176 page format, this value guide features beautiful black and white photographs with detailed descriptions of the pieces featured. A short history of the furniture is also included.
#1965, 8½ x 11, 152 Pgs., PB $14.95

Victorian Furniture
by Kathryn McNerney
With the same pleasant style and format of her other books, Kathryn McNerney presents a detailed informative look at this beautiful style of furniture. Useful information and an abundance of photographs are included in this fully illustrated, handy value guide.
#1885, 5½ x 8½, 256 Pgs., PB $9.95

Paper Collectibles & Records

American Premium Record Guide 1900-1965
by Les Docks
The #1 reference for collectors of old records. Thousands upon thousands of listings from over 7,500 artists. 1,500 photos of labels. Jazz, Big Bands, Blues, Rhythm & Blues, Country & Western, Hillbilly, Rock & Roll, Rock-a-Billy, etc. 78's & 45's, LPs and EPs.
#2386, 8½ x 11, 400 Pgs., PB $22.95

Collecting Little Golden Books
by Steve Santi
Since 1942, *The Poky Little Puppy*, and his cohorts, the *Saggy Baggy Elephant*, *Scuffy the Tugboat* plus hundreds of others have delighted all of us at one time. This guide illustrates approximately 700 books, each is fully described and priced. Several hundred others are listed and priced.
#2049, 5½ x 8½, 266 Pgs., PB $10.95

Collector's Guide To Post Cards
by Jane Wood
Over 2,000 post cards are included in this illustrated value guide. It contains 16 pages of full color and features post cards on the subjects of Christmas, Easter, railroad, children, military, and many more. An interesting and informative look at this collectible field.
#1441, 8½ x 11, 176 Pgs., PB $9.95

Comic Book Price Guide
22nd Edition • by Robert Overstreet
Since 1970 the Overstreet Price Guide has been known and accepted as the most comprehensive & reliable source of information in the comic book market. Every known American comic book from 1901 to present is listed and all major artists are pointed out. The information in this guide is as complete as 20 years of research can allow.
#2249, 5½ x 8½, 520 Pgs., PB $15.00

Florence's Standard Baseball Card Price Guide
5th Edition • by Gene Florence
This guide is so easy to use, the advanced collector, beginner or even a child can find a card in seconds. With over 60,000 listings in alphabetical order, it has become a best seller in its field. A color section showing the front and back of the card identifies cards throughout the years.
#3317, 5½ x 8½, 576 Pgs., PB $9.95

Price Guide To Cookbooks
by Colonel Bob Allen
Allen has formed an extensive collection and has been studying and researching cookbooks for many years. This comprehensive study, loaded with histories, dates and current values, features a wealth of information about cookbooks and booklets over the years.
#2081, 8½ x 11, 216 Pgs., PB $14.95

Huxford's Old Book Value Guide
5th Edition
This informative annual guide lists 25,000 titles with current values. More than just a price guide – you'll find actual buyers listed by the subject matter they are looking for, so it's a selling guide as well.
#3439, 8½ x 11, 384 Pgs., HB $19.95

Maxfield Parrish
A Price Guide
This book has 120 pages with 40 pages of full color photos. There are over 932 items plus book plates listed & priced. This book will help anyone who is just starting to collect Maxfield Parrish and it will also help price and identify items that you already have.
#3473, 5½ x 8½, 112 Pgs., PB $12.95

Price Guide To Cookbooks & Recipe Leaflets
by Linda Dickinson
This author has been collecting and studying the history of cookbooks for years and now has completed a very needed price guide to thousands of cookbooks. Included are many large photos to aid the collector in identification. The cookbooks are arranged in alphabetical order to make locating simple.
#2080, 5½ x 8½, 190 Pgs., PB $9.95

Sheet Music Reference & Price Guide
by Marie-Reine A. Pafik & Anna Marie Guiheen
This full color price guide lists the song titles alphabetically with as much information as is available to make identifying quick and simple. You don't have to be able to read music to be an enthusiast of this beautiful and fanciful art form. From Dixie to Jazz, Blues to Ragtime, this is a most enjoyable book.
#2346, 8½ x 11, 296 Pgs., PB $18.95

Advertising Playing Cards
by Everett Grist

This colorful book includes nothing but advertising playing cards. The author has been collecting cards for several years and has bought and sold over 10,000 decks. Included are hundreds of photos with the bulk of the cards from 1940-1970.
#2280, 8½ x 11, 232 Pgs., PB................................$16.95

American Sporting Advertising
Volume I • by Bob & Beverly Strauss

Included are 100's of old calendars and posters that will bring back memories of days past. These advertising items all include some type of sporting item. Guns, shells, and powder advertisers are all included from many different manufacturers. Also included are current values.
#3335, 8½ x 11, 228 Pgs., PB................................$12.95

Antique Advertising Encyclopedia
Volume I • by Ray Klug

This book has long been considered the authority on advertising collectibles. Includes tins, trays, signs and much more. If you are an antique advertising enthusiast, you must have this book for reference and pricing.
#1520, 8 x 10, 327 Pgs., PB................................$17.95

Antique Brass & Copper
by Mary Frank Gaston

Brass and copper collectibles are sought after in today's market and this book will help both the buyer and seller make accurate evaluations. Over 500 full color examples are included, each containing complete descriptions and current values.
#2269, 8½ x 11, 208 Pgs., PB................................$16.95

Black Collectibles
by P. J. Gibbs

Over 500 color photos including advertising items, containers, dolls, entertainment, figural images, folk art, literary collectibles, novelties and souvenirs, pictorial images, toys and more are included in this volume with current values.
#1714, 8½ x 11, 296 Pgs., PB................................$19.95

Classic TVs
Edited by Scott Wood

One of the newest collectibles to hit the market is old television sets. This book is full of information and photos on those sets. It includes 32 old catalog pages plus 50 pages of color photos of collector's own sets. You may just have one old TV and chances are you will find it in this book.
#2387, 8 x 11, 86 Pgs., PB................................$16.95

Collecting Antique Bird Decoys and Duck Calls
2nd Edition • by Carl F. Luckey

The author has traveled throughout the country researching this reference guide and has photographed over 230 decoys and approximately 100 calls. Along with the photos are full descriptions and values. Each is identified as to its maker, school of carving, etc.
#3361, 8½ x 11, 240 Pgs., PB................................$22.95

Collecting Transistor Novelty Radios
by Robert Breed

A brightly colored book on the novelty radios. Includes everything from cars to sports to McDonalds to celebrities to cartoon characters and more. A must book for the collector, dealer or anyone with that one special radio.
#2196, 8 x 11, 217 Pgs., PB................................$24.95

American Sterling Silver Flatware
1830's-1990's

Featuring patterns and values of thousands of pieces from the early silversmiths to current manufacturers. Also includes historical information on all companies.
#3418, 8½ x 11, 230 Pgs., PB................................$22.95

American Sporting Advertising
Volume II • by Bob & Beverly Strauss

The goal of this 2nd edition is to make Volume I more complete while trying not to duplicate any collectible in the 1st edition. Included are 100's of current values and photographs in both full color and black & white. Collectors have once again welcomed this edition.
#3387, 8½ x 11, 224 Pgs., PB................................$19.95

Antique Advertising Encyclopedia
Volume II • by Ray Klug

A very lovely book on advertising with 117 pages in full color. This book is good for the hard-to-find items and very expensive items. If you can't find it in volume one, chances are that you will find it here.
#1687, 8 x 10, 240 Pgs., HB................................$39.95

Antique Iron
by Kathryn McNerney

Included in this identification and value guide are farm tools, furniture, kitchen items, toys, banks and many more cast iron collectibles. Over 400 different photos fill this informative value guide.
#1880, 5½ x 8½, 232 Pgs., PB................................$9.95

Christmas Ornaments, Lights & Decorations
by George W. Johnson

This book lists information on identifying, storage, repairing, histories, types and much more. Over 750 full color photographs with the name of the item, interesting facts and current values are all listed.
#1752, 8½ x 11, 320 Pgs., HB................................$19.95

Collectible Cats: An Identification & Value Guide
by Marbena "Jean" Fyke

This is a comprehensive value guide to cats made of wood, bronze, glass and china; cat jewelry; black cats of the 1940's; Garfield; prints & paintings; salt & pepper shakers; kitchen items; and a large miscellaneous section. This fun, colorful guide features over 500 photos with complete descriptions & current values.
#3445, 8½ x 11, 160 Pgs., PB................................$18.95

Collecting Baseball Player Autographs
by Don Raycraft

Included are chapters on baseball card shows, autograph sessions at shows, paying for autographs, autographs by mail, value guide to Hall of Fame autographs, questions and answers, 100's of photos and current values.
#2183, 5½ x 8½, 128 Pgs., PB................................$9.95

Collector's Encyclopedia of Granite Ware
by Helen Greguire

This comprehensive work includes pattern and color descriptions, shades of color, enameling types, names and makers, age, construction, popularity, care and preserving instructions and more. Over 180 color photographs make this a truly necessary guide to investing in this collectible.
#2018, 8½ x 11, 416 Pgs., HB................................$24.95

Collector's Guide to Antique Radios
2nd Edition • by Marty & Sue Bunis
This all-new revised 2nd edition includes over 5,000 model numbers & over 600 full color photos not found in the 1st edition. This new edition covers literally 1,000's of sets made between the years of 1920-1960. Collectors will enjoy the easy-to-use format with the radios listed alphabetically by company. All manufacturers are included with complete descriptions.
#2336, 8½ x 11, 216 Pgs., PB.................................$17.95

Collector's Guide to Coca-Cola Collectibles
Volume I • by Al Wilson
A very nice book by one of the foremost authorities on Coca-Cola collectibles. From signs to trays to calendars to toys to thermometers, it is all in this book. Fine quality all color pictures. Also includes 1992 current values.
#1677, 5 x 8, 95 Pgs., PB.................................$10.95

Collector's Guide to Decoys
Books I & II • by Bob & Sharon Huxford

These books cover miniature, decorative, factory and artists' decoys. Actual prices, characteristics and conditions are listed with hundreds of color and black and white photographs. These two volumes will be a valuable addition to any sports enthusiast's library and will help in dating and pricing a collection. Both advanced and beginning collectors will enjoy these books.

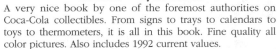

Book I, #1962, 8½ x 11, 232 Pgs., PB $14.95
Book II, #2337, 8½ x 11, 232 Pgs., PB $16.95

Collector's Guide to Keywind Coffee Tins
by James H. Stahl
Over 1,200 one pound coffee tins are pictured and priced. This is the only book you will ever need if you are a collector of coffee tins. It shows over 150 coffee tins in full color; the rest in fine quality black and white, and includes a history of the coffee tin.
#2250, 8 x 11, 172 Pgs., PB....................................$19.95

Doorstops
Identifications & Values • by Jeanne Bertoia
Collectors will learn detection of reproductions and care and preservation as well as history, manufacturers, designers, and pointers in valuing doorstops. Figural examples include Uncle Sam, black mammies, art deco ladies and more. Over 300 color photographs are included.
#1629, 5½ x 8½, 176 Pgs., PB $9.95

Evolution of the Bicycle
Edited by Neil S. Wood
A beautiful price guide on collecting bicycles. Includes bicycles from the 1800's to the 1960's. High wheelers to whizzers! You'll find them all in this "must have" book. Also includes a 4 page color section.
#2311, 8 x 11, 204 Pgs., PB....................................$29.95

A Guide To Easter Collectibles
by Juanita Burnett
This pictorial guide is designed for the beginning or advanced collector, with many categories covering a time span from the 1800's to the present. History, care instructions and tips on dating your collection, color photos and current values are included.
#2340, 8½ x 11, 128 Pgs., PB.................................$16.95

Collector's Guide to Art Deco
by Mary Frank Gaston
The distinctive lines of Art Deco come alive in this full color value guide. The 318 color photos are divided into categories including Clocks, Dress Accessories, Lamps, Smoking Accessories, Statues, Tablewares, and Vases.
#1916, 8½ x 11, 136 Pgs., PB.................................$14.95

Collector's Guide to Coca-Cola Items
Volume II • by Al Wilson
Coca-Cola collectibles are one of the more popular collectibles on the market today. Al Wilson is one of the foremost authorities of this popular collectible. Included in this new Volume II is virtually every Coca-Cola category. This book is produced in full color and contains current values.
#1824, 5½ x 8½, PB.................................$10.95

Collector's Guide to Country Baskets
by Don & Carol Raycraft
This book has interesting information and hundreds of photos on this popular collectible, with current values.
#1537, 5½ x 8½, 128 Pgs., PB $9.95

Collector's Guide to Hopalong Cassidy Memorabilia
by Joseph J. Caro
There are several hundred items in this book ranging from Advertising to Toys to Playsuits with many items in between. The author is a very respected Hoppy collector and has been collecting since 1977. Mr. Caro has collected over 600 items of "Hoppy" memorabilia. Rare and common items are pictured in this book.
#3458, 8½ x 11, 190 Pgs., PB.................................$17.95

Decoys
by Gene & Linda Kangas
The scope of this manuscript is very complex and includes every aspect of decoy collecting. This is much more than just an identification and value guide. This full color hardbound book includes 600+ photographs with chapters on North American Indian decoys, non-native decoys, transportation, influences and decoy painting, care & maintenance, decoratives, miniatures, fish decoys and much much more!
#2276, 11 x 8½, 336 Pgs., HB $24.95

The Encyclopedia of Golf Collectibles
by Mort & John Olman
This book is a comprehensive guide dealing with the identification, dating and valuation of all sorts of golf memorabilia from clubs and balls to books, paintings, prints and more. Among its features are over 2,000 items fully illustrated, names of craftsmen, manufacturers, artists and authors.
#1559, 8½ x 11, 328 Pgs., PB.................................$14.95

Goldstein's Coca-Cola Collectibles
by Shelly Goldstein
If you have any interest in Coca-Cola memorabilia, you will want and need this full color price guide. Previously offered as a four volume set, we have taken these four volumes and combined them into one book. This edition is a must for both the serious collector and the novice.
#2215, 8½ x 11, 128 Pgs., PB.................................$16.95

Huxford's Collectible Advertising
by Bob & Sharon Huxford
Thousands of listings and hundreds of photos are included with the bulk of them produced in full color. The format is amazingly simple and the book very easy to use. Each item is described in full so that even subtle variations are easy to spot; condition, an all-important factor to consider as you evaluate your collectibles, is well defined.
#3319, 8½ x 11, 144 Pgs., PB.................................$17.95

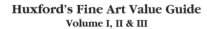

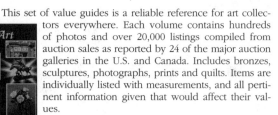

Huxford's Fine Art Value Guide
Volume I, II & III

This set of value guides is a reliable reference for art collectors everywhere. Each volume contains hundreds of photos and over 20,000 listings compiled from auction sales as reported by 24 of the major auction galleries in the U.S. and Canada. Includes bronzes, sculptures, photographs, prints and quilts. Items are individually listed with measurements, and all pertinent information given that would affect their values.

Volume I, #1966, 8½ x 11, 560 Pgs., HB..............$29.95
Volume II, #2085, 8½ x 11, 925 Pgs., HB..............$29.95
Volume III, #2232, 8½ x 11, 584 Pgs., HB $39.95

Pictorial Price Guide to Metal Lunch Boxes
by Larry Aikins

This is the book everyone has been waiting for. Almost every metal lunch box that was ever made is included in this full color publication. Over 800 boxes pictured. Every box has a front and back view plus a photo of the thermos. You must have this book!
#3334, 5 x 8, 218 Pgs., PB......................$19.95

Old Lace & Linens Including Crochet
Identification & Value Guide • by Maryanne Dolan

This reference guide features the intricate artwork found in handstitched items over the past century. Featuring tablecloths, centerpieces, doilies, collars, bedspreads, napkins, pillowcases, hand & tea towels plus more. Fully illustrated.
#2041, 5½ x 8½, 200 Pgs., PB $10.95

Evolution of the Pedal Car
Volume I • Edited by Neil S. Wood

Includes Pedal Cars and other riding toys from 1884 to 1970's. Contains old catalog pages and color photos of private collections. This is possibly the hottest new collectible in the antique market today. With the aid of this book you will keep in touch with realistic prices for any pedal car you will find.
#2060, 8 x 11, 218 Pgs., PB......................$29.95

Evolution of the Pedal Car
Volume II • Edited by Neil S. Wood

Same format as volume one with completely different information and photos. Includes pedal cars, sleds, scooters, tricycles and more from pre 1900's to 1980's. A must book for your pedal car library.
#2197, 8 x 11, 185 Pgs., PB......................$29.95

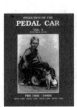

Evolution of the Pedal Car
Volume III • Edited by Neil S. Wood

The best one yet! Another completely different book on pedal cars. This book is on pedal cars from pre 1900 to 1990's. Add this one to your other two books on pedal cars and you shouldn't have to look any further.
#2388, 8 x 11, 250 Pgs., PB......................$29.95

Jukeboxes & Slot Machines
Plus Gum Balls, Arcade, Trade Stimulators
3rd Edition • by Jerry Ayliffe

Includes Wurlitzer, Seeburg, Rockola, AMI, Mills, Fey, Caille, Jennings, Pace, Watling, Northwestern, Columbus, Advance, Leebold, Master plus many more.
#2332, 5½ x 8½, 400 Pgs., PB $14.95

Jukeboxes: A Blast From the Past
Edited by Scott Wood

You will never find another book on jukeboxes with this many photos and prices. Over 100 jukeboxes in beautiful color. Wurlitzer and AMI to Seeburg, Rockola and more. Also includes some wall boxes and speakers.
#3388, 5 x 8, PB $14.95

Kitchen Antiques 1790-1940
by Kathryn McNerney

This outstanding reference includes over 650 photographs containing virtually every kitchen item since the 1790's. Every kitchen item picture or listing in this book contains complete descriptions, sizes, dates, histories and of course a current value guide.
#2216, 8½ x 11, 224 Pgs., PB $14.95

Old Fishing Lures & Tackle
3rd Edition • by Carl Luckey

This very popular book has now added over 400 lures to the existing photos and illustrations in the 2nd edition. Many more manufacturers have been added and all prices have been updated. "Tremendous job...very well written and illustrated. Believe, Uncle Homer will help spread the word...you've earned it."
#2194, 8½ x 11, 472 Pgs., PB $22.95

Ornamental & Figural Nutcrackers
by Judith Rittenhouse

At long last, a book about decorative nutcrackers covering their history from the very earliest use to the production of colorful and elaborate figurals of today. Over 100 color photos of over 150 nutcrackers, along with a variety of illustrations. Basic types of nutcrackers, their composition, dating and pricing are discussed.
#3321, 8½ x 11, 144 Pgs., PB $16.95

Pepsi-Cola Collectibles
Volume I • by Bill Vehling & Michael Hunt

Pepsi-Cola collectibles are now as popular as Coca-Cola items. You need this book to find the price of the items you have just purchased or are looking for. Very accurate pricing on trays to openers to jewelry to signs to coolers. Includes current values.
#1800, 8 x 11, 150 Pgs., PB..............................$14.95

Pepsi-Cola Collectibles
Volume II • by Bill Vehling & Michael Hunt

Another fine book by the experts in the Pepsi-Cola field. Completely different items found in this book than are pictured in volume one. Aprons to carriers to fans to magazine ads, this book will price them for you.
#2142, 8 x 11, 192 Pgs., PB..............................$17.95

Railroad Collectibles
Revised 4th Edition • by Stanley Baker

Stanley Baker, the well-known & popular collector of America's railroad memorabilia has completely revised his popular value guide. This edition has new illustrations and is completely updated. From dining car china to switch keys this book is invaluable to thousands of railroad buffs. It is not only a must but is considered *the* book on the subject.
#2026, 8½ x 11, 200 Pgs., PB $14.95

R. Atkinson Fox, His Life & Works
by Rita C. Mortenson

A very nice book on the history of R. Atkinson Fox with pictures and prices. Eight pages of full color with the rest of the book in fine black and white. One of the fastest growing collectibles in the art field today.

#2247, 8 x 11, 150 Pgs., PB.....................$17.95

R. Atkinson Fox
Volume II • by Rita C. Mortenson

The second volume that everyone has been waiting for. Completely different from volume one. Anyone interested in the works of R. Atkinson Fox will want this book.

#3350, 8 x 11, 308 Pgs., PB.....................$24.95

Roycroft Collectibles
by Charles F. Hamilton

This book remains the most popular and comprehensive history of Roycroft Arts & Crafts collectibles. Included are many photographs with several in full color. Complete descriptions, histories, and current values are also included. A nice presentation of this collectible.

#3352, 8½ x 11, 250 Pgs., HB $24.95

Schroeder's Antique & Collectibles 1994 Engagement Calendar

This 1994 edition includes 54 of the most beautiful full color photos you have ever seen of your favorite antiques. It features a collectible to enjoy each week of the year, plus plenty of room to write daily appointments.

#3394, 7 x 9, 112 Pgs., SB.......................$9.95

Silverplated Flatware
Revised Fourth Edition • by Tere Hagan

This 4th edition has been expanded to 372 pages with updated values. As in the previous edition, each pattern has current values for the fork, knife and spoon with each illustration. A price code remains in the front of the book for the other pieces in each pattern. Over 1,500 patterns are included in this fully illustrated guide.

#2096, 8½ x 11, 372 Pgs., PB.................$14.95

Sterling Silver, Silverplate & Souvenir Spoons
Edited by Neil S. Wood

A very nice book to identify and price your silver, silverplate and souvenir spoons. Includes everything from flatware to thimbles to napkin rings to match boxes.

#1875, 8 x 11, 188 Pgs., PB.....................$12.95

Identification & Value Guide To Textile Bags
by Anna Lue Cook

Many of us remember their mother carefully selecting her flour or feed sacks for the printed design. It was from these brightly printed bags that much of our inner and outerwear came. These articles of clothing, quilts, tablecloths, etc., along with the bags that have colorful labels attached are now being sought by collectors.

#2144, 5½ x 8½, 220 Pgs., PB $12.95

The Book of Moxie
by Frank N. Potter

This huge book by America's Moxie expert is full of information about the company, its products, advertising and collectibles. Hundreds of vintage photographs plus hundreds of color photos of collectible items are included. Moxie, a bitterish concoction of gentian root extract and about 20 other flavorings was once the nation's No. 1 soft drink.

#1811, 8½ x 11, 304 Pgs., HB $29.95

300 Years of Housekeeping Collectibles
by Linda Campbell Franklin

You already know her *300 Years of Kitchen Collectibles*; this new collector's guide is just as comprehensive and exciting with well illustrated sections on Laundering, House Cleaning, Closeting, Bathrooms. You'll know what all those "Whatzzit" gadgets were used for. 216 pages loaded with illustrations and full descriptions.

#3359, 8½ x 11, 216 Pgs., PB.................$22.95

300 Years of Kitchen Collectibles
3rd Edition • by Linda C. Franklin

Four years ago, Linda Franklin decided to take the extra time to move this reference work to a much higher plane. The number of illustrations, listings and the size of the book has doubled. (Patent date charts and a recipe index are also included.) Now in a large format.

#2299, 8½ x 11, 640 Pgs., PB.................$22.95

Value Guide To Baseball Collectibles
by Don & Craig Raycraft

Until the publication of this *Value Guide To Baseball Collectibles* there have been few sources for collectors seeking detailed & current information about baseball related memorabilia. Now you can even locate a value for a copy of *Newsweek* magazine from the 1930's with Carl Hubbell on the cover. The authors have been serious collectors of baseball memorabilia for 15 years.

#2349, 8½ x 11, 216 Pgs., PB.................$16.95

Wanted To Buy
4th Edition

The perfect reference book for both selling your collectibles and determining the actual current market value, because it lists actual buyers along with the price they're willing to pay. This book creates a marketplace for both the collectors and dealers.

#3444, 5½ x 8½, 416 Pgs., PB $9.95

Order From:

Nostalgia Publishing Co., Inc.
P.O. Box 277
La Center, KY 42056

NOSTALGIA PUBLISHING ORDER FORM

Method of Payment

☐ Check   ☐ VISA   ☐ MasterCard

Name_____
(please print)

Cardholder's Name_____

Address_____

City_____State____Zip_____

Card #_____Expiration Date_____

POLICY

- **Send check or charge card information with order.**
- **NO OPEN ACCOUNTS**
- **Postage & Handling: Add $2.00 for 1st book & .30¢ for each additional book.**
- **We will ship your order the day we receive it.**
- **Mail order only – no showroom.**
- **Due to high postage rates we only accept orders from U.S. customers.**

ITEM #	QTY	TITLE	PRICE	TOTAL

Send Order To:

Nostalgia Publishing Co., Inc.
P.O. Box 277
La Center, KY 42056

SUBTOTAL	
Postage & Handling: Add $2.00 for 1st book & .30¢ for each additional book	
TOTAL ENCLOSED	

This form may be photocopied